I0819850

The Complete Seymour

Colville Storyteller

Native Literatures of the Americas Series

The Complete Seymour
Colville Storyteller

Peter J. Seymour

Compiled and Edited by Anthony Mattina

Translated by Madeline DeSautel and Anthony Mattina

University of Nebraska Press
Lincoln & London

Manufactured in the United States of America

Publication of this volume was assisted by the generous contribution of The Confederated Tribes of the Colville Reservation and The Salish Research Foundation.

Library of Congress Control Number: 2015932782

Peter J. Seymour (late 1960s). Courtesy Ada Holford.

Dedicated to the memory of *kʷikʷitás*

Table of Contents

Acknowledgments

I thank the many individuals who have made it possible for me to study the language and literature of the Colville-Okanagan, and especially Dale Kinkade, my first linguistics teacher, who introduced me to Salish; Larry Thompson, who sponsored my doctoral studies and shared his deep knowledge of the Salish family; and Terry Thompson, who provided practical support of many kinds, including the use she and Larry gave me of their beautiful home in Kailua for a whole year. I am especially grateful to Terry Thompson who, as President of the Salish Research Foundation, has made possible the publication of this book, and several others books before this, with substantial financial contributions.

I owe special thanks to Bob Hsu who showed me how computers can aid in the processing of linguistic data, and to Tim Montler who worked by my side for several years processing Colville data in his quiet and expert way, showing me how he did it. I have learned much from them, and I value not only the expertise and instruction they offered me, but also their friendship.

I also thank the various institutions that over the years made it comfortable for me to study Colville-Okanagan: the American Council of Learned Societies, the American Philosophical Society, the National Endowment for the Humanities, the National Science Foundation, and the University of Montana.

For the past 45 years collectively the Colville Culture Committee and the Colville Tribal Council have welcomed me and supported my work. Their subvention for the publication of this book has helped greatly and is much appreciated. The Okanagan have been similarly generous to me, first the Penticton Band, represented by its Chief, with whom I entered into a formal *Relationship of Trust*, then other bands, and eventually the En'owkin Centre, where I had the privilege of being in residence for two years, and where I still hold a professional affiliation.

For a couple of weeks in the early summer of 1968, Sophie McDonald of Coeur d'Alene, Idaho, was my first teacher of the language, and she recorded for me a word list. She then wrote a letter of introduction to her relative Mrs. Helen Toulou of Kewa, Washington. When I showed up in Kewa, Mrs. Toulou agreed to start teaching me the language, and I studied with her for two summers. She is the one who with extreme patience taught me how to pronounce the sounds of the language and encouraged me. Her great-grandchildren were playmates of my daughter Lori, and her great-granddaughter Shelly Boyd is now studying the language of her t'aʔt'úpaʔ (or túpa), and I am grateful for her commitment.

In the same summer of 1968 I started working with several other Colvilles, whose help I acknowledge gratefully: Mary Lemery, Julia Quintasket, Cecilia Smith, Cecilia Andrews, Charlie Quintasket, George Quintaket, Martin Louie, Louie Pichette, and Albert

Louie, the last who would not speak Colville[1] to me, but helped in other ways—every time I visited him in Rogers Bar I learned something from him.

That summer and the next two I met three Colvilles who became instrumental in my work of documentation of the language and of the literature of its people: Peter J. Seymour, Madeline DeSautel, and Dora DeSautel, all three of Inchelium, Washington.

The narrative art of Pete Seymour is what this book is about. I spent many months over ten years with Madeline DeSautel studying the Colville language. She is the person with whom I transcribed and translated Pete Seymour's texts, and even though, after her death in 1979, I have continued to spend countless hours on the preparation and edition of this anthology, I consider her my co-editor. Dora DeSautel helped me check many recordings and transcriptions and I learned much from her. I became close to all three, but especially the first two, who felt comfortable enough to visit me in Missoula, Montana, and Honolulu, Hawaii, respectively. All three let me record their narrations, and I have compiled anthologies of these. In Missoula I collaborated with Herb Manuel, from spáx̌mən, British Columbia, who remained in residence at the University for one academic quarter.

The years went by, and one by one all these individuals passed away, and I stayed away from Inchelium. But I went to Okanagan country in British Columbia and started working first with Clara Jack of Penticton who was of critical importance for the progress I made. At the Jack residence I had the pleasure and good luck of recording some narratives of cəm̓xnálqs[2] (Edna Jack) and Mary Louise Powers. Clara introduced me to Harry Robinson from whom we recorded some important texts, and I enjoyed the contributions of Herman Edwards and Punky Pierre.

I attribute great importance to the work I did with all the members of the literacy classes we held at the En'owkin Centre, first of all of saʕmtíc̓aʔ (Sarah Peterson), with whom I had the pleasure of working not only there, but also at the Colville Language Preservation Program in Nespelem and Omak, Washington. There she led all the activities of the group and was instrumental in setting up and running that program. I also acknowledge the contribution of the participants in the En'owkin group: kiʔláwnaʔ (Andrew McGinnis), mx̌ikn̓átkʷ (Sophie Alec), ɬəkmxnálqs (Delphine Derrickson), syanátkʷ (Margaret Tom), q̓iw̓sálxqən (Herman Edwards), snəmtpíc̓aʔ (Theresa Dennis), x̌ʷnámx̌ʷnəm (Theresa Tom), caylx (Richard Armstrong), sklítaʔ (Hazel Squakin), Maxine Baptiste, Jonas Manuel, Shirley Paul, uɬmánc̓aʔ (Grace Greyeyes) cucuwálqs (Ramona Allison), ɬk̓əmpíc̓aʔ (Sarah Pierre), c̓c̓rímtqən̓ (William Qualtier), Clare Manuel, Jeannine Terbasket, Kel Gottfriedson, Carol Allison, Nancy Allison. I appreciate the assistance of the following speakers: suʔq̓ím (Sandy Lezard), Andy Joseph, William Charley, and Modesta Batterman.

My work at the En'owkin Centre wouldn't have been possible without the support of its directors, first Don Fiddler, and later Jeannette Armstrong, to whom I am greatly indebted. And I want to acknowledge the special help I received there from Richard Armstrong, Delphine Derrickson, Chris Armstrong and Brody Armstrong. The staff of the Centre has always been helpful, courteous, friendly, and fun to be around.

1 To refer to the language of both the Colville and the Okanagan I use Colville-Okanagan (Cv-Ok). Otherwise, Colville if spoken on the Colville Reservation, Okanagan if spoken in the various Okanagan Reserves. These dialects are close to each other.

2 I provide Okanagan names for those who volunteered them.

In Omak and then in Nespelem, where I worked for and with the Colville Language Preservation Program I am indebted, first of all, as I wrote above, to Sarah Peterson, and then to administrators Rodney Cawston, Colleen Cawston, John Sirois, and Sharon Covington, and speakers Hazel Burke, Millie Steele, Elaine Emerson, Ted Moomaw, Kenny Condon and Eva Orr. I appreciate the help, support and hospitality I received from my good friend Mike Somday over many years.

I want to acknowledge the contribution of Lori Mattina, who commented with acuity on my draft of "The texts." Two anonymous reviewers provided insightful comments, and I thank them for their help.

Aaron Carden, Pete Seymour's grandson, son of Pete's daughter Tilly (Matilda), has kept me virtual company much of the time I have been assembling this anthology, and has been something of a reward and an inspiration for the interest he has demonstrated in his grandfather's stories, in the language, and in all things Colville. He wrote to me: "[I] was told you were trying to get a book published the work you did with my grandfather, i am interested in getting any of the language you have from pete and i believe that there was a reason you worked with him i am working on my language here in omak. i read one of your [texts] pete had mentioned how he was talking the language to you and not his grandchildren, i felt pain for i was at the age of nine when he passed i heard little of the language in stories but i was one of the little coyotes that would run all the farm animals out of the country so i was not brought over too many times. this is not an excuse of my language but a passion to continue it as my grandfather did i feel very proud to say he helped the language reach me. i have been working to learn my language for three years on my own time i would like to help you get the book published with approval of our council."

My wife Nancy has supported and encouraged me unconditionally, and for this I am and will always be grateful.

Finally, all errors and oversights are mine alone.

Preface

Whoever will read this book, Colville Indians or linguists or others, I owe them my story of who Pete Seymour is.

Pete Seymour was a farming family man, a hunter, a jockey, and a storyteller. The texts I have put together in this anthology (all that I recorded except for "The Golden Woman"[3]) address these facets of Pete's life. The lines that tell us what he thought about his storytelling can be found in "Coyote and Grizzly" (q.v.), where, having been lost in his narration for one hour and twenty minutes, he closed with what translates in English as "I just now realized I am teaching. My pupil is sitting by me. The one I am teaching is not anybody. The one getting taught is not my grandchild, it's a white man." Why wasn't he telling his story to his grandchildren? Had he ever told them, or tried to tell them, these stories? Who had he ever told these stories to? Surely, I wasn't the first to hear Pete tell stories.

In October 2007 I met with Ada, Pete's eldest child, and with two of her children, Anna Jean and Clarence ("Turk"), to talk about Pete, and I recorded our conversation. I asked if the stories Pete told in my presence were "told often in the household," and Anna Jean (64 years old at that time),[4] replied: "No, because when we were born they [the elders] wouldn't even talk Indian. When we went huckleberrying, they talked [Indian], but they wouldn't talk to us." Later she added, "but they did pass their stories around, and they did have their sweats, and they did have Big Louie[5] ..." When Clarence replied in the positive to my question "Do you remember his storytelling at all?" I added "You do! What sort of setting was it, was it in the evening, in the living room?"

Clarence: "Evening in the living room, yeah." And he added that he had heard his uncle Eneas, Pete's older brother by about 20 years, tell more stories than Pete.

Clarence: "Dad [Pete Holford, Ada's husband and Pete Seymour's son-in-law] was a favorite of Uncle Eneas, ... and we'd go to his house, and sit in the living room, and he'd start telling stories, in the evening..."

"When Pete told stories did he tell them in Indian or in English?"

Clarence: "In English." ...

"Were they aimed at the children, or the adults, or didn't matter?"

Clarence: "I'm not sure whether it mattered. They just told stories."

At this point Ada interjected: "They were really interesting stories that would take your attention and you would listen until it was ended."

"Would it go well into the night?"

Ada: "Well, yes, the children, they'd be going to sleep, tired, and pretty soon the last one ... and they'd give up, because there'd be nobody to talk to anymore. So they'd quit for the night. In Indian they call them captíkʷɬ, and that means, I guess, stories. That's what we do every night, captíkʷlm, and he told good interesting stories."

---

3 Published by the University of Arizona Press (Mattina 1987).

4 Pete Holford, Ada's husband, was also present, but was not an active participant.

5 We would later return to Big Louie.

I asked "All his stories are so good that I wonder, who did he practice with, who was he conversing with in Indian?"

Ada: "See, he was a little boy, he had elders, and he listened to them and he got the stories from his elders, it went back like that. I remember stories that they called nʔałnaʔsqílx^{w}tn, that means cannibal, man-eater, ... the word means "eat," ʔiłn means "eat you" it was a word that children wondered about, you got excited, you wanted to listen. So, I used to think, it'd be nice if they got all those stories because some of them are magic, some of them were really exciting..."

I pushed on and asked Ada, "Did your dad have a reputation for being a good storyteller, or not?"

Ada: "He loved to go places where they told stories and he told stories too and they told stories to him and they got together and they talked and they exhanged stories and he learned a lot and he loved them because it was about his people and he wanted to know."

"Was he recognized as a person who could tell wonderful stories? Did the people know about him?"

Ada: "Well, he could talk English and so they would talk English with him a lot. And then once in a while some of them would ask for words, you know, how do you say this, how do you say that, and he'd say it."

I persisted: "The reason I'm asking, I'm sort of surprised, because when I ask, is Pete Seymour [well known as a story teller] ... Now it's too late because youngsters don't remember. But when I was here 35 years ago, it's not like everybody knew Pete's stories were so wonderful, and I wondered why, because his stories are beautiful."

Ada: "Oh, yes, because he talked with the old timers that knew stories and had good stories, how to hunt, how to fish, and they were good, interesting stories, and he listened, because he could understand."

Pete had mentioned Lisette as one of the people he had learned these stories from, but only recently have I connected this name with his grandmother.[6] Pete had also told me that he used to visit Joe Boyd to hear Joe's stories, but I am still not clear who Joe Boyd was and how he was related to the Boyds I know. In fact, I am beginning to think that I am mistaken about the identity of this storyteller. Earlier on in the conversation from which I am quoting, I had heard Anna Jean say that "they [the family] had Big Louie."[7] And Clarence had said that when the family lived at Smoke Ranch, his father, Pete Holford, "didn't learn this stuff [what he knew of Indian things] from Grandpa, either. He learned it from Big Louie." I wonder, then, if Pete's storytelling partner was Big Louie, and not Joe Boyd.

Clarence: "I don't know what Big Louie's real name is."

Ada: "We always called him Big Louie, that's all I know. He knew a lot of magic stories. He could tell a lot of stories, you couldn't hardly believe."

Anna Jean: "Actually they told all [kinds of] stories. I can remember them coming to the old house, they all got around the table and they would tell stories. But at that time I didn't know the significance of them. I was young."

No one I have interviewed has had much to say about Pete the storyteller, and my many inquiries, over the years, aimed at finding out if he was a renowned storyteller on

6 From the conversation from which I am quoting here.
7 Quoted above.

the Reservation have not confirmed what one might have expected—but, even though I said to Ada that I am surprised, I am not, because circumstances have deprived all narrators (not only Pete) of the opportunities to perform as they would have several generations ago. His reputation on the Colville Reservation suggests that, except for his family perhaps, he was a closet storyteller.

What about his personal life? We recorded several narratives of autobiographical content, and I have included all of them in this anthology; and Pete and I did have some conversations in English about his past. We were good friends, we went places together, took car rides, drank a few beers, and we talked. Sometimes Pete talked even when I couldn't hear, as when, once, in one of our rides, with the top of my Volswagen convertible down I hollered "Pete, I can't hear what you are saying" and he mouthed back "Oh, it's OK", and resumed his story, whatever it was.

When I met him, in Inchelium, Washington, he had been widowed for a short time (Lina Camille had died the year before, 1967), and he was mourning, and he missed his wife. We didn't talk much about that, but Lina and Pete had eleven children, "one shy of a dozen," Pete would say, and they had a long life together. His life was the hard life of a farmer and a hunter, and, like the lives of most of us, it must have had its ups and downs, and its joys and sorrows. One of their children died as an infant; and their youngest son was born with a cleft palate and needed long-term hospitalization and care. The family had at one point been evicted from a place they would have owned if they could have paid a balance of one hundred dollars. Their first house had had to be moved to higher ground when Grand Coulee dam was built and the old Inchelium was flooded. In sum, a regular hard life.

Pete was born in Kelley Hill, on the "North Half" of the Reservation, May 1, 1896 to Joseph (Joe) and Rosalie (Rosie). In his "Autobiography" (q.v.) he tells us he had eleven brothers and sisters. With Ada I could confirm that he had three brothers, Eneas, Charlie, and John, and two sisters, Adeline and Christine.[8] While Eneas figures prominently in the autobiographical accounts Pete gave me, the others do not. For a good part of his youth he lived with his grandparents in Kelley Hill. Of school age he went to "day school."[9] Ada explained, "See, he lived up to North Half, and he talked about, they went to school, I don't know how, they went to school some place, but he said he got to go to school, he called it white man's school... He got with some other kids and they go to school, just, you know, before the winter sets in. When the winter set in they quit going to school."

"But we're not sure where this school was?"

Ada: "No, because he'd say 'I'd get with the white people and go to their school.'"

"Do you think it might be at Marcus?"

Clarence: "I really don't know."

Anna Jean: "I don't know where the old time schools are, around there ..."

Clarence: "It would have been a big trip, in those days."

"From Kelly Hill to Marcus?"

Clarence: "Yeah."

From an early age Pete rode horses well, having been trained by his older brother and mentor Eneas (see "Racing Horses"). Apparently, beginning in his late youth he started

8 The kin terms that refer to brothers also refer to first cousins. This probably explains the discrepancy. See "Racing Horses."

9 See "Autobiography."

racing horses, quite successfully. Some of his prowess Ada attributes to the strong powers he had.

Ada: "He loved to race, he was kind of a jockey... He had magic. He could go out get some weeds and they'd put it on their horse and they would really race. Nobody else could do that. He'd win more races ..."

Pete's wife Lina was also a good rider, and Anna Jean recounted this episode.

Anna Jean: "Remember the story what Bud told us about his [Bud's] tima [stəmtímaʔ, *grandmother*], and I didn't know this until..., he just told me the other day. He said, 'You know, Tima and Tupa [t'aʔt'úpaʔ *grandfather*] were coming down, and she was on a big grey ... [that's] what she called him. But anyway, she was on the big grey, and Tupa was on this other horse, and he told his Tima, 'Tima, how come you got Tupa riding that gentle horse and you are on the high stepping one?' She just looked at him and said, 'I could outride that old man any time of the day'" [general laughter].

Ada: "She was a good rider when she was young. Well, she was just skin and bones, but then she turned into a big woman, and she kinda quit riding."

When Pete became of age he courted Lina, and eventually joined her at Smoke Ranch, near Kewa, where they started their family. Pete provided for his family in different ways: he was a good hunter, and he learned how to farm. In the old days, Ada explains, "You could make a living, see, that's how they made a living, how their grandfathers made their living. They were good hunters, they were good fishermen, they were good [at] this or that..."

As I have been reminded often, by my Colville friends and by life itself, being good at something isn't all one's doing. There is luck, and then there are different kinds of help:

Ada: "And lot of them had magic, and they had medicine partner, and you didn't just get that medicine partner. You were lost in the mountains and something came to you, and it was your medicine partner. And then when you got older... The elders would tell you 'Just be quiet, don't talk about it until you get to be an old man, and then you'll be an Indian doctor, and you'll sing. That's when you sing. But if you talk about it now you'll die.'"

Clarence: "Is that why Bugs [Clarence's younger brother Robert] never talked about it?"

Ada: "I guess" [general laughter].

Ada persisted. "Well, one of these days he'll have to sing. It'll come to you [him], and it'll be time to sing."

Anna Jean: "How shall we sing? [if] we never heard the song?"

Ada: "The song'll come to you. It'll come to you, and you will sing it, and that'll be your song. That's the way it was... You know, I was such a big coward that I didn't get out of sight [laughs]. There is no way I could get a sumíx [spirit power]. My grandmother had a sumíx. I call it sumíx. Well, that's your medicine partner... And your medicine partner, if you were lucky enough to get one, accompanies you in your life."

I do not know if Pete had received his sumíx—I had never asked him nor did I ask Ada.

I asked: "Were you encouraged to talk Indian? You [Ada] speak Indian."

And with a reticence I know well, Ada went around the question: "My grandmother couldn't talk English. I loved her so much, I went berry picking with her, we always traveled on horses and she was always telling me how to saddle, how to do this, how to make your basket, and you know, I was always making mistakes and she was always telling me... 'Oh, you're so x̌ʷupt [feeble]'."

I asked again: "Did you get to talk Indian with anybody?"

Ada: "No. I hear people talking Indian, and I'll sit and listen."

"But you won't talk because you're shy?"

Ada: "Well, I'll hear them talk and I'll just listen to hear what they're saying. If someone'd come, you know, I wouldn't be rude, you know, get in and talk with them, if two of them were talking. But if somebody came and talked with me, then I would talk."

Anna Jean: "You talk with Tootie all the time. When you and Tootie see each other you talk Indian."

Ada: "Yeah, because we both can talk Indian and so we do."

I asked: "And your siblings? ... I know Ed [eldest of the Seymour boys] talked Indian..."

Ada: "A little. Yeah, he can understand a lot, you'll talk to him, he understands, talks a certain amount."

"But the younger ones didn't?"

Ada: "No. You know, if you wanted to, you take interest, some of them did. It seemed too hard for them, so they wouldn't try. And some would take interest, and like me, if I wanted to quit talking they'd get after me because I wasn't, you know, smart or something, they'd say 'Oh, you're x̌ʷupt', or something... If you did something good they'd say 'sysyus, sysyus [*smart*]', you know, they'd compliment you. But if you weren't they'd say 'x̌ʷupt, x̌ʷupt' and that means just *impossible*. You can't do it. They're just letting me know."

"How did [Pete] spend most of his time?"

Ada: "Well, I could say he had a big family, and he liked to hunt... He'd get meat, dry it ... they put all that dried meat, larder for the wintertime, and then they'd raise big gardens, and they'd put that in the cellar."

"Did he encourage his children to [use the sweat house]?"

Ada: "Well, he'd explain it to them. 'You got to clean yourself off. [If you are racing you] must have nothing to do with women, can't hold their hands or nothing. Stay away from them. Spoils your luck.' So when he was going to go to a big doings, he'd go sweat and everything, he'd be all cleaned up and ready to go and then he'd win. He'd gamble, and play stick games or gamble, just gamble, and he'd win money. And he rode horses, he'd win races, and they couldn't figure it out, how he could win, you know, his horse wasn't all that good, but he won."

"Did the children in the family do things like sweating?"

Ada: "If you wanted to."

"Did he have a favorite son or daughter, that you know of?"

Ada: "Not really, he liked them all, and spanked them all, and told them what was right and what was wrong."

"Same with your mom?"

Ada: "Well, my mother, she was big hearted. She loved us, and we ... loved her. She'd hug us and you know, make you feel that she had a lot of love. She was a big woman and she just loved her children, so we loved our mother. But our father, he was a little bit on the strict side, and if we did something wrong we got a hard paddling, so we were just a little bit afraid of him" [laughs].

"Did the children have Indian names?"

Ada: "Well, a lot of them, they had to have an Indian partner and their Indian partner gave them their name. But that's something unusual. You don't get it, there's very few that gets it. And then when they do get it, they won't let them talk about it. You gotta wait to be old, and then it'll come to you, and you'll hear it singing. Then you're sick, and then you tell people. 'Well, I'll have a dance and I'll tell you my story'. Then he'll tell where he got the power, his partner."[10]

"This is interesting about names being private and you can't repeat them. Why is that?"

Ada: "Well, lot of times they don't want you to know. It's just your own name, and it's just yours. Well, like me, I never hardly say my name to anybody."

"Oh?"

Ada: "Because it's kinda hard to say, and I hate to say it because nobody knows it, so why say it? But if I was with a bunch of Indians and they'd talk, and they'd come and say my name, then I'd feel at home, and I'd feel good that they know my name. Your name [directed to Clarence], what is it?

Clarence: [chuckling] "You know, you remember it. You forgot it, huh?"

Ada: "I forgot it."

Clarence: "You forgot it."

...

And I pushed Clarence on the topic of his name: "So you're not going to tell us, huh?"

Clarence: [laughs] "It'll come to me here in a minute."

and at an appropriate break in the conversation I asked: "Did you come up with your name?"

Clarence: "Yeah, I know what it is [laughter] it's q̓ʷʕay kʷukʷús[11] [Black Pig]."

And Ada commented: "You know, we don't say it very often, and we kind of forget it. I can't ... I don't forget mine, because, you know, I always remember it, because it's mine."

Pete and Lina had eleven children. As of the date of my conversation with Ada, Clarence and Anna Jean, only two were still alive, Ada, the eldest, and Philomena (Pinky, also known as Theresa) the youngest. Ada passed away some time after our converstion, and so did Pinky. The Seymour children had their lives: some married; young Ada went to school in DeSmet, Idaho, and stayed there all year. Rose Frances joined a religious order and suffered her rheumathoid arthritis in silence. Ten made it to maturity and all ten have passed on: Ada, Ed, William, Tillie, Jim, Dave, sister Rose Frances, Paul, Ricky and Francis.

The context of all their lives, parents and children, is a familiar one:

Ada: "The life of the family, the religious [people], when they got here, they kind of converted the Indians. Before that the Indians had their own way of living, they had

10 Ada said that it is the sumíx to give a person a name. But she might be referring to a special name-giving by the sumíx. In a recent e-mail message to me, Aaron Carden, Pete's grandson, reacted as follows: "Conversations with elders and my teachers suggest that Indian names were given within 10 days of birth by the grandparent heading the family[.] with my conversations with aunt Ada she would go off track at times refusing to involve some indian ways[.] not until we visited many times she would open up, but her daughter would distract her and I was left incomplete with some information but realized she had more to tell, then she had her stroke and i visited and we spoke the language and she mistook me for pete seymour (thinking i was her father) so I realized that i could not lead her back into time at a time of her weakness so i stopped visiting for her health and mind reasons." What Pete told me is that his childhood name was ɬyaʕlxʷ, that kʷikʷitás was the name given to him by his parents, and that one of his old-age names was ɬcánmən. Such multiple names were the norm in earlier times.

11 I do not follow the capitalization conventions of English for Colville-Okanagan.

their own magic, they had their own way of hunting, they had their own way of living, all that, but when the white man come he just destroyed it... They had magic, they had a lot of magic. And they [the religious people] didn't like the magic. See, he could make his horse win when his horse wasn't all that good, but he'd win, because he had magic."

For a while the family lived in Nespelem.

Ada: "Ed and I would sit in the window watching for Mama to come back. Of course she had a little buggy and she'd go down to Nespelem to get groceries, and she'd leave us home, so we sat in the window and watched for her to come back. I always remember that. Oh, I hated it. We were just little and we were scared, but she'd get back and everything was fine again. But she wouldn't take us, because she had to buy groceries, you know, and the little buggy, the back was about that big, and it'd be loaded with groceries. She'd get back, and she'd put her horses away, unload her groceries. We got by until the next time she had to go ... I remember they used to buy stacks of flour, and they were in these little bags, white bags, and she made white bread, and she was good baker."

Clarence: "What was the name of those sacks?"

Ada: "We called them flour sacks. We made lot of things out of them, dish towel, made clothing, made shirts, everything ... we managed. My mother was a smart woman; my dad, he was always hunting and he kept us in meat; and we had soup, and dumplings, and sometimes they'd buy macaroni, and that was a treat, or rice, or anything that you can bring from the store. We enjoyed everything. Then it was time to go to school, and we always went to Idaho and we never come back til school was out. That's the way it was for me."

And that's the way it was for Pete. After his wife died Pete moved in with Ada and Pete Holford and helped with the chores of the ranch. He tended a big garden, and looked after the horses. Much of the storytelling he did for me took place in their kitchen. Pete Seymour died September 26, 1979.

Symbols and Abbreviations

Symbols

1	first person singular
2	second person singular
3	third person singular
4	first person plural
5	second person plural
=	lexical affix boundary
-	inflectional affix boundary
+	non-inflectional affix boundary
•	reduplicative affix boundary
ˆX	suffixal part of the circumfix
Xˆ	prefixal part of the circumfix
[X]	editorial addition
{X}	false starts, incomplete or other intrusive matter
[?]	inchoative infix

Text titles

2gts	The two goats	HnTrp	A hunting trip
Aut	Autobiography	Hrvst	Harvesting
BJ	Blue Jay and Wolf	Lynx	Lynx and the virgin
blkpg	Black Pig	Marry	Marriage customs
Brth	After the birth of a child	Nams	How Coyote got his powers
Butch	Parnership Hunting	Prov	Provisions
CoGr	Coyote and Grizzly	RHorse	Racing Horses
Dvl	The devil and the black face	RnTrp	The rainy trip
GDd1	The grateful dead version 1	Whal	Coyote and Whale
GDd2	The grateful dead version 2		

Grammatical labels

1x	1st singular of x...	inch	inchoative
2x	2nd singular of x...	incp	inceptive
3x	3rd singular of x...	indef	indefinite
3e2obj	third ergative and second singular object	intj	interjection
3e4obj	third ergative and first plural object	intt	intent (forms)
4x	1st plural of x...	ipftv	imperfective
5x	2nd plural of x...	ipftvp	imperfective of present relevance
6x	3rd plural of x...	ipimptv	intransitive plural imperative
act	actual	isimptv	intransitive singular imperative
agInst	agent-instrument	kn	kn- paradigm
apsv	antipassive	$k^{w}u$	$k^{w}u$- paradigm

art	article
benf	benefactive
caus	causative
cisl	cislocative
comp	complement
comptv	comparative
cpd conn	compound connector
cust	customary
dim	diminutive
dub	dubitative
dur	durative
dvel	developmental
erg	ergative
evid	evidential
fut	future
futi	future intransitive
futImp	future imperative
futNeg	future negative
futPerf	future perfect
futPerfCust	future perfect customary
furPerfi	future perfect (i(n)-)
furPerfkn	future perfect (kn‿)
futt	future transitive
gpat	get-passive
hab	habitual / durative
habCisl	habitual cislocative
i-	i- paradigm
in-	in- paradigm
-ɬt	-ɬt transitive
mdl	middle
negEmph	negative emphatic
negFac	negative factual
nom	nominalizer
nom4	1st pl of nominalized verbs
-nt	-nt transitive
obj	object
obj itr	object of intransitive
obj tr	object of transitive
perf	perfective
pl	plural
pperf	past perfect
prttv	partitive
psv	passive
rec	reciprocal
refl	reflexive
rel	relative
sg	singular
s.o.	someone
s.t.	something
-st	-st transitive
subord	subordinate
tpimptv	-y imperative
tran	transitive
tsimptv	-sk^{w} imperative
-tuɬt	-tuɬt transitive
-ẏ	-ẏ transitive

Miscellanea

bro	brother
Cm	(Moses) Columbian
Cr	Coeur d'Alene
ex	example
fa's	father's
Fl	Flathead
H.B.	Hudson's Bay
inaud	inaudible
indec	indecipherable
JC	Jesus Christ
Ka	Kalispel
Li	Lillooet
MD	Madeline DeSautel
m's	man's
onom	onomatopoeic
Sh	Shuswap
Sp	Spokane
s.t.	something
Th	Thompson
unfin	unfinished
w's	woman's

Introduction

Colville-Okanagan (Cv-Ok) is one of twenty-three Salishan languages[1] spoken in north-west North America. The territory occupied by speakers of Salishan languages consists of a large, contiguous mass of land, and two non-contiguous pockets, one situated north-west of the main territory,[2] the other south-west.

The Colville-Okanagan land and its people

The area where Cv-Ok has been spoken, and is now spoken by perhaps as many as one thousand speakers of mostly mature age (if we includes semi-fluent speakers and intermediate students of the language) spans along the north-south expanse of the Okanagan valley from just south of what is now Enderby to south of Okanogan,[3] Washington, and westward in the Similkameen and Methow valleys; along the north-south expanses of the Sanpoil and Kettle rivers, and the area west of the Columbia river as far as the bend around Wilbur, Washington. Dialectal differences are minor but remain to be described.

Cv-Ok is also the term I use in this book to refer to all the people who speak it,[4] to wit, the suqnaqínx,[5] who live from just south of Enderby to Oroville, the sʔaltítkʷ, who live in the Arrow Lakes area, the sx̌ʷyʔiɬpx, who live along the Kettle River from above Rock Creek to the confluence with the Columbia River, the sənʕíckstx, who live from Slocan to north of Chewelah, the sməlqmíx, who live along the Similkameen River, the sənqʕáytkʷ, who live south of Oroville to Brewster, the mitxʷúʔ, who live along the Methow River, and the sənpʕʷílx, who live along the San Poil River. Collectively, these eight groups form what we call the siylx nation.[6] Peter J. Seymour is sx̌ʷyʔiɬpx.

1 The family divides in five branches, the result of migrations. A single group is thought to have headed northwest and settled in the area where Bella Coola is now found, surrounded by non-Salishan languages, Wakashan sea-side, and Athapascan inland-side. Another group is thought to have settled along the coast, and then spread further, one sub-group going southward to where Tillamook, now extinct, was spoken, and formed the third branch of the linguistic family. This language, too, is surrounded by non-Salishan languages, clockwise from the north, Chinookan, Athapascan, Takelman, and Maidu. A fourth group, forming the Tsamosan branch, also moved southward, and a fifth group, forming the Interior branch, moved eastward. One now extinct Athapascan language, Nicola, was spoken in the approximate geographic center of the Salish area.

2 The Salish territory extends longitudinally from about 123^0 West to about 113^0 West, and latitudinally from about 52^0 North to about 45^0 North. The extent of the territory is such that it spans two different culture areas: the Pacific Northwest, and the Plateau.

3 This is the spelling used in the US.

4 Many individuals feel that the term "Okanagan" should be reserved for the Native population that lives along the Okanagan River. These same individuals prefer to use the word nsíylxcən to refer to the language spoken not only by those who live along the Okanagan River, but also to other Natives of the same linguistic group,

5 As I have mentioned, I do not follow the capitalization conventions of written English when writing Cv-Ok, and many of the individuals I have worked with and conducted research among do not, either—but occasionally forget not to.

6 This is the word on which nsíylxcən is based. The combination n-...-cən signal *mouth, language.*

The map shows the territory where Salishan languages are spoken in white; and the territory where non-Salishan languages are spoken, either striped or, in the case of the Nicola Athapascan enclave in the approximate center of Salish territory, in gray. The non-contiguous languages are Bella Coola, to the north and west of the main body of Salishan languages, and Tillamook, to its south and west. The eastern-most Salish language is Flathead, spoken in the Bitterroot and Mission valleys of Montana. Flathead is also the southern-most Salishan language, and it forms a dialect continuum with Kalispel and Spokane.

Languages of the area (adapted from Aert H. Kuipers' *Salish Etymological Dictionary*).

The notion of "land", or, in Cv-Ok sqilxʷ iʔ təmxʷúlaʔxʷtət, "Our Indian Land" is as felt a notion as any in Cv-Ok culture.[7] The Cv-Ok have always relied on the natural resources of their lands to survive. Until the encroachment of the Anglo-Americans, the traditional culture of the Cv-Ok was based almost entirely on subsistence. The Cv-Ok have always lived off the land and its products: fruits, berries and vegetation that grow above ground; tubers and roots that grow underground; fish and creatures that dwell in the water, and land and sky creatures. And they also exchanged goods with their neighbors, often at specific times of the year, and in specific meeting places.[8]

7 I know of many Okanagan speakers who have cooperated with linguists and other researchers to compile extensive ethnogeographic records. They want to preserve for posterity the names their ancestors had given to the various landmarks, as demonstration that, in fact, all these places were, once, theirs, their communal land.

8 The purposes of these gatherings and exchanges are more social than economic.

The languages

From the distribution of the languages, the size of the territory, the divergences of the various language, the vocabulary common to these languages, we make inferences about the original homeland, and the directions and chronology of the movements. In contrast to early speculations that the Salishan languages had spread from an inland location (Boas 1905), recently scholars have demonstrated with convincing evidence that speakers of the original language occupied a maritime area, and migrated outward from there, following routes to the interior along such major rivers as the Fraser and Thompson (Suttles & Elmendorf 1963, Suttles 1987). The linguistic evidence adduced focuses on terms of flora and fauna (Kinkade 1991). The discontinuity of the territory points to ancient migrations[9] of the Proto-Salish, the ancestors of all Salishan people, and suggests that splinter groups of Salish people, at various times, moved to their respective territories. In sum, the homeland of the original Salish peoples must have been along the Northwest coast, and around the 49th north parallel. The linguistic evidence shows as well that the Cv-Ok descended from the Proto-Salish, and, once separated from the other Salish people, spoke a language that eventually differentiated from the languages of the other groups of Salish people.

The Salishan languages divide into five branches: the Interior branch, and four others.[10] Cv-Ok (nsíylxcən) is one of seven languages that belong to the Interior branch of the family, along with (northwest to southeast) Lillooet, Shuswap, Thompson, Moses-Columbian, Kalispel-Flathead-Spokane, and Coeur d'Alene. The comparative evidence I have studied shows that Cv-Ok's closest relative in the Interior branch of the family is Kalispel-Flathead-Spokane, as evidenced by the lexical and morpho-syntactic facts of the languages, and in spite of the phonological differences, that consist of two primary traits: (1) the palatal series in Ka-Fl-Sp corresponding to the velar series in Cv-Ok (Ka-Fl-Sp č̓, č, š = Cv-Ok k̓, k, x); (2) the five-vowel system of Ka-Fl-Sp, and the three-vowel system of Cv-Ok. These two languages, together with Coeur d'Alene and Moses-Columbian[11] form the Southern Interior subgroup of the branch.

The phonological inventory of Cv-Ok includes three distinctive vowels and a fourth, automatic variant of the other three, and thirty-nine or forty-one consonants, depending on the dialect—Northern Okanagan has ɣ̓ and ɣ corresponding to Southern Okanagan ẏ and y. I have also recorded a rare ḥ, which remains marginal.

9 Better known than the migrations of the Salishan people are the migrations of the Na-Dene people, with representatives in discontinuous territories: the Yukon and Alaska, Northern California, and the American Southwest.

10 The non-Interior Salish languages are grouped by Salishanists into four subgroups. Two of these consist of a single language: Bella Coola, spoken on the coast of British Columbia north of Vancouver Island, and Tillamook, now extint, but earlier spoken on the coast of Oregon. The other two subgroups are labeled Central Salish, and Tsamosan respectively. Ten languages comprise the Central Salish branch of the family (Comox, Pentlach, Sechelt, Squamish, Halkomelem, Straits, Klallam, Nooksack, Lushootseed, and Twana), and four language comprise the Tsamosan branch (Quinault, Lower Chehalis, Upper Chehalis, and Cowlitz).

11 Moses-Columbian shares more phonological features with Cv-Ok (the velar series and the several pharyngeals), while Coeur d'Alene is phonologically closer to Ka-Fl-Sp (palatal series and five vowels). These two languages seem to be equally distant from Cv-Ok.

Table 1: The phonological inventory of Cv- Ok

p̓	t’	c̓	ƛ̓	k̓		k̓ʷ	q̓	q̓ʷ	
p	t	c		k		kʷ	q	qʷ	ʔ
	s		ɬ	x		xʷ	x̌	x̌ʷ	h
m̓	n̓	r̓	l̓	(γ̓)	y̓	w̓	ʕ̓	ʕ̓ʷ	
m	n	r	l	(γ)	y	w	ʕ	ʕʷ	
					i	u			
					(ə)				
					a				

I use this order of the Cv-Ok alphabet: a c c̓ ə γ γ̓ h ḥ i k k̓ kʷ k̓ʷ l l̓ ɬ ƛ̓ m m̓ n n̓ o p p̓ q q̓ qʷ q̓ʷ r r̓ s t t’ u w w̓ x xʷ x̌ x̌ʷ y y̓ ʕ ʕ̓ ʕʷ ʕ̓ʷ ʔ.

Cv-Ok morphosyntax is polysynthetic, and, analogous to other languages, Cv-Ok words that are related may have a wide range of meanings. For example a Cv-Ok set of words based on the root √xt’, may translate as *take care, be pregnant, fool with, aim*, etc., as in these examples: txt’ntim *to take care of someone or to aim at something*; txt’t’iʔst *to become pregnant*; stxt’miʔst *to be pregnant*; nxt’iw̓sm *to join in to help*, or *to compartmentalize*; txxaʔt’mínm *to fool around with something*; xxát’wyaʔ *to be a joker*; xaʔt’mín *to play tricks on*; xt’uʔsús *to go full circle*; xat’lsmíst *to think little of oneself*; txt’ncutn *protector, caretaker*; txt’tmist and txt’mscut *to take care of oneself*; txt’iltm *to look after a child*; txt’xitms *to protect on behalf of someone*; txt’t’nuɬtm *to manage to take care of someone's things*; nxt’ɬq̓itm *to let go or shoot an arrow at the neck*; k̓ɬxt’xt’ax̌n *to aim to hit under the arm*; etc.

The meanings of these words (and others), all based on the root √xt’, are determined by the combinations of the root with the various derivational affixes that form them (as well as by their sentential and discourse context). The meanings of these words are far from transparent—they are not the predictable sum of all their morphs, and I will address this question in detail below (pp. 95-125). The polysynthetic nature of Cv-Ok makes it possible, indeed easy, for the language to form hundreds, if not thousands, of words based on a single root. The language has more than two thousand roots, most of these with the potential to form hundreds of lexical items, so that the language has tens of thousands of words, as a look at the appropriate evidence teaches. And, of course, Cv-Ok words, like the words of other languages, have various functions; denotative and connotative meanings; metaphorical extensions; and contextual interpretations.

Colville-Okanagan social organization

The terminology that encodes the various social relationships of the Okanagan, the traditional ones as well as some recent ones, is more elaborate than the corresponding

English one. While English makes use of bi-nomial (or greater) nomenclature[12] to refer to several kin members (e.g. brother-in-law, grandfather, great-grandfather, second cousin, etc.), the Cv-Ok have different monomial terms for such relationships as older female sibling (ɬkíkxaʔ), younger female sibling (ɬcəcʔúps), older male sibling (ɬqáqcaʔ), younger male sibling (ɬsísəncaʔ), and two dozen other kinship terms.[13]

A *nation* is called iʔ‿nək̓ʷcwílxʷtən,[14] a *community* is called iʔ‿nəqscwílx or iʔ‿nəqɬcwílx and a *family* is called iʔ‿snəqsílt. The terminology that refers to units larger than the (extended) family reveals a social organization that recognizes first iʔ‿ƛ̓ax̌əx̌ƛ̓x̌áp (the *elders*), whose counsel is sought at all group meetings, then the xaʔtús, (the extended family's *leader*), who directs the family in hunts and expeditions.

The ylmíxʷəm (the *chief*) is higher in the socio-political hierarchy. The ylmíxʷəm calls the meetings that the elders hold, as well as the assemblies attended by all members of the community. A separate term, based on the stem for chief, refers to the office of the chief, ylyaʔlmíxʷəm. Another term has plural reference (a regular plural formation), *chiefs*: ylylmíxʷəm. Yet another term refers to a *congregation of chiefs*, həɬylmíxʷəm, and, finally, another term refers to the *class of chiefs*, qaʔɬylmíxʷəm, and the nomenclature correlates with the current socio-political organization. A meeting of həɬylmíxʷəm constitutes a meeting of the chiefs of the Nation. The notion of ylmíxʷəm in all its forms, is parallel in function to the English notion of "president", as evidenced by its use in mythological narratives and historical accounts. The lexical root √yl of the word ylmíxʷəm is also found in the word ck̓əɬyál, which means *to protect*, paralleling the English word *president* which can be traced to the lexical root sede- (with the meaning *to sit*) in conjunction with the prefix pre- (with the meaning *before*). The Okanagan ylmíxʷəm is the protector, the English president is one who sits before others.

The səxʷk̓ɬxʷám, the equivalent of the *town crier*, goes from dwelling to dwelling to announce the various assemblies. These are held to discuss matters of concern and interest common to all members of the community: to organize a hunt, to discuss an expedition, to defend against enemies, to celebrate a feast, to relay news of death.

Within the community the ƛ̓aʔkʷílx (*Indian doctor*) is recognized as possessing special healing powers. Special rituals accompany the various celebrations of the community.

The Cv-Ok social organization is based on a hierarchical layering of increasing scope: individuals (the sqilxʷ) are members of a family (the snəqsílt), the family belongs to the nəqscwílx or nəqɬcwílx (the community), and the community is part of the nək̓ʷcwílxʷtən (the nation).

12 The use of two or more basic terms (words) to qualify a given relationship.

13 For details see Mattina and Jack 1992. For earlier accounts of kin terms and of the social organization of the Southern Okanagan, see Walters in Spier 1938. Several Cv-Ok kinship terms suggest relationships that aim to preserve and enhance the integrity and success of a family. Thus, for example, the term nq̓ʷíctən refers to the brother of a widow's husband, who, after the death of his brother, is expected to care for the wife (or wives) he left behind, as well as the children born from that union. The word sk̓ʷúk̓iʔ, which refers to an individual's father's sister, has the alternate pronunciation sk̓ʷúkʷiʔ, obviously an interpretation of the term as based on sk̓ʷuy *man's mother*, and reflexive of the social function of the referent.

14 I generally use the undertie to connect clitics with their head-words but I omit it from my interlinearizations.

Colville-Okanagan knowledge

The sum of all the Okanagan practices and beliefs constitutes Okanagan knowledge in the broadest sense. Not all the material, behavioral and cultural characteristics of the Okanagan have been documented—there is no Okanagan encyclopedia available—but the documents that have been compiled for several such demonstrate a complex social organization, a complex system of beliefs, and a sophisticated knowledge of nature.[15]

At the center of Okanagan cosmogony is the concept of Creator. The Cv-Ok term that translates "Creator" is k̓ʷl̓əncútən. The etymology of this word is transparent: the root is √k̓ʷl̓ *make, do*; the suffix –ncút is a reflexive morpheme; and the suffix –(t)n is an instrumental suffix. The literal English rendition of the word is *one who made oneself.*

Cultural norms are transmitted in different ways, and the telling of captíkʷɬ (*invaluable stories*) is one such.[16] These are the tenets and principles that guide Cv-Ok life: the inhabitants of the earth, human and animal, undifferentiated[17] when first created, were given specific characteristics and charges by the Creator. The most important such charge is to protect the world, and, more narrowly, the land on which the inhabitants were placed.[18]

Okanagan elder Harry Robinson (now deceased), in one of a series of interviews with ethnographer Wendy Wickwire, tape recorded in 1977 (copies deposited at the archives of the American Philosophical Society), so characterizes these captíkʷɬ (cəpcaptíkʷɬ in the plural):[19]

[Robinson] "Coyote. You might did not know this, this cəpcaptíkʷɬ, the first, you know cəpcaptíkʷɬ, that means, that means invaluable stories.

[Wickwire] Oh.

[Robinson] cəpcaptíkʷɬ, that's an Indian word.

15 In 1911 Charles Hill-Tout published his *Report on the Ethnology of the Okanák•ēn of British Columbia, an Interior Division of the Salish Stock*. In 1917 Franz Boas published a collection of the oral tradition of the Interior Salishan peoples, and in 1927-28 ethnographic accounts of the same peoples. In 1932 Verne Ray published an ethnographic account of the Nespelem and Sanpoil Okanagans of Washington State, and the following year he published a collection of the oral traditions of the same peoples. In 1933 Mourning Dove, herself an Okanagan, published a collection of the oral traditions of her people. In 1938 Leslie Spier published a collection of ethnographic essays on the Southern Okanagan. In 1979 Bouchard and Kennedy published an ethnogeography of the Roosevelt Lake region; in 1980 Turner, Bouchard, and Kennedy published an ethnobotany of the Okanagan. In 1985 I published in book form an edition of an important literary text by Peter J. Seymour, and in 1987 I published the dictionary of Cv-Ok I had been compiling since 1968. In the past two decades Wendy Wickwire has compiled and edited into three volumes the oral narratives of Harry Robinson, a sməlqmíx Okanagan. All these works are listed in the references. Five PhD and one EdD dissertations have been written on the language of the Okanagan.

16 For some details see my compilation and edition of *Dora Noyes DeSautel ɬaʔ kɬcaptíkʷɬ*. For my account of an important literary document, see *The Golden Woman.*

17 For John Bierhorst this ambiguity "defines the so-called myth age" (p. 12).

18 This is how John Bierhorst characterizes myths: "Myths … are inherited from the past. Viewed at a distance, myths create a luxuriant configuration that gradually changes from region to region. At close range, these same myths reflect the desires and fears of distinct peoples, granting them *trusteeship of the land* with the consent of unseen powers" (pp. 1-2, emphasis mine).

19 This is a verbatim transcription of the tape which opens abruptly. I do not make any emendations to the words of either Robinson or Wickwire.

[Wickwire] Improbable stories?

[Robinson] cəpcaptíkʷɬ, that's, that's, this one here that

[Wickwire] Oh, yeah.

[Robinson] cəpcaptíkʷɬ sənk̓líp, that's Coyote, sənk̓líp

[Wickwire] Right, oh, yeah.

[Robinson] Yeah, cəpcaptíkʷɬ sənk̓líp, that means invaluable stories Coyote.

[Wickwire] So does that mean that they're true stories, or not? Are they true stories?

Did they really happen?

[Robinson] That's invaluable stories, that's from way back that we can't guarantee if it's true stories or not. But it's the stories. The way I heard that stories

[Wickwire] yeah

[Robinson] is that I don't know if it's true

[Wickwire] ah ah

[Robinson] or may not. We cannot tell

[Wickwire] uh uh

[Robinson] that's too far back. Invaluable stories that's when they're animal instead of human. sənk̓líp at that time he's the leader and. See this one here cəpcaptíkʷɬ sənk̓líp are invaluable stories Coyote. That's what it is. And at this time...[20]

As Robinson implies, Coyote is the Okanagan culture hero. This character, also found in much of the mythology of the West, is what is commonly called the "trickster," the protagonist of a "cycle" (or set) of myths.[21]

Collectively, the cəpcaptíkʷɬ constitute the beliefs and the laws of the Okanagan, and their origin is ancient (cf. Robinson's explanation quoted above). The creator (k̓ʷl̓əncútən) put on earth the representatives of four groups of living things: the four-legged (kmúsxən), the flyers (a‿ct̓əxʷt̓əxʷtílx), the water-dwellers (la‿nixʷítkʷ), and the plants and roots (spəl̓l̓áɬq uɬ iʔ‿saʕx̌ʷíp). The first creatures to be formed were the st̓əlsqílxʷ, literally, those "sprung or torn" from each of these groups, each incomplete by itself, and united into a single being. The four-legged and the water-dwellers would provide sustenance, the flyers would provide the means to obtain the sustenance,[22] and the plants and roots would complete the sustenance of the st̓əlsqílxʷ. Thus we have interconnections between humans, animals, and the rest of the natural world, interconnections felt by modern day Cv-Ok.

The hunter who kills the deer, and the family members who share it, give ritual thanks

20 Harry Robinson spoke English with an accent, and Wickwire did not make out the word "invaluable." She transcribed it "imbellable" and added this footnote: "This is the English translation Harry was given for *chap-TEEK-whl*, stories from 'way back' during 'the time of the animal-people.' Once, when seeking an English translation for *chap-TEEK-whl*, Harry was told these stories are 'unbelievable.' Since that time, Harry has called them 'imbellable' stories" (Robinson 1989 p. 282; also footnotes in Robinson 1992 p. 240, and Robinson 2005 p. 36.

21 Other such tricksters are Raven, also typical of West Coast mythology, Spider, found in portions of the West and the Plains, and Hare and Rabbit in the cycles of the Midwest and East. All such trickster characters range "from the playful to the outrageous" (Bierhurst p. 12). Culture heroes can also be "transformers" because they can transform monsters and other creatures into harmless animals.

22 To elaborate a bit on the contribution of the flyers, perhaps not obvious, I should explain that the flyers offer their contribution in various ways, for example, they provide the feathers that guide the arrows to their targets (sk̓ʷaʔkʷúɬ), and the oil that waterproofs the fishing line. In each human activity, an acknowledgment of these interconnections is (or should be) made.

to the fallen animal that has sacrified its life for the survival of the people; the gatherers of the roots and berries, staples of the Okanagan, offer prayers to these fruits, and to the leaf or bud that serves as medicine. Special words designate all the elements of these interactions. Practices that might seem only rituals turn out to have ecological significance. For example, the Saskatoon or service berry bush, which carries the síyaʔ, a Cv-Ok staple, is beaten with a special stick after the harvest. The stick is called ksaʔṗústən, and it is not just an ordinary stick.[23] It turns out that knocking all the berries off the bush ensures a strong production in the following season.

The st̓əlsqílxʷ (the *original people*) were followed by the xatmaʔsqílxʷ (the *first generation*) of humans. All are sqílxʷ, *humans, Indians*. Animals and humans have equal rights on earth, and human individuals may have (some of) the characteristics of a certain animal. According to some elders, as predicted in the cəpcaptíkʷɬ, after contact the sqilxʷ became ʔawtmaʔsqílxʷ (the *generations that follow*). The make-up of this word suggests two etymologies or interpretations, one based on the lexical root √ʔawt *to follow*, and the other based on the complex form ʔawtús *opponent*, with these two resulting readings: "those who follow," and "those who are divided."[24]

Whatever the variants of the Christian views about good and evil, and who is good and who is evil, in a world with sinners and saints, Cv-Ok philosophy sees all individuals as being capable of doing good and bad things, beautiful and ugly, heroic and cowardly, rare and commonplace. The prototypical such creature, and the most important in Cv-Ok cosmogony, is Coyote, who is ridiculous on the one hand, and therefore not special, and on the other is endowed with special powers because he has the special responsibility of ridding the earth of man-eaters, symbolic of all dangerous and bad things.

The spirit quests are among the religion-based practices of the Cv-Ok. All adolescents must search for guidance in life by fasting and exposing themselves to the hardship of a solitary stay in the wilderness. Another religion-based practice is one's cleansing in the steam of their most sacred structure, the Sweat Lodge. Elaborate rituals accompany the arrangement and preparation of the rocks, including songs and prayers. The oral traditions of the Cv-Ok, known as the cəpcaptíkʷɬ, and which constitute the cosmogony of the Okanagan, are rich and extensive, and as old or older than the analogous Western (Christian) or Islamic cosmogonies.

I hope that the information about the cəpcaptíkʷɬ and the other pertinent Cv-Ok cultural traits that I have provided in this introduction will prove helpful in the reading of the texts.

In the next chapter I will provide the English translations of the texts because the translations are accessible to all readers, and they give readers a good sense of the artistic worth of the texts. I will put the texts in context, and explain the organization of this anthology.

23 Based on the same root √sṗ *to hit* two terms that refer to an ordinary stick are sṗústən and ksṗíkstən.

24 The elders suggest that the "division" is one of religious belief: some Okanagan have remained faithful to their religious beliefs, others have come to respect the Christian ones.

The Texts

This anthology comprises nineteen texts Pete Seymour narrated to me and I recorded between 1968 and 1974. It was I who prompted Pete to talk about himself, and his personal history, so "Autobiography," "Man's activities after the birth of a child," "Marriage customs," are my prompts. When I asked him to "tell me a story," Pete did some thinking, and then announced the topic and provided an informal title. For the reasons I now explain I changed some of these. What he called "The king with one boy" I retitled "The grateful dead version 1;" and what he called "The chief's family," I retitled "The grateful dead version 2." It is clear these are two versions of the same story, and I picked "grateful dead," the label given to type 505 in the Aarne-Thompson classification of tale types. When he had to "splice the story" as Pete would say, he would make an informal reference to it, so that, for example, "Coyote and his family" and "Coyote and his sons," refer to one and the same story, which I retitled "Coyote and Grizzly." All such changes can be inferred by comparing the "Index and chronology of Pete Seymour's narrations" with the titles that precede each narrative in the anthology. The recordings of these texts can be downloaded from http://www.colvilletribes.com/mattina.php.

Madeline DeSautel and I worked together to transcribe and translate the texts as I described in *The Golden Woman*[1] (p. 9): I played a stretch of tape, she repeated it, I wrote it, then she translated it into the English she normally spoke and I wrote that.

Here I want to celebrate Pete Seymour's tales and myths as literary productions, and not just specimens of Cv-Ok discourse. Though these are narratives told in Cv-Ok, I start with their English translations because I assume English is the language shared by my intended audiences. Were I to begin with the Cv-Ok texts, I would stand to turn away all Okanagan who are not familiar with Salish orthography (a large majority of them), and most other readers, who I do not expect to read or speak Cv-Ok, except, perhaps, the most dedicated Salish scholars. Therefore in this chapter I present, in translation, first the autobiographical material, then other ethnograpic material that serves as cultural context, and then the tales and the myths. In this way I intend to draw readers in, so that, once they have appreciated their literary worth, they will want to study the texts in the original provided later.

For this anthology I have decided to organize Pete's texts thematically, and not in chronological order. The texts divide into autobiographical and ethnographic accounts; tales of European origin; and Colville-Okanagan myths. I have grouped together as having ethnographic content nine texts; four texts are Pete's renditions of European fairy tales; and the remaining six are Colville-Okanagan mythological texts.

The ethnographic accounts are shorter than the others and range in duration from three to forty-two minutes, averaging seventeen minutes.[2] The topics that Pete dwells on most are farm-related accounts, and hunting and horse racing stories. The text titled "Racing horses" is about twenty minutes long, but is unfinished.[3] In contrast to these

1 Pete had narrated and I recorded a text with that title. The University of Arizona Press published our edition in 1985, and therefore I do not include it here.
2 I mark the time elapsed (in intervals of one minute) in the interlinearization.
3 I give more information in a later section.

shorter ethnographic texts, the remaining narratives (with the exception of "Black Pig," the earliest story I recorded, which is about ten minutes) are longer, and range from 27 to 81 minutes.

Four narratives comprise the collection's tales of European origin: the brief "Black Pig" (an adaptation of Cinderella); two versions, one unfinished, of "The grateful dead;" and "The Devil and the Black Face." This latter story lacks its opening lines—I turned the tape-recorder on some minutes after Pete had begun his story.

"How Coyote got his powers" (26:53) is the first text in a series of narratives about Coyote's efforts to rid the earth of man-eaters that make-up the "man-eater saga." Two other texts from this saga are included here, "Coyote and Whale;" and "Coyote and Grizzly." A fourth captíkʷɬ of the collection, "The two Goats," has also a man-eater element, but in a reversal of roles, it's Coyote who is the man-eater (but fails to defeat his opponents the Goat brothers). The man-eater narratives, in turn, are part of the myths called "captíkʷɬ," a complex of stories that feature the entire pantheon of Colville-Okanagan pre-human characters. "Lynx and the virgin" is one such text, with Coyote a minor character. Finally, Coyote does not figure in the sixth text, the sparkling "BlueJay and Wolf."

In the pages that follow I introduce each of the texts with some remarks I have deemed appropriate, and because the stories speak for themselves, I have kept the introductory notes, as well as the footnotes, concise. Then I provide the English translation of the text, and here I have endeavored to keep the flavor of Madeline DeSautel's diction.

Presented in this order, first the more mundane autobiographical and ethnographic accounts, then the acculturated tales of Western origin, and finally the myths, the texts should give readers some acquaintance with the author and with the life of the Colvilles. Pete's artistic gifts manifest themselves best in the fictional accounts.

I consider the texts of Western origin rich specimens that demonstrate the narrator's ability to address and reach his audience, western or not. Seymour is, in John Greenway's terms, a gleeman and maker who knows how and when to engage his audience with subtle and apt adaptations of the original material. Pete knows how to integrate these foreign stories into the Colville tradition.

Pete also knows how to regale his audience with the captíkʷɬ of his Colville tradition. Indian myths, it has been pointed out before, may seem alien, and often impenetrable and strange, and many have attempted to advance the explication of such texts with special orthographic conventions, hoping that these could reveal the structure of the stories and celebrate the power of the voice. Pete Seymour's texts need no versification, whether in translation or in the original Colville. And this leads me to another point.

As I have already reported in the "Preface," since the time I became convinced that Pete Seymour's narratives are exceptionally artful, I have searched the Colville landscape for confirmation of this fact: I searched for Colvilles acquainted with his narratives and found none who could vouch that he had the reputation of a good story teller. I have interviewed several of Pete Seymour's children (his oldest daughter Ada Holford more than the others) and I have interviewed several of his contemporaries—now all deceased, along with Pete—and I have had to conclude, not that he was not valued as a story teller, but that, in the community, he was little known or not known at all as a story teller. This is an indictment of the effects of white contact, with all its unfortunate consequences, however unintended. Pete Seymour learned these stories from his grandparents, but didn't get a chance to tell his grandchildren. The story I just told is sad indeed, but, fortunately, it doesn't end there.

In my search for evidence of his fellow Colvilles' appreciation of Pete's literary gifts, I have discovered (and continue to discover) signs of it in the unlikely person, among others, of one of Pete's grandchildren. Unlikely because Aaron Carden is of a generation that, until recently, I had judged as not particularly interested in traditional Colville literature. This is changing, and Aaron is not the only evidence I have of this revival of interest. Four or five years ago he asked me for transcripts and tapes of some of his grandfather's stories. We began a correspondence that has given me the extra incentive I needed to complete this anthology.

Autobiographical and ethnographic texts

Autobiography (42')

On July 21, 1969, I recorded three texts, and "Autobiography" is the third of these. As I often did, I announced the title of the narrative, and waited for Pete to start talking. On this occasion he hesitated, then said "Oh... Well, how... You mean just a history from ..." and I interjected "from birth on."

"When I was born?"

"Yeah!"

"Or after I was married?"

"No, all the time."

"I don't know if I can remember ... Oh well, I guess ... See, I was ... Oh, you already got it [the tape recorder going] ..."

"Yeah."

"You recording it now?"

"You don't want to?"

"No, but I was gonna tell you before you record."

"Ok."

I turned the tape recorder off, and can't remember even the gist of that conversation. When I resumed the recording Pete said "All right" and then shifted to Colville and said the words I have transcribed for this anthology, the translation of which I present here. Pete focuses on a few high points: his growing up with his grandparents and the awe in which he held his grandfather; his drive to marry and have a family; and his determination to be a self-reliant provider. His story tells us that his adult life has been that of a farmer and that he has mourned the loss of one of his children in its infancy.

> I'm going to tell a story, but it's not Coyote's legend, it's about my growing up, that's what I am going to tell about. I got my senses, I could think, [I'll start] from then. I cannot tell from the time I was born (5)[4] because a baby doesn't know what he does. What I did only from the time I got my senses.
>
> I got my senses, I don't know just how old I was, I hadn't gone to school yet, I must have been six when my uncle died, they call him Sharp Bones, he died. (10)

4 The numbers, in increments of five, match the line numbers in the Cv-Ok transcriptions beginning with "Autobiography."

And all that's left is my maternal grandfather and my paternal grandmother; that's who is living with my uncle. Their houses were side by side at lower bottom, right there. And my parents said to me, "You keep company with your grandparents. (15) You aren't able to do much, but you can keep company with them, stay with them." I said to them, "That's how I am going to get the best of you folks: my grandparents will tell me legends." Then I stayed with my grandparents.

And my uncle had two horses, work horses, medium sized. (20) And my grandmother and my grandfather had two milking cows, and they each had a calf, and they had three saddle horses. And my grandmother had a saddle horse, and my grandfather had a saddle horse, and they had one pack horse, that's the only way they can get around. At that time they didn't have cars, (25) they didn't have airplanes, or railroads, no. At that time there was only horses that they could travel with.

My grandparents pitied me. Morning came and my grandfather threw me out of bed, woke me up. I built the fire, and after I got done making fire I went fed the horses. (30) Sometimes I wanted to sleep more, I got lazy, and then they yelled at me. And it's just one room, and my bed is on one side, and theirs is on the other side. They yell at me with no results, and then he ties me around the wrists and drags the rope across to where he sleeps, and he ties it to his bed. (35) And when daylight comes he jerks the rope over and over. And if I had had any sense at all I could have untied it from my wrist and tied it to my bed. And then I wouldn't have had to wake up. That's how long ago the Indians trained their children to be early risers and bathers. (40) And they are smart and spry, they don't get old in a hurry. And my grandparents pitied me, that's why they woke me up early and then I had to bathe.

And I must have stayed there with them more than a year. And then my grandfather died. (45) He was blind and getting old, like they would say in English, he was close to one hundred years old, or maybe past. And they say that he had been blind for more than thirty years.[5] But he is spry, I guess he bathes often. (50) On Saturday my grandmother gave us... I mean my mother, she brought us our clothes, because it's my mother that washes them for us. She brings our clothes there. Then we bathe, we change our clothes.

(55) And whenever my paternal grandfather takes off his clothes, strips, his body... I made a mistake, I said paternal grandfather, it's maternal grandfather.[6] His body is nothing but scars, and I got puzzled. And I asked my grandfather, I said, "Gee, your body is nothing but scars; how is it that it's like that?" (60) He wouldn't tell me. My grandmother stopped me. She said to me, "Stop asking your grandfather about the scars." They are scars all right. I said, "They are fierce looking, that's why I have been puzzled. (65) I'd like to know." My grandmother said to me, "I will tell you, and then don't ask him any more."

"After he stopped growing and he was hunting, his game, a grizzly, got away from him. He had a friend, and the grizzly went in the brush. He said to his friend... (70) At that time they must have had a gun loader, not a bow and arrow, they already had gun loaders. He said to his friend, "I'll follow him in the brush.

5 Here Pete interjects " I guess you can shut that off ask you for..."

6 The narrative would be smoother if I edited out such parenthetical remarks, but they are part of the record. A literary edition of these translations may be called for at some later time.

And from outside the brush you listen for me, and I'll holler for you. (75) Don't get scared if you hear the grizzly." My grandfather was tall but not fat, not large. He must have great muscles, he's strong. He said, "Whenever I get hold of the bear tight, I'll holler for you. Then you come and kill him, you shoot it under the arm or stab it under the arm." (80) His partner tried to stop him, he said "No, no, I am scared, he's too fierce." He said "No." "He went into the brush and I stayed there.[7] And then I heard, I guess that's when they met. The bear was sure hollering. (85) I heard my partner holler for me, but no, I couldn't help it, he would kill the both of us. He's going to kill my partner."

His friend got scared, my grandfather's partner got scared out. (90) He ran back. They were fall hunting, lots of them. He ran all the way and got back to their camp. Some of the hunters were back in camp. He was all tired and chocked up because he ran all the way. (95) "What's the matter with you that you are so scared and tired? Where is your partner?"[8] He got to talking, he said, "He had gained a grizzly. He went after it in the brush, because the bear went in the brush. I tried to stop him, I said to him, 'Don't go in the brush, (100) he'll just kill you,' but no. He told me 'No. I'll go in the brush after him, and then we'll catch hold of one another. When I get hold of him I'll holler for you, then you'll come. (105) You get in the brush and stab him under the arm.' That's what he told me, and he went in the brush. And then the bear howled fierce. Then he hollered for me, and I got scared to help my partner, and then I ran back. I thought my partner'll get killed, (110) and there is no doubt he'll kill me too, he'll track me" [end of tape].

I am going to splice, like they say in my language, in the Indian language. The young hunter started running, the one that had gotten back. (115) "Take us where you left your partner." They went and they got to the swamp. He said, "That's where he went in the brush." They went in the brush, they saw him. My grandfather was sitting there, his body is like it's been butchered, his body is nothing but blood. (120) The bear tore him apart. They asked him, they said, "How are you?" He said "I'm feeling better."[9] They asked, "What happened to the bear?" He told them, "I don't know what happened, because I passed out." (125) He said, "When I got hold of the grizzly's ears, when I overtook him, I got hold of his ears, and I hollered for my partner. I kept yelling for him. It was a little too long, and my arms gave out. The grizzly was strong. The grizzly turned his face, and he bit me in the arm, (130) and I lost strength in my arm. Then he bit my other arm; that killed the strength of my other arm. Both my arms are dead-like. That's the last I know." (135) He said, "Then I came to. You just saw what happened to my body." He said, "And the grizzly is gone."

They rushed and they tracked him, because there is blood, there is lots of blood. (140) Not far, he never got out of the brush, they overtook the grizzly. He was lying there dead too.

That's what my grandmother told me. Because I was always asking questions the time I was with them. When he changes his clothes his body is nothing but scars. (145) And then I asked my grandfather, I said. "What happened to your body that's it's all scars?" He never told me, he hid it from me. And then my grandmother

7 Spoken as the partner.

8 It's Pete's grandmother talking.

9 Literally "my heart has fallen in place."

stopped me. She said to me, "Stop asking your grandfather, he is ashamed of it, (150) that's why he didn't tell you." I said "And why is he ashamed of it, what happened?" "He was still growing up when the bear tore him to pieces, he was fought by the grizzly. That's why he is ashamed to tell about it. (155) And he told me secretely." I said, "Oh, now I'll leave him alone." I stayed with them longer than a year, maybe a year and a half, and then my grandfather died of old age. Maybe his age was past one hundred. (160) His hair was white; at first, gray hair, then it turned yellow when he died.

And my grandmother had two daughters left. My mother is the older and my aunt is the younger. I guess she likes the youngest one better. Then she changed country to Inchelium; (165) my aunt was in Inchelium. She had quite a big family, and we were here at the Kettle River. We were here, we are Kettle River people. I got my senses then, and I went to school.

Oh, I took a shortcut, I forgot. (170) My oldest brother, they call him Eneas, he came downriver. He said to my parents, "I'm leaving you. I am going to make a ranch of my own at Inchelium." That's before they surveyed the land. (175) "I am going to look for some land for me. When the surveyors come along, that will be my allotment." And they already had a child, a boy, and he's already able to sit around. And then my brother asked me, (180) he said to me, "It's better you come with me for my company; your little nephew might get lonesome if he's alone." And then we came downriver. We came as far as Inchelium, we got here, we went downriver, they call it "little lump in the woods," (185) there is a house there. Then we went up to a creek, they call it "Cut Something." That's the end of the places where people are, "Cut Something."

Smoke and his brother máʕ̓ʷtət picked that for their home place, and it's not fenced. My brother bought the rights from them. And my brother started fencing it; (190) and he started to plow it, and built a house, a barn. I don't know how many years, then my nephew grew up, the first one; then he went to school, and the school is far from there. They call it "Rogers Bar." (195) And we weren't able to go to school that far to go back and forth. Not from sənx̌ʷúc̓əc̓tən, because it's far. Then we went back, my nephew went back with me too, they call it, my parents' country, "Little Summit." That's the little summit that goes from səntqəlɬxəwíltən, (200) and from here it's the Kettle River. It goes up to the summit, and then it's level land, a valley. That's why they call it "Little Summit." From there we go to school. Maybe the distance is five miles. (205) And there is a road, a wagon road; and we always get to school on time. School ended and then we went back to his parents, I went back with him. Then we stay with them all summer.

At that time there were threshing machines that go by horse power, (210) they say in English "horse power." And the feeder must have a cutter. And with my nephew he and I cut the bundles. When we were small a box went with us, an apple box. (215) They put it under our feet, and we stand on it. Then we can reach the bundles. And then my older brother, next to the oldest, got married. Then he left his folks, and he got a ranch of his own. And he has a house, and everything.

(220) Then my folks asked me back. They said to me, "Come back to take care of us. The one who takes care of us left us, he got married, he's got a home." That's when I got back home to my parents, (225) and then I continued from there

planting crops, harvesting them in the fall.

Then I came of age, and I said to my parents, "I want to get a woman." They said to me, they laughed at me, they said to me, "You poor pitiful thing. It takes a good smart man to get a woman nowadays, (230) smart in work; and you are good for nothing, you are lazy, you are pitiful. It takes a lot of money to keep a woman nowadays." I said to them "No, I want to, I am of age. Like they say in Indian about horses, (235) in the spring, when he eats well in the winter, in the spring he itches in the back. Then he runs around, and he wants the old hair off. And if that's what I am going to do, I'll get you embarrassed if I start running around and bother people (240) because I want a wife. That's why I told you it's better I don't do that, and get a woman. And from then on I'll get back to work again." My parents said to me, "Ok, if that's how you feel. (245) But we are going to tell you one thing, we are very old, and we cannot feed your wife or when you get them, children. We are not able; when you get children you have to feed them, you and your wife will have to take care of them." I told them "I wasn't going to depend on you, that's why I will leave the country." (250) That's why I moved plum to Nespelem and that's where I settled down.

I rented a place from Antoine, it's a big place, but that ranch deceived me. The good soil is [only] right on top of the ground. I got done putting the crops in, and I fenced it. (255) I was digging post holes, and that's when I found out this land is no good. It's just good to look at. Then I harvested, but no. At that time we had a wrapper machine to cut the grain to tie bundles. The hay I harvested was one hundred and six acres, (260) and the hay I got was about eighty tons that I stacked. And there was a big garden of small stuff, potatoes, corn, beans. And I thought I could sell some of that, and get money from that. (265) And we had milk cows, and we could milk them and sell the cream. And at that time cream wasn't worth much, cream was maybe ten cents a pound, and at that time there was no delivery. As they say in White people's language there is no truck or anything. (270) It's only with horses that they deliver food and things, sacks, like they say in English "freight." And that's why it's so high priced, and this grain has got no price. It's far, far that they have a mill, across the Columbia River, (275) they call it Davenport. And when you haul wheat it's two or three days to get back, and that's why there is no price for anything in Nespelem.

And I started to work for a white man next door on the threshing machine; I worked there six weeks. (280) It's horses that pull it, I think sixteen horses, that's what pulls the thresher. And that white man has lots of horses. Look, sixteen for the thresher, and nine colts, all mules. (285) And all the implements, the plow, all the tools for planting. He takes care of all that, and then he has cows, and also milk cows for milk. And that white man said to me: (290) "You are a smart Indian, you are a good worker, and you are handy. All I got to do is tell you, and you'll do the rest. I don't have to rush you, or to tell you, and you'll work. That's why I feel sorry for you, and I'm telling you. (295) Look, you see all my implements, my horses, everything? I borrowed [for] everything. It's five years since I rented the place, and every year I lose one thousand dollars. Then I borrow money again, and I plant a garden again. (300) And when I get done harvesting, and get done selling it, then I get behind one thousand again." He said "And now it's five years and this is the last, and I am five thousand behind. And I borrowed [for] everything: (305) I borrowed for my implements, my horses, everything. And it's just my wife and my children, just what we have on our backs. The bank will drive us out, they will sell everything we have. (310) And that's why I am telling you, you are smart in working, you'll go just like me. It's better that before it's too late you get away from here. This place fooled my eyes; I think you must have done the same." (315) I said, "Fall is coming. I sold the wheat I harvested, only half dollar for a bushel; and I couldn't sell the hay; and the potatoes, the beans, the corn. (320) I hired a helper to dig potatoes, and he threshed the beans for me, and he shucked the corn. And when I sold the potatoes the price was just six bits a sack, and corn twenty five cents a sack, (325) and the beans two and a half a hundred pounds. I broke even, I sold everything, I broke even with all I owed."

I moved back from there, and I settled in Inchelium. That's where my in-laws are, and I wintered there. (330) Spring came and I got lonesome for the country, I went to see my folks. I had a garden there, and I had turned it over to my folks. That's their land, their allotment; (335) and as for my allotment, I gave that to my brother the oldest one. I said to him, "You work it. You cut it and thresh it, and we'll share in half." When I got back my brother said to me: (340) "All your crop is loose in the granary." I said, "And didn't you take your half?" "I already took it, it's just your half I put there loose." I said, "I guess it must have turned out good." (345) He told me "Yes, 35 bushels an acre." I said "Thanks." That's how I pulled through the winter. I sold it and kept only enough for feed for the winter. I had about forty heads, cows and horses.

(350) Then we moved to sənx̌ʷúc̓əc̓tən. And it's a good many years that my brother has been renting his place, and it's not even fenced, and the posts are rotten, and the barn has got no more stalls or feed places. I fixed it all up and put in a crop, I fenced it. (355) And I thought I was going to stay there forever, stay there in that country. And we had a baby and then it got sick and we took him to Hunters. It's far, across the river; there is a doctor there. He doctored him, and we brought him home. (360) The baby never went to sleep, and towards morning he died. And that's why I hate that place. It's too far from the doctor, and if we had been closer, he wouldn't have died. (365) I have eleven children, and that's the only one that's dead. There is ten left, I still got them yet. And from my oldest daughter I have about six great-grandchildren.

And my parents asked me, they said to me, "It's better that you come home. (370) And why is it that you told us, when the rest of your sisters and brothers get married and when we cried, when we confessed, you petted me and you told me, 'I will take care of you,' and then you left us? It's best that you come back home, and take care of us." (375) I said, "Yes, that's what I told you." I said, "And what is it that you told me? You told me you are too old, for you to feed my wife, or if I get kids, and that's why I went away. And so I went far, and there is no two things about it. (380) I have to work to take care of my children, to feed them and my wife. Stop talking to me like that, that's what we agreed." Then they stopped talking to me like that.

And I have eleven brothers and sisters, (385) and with me there is twelve of us. Then my parents died, and then my sisters and brothers died too. I am the only one left of twelve. And my wife died too. (390) And if it hadn't been for my oldest daughter, they stopped me there,[10] and now I'm staying with them, I'm there yet. That finishes it.

Harvesting (29')

This text is unfinished. If we recorded a sequel I have lost it. What we have of this text continues the story of Pete as a farmer. Pete titled it "Harvesting." He starts with the disastrous flood of 1890, then tells us his father was a packer, and finally gets to the topic of his title. Unfortunately we don't have the rest of the story.

I'll tell a story about myself. I already had my senses, feelings. I was looking for a horse, they call the place, in English they call it Bossborg. And I saw both sides of the river, the Kettle River, the marks of the high water, there are marks on both sides [shores]. There is a mark past the road on this side, and below.

I got back and I asked my folks. I asked, "What is that [mark], the water, is it when there is lots of water, too much water that the water leaves marks?" They told me, "Yes." They said, "It was in 1890 (as they say in English) that it snowed four feet in a week before it stopped. My father[11] went out and measured the snow, an even four feet. When it thawed at spring time, then the water rolled up; and many people on the ridge, their dwellings, their gardens, their barns, they all floated down. When the snow went away, and when summer came, the water went back down, and there is only sand, white sand, and then their gardens didn't grow any crop. Only corn grew." (Oh, I guess I'll take a five now.)

That's the time when there was lots of snow,[12] that's what I was saying, the Columbia River came up over the bank. That time the people lost their stock. All the people had a few head of animals. At that time they didn't have plows, neither two-pointed nor three-pointed, only the walk behind type. And what they cut with, they call it "bundling scythe," and the scythe for hay. The bundling scythe is the kind that bundles. And they thresh what's bundled, the wheat or the oats. They drive the horses in the corral, the horses go around, they clean the grain.[13] And that's what they trade for groceries at the flour mill, at Kettle Falls—no, at Meyers Falls.

There are falls, there are falls from the Colville River, and that's where they made a flour mill, and it's the water that runs the mill. At that time there was no price for wheat or oats,[14] they only traded for flour the wheat that they had threshed by hand.[15] Oats is only for feeding the stock. That's all what they

10 "They hosted me."

11 Pete's paternal grandfather.

12 Pete restarts his narrative by reminding us that it refers to the 1890 flood.

13 A practice similar to that witnessed by me in Sicily in my childhood. The harvest is collected in a circle 30 or so feet in diameter. Standing in the middle, the farmer directs a horse on a leash to go in circles over the grain, causing the kernels to detach from the sheafs. Then the kernels are separated from the stomped-on material by lifting this material three or four feet in the air with a pitch fork. The breeze carries the chaff to a side, where it settles in graceful dunes. The heavier wheat does not shift its position and, eventually quite clean of chaff, is ready to be shoveled into sacks and transported to the flour mill.

14 The grain was traded for flour, not sold.

15 Apparently only the working stock were fed grain, and the others were left in the open range.

feed stock with, their saddle horses. Because there weren't wagon roads for wagons. It's only work horse or milking cow [trails], because there wasn't much snow, and they didn't feed the stock. The horses pull through winter, they don't die.

But that time it snowed lots. And my father must have had more than 300 horses, some good ones, and a stallion race horse, and one work horse, as they call it in English, a Persian, dappled grey, a big work horse. The horses went to nothing.

The snow was going to crust. He had a working man, they called him spapuʔúl, he said to him... My eldest brother, twenty years older than I, was already getting awareness and he remembers that.[16] He went with them at that time.

Maybe a mile from our house up the hill there was a flat area and a swamp. And my father said, "We'll go up there. There might be where the horses are snowed in; maybe we'll find them there." He took the stallion and the work horse, big and fat, and the race horse followed. My father and his working man put snowshoes on. My brother was small, but already smart, and he ran on the snow crust. They went and where they went is wide open. They got close. The work horse and the stallion's bodies are covered in sweat, getting tired.

He said to his working man, "You go ahead with your race horse, the leading horse is getting tired." He stepped out of the way and the race horse went ahead again. [There was] one place the race horse could only jump, and it got stuck in the snow, and couldn't move, there was so much snow. The big stallion continued to lead. They got there, my, the horses are pitiful. My, the bushes, the big poplars and the cottonwoods, and the wire bushes, they are big around, and up to way up in the tree they didn't have any bark because the horses got so hungry they chewed the bark. And as soon as a colt dies the mothers eat their tails, their manes. There is nothing but bones lying there. It's only the oldest horses that are alive, and they were coming to an end.

My father picked 25 mares, that's what he picked, and four geldings, maybe three years old, or four years old (they make saddle horses out of them), and one mule, and that made it 30 head he pulled out of there. They drove them out because they already had cleared a good road, and they ran down the hill. They went and got home.

And my father also had cattle, a fair number of cows, corraled or under the shed. He drove the cows out and he drove in his mares. And he tied up the geldings in the barn. The mule was right in with the mares. He loaded the hay, hooked up the team to the sleigh, loaded it on the hay rack, and he filled it with hay and put it down. He said to the horses, "You have had too hard a time with hunger. Now you have good things to eat, you are going to hoard food." It was late when he finished putting it down.

In the morning he went to the barn. All the animals he had fed, his mares, they were all lying on the ground [dead]. It's only the mule that is alive. But those that were standing in the barn, they were alive.

My folks had a barn, and my father had hay for the winter. And my mother, she is smart at cooking, and they had a bed there, an overnighter for

16 Pete is saying that the facts are confirmed by his oldest brother's eye witness accounts.

white people, and at that time they had one overnighter. (125) The next day he said to my dad... It's my father who said to the white man, "What happened to my horses that they are dead, gone, twenty five of them, all mares?" He said to him, he asked him, (130) he said, "Do you always feed them?" He said "No, I just got them down yesterday. They have been snowed in up there." He said to him, "Well, you just murdered them. They were snowed in and they hadn't eaten for many days (135) and their stomachs are all tied up. Then you fed them lots suddenly and their stomachs busted inside. And that's why they died." My father said, "What about the mule, he was among them and he didn't die." He said, "Yes, they say the mule has a lot of sense. (140) He thinks, and when he ate he ate just so much. He felt it was going to harm him and he quit. That's why it didn't harm him. But the horse got no sense. He eats and eats, and his stomach busts, and he dies." (145) He said, "And why is it that the horses in the barn, the four year olds, the four [year olds] didn't die?" He asked, "Could they be lead when you put them inside?" He said "No, I just caught them and pushed them in and tied them." He said "Yes, because they pulled back, they are not broken in to lead. (150) How could they eat, they kept pulling back and never got to eat until daylight. That's why they didn't die." Then my father believed, it's so.

Everybody at that time lost horses because at that time they didn't have balers (155) or horse drawn mowers. [They work] only by hand, [with] a scythe. And what they tie with, what they call a grain cutter with prongs. Now there are mower machines for hay. They cut, it falls there, and it's already baled. (160) Same with dry grain. They call this, I don't know in Indian what "combine" is. They combine it, they cut it. It falls the other way, and it's already tied or sewn. At that time, a long time ago the Indians [worked] only by hand, (165) and they call it grain cutter with prongs, that's their hand cutter. Long ago, when my father and mother got married, my grandfather had only one child, my father, and he fed his horses, anything, cows. Because at that time there were no wagon roads or railroads.

(170) Like I said, there was only one store at Marcus [at the shore]. They call it Open Hammer. My father worked there, packing. Thirty of his pack horses. He goes across the line, (175) they call it above the rails to Port [Fort] Hope. It's from there that they pull their groceries and merchandise out of the water from across. At that time there was no border. My father packed it and took it to Marcus. Other times he goes from there to, (180) they call in Indian púłən, that's Portland. He packs from there and he comes, and it takes him many days to get back. And that's my father's job, packing. All my father is is a gardener with my grandmother. And my mother lives with them and they farm hay.

(185) Like I said, they don't have hay mowers pulled by horses, only by hand. In the morning they walk, my grandfather, and my grandmother, and my mother. My grandfather cuts with a hand grain mower (190) for the dry [grain] to be tied. And my grandmother is smart at tying grain. It's not with rope that it's tied, but with hay. She twists it, and then she ties the bundle. And my mother is the one that stands them up. (195) My grandfather gets done cutting, and my grandmother gets done tying right behind him, and my mother gets done standing them up. Then they start hauling bundles, stacking them. They stack, and they get done stacking the hay. (200) In the fall it snows and my father gets back from packing.

He packs things from here, from the store, from Marcus, they call it "Open Hammer" or "Beard." From Portland he turns around, that's what they call in English "Portland" and in Indian "púłən." From here he goes up the Kettle River, he goes back across the line, over there to the big water. They call the place "Port Hope." From there they pack, they bring the groceries across on the boat. They call him "Beard." They unload his groceries and my father packs them, and then he brings them. He had about thirty horses and one mule; and he isn't the only one [packing]. He had packers, he had hired two, they are his hired hands, the packers. And he has a cook, and he is just the boss.

They they got snowed in, it's winter, and my father quits working [packing], because at that time they don't plow the roads. Because at that time there are only trails for horses. They didn't have wagon roads, they didn't have wagons at that time, that's how it was. Now there are wagon roads and railroads and airplanes. Horse packing is all gone now.

When I was born the only way Indians travel is on horses. Now that's when we got white people, and lot of sense. Then they got cutting machinery for horses, machinery to cut, and machinery to bundle. They also got hay mowers, and they got threshers.

And when I first worked I got paid two bits a day, maybe ten hours. I was on foot when I was driving the team to stack—I can't say "derrick fork" in Indian. And I thought that what I earned is a lot. The older ones get paid one dollar. At that time everything was cheap, food, shoes, clothes; and we sure had a good time. But now we have high wages and you only work eight hours. 15 or 20 [dollars] is the lowest you can pay. Now tobacco is 37 cents a package. And at that time, when I was working for a quarter, it was ten packages for one dollar. At that time we were satisfied, no matter how small our pay for work was. Now wages are very high and those who are working never come to the top of the water,[17] especially those with lots of children.

Long ago they got done haying, they got done stacking the hay, and then in the late fall they bale it with horses. That's when I worked driving the team to bale hay. Christmas is when we finish. They also didn't have threshing machines. They thresh in the fall when they get done cutting. And like I said, when they got horse-powered balers then they get done with the baling.

Racing horses (20')

This text is also unfinished. Pete told me more about his horse racing, but I must not have recorded the rest of the story. He told me of his talking with his wife before a race (I can find no written record that confirms my memory), and telling her that he had to sleep alone as long as he was in the races. And the story went that Lena laughed at him and told him she wouldn't miss him—a remark not atypical of Pete's self-effacing style. But he can also give himself credit when he deserves it, and he did deserve it for jockeying, as we hear in this text. Starting from the lessons his older brother Eneas gave him, the story continues with a shaky start as a jockey, and concludes with his success,

17 The metaphors are similar in the two languages, "keep one's head above water," and "one['s boat] comes to the top of the water."

not only at racing, but also at always running an honest race.

I got my senses. My oldest brother, they call him Eneas, he pitied me. Like they say in Indian, he trained me in riding.

(5) As you know youngsters like to ride horseback, and I didn't know how to ride. We got the horses corralled with another older brother of mine, his name is Peter Pichette, and the oldest one is my close older brother. The other one is, as they say in English, my "first cousin," (10) and in Indian also "qick." They put the horses in the corral and they roped a colt. And I had just come to my senses, and I remember. But I didn't know how to ride horses. My brother Eneas put me on the horse, on the colt, (15) and my other brother is holding it. And then they turned me loose. Then the colt would just buck, and I'd fall off. Sometimes I'd get hurt, and I'd cry. My older brother said to me, "Don't cry. (20) If you cry I'll whip you. Why is it, you'd like to ride and you don't get hurt, and still you cry." And I am dead scared of my brother the oldest one because it's strong when he whips me. (25) And then I ride again, he puts me back on. He'll just buck a couple of times, and I fall off again. And there is no saddle and no strap, the only hold I have is the mane. I'd fall off maybe ten times in one day. (30) Then I got used to it, got smarter at riding.

Then he fixed a bed to train horses; as they say in Indian, they train horses for races, and they train there. Then he finished the bed to train horses, (35) and then he put me on one. And there were maybe two or three who were trained to ride, boys like me. Then we run, we train. From where we jump to start my friends are gone; just me, my horse trots for a while before it starts to gallop, (40) and my friends are gone. Then my horse starts to run, and they beat me. Maybe twice, then I got used to it, and then I beat them.

At that time we gathered a lot. (45) When the grass starts to sprout, the horses get done shedding hair, they turn sleek, then they race here at Inchelium for one week. The Indians gather there and they race there until dark. I ride all day long, and when that finishes, then [they go] to Meteor, (50) and they gather there another week. There is where I rode [raced] the first time.

My brother got horse whips, two horse whips. He gave me one, and he kept the other. I said to him, "What are you going to do with the other one? (55) I don't want you to whip my horse, we are up to date now." (It used to be the old timers' custom to whip each other's horses.) He said to me, "No, it's true that now we don't whip one another's horse; I am keeping the other whip for you. If you pull the reins on the horse and get beat, if you cheat, (60) then I will whip you with the whip. That's why I kept it, and I gave you one. That's for you to whip the horse, for your race horse." (65) He said to me, "That's why I told you, I taught you, that if you are smart, your friends will hire you [to ride]. If you ride for someone who has horses, race horses, it's because you are good. And if you don't cheat you'll have lots of friends, everybody will be your friend. (70) But if you cheat and pull the reins, nobody will be your friend, even we who are your brothers, or your parents, nobody will bet on you." I said "Ok," and I never did pull the reins, and I always came ahead. I am good at jockeying.

(75) And the white man who owns a store in Meteor, they call him Coleman, and Pete Noyes, a half-breed, they are against one another. They argue and then they

race, they ask [challenge] one another to race. (80) I got to be friends with the white man Coleman, and he said to me, "Come jockey for me." And then I rode, and I won. As soon as we run, they'll have an argument Pete Noyes and Coleman. (85) They'll challenge one another, they'd say, "Let's exchange horses. You take the one that got beat and I the one that won, and we'll race again," he [Pete Noyes] won't give up [arguing]. Pete Noyes said to Coleman, "Ok," and they make bets again. (90) Then Coleman put me on his horse and I won again, because I got used to horses, I got used to running races. They'll do that until the 4th of July. That's when they gather here at Inchelium.

(95) For six days they race and they celebrate, lots of people, from Canada, from Idaho, from Montana, lots of tribes. They gather there, lots of people. Every day they have races. We have an older brother, as they say in English our "cousin," (100) and in Indian our "qick," from Republic, and he's an important person, a boss, they call him Baptiste Tonasket. He bought maybe four race horses, white people's race horses, (105) and then he came to the Indians, came to Inchelium. And he never won. His horses are good looking, he paid big money for one. And my brother asked his friend, he said, "What is the matter with your horses? (110) They are good looking, and you paid a good price for them, and you are a good trainer, and you haven't won yet." Tonasket said, "That's true, I am puzzled by it too. Why is it that I don't win? I give good training to my horses, (115) and I haven't won." My brother said to him, "Have you changed your jockey?" He said, "No," he said, "I am not acqainted with the people, I only know the white man I brought, my jockey, he's the one that rides for me all the time." (120) My brother said to him, "It's best you change him; then you'll find out what the matter is. Maybe your jockey is cheating you." He said, "Well, I don't know who to hire, who to change." He said, "And who?" and he said, "Our partner, my little brother. (125) He should be jockeying for you." He said, "I'm not acquainted with our young brother; it's only you I know. Ask him." Then my brother came to me, he said, "Well, (130) would you ride for our friend in the race, in the quarter mile?" (Quarter of a mile and in English that's 400 yards.) I said, "If that's what you want." So I rode, they put me on the horse. (135) It was a chestnut horse for short distances. He is sure a good looking horse, no wonder he's a race horse.

And I always lope it [a horse] around, and I find out what strength he has, or if he is stiff necked, or if he can stand a whipping. And I loped him around. (140) And a white man got side by side with me, and he engaged me. He said to me, "Thirty five if you hold him back, that's what I'll pay you." I wasn't acquainted with the white man, and I just laughed at him. We ran. (145) I held him back,[18] and we ran to the finish [and won]. I never whipped my horse. My brother put three dollars in my hand. He said to me, "I thank you for riding the horse." And I don't know how much he won, what he bet. (150) And, look, if I had pulled the reins my pay would have been 35. And I didn't pull the reins, I won the race, and I only got three dollars from the one that owns the horse. But from my friends (and everybody is my friend), (155) when I ride they bet on me. And they bet whatever, and when I win they put [money] in my hand, one puts half, or one dollar, from one who bets lots ten; and from one race I won more than one

18 "I didn't have to push him."

hundred. That's from what my friends gave me. That's what happened to me, and what my brother told me is true: If I am honest I'll have lots of friends; but if I am crooked I won't have any friends.

Then a man came to me, they call him Chaps, white man, must be a cowboy, he always wears chaps and that's why they call him Chaps. He's got an Indian wife. My friend came to me, and he said to me: "I am going to tell you this, my partner: If you ride for me, I am going to challenge a race at the race track.[19] If you ride for me." I turned him down, I said to him, "Why did you say 'you are my partner?' Are you making fun of me?" He said to me, "What makes you think that, that you say that to me?" I said, "Well, you have three sons, is that right?" He said "Yes," and I said, I named them. I said to him, "And they are smarter than I at riding and then it's me you hire to ride for you?" He said to me, "Yes, it's true." He said to me, "The boys you named are only in it for the money; they are not for their relatives. Even if I am their father, they'll pull the reins on my horse." [End of tape.]

A hunting trip (34')

This text tells of a hunting episode in Pete's long life as a hunter. Pete and his brother are good hunters, but the same cannot be said of the other members of the party—one goes without snowshoes and can't shoot, another is too fat to move around with the agility required by the circumstances. What game is collected has all been Pete's doing.

When I used to live at sənx̌ʷúc̓əc̓tən, there was snow on the ground, as they say in Indian, it was winter, and there was lots of snow. All at once some friends came to me, my oldest brother and Cricket [Idaho Fry]. And they said to me, "Let's go hunting." I told them, "You got me on surprise and I have nothing ready. Give me this one day to get ready. I'll go to town, get me some groceries, and then we'll go. I go to the store, I get some grub, and I'll have everything ready."

Night came, daylight came, then we started to move. Ah,[20] Cricket said to us, "I'd like to go with you, but I haven't got a gun." I said to Cricket: "I have two guns and lots of cartridges, pick one." One gun they call Winchester in English; and the other gun they call Marlin in English. He said to me, "I'll take the Winchester." I said "Ok." My belt is full of cartridges, my hunting knife. And I took the other gun, the Marlin.

We went up in the mountains. We went and stopped at "Push Pack." It got daylight. We got done eating. And my brother knows the country, it's his cache. He said to us, "Just after you cross, there are deer all over. There are gulches, and that's where we'll hunt." And my brother and I had snowshoes, but our friend Cricket didn't have snowshoes.

We crossed the little creek, and then my brother told us where to go. He said, "We'll hunt this gulch." There is a low place, the head of the gulch; that's where to sit and watch, that's the deer's trail. They go down to another gulch,

19 Not clear. Probably "I am going to bet on you to win."
20 The interjection signals that Pete had failed to mention something. Here he backtracks.

or to [Wilmont Creek].[21] They'll go down there. I said to my brother, "You go sit and watch" (as they say in Indian), "you be the one to sit and watch. We'll do the driving." He told us "Ok," and he went.

And I said to Cricket, "You haven't got showshoes. I have showshoes and I'll go the lower route. There is no crust on the snow [there]. But there is a crust in the upper place, and you won't break through the snow." He went. I waited for him a little while, then I went.

I came in sight; where we were headed was open country. I heard our partner's shot. I came in sight to where I was going. He was shooting around, shooting with his gun pointed up. And I saw the deer, a whole bunch, running. He was shooting, and I got disgusted. I turned away to where he was supposed to go, that's where I went. There I saw tracks. The deer had scattered, seven had gone towards the side hill. They ran on the side hill. I started to run after them, I overtook them. I killed two. That's enough. Then I came back, I came back and I got back after dark.

My partners were back at camp, and they started telling stories. My brother said, "The deer went ahead of me. When I got back they are already gone, and I saw nothing." Cricket said, he started his story, he said, "I used every one of my shells, I am embarrassed [to say]. I shot and shot and ran out of ammunition. I never hit one, and they're gone. I guess my gun must be no good." And I had been watching him. He was shooting at the sky, his gun pointed upward.[22] He must have had the buck fever, as they say in English. We went to bed, daylight came.

Oh, I forgot, in the evening two others overtook us. sqəmqmmín and his distant son, that was my brother Eneas's date.[23] And they followed us hunting. Little ways from there they made a fire, and we said to them, "What's the matter, there is a good fireplace here! We got the snow cleared away, heck, this is good. We should eat all together here." No, we got our lunch. They spread a tablecloth, and they put a lard bucket on it. It was nothing but a little sandwich. Like they say in English, sandwiches, that was their lunch. And my brother said to them... sqəmqmmín said "We never drink coffee. But do you have warm water?" My brother told him, "We have lots of warm water." He said "We just drink Postum." They made coffee with Postum. It got daylight and they ran out of grub. We ate with them. They drank the coffee. Daylight came and we went hunting.

We came in sight of the place where the deer winter. It's a big pocket, a big place. My brother told us, because he is the guide, "We are going to scatter. And who is going to be, like they say in Indian, those that sit up and watch to where the deer are going, [who is going to] go to sit and watch?" I said to my brother, "You go. You know the country well. We'll drive the deer to you." He said to us, "I and my partner sqəmqmmín, the two of us will go set up watch. You and your friend will drive them. Then you will split up. Wait for us because it will take us a little while for us to go, for us to get in the lead. Then you go, and we will get the deer, the ones you drive." I said "Ok."

21 Is this an incidental remark?
22 An exaggeration. See 169-177.
23 Hunting companion.

We were there a while, and I said to my partner, "It's been long enough, even if they were crawling, they'd be there by now. Now we'll part." I told him, "You have no snowshoes. You go on the open side hill, you'll be between, you go [there]. And I'll go in the center. [There] the snow doesn't have a crust, and I have snowshoes." And I said, "If any of us shoots, do you know what to do?" He said, "Yes," he said, "I stop and then I look for it." I said "No," I said, "Look, [walking on] snow makes lots of noise. Look for the closest tree. Go there and stand next to it." And I said, "And if the deer comes towards you he won't see you, it'll get right up to you before it sees you. But if you stand in the open as soon as he comes in sight he'll see you and run the other way. And you won't [get to] shoot." "Ok." Then we parted.

I went, and I was in the center of that pocket, and then I started to go up the hill, and I saw the deer lying there, four. And they didn't see me. And I waited for my partners,[24] and I thought it had been long enough. They would just run to where they're watching. I shot. The deer jumped up. I shot and I broke the front leg off one. They ran up the hill. Then I went and I came in sight, and I didn't see the deer. They were already out of sight.

And I started looking for my partner. I saw him standing right next to a tree. I saw the crippled deer running on the side hill. And the old timers say when you shoot a deer if he is hurt he will try to follow the others, but can't go up the hill. He'll turn around to go down. That's the one I shot and it's running on the side hill. It went straight for my partner who was standing behind a tree. It got right to him, then he saw him. The deer stopped. My partner shot him, four times. He didn't hit him. The deer was standing there, and he started loading his gun. He kept watching him. I thought the deer I crippled might go far. I shot, I shot it from down below, it fell. I went and I got there.

I said, "You shot four times, how many did you hit?" He laughed at me, and he said, "That's the one I was shooting at." He said, "He got right up to me. I shot him four times, and I never hit it. I got disgusted, and after I got done loading I just stood there. And then you shot it from below. And it fell right in front of me." And I said to him, "Where did you point the gun?" He said "Right at the knees." He said, "I borrowed a gun, and that's what the owner of the gun told me. 'My gun shoots high, six inches. You have to shoot half a foot below, and then you'll hit it.'" I said to him, "Maybe from a distance, but from close it won't shoot that high. And if you hit it [it will be] on the legs, break his legs."

I said to him, "You follow the rest, go. The ones that are watching will shoot and they [the deer] will run back down. They'll run into you, they'll follow their own tracks." Then he went. And I gutted the deer, took out the insides.

Oh, I forgot my snowshoes. And I had to go after them. Then I went, I went and overtook them [my partners]. They were sitting there, they never even got a shot. I asked them, "Have you got a bow and arrow, have you a bow and arrow to kill the deer I drove?" They said to me, "You killed them, they never went by here." I told them "No, here are the tracks I have been following, and these are their tracks, and they never turned back."

My brother was disgusted, he said, "I'm disgusted with myself." He said, "My

24 To get to the waiting place.

partner and I got here. (195) And my partner is so fat, we take two steps and he gets so tired, he gets choked[25], and I have to wait for him. And I got to thinking I am a fool. We are here to watch for deer, and [instead] I'm waiting for him. I think the deer will go ahead of us. (200) And I did my best. I hadn't gotten here, and you started shooting. And they went ahead of us, they got ahead of me before I got here."

sqəmqmmín said to his grown child, "Tell about yourself. (205) You shot four times, how many [did you get]?" He said, "I never even hit it. My partner crippled him, I was going to shoot it under the arm." He said, "He got right up to me and I singed him with black powder.[26] I shot him four times, and I never hit it. (210) I got so disgusted, I didn't try to shoot any more. It was my partner that shot it from below; then it fell. He got to me and he said to me: 'Go ahead, if they shoot one of the bunch they'll run back down, they'll follow their own tracks.'"

(215) Then we went to another gulch. My brother told us, "The deer winter here too. And the ones we drove, I guess they settled here, we'll hunt this ground." They instructed us to where we should go. (220) He asked us, "Who is going to do the watching?" I said to my brother, "You know the country; we will drive the deer." "Ok;" he went. He said "I'll go alone." (225) sqəmqmmín said to us, "I'm going to tell you, don't get fooled if I shoot four times. I'm letting you know I'm going home. I am tired from breaking through the crust of the snow too many times. I'll go back." (230) We said "Ok," and we just thought he was joking. We scattered, we went.

We didn't see a deer, and we got back all together, the three of us. sqəmqmmín was gone, and we waited and waited for him. We started hollering, he never gave an answer. (235) I forgot, we heard him shoot four times. I said to my brother, "sqəmqmmín told us if he gets tired he'll shoot four times. He said, 'That's when I am going home, I am tired.' And he went back, he told me, that's true."

(240) We came back, and the snow got warm, and our friend breaks through the crust, he doesn't have snowshoes. "Let's go back, we'll hunt on the way back to the camp."

Oh, I forgot about my partner Cricket, I forgot that. The morning after he said, "I'm all out of cartridges," (245) I said to him, "I have more cartridges, our guns are the same." He said "No, I am too disgusted. I shot too many times, and I hit nothing. But you are lucky, I'll just go after the deer that's killed. Where did you kill it?" (250) I told him it was over at "big slabs of rock," across from kɬxənxən̓ín̓k. "That's where I overtook them, that's where I shot. I already skinned it, and I left it there." I said to him, "When you get on my snoeshoe tracks, follow them." (255) He asked me, "Do you have rope for when I tie it onto the back of the horse?" I said "Yes, be sure and take my pack horse." Then he went.

We got back, our friend Cricket is gone. (260) sqəmqmmín was back at camp. Then my brother started to cook because he is good at cooking. He cooked and it was getting dark. We heard a noise, it's Cricket coming. He got back, he had no pack on the horse. (265) He took the saddle off, he tied it up. He fed the horse, and we asked him, "What happened to your dead deer?" He said to me, "Your tracks are just like a coyote's, and I lost your tracks, (270) and I didn't find the deer." I

25 He can't breathe.
26 "I was so close that ..."

said to him, “What’s the matter, I never took my snowshoes off, I kept them on all the time until we got back.” And there is plenty of snow for me to be taking my snowshoes off.[27] The next day I said to my brother (275) Coyotes might... [unfinished]. That evening my brother said to me, “We are running out of bacon. I thought it’s just two of us, and I got food enough for two; and now we got partners, three of them. (280) And we ate our grub in one meal.” He asked me, “Is it far where you shot the deer?” I said “No,” and he said to me, “It’s better we get some meat.” I said “In the dark?” He said to me, “We have moonlight.” (285) I said, “The horse will not reach it, the snow is crusted.” He said to me, “We’ll use snowshoes. We’ll take our horses as far as the river to kyríptən, we’ll tie them up there, and from there we’ll go on the side hill. (290) We’ll drag it as far as the horses, then we’ll pack it on the horse. And then we’ll come back up the hill.” I said “Ok.”

We went, we went and got to the bottom; we tied our horses there; (295) from there we went on snowshoes; then we went up the hill, then we walked on the side hill. We went, and we got to the deer I shot. He tied up his feet and he tied around the neck. He said to me, “I’ll go first, because I got to pick our way out. (300) You hold it so it won’t slide down the hill. And then we’ll just walk on the side hill.” I said “Ok,” and then we dragged it, because it’s big. And I held it with the rope so it won’t slide down. We came down the hill and then we got back to our horses. (305) Then we put it on the horse, we tied it to it again, and we came back up the hill.

The next morning I said to my brother, “I’ll go after my deer. Coyotes might steal it from us, it’s been overnight and all day.” He said “I’ll go with you,” and I said “Ok.” (310) Cricket said, “I’m going to stay here.” Then we went, we went and we hit a road, a trail. If it were summer the deer would go there. We got on the snowshoe trail where I and the deer had been. We went and we got there. (315) I said to my brother, “It’s right here that I was skinning, and that I piled the meat.” It’s gone. I looked around, and there was a fire built there. (320) I saw my partner’s tracks. His tracks didn’t have snowshoes. I told my partner, “Here are our partner’s tracks.” I looked around and up on the side of the hill there was a lump. (325) It had snowed that night and it had covered everything. I went to look. That was the deer. He must have prepared it for packing, because he had left his horses a little above on the hill. (330) It was too heavy. I started to untie it, we were going to divide it up to put it on our horses. There was only the legs, the back and the neck. It didn’t have ribs. I laughed and I said to my partner: (335) “Our partner must have eaten it. That’s why he couldn’t pack it. He must have burned the ribs.” The bones wouldn’t burn, they were lying in the fireplace. We tied them on the horse and we went and we got back. (340) We went back home. We went back and we got back there to sənx̌ʷúc̓əc̓tən. I passed the meat around to my partners. Then they came back. That’s the end.

27 The import of this utterance is unclear. Perhaps “I couldn’t have taken them off.”

Marriage customs (10')

Pete responded with this text when I asked him to tell me about traditional marriage customs. It's a text about then and now, as matter-of-fact a narration as I had learned to expect from Pete, always restrained about the past, and not given to celebrating the ancient ways or condemning the present when I was his audience.

I am going to tell a story about my ancestors' ways, about marriage, when a man gets a woman, or a woman gets a man, or a man gets a woman.

(5) At that time there were no white people, no laws. That's real old timers. They don't take papers when they get married, no. They pick one another. The parents are the bosses of their children. (10) And even if they are of age, they still have to think for their children. But now we are all turning white: when we are 21 we are of age. Not so a long time ago; the parents are the boss all the time. Those smart at getting things to eat, getting fish, or deer, (15) the smart ones are those they make boss. And they tell their daughter, "That will be your man, then you'll be satisfied. Whether he is not good looking, or he's handsome, you'll never get hungry. Look, he is smart in getting things to eat. (20) And another thing, we old people will get benefit too from your man. You will feed us fish or deer meat."

At that time there was no money, or stores, or anything, only Indian things, just us Indians at that time. Our clothes are just buckskin, (25) buckskin that they tan. And the women fix bukskin clothes, their dresses are buckskin clothes. And the men the same: the women fix their buckskin clothes. (30) And they have leggings and that's buckskin. That's what they call pants now, that's leggings. But now we are the now people, we are turning white people, and we follow the white people's ways. (35) From the white people we learn money, and we have stores, we buy groceries or our clothes. And buckskin clothes are out of date, [we wear them] only at gatherings. If anybody is ambitious enough to make buckskin clothes, or skin clothes, (40) for the war dance, it's only for show at a gathering. Long time ago that's all they had to wear. Like I said, there was no store, there were no white people. {Well that's about all.}[28] Their clothes were all Indian clothes.

Like I said, they pick out one another, (45) and that's why some of them got more than one wife, those that are smart at getting things to eat. They told me about it, my great-grandfather from my father, maybe his paternal grandfather or maybe his maternal grandfather. He had ten wives. That's why, and my parents told me (50) when they were alive, that we got relatives in Montana and in Idaho. We have relatives there, and in Canada, there too we have relatives. My great-great-grandfather had many wives. Then they scattered and their children had wives, and children were born, (55) and that's why we got relations in all the places I mentioned. But the good for nothing didn't take what they were taught, they only sleep and eat, and that's all. Somebody just feeds them. Them kind don't get picked out to be a son-in-law, (60) or put down for them somebody to be his wife, because they are too lazy.

Like I said, it's just for eats, those smart at getting things to eat, fish, or deer. At

28 This is what Pete interjects in English, and then continues.

that time they didn't cultivate potatoes or corn, or watermelon, no. (65) It's not long ago that the Hudson Bay people, as they call them, brought here corn and potatoes. That's when the Indians learned how to plant corn and potatoes and oats, wheat. That's for the horses, and they also brought the horses. We Indians were pitiful at first. (70) We only went afoot or by water. They made bark boats and that's their transportation; they didn't have horses at the time, or cows. And like they say in the Indian language, the Hudson's Bay people are white people, (75) they are the ones that brought horses and cows here, and corn, potatoes, and oats. They brought all that, and they taught the Indians how to put in gardens and how to harvest.

And now we turned White people. And another thing, we got to believing in prayers. (80) And now we take papers when we marry. And there is no divorce until one dies, the man or the woman dies. Then for a year one gets to feeling better and get somebody in their place, take another woman, or take another man. (85) That's all.

After the birth of a child (8')

Like the previous text, this is what Pete came up with when I asked him to talk about the topic, and tells about an episode he had witnessed as a youngster. His final comment is that things have changed: that was then, and now it's different.

The customs of the Indians long ago.

I gained knowledge, and when they have a baby they respect the baby, both of them, the man, and the woman. (5) The man does not hunt, shoot a deer, or kill anything; or even if he rides a horse, if it sweats, that's not [good], it's bad. Or fishing, anything that he kills, dead, the child might react [negatively]. (10) They say "it has a curse."

I had gained some smarts when my oldest brother's wife had a child. And my mother said to him, she stopped him and said to him, "Don't do anything (15) for the duration, that's ten days. Your child might get the curse." He didn't do anything for several days, [but] not the complete period. Maybe he got bored just sitting around, doing nothing, maybe also he forgot, he did some blacksmithing (20) maybe for the point of his plow. Maybe he was going to hammer it. So he made a fire in the forge; he placed what he was going to work across the fire, and when it became red hot he hit it. (25) He hammered the plow on the point. Suddenly my mother dashed out, and I was there outside, and (30) she said to me, "What did your brother do?" I said, "He was messing around in the shop." She said to me, "Go, run, tell him, 'come, hurry.'"

I rushed and I said to my older brother, "They are calling you, hurry, go. They are worried about something." (35) I followed him back, and I saw [this]: We went back in, I and my brother, and my mother said to him, "Now look, for your stubborness your son has the curse; (40) and if it dies, it's your doing." And I saw the baby act like the iron when he first lay it on the fire. It warms, and it's black, it's like the iron, it doesn't glow when it heats. (45) It looked just like it. The child was crying steadily. Then the baby's looks changed. It turned red, acted like the iron when it glows. It turned red, [with] its brightness. The baby's breath went out.

She said to my brother, "Now, see, you doubted. If you had listened to me this wouldn't have happened, your son wouldn't be dead. And it's like your fault that the baby is dead. You didn't show respect for it and he got the curse." She said, "There is a remedy, they call it the "Indian enema." But if you cannot succeed in respecting the ten days you have to doctor yourself. If in hunting, pour water in a lard bucket, a little bucket. Move back and shoot a hole through it [so] the water will drain out, and your child won't have the curse. Even if you shoot a deer and see its blood spill, he won't react, won't fall under the curse. Or when you ride a horse and you push him hard and he sweats til he foams, scoop the sweat with your hand and rub it on your chest, on your eyes, on your face, and this way too your child won't have the curse." That's what I saw in my early childhood, that's what I saw.

At that time the Indians believed in these ways. But now this generation, nobody believes it, there is no curse. When they have a child they don't respect the days. {That's about just the end of that.}[29]

Partnership butchering (3')

The briefest of Pete's texts, this is a short statement about the practice of sharing the game hunted.

Well, this, as they say in Indian, shooting deer... They skin it, then they cut it. They cut off the front foot, and the feet, and the ribs on both sides, and only the backbone, and the nape of the neck.

And when you have friends you pass it around to them; or if you have only one partner, you give him the backbone and one foot and half the ribs and the hind quarter, and that's your partner's share. And if you shoot two, you put down one deer for your partner and you take one, and then you both go back.

The attainment of provisions (6')

Pete is a hunter, and neither a fisherman nor a trapper.

Long ago the Indians' food was deer, things they hunt, fowl. When I grew up and gained some knowledge, I followed my oldest brother when we went hunting. A group at fall time, they fall hunt and they dry the meat; and when they have enough meat to last them the winter, then they move back home, they get back. And they store it, they have a storing place for dry stuff. They make a platform up high in the trees, then they cover it, and they store the meat. And no birds or anything can steal it from them. That's the way the Indians did it long ago.

As for myself, I have grown. Then they found out, they got a storage device, a white people's storage device with electricity, what they call in English "deep freezer."

29 Pete concludes with this remark in English.

I have always hunted: deer and bird [hunting] is open on the Reservation to us Indians. I have always hunted, and I have deer meat. Anytime I run out I hunt and I get fresh meat again. And now I am going blind, and I can't see my sights, and I can't hunt. Hunting is very enjoyable, I enjoyed it in my youth, even if it was tiring and we had to walk. Or we rode on horses, or in the winter when there is lots of snow we snowshoed.

But about fishing, my oldest brother, he got a lot of fish, but I don't know fishing--only hunting.

Also long ago, as they call it, raw hides, they trapped and they sold the hides. That's what they call raw hides. I did not practice trapping [for] raw hides, what they call beaver, beaver hides. These are the skins they sell, or the weasel, that's money. Brown bear, grizzly, their hides don't have a good price, only the skins of the weasel and the beaver [do]. There are more animals, creatures, and, like I said, I don't know trapping, I don't know them, I have seen only the bear, and the grizzly, and the deer.

The rainy hunting trip (8')

This is about the social interaction of a hunting party kept idle by persistent rain. The men challenge one another to see who could make the rain stop. The only single man in the party volunteers and has himself whipped by one of the women. The trick works and the rain stops. We are then told that the man subjected himself to the whipping because he wanted to find out if one of the women, otherwise always quiet, would laugh at his antics.

I'm going to tell an Indian story. Like they say in Indian, we North Halfs, we Colvilles, that's where I was born. When fall came they went fall hunting, I don't know how many. They had their wives along, and there's one that doesn't have a woman. They call him Freckled.

They settled down, they went up the sənʔaw·tíɬxʷtən river. They went up and settled down. That creek is the fall hunting place. They settled down, they got done fixing their lodges, their tipis. The rain got there, it poured on them. I don't know how many days it rained. They can't do anything about hunting; they'll either get wet or get lost in the rain. They stayed put, and they started challenging one another. They said, "Now who is going to stop the weather? Maybe somebody knows how to stop the weather, to end the rain." The ones that had wives said, "You are talking pitifully. We don't know anything about stopping the weather." They said to the one that didn't have a woman: "You do it, q̓ẏpyawt," (because that's his name).

He said, "Ok, I'll stop the rain. But don't let me spook you; if you do what I'm telling you, what [I'll ask] you to do to me, if it fits, it will stop raining. But if you don't do what I'm telling you, what you have to do to me, then it won't stop raining." They said "Ok." He said, "All right, but I'll have to have a woman that plays with me. I'll be getting things ready. They call those Oregon Grape bushes, those that have thorns just like rose bushes have thorns. I'll get them and I'll tie them in a bundle, and she will heat them up in the fire." (Their fire is outside the tipi, they're drying themselves.) "And I'll take all my clothes off, and she will whip me [with the bundle] when it has sparks, then with the thorns. And I'll be naked, and I'll be hurting. I'll jump from one side of the fire to the other, I'll jump over the fire. And if I go around she always has to whip me. That's when it'll stop raining. Don't pity me." They said "Ok."

The women started challenging one another. Then one woman said, "Ok, I'll do it." She said, "Ok, ok, I'll do it." They said "Ok." q̇ẏ̓pyawt took his clothes off. She already had put the oregon grape there [on the fire], he already had his clothes off, and the woman had already put [the Oregon Grapes] on the fire. It's sparking, ready to burn. She hit q̇ẏ̓pyawt on the back, ih, he groaned, jumped up. She followed him right up, and he jumped back and forth over the fire. She kept following him and whipping him on the back. He just groaned. They all laughed, because they looked funny, they went on like little kids. Well, it quit raining, and they went hunting. They had good days and they fall hunted.

Ah, I forgot one thing: I forgot that q̇ẏ̓pyawt liked only one woman, the chief's wife. She never talks, she's like deaf and dumb, she never laughs or talks to anybody. He wanted to find out if she could talk or not. That's why he got himself whipped. Well, the woman laughed. She wasn't deaf and dumb. "She laughed at me." Well, it quit raining. Well, it's the end of the story, that's all.

Tales of European origin

The texts that comprise this part of the anthology are: Black Pig; The grateful dead version 1; The grateful dead version 2; and The Devil and the Black Face. "The grateful dead" is my title of this tale—Pete referred to the first version as the story of "The king with one boy" and to the second version as the story of "The chief's family." The recording of the first version is unfinished, and the transcription reflects that fact. Recordings went unfinished when I had not brought with me enough blank tapes.[30]

Black Pig (10')

Black Pig is the first of these texts Pete narrated for me to record. It is also the shortest text, and I judge it to be the least cohesive. Black Pig is an eligible bachelor born to an important family, and quite a catch, judging from the report that young maidens are dry-mouthed about him. His parents arrange a marriage for him, and he seems to go along with the plan. He acts incongruously self-effacing when he reminds his promised bride that he is only a "black pig." The bride-to-be is undeterred and wants him as a husband, but Black Pig asks her to wait a while. She complies, and soon after she discovers that Black Pig has disappeared. Disconsolate she wanders to a town where an old woman takes her under her wing, and coaches her on how to win back Black Pig, who, fate wants it, is a boss of the town. The rest is a Cinderella story.

They had a son, an only child. They had named that child "Black Pig." He was a chief. And the women are just about dry mouthed. They propose to Black Pig

30 Five-inch reels, 600 or 900 feet. The latter hold 45 minutes.

every day. His parents consented to this one woman. They told her "Ok."

Black Pig said to this woman, "Well, I guess it's your wish that we marry. You see me, I'm just a black pig, and then you want to marry me. Aren't you going to be ashamed of me?"

And the woman said, "No, I'm not going to be ashamed of you, I like you."

"Well," he told her, "Don't get in a hurry. At bed time you'll sleep by yourself. Then [later] we'll get married, and you'll have a husband." "Ah, ok."

It wasn't long, the woman got anxious. "What's wrong with my husband-to-be, the one I am wishing for?"

The man was staying behind a curtain. She pulled it open. Her husband-to-be Black Pig was gone. The woman was left standing in the dust. The couple had moved away with their son Black Pig. That woman started to cry. She cried and cried. She started to walk the country. She looked for her man. She went, and she got to where some people live, it's a town, a big town, but I don't know the name of the town. There was a little house all by itself, a little building, an old lady['s]. She stopped there. And because it had been quite a few days her body was dirty and the clothes she had outfitted herself with looked bad.

Then her grandmother[31] said to her, (because she had started calling her granddaughter), "Well, you have come to see me, granddaughter. Keep company here with me. In a while our head boss Black Pig is going to get married. They are summoning the people, because he's a boss, he's the boss of all the world. They'll gather here; they are going to come and dance at his wedding."

"Ah," she said "ok."

Then the grandmother bathed her, she got her ready with nice clothes, she dolled her up. And the girl looked different, good looking. So they went to the boss's house. Her grandmother said to her, "Now we go in. Black Pig will see you. He's the one who's getting married, he has turned into a human.[32] He'll ask you to dance and you'll dance, and you'll be a good dancer. He'll see that you are very beautiful. You are more beautiful than the one he's about to marry. And if when you dance you dance well, before the dance is over, pretend you trip. Say to him, 'Stop, let me go. I have hurt my foot.' Then he'll let you go, and you'll run out. And your shoe'll come off. But don't stop for that, come back home. And that's when Black Pig will change his mind."

"His love'll go to you, he'll get stuck on you again, you'll be his woman. And he'll say, he'll tell the people gathered here from all over: 'I've changed my mind, I'm not going to get married now. Maybe tomorrow night, I'm still studying it.' Because he would still be holding the shoe. And just as soon as [the dance] is over, Black Pig will start asking the people. He'll tell the women: 'Whoever this fits, whoever can put this shoe on, that's the one I'm going to marry.'"

The one he was going to marry is the first one [to try it]. She tried to fit it, but she has big feet, and it won't [fit]. She tried to force it, and Black Pig said to her, "No, your feet are too big, you might bust the shoe."

It got late. All the people had tried [the shoe] on. Black Pig asked, "Have all of you tried putting the shoe on?" They said, "Yes." He said to them, "Mm, yes."

The old woman said: "Oh, I forgot, I have a grandchild. She stayed home,

31 "Grandmother" is generic reference (and address) term for an elderly woman.

32 Probably to be interpreted as a parenthetical remark.

she didn't come." They said to her, "Go get her." She went and got her. She talked to her granddaughter, and she came.

She came in, and they gave her the shoe. And because it's her shoe, she took it, slipped it on, and it fit. Black Pig thought, "Yes, that's just what I thought. The one who can make it fit, that's her shoe, that's the one who lost it. That's the one I'm going to marry."

He said to the people, "This is why I said that whoever this shoe fits, that's the one I'm going to marry."

They started to dance. They got married, and then they started to dance. They danced until daylight. And I told them, "I'm going to school.[33] My school boy is waiting for me. I'm leaving you, but then I'll come back home." That's the end of it.

The grateful dead version 1 (unfinished: 68')

This is the text Pete called "The King with One Boy." There are several places in this version of the story where Pete has to backtrack and provide important details that he had missed, and, unfortunately the story is unfinished, but such missteps do not detract from the narrative, full of signs of Seymour's superior skills as a narrator.

A young man goes out to search for a woman he knew only from a picture he had seen. On the way he witnesses a crowd abusing a corpse because the man had failed to pay his debts before he died. The young man pays the dead man's debts and remains penniless. He continues his journey and is joined by what turns out to be the spirit of the dead man. The two arrive at a beautiful house that turns out to be where the woman object of the young man's desires lives. This woman is as evil as she is beautiful, and in cahoots with the devil devours human victims. The dead man's spirit know this, and coaches his traveling companion to defeat her. We will find out how the story ends in the second version of the story, following this.

There lived a king. Because my fairy tales [have] a boss, or Coyote. This is what I am going to tell, [about] a grown [young man]. This chief had a son, I had forgotten, and their son was grown. And he told his father, "I am grown, and I am bored of staying here, and I want to travel the world, I want to see places. And if I stay here with you, if I stay here I won't see the world, and I won't get acquainted with different people. But if I travel around I'll see the world, I will see different tribes." His father said to him, "Ok, if it's your wish. It's true you are old enough, and we're not tired of you; it's all right if you go, it's your wish. I hate to see you go. Something might happen to you, you might die, and that's no good. We feel bad, because you are the only child we have." His son said, "Yes, that's true. As I said, I am bored staying here with you. And you know that I always listen to you. Be at ease, I am not wild, and I won't do anything wrong." He said, "Ok."

The chief put something [down] for him. He opened his money bank, in a trunk. He put down money for him, lots. He said, "This is for your grub," he said, "because you can't go without money. This is what you'll have for food. Or

33 Pete is referring to the fact that he is teaching (telling stories to) his school boy (Mattina).

you might get hard up for your wages if you hire somebody. (35) Or you might wear your clothes out and this is to buy clothes. Or you will hire to get your clothes washed." He said, "Ok." He shook hands with his father and his mother, then he walked out.

(40) And he didn't kow just where he was going, he just went out. And he arrived at a place. He started walking and where he was facing, he just went. He went and he came in sight in level country. Gee, what did he see, like people gathered. (45) And because it's right in his path, he just went straight for it. And because that's where he is going, he got close. It's people running around, they are playing, and they gather, and what is it they are kicking? (50) What they are kicking is not like a football. They take it, and they fight over it. One gets hold of it and runs with it, and he drags it. And they kick what they are dragging from behind. He went, got close, made out what it was. (55) It's a human what they are doing that to, it's a body that they are kicking. He went, got there, and made out what it was. This person is not alive. What they are doing that to is a corpse, is what it is. Then the boy stopped them.

(60) He said to them, "Wait a minute, stop!" The people stopped. He said, "I want to ask you. And why is it, it's a corpse, a human being, one of you. (65) A corpse is respected in the country where I come from. When we have dead ones we respect them, we put them away, we bury them. But you folks treat this corpse pitifully." They said, "Are you done talking?" "Yes." They told the boy: (70) "When he was alive he asked for credit from the store, he has debts with everybody; and he didn't pay his debts. And when he died we lost all of that. He hasn't got relatives, and we lost all our money. (75) He's got no living relatives for us to ask money of. And one has to have money to buy clothes and a coffin, to make a coffin. And one has to pay to have diggers to bury him. And he doesn't have any money. (80) So we are figuring his debts, and that's why each is kicking him. When he gets tired of kicking him, he thinks, 'You are paid up, now it's your turn.' And then the next takes him, and he kicks him more. (85) He does that, until he too is satisfied that his debt is paid. Then he gives him to another one, until those he owes to all take their turn. And then you got here. (90) But this is only for his clothes, for his coffin, and for the grave diggers. He is going to have to pay for that. We were going to figure all that out, and then you stopped us."

He said to them, "All of you, stand in a row." They all stood in a row. (95) The boy took out his purse. He said to the one in front of him, he asked him, "How much did he owe you?" He told him how much, and he gave it to him. And then another one, and he told him, and he gave it to him. (100) He paid all the ones he owed. He asked them, "And how much is his coffin?" The coffin-makers told him. One [of them] said "This is how much I get for it." He paid him that. (105) He told him, "Now make him a coffin." He said to the store keeper, he said, "And you, how much do you charge for clothes for dead people? A complete outfit, a suit, (110) shoes, socks, shirts, and a handkerchief for his neck." In English they call this "necktie" and in Indian "k̓łir̓cín." "Everything." The store keeper told him, and he paid. (115) He asked, "Who is the digger?" They named the grave digger, or maybe three or four. They told him, "We take turns, we don't stop. (120) When one is out of breath, then another joins in. We all take our turn, and then the first one again, because he is rested, and then he'll join in and dig. We never stop, and in just a little while we have our grave dug. And when we fill the grave we do the same thing. (125) Two will start filling it, and their partners wait. When they figure they must be tired, the two will push their partners aside and they will take their turns filling in the grave. When they finish burying they fix the grave." And he asked them, "How much do you charge?" (130) They told him, for the four of them. And the boy is flat broke when they are done with the burying. They all put their money in their pockets. They picked him up on both sides. They told him (there must be a graveyard)... (135) He said to them, "Now you fix him for the grave, with clothes, with a coffin." They took him, and they took him to the cemetery. They bathed him, washed his body well. They got clothes from the store, everything new. (140) They got him ready with underwear, stockings. They got him ready, they put pants on him, a shirt, a tie, and they put a coat on him, a suit. He had on a beautiful outfit. (145) And his shoes, everything new. They finished putting him in the coffin. He finished the coffin, and they put him in it. They closed the cover. They were having a funeral now. There were four grave diggers. (150) The white people now do the same thing. Now they have poll bearers, four or six, the white people call these "pall bearers." They took him and they put him down on the edge of the grave. They rested, and then they put him in the ground. (155) Then they filled in the grave. They got done filling in the grave, and then the boy left.

Oh, I just thought of something, I forgot one thing. When the boy was reading books, when he was at his parents, he had seen a picture, a woman, a maiden. (160) Gee, she's good looking. He had only seen it, and he got stuck on her. He is growing up, and he has already lots of sense, and a desire for women. And he said, "I am going to look for [the one in] this picture. If I find her, she's going to be my wife. (165) I am going to travel the world until I find her before I turn back." That's what I thought of, that's what I forgot. He hid this from his parents, he didn't tell them about the one in the picture, only how tired he was of staying at home. (170) He is going to loosen up and see the world, he is going to walk the world over. But it's that he is going to look for the woman in the picture in the book.

This is what I thought of, what I forgot. (175) Because my grandma maybe sixty years ago told me this story. And that's why I forget.

They got done with the funeral, and now I'm going to continue. They got done with the funeral, and he started on. He went, and I guess there is a road now. (180) He got hungry, and when people get hungry that's when they want food. I guess wishing for food is being hungry. People also get tired when they are hungry, and he got tired. This boy got hungry and tired. And he thought, "Even if I do see people (185) I don't have money to buy food, I spent all my money." That's what he thought.

He came in sight of flowing water. There is a bridge right where he is going. From the time he walked from over there from his parents, (190) the way he was facing he continued straight in the same direction. He doesn't recognize the country, he doesn't know the country. He doesn't know where he is going. He is just going for nothing. [End of tape]

Now I am going to splice my story. (195) I am smoking, as they say in the white people language, I lit my peace pipe. I just got done smoking, and now I'll splice.

The boy got next to the river, and he felt, “I am really tired.” (200) When a person gets tired he wishes for food. But he paid all his money out, and he thought, “That’s pitiful, and what can I do? Even if I get to a town I can’t get anything to eat.” That’s just what he thought when he walked on the bridge over running water. (205) Just as he got to the middle of the bridge, he did like that,[34] and there was a boy sitting there, a boy, small, but able to run around, strong, but very young. The little one sitting there said to him, “So you are traveling around, pilgrim[35].” (210) He said to him, “Yes.” “Where are you going?” “I don’t know where I am going, I am just traveling around the world.” “Ah,” he said, “Can I go with you?” (215) The boy thought, “Heck no. I haven’t got any money, and he is too small. How can we get food, even if we get to a town? And besides, he might slow me down. He is too small, (220) he could never walk the whole day and night. And I haven’t got a place to stop, we haven’t got any money, even if we get to a town, if we go to an eating place, or to a hotel.” He said to him “No, you are too small, you are helpless, (225) you might slow me down, I am going far.”

He said to him “No, I am strong, I am smart. I always wanted to go with you.” He tried to discourage him. He thought, “Well, I pity him, he might be an orphan.” (230) Then he asked him, “What’s the matter, don’t you have any parents?” “No, I haven’t got any parents, I don’t have a place to stay. And I walked here, and then I looked for someone to go with. Then I saw you, and I want to go with you.” (235) The boy thought he must be running away. He said, “Aren’t you running away?” “No.” “Or are you lost?” (240) “No,” and he thought, “Maybe he wouldn’t bother me.” He told him, “Just for one thing I don’t want you with me. Even if I am a grown man, I get tired and I get hungry, and I don’t have money. And you are little, and you will get tired, and you will get hungry. (245) And then you will bother me.” The little boy said, “Don’t think that way. I am used to getting hungry, we’ll just go partners.” He said “Ok,” and so they went.

The boy, the king’s son said to him: (250) “I am tired and hungry. I won’t be able to pack you if you get tired.” He said to him, “No, don’t think that way. I am smart, you won’t have to pack me. I won’t get tired, I just want to go with you.” (255) He said “Ok,” then they joined hands and they walked. They joined hands, he and the little boy, and they started telling stories. Then he thought, “Now I got company. I am worried, I think maybe he’ll get me in trouble. Maybe he ran away, maybe he has parents. (260) They might miss him and look for him, and they’ll find him following me. And what will I do, what will I say? They might arrest me, and what can I do to pay my fine?” (265) But he [also] thought, “He has no parents, and no place to stay, and he is not running away, and I wonder why. Maybe he is orphaned, I wonder what can be.” That’s what the boy has been thinking.

They went, they hadn’t gone far (270) and they saw a house. My, that’s a big house, a beautiful house. It’s right in their path to where they are going. They went and they got right opposite to it. And the boy thought: (275) “I am really tired, and I am hungry. Maybe the people will feel sorry. I’ll ask for left overs or for garbage, and that’ll be all right. And maybe in the barn, or whatever it is they’ll give us to sleep. (280) They don’t have to put us up in the house.” That’s

34 A head motion probably accompanied this utterance.
35 Madeline’s appropriate rendition.

what he was thinking. They went and they got to where the road forks, and the chief's son thought, "This is what I figured: I am too tired. I am not going to be particular, people take chances. I'll take a chance, maybe they are merciful." They went there. He said to his friend, "Let's turn to where that house is." He [the little one] said to him, "You are the boss, I am following you. Whatever you do I'll do."

They turned off the road. They knocked on the door, they opened the door for them. Goodness, she's beautiful. She said to them, "You got here, boys." They said, "Yes." She said to them, "Maybe it's from somewhere far that you come. I haven't seen you before. I know everybody here, the children, and the old people, and I have never seen you." The boss's son said, "Yes, that's right, I come from very far." She said to them, "Come in, you must be hungry and tired. I'll cook for you, it's close to my cooking time. Then I am going to be gone." And the boy thought, "We're lucky to get pitied. We are being given a good thought, and we are not worth it. We would have come up short if we'd gone straight, and we would have starved. She must be merciful that she took pity on us." We went in, my partner and I.[36] I said to him, "We'll go in the house." We went in and the woman followed us.

Then she gave us chairs. She told us, "In the other room (there is a door) there is a wash basin there, a bath tub. Go there and wash your face. Then I'll cook for you, do whatever, bathe." They went in.[37] She told them, "I also got an outhouse." They used it, but they didn't bathe. They washed and they drank some water. Goodness, it's real nice water, cold. They washed, they drank, they wiped their faces, they combed with a comb. They went into another room, they sat down in a sitting place. They just got settled in the chairs, and she brought them in {unfinished}.

He thought of..., no, he hadn't thought of the picture yet. Because he is still tired, and he didn't think about anything. She came in to them, and said to them, "I'm done with cooking for you, come in. Have you washed?" "Yes." They went in. My, their food is steaming. I suppose her cooking stove is electric, it's too quick [for her] to have started the fire, to get it hot, to get things cooked. They had just finished washing when they were called. They sat down, there are all kinds of things to eat. "Gee, it's only at my father's that I have seen this kind of food. Now I see it here." They thought she was a really important woman. And they didn't see or hear any [other] people, it's a big house. They ate and they got filled up. They, the king's son, said to the woman, "Well, we are done eating." She asked them, "Did you really get enough, or maybe you are bashful, maybe you didn't eat enough." He said, "No, we got plenty, we got filled up. We were plenty hungry and we got lots to eat. We are filled up. We can't eat any more. We didn't even get most of the food." She said to them, "Now I am going to show you where you are going to stay. Because, as I told you, I am going to be gone. A little bit more and you would have missed me, because I have a date. And now I'll show you where you are going to stay. And you'll be there. Whatever you want, you can go to bed, or rest."

She took them there, they went out. And there is another building, a little house,

36 For a few lines it's the boss's son who is telling the story.

37 Pete resumes the story in the third person.

(365) not big, just enough. They went in, they opened the door. It's locked. They opened the door, they went in. It's fixed beautifully, and it's just the same on the outside. (370) It's made well and the paint is good. There are chairs, two chairs, and there is a table, and there is a bed, two beds. She told them, "Next door there is a bathroom and a bathtub. And there you can bathe. (375) When you are done bathing, your night clothes are there. And here is also a change of top clothes. And when you take off your clothes, throw what you take off in the box, and get dressed with your change of clothes. (380) Put your sleeping clothes on. That's what you are going to do, and don't be backwards. Then go in there when you are done bathing and changing your clothes, don't be bashful about using the beds. Don't think that you'll get them dirty, because you've already bathed. (385) Don't be backward, you are tired. Just lay around on the bed, rest. When you get sleepy go to bed. Tomorrow I'll call you to eat, and you can get up. Or, if you are already awake, (390) and already washed, and dressed, wait for me to call you. Then you come out and come to the house. You will eat, we will eat." That's what the woman told them. (395) Then the woman went out. "I have to go wash dishes before I go." She went out.

He went in, and said to his little brother, "You better go bathe." (400) The little boy said to him, he said, "You are the oldest, and I am the little one; I'll be last, you bathe first. I'm following you, that's why I let you do things first, because I am the youngest." He went into the bath. (405) He poured water in, it's warm, and it's just right. There is everything there, a towel, soap, a comb. He bathed and bathed, got done bathing and dried himself. He looked around and also a change of clothes was put there. He took them and put them on, they fit perfectly, (410) like measured. His shirt, his trousers, his shoes, everything new. There is also a coat, a house coat. Look, at the hospital they have those, they are like a sleeping coat. (415) He went back in, said to his little brother, "It's your turn, I'm done bathing." The little one went in, in a little while he came out. He is done bathing too, he too had different clothes on, he also had a house coat, (420) a long white coat. The boy had just settled down when the woman that owned the house came in.

She's fixed up to the max. Her dress is beautiful, (425) and everything how she was fixed was beautiful, her hair. . . Gee, her rings were blinding with shine. The woman said to the oldest boy, the king's son, she said to him, she took off her ring and said to him, "Take care of my ring for me, (430) because it's expensive and I might lose it. Tomorrow morning when you get up you give it back to me, when I ask for it. When we eat you give it back to me. When I come after you for breakfast you give it to me." There is a small table there by the bed. (435) He said to her, "Lay it down there." Then the woman went out, the woman left.

In a little while, just before he went to bed he glanced at it, the boy looked at the ring, (440) where she had put it on the table. Gee, it's gone. And he and his partner hadn'd made a move. His partner was across the room lying down, and he is lying on this side. And she had hired him to take care of the ring. (445) He had told her, "Put it on the table." Something queer is going on, she played a trick on him. He doesn't know what to think. So he says to his partner, his younger brother...

Oh, no, I took a shortcut. (450) I forgot. They went to bed. Daytime came and they got up. They got done washing, and they are waiting. That's the time he thought of the ring. They had locked the door. They don't have any money that might be stolen for them to lock; it's on account of the ring, it doesn't cost just a little. "There might be some no good people get here, they might catch us asleep, and steal from us." That's why they locked, and the key was on the table. They got done washing and combing. He opened the door of the house, and he hung the key there. He looked at the table (he had told the woman to put it down there, the good looking woman). It's gone. He got puzzled. "What is the matter? We were locked in, and two of us watched when she put it down there herself." Then she went out and they locked the house, and it's gone. "Nobody has got here to us. I am going to ask my little brother, maybe he knows." He said ...

No, I am lying.[38] I forgot, first it was her watch, not her ring, her watch that goes around the wrist. Because it's been too many years that my old relatives told me the stories. I forget them, I get the stories mixed up, I forget. Then I thought of it, I remembered it was a watch.

Then he asked his partner, he said, "Were you watching the woman when she put me in charge of her watch, and I told her to put it down? And she took it off her wrist?" He said to him, "Yes, I was watching." He said, "And she went out, and I locked our house. And we are tired, and we might fall asleep, and somebody might get to us, and steal from us. We have nothing like money for them to steal from us. We are just thinking they might steal the watch from us. That's why we locked ourselves in. And we didn't notice anyone. Did you?" "No, I was asleep too." He [the little one] said "Yes," he stuck his hand, pulled it out, there is the watch. The boy uncovered his wrist. He took it off and gave it to his partner. He said, "Here is the watch." "Oh, you took it!" "Yes, because I was afraid we might lose it. That's why I kept it. That's why I put it around my wrist. And there is no two ways about it, I'll wake up if they [try to] take it off my wrist." He just took it and put it on the table. The woman came in. She asked "Where is the watch I gave you to keep for me?"

I thought of something.[39] This woman is like a cannibal. She went back out and wished her watch back to herself. Her watch went to her. She went upstairs, three stories, the fourth floor of the house. That's where she stores her things, all locked. She went up and got to the top where she stores her things. She opened the trunk where her clothes are, and she put it there. She covered it and locked it. Then she went out and locked the door. She came down to another door, and [locked it]. She locked them all to the bottom. And then she left.

Then she asked, she said, "Where is the watch I gave you to take care of? I am back, I want it." "Ah, and where did I tell you to put it? I guess it's there, wherever you put it." The woman looked there, and there was the watch. The woman took it. My, she was surprised. "Since I got here to this world nobody has ever done this to me. Nobody has found, or given back what I have given them to look after. He must be real smart."

She stepped outside, she asked them, "Are you freshened up?" They told her "Yes." "Well, come back with me, we are going to eat." They went with her,

38 Here it's Pete talking, making a correction to the story.
39 The import of this utterance is "I should have mentioned this before."

they followed her. They went into the woman's house. The food is already laid out, it's steaming. It wasn't just ceral, rolled oats, white man's food, [the kind] that they don't cook, the kind with milk, the kind they pour [milk] on and eat. But hot cakes, bacon, eggs, cooked food. They ate, and not much, because they had overtaken their hunger, they ate lots already the day before.

They got done eating and the woman said to them, "Just like I said to you, you must be very tired. Stay here and rest as many days as you wish. If you wish four days or two days, whenever you are rested then you go wherever you are going." And the woman thought, (she is a man-eater), she thought, "Later this evening I'll go to my boss, in a while I'll get to my boss. I'll call him on the phone and my boss'll get back to me. Then I'll ask him, it's not for nothing that he is my boss, he is smart, that's why I am his bait to kill humans. He'll thing of something and we'll kill these boys."

They got done eating, and the woman said to them: "You stay here and rest. Like I said to you, far, you must come from far. You must be tired, and foot-sore; or maybe your feet are full of blisters (and you would hide that). Get rested, just as you like, two days, four days, whatever, for you to get rested. Then you can go wherever you are going." They said, "Yes." She said, "As you wish, you can lay around, sleep, or talk. Or you can walk outside, walk around, or play. But don't go far, because you are tired, or you might get lost, you don't know the country. Look, you were saying you don't know the country, you are just going for nothing, just looking the country over. Don't go far, and when you are rested then you can go, you won't bother my mind."[40] They told her, "Yes, thank you." They sat around, then they went back out.

She washed the dishes, she called her boss. She said, "Boss, I told you last night two boys were my guests. They may be brothers; one of them is grown, but the other is small. But he must be smart, and they come from a long ways, from another country, he's a king's son, his lineage is king. They are traveling the country over." And she said, "And you said that I was to use as bait my watch for them to keep. Then we will kill them if the watch is gone. I gave it to them to keep, and I came over to see you. I gave it to the oldest one to keep, and he said to me, 'Put it on the table,' and I put it on the table. Then I went back out, and I wished my watch back, and I had it come to my wrist. I went upstairs and went to the door. I had the key with me (it was locked), and I unlocked it. I continued for four floors, the doors were all locked. There is my storage place, the trunk for clothes, and I put my watch there. I closed it and I locked it. Then I went out and I locked, I locked everything; I got to the bottom and then I came, I came to you. And I was here all night, I was here with you. Then I went back and I asked the boy for what I gave him. And he said to me, 'Oh, wherever you put it, it must still be there.' I looked on the table where I had put it, and I was sure I had locked it in the trunk and I just asked for nothing. And if it's not there we kill them. I looked there, and my watch was there! Gee, was I puzzled. And there are lots of doors, four levels in the house, they all have a door, and they were all locked. And my clothes, I had locked that too. That's where I store things. And I locked all back, and I came back down. And how did

40 "You won't have me worried."

he get it back? (615) The boy, the oldest one, must be powerful, great."

He said to her, "Now your ring is what you are going to have him keep. Even if this boy is powerful he can't hang on to the ring. Put your mind at ease, don't feel bad because we didn't kill them. (620) They'll be more rested now. Go, sleep, you might get tired. This evening you come back, come back to me."

The youngest one said to him, said to his older brother, "Brother, are you tired of sitting around? I am bored. (625) She told us if we want to we can walk around, we can walk around outside so we won't get bored." He said "Yes." So they went out. The young one said to him, (630) he asked his older brother, "Do you have a knife?" He said, "Yes, I got a knife." "Good, this is what we want." "And what are you going to do with it?" He said, "We are going to get a weapon. (635) We are going to do something important." He said "Ok."

They came, they saw that there was brush, not bad brush. They saw it, they weren't going to get lost or be afraid of it. They went in there. (640) What grows there is thorn bush, only thorn bush. Gee, the young shoots, nice shoots, just the right size, just like my little finger. (645) They started cutting because both had knives. He said to his big brother, "Get enough, get so much, enough to hold in your hand. Wrap it, and that's one bundle. (650) We will get four packages." "And what are we going to do with it?" His little brother said to him, "When we finish getting them then I will tell you what we'll use it for." He said to him, "Hurry up." [tape ends]

The grateful dead version 2 (70')

Pete announced this story as "The Chief's Family." It differs in a detail from the previous text (a watch in the first, a key in this), but it is otherwise substantially identical to the previous text, and complete. There are fewer backtracks in this story, possibly because Pete had already told the story, and it was now fresher in his mind. So, for example, we know off the bat that the young man is bent on finding the woman of the picture, and he keeps his intent from his parents.

Picking up the story where the recording of first one abruptly ended (the little fellow had just instructed his big brother to gather four bundles of thorn bushes), their task is to beat the devilish out of the woman—a visible puff of something exits her body once she has reached her limit of tolerance. She is done being a man-eater. Immediately she joins the young man in his bed, and they marry. In the morning the little fellow announces that he is god, and that in exchange for the help he had provided the couple, he expects to collect their first born child. The pair does indeed get a son, and when the little fellow comes to claim his prize, with an attitude reminiscent of Abraham's, he consents to have his young boy split in half. The result of the blow of the sword over his head is not his death, but the splitting of his body into two healthy bodies—the origin of twins. The young fellow leaves without taking either twin, and the happy family returns to the young man's parents where the whole bunch and guests celebrate their happy reunion.

I'm going to tell a fairy tale. The boss had a son. Maybe he [the son] was doing something, and he saw a picture. It was a good looking maiden, (5) a young virgin or a woman. He got stuck on her. He saw her and got stuck on her. "I'm going to look for her. If I find her I'm going to propose. She's going to be my wife, she's beautiful." He thinks he can do it, because he's the chief's son. So he told his parents, "I'm going to leave you." They said, "And why? We baby you a lot; you are our only son, and you are going to leave us? Maybe something is bothering you; you don't like the way we take care of you and..." He said "No," he said "I've been here with you and I now I've grown, I'm a man; and I won't see the world. I only want to travel around and see the world. That's why I am leaving. And I am going to tell you that, if I am alive, I'll come back in one year just about this time." His father said to him, "If that's what you want, I'm not sending you away." He said "We will get lonesome. Just as you said, you are of age, and you can decide what you're going to do, if that's what you want." He told his father, "Yes, yes, that's what I've decided. I want to see the country."

So the chief took his money box and maybe he counted, but I don't know how much money. He gave it to him, he said "I give you this for your lunch. You might be hard up or get hungry, or your clothes might wear out. And this is for your clothes and for your food, that's why I'm giving you money." He said "Ok." He took it, he saved it in his money pouch. He shook hands with his elders, he left.

And he didn't know where he was going; wherever he was facing when he walked out of the house, no trail or nothing, he just walked. Maybe it's level ground, open and level, there's no road. He went and came in sight. There are people there on the level. He saw lots of people, and what are they doing? They are playing, or running around, or something. He doesn't know, because it's far. "I am going to go and see. I'm going to go see." He went straight for them; he got close, then he was right in the crowd of people. What are they kicking and taking away from each other? And when it's one's turn he kicks it. It's not a baseball. He came closer, he got close and recognized what it was. He got close and recognized it: it's something, a person, dead. What they're grabbing from one another is a corpse. Each takes his turn at kicking. It's a corpse and they are making a ball our of it and playing with it.

He said to the people: "Wait, stop for a minute, I want to ask you something." They stopped and stopped playing with the corpse. He said to them "What's the matter? What's the matter with the corpse that you are playing with it? That you are killing it, like? No, you're not playing, you are kicking it." One of them said, he said "When he was alive we lent him money and paid his debts, and he didn't pay his debts or the money he borrowed. And when he died he didn't have anything. And how are we going to get our money back? What he owes us? And that's why we are playing with him. So when he pays all his debts then we'll let him go. We'll take a collection and we'll bury him, we'll get him a coffin." He said "Well, all of you that he owes get in a row. Stand up and get in a line, and from one end I'll start a-questioning you. However much he owes you I'll pay it." They said "Ok."

They got in a line, they stood. He went from one end and asked the first one, he said, "How much does he owe you?" He said, well, he named how much. He paid him. Then he went on, and he asked the one next to him. He said, "How much does he owe you?" He told him how much, and he paid him. He paid everybody. He said to them (and there is a store), he said to them "Give him clothes, a new change of clothes. I'll pay for it, you name the price." He took it down, and said what it was; he paid for it. He said (and at that time there was no undertaker), he said, "Whoever will bury him can dig the grave and take him to the graveyard." I guess there is a graveyard, and there they dug a grave, and they got a coffin ready, I forgot, they put him there. "You take him there and bury him. Tell me your price." They told him. And he ran out of money. He went on.

Then there were roads, and he went in the same direction, he walked there. He went and got to a shore, he came in sight to a shore, it's running water, it's not a big river, and it has a bridge. That's the road he's been walking on, because he's on foot. He went and got to the bridge, and he walked on it to half way. Suddenly a child spoke to him. He looked around and on the side of the bridge a boy was sitting there on the rail of the bridge. He asked him, "Aren't you scared?" He said to the boy, "Aren't you scared? You might get dizzy and fall in the water." The boy said "No. No, I'm not scared, I don't get dizzy." He said "All right then, get off. Let's talk and understand one another. You are too far and I can't make out every word you say, I can't hear you." Then the boy climbed down and got there and he asked him, "Where are you going?" He said "I don't know where I am going. I'm just walking the country over, I want to see the country. Whatever direction I face, wherever it goes, I follow the road there; and where there is a clear road that's what I follow. And here I have come to this shore and I saw you." The little boy said, "I'll follow you." He said to him, "And what's the matter, maybe, maybe you have parents, and they'll miss you." He said, "No, I don't have parents. It's best I follow you." He said "No, I don't know where I am going; maybe you'll get hungry or tired, and I don't have any money. And if we get to a town, how can we eat at a restaurant or stay at a sleeping place. You are too pitiful." He told him "No, I'll follow you." "Well, if that's how you feel." So he followed him.

They went, I don't think they overnighted, they came in sight. A beautiful house stood there, a big house. It wasn't sundown yet, wasn't evening yet. And this traveling person commenced to get tired, and he hadn't eaten since morning, he hadn't had any lunch, and he's got no money. And he thought, "Well, maybe they'll have pity. We'll stop at that house; we are going to inquire. Maybe they'll give us a job, maybe they'll feed us, give us a place to stay." And he asked his partner, the little boy, his little brother (he claims him as his little brother because he is a man, and the boy is little), he asked him, "Are you tired?" He said "No, I haven't come very far for me to be tired." He asked, "Ain't you hungry?" "No, I'm not hungry, either." He said to him, "But I am tired, and I'm hungry. I have come far, and it's morning since I've eaten. We are going to go over to this house. Maybe they'll have pity, have pity on us, feed us." He said, "If that's how you feel."

They went, got there, knocked on the door. A woman opened the door for them, a good looking woman. She said to them, "You folks are traveling around. It's not often that people visit here, and then you folks got here. And where are you folks going?" The older one said, "We don't know where we are going, we are just traveling around the country, sightseeing. We are tired." She said to them, "You must be tired." He told her, "Yes we are tired and hungry. I am hungry, (205) and my child follower must really be hungry, tired. Can we camp here?" She told them "Yes, yes, when you are done eating ... I'll cook for you and I'll give you a place to stay, a bed." She said to them, "Come in." (210) Oh, no, wait a minute.

She took them a way away, not too far; just outside there was a small building there. She took them there, she opened the door. She said to them, "That house has everything." (215) She told them, "There is a bath there, there is soap there; if you want to, you can bathe and wash. I am going to go cook for you; and that'll be your house and that'll be your beds.You can camp there, you must be tired. I'm going back to cook for you. (220) When my cooking is done I'll bring you what you are going to eat." Then the woman went back out. And secretely, when the good looking woman turns her back, he takes the picture out of his clothes. Goodness, it's just like that woman's picture.

(225) When she opened the door they are all washed up and combed. She opened the door, their food is steaming. There is a table there. She put it down on the table. She went got ...; there were dishes there. (230) She said to them, "Eat." They ate, they got done eating. She took back their plates. She knocked on the door. He told her, "Come in." (235) The woman came in to them. She said "I am going there to the gathering, to the dance. They invite me to go there; and I am alone and then I might lose my key. And I want you to take care of my key to the house, (240) I might lose it, and I might have to break my door before I can get in the house." He said to her, "There, put it there on the table." The woman thought, "What's the matter? When I ask him to take care of it for me he should put it away. (245) And it's there on the table." She put it down there, and she went out. She said, "Tomorrow morning I'll come back and ask you for the key." "Any time." (250) She went out.

Then his little brother said to him, he said to him, "That woman is a man-eater. Look here. When she'll have wished it back, the key'll be gone. (255) Look, it's really gone." He looked at the [key], and sure enough, it's gone. He told him "Yes, yes, it's gone, I lost it." His little brother told him, "We'll follow her, we'll get it, maybe she hasn't gone yet. (260) She'll put it away." In a little while his little brother came back. He told him, he told his little brother, his little brother told him, "I got the key, I got it back. She put it away where she puts things away. (265) I'll take care of it. Tomorrow we'll wait for her to come back, and you'll put it back there. She'll come back in and ask you, 'I'm after my key.' You'll tell her, 'Ah, I told you to put it down there. (270) Go there, and it must be there.' When she sees the key lying there she'll be surprised; never has anyone taken it back when she puts it away." They went to bed. (275) Ah, they took a bath, finished, went to bed. They are tired, they went to sleep.

Towards daylight, when it's daylight all over he elbowed him, because he went to bed with his little brother. His little brother elbowed him; he said to him, (280) "Ah, wake up, take the key; put it back down there. It's daylight, she's about to show up." He put the key there; they started washing their faces, (285) they washed, they combed their hair. All of a sudden somebody knocked in the daylight. They opened the door for her, she came in. She said, "I am after the key, I came back." The grown boy said to her, "Ah, (290) I told you to put it there, I guess it's there. Go there, go look for it." She went in there. Where she had put it down, the key was lying there. The woman was sure surprised. (295) She took the key. Nobody ever had done that to her, no. She had put it away, she had got it back with a wish, she had taken the key and forgotten about it. She took her key back and went back out. She said to them, "I'm going to cook for you in a while. (300) When you are done with your eating then I'll take my nap because I was out at the dance all night, I haven't slept yet." She said to them, "Don't be backwards; you are tired. Stay here two nights; get rested and then continue your trip. (305) Don't be backwards, this is your house, you can stay here. You can walk around. I am going to bed, I'm going to take a rest. You don't have to pay me. You've already paid me, you took care of my key. (310) It's just like you're working for your board and room," she said. She went back out, a little while she came back in.

The woman was surprised. She thought, "Gee, that man must be really smart. It never happened that anybody could take care of my key. (315) And he... I put it down there, and I got it back with my wishing, and he overtook the key. And I had put it away in my box." The man-eater, the woman, thought, "Well, not this time, this evening. (320) I'm going to win, they're not going to find what I'll give them to keep." She cooked for them. She cooked, she took the food back. She didn't ask them to the house, they hadn't seen her house. She put it down, set the table for them. (325) They ate, they got done eating. She took the dishes back. In a while the sun came up. His little brother said, "Ok, do something smart. Let's get something to fight with. (330) Do you have a knife?" The old one said, "Yes, I have a knife." He asked, "Is it sharp?" "Yes, sharp enough. Are we going to butcher, or what are we going to do?" (335) "No, we are going to get something." He said to him, "We are going quite a ways." They started to walk, they walked. They didn't go far, they got out of sight, and they came in sight of a swamp. (340) Not a big swamp. They went and got to the edge. They walked in the swamp. My the thornbushes, they are just grown. He said, "Now your knife, (345) start cutting these thornbush shoots." He said to him, "And what are we going to do with them? Are we going to make arrows?" He told him "No, we got a use for it, I'll tell you. (350) You have to get four bundles, just as much as you can hold, tie these thornbushes. And where you are going to hold it cut the thorns off, because that will prick your hands. (355) Halfway the stem.[41] Don't cut the thorns off, leave the thorns on." The big one got puzzled again. He started cutting. He cut until he was holding enough; (360) and he had been cutting the [thorns off the] handle. He got his four bundles. He said, "Is this enough?" "That's enough. Our boss will soon wake up." (365) They went and got back. He said, "Put it away, don't let it show, don't let our boss see it. Maybe she'll get wise." The oldest one keeps getting puzzled. They got back, and he covered it (370) with something so it would't show in another room.

In the evening she fed them again. They finished eating and she washed their dishes. In a little while she came back. She told the oldest one, "I'll be gone again. (375) I want you to keep this ring for me." She took it off. Her ring is gold, and it shines, what do they call it, "diamond ring." (380) It shines, it's valuable. "I might

41 "Peel the thorns off the bases of the stem where you will be holding them."

lose my ring; I'll have you keep it. And tomorrow when I get back you'll give it back to me." "Put it there on the table, (385) or in the cupboard." The woman put it down there. She took it off and put it there. She went out, went out and wished back her ring. It was back on her finger. (390) She went back, went back in. He told his older brother, the older one, "Now we'll be dead if we don't catch up with it. I'm going to follow her [and see] if I can get it back from where she's going to store it." (395) He said to him, "Well, you are smart," he told the young one, the oldest one told him, he told his little brother.

The boy, the little fellow, went out. In a while after he'd been gone he came back in; (400) he was holding the ring. He said, "She really hid it," he said "in the fourth floor of the house." All of them, the first floor has a key; they are all locked to the top of the house. And there is a thing to store things in, (405) a trunk, and that's where she puts her ring. And she locks the trunk back. She locked all the doors and she went back down. And then she went back out. (410) That makes four doors, maybe her house has three thicknesses [stories]. And she left. She said to him, "Here it is." He said to her, "There," and she put it in the cupboard. "Put it there." (415) They went back to bed.

When daylight comes, daylight came, and his older brother woke back up. He said to him, "Wake up, you might get caught. Our boss is coming back." He said to him, "When she asks you for her ring you'll tell her, (420) 'Wherever I said to you to put it, it must be there. Nobody gets here to us; and we locked the house, the door.'" The man-eater went back to the cupboard, she looked, the ring is there. (425) Gee, the woman is real surprised. She thought, "My, he is smart; he is smarter than I am. He has beaten me." She put it back on, (430) she said to them, "I'll cook for you. When you are done eating then I will go to bed. I was up all night." She went, she went back out. In a little while, it wasn't very long, it was just a little while, she came back. (435) Their food was all steaming, the hot cakes, the oatmeal, or the eggs. I suppose she had electric stove at the time, she is a man-eater. She brought their food in, it's steaming. (440) They ate, they got done eating. She asked them, "Are you satisfied with what I cooked for you? Maybe I don't cook enough for you, don't feed you enough." They said "No, we are plenty filled up. We don't want to hurt your feelings and we eat everything." (445) They picked up their dishes.

The little one jumped up, grabbed the woman. He asked his big brother, "Where is the whip[42] you are going to whip with? Bring them in, and take one, and start whipping her. She will say it's enough; (450) she'll feel it and she'll groan; and she'll say 'enough,' that's when you stop. I'll tell you 'quit.'" The young fellow grabbed the man-eater. He took the four bundles, (455) that's his whip. He told him "Don't take pity on her." He told him, "That's a man-eater. If we don't defeat her she'll kill us. She'll kill us, she's trying her best to get us with her ring, (460) with her key and her ring." He whipped her, and the first bundle got to the end; and he took another bundle. She doesn't even groan. That woman is laughing at them. (465) He beat her, and that's the second bundle. He beat her; he took the third bundle, he beat her; and that's gone too, and no, she just laughs at them. The woman doesn't even groan. (470) That's his fourth one, and that's all gone. I

42 The thornbush bundles.

don't know how many times with the fourth whip, and that's when the woman groaned. He still whipped her; then she tried to stop him. He saw something but he couldn't make out what it was. It came out from where he was hitting, and it was sucked in.[43] He couldn't make out what it was, it flew. The woman tried to stop them. She said, "I'm really hurt, you win me." So he stopped.

She asked them to her house, she asked them. They went, went in, went to bed. The woman took a bath. She changed, they went to bed. They went to bed, he and the woman. The little one was under another blanket. The next morning they got married. The young one married them. The little one said, "Well, now you found her." He asked "What did you do with your picture?" The young one didn't know. The older one thought, "He doesn't know I have a picture for him to ask me about. Only I know it, and I've been hiding it. And for him to ask me..." He gave it to him. He pulled it from under his clothes. He asked, "Is this, the one sitting here, your woman? Is this her picture that looks like her?" He said "Yes." "Is this the one you've been looking for?" He said, "Yes, that's the one I'm looking for." "And you hadn't seen this woman before, you had only seen this picture. You didn't know whose picture it was. And you looked for her for nothing." He told him, "I pitied you. You would have been dead, the woman is a man-eater. And your father gave you money for your eats and for your clothes if you wear them out; and you pitied the corpse, you paid his bills. And then you were broke. That's why I pitied you, I am god. That's why I helped you, and you found what you are looking for. Now she's turned into a human." He[44] said, "No, she doesn't go to the straight people when she goes to the dance. She goes to her lover, because the devil had won her. That's where she goes every night. She goes to the dance. And then the first time she let you take care of her key. Because I am god, I know. And that's why I told you; and you don't put the key away, and she thinks it back; and the key is gone again. When you look the key is gone again. And I said 'I'm going to follow her.' She locks the key in the trunk, she locks the key there. And she did the same with her ring, to the three rooms. They are locked, she locks all of them. I got them from there because I pitied you; you pitied the corpse and paid his debts." He said, "Now I am going to instruct you.

I pitied you, and now you got what you were looking for. And now I'm leaving you, I am going back to the sky. When you get your child, I think you'll get a child, the woman's child will be a boy. That's what you'll pay me for helping you. You'll give me your son, her first son. From then on they'll be all your children." He said "Ok." "Now I'm leaving you." He agreed. "And when it comes to the same day next year I'll come back here, and you'll have a child, and I'll collect my pay." "If that's how you feel. I'm sure going to miss you. I'm going to miss you when you leave me. [If] that's what you want to do." He said, "Yes, because I am god. But no, I'll be with you all the time. I'll look after you, and you can't see me." He went out. They followed him and he went out.

This woman turned into a real woman, she's not a man-eater any more. She likes the man she got. They went out, and as soon as he went out the door and on the

43 Whatever spirit possessed her is now sucked out of her body.
44 The little fellow continues his account.

porch (560) the boy's feet left the ground; he changed, he turned into Jesus Christ.[45] They looked, and he was gone to the sky. It was shiny, and then it got out of sight.

They were getting along well. (565) His wife started to love him, and he her. They don't have any trouble of any kind. They don't get any company. Then the woman got a baby, a boy. And because it's a fairy tale (570) he was born and it wasn't long after that, he grew up, and was running around and playing, running around. Then it came to that time, he thought of it, that his friend is going to get back. He said to his wife, "I am all prepared. (575) That's right, my partner is going to get here, that's our date. I want you to cook the best things to eat, and clean the house; clean the house and the table." The woman did just that, (580) because she likes her husband. She cleaned house and got done cleaning house. She cooked pie and cake, because she had canned fruit. She just got done setting the table, and the clock rang twelve o'clock.

(585) Somebody knocked on the door. They opened the door. That's his friend, the boy; he had turned back into a boy. They were glad to see him again, he shook hands with his brother, took him on his lap. (590) The woman did the same, she shook hands with him, she kissed him, was tickled. He said to him, "The table is already set. We know you, and this is what we do. We'll eat." And the child[46] is sitting right by his side. (595) They got done eating. His little brother said to him, "I'm not going to camp with you. I just ate with you. And our bargain, (600) I'm after my pay. That's what you pay me, what I asked you to pay, your first born child, a little boy. Now I'm after it. That's the deal we made, do you remember?" (605) The oldest one said "I remember." But he got stingy of his son. "It's a pity, and it's what you pay me." And god knew all his thoughts; he said to him, "Well, you are stingy of your son, and you are keeping[47] it to yourself." (610) He said, "It's true, I am stingy of him. It's a pity, but that's our bargain." He asked, "Where is your sword? Have you got a sword?" He said "Yes," and gave it to him. (615) He asked "Will your feelings be good if I hit him on the head and then we divide him? You take one half and I take the other half?" He said "If they were two, and alive, (620) I'd take one, and you the other." The oldest one thought, "And what's the matter, split in two, it can't be alive split in two. But that's what he said. (625) I guess it's not for nothing that he said that, that he talked like that." He said "Go ahead, if that's what you think. I told you that's the bargain we made. I agreed with you with what you asked for pay. (630) Go ahead, do what you think best." "Ok."

He took the sword, he hit him on top of the head. The half flew off (635) and a boy stood there; another flew and it stood there too. Their faces are alike, and their heights too; their clothes are the same. He said to him, "Your thoughts are very strong; (640) you really believed. Nobody'd give away his son to have him split in two, but you [did]." He said "Yes," "And then we split it. You take one; (645) and I'll take one. And when the next generation comes it won't always be one child born. There will be twins." He said, "I'm going to leave you." (650) He said "They are your children." And god rose up. It went a little way and it shone;

45 The character is best viewed as a generic Western supernatural being.
46 The couple's son.
47 The gist is "you want to keep it."

they looked, and he got out of sight in the sky.

They were sitting around I don't know how many days, and the woman felt surprised. And the man felt surprised too. He said to his woman, "I am lonesome for my folks. The day has come that I told them if I am alive I'm supposed to get back, I am lonesome for my elders, and they'll be lonesome for me too. I guess they are looking for me. Let's go. And I want them to see their grandchildren, and to see you. You can get acquainted with your father-in-law and mother-in-law." The woman said "All right. You are my man, I'm married to you. That'll be fine, I'll go with you. I won't refuse. Sure, I'm glad to see my relatives."

Daylight come, and because the woman he won is important, he got the best horses and the little buggy. Because at that time they didn't have cars or airplanes. They got in the rig, they went. Their horses prance and they're well matched, and the buggy has a top, and it's a two-seater. The boys are in the back and the parents sit in front. The elders have been searching and they are lonesome for their son, because he's their only son; they are always looking for him. All of a sudden they saw the wagon come in sight. They said "Maybe that's our son, the one we've been looking for." He got closer and they recognized him. They said "No, maybe we are mistaken." Maybe the father [said], "Maybe that's a fellow chief, he's got too much of a good outfit, horses, wagon. And he has a companion, a woman, and boys. It must be a boss like me." They [the visitors] got close to the door, they got off. They went to meet them, that's their son.

Gee, his parents are tickled to see him! They shook his hand and kissed him. He said to his father and mother, "This is your daughter-in-law, that's the one I got for a woman, she's the one I was looking for. I told you I am going to travel the country, I'm going to see the country over. And these are my children, they're twins, they're alike." Gee, they're glad. They shook hands with their daughter-in-law, they shook hands with the boys, took them on their lap. The woman took one boy in her lap, and the man took the other boy. They picked them up and petted them. They were glad. They asked them to the house. And the boss told his working man: "Fix his horses, take them to the barn." They fed them and they got done eating.

The boss, the father, is going to call on the telephone the whole neighborhood. He said "My son is back. You are going to gather, we are going to play. He has children and you are going to get acquainted with them." At that time the people are always looking for an excuse to gather and to dance.

Gee, all the boss's children gathered, they all gathered. The boss's house, the dance hall, filled up. Gee they are happy. They shook hands with the son and his wife's in-laws; and with the boys, his children. They danced. And I was right there with them.

It's not quite daylight. Things commence to be different and then daylight comes, the first light comes on. I am tired. Then I tell them, "I am weeding, I should go back home. I am tired. It's the end of the story."

The Devil and the Black Face[48] (53')

I recorded this story (minus its first few utterances) in 1974. While that summer I recorded a few conversations I had with Pete (in English), it had been three years since the recording of his previous narrative. This is a story in the Seymour tradition of Western tales. The tale[49] revolves around the two characters of the title who have partnered up, and starts with a developed motif K171.1 "*Deceptive crop division: above the ground, below the ground.* Of root crops the [Devil] chooses the tops; of other crops the roots." After two disastrous choices, the Devil opts out of the partnership and pays the Black Man to build him a see-through house. The motif here is subsumed under J730 "*Forethought in provision for shelter,*" and the material provided by the Black Man is ice, destined to melt at the end of winter. The ironic conclusion of the tale is that when the Black Man dies and the Devil refuses to let the Black Man into, presumably, hell, he deceptively works his way into, presumably, heaven. His deceipt, however, is punished by the heavenly higher-ups, and he is confined to the vehicle[50] of his deceitful entry until "the last day."

And he said to his friend, "Might as well we go partners. I don't think there are people around here, and it's just you (and) I here. (5) It's just as well we go partners." "Ah, if that's how you feel," said the Black Face to the Devil. The Devil is the one that does the talking.

Spring came, somehow they made it through winter, maybe with moss (long ago moss was food). (10) Spring came, and the snow was gone, and the frozen earth thawed and it's getting time for the grass to sprout, and the Devil said, he said to the Black Man, "Well, being that we are partners, and now there is no more snow..." And they live in one house, and just it's one inside, it's not partitioned; there's only the fireplace that burns between them. (15) And on one side of the room is the Black Face. That's where he stays, and that's where he cooks. And the Devil is on the other side, and that's where he cooks. And when they cook, they eat separately. One stays on one side, and the other on the other side. (20) The snow came off the ground, the frost is out of the ground, and then garden time came.

And the Devil said to the Black Face, "Well, since we are partners, and the snow is all gone, just as well we put in a garden. (25) We might reach winter again, we might stay alive until winter. Let's put in a garden for our winter supply." The Black Face said, "All right. You are the oldest, you do the thinking, your thinking is good. And you name what we're going to plant." (30) And the Devil said, "Well, let's plant potatoes." "Ah, if that's how you feel. And from where will we get potatoes for our garden?" "Ah, said the Devil, I will rustle them." He said, "OK, and I will do the plowing, and fix the surface in our garden. (35) And just when I'll be done plowing you will be ready for planting. Just then we will put in a garden."

Well, the Black Face plowed, but I don't know what it is, mules, or oxen, that

48 MD used "Black Man" interchangeably with "Black Face."

49 Tale type 1030.

50 See motif D1520 Magic object affords miraculous transportation.

they use for plowing. It grew. They weeded, and because it's new ground there are hardly any weeds. They hilled the garden; after they got done hilling the garden it started to grow. The potatoes flowered, then they hilled it, the blooms are beautiful. Then fall came. They said, "Now we will harvest our crop."

The Black Face said to the Devil, "You are the oldest, you are smart. Ok, let's divide in half our crop, which do you like?" The Devil said, "Yeah, how are we going to divide it? Maybe you have figured it out," he said to the Black Face. The Black Face said, "There's nothing to it. It'll be easy to figure it out, for me to figure it out. One will take the tails, and that will be his share. And then just the roots, that will be the other one's share." He said, "Yeah, that's good thinking." The Black Face said to the Devil, "You are the oldest, and you will be the first one. You name what you want to harvest, and I will take what's left."

When the Devil saw from the time they grew, the potatoes sprouted, my the blooms! Truly beautiful blooms. He said to his partner, "Is it true that you want it that way?" "Yes, I am not going to change my mind. I told you, you are the oldest one, you will have your pick, whatever you want, and we'll divide it up." The Devil said, "All right, I will take the tops, and you the roots. Are you well satisfied?" The Black Face said, "Of course. You are the oldest, that's why I told you to go first. Ok, now let's take our crop in."

The Devil said to the Black Face:[51] "Well, you wait for me. I'll do my work first, since you take the tops of our garden and I what's underground. Since the tails are on top it's easy for you to take your crop, but I can't see where they [the roots] are. That's why I wanted to go first. I will dig my crop [first], I will dig the roots. When I get done taking them then I will pile together the tops of the potatoes. I'll pile them there, and it'll be easy for you to put away your share. Mine is the hardest because it just has to have its tail before I know where to dig." "Ok," he said, "Go."

The Black Face went, he started to dig. He dug the potatoes, and piled them up. He got done piling what he dug and then he put the tails to one side, he piled them. He finished digging and then he said to his partner, "Well, I am done; do whatever you want to do with your share, and I too will do the same. That's for the winter." And this Black Man, I guess he wrote somewhere, and sent for sacks. He filled the sacks. He filled the sacks, he had just enough sacks. He brought them to their house. And the Black Man had his place to one side of the house, and the Devil to the other. And the Devil brought the potatoes to his side. He put them there, lots of potatoes. And the Devil took his tops, and he put them also to one side. That too was lots of tails, his crop, he slices them.[52]

Then winter time came. The ground froze, and the snow fell. And the Black Face started to cook. He washes the potatoes, and then he boils them. He doesn't have a particular way; he peels them and he slices them. I don't know where he gets his meat, and he slices the meat. And it's excellent chop suey. And all the Devil has from his garden is nothing: the tails of the potatoes are not edible. He sure had a hard time to pull through winter. The Devil lost lots of weight. Gee, but the Black Man got big and fat. He had good things to eat, potatoes, roots.

Spring time came. The Devil sure had a hard time pulling through winter,

51 This is backwards: the Black Face is the one talking.

52 Not clear what Pete had in mind.

and the Black Face got big and fat. "Now we will put in a garden again, because we are partners, we are acquaintances. We are good friends, we have done good. We will put in a garden again. (125) But this time we'll change what we're going to plant, because the weeds will spoil the ground." He said, "All right, but what are we going to plant?" The Black Face said, "Wheat, we'll plant wheat. We will change grub. Look, we've had potatoes, now let's have wheat." (130) They didn't have to plow, because they kept pulling the weeds, it's clean soil, but they just harrowed it, and they sowed the wheat. It grew, because that land is good land. Goodness there are no weeds, or anything because all summer long they pulled weeds.

(135) And it's fall again, and the Black Man said to his partner, "It's fall, soon it will snow, winter starts. We might get caught in the snow, we better hurry. Well, it's a pity that you are the oldest." The Black Face said to the Devil, (140) "You are the older one, you pick out what you want, the roots, or the tops." The Devil thought, "Haven't I taken the tops before, the stalks? And the flowers were beautiful, and sure enough I had a hard time to pull through winter, I was the loser all the way. (145) But the Black Face got fat on the roots. This time I will take the roots. I am not going to be the loser this time." He told his partner, "This time I will take the roots and you the tops of the wheat." (150) "Ah, are you sure that you want it that way, my partner?" "Yes, yes, I am satisfied." "Ah, you are well satisfied, and we are good partners; you are the oldest." The Black Face said to the Devil, "But I'm going to say to you one thing: (155) I don't know what to do for us two to harvest together. We will wait for one another. I will go ahead because I have the stalks, the meat of it, like. I am the one who is going to take that, and you the things under ground, the roots. (160) You will take that for your own. You'll be the first to cut the grain[53] and put away your winter supply. And I can't find..." Oh, no![54]

The Devil said, "Ok," and he took the cutter... (165) But I forget. The mower has a name, "cradle scythe," "cradle scythe," that's the name. You cut it and it hits the ground; and when it cuts, because it has finger-like things, it stops right there. You let go there, (170) and it's just enough for a bundle. He cut it and got done cutting, and he was bundling. And then he said to his partner, "I am done harvesting; now it's your turn." He took the shovel, and he tried, he remembered what his partner did--(175) or the potato digger. He dug, but it didn't do any good, it didn't work. He pulled them by hand, then he got done. He packed them and stored them. Lots of roots on one side of the room for winter.

(180) And the Black Face started looking for something to put under [the wheat]. He got something to spread down, and he started threshing the wheat. He filled the sacks, he lay them down. He had lots of wheat. Then they cooked. The Black Face washes the wheat, (185) then he mixes it with bacon, then he eats. Or [he grinds it] in the coffee mill. He gets it ground and then he makes biscuits; or he'll make bannock. Goodness, the Black Face has good things to eat. (190) But the Devil, he tries to work the roots. It doesn't work. He's going to die of starvation. He's going very much to nothing. And it was past mid winter.

Then the Black Face said... no, the Devil said to the Black Man, "Well, partner,

53 This is backwards: the Black Face goes first and cuts the wheat.
54 Pete realizes he has said it backwards.

we are going to quit one another." The Black Face said to him, "And what's the matter? We are real partners, and then you're going to throw me away?" He answered, "No, it's two winters you get the best of me in our crops. This time I sure had a hard time pulling through winter." It's past mid-winter, and there is still ice, lots of ice. The Devil said to the Black Face, he said, "Well, partner, now we're going to leave one another. If I live, or if I don't make it to when the warm weather arrives, we have been partners two years, and every year you get the best of me. And now I can't make it to spring. I'm telling you, we are quitting our friendship. Even if you were to die, I would't take you." The Black Face said to the Devil, he said, "No, don't feel that way. I didn't get the best of you. It's always you [who did]. I told you, you are the oldest one. I always had you go first when we divided the garden. You go first, and it's you that makes yourself lose." The Devil said, "What I said goes. Even if you were to die, I wouldn't take you." He said, "Well, if that's how you feel."

The Devil said, he said to the Black Face, he said, "I'm going to say one thing to you. Now I want you to fix me a house, then we will part." And the Black Face said to the Devil: "Ok, if you want it that way. I don't want to get rid of you, nor did we quarrel. Do as you please. And now I'm going to ask you, what kind of house would you like?" The Devil told him: "I want my house to be all glass, all around. Wherever I look I'll see the outside, and up above there the same, and down below. And I'll give you all my money." The Black Face said to him: "Certainly not I'm going to fool you and tell you [right away]. I will stay with the job. I will think about it, maybe I'll get the right idea and I'll fulfill your wish. That's what I'm going to tell you."

The Black Face got thirsty, maybe he wants to drink cold water, he went to the water, he got there, he tipped his head to drink. Ah, what did he see there down in the water? Gee, he saw his image. It was then that he got the idea: "I will build a house just like that for my friend." The Black Face started sharpening the ice saw, one could call it "sxʷúyənt naʔník̓mən" in Indian. He got done sharpening it, he went, he cut the ice. He measured the ground where the house was going to be. He asked his friend, "Where would you like your house?" He said "Here," and so he marked the ground. He laid the ice up to the ceiling, he got done. He looked around, it's just like window: wherever he looks it's like outside.

He went after his partner, and the Black Face brought the Devil into the house. He said, "Well, I finished your house, and I am not forcing you. It was you who wanted to hire me. And that's why I told you. If you go look and you are satisfied, then you can pay me. But if you are not satisfied, then don't pay me. Come!" And they went out there. They went in, and it has a door and windows all around. The Devil walked all around. "Yes, yes, I am satisfied, thank you." He gave him all his money. The Black Man got the money, and the Devil got the house. They shook hands. The Devil said, "Two years you starved me with our garden. I had a hard time pulling through winter, and that's why I said to you build me a house, and when you finish it we will part, we won't be partners any more." The Black Face said to him, "No, don't think that way. You are the one who always picked our crop, corn [wheat] or potato, and you that beat yourself." He said, "That's what I think." They parted.

The Black Face was all alone at his house and the Devil got settled. When it gets warm... The Devil is bragging how beautiful the house he got is. Wherever he looks, there it's bright like; and the doors are also like that, and the ceiling, and the floor. The Devil was well satisfied. At once it got warm from the sun; the snow and the ice melted, and the house melted and the water started running. And the Devil got scared. "Now it's going to fall on me." He went out fast, he just got out when the house caved in. "Ah," thought the Devil, "Again my partner beat me. When he dies I am not going to take him, he gets the best of me too much." Then he moved to where he belongs. When daylight came to the Black Face, he looked over to his partner's. His house is gone, his partner is gone. "And what's the matter, he must have moved in the night. He didn't even say, 'I'm leaving you.' I wonder where he went."

After he was figuring around, he got sick maybe because he got lonesome, because he's all alone. It was no time, and the Black Face died. His life went out of his body. His soul went, like they say in English, "his soul went out of his body." He saw two roads. One is steep uphill, the road to his right. It's dim, and there aren't many tracks on it. And the one to the left is downhill. Goodness, it's nothing but dust[55] there, it's a beautiful road. The Black Face thought, "I am going to the good road. It doesn't look like people go to the right often." He went to the left, downhill.

He went, he came in sight, gee, there is a beautiful gate, it glitters. He got closer, and he started feeling the heat. He got right to the door, he knocked on it, he played white man. He opened the door, he had a fork in his hand. He recognized him, "That's my partner." He said, "Well, partner, here I am." He said, "No, we're not partners. I told you while we were living on earth, you got the best of me twice in the garden, and in the house, there too you got the best of me. And then I left that country and now I have made my home here." He said, "Partner, I am dead. I don't have where to go, only here." He said, "You're not my friend," and he shut the door.

He stood there, and he thought, "Well, it's a pity I can't go back to life, I am dead." Then he turned around, went up the hill in the road where all kinds of things grow. It's not often that they travel there. He went up the hill, got to the top, gee there's a shining door, and it's far. He went, he got there, he knocked on the door. Saint Peter opened the door (it's "pyar" in Indian). Peter, he's the one who opened the door. He asked, "What do you want?" He said, "I am dead, and I am hard up for a place to stay. That's why I came here. Let me in." Saint Peter said, "I just work here. And it's not anybody who can get in here, only the good. Look, when you were still alive you were partners with the Devil. And you never thought about your prayers. Go to your partner, to the Devil." He was going to close the door and he said, "When you were still alive you were partners with the Devil." "No, my friend doesn't want me either, and I can do nothing to go back to life. I have got to have a place to stay. Come on and open the door, I only want to see inside there, and then I will be satisfied." He said, "Ok," and he opened the door. The Black Face jumped in his glove, he threw his glove in there. The glove landed inside there, and there it sat.

55 The sense is "well-traveled."

Saint Peter closed the door, and he looked behind himself, and he saw him there sitting in the glove. He said, "I told you not to come in, and you came in!" He said to Saint Peter, "Now I am in, and you can't do anything to throw me back out." He had just said that when JC was standing there. He said to St Peter, "Go, I'll talk to him. You go to your work." St Peter went. And that's God himself, God said, "Well Black Man, I am God. And you forced yourself here. He didn't tell you to come here and then you came here. And now I'm going to give you a sentence. You got in with your glove. You went in your glove and you threw it in. So you are going to stay in your glove until the last day."

captíkʷɬ

This section includes the six captíkʷɬ Pete had me record. The first text ("Coyote gets his powers") is a version of the important story of how the Creator assigned names (and attendant charges) to the animals that populate the earth. This text is the prelude to the stories that constitute what I call the "man-eater saga," to which the second text, "Coyote and the whale," belongs. This is Pete's account of how Coyote disposed of a man-eating water monster and rescued the creatures the whale had swallowed. One of the rescued is Buffalo Woman, the daughter of a powerful chief who rewards Coyote by giving him his daughter in marriage. In the third story, "Coyote and Grizzly," Seymour tells us how Muskrat avenges the death of Coyote and Gopher's four sons (Muskrat's half brothers) at the hand of a man-eating she-Grizzly, and how Coyote manages to dispatch the man-eater. The fourth text, "The two goats," is the text with the twist that Coyote is the man-eater who uses his daughter as bait for her suitors, Coyote's would-be victims. The goat brothers manage to defeat Coyote. The next two texts, not part of the man-eater saga, are versions of well-known captíkʷɬ. They are both stories about apparently unremarkable non-entities who end up ouperforming their peers. In "Lynx and the virgin" Lynx secretely (and with slight of hand) impregnates a most desirable maiden and thus beats his many competitors. He and the young woman are punished and banished by the community, but eventually Lynx rescues them from starvation and rejoins the group. Finally, in "BlueJay and his brother-in-law Wolf," BlueJay is a seemingly lazy playboy who ends up outperforming his wife's older sister's husband Wolf, the best hunter in the community.

How Coyote got his powers (27')

This is the shortest of the six texts in this section. All the four-legged and winged creatures of the earth are assembled one morning by the Creator to be given their names and relative powers.[56] Coyote wants to be first in line (and therefore the most powerful of the quadrupeds), and he tries to stay up the night before the meeting, ending up oversleeping, missing the ceremony altogether, and becoming the incarnation of foolish pride. The Creator designates Coyote as the one who will rid the earth of man-eaters,

56 See "The spirit chief names the animal people" (Mourning Dove 1933 pp. 17-26); "Naming the animals" (Andrist 1971 pp. 41); "The origin of the people" and "The naming of the animals" (Spier 1938, p. 176 and pp. 197-200).

and gives Coyote four special powers who will help him in this enterprise. The story is known in all parts of the Colville-Okanagan world, and published versions of it abound.

The story has an interesting epilog. Seymour repeats what Coyote's charges are, and he tells us that Coyote did complete them successfully. We also infer that the Creator wants Coyote not to become too full of himself: disguised as a little boy he challenges (and defeats) Coyote at an extraordinary feat. Then he banishes him to a remote and unreachable island til the "judgment day."[57]

I am going to tell a story. When JC[58] was first born and he got here on earth, he called all the birds, and the ones that walk on the ground, coyotes, lynxes, wolves, all those that walk on the ground. He asked all of them to come, not the human beings, only what they call in English "animals," and the fowl, the birds. He said to them, "Now we are going to gather. Just now this world is going to come to life and I am going to change you. You birds that fly in the air, you are going to be birds, and you are going to be those that fly in the air. And you that stand on four legs, you that don't have wings, the coyotes, and the grizzlies, and the black bears, and the deer, everything that is on this earth, but high [in the mountains], you are not going to be mixed up with the people." They all agreed. He said to them "Tomorrow, just when the sun is turning, we'll gather back here. That's when I'll give you what's going to be your arrows.[59] That's when you'll scatter to the mountains. You won't be mixed up with the people." They all agreed. He said to them, "You can scatter, go to bed. When daylight comes on you, and the turning fits again[60] you will all gather here again, and I'll give you the arrows."[61] They said "Ok," and they scattered to where they are going to camp.

I guess their camping place is all together. And then Coyote, because he is Coyote, he started thinking up things. He thought, "I am going to win the first arrow, the longest. I am not going to sleep." Well, Coyote started walking back and forth. In no time he got tired from walking back and forth. And the others all went to bed, it's only Coyote fooling around. In no time he got tired from his walking back and forth; then he sat down, he sat down and he got sleepy. Heck no, he got tired walking. He holds one eye down, just one eye, but no, still no; he is still sleepy. He presses one down, even when he turns to the other eye and he presses the other down, it still doesn't work. Whatever he does is to no avail. And his partners, the rest of them, are asleep, snoring. Then he thought of something. He broke a stick, he propped his eyes open. What he fixed is still the same. He lay down, and he fell asleep.

He slept and slept, and he must have overslept. The sun must have been high when he woke up. Heck, he could not see, because his eyes went dry. He

57 We have encountered this motif in the story of the Devil and the Black Face. Both the glove of the first story, and the island of the current text, remind us of purgatory. For a brief discussion of biblical and new testament motifs in Okanagan mythology see Boas 1917 pp. 81-82.

58 Seymour often resorts to westernizing the Creator. I interpret this to be Pete's way of deflecting the (western) audience's attention from the Colville supernatural, redirecting it to the familiar catholic supernatural. As we know, the jesuits, the oblates, and other missionaries have had some important influences on the Colville-Okanagan and other Indians of the Plateau.

59 The symbol of each animal's power.

60 The sense is "at this same time."

61 Arrows vary in length in direct proportion to the importance of the recipient.

tried to listen. They are gone, he can't hear anything. He lay there still, lying down. He stayed there, he was awake, awake. (55) They gathered there at the gathering place. JC was there to give them their arrows. They gathered there, they got there, all got there. Then JC got there, then it was time. He asked them, "Are you all here?" (60) They said, "Yes, we are all here." He said to them "Ok."

He would give one the longest [arrow]. JC was holding the arrows. He gave the longest one to Grizzly. He said to him, "You'll be the head boss on earth of you that walk; you will be the boss." (65) He was given it, and he took it. And then another. He put it in Eagle's hand. He was told, "You will be the chief of the birds, those that fly, you will be their boss, take this and go. That will be your home, up high. (70) You won't be mixed up with people." He gave them all out, except one arrow, the shortest one [that was left]. So JC asked them, "Is it all of you?" They said, "It's all of us." (75) He said to them, "And what's the matter, you are all here and there is one arrow left? One person must not be here."

Then they thought of Coyote. They said, "Coyote is not here." "And why?" (80) They said, "He must have overslept. He was walking up and down when we went to sleep. Then he must have gone to bed and overslept. When we woke up we came, because [otherwise] we might get behind. (85) It's written down just what time in the morning we gather here. We just got settled here, and then you came." JC said, "Go and get him. Even if he gets lazy, pack him! There is no no about it, he has to be here." (90) He told the young folks. The young people ran. They went and they got there.

Coyote was rolling around. He is trying his best to see, (95) but he can't see, because his eyes have dried out. They went and they got him there, they sat him down there, they sat him in front of the Creator. They were told, "Go, scatter. Take the arrows I gave you. (100) And I will give the arrow that's left to Coyote. Now go." Then they scattered.

He put it right in Coyote's hand, he said, "Coyote, it's a pity you got behind. (105) This is the only arrow left. Take it, this will be your arrow, and Coyote will be your name. Now you can go, that's all of them." Coyote took it. He took it and went a little ways, and Coyote started being a coyote. (110) He thought, "Heck no. What's up with that, I'm way up in class, and this is the shortest arrow and I took it? He gave it to me. I am going to follow Grizzly." I guess he found out Grizzly is the one who took the longest arrow. (115) He followed him, his tracks are plain. He crossed a big valley and he overtook him. He started coaxing Grizzly. He said to him, "Let's trade our arrows." He stopped Grizzly. (120) He [Grizzly] said to him "No," he said, "JC gave me this arrow, and he told me always to take care of it. He didn't tell me to trade it. I am not going to trade it off, I am not going to throw away my word to JC." (125) Coyote said, (he started coaxing him), he said to him, "Just lend me your arrow. I'll give it back to you." Grizzly said to him, "No. I can never make myself lend it to you (130) because JC told me to keep it, to keep it forever. He didn't tell me to lend it out. He gave it to me as judgment."

Then JC stood over them and he said to Grizzly, "What is Coyote saying to you?" (135) He said "He has been coaxing me to lend him my arrow, the one you gave me. And I told him no, and he coaxed me more for me to lend it to him. And I said to him, 'I can't make myself loan it to you, the Creator told me to keep this arrow, (140) not to lend it out.'" He said to him, "Go, go, don't pay attention to

Coyote. I'll talk to him." Grizzly went on, he went.

There is only Coyote there. He said to him, "Sit down, I am going to talk with you." Then Grizzly got out of sight and the Creator said to Coyote, "You are pitiful, Coyote. You haven't got any training. You keep putting yourself higher than others. If you had gone to sleep right away it wouldn't have gone this way. Then you thought all kinds of things. I am the Creator, you can't outwit me. Then you did all kinds of figuring to get the best of my decisions. And you wanted to be first and you propped your eyes with sticks and that's how your eyes got dried up." He said to him, "Now take those sticks out of your eyes." Coyote took out the sticks that he had propped his eyes with. He went like that, (there must have been water there), he did like that, he dipped from the water with his hand. Coyote washed his eys, just like that he could see.

He said to him, "Now you got back your eyesight. I am telling you, don't bother any of the animals or of the birds, or the animals that walk the earth. Don't bother them; I pity you." That's when he gave him wrapped up things for his powers, four packages. He said to him, "Take these four packages for my pitying you." He said to him, "It's not for nothing that I pity you: I want to hire you. Swallow these four packages. Whenever you get crowded with man-eaters you summon these four packages and they will help you. Tell them your troubles and they will tell you what to do. They are going to be your powers, and you will be able to kill man-eaters. And all over the world you will kill man-eaters. That's when you are done,[62] this is what I am telling you." JC said. He gave him the four packages. Coyote swallowed them, he had said "Swallow them." He swallowed them. He was told, "Go, don't bother with talk the bears or anybody. I have already settled all that. They will never lend the arrows." Then he gave him the arrow. He went, he said to him "Go." Then JC rose to the sky.

Coyote went, he wouldn't believe JC. "Maybe he is fooling me. I'm going to get to the truth of it." He stopped and sat down. He summoned what was given to him, the bundles. He said "ṗs ṗs ṗs ṗs k̓ʷƛ̓up!" All at once it fell, what is it? Then he called another one, "ṗs ṗs ṗs ṗs k̓ʷƛ̓up!" He also fell out, another person. He called four of them, all turned into humans. They said to him, "Why are you bothering us, Coyote? What is your trouble?" Coyote said, "No, I have no trouble." They said, "Hurry up with us, we are chilled, we are cold." Coyote swallowed them back, then he went on. Then he believed.

Then Coyote started traveling the world. Then he started killing man-eaters. His friends [powers] had given him something to be powerful with. See, when he gets in a corner he calls them, and they get to him, and they ask, and he tells the little people what his trouble is. He killed and killed man-eaters until he cleaned them up.

Coyote went, he ran into a boy.[63] He stopped, they both stopped. Coyote said to the boy: "Well, young brother, you are traveling around, where do you come from?" The little boy said to him, "No, I'm not your younger brother. You are the younger one, I am the older." "Ah," Coyote said, he shook his head and said "No. Don't you know that when you were a baby I used to pack you around, I walked the floor with you? I am the oldest, and you are the youngest one." The

62 "When you kill all the man-eaters."
63 This segment of the story is similar to one found in Andrist 1971, p. 40.

boy said to him, "All right, if that is true, Coyote, move this mountain,[64] put it down over here." Coyote said, "That's nothing. I told you I am the oldest." He moved it over. Coyote pointed, he turned it around and was going to put it down. And the mountain followed and settled there. He said to him, "See, I am the oldest one." His interlocutor said to him, "Ok, move it back now to where it was down before." "Ah, that's nothing." Coyote pointed for nothing, heck no. He even scratched it with his hand. No, it's a mountain, no, he had no show. Then JC told him, he said to him, "I am JC. It was I who gave you your smarts, your powers, the bundles, the four packages. Then I hired you to kill all the man-eaters. And you killed them all. And now you want to beat me too. It is I who is your boss, I am JC, and you can't beat me. The first time I pitied you and you moved the mountain. And you are going to learn. I told you to put the mountain where it belongs and you tried and couldn't move it. And what can you do, I am the boss. I am the one who has smarts."

He said to him, "Now you didn't listen to me. I am going to judge you. You will be in prison until the last day.[65] That's when you will get back where there are people on earth." Then he took him somewhere, maybe to the water, to the big water, the ocean. Maybe there is an island there, that's where he put him. He told him, "That's your place until judgment day." And they say that with the white people's binoculars one can see Coyote walk around there on the island. And even if they go there in a boat, they can never reach him. They get close and their eyes lose it. That's the end of it.

Coyote and Whale (70')

Having received the four critters who will help him in his hunt for man-eaters, Coyote travels the country by foot and boat, and is swallowed by a man-eating sea monster. One of the swallowed victims is the daughter of an important chief, who has promised her as wife to the one who rescues her. Coyote dispatches the man-eater and rescues the maiden and the other victims. He then accompanies the woman to where she comes from, the country of Buffalo Cows, receives her as wife, and with her fathers two children. He then returns to his own home alone, leaving his wife and children behind.

I am continuing with my Coyote story. He [Coyote] had got an arrow, a short arrow; and the Creator pitied him because his eyes went dry. And he wrapped it up for him, he pulled it from the grass, he wrapped that, four bundles. He told Coyote, "Because I pity you these are what is going to help you, your partners, four of them. Now you are going to work, this is what I give to you. You are going to destroy all the man-eaters, those that kill people, you are going to kill all of them. That's why I'm hiring you and I gave you these for your powers. When you get cornered you call them and then they'll say to you 'What is it you want that you called us?' and you tell them, 'Yes, I am cornered. I am going to beat the man-eater, I'm going to kill him.' And they'll say 'Ok,' and they'll show you what

64 A variant of this motif was described by Teit as follows, "Old-One and Coyote meet each other, and have a contest trying to move a mountain" (Boas 1917, p. 79).

65 An allusion to purgatory.

to do, and they'll help you." And then he can kill the man-eater. Then JC said to Coyote, "Go, and don't bother the Grizzly Bear or anybody. You are first. You are more powerful than anybody that has a longer arrow." Then he left him.

Then he went. He went and got a ways away. And JC went up to the sky. Coyote thought, "I think God's just fooling me. No, it doesn't make sense. I'm going to get the story of this." Coyote stopped. He said "ṗs ṗs ṗs ṗs k̓ʷƛ̓up!" They dropped on the ground. They asked him, "What do you want?" "Nothing, I just want to find out." Again he said "ṗs ṗs ṗs ṗs k̓ʷƛ̓up!" And again one dropped to the ground. He asked him, "Coyote, what do you want?" "Oh, nothing, I just want to get the story out of you." Again "ṗs ṗs ṗs ṗs k̓ʷƛ̓up!" Then another one; he asked him too. He said, "No, I just want to get the story from you. Is it true?" Again "ṗs ṗs ṗs [ṗs] k̓ʷƛ̓up!" The fourth one. He said "What did you want, Coyote, and you are getting us chilled?" He said, "No, I just want to find the story out from you. Is it true?" They told him, "Sure it's true. That's what God told you and it's true." "Oh, ok." Then he swallowed the bundles back, then he went on.

He went, and he got to the Lakes tribe. He got there. He heard that there was a maiden from Montana. She had disappeared from there. They don't know where she went. She is not dead. Her clothes were right close to the shore, a bundle right close to the water where the water runs. Her clothes are close to the water, and the woman is gone. And it's the chief's daughter that disappeared. She went after water and then she disappeared. Morning came. They looked for her, and that's when they saw her clothes: they were lying close to the shore. And her bucket.

Then he said, the boss from Montana hollered, the chief, he hollered and said, "My daughter has disappeared. You will search for my daughter. She is not dead, we didn't see her body that she is dead, we saw only her clothes bundled by the water. She was dipping water, and she disappeared. Maybe she is alive. And this is what I am offering to pay" (because his daughter is good looking). He said, "Whoever finds her, he can have her for his wife." Gee, these young fellows were horny for the girl, because she is good looking, and they don't think they are good enough and she wouldn't consent if they proposed for her to the chief.

They all rushed and looked for her. They looked on both sides of the running water by the big water, but they didn't find her. And they didn't hear where she went. And they got tired, and they gave up.

Coyote heard about it. And because, because he's Coyote he wants her, even if he had never seen the girl; he wants to get a taste of the maiden. So he looked for her. He went, Coyote went upstream, maybe in his bark canoe. He got over a falls, in Indian they call it the "Kutenai River." It's from the lake, the head of this big river is from there. They call it "Roosevelt Lake" in English, and in Indian "nx̌ʷəntkʷítkʷ." The head of the river is from there. From there he came back downriver.

He came back, and at Kettle Falls he came back in sight. He came back, downriver, at Kettle Falls. He was swallowed by the whale. Maybe Coyote had a bark canoe, and she swallowed him. He saw in the insides, the insides of the sea monster, that there were lots of people there. The people there are still alive, maybe the newly swallowed, and these are alive. But the ones that have been there a long time, they have died of starvation. And some of them are dead. They still have some meat on. But the ones before that, they are just bones. The first ones are dead. The sea monster is a man-eater. Coyote found out.

He started traveling around there in the insides of the sea monster, [he saw] its fat. Coyote took out the knife. He started cutting the fat off, and he ate it. The people who are still alive wished for it. He gave each some and they started to eat, because it's been many days since they ate. The sea monster got sick to the stomach. He[66] said, "What's the matter Coyote? I don't get sick, I never felt like that until you got here. I swallowed you and I am sick to the stomach." Coyote [said], "No, we are just telling stories here. And then you interrupt me!" Then the sea monster quieted down. Then he'd take another slab from the fat. Gee, it's hanging down uneven. Because he ate lots. The sea-monster said, "You are coyoteing, Coyote." The sea monster thought, "It must be Coyote that is doing this to me." So he squirted Coyote out. He fell way up on the shore, he fell. He thought "Ok."

He had seen a curtain there in the inside. There was a curtain, but there was no door, or window. And he had asked the kidnapped ones that were still alive: "What is that curtain?" They had said "We don't know. We got here and we saw the curtain there. We don't know what is in there." Coyote thought: "I bet that's the kidnapped one, the girl from Montana." "I hadn't found out and he threw me out. I'm going to have to find out. I'll ask my partners."

He started to go up the river. He went and got back above Kettle Falls, way up North. Then he called his partners. He said to the first one, he was getting ready to ask, then he said: "p̓s p̓s p̓s p̓s k̓ʷƛ̓up!" He fell to the ground, that's the first one. They don't have names. He said, "Why is it you called me?" "No, I am in a heap of trouble. This sea monster is a man-eater, and it threw me out of there. And there are lots he kidnapped, and some are dead; and those that are alive are starving to death. And I want you to help me, that's why I called you. The sea-monster threw me out of there." "Ah," he said, "I'll help you. I'll be your bark boat. I will be a whole, a whole driftwood. It'll stay on top of the water, and I'll be your transportation." He said "Ok." "p̓s p̓s p̓s p̓s k̓ʷƛ̓up!" Another one fell on the ground. He said, "You are getting me chilled. What is it you want?" He said, "I am cornered. The sea-monster is going to kill me. That's why I am calling you. I want you to help me, we will kill the sea-monster." "I am going to be a big knife, that's the help I'm going to give you." The he called another one, "p̓s p̓s p̓s [p̓s] k̓ʷƛ̓up!" He too fell to the ground. "You call me? What do you want, Coyote?" He said to him, "Keep quiet! You are going to help me, I am cornered. I am going head to head with the sea-monster. He has lots of people kidnapped. The others, the bones of the dead ones are bleached. And the ones who are alive are dying too." "Ok, I am going to help you. I'll also be a knife." He said to him, "The sea-monster is a man-eater." "My brother will think about you. If that doesn't work and the [first] knife breaks, then I'll go next." He said "Ok." Then he called the other one, he told him the same thing. He said, "I'll be a knife too." So he's going to have four knives because there were

66 The translator's switch of 3rd person gender is not uncommon.

four bundles.[67] It went just the way they told Coyote.

He saw the driftwood, a whole thing with its roots. The whole thing uprooted and fell in the water, the whole tree is in the water. (210) His friends told him, "This is your canoe, Coyote. They told him, "Sit on that log; then you can say whatever you want. Talk smart to the whale. Then the sea-monster will get mad at you (215) and then he will swallow you. And you will have weapons." They all told him, "We will help you, us knives. We are going to be your help. You wouldn't be capable if you have just one knife. (220) The sea-monster is very smart. That's why he is a man-eater." Then they quit preaching to him. Then Coyote pushed away from shore. He was sitting on the driftwood. (225) He started to sing a love song, and he sang. He started to insult the sea-monster. He got close to the falls, Kettle Falls. The sea-monster tried to control its temper. He didn't like what Coyote said, (230) because he was giving him bad hints. He swallowed Coyote back. He said, "Now I am not going to let him loose again. He'll be there and die like the rest." He didn't swallow it, the canoe, the whole thing. (235) He pushed it to one side and swallowed only Coyote.

Coyote fell in there, he fell back in with his partners. They had started to pick up.[68] (240) They were glad that he got back, and they said, "We are hungry again. We were just picking up when you left. We are hungry again." He started cutting some of its fat again. (245) He passed it around, they all rushed again, and they ate again. He passed that around, and then Coyote [got] to the heart of the sea-monster; it's big, because cannibals have big hearts. He cut its heart out. He cut it with a knife. (250) Before long the knife broke in two. Then another one, and he starts cutting again. Before he gets anything done, it wasn't quite half, and the knife breaks in two again. He took another from where it was fastened (255) and he started cutting again. He kept cutting and it also broke in two. That also broke in two. The sea-monster groaned. "What is the matter with you, Coyote? (260) Since you got here I have been sick to my stomach." Coyote said, "No, I am denying it. I got diarrhea, and maybe that makes you sick to the stomach." That's the last knife. The sea-monster thought: (265) "This is not good for me, I am going to die. I am going back to my country. There I'll doctor myself, and then I'll get well, there at the big water." (270) They call it "ocean" in the white man's language. "I'm going back there, there I'll get well, I'll doctor myself." Then he went downstream.

He went... and I just thought of something. His friends gave Coyote something to make a hoop with, (275) a stick's big hoop. They said to him, "If you get a chance to kill the man-eater, to kill him, before he dies put the hoop to his hind part. That will be your way to get out, and you will get out." (280) Then the man-eater went by Coulee Dam. I suppose Coyote can talk English and he knew Coulee Dam. There is a dam there, he'll never reach the ocean, (285) his hospital. He is going to take a shortcut to make it. He went straight and the water ran through. He was just half way when Coyote cut off his heart. (290) The man-eater died there.

And just before he died Coyote put that hoop there in the sea-monster's back side. And then he died. And as soon as he died the water backed up (295) and went back to where it was running and the river went dry. [end of tape]

67 Actually three knives, because the first helper is a driftwood boat.
68 Because Coyote had fed them the monster's fat.

I continue my story. Like I said, the monster from the ocean is dead and Coyote already put a hoop around the whale's back-end. He said to the people, "Go on, get out. We might get caught." They all got out. They all went out, the whole bunch. It was going to be all of them, and Woodtick is the last of them. Woodtick was half-way out when that hoop broke. It pinched Woodtick right in the center. He had a hard time before he got out because he was the last one.

First Coyote inquired about another part,[69] the curtain, in the whale. It's another part, and he inquired about it of those people kidnapped. And they told him, "We haven't seen anything; we've been here, what we saw is here." I guess that's another part. That's when he took his knife, and cut wide open that part. I guess it's just skin, or something, that curtain is not board. A beautiful girl was sitting there. He went in there and asked her, "Why is it that you are sitting here?" She said, "You talk pitiful. I come from long ways away. It's from there that this here whale kidnapped me, he got me prisoner in here." He said, "I know everything in the world. Name your country. I will know the name." She said "From Montana, I am an Indian from there. That's where he kidnapped me, this here cannibal, the whale." He said, "Well, yes, I know that country. I've been through there and I know your people and your country." So he said, "Come on, let's get out and then I'll take you back to your country."

He took her by the hand, and the woman, the virgin said to him, she said, "And this here monster, don't you think he'll kill us?" "Why no, he's already dead, pity him, he'll not come to life. Hurry." And then she followed him. They hurried, and they went out. They went out and that's when Woodtick got behind, and that's when that hoop broke. Then he got pinched. Woodtick had an awful time before he got out. That's why if you see Woodtick today he is flat. Because he got pinched there, that's how it happened.

After they went a ways, Coyote said to the girl, he said, "Well, you know the way to your country. As long as we go the right way, we won't go around curves, you go straight." The virgin said to him, "Yes, yes, I know the way, because it's my country. But let me tell you, if you get tired it's better if I pack you on my back." That's what the girl said to Coyote. Coyote laughed at the girl, he laughed at her. He said, "What are you saying? I am a man. You are the woman, and you'd be packing me! It's because I am smart that I found you. It's your parents that sent me over here and that's why I looked for you. And then you'd pack me around? I should be packing you." He said, "Let's go, let's walk." The woman jumped up. She turned into a cow, a Buffalo Cow. She raised her tail up, and she trotted.

Coyote was running alongside her. He was running alongside her, and they got to the top over a valley. The cow never did slack up; she got down to the bottom, then up the hill, and she's always trotting. She's always fast. They went. Then they got to the top, they kept on going, then they went down again. I don't know how many times, maybe three times they went down deep gulches. Coyote is getting tired. Coyote is falling behind. They were about to get to the top and Coyote gave out with tiredness. And Coyote sat right down. "Heck, I am going to lose what I kidnapped." He sat there a little while until he got rested. He

69 Seymour has to backtrack here.

is going to follow for nothing. Then he went. He went and took his time, went and got on top of the hill. (385) The woman was sitting there. She said, "You are taking too long on me. And I thought maybe something happened to you, you got hurt and that's why you didn't get to the top." He said "No, I'm ok." She said "You are tired." (390) "Yes, yes," Coyote said; he didn't deny it. He said, "Yes, yes, I got tired." She said, "I told you. Go ahead and ride on me, lie flat on my back. Put your arms around me and don't look around. (395) If you look around you'll get dizzy, and you'll fall off. And then I'll leave you for ever, I won't wait for you. But if you listen to what I am telling you then we'll both get back to my people." He said "Ok." (400) Then he climbed on the woman, on the maiden. He lay flat on her back and put his arms around her neck.

Then the Black Cow continued to run. She kept her speed, she won't go slow even if she goes uphill or on the level. (405) She is always fast. My, the trees, the shadows are running by fast. He closed his eyes tight again. They go through a valley, they go straight for it. They go to the bottom, and back up, to the top. (410) The Black Cow stopped. She said, "Now get off." The woman lay down. Coyote got down. "Look around. (415) The Cows, the Black Buffaloes, are over there in the open. They call them "Black Cows," they call those "Buffalo Robes," they are my people." Coyote said, "Leave me here. Go by yourself to your people." (420) She asked him "Why?" He said, "No; I'm going to rest. When I get rested you can come back and get me, they can come back after me." She said, "If this is how you feel." The Black Cow raised her tail, she ran down the hill.

(425) She hollered at her people. It was their holler, a herd of cows. They turned around. My, the dust just rose. (430) Next day, just at daylight, the virgin was back in the herd. Boy, were the cows tickled! They were glad, her grandparents and her parents; her relatives licked her. They started to walk and they got out of sight; they went to a hidden place.

Coyote was there, and it was a long time, and he thought: (435) "Well, I guess that's it. She got away from me, I didn't get rewarded. The chief stole it from me." All at once little calves came back in sight. They were little black calves, two of them. They are coming, they came up the hill, they got to Coyote. (440) They said to Coyote, "Our elders sent us, and we came after you." He said to them, "Go on, or I'll club you. It's not babies I want to come after me. Why, I am a big boss." So Coyote started his powers. (445) His friends already got to him. They said to him, "Why it is you are getting us chilled?" He said to them, "Hurry, hurry! I got to a different tribe, the Black Cows. Give me something to wear, something to be strong. (450) A cane and some arrows." They said, "Here is a knife." He got everything. They told him, "Go ahead, put your things on, and then go. You are fully outfitted." (455) Coyote got ready. He got ready. Where are the people that came to him? Some yearlings came to him, calves, cow calves. Again he threatened to lick them. And he said to them, "My own kind is to come after me, (460) important people, not you little nothings." And they ran back down. They got scared, and they ran down, got back to the herd, to their relatives. And they asked, "What's the matter, where is the one you went to get?" They said "He threatened to club us. (465) He sent us back here, and he told us: 'I want my kind to come and get me, not you kids.' And that's how we were run back." Then they sent the two year olds. (470) Then they went. They got to Coyote. The same happened to them, he threatened to club them. They ran down the hill, they got back. They said the same thing. (475) The boss sent the three year olds. The three year olds went. They got there too. Coyote told them the same thing, he sent them away. They went back down the hill. (480) The chief told them, "You four year olds, now it's your turn." They said "Ok." [pause]

I am going to continue, I am going to rest, and I am rested. (485) Then the four year old bulls. The boss sent them. He told them, "Now you. I guess that's when that boss will consent and come to see." So the four year olds ran up the hill. (490) They went and got to Coyote. He was sitting there singing a war song. They said to him, "We've come after you, boss. Now don't you get talking funny again." Coyote looked them over. (495) (495) Then Coyote said "Now I'm satisfied, they're my kind and I am satisfied. The first times it was kids, and they haven't got sense. And I don't like that, and I didn't go with them. I wasn't lazy to go or I wasn't trying to be hard to get." (500) They said "Ok." They were on each side of him. They went right in the herd, it's a big ground pocket, a hollow in the ground. There are lots of tipis. Then he saw lots of people walking around. (505) He looked on one side, and those that had come after him, they are people. He looked on the other side, they are also people. "What's the matter, they were Black Cows that came after me. They turned into people. They must be powerful."

(510) They took him, and right in the center there was a tipi there, four tipis put together. They went in there. They already have a place for him. They had fixed a bed because Coyote is a boss, a great man. (515) They said to him, "You are the boss. Here is a place for you to sit down, for you to lay down on." They had spread around black hides that are tanned, the ones they call "qʷəspíċaʔ." They said to him, "You'll sit down here." (520) Then they gave him something to eat. They ate and they got done eating. And the chief said to him, "I suppose you are rested now." He said, "We respect you and we didn't ask you yet. (525) But now you are rested and now we are going to ask you where you found my daughter." And his daughter introduced him. She said, "This is my father, that's the boss; and this is my mother, she's the boss's wife. (530) And these are the others." Then the great one said, "I had heard about your daughter getting lost; and then I heard that you'd give a reward to whoever finds her, and he is going to get money." (535) The chief said, "Yes, that's what I said." The chief said to him, "Not only money; money is nothing. This is my reward, I am so glad. We had her for dead. (540) This is what I give to boot, this is what I said: whoever finds her, she'll be his wife. I would be so glad that my daughter is alive." He said "Ok."

And then he said to his daughter, "Go sit by his side, and he becomes your man. (545) He's the one that brought you back alive, and then we saw you again." And the woman jumped up, and sat down by the great man's side. And he is handsome with his clothes, good things to wear, how he was fixed, the way he was dressed. Coyote got law relation. (550) Then at daylight they go out on the prairie. They go a little ways and the people turn into cows when they go away. In the evening they go back.

A year went by and the woman got a baby. (555) Goodness, the elders, their elders, are glad, they make over the baby. Then the next year she got another baby. They were tickled to death again, and the first one got to be sitting around. And Coyote said to his law relations, "You are my law relation. (560) It's two years since I left my folks, my country. I am lonesome for my country, I am lonesome for my people. And tomorrow morning I am leaving you. This is what I telling you, my father-in-law." He told him, "Ok, if that's how you feel. We didn't send you away, it's your wish. Look, as you said, you have relatives. I suppose your relatives are worrying about you. They must be thinking lots of things; they must wonder whether you are alive, or maybe you are dead. It's been a long time since they have seen you. And look, that's just the way we figured about our daughter. We wondered about lots of things, we felt bad if we would find out if she was alive or dead. And now we got her back, you brought her back alive. And now this is what I am going to say to you, my son-in-law. [end of tape]

Daylight came. His father-in-law said to Coyote, "Half of my children... I am the one who is boss, and whatever I say to my children they consent to it. Half of my children is my bonus to you. My grandchildren are going to be their companions. It's a pity; I love my grandchildren. Because they are your children you'll take them back with you. They might get lonesome because we are different people. We are Black Buffaloes and you are people. And they won't get acquainted [quickly] with their relatives; that's why they might get lonesome. Half of my children will be going back; they are going to be companions to my grandchildren. This is what I am telling you, you are the chief."

Coyote said, "What you are thinking is not right. It's your people, they'll stay here. And your children will stay here. And your grandchildren will also stay here. And even my wife stays here. I'll go back alone." The chief said to him, "And why? Why, it's your wife, your woman, and your children, that you leave here with me." Coyote said, "Well, no, this is what I have figured. Look, I didn't dispute what you were telling me. Don't you dispute my word. This is what I figured." The Black boss said to him, he said to him, "Well, if that's how you feel. Thank you. I didn't think you'd leave your married woman. Look, you earned her, and if it's the way you want it..." He said "Yes," "But don't ever forget your woman. Come over and see your children whenever." Coyote said, "Ok, I'll be over to see you all. It's only that I got lonesome for my people." Coyote didn't tell him that he already has a wife, that's the one they call Gopher, "blow the dirt." And he calls her "alapúl." That's the end of the story.

Coyote and Grizzly (82')

Variants of this text can be found in Maud 1978 (Hill-Tout 1911) p.147-149; Boas 1917, pp. 79-80 ("Coyote and Grizzly Bear"). Coyote and Gopher's four sons, in turn, propose for the daughter of a man-eating she-grizzly, each perishing at the very hands (or claws) of the object of their desire. Coyote's fifth son, Muskrat, avenges the death of his four half-brothers and presents Coyote with the head of the grizzly killer. The mother grizzly is furious and wants to kill Coyote, but he is able to humiliate her further with the help of this four helpers.

Coyote and his family were sitting around, and I am going to announce their names.

All I know is Coyote's wife's [name]. Coyote's name is Coyote. And the woman is Pul, Gopher, and for short Pul. And he has four, [no] five sons. The oldest one is Muskrat, his son from another woman; and these four here are from Gophie, they are Gopher's sons. And the brothers are grown up. And Grizzly, Grizzly is a woman, a man-eater. And Grizzly has a daughter. She is good looking and she is her bait. That's how she kills people, because she is a cannibal.

Madeline[70] from Kettle River was living right close to the river, this here Grizzly. But I don't know just where Coyote was. His children are all grown up and then one morning the oldest one is thinking about a mate. He started flirting with Grizzly's daughter. And he said to his parents, "I am going to leave you now, I am going to propose to Grizzly for her daughter." They said to him "Ok, go."

He started to doll himself up. He changed his clothes, I suppose he shaved, maybe cut his hair too. Then he went in the boat. He paddled. And I guess he was going south, that's why he had to go up the Kettle River.[71] He went and landed in front of Grizzly's. He tied his boat and he took his bow and arrows. He took his bow and arrow and he looped it over his shoulder. He went up the bank, got up there. That's where Grizzly's house is. He knocked on the door because that's the proper way[72] even though it's just a tipi. He knocked on the pole. Grizzly said "Come in!" He leaned his weapons there, his arrow and his bow, because Indians have scabbards just like white people. And look, white people too have scabbards for their guns just like for arrows. That's how the arrows and the bow are stuck in [the scabbard]. Promptly he looped it over his shoulder and over his head. He doesn't hold them in his hand. Grizzly said "Come in!" He went in.

Grizzly said "You arrived here to me, you surprise me." He said "It's not important. I have come to propose to you for your daughter." And she was sitting right there on the other side of the room. My she's good looking. She [the mother] said to him "All right. But I am going to tell you one thing." She made a motion to her daughter to go out. And the woman [the daughter] went out. She went out and she stepped on his arrows.[73]

Hard points are stuck on the ends. He fastens the hard points with sinew, he wraps it around [the points]. Then he melts pitch and he smears it around and when it gets dry it's glued strong. It's just like a gun, straight. And it has the hard points, that's the kind that don't break. They are sharp as a knife. One with strong arms, whatever it hits it goes right through it, goes right through deer or anything.

Grizzly said to him, "Ah, your heart is in a good place. I am going to tell you one thing. Over at that open place on the other side of the hill, that is where a grizzly stays. I want you to get it for me to put [its hide] under my hip to lay on. Go after her hide. Then after you bring it to me you can take my daughter, you can have my daughter." He said "All right, that's what I like to hear."

And he thought that the arrows and the bow he had fixed are good. And that he is good at hunting. He isn't afraid of grizzlies or of anything.

70 Apparently the man-eater's name.
71 The geography is not clear. The Kettle river runs north to south.
72 Actually, this is not the proper Colville way but it is the proper way for a white audience.
73 Apparently breaking the points off.

He went to his boat. He went out and put his weapon over his neck looped it under his arm. He sat in his boat and [went upstream]. He crossed to the other side; he landed on the other side.

Oh, I forgot.[74] Grizzly had told him, "Don't try to shoot it [the grizzly] from above. She [the grizzly] might hurt you if she sees you. Before you get close to her she'll hear you. Go towards her from below. That's how you can get close to her and she won't hurt you." "Oh, ok." That's what I just thought of, what Grizzly had said.

Then he landed. He tied his boat and went up the hill. Maybe he'll get her in sight in the open ground. Grizzly was fooling around there, digging for roots. I don't know what grizzlies eat, but what she was digging is what they eat. He fooled around from below and [sneaked up to it]. He was watchful. He went and got close to it. Then he stopped. He whistled at the one that's fooling around [at the grizzly]. She turned around and looked at him. He aimed and shot her under the arm. But the hard points are broken, they are split, they barely stuck there. The arrow went and hit her under the arm but it didn't even go through the hide. It [the point] fell off of the arrow. The arrow won't go through the skin. Grizzly jumped towards him. He took another arrow and then he shot again. He was shooting, and she got to him and started to kill him.

It's late in the evening and he [Coyote's son] is still gone [from Coyote's place]. It's dark and [Coyote][75] started to feed bad. He said "Well, my son is dead. If he were alive he would have been back by sundown. He's dead, that's why he is gone."

Then it got to be the next day and [the son] next to the oldest one said, "Well I am going to leave you. I am going to look for my older brother. If he is still alive then I'll come back. [Or] I might be his replacement husband. I'll still get back if I am alive. But I won't come back if I am dead." His father and mother said to him, "Well, all right, if that's how you feel. It's good that you find out about your brother. Then we'll know if he is dead and we can give up. [But] we still have hopes."

He [the second oldest] went and got to the boat. He went and got to Grizzly. He landed. He tied his boat, took his weapon and slung it over his shoulder. He went up the hill and got on the bank. There was Grizzly's place. He went and got next to the door [flap] of the tipi. He knocked on the poles. Grizzly said "Come in!" He went in.

Grizzly said, "Well you got to me, human. It's not often that people get here to me." She said "Well, what is on your mind?" "Well, it's your daughter, the one sitting here. I came over to propose." She said "Well if that's what you want." She was sitting there. She motioned to her daughter to go out, and the woman got up and went out. And right there where his older brother had leaned his scabbard, he too leaned his scabbard there. It's not like there is a place there for storing things, that's where they put things. Grizzly said to him, "But I am going to tell you one thing. I am going to hire you. I suppose you are going to be my son-in-law, that's why I'm going to send you on an errand." She said "Right across there in that open place, that's where a grizzly dwells. Get it for me

74 "I forgot to mention what I am about to relate."
75 Pete here says "Grizzly." An obvious slip of the tongue.

to put under my hip. Where I lay is too hard." (165) She wants the hide to put under her. He said to her "Ok, if that's your wish I'll go after it for you."

He went out and it never entered his mind that where he had leaned it [might not be good]. He took his scabbard, looped it over his shoulder; (170) he went down to his boat he sat in his boat. He crossed and landed. He tied [the boat], then went up the hill.

I forgot. She said the same thing to Coyote's son. She said "Don't go around from above. (175) Before you get there she will notice you. She might hurt you. Go towards it from below and she will not notice you." "Ah, ok."

(180) So he was going from below and he came in sight and saw her. He climbed from below; he went slowly and got pretty close. Then he wistled to the one that was digging. She looked at him. (185) He stopped there. She looked at him, he shot her. [But] his hard points are broken. She gave a yell and jumped after him. He kept shooting and she got to him. She slapped him on top of the head, fought him, and killed him. (190) That's two of them she killed, Coyote's sons. Then the woman, Grizzly's child, swam across. Coyote's son is gone.

It got late, got dark. They thought, Coyote said "Well, my son is dead. (195) If he were living he'd been back before sundown." They went to bed. It got daylight, they got up early—the Coyotes are early risers. They got done breakfasting, and the middle one said, "Well, I'll just track down my brothers. (200) How is it that both of them are lost? I am going to look for them. I want to find out. And if I'm gone until dark, then I'm dead. But if I am alive I'll be back before sundown." Coyote said "Well, yes, go. (205) We are very worried. We have hopes. Even though he's gone overnight we still have hopes. It'll be good and our feelings will be settled when we hear if he is still alive or dead. If he is dead we'll give up."

Then he went. He went in the boat again. (210) He paddled and he landed right below Grizzly's house. He tied his boat, took his scabbard, and looped it around his neck. He went up the hill, up the bank. Grizzly lived right there on the bank. He got right close to the door, and there he hung up his scabbard. (215) He knocked on the pole because Coyote {correction} Grizzly lives in a tipi. She said "Come in!" and he went in. She said to him "You got to me. People don't often, and now you got to me. You surprise me." (220) He said "No. Your daughter sitting there, that's why I came to propose to you." She said "Ah, that's what you have to say. You can take her." She motioned to her daughter to go out. (225) And when her daughter goes out Grizzly tells him [what she wants].

She [the daughter] does the same thing with his arrows leaning there: she breaks their hard points. Then she crosses and goes up the hill to get herself some grub roots.

Then Grizzly says to him: (230) "You are going to be my son-in-law. [Tape ends.]

Three sons are already dead. Well, I am going to continue my story about Coyote. Only two are left. I don't know the youngest boy's name, maybe it's k̓łttiʔłálqʷpxən. (235) And the oldest one, his distant son's name is Muskrat. That's all that's left alive.

Daylight came and the youngest one said, he said to his parents "I am leaving you, parents. I am lonesome for my older brothers. (240) How come they disappeared? Something must be the matter. I am going to track them, I am going to find out. Then I'll be satisfied." His parents said to him "If that's how you feel...

We are not sending you. It's your wish. We too are bothered in the mind, but what can we do? We are old and we can't trust ourselves to go looking for them. But you are a young boy. Go."

Then he got ready, he went. I guess they each had a boat. He went in his boat, he went. He landed in front of Grizzly's house. He tied his boat, took his weapon and slung it around his neck. He went up the hill and got up on the bank. That's where Grizzly lives. He went right up to the door and he hung his scabbard outside the door. He knocked on the pole. Grizzly said "Come in!" He went through the curtain (because it's a tipi). Grizzly said "You surprise me. It isn't often that people come to visit me. And then you got here to me." "Your daughter sitting on the bed across there, that's what I came after, I am proposing for her." "Oh, well. Thanks for asking me. You didn't hide around and you didn't kidnap her from me, you didn't just take her. You proposed to me, you showed respect to me." Then she motioned to her daughter.

The woman [the daughter] thought "It's no good. She is killing too many people. And then I am helping my {father} [mother][76]. It's a pity [she is my mother]. She is not satisfied with her son-in-law to-be. As for me, I am satisfied even if it is just Coyote's son." She [the old Grizzly] made a motion to her and she [the young Grizzly] just dragged her feet.[77]

Then she [old Grizzly] said to Coyote's youngest son, "Well I got you as a son-in-law now. And I am going to hire you. Well, across the water on the side hill, that's where a grizzly is staying. Go after it for me so I can put it[s tanned hide] under my hip. When I go to bed I [lie on] too many hard lumps. That [hide] is to put under me." Her son-in-law said to her, "Well, yes, just like you asked me, I'm going to rustle for you what you want, what you send me for. I will go, that's nothing." The woman [the young Grizzly] went out and did the same thing: she broke the hard points. Then she went across and got on the side hill.

Then Coyote's son went out. He took his scabbard and looped it over his arm. It never came close to his mind, he never thought about [what might happen]. That's how his brothers got killed. Well, he crossed, got on shore, tied his boat, and went up the hill. He never even looked at his arrows [to see] if they are good or what. Oh, [I should mention that the old] Grizzly also said to him, she said "Don't shoot from above. She might hurt you, she might notice you before you get close, she might notice you from afar. But [if you go] from below you might get close to her. And then you can shoot her and you'll have a good aim." He said "Ok," and that's what he did. He went up from below.

He climbed and he saw her [the grizzly] standing there. He kept going up from below. He went, he stepped softly, and he got close to her. He stopped, he took out his arrows. He started to aim. After he aimed he whistled at her. She looked at him and she saw him. He shot her right under the arm. [The point] didn't even go through her hide. The hard point broke off and the arrow just fell there. She jumped on him, she yelled and jumped on him. He tried to shoot her, kept shooting at her, and then she got to him. She slapped him on the head,

76 At the beginning of the story Pete announced that the Grizzly is a woman. Here the young grizzly talks about her "father." Later in the story there will be more evidence that the Grizzly is a woman.

77 i. e. she leaves begrudgingly.

killed him, scalped him. The woman went back down the hill and crossed the river.

(320) Coyote had no more children, except for his distant son Muskrat. The oldest one is gone, and so is Coyote's youngest.

It got late, it got dark. Then they said "Yes, my son died too." (325) And Coyote started to bawl, and I guess he blamed Gopher[78] as if it were all her fault that the children are dead. Gopher tried to tell him, "No, you are the man, you are supposed to guide your children. (330) And you went along with your children. You didn't stop them, and now you put the blame on me. Heck no, Coyote." Maybe he got lonesome, so he beat his wife up. She ran away from him, she got away. (335) And Coyote is all by himself.[79] He and his distant son are by themselves.

Daylight came and Muskrat likes to sweat bathe. Muskrat likes to sweat bathe, he likes to bathe. Sometimes before daylight he goes bathing. (340) And it's just he and his father. Coyote is smart at cooking. He doesn't make hot cakes, just toast, bread roasted in the ashes, that's what he fixes, toast.[80] They got done eating, and he said to his father, "Father I'm leaving you. (345) I am troubled about my brothers. Why it is that they all disappeared? Not one of them has come back. Something must be wrong. I am going to find out." He [Coyote] said to him "I am troubled too, but what can I do? (350) I am too old. You are young, and you can do something. And that is good." And as I said, Muskrat likes to sweat bathe and bathe. He is spry, and he has something to live for.

(355) And I guess he had seen what was wrong, what had caused his brothers' death. I guess he had a dream about it.[81] That's why he is going to look for his brothers and why he prepared what he is going to take with him. (360) Muskrat took some pitch with him. In his dream he figured out their deaths. Their hard points had been broken and when they do shoot the grizzly it doesn't even go through the hide (365) and the hard point breaks and the arrow falls off. It doesn't even hurt the grizzly, the grizzly's child. And that's why he is going to take pitch along. Because he is going to repair the hard points solid.

(370) Muskrat went upstream. He went and he got right in front of Grizzly's house. He stopped there. He tied his boat and looped his weapon around his neck, but he left his pitch there. (375) Or maybe he stuck it under his shirt, because the woman looks in his boat to see what he has. And so she can't see his pitch.

He got right close to the door, he got on top of the bank. There was a house there, that's Grizzly's house. (380) He went there, got right outside the house, hung up what he had looped around his arm, and his arrows. He knocked on the poles. Grizzly said "Come in!" He raised the curtain, he went in. (385) Because at that time they didn't have bungalows, no. Their houses are tipis. Grizzly said "Well, you surprise me. Nobody ever gets here, and then you got here." "Ah," he said "I came here for your daughter, the one sitting there. (390) That's what I come to you for. I'm going to propose to you for her. I am not a match for your

78 Coyote typically shifts blame as he wants.
79 Having made the situation even worse.
80 Coyote is making breakfast.
81 Dreams foretell and help prepare.

daughter and so I want my thoughts to come to an end.[82] I have been wishing for your daughter, and that's why I came to you." "Ah, you are doing something good for me, you are going to be my son-in-law. (395) My daughter has been single for too long. I guess that's because there are no people here, and she hasn't eloped yet." She motioned to her daughter.

The maiden saw Muskrat. (400) She is plum satisfied with him and she thought, "Gee that's going to be my husband and he's handsome and he's spry." Muskrat likes to sweat bathe and to bathe; Muskrat never gets mopey; he likes to hunt for things to eat. She motioned to her daughter but she didn't go. (405) She motioned a few times, finally she came out with words. And then [the daughter] went out, the woman got forced. She went out. She broke the arrows and then she crossed and went up the hill. (410) She went up the hill and started digging for roots.

She said (I forgot to say) "There is one thing I am hard up for. I guess you are going to be my son-in-law, you are my son-in-law, and you are going to get me something to put under my hip. Right across there on that bare side hill, (415) that's where a grizzly hangs out getting things to eat. That's what I want you to get me to put under my hip. The floor is too hard for me." That's a mat for you to lie on, that is Grizzly's mattress. (420) Muskrat said, "It's like you are my [mother-in-law][83]. You can send me for whatever you are in need of and I'll go get it for you. I think I am a match [able enough] to get things to eat. I'll go after it for you."

(425) Muskrat got up and [Muskrat] took a stick from the fire. Then Grizzly said, Grizzly started to howl. She said "What's the burning stick you took for?" (430) He said "I am going to fix my boat. Just when I got here on shore that's when my glue, my pitch, came undone. That's when it [the boat] started to leak. It got filled up when I landed. If it had happened before where it's deep I would have drowned. I don't know how to swim. That's what I am going to fix, to glue back. I can't sail. I might drown, (435) I don't know how to swim. That's what I am going to fill with clay." (440) She asked, "And do you have some pitch?" "Yes I got some pitch." Then he went. Grizzly got satisfied.

Muskrat wet out. He looped his bow and arrow, looped it around his arm. (445) He untied the boat and he went across. The [old] grizzly got chills of premonition. She went out, stood on the edge of the bank, and she watched him. He crossed. He started pulling out his arrows. Well, the hard points were broken. (450) He straightened them out. Then he heated the pitch and dabbed it on. Grizzly started hollering. She asked, "What is it you are fixing?" He started answering, (455) he said "I told you, my boat. I was in a hurry, the grizzly might go back in the brush. That's why I didn't fix it there, and then I crossed. When I come I'll fix it." He fixed every one of the arrows, and he got to shore. (460) He tied his boat. He saw his brothers' boats. They are all tied there, four boats. He too tied his boat and thought, "Yes, yes, my dream was true. (465) It must be on this hill that my brothers died. They got killed, Grizzly is a cannibal." He started to climb, he climbed sneaking. And Grizzly had told him, she had said, "Don't go from above to come down on her. (470) She'll notice you before you get near, the Grizzly is very smart. But if you go from below she won't see you. You will get very close to

82 "I may not be worthy of your daughter but I want to find out if you will consent."
83 Pete says "father-in-law."

her before she sees you. You will surely kill her. (475) But if you go from above you'll be just half way and she will notice you. Just the minute you get in sight she will see you. She has been expecting you." He said "Yeah." (480) He didn't believe her.

He went out of sight and climbed. And the Grizzly, "I have been telling you to go towards her from below. She will hurt you from above!" He didn't pay any attention, he pretended not to hear her. (485) He went from above; he just guessed it and he saw the grizzly standing on the side hill. He just figured it out, then he started stepping lightly. He's always sweating and bathing and he is light on his feet. He doesn't make noise when he walks, sneaks. (490) He came in sight, he saw the grizzly. He went straight towards her, got close. He whistled, a small whistle. [The old] Grizzly has been hollering from below for nothing. The young grizzly turned around, raised her head, she saw him. (495) The grizzly girl gave Muskrat a smile. Muskrat thought, "Tomorrow you won't be smiling at people. It was you that killed my brothers and then you smile at me! (500) You are covering up now and you smile at me." He let the arrow go at Grizzly. And the arrow went in all the way to the feather. The Grizzly let out a big grunt, she jumped at him. And being that it's uphill and pretty steep (505) the grizzly girl had no show. Muskrat got very close. He shot again at the other side. It's like Grizzly is paralized in both arms. Grizzly fell face down. (510) All what's alive is her feet. She fell down. Muskrat jumped on her. He got close to her, grabbed her by the top of the head, cut it off. There is no question that Muskrat's knife is sharp. (515) He cut off her head, got done cutting it off. The grizzly girl lay still. She's dead, her head cut off. He skinned her, just pulled off her skin. He just took her hide and threw it over his shoulder. (520) And he packed her head on the other side. And he also had his bow and arrow over his shoulder, and he had a knife case.

He ran down the hill, he went to his boat. He threw in the hide and threw in the head. He went back across. (525) And Grizzly must have already given up. She hollered and hollered for nothing, then she went back into her house. "My daughter can do wonders, he can't kill her." She went in and Muskrat got to the shore. At its tying place he only looped it. (530) He didn't tie it because he thought "It takes me too much time, Grizzly might kill me, might overtake me. I will do everything in a hurry and get away from her. Maybe I'll get away." He threw only her hide over his back, (535) he ran up the bank. He's the one that sweat bathes, he is ligh footed, doesn't get tired, his breaths are good, he likes to bathe. He got up on the bank. Grizzly was humming a tune. She was glad that Coyote's sons are all gone, (540) even his distant son. Just when she was thinking that, he [Muskrat] raised the door flap. He put it plum out of the way. He threw in the grizzly [hide]. He said, "This is what you sent me for, for you to put under your hip. (545) Do as you please with it." He put the flap back down, he turned around.

He ran down the hill to his boat. Because he had only looped it around he unlooped it. He sat in his boat, went downstream. (550) It's swift water, shallow water; the Kettle River is swift when it's shallow. He went down the river. Gee, when Grizzly saw her daughter's hide she started bawling. (555) She bawled and bawled, screamed, cried loudly. She bawled, it was like her mind was made up. Grizzly thought "It's all my fault. My daughter was satisfied. Here I am, a man-eater, and I always forced her, (560) wanting to kill more and more. But I am going to kill the one who killed my daughter. Then I will be satisfied." She raised her dress up, ran out of the house. She got on the bank facing the water. (565) Well, Muskrat was just about out of sight coming downstream. The water went around a bend. Grizzly took a shortcut, went straight where the water bends. "I'll be waiting there, I'll get ahead of him there." (570) She went, got there. Muskrat's tracks are riley water.[84] She looked at the water. There is another bend. She took another shortcut. She got there, Muskrat's tracks are riley water.

(575) Gee she was mad! She went on doing her best. She thought "At his father's house. I will catch up with him when he gets there. Then Coyote, too, and Gopher. I will finish every one of them." (580) Grizzly wasn't satisfied. She had killed all of Coyote's children and she is also going to finish Coyote and Gopher. These are Grizzly's thoughts. And Gopher had already run away from trouble, (585) there is only Coyote.

Muskrat went,[85] he pulled the curtain back. He said to his father, "Coyote, this is the head that wiped out your children, my brothers. This is Grizzly's daughter. (590) She is her bait." He [Muskrat] said to him "Now what is going to become of you? She is coming following my tracks, she is coming right behind me. I am going to run away. Whatever will become of you?"

(595) Coyote took the head. There must be something to climb on. He climbed to where the poles of the tipi are tied. That's where he tied it [the head], then he went back in the tipi. Then Coyote threw pitchwood on the fire. (600) And you know how pitchwood gets black when it blazes. When it blazed the smoke was black. Then Coyote started to sing. This is what his song says, it says "saʔlisáw saʔlisáw saʔlisáw saʔlisáw saʔlisáw saʔlisáw." (605) "It isn't for nothing that I act crazy. Even if you are a Grizzly, you killed all my children." Then Coyote started to say how he felt. "You are pitiful that you think you are going to kill me too, and that you are going to kill my Gopher too." (610) Grizzly got to the door.

All this time Grizzly was listening. Boy, did Grizzly get mad. She heard him; she said to Coyote, "Wherever you are I will kill you. (615) You are saying all these things for nothing." Boy, did Coyote get scared then, for sure. And she is right at the door. There is nothing he can do to escape. So then he pulled his old tricks [powers] out. (620) "p̓s p̓s p̓s p̓s k̓ʷƛ̓up p̓s p̓s p̓s p̓s k̓ʷƛ̓up." Four of them came out, his powers. They said to him, "You are getting us chilled, what is troubling you?" He said to them "Hurry up, think of something for me. I am going to die at the hand of the man-eater Grizzly. She is right at my door." (625) They said to him "You are always putting yourself ahead of everything. You have done something pitiful to his daughter, you tied her [head] at the top of the tipi." He said "Hurry up!" They [the first one] said "I will turn myself into meat, good meat." (630) Another said "I will turn into maggots." Another said "I will turn into. . . I am going to make it her business to hate me. This meat, the meat will maggot. As mad as she is, she is going to bite it, (635) and she'll get sick with the maggots. 'Heck no' [she will yell] she will turn, and you [can] get away. You'll go quite a little ways and then you'll laugh at her. Then she'll continue to run after you."

She got right to the door and [Coyote] was singing about his power. (640) Grizzly got right to the door, she went right in. And Coyote was saying these other

84 Muskrat has already gone by.
85 Having arrived at Coyote's.

things he had done. “I tied the Grizzly’s bait on top of the tipi, her daughter’s head.” That’s what Coyote is saying he did. He said “I am smiyaw” (that’s Coyote’s name in a different language), that means Coyote, this smiyáw. Grizzly went right in; he [Coyote] is gone. He did something magic again. He’s not Coyote for nothing. She did like that[86] and then she remembered what Coyote had been saying he did. She heard him, she did like that. It’s true he had tied her daughter['s head] on top of the tipi. And it’s black beyond limit.

Boy, was Grizzly angry, yes. “No matter what you turn into I will bite you. I am going to kill you with my mouth. I am going to gnaw on you.” She looked around, all around, and saw beautiful meat. That’s Coyote. He must have turned into that meat. She jumped at it, was going to bite it, then she realized what it was. The meat is nothing but maggots. Grizzly drew back, a thought was thrown to her. She said “No I’m too sick to the stomach. I am feeling bad. I’ll kill him before I get sick.” From a distance Coyote was laughing, making fun of Grizzly. No, Coyote.[87] “He is making fun of you. You are scared that the maggots might beat you.” He got done singing that’s what he is saying he is going to do.

Goodness, Grizzly was madder than ever. “Whatever you might turn into I am going to kill you.” Then the maggots disappeared. Gee, Grizzly bolted out of there. She ran towards where she heard that. She went there, and looked for tracks. Yes, here are Coyote’s tracks. She started running, Grizzly is fast. And, no, Coyote. “Grizzly is going to overtake me.” He heard her because a grizzly is never quiet when tracking something, she roars. Coyote is going to be overtaken. While she was out of sight he asked for his powers, his wishes. He sat down. “p̓s p̓s p̓s p̓s k̓ʷƛ̓up.” Here is the first one, and then they all came, the four of them. They said “You are getting us chilled, what do you want?” He said “hurry up and do something for me. The man-eater is right on to me. Grizzly is going to kill me.” They said “We will help you. We will turn ourselves into thorn bushes, not these thorn bushes, the short ones, the ones with sharp thorns, the ones they call red thorn bushes, just like young brush. They’ll be thick right where you are moving. We’ll settle right there and she’ll have a tough time getting out of there. Even though Grizzly has a lot of wool she’ll get all torn up, nothing but blood. Before she gets through she’ll be all torn up, bloody.” They said “That’s what’s going to happen to you. And when she stops being mad, then you can laugh some more at her. That’s when you can kill her.” He said “Ok.” Then Coyote went a little ways, then he stopped, he waited for Grizzly. Gee Grizzly is coming downriver. [tape ends]

(Well I continue.) Coyote started to sing his song again, and he went “saʔlisáw saʔlisáw saʔlisáw saʔlisáw saʔlisáw.” “It isn’t for nothing that I am tricky. I am a man, even if I am a Coyote. Even if I know that I’m going to die, I am going to sing anyway.” He was making noise singing and Grizzly came in sight. Gee, Coyote makes noises again. “I am going to chew him up whatever he turns into. I’m still going to kill him, I won’t get sick in the stomach again. I’m going to kill him with my eyes shut tight. Ah, here are his tracks, I’m tracking him.” My, the thorn bushes. Coyote went through there. And she thought “Coyote went

86 A motion or gesture might have accompanied this utterance.
87 The rhetorical value of this utterance is not clear.

through there, and I am a man-eater. I am not going to back down, I am not going to go around it. I suppose that's Coyote's doings, but I am still going to kill him." She kept on tracking, walked right through. Gee, Grizzly is all scratched up, she suffered. She is still going strong, angry. From a little ways Coyote is laughing at her. He laughs, and then he'll say, "My, Grizzly thinks she's important, she's a man-eater." Coyote[88] scratched her all over her hind end as she went through.

My, did Grizzly get angry. Then she got out of the brush. She went some more, went after him. Coyote started running, ran away from there. He got out of sight, she is tracking him again. She gets a glimpse of him, then Coyote gets out of sight again. And because Grizzly is fast, Grizzly overtook him finally. He is out of sight. Coyote sat down again. Now he is going to make his tricks; he calls his tricks out again. They are his tricks, four packages. He called them. They all came out, four of them. They said to him "You are getting us chilled, what is your trouble?" He said to them "Hurry. The one who is going to kill me is just about in sight of me, Grizzly the man-eater. Now she is going to kill me, kill me dead, even if I turn into something else." They told him "You know she is a man-eater and then you made fun of her again." They said to him "Ok," and then the oldest one said to him, "I'll turn into a trap." And another one said "I'll turn into bait." Another one said "I too will turn into... I'll grab her if this trap is strong enough and won't break." The youngest one said the same thing. That's all of them, four of them.

Coyote went a little farther, he hid there. Grizzly came in sight. She looked around for Coyote. She kept coming on his tracks. She saw the trap. "Well, that's Coyote playing tricks on me. That's Coyote playing tricks again. I am not afraid of him, I am still going to kill him." Grizzly is fierce and strong. She is a man-eater. She fears nothing. I suppose that bait is Coyote['s doing]. The bait is really good, maybe meat. Grizzly went right up to it, went right into it. She bit the bait, and the whole thing [trap] came down on her. Two of them [the powers] sat down on her. She had no show. It [the trap] was right on her back, half way on her back. The trap just held her down. Only her hind end was outside [the trap]. Then Coyote got there to her. Then Coyote humiliated her. He did all kinds of things to the old lady, the Grizzly. He showed no respect to her old ladyhood. When he got done humiliating her, he hit her in the eye.

Then Coyote started his song again. He got done cutting her head off, fighting her, killed her dead.[89] Coyote started singing his song "saʔlisá·w saʔlisá·w saʔlisá·w saʔlisá·w saʔlisá·w hu·y hu·y huyawáw huyawáw huyawáw huyawáw huyawáw." He started to say what he did to her. He said "You are so pitiful, you man-eater. You disposed of lots of people, and you did pitiful things to me. You wiped out all my children. Now I am getting back on you, that's why I played tricks on you, and then I killed you. You are pitiful, you are an old lady Grizzly. I am a better man. And then you thought you were going to bite me on the wrist, no! That's why I made fun of you. I didn't even respect your old ladyhood. That's why I killed you." He said [that], and then Coyote scalped Grizzly. When he got done scalping her, he tied her scalp, Grizzly's hair.

88 By means of the thornbushes.
89 The logical order is "Coyote fought her, killed her, cut her head off."

Then he sang, started to sing again "saʔlisáw saʔlisáw saʔlisáw saʔlisáw saʔlisáw." I[90] say to them "I am taking a lot of your time. I just now realized I am teaching. My pupil is sitting by me. The one I am teaching is not anybody. The one getting taught is not my grandchild, it's a white man. Well I have to go to the toilet,[91] it's the end of the story.

The two goats (37')

This story matches the first part of "Race along the Okanagan river" (Andrist 1971, p. 57-59) where Mountain Goat sends his two younger brothers to win Coyote's daughter, a fast runner, for his wife. The goats do beat the fast runner by magic: they pour some incapacitating magic liquid in the racer's foot tracks. While in the Andrist version it is not said whether Coyote is to kill the losers of the race, in his retelling of the story Seymour adds the twist that the punishment for losing the race is death.

Seymour's version opens with an introduction that contextualizes it, then tells of a goat who covets Coyote's daughter and, along with his brother and some magic help, wins her.

Well, my friend told me a fairy tale story. At ..., I don't know the Indian name, the name of the country; I'm going to say it only in English: they call it "Monse." This lake down south, the Okanagan river runs this way, and goes past Okanagan town. That's what they call "Monse." And my friend is just housekeeping. He has a name, but I am forgetful, and I forget, I forget his name. They asked him, they said, "You better come with me. We are going to look for the place." They call it "Goose Lake." I expect it has an Indian name, but we'll talk White Man's talk. That's all I remember, "Goose Lake." Omak Lake is a big lake. From there it goes southward, and over there there are some small lakes, and one of them is what they call "Goose Lake." And they asked my friend, I think his name is Sam, he said, "I have seen that country; but it's been many years since I traveled around there; but maybe I'll remember the place." "I'll go with you." He said, "I have some beer." And my friend doesn't drink. His Indian name is "cəwáylx," and with the White folks "Henry Nelson," he's a half-breed.

We went and we drank, my friend and our guide. We came in sight of the woods and we saw a big mountain. At the end of the mountain there is another mountain. I got puzzled and I asked our guide, I said, "Is that a mountain?" That is the end of the mountain, and it's high. He laughed at me, and he said to me: "No, that's not a mountain. That's the Big Bend [Wilbur]. In Indian that's "spíləm," that level ground country, and in English it has the name 'Big Bend Country.'" And he said, "That's where it ends, right next to the river." That's the main river, the Columbia, that's before they put the dam in. And that's the edge of the level land, and it's just like a mountain. All kinds of things grow there, Indian fruit, foamberries, huckleberries, white camas, camas, all kinds of things the Indians eat. And now I am going to tell you the fairy tale story.

Coyote lived there, and Coyote was there. A man-eater is killing the people,

90 Pete speaking now.
91 This is what Madeline says the literal meaning of this closing formula is.

and that's why he is there. And when they get there to him they can't come away from there. They can't come away alive from Coyote. Coyote kills them. (60) That's the story of that. And Coyote has already killed lots of people. And Coyote's bait is Coyote's daughter. His daughter is good looking, and she is Coyote's bait. The young folks go over there to flirt with her; (65) they go there and they flirt with Coyote's daughter so they can marry her. They do every which thing, they race, they do anything, and they bet, and Coyote tells them: (70) "If you beat me you win my daughter. But if I beat you, you'll be dead, I'll kill you."

And from across the line came two brothers. They are goats, brothers. They went, they said, "Let's go downstream on the Okanagan River (75) and get to Coyote. That's the way people do. We are going to satisfy ourselves. They are not going to get stuck on us;[92] we are going to satisfy ourselves; (80) we are going to propose. If she turns us down, we're not going to feel bad." They said "Ok." Then they went downstream in the Okanagan River.

They went, and at the mouth of the Okanagan river into the Columbia (85) they made a raft, and they crossed to the other side. They came to shore and got on the bank. They went, they went, and they arrived at Coyote's house. Coyote said to them, "You got here, folks! (90) Where are you folks from? It isn't often that people get here, and then you folks got to me." They said "Yes. We are just traveling around (95) and we got here to you." He said to them, "What are you traveling around for?" They said, "We're up to your daughter. We heard that you have a daughter and we came for your daughter. (100) We are going to satisfy ourselves, we are going to propose to your daughter." Coyote said to them, "I am not going to give you the answer now. You have come from long ways away; (105) you are tired and hungry. When we get done eating our lunch then I will talk to you, I will give you your answer." They said "Ok."

(110) Then maybe in a while Coyote told the cook... (The cook cooked for them.) The cook set the table, then the chief said (and Coyote is the chief), (115) he said, "The cook is done cooking. He is asking us to go eat." They went and sat down. There is all kinds of food, bitterroot, camas, white camas... All kinds of Indian food. (120) They ate, got done eating, then Coyote said to them, he said, "Well, you are done eating. When you are rested, when you feel better, that's what I was going to tell you: we are going to play games. (125) We play, and when we get done playing if you beat me then you take back my daughter, and she will be your wife. I guess that's what you want and that's why you came to me, that's why you traveled so far, (130) from wherever you are." He said, "But if I beat you, you are dead. Are you satisfied with the bargain?" They said, "Yes, that's why we came, to take a chance. We didn't think we'd take your daughter for nothing. (135) And if we die, we got our satisfaction for your daughter if we die." Coyote said "Ok."

The brothers asked him, "And what is the game you figured? (140) You are the chief, Coyote." He said, "We are going to race," Coyote said to them. "And where is the turn-around place?" "Where you came downriver (145) you saw the country. They call it "go around a tree," that's the turn-around. That's where you turn around and then you get back here. Whoever is first, if you folks are first then you beat me; (150) but if our race horse comes first then I have beaten you and you are

92 The sense is that the brothers take the initiative and do not wait for the woman to propose to them.

dead. But if you beat me, then you win my daughter." They said, "We are going to be satisfied. If we die, we aren't going to say that we win. [And if] we lose, we are [still] satisfied. For sure we are stuck on your daughter, that's why we came." And Coyote's daughter [thought], "My father is sure no good." She had alredy consented to who she is running against, to the Goats. His daughter is stuck on the goats.

They got up, he said to them, "Go on, run. You go, and when you get to the turn-around point that's where you turn around; that's the turn-around place. Whoever wins wins; and if you beat me you win my daughter. But if I win, you are dead." "Ok." Coyote shot the [starting] gun and they ran.

When they first jumped, the girl, the woman, is fast, she has the lead.[93] They hadn't gone halfway and she is out of sight, the woman is out of sight. But the goats are just trotting. They don't move [fast], they just trot. They went and they went to the turn-around place. And now in English they call it Ellisford, they call it the turn-around place. I have seen it. The girl has already gone around, Coyote's daughter. She has come half way around again when she met her competitors, the goats. They are just a-trotting along. She just smiled at them, and she winked at them. Coyote's daughter, his race horse, kept running.

Then he said to him, maybe the oldest said to his younger brother, he said, "What's the matter with you, you are not doing anything. We are going to be dead now." He said, "And what should I do? I am at the limit." He said "No, it isn't for nothing that we came here to propose. You must be worth something. You must think more of yourself."[94] He said "No, pity me. I'm just keeping you company that I came with you, I am in your same boat. I was sure you are going to die. You don't come close to Coyote, because he is a man-eater, and his daughter is his bait [lit. 'trap']. He never loses."

Then his partner challenged him to do something. He said to him, "Ok, I will try to do something. But you have to look after yourself. Don't minimize what I tell you. I am going to do some preaching to you. Then you do what I tell you. Don't step on her tracks. Keep staying alongside her tracks; and don't cross her tracks, either. We might be able to do something, we might get the best of them." He said "Now you are talking." He took from under his clothes... [tape ends].[95]

They came around from around the swamp. They turned around and his partner said to him, "What is the matter with you? She had [already] come half way [back] when we met our opponent again, and we are dragging our feet? We are going to die, we know we are going to die. And you don't try to do anything." He said "No, maybe you were going to think about what to do." He said "No, I'm just going to stick by you, because I like you, you're my friend. And I know we're going to die. But I was going to stick with you, that's why I came with you. And you, I'll put you before me, maybe you can do something." He said "Ok."

He took something wrapped up from under his clothes, he unwrapped it.

93 Coyote's daughter is the racer.

94 The sense is "try harder."

95 Usually Pete announces that he is "splicing" his story. This time he retraces the steps of his story without the announcement.

He put it down, he got done unwrapping it. There are sticks there, just common wood sticks. That's what's wrapped up. He said to his partner, "That's what I depend on, that's my power. If this doesn't help us, we are dead. And that's what I'm going to preach to you: you mustn't step over our opponent's tracks. Stay always on one side, and I on the other side. That's what I am telling you: we're on each side of her, we won't cross her tracks. That's how we stay alive. But if we step over her tracks my good luck charm will go against us and we will die." He put [sticks] down in the racer's tracks, footprints. He put one of the little sticks across it and then another on the other side. He also put one across there. Then they started to run again, they trotted.

They went and they came in sight. Their opponent, the virgin, was sitting down. His friend said, maybe it's the older brother, maybe the younger brother... Maybe the older brother, "What's the matter with our opponent that she's sitting in the middle of the road, maybe waiting for us? She must be making fun of us. Why would she wait for us?" Because the goats were just trotting.

They got to her, they passed her. The girl, the foot racer, gave them a pretty smile. She didn't move even to stand. They passed her. One of them said, maybe the one that wanted her, the one that had the amulet,[96] he said "How is it that we passed our opponent? There must be something the matter. And it's better we wait for her, we turn back, we find out what's wrong." His partner said "No sir. We are half way around the turn-around point and she's already met us. She's just making fun of us. Then she'll keep on running. She won't even bother with us." He said "No. Even if we are going to die, we are going to find out." He coaxed his partner, they stopped, they turned back.

That girl is still sitting there. They got back to her. They said to her "What's the matter with you, did you break your leg? What happened to you?" "No, it's just leg cramps that got to me and I couldn't keep on going. I just had to sit down." They hooked her under the arms, on both sides. They started trotting along. They went. And Coyote had binoculars and he's been watching the foot racers all the time. They got there. What's the matter with Coyote's racer? The two brothers hooked her under her arms. Then so...

Just before they crossed the finish line they dropped the fast girl, Coyote's race horse, they dropped her. She fell down flat. She sat down as she couldn't even walk, she had cramps. "You won my daughter from me." And the Goats went over the mark on the ground, the finish line. Coyote said to them, "You beat me. You take her back." Coyote didn't argue about his bet. Coyote just gave up. That's the end of the story.

Lynx and the virgin (53')

This is the story[97] of a beautiful maiden who has many suitors, but is not yet willing to

96 The sticks.

97 This story is well known around Inchelium and I have recorded two other versions, each embedded in a longer narrative (Mattina and DeSautel 2002 pp. 19-21; and Mattina and DeSautel MS, pp. 8ff.)

marry. Lowly Lynx impregnates her with a subterfuge, and when he is found out the young woman is banished, and he is smashed to smithereens by the envious suitors. Endowed with special powers, Lynx manages to come back to life, and almost starves the group jinxing them into harvesting no meat, fish, or fowl, while he accumulates lots of cached food. He then invites the group to reunite with him and his wife, shares his food with them, and all is well.

There were lots of people and they had a leader, a boss, but I don't know his name. He's their leader, their boss, and he had a daughter, and she was in her puberty. His daughter is already a woman, and good looking, and the boys and the young men are proposing for that girls to the boss. And the boss says to them, "I am not going to choose for my daughter if I am satisfied with you." And he reported for nothing what the suitors said. He said to his daughter, "They are proposing for you." But the woman would shake her head, the virgin says "No, I haven't thought yet about marrying." And she refused. The boss said to them, "I've told you, she's got to boss her own self, I am not going to force her, and I'm not going to do the thinking for her."

The whole tribe proposed, except (I forgot) Lynx who hadn't yet. . . Lynx is not good enough, and he put himself back, and doesn't propose. Lynx is going to think of something. They are not white people, that's the Indian way, it isn't French. That's why they have tipis, buckskin tipis, and tipis. When night comes the chief ties the curtain with a string and he locks it, and he ties it from inside. And nobody can get in. Because they might fall in bed with the woman, and they'll crawl in bed with the virgin. That's why they have to watch their daughter.

And Lynx thought of something. I guess Lynx goes visiting over there and he's seen the house and their beds. And the virgin, way in the back on one side is where she lays. And the boss, as soon as you get in the door that's where he lays. They lay right in front of the door because they got to watch her. Night time comes. That's when Lynx is going to crawl in bed with her. He went there, it's long after dark because the people, the young people don't go to bed early. They play, the last ones go to sleep long after dark, and they make all kinds of noise. And Lynx went there to crawl in bed with her. He got right to the edge. He listened for the chief. The chief was snoring, he's asleep. He listened for the one on the other side, the girl. She's snoring too. It's a soft sound when she snores, not like her father; her father is very loud when he snores. He figured where she would be, and started climbing. He must have had climbing shoes.

He took his shoes, he climbed on the tipi poles right to the top of the tipi; he settled there. Lynx raised his leg. She was lying with her head up. It was like moonlight and there was dim light in the tipi. His pee traveled.[98] The girl was there head up, mouth wide open; she was asleep. The drop dropped right down the pole, it dropped in the virgin's mouth, it spilled in her mouth. And so she swallowed, and she never felt anything. Not long after that she started to get big. She was carrying.

And the virgin thought, "And what is the matter?" And her parents got puzzled too. And they started asking her questions, put her on trial. They asked her

98 The form is not clear and it probably is a euphemism. The root seems to be √x^{w}č *give*.

daughter "Did somebody get to you (80) that then you got pregnant?" "No." They said "Don't lie." She said "No, and why should I make up a lie? And even if I did lie, I'd get caught anyway. (85) It's the truth, no man ever got to me, I have been alone." "Well, how is it that you are carrying?" She said, "Well, I don't know how. Nobody got to me for me to know I am pregnant." (90) They got puzzled.

It wasn't long a child was born. Because the chief is way up in society and it's shameful and they might laugh about it, (95) they might say "The boss got a child, got a child who is a bastard," they might get ashamed. Then the baby was born. And the boss thought: (100) "We don't know who his father is, and also we are very ashamed to take care of our daughter. It's better that we give her away."

The announcers started to holler. In the evening they said, "The chief is calling you, (105) all of you people, there is no no about it. He is asking all of you to have a meeting. Or maybe you'll eat some foam berries." The people agreed. They got ready, they all went. (110) They all are gathered there, and the chief's house is four tipis together, it's big. The people sat down in a circle, and right in the center. . . [unfinished] Lynx was the last one. (115) There is only a little place by the door, and Lynx sat there.

They finished smoking, the chief said to them, "It's not that we are going to tell stories, or do something else that I called you. My daughter got a baby. (120) And we asked her who its father is for nothing. She denied it, she said 'I don't know, no man got to me. I don't know who its father is.' And I am going to satisty myself, that's why I called you. (125) And when somebody. . . [unfinished] The baby is crying. Whoever holds it and it stops, that's his son, he takes my daughter."

The people started holding the baby. (130) They went in a circle. It was Coyote's turn and he held the baby, he tried to humor it. The child cries and cries. He sticks his index finger so the baby will be quiet. (135) But no the baby. The people tried to tell him. "Coyote, pass their child on, don't be a dog, pass it on." Then he gave it to them. (140) They took it from Coyote, and then to another, and Coyote goes back around another person and sits down again.[99] Then the baby comes back and he takes it again. (145) And they say "Coyote, how many times are you holding it? You've already held him." They all went around. Nobody made the baby be quiet. The boss asked them: (150) "Did you all [hold him]?" "Yes, " they said, "Yes, we all did, we've gone around."

I don't know who the one next to Lynx was, by the door, the one next to Lynx. (155) He said, "Ah, Lynx never held it. I was close to him. I held him, I tried to give it to him, but no. And the baby is still a-crying." They said "Give it to Lynx." (160) "I said everybody is going to hold the baby, and whoever makes it stop, that's his baby, and he's going to take my daughter." They took it to Lynx, they said to him, "The chief told you, you have to hold the baby." (165) "Heck, have pity on me." They said to him "No, you've got to, the chief said so. If you don't hold the baby, if you don't listen to the chief, you'll be sentenced." Then Lynx got scared, (170) and he held the baby. Lynx took it, the baby stopped. The baby yawned, went to sleep. The chief said, "When the human beings come on earth (175) there will be good looking people, and anyone good looking can have an

99 To get another turn at holding the baby. He wants the young woman.

ugly mate.[100] He won my daughter, that's his child." He said "We'll scatter. This woman my daughter is married. Lynx took my daughter. (180) Let's scatter."

Maybe Grizzly was first, and Grizzly was disgusted because he thought he was going to win the chief's daughter, and that's going to be his wife, but no. (185) Lynx at the end won the chief's daughter. Grizzly got up and he went out; as he passed Lynx he kicked him where his heart should be, and Lynx fell on his back. He [Grizzly] just rubbed his feet on him and then he went out. (190) And then another one, they all did the same thing, they smashed him all up.

The chief took the clothes off his daughter.[101] I don't suppose it was a silk wedding dress, maybe buckskin. All the girl had on was the breech cloth. (195) They were all gone. The chief said, "We're going to move." He named the place where they were goint to settle. They had lived there before, it's an Indian campground. (200) They started getting ready. It didn't take long to get ready. The women fixed the blankets for their packs and the men took down the buckskin tipis. In a little while things are ready tied with strings around. (205) They started walking, they moved.

They had smashed Lynx to death when they kicked him around; only his fur was left; maybe they busted that too. I don't know what else, only his bones...[102] (210) And the virgin started feeling bad. She is not a virgin any more, because she had a virgin-baby. Her parents and the people threw her away. Night came, and she was crying. Just from that pile of bones words come out. (215) He said, "Don't feel too bad. Go to my house. There on my bed mattress are my sheets; under that there you'll find some clothes. Take them, put them on yourself. (220) Don't feel too bad." The woman got surprised. It's his ghost that's talking to her, a pile of bones. He told her "Go, don't be afraid of me. I sympathize with you."

(225) The woman went. She went to Lynx's house. Under the pillow where he put it that's where her clothes are, her buckskin dress. She put it on and it fit perfectly, (230) just like fitted. She put it on, [then] her shoes. The woman got in a better humor. He asked "Are you done dressing?" She said "Yes." (235) He said, "Ok, gather my body, all of it, don't leave anything. And that smoked piece of tipi that's thrown away" (because they cut that off and they threw away the [top of the] buckskin tipi) (240) "You take that and put a curtain in front of me. Don't be in a hurry. If you hear something don't get scared, and don't get in a hurry. (245) I'll let you know when you can take away my curtain. Then I'll be your husband." The woman thought "Lynx sure must be powerful. (250) He never did get to me. I wonder how it happened that I got pregnant from him. He never got to me. He's sure smart."

She gathered all his body parts and his fur, (255) she put it all in a pile. She started looking for the smoked top of the tipi they had thrown away, the old top of the tipi that they cut off. She put the curtain in front of him. It was getting dark; (260) a little after dark, when light disappears some birds could be heard. They were making noise from behind the curtain. [end of tape]

His wife got in a hurry. She got lonesome because she's alone. (265) She's in a hurry for her man. She said to him "Hurry, I'm in a hurry, I'm lonesome." "I'm not

100 Lynx is considered ugly.
101 To shame her.
102 All that's left of Lynx is a pile of bones.

put together yet, I am not finished with my medicine." "That's good enough." He said "Well, if you think so. You must be in a hurry. Take down the curtain." She took the curtain off, and it's only his face that wasn't healed up yet. That's why they say Lynx is "wrinkled face." And if his wife hadn't got anxious his face wouldn't be puckered like that. This woman's man was a real handsome man. The woman is well satisfied. She said "Come on now to my bed."

The man took the baby. They had a baby boy. He took the baby and his wife hooked up with him in the arm, she took his other arm. They went. They went to... All the people had moved away. Only her little tipi is left. They went and they went in. Lynx had gotten lots of grub, because he was smart at getting grub, in hunting, and getting fish. And that's his grub, lots of grub. The woman was happy. It got daylight, and Lynx is ready to go hunting. Lynx is really smart, he knows all about deer. He had wished bad luck hunting for those that moved from there, and he turned the deer towards him.[103] And the chief and his tribe don't see them [the deer] when they hunt. They never get to shoot deer. They ran out of grub.

Lynx goes hunting every day and he kills lots of deer, lots of deer. The woman has enough. She dries meat every day. At that time they didn't have fridge or freezer; they only dried the meat and it didn't spoil. She said to her man: "I have enough meat, and what will I do with it? The cache where we store our food is getting crowded with dry meat." He said "No, don't say that. That's for your people. You'll give them some meat for their cache. You can store it in their cache. And if you think it's enough then put it in another one. Put it in all the caches (everybody has got caches). They might come back to us, it's their homes. They are hard up, they won't get what they want to eat every day." The woman kept on drying meat, and Lynx hunts every day. He shoots deer or bear; every day he gets stuff off his back.[104] Then the wife said, "Well, all the people's caches are full with grub; it's already lots." He said "Pretty soon they'll get to us; they're going to come and see what's happened to us. When your cousins, your relation come to us they'll want to find out what's happened to us, if you're alive or if you're dead."

Their elders sent them to come over and see them.[105] "And whenever they get here to you,[106] treat your cousins well and feed them. And when they're ready to go back give them grub, deer to pack, just to pack. And then you tell them 'When you get back you tell our elders I am doing real good, I'm doing good, you see me. Look, I'm well, and I eat; and look, I feel well, I am fat. And you tell the elders I'm asking them back, I am lonesome for them. Come and visit us again, come see us again.'" They said "Ok," they went back.[107]

They went, they got back home. And they packed lots of dried meat. Two of them and both had packs, enough for a big pack, all dried meat. And their elders asked them, "And where did you get this?" They said "From our relative, from our relative. Our young relative is very good, she has lots of meat, she

103 Lynx ensured the group's failure and his success hunting.
104 Back from hunting he unloads his pack.
105 A delegation of two will be sent.
106 Lynx is talking to his wife.
107 It's implied that the events took place as Lynx foretold.

dries meat every day. And we were coming back, and they fed us, and they told us 'Now I'm going to tell you something. Tell my elders to come and visit me.' She is lonesome for you. 'And another thing, I want you to see your grandchild'" (the child is already growing). And it's a fairy tale, and he's already running around.

Then the boss started hollering. He went out and hollered, he called his people. And he's the boss, a big boss; they don't dispute his words. He said to them "I'm asking you to come. My children got back. My sons went to check up on their sister. Their sister is doing all right and they're going to tell their story." They gathered. They were starving. They all gathered in there. Maybe there are four tipis together, because he's the boss, four tipis. It's jam full.

He didn't untie his sons' bundles. They unwrapped one. He said, "Are you all here?" They said, "Yes, yes, we're all here." He said "This was given to us by our son-in-law. Our daughter fed it to us. And I'm not going to eat it alone, and that's why I called you. We are going to share. We all are going to chew from what's given to us." They were all starving because they never got any deer [though] they tried to hunt. He untied a bundle; he passed it around in their hands. He gave it to them, and maybe went half way around and the first bundle was all gone. Then another bundle, he passed it around. He passed it around and joined where he started from, dry meat. He said to them "Well, when daylight comes (you got enough to eat) we're going to move. Our daughter asked us to come back, and we are going to visit her; we are going over to see our grandchild. Their uncles are saying, they said he's already running around. We are going to go and make over him." They're all starving, and they didn't sleep until daylight.

Daylight came, and maybe they warmed up some cocoa. They got done eating, they started tying their stuff in bundles, and they started moving back. They went and got in sight. My, there is smoke at their daughter's. They got back, their daughter is busy drying meat. Gee, they rushed to their grandchild. The boss and his wife started loving him. The people tried to get back to their houses their camping places, and because there is meat in the dry cache where they had put it, they went to ask.[108] They asked the woman, they asked "And where shall we put our place to stay?" The woman laughed at them. She said "What are you saying? This is your own place and you are backward. It's your own place to stay." They said "And the meat? Maybe it's somebody else's." She said "What are you saying? That's your storage cache, that's your meat, and then you're backward."

They're sure tickled, and they started setting up their houses. In the evening Lynx came back. He threw his pack in the back, with deer, fresh meat. That's the end of the story.

BlueJay and Wolf (63')

This is the story of a newcomer who marries into the family of a chief whose eldest

108 The camping spots are presumed occupied and the full caches presumed to belong to others.

daughter is married to Wolf, the best hunter and provider of the group. BlueJay acts quite the lazy fellow, until spurred by his wife to join the other men in a hunt. Departing for the hunt he acts incompetently, but soon outperforms Wolf and shames him in front of everyone.[109]

Well, this here BlueJay and his brother-in-law the Wolf, that's what I'm going to talk about. Wolf was married with the oldest one. And he was the leader of this group. There were also others, such as the chief's children, and the chief's law relations. And so, long ago that's what comes first for the people: their riches, those who are good providers, of fish, or deer. At that time they didn't know what money was, so they put them above all else. Obtaining food, yes indeed, they put above all else these providers, they are the highest.

And that's why when Wolf proposed to the chief for his daughter he consented, because Wolf is smart at getting food, deer. He was told, "Alright." And so he and the [chief's] daughter got married. And when they go hunting they put Wolf at the head. Because at that time the people didn't stay alone, but in a group. And they stick together in winter. They winter, they call it wintering place. They don't have buckskin tipis, board houses or tule [houses]. They cover houses with tree bark, or anything, boughs, cedar boughs. Those which sprout from the limbs, these they call palm boughs, they grow from cedar trees. That's why, look at fir trees; these they call fir boughs; that's how it grows. And that which grows on the cedar. . . Well, no, I can't name [i. e. remember its name] what grows on cedar, that's how they cover their houses. And they don't get wet, and it's warm. And those that are board houses that's bark; they board these up, and they board them on top. And they call them boarded houses.

Well, BlueJay got to them. Well, he proposed to the chief. Yes, since the youngest one also had grown up. One should say in Indian she was a young maiden, she had grown up. Yes, she wants a man. Well, he began to flirt. BlueJay likes his daughter, the chief's daughter. He got stuck on her, and she said to her father, "Well, you had better consent." To no avail her father said to her, "But we don't know him. We don't know in what things he is smart, in getting things to eat, maybe you'll suffer from it. It might not be long and you will throw him away if it turns out that he's good for nothing. One who will do us good, take him for your husband." "He's going to be MY husband, not your husband; even if I get hard up, it is I who would be hard up." He told her, "Well, if that's how you feel." That was that, BlueJay got his answer.

So he got married. So BlueJay honeymooned. So they were gathered together; Wolf and his wife, and BlueJay and his wife, and his law-relations, the couple of the chief. And there they are all together, in one house, I don't know in how many tipis put together, maybe four, maybe three, since there are three couples. Well, all BlueJay does is play with his wife. He sleeps until noon, then he wakes, then he and his wife get up, because they are honeymooning. By that time the others are gone, those that hunt, and get things to eat.

And Wolf is their leader because he sure is smart at getting things to eat. He

109 The story is cognate with "Blue Jay and Eagle." William Burke told this story to Verne Ray in August 1930, and Ray included it in his "Sanpoil Folk Tales," published in the Journal of American Folklore Vol. 46 (1933), pp. 129-87).

knows where the deer's wintering places are, (60) and he's smart with snowshoes. When they make a drive for the deer, Wolf chases them. The deer don't go far, and he catches up with them, and then he slaughters them. Then he overtakes his law relations, the other people. (65) And then he gives them the deer. And then they drag the meat home, they don't even have to shoot, and that's how Wolf feeds them. Because he's great, smart at hunting. That's why he was their leader.

(70) Well, the oldest daughter started eating her feelings, Wolf's wife. She's always watching her brother-in-law. She even said to her younger sister, "What's the matter? It's been many days, and still you two are honeymooning. (75) You should be getting tired of one another. And your husband should get things to eat. And all you do is play. But no. You know that your brother-in-law gets very tired. All you do is play, and he doesn't get things to eat. (80) Even if he doesn't shoot, just so he goes along. And his brother-in-law would sure feel good." I guess she has all kinds of different thoughts. Well, she kept nagging at her younger sister. Well, she believed her. (85) At first she tried to take up for her husband; finally she believed, she understood. "That's true, my older sister is telling the truth."

The parents never say anything. They tried to stop their oldest daughter when she hates her brother-in-law, and she backbites him. (90) Well, she said to BlueJay, "Listen here. It's been too many days, and we're still honeymooning. Listen, think about getting something to eat. We have sponged too much. Maybe they are getting tired of us. (95) Just look at your sister-in-law. They hate us very much. And your law relations tried to take up for you. They tried to stop their daughter, the oldest one. They said to her: 'Listen, leave your brother-in-law alone.'"

He [BlueJay] said to his wife, "Give me a piece of skin, (100) since you complain with me. I haven't any snowshoes, or bow and arrow. I'm going to prepare myself." Well, BlueJay got a bow. Well, the bow he made wasn't even that, it was awful. (105) It wasn't any good. And the arrows he got are just the same. And when he puts the feathers on the arrows, he just sticks them on. And his arrows are not good enough. His things are bad; the snowshoes, (110) no, they're bad, they weren't much. Well, they are not fit, he made the frame with new shoots. Well, it's not even fit.

She asked her mother for some lacing skin. She asked her, "And what is it for?" (115) She said, "Your son-in-law, the one I'm married to, he's going with the hunters and he doesn't have snowshoes, and now he's prepared sticks, and made frames, but he doesn't have anything to lace them with. That's why he told me, and I interpret him to you, maybe you have some hide." She said to her, "Yes, I keep some in stock. I'll give you some." (120) She started cutting it.

BlueJay started stringing the shoes. It took him one day to fix his bow and arrow and his snowshoes. And it takes those who are used to it (125) several days to finish shoe work or arrow work. But he in one day already had finished his arrows and his snowshoes. They can't be good enough. Those who know how to fix them take pains. The sticks for the arrows have to be dry, and then they straighten them. (130) Then they fix the feathers on, they fix the arrows, and the bow the same way. They dry the sticks dry, they whittle them, and they dry them. They make it shine in the center of the bow, and then they wrap it with sinew, and with pitch (135) they glue it, and it doesn't come loose, and it's solid, the bow is good and strong. But because BlueJay maybe has weak arms, what he made is no good.

The next day it was still dark when Wolf hollered: "Daylight will overtake us, we will be late, we are going far, get up." Goodness, the people, the young people got up. They ate, they drank, they were all ready. Wolf hollered, he was proclaiming. "Alright. We are going." The young folks started coming out. BlueJay came out too. From inside BlueJay coaxed his wife to put his snowshoes on him, because he doesn't even know how to tie his shoes, the loops around the ankle, that's what we call it. Well, it was his woman who put his snowshoes on him, right from inside he put his snowshoes on. These young folks that are used to it..., they go far, like where there is no road, and then they put their snowshoes on. Goodness, they made fun of him. The people laughed at him because he put his snowshoes on from inside. BlueJay takes just one step and he hooks on something, and he has to protect himself with his hands. It must have been that his hands got cold from the snow, because I don't suppose he has gloves, wool gloves. He started sucking his fingers because they are cold. Then the young ones said, "Well, no, maybe he'll get out of sight and then he'll come back, because BlueJay is way behind, there he will give up, he'll come back. He's making us lose time."

They walked away, and Wolf is way ahead, he breaks the trail for his friends. He breaks the trail for his friends. Then they find tracks, then they scatter. Wolf'll point to where to go. This Wolf is the leader, the smartest of all; and then he goes where the deer go. Because he's smart and strong. And he can go fast. They were going. Then they see the tracks. Lots of deer where they are feeding. They scattered. There were very many deer. He stopped. There's a hollow place, it's a big place. The deer must be there, "We didn't scare them. Here are their tracks, they might still be eating." It was broad daylight. They stopped and he asked them, "Are you all gathered here?" They said, "Yes, we are all here. Just your brother-in-law BlueJay hasn't yet come in sight. Just as we left, he was falling around, because he doesn't know anything about snowshoes, he might have turned back. Let's not wait for him. We are wasting time."

Wolf said, "Well, that's right. We saw tracks of deer, fresh tracks. I don't think they went anywhere far. Maybe they're in that hollow, in those slate rocks. We are going to scatter. There on the top there's a hollow. That's where we will get back together. If they've gone over, then we'll think more how they're going to scatter." They agreed, "Yes." He pointed for them where to drive the deer. "And those on the outside, half of them will go where they'll be watching (for deer) to walk under: there will be two of them; and as for me, I'll be from this half, I will be on the outside, I am going to walk under." Only the smart ones can be on the outside, because they're going to have to work hard to get to where the deer go. That's where they always go, it's a low place where the deer go. And these who drive the deer take their time; when they see tracks they follow them, they drive them. The deer tracks go straight to the low pass, and those who went to watch, these will kill them. When he who drives the deer accidentally catches a glimpse of it, he shoots it, or when they come down and turn around, they see the ones who are watching, and they come down on their same tracks, they run across the others, then they kill them. That's when the ones that are driving kill their own deer. And that's what's called in the language "the ones that go and set watch," the smart ones, those who watch.

They said, "Maybe when BlueJay comes out of sight he gets tired, his hands'll get cold, he might turn back. He doesn't know anything about snowshoes. We'll waste too much time if we wait for him." They scattered. He told them, "You know the place where I told you to go, we will gather there." They scattered. BlueJay's been watching for them. He saw his friends scatter. He must have good hearing, he heard every word of it. His brother-in-law is the one who's going to watch.

BlueJay was just putting on, and that's why he fell deep in the snow, like he didn't know snowshoeing. BlueJay rose, he kicked the trees. The wind started blowing, it came down on the trees, the snow to the ground. The snow was floating around the earth. He went up the hill. The deer... The same thing there, the earth... They did their best to get where they could get shelter, to a place for shelter, and there is no air there. The snow didn't reach there, the wind is still. BlueJay went up the hill. He went. He got there to the top of the mountain where that low place is. The deer had already gone over. His partner, his brother-in-law has already gone over behind. He started following, he was right on the tracks of his brother-in-law.

Wolf hadn't gone very far, he heard something. He got the chills. He looked behind him, well, he was being overtaken by his brother-in-law BlueJay. Then he runs, he's doing his best. He thinks, "Ah. And we thought he couldn't make it. And I am the best in hunting, and then he overtakes me. It won't be far he will give out." Until he overtakes the deer, that's when Wolf'll turn back. Well, Wolf ran down the hill. "Dust, dust, dust, dust, dust" go his snowshoes. And with the corner of his eye he saw his brother-in-law. "Dust, dust, dust" go his snowshoes. He had got used to his snowshoes. He didn't get to the bottom and he got give out,[110] because it isn't for nothing that he's BlueJay. Wolf used to not get tired. He just overtakes the deer, he slaughters them, and he doesn't get tired, and he gets back. I suppose BlueJay changed him around, that's why he's tired.

Wolf tried but could't do it, and he turned around. He was too tired. He told his brother-in-law, "Go ahead, maybe you are a little better off. I am plum to the end with tiredness. You are stronger." He said, "Ok." Wolf gave him the way. BlueJay jumped. Like Wolf didn't make a move.[111] He started to go. Just like that BlueJay was out of sight. He tried his best, finally Wolf got to the bottom, because he always tracks the deer. BlueJay's tracks are right along. It got dark, it was dusk when he got to the bottom. There are deer laying all over. Well, he was busy doing something. That was the last. And BlueJay got done taking the guts out. That's when he [Wolf] overtook him. He has the deer all killed. Wolf thought, "From the time I was born, from the time I got my senses, there is not anybody who could step in front of me. Now this brother-in-law of mine steps in front of me. I'm not going to believe it. Maybe I am just dreaming."

BlueJay said to him, "Hurry, let's turn back. We might be very late. Our women and our staying place are far away." Wolf told him, and he figured, it's all uphill to the top, then it's downhill to their houses, he said, "No. I fear it. I have

110 BlueJay has the power to cause Wolf to get tired. See 253.
111 BlueJay outdistances Wolf as though Wolf weren't moving.

no more breath from fatigue. All I could do was catch up with you. I can't make it up the hill. I am going to camp here." (285) "Ah." He said, "Ok," and BlueJay had already figured out what to do. The biggest, the leader of the deer that he had killed, there was very much fat in the inside of it, he thought; he lay down the deer gift. They dug until the deer came in sight. (290) He broke up the stitches on the deer, because he had stitched the deer up. He told his brother-in-law, "Here, get into this deer." He said to him, "And then you will live. Well, look how clear it is, it's very cold. (295) You will freeze. What can you do to make fire, what can you do to get wood. There's snow on trees, lots of snow. What can you do to get fir boughs in the dark. And you are tired besides. That's the only way you can save your life. Don't refuse. If you refuse, you will die. (300) Don't you get stingy of your wife? You want to stay alive." He coaxed his brother-in-law.

He believed him. He thought, "Well, I am too tired. I can't even try to get fire; and if even I make fire, I still have to get wood. No. It's still early in the night. And I have got to have something under me. (305) And I am done in from being tired. What he figured out for me is true." He said, "I'll take your advice." He told him, "Get in." He went into the deer, because it's big. He stitched the deer back, and he put snow back on it. (310) After he got snow on top of him, Wolf got warmed up. Because he still wasn't too cold, he was warm; he hadn't gotten cold. He really liked how he was getting warm. It was very warm.

But he's very hungry. (315) He felt something, fat. He cut some off. And then he ate it. It was delicious. He cleaned off the inside of his deer gift. In a little while since it's fresh meat, he got diarrhea. He couldn't do anything to get out, because he's sewn up in there. (320) Then Wolf did something pitiful, he that used to be boss.

BlueJay ran up the hill. He ra··n, got to the top, he ran down the hill. [end of tape]

Now I am going to splice my story. The BlueJay group with Wolf, they are brothers-in-law. (325) They were hunting when Wolf got tired. And BlueJay was newly wed. And he wasn't tired, and he was lonesome.[112] He didn't like to camp by his brother-in-law. And he picked out the biggest fattest deer. That's where he put his brother-in-law. (330) And he said, "You might freeze, you are tired, what can you do to make fire, or to get wood, or to get the boughs. It's too cold. You will freeze. The place for you here is nice and comfortable." Wolf thought, "Yes, he's telling the truth." He said, "Ok." (335) He put him in the biggest deer. He sewed him up there with a twisted twig, then he covered it with snow. In a little while Wolf felt warm, I guess from his breath, from where else could the air come, the deer in his insides, and besides he had snow on it.

(340) BlueJay ran up the hill, got to the top; he ran down the hill. He got half way, closer to home. He hollered repeatedly, because that's the way the hunters go when they get late. They don't go to sleep when they have relatives. They always wait up for them. They sit around. (345) If nobody shows up, then the next daylight they go looking for them. Something could have happened to them, they're either hurt or give out. They heard. He was hollering. They answered him. They thought, "That's Wolf."

112 Lonesome for his wife and eager to get back to camp.

(350) Wolf's wife pushed her. She pushed her younger sister. She said, "Fix the fire. That might be your husband that is hollering. Put the coffee pot on the fire. He must be awful hungry." Now she's making fun of her younger sister, because BlueJay put his snowshoes on from inside. (355) He didn't know his snowshoes. He was falling around and then he got out of sight. Because the oldest one is sure that the smartest one is her husband. That's why she was making fun of her younger sister. The younger sister jumped up, stood up. (360) She fixed the fire. And she started supper. She warmed up some leftovers, some soup, what was cooked for them. She warmed it over. The hollering continued. They answered it. Then she rushed her younger sister. She said, "Fix that fire, that's your man." (365) Their parents tried to stop her, their parents are sure that she's making fun of her younger sister when she says, "That's your husband." Because it never came close to their minds. They thought, "The one who gave up is BlueJay, because he's new at hunting, since he got married."

Well. They heard him, because the snowshoes are loud, because it's frozen. (370) "px̌, px̌, px̌, px̌, px̌, px̌." That's snowshoes. The snowshoes make a good, clear sound. He came in. He raised the curtain. He came in. He had snowshoes still on. And he sat down. His wife rushed to him. He told his wife. (375) She hugged him and kissed him on the face. She said to him, "I bet you are tired." He said, "Yes, yes, I am tired. I have travelled far. I was done in when I got back. Take off my snowshoes." (380) She took off his snowshoes, and then he said, "Also my moccasins, because my feet got wet (because he had moccasins on) when I covered the deer with snow." Well, she took his moccasins off, she dried them. (385) She gave him bedroom slippers. They say in English "house slippers." She set dishes up. They don't have a table, she set down dishes for him. She just spread something down for him. And then she put a whole pot of food for him.

(390) BlueJay was about to eat and he pulled something from his vest. And he threw it at his father-in-law. He said, "Look at this. Then you'll know what this is, you'll wonder what it is." His father-in-law took it. He started to unwrap it. What part of the deer is it? (395) He laid it down, he did like that, shook it, and put it down; he can't figure out what it is. It doesn't come out right. He started to eat. BlueJay ate. He got done eating. My, his sister-in-law, the one that made fun of him, had a frown on her face. And sure enough the older sister was making fun of him, and it was he who came in. (400) She was saying, "Your husband is coming. Fix that fire." And true enough, BlueJay came in. His sister-in-law was disappointed. She got ashamed, felt cheap for making fun of her brother-in-law. BlueJay got done eating.

The old man went out, and because he's chief he yelled. (405) He hollered, and everybody is listening. It was all of them and they said, "Ah, the chief is talking. It's important." He said to them, "I am calling all of you. My son-in-law BlueJay came back. (410) And he gave me this thing that is tied up. And I can't get them together, and I can't get it right. I want you to figure it for me, that's why I am calling you." My, the people ran over there, because that's surprising news. They all came in, at the chief's. It was a house full with young folks. (415) The old man gave it to them. They tried to figure it out. No, they couldn't figure out the ears. They knew it's deer's ears, but they didn't match. They even laid them out. One half doesn't fit with the other. (420) Well, no, it doesn't match.

Then they asked BlueJay. They said, "We are puzzled. What is wrong with this ear that it doesn't match?" BlueJay laughed at them, and he said to them, "You got no sense. You know that it won't match. And each deer has one ear. I marked all of them to one side. And if it comes out right, it will show. And it will be easy to count." That's when they all agreed. They understood, and they knew the ears. They counted them. There were lots of deer if there are so many ears. The brother-in-law told them this.

Because maybe the oldest one got over her shame, his sister-in-law asked him, she said, "And what became of your brother-in-law? Didn't you see him?" He said, "Yes, we scared the deer, and then I did my best to where they're going, to a low place where it joins the little mounds, that's where the deer went. And he went to the outside of those who drive. I got there. The deer had left, gone over the mountain. I was late. He also was tracking behind. I guess he didn't even get a shot at it, and then he started chasing the deer, many of them. And I started chasing too. I followed the tracks. They hadn't got to the bottom yet on the other side of the mountain. There was a bigger valley from there to the other side. They hadn't yet got to the bottom, they were gone half way when I overtook my brother-in-law. He didn't go far, and he made room, he told me: 'I am getting tired. I will never get near them. You go ahead.'" He said, "'Ok.' I went ahead of him. I left him. The deer just got to the bottom and I overtook them. I killed them, finishem them all, and these are their ears. And I just had got done gutting them, I was going to bury them when my brother-in-law overtook me. He's played out with fatigue, he's just walking. Then he told me: 'You cleaned the deer all out.' I said: 'Yes.' And he said to me: 'Well, with me, I got tired. And I am discouraged to go back. And I'll camp here with these deer.' And I said to him: 'No.' He told me: 'I am too tired.' And I said: 'No. You will freeze to death. It's late and dark. Gee, the stars are bright.' I said to him: 'You just said you are tired, tired. And what can you do to make fire? And if even you did make fire, what can you do to get wood in this dark night? And also things to put under you? You will freeze to death. You want to camp, and I will store you here, in the biggest of the deer, because they are all cut open. I will put you here and you won't freeze to death. The deer is quite warm, still warm. And then I'll bury you, and you won't freeze to death.' I put him there, and I sewed him up. I twisted a stick. I sewed up the deer. I stamped on the snow and it made a hole there. I stuck him there, and I buried him with snow. And then I stepped away."

He told the chief. He told his father-in-law, BlueJay told them, "All of you that are related will get up early, also the women folks, we are going to get the dead deer. Because it's far." They said, "Ok." The folks didn't go to sleep. Morning came, and they woke up, and started hollering. They did that, and got done eating. Then the chief went out. He said, "Now we will walk." They said, "We are all ready."

It got broad daylight. "You women folks whose husbands have gone along." Because the women are smart with snowshoes, and that's the only way they can travel anyway, they don't have horses, who does in wintertime. That's all they travel on, snowshoes. Especially the North Halfs. They went. And they got a leader, BlueJay. BlueJay is really smart on snowshoes. He didn't used to know how. And they made fun of him. BlueJay's wife had gone along. And his sister-in-law was right behind him, his father-in-law and mother-in-law are also behind. And then the rest of the folks string along.

They went, there in a big valley, and at the end a little mountain, that's where the low place is. They went right over that hill. Then they went down the hill. They went. They got to the bottom. He told them, "It's right here." There are snow mounds all over where the deer are buried. He told his father-in-law, "You are the boss, my father-in-law. You distribute the meat. That's the whole catch." The father-in-law said, "No, even if I am the chief. It's you that killed them, you're the one that worked hard. You pass it around. And here I only was sitting around, lying on my back, pulling my whiskers with tweezers, and for me to take the lead to pass it around... You do it." He said, "Ok," and he passed it around.

He knew what deer he put him in. He told his sister-in-law: "That's what I'm going to give you, this is your lump. You dig that out, do what you please, drag it home, or skin it, pack it back, do what you want. Whatever you think." My, his sister-in-law was glad. I suppose his sister-in-law kissed BlueJay, she was so tickled. His sister-in-law used to hate him because he was good for nothing. She started digging the deer. She took off the snow, she got to the deer. It was sewn up twisted with the sprig. She undid the stitches, she did like that, she opened it where it was cut open and sewn up. She opened it. All of a sudden out came her husband. He's nothing but shit.

Goodness, the stench hit the woman's nose. Her husband really stank. She tried. She's going to try to skin it. She couldn't stand it. The deer is nothing but shit. Her husband got tired, and people get hungry when they get tired. He got warmed up there when he got rested and then he realized he was hungry. He felt around, he felt the fat. He cut off from there and he ate it. It's fresh meat that bulged here and there. In a while after he was done eating he started to ache with diarrhea. He tried to get out. He couldn't. It's sewn from the outside, and there isn't anything to do to get out. He came to the end. He crapped right in there, in the deer. He crapped in the deer until daylight. That's why it stank, it's nothing but shit.

Goodness. the woman just frowned. She got after her husband. She said, "You have done something awful. Why, that's our eats, and you messed it up." He told his wife, "You talk pitifully. I didn't do it on purpose. I got give out, I was tired. If I hadn't slept inside the deer (my brother-in-law did my thinking) I would have frozen to death. He left me. In a while I got rested, and that's when I felt hungry. And I ate the fat. That's what did me bad, and then I got diarrhea. There isn't any way for me to get out. That's when I did that pitiful thing inside there, I didn't do it on purpose."

They started packing the deer. BlueJay became boss. They got the meat home. The men folks started drying meat, roasting it. And the women started cutting it open, they started drying it over the fire. Lots of deer, each one gets a whole deer. And Wolf's woman, she will not throw it away, whatever she did with it, maybe she washed the deer. She aired it out and when it had no more smell then she roasted it. And because it's fairy tales I tell them, "The sun is coming high on me, I am going to end, as they say in Moses (Columbian) language." With us we say "It's the end of the story." That's the end.

The transcription and analysis of the texts

Here I describe how I write the texts.[1] Because audiences with different interests in technical linguistic explanations may read the book, I will try to be as clear as I can without sacrificing salient details. This section can be used as a reference resource as wished, and needn't be read through at once.

Each text is divided into lines; each line is a convenient discourse unit that may correspond to a sentence, complex or otherwise, but only approximately. There may be lines that consist of fragments of sentences, such as lists, for example, if I saw fit to do so for such practical reasons as to constrain the length of a line. Each word of the line is divided into its stem and inflectional affixes, with some exceptions, as explained here. Each stem and each inflectional affix is given a gloss, and the whole Cv-Ok line is translated into English. I do not gloss any derivational material (see below). I enclose editorial comments, additions, or corrections in square brackets; and I enclose in curly brackets false starts, repetitions, unfinished words, and other intrusive matter.

Approximate phonemic transcriptions

Each Colville line is in approximate phonemic transcription. Three details make it approximate: (a) the use of schwa, which marks mostly predictable epenthesis; (b) the use of vowels in place of underlying semi-consonants; (c) the transcription of phonetic [c] as [ts].

I use schwa because the Colville and Okanagan speakers I have worked with approve of its use, inconsistent though it might (appear to) be. It hurts nothing to insert it, and it helps with the reading of the form, especially if it is long. Thus, for example, we prefer ƛ̓axəxƛ̓x̌áp to ƛ̓ax̌x̌ƛ̓x̌áp.

The initial vowel of a form like [ilmíxʷum] is an underlying semi-consonant, as the plural [ililmíxʷum] demonstrates: the plural reduplicative prefix is C_1C_2-, not VC_1-. What to write? In my approximate phonemic line I write ilmíxʷəm and ililmíxʷəm; in the line below I write ylmixʷm and yl•yl=mixʷ+m (with morph boundaries marked as appropriate —more on the use of the symbols [+], [=], and [•] below). Notice, incidentally, that the epenthetic vowel between xʷ and m is phonetically [u]. I write ə in the approximate phonemic line in an attempt to remind readers and writers of the language that this is an epenthetic vowel, the shape of which is determined by the rounded consonant that precedes (and/or follows) it. An analogous example with [u] (underlying /w/) is uksqílxʷ /wk+s+qilxʷ/ (√wik). These practices are subject to criticism, I realize, because they represent neither a phonetic nor a phonemic reality. The theoretically most consistent alternative would be to write underlying forms; the reason that is not acceptable can be summed up as follows: many underlying forms are too abstract to be recognized easily by the speaker / reader / writer (more on the subject later). In sum, I

1 Parts of this chapter are modifications of the introductory chapter in my editions of Madeline DeSautel's texts *matlán kʷu̯ m̓ayxíts. Madeline told me.* and of Dora DeSautel's texts *Dora Noyes DeSautel ɬaʔ kɬcaptíkʷɬ.*

have compromised in a number of cases for the benefit of the Cv-Ok speaker / reader / writer.

My approximate phonemic transcription of a form like [wíkəncən] (where c is somewhat palatalized), is wíkəntsən, a compromise in the interest of morphological transparency. All sequences of /ts/ are realized as [c], indistinguishable from /c/[2]. The make-up of this word, and analogously, of every other transitive form like this, is /wik-nt-s-n/ *I saw you*, with wik *see*, -nt[3] *transitive*, -s *2sgObj*, and -n *1erg*. Similarly, I write iʔ‿skʷists[4] /s+kʷist-s/ *his name*, (-s *3rd poss*) and not iʔ‿skʷisc.

Whatever the inconsistencies and the shortcomings of the approximate phonemic transcription, each form is given its underlying composition in the second line of the interlinearization, morph by morph. This, too, is an approximation, because I try to stay as close to the surface as possible. I can explain with this example: I write surface uksqílxʷ and approximate underlying form /wk+s+qilxʷ/. This is only approximately an underlying form, because I don't write the vowel of the strong root /wik/. Writing the vowel (/wik+s+qilxʷ/) would make it less transparent to the reader that the stressed vowel is the /i/ (of sqilxʷ) that follows (without further complicating the transcription). One of the alternatives, to expect one to know strong and weak stems and affixes, imposes an intolerable burden on the reader because the stress valence of a stem does not fall from the valence of the lexical root and its interplay with the valence of the affixes. Otherwise stated, the stress valence of roots is only of relative value: some otherwise identical roots behave as strong in some forms, and as weak in others, and similarly with some affixes: c-my-st-ín (weak) means *I know it*, and miy-st-n (strong) mean *I am sure of it*. Therefore I do not write stem vowels that reduce to zero.

Phrasal words and amalgams

Constructions that consist of more than one independent word, yet function lexically as single words, are *phrasal words*. These include combinations of two stems (Table 1); combinations of particle and stem (Table 2); and combinations of two particles (Table 3). *Amalgams* consist of a clitic and a stem (Table 4). *Amalgams* are so perceived by native speakers as single words that I list each in the index of stems as such.

yaʕ•yáʕ+t s+tim̓	*everything*
yaʕ•yáʕ+t swit	*everybody*
lut kmʔ=ikxt+m	*do things*
lut k+s+lut+s	*no exceptions, there is no no about it*
lut pn+ʔkin̓	*never*
lut s+lkʷ=ut+s	*not far*
lut s+q̓sápiʔ+s	*not long after*
lut s+qʷay+s	*not often*
lut s+tim̓	*nothing*
lut swit	*nobody*
lut t’ xʷuy	*never*

2 However, the phonemic reality of /c/ distinct from the sequence /ts/ is undisputed. Thus, for example, citxʷ *house* reduplicates as ct•citxʷ with C_1C_2-.

3 It is not my practice to segment this and other transitivizers further.

4 In non-interlinearized writing I use the undertie between clitics and stems.

lut xʷuy pn+ʔkin̓	*never*
lut+m swit	*not anybody*
sic+m put	*especially*

Table 1: Two or more stems (phrasal words)

aɬíʔ swit	*in fact*
t̓a wnixʷ	*for sure*
t̓iʔ c+ʔx̌iɬ	*like*
t̓iʔ lut	*in no time*
t̓iʔ n+y̓ʕ=íp	*always, continuously*
t̓iʔ put	*just enough*
t̓iʔ x̌as+t	*as well*
kmix k̓m	*that's all, only*
lut cmay	*everywhere, every which way*
lut ití?	*good about one*
lut k̓im	*no more*
lut nixʷ	*no more*
swit aɬíʔ	*in fact*
lut t̓	*neg emph*

Table 2: Particle and stem (phrasal words)

mi sic	*then*
pnaʔ cmay	*maybe*
t̓iʔ kmix	*only*
t̓iʔ kʷm̓iɬ	*at once*
t̓iʔ wim̓	*powerless*
t̓xʷ mat	*maybe*
xʷm t̓iʔ	*evidential*
t̓iʔ ʔayxáxaʔ	*a little while*

Table 3: Particles in combination (phrasal words)

Cv-Ok has a closed set of clitics that include the article iʔ‿ and its allomorphs, two person marker sets (kn‿ and kʷu‿--see below), and five directional markers (t‿ *source* or *agent/instrument,* l‿ *in, at,* k̓‿ *to,* tl‿ *from,* k̓l‿ *to*)[5]. Clitics combine with stems normally: kən‿xʷuy *I went,* consists of the clitic kn‿ and the stem xʷuy. These forms needn't receive special treatment in the dictionary of the language or in the index of this volume.

la‿c+xʔít	*at first*
la‿c+xʔít+iʔ	*at first*
la‿c+ʔiwt	*last (in a series)*
la‿n+yxʷ=ut	*inside*
ta‿c+k̓	*in the direction of*

5 These are proclitics that attach to the head noun, thus iʔ‿l‿citxʷs *art, at, house-his* "at his house."

ta‿c+k̓l	*in the direction of*
ta‿c+k̓líʔ	*in that direction, that way*
ta‿n+y̓ʕip	*keep on, forever*
tla‿ʔkín	*from there*
tla‿ʔx̌iʔ	*from there*
incá‿kn[6]	*I*

Table 4: Clitics and stems (amalgams)

Alternate forms

Alternate forms are of several different kinds. First, there are dialectal or idiosyncratic differences with words that differ in one or two sounds, as the examples I chart in Table 5.

yutlx^{w}	yutlx	*raven*
kmix	kmax	*only*
uníx^{w}	unáx^{w}	*true*
limlmtx	limlmt	*thank you*
níkxna	níkna	*goodness*
nstils	ntils	*he thinks*
taʔx^{w}-	taw-	*get (in compounds)*

Table 5: Forms that differ in one or two sounds

In my less than systematic survey of the matter, yutlx^{w} is the prevalent pronunciation, but I have heard more than one speaker from Douglas Lake insist that they say yutlx. kmix and uníx^{w} are typical of Southern Okanagan speakers (as are all pairs of words that show the i/a correspondence), and so are limlmtx, níkxna, nstils, and taʔx^{w}-, while the other forms prevail among the Northern Okanagan. But there is also significant idiosyncratic variation, not least because of the common interactions, travel, and intermarriage among members of all Okanagan groups.

Second, there are basic lexical items with resonants (laryngealized or not) that differ in the pronunciation of individuals: one hears, for example, sl̓ax̌t and slax̌t *friend*, skm̓xist and skmxist *black bear*, sql̓tmix^{w} and sqltmix^{w} *man, husband*, and I have detected no regional or other correlates of the variants. I have remarked that speakers are fickle when it comes to the laryngealization of resonants, and the fact that laryngealization of resonants is one of the mechanisms that mark diminutive and hypocoristic forms, contributes to the matter.[7] Many kin terms contain laryngealized resonants, and an analogous phenomenon is well known: in Shuswap first person forms of reference are diminutivized. I record the forms as I have heard them in their context.

6 Interior Salish languages have one (or more) set(s) of clitic person markers. In some languages these are postclitics, in others proclitics, and in yet another (Moses Columbian) they can be either. The Cv-Ok example incá‿kn kn‿x^{w}uy *I (emphatic) went, It is I who went*, shows a Cv-Ok instance of a person marker that can be a pro- or a postclitic.

7 See Footnote 14 below, and other remarks that address this phenomenon in the other Interior Salish languages in the "Index of roots."

Third, the word-internal glottal stop of several common items often disappears in casual speech, so that one hears caʔkʷ and cakʷ *if, should,* taʔlíʔ, talíʔ (and taʔlí, talí) *much, many.* In such cases the near-phonemic transcription reflects what I heard, and the morpheme line reflects the standard form.

Fourth, the initial or final glottal stop of several common words also disappears in casual speech, and one hears such variants as iʔ‿ and i‿ *article.* In such cases too, the near-phonemic transcription reflects what I heard, and the morpheme line the standard forms.

Fifth, epenthetic a is attached to a number of proclitics before words that begin with resonants, and the grammatical prefix c- *habitual / durative.* The relative marker kiʔ has the variant kaʔ in these environments. I list some other examples in Table 6.

/iʔ‿t‿ylmixʷm/	i ta ylmíxʷəm	*by the chief*
/k̓‿nspilm/	k̓a nspíləm	*to Nespelem*
/kiʔ cwix/	kaʔ cwix	*where he lives*
/iʔ‿ylmixʷm/	ya ylmíxʷəm	*the chief*
/iʔ‿lʔiw-s/	ya lʔiws	*his father*
/t‿nqilxʷcn/	ta nqílxʷcən	*in Indian*

Table 6: Epenthetic a

Finally, there are several cases where I am unsure of the phonetics of the variants. One such is the repetitive infix, which may be –a- or –aʔ-. Another is uncertainty about the presence of a pharyngeal in such forms as lṗ+la(ʕ)ṗ=qn. My transcriptions reflect my uncertainties, and I list some of these in Table 7.

ya	yaʔ	*article*
hɬ=	haɬ=	*group*
ɬ	aɬ	*comp*

Table 7: Other indeterminacies

Inflectional and non-inflectional material

Over the course of my work with Colville-Okanagan I have grown more and more concerned with the appropriateness of interlinear representations that discriminate between inflectional morphemes and other morphemes. In the interinearizations I separate a Cv-Ok word into a stem and its inflectional affix(es); and I separate the stem into its root(s) and derivational affixes. I do not label any of the derivational members of the stem because I do not want to clutter the interlinearization and I want to stay focused on the syntax. However, I provide an exhaustive list of derivational affixes and those who, having studied and understood the syntax of the sentence, want to study the derivational morphology of the individual words, can do so by referring to these lists.

One who wants to understand how the syntax of the language works must know the inflectional categories of the language. If an affix forms a new word that needs to be included in the inventory of words, then that affix is derivational; if an affix differentiates between forms like cat and cats (-s), then the affix is inflectional: -s is (simplifying the matter) the English inflectional suffix that signals *plural of regular*

English nouns. And, in the Cv-Ok example kilx *hand*, inkilx *my hand*, in- is the Cv-Ok inflectional prefix that signals *first person singular possessive*. One must know all the inflectional affixes of the language to make sense of sentences. But to say that one knows the language, one must also know the derivational affixes, and these, though often productive, often are not (and so a good knowledge of the derivational morphology requires years of study). In English for example, *indifferent* is not the sum of in- *not* and *different*—the word doesn't mean *same*. Similarly, in Cv-Ok ɬcəcʔúps is *younger sister* and (s)caʔpsíw̓s is *two sisters*; síncaʔ is *younger brother* and səncʔíw̓s is *two brothers*; nkʷəlmút is *brother-in-law* and *nkʷəlmtíw̓s* is *two brothers-in-law*; (s)əntxʷús is *sibling* and (s)əntxʷsíw̓s is *two siblings*; but náx̌ʷnəx̌ʷ is *wife* and nəx̌ʷnx̌ʷíw̓s is not the expected *two wives*, but rather *a (married) couple*. In the interlinearizations I identify all inflectional material, but I also try to foreshadow the morphology of the language by writing these stems with internal boundaries as follows:

	word	analysis	word	analysis
	ɬcəcʔúps	ɬ+c•cʔ=ups	(s)caʔpsíw̓s	(s)+caʔ=ps=iw̓s
gloss	*younger sister*		*two sisters*	
	síncaʔ	síncaʔ	səncʔíw̓s	sncʔ=iw̓s
gloss	*younger brother*		*two brothers*	
	nkʷəlmút	n+kʷlmút	nkʷləmtíw̓s	n+kʷlmt=íw̓s
gloss	*brother-in-law*		*two brothers-in-law*	
	(s)əntxʷús	(s)ntxʷ=us	(s)əntxʷsíw̓s	(s)n+txʷ=s=iw̓s
gloss	*sibling*		*two siblings*	
BUT				
	náx̌ʷnəx̌ʷ	nax̌ʷ•nx̌ʷ	nəx̌ʷənx̌ʷíw̓s	nx̌ʷ•nx̌ʷ=iw̓s
gloss	*wife*		*a (married) couple*	

Table 8: Singular – plural pairs

The plus sign (+) is the boundary of a derivational affix; the double hyphen (=) is the boundary of a lexical affix; and the bullet (•) is the boundary of a reduplicative affix. In an interlinearization, the forms iɬcəcʔúps, isíncaʔ, inkʷəlmút, isəntxʷús, all with the inflectional prefix i(n)- *first person singular possessive*, are written with a hyphen that separates the inflectional prefix from the stem, while the stem is written as in the above chart. To reiterate, the chart illustrates my practice of separating a word into a stem and its inflectional affix(es); and a stem into its root(s) and its derivational affixes (and not glossing the latter for the reasons given).

With my orthographic practices I tell the student of the text, for example, that sxʷiplp means *mat, rug*. I also alert the reader that this stem is analyzable into three morphs: s+xʷip=lp, where s- is a *nominalizer*, xʷip means *cover with a sheet-like object*, and =lp is the lexical suffix glossed *floor*, and this information is retrievable from my lists. I think that, in interlineared texts, the labeling of all morphs, here, for example, *nom+cover with a sheet-like object+floor* would be clutter. However, it goes without saying, there are circumstances, specifically when studying and analyzing derivational morphology, when *nominalizer+cover with a sheet-like object+floor* is appropriate.

Affixes that prepare stems for transitivization are derivational suffixes. (Variants of at least) two such are commonly recognized for the (Southern) Interior languages, +min, and -nu(n), which I mark as shown here: the former with a plus sign, the latter with a hyphen. The meaning of the former is unpredictable; that of the latter consistently *success, manage*. Similarly, all transitivizers are derivational suffixes, but I have been marking them as though they were inflectional—except as I describe below.

Verb stems may have intransitive, middle, and transitive forms as I exemplify here: ʔiɬn is an intransitive stem, conjugated with the intransitive person markers (kʷ‿ʔiɬn *you ate*); it can be transitivized, (ʔiɬn-(n)t-xʷ *you ate it*); and, in certain constructions, can be intransitive or middle (lut a-ks-ʔíɬn *don't eat*; lut a-ks-ʔíɬn+m *don't eat it*). The root √tx *comb* can be transitivized (tx-nt-in *I combed her*)[8], and it can occur as a middle stem (kən txa+m[9] *I combed (my hair)*). Here, too, I mark these affixes inconsistenly, as I have shown, the transitive suffixes with a hyphen, and the middle suffix with a plus sign.

The transitivizer -st / +st has three functions. Together with the prefix c- it marks the customary: c-wik-st-xʷ *you always see him* (cf. wik-nt-xʷ *you saw him*); in a number of specific stems which have no corresponding -nt transitivizer, it functions as a simple transitivizer (wẏ-st-ixʷ *you finished it*; miy-st-xʷ *you are sure of it*; *wẏ-nt-ixʷ, *miy-nt-xʷ)[10]; and, in a number of specific stems it marks causative: xʷuy+st-xʷ *you took it (there)* (kʷ‿xʷuy *you went*; *xʷuy-nt-xʷ); ʔácqaʔ+st-xʷ *you took it out(side)* (kʷ‿ʔácqaʔ *you went outside*, *ʔácqaʔ-nt-xʷ). I write with the plus sign the affix of the causative stems, but not so the affixes of the other two stems, as I have shown.

In this anthology I have reversed my earlier practice to mark with a hyphen the highly productive prefix kɬ+ *have, there be.*[11] This prefix derives verb stems from nouns, and I have listed each such "have" verb in the index of stems, a total of approximately 200 such.[12]

I mark all reduplicative affixes with the bullet (•), but I do not give examples of these, except for •VC$_2$ *patient.*[13] (See below).

While there are some discernible patterns in stems with •C$_2$ *plural* reduplication (ʔickn: ʔic•c•kn *play: pl play*; ʔácqaʔ: ʔác•c•qaʔ *go out: pl go out*, xʷl•xʷalt: xʷl••xʷalt *alive: alive pl*), this reduplicative suffix is stem-specific. I write the variants of such plural stems with the bullet, for example, kl•kil•l+x and kl•kiľ•l+x[14] *hands*. The referent of suxʷ(•xʷ) is always plural, but the distribution of the two variants is not straight-forward. Similarly with the distribution of xʷuy and xʷuẏ•y *they went*, and other stems.

8 This form, based on a weak stem, is suffix-stressed.

9 The vowel /a/ of this and other weak stems is analogous to the epenthetic /a/ mentioned above.

10 Here I have given an example of a form based on a weak (suffix-stressed) stem, and one based on a strong (stem-stressed) stem.

11 In the "Index of stems and inflectional affixes" I give the gloss *have...* (and not *there be...*) almost exclusively.

12 This may not be the best choice, but it's the one I have made, at least for now.

13 I do not include a description of all Cv-Ok reduplicative affixes in this volume.

14 Here and in many other forms, especially diminutives, the laryngealization of resonants is not as regular as one might wish it to be. As I have mentioned, many lexical items have alternate pronunciations, with and without laryngealization of resonants. In my interlinearizations I write either the plain or the laryngealized form as I heard it (for example, ckʷ=ink and ckʷ=iṅk *bow*; c+yaʕ, c+yaʕ̓ *all, lots)*. See also my discussion of alternate forms, above. I should add that fickle laryngealization is not peculiar to Okanagan. Entries in the Spokane and Coeur d'Alene dictionaries, authored or co-authored by native speakers, confirm the analogous phenomenon. For example, Sp √yaʕ̓ (yaʔ) *gathered, accumulated* ... yʕ̓-áʔp *they all arrived together* ... c-yʕ̓-áʔp *they've all gotten here*; Cr yaʕ+aʕ *assemble, congregate (lit. they gathered together in a group)* ... yaʕ̓+aʕ *assemble, congregate, (lit. they gathered together in a group)*. See also, for example Th xwéɬ, xẇeɬ *road.*, zʕ ~ zʕ̓ *group*.

The C_1C_2• plural prefix is also a derivational prefix, with various references such as repeated action or plural participants. Likewise for C_1a•, that signals repeated action. I list separately the pairs of both cases in the index of stems and inflectional affixes.

I segment lexical affixes with a double hyphen[15], but because these are stem-forming affixes, I do not gloss them. I have tabulated all occurrences of lexical affixes and sequences of lexical affixes in "Lexical affixes."

I gloss compounds as single stems, even though some roots participate in many such, as does wỳ *finish.*[16] More than 60 compounds with wỳ as first member are listed in the "Index of stems and inflectional affixes."

I do not write any morph boundaries in the independent personal referents, which are otherwise transparently made up of four separate stems, the amalgamated markers that belong to what I call the in- set (*possessive*—see below), and, in the third plural, the plural marker, as shown in Table 9.

in-cá	*1sg*
an-wí	*2sg*
cniɬ-c	*3sg*
mnimɬ-tt	*1pl*
mnimɬ-mp	*2pl*
mnimɬ-c-lx	*3pl*

Table 9: Independent person markers

The most complex of my current transcriptions of verb forms have six fillers: (1) a prefix, commonly the *habitual / durative,*[17] the *customary,* and the *future*), (2-3) a stem with a transitivive marker, (4) an object marker, (5) a subject or (anti)passive marker; and (6) the plural suffix -lx. I give an example of the most complex forms in this anthology in Table 10

cwíkstəmsəlx						Whal 570
c	-wik	-st	-m	-s	-lx	
cust^	-see	-^cust	-2obj	-3erg	-pl	
they used to see you						

Table 10: Example of a complex form in this anthology

Finally, I use the question mark symbol to gloss those morphs I do not understand, or for which I have yet to propose an analysis. Foremost among these is a particle ɬ that I am not able to assign to any of the homophonous particles.

Derivational affixes

Having laid out my analytical and presentational choices, I now provide a list of all the derivational affixes that occur in the Seymour texts. Some are well identified, with

15 But I am not always certain if a specific form is or not a lexical affix.

16 This root participates in such transitive forms as wỳ-st-in *I finished it,* and may be on its way to becoming a gram (or gramming) in compounds.

17 This label is not satisfying, but may be satisfactory. The prefix is cognate with what others have called *actual,* but I use this label for a homophonous prefix as I point out below.

cognates in the other languages of the Interior; others not. The form of my presentation copies that found in Kuipers 1974 pp. 61 ff., N. Mattina et al. (no date and no page numbers), and Vogt 1940 pp. 48 ff. In cases where I am not interested in glossing an affix, I provide the available glosses of cognate forms in IS languages.

1. Cv-Ok has two directional prefixes, c+ cislocative (toward the speaker), and ɬ+ back, again. These may cooccur as the sequence ɬ+c+ as I exemplify in Table 11.

xʷuy	*go*
c+xʷuy	*come*
ɬ+xʷuy	*go back*
ɬ+c+xʷuy	*come back*

Table 11: Directional stems based on xʷuy

The sequence ɬ+c+ is found in many stems, some based on roots of motion as shown in table 11, others not. ɬ+ carries the notion *back, again*, and c+ the *cislocative* notion. The latter extends to a general notion of *non-remote* or of *contextual relevance*, as seen in the examples in Table 12:

stem	root	*gloss*	source
ɬ+c+kʷum	(√kʷm)[18]	*store again cisl.*	In GDd2 273.
ɬ+c+laklí	(√lkl)	*lock again cisl.*	In GDd1 613.
ɬ+c+laʕ̓ʷ=qín=kst	(√lʕ̓ʷ)	*fit back on finger.*	In GDd2 389.
ɬ+c+n+xỷ	(√xỷ)	*be mixed with again.*	In Nams 70.
ɬ+c+t+xt̓•t̓	(√xt̓)	*take care of again.*	In GDd2 314.
ɬ+c+t̓aqʷ=cin+m	(√t̓qʷ)	*holler again.*	In BJ 362.

Table 12: ɬ+c+

There is semantic affinity between the c+ of the examples in Table 12 and c- *habitual / durative* (corresponding to cognate forms glossed as *actual*). I note it, but I make no effort to try and connect the two.

2. A prefix c+, homophonous with the *habitual / durative* prefix (inflectional) occurs with non-predicative elements as in lkʷut iʔ‿c+maq̓ʷ *the mountain is far.*

3. k+ derives stems that add subtle, but not predictable or discernible semantic content: lkʷ•akʷ far, k+lkʷ•kʷ+mi *remove*; k+lkʷ•kʷ=ína?[19] *uncover (remove a cover)*. k+ has an allomorph t+ before stems that begin with a (post)velar. Of course, in cases where no semantic connection can be established, t+ would be more sensibly set up as a prefix with no connection to k+:

root	*gloss*	k-stem	*gloss*
√c̓l	*stand up*	k+c̓l•l+min	*stand close, reach*
√mt	*sg. sit*	k+mut+m	*sit by*
√pl	*camp*	k+pul+x+m	*camp by, with*

18 It is my practice, here and elsewhere, to list root scheleta, without vowel.

19 Lexical affixes always add their own semantic baggage, thus making problematic the unequivocal identification of k+.

√lq̓	*bury*	k+liq̓	*bury*
√c̓p̓q̓	*glue, stick*	k+c̓p̓q̓	*glue, stick*
√xʷy	*go*	t+xʷuy+m	*go toward*
√kc	*arrive*	t+kic	*meet with*
√xƛ̓	*complete*	t+xƛ̓a+p	*all*
√qʷy	*often*	t+qʷay	*discend*

Table 13: k+

4. kɬ+, with primary meaning *on*, is productive, as in s+n+kɬ+mut+n (√mt) *chair*, c+kɬ+c̓l•l=us (√c̓l) *stand on the bank*, and kɬ+maʕ=ítkʷ (√mʕ) *float*. In other stems this sense is lost and there is no good reason to assign a label (other than the form itself) to it:

stem	root	*gloss*	source
kɬ+ʕac=cí	(√ʕc)	*tie around the neck.*	HnTrp 298.
s+kɬ+ck̓a+p	(√ck̓)	*cream.*	Aut 265.
s+kɬ+caw+t	(√cw)	*effort.*	2gts 189.

Table 14: kɬ+

5. kɬ+ *have, there be*. All forms that include the productive prefix kɬ+, are listed in the index of stems. This prefix has allomorphs aʔk(ɬ)- *there be, have*, the distributions of which I do not fully understand.

6. k̓ɬ+ *under* is seen is such examples as k̓ɬ+cq̓•cq̓=ax̌ (√cq̓) *hit under the arm*, and k̓ɬ+ciq (√cq) *dig*. In other stems, and in combination with other prefixes, this sense is lost. I add here cases of k̓+√ɬ... with a simplification of k̓ɬ+ɬ:

stem	root	gloss
k̓ɬ+c̓sa+p	(√c̓s).	*finished.*
k̓ɬ+kʷinxʷ=cn	(√kʷnxʷ)	*answer.*
k̓ɬ+kʷukʷ	(√kʷkʷ)	*benefit.*
k̓ɬ+k̓ʷul̓	(√k̓ʷl̓)	*fix.*
k̓ɬ+n+caʔq•q=íp	(√cq)	*come close to door*
k̓ɬ+n+cʔ=ip	(√cʔ)	*knock on door*
k̓+ɬʔ=al·qʷ	(√ɬʔ)	*next to shore*
k̓+ɬʔiq̓ʷ	(√ɬq̓ʷ)	*come in sight*

Table 15: k̓ɬ+

7. ɬ+ precedes the stems of many kin terms: ɬ+c•cʔ=ups *younger sister*; ɬ+ci•ck *mother-in-law*; ɬ+qá•qcaʔ *older brother*; ɬ+sí•sncaʔ *younger brother*.

8. ɬɬ+ is reserved for some kin terms and derives plural stems: ɬɬ+qá•qcaʔ *elder brothers*; ɬɬ+qick *brothers*; ɬɬ+s•siʔ (√sʔ). *uncles*.

9. n+ has a vague locative sense, as in these forms: n+k+ʔamt=íw̓s+tn *saddle horse*; s+n+citxʷ+tn *camping place*; s+n+c̓iqʷ+mn *skinning place*; s+n+ilíʔ+tn *dwelling place, allotment*. Otherwise this sense is hard to reckon:

stem	root	gloss
n+t̓q+mi	(√t̓q)	*throw sheet like obj.*
n+c̓aʕp=s	(√c̓ʕp)	*wink.*
n+kcn=ik	(√kcn)	*overtake.*
n+paʔq=cín	(√pq)	*dawn.*
s+n+xʷʔit	(√xʷʔt)	*lots.*
n+t̓aʕp-nt-ís	(t̓ʕp)	*load (to shoot)*
n+xl=aw̓s=q	(√xl)	*chop head*

Table 16: n+

10. naʔ+ derives nouns that occasionally, but not regularly, add a notion of *inside* and/or *other side*:

root	gloss	naʔ+ stem	gloss
√łʔ	?	na+łáʔ	*other side*
√mt	*sg. sit*	na+mút	*sit inside*
√c̓n	*say what*	na+c̓n+t=íls	*think, worry*
√yʕ	*in need*	na+yaʕ̓+p=cín	*hard up*
√nq	*satisfied*	na+naʕ•nq=cín	*filled up*

Table 17: naʔ+

11. s+ derives nouns from verbs: ʔiłn *eat*, s+ʔiłn *food*; ʔitx *sleep (v)*, s+ʔitx *sleep (n)*; c̓ał +t *cold*, s+c̓ał•ł+t. *freeze (n)*.

12. sc+ also derives nouns from verbs (I do not segment s+c+) perhaps signaling some aspectual notion that carries to the noun:

root	gloss	sc+ stem	gloss
√km̓	*take pl.*	sc+km̓=ax̌n	*kidnapped pl.*
√kʷn	*take sg.*	sc+kʷan=x̌n	*kidnapped sg.*
√k̓ʷl̓	*make, do, work*	sc+k̓ʷul̓	*work*
√ƛ̓xʷ	*kill pl.*	sc+ƛ̓axʷ	*killing*
√q̓ʔ	*concern*	sc+n+q̓aʔ=íls	*problem*
√ʔx̌ł	*do like*	sc+ʔx̌ił	*like, as*

Table 18: sc+

13. s+n+ is another nominalizer, as shown in Table 19 (the + recognizes the likely composition of the form):

root	gloss	s+n+ stem	gloss
√c̓x̌ʷ	*promise*	s+n+k+c̓x̌ʷ=íplaʔ+tn	*laws*
√qlw	*money*	s+n+qlaw+tn	*bank*
√ʔys	*change*	s+n+ʔiys	*price*
√qʷn̓	*pity*	s+n+qʷn̓•an̓	*pity*

Table 19: s+n+

14. Several other (sequences of) prefixes, listed in Table 20 are identified only tentatively or remain obscure:

caʔ+	?	caʔ+síw̓+st (√sw̓).	*drink pl.*
kaʔ+	?	kaʔ+kíc[20] (√kc)	*find*
k+n+	?	s+k+n+xʷaʔt=ús (√xʷt)	*big money*
k+s+...+s	?	lut k+s+lut+s (√lt)	*no exceptions, there is no no about it*
ks+	?	ks+xt̓ (√xt̓) ks+x̌l+p (√x̌l) ks+mẏ•may+t (√mẏ)	*aim* *all night* *proper way*
k̓a+	*k̓‿*	k̓a+ɬáʔ[21] (ɬʔ)	*on that side, other side*
k̓l+	?	k̓l+s+qlt=mixʷ (√qlt)	*better man*
k̓l+n+	*k̓l‿*	c+k̓l+n+ixáʔ[22] (√xʔ)	*this side*
la+	*l‿*	la+ʔkíń[23] (√kń)	*when, whenever, wherever, how, from time to time, sometime*
ml+	?	ml+q̓m (√q̓m)	*swallow*
naʔɬ+	?	naʔɬ+t+xt̓+st=íʔst (√xt̓)	*become pregnant*
syɬ+	?	syɬ+kʷ•kʷ=ʕast (√kʷʕst)	*early morning*
t+	?	k̓ɬ+t+k̓m=ax̌n (√k̓m) t+haht+m (√hht) t+mut (√mt)	*outside* *laugh at* *sit*
ta+	*t‿*	ta+ʔkíń (√ʔkń) ta+ʔx̌íl+m (√ʔx̌l)	*from where; sometimes; how far* *do so*
x+	?	x+kin (√ʔkn)	*do what, do how*
ʔax+	?	ʔax+kín+m (√ʔkn)	*do what, how*

Table 20: Obscure prefixes

15. There are two compound connectors,[24] here given with some examples:

+ɬ+	c+kʷn+ɬ+q̓ẏ+min+m (√kʷn, √q̓ẏ). *take papers*; c̓s+p+ɬ+kʷu•kʷús (√c̓s, √kʷs). *run out of bacon*; my+ɬ+s+wẏ+numt=x (√my, √wẏ). *more beautiful*; s+nk̓ʷ+ɬ+cwix (√nk̓ʷ, √cwx). *house mate*; s+nk̓ʷ+ɬ+mrim (√nk̓ʷ, √mrm). *spouse*; s+taʔxʷ+ɬ+tkɬ+m=ílxʷ[25] (√txʷ, √tkɬm). *acquired wife.*
+s+	c+ʔaw+s+k+síw (√ʔw, √sw). *come ask*; c̓s+p+s+ɬiqʷ (√c̓s, √ɬqʷ). *run out of meat*; c̓s+p+s+t̓ík̓l (√c̓s, √t̓k̓l). *finish grub*; ɬ+ʔaw+s+n+c̓íw̓+m (√ʔw, √c̓w̓). *go back and wash dishes*; mlx̌aʔ+s+t+q̓l•q̓lxʷ=us=xn (√mlx̌ʔ, √q̓lxʷ). *pretend to trip*; s+taʔxʷ+s+tkɬ+m=ílxʷ *acquired wife.*

Table 21: Compound connectors

16. +aʔ+ *diminutive* follows the pattern exemplified here:

20 kaʔ+ could be reduplicative, but the sense of the word is neither diminutive nor repetitive.
21 An amalgam that incorporates the particle k̓‿.
22 Has the appearance of an amalgam that incorporates the particle k̓l‿.
23 An amalgam that incorporates the particle la‿.
24 See below for compounds without connector.
25 See also s+taʔxʷ+s+tkɬ+m=ílxʷ *acquired wife,* with connector +s.

√ws	ẇí•ẇaʔs+t (√ws)	*high dim.*
√wx	ẇí•ẇaʔx (√wx)	*live dim.*
	waʔx=útyaʔ	*dwelling dim.*
√k̓t	k̓í•k̓aʔt (√k̓t)	*near*
nixʷ	ṅí•ṅaʔxʷ	*more dim.*
=aqs	=áqaʔs	*road*
=tk	taʔk as in nk̓ʷ•nk̓ʷ+s+pín=aʔtk	*yearlings*

Table 22: +aʔ+

Diminutive +aʔ+ is also inferred in cases like s+n+ʔím+aʔ+t *grandchild*, where the basic stem always shows +aʔ+ (in this case, *s+n+ʔim+t). maʔ•mṅxʷ (√mnxʷ) *smoke dim.* (see s+manxʷ *smoke*) is probably best analyzed as the reduplicative prefix m•, the infix +aʔ+, and the root with the attendant laryngealization of the stem vowel. Other cases are listed in the finderlist as they occur in the texts.

17. •(V)C_2 derives *patient* forms[26] (kn‿ verb+VC_2) kn‿t̓k̓ʷ•ak̓ʷ *I fell.* (Cf t̓k̓ʷ-nt *put something down*).

18. The suffix +a(ʔ) derives negative counterparts of several particles:

+á	ałi+á *because not, so not*
	km+a *or not*
	lut+á (√lt). *not*
	nixʷ+á *also not*
	uł+á *and not.*

Table 23: +á

19. +amn with variants +imn (the more common variant) and +ʕamn (with pharyngeal intrusion), carries an *habitual* notion:

+amn	x̌•x̌s+t+m+amn (√x̌s) *talk funny, entertaining*
+imn	caʕʷ+lx+ímn (√cʕʷ) *(like to) bathe often*
	kʷls+tn+imn (√kʷls) *(like to) sweat bathe often*
+ʕamn	kʷc+t+aʕmn (√kʷʕc) *rise early often*

Table 24: +amn, +imn, +ʕamn

20. +a+m, where +m is verb-forming, carries the stress of weak (vowelless) stems as in n+t̓p=qs+a+m (√t̓p) *tip head*; and my+n+a+m (√my). *find out.*

21. Stem-internal +aʔ+ carries a diminutive notion: n+k̓•k̓aʔlí=cn (√k̓ʔl) *soft talk, slow talk*; t̓•t̓áʔq̓aʔ+t (√t̓q̓) *short, abstract.*

22. +aʔ+ *repetitive / continuative* should not be confused with epenthetic a of reduplicated (plural) forms with ʔ in C_1 position: ʔiłn, ʔał•ʔíłn *eat, pl. eat*; ʔitx, ʔat•ʔítx *sleep, pl. sleep*. A form like qʷaʔ•qʷʔál+ *they talk* is the plural of qʷl•qʷil+t *he talks*. +aʔ+ *repetitive* occurs in simple and reduplicated stems, always unstressed, as follows:

26 Cognates of which others have labeled *out-of-control*.

k̓ʷaʔ•k̓ʷúl̓+m	(√k̓ʷl̓)	*practice*
xʷaʔ•xʷíst	(√xʷst)	*walk back and forth*
s+xʷaʔ•xʷúy+tn	(√xʷy)	*many tracks, usual tracks, place of repeated walking*
t̓qʷ•t̓aʔqʷ=cín	(√t̓qʷ)	*holler repeatedly*
n+k̓ʷaʔ•k̓ʷín	(√k̓ʷn)	*pick*
paʔ•pút	(√pt)	*match*
t̓qʷ•t̓aʔqʷ=cín	(√t̓qʷ)	*holler repeatedly*

Table 25: +aʔ+ repetitive

The *continuative* notion is discernible in forms like the following:

k+caʔx=ísxn	(√cx)	*glow*
k+c̓aʔlmt̓=íc̓aʔ	(√c̓lmt̓)	*get chills*
k+c̓aʔx=qín	(√c̓x)	*be ashamed*
n+c̓aʔr=ínk	(√c̓r)	*diarrhea*
n+c̓aʔxʷ=íɬc̓aʔ+m	(√c̓xʷ)	*make hot cakes*
n+kaʔx+m=útyaʔ	(√kx)	*go on foot*

Table 26: More +aʔ+

23. +ayn, rare, may be a variant of +tan, itself related to +tn *instrumental*, in the form s+ʔayx̌ʷ+t+áyn (√ʔyx̌ʷ). tiredeness.

24. +aʔ, of indeterminate function, occurs in forms such as k̓ɬʔ=álqʷ+aʔ (√k̓ɬʔ) *shore*; ʕa•ʕím+aʔ (√ʕm) *hate*; ʔíckn+aʔ (√ʔckn) *play*; ɬ•ɬkáp+aʔ (√ɬkp) *bucket* (see also ɬkap); n+pút+aʔ+tn (√pt) *respected*; q̓ʷ•q̓ʷúƛ̓+aʔ=xn+m (√nk̓ʷ, √q̓ʷƛ̓) *race*; n+ʔaɬn+aʔ+s+qílxʷ+tn (√ʔɬn) *man-eater.*

25. +aʔt is the diminutive of +t *stative*, as in t̓k̓ʷ•t̓ík̓ʷ+aʔt (√t̓k̓ʷt) *small lakes*; c•cám̓+aʔt (√cm̓) *small.*

26. +cut *reflexive* more often than not conveys no reflexive notion. I have chosen not to segment further +mncut and the remaining variants though one can discern some form of the transitivizer to precede it.

+cut	n+kʷn+cut (√kʷn)	*sing*
	k̓ʷl̓=cn+cut (√k̓ʷl̓)	*cook*
	k̓ɬ+wk+cut (√wk)	*see, realize*
	k̓ɬ+paʔx̌+cút (√px̌)	*decide*
	kn+x+cut+n (√knx)	*help*
+mncut	ckʷ+mncut (√ckʷ)	*pull back*
	saʕ+mncút (√sʕ)	*go downhill*
	c+saʕ+mncút (√sʕ)	*dismount cisl.*
	q̓ʷy+mncút (√ʔw, √q̓ʷy)	*dance*
	k+maʔ+mncút (√mʔ)	*run away*
	k+ʕʷy+mncut+m (√ʕʷy)	*laugh about*
	k+ʔax̌l+mncút+m (√ʔx̌l)	*turn against self*
	lk̓+mncut (√lk̓)	*force oneself*
	lq̓+mncut (√lq̓)	*go strong*
+mncaʕt[27]	sy+mncaʕt (√sʕy)	*make noise*

27 With pharyngeal intrusion.

+mscut	ċx+mscut (√ċx)	*embarrassed*
	k+łṗ+mscut (√łṗ)	*awful*
	pcxʷ+mscut (√pcxʷ)	*disgusted with self*
	wal̓+mscút (√wl)	*do magic, puzzle*
	xẏ+mscut (√xy)	*done in*
+ncut	s+x̌q̇+ncut (√x̌q̇)	*pay*
	c+xʷt̓+p+ncut (√xʷt̓)	*run cisl.*
	ċs=lxʷ+ncut (√ċs)	*strip*
	k+lq̇=naʔ+ncút (√lq̇)	*cover up*
	k+ʕʷy+ncut+m (√ʕʷy)	*laugh at*
	k+ʔam=plaʔ+ncút+m (√ʔm)	*name oneself, call by a name*
	k̓ʷl̓+ncut+n (√k̓ʷl̓)	*god, creator*
+scut[28]	k+łw+scut (√łw)	*divorce, part ways*
	k̓ł+wẏ=naʔ+scút (√wẏ)	*be ready*
	ł+wẏ=naʔ+scút (√wẏ)	*prepared again*

Table 27: +cut forms

27. +icíʔ, which may be better classified as a lexical affix, occurs in the form pn+icíʔ (√pn) *at that time*.

28. +(í)lx and its allomorph +ʕalx (with pharyngeal intrusion) often carries the notion *motion, change.*[29] See also +lilx.

(Stressed)	caʔqʷ•qʷ+ílx (√cqʷ)	*summer comes*
	k̓aʔ+ílx (√k̓ʔ)	*turn fall*
	k̓w+ilx (√k̓w)	*go upstream*
	cn•cn+ilx (√cn)	*roar*
	s+łq̇+ilx (√łq̇)	*bedroom*
	k̓ł+n+ws+lx+ilx[30] (√ws)	*jump over*
(Vowelless)	sy•syaʕ+lx (√sʕy)	*make noise*
	caʕʷ+lx (√cʕʷ)	*bathe*
	k̓aẏ•y+lx (√k̓ẏ)	*fall comes*
	k̓iw+lx (√k̓w)	*old*
	six̌+lx (√sx̌)	*move*
	t+k̓ʷit̓+x+lx+m (√k̓ʷt̓x)	*walk across*
	sx̌+lx=úlaʔxʷ (√sx̌)	*change country*
	sy•sy+ʕalx (√sʕy)	*make noise*
	k̓ł+n+ws+lx+ilx (√ws)	*jump over*

Table 28: +(í)lx

29. +it occurs in the form k̓aẏ+ít (√k̓y). cold.

28 +cut and +scut are sometimes interchangeable as in **n+t̓y=naʔ+cút, n+t̓y=naʔ+scút (√t̓y).** *dispute*.

29 See Cr -ilc motion in horseshoe curve (Reichard p. 606) and -il̓c (-äl̓x) *grow, become through growth* (Reichard p.605).

30 This form is listed twice in this chart as it includes both +lx and +ilx. nwis+lx *high* functions as the unit to which +ilx is added.

30. +iʔ, the form of which I let stand for its function, occurs most commonly in these forms:

c+xʔít+iʔ (√xʔt)	*at first*
la‿c+xʔít+iʔ (√xʔt)	*at first*
lút+iʔ (√lt)	*before, not yet*
pút+iʔ (√pt)	*still*

Table 29: +iʔ

31. +ʔis, +k, +kaʔ remain identified no further than their form in stems such as the following

+iʔs	c+xlk+iʔs (√xlk)	*turn around*
+k	t+qlt+k=alqʷ (√qlt)	*Canada, across the line*
+kaʔ	s+xʷús•s+kaʔ+m (√xʷs)	*rush*

Table 30: +iʔs, +k, +kaʔ

32. +lilx is the plural of +ilx:

t̓xʷ•t̓xʷt+lilx (√t̓xʷt)	*fly pl.*
łq̓+lilx (√łq̓)	*in bed pl.*
n+łxʷt+lilx (√łxʷt)	*go in bush pl.*

Table 31: +lilx

33. +líxʷ has the looks of a lexical affix, possibly related to =ilxʷ, but I cannot confirm this analysis: mya+líxʷ **(√my)** *guide.*

34. +lwis *here and there* is quite common:

sx̌+lwis (√sx̌)	*move s.t.*
t̓xʷt+lwis (√t̓xʷt)	*airplane*
k̓ł+paʔx̌+m+lwís (√px̌)	*be thinking*
k̓ł+ʔam+lwís (√ʔm)	*sit around*
kʷl=wt+lwis (√kʷl)	*sit around*
n+xʷy+lwis+tn (√xʷy)	*vehicle*
q̓ʷłt+lwis (√q̓ʷłt)	*pack around*

Table 32: +lwis

35. +m derives verbs from nouns.

ilíʔ	*there*	ilíʔ+m (√lʔ)	*stay with*
captíkʷł	*legend*	captíkʷl+m (√cptkʷl)	*tell stories*
s+k̓ʷan=łq	*garden*	k̓ʷan=łq+m (√k̓ʷn)	*plant a garden*

Table 33: Verb-forming +m

36. A suffix, homophonous with the previous+m, occurs in many forms with obscure function, seemingly an optional suffix:

ałíʔ	*so, because*	ałíʔ+m	*so, because*
iwá	*even though, try to*	iwá+m	*even though, try to*
ixíʔ	*that*	ixíʔ+m	*that*
myał	*too much*	myał+m	*too much*
uł	*and*	uł+m	*and*
t̓xʷ	*emph.*	t̓xʷ+m	*emph.*
anwí	*you*	anwí+m (√nw)	*you*

Table 34: Optional (?) +m[31]

37. Another suffix +m[32] also occurs in a great many nouns, sometimes (almost) predictably, as in forms with the lexical prefix sxʷ=, sometimes not.

sxʷ=k̓ʷan=łq+m (√k̓ʷn)	*gardener*
sxʷ=k̓ʷul̓+m (√k̓ʷl̓)	*worker*
sxʷ=k+ʕac=qáx̌aʔ+m (√ʕc)	*packer*
s+x̌ʷus+m (√x̌ʷs)	*foam berry*
s+ƛ̓aʔ=cín+m (√ƛ̓ʔ)	*deer*
s+t+kl•klx+m=iks+tn (√klx)	*sticks*

Table 35: Nouns with +m

38. +mi(n) is a common stem formative, one that, with two others (-nun and +xix, q.v., the first listed with the inflectional affixes), prepares stems for transitivization. Kinkade labeled its Cm cognate *relational* (Kinkade 1982, p. 53), and Kuipers described its Sh cognate as follows: "The suffix -m(í)nt- refers to an object which is affected indirectly, superficially or malefactively by the action ('look for', 'spill', 'accuse', etc.)" (Kuipers p. 46). Because Ok forms with +mi(n) often include other morphological material, I prefer not to try to assign a label to +mi(n), listing examples of pairs or sets of Ok forms, with and without +mi(n). -min, often as the circumfix k+/t+...+min:

	√tq	*touch, stack*	tq+mi	*put down*
	√cq̓	*hit*	cq̓+mi	*throw*
	√c̓x	*bashful, ashamed*	c̓aʔx+mín+m	*be ashamed of*
	√k̓t	*near*	k̓t+min+m	*get close to*
	√mʔ	*bother*	maʔ+mín+m	*send away*
	√qm[33]	*calm*	kł+qm+(m)ín+miʔst	*lie on*
	√ʔyx̌ʷ	*tired*	ʔayx̌ʷt+mn	*tire of*[34]
k+/t+...+min	√lkʷ	*far*	k+lkʷ•kʷ+mi	*remove*
			k+lkʷ•kʷ=xn+mi	*travel far*
	√c̓l	*single upright object*	k+c̓l•l+min	*stand close to*

31 The following remark, that Reichard made about a different form, could well apply to these Cv-Ok forms: "Like some other elements of Coeur d'Alene the suffix -ał seems to have several functions none of which is so definite that it may not be mistaken for another" (Reichard p. 620).

32 An example of sxʷ= not cooccurring with +m is sxʷ=k+ʔam=t=íw̓s *jockey*.

33 There is probably a connection between this root and √cq *lie (on)*.

34 See tałt ʔayx̌ʷt+ m(n)-nt-s-n *I am tired of you.* (Cf. kn‿ʔayx̌ʷt *I am tired*; ʔayx̌ʷt-st-n *I made him tired.*)

	√plx	*camp*	k+pulx+mn	*camp with s.o.*
	√c̓l	*single upright object*	k+c̓l•l+min	*stand close to s.o.*
	√xʷy	*go*	t+xʷuy+mn	*go up to s.o.*

Table 36: Verbs with +mi(n)

39. +m(i)n forms nouns that most commonly (not always) carry an *instrumental* meaning:

kɬ+cq+min (√cq)	*rack*
k+txʷ+min (√txʷ)	*contribution*
k̓ɬ+paʔx̌+mín (√px̌)	*memory*
s+x̌ʷil+mn (√x̌ʷl)	*devil*
x̌aq̓+mn (√x̌q̓)	*reward*
ʕac̓+mn (√ʕc̓)	*binoculars*
k̓ɬ+xar+mn (√xr)	*curtain*
ṅi•ṅk̓+ṁṅ (√nk̓)[35]	*knife dim.*
s+n+c•ckʷ+ṁiṅ (√ckʷ)	*buggy dim.*

Table 37: +m(i)n Instrumental

40. Three suffixes, or perhaps a single suffix, one stressed (+míst), another unstressed (+mist), and a third with a glottal stop (+miʔst), carry a vague *reflexive* meaning in intransitive verbs:

+mist	wkʷ+mist (√wkʷ)	*keep secret*
	xíʔt+mist (√xʔt)	*run*
	c̓lp=cn+mist (√c̓lp)	*holler fiercely*
	ha•háʕʷ+mist (√hʕʷ)	*loosen up*
	klm=íls+mist (√klm)	*think highly of self*
	k+mx̌=qn+mist (√mx̌)	*give up*
	km=ls+mist (√km)	*not good enough*
	k̓aʕʷ+míst (√k̓ʕʷ)	*hire*
	ɬt̓p+mist (√ɬt̓p)	*jump pl.*
	s+tw+mist (√tw)[36]	*merchandise*
+míst	t+x̌q̓=plaʔ+míst (√x̌q̓)	*pay a fine*
	wkʷ+mist (√wkʷ)	*keep secret*
+miʔst	cí•cl+miʔst (√cl)	*trot slowly*
	kɬ+qm+(m)ín+miʔst (√qm)	*lie on*
	k̓ɬ+xt+miʔst=ínk (√xt)	*run on the side hill*
	ƛ̓íl+miʔst (√ƛ̓l)	*stay put*
	wíkʷ+miʔst (√wkʷ)	*hide oneself*
	xt•xít+miʔst (√xt)	*run around*

Table 38: Forms with +mist, míst, and +miʔst

35 This (and the following) diminutive form shows the laryngealization of its resonants.
36 The prefix s+ makes this a noun.

41. +m(i)x could be classified a lexical suffix[37] meaning *people*; some forms with +mix, however, seem to have nothing to do with *person*:

+m(i)x	s+ťy+mix	*lazy*
	sc+yaʕ̓+míx	*gathering*
	s+ťaʔk̓+míx	*virgin*
	k+ťaʔk̓+mx=áqs (√ťk̓)	*taste of maiden*
	xiʔ+míx	*whatever*

Table 39: +m(i)x

42. +na ?. In the form my+na+m (√my) *find out*, where +na is the combination of +n and the vowel a which forms middle verbs of weak stems, e.g. n+kxa+m *go on foot*; q̓ya+m *write*.

43. +nap ?. In the form n+wk+nap=ánaʔ=qn+m (√wk) *see with the corner of the eye*.

44. +numt. In my Cv-Ok dictionary I had given a gloss *endowed with, have without effort*. IS cognates and the labels assigned them include Cr -numt *desire* (Reichard p. 601); Ka -numt *intransitive success*. (Speck p. 73); Cm -numt *characteristic* (N. Mattina et al. no page number). Sp -numt is easily found in the Carlson, Flett and Black dictionary in forms like čn x̣n-númt *I had an accident, I hurt myself*. These facts bespeak the futility of the search, however valiant, for the perfect label: the only such could be the form itself.

+numt	wy̓+numt (√wy̓)	*handsome, ready*
	s-k̓əɬ+my+p+númt-s	*he thought about it*
	xʷəťťpnúmt (√xʷť)	*get up*
	k̓ɬ+ʔat•t•x+númt (√ʔtx)	*fall asleep*
	k̓w•k̓w+p+numt (√k̓w)	*get lonesome*
	na•nak̓+númt (√nk̓)	*feel*
	x̌n̓+numt (√x̌n)	*get hurt*

Table 40: +numt

45. +p. "The [Cr] suffix -p indicates that the action was not voluntary on the part of the subject" (Reichard p. 579).

+p	s+x̌la+p (√x̌l)	*morning*
	ca•cáʕy+p+m (√cʕy)	*cry*
	k+ɬaʔ+p=ínk (√ɬʔ)	*close*
	c+yaʕ̓+p (√yʕ)	*arrive here pl.*
	ɬx̌ʷa+p (√ɬx̌ʷ)	*slip away*

Table 41: +p

46. +pnaʔm occurs in the following form, and remains obscure: n+maʔ•múkʷ•kʷ+pnaʔm (√mkʷ) *bulge*.

47. +s. In negative constructions +s cooccurs with the prefix s+:

37 There is connection, in Ok and in other IS languages, between (cognates of) this suffix and (cognates of) =mixʷ (q.v.). For the moment this mention will suffice.

lut s+lkʷ=ut+s (√lkʷ)	*not far*
lut s+q̓sápiʔ+s (√q̓sp)	*not long after*
lut s+qʷay+s (√qʷy)	*not often*

Table 42: s+...+s

The +s of the following form may also be this suffix: xil+s (√xl). *go to the edge.*

48. +st *causative.*

+st	caʕn+m+st (√cʕn)	*make tight*
	c+kic+st (√kc)	*bring*
	lkʷ+ilx+st (√lkʷ)	*remove*
	λ̓l+p+st (√λ̓l)	*stop s.o.*
	mrim+st (√mrm)	*doctor*
	mut+st (√mt)	*set down*

Table 43: +st causative

49. +st remains unidentified in these intransitive forms:

caʔ+síẃ+st (√sẃ)	*drink pl.*
k̓ʷul̓+st (√k̓ʷl̓)	*train, turn into*
sc+mrim+st (√mrm)	*recover(y)*
sx̌ʷ+st=us (√sx̌ʷ)	*downhill.*

Table 44: +st

50. +t *state.* With cognates throughout the sub-family, and congruous glosses, the suffix also derives forms that seem to have little to do with *state.* See Cr -t: "The suffix -t indicates that a person or object has a characteristic innately, rather than within but not inherent ... A suffix -t which may not be the same is also used with some verbs of action" (Reichard p. 578).

+t	x̌ʷup+t (√x̌ʷp)	*worthless*
	cix̌•cx̌+t (√cx̌)	*hot*
	cnaʕm+t (√cnm)	*deaf mute*
	c+n+ɬuxʷ+t (√ɬxʷ)	*come in the brush*
	c+ʔx̌iɬ+t (√ʔx̌ɬ)	*like, amen, plain*

Table 45: +t

51. +t(a)n *instrument.* The variants of the suffix are +an (after t),+tan, +tn, and +tayn. This gloss, too, does not capture the range of meanings carried by the suffix.

+an	wt+an (√wt)	*placed*
+tan	s+t̓k̓ʷ+tan (√t̓k̓ʷ)	*resting place*
	n+λ̓xʷ+tan (√λ̓xʷ)	*death*
	n+x̌s+tan (√x̌s)	*good, well being*
	s+n+kxn+tan (√kxn)	*travel companion*
	s+n+k̓aʔy+tán (√k̓ý)	*fall hunting place*

	s+n+ɬx̌m+tan (√ɬx̌m)	*in-law*
	s+n+t+xlk+tan (√xlk)	*race track*
	s+n+t̓k̓ʷ+tan (√t̓k̓ʷ)	*resting place*
+táyn	s+ʔayx̌ʷ+táyn (√ʔyx̌ʷ)	*tiredness*
+tn	kl•kl+nwixʷ+tn (√kl)	*go over*
	k+lk̓=íċaʔ+tn (√lk̓)	*baler*
	lk̓=iw̓s+tn (√lk̓)	*baler*
	s+n+caʕʷ+lx+tn (√cʕʷ)	*bath tub*
+(t)n	k̓ʷl̓=cn+cut+n (√k̓ʷl̓)	*cook*
	s+mut+n (√mt)	*place to sit*
	s+tkʷ•tkʷʔ=ut+n (√tkʷʔ)	*tracks*
	n+ċxʷi+n+tn (√ċxʷ)	*enema*

Table 46: +t(a)n

52. +uɬ *does often, likes to.* Ex: txʷ•txʷ=cn+uɬ (√txʷ) *provision seeker*; t̓y•t̓y+m+uɬ (√t̓y) *lazy*; k̓ʷl̓•k̓ʷl̓+uɬ (√k̓ʷl̓) *good worker.*

53. +wilx *development.* I list two allomorphs of +wilx besides the main one: wílaʔx is the *diminutive*; +twílx includes a +t which I am not prepared to associate with another suffix.

+wílx	t̓alaʔx+wílx (√t̓lʔ)	*next generation*
	kw̓t+wilx (√kwt)	*lose weight*
	k̓s+t+wilx (√k̓s)	*become bad, spoil*
	ɬ+t̓x̌=iwt+wílx (√t̓x̌)	*year again*
	ɬ+x̌s+t+wilx (√x̌s)	*get well again*
	px̌•px̌+t+wilx (√px̌)	*get, gain one's senses*
	slxʷaʔ+t+wílx (√slxʷʔ)	*get big*
	t̓aʔk̓+mx+wílx (√t̓k̓)	*maiden*
+wílaʔx	p•px̌•px̌+t+wílaʔx (√px̌t)	*grow aware dim.*
	px̌•px̌+t+wílaʔx (√px̌)	*get, gain one's senses dim.*
+twilx	sy̓•sy̓+twilx (√sy)	*smart dim.*

Table 47: +wilx and its variants

54. A reciprocal +wixʷ, with cognates in the other IS languages, occurs in combination with other transitivizing suffixes, but I do not segment these and prefer to list all of them as units:

+wixʷ	n+x̌lt=cn+wixʷ (√x̌l)	*ask rec.*
	ɬwn+wixʷ (√ɬwn)	*part*
+mnwíxʷ	n+sxʷ=naʔ+mnwíxʷ (√sxʷ)	*acquaint rec.*
	ʕac•c=qn+mnwíxʷ (√ʕc)	*go head to head*
+nwixʷ	kc+nwixʷ (√kc)	*meet, be with one another*
	kl•kl+nwixʷ (√kl)	*chase*
	k̓ɬ+ʔam+nwíxʷ (√ʔm)	*wait rec.*
	kʷn=ks+nwixʷ (√kʷn)	*shake hands*
	kʷn•kʷn=ks+nwixʷ+m (√kʷn)	*hold two sides*
	ɬ+x̌c+nwixʷ (√x̌c)	*bet again rec.*
	qʷaʔm+nwíxʷ (√qʷʔ)	*introduce rec.*

+stwixʷ	x̌ʷl+stwixʷ (√x̌ʷl)	*discard rec.*
+twixʷ	c̓x̌ʷ+twixʷ (√c̓x̌ʷ)	*appointment*
	kʷn•kʷn+twixʷ (√kʷn)	*grab one another*
	x̌c+twixʷ (√x̌c)	*be companions*
+xtwixʷ	m̓ay+xtwixʷ (√my or √m̓y̓)	*tell stories rec., have meeting*
	s+c̓x̌ʷ+xtwixʷ (√c̓x̌ʷ)	*arrangement*

Table 48: +wixʷ and its variants

55. +wx ? In the form s+kic+wx (√kc) *Idaho.*

56. +x is attached to a few verbs to form intransitive stems, and remains unexplained in several cases:

kic	*reach*	c+kic+x (√kc)	*arrive here*
ʔx̌il	*do a certain way*	c+ʔx̌il+x (√ʔx̌l)	*how*
kʷni+m	*sing*	n+kʷni+x (√kʷn)	*sing*

Table 49: +x

It is not clear that the stem final x of n+p•pilx(√pl(x)) *pl. enter* and ʔimx (√ʔm(x)) *move,* and k̓ʷɬx (√k̓ʷɬ(x)) *startle* is the same suffix.

57. +xix(+m). See Cm -x, -xáx, -xíx *developmental*; Cr "-cic (-căc, -cᴇc), *something, for someone.* When used with an intransitive verb, this suffix is used to complete ... the meaning and may be translated as an indefinite pronoun. If used with the transitive it means 'for someone'" (Reichard p. 626). Cv-Ok -xix(m), with unclear allomorphy, changes the roles of the arguments (not fullly understood) of the verb as well as the meaning of the verb: kʷɬn+xixm-st-xʷ You lent it out to her. (Cf. kʷuɬ-nt-xʷ You borrowed it.)

kʷáɬn+xix (√kʷɬn)[38]	*lend out.* In Nams 140.
kʷɬn+xix+m (√kʷɬn)	*lend, rent out.* In Nams 131, Aut 351.
t+kʷp+xix+m (√kʷp)	*pass along.* In Lynx 137.

Table 50: +xix

Inflectional affixes

Here I begin with the various sets of person markers, then I present the transitive suffixes, which, it will be remembered, are derivational suffixes, and for convenience I mark with the hyphen (ex: -nt *nt transitive*), and then, in tabular form, the remaining inflectional affixes.

Person Marking

Okanagan has four main sets of person reference markers: the kn‿ set (intransitive), the i(n)- set (possessive), the -(í)n set (transitive subject), and the (transitive) object set.

38 I do not know why this form is stem-stressed, and the following one, based on the same root, is suffix-stressed; and I cannot explain the retention of the vowel of the suffix in the strong (stem-stressed) form.

The kn‿ set consists of clitics (marked with the undertie), and a suffix:

kən‿	*1sg*	kʷu‿	*1pl*
kʷ‿	*2sg*	p‿	*2pl*
Ø	*3sg*	Ø ...-lx	*3pl*

Table 51: kn‿ set

These markers accompany stems that in English translate as intransitive verbs, nouns, and adjectives, as in kn‿ʔitx *I slept*; kʷ‿sqilxʷ *You are an Indian / a person*; ʔayx̌ʷt (axáʔ) *This one is tired.*

A subset of these markers, identical in all persons except for 1sg kʷu‿, co-occurs with the possessive set of person markers, and is reserved for double possessives and verb nominalizations, as in kʷu‿an-lʔíw *I am your father (man speaking)*; kʷ‿in-x̌mínk *I like you* (see below).

kʷu‿	*1sg*	kʷu‿	*1pl*
kʷ‿	*2sg*	p‿	*2pl*
Ø	*3sg*	Ø ...-lx	*3pl*

Table 52: kʷu‿ subset of kn‿ set

The possessive set has two subsets, one used with nouns and psych verbs, and the other with verb nominalizations. I abbreviate members of the former *1in, 2in, 3in*; and members of the latter *1i, 2i, 3i*, in a fashion that captures the phonology of the forms: verb nominalizations never have the nasal in the first and second persons, while nouns and psych verbs do, except for stems that begin in s and kin terms that begin in ɬ:

i(n)-	*1sg*	-tt	*1pl*
a(n)-	*2sg*	-mp	*2pl*
-s/-c	*3sg*	-s-lx / -c-lx	*3pl*

Table 53: Possessive markers

These person markers yield such forms as an-lʔíw *your father* and in-x̌mínk *I like / want it*, which, in turn, may combine with members of the kn‿ set (kʷu‿ subset) to yield forms such as kʷu‿an-lʔíw *I am your father*; kʷ‿in-x̌mínk *I like / want you (you are my wanting)*; kʷ‿i-ks-ʔam-ɬt-ím an-lʔíw *I am going to feed your father*, the last of which is the nominalization of a future (ks-) possessor applicative (-ɬt) verb form (see below—root ʔam, *feed*), in which the suffix -(i)m, sometimes referred to as the *antipassive*, is required.

The transitive subject set, often called the *ergative* set, consists of the following suffixes (parentheses abbreviate stressed and unstressed variants):

-i(n)	*1sg*	-(í)m / -t	*1pl*
-(í)xʷ	*2sg*	-(í)p	*2pl*
-(í)s	*3sg*	-(í)s-lx	*3pl*

Table 54: Transitive subject markers

These markers follow the object markers, which, in turn, follow one of several obligatory transitive markers (see below).

The (transitive) object set consists of the following markers (one proclitic and suffixes):

kʷu	*1sg*	kʷu...-m	*1pl*
-s / -m	*2sg*	-ɬ(úl)m	*2pl*
-Ø	*3sg*	-Ø...-lx	*3pl*

Table 55: Object markers

The allomorphy of the second singular object is transitivizer-dependent: -m is the 2sg object marker with -st and -xt transitives; -s occurs with -nt and -ɬt transitives.The disambiguation of number in the first person object is accomplished by the suffix -m and such forms are interpreted as *3rd indef subject - 1pl object*: kʷu‿sp̓-nt-is *He whipped me* (-nt transitivizer); kʷu‿sp̓-nt-im *They whipped us / We were whipped.*

-(í)m occurs also with Ø, and the interpretation of these forms can be indefinite subject, or passive: sp̓-nt-is *3rd person whipped 3rd person*; sp̓-nt-im *3rd person indef whipped 3rd person / 3rd person was whipped.*

Transitive forms and transitive suffixes

Three suffixes prepare stems for transitivization. I exemplified +min and +xix with the other derivational affixes. And, as I have written, I list the third such pre-transitivizer as -nu(n) *manage to, success* (as though it were inflectional). Here I exemplify this suffix, which is most commonly added to stems with the •C_2 reduplicative suffix (see 17 above) cognates of which have been labeled *out-of-control.*

tq•q-nun+m (√tq)	*manage to fool s.o.*
taɬt iʔ‿x̌s•s-nu-nt-xʷ	*You did well (x̌ast good).*
talíʔ x̌ast iʔ‿k̓ʷl̓•l̓-nu-nt-xʷ	*You did / got it done very well.*
taɬt x̌ast iʔ‿k̓ʷl̓-nu-nt-xʷ	*You did very well.* (k̓ʷul̓-nt-xʷ *You fixed it.)*

Table 56: -nu(n)

Cv-Ok has two transitivizers, -nt and -st; a causative -st; and three applicatives -ɬt, -x(í)t, -túɬt. -nt is the suffix that derives most transitive stems, but a few stems take -st. -ɬt is the *possessor applicative*, and -x(i)t the *benefactive applicative*. With some stems these last two are interchangeable (ex: kʷu‿m̓aẏ-xít-s ~ kʷu‿m̓aẏ-ɬt-ís *he told me*). -tuɬt, with its various allomorphs is the least understood of these affixes—what is certain is that its use entails changes to the roles of the arguments.

	Form	Function / variant of	*Translations*
	-nt	*nt* Accompanies most stems	
ex		wik-nt-xʷ	*you saw it*
ex		ƛ̓aʔ-nt-ín	*I fetched it*
	-áʕnt	-nt with pharyngeal intrusion	
ex		p̓c̓+am-áʕnt-m	*he was squirted out*
	-t.	-nt with the stem ʔam feed	
ex		ʔam-t-ín	*I fed him*
	-t	-nt after stems ending in n	
ex		x̌aʔn-t-im-lx	*they were stopped*

	ẏ	Optional (?) variant of -nt in strong stems	*See Table 58*
	-st.	*st tr.* Accompanies several stems	
ex		pul-st-n	*I beat him up*
ex		qʷl•qʷil-st-m-s	*He talks to you*
	-t	-st trans after stems ending in s	
ex		c-lk̓=iẇs-t-s-lx	*they bundle it*
	-st	*cust.* With c-, *customary*	
ex		c-k̓ɬ+q̓m-st-in	*I wish for him*
	-t	-st ˆ*cust.* after stems ending in s	
ex		c-n+ʔiys-t-m	*we trade*
	+st[39]	*caus.* causative	
ex		ʔayx̌ʷt+st-m-n	*I made you tired*
ex		(Cf. kʷ‿ʔayx̌ʷt	*you are tired).*
	-ɬt,	*ɬt.* possessor applicative[40]	
	-t	-ɬt after stems ending in ɬ.	
ex		ʔiɬ-t-m-lx	*they ate the others' ...*
	-xit	*xit tr.* benefactive applicative	
ex		kʷu‿q̓ẏ-xit-s t‿i-ks...	*he wrote the X for me*
		(Cf. q̓ẏ-nt-is	*he wrote it.)*
	-xt.	Unstressed variant	
ex		kʷu xʷic̓-xt-xʷ	*you gave it to me*
	-tuɬt	*tuɬt tr.* changes the roles of the arguments	
ex		kʷu‿ʔam-tuɬt-xʷ iʔ‿spapáʕɬaʔ	*you fed me to the monster*
ex		(Cf. kʷu‿ʔam-t-ixʷ	*you fed me*
ex		kʷu‿ʔam-ɬt-ís i-sqʷsíʔ	*you fed my child)*
ex		kʷu k+tl+mn-tuɬt-s	*she put me in charge of it*
	-uɬt	After stems ending in t	
ex		kʷu ks-kʷlst-uɬt-xʷ	*you sent me for it*

Table 57: Transitive suffixes

The suffix -ẏ

This suffix –ẏ is cognate with Kalispel –i of such forms as kúpis *he pushed it* (see Vogt 1941 p. 36), and can be analyzed as an (optional) allomorph of the transitive –nt in forms based on strong stems (forms where the stress is born by the stem and not by the person markers). I give a substantial list of such forms in Table 58.

ks-	c̓iqʷ	-ẏ	-s	*she'll [try to] skin it.*
	kaʔ•kíc	-ẏ	-s-lx	*they find him*
ks-	my+p-nu	-ẏ	-s	*he wants to find out*
ks-	n+cq̓=aqs	-ẏ	-s	*he was going to hammer it*
ks-	k̓ʷan=ɬq	-ẏ	-s-lx	*they are going to plant a garden*
kʷu‿ks-	t̓qʷ=cin+m	-ẏ	-s	*he will yell at me*

39 Included in this chart for convenience.

40 Ex: uc kʷu‿wik-ɬt-xʷ i-sqʷsíʔ *Did you see my son?* (Cf. uc kʷu‿wik-nt-xʷ *Did you see me?*)

lut ks-	wík	-ẏ	-s	*he won't see it*
ks-	ƛ̓xʷu+p	-ẏ	-s	*he will win her*
	kaʔ•kíc	-ẏ	-s	*they find her*
	ʔa+ʔúkʷ	-ẏ	-s	*he carried them*
ks-	m̓ẏ+p-nu	-ẏ	-s-lx	*they will find out*
c-	ʔiq̓	-ẏ	- s	*she scraped it*
ks-	wic̓	-ẏ	-s	*he will dig it*
	c+ʔa+ʔúkʷ	-ẏ	-s	*he brought them*
	kaʔ•kíc	-ẏ	-s-lx	*they found it*
	n+k̓ʷaʔ•k̓ʷín	-ẏ	-s	*he picked it*
kɬ-	ɬ+k̓ʷul̓	-ẏ	-s	*he'll fix it again*
kʷu ks-	ɬx̌ʷ+p-nu	-ẏ	-s	*she'll lose me*
kʷu c-	n+k̓aʔt=ík	-ẏ	-s	*she is coming behind me*
kʷu ɬ ks-	kim̓	-ẏ	-s	*... that she will hate me*
kʷu ks-	ƛ̓l•l-nu	-ẏ	-s	*she will kill me*
	ʔaw+t=íp	-ẏ	-s-lx	*they followed her*
ks-	kʷum	-ẏ	-s	*she is going to store it*
	ʔaw+t=íp	-ẏ	-s	*they followed him*
kʷu kɬ-	ɬ+c+kíc	-ẏ	-s	*he is going to join me again*
ks-	wík	-ẏ	-s-lx	*they will see them*
ks-	x̌lít	-ẏ	-s	*he was going to ask*
	cucm̓	-ẏ	-s	*?*

Table 58: -ẏ

List in tabular form of remaining inflectional affixes

	Affix	Function – Variant (Person-marking paradigm)	Examples
	c- [c-...-st-...]	*cust˄.* (-(í)n)	
ex		c-wik-st-n *I always see it*	
	c- [c-...-st-...]	*cust˄.* [s-...-st-...]. Variant of c-...st before stems that begin in c, t. (-(í)n)	
ex		s-tẇ•tíẇ+aʔ-st-m *We baby you a lot*	
	c-	*gpat.* (kn‿)	
ex		uɬ ilíʔ kn‿c-lak̓ *I was in jail a long time* (cf. lk̓-nt *tie something*)	
	c-	*hab.* habitual / durative forms (kn‿c+verb) (kn‿)	
ex		kn‿c-nqilxʷ=cn-m *I (regularly) talk Indian* (Cf. kn‿nqilxʷ=cn-m *I talked Indian*) kn‿c-málx̌aʔ *I (regularly) lie* (Cf. kn‿málx̌aʔ I lied)	
	c-	*act.* actual (-(í)n)	

ex		kʷu a c-xar=kst+m-s *He is making us lose time* lut cx̌əstmíntxʷ a ctxət'stúmt *You don't like the way we treat you*
	kc-	*futImp.* future imperative forms (i+kc+verb) (i(n)-)
ex		lut a-kc-náq̓ʷ *You will not steal* x̌ast a-kc-k̓ʷúl'-m *You will work well* kc-n+miƛ̓-mp *you will be mixed with ...*
	kɬ-	*to be.* (kʷu˯,[41] i(n)-)
ex		kɬ-ilmíxʷm snk̓lip. *Coyote will be chief / is chief-to-be*
		k- Variant of kɬ- before stems that begin with s. (kʷu˯, i(n)-)
ex		kʷu a-k-s+nk̓ʷ+ɬ+mr•r•im *I am going to be your spouse*
	ks-	*futi.* (kʷu˯, i(n)-)
ex		lut a-ks-xʷúy *Don't go* kʷ˯i-ks-(s)íw-m *I'll ask you.* i-kɬ-ɬ+x̌iƛ̓+m *I will climb back*
	ks-	*futt^.* future applicative forms (i-ks-verb-t-m) (kʷu˯, i(n)-)
ex		kʷ˯i-ks-maẏ-xít-m ... *I am going to tell you ...*
		kɬ-. Variant of ks- before stems that begin with ɬ
ex		kɬ-ɬ + kic-nt-m *he will be reached again by him*
	ks-	?.
ex		ks-kl•kl+nwixʷ+tn *chase*
	ks- [ks-...(-mí)x+aʔx]	*incp^.* kɬ-[kɬ-...(-mí)x+aʔx]Variant of ks-...-(mí)x-aʔx before stems that begin with ɬ. (kn˯)
ex		kɬ-ɬ+c+kic+x-aʔx *she will be getting back*
	ksc-	*futPerfi. (i(n)-)*
ex		ksc-mrím-s *They will be married*
	ksc-... -ʔax	*futPerfkn^.* (kn˯)
ex		kʷu ksc-mrim-aʔx *We will be married*
	ksc-[42]	*pperf.* past perfect forms (kn˯ksc+verb) (kn˯, i(n)-)
ex		kn˯ksc-k̓ʷul' ta˯ńcaqkʷ *I have some sour dough bread made / I have made some sour dough bread* kn˯ksc-nik̓ *I have some cut / I have cut some*
	ɬ-.	*ipftv^.* ɬ-[ɬ-...-x] Variant of s-...-x before stems that begin with ɬ. (kn˯)
ex		kən ɬ-ɬ+xʷúy-x *I am going back*
	ɬ-	*nom.* ɬ- Variant of s- before stems that begin with ɬ. (i(n)-)
ex		i-ɬ-ɬ+c+xʷuy *my coming back* ɬ-ɬ+x̌c+nwixʷ-s-lx *their betting again*
	ɬɬ-	*pl.* (i(n)-)
ex		a-ɬɬ-s+qʷsiʔ *your sons*

41 Here and following, kʷu˯ subset of kn˯.
42 These forms have the looks of *have-verbs*.

	s-	*hab.*[43] Variant of c-...-st before stems that begin in alveolars.
ex		s-cí•cl+mi?st-lx *they just trot*
	s- [(k)s-...-a?x].	*incp^.* inceptive forms (kn͜ks+verb-(mí)xa?x). Variant of ks-..-a?x after kʷ͜, kʷu͜. (kn͜)
ex		kn͜ks-ƛ̓a?+ƛ̓a?-míxa?x *I'm going to look for something.* kn͜ks-xʷúy-a?x *I'm going (away)*
	s-	*intt. durative / intent* forms (i+s+verb) (i(n)-)
ex		s-q̓sápi?-s ilí? i-s-ilí? *I lived there a long time.* (root ilí? *there,* lit. *long-time there I-there)*
	s- [s-...-(mi)x].	*ipftv^.* imperfective forms (kn͜s-verb-(mi)x (kn͜)
ex		kn͜s-k̓ʷl̓=cn+cut-x *I am cooking* s-?itx-x pit *Pete is sleeping* kn͜s-q̓ẏ-mix I *am writing* s-n+sw=cn+mist-x *They propose*
	s-	*nom.* nominalizer of verb forms
ex		s-ckʷ=íɬc̓a?-s-lx *their dragging of the body*
	s- [kʷu͜s-...-s]	*nom4^.* nominalizer of verb forms in the first plural
ex		kʷu s-c•cám̓+a?t-s *We are children*
	sc- [sc-...-(mi)x].	*ipftvp^.* imperfective of present relevance[44] ((kn͜sc-verb-(mi)x)
ex		kn͜sc-k̓ʷl̓=cn+cut-x *I have been cooking* sc-?itx-x pit *Pete has been sleeping* kn͜sc-q̓ẏ-mix *I have been writing*
	sc-[45]	*pftv.* perfective forms (i+sc+verb) (i(n)-)
ex		in-x̌ást i-sc-?ítx *I slept well (my-good my-having-slept)*
	ss- [sc-...-(mi)x].	*ipftvp^.* Variant of [sc-...-(mi)x] (kn͜)
ex		kʷ͜ss-c̓int-x *What are you saying?*
	ss-	*pftv.* (kʷu͜, i(n)-)
ex		kʷ͜i-ss-cun+m *I've been telling you*
	t̓c-	*habCisl.* (kn͜)
ex		t̓c-xʷuy (√xʷy) *habitual come* t̓c-n+?uc=xn+m *follow tracks cisl.*
	t̓s-	*habCisl.* Variant of t̓c- before stems that begin with alveolar (kn͜)
ex		t̓s-tiyáp (√typ) *run cisl.* t̓s-t+xʷuy+m *come toward*
	[?]	*inch.*
ex		c[?]axʷ (√cxʷ). *get tired* c[?]ix (√cx). *get warm* c̓[?]ax (√c̓x). *shame inch.* q̓ʷ[?]uɬ (√q̓ʷɬ). *blacken*

43 The label *habitual / durative* will have to do for now.
44 Compare with imperfective forms.
45 Connection with sc + *nominalizer*?

	-am	*psv.* (-(í)n)
ex		q̓ʷʕay-ɬt-am *they (theirs) are blackened*
	-aʔx [ksc-...-(míx)aʔx]	*ˆfutPerfkn.* (kn‿)
ex		kʷu‿ksc-mrim-aʔx *we will be married* ksc-yaʕ̓-míx+aʔx *they will be gathered there*
	-aʔx [ks-...-(míx)aʔx]	*ˆincp.* (kn‿)
ex		kn‿ks-ʔaw+s+n+sw=cn+míst-aʔx *I am going to propose* kn‿ks-ƛ̓l-míx+aʔx *I am going to be killed*
	-aʔx [s-...-aʔx]	*ˆipftvDim.* (kn‿)
ex		s-k=na•nqs-aʔx *she is single*
	-ikʷ	*imptv.*
ex		kʷu‿ƛ̓aʔ-ɬt-ikʷ *find me one!*
	-lx	*pl.*
ex		s+my+s+qilxʷ-lx *they are important people*
	-m	*apsv.* (kʷu‿, i(n)-)
ex		kʷu‿a-k+s-c̓aʔx+mín-m *you will be ashamed of me* i-s-ʔam•ʔúm-ɬt-m *I am going to announce their [names]*
	-m	*psv.* (-(í)n)
ex		cu-nt-m *he was told*
	-(mi)x [s-...-(mi)x]	*ˆipftv.* (kn‿)
ex		s-yaʕ̓•ʕ̓-míx *they are all gathered* s-kɬ+xʷl•xʷilt-x *he owes them*
	-(mi)x [sc-...-(mi)x]	*ˆipftvp.* (kn‿)
ex		sc-xaʔt-mix *he is the first* p‿sc-súxʷ=maʔ-x *you have been ttrying it on*
	-míx+aʔx [ksc-...-míx+aʔx]	*ˆfutPerfkn.* (kn‿)
ex		ksc-yaʕ̓-míx+aʔx *they will be gathered here*
	-míx+aʔx [ks-...(-mí)x+aʔx]	*ˆincp.* (kn‿)
ex		kn‿ks-ƛ̓l-míx+aʔx *I am going to be killed*
	-naʕ	*manage.* Allomorph of -nu(n), with pharyngeal intrusion (-(í)n)
ex		c̓n+p-naʕ-n *I manage to hold him tight*
	-nu(n)	*manage.* (-(í)n)
ex		lʕ̓ʷ+p-nu-s *he made it fit* ks-lxʷ+p-nun-t-s *she will hurt you*
	-skʷ	*tsimptv.*
ex		way̓-skʷ *stop it!*
	-s [kʷu‿s(c)-....-s]	*ˆnom4.*
ex		kʷu‿s-c•cám̓+aʔt-s *[when] we were small* lut kʷu‿sc+ƛ̓la+p-s *we don't stop*
	-s [ks-...-s]	*ˆfuti4.*
ex		kʷu‿ks-ʔiɬn-s *we will eat.*[46]
	-wy	*ipimptv.*
ex		xʷus+t-wy *hurry up!*

46 In context this is ilíʔ nixʷ qɬ-nu-nt-m itlíʔ nixʷ kʷu‿ks-ʔiɬn-s. *We can't eat any more.*

	-x, -x^{w}	*isimptv.*
ex		x^{w}uy-x *go!* c+n+ʔuɬx^{w}-x^{w} *come in!*
	-x^{w} [s-...-x]	*ˆipftv.* Variant of s- [s-...-(mi)x] after stems that end in x^{w} (kn‿)
ex		s-wnix^{w}-x^{w} *he is being truthful*
	-x^{w} [sc-...-x]	*ˆipftvp.* Variant of sc- [sc-...-(mi)x] after stems that end in x^{w} (kn‿)
ex		p‿sc-wík=laʔx^{w}-x^{w} *You have been looking the country over*
	-y[47]	*tpimptv.*
ex		k^{w}u‿k̓ɬ+paʔx̌-xit-y *figure it out for me*

Table 59: Remaining inflectional affixes

Word classes

Aspectual criteria can be established to distinguish word classes, and, as expected, these may derive forms of other classes--nouns can derive verbs and verbs can be nominalized, for example (N. Mattina 1996). A prototypical noun like k^{w}ilstn *sweat lodge*, culturally relevant and categorially marked (+tn *instrumental*), derives a verb with +m: kn‿k^{w}ilstn+m *I sweat bathed.* Similarly, q^{w}acqn *hat* derives q^{w}acqn+m *wear a hat* (intransitive); ntx̌^{w}x̌^{w}qin *noon* derives ntx̌^{w}x̌^{w}qin+m *do lunch* (intransitive).

Analogously qiʔs *to dream* (intransitive) derives s+qiʔs *a dream*, and the latter form can be inflected with possessive markers and interpreted as a possessive noun form, or as a nominalized verb form.

Most Okanagan stems can also be transitivized.

Nominal and pronominal arguments

Scholars have argued that Salishan languages are pronominal argument languages: a form like wik-nt-x^{w} *You saw it* is a full sentence with a third person object (Ø), and second person subject (-x^{w}). In this interpretation, any object expressed in nominal form is an adjunct, not a (nominal) argument. The claim is countered with the suggestion that in applicative sentences like k^{w}u‿tq-ɬt-is in-kílx *He touched my hand* the noun phrase in-kílx *my hand* functions as one of the arguments of the possessor applicative verb form k^{w}u‿tq-ɬt-is *He touched my ...* and this argument is not, and cannot be, referenced in pronominal form on the verb.

Intransitive forms are most often also analyzed as fully predicative: kn‿x^{w}uy *I went*; k^{w}‿ilmíx^{w}m *You are a boss*; k^{w}‿x̌ast *You are fine*. In these sentences, the clitics kn‿ and k^{w}‿ are the subjects, and the word to which the clitics are attached are the predicates. Third person forms have Ø subject person marking, and forms like sql'tmix^{w} have been analyzed as full predications that should be translated as something like *He is a man* or *It's a man*. In the stream of discourse such words can function as predicative elements. The normal way to express either of the isolated propositions *He's a man*, and *It's a man* is with utterances like ixíʔ sql'tmix^{w} *That's a man*, or sql'tmix^{w} yaʔx̌ís *That one over there*

47 This is -i on the surface.

is a man; that is, by juxtaposing (in either order) the stem sql'tmix^{w} and a deictic stem (ixíʔ, yaʔx̌ís). In traditional terms these sentences would be analyzed as exocentric equational constructions consisting of a subject and a predicate. The participant persons kn‿ and k^{w}‿ are pronominal subjects; third person forms can be analyzed as having a nominal subject of the classes mentioned, which, in context, can be deleted. Another complication for the interpretation of all full words as predicative is presented by the different markings for morphological and syntactic plurals: the morphological plural of citx^{w} house is the reduplicated form ct•citx^{w} *houses*, while the syntactic plural of the same form is citx^{w}-lx (ixíʔ) *(Those) are houses*.

In recent times, when scholars are preferring to view all constructions to have heads (or centers, in the older terminology) the question is raised as to what constitutes the head of such a sentence as kn‿sql'tmíx^{w}. Most common is the hypothesis that the verb is the head of the sentence (here it would be the predicate nominal), but because the identification of head with lexical head can be dispensed with, just as abstract features within the Inflection or Agreement nodes have been proposed to head sentences, and just as the determiner has been proposed to head Determiner Phrases, so can kn‿ be proposed to head the sentence kn‿sql'tmíx^{w}. An utterance like x^{w}uy *He went*, then, can be viewed as the abbreviation of x^{w}uy ixíʔ *That one went*, and analyzed either as having a null subject, or as requiring a third person nominal subject which undergoes deletion in the appropriate circumstances.

Autobiography

1 waẏ kən kscaptíkʷlaʔx axáʔ t̓əxʷ lútəm sənk̓líp ikɬcaptíkʷɬ
waẏ kn ks -captíkʷl -aʔx[1] axáʔ t̓xʷ lut+m sn+k̓l̓=ip i -kɬ -captíkʷɬ
well 1kn incp^ -tell_stories -^incp this emph no Coyote 1i -to_be legends
I'm going to tell a story, but it's not Coyote's legend,

2 waẏ t̓əxʷ axáʔ incá {is} incá {is} iscƛ̓x̌áp, ixíʔ mi
waẏ t̓xʷ axáʔ in+cá in+cá i -sc -ƛ̓x̌a+p ixíʔ mi
well emph this I I 1i -pftv -grow_sg that fut
it's about my growing up, that's what I am going

cṁáyaʔstən 3 waẏ t̓əxʷ kən staʔxʷspəx̌páx̌t {kən taʔxʷ} kən
c -ṁáyaʔ -st -n waẏ t̓xʷ kn s -taʔxʷ+s+px̌•páx̌+t kn
cust^ -tell -^cust -1erg well evidently 1kn hab -get_senses 1kn
to tell about. *I got my senses,*

k̓əɬpaʔx̌mín kiʔ ixíʔ {itlíʔ məɬ kən} 4 lut iksṁayám təl
k̓ɬ+paʔx̌+mín kiʔ ixíʔ lut i -ks -ṁáyaʔ+m tl
memory rel that not 1i -futi -tell from
I could think, [I'll start] from then. *I cannot tell from*

isck̓ʷúl̓l̓ 5 uɬ aɬíʔ kʷa iʔ uʔx̌tílaʔt uɬá cmistís {awa}
i -sc+k̓ʷúl̓+l̓ uɬ aɬíʔ kʷa iʔ ẁx̌t=ílaʔt uɬ+á c -my -st -is
1i -being_born and because intj art newborn not cust^ -know -^cust -3erg
the time I was born *because a baby doesn't know*

iʔ cawts {is} 6 waẏ axáʔ t̓i_kmix incá incáwt {təl isckʷ} təl
iʔ cawt -s waẏ axáʔ t̓iʔ_kmix in+cá in -cawt tl
art doing -3in well this only I from
what he does. *What I did only from the time*

iscpəx̌pəx̌twílx 7 waẏ axáʔ {kən} kən cpəx̌pəx̌twílx, lut t̓a
i -sc -px̌•px̌+t+wilx waẏ axáʔ kn c -px̌•px̌+t+wilx lut t̓
1i -pftv -get_senses well this 1kn hab -get_senses not negfac
I got my senses. *I got my senses, I don't*

cmistín náx̌əmɬ {put} put kən sk̓ʷənxspíntk 8 lúti
c -my -st -in nax̌mɬ put kn s+k̓ʷn+x+s+pin=tk lút+i
cust^ -know -^cust -1erg but just 1kn how_many_years not_yet
know just how old I was, 1:06[2] *I hadn't*

1 I parsed words into stems and inflectional affixes with Shoebox (and later Toolbox), applications that, after the first morpheme of a word, insert a hyphen before each morpheme, and make no distinction between stems and affixes.

2 Marks time on the tape, which, at, or just past every minute, I mark at the end of the utterance in all texts.

isṁaʔṁaʔyám, mat kən sť̓əq̓əmkspínk ki? ƛ̓lal isəsíʔ
i -s+ṁaʔ•ṁáʔya+m mat kn s -ť̓q̓m=ks+pin=tk kiʔ ƛ̓l•al i -s•siʔ
1i -going_to_school maybe 1kn hab -six_years rel dead 1in -uncle
gone to school yet, I must have been six when my uncle died,

9 scústsəlx x̌ʷəyx̌ʷəysċím, ixíʔ ƛ̓lal 10 uł k̓im axáʔ {in in}
s -cu -st -s -lx x̌ʷy•x̌ʷy+s+ċim ixíʔ ƛ̓l•al uł k̓im axáʔ
custˆ -tell -ˆcust -3erg -pl m's_name that dead and left this
they call him Sharp Bones, he died. *And all that's left is my*

ink̓ík̓waʔ uł inqáqnaʔ 11 ixíʔ ałíʔ sənk̓ʷłcwíxc {axáʔ}
in -k̓í•k̓waʔ uł in -qá•qnaʔ ixíʔ ałíʔ s+nk̓ʷ+ł+c+wix[3] -s
in -mother's_father and 1in -father's_mother that so house_mate -3in
maternal grandfather and my paternal grandmother; *that's who is living*

axáʔ isəsíʔ 12 ilíʔ ck̓əłuxsíłxʷəlx i l sʔixʷəxʷəlxíp kiʔ
axáʔ i -s•siʔ ilíʔ c -k̓ł+wx+s=iłxʷ -lx i l s+yxʷ•xʷ+lx=ip kiʔ
this 1in -uncle there hab -houses_side_by_side -pl art at lower_bottom rel
with my uncle. *Their houses were side by side at lower bottom, right*

ixíʔ 13 uł axáʔ kʷu cúsəlx axáʔ inƛ̓ax̌əx̌ƛ̓x̌áp 14 way̓
ixíʔ uł axáʔ kʷu cu -s -lx axáʔ in -ƛ̓ax̌•x̌•ƛ̓x̌á+p way̓
that and this 1obj tell -3erg -pl this 1in -elders yes
there. *And my parents said to me:* *"You keep*

ntkʷílsəntxʷ anxaxʔít 15 ixíʔ ť̓əxʷ iwá kʷ x̌ʷupt
n+t+kʷil=s -nt -xʷ an -xaʔ•xʔít ixíʔ ť̓xʷ iwá kʷ x̌ʷup+t
keep_company -nt -2erg 2in -older_relative then emph to_no_avail 2kn weak
company with your grandparents. *You aren't able to*

uł way̓ {ť̓əxʷ i} ntkʷílsəntxʷəlx uł ilíʔ kilíʔməntxʷəlx
uł way̓ n+t+kʷil=s -nt -xʷ -lx uł ilíʔ k+ilíʔ+m -nt -xʷ
and yes keep_company -nt -2erg -pl and there live_with -nt -2erg
do much, but you can keep company with them, stay with them." 2:01

16 a·· cúnəlx way̓, səċkínx a p ikskk̓əłkʷúkʷəm
a cu -n -lx way̓ sc -ʔkin -x a p i -ks k̓ł+kʷukʷ+m
intj tell -1erg -pl yes ipftvpˆ -indef -ˆipftvp art 5kn 1i -futi benefit
I said to them, "That's how I am going to get the best of you

ṅíṅw̓iʔ 17 kʷu ł captíkʷlxtsəlx {in} inxaxʔít 18 ixíʔ uł
ṅíṅw̓iʔ kʷu ł captíkʷl -xt -s -lx in -xaʔ•xʔít ixíʔ uł
a_while 1obj when tell_stories -xit -3erg -pl 1in -older_relative then and
folks: *my grandparents will tell me legends."* *Then*

ik̓líʔ kilíʔmnəlx {inƛ̓ax̌} inxaʔxʔít 19 uł ałíʔ axáʔ isəsíʔ
ik̓líʔ k+ilíʔ+m -n -lx in -xaʔ•xʔít uł ałíʔ axáʔ i -s•siʔ
there live_with -1erg -pl 1in -older_relative and so this 1in -uncle
I stayed with my grandparents. *And my uncle had*

3 This compound has in it the inflectional prefix c- *hab.*

ʔasíl {i an} i kəw̓wáps a nk̓ʷúl̓məns, t̓əxʷ púti 20 uł
ʔasíl i kw•w•ap -s a n+k̓ʷul̓+mn -s t̓xʷ put+iʔ uł
two art horses -3in art custom -3in evidently just and
two horses, work horses, medium sized. *And*

axáʔ {in} istəmtímaʔ naʔł ink̓ík̓waʔ ʔasíl iʔ sk̓əłp̓aʔp̓áʔsəlx
axáʔ i -s+tm•tímaʔ naʔł in -k̓ík̓waʔ ʔasíl iʔ s+k̓ł+p̓aʔ•p̓aʔ -s -lx
this 1in -grandmother and 1in -mother's_father two art milking_f -3in -pl
my grandmother and my grandfather had two milking

iʔ st̓máʕlt 21 uł kłkʷəl̓kʷl̓álxʷ, uł axáʔ {an a} nk̓amtíw̓stən {kaʔ} kaʔłís iʔ
iʔ s+t̓m=ʕalt uł kł+kʷl̓•kʷl̓=alxʷ uł axáʔ n+k+ʔam=t=iw̓s+tn kaʔłís iʔ
art cow and have_calf and this saddle_horse three art
cows, *and they each had a calf, and they had three*

kəw̓wápsəlx 22 axáʔ {in} istəmtímaʔ kłənk̓amtíw̓stən uł axáʔ
kw•w•ap -s -lx axáʔ i -s+tm•tímaʔ kł+n+k+ʔam=t=íw̓s+tn uł axáʔ
horses -3in -pl this 1in -grandmother have_saddle_horse and this
saddle horses. 3:04 *And my grandmother had a saddle horse, and*

ink̓ík̓waʔ kłənk̓amtíw̓stən 23 uł axáʔ {i} kłənq̓ʷəłcqáx̌aʔtnəlx,
in -k̓ík̓waʔ kł+n+k+ʔam=t=íw̓s+tn uł axáʔ kł+n+q̓ʷł+t=sqáx̌aʔ+tn -lx
1in -mother's_father have_saddle_horse and this have_pack_horse -pl
my grandfather had a saddle horse, *and they had one pack horse,*

ałíʔ ixíʔ t̓i_kmix a ntkʷtkʷʔútənsəlx 24 uł ałíʔ nak̓ʷáʔ way̓
ałíʔ ixíʔ t̓iʔ_kmix a n+tkʷ•tkʷʔ=ut+n -s -lx uł ałíʔ nak̓ʷ+á way̓
because that only art means_of_travel -3in -pl and so not yes
that's the only way they can get around. *At that time*

pnicíʔ uł {a} way̓ {akł} kłənʔakʷtáqs 25 kəm̓ kłt̓xʷtəlwís kəm̓
pn+icíʔ uł way̓ kł+n+ʔakʷ=t=áqs km̓ kł+t̓xʷt+lwis km̓
at_that_time and yes have_car or have-fly_around or
they didn't have cars, *they didn't have airplanes, or*

kłtłtqcəlxálqʷ xəwíł, lut 26 pn̓icíʔ way̓ t̓i_kmix iʔ sənkłc̓aʔsqáx̌aʔ
kł+t+qc+lx=alqʷ xwił lut pn+icíʔ way̓ t̓iʔ_kmix iʔ sn+kł+c̓aʔ=sqáx̌aʔ
have_run_over_logs road not at_that_time yes only art horse
railroads, no. *At that time there was only horses that*

a ntkʷtəkʷʔútənsəlx {i} 27 way̓, way̓ ixíʔ {wa} kʷu nqʷən̓mísəlx
a n+tkʷ•tkʷʔ=ut+n -s -lx way̓ way̓ ixíʔ kʷu n+qʷn̓+mi -s -lx
art means_of_travel -3in -pl well yes then 1obj feel_sorry_for -3erg -pl
they could travel with. *Well, my grandparents*

axáʔ inxaxʔít 28 t̓əxʷ axáʔ ink̓ík̓waʔ way̓ t̓iʔ cxʷuy
axáʔ in -xaʔ•xʔít t̓xʷ axáʔ in -k̓ík̓waʔ way̓ t̓iʔ c+xʷuy
this 1in -older_relative emph this 1in -mother's_father yes evid come
pitied me. *Morning came and my grandfather*

sx̌lap məł way̓ kʷu c̓əq̓mís kʷu qiłs 29 kən ur̓ísəlp̓əm, {kən ay}
s+x̌la+p mł way̓ kʷu c̓q̓+mi -s kʷu qił -s kn wr̓=islp̓+m
morning and yes 1obj throw -3erg 1obj awake -3erg 1kn build_fire
threw me out of bed, woke me up. 4:00 *I built the fire,*

kən wiʔsuṙísəlṗəm məɬ kən ʔawsʔamənsqáx̌aʔm {a} 30 məɬ laʔkín uɬ kən
kn wẏ+s+wṙ=islṗ+m mɬ kn ʔaw+s+ʔamn=sqáx̌aʔ+m mɬ la+ʔkíṅ uɬ kn
1kn finish_building_fire and 1kn go_feed_horse and when and I
and after I got done making fire I went fed the horses. Sometimes

sq̓əx̌əx̌sʔítx[x] kən t̓iyám, {əɬ} iwá kʷu t̓qʷcínəms
s -q̓x̌•x̌+s+ʔitx -x kn t̓ya+m iwá kʷu t̓qʷ=cin+m -s
ipftv^ -want_to_sleep -^ipftv 1kn be_lazy to_no_avail 1obj yell_at -3erg
I wanted to sleep more, I got lazy, and then they yelled at me.

31 uɬ aɬíʔ t̓iʔ ilíʔ {il} iʔ l nəqsíɬċaʔ iʔ k̓la nsək̓ʷtílp incá
uɬ aɬíʔ t̓iʔ ilíʔ iʔ l nqs=íɬċaʔ iʔ k̓l n+s+k̓ʷt=ilp in+cá
and so evid there art in one_room art to across_bed I
And it's just one room, and my bed is

isənɬq̓ʷútən 32 uɬ mnímɬcəlx k̓la nsək̓ʷtílp {wayl} 33 wi··ṁ kʷu
i -sn+ɬq̓ʷ=ut+n u mnimɬ+c+lx k̓l n+s+k̓ʷt=ilp wiṁ kʷu
1in -bed and they to across_bed in_vain 1obj
on one side, and theirs is on the other side. They yell

kst̓əqʷcínmiʔs, waẏ {kʷu} kʷu k̓əɬʕacəcníksəs 34 məɬ
ks -t̓qʷ=cin+m -iʔ -s waẏ kʷu k̓ɬ+ʕac=cn=íks -s mɬ
futt^ -yell_at -nt -3erg yes 1obj tie_around_wrist -3erg and
at me with no results, and then he ties me around the wrists and

nʕʷx̌ʷíw̓səs məɬ iʔ k̓əl sənɬq̓ʷútəns {məɬ il sənɬq̓ʷútəns} məɬ kʕacálqʷs
n+ʕʷx̌ʷ=iw̓s -s mɬ iʔ k̓l sn+ɬq̓ʷ=ut+n -s mɬ k+ʕac=álqʷ -s
drag_across -3erg and art to bed -3in and tie_to_post -3erg
drags the rope across to where he sleeps, and he ties it to his bed.

35 ixíʔ uɬ x̌lap məɬ ixíʔ cəkʷcaʔkʷəntís {məɬ a} 36 uɬ caʔkʷ kən ɬaʔ
ixíʔ uɬ x̌la+p mɬ ixíʔ ckʷ•caʔkʷ -nt -is uɬ caʔkʷ kn ɬaʔ
then and morning and then pull_repeatedly -nt -3erg and if 1kn if
And when daylight comes he jerks the rope over and over. And if I had had any

kspəx̌páx̌t pnicíʔ 37 uɬ caʔkʷ axáʔ q̓ʷíxʷən {il il} i l
k+s+px̌•pax̌+t pn+icíʔ uɬ caʔkʷ axáʔ q̓ʷixʷ -n i l
have_smarts at_that_time and could this untie -1erg intj on
sense at all I could have untied it from

ink̓əɬk̓əmcníkst uɬ iʔ l isənɬq̓ʷútən ckʕacstín {iʔ} 38 ixíʔ
in -k̓ɬ+k̓m=cn=ikst uɬ iʔ l i -sn+ɬq̓ʷ=ut+n c -k+ʕac -st -in ixíʔ
1in -wrist and art on 1in -bed cust^ -tie -^cust -1erg then
my wrist and tied it to my bed. 5:02 And

uɬ lut kiʔ {k} ikscqíɬt {uɬ aɬíʔ} 39 uɬ aɬíʔ ixiʔ a nc̓x̌ʷíltəns
uɬ lut kiʔ i -ksc -qiɬ+t uɬ aɬíʔ ixíʔ a n+c̓x̌ʷ=ilt+n -s
and not rel 1i -futPerfi -awaken and so that art child_training -3in
then I wouldn't have had to wake up. And that's how long ago the Indians

q̓sápiʔ iʔ sqilxʷ iʔ kʷəctʕámən, uɬ iʔ caʕʷlxímən 40 ixíʔ uɬ {əc}
q̓sápiʔ iʔ s+qilxʷ iʔ kʷc+t+ʕamn uɬ iʔ caʕʷ+lx+ímn ixíʔ uɬ
long_ago art Indian art rise_early_often and art bathe_often then and
trained their children to be early risers and bathers. And they

əcsisyús cxík̓xək̓[t], {kəm} lut xʷust tʼa ck̓iwlx 41 uł ixíʔ iwá
c -sy•sy=us c -xik̓•xk̓+t lut xʷus+t tʼ c -k̓iw+lx uł ixíʔ iwá
hab -smart hab -spry not hurry negfac hab -old and then even
are smart and spry, they don't get old in a hurry. *And*

kʷu scənqʷən̓mínəms axáʔ inxaxʔít 42 kiʔ {kʷu ac} kʷu a
kʷu sc -n+qʷn̓+min+m -s axáʔ in -xaʔ•xʔít kiʔ kʷu a
1obj pftv -pity -3i this 1in -older_relative rel 1obj art
my grandparents pitied me, *that's why*

cqíłstsəlx i l {łi} skʷkʷaʕst {i} məł axáʔ kən
c -qił -st -s -lx i l s+kʷ•kʷaʕst mł axáʔ kn
cust^ -awake -^cust -3erg -pl intj in early_morning and this 1kn
they woke me up early and then I had

kscáʕʷlxaʔx 43 way̓ uł mat ksx̌an tla nək̓ʷspíntk kiʔ
ks -caʕʷ+lx -aʔx way̓ uł mat k+sx̌a+n tla nk̓ʷ+s+pin=tk kiʔ
incp^ -bathe -^incp yes and maybe past from one_year rel
to bathe. *And I must have stayed there with them*

ilíʔmnəlx 44 ixíʔ uł_iʔ {i} ƛ̓lal ink̓ík̓waʔ 45 uł way̓
ilíʔ+m -n -lx ixíʔ uł_iʔ ƛ̓l•al in -k̓ík̓waʔ uł way̓
stay_with -1erg -pl then and_then dead 1in -mother's_father and yes
more than a year. *And then my grandfather died. 6:01* *He was*

cknəmqín way̓ k̓əl ƛ̓əx̌ƛ̓x̌áp 46 caʔkʷ cus ia nuyápəxcən mat way̓
c -k+nm=qin way̓ k̓l ƛ̓x̌•ƛ̓x̌a+p caʔkʷ cu -s iʔ n+wyap=x=cn mat way̓
hab -blind yes to elder as tell -3erg art say_in_English maybe yes
blind and getting old, *like they would say in English,*

k̓əłkícəs {i} iʔ x̌əcckspíntk 47 kəm̓ mat ksx̌an 48 uł cútəlx
k̓ł+kic -s iʔ x̌c•c=ks+pin=tk km̓ mat k+sx̌a+n uł cut -lx
reach -3erg art one_hundred_years or maybe past and say -pl
he was close to one hundred years old, *or maybe past.* *And they say*

way̓ mat ksx̌an təl kaʔłlʔapənkspíntk kiʔ sknəm̓qín[x] 49 uł
way̓ mat k+sx̌a+n tl kaʔłl+ʔapn=ks+pín=tk kiʔ s -k+nm=qin -x uł
yes maybe past than thirty_years rel ipftv^ -blind -^ipftv and
that he had been blind for more than thirty years. *But*

náx̌əmł xík̓xək̓t, ałíʔ mat cəcaʕʷlxímən {uł ixíʔ uł kʷu ks} 50 axáʔ tʼəxʷ
nax̌mł xik̓•xk̓+t ałíʔ mat c -caʕʷ+lx+ímn axáʔ tʼxʷ
but spry because maybe hab -bathe_often this evidently
he is spry, I guess he bathes often. *On Saturday*

i l skłaʔásq̓ət ixíʔ məł axáʔ {kʷu} kʷu xʷíc̓xtəm axáʔ iʔ {t} t
iʔ l s+k+łaʔ=ásq̓t ixíʔ mł axáʔ kʷu xʷic̓ -xt -m axáʔ iʔ t
art on Saturday then and this 3e4obj give -xit -3e4obj this art agInst
my grandmother

inqáqnaʔ 51 tʼəxʷ t isk̓ʷúy kʷu ʔúkʷłtəm
in -qá=qnaʔ tʼxʷ t i -s+k̓ʷuy kʷu ʔukʷ -łt -m
1in -fa's_mother emph agInst 1in -man's_mother 3e4obj take -łt -3e4obj
gave us... 7:06 *I mean my mother, she brought us*

iʔ stətəmtímtət 52 uł ałíʔ t isk̓ʷúy {kʷu c} kʷu
iʔ s+t•tm̓•tim̓ -tt uł ałíʔ t i -s+k̓ʷuy kʷu
art clothes -4in and because agInst 1in -man's_mother 3e4obj
our clothes, *because it's my mother that*

cənq̓ʷʔítkʷxtəm 53 ixíʔ uł kʷu ʔúkʷłtəm ik̓líʔ iʔ
c -n+q̓ʷʔ=itkʷ -xt -m ixíʔ uł kʷu ʔukʷ -łt -m ik̓líʔ iʔ
cust^ -launder -xit -3e4obj then and 1obj take_around -łt -3e4obj there art
washes them for us. *She brings*

stətəmtímtət 54 ixíʔ uł {kʷu kʷu kł} kʷu cʕawlx kʷu k̓əłʔaysəlscút
s+t•tm̓•tim̓ -tt ixíʔ uł kʷu caʕʷ+lx kʷu k̓ł+ʔays=lscút
clothes -4in then and 4kn bathe 1obj change_clothes
our clothes there. *Then we bathe, we change our clothes.*

55 ixíʔ uł axáʔ łaʔ c{k̓ʷəƛ̓s}k̓ʷəƛ̓stís ckəłtməlxʷəncút
ixíʔ uł axáʔ łaʔ c -k̓ʷƛ̓ -st -is c -kł+tm=lxʷ+ncut
then and this when cust^ -take_off -^cust -3erg hab -strip
And whenever my paternal grandfather takes off his clothes, strips,

isx̌áx̌paʔ way̓ {is} iʔ sqiltks {k} 56 way̓ kən xík̓ək̓, kən cut
i -s+x̌á•x̌paʔ way̓ iʔ s+qil=tk -s way̓ kn xik̓•k̓ kn cut
1in -grandfather well art body -3in yes 1kn mistake 1kn say
his body... *I made a mistake, I said paternal*

isx̌áx̌paʔ, ink̓ík̓waʔ 57 way̓ sqiltks way̓ uł kmix sqt̓am
i -s+x̌á•x̌paʔ in -k̓ík̓waʔ way̓ s+qil=tk -s way̓ uł kmix s+qt̓a+m
1in -grandfather 1in -mother's_father yes body -3in yes and only scar
grandfather, it's maternal grandfather. *His body is nothing but*

nt̓aʔ uł ixíʔ nwaʔlílsmən 58 ixíʔ uł síwən {is} ink̓ík̓waʔ
nt̓a uł ixíʔ n+waʔl=ils+m -n ixíʔ uł siw -n in -k̓ík̓waʔ
intj and then puzzle -1erg then and ask -1erg 1in -mother's_father
scars, and I got puzzled. *And I asked my grandfather,*

cun, nt̓a·· asqíltk uł kmix sqt̓am 59 uł laʔkín_sc̓kínk uł
cu -n nt̓a a -s+qil=tk uł kmix s+qt̓a+m uł la+ʔkín_sc+ʔkin+x uł
tell -1erg intj 2in -body and only scar and how_come and
I said, "Gee, your body is nothing but scars; *how is it that*

ilíʔ ła c̓x̌ił 60 way̓ uł lut {kʷu} kʷu t̓a cm̓áyaʔłts
ilíʔ łaʔ c+ʔx̌ił way̓ uł lut kʷu t̓ c -m̓áyaʔ -łt -s
there one_that like well and not 1obj negfac cust^ -tell -łt -3erg
it's like that?" 8:00 *He wouldn't tell me.*

61 ixíʔ uł kʷu x̌aʔntís axáʔ {i i} istəmtímaʔ 62 kʷu cus
ixíʔ uł kʷu x̌aʔn -t -is axáʔ i -s+tm•tímaʔ kʷu cu -s
then and 1obj stop -nt -3erg this 1in -grandmother 1obj tell -3erg
My grandmother stopped me. *She said to me,*

way̓ k̓əwpmíntxʷ ank̓ík̓waʔ ł aksíwm ixíʔ iʔ
way̓ k̓w+p+mi -nt -xʷ an -k̓í•k̓waʔ ł a -k -siw -m ixíʔ iʔ
yes stop_asking -nt -2erg 2in -mother's_father when 2i -futi -ask -apsv that art
"Stop asking your grandfather

l sqťam 63 way̓ uníxʷ sqťam 64 cun aɬíʔ way̓
l s+qťa+m way̓ wnixʷ s+qťa+m cu -n aɬíʔ way̓
about scar yes true scar tell -1erg because yes
about the scars." They are scars all right. I said, "They are

myaɬ c̓əlc̓álpt, sc̓x̌ilx uɬ a cnwaʔlílsmstən
myaɬ c̓l•c̓al+p+t sc+ʔx̌il+x uɬ a c -n+waʔl=ils+m -st -n
too_much fierce reason_why and art cust^ -puzzle -^cust -n^ils
fierce looking, that's why I have been puzzled.

65 uɬ inx̌mínk iksmipnúnəm 66 ixíʔ kʷu cus
uɬ in -x̌m=ink i -ks -my+p -nun -m ixíʔ kʷu cu -s
and 1in -like 1i -futi -learn -manage -apsv then 1obj tell -3erg
I'd like to know." My grandmother

istəm̓tímaʔ, way̓ t incá mi m̓áyaʔɬtsən, uɬ way̓
i -s+tm•tímaʔ way̓ t in+cá mi m̓áyaʔ -ɬt -s -n uɬ way̓
1in -grandmother well agInst I fut tell -ɬt -2obj -1erg and yes
said to me "I will tell you, and then

k̓əwpmíntxʷ 67 axáʔ {i ls} iʔ l scənwiʔqíns ixíʔ ɬaʔ
k̓w+p+mi -nt -xʷ axáʔ iʔ l sc+n+wy̓=qin -s ixíʔ ɬaʔ
stop_asking -nt -2erg this art at stop_growing -3in then when
don't ask him any more. After he stopped growing and he was hunting,

cpíx̌əm kiʔ ixíʔ náʔx̌ʷaʔst t səmx̌íkən 68 uɬ ksl̓ax̌t, uɬ ixíʔ
c -pix̌+m kiʔ ixíʔ náx̌ʷ=aʔst t s+mx̌=ikn uɬ k+s+l̓ax̌+t uɬ ixíʔ
hab -hunt rel then game_gets_away obl grizzly and have_friend and then
his game, a grizzly, got away from him. He had a friend,

nɬuxʷt iʔ səmx̌íkən 69 uɬ ixíʔ cus iʔ sl̓ax̌ts 70 uɬ
n+ɬuxʷ+t iʔ s+mx̌=ikn uɬ ixíʔ cu -s iʔ s+l̓ax̌+t -s uɬ
enter_brush art grizzly and then tell -3erg art friend -3in and
and the grizzly went in the brush. He said to his friend... 9:00 And

aɬíʔ pn̓icíʔ uɬ mat ta nťaʕpmútyaʔ {mat wa m} 71 lútəm t
aɬíʔ pn+icíʔ uɬ mat t n+ťaʕp+m=útyaʔ lut+m t
because at_that_time and maybe obl gun_loader no obl
at that time they must have had a gun loader, not

cəq̓əlnútyaʔ, way̓ ixíʔ ɬ taʔxʷɬənťaʕpmútyaʔlx 72 cus
cq̓+ln=útyaʔ way̓ ixíʔ ɬ c -taʔxʷ+ɬ+n+ťaʕp+m=útyaʔ -lx cu -s
bow_and_arrow yes then when hab -have_gun_loaders -pl tell -3erg
a bow and arrow, they already had gun loaders. He said

iʔ sl̓ax̌ts, way̓ t incá_kən nɬúxʷtmən 73 uɬ axáʔ t
iʔ s+l̓ax̌+t -s way̓ t in+cá_kn n+ɬuxʷ+t+m -n uɬ axáʔ t
art friend -3in well agInst I follow_in_brush -1erg and this from
to his friend, "I'll follow him in the brush. And from

k̓míkən mi kʷu ck̓əɬk̓níyaʔmstxʷ 74 uɬ {ńińw̓iʔ} ńińw̓iʔ c̓x̌iɬ
k̓m=ikń mi kʷu c -k̓ɬ+k̓níyaʔ+m -st -xʷ uɬ ńińw̓iʔ c+ʔx̌iɬ
outside fut 1obj cust^ -listen_for -^cust -2erg and a_while like
outside the brush you listen for me, and I'll holler

ťqʷcínməntsən 75 lut aksənx̌íləm ńíńẃiʔ ɬ níxlməntxʷ iʔ
ťqʷ=cin+m -nt -s -n lut a -ks -n+x̌il+m ńíńẃiʔ ɬ nixl+m -nt -xʷ iʔ
yell_at -nt -2obj -1erg not 2i -futi -fear a_while if hear -nt -2erg art
for you. *Don't get scared if you hear*

iʔ səmx̌íkən 76 uɬ aɬíʔ axáʔ isx̌áx̌paʔ ťíqʷəlqʷ, uɬ {lut s} lut
iʔ s+mx̌=ikn uɬ aɬíʔ axáʔ i -s+x̌á•x̌paʔ ťiqʷ=lqʷ uɬ lut
art grizzly and so this 1in -grandfather tall and not
the grizzly." *My grandfather was tall*

sq̓ʷucts, ťəxʷ lut səlxʷaʔálqʷs {uɬ náx̌əmɬ aɬíʔ} 77 náx̌əmɬ taʔlíʔ
s -q̓ʷuc+t -s ťxʷ lut slxʷaʔ=álqʷ -s naxmɬ taʔlíʔ
nom -fat 3i emph not large -3i but very_much
but not fat, not large. *He must have*

mat kɬtətínx, k̓ʷəck̓ʷáct 78 ixíʔ cut, waẏ ńíńẃiʔ c̓ənpnáʕn iʔ
mat kɬ+t•tinx k̓ʷc•k̓ʷac+t ixíʔ cut waẏ ńíńẃiʔ c̓n+p -naʕ[4] -n iʔ
maybe have_muscle strong then say well a_while tight -manage -1erg art
great muscles, he's strong. *He said, "Whenever I get hold of the bear*

səmx̌íkən {mi ta} ixíʔ ťqʷcínməntsən 79 ixíʔ məɬ {kʷ} kʷ
s+mx̌=ikn ixíʔ ťqʷ=cin+m -nt -s -n ixíʔ məɬ kʷ
grizzly then yell_at -nt -2obj -1erg then fut 2kn
tight, I'll holler for you. 10:03 *Then you come*

cxʷuy məɬ sic pulstxʷ t anwí nťaʕpáx̌əntxʷ {t}
c+xʷuy mɬ sic pul -st -xʷ t anwí n+ťaʕp=áx̌n -t -xʷ
come and then kill_one -st -2erg agInst you shoot_under_arm -nt -2erg
and kill him, you shoot it under the arm

kəm̓ k̓əɬwáx̌əntxʷ 80 uɬ iwá x̌aʔntím iʔ t sl̓ax̌ts
km̓ k̓ɬ+ɬẃ=ax̌n -t -xʷ uɬ iwá x̌aʔn -t -im iʔ t s+l̓ax̌+t -s
or stab_under_arm -nt -2erg and try_to stop -nt -psv art agInst friend -3in
or stab it under the arm." *His partner tried to stop him,*

cúntəm waẏ lut, waẏ lut {way kʷ} 81 waẏ nx̌ílmən waẏ myaɬ
cu -nt -m waẏ lut waẏ lut waẏ n+x̌il+m -n waẏ myaɬ
tell -nt -psv well not well not yes fear -1erg yes too_much
he said "No, no, *I am scared, he's too*

c̓əlc̓álpt, cus sta lut. 82 ixíʔ {ɬ} sənɬúxʷts, uɬ ixíʔ kən
c̓l•c̓al+p+t cu -s sta lut ixíʔ s -n+ɬuxʷ+t -s uɬ ixíʔ kn
fierce tell -3erg intj no then nom -enter_brush -3i and then 1kn
fierce." He said "No." *He went into the brush and I*

ilíʔ {uɬ waẏ} 83 ixíʔ kiʔ k̓əɬníxəlmən waẏ mat {iʔ} iʔ kcənwíxʷ 84 nťa
ilíʔ ixíʔ kiʔ k̓ɬ+nixl+m -n waẏ mat iʔ kc+nwixʷ nťa
there then rel hear -1erg well maybe art meet intj
stayed there.[5] *And then I heard, I guess that's when they met.* *The*

4 Variant of -nu(n), with pharyngeal intrusion.
5 Spoken as the partner.

uníxʷ kɬcucín iʔ səmx̌íkən iʔ scaʕcaʕcáʕs {uɬ i} 85 way̓ uɬ
wnixʷ kɬ+cw=cin iʔ s+mx̌=ikn iʔ s -ca•ca•cáʕ -s way̓ uɬ
true good_word art grizzly art nom -holler -3i well and
bear was sure hollering. *I heard*

k̓əɬníxlmən axáʔ isl̓áx̌t kʷu t̓əqʷcinəms 86 uɬ way̓ lut, way̓
k̓ɬ+nixl+m -n axáʔ i -s+l̓áx̌+t kʷu t̓qʷ=cin+m -s uɬ way̓ lut way̓
hear -1erg this 1in -friend 1obj yell_at -3erg and well not well
my partner holler for me, *but no, I couldn't*

lut qəɬnún {way̓} way̓ cəm̓ kʷu tk̓səlmíst kʷu ƛ̓əxʷəntím
lut qɬ -nu -n way̓ cm̓ kʷu tk=ʔasl+míst kʷu ƛ̓xʷ -nt -im
not able -manage -1erg yes maybe 4kn two_people 3e4obj kill_many -nt -3e4obj
help it, he would kill the both of us.

87 way̓ púlstəm isl̓áx̌t 88 way̓ uɬ_i {k̓ɬənx̌ílmən}
way̓ pul -st -m i -s+l̓áx̌+t way̓ uɬ_iʔ
yes kill_one -st -psv 1in -friend well and_then
He's going to kill my partner." *His friend*

k̓ɬənx̌íləms iʔ sl̓ax̌ts 89 way̓ ink̓ík̓əwaʔ k̓ɬənx̌ílməntəm
k̓ɬ+n+x̌il+m -s iʔ s+l̓ax̌+t -s way̓ in -k̓í•k̓waʔ k̓ɬ+n+x̌il+m -nt -m
get_scared -3erg art friend -3in yes 1in -mother's_father get_scared -nt -psv
got scared, 11:01 *my grandfather's partner got*

iʔ t sl̓ax̌ts 90 way̓ uɬ ixíʔ xʷət̓pəncút ɬxʷuy {si k} 91 uɬ aɬíʔ
iʔ t s+l̓ax̌+t -s way̓ uɬ ixíʔ xʷt̓+p+ncut ɬ+xʷuy uɬ aɬíʔ
art agInst friend -3in well and then run go_back and so
scared out. *He ran back.* *They*

sck̓ay̓míxəlx mat, txʷaʔxʷʔítəlx {uɬ} 92 way̓ niʕ̓íp xʷət̓pəncút
sc -k̓ay̓ -mix -lx mat t=xʷaʔ•xʷʔí+t -lx way̓ nyʕ̓ip xʷt̓+p+ncut
ipftvp^ -fall_hunt -^ipftvp -pl maybe many_persons -pl well always run
were fall hunting, lots of them. *He ran all the way*

uɬ ɬkicx iʔ k̓əl sənpúlxtənsəlx 93 way̓ ɬiyáʕ̓p axáʔ iʔ
uɬ ɬ+kic+x iʔ k̓l sn+pul+x+tn -s -lx way̓ ɬ+yaʕ̓+p axáʔ iʔ
and arrive_again art to camping_place -3in -pl yes arrive_again this art
and got back to their camp. *Some of the hunters*

k̓ʷiƛ̓t iʔ scpəx̌píx̌əx 94 nt̓a·· uɬ_i sʔayx̌ʷts iʔ stkʷaps
k̓ʷiƛ̓+t iʔ sc -px̌•pix̌ -x nt̓a uɬ_iʔ s+ʔayx̌ʷ+t -s iʔ s+tkʷa+p -s
others art ipftvp^ -hunt_pl -^ipftvp intj then tiredness -3in art choking -3in
were back in camp. *He was all tired and chocked up because*

uɬ aɬíʔ niʕ̓íp sxʷət̓pəncútx 95 way̓ cúsəlx uɬ
uɬ aɬíʔ nyʕ̓ip s -xʷt̓+p+ncut -x way̓ cu -s -lx uɬ
and because always ipftv^ -run -^ipftv well tell -3erg -pl and
he ran all the way. *"What's*

sc̓kinx t̓i way̓ kʷ scənx̌ílx {kʷsə} myaɬ iʔ kʷ
sc -ʔkin -x t̓iʔ way̓ kʷ sc -n+x̌il -x myaɬ iʔ kʷ
ipftvp^ -indef -^ipftvp evid yes 2kn ipftvp^ -fear -^ipftvp too_much art 2kn
the matter with you that you are so scared

ɬ ʔayx̌ʷt 96 kínəm asl̓áx̌t 97 wai̓ qʷəlqʷəltíʔst, cut wai̓
ɬ ʔayx̌ʷ+t kiṅ+m a -s+l̓ax̌+t wai̓ qʷl•qʷl+t=iʔst cut wai̓
subord tired indef 2in -friend well manage_to_talk say yes
and tired? Where's your partner?"[6] *He got to talking,*

wai̓ náx̌ʷaʔst t səmx̌íkən 98 uɬ ixíʔ knɬúxʷtəms,
wai̓ náx̌ʷ=aʔst t s+mx̌=ikn uɬ ixíʔ k+n+ɬuxʷ+t+m -s
yes almost_gain obj_itr grizzly and then go_after_in_the_brush -3erg
he said, "He had gained a grizzly. He went after it in the brush,

nɬuxʷt aɬíʔ iʔ səmx̌íkən 99 uɬ iwá x̌aʔntín, cun wai̓
n+ɬuxʷ+t aɬíʔ iʔ s+mx̌=ikn uɬ iwá x̌aʔn -t -in cu -n wai̓
enter_brush because art grizzly and try_to stop -nt -1erg tell -1erg well
because the bear went in the brush. I tried to stop him, I said to him,

lut wai̓ lut t̓ t̓ akskənɬúxʷtəm 100 wai̓ cəm̓
lut wai̓ lut t̓ t̓ a -ks -k+n+ɬuxʷ+t+m t̓ wai̓ cm̓
not yes not negfac negfac 2i -futi -go_after_in_the_brush negfac yes maybe
'Don't go in the brush, 12:02 he'll just

t̓i púlstəms, uɬ lut 101 kʷu cus, staʔ 102 wai̓ ṅíṅw̓iʔ
t̓iʔ pul -st -m -s uɬ lut kʷu cu -s staʔ wai̓ ṅíṅw̓iʔ
evid kill_one -st -2obj -3erg and not 1obj tell -3erg intj yes a_while
kill you,' but no. He told me 'No. I'll go

kənɬúxʷtmən ik̓líʔ {kʷu} mi kʷu kʷənkʷəntwíxʷ 103 ṅíṅw̓iʔ
k+n+ɬuxʷ+t+m -n ik̓líʔ mi kʷu kʷn•kʷn+twixʷ ṅíṅw̓iʔ
go_after_in_the_brush -1erg there fut 4kn grab_one_another a_while
in the brush after him, and then we'll catch hold of one another. When

c̓ənpnáʕn, mi t̓qʷcínməntsən, ixíʔ məɬ kʷ cxʷuy 104 kʷ
c̓n+p -naʕ -n mi t̓qʷ=cin+m -nt -s -n ixíʔ mɬ kʷ c+xʷuy kʷ
tight -nu -1erg fut yell_at -nt -2obj -1erg then and 2kn come 2kn
I get hold of him I'll holler for you, then you'll come. You

cənɬúxʷt ṅíṅw̓iʔ t anwí {k̓əɬ} k̓əɬwáx̌əntəm 105 ixíʔ
c+n+ɬuxʷ+t ṅíṅw̓iʔ t anwí k̓ɬ+ɬw=ax̌n -t -m ixíʔ
come_in_the_brush a_while agInst you stab_under_arm -nt -psv that
get in the brush and stab him under the arm.' That's

kʷu cus, uɬ wai̓ ixíʔ ɬaʔ nɬuxʷt 106 uɬ_i c̓əlpcənmíst
kʷu cu -s uɬ wai̓ ixíʔ ɬaʔ n+ɬuxʷ+t uɬ_iʔ c̓l+p=cn+mist
1obj tell -3erg and yes then the_one_that enter_brush and_then fierce_holler
what he told me, and he went in the brush. And then the bear

axáʔ iʔ səmx̌íkən 107 uɬ_i kʷu st̓əqʷcínəms uɬ wai̓
axáʔ iʔ s+mx̌=ikn uɬ_iʔ kʷu s -t̓qʷ=cin+m -s uɬ wai̓
this art grizzly and_then 1kʷu nom -yell_at -3i and yes
howled fierce. Then he hollered for me, and I

6 It's Pete's grandmother talking.

k̓ɬənx̌ílmən isláx̌t
k̓ɬ+n+x̌il+m -n i -s+l̓ax̌+t
get_scared -1erg 1in -friend
got scared to help my partner,

108 ixíʔ uɬ_i kən {a} ɬcx^{w}ət̓pəncút {i}
ixíʔ uɬ_iʔ kn ɬ+c+x^{w}t̓+p+ncut
then and_then 1kn run_back_cisl
and then I ran back.

109 kən nstils uɬ a[xáʔ] cəm̓ {pul} púlstəm axáʔ isl̓áx̌t
kn n+st=ils uɬ axáʔ cm̓ pul -st -m axáʔ i -s+l̓ax̌+t
1kn think and this maybe kill_one -st -psv this 1in -friend
I thought my partner'll get

púlstəm axáʔ isl̓áx̌t
pul -st -m axáʔ i -s+l̓ax̌+t
kill_one -st -psv this 1in -friend
killed,

110 uɬ way̓ incá lut_ksluts
uɬ way̓ in+cá lut_k+s+lut+s
and yes I there_is_no_no_about_it
and there is no doubt he'll

nix^{w} {k^{w}u} k^{w}u kspulsts, k^{w}u ksənʔúcxiʔs
nix^{w} k^{w}u ks -pul -st -s k^{w}u k+s -n+ʔuc=xiʔ -s
also 1obj futt^ -kill_one -st -3erg 1obj futt^ -follow -3erg
kill me too, he'll track me" [end of tape]. 13:00

111 way̓ itlíʔ t̓əx^{w} kən nc̓əp̓q̓síw̓səm
way̓ itlíʔ t̓x^{w} kn n+c̓p̓q̓+s=iw̓s+m
well from_there emph 1kn splice
I am going to splice

112 caʔk^{w} cus inq^{w}əlq^{w}íltən a nqílx^{w}cən
caʔk^{w} cu -s i -n+q^{w}l•q^{w}il+tn a n+qilx^{w}=cn
as tell -3erg 1in -language art Indian_language
like they say in my language, in the Indian language.

113 way̓ axáʔ {is·· } sxíʔtmistsəlx axáʔ {is} iʔ splal iʔ scpíx̌əx, ia ɬyaʕp
way̓ axáʔ s -xít+m=iʔst -s -lx axáʔ iʔ s+pl•al iʔ sc -pix̌ -x iʔ ɬ+yaʕ+p
well this nom -run_pl -3i -pl this art young_growth art ipftvp^ -hunt -^ipftvp art arrive_again
The young hunter started running, the one that had gotten back.

114 way̓ cúsəlx huhúy k^{w}u x^{w}istúɬt laʔkín {i} kiʔ cɬəwíntx^{w} asl̓áx̌t
way̓ cu -s -lx hu•húy k^{w}u x^{w}y -stuɬt la+ʔkín̓ kiʔ c -ɬwi -nt -x^{w} a -s+l̓ax̌+t
well tell -3erg -pl Ok 1k^{w}u go -stuɬt wherever rel act -leave -nt -2erg 2in -friend
They said to him: "Take us where you left your partner."

115 way̓ {x^{w}u··yl ə} x^{w}u··ylx, k̓liʔ yáʕpəlx iʔ k̓əlá cɬak
way̓ x^{w}uy -lx ik̓líʔ yaʕ+p -lx iʔ k̓l c+ɬak
well go -pl there arrive_pl -pl art to swamp
They went and they got to the swamp.

116 way̓ cut aláʔ {kiʔ} kiʔ nɬúx^{w}təms
way̓ cut aláʔ kiʔ n+ɬux^{w}+t+m -s
well say here rel follow_in_brush -3erg
He said, "That's where he went in the brush."

117 way̓ ixíʔ sənɬəx^{w}tlílxsəlx, ixíʔ wíksəlx {way̓}
way̓ ixíʔ s -n+ɬx^{w}+t+lilx -s -lx ixíʔ wik -s -lx
well then nom -go_in_bush_pl -3i -pl then see -3erg -pl
They went in the brush, they saw him. 1:03

118 mu··t axáʔ ink̓ík̓əwaʔ t··a uɬ iʔ sqiltks
mut axáʔ in -k̓í•k̓waʔ ta uɬ iʔ s+qil=tk -s
sit_sg this 1in -mother's_father intj and art body -3in
My grandfather was sitting there, his body

way̓ uɬ xʷəm_t̓i {sca} scc̓iqʷ 119 kmix məɬ̓kíyaʔ iʔ sqiltks
way̓ uɬ xʷm_t̓iʔ sc -c̓iqʷ kmix mɬ̓kíyaʔ iʔ s+qil=tk -s
yes and evid pftv -butcher only blood art body -3in
is like it's been butchered, *his body is nothing but blood.*

120 uɬ axáʔ {is} iʔ t̓ílx̌ʷəntəm iʔ t səmx̌íkən 121 way̓
uɬ axáʔ iʔ t̓ilx̌ʷ -nt -m iʔ t s+mx̌=ikn way̓
and this art tear_apart -nt -psv art agInst grizzly well
The bear tore him apart. *They*

síwsəlx cúsəlx way̓ uɬ c̓knútyaʔ 122 cut way̓ kən
siw -s -lx cu -s -lx way̓ uɬ c+ʔkn=útyaʔ cut way̓ kn
ask -3erg -pl tell -3erg -pl well and what_bad_state say well 1kn
asked him, they said, “How are you?” *He said “I’m*

t̓ək̓ʷk̓ʷspuʔús 123 cúsəlx uɬ xkínəm iʔ səmx̌íkən 124 cúntəm {a t}
t̓k̓ʷ•k̓ʷ+s+puʔ=ús cu -s -lx uɬ x+kin+m iʔ s+mx̌=ikn cun -nt -m
feel_better tell -3erg -pl and do_what art grizzly tell -nt -psv
feeling better”[7] *They asked, “What happened to the bear?”* *He told them,*

aɬíʔ uɬ lut t̓a cmistín əxkínəm uɬ aɬíʔ {kən} kən
aɬíʔ uɬ lut t̓ c -my -st -in x+kin+m uɬ aɬíʔ kn
so and not negfac custˆ -know -ˆcust -1erg do_what and because 1kn
“I don’t know what happened, because I

qʷəńíwtəm 125 cut ixíʔ a nkəm̓km̓ínaʔn axáʔ iʔ səmx̌íkən, a
qʷń=iwt+m cut ixíʔ a n+km̓•km̓=ínaʔ -n axáʔ iʔ s+mx̌=ikn a
pass_out say then art grab_ears -1erg this art grizzly art
passed out.” *He said, “When I got hold of the grizzly’s ears, when*

nkəcníkənn 126 kiʔ a nkəm̓km̓ínaʔn uɬ_iʔ t̓qʷcínmən
n+kc+n=ikn -n kiʔ a n+km̓•km̓=ínaʔ -n uɬ_iʔ t̓qʷ=cin+m -n
overtake -1erg rel art grab_ears -1erg and_then yell_at -1erg
I overtook him, *I got hold of his ears, and I hollered for my*

isl̓áx̌t 127 cut uɬ wim̓ t̓qʷcínmən, hoy uɬ q̓əssápiʔ {uɬ}
i -s+l̓ax̌+t cut uɬ wim̓ t̓qʷ=cin+m -n hoy uɬ q̓s•s•ápiʔ
1in -friend say and in_vain yell_at -1erg finish and a_little_too_long
partner. 2:00 *I kept yelling for him. It was a little too long,*

uɬ kən ƛ̓əxʷƛ̓xʷáx̌ən 128 uɬ aɬíʔ k̓ʷəck̓ʷáct iʔ səmx̌íkən 129 way̓
uɬ kn ƛ̓xʷ•ƛ̓xʷ=ax̌n uɬ aɬíʔ k̓ʷc•k̓ʷac+t iʔ s+mx̌=ikn way̓
and 1kn paralized_arms and so strong art grizzly well
and my arms gave out. *The grizzly was strong.* *The grizzly*

ʔax̌lúsəm iʔ səmx̌íkən, kʷu k̓ʷaʔɬtís {axáʔ iʔ} isək̓ʷtáx̌ən 130 ixíʔ uɬ kən
ʔax̌l=ús+m iʔ s+mx̌=ikn kʷu k̓ʷaʔ -ɬt -is i -s+k̓ʷt=ax̌n ixíʔ uɬ kn
turn_face art grizzly 1obj bite -ɬt -3erg 1in -one_arm then and 1kn
turned his face, and he bit me in the arm, *and I*

7 Lit. “my heart has fallen in its place.”

kƛ̓əllíkst ik̓lí? 131 uɬ axá? k̓əl sk̓ʷut nixʷ kʷu k̓ʷa?ɬtís
k+ƛ̓l•l=ikst ik̓lí? uɬ axá? k̓l s+k̓ʷut nixʷ kʷu k̓ʷa? -ɬt -is
strengthless_arm there and this to other_side also 1obj bite -ɬt -3erg
lost strength in my arm. *Then he bit my other arm;*

132 ixí? uɬ nixʷ ki? ilí? kən kƛ̓əllíkst 133 uɬ ctxəmníw̓s {k̓əl ks k̓əl}
ixí? uɬ nixʷ ki? ilí? kn k+ƛ̓l•l=ikst uɬ c -t+xmn=iw̓s
then and also rel there 1kn strengthless_arm and hab -each_side
that killed the strength of my other arm. *Both my arms*

t̓əxʷ {k̓əl} ƛ̓lal inkəlkíl·x c̓x̌iɬ 134 ixí? uɬ way̓ ɬa?
t̓xʷ ƛ̓l•al in -kl•kil•l•x c+?x̌iɬ ixí? uɬ way̓ ɬa?
emph dead 1in -hands like that and all the_one_that
are dead-like. *That's the last*

cmistín {tx} 135 ixí·? ɬ iksənt̓ək̓ʷk̓ʷspu?ús 136 way̓ uɬ
c -my -st -in ixí? ɬ i -ks -n+t̓k̓ʷ•k̓ʷ+s+pu?=ús way̓ uɬ
cust^ -know -st -1erg there when 1i -futi -come_to well and
I know." *He said, "Then I came to.* *You just*

taɬt uɬ kɬcawt aɬí? {t} kʷu wikɬtp isqíltk {i} 137 cut, {x}
taɬ+t uɬ kɬ+cawt aɬí? kʷu wik -ɬt -p i -s+qil=tk cut
surely and quite_something so 1obj see -ɬt -5erg 1in -body say
saw what happened to my body." 3:00 *He said,*

uɬ t̓i? k̓aw i? səmx̌íkən 138 way̓ {is} tkʷúpxənsəlx, {s·} n?úcxsəlx
uɬ t̓i? k̓aw i? s+mx̌=ikn way̓ t+kʷup=xn -s -lx n+?uc=x -s -lx
and evid gone art grizzly well rush_to -3erg -pl follow -3erg -pl
"And the grizzly is gone." *They rushed and they tracked him,*

uɬ aɬí? kɬməɬk̓íya? 139 sənxʷ?ít i? ta məɬk̓íya? 140 way̓ t̓i?
uɬ aɬí? kɬ+mɬk̓íya? sn+xʷ?i+t i? t mɬkíya? way̓ t̓i?
and because have_blood lots art prttv blood well evid
because there is blood, *there is lots of blood.* *Not far,*

lut_səlkʷúts lut sənpúƛ̓əms nkcníki?səlx i? səmx̌íkən
lut_s+lkʷ=ut+s lut s -n+p̓uƛ̓+m -s n+kc+n=íki? -s -lx i? s+mx̌=ikn
not_far not nom -come_out -3i catch_up_with -3erg -pl art grizzly
he never got out of the brush, they overtook the grizzly.

141 way̓ ct̓ak̓ʷ, way̓ ƛ̓lal nixʷ {ixí?} 142 ixí? {kʷu·} kʷu may̓ɬtís
way̓ c -t̓ak̓ʷ way̓ ƛ̓l•al nixʷ ixí? kʷu m̓ay -ɬt -is
yes hab -put_down yes dead also that 1obj tell -ɬt -3erg
He was lying there dead too. *That's what*

aɬí? axá? {in} istəmtíma? 143 kʷa aɬí? uɬ kən
aɬí? axá? i -s+tm•tíma? kʷa aɬí? uɬ kn
so this 1in -grandmother intj because and 1kn
my grandmother told me. *Because I was*

sənsáw̓su?cna?x ilí? ɬ kilí?mnəlx 144 uɬ ɬa?
s -n+saw̓•sw̓=cn -a?x ilí? ɬ k+ilí?+m -n -lx uɬ ɬa?
ipftv^ -ask_questions -^ipftvDim there when live_with -1erg -pl and when
always asking questions the time I was with them. *When he*

ck̓əɬʔaysəlscút náx̌əmɬ {a} axáʔ iʔ sqiltks waẏ kmix sqt̓am {uɬ}
c -kɬ+ʔays=lscút nax̌mɬ axáʔ iʔ s+qil=tk -s waẏ kmix s+qt̓a+m
hab -change_clothes so this art body -3in yes only scar
changes his clothes his body is nothing but scars.

145 uɬ ixíʔ {i it} iʔ síwən {in} ink̓ík̓əwaʔ 146 cun uɬ
uɬ ixíʔ iʔ siw -n in -k̓í•k̓waʔ cu -n uɬ
and then art ask -1erg 1in -mother's_father tell -1erg and
And then I asked my grandfather, I said:

sc̓kinx haʔ uɬ asqíltk uɬ kmix {a} sqt̓am 147 uɬ lut
sc -ʔkin -x haʔ uɬ a -s+qil=tk uɬ kmix s+qt̓a+m uɬ lut
ipftvp^ -indef -^ipftvp inter and 2in -body and only scar and not
"What happened to your body that's it's all scars?" 4:03 He never

kʷu cuɬts, kʷu ukʷtúɬts 148 ixíʔ uɬ kʷu x̌aʔncís
kʷu cu -ɬt -s kʷu wkʷ -tuɬt -s ixíʔ uɬ kʷu x̌aʔn -t -s -is
1obj tell -ɬt -3erg 1obj hide -tuɬt -3erg then and 1obj stop -nt -2obj -3erg
told me, he hid it from me. And then my grandmother

axáʔ istəmtímaʔ 149 kʷu cus waẏ, waẏskʷ ɬ
axáʔ i -s+tm•tímaʔ kʷu cu -s waẏ waẏ -skʷ ɬ
this 1in -grandmother 1obj tell -3erg well finish -tsimptv subord
stopped me. She said to me, "Stop

aksíwm ank̓ík̓əwaʔ, səsc̓aʔxmínəms 150 sc̓x̌ilx
a -k -siw -m an -k̓í•k̓waʔ sc -c̓aʔx+mín+m -s sc+ʔx̌il+x
2i -futi -ask -apsv 2in -mother's_father pftv -be_ashamed_of -3erg reason_why
asking your grandfather, he is ashamed of it, That's why

uɬ lut ksmáẏaʔɬts 151 cun ha uɬ sc̓kinx kaʔ
uɬ lut ks -m̓áyaʔ -ɬt -s cu -n haʔ uɬ sc -ʔkin -x kiʔ
and not futt^ -tell -ɬt -3erg tell -1erg inter and ipftvp^ -indef -^ipftvp rel
he didn't tell you." I said "And why is he

ɬ cc̓aʔxmísts uɬ səxkínx kʷaʔ
ɬ c -c̓aʔx+mí -st -s uɬ s -x+kin -x kʷaʔ
when cust^ -be_ashamed -^cust -3erg and ipftv^ -do_what -^ipftv intj
ashamed of it, what happened?"

152 cúntəm waẏ {i l} púti l swínumtaʔxs kiʔ ixíʔ {t s} t
cu -nt -m waẏ pút+iʔ l s+wẏ+numt=aʔx -s kiʔ ixíʔ t
tell -nt -psv well still in youth -3in rel that agInst
She said "He was still growing up when

səmx̌íkən iʔ t̓ílx̌ʷəntəm {iʔ} 153 nk̓ʷəɬtyáqʷtməntəm iʔ t səmx̌íkən
s+mx̌=ikn iʔ t̓ilx̌ʷ -nt -m nk̓ʷ+ɬ+tyaqʷ+m -nt -m iʔ t s+mx̌=ikn
grizzly art tear_apart -nt -psv fight_with -nt -psv art agInst grizzly
the bear tore him to pieces, he was fought by the grizzly.

154 itlíʔ uɬ {ac} acc̓aʔxmísts {tks} ɬ ksmaẏncúts
itlíʔ uɬ c -c̓aʔx+mí -st -s ɬ ks -m̓ay+ncút -s
from_there and cust^ -be_ashamed -^cust -3erg subord futi -tell_story -3i
That's why he is ashamed to tell about it.

155 uł t̓i incá iʔ kʷu m̓ayncútmiʔs 156 cun, a·· way̓ ixíʔ
uł t̓iʔ in+cá iʔ kʷu m̓ay+ncút+mi -s cu -n a way̓ ixíʔ
and evid I art 1obj tell_confidentially -3erg tell -1erg intj well then
And he told me secretely." 5:00 *I said, "Oh, now*

k̓əwpmín 157 uł kilíʔmən kilíʔmən mat ksx̌an tla
k̓w+p+mi -n uł k+ilíʔ+m -n k+ilíʔ+m -n mat k+sx̌a+n tla
stop_asking -1erg and live_with -1erg live_with -1erg maybe past from
I'll leave him alone." *I stayed with them longer than a year,*

nk̓ʷspintk, mat nək̓ʷəspíntk kłtx̌ʷəx̌ʷspíntk 158 ixíʔ uł ƛ̓lal
nk̓ʷ+s+pin=tk mat nk̓ʷ+s+pin=tk kł+tx̌ʷ•x̌ʷ+s+pin=tk ixíʔ uł ƛ̓l•al
one_year maybe one_year half_year then and dead
maybe a year and a half, *and then*

ink̓ík̓waʔ i t sƛ̓əx̌ƛ̓x̌áps mʕ̓an {ił} 159 mat ksx̌an iʔ
in -k̓ík̓waʔ i t s+ƛ̓•ƛ̓x̌a+p -s mʕ̓an mat k+sx̌a+n iʔ
1in -mother's_father art agInst old_age -3in intj maybe past art
my grandfather died of old age. *Maybe his age*

təl x̌əccíkst iʔ sƛ̓əx̌ƛ̓x̌áps 160 mʕ̓an {i} iʔ qəpqíntəms uł laʔcxʔítiʔ
tl x̌c•c=ikst iʔ s+ƛ̓x̌•ƛ̓x̌a+p -s mʕ̓an iʔ qp=qin+tn -s uł la_c+xʔít+iʔ
of hundred art age -3in intj art hair -3in and first,
was past one hundred. *His hair was white;*

t̓iʔ pa··yq, i t spqmúsc hoy uł c̓x̌ił t
t̓iʔ payq i t s+pq+m=us -c hoy uł c+ʔx̌ił t
evid white art agInst white_hair -3in well and like obj_c̓x̌ił
at first, gray hair, then it turned yellow when

skʷər̓r̓íʔx {i s} kiʔ ƛ̓lal 161 ixíʔ {uł} uł ałíʔ istəmtímaʔ
s -kʷr̓•r̓•iʔ -x kiʔ ƛ̓l•al ixíʔ uł ałíʔ i -s+tm•tímaʔ
ipftv^ -yellow -^ipftv rel dead then and so 1in -grandmother
he died. *And my grandmother*

tk̓asʔasíl k̓im iʔ st̓əmt̓əmkʔílts 162 axáʔ isk̓ʷúy iʔ sxʔitx
tk=ʔas•ʔasíl k̓im iʔ s+t̓m•t̓mkʔ=ilt -s axáʔ i -s+k̓ʷuy iʔ s+xʔit=x iʔ
two_persons left art daughters -3in this 1in -mother art oldest_one art
had two daughters left. *My mother is the older*

iʔ sxʔitx uł axáʔ {i} inwásaʔ ixíʔ iʔ stʔiwtx 163 uł ixíʔ
iʔ s+xʔit=x uł axáʔ in -wásaʔ ixíʔ iʔ s+tʔiw+t=x uł ixíʔ
art oldest_one and this 1in -aunt that art young_one and then
and my aunt is the younger. 6:02 *I guess*

miłx̌mínks mat iʔ stʔiwtx 164 ixíʔ uł {its} iʔ t səx̌lxʷúlaʔxʷ
my+ł+x̌m=ink -s mat iʔ s+tʔiw+t=x ixíʔ uł iʔ t sx̌+lx=úlaʔxʷ
like_better -3erg maybe art young_one then and art obl change_country
she likes the youngest one better. *Then she changed country*

k̓laʔ ncaʔlím 165 ałíʔ aláʔ la ncaʔlím kiʔ ilíʔlx axáʔ inwásaʔ
ak̓láʔ n+caʔlím ałíʔ aláʔ l n+caʔlím kiʔ ilíʔ -lx axáʔ in -wásaʔ
here Inchelium so here at Inchelium rel there -pl this 1in -aunt
to Inchelium; *my aunt was in Inchelium.*

166 uɫ aɫíʔ t̓əxʷ txʷaʔxʷʔílt, uɫ axáʔ mnímɫtət uɫ aɫíʔ kʷu {k̓əls}
uɫ aɫíʔ t̓xʷ t=xʷaʔ•xʷʔ=ílt uɫ axáʔ mnimɫ+tt uɫ aɫíʔ kʷu
and so evidently many_offspring and this we and because 4kn
She had quite a big family, and we were here

kʷu {k̓əls} k̓la nx̌ʷyaʔɫpítkʷ 167 ik̓líʔ kiʔ kʷu ilíʔ, kʷu sənx̌ʷyaʔɫpítkʷx[8]
kʷu k̓l n+x̌ʷyaʔ=ɫp=ítkʷ ik̓líʔ kiʔ kʷu ilíʔ kʷu sn+x̌ʷyaʔ=ɫp=ítkʷ=x
4kn to Kettle there rel 4kn there 4kn Kettle_people
at the Kettle River. *We were here, we are Kettle River people.*

168 ixíʔ uɫ way̓ incá {kən} kən pəx̌pəx̌twílx ixíʔ uɫ {kən} kən xʷuy k̓əl
ixíʔ uɫ way̓ in+cá kn px̌•px̌+t+wilx ixíʔ uɫ kn xʷuy k̓l
then and yes I 1kn get_senses then and 1kn go to
I got my senses then, and I went

sənm̓aʔ•m̓áyaʔtən {uɫ t̓i} 169 ah way̓ kən k̓əɫk̓ʷít̓ət̓ ixíʔ naɫcəcám 170 ixíʔ
sn+m̓aʔ•m̓áyaʔ+tn a way̓ kn k̓ɫ+k̓ʷit̓•t̓ ixíʔ naɫc•c•ám ixíʔ
school intj well 1kn shortcut that forget that
to school. *Oh, I took a shortcut, I forgot.* *My*

uɫ axáʔ inqíck iʔ sxʔitx scústsəlx nyas
uɫ axáʔ in -qick iʔ s+xʔit=x s -cu -st -s -lx nyas
and this 1in -older_brother art oldest_one cust^ -tell -^cust -3erg -pl Ignace
oldest brother, they call him Eneas, 7:03

171 ixíʔ uɫ ak̓láʔ {c} cənʔáx̌ʷt {c} 172 cus axáʔ inƛ̓ax̌əx̌ƛ̓x̌áp,
ixíʔ uɫ ak̓láʔ c+n+ʔax̌ʷ+t cu -s axáʔ in -ƛ̓ax̌•x̌•ƛ̓x̌á+p
then and here come_downriver tell -3erg this 1in -elders
he came downriver. *He said to my parents,*

way̓ {kə} ɫəwíɫmən 173 way̓ kən ksk̓ʷəl̓ɫtəmxʷúlaʔxʷaʔx k̓liʔ
way̓ ɫwi -ɫm -n way̓ kn ks -k̓ʷl̓+ɫ+tmxʷ=úlaʔxʷ -aʔx ik̓líʔ
yes leave -5obj -1erg yes 1kn incp^ -make_ranch -^incp there
"I'm leaving you. *I am going to make a ranch of my own*

k̓la ncaʔlím 174 ixíʔ púti lúti sq̓əy̓úlaʔxʷəmsəlx 175 məɫ nixʷ
k̓l n+caʔlím ixíʔ pút+iʔ lút+i s -q̓y̓=úlaʔxʷ+m -s -lx mɫ nixʷ
at Inchelium that still before nom -survey_land -3i -pl and also
at Inchelium." *That's before they surveyed the land.* *"I am*

kən ƛ̓aʔƛ̓ʔám t ikɫtəmxʷúlaʔxʷ {ixíʔ məɫ} 176 ixíʔ n̓ín̓w̓iʔ ɫ
kn ƛ̓aʔ•ƛ̓ʔá+m t i -kɫ -tmxʷ=úlaʔxʷ ixíʔ n̓ín̓w̓iʔ ɫ
1kn look_for obj_itr 1i -to_be -land then a_while when
going to look for some land for me. *When*

q̓əy̓úlaʔxʷməlx uɫ ixíʔ iksnilíʔtən 177 uɫ axáʔ {way̓ ks}
q̓y̓=úlaʔxʷ+m -lx uɫ ixíʔ i -k -sn+ilíʔ+tn uɫ axáʔ
survey_land -pl and that 1i -to_be -dwelling_place and this
the surveyors come along, that will be my allotment." *And they*

8 I have also recorded this form as sənxʷyaʔɫpítkʷx.

way̓ {taʔxʷs} taʔxʷsqʷəsqʷsíʔlx tətw̓ít 178 ixíʔ uɬ way̓ mat
way̓ taʔxʷ+s+qʷs•qʷsíʔ -lx t•tw̓it ixíʔ uɬ way̓ mat
yes get_baby -pl boy that and yes maybe
already had a child, a boy, *and he's already able to*

c̓amtlwís 179 ixíʔ uɬ kʷu cx̌líts axáʔ inqíck
c -ʔam=t+lwís ixíʔ uɬ kʷu c -x̌lit -s axáʔ in -qick
hab -sit_around then and 1obj act -call -3erg this 1in -older_brother
sit around. *And then my brother asked me,*

180 kʷu cus way̓ x̌ast kʷu ɬ kxəntíxʷ, ixíʔ kʷ
kʷu cu -s way̓ x̌as+t kʷu ɬ kx+n -t -ixʷ ixíʔ kʷ
1obj tell -3erg well good 1obj subord follow -nt -2erg then 2kʷu
he said to me, "It's better you come with me

i{kɬ a}kɬəntkʷíls 181 cəm̓ nk̓əwpíls axáʔ asɬwílt ɬ knánaʔqs
i -kɬ -n+t+kʷil=s cm̓ n+k̓w+p=ils axáʔ a -s+ɬw=ilt ɬ k+ná•naʔqs
1i -to_be -keep_company maybe lonesome this 2in -niece if alone
for my company; *your nephew might get lonesome if he's alone." 8:00*

182 ixíʔ uɬ kʷu cənʔax̌ʷʔáx̌ʷt 183 kʷu cxʷu··y uɬ aláʔ la ncaʔlím
ixíʔ uɬ kʷu c+n+ʔax̌ʷ•ʔáx̌ʷ+t kʷu c+xʷuy uɬ aláʔ l n+caʔlím
then and 4kn come_downriver 4kn come and here at Inchelium
And then we came downriver. *We came as far as Inchelium,*

kʷu cyaʕp uɬ itlíʔ {kʷu} kʷu nʔax̌ʷʔáx̌ʷt 184 ixíʔ uɬ
kʷu c+yaʕ+p uɬ itlíʔ kʷu n+ʔax̌ʷ•ʔáx̌ʷ+t ixíʔ uɬ
4kn arrive_here and from_there 4kn go_downstream that and
we got here, we went downriver, *they*

c̓úmlaʔxʷstsəlx {ta nʕapt lut} ta nm{m̓}kʷutálaʔqʷ 185 ilíʔ cwix
c -ʔúm=laʔxʷ -st -s -lx t n+m̓kʷ+wt+álaʔqʷ ilíʔ cwix
cust^ -call_a_place -^cust -3erg -pl obl little_lump_in_woods there live
call it "little lump in the woods," *there is*

itíʔ uɬ {kʷu} kʷu {nʔaw} nʔawcínəm ik̓líʔ uɬ {k̓l} c̓úmstsəlx
itíʔ uɬ kʷu n+ʔaw=cín+m ik̓líʔ uɬ c -ʔum -st -s -lx
that and 4kn go_upstream there and cust^ -call -^cust -3erg -pl
a house there. Then we went up to a creek, they call it

t sənx̌ʷúc̓əc̓tən 186 ixíʔ uɬ sk̓máx̌əns {i s} i tla ksqilxʷ, kiʔ ixíʔ
t sn+x̌ʷuc̓•c̓+tn ixíʔ uɬ s+k̓m=ax̌n -s i tla k+s+qilxʷ kiʔ ixíʔ
obl cut_something that and end -3in art from have_person rel that
"cut something." *That's the end of the places where people are,*

sənx̌ʷúc̓əc̓tən 187 ixíʔ spaʔpʔúl naʔɬ qicks máʕʷtət ixíʔ
sn+x̌ʷuc̓•c̓+tn ixíʔ s+paʔ•pʔúl naʔɬ qick -s maʕʷt•t ixíʔ
cut_something that m's_name and older_brother -3in m's_name that
"cut something." *Smoke and his brother máʕ̓ʷtət*

ɬaʔ ksckʷínəlx ixíʔ kɬtəmxʷúlaʔxʷsəlx 188 uɬ lut t̓a
ɬaʔ ksc -kʷin -lx ixíʔ kɬ -tmxʷ=úlaʔxʷ -s -lx uɬ lut t̓
the_one_that pperf -take -pl that to_be -land -3in -pl and not negfac
picked that for their home place, *and it's not*

cḱəłʕáľ, ťiʔ waẏ kmix {unfin} uł ixíʔ nʔíyłtməlx axáʔ t
c -ḱł+ʕaľ ťiʔ waẏ kmix uł ixíʔ n+ʔiy[9] -łt -m -lx axáʔ t
hab -fence evid yes only and then buy -łt -psv -pl this agInst
fenced. My brother bought the rights

inqíck 189 waẏ ixíʔ {s} ḱəłʕaľəntís axáʔ inqíck
in -qick waẏ ixíʔ ḱł+ʕaľ -nt -is axáʔ in -qick
1in -older_brother well then fence -nt -3erg this 1in -older_brother
from them. *And my brother started fencing it; 9:00*

190 uł ixíʔ sťəlúlaʔxʷəms uł ḱʷəľłcítxʷəm sənťəwscqáx̌aʔtən {uł}
uł ixíʔ s -ťl=úlaʔxʷ+m -s uł ḱʷľ+ł+citxʷ+m sn+ťwst=sqáx̌aʔ+tn
and then nom -plow -3i and make_house barn
and he started to plow it, and built a house, a barn.

191 ixíʔ uł mat ḱʷənxspíntk 192 ixíʔ uł axáʔ ƛ̓x̌ap axáʔ
ixíʔ uł mat ḱʷn+x+s+pin=tk ixíʔ uł axáʔ ƛ̓x̌a+p axáʔ
then and maybe some_years then and this grow_sg this
I don't know how many years, *then my nephew*

isłwílt, iʔ sxʔitx 193 ixíʔ uł ḱəl sənmaʔmáyaʔtən uł ałíʔ
i -s+łw=ilt iʔ s+xʔit=x ixíʔ uł ḱl sn+m̓aʔ•m̓áyaʔ+tn uł ałíʔ
1in -niece art oldest_one then and to school and because
grew up, the first one; *then he went to school,*

kəlkʷút iʔ sənmaʔmáyaʔtən itlíʔ mat 194 ḱəl
k+lkʷ=ut iʔ sn+m̓aʔ•m̓áyaʔ+tn itlíʔ mat ḱl
far art school from_there maybe at
and the school is far from there. *They*

ċúmlaʔxʷstsəlx t kʷkʷáṙkʷəṙxnəm 195 uł lut ť
c -ʔúm=laʔxʷ -st -s -lx t kʷ•kʷaṙ•kʷṙ=xn+m uł lut ť
cust^ -call -^cust -3erg -pl obl Rogers_Bar and not negfac
call it "Rogers Bar." *And we weren't able*

qəłnúntəm iḱliʔ kʷu ł ksmaʔmáyaʔms kʷu ł
qł -nu -nt -m iḱlíʔ kʷu ł ks -m̓aʔ•m̓áyaʔ+m -s kʷu ł
able -manage -nt -4erg there 1kʷu subord futi -school -futi^4 1kʷu subord
to go to school that far to go

ksxʷaʔxʷúyiʔs 196 lut təl sənx̌ʷúċəċtən, uł ałíʔ lkʷut
ks -xʷaʔ•xʷúy•iʔ -s lut tl sn+x̌ʷuċ•ċ+tn uł ałíʔ lkʷ=ut
futi^4 -go_repetitive futi^4 not from cut_something and because far
back and forth. *Not from sənx̌ʷúċəċtən, because it's far.*

197 ixíʔ uł kʷu łxʷuy kʷu łkxəntís axáʔ isłwílt ḱəl
ixíʔ uł kʷu ł+xʷuy kʷu ł+kx -nt -is axáʔ i -s+łw=ilt ḱl
then and 4kn go_back 4kn follow_back -nt -3erg this 1in -niece to
Then we went back, my nephew went back with me too, to

9 The s of the root √ʔys is lost before -łt.

198 ċúmlaʔxʷstsəlx {k} axáʔ iʔ k̓ inƛax̌əx̌ƛx̌áp iʔ
c -ʔúm=laʔxʷ -st -s -lx axáʔ iʔ k̓ in -ƛax̌•x̌•ƛx̌á+p iʔ
cust^ -call_a_place -^cust -3erg -pl this art to 1in -elders art
a place they call, my parents' country,

təmxʷúlaʔxʷsəlx t sənqəql'tús 199 uɬ aɬíʔ ixíʔ sənqəltúsx {k təl}
tmxʷ=úlaʔxʷ -s -lx t sn+q•ql'tʼ=us uɬ aɬíʔ ixíʔ s -n+qlt=us -x
land -3in -pl obl Little_Summit and so that ipftv^ -summit -^ipftv
'Little Summit." 10:02 *That's the little summit that goes from*

təl səntqəlɬxəwíltən 200 kiʔ ixíʔ uɬ axáʔ atláʔ {x̌ʷəyaʔɬpə} nx̌ʷəyaʔɬpítkʷ
tl sn+t+qlɬ+xwil+tn kiʔ ixíʔ uɬ axáʔ atláʔ n+x̌ʷyaʔ=ɬp=ítkʷ
from place_name rel then and this from_here Kettle_River
səntqəlɬxəwíltən, *and from here it's the Kettle River.*

201 ixíʔ uɬ nqəltús ixíʔ uɬ xíƛ̓laʔxʷ ixíʔ iʔ
ixíʔ uɬ n+ql+t=us ixíʔ uɬ xiƛ̓=laʔxʷ ixíʔ iʔ
then and summit then and level_land that art
It goes up to the summit, and then it's level land,

scələʕ̓ʷútx {ixíʔ uɬ} 202 sċx̌ilx uɬ a ċúmstsəlx t
sc -lʕ̓ʷ=ut -x sc+ʔx̌il+x uɬ a c -ʔum -st -s -lx t
ipftvp^ -valley -^ipftvp reason_why and art cust^ -call -^cust -3erg -pl obl
a valley. *That's why they call it*

sənqəqəl'tús 203 ixíʔ itlíʔ kʷu ɬ ċawsmáʔmáyaʔm
sn+q•ql'tʼ=us ixíʔ itlíʔ kʷu ɬ c -ʔaw+s+maʔ•máyaʔ+m
Little_Summit then from_there 4kn subord hab -go_to_school
"Little Summit." *From there we go to school.*

204 mat ċkin mat cilkst səxʷmʔúlaʔxʷtən iʔ səlkʷúts 205 uɬ
mat c+ʔkin mat cil=kst sxʷ=mʔ=úlaʔxʷ+tn iʔ s+lkʷ=ut -s uɬ
maybe how maybe five mile art distance -3in and
Maybe the distance is five miles. *And*

náx̌əmɬ kʷu ctkʷəllíw̓s uɬ iʔ kɬxəwíɬ ncəkʷmnáqs 206 uɬ
nax̌mɬ kʷu c -t+kʷl•l=iw̓s uɬ iʔ kɬ+xwiɬ n+ckʷ+mn=aqs uɬ
but 4kn hab -pl_on_horseback and art have_road wagon_road and
there is a road, a wagon road; *and*

put {kʷu c} kʷu cpənhíw̓səm iʔ k̓əl sənm̓aʔmáyaʔtən {uɬ} 207 ixí··ʔ məɬ
put kʷu c -pnh=iw̓s+m iʔ k̓l sn+maʔ•máyaʔ+tn ixíʔ mɬ
just 4kn hab -be_on_time art to school then and
we always get to school on time. *School*

np̓əƛ̓mús iʔ sənmaʔmáyaʔtən ixíʔ uɬ kʷu ɬxʷuy iʔ {k̓əl} k̓əl ƛax̌əx̌ƛx̌áps
n+p̓ƛ̓+m=us iʔ sn+m̓aʔ•m̓áyaʔ+tn ixíʔ uɬ kʷu ɬ+xʷuy iʔ k̓l ƛx̌•x̌•ƛx̌a+p -s
end art school then and 4kn go_back art to parents -3in
ended and then we went back to his parents, I went back

tkxəntín 208 uɬ ilíʔ {kʷu ɬ} kilíʔməntəm nk̓ʷəscaʔáqʷəm
t+kx -nt -in uɬ ilíʔ k+ilíʔ+m -nt -m nk̓ʷ+s+caʔáqʷ+m
follow -nt -1erg and there stay_with -nt -4erg all_summer
with him. 11:06 *Then we stay with them all summer.*

209 way̓ məł ałíʔ axáʔ pnicíʔ uł iʔ səp̓qíntəm uł sənkłc̓aʔsqáx̌aʔ
way̓ mł ałíʔ axáʔ pn+icíʔ uł iʔ sp̓=qin+tn uł sn+kł+c̓aʔ=sqáx̌aʔ
well and so this at_that_time and art thresher and horse
At that time there were threshing machines

kiʔ {c ki cə} cxʷists
kiʔ c -xʷy -st -s
rel cust^ -go -^cust -3erg
that go by horse power,

210 caʔkʷ cus iʔ {tan} ta
caʔkʷ cu -s iʔ t
as tell -3erg art agInst
they say

nuyápəxcən *horse power*
n+wyap=x=cn
say_in_English
in English 'horse power.'

211 way̓ uł ixíʔ {ts axáʔ ts} sənq̓ʷmám uł axáʔ
way̓ uł ixíʔ sn+q̓ʷma+m uł axáʔ
yes and that feeder[10] and this
And the feeder must have

ksəxʷník̓uʔsəm
k-sxʷ=ník̓=w̓s+m
have_cutter
a cutter.

212 uł axáʔ {a} naʔł isłəwílt uł ixíʔ kʷu
uł axáʔ naʔł i -s+łw=ilt uł ixíʔ kʷu
and this with 1in -niece and then 4kn
And with my nephew he and I cut

cník̓uʔsəm {inaud}
c -nik̓=w̓s+m
hab -cut_bundles
the bundles.

213 kʷu scəcámaʔts uł ixíʔ kʷu
kʷu s -c•cám̓+aʔt -s uł ixíʔ kʷu
4kn nom4^ -small -^nom4 and then 3e4obj
When we were small

ckəxstím {axáʔ iʔ t} axáʔ i tə lkasát
c -kx -st -im axáʔ i t lkasát
cust^ -follow -^cust -3e4obj this art agInst box
a box went with us, 12:02

214 lipúm a
lipúm a
apple art
an apple

lkasáts {ti}
lkasát -s
box -3in
box.

215 məł {kʷu} kʷu q̓aʔxəntím məł kʷu kt̓əwstíw̓s
mł kʷu q̓aʔ=xn -t -im mł kʷu k+t̓wst=iw̓s
and 3e4obj shoe -nt -3e4obj and 4kn stand_on
They put it under our feet, and we stand on it.

216 ixíʔ məł put k̓əłkícəntəm {i i} i l kscník̓uʔstət
ixíʔ mł put k̓ł+kic -nt -m iʔ l ksc -nik̓=w̓s -tt
then and just reach -nt -4erg art for futPerft^ -cut_in_middle -4in
Then we can reach the bundles.

217 ixíʔ
ixíʔ
then
Then

uł axáʔ inqíck itlíʔ iʔ knaqs {iʔ t} iʔ t k̓ík̓aʔt ixíʔ {c}
uł axáʔ in -qick itlíʔ iʔ k=naqs iʔ t kí•k̓aʔt ixíʔ
and this 1in -older_brother from_there art one_person art obl near that
my older brother, next to the oldest,

cmərím
c -mrim
hab -marry
got married.

218 ixíʔ uł łwis axáʔ {in} iʔ ƛ̓ax̌əx̌ƛ̓x̌áps uł ałíʔ
ixíʔ uł łwi -s axáʔ iʔ ƛ̓ax̌•x̌•ƛ̓x̌a+p -s uł ałíʔ
then and leave -3erg this art parents -3in and so
Then he left his folks, and he got a ranch

10 Is this a rake? The root suggests "pile."

way̓ cniłc kłtəmxʷúlaʔxʷ 219 uł ilíʔ kłcitxʷ, kłxƛ̓ap
way̓ cnił+c kł+tmxʷ=úlaʔxʷ uł ilíʔ kł+citxʷ kł+xƛ̓a+p
yes (s)he have_land and there have_house have_everything
of his own. *And he has a house, and everything.*

220 way̓ ixíʔ kʷu łx̌əlítsəlx axáʔ inƛ̓ax̌əx̌ƛ̓x̌áp 221 kʷu
way̓ ixíʔ kʷu ł+x̌lit -s -lx axáʔ in -ƛ̓ax̌•x̌•ƛ̓x̌á+p kʷu
well then 1obj summon_again -3erg -pl this 1in -elders 1obj
Then my folks asked me back. *They*

cúsəlx way̓ uł kʷu łtxətʼəntíxʷ anwí 222 way̓ axáʔ iʔ
cu -s -lx way̓ uł kʷu ł+t+xtʼ -nt -ixʷ anwí way̓ axáʔ iʔ
tell -3erg -pl yes and 1obj take_care_of_again -nt -2erg you yes this art
said to me, "Come back to take care of us. *Well, the one*

txətʼənxcútəntət way̓ uł kʷu łwíntəm 223 ałíʔ way̓ {taʔxʷ}
t+xtʼ+ncut+n -tt way̓ uł kʷu łwin -t -m ałíʔ way̓
care_giver -4in yes and 3e4obj leave -nt -3e4obj because yes
who takes care of us left us, *he*

taʔxʷstkəłmílxʷ, taʔxʷsnilíʔtən 224 ixíʔ uł {si} łkícən
taʔxʷ+s+tkł+m=ilxʷ taʔxʷ+sn+ilíʔ+tn ixíʔ uł ł+kic -n
get_wife get_place then and arrive_back -1erg
got married, he's got a home." 13:00 *That's when I got back home*

inƛ̓ax̌əx̌ƛ̓x̌áp 225 ixíʔ uł incá isənxətʼsíw̓səm isk̓ʷánłqəm uł
in -ƛ̓ax̌•x̌•ƛ̓x̌á+p ixíʔ uł in+cá i -s i -s -k̓ʷan=łq+m uł
1in -elders then and I 1i -intt 1i -intt -grow_crop and
to my parents, *then I continued from there planting crops,*

istáʔxʷłqəm iʔ l sk̓ʔáy 226 xi··ʔ uł kən xəƛ̓pspíntk ixíʔ uł
i -s -taʔxʷ=łq+m iʔ l s+k̓[ʔ]ay ixíʔ uł kn xƛ̓+p+s+pintk ixíʔ uł
1i -intt -get_crop art in autumn then and 1kn mature_age then and
harvesting them in the fall. *Then I came of age, and*

cun axáʔ {i} inƛ̓ax̌əx̌ƛ̓x̌áp 227 way̓ {kən ks} kən
cu -n axáʔ in -ƛ̓ax̌•x̌•ƛ̓x̌á+p way̓ kn
tell -1erg this 1in -elders yes 1kn
I said to my parents: *"I*

ksk̓ʷəl̓łtəkłmílxʷaʔx, kʷu cúsəlx, kʷu kəʕʷyncútmsəlx
ks -k̓ʷl̓+ł+tkł+m=ilxʷ -aʔx kʷu cu -s -lx kʷu k+ʕʷy+ncut+m -s -lx
incp^ -get_wife -^incp 1obj tell -3erg -pl 1obj laugh -3erg -pl
want to get a woman." They said to me, they laughed at me,

228 kʷu cúsəlx way̓ uyá kʷ qʷəňcənmíst 229 taʔlíʔ sisyús iʔ
kʷu cu -s -lx way̓ uyá kʷ qʷň=cn+mist taʔlíʔ sy•sy=us iʔ
1obj tell -3erg -pl well intj 2kn pitiful_thing very_much smart art
they said to me, "You poor pitiful thing. *It takes a good smart*

sqilxʷ kaʔ ck̓ʷəl̓łtkəłmílxʷəm ʕapnáʔ 230 sisyús i l sk̓ʷúl̓əm, uł
s+qilxʷ kiʔ c -k̓ʷl̓+ł+tkł+m=ilxʷ+m ʕapnáʔ sy•sy=us iʔ l s+k̓ʷul̓+m uł
person rel hab -get_wife now smart art at fixing and
man to get a woman nowadays, *smart in work;*

axáʔ maɬ anwí kʷ x̌ʷupt 231 kʷ t̓iʔt̓iʔmúɬ waẏ kʷ qʷəṅcənmíst
axáʔ maɬ anwí kʷ x̌ʷup+t kʷ t̓y•t̓y+m+uɬ waẏ kʷ qʷṅ=cn+mist
this too_much you 2kn weak 2kn lazy yes 2kn pitiful_thing
and you are good for nothing, you are lazy, you are pitiful.

232 taʔlí sqlaw {iʔ} iʔ təkɬmílxʷ ʕapnáʔ 233 cúnəlx lut,
taʔlíʔ s+qlaw iʔ tkɬmilxʷ ʕapnáʔ cu -n -lx lut
very_much money art wife now tell -1erg -pl not
It takes lots of money to keep a woman nowadays." 14:03 I said to them "No,

aɬíʔ ispuʔús waẏ kən xəƛ̓pspíntk 234 uɬ caʔkʷ cus axáʔ {a}
aɬíʔ i -s+puʔ=ús waẏ kn xƛ̓+p+s+pintk uɬ caʔkʷ cu -s axáʔ
because 1in -heart yes 1kn mature_age and as tell -3erg this
I want to, I am of age. Like they say

ia nqílxʷcən aɬíʔ {kʷu axáʔ is} iʔ sənkɬċaʔsqáx̌aʔ 235 kstaʔmínaʔ uɬ
iʔ n+qilxʷ=cn aɬíʔ iʔ sn+kɬ+ċaʔ=sqáx̌aʔ k+s+taʔm=ínaʔ uɬ
art Indian_language so art horse have_spring and
in Indian about horses, in the spring,

ɬaʔ cx̌ast ɬaʔ ċiɬnəm i l sʔistk 236 ixíʔ kstaʔmínaʔ məɬ
ɬaʔ c -x̌as+t ɬaʔ c -ʔiɬn+m iʔ l s+ʔis=tk ixíʔ k+s+taʔm=ínaʔ mɬ
when hab -good when hab -eat art in winter then have_spring and
when he eats well in the winter, in the spring he

ixíʔ kɬsəwpílxʷ 237 a· məɬ ixíʔ sqəcqíclxs, uɬ aɬíʔ {ks}
ixíʔ kɬ+sw+p=ilxʷ a mɬ ixíʔ s -qc•qic+lx -s uɬ aɬíʔ
then have_itchy_back intj and then nom -run -3i and so
itches in the back. Then he runs around, and he wants

ksláqʷnaʔx {hoy məɬ} 238 uɬ ilíʔ waẏ {kən} cəṁ kən x̌íləm {uɬ} uɬ aɬíʔ
ks -laqʷ=naʔ -x uɬ ilíʔ waẏ cṁ kn x̌il+m uɬ aɬíʔ
incp^ -shed_hair -^incp and there yes maybe 1kn do_like and so
the old hair off. And if that's what I am going to do,

cəṁ nċəxċíxəlɬmən 239 itíʔ kən ɬaʔ cqəcqícəlx kən ɬaʔ
cṁ n+ċx•ċix -ɬm -n itíʔ kn ɬaʔ c -qc•qic+lx kn ɬaʔ
maybe embarrass -5obj -1erg from_that 1kn when hab -run 1kn when
I'll get you embarrassed if I start running around

cmaʔkstəmɬtíɬən 240 uɬ aɬíʔ waẏ {kən} kən nnəx̌ʷnəx̌ʷíls
c -maʔ=kst+m=ɬtíɬn uɬ aɬíʔ waẏ kn n+nx̌ʷ•nx̌ʷ=ils
hab -bother_people and because yes 1kn want_wife
and bother people because I want a wife.

241 sċx̌ilx uɬ_i cúɬmən waẏ x̌ast lut iksx̌íləm 242 məɬ
sc_ʔx̌il+x uɬ_iʔ cu -ɬm -n waẏ x̌as+t lut i -ks -x̌il+m mɬ
reason_why and_then tell -5obj -1erg yes good not 1i -futi -do_like and
That's why I told you it's better I don't do that, 15:03 and

kən k̓ʷəl̓ɬtkəɬmílxʷəm 243 məɬ waẏ t̓iʔ_kʷṁiɬ uɬ itlíʔ kən nxət̓síẇsəm
kn k̓ʷl̓+ɬ+tkɬ+m=ilxʷ+m mɬ waẏ t̓iʔ_kʷṁiɬ uɬ itlíʔ kn n+xt̓+s=iẇs+m
1kn get_wife and yes at_once and from_there 1kn care_for
get a woman. And from then on I'll get back

kən k̓ʷúl̓əm {kən} 244 ixíʔ kʷu cúsəlx axáʔ inƛ̓ax̌əx̌ƛ̓x̌áp, way̓ way̓
kn k̓ʷul̓+m ixíʔ kʷu cu -s -lx axáʔ in -ƛ̓ax̌•x̌•ƛ̓x̌á+p way̓ way̓
1kn work then 1obj tell -3erg -pl this 1in -elders well well
to work again.” *My parents said to me, “Ok, if that's how*

mat aspuʔús. 245 náx̌əmɬ axáʔ iʔ kscúntsət way̓ taʔlí
mat a -s+puʔ=ús nax̌mɬ axáʔ iʔ ks -cun -t -s -t way̓ taʔlíʔ
maybe 2in -heart but this art futt^ -tell -nt -2obj -4erg well much
you feel. *But we are going to tell you one thing,*

kʷu ƛ̓ax̌əx̌ƛ̓x̌áp 246 uɬ lut qəɬnúntəm ksʔamɬtsít {a}
kʷu ƛ̓ax̌•x̌•ƛ̓x̌á+p uɬ lut qɬ -nu -nt -m ks -ʔam -ɬt -s -it
4kn elders and not able -manage -nt -4erg futt^ -feed -ɬt -2obj -4erg
we are very old, *and we cannot feed*

antkəɬmílxʷ kəm̓ kʷ ɬə taʔxʷsqʷəsqʷasíʔa 247 uɬ aɬíʔ way̓ uɬ kʷu
an -tkɬ+m=ilxʷ km̓ kʷ ɬ taʔxʷ+s+qʷs•qʷasíʔa uɬ aɬíʔ way̓ uɬ kʷu
2in -wife or 2kn if have_children and because well and 4kn
your wife or when you get them, children. *We are*

x̌ʷəptwílx, uɬ way̓ náx̌əmɬ t anwí ʔamtíxʷ {as} kʷ ɬ taʔxʷsqʷəsqʷasíʔa
x̌ʷp+t+wilx uɬ way̓ nax̌mɬ t anwí ʔam -t -ixʷ kʷ ɬ taʔxʷ+s+qʷs•qʷasíʔa
grow_weak and yes so agInst you feed -nt -2erg 2kn if have_children
not able; when you get children you have to feed them,

248 t anwí txət̓əntíxʷ naʔɬ antəkɬmílxʷ 249 cúnəlx
t anwí t+xt̓ -nt -ixʷ naʔɬ an -tkɬ+m=ilxʷ cu -n -lx
agInst you watch_so -nt -2erg and 2in -wife tell -1erg -pl
you and your wife will have to take care of them.” *I told them*

way̓ {kəma} kma p ist̓k̓ʷílsəm, way̓ ixíʔ uɬ_i {kən i} kən
way̓ km+a p i -s -t̓k̓ʷ=ils+m way̓ ixíʔ uɬ_iʔ kn
well or_not 5kʷu 1i -intt -depend_on well then and_then 1kn
“I wasn't going to depend on you, that's why I will leave

cənkʷlxʷúlaʔxʷ 250 ixíʔ uɬ kən c̓imx uɬ {k̓əl} k̓la nspíləm kiʔ kən
c -n+kʷl+x=úlaʔxʷ ixíʔ uɬ kn c -ʔimx uɬ k̓l n+s+pil+m kiʔ kn
hab -leave_country then and 1kn hab -move and to Nespelem rel I
the country.” 16:07 *That's why I moved plum to Nespelem and that's where I*

ƛ̓əlpúlaʔxʷ 251 ilíʔ kən kʷəɬnúlaʔxʷ təl̓ swaʔwílaʔxʷ 252 sílxʷaʔ
ƛ̓l+p=úlaʔxʷ ilíʔ kn kʷɬn=úlaʔxʷ tl̓ s+waʔ•wílaʔxʷ sílxʷaʔ
settle there 1kn rent_a_place from m's_name big
settled down. *I rented a place from Antoine,* *it's a big*

təmxʷúlaʔxʷ, uɬ {k} ksl̓úsaʔmən ixíʔ iʔ təmxʷúlaʔxʷ 253 uɬ nák̓ʷəm t̓iʔ
tmxʷ=úlaʔxʷ uɬ k+sl̓=úsaʔ+m -n ixíʔ iʔ tmxʷ=úlaʔxʷ uɬ nakʷ+m t̓iʔ
land and be_deceived -1erg that art land and evid evid
place, but that ranch deceived me. *The good soil*

ckɬpəpq̓ʷúsaʔx iʔ t x̌ast {iʔ t} iʔ t ɬúkʷlaʔxʷ 254 ixíʔ kən
s -kɬ+p•pq̓ʷ=úsaʔ -x iʔ t x̌as+t iʔ t ɬúkʷ=laʔxʷ ixíʔ kn
ipftv^ -on_top -^ipftv art obl good art obl dirt then 1kn
is [only] right on top of the ground.

ɬ wiʔsk̓ʷánɬqəm {a kəl a ɬ} k̓ʷúl̓ən iʔ k̓əɬʕal̓mín 255 uɬ kən
ɬ wy̓+s+k̓ʷan=ɬq+m k̓ʷul̓ -n iʔ k̓ɬ+ʕal̓+mín uɬ kn
when finish_planting make -1erg art fence and 1kn
I got done putting the crops in, and I fenced it. I was

ɬaʔɬaʔx̌ʷúlaʔxʷəm ixíʔ kiʔ mipnún way̓ lut nák̓ʷəm axáʔ iʔ
ɬaʔ•ɬaʔx̌ʷ=úlaʔxʷ+m ixíʔ kiʔ my+p -nu -n way̓ lut nak̓ʷ+m axáʔ iʔ
dig_post_hole then rel learn -manage -1erg yes not evid this art
digging post holes, and that's when I found out this land is

təmxʷúlaʔxʷ 256 tanm̓ús kiʔtlaxʷs {s sx̌} sx̌əsʕáċəċx 257 way̓
tmxʷ=úlaʔxʷ tanm̓=ús ? s -x̌s+ʕaċ•ċ -x way̓
land nothing ? ipftv^ -good_to_look_at -^ipftv well
no good. It's just good to look at. 17:02 Then

ixíʔ kən {ɬ} táxʷɬqəm uɬ way̓ lut 258 uɬ aɬíʔ pnicí uɬ axáʔ
ixíʔ kn taxʷ=ɬq+m uɬ way̓ lut uɬ aɬíʔ pn+icíʔ uɬ axáʔ
then 1kn harvest and well not and so at_that_time and this
I harvested, but no. At that time we had a

kɬʔaʔáx̌ʷəx̌ʷ {iʔ} iʔ x̌ʷíc̓laʔxʷtən {i l} i l səlk̓íw̓səm 259 uɬ axáʔ {i s} iʔ
kɬ+ʔa•ʔáx̌ʷ•x̌ʷ iʔ x̌ʷíc̓=laʔxʷ+tn iʔ l s+lk̓=iw̓s+m uɬ axáʔ iʔ
have_wrapper art mower art in tie_bundles and this art
wrapper machine to cut the grain to tie bundles. The hay

səsp̓qín isk̓ʷánɬq x̌əcəcíkstɬt̓áq̓əmkst *acre* 260 ixíʔ uɬ axáʔ
s•sp̓=qin i -s+k̓ʷan=ɬq x̌c•c=ikst+ɬ+t̓áq̓m=kst ixíʔ uɬ axáʔ
wheat 1in -harvest one_hundred_six then and this
I harvested was one hundred and six acres, and

iscksupúlaʔxʷ mat k̓əl təmɬʔúpənkst sənckʷmín isct̓əqt̓áq
i -sc -k+s+wp=úlaʔxʷ mat k̓l tmɬ+ʔupn=kst sn+ckʷ+min i -sc -t̓q•t̓aq
1i -pftv -have_hay maybe about eighty ton 1i -pftv -stack
the hay I got was about eighty tons that I stacked.

261 uɬ axáʔ sílxʷaʔ axáʔ iʔ sənk̓ʷánɬqtən axáʔ i l cəcámaʔt 262 axáʔ {ɬ}
uɬ axáʔ sílxʷaʔ axáʔ iʔ sn+k̓ʷan=ɬq+tn axáʔ i l c+cám̓aʔ+t axáʔ
and this big this art garden this 1i in small this
And there was a big garden of small stuff, potatoes,

patáq uɬ liplí {uɬ} uɬ pins 263 uɬ aɬíʔ yaʕyáʕt itlíʔ kən nstils
patáq uɬ liplí uɬ pins uɬ aɬíʔ yaʕ•yáʕ+t itlíʔ kn n+st=ils
potato and corn and beans and so all from_there 1kn think
corn, beans. 18:00 And I thought I could sell

ńíńw̓iʔ tumístmən 264 ixíʔ itlíʔ ńíńw̓iʔ kən taʔxʷsqláw {uɬ}
ńíńw̓iʔ tw+mist+m -n ixíʔ itlíʔ ńíńw̓iʔ kn taʔxʷ+s+qláw
a_while sell -1erg then from_there a_while 1kn get_money
some of that, and get money from that.

265 uɬ axáʔ {kʷu} kʷu ksck̓əɬp̓ap̓áʕʔ[11] kʷu k̓əɬp̓aʔp̓ʔʕám {s} tumístməntəm
uɬ axáʔ kʷu k+sc+k̓ɬ+p̓a•p̓áʔ kʷu k̓ɬ+p̓aʔ•p̓ʔá+m tw+mist+m -nt -m
and this 4kn have_milk_cow 4kn milk_cows sell -nt -4erg
And we had milk cows, and we could milk them and sell

iʔ skɬc̓káp 266 uɬ aɬíʔ pnicíʔ uɬ ɬaʔ ksnʔiys iʔ
iʔ s+kɬ+c̓ka+p uɬ aɬíʔ pn+icíʔ uɬ ɬaʔ k+sn+ʔiys iʔ
art cream and so at_that_time and the_one_that have_price art
the cream. *And at that time cream wasn't*

skɬc̓kap 267 mat ʔúpənks sens i 1 naqs nʕast axáʔ iʔ skɬc̓kap
s+kɬ+c̓ka+p mat ʔupn=kst sens iʔ 1 naqs naʕs+t axáʔ iʔ s+kɬ+c̓ka+p
cream maybe ten cents art for one pound this art cream
worth much, *cream was maybe ten cents a pound,*

268 uɬ aɬíʔ pnicíʔ uɬ {lut'a kʷa} lut {t'akɬ} t'a kɬnʔaʔúkʷmən
uɬ aɬíʔ pn+icíʔ uɬ lut t' kɬ+n+ʔa•ʔúkʷ+mn
and so at_that_time and not negfac have_delivery
and at that time there was no delivery.

269 caʔkʷ cus iʔ ta nuyápəxcən lut t'a kɬtrək, t'a
caʔkʷ cu -s iʔ t n+wyap=x=cn lut t' kɬ+trək t'
as tell -3erg art agInst say_in_English not negfac have_truck negfac
As they say in White people's language there is no truck or

kstiṁ 270 waẏ kmix t sənkɬc̓aʔsqáx̌aʔ sənkɬc̓aʔsqáx̌aʔ kiʔ
k+s+tiṁ waẏ kmix t sn+kɬ+c̓aʔ=sqáx̌aʔ sn+kɬ+c̓aʔ=sqáx̌aʔ kiʔ
have_something well only obl horse horse rel
anything. *It's only with horses that*

sc̓akʷstísəlx iʔ sc̓íɬən iʔ stiṁ {iʔ} iʔ ƛ̓áqnaʔ
c[12] -ʔakʷ -st -is -lx iʔ sc+ʔiɬn iʔ stiṁ iʔ ƛ̓áq=naʔ
cust^ -haul -^cust -3erg -pl art groceries art whatever art bag
they deliver food and things, sacks,

271 t'əxʷ iʔ caʔkʷ cus iʔ ta nuyápəxcən iʔ *freight* 272 uɬ
t'xʷ iʔ caʔkʷ cu -s iʔ t n+wyap=x=cn iʔ uɬ
evidently art as tell -3erg art agInst say_in_English art and
like they say in English "freight." 19:01 *And*

sc̓x̌ilx kaʔ nsəlxʷaʔáqsəm, uɬ axáʔ iʔ sk̓ʷanɬq lut t'a ksnʔiys
sc+ʔx̌il+x kiʔ n+slxʷaʔ=áqs+m uɬ axáʔ iʔ s+k̓ʷan=ɬq lut t' k+sn+ʔiys
reason_why rel expensive and this art harvest not negfac have_price
that's why it's so high priced, and this grain has got no price.

273 uɬ aɬíʔ k̓la lkʷut lkʷut kiʔ aʔksnx̌ʷáq̓ʷmən[13] 274 k̓la nsq̓ʷut axáʔ ta
uɬ aɬíʔ k̓l lkʷ=ut lkʷ=ut kiʔ k+sn+x̌ʷaq̓ʷ+mn k̓l n+s+q̓ʷut axáʔ t
and so to far far rel have_mill to other_side this obl
It's far, far that they have a mill, *across the Columbia*

nx̌ʷəntkʷítkʷ 275 c̓úmlaʔxʷɬtsəlx t *Davenport* 276 uɬ ixíʔ
n+x̌ʷn=tkʷ=itkʷ c -ʔúm=laʔxʷ -ɬt -s -lx t uɬ ixíʔ
Kettle_River cust^ -call_a_place -ɬt -3erg -pl obl and then
River, *they call it Davenport.* *And when*

11 The pharyngeals of this stem are uncertain.
12 This is the expected form. The s- is unexplained.
13 The aʔ- of this and similar forms seems to be an amalgam of the article and kɬ+.

mat ʔaslásq̓ət kaʔɬlásq̓ət mi kʷ ckʷam iʔ t səsp̓qín mi kʷ
mat ʔasl=ásq̓t kaʔɬl=ásq̓t mi kʷ ckʷa+m iʔ t s•sp̓=qin mi kʷ
maybe two_days three_days fut 2kn pull art obj_itr wheat fut 2kn
you haul wheat it's two or three days to

ɬckicx 277 uɬ sc̓x̌ilx lut t̓a ksənʔíys axáʔ {la} la nspíləm
ɬ+c+kic+x uɬ sc+ʔx̌il+x lut t̓ k+sn+ʔiys axáʔ l n+s+pil+m
arrive_cisl_again and reason_why not negfac have_price this in Nespelem
get back, *and that's why there is no price for anything in Nespelem.*

278 way̓ uɬ ilíʔ kən k̓ʷúl̓əm i l snəqsíɬxʷəm suyápix axáʔ { i l an}
way̓ uɬ ilíʔ kn k̓ʷul̓+m i l s+nqs=iɬxʷ+m s+wyapy=x axáʔ
well and there 1kn work intj for neighbor white_person this
And I started to work for a white man next door on

i l səp̓əp̓qíntən 279 t̓áq̓əmkst skaʕcíw̓s ilíʔ isk̓ʷúl̓əm
iʔ l sp̓•p̓=qin+tn t̓aq̓m=kst s+k+ʕac=íw̓s ilíʔ i -s -k̓ʷul̓+m
art on threshing_machine six week there 1i -nom -work
the threshing machine; *I worked there six weeks.*

280 uɬ t sənkɬc̓aʔsqáx̌aʔ kiʔ cəcəkʷstís mat kən nstílsəm
uɬ t sn+kɬ+c̓aʔ=sqáx̌aʔ kiʔ c -ckʷ -st -is mat kn n+st=ils+m
and agInst horse rel cust^ -pull -^cust -3erg maybe 1kn think
It's horses that pull it, I think

ʔupənkstɬt̓áq̓əmkst iʔ sənkɬc̓aʔsqáx̌aʔ 281 ixíʔ cəcəkʷstís axáʔ iʔ
ʔupn=kst+ɬ+t̓áq̓m=kst iʔ sn+kɬ+c̓aʔ=sqáx̌aʔ ixíʔ c -ckʷ -st -is axáʔ iʔ
sixteen art horse that cust^ -pull -^cust -3erg this art
sixteen horses, 20:07 *that's*

səp̓əp̓qíntən 282 a uɬ axáʔ iʔ suyápix xʷʔit iʔ
sp̓•p̓=qin+tn a uɬ axáʔ iʔ s+wyapy=x xʷʔi+t iʔ
threshing_machine intj and this art white_person many art
what pulls the thresher. *And that white man has lots of*

kəw̓wáps 283 ixíʔ ʕác̓ənt ʔupənkstɬt̓áq̓əmkst {i l} i l səp̓p̓qíntən
kw•w•ap -s ixíʔ ʕac̓ -nt ʔupn=kst+ɬ+t̓áq̓m=kst iʔ l sp̓•p̓=qin+tn
horses -3in then look -nt sixteen art for threshing_machine
horses. *Look, sixteen for the thresher,*

284 uɬ axáʔ {i} x̌əx̌n̓út iʔ sq̓əq̓əyksqáx̌aʔ yaʕyáʕt stúɬc̓aʔ 285 uɬ
uɬ axáʔ x̌•x̌n̓ut iʔ s+q̓•q̓y̓k=sqáx̌aʔ yaʕ•yáʕ+t s+túɬ=c̓aʔ uɬ
and this nine art colts all mule and
and nine colts, all mules. *And*

yaʕyáʕt {iʔ} iʔ kɬk̓ʷúl̓məns, axáʔ iʔ t̓lúlaʔxʷtən 286 yaʕyáʕt {il} i l
yaʕ•yáʕ+t iʔ kɬ -k̓ʷul̓+mn -s axáʔ iʔ t̓l=úlaʔxʷ+tn yaʕ•yáʕ+t iʔ l
all art to_be -tool -3i this art plow all art for
all the implements, the plow, *all the tools*

sk̓ʷánɬqəm iʔ k̓ʷúl̓məns 287 yaʕyáʕt ixíʔ ctxət̓stís uɬ
s+k̓ʷan=ɬq+m iʔ k̓ʷul̓+mn -s yaʕ•yáʕ+t ixíʔ c -txt̓ -st -is uɬ
planting art tool -3in all that cust^ -watch_so -^cust -3erg and
for planting. *He takes care of all that, and then*

sic nixʷ 288 uɬ nixʷ cḱəɬp̓aʔp̓ʔʕam iʔ x̌əl sqʔim 289 uɬ ixíʔ kʷu
sic nixʷ uɬ nixʷ c -ḱɬ+p̓aʔ•p̓ʔʕám iʔ x̌l s+qʔim uɬ ixíʔ kʷu
then also and also hab -milk_cow art for milk and then 1obj
he has cows, and also milk cows for milk. And that

cus axáʔ ixíʔ t suyápix 290 way̓ kʷ sisyús kʷ sqilxʷ way̓
cu -s axáʔ ixíʔ t s+wyapy=x way̓ kʷ sy•sy=us kʷ s+qilxʷ way̓
tell -3erg this that agInst white_person yes 2kn smart 2kn Indian yes
white man said to me: "You are a smart Indian, you

kʷ ḱʷəl̓ḱʷl̓úɬ, uɬ {kʷ ə} kʷ mymyikst 291 way̓ t̓iʔ máyaʔɬtsən
kʷ ḱʷl̓•ḱʷl̓+uɬ uɬ kʷ my•my=ikst way̓ t̓iʔ m̓áyaʔ -ɬt -s -n
2kn good_worker and 2kn skilled yes evid tell -ɬt -2obj -1erg
are a good worker, and you are handy. 21:04 All I got to do is tell you,

aksck̓ʷúl̓ məɬ t anwí ḱʷúləntxʷ 292 lut t̓a
a -k+s+c -ḱʷul̓ mɬ t anwí ḱʷul̓ -nt -xʷ lut t̓
2i -futPerfi -do and agInst you do -nt -2erg not negfac
and you'll do the rest. I don't

cxʷəsmaʔcínmstmən kəm̓ t̓a cəcústmən
c -xʷs=maʔ=cín+m -st -m -n km̓ t̓ c -cu -st -m -n
cust^ -rush -^cust -2obj -1erg or negfac cust^ -tell -^cust -2obj -1erg
have to rush you, or to tell you,

293 way̓ ixíʔ ńíńw̓iʔ aksck̓ʷúl̓ 294 uɬ sc̓x̌ilx kiʔ
way̓ ixíʔ ńíńw̓iʔ a -k+s+c -ḱʷul̓ uɬ sc+ʔx̌il+x kiʔ
yes then a_while 2i -futPerfi -work and reason_why rel
and you'll work. That's why

nqʷəńmíntsən uɬ axáʔ iʔ c̓əx̌ʷəntsín 295 ʕác̓ənt
n+qʷń+mi -nt -s -n uɬ axáʔ iʔ c̓x̌ʷ -nt -s -in ʕac̓ -nt
feel_sorry_for -nt -2obj -1erg and this art lecture -nt -2obj -1erg look -nt
I feel sorry for you, and I'm telling you. Look,

axáʔ kʷu wikɬtxʷ ink̓ʷúl̓mən inkəw̓wáp yaʕyáʕt {iʔ} iʔ stim̓
axáʔ kʷu wik -ɬt -xʷ in -ḱʷul̓+mn in -kw̓•w•ap yaʕ•yáʕ+t iʔ stim̓
this 1obj see -ɬt -2erg 1in -tool 1in -horses all art thing
you see all my implements, my horses, everything?

296 yaʕyáʕt ixíʔ isckʷúɬən 297 a cəlkspíntk {ki} kiʔ kən
yaʕ•yáʕ+t ixíʔ i -sc -kʷuɬn a cl=ks+pin=tk kiʔ kn
all that 1i -pftv -borrow intj five_years rel 1kn
I borrowed everything. It's five years since

skʷɬənúlaʔxʷəxʷ 298 uɬ ʔax̌əlspíntk naqs *thousand* sqlaw
s -kʷɬn=úlaʔxʷ -xʷ uɬ ʔax̌l+s+pín=tk naqs s+qlaw
ipftv^ -rent_a_place -^ipftv and every_year one money
I rented the place, and every year I lose one thousand

iksk̓əɬʔilál 299 way̓ məɬ itlíʔ nixʷ kən ɬkʷúɬən t sqlaw
i -ks -ḱɬ+y̓l•al way̓ mɬ itlíʔ nixʷ kn ɬ+kʷuɬn t s+qlaw
1i -futi -lose well and from_there again 1kn borrow_again obj_itr money
dollars. Then I borrow money again, and I plant

kən ɬk̓ʷánɬqəm 300 way̓ məɬ ixíʔ {kən tliʔ} ixíʔ {kən tliʔ} kən ɬ
kn ɬ+k̓ʷan=ɬq+m way̓ mɬ ixíʔ ixíʔ kn ɬ
1kn plant_again well and then then 1kn when
a garden again. *And when I get done harvesting,*

wiʔstáxʷɬqəm wiʔstumístmən 301 məɬ itlíʔ nixʷ naqs *thousand*
wy̓+s+taxʷ=ɬq+m wy̓+s+tw+mist+m -n mɬ itlíʔ nixʷ naqs
finish_harvest finish_sell -1erg and from_there again one
and get done selling it, 22:02 *then I get behind one thousand*

iksk̓əɬʔilál 302 cut ʕapnáʔ uɬ cəlkspíntk {kiʔ} ixíʔ uɬ np̓ƛ̓mus
i -ks -k̓ɬ+y̓l•al cut ʕapnáʔ uɬ cl=ks+pin=tk ixíʔ uɬ n+p̓ƛ̓m=us
1i -futi -lose say now and five_years then and end
again." *He said "And now it's five years and this is the last,*

303 ixíʔ uɬ cilkst *thousand* iksk̓ɬʔilál 304 uɬ aɬíʔ yaʕyáʕt
ixíʔ uɬ cil=kst i -ks -k̓ɬ+y̓l•al uɬ aɬíʔ yaʕ•yáʕ+t
then and five 1i -futi -lose and so all
and I am five thousand behind. *And I borrowed*

isckʷúlən 305 tkʷúɬnmən axáʔ {is} ink̓ʷúl̓mən, inkəw̓wáp,
i -sc -kʷuln t+kʷuɬn+m -n axáʔ in -k̓ʷul̓+mn in -kw̓•w•ap
1i -pftv -borrow borrow_for -1erg this 1in -tool 1in -horses
[for] everything: *I borrowed for my implements, my horses,*

yaʕyáʕt iʔ stim̓ 306 uɬ cəm̓ t̓iʔ_kmix naʔɬ intkɬmílxʷ uɬ
yaʕ•yáʕ+t iʔ stim̓ uɬ cm̓ t̓iʔ_kmix naʔɬ in -tkɬ+m=ilxʷ uɬ
all art thing and maybe only with 1in -wife and
everything. *And it's just my wife and*

isqʷəsqʷasíʔa 307 kmix cəm̓ t̓iʔ kʷu cɬəɬáxʷ 308 məɬ atláʔ {kʷu}
i -s+qʷs•qʷasíʔa kmix cm̓ t̓iʔ kʷu c -ɬ•ɬaxʷ mɬ atláʔ
1in -children only maybe evid 4kn hab -dress and from_here
my children, *just what we have on our backs.* *The bank*

kʷu qíxʷəntəm axáʔ iʔ {ti} ta ksnqláwtən 309 iʔ {kʷu} kʷu
kʷu qixʷ -nt -m axáʔ iʔ t k+sn+qlaw+tn iʔ kʷu
3e4obj drive -nt -3e4obj this art agInst bank art 3e4obj
will drive us out, *they will*

tumístməɬtəm yaʕyáʕt iʔ stímtət 310 uɬ sc̓x̌ilx kiʔ
tw+mist+m -ɬt -m yaʕ•yáʕ+t iʔ stim̓ -tt uɬ sc+ʔx̌il+x kiʔ
sell -ɬt -3e4obj all art thing -4in and reason_why rel
sell everything we have. *That's why I'm*

c̓əx̌ʷəntsín uɬ way̓ myaɬ kʷ sisyús {kʷ} i l sk̓ʷúləm
c̓x̌ʷ -nt -s -in uɬ way̓ myaɬ kʷ sy•sy=us iʔ l s+k̓ʷul̓+m
lecture -nt -2obj -1erg nd yes too_much 2kn smart art at fixing
telling you, you're smart in working,

311 uɬ way̓ t̓iʔ kʷu qəpəntíxʷ 312 way̓ t̓iʔ x̌ast kʷ ɬaʔ
uɬ way̓ t̓iʔ kʷu qp -nt -ixʷ way̓ t̓iʔ x̌as+t kʷ ɬaʔ
and yes evid 1obj predicament -nt -2erg well evid good 2kn when
you'll go just like me. *It's better that*

nk̓ətpmíst mi atláʔ kʷ ɬ kʷəlxʷúlaʔxʷ 313 taʔlíʔ {ɬ}
n+k̓t+p+mist mi atláʔ kʷ ɬ kʷl+x=úlaʔxʷ taʔlíʔ
still_time fut from_here 2kn subord leave_country very_much
before it's too late you get away from here. *This place*

kcəxʷʔúsaʔmən axáʔ iʔ təmxʷúlaʔxʷ 314 uɬ mat anwí ilíʔ nixʷ kʷ
k+cxʷʔ=úsaʔ+m -n axáʔ iʔ tmxʷ=úlaʔxʷ uɬ mat anwí ilíʔ nixʷ kʷ
be_fooled -1erg this art land and maybe you there also 2kn
fooled my eyes; 23:02 *I think you must have done*

sənʔaxəlílsx 315 waẏ cun waẏ ixíʔ k̓áẏilx 316 ixíʔ uɬ
s -n+ʔaxl=íls -x waẏ cu -n waẏ ixíʔ k̓aẏ•y+lx ixíʔ uɬ
ipftv^ -think_so -^ipftv well tell -1erg yes then become_fall then and
the same." *I said, "Fall is coming.* *I sold*

tumístmən iʔ səsp̓qín isctáxʷɬq 317 kmix sk̓ʷut i l naqs
tw+mist+m -n iʔ s•sp̓=qin i -sc -taxʷ=ɬq kmix s+k̓ʷut iʔ l naqs
sell -1erg art wheat 1i -pftv -harvest only half art for one
the wheat I harvested, *only half dollar*

kilʼwíc̓aʔ 318 uɬ axáʔ iʔ supúlaʔxʷ uɬ lut t̓ tumstnún
k+ylw=íc̓aʔ uɬ axáʔ iʔ s+wp=úlaʔxʷ uɬ lut t̓ tw+mst -nu -n
bushel and this art hay and not negfac sell -manage -1erg
for a bushel; *and I couldn't sell the hay;*

319 uɬ axáʔ {iʔ} iʔ patáq uɬ iʔ pins iʔ liplí 320 ixíʔ kən k̓aʕʷmíst
uɬ axáʔ iʔ patáq uɬ iʔ pins iʔ liplí ixíʔ kn k̓aʕʷ+míst
and this art potato and art beans art corn then 1kn hire
and the potatoes, the beans, the corn. *I hired*

t ikɬkənxcútən kən ɬ ƛ̓qáɬqəm {uɬ} 321 uɬ axáʔ iʔ pins
t i -kɬ -kn+x+cut+n kn ɬ ƛ̓q=aɬq+m uɬ axáʔ iʔ pins
obj_itr 1i -to_be -help 1kn subord dig_crop and this art beans
a helper to dig potatoes, *and he threshed*

ixíʔ {kʷuksəp̓} kʷu ksəp̓ɬtísəlx 322 uɬ axáʔ iʔ liplí k̓əɬx̌ʷíƛ̓səlx
ixíʔ kʷu k+sp̓ -ɬt -is -lx uɬ axáʔ iʔ liplí k̓ɬ+x̌ʷiƛ̓ -s -lx
that 1obj thresh -ɬt -3erg -pl and this art corn shuck -3erg -pl
the beans for me, *and he shucked the corn.*

323 uɬ axáʔ iʔ patáq kiʔ ɬ tumístmən uɬ kmix kaʔɬís kʷaʕtá iʔ
uɬ axáʔ iʔ patáq kiʔ ɬ tw+mist+m -n uɬ kmix kaʔɬís kʷaʕtá iʔ
and this art potato rel when sell -1erg and only three quarter art
And when I sold the potatoes the price was just six bits

sənʔíysc {iʔ} iʔ k̓əɬnáqs 324 uɬ axáʔ iʔ liplí kʷaʕtá iʔ k̓əɬnáqs 325 uɬ
sn+ʔiys -c iʔ k̓ɬ+naqs uɬ axáʔ iʔ liplí kʷaʕtá iʔ k̓ɬ+naqs uɬ
price -3in art one_sack and this art corn quarter art one_sack and
a sack, 24:05 *and corn twenty five cents a sack,* *and*

axáʔ {iʔ} iʔ pins ʔasilɬsk̓ʷút {iʔ} iʔ l x̌əccíkst 326 waẏ ixíʔ {kən ɬ}
axáʔ iʔ pins ʔasl+ɬ+s+k̓ʷút iʔ l x̌c•c=ikst waẏ ixíʔ
this art beans two_and_half art for hundred well then
the beans two and a half a hundred pounds. *I broke even,*

nxəƛ̓púsən, yaʕyáʕt tumístmən 327 nxəƛ̓púsən yaʕyáʕt i
n+xƛ̓+p=us -n yaʕ•yáʕ+t tw+mist+m -n n+xƛ̓+p=us -n yaʕ•yáʕ+t iʔ
break_even -1erg all sell -1erg break_even -1erg all art
I sold everything, *I broke even*

l inxʷəlxʷílt ilíʔ 328 ki waẏ kən ɬc̓imx itlíʔ ixíʔ aláʔ
l in -xʷl•xʷilt ilíʔ kiʔ waẏ kn ɬ+c+ʔimx itlíʔ ixíʔ aláʔ
with 1in -debt there rel yes 1kn move_back_cisl from_there then here
with all I owed." *I moved back from there,*

la ncaʔlím {kən ɬc} kən ɬct̓qlímx 329 ilíʔ isənɬx̌əmtán, ilíʔ uɬ
l n+caʔlím kn ɬ+c+t̓ql=imx ilíʔ i -sn+ɬx̌m+tan ilíʔ uɬ
in Inchelium 1kn settle_back_cisl there 1in -in_law there and
and I settled in Inchelium. *That's where my in-laws are, and*

kən ʔístkəm 330 uɬ ixíʔ taʔmúlaʔxʷ uɬ iʔ ah 331 ixíʔ uɬ kən {ɬ}
kn ʔis=tk+m uɬ ixíʔ taʔm=úlaʔxʷ uɬ iʔ ah ixíʔ uɬ kn
1kn winter and then snow_melt and art intj then and 1kn
I wintered there. *Spring came* *and I*

nk̓əwpəlsúlaʔxʷ, ɬtxʷúymən axáʔ inƛ̓ax̌əx̌ƛ̓x̌áp̓ 332 uɬ aɬíʔ ilíʔ kən
n+k̓w+p=ls=úlaʔxʷ ɬ+t+xʷuy+m -n axáʔ in -ƛ̓ax̌•x̌•ƛ̓x̌á+p uɬ aɬíʔ ilíʔ kn
miss_country go_back_to -1erg this 1in -elders and so there 1kn
got lonesome for the country, I went to see my folks. 25:02 *I had*

ksk̓ʷánɬq {əʔ} 333 t̓əxʷ {yə} yaʕyáʕt iʔ sk̓ʷanɬq ilíʔ ʔax̌əltúɬtən axáʔ
k+s+k̓ʷan=ɬq t̓xʷ yaʕ•yáʕ+t iʔ s+k̓ʷan=ɬq ilíʔ ʔax̌l -tuɬt -n axáʔ
have_harvest emph all art garden there turn -tuɬt -1erg this
a garden there, *and I had turned it over to*

inƛ̓ax̌əx̌ƛ̓x̌áp̓ 334 ixíʔ təmxʷúlaʔxʷsəlx, aɬíʔ q̓əẏúlaʔxʷtənsəlx
in -ƛ̓ax̌•x̌•ƛ̓x̌á+p ixíʔ tmxʷ=úlaʔxʷ -s -lx aɬíʔ q̓ẏ=úlaʔxʷ+tn -s -lx
1in -elders that land -3in -pl so allotment -3in -pl
my folks. *That's their land, their allotment;*

335 uɬ axáʔ kmix incá kən i l inq̓əẏúlaʔxʷtən {ixíʔ} 336 ixíʔ
uɬ axáʔ kmix in+cá kn iʔ l in -q̓ẏ=úlaʔxʷ+tn ixíʔ
and this only I 1kn art in 1in -allotment that
and as for my allotment, *I gave*

xʷíc̓əɬtən axáʔ inqíck iʔ sxʔitx 337 cun waẏ anwí
xʷic̓ -ɬt -n axáʔ in -qick iʔ s+xʔit=x cu -n waẏ anwí
give -ɬt -1erg this 1in -older_brother art oldest_one tell -1erg well you
that to my brother the oldest one. *I said to him,*

ixíʔ k̓ʷúləntxʷ 338 x̌ʷíc̓laʔxʷəntxʷ uɬ səp̓qíntxʷ uɬ
ixíʔ k̓ʷul̓ -nt -xʷ x̌ʷic̓=laʔxʷ -nt -xʷ uɬ sp̓=qin -t -xʷ uɬ
that work -nt -2erg mow -nt -2erg and thresh -nt -2erg and
"You work it. *You cut it and thresh it, and we'll share*

tx̌ʷíw̓səntəm 339 waẏ kən ɬkicx ik̓líʔ, kʷu cus axáʔ
tx̌ʷ=iw̓s -nt -m waẏ kn ɬ+kic+x ik̓líʔ kʷu cu -s axáʔ
middle -nt -4erg well 1kn arrive_again there 1obj tell -3erg this
in half." *When I got back my brother*

inqíck waỷ 340 waỷ ixíʔ {a} asḱʷánɬq cənpákʷ ilíʔ, i l
in -qick waỷ waỷ ixíʔ a -s+ḱʷan=ɬq c -n+pakʷ ilíʔ iʔ l
1in -older_brother well *well* that 2in -harvest hab -loose there art in
said to me: *"All your crop is loose in*

səlawántən 341 a˙˙ cun, waỷ uɬ lut ha anwí {an}
s+lawán+tn a cu -n waỷ uɬ lut haʔ anwí
granary intj tell -1erg well and not inter you
the granary." *I said, "And didn't you take*

antx̌ʷíẁs, ha waỷ kʷintxʷ 342 kʷu cus waỷ pnicíʔ ixíʔ
an -tx̌ʷ=iẁs haʔ waỷ kʷin -t -xʷ kʷu cu -s waỷ pn+icíʔ ixíʔ
2in -half inter yes take -nt -2erg 1obj tell -3erg yes at_that_time then
your half?" *"I already*

kʷin 343 ḱim axáʔ anwí antx̌ʷíẁs aláʔ npkʷəntín 344 cut nt̓a
kʷi -n ḱim axáʔ anwí an -tx̌ʷ=iẁs aláʔ n+pkʷ -nt -in cut nt̓a
take -1erg only this you 2in -half here pour -nt -1erg say intj
took it, *it's just your half I put there loose." 26:03* *He said,*

mat waỷ axáʔ x̌ast iʔ sḱʷul̓s 345 kʷu cus waỷ {at} ḱəl
mat waỷ axáʔ x̌as+t iʔ s -ḱʷul̓ -s kʷu cu -s waỷ ḱl
maybe yes this good art nom -work -3i 1obj tell -3erg yes about
"I guess it must have turned out good." *He told me "Yes, 35 bushels*

kaʔɬlʔupənkstɬcílkst kylwíċaʔ i l naqs *acre* 346 a˙, cun waỷ
kaʔɬl+ʔupn=ks+ɬ+cil=kst k+ylw=íċaʔ iʔ l naqs a cu -n waỷ
thirty_five bushel art for one intj tell -1erg well
an acre." *I said*

límləmtx 347 waỷ caʔkʷ lut ixíʔ iʔ kən kstaʔmínaʔ 348 ixíʔ
lim•lm+t+x waỷ caʔkʷ lut ixíʔ iʔ kn k+s+taʔm=ínaʔ ixíʔ
thank_you well if not that art 1kn have_spring that
"Thanks." *That's how I pulled through the winter.* *I sold*

tumístmən uɬ iʔ {kən} kən təxʷsʔamənsqáx̌aʔm x̌əl sʔistk 349 uɬ
tw+mist+m -n uɬ iʔ kn txʷ+s+ʔamn=sqáx̌aʔ+m x̌l s+ʔis=tk uɬ
sell -1erg and art 1kn have_feed for winter and
it and kept only enough for feed for the winter. *I had*

aɬíʔ mat ḱəl məsɬʔúpənkst {is} ist̓máʕlt uɬ iʔ {s} naʔɬ sənkɬċaʔsqáx̌aʔ
aɬíʔ mat ḱl ms+ɬ+ʔupn=kst i -s+t̓m=ʕalt uɬ iʔ naʔɬ sn+kɬ+ċaʔ=sqáx̌aʔ
so maybe about forty 1in -cow and art and horse
about forty heads, cows and horses.

350 ixíʔ uɬ_iʔ kʷu ʔimx {ḱəl} ḱəl sənx̌ʷúċəc̓tən 351 ixíʔ {uɬ} uɬ aɬíʔ
ixíʔ uɬ_iʔ kʷu ʔimx ḱl sn+x̌ʷuċ•ċ+tn ixíʔ uɬ aɬíʔ
then and_then 4kn move to cut_something then and so
Then we moved to sənx̌ʷúċəc̓tən. *And it's*

mat xʷaʔspíntk {waỷ təl} waỷ ɬaʔ ckʷɬənxíxəmsts axáʔ
mat xʷaʔ+s+pin=tk waỷ ɬaʔ c -kʷɬn+xix+m -st -s axáʔ
maybe many_years yes when cust^ -lend -^cust -3erg this
a good many years that

inqíck {i?} i təmxʷúla?xʷs 352 way̓ uɬ lut k̓əm t̓a
in -qick i? tmxʷ=úla?xʷ s way̓ uɬ lut k̓m t̓
1in -older_brother art land 3in well and not except negfac
my brother has been renting his place, 27:04 *and it's not even*

ck̓əɬʕál uɬ yaʕyáʕt nitkʷíp 353 uɬ axá? i? sənt̓əwscqáx̌a?tən uɬ
c -k̓ɬ+ʕal̓ uɬ yaʕ•yáʕ+t n+ytkʷ=ip uɬ axá? i? sn+t̓wst=sqáx̌a?+tn uɬ
hab -fence and all rotten and this art barn and
fenced, and the posts are rotten, *and the barn has got no more*

t̓əxʷ lut t̓a ksənt̓wístən t̓a ksn?amənsqáx̌a?tən {uɬ s} 354 uɬ ixí?
t̓xʷ lut t̓ k+sn+t̓wist+n t̓ k+sn+?amn=sqáx̌a?+tn uɬ ixí?
emph not negfac have_horse_stall negfac have_manger and then
stalls or feed places. *I fixed it*

yaʕyáʕt k̓ʷú··l̓ən uɬ ixí? kən k̓ʷánɬqəm k̓əɬʕaləntín 355 way̓ uɬ kən
yaʕ•yáʕ+t k̓ʷul̓ -n uɬ ixí? kn k̓ʷan=ɬq+m k̓ɬ+ʕal̓ -nt -in way̓ uɬ kn
all fix -1erg and then 1kn grow_crop fence -nt -1erg well and 1kn
all up and put in a crop, I fenced it. *And I*

nstils kən ṅíṅw̓i? alá? mi kən niʕ̓íp {kən ya} kən ilí? 356 ixí? i? l
n+st=ils kn ṅíṅw̓i? alá? mi kn nyʕ̓ip kn ilí? ixí? i? l
think 1kn a_while here be_sure 1kn always 1kn there there art in
thought I was going to stay there forever, *stay there*

təmxʷúla?xʷ 357 way̓ uɬ kʷu kɬux̌tíla?t, ixí? q̓ilt uɬ xʷyúsəntəm k̓əl
tmxʷ=úla?xʷ way̓ uɬ kʷu kɬ+wx̌t=íla?t ixí? q̓il+t uɬ xʷy=us -nt -m k̓l
country yes and 4kn have_baby then sick and take -nt -4erg to
in that country. *And we had a baby and then it got sick and we took him to*

px̌ʷpəx̌ʷx̌ʷíls 358 lkʷut aɬí? {uɬ} k̓a nsq̓ʷut, ilí? i? səxʷmrím 359 way̓
px̌ʷ•px̌ʷ•x̌ʷ=ils lkʷ=ut aɬí? k̓ n+s+q̓ʷut ilí? i? sxʷ=mrim way̓
Hunters far so to other_side there art doctor well
Hunters. *It's far, across the river; there is a doctor there. 28:02* *He*

ixí? mərímən təm, way̓ {uɬ} uɬ ixí? ɬcxʷúystəm 360 way̓
ixí? mrim -nt -m way̓ uɬ ixí? ɬ+c+xʷuy -st -m way̓
then doctor -nt -psv well and then come_again -caus -4erg well
doctored him, and we brought him home. *The baby*

uɬ lut̓ ?itx i? sk̓ʷək̓ʷíməlt {uɬ x̌əlap} 361 k̓əl ksx̌lap ki? uɬ
uɬ lut_t̓ ?itx i? s+k̓ʷ•k̓ʷim=lt k̓l k+s+x̌la+p ki? uɬ
and neg_emph sleep art baby about have_morning rel and
never went to sleep, *and towards morning*

ƛ̓lal i? sk̓ʷək̓ʷíməlt 362 way̓ ixí? ki? uɬ_i? {i?} kím̓ən ixí? i?
ƛ̓l•al i? s+k̓ʷ•k̓ʷim=lt way̓ ixí? ki? uɬ_i? kim̓ -n ixí? i?
dead art baby well that rel and_then hate -1erg that art
he died. *And that's why I hate*

təmxʷúla?xʷ {inaud} 363 myaɬ {tlalkʷu} k̓əɬlkʷút i? təl səxʷmrím 364 uɬ
tmxʷ=úla?xʷ myaɬ k̓ɬ+lkʷ=ut i? tl sxʷ=mrim uɬ
country too_much as_far_as art from doctor and
that place. *It's too far from the doctor,* *and*

ixíʔ caʔkʷ kʷu k̓əɬk̓íkaʔt uɬ lut ixíʔ {ks} ksƛ̓lals 365 ixíʔ
ixíʔ caʔkʷ kʷu k̓ɬ+k̓í•kaʔt uɬ lut ixíʔ k+s -ƛ̓l•al -s ixíʔ
then if 4kn as_close_as and not that futi -dead -3i that
if we had been closer, he wouldn't have died. *I*

k̓upənkstɬknáqs isqʷəsqʷasíʔa, uɬ iʔ knaqs kmix iʔ ƛ̓lal {i}
k+ʔupn=kst+ɬ+k=náqs i -s+qʷs•qʷasíʔa uɬ iʔ k=naqs kmix iʔ ƛ̓l•al
eleven_persons 1in -children and art one_person only art dead
have eleven children, and that's the only one that's

itlíʔ 366 uɬ k̓im k̓im k̓úpənkst, ixíʔ ctxət̓stín
itlíʔ uɬ k̓im k̓im k+ʔupn=kst ixíʔ c -txt̓ -st -in
from_there and left left ten_persons that cust^ -watch_so -^cust -1erg
dead. *There is ten left, I still got them yet.*

367 uɬ itlíʔ uɬ axáʔ iʔ təl sxaʔtmíxəlt way̓ uɬ {kən} mat
uɬ itlíʔ uɬ axáʔ iʔ tl s+xaʔt+míx+lt way̓ uɬ mat
and from_there and this art from first_child yes and maybe
And from my oldest daughter I have about

kt̓áq̓t̓əq̓əmkst int̓at̓úpaʔ 368 ixíʔ uɬ {kʷu ɬ} kʷu
k+t̓aq̓•t̓q̓m=kst in -t̓aʔ•t̓úpaʔ ixíʔ uɬ kʷu
nine_persons 1in -great_grandfather then and 1obj
six great-grandchildren. 29:08 *And my parents*

ɬx̌əlítsəlx axáʔ inƛ̓ax̌əx̌ƛ̓x̌áp 369 kʷu cúsəlx way̓ x̌ast
ɬ+x̌lit -s -lx axáʔ in -ƛ̓ax̌•x̌•ƛ̓x̌á+p kʷu cu -s -lx way̓ x̌as+t
summon_again -3erg -pl this 1in -elders 1obj tell -3erg -pl yes good
asked me, *they said to me, "It's better*

kʷu ɬaʔ ɬtxʷúyməntxʷ 370 uɬ ƛ̓əm kʷu c̓əx̌ʷxítxʷ
kʷu ɬaʔ ɬ+t+xʷuy+m -nt -xʷ uɬ ƛ̓m kʷu c̓x̌ʷ -xit -xʷ
1obj if go_back_to -nt -2erg and past 1obj promise -xit -2erg
that you come home. *And why is it that you told us,*

371 axáʔ {ɬa} ɬaʔ cmrəmmrím {i} ask̓ʷíƛ̓təm asəntəxʷtxʷús uɬ axáʔ
axáʔ ɬaʔ c -mrm•mrim a -s+k̓ʷiƛ̓t+m a -sn+txʷ•txʷ=us uɬ axáʔ
this when hab -marry_pl 2in -brothers 2in -cousins and this
when the rest of your sisters and brothers

aɬəɬqíck 372 uɬ kʷu ɬaʔ cc̓qʷaqʷ kʷu ɬaʔ
a -ɬɬ+qick uɬ kʷu ɬaʔ c -c̓qʷ•aqʷ kʷu ɬaʔ
2in -brothers and 4kn when hab -cry 4kn when
get married *and when*

c[nmimipmíst] {uɬ kʷu cuntxʷ} kʷu ɬməntíxʷ uɬ kʷu cuntxʷ 373 uɬ
c -n+my•my+p+mist kʷu ɬm -nt -ixʷ uɬ kʷu cu -nt -xʷ uɬ
hab -confess 1obj pet -nt -2erg and 1obj tell -nt -2erg and
we cried, when we confessed, you petted me and you told me, *'I*

way̓ n̓ín̓wiʔ t incá txət̓ɬúlmən uɬ ʕapnáʔ uɬ_i kʷu a
way̓ n̓ín̓wiʔ t in+cá txt̓ -ɬulm -n uɬ ʕapnáʔ uɬ_iʔ kʷu a
well a_while agInst I watch_so -5obj -1erg and now and_then 1obj art
will take care of you,' and then

ɬwintxʷ 374 uɬ way̓ t̓iʔ x̌ast kʷu ɬaʔ ɬtxʷúyməntxʷ məɬ ixíʔ
ɬwi -nt -xʷ uɬ way̓ t̓iʔ x̌as+t kʷu ɬaʔ ɬ+t+xʷuy+m -nt -xʷ mɬ ixíʔ
leave -nt -2erg and yes evid good 1obj if go_back_to -nt -2erg and then
you left us? *It's best that you come back home, and*

kʷu txət̓əntíxʷ 375 cúnəlx way̓, cun way̓ ixíʔ ƛ̓əm
kʷu t+xt̓ -nt -ixʷ cu -n -lx way̓ cu -n way̓ ixíʔ ƛ̓m
1obj watch_so -nt -2erg tell -1erg -pl yes tell -1erg yes that past
take care of us." 30:02 *I said, "Yes, that's what*

c̓əx̌ʷxíɬmən 376 cun uɬ stim̓ axáʔ náx̌əmɬ iʔ kʷu
c̓x̌ʷ -xi -ɬm -n cu -n uɬ stim̓ axáʔ nax̌mɬ iʔ kʷu
promise -xit -5obj -1erg tell -1erg and what this but art 1obj
I told you." *I said, "And what is it that*

cuntp 377 kʷu cuntp way̓ way̓ taʔlíʔ p ƛ̓ax̌əx̌ƛ̓x̌áp
cun -t -p kʷu cun -t -p way̓ way̓ taʔlíʔ p ƛ̓ax̌•x̌•ƛ̓x̌á+p
tell -nt -5erg 1obj tell -nt -5erg well well very_much 5kn elders
you told me? *You told me you are too old*

kʷu ɬə ksʔamɬtíp intəkɬmílxʷ 378 kəm̓ kən ɬ
kʷu ɬ ks -ʔam -ɬt -ip in -tkɬ+m=ilxʷ km̓ kn ɬ
1obj subord futtˆ -feed -ɬt -5erg 1in -wife or 1kn if
for you to feed my wife, *or if*

taʔxʷsqʷəsqʷasíʔa uɬ aɬíʔ sc̓x̌ilx {ki kən} kiʔ kən {a} lkʷilx 379 uɬ aɬíʔ kən
taʔxʷ+s+qʷs•qʷasíʔa uɬ aɬíʔ sc+ʔx̌il+x kiʔ kn lkʷ+ilx uɬ aɬíʔ kn
have_children and so reason_why rel 1kn leave and so 1kn
I get kids, and that's why I went away. *And so I went*

lkʷakʷ uɬ aɬíʔ lut_ksluts 380 incá {k} kən ksk̓ʷúl̓aʔx iʔ
lkʷ•akʷ uɬ aɬíʔ lut_k+s+lut+s in+cá kn k+s -k̓ʷul̓ -aʔx iʔ
far and so there_is_no_no_about_it I 1kn incpˆ -work -ˆincp art
far, and there is no two things about it. *I have to work to take care*

l isqʷəsqʷasíʔa 381 iksʔamníltəm kəm̓ axáʔ iʔ l
l i -s+qʷs•qʷasíʔa i -ks -ʔamn=ílt+m km̓ axáʔ iʔ l
with 1in -children 1i -futi -feed_children or this art with
of my children, *to feed them and*

intəkɬmílxʷ 382 uɬ way̓ kʷu k̓əwpmínti, ixíʔ kʷa {i} iʔ
in -tkɬ+m=ilxʷ uɬ way̓ kʷu k̓w+p+min -t -y ixíʔ kʷa iʔ
1in -wife and yes 1obj stop_talking_to -nt -tpimptv that intj art
my wife. *Stop talking to me like that,*

scqʷaʔqʷʔáltət 383 way̓ ixíʔ kʷu k̓əwpmísəlx 384 way̓ uɬ
sc -qʷaʔ•qʷʔál -tt way̓ ixíʔ kʷu k̓w+p+mi -s -lx way̓ uɬ
pftv -talk -4i yes then 1obj stop_asking -3erg -pl well and
that's what we agreed." *They stopped talking to me like that.* *And I*

aɬíʔ k̓upənks{ɬtk̓asʔasíl is}ɬknaqs isk̓ʷíƛ̓təm {a i} iʔ tuʔtw̓it uɬ axáʔ iʔ
aɬíʔ k=ʔupn=ks+ɬ+k=náqs i -s+k̓ʷiƛ̓+t+m iʔ tw̓•twit uɬ axáʔ iʔ
so eleven_persons 1in -brothers art boys and this art
have eleven brothers and

smaʔmʔím 385 uł axáʔ {i} t incá uł kʷu ł k̓upənkstłk̓asʔasíl
s+maʔ•mʔím uł axáʔ t in+cá uł kʷu ł k+ʔupn=kst+ł+k=ʔas•ʔasíl
women and this obl I and 4kn comp twelve_persons
sisters, 31:08 *and with me there is twelve of us.*

386 ixíʔ uł ƛ̓axʷt axáʔ inƛ̓ax̌əx̌ƛ̓x̌áp 387 ixíʔ uł axáʔ {i}
ixíʔ uł ƛ̓axʷ+t axáʔ in -ƛ̓ax̌•x̌•ƛ̓x̌á+p ixíʔ uł axáʔ
then and dead_pl this 1in -elders then and this
Then my parents died, *and then*

isk̓ʷíƛ̓təm nixʷ {t} ƛ̓áxʷtəlx 388 way̓ uł k̓əm t̓i kmix incá kən
i -s+k̓ʷiƛ̓+t+m nixʷ ƛ̓axʷ+t -lx way̓ uł k̓m t̓iʔ kmix in+cá kn
1in -brothers also dead_pl -pl well and except evid only I 1kn
my sisters and brothers died too. *I am the only one*

sknaqsx ixíʔ kʷu təl k̓upənkstłk̓əsʔasíl 389 uł axáʔ nixʷ
s -k=naqs -x ixíʔ kʷu tl k+ʔupn=kst+ł+k=ʔas•ʔasíl uł axáʔ nixʷ
ipftv^ -one_person -^ipftv that 4kn of twelve_persons and this also
that's left of twelve. *And my wife*

intkłmílxʷ intkłmílxʷ ƛ̓lal 390 uł axáʔ caʔkʷ lut tl
in -tkł+m=ilxʷ in -tkł+m=ilxʷ ƛ̓l•al uł axáʔ caʔkʷ lut tl̓
1in -wife 1in -wife dead and this if not from
died too. *And if it hadn't been for*

isxaʔtmíxəlt ist̓əmkʔílt 391 ilíʔ kʷu máqsəlx ilíʔ uł
i -s+xaʔt+míx+lt i -s+t̓mkʔ=ilt ilíʔ kʷu maq -s -lx ilíʔ uł
1in -first_child 1in -daughter there 1obj stop -3erg -pl there and
my oldest daughter, *they stopped me there,*[14]

ʕapnáʔ {ik̓líʔ} ł kilíʔmnəlx ilíʔ {kən} kən ł ilíʔ 392 ixíʔ
ʕapnáʔ ł k+ilíʔ+m -n -lx ilíʔ kn ł ilíʔ ixíʔ
now subord live_with -1erg -pl there 1kn subord there that
and now I stay with them, I'm there yet. *That*

way̓ nc̓ayxʷápəlqs
way̓ n+c̓ayxʷ=áp=lqs
yes end_of_story
finishes it. 32:00

14 "They hosted me."

Harvesting

1 waỷ axáʔ kən ksmaỷncútaʔx
waỷ axáʔ kn ks -m̓ay+ncút -aʔx
well this 1kn incp^ -tell_story -^incp
I'll tell a story about myself.

2 waỷ axáʔ kən cpəx̌pəx̌twílx [kən]
waỷ axáʔ kn c -px̌•px̌+t+wilx kn
well this 1kn hab -get_senses 1kn
I already had my senses,

taʔxʷspuʔús
taʔxʷ+s+puʔ=ús
gain_feelings
feelings.

3 uɬ ixíʔ kən səsƛ̓aʔsqáx̌aʔx
uɬ ixíʔ kn sc -ƛ̓aʔ=sqáx̌aʔ -x
and then 1kn ipftvp^ -search_for_horse -^ipftvp
I was looking for a horse,

c̓úmlaʔxʷstsəlx səntqəɬxwíltən
c -ʔúm=laʔxʷ -st -s -lx sn+t+qɬ+xwil+tn
cust^ -call_a_place -^cust -3erg -pl place_name
they call the place "səntqəɬxwíltən"

4 axáʔ iʔ caʔkʷ cus iʔ
axáʔ iʔ caʔkʷ cu -s iʔ
this art as tell -3erg art
in English they call it

ta nuyápixcən *Bossborg*
t n+wyap=x=cn
agInst say_in_English
"Bossborg."

5 uɬ ixíʔ wíkən i {s} cənxmníw̓s {i}
uɬ ixíʔ wik -n iʔ c -n+xmn=iw̓s
and then see -1erg art hab -both_sides
And I saw both sides of

ia ntx̌ʷitkʷ
iʔ n+tx̌ʷ=itkʷ
art river
the river,

6 axáʔ a nx̌ʷəntkʷítkʷ {i i s k̓əɬ} i sk̓əɬq̓əỷáỷs iʔ síwɬkʷ
axáʔ a n+x̌ʷn=tkʷ=itkʷ iʔ s+k̓ɬ+q̓ỷ•aỷ -s iʔ siwɬ=kʷ
this art Kettle_River art marks -3in art water
the Kettle River, the marks of

axáʔ i l st̓ík̓ət {indec}
axáʔ iʔ l s+t̓ik̓+t
this art at high_water
the high water,

7 ilíʔ k̓əɬq̓əỷáỷ {ə} cənxmníw̓s {uɬ k}
ilíʔ k̓ɬ+q̓ỷ•aỷ c -n+xmn=iw̓s
there marks hab -both_sides
there are marks on both sides [shores].

8 uɬ
uɬ
and
There

nɬəx̌ʷmáqs iʔ t xəwíɬ ck̓əlnixáʔ aɬíʔ uɬ syxʷútaʔx[1]
n+ɬx̌ʷ+m=aqs iʔ t xwiɬ c+k̓l+n+ixáʔ aɬíʔ uɬ s -yxʷ=ut -aʔx
cross_road art obl road this_side so and ipftv^ -below ^?
is a mark past the road on this side, and below. (1:00)

9 uɬ ixíʔ kən
uɬ ixíʔ kn
and so 1kn
Then

ɬkicx uɬ ixíʔ síwən inƛ̓ax̌əx̌ƛ̓x̌áp
ɬ+kic+x uɬ ixíʔ siw -n in -ƛ̓ax̌•x̌•ƛ̓x̌á+p
arrive_again and then ask -1erg 1in -elders
I got back and I asked my folks.

10 cun uɬ stim̓ ixíʔ
cu -n uɬ s+tim̓ ixíʔ
tell -1erg and what that
I asked, "What is that [mark],

11 {as} siwɬkʷ ha ixíʔ {as'} ɬaʔ cxʷʔítkʷəm maɬ əcxʷʔítkʷəm
siwɬ=kʷ haʔ ixíʔ ɬaʔ c -xʷʔi+t=kʷ+m maɬ c -xʷʔi+t=kʷ+m
water inter that when hab -much_water too_much hab -much_water
the water, is it when there is lots of water, too much water

1 This form is unclear to me. Could -aʔx be a diminutive of -x ^ipftv?

12 kiʔ ixíʔ əck̓əɬq̓əy̓áy̓ iʔ siwɬkʷ 13 ki kʷu cúsəlx way̓
kiʔ ixíʔ c -kɬ+q̓y̓•ay̓ iʔ siwɬ=kʷ kiw kʷu cu -s -lx way̓
rel then hab -marks art water yes 1obj tell -3erg -pl yes
that the water leaves marks?" *They told me, "Yes."*

14 cútəlx axáʔ i l caʔkʷ cus i ta nuyápixcən i l *1890* kiʔ
cut -lx axáʔ iʔ l caʔkʷ cu -s i t n+wyap=x=cn iʔ l kiʔ
say -pl this art in as tell -3erg art agInst say_in_English art in rel
They said, "It was in 1890 (as they say in English)

ixíʔ a mqʷaqʷ 15 t mus sc̓uʔxán i l naqs skaʕcíw̓s ki
ixíʔ a mqʷ•aqʷ t mus s+c̓w̓=xan iʔ l naqs s+k+ʕac=íw̓s kiʔ
then art snow_fall obl four animal_hind_leg art in one week rel
that it snowed *four feet in a week before*

k̓ət̓píys 16 uɬ axáʔ ʔácqaʔ inlʔíw uɬ súxʷmaʔs {iʔ} iʔ
k̓t̓+p=iys uɬ axáʔ ʔácqaʔ in -lʔiw uɬ súxʷ=maʔ -s iʔ
stop_snowing and this go_out 1in -m's_father and measure -3erg art
it stopped. *My father went out and measured*

smik̓ʷt 17 uɬ xiƛ̓ mus sc̓uʔxán 18 ixíʔ uɬ iʔ {l}
s+mik̓ʷt uɬ xiƛ̓ mus s+c̓w̓=xan ixíʔ uɬ iʔ
snow_on_ground and even four animal_hind_leg then and art
the snow, *an even four feet.* *When it thawed*

ɬʕamáp staʔmúlaʔxʷ ixíʔ kiʔ k̓ʷəlk̓ítkʷəm iʔ siwɬkʷ 19 uɬ
ɬ+ʕamá+p s+taʔm=úlaʔxʷ ixíʔ kiʔ k̓ʷlk̓=itkʷ+m iʔ siwɬ=kʷ uɬ
thaw_again spring_time then rel water_rolls_back art water and
at spring time, then the water rolled up; *and*

txʷaʔxʷʔít {iʔ} iʔ sqilxʷ iʔ l skəɬqəltús 20 ia ccuxwíx ia
t=xʷaʔ•xʷʔí+t iʔ s+qilxʷ iʔ l s+kɬ+qlt=us iʔ c -c+wx•wix iʔ
many_persons art person art on ridge art hab -dwellings art
and many people on the ridge, (2:04) *their dwellings,*

ksənk̓ʷánɬqtən uɬ ia ksənt̓əwscqáx̌aʔtən yaʕyáʕt ixíʔ sək̓ʷtlílx {i} 21 uɬ
k+sn+k̓ʷan=ɬq+tn uɬ iʔ k+sn+t̓wst=sqáx̌aʔ+tn yaʕ•yáʕ+t ixíʔ s+k̓ʷt+lilx uɬ
have_garden and art -have_barn all that float_down and
their gardens, their barns, they all floated down. *When*

ixíʔ {ɬɬa·} ɬə taʔmúlaʔxʷ a ixíʔ {ɬaɬə·} ɬə caʔqʷqʷílx ɬsw̓aw̓ 22 uɬ
ixíʔ ɬ taʔm=úlaʔxʷ a ixíʔ ɬ caʔqʷ•qʷ+ílx ɬ+sw̓•aw̓ uɬ
then when snow_melt art then when summer_comes recede and
the snow went away, and when summer came, the water went back down, *and*

ixíʔ kmix sq̓aʔpínaʔxʷ axáʔ npíqlaʔxʷ {iʔ sƛ̓aʔ} iʔ {s} sq̓aʔpínaʔxʷ 23 ixíʔ uɬ
ixíʔ kmix s+q̓aʔpínaʔxʷ axáʔ n+piq=laʔxʷ iʔ s+q̓aʔpínaʔxʷ ixíʔ uɬ
then only sand this white_on_ground art sand then and
there is only sand, white sand, *and then*

lut {t̓a c} t̓a cpəllálɬqəlx iʔ t sk̓ʷanɬq {i t} 24 kmix axáʔ iʔ t
lut t̓ c -pl•l=aɬq -lx iʔ t s+k̓ʷan=ɬq kmix axáʔ iʔ t
not negfac hab -crop_grows -pl art obl garden only this art prttv
their gardens didn't grow any crop. *Only corn grew." {Oh*

liplí kiʔ cplal
liplí kiʔ c -pl•al
corn rel hab -grow
I guess I'll take a five now.}

25 way̓ ixíʔ pnicíʔ {i s} ixíʔ {iʔl s·} iʔ xʷaʔsmík̓ʷtəm
way̓ ixíʔ pn+icíʔ ixíʔ iʔ xʷaʔ+s+mík̓ʷt
well that at_that_time that art much_snow
That's the time when there was lots of snow, (3:09)

26 kiʔ ixíʔ a ccústən i {it̓i} t̓ík̓ət {iʔ} ia nx̌ʷəntkʷítkʷ uɬ_i
kiʔ ixíʔ a c -cu -st -n iʔ t̓ik̓+t iʔ n+x̌ʷn=tkʷ=itkʷ uɬ_iʔ
rel then art cust^ -tell -^cust -1erg art high_water art Kettle_River then
that's what I was saying, the Columbia River came up over

kɬqəltús
kɬ+qlt=us
hill_top
the bank.

27 ixíʔ uɬ pnicíʔ uɬ c̓əspsqáx̌aʔ iʔ sqilxʷ
ixíʔ uɬ pn+icíʔ uɬ c̓s+p=sqáx̌aʔ iʔ s+qilxʷ
then and then and stock_gone art person
That time the people lost their stock.

28 yaʕyáʕt ilíʔ iʔ sqilxʷ xʷaʔxʷaʔsqáx̌aʔ
yaʕ•yáʕ+t ilíʔ iʔ s+qilxʷ xʷaʔ•xʷaʔ=sqáx̌aʔ
all there art person pl_have_stock
All the people had a few head of animals.

29 uɬ aɬiá pnicí uɬ aɬiá kɬt̓lúlaʔxʷtən t nʔasʔasláqs kəm̓ nkaʔɬláqs
uɬ aɬi+á pn+icíʔ uɬ aɬi+á kɬ+t̓l=úlaʔxʷ+tn t n+ʔas•ʔasl=áqs km̓ n+kaʔɬl=áqs
and because_not at_that_time and because_not have_plow obl two_headed or three_pointed
At that time they didn't have plows, neither two pointed nor three-pointed,

30 way̓ t̓i_kmix axáʔ ta nkaʔxmútyaʔ
way̓ t̓iʔ_kmix axáʔ t n+kaʔx+m=útyaʔ
yes only this obl go_on_foot
only the walk behind type.

31 uɬ axáʔ iʔ x̌ʷíc̓laʔxʷtəns axáʔ ʔúmsəlx axáʔ iʔ kc̓álálqʷ
uɬ axáʔ iʔ x̌ʷíc̓=laʔxʷ+tn -s axáʔ ʔum -s -lx axáʔ iʔ k+c̓l=alqʷ
and this art mower -3in this call -3erg -pl this art bundling_scythe
And what they cut with, they call it "bundling scythe,"

32 uɬ axáʔ iʔ sap̓mútyaʔ i l supúlaʔxʷ
uɬ axáʔ iʔ sap̓+m=útyaʔ iʔ l s+wp=úlaʔxʷ
and this art scythe art for hay
and the scythe for hay.

33 axáʔ iʔ kc̓álálqʷ ixíʔ {ac} a cəlk̓íw̓stsəlx
axáʔ iʔ k+c̓l=alqʷ ixíʔ a c -lk̓=iw̓s -t -s -lx
this art bundling_scythe that art cust^ -bundle -st -3erg -pl
The bundling scythe is the kind that bundles.

34 məɬ ixíʔ qəlwátqsəlx axáʔ a cəlk̓íw̓s iʔ t wiʔsəsp̓qín kəm̓ i t lawán
mɬ ixíʔ ql=wat=q -s -lx axáʔ a c -lk̓=iw̓s iʔ t wy̓+s•sp̓=qin km̓ i t lawán
and then thresh -3erg -pl this art hab -bundle art obl finish_wheat or art obl oats
And they thresh what's bundled, the wheat or the oats. (4:01)

35 axáʔ iʔ {l} sənkɬc̓aʔsqáx̌aʔ iʔ l sənʕacqáx̌aʔtən {məɬ} məɬ ilíʔ nyx̌əntísəlx
axáʔ iʔ sn+kɬ+c̓aʔ=sqáx̌aʔ iʔ l sn+ʕac=qáx̌aʔ+tn mɬ ilíʔ n+yx̌ -nt -is -lx
this art horse art in corral and there drive_into -nt -3erg -pl
They drive the horses in the corral,

36 məɬ iʔ sənkɬc̓aʔsqáx̌aʔ xəlkməncútəlx {i iə məɬ məɬ ə}
mɬ iʔ sn+kɬ+c̓aʔ=sqáx̌aʔ xlk+mncuta
and art horse turn
the horses go around,

37 nəxʷk̓ʷíw̓sslx ixíʔ uɬ a cnʔayxʷuʔscínəmstsəlx {i k̓əl} i
n+xʷk̓ʷ=iw̓s -s -lx ixíʔ uɬ a c -n+ʔayxʷ=w̓s=cín+m -st -s -lx iʔ
clean -3erg -pl that and art cust^ -trade_for_groceries -^cust -3erg -pl art
they clean the grain. And that's what they trade for groceries

k̓əl sənx̌ʷáq̓ʷmən 38 uɬ aɬíʔ axáʔ {k̓əl} k̓əl scáʕycup, lut, k̓əl skɬp̓úpƛ̓əm
k̓l sn+x̌ʷaq̓ʷ+mn uɬ aɬíʔ axáʔ k̓l s+caʕycwp lut k̓l s+kɬ+pu•p•ƛ̓m
at mill and so this at Kettle_Falls not at Meyers_Falls
at the flour mill, *at Kettle Falls—no, at Meyers Falls.*

39 ixíʔ a cyxʷitkʷ[m], təl kɬtx̌ʷʕʷtíw̓s iʔ ctyap ixíʔ uɬ a
ixíʔ a c -yxʷ=itkʷ+m tl kɬ+tx̌ʷ=wt=iw̓s iʔ c -tya+p ixíʔ uɬ a
that art hab -water_fall from Colville_River art hab -water_runs that and art
There are falls, there are falls from the

cyxʷítkʷəm 40 ixíʔ ilíʔ uɬ iʔ k̓əɬk̓ʷúl̓səlx {iʔ} iʔ sənx̌ʷáq̓ʷmən
c -yxʷ=itkʷ+m ixíʔ ilíʔ uɬ iʔ k̓ɬ+k̓ʷul̓ -s -lx iʔ sn+x̌ʷaq̓ʷ+mn
hab -water_fall that there and art fix -3erg -pl art mill
Colville River, *and that's where they made a flour mill,*

41 uɬ axáʔ iʔ t siwɬkʷ {ki c} ki cxʷists iʔ sənx̌ʷáq̓ʷmən
uɬ axáʔ iʔ t siwɬ=kʷ kiʔ c -xʷy -st -s iʔ sn+x̌ʷaq̓ʷ+mn
and this art agInst water rel cust^ -go -^caus -3erg art mill
and it's the water that runs the mill.

42 uɬ aɬíʔ nak̓ʷá pnicí uɬ ksənʔíys a[xáʔ] iʔ səsp̓qín iʔ
uɬ aɬíʔ nak̓ʷá pn+icíʔ uɬ k+sn+ʔiys axáʔ iʔ s•sp̓=qin iʔ
and because indeed_not at_that_time and have_price this art wheat art
At that time there was no price for wheat

lawán {iʔ} 43 uɬ t̓i_kmix cənʔayxʷuʔscínəmstsəlx {iʔ} x̌əl
lawán uɬ t̓iʔ_kmix c -n+ʔayxʷ=w̓s=cin+m -st -s -lx x̌l
oats and only cust^ -trade_for_groceries -^cust -3erg -pl for
or oats, (5:00) *they only traded for flour the wheat*

a lparín axáʔ iʔ scqəlwátqəns {iʔ} iʔ səsp̓qín 44 uɬ axáʔ iʔ lawán t̓əxʷ
a lparín axáʔ iʔ sc -ql=wat=qn -s iʔ s•sp̓=qin uɬ axáʔ iʔ lawán t̓xʷ
art flour this art pftv -thresh -3i art wheat and this art oats emph
that they had threshed by hand. *Oats is only for*

axáʔ t̓i_kmix c̓amənsqáx̌aʔmstsəlx 45 uɬ ixíʔ itíʔ kiʔ
axáʔ t̓iʔ_kmix c -ʔamn=sqáx̌aʔ+m -st -s -lx uɬ ixíʔ itíʔ kiʔ
this only cust^ -feed_stock -^cust -3erg -pl and that from_that rel
feeding the stock. *That's all what they*

a c̓amənsqáx̌aʔmstsəlx t̓i_kmix axáʔ iʔ la
a c -ʔamn=sqáx̌aʔ+m -st -s -lx t̓iʔ_kmix axáʔ iʔ l
art cust^ -feed_stock -^cust -3erg -pl only this art on
feed stock with,

nk̓amtíw̓stənsəlx {kəm̓ i la} 46 aɬíʔ nak̓ʷáʔ kɬənckʷmnáqs {məl} məɬ iʔ
n+k+ʔam=t=íw̓s+tn -s -lx aɬíʔ nak̓ʷ+á kɬ+n+ckʷ+mn=aqs mɬ iʔ
saddle_horse -3in -pl because indeed_not have_wagon_road and art
their saddle horses. *Because there weren't wagon roads for*

l sǝncǝkʷmín ixíʔ {i} la nckʷmínsǝlx 47 t̓i way̓ la
l sn+ckʷ+min ixíʔ l n+ckʷ+min[2] -s -lx t̓iʔ way̓ l
in buggy that in buggy -3in -pl evid yes for
wagons {not clear}. *It's only*

nt̓ǝllúlaʔxʷtǝnsǝlx kǝm̓ axáʔ ck̓ǝɬp̓aʔp̓áʔ axáʔ {is} iʔ tqǝlwátqǝntǝn
n+t̓l•l=úlaʔxʷ+tn -s -lx km̓ axáʔ c -k̓ɬ+p̓aʔ•p̓áʔ axáʔ iʔ t+ql=wat=qn+tn
plow_horse -3in -pl or this hab -milk_cows this art threshing_horse
work horse or milking cow [trails],

48 uɬ aɬíʔ lut {t̓a} t̓ xʷaʔsmík̓ʷǝt pnicíʔ uɬ lut t̓a
uɬ aɬíʔ lut t̓ xʷaʔ+s+mík̓ʷt pn+icíʔ uɬ lut t̓
and because not negfac much_snow at_that_time and not negfac
because there wasn't much snow, and they didn't

ċamǝnsqáx̌aʔmǝlx 49 ilí··ʔ mǝɬ kstaʔmínaʔ sǝnkɬċaʔsqáx̌aʔ, lut t̓a
c -ʔamn=sqáx̌aʔ+m -lx ilíʔ mɬ k+s+taʔm=ínaʔ sn+kɬ+ċaʔ=sqáx̌aʔ lut t̓
hab -feed_stock -pl there and have_spring horse not negfac
feed the stock. *The horses pull through winter, they*

cƛ̓axʷt 50 ixíʔ náx̌ǝmɬ iʔ xʷaʔsmík̓ʷǝtǝm {uɬ} 51 uɬ axáʔ {in}
c -ƛ̓axʷ+t ixíʔ nax̌mɬ iʔ xʷaʔ+s+mík̓ʷt+m uɬ axáʔ
hab -dead_pl then but art snow_lots and this
don't die. *But that time it snowed lots. (6:00)* *And*

inlʔíw mat ksx̌an tǝl kaʔɬís x̌ǝccíkst iʔ kǝw̓wáps 52 sic
in -lʔiw mat k+sx̌a+n tl kaʔɬís x̌c•c=ikst iʔ kw•w•ap -s sic
1in -m's_father maybe past than three hundred art horses -3in then
my father must have had more than 300 horses, *some*

nx̌siw̓s, uɬ aɬíʔ axáʔ nmǝlk̓ʷápaʔst sƛ̓ǝx̌sqáx̌aʔ 53 uɬ axáʔ {iʔ} iʔ naqs ixíʔ
n+x̌s=iw̓s uɬ aɬíʔ axáʔ n+mlk̓ʷ=ápaʔst s+ƛ̓x̌=sqáx̌aʔ uɬ axáʔ iʔ naqs ixíʔ
good and so this stallion race_horse and this art one that
good ones, and a stallion race horse, *and one*

nk̓ʷúl̓mǝn 54 axáʔ {iʔ} iʔ caʔkʷ cus ia nuyápixcǝn iʔ *Persian,*
n+k̓ʷul̓+mn axáʔ iʔ caʔkʷ cu -s iʔ n+wyap=x=cn iʔ
work_horse this art as tell -3erg art say_in_English art
work horse, *as they call it in English a "Persian,"*

tx̌ilps, cksǝl̓íċaʔ 55 sílxʷaʔ nk̓ʷúl̓mǝn 56 way̓ ixíʔ uɬ iʔ
tx̌=ilps c -k+sl̓=íċaʔ sílxʷaʔ n+k̓ʷul̓+mn way̓ ixíʔ uɬ iʔ
gray_horse hab -dappled_grey big work_horse well then and art
dappled grey, *a big work horse.* *The horses went*

nċǝspúlaʔxʷ iʔ sǝnkɬċaʔsqáx̌aʔ 57 uɬ ixíʔ {iʔ ixíʔ uɬ} way̓ uɬ
n+ċs+p=úlaʔxʷ iʔ sn+kɬ+ċaʔ=sqáx̌aʔ uɬ ixíʔ way̓ uɬ
kill art horse and then yes and
to nothing. *The snow*

2 Note the two forms of the word translated as *buggy*.

ksúltaʔx i? smík̓ʷt 58 ixíʔ uł scuts
k -sul+t -aʔx iʔ s+mík̓ʷt ixíʔ uł s -cut -s
incp^ -snow_crust -^incp art snow_on_ground then and nom -say -3i
was going to crust. *He had*

inlʔíw ixíʔ ałíʔ ksəxʷk̓ʷúləm scústsəlx spapuʔúl
in -lʔiw ixíʔ ałíʔ k+sxʷ=k̓ʷul̓+m s -cu -st -s -lx s+paʔ•pʔúl
1in -m's_father that so have_worker cust^ -tell -^cust -3erg -pl m's_name
a working man, they called him "spapuʔúl," he said to him... (7:02)

59 uł axáʔ inqíck iʔ sxʔitx 60 ʔasəlʔapənkspíntk iʔ
uł axáʔ in -qick iʔ s+xʔit=x ʔasl+ʔapn=ks+pin=tk iʔ
and this 1in -older_brother art oldest_one twenty art
My eldest brother, *twenty years*

sxʔitxs tl̓ incá 61 uł ixíʔ way̓ cppəx̌pəx̌twílaʔx uł mʕan
s -xʔit=x -s tl̓ in+cá uł ixíʔ way̓ c -p•px̌•px̌+t+wílaʔx uł mʕan
nom -oldest -3i than I and then yes hab -grow_aware_dim and intj
older than I, *was already getting awareness and he*

way̓ ixíʔ cmistís 62 uł ixíʔ kxan pnicí 63 uł
way̓ ixíʔ c -my -st -is uł ixíʔ kxa+n pn+icíʔ uł
yes that cust^ -know -^cust -3erg and then go_along at_that_time and
remembers that. *He went with them at that time.* *Maybe*

mat naqs sxʷmʔúlaʔxʷ[tən] təl cítxʷtət ksxw̓íw̓stəms {is} 64 ilíʔ
mat naqs sxʷ=mʔ=úlaʔxʷ+tn tl citxʷ -tt ? ilíʔ
maybe one mile from house -4in ? there
a mile from our house up the hill *there*

ct̓iwsx[3] ixíʔ cłak ilíʔ 65 way̓ {kna} cut inlʔíw way̓ ixíʔ ik̓líʔ
c -t̓iws -x ixíʔ c+łak ilíʔ way̓ cut in -lʔiw way̓ ixíʔ ik̓líʔ
? -flat -? that swamp there well say 1in -m's_father well then there
was a flat area and a swamp. *And my father said, "We'll*

mi kʷu xʷuy {ilíʔ way̓ mi} 66 ilíʔ mat ki mík̓ʷk̓ʷt iʔ snkłc̓aʔsqáx̌aʔ
mi kʷu xʷuy ilíʔ mat kiʔ mik̓ʷ•k̓ʷ•t iʔ sn+kł+c̓aʔ=sqáx̌aʔ
fut 4kn go there maybe rel snowed_in art horse
go up there. *There might be where the horses are snowed in;*

67 ilíʔ mat mi kaʔkícəntm 68 aláʔ xʷuysts ia
ilíʔ mat mi kaʔ•kíc -nt -m aláʔ xʷuy -st -s iʔ
there maybe fut find -nt -4erg here go -caus -3erg art
maybe we'll find them there." *He took the stallion and*

nməlk̓ʷápaʔst {ia} ia nk̓ʷúl̓mən 69 sílxʷaʔ ałíʔ uł q̓ʷúc̓təlx 70 uł axáʔ
n+mlk̓ʷ=ápaʔst iʔ n+k̓ʷul̓+mn sílxʷaʔ ałíʔ uł q̓ʷuc̓+t -lx uł axáʔ
stallion art work_horse big so and fat -? and this
the work horse, *big and fat,* *and the*

3 This form is unclear.

i? sƛ̓əx̌sqáx̌a? ixí? ?awtpáɬq {əl} 71 aɬí yríwa?xnməlx axá?
i? s+ƛ̓x̌=sqáx̌a? ixí? ?aw+t+p=áɬq aɬí? yr=íwa?=xn+m -lx axá?
art race_horse that follow so wear_snowshoes -pl this
race horse followed. *My father and his working man*

inl?íw i? na?ɬ səxʷk̓ʷúl̓əm 72 uɬ axá?m inqíck uɬ aɬí?
in -l?iw i? na?ɬ sxʷ=k̓ʷul̓+m uɬ axá?+m in -qick uɬ aɬí?
1in -m's_father art and worker and this 1in -older_brother and so
put snowshoes on. (8:00) *My brother was small,*

t̓i k̓ʷək̓ʷyúma? uɬ náx̌əmɬ way̓ pəx̌páx̌t 73 way̓ kɬqcəlxíkən
t̓i? k̓ʷ•k̓ʷy=úma? uɬ nax̌mɬ way̓ px̌•pax̌+t way̓ kɬ+qc+lx=ikn̓
evid small and but yes smart yes run_on_crust
but already smart, *and he ran on the snow crust.*

74 way̓ xʷu··ylx taɬ[t] xʷəm_t̓i sckt̓l̓íw̓sx i?
way̓ xʷuy -lx taɬ+t xʷm_t̓i? sc -k+t̓l=iw̓s -x i?
well go -pl surely evid ipftvp^ -split_lengthwise -^ipftvp art
They went and where they went is

sxʷúytənsəlx 75 way̓ k̓a?k̓a?íttəlx 76 ixí? uɬ txəƛ̓píc̓a? axá? {i} ia
s+xʷuy+tn -s -lx way̓ k̓a?•k̓a?ít•t -lx ixí? uɬ t+xƛ̓+p=íc̓a? axá? i?
step -3in -pl well get_close_pl -pl then and entire_body this art
wide open. *They got close.* *The work horse and the stallion's*

nk̓ʷúlmən a nməlk̓ʷápa?st i? t skskʷálts 77 way̓ uɬ
n+k̓ʷul̓+mn a n+mlk̓ʷ=ápa?st i? t s -k+s+kʷal̓+t -s way̓ uɬ
work_horse art stallion art agInst nom -be_sweaty -3i yes and
bodies are covered in sweat, *getting*

n?ayx̌ʷtíls 78 cus axá? i? səxʷk̓ʷúl̓əms 79 huhúy anwí [u]ɬ
n+?ayx̌ʷ+t=íls cu -s axá? i? sxʷ=k̓ʷul̓+m -s hu+húy anwí uɬ
get_tired tell -3erg this art worker -3in OK you and
tired *He said to his working man:* *"You go ahead*

k̓əɬxá?txna?x i? t asƛ̓əx̌sqáx̌a? 80 way̓ n?ayx̌ʷtíls axá? {inca} i?
k̓ɬ+xá?t=xna -x i? t a -s+ƛ̓x̌=sqáx̌a? way̓ n+?ayx̌ʷ+t=íls axá? i?
go_ahead -isimptv art obl 2in -race_horse yes get_tired this art
with your race horse, *the leading horse is*

stkən̓pla?sqá[x̌a?] 81 way̓ way̓ ixí? k̓əɬx̌əqəntís way̓ ixí?
s+t+kn̓=pla?=sqáx̌a? way̓ way̓ ixí? k̓ɬ+x̌q -nt -is way̓ ixí?
lead_horse well well then step_aside -nt -3erg well then
getting tired." *He stepped out of the way and the race horse*

ɬk̓əɬxətxnáms axa? i? sƛ̓əx̌sqáx̌a? 82 way̓ t̓i i l nəqslúp way̓
ɬ+k̓ɬ+xt=xna+m -s axá? i? s+ƛ̓x̌=sqáx̌a? way̓ t̓i? i? l nqs=lup way̓
go_ahead_again -3erg this art race_horse well evid art in one_place well
went ahead again. *[There was] one place the race horse*

t̓i_kmix nwí··səlx axá? {is} i? sƛ̓əx̌sqáx̌a? 83 ilí? uɬ nɬpak lut uɬ
t̓i?_kmix n+wis+lx axá? i? s+ƛ̓x̌=sqáx̌a? ilí? uɬ n+ɬpak lut uɬ
only jump this art race_horse there and stuck_in_snow not and
could only jump, *and it got stuck in the snow, and*

t̓ q̓aʕp 84 uł ałíʔ iʔ sxʷʔits iʔ smik̓ʷt 85 way̓
t̓ q̓aʕ+p uł ałíʔ iʔ s -xʷʔi+t -s iʔ s+mik̓ʷt way̓
negfac move and because art nom -much -3i art snow_on_ground well
couldn't move, there was so much snow. (9:04) The

itlíʔ {itlí} łk̓əłkxám axáʔ iʔ t sílxʷaʔ ta nməlk̓ʷápaʔst 86 way̓
itlíʔ ł+k̓ł+kxa+m axáʔ iʔ t sílxʷaʔ t n+mlk̓ʷ=ápaʔst way̓
from_there follow_again this art agInst big agInst stallion well
big stallion continued to lead. They

kícxəlx nt̓a··, way̓ qʷən̓qʷán̓t iʔ sənkłċaʔsqáx̌aʔ 87 axáʔ maʕn {iʔ} ia
kic+x -lx nt̓a way̓ qʷn̓•qʷan̓+t iʔ sn+kł+ċaʔ=sqáx̌aʔ axáʔ m̓ʕan iʔ
arrive -pl intj yes pitiful art horse this intj art
got there, my, the horses are pitiful. My, the bushes,

ct̓əkʷt̓ákʷ iʔ yult axáʔ t̓əxʷ {iʔ} iʔ məl̓məl̓tíłp uł iʔ mulx
c+t̓kʷ•t̓akʷ iʔ yul+t axáʔ t̓xʷ iʔ ml̓•ml̓t=iłp uł iʔ mulx
bushes art big_around this evidently art poplar and art cottonwood
the big poplars and the cottonwoods,

88 uł axáʔ iʔ ċáq̓ʷċəq̓ʷłp uł ixíʔ taʔlíʔ kʷa ł ilyúlt 89 ixíʔ uł
uł axáʔ iʔ ċaq̓ʷ•ċq̓ʷ=łp uł ixíʔ taʔlíʔ kʷa ł yl•yul+t ixíʔ uł
and this art wire_bush and that very_much intj ? big_around then and
and the wire bushes, they are big around, and up to

miʔmiw̓sálqʷ {is} lut {t̓a kłk̓íʔlaʔlxʷ} t̓a kłk̓iʔlílxʷ 90 uł ałíʔ axáʔ
mi•miw̓s=álqʷ lut t̓ kł+k̓yl=ilxʷ uł ałíʔ axáʔ
half_way_up_tree not negfac have_tree_bark and because this
way up in the tree they didn't have any bark because the horses

iʔ sənkłċaʔsqáx̌aʔ {ic} ksq̓míltən uł ixíʔ txpálqʷsəlx {uł ixíʔ} axáʔ iʔ
iʔ sn+kł+ċaʔ=sqáx̌aʔ k+s+q̓m=ilt+n uł ixíʔ t+xp=alqʷ -s -lx axáʔ iʔ
art horse have_hunger and then chew_tree -3erg -pl this art
got so hungry they chewed

k̓iʔlílxʷ 91 uł axáʔ {iʔ} iʔ q̓iʔq̓ʔík way̓ t̓iʔ ƛ̓lal 92 məł ixíʔ iʔ t
k̓yl=ilxʷ uł axáʔ iʔ q̓y̓•q̓y̓ik way̓ t̓iʔ ƛ̓l•al mł ixíʔ iʔ t
tree_bark and this art colts yes evid dead and then art agInst
the bark. And as soon as a colt dies (10:00) the mothers

túm̓təm̓ ixíʔ ʔíłtməlx iʔ syúpscəlx iʔ qəpqíntəns 93 way̓
tum̓•tm̓ ixíʔ ʔił -t -m -lx iʔ sy=ups -c -lx iʔ qp=qin+tn -s way̓
mothers then eat -łt -psv -pl art tail -3in -pl art hair -3in well
eat their tails, their manes. There is

uł t̓iʔ_kmix sċim̓lx k̓im ilíʔ cəqmín 94 k̓im t̓iʔ {ƛ̓ə} iʔ ƛ̓ax̌əx̌ƛ̓x̌áp iʔ
uł t̓iʔ_kmix s+ċim -lx k̓im ilíʔ cq+min k̓im t̓iʔ iʔ ƛ̓ax̌•x̌•ƛ̓x̌á+p iʔ
and only bone -pl only there lie only evid art elders art
nothing but bones lying there. It's only the oldest horses

sənkłċaʔsqáx̌aʔ kiʔ cxʷəl·xʷált {uł way̓ náx̌əmł} 95 way̓ uł łaʔłʔápəlx
sn+kł+ċaʔ=sqáx̌aʔ kiʔ c -xʷl·•xʷal+t way̓ uł łaʔ•łʔá+p -lx
horse rel hab -alive_pl well and come_to_end -pl
that are alive, and they were coming to an end.

96 waẏ sənk̓ʷínəms inl?íw ?asəl?upənkstłcílkst i?
waẏ s -n+k̓ʷin+m -s in -l?iw ?asl+?upn=kst+ł+cíl=kst i?
well nom -pick -3i 1in -m's_father twenty_five art
My father picked

ksəm̓m̓cxənsqáx̌a?s 97 ixí? {is is} i? scənk̓ʷíns, uł axá? mus {i} ia
s+sm̓•m̓cxn=sqáx̌a? ixí? i? sc -n+k̓ʷin -s uł axá? mus i?
mares that art pftv -pick -3i and this four art
25 mares, *that's what he picked, and four*

nq̓ʷa?q̓ʷ?ápa?st 98 mat ska?ka?łəlspíntk kəm̓ sm̓əm̓əspíntk ixí? i?
n+q̓ʷa?•q̓ʷ?=ápa?st mat s+ka?•ka?+l+s+pin=tk km̓ s+m̓•m̓s+pin=tk ixí? i?
geldings maybe three_year_olds or four_year_olds that art
geldings, *maybe three years old, or four years old (they make*

kłənk̓amtíw̓stən[s] 99 uł naqs sťúlc̓a?, ixí? uł ka?łəl?úpənkst i?
kł -n+k+?am=t=íw̓s+tn -s uł naqs s+ťúl=c̓a? ixí? uł ka?łl+?upn=kst i?
to_be -saddle_horse -3i and one mule that and thirty art
saddle horses out of them), *and one mule, and that made it 30 head he pulled*

sck̓əłkəłmíksts 100 ixí? uł cyx̌əntísəlx uł ałí? kʷa
sc -k̓ł+kł+m=ikst -s ixí? uł c -yx̌ -nt -is -lx uł ałí? kʷa
pftv -separate -3i then and act -drive -nt -3erg -pl and because intj
out of there. (11:01) *They drove them out because they had cleared*

qʷámqʷəmt waẏ i? scwi?sk̓əłqáx̌səlx 101 waẏ ałí?
qʷam•qʷm+t waẏ i? sc -wẏ+s+k̓ł+qax̌ -s -lx waẏ ałí?
excellent yes art pftv -finish_clearing -3i -pl well so
a good road, *and they*

[s]tqʷáysəlx 102 xʷu··ylx łciyáʕpəlx uł ałí? nixʷ
s -t+qʷay -s -lx xʷuy -lx ł+c+yaʕ+p -lx uł ałí? nixʷ
nom -run_down -3i -pl go -pl arrive_cisl_again -pl and so also
ran down the hill. *They went and got home. And my father also*

ksťmáʕlt inl?íw 103 put i? xʷəxʷ?ít i? sťmáʕlt 104 uł ałí?
k+s+ťm=ʕalt in -l?iw put i? xʷ•xʷ?i+t i? s+ťm=ʕalt uł ałí?
have_cow 1in -m's_father just art several art cow and so
had cattle, *a fair number of cows,* *corraled*

ck̓əłʕáľ uł k̓əłkłcáw 105 waẏ ixí? yx̌əntís i? sťmáʕlt uł
c -k̓ł+ʕaľ uł k̓ł+kłcaw[4] waẏ ixí? yx̌ -nt -is i? s+ťm=ʕalt uł
hab -fence and under_shed well then drag -nt -3erg art cow and
or under the shed. *He drove the cows*

?ácəcqa?sts 106 waẏ {an} nyx̌əntís axá? {i?} i?
?ác•c•qa? -st -s waẏ n+yx̌ -nt -is axá? i?
go_out_pl -caus -3erg well drive_into -nt -3erg this art
out *and he drove in*

4 Analysis not clear.

sṁəcṁəcxənsqáx̌aʔs 107 uɬ axáʔ iʔ sqəlqəltmxʷsqáx̌aʔs ixíʔm
s+ṁc•ṁcxn=sqáx̌aʔ -s uɬ axáʔ iʔ s+ql•qlt=mxʷ=sqáx̌aʔ -s ixíʔ+m
mares -3in and this art male_horses -3in that
his mares. *And he tied up the geldings*

náx̌əmɬ nʕacʕacəntís iʔ l sənt̓əwscqáx̌aʔtən 108 uɬ axáʔ iʔ {s}
nax̌mɬ n+ʕac•ʕac -nt -is iʔ l sn+t̓wst=sqáx̌aʔ+tn uɬ axáʔ iʔ
but tie_inside -nt -3erg art in barn and this art
in the barn. *The mule was*

st̓úɬċaʔ ilíʔ nʔaksuxíẇs axáʔ iʔ l sṁəcxənsqáx̌aʔ 109 axáʔ
s+t̓úɬ=ċaʔ ilíʔ n+ʔaks+wx=íẇs axáʔ iʔ l s+ṁcxn=sqáx̌aʔ axáʔ
mule there stand_amongst this art with mare this
right in with the mares. *He loaded [the*

kɬt̓qam kləʕʷsqáx̌aʔm iʔ laslí {u} 110 i kɬt̓qa··m axáʔ iʔ l kɬcqmín
kɬ+t̓qa+m k+lʕ̓ʷ=sqáx̌aʔ+m iʔ laslí i kɬ+t̓qa+m axáʔ iʔ l kɬ+cq+min
load hitch_team art sleigh intj load this art on rack
hay], hooked up the team to the sleigh, *loaded it on the hay rack, (12:02)*

111 uɬ q̇ʷíċəsts waẏ ixíʔ t supúlaʔxʷ ixíʔ təqmí··s
uɬ q̇ʷiċ -st -s waẏ ixíʔ t s+wp=úlaʔxʷ ixíʔ tq+mi -s
and full -st -3erg well that agInst hay then put_down -3erg
and he filled it with hay and put it down.

112 cus axáʔ iʔ sənkɬċaʔsqáx̌aʔ waẏ mya··ɬ {mət} p ɬa
cu -s axáʔ iʔ sn+kɬ+ċaʔ=sqáx̌aʔ waẏ myaɬ p ɬaʔ
tell -3erg this art horse yes too_much 5kn when
He said to the horses,

cqʷəṅqʷəṅnməscút iʔ t sq̇míltən 113 mat ʕapnáʔ
c -qʷṅ•qʷṅ+mscut iʔ t s+q̇m=ilt+n mat ʕapnáʔ
hab -hard_time art agInst hunger maybe now
"You have had too hard a time with hunger. *Now you have*

kstqʷámqʷəmqsəmp {p ks} p ksənʔakʷmaʔscínaʔx 114 a
k -s+t+qʷam•qʷm=qs -mp p ks -n+ʔakʷ=maʔ+s=cín -aʔx a
to_be -good_things_to_eat -5in 5kn incp^ -hoard_food -^incp intj
good things to eat, you are going to hoard food." *It was late*

wiʔstəqmís {ay i} ixíʔ uɬ k̓laxʷ 115 waẏ ksx̌əlpínaʔ {a} xʷuy k̓əl
wẏ+s+tq+mi -s ixíʔ uɬ k̓laxʷ waẏ k+s+x̌l+p=ínaʔ xʷuy k̓l
finish_stacking -3erg then and evening well have_daylight go to
when he finished putting it down. *In the morning he went*

sənt̓əwscqáx̌aʔtən 116 yaʕyáʕt t̓i qmní··waʔt axáʔ {i s} iʔ
sn+t̓wst=sqáx̌aʔ+tn yaʕ•yáʕ+t t̓iʔ qmn=íwaʔt axáʔ iʔ
barn all evid lying_around this art
to the barn. *All the animals he had fed,*

sʔamənsqáx̌aʔs iʔ sṁəcxənsqáx̌aʔs 117 waẏ t̓i_kmix iʔ {st̓uɬ ka}
s+ʔamn=sqáx̌aʔ -s iʔ s+ṁcxn=sqáx̌aʔ -s waẏ t̓iʔ_kmix iʔ
animal_fed -3in art mare -3in well only art
his mares, they were all lying on the ground. *It's only the mule*

sťúłċaʔ ka cxʷəlxʷált {uł axáʔ} 118 axáʔ náx̌əmł a nťwist {i l sənkł} iʔ l
s+ťúł=ċaʔ ka c -xʷl•xʷal+t axáʔ nax̌mł a n+ťwist iʔ l
mule rel hab -alive this but art stand_up_pl art in
that is alive. *But those that were standing*

sənťəwscqáx̌aʔtən 119 náx̌əmł ixíʔ cxʷəl·xʷált 120 uł ałíʔ axáʔ
sn+ťwst=sqáx̌aʔ+tn nax̌mł ixíʔ c -xʷl·•xʷal+t uł ałíʔ axáʔ
barn but that hab -alive_pl and so this
in the barn, *they were alive. (13:03)* *My folks*

inƛ̓ax̌əx̌ƛ̓x̌áp̓ uł ałíʔ ksənťəwscqáx̌aʔtən 121 uł ksupúlaʔxʷ axáʔ
in -ƛ̓ax̌•x̌•ƛ̓x̌á+p uł ałíʔ k+sn+ťwst=sqáx̌aʔ+tn uł k+s+wp=úlaʔxʷ axáʔ
1in -elders and so have_-barn and have_hay this
had a barn, *and my father*

inlʔíw iʔ l sʔistk 122 uł axáʔ isk̓ʷúy {ks} sysyus iʔ l
in -lʔiw iʔ l s+ʔis=tk uł axáʔ i -s+k̓ʷuy sy•sy=us iʔ l
1in -ṁs_father art for winter and this 1in -mother smart art at
had hay for the winter. *And my mother she is smart at*

sk̓ʷəlcəncút 123 uł ksənłq̓ʷútənəlx ilíʔ {uł} uł ilíʔ sənpaʔpúlxtənlx
s+k̓ʷl̓=cn+cut uł k+sn+łq̓ʷ=ut+n -lx ilíʔ uł ilíʔ sn+paʔ•púl+x+tn -lx
cooking and have_bed -pl there and there place_to_overnight -pl
cooking, *and they had a bed there, an overnighter for*

iʔ t suyápix 124 uł ixíʔ ilíʔ ksənpəpúlxəlx pnicíʔ
iʔ t s+wyapy=x uł ixíʔ ilíʔ k+sn+p•pul=x -lx pn+icíʔ
art obl white_person and then there have_overnighter -pl at_that_time
white people, *and at that time they had one overnighter.*

125 uł ixíʔ ksx̌əlpínaʔ {uł} uł ixíʔ {cuł} cus inlʔíw 126 ťəxʷ
uł ixíʔ k+s+x̌l+p=ínaʔ uł ixíʔ cu -s in -lʔiw ťxʷ
and then have_daylight and then tell -3erg 1in -m's_father emph
The next day he said to my dad... *It's*

t inlʔíw iʔ cus axáʔ iʔ suyápix 127 a mat uł
t in -lʔiw iʔ cu -s axáʔ iʔ s+wyapy=x a mat uł
agInst 1in -ṁs_father art tell -3erg this art white_person intj maybe and
my father who said to the white man: *"What*

səxkínx uł inkəẃwáp uł ał ƛ̓axʷt nċəspúlaʔxʷ
s -x+kin -x uł in -kẃ•w•ap uł ał ƛ̓axʷ+t n+ċs+p=úlaʔxʷ
ipftv^ -do_what -^ipftv and 1in -horses and compl dead_pl kill
happened to my horses that they are dead, gone,

128 ʔasəlʔupənksłcílkst {iʔ} yaʕyáʕt iʔ sṁúṁcxən 129 ah cúntəm
ʔasl+ʔupn=kst+ł+cíl=kst yaʕ•yáʕ+t iʔ s+ṁu•ṁcxn ah cu -nt -m
twenty_five all art mare intj tell -nt -psv
twenty-five of them, all mares?" *He said to him,*

waẏ uł, cúntəm uł síwəntəm 130 cúntəm uł ha niʕíp̓ ha
waẏ uł cu -nt -m uł siw -nt -m cu -nt -m uł haʔ n+yʕ=ip haʔ
well and tell -nt -psv and ask -nt -psv tell -nt -psv and inter always inter
he asked him, (14:02) *he said, "Do you always*

ċamstíxʷ ha 131 cut lut, sic iscəntkɬíkstəm
c -ʔam -st -ixʷ haʔ cut lut sic i -sc -n+tkɬ=ikst+m
cust^ -feed -^cust -2erg inter say not then 1i -pftv -bring_down
feed them?" *He said "No, I just got them down*

tə_spiʔsċíɬt 132 ik̓lí stk̓əɬmík̓ʷk̓ʷtxəlx 133 ah, cúntəm
t_s+piʔ+s+ċíɬt[5] ik̓líʔ s -t+k̓ɬ+mik̓ʷ•k̓ʷ•t -x -lx ah cu -nt -m
yesterday there ipftv^ -snowed_in -^ipftv -pl intj tell -nt -psv
yesterday. *They have been snowed in up there."* *He said to him,*

way̓ t̓əxʷ aɬíʔ uɬ asƛ̓xʷám nák̓ʷəm 134 uɬ aɬíʔ kʷa {iʔ}
way̓ t̓xʷ aɬíʔ uɬ a -s+ƛ̓xʷa+m nak̓ʷ+m uɬ aɬíʔ kʷa
well evidently so and 2in -murder evid and because intj
"Well, you just murdered them. *They were snowed in*

mík̓ʷk̓ʷtəlx uɬ lut t̓a ċaɬʔíɬənəlx xʷʔásq̓ət 135 uɬ axáʔ {iʔ iʔ sə}
mik̓ʷ•k̓ʷ•t -lx uɬ lut t̓ c -ʔaɬ•ʔíɬn -lx xʷʔ=asq̓t uɬ axáʔ
snowed_in -pl and not negfac hab -eat_pl -pl many_days and this
and they hadn't eaten for many days *and their stomachs*

iʔ sqʷəlcnínksəlx uɬ ixíʔ q̓p̓axʷ 136 way̓ uɬ t̓i_kʷmiɬ kiʔ
iʔ s+qʷl=cn=ink -s -lx uɬ ixíʔ q̓p̓axʷ way̓ uɬ t̓iʔ_kʷm̓iɬ kiʔ
art belly -3in -pl and that tied_up well and at_once rel
are all tied up. *Then you fed them*

xʷʔit {iʔ amt} iʔ ʔamtíxʷəlx uɬ ixíʔ {i} kt̓íliʔs uɬ axáʔ iʔ
xʷʔi+t iʔ ʔam -t -ixʷ -lx uɬ ixíʔ kt̓=íliʔs uɬ axáʔ iʔ
much art feed -nt -2erg -pl and then stomachs_burst and this art
lots suddenly and their stomachs

sqʷəlcnínksəlx 137 ixíʔ uɬ aɬíʔ ƛ̓axʷt 138 scuts axáʔ
s+qʷl=cn=ink -s -lx ixíʔ uɬ aɬíʔ ƛ̓axʷ+t s -cut -s axáʔ
belly -3in -pl that and because dead_pl nom -say -3i this
busted inside. *And that's why they died."* *My father said,*

inlʔíw uɬ sċkinx kʷa axáʔ iʔ st̓úɬċaʔ {u} ixíʔ nʔaksuxíw̓s lut
in -lʔiw uɬ sc+ʔkin+x kʷa axáʔ iʔ s+t̓úɬ=ċaʔ ixíʔ n+ʔaks+wx=íw̓s lut
1in -m's_father and why_is_it intj this art mule that stand_amongst not
"What about the mule, he was among them and he

sƛ̓lal[s] 139 cúntəm way̓ aɬíʔ kʷa scútəlx iʔ st̓úɬċaʔ
s -ƛ̓l•al -s cu -nt -m way̓ aɬíʔ kʷa s -cut -lx iʔ s+t̓úɬ=ċaʔ
nom -dead -3i tell -nt -psv well because intj hab -say -pl art mule
didn't die." *He said, "Yes, they say the mule has*

talí pəx̌páx̌t 140 uɬ aɬíʔ spəx̌pəx̌tmíx uɬ mat t̓i
taʔlíʔ px̌•pax̌+t uɬ aɬíʔ s -px̌•px̌+t -mix uɬ mat t̓iʔ
very_much smart and because ipftv^ -think -^ipftv and maybe evid
a lot of sense. (15:03) *He thinks, and when he ate he ate*

5 This analysis is unconfirmed. But see Sp s-piʔ-s-ċeʔ; also Th s/piʔh=éwt.

ʔíɬən put iʔ sċíɬəns 141 uɬ ʔanwís {iʔ s} ksənk̓əstmís ixíʔ uɬ
ʔiɬn put iʔ sc+ʔiɬn -s uɬ ʔanwí -s ks -n+k̓s+t+mi -s ixíʔ uɬ
eat just art food -3in and feel -3erg futt^ -harm -3erg then and
just so much. *He felt it was going to harm him and he*

wáy̓sts 142 sċx̌ilx uɬ lut t̓a nk̓əstmís 143 kʷa axáʔ
way̓ -st -s sc+ʔx̌il+x uɬ lut t̓ n+k̓s+t+mi -s kʷa axáʔ
quit -st -3erg reason_why and not negfac harm -3erg intj this
quit. *That's why it didn't harm him.* *But*

aɬíʔ iʔ sənkɬċaʔsqáx̌aʔ lut t̓a kspəx̌páx̌t 144 way̓ t̓i ʔí··ɬən uɬ
aɬíʔ iʔ sn+kɬ+ċaʔ=sqáx̌aʔ lut t̓ k+s+px̌•pax̌+t way̓ t̓iʔ ʔiɬn uɬ
so art horse not negfac have_smarts well evid eat and
the horse got no sense. *He eats and eats,*

kt̓əlt̓líw̓s iʔ sqʷəlcnínks uɬ ƛ̓lal 145 cut uɬ sċkinx kʷa a
k+t̓l•t̓l=iw̓s iʔ s+qʷl=cn=ink -s uɬ ƛ̓l•al cut uɬ sc+ʔkin+x kʷa a
burst art belly -3in and dead say and why_is_it intj art
and his stomach busts, and he dies." *He said, "And why is it*

nt̓wist iʔ sənkɬċaʔsqáx̌aʔ 146 iʔ sməsməspíntk uɬ lut sƛ̓axʷts
n+t̓wist iʔ sn+kɬ+ċaʔ=sqáx̌aʔ iʔ s+ms•ms+pin=tk uɬ lut s -ƛ̓axʷ+t -s
stand_up_pl art horse art four_year_olds and not nom -dead_pl -3i
that the horses in the barn, *the four year olds, the four [year olds] didn't*

iʔ mus 147 cúntəm way̓, uɬ ha stkəṅkṅípləʔ {iʔ} kiʔ ia
iʔ mus cu -nt -m way̓ uɬ haʔ c -t+kṅ•kṅ=ípləʔ kiʔ iʔ
art four tell -nt -psv well and inter act -be_lead rel art
die?" *He asked, "Could they be lead when you put them*

npəpílxstxʷ 148 cut lut, {sic} t̓iʔ ʕacəntín məɬ nʔúɬxʷstən
n+p•pilx -st -xʷ cut lut t̓iʔ ʕac -nt -in mɬ n+ʔuɬxʷ -st -n
enter_pl -st -2erg say not evid tie -nt -1erg and enter -st -1erg
inside?" *He said "No, I just caught them and pushed them in*

uɬ_iʔ kʕacálqʷən 149 cúntəm way̓, cúntəm uɬ aɬíʔ
uɬ_iʔ k+ʕac=álqʷ -n cu -nt -m way̓ cu -nt -m uɬ aɬíʔ
and_then tie_to_post -1erg tell -nt -psv yes tell -nt -psv and because
and tied them." *He said "Yes,*

scəkʷməncútx uɬ aɬíʔ lut t̓a cənqʷaʔmús 150 xkínəm
s -ckʷ+mncut -x uɬ aɬíʔ lut t̓ c -n+qʷaʔm=ús x+kin+m
ipftv^ -pull_back -^ipftv and because not negfac hab -used_to_lead do_what
because they pulled back, they are not broken in to lead. (16:00) *How could*

mi ʔíɬən uɬ t̓iʔ_niʕíp̓ cəkʷməncút uɬ lut t̓a ʔaɬʔíɬniʔst uɬ ixíʔ
mi ʔiɬn uɬ t̓iʔ_n+yʕ=ip ckʷ+mncut uɬ lut t̓ ʔaɬ•ʔiɬn=iʔst uɬ ixíʔ
fut eat and always pull_back and not negfac manage_to_eat and then
they eat, they kept pulling back and never got to eat until

x̌əláp 151 ċx̌ilx uɬ lut iʔ ƛ̓axʷt 152 way̓ ixíʔ nunxʷínaʔ axáʔ {iʔ}
x̌la+p c+ʔx̌il+x uɬ lut iʔ ƛ̓axʷ+t way̓ ixíʔ n+wnxʷ=ínaʔ axáʔ
morning how and not art dead_pl well then believe this
daylight. *That's why they didn't die."* *Then my father*

inlʔíw uɬ waẏ uníxʷ 153 ixíʔ uɬ yaʕyáʕt_swit pnicíʔ
in -lʔiw uɬ waẏ wnixʷ ixíʔ uɬ yaʕ•yáʕ+t_swit pn+icíʔ
1in -m's_father and yes true then and everybody at_that_time
believed, it's so. *And everybody at that time*

c̓əspsqáx̌aʔ 154 aɬíʔ uɬ nak̓ʷá pnicíʔ uɬá waẏ {aʔkɬ}
c̓s+p=sqáx̌aʔ aɬíʔ uɬ nak̓ʷá pn+icíʔ uɬ+á waẏ
stock_gone because and not at_that_time and_not yes
lost horses *because at that time they didn't have*

kɬkəlk̓íc̓aʔtən 155 kəm̓ {a} kɬx̌ʷíc̓laʔxʷtən iʔ t sənkɬc̓aʔsqáx̌aʔ
kɬ+k+lk̓=íc̓aʔ+tn km̓ kɬ+x̌ʷíc̓=laʔxʷ+tn iʔ t sn+kɬ+c̓aʔ=sqáx̌aʔ
have_baler or have_mower art agInst horse
balers *or horse drawn mowers.*

156 waẏ t̓əxʷ ixíʔ t̓iʔ_kmix t kalxútyaʔ sap̓mútyaʔ
waẏ t̓xʷ ixíʔ t̓iʔ_kmix t kalx=útyaʔ sap̓+m=útyaʔ
well evidently then only agInst hand_tool scythe
[They work] only by hand, [with] a scythe.

157 uɬ axáʔ {iʔ i t} sc̓úmstsəlx axáʔ t̓əxʷ i la cəlk̓íẃs,
uɬ axáʔ c -ʔum -st -s -lx axáʔ t̓xʷ iʔ l c -lk̓=iẃs
and this custˆ -call -ˆcust -3erg -pl this emph art with hab -bundle
And what they tie with, what they call

ixíʔ t kc̓lálqʷ 158 uɬ aɬíʔ ʕapnáʔ kʷa {iʔ} iʔ x̌ʷíc̓laʔxʷtən aɬíʔ
ixíʔ t k+c̓l=alqʷ uɬ aɬíʔ ʕapnáʔ kʷa iʔ x̌ʷíc̓=laʔxʷ+tn aɬíʔ
that obl bundling_scythe and so now intj art mower so
a grain cutter with prongs. *Now there are mower machines*

iʔ l supúlaʔxʷ {waẏ t̓i k̓ax̌íʔ t̓k̓ʷakʷ məɬ ə} 159 t̓iʔ x̌ʷíc̓əlx axáʔ məɬ
iʔ l s+wp=úlaʔxʷ t̓iʔ x̌ʷic̓ -lx axáʔ mɬ
art for hay evid cut -pl this and
for hay. *They cut, it falls there, and*

k̓ax̌íʔ t̓k̓ʷak̓ʷ məɬ waẏ cwiʔskəlk̓íc̓aʔ 160 uɬ axáʔ nixʷ {iʔ iʔ l s} iʔ
k̓a+ʔx̌íʔ t̓k̓ʷ•ak̓ʷ mɬ waẏ c -wẏ+s+k+lk̓=íc̓aʔ uɬ axáʔ nixʷ iʔ
over_there fall and yes hab -finish_bundling and this also art
it's already baled. *Same with*

l x̌əẃáẃ iʔ l sk̓ʷanɬq 161 axáʔ {i t} sc̓úmstsəlx {aɬ} lut
l x̌ẃ•aẃ iʔ l s+k̓ʷan=ɬq axáʔ c -ʔum -st -s -lx lut
with dried art with harvest this custˆ -call -ˆcust -3erg -pl not
dry grain. (17:00) *They call this, I don't*

t̓a cmistín iʔ ta nqílxʷcən {i t} 162 stim̓ ixíʔ
t̓ c -my -st -in iʔ t n+qilxʷ=cn s+tim̓ ixíʔ
negfac custˆ -know -ˆcust -1erg art agInst Indian_language what that
know in Indian *what*

ɬ *combine* ixíʔ tkampáyntəm uɬ aɬíʔ waẏ t̓iʔ x̌ʷíc̓əc̓ ixíʔ
ɬ ixíʔ t+kampáyn -t -m uɬ aɬíʔ waẏ t̓iʔ x̌ʷic̓•c̓ ixíʔ
one_that that combine -nt -psv and so yes evid cut that
"combine" is. They combine it, they cut it.

163 məł way̓ k̓aʔx̌í saʕsáʕt way̓ cwiʔsk̓əłlák̓ək̓ kəm̓ ck̓əłt̓áq̓ʷ
mł way̓ k̓a+ʔx̌íʔ saʕ•sáʕ+t way̓ c -wy̓+s+k̓ł+lak̓•k̓ km̓ c -k̓ł+t̓aq̓ʷ
and well there fall_off yes hab -already_tied or hab -sewn
It falls the other way, and it's already tied or sewn.

164 uł ałíʔ pnicíʔ uł way̓ t̓iʔ q̓sápiʔ iʔ sqilxʷ way̓ kmix t̓iʔ
uł ałíʔ pn+icíʔ uł way̓ t̓iʔ q̓sápiʔ iʔ s+qilxʷ way̓ kmix t̓iʔ
and because at_that_time and yes evid long_ago art Indian yes only evid
At that time, a long time ago the Indians [worked]

iʔ t sap̓mútyaʔ 165 uł axáʔ ʔúmsəlx iʔ t kc̓lalqʷ t̓iʔ
iʔ t sap̓+m=útyaʔ uł axáʔ ʔum -s -lx iʔ t k+c̓l=alqʷ t̓iʔ
art agInst scythe and this call -3erg -pl art obl bundling_scythe evid
only by hand, *and they call it grain cutter with prongs,*

t kalxútyaʔ {i ki c c̓x̌ʷi i} x̌ʷíc̓laʔxʷtənsəlx {uł ał} 166 uł ałíʔ ixíʔ q̓sápiʔ
t kalx=útyaʔ x̌ʷíc̓=laʔxʷ+tn -s -lx uł ałíʔ ixíʔ q̓sápiʔ
agInst hand_tool mower -3in -pl and so then long_ago
that's their hand cutter. *Long ago, when*

ixíʔ uł ałíʔ kʷa a cmrim {in} inlʔíw naʔł isk̓ʷúy
ixíʔ uł ałíʔ kʷa a c -mrim in -lʔiw naʔł i -s+k̓ʷuy
then and so intj intj hab -marry 1in -m's_father and 1in -mother
my father and mother got married, (18:05)

167 uł ałíʔ kʷa t̓iʔ sknəqsəltílt axáʔ iʔ t isx̌áx̌paʔ
uł ałíʔ kʷa t̓iʔ s+k=nqs=lt=ilt axáʔ iʔ t i -s+x̌á•x̌paʔ
and because intj evid only_child this art obl 1in -grandfather
my grandfather had only one child,

inlʔíw 168 ixíʔ uł i ʔamtúłtəm iʔ kəw̓wáps iʔ stim̓s
in -lʔiw ixíʔ uł iʔ ʔam -tułt -m iʔ kw•w+ap -s iʔ stim̓ -s
1in -m's_father then and art feed -tułt -psv art horses -3in art thing -3in
my father, *and he fed his horses, anything,*

iʔ st̓máʕlts 169 ixíʔ uł ałíʔ pnicíʔ uł {ał} nak̓ʷáʔ {kł}
iʔ s+t̓m=ʕalt -s ixíʔ uł ałíʔ pn+icíʔ uł nak̓ʷ+á
art cow -3in then and because at_that_time and not
cows. *Because at that time there were no*

kłənckʷmnáqs kəm̓ kłtqcəlxálqʷ xəwíł 170 uł ixíʔ iʔ t cun[6] way̓
kł+n+ckʷ+mn=aqs km̓ kł+t+qc+lx=alqʷ xwił uł ixíʔ iʔ t cu -n way̓
have_wagon_road or have_rail road and then art say 1erg yes
wagon roads or railroads. *Like I said, there was*

t̓i_kmix naqs səntumístən ilíʔ iʔ l sk̓əłʔál·qʷaʔ
t̓iʔ_kmix naqs sn+tw+mist+n ilíʔ iʔ l s+k̓ł+ʔál·qʷaʔ
only one store there art in border
only one store at Marcus [at the shore].

6 Here I have kept the three words separate; elsewhere I have also interlinearized the phrase, inconsistently as I realize, as a single idiomatic unit.

171 scústsəlx t *Open Hammer* 172 uɬ ixíʔ ilíʔ
s -cu -st -s -lx t uɬ ixíʔ ilíʔ
custˆ -tell -ˆcust -3erg -pl obl and then there
They call it Open Hammer. *My father*

inlʔíw k̓ʷúləm ixíʔ uɬ kaʕcám {kaʔɬ} 173 kaʔɬəlʔúpənkst ia
in -lʔiw k̓ʷul̓+m ixíʔ uɬ k+ʕacá+m kaʔɬl+ʔupn=kst iʔ
1in -m's_father work that and packing thirty art
worked there, packing. *Thirty of*

nq̓ʷəɬtsqáx̌aʔtəns 174 ixíʔ məɬ xʷuy məɬ k̓aʔx̌íʔ k̓əl k̓aɬʔálqʷ
n+q̓ʷɬ+t=sqáx̌aʔ+tn -s ixíʔ mɬ xʷuy mɬ k̓a+ʔx̌íʔ k̓l k̓a+ɬʔ=álqʷ
pack_horse -3in then and go and over_there to over_the_line
his pack horses. *He goes across the line, (19:00)*

175 c̓úmstsəlx tqəltkálqʷ {k̓əl} k̓əl *Port_Hope* {tli mi}
c -ʔum -st -s -lx t+qlt=k=alqʷ k̓l
custˆ -call -ˆcust -3erg -pl across_line to
they call it "above the rails" to Port [Fort] Hope.

176 itlíʔ mi ct̓íxəlxstsəlx tla nsq̓ʷut {iʔ} iʔ
itlíʔ mi c -t̓ix+lx -st -s -lx tla n+s+q̓ʷut iʔ
from_there fut custˆ -come_to_shore -ˆcust -3erg -pl from other_side art
It's from there that they pull their groceries and merchandise

stíwcəns iʔ stumísts 177 uɬ aɬiá pnicíʔ uɬá
s+tiw=cn -s iʔ s+tw+mist -s uɬ aɬi+á pn+icíʔ uɬ+á
groceries -3in art merchandise -3in and because_not at_that_time and_not
out of the water from across. *At that time there was*

kɬp̓úlaʔxʷtən 178 ixíʔ məɬ axáʔ inlʔíw ckaʕcəntís {li}
k+ɬp̓=úlaʔxʷ+tn ixíʔ mɬ axáʔ in -lʔiw c -k+ʕac -nt -is
have_border then and this 1in -m's_father act -pack -nt -3erg
no border. *My father packed it*

cxʷuysts aláʔ l sk̓əɬʔál·qʷaʔ 179 kəm̓ laʔkín̓ məɬ {kə} itlíʔ {ɬ}
c+xʷuy+st -s aláʔ l s+k̓ɬ+ʔál·qʷaʔ km̓ la+ʔkín̓ mɬ itlíʔ
bring_st -3erg here at Marcus or when and from_there
and took it to Marcus. *Other times he goes from*

cxʷuy məɬ k̓əl {sc̓um} 180 sc̓úmstsəlx iʔ ta
c -xʷuy mɬ k̓l c -ʔum -st -s -lx iʔ t
hab -go and to custˆ -call -ˆcust -3erg -pl art agInst
there to, *they call in Indian*

nqílxʷcən púɬən, ixíʔ uɬ *Portland* 181 itlíʔ mi ckaʕcám
n+qilxʷ=cn puɬn ixíʔ uɬ itlíʔ mi c -k+ʕacá+m
Indian_language Portland that and from_there fut hab -packing
"púɬən," that's "Portland." *He packs from there*

cxʷuy məɬ taʔlíʔ cxʷʔásq̓ət {n} məɬ t̓əckícx 182 uɬ ixíʔ
c+xʷuy mɬ taʔlíʔ c -xʷʔ=asq̓t mɬ t̓c -kic+x uɬ ixíʔ
come and very_much hab -many_days and habCisl -arrive and that
and he comes, and it takes him many days to get back. *And that's*

sck̓ʷúl̓s inlʔíw ałíʔ iʔ {s} skaʕcám 183 uł axáʔ kmix
sc+k̓ʷul̓ -s in -lʔiw ałíʔ iʔ s+k+ʕacá+m uł axáʔ kmix
work -3in 1in -m's_father so art packing and this only
my father's job, packing. *All my father is*

isx̌áx̌paʔ iʔ səxʷk̓ʷánłqəm {naʔ} naʔł inqáqnaʔ 184 uł axáʔ
i -s+x̌á•x̌paʔ iʔa sxʷ=k̓ʷan=łq+m naʔł in -qá•qnaʔ uł axáʔ
1in -grandfather art gardener with 1in -fa's_mother and this
is a gardener with my grandmother. (20:02) *And*

isk̓ʷúy i·· kʷlíwtəlx iʔ sck̓ʷánłqxəlx iʔ t supúlaʔxʷ
i -s+k̓ʷuy i·· kʷl=iwt -lx iʔ sc -k̓ʷan=łq -x -lx iʔ t s+wp=úlaʔxʷ
1in -mother intj live -pl art ipftvp^ -grow_crop -^ipftvp -pl art obl hay
my mother lives with them and they farm hay.

185 axáʔ iʔ_t_cun uł ałíʔ {nak̓ʷá} nak̓ʷá uł a kłx̌ʷíc̓laʔxʷtən {i ts} iʔ t
axáʔ iʔ_t_cun uł ałíʔ nak̓ʷá uł a kł+x̌ʷíc̓=laʔxʷ+tn iʔ t
this as_I_said and so not and intj have_mower art obl
Like I said, they don't have hay mowers

supúlaʔxʷ axáʔ iʔ t sənkłc̓aʔsqáx̌aʔ 186 kmix t kalxútyaʔ
s+wp=úlaʔxʷ axáʔ iʔ t sn+kł+c̓aʔ=sqáx̌aʔ kmix t kalx=útyaʔ
hay this art agInst horse only agInst hand_tool
pulled by horses, *only by hand.*

187 way̓ uł ałíʔ axáʔ ksx̌əlpínaʔlx tkʷʔútəlx 188 axáʔ {iʔ is}
way̓ uł ałíʔ axáʔ k+s+x̌lp=ínaʔ -lx tkʷʔ=ut -lx axáʔ
well and so this have_daylight -pl walk_pl -pl this
In the morning they walk, *my*

isx̌áx̌paʔ uł axáʔ inqáqnaʔ uł axáʔ isk̓ʷúy 189 axáʔ {i}
i -s+x̌á•x̌paʔ uł axáʔ in -qá•qnaʔ uł axáʔ i -s+k̓ʷuy axáʔ
1in -grandfather and this 1in -fa's_mother and this 1in -mother this
grandfather, and my grandmother, and my mother. *My*

isx̌áx̌paʔ ixíʔ x̌ʷíc̓laʔxʷəm axáʔ iʔ t kc̓lalqʷ 190 ixíʔ uł
i -s+x̌á•x̌paʔ ixíʔ x̌ʷíc̓=laʔxʷ+m axáʔ iʔ t k+c̓l=alqʷ ixíʔ uł
1in -grandfather that mow this art agInst bundling_scythe that and
grandfather cuts with a hand grain mower *for*

ałíʔ {a} iʔ l x̌əw̓áw̓ iʔ l cəlk̓íw̓s 191 uł axáʔ inqáqnaʔ
ałíʔ iʔ l x̌w̓•aw̓ iʔ l c -lk̓=iw̓s uł axáʔ in -qá•qnaʔ
so art for dried art for hab -bundle and this 1in -fa's_mother
the dry [grain] to be tied. *And my grandmother*

sisyús iʔ l səlk̓íw̓səm 192 nak̓ʷa axáʔ {iʔ t i t} iʔ t sp̓íc̓ən a kaʔ
sy•syus iʔ l s+lk̓=iw̓s+m nak̓ʷ+á axáʔ iʔ t s+p̓ic̓n a kiʔ
smart art at tie_bundles not this art agInst rope intj rel
is smart at tying grain. *It's not with rope that it's*

cəlk̓íw̓s 193 sta axáʔ iʔ t sksp̓qíntən, ixíʔ íylw̓əs, íylw̓əs
c -lk̓=iw̓s sta axáʔ iʔ t s+k+sp̓=qin+tn ixíʔ yilw -s yilw -s
hab -bundle intj this art agInst wheat_stem that twist -3erg twist -3erg
tied, (21:08) *but with hay. She twists it, and then she ties*

məɬ ixíʔ kʕacíc̓aʔs 194 uɬ axáʔ isk̓ʷúy iʔ səxʷc̓al̓ám
mɬ ixíʔ k+ʕac=íc̓aʔ -s uɬ axáʔ i -s+k̓ʷuy iʔ sxʷ=c̓al̓á+m
and then tie_bundle -3erg and this 1in -mother art one_who_stands_it
the bundle. *And my mother is the one that stands them up.*

195 i·· məɬ wiʔsx̌ʷíc̓laʔxʷəm axáʔ isx̌áx̌paʔ 196 məɬ axáʔ
i·· mɬ wy̓+s+x̌ʷíc̓=laʔxʷ+m axáʔ i -s+x̌á•x̌paʔ mɬ axáʔ
intj and finish_mowing this 1in -grandfather and this
My grandfather gets done cutting, *and my*

wiʔsəlk̓íw̓səm t̓i ilíʔ c̓awtípstəm axáʔ in{ti}qáqnaʔ
wy̓+s+lk̓=iw̓s+m t̓iʔ ilíʔ c -ʔaw+t=íp -st -m axáʔ in -qá•qnaʔ
finish_bundling evid there cust^ -follow -^cust -psv this 1in -fa's_mother
grandmother gets done tying right behind him,

197 məɬ axáʔ isk̓ʷúy nixʷ wiʔsc̓al̓ám 198 ixíʔ məɬ ixíʔ
mɬ axáʔ i -s+k̓ʷuy nixʷ wy̓+s+c̓al̓á+m ixíʔ mɬ ixíʔ
and this 1in -mother also finish_standing_st_up then and then
and my mother gets done standing them up. *Then they*

sckʷámsəlx stqámsəlx 199 uɬ ixíʔ tqəntí··səlx məɬ
s -ckʷa+m -s -lx s -tqa+m -s -lx uɬ ixíʔ tq -nt -is -lx mɬ
nom -haul -3i -pl nom -stack -3i -pl and then touch -nt -3erg -pl and
start hauling bundles, stacking them. *They stack, and they*

wiʔstqəntísəlx iʔ supúlaʔxʷ 200 i·· məɬ k̓aʔílx mqʷaqʷ mi
wy̓+s+tq -nt -is -lx iʔ s+wp=úlaʔxʷ i·· mɬ k̓ay̓•y+lx mqʷ•aqʷ mi
finish_stacking -nt -3erg -pl art hay intj and turn_fall snow_fall fut
get done stacking the hay. *In the fall it snows and*

uɬ {i} inlʔíw ɬckicx uɬ aɬíʔ scq̓ʷaɬtsqáx̌aʔx
uɬ in -lʔiw ɬ+c+kic+x uɬ aɬíʔ sc -q̓ʷaɬ+t=sqáx̌aʔ -x
and 1in -m's_father arrive_cisl_again and because ipftvp^ -pack_horse -^ipftvp
my father gets back from packing. (22:00)

201 a· atláʔ q̓ʷiɬt tla ksəntumístən təl sk̓əɬʔál·qʷaʔ
a atláʔ q̓ʷiɬ+t tla k+sn+tw+mist+n tl s+k̓ɬ+ʔál·qʷaʔ
intj from_here pack_on_back from have_store from Marcus
He packs things from here, from the store, from Marcus,

c̓úmstsəlx t *Open Hammer* kəm̓ axáʔ upcín 202 a[xáʔ] təl
c -ʔum -st -s -lx t km̓ axáʔ wp=cin axáʔ tl
cust^ -call -^cust -3erg -pl obl or this beard this from
they call it "Open Hammer" or "Beard." *From*

pú··ɬən itlí··ʔ mi cxəllákək 203 ixíʔ caʔkʷ cus iʔ ta
puɬn itlíʔ mi c+xl•l•ak•k ixíʔ caʔkʷ cu -s iʔ t
Portland from_there fut turn_around_cisl that as tell -3erg art agInst
Portland he turns around, *that's what they call in English*

nuyápixcən *Portland* ixíʔ uɬ aɬíʔ ta nqílxʷcən uɬ púɬən 204 way̓ uɬ
n+wyap=x=cn ixíʔ uɬ aɬíʔ t n+qilxʷ=cn uɬ puɬn way̓ uɬ
say_in_English that and so agInst Indian_lg and Portland well and
"Portland" and in Indian "púɬən." *From*

atláʔ {ɬ} ɬənk̓əwílx ta nx̌ʷyaʔɬpítkʷ 205 ɬxʷuy {ɬ} məɬ yaʔx̌í k̓əl
atláʔ ɬ+n+k̓w+ilx t n+x̌ʷyaʔ=ɬp=ítkʷ ɬ+xʷuy mɬ yaʔx̌í k̓l
from_here go_back_upriver obl Kettle go_back and that_one to
here he goes up the Kettle River, *he goes back across*

k̓aɬʔál·qʷ 206 yaʔx̌í {k̓əl s··} k̓əl sílxʷaʔ iʔ k̓əl siwɬkʷ {i s}
k̓a+ɬʔ+alqʷ yaʔx̌í k̓l sílxʷaʔ iʔ k̓l siwɬ=kʷ
across_border that_one to big art to water
the line, *over there to the big water.*

207 c̓úmlaʔxʷstsəlx {t} t *Port_Hope* {thop} itlíʔ məɬ
c -ʔúm=laʔxʷ -st -s -lx t itlíʔ mɬ
custˆ -call_a_place -ˆcust -3erg -pl obl from_there and
They call the place "Port Hope." From there

cq̓ʷəɬtsqáx̌aʔm 208 məɬ aɬíʔ cənyak̓ʷstísəlx {iʔ s} iʔ l stáɬəm
c -q̓ʷɬ+t=sqáx̌aʔ+m mɬ aɬíʔ c -n=y̓akʷ -st -is -lx iʔ l s+taɬm
hab -horse_pack and so custˆ -cross -ˆcust -3erg -pl art in boat
they pack, *they bring the groceries across on*

axáʔ iʔ stíwcəns 209 axáʔ sc̓úmstsəlx t upcín
axáʔ iʔ s+tiw=cn -s axáʔ c -ʔum -st -s -lx t wp=cin
this art groceries -3in this custˆ -call -ˆcust -3erg -pl obl beard
the boat. (23:03) *They call him "Beard."*

210 way̓ a ct̓íxəlxsts iʔ stíwcəns ixíʔ məɬ
way̓ a c -t̓ix+lx -st -s iʔ s+tiw=cn -s ixíʔ mɬ
well intj custˆ -come_to_shore -ˆcust -3erg art groceries -3in then and
They unload his groceries and my father

ckʕacəntís inlʔíw 211 məɬ ixíʔ cxʷuysts
c -k+ʕac -nt -is in -lʔiw mɬ ixíʔ c+xʷuy+st -s ixíʔ
act -tie -nt -3erg 1in -m's_father and then bring_st -3erg then
packs them, *and then he brings them.*

212 uɬ aɬíʔ mat k̓əl kaʔɬəlʔúpənkst a nq̓ʷəɬtsqáx̌aʔtəns 213 iʔ t
uɬ aɬíʔ mat k̓l kaʔɬl+ʔupn=kst a n+q̓ʷɬ+t=sqáx̌aʔ+tn -s iʔ t
and so maybe about thirty art pack_horse -3in art obl
He had about thirty horses *and*

st̓úɬc̓aʔ iʔ ɬ naqs, uɬ ixíʔ lut knánaqs 214 i[xíʔ] {ksəxʷ}
s+t̓úɬ=c̓aʔ iʔ ɬ naqs uɬ ixíʔ lut k=ná•naqs ixíʔ
mule art one_that one and that not alone that
one mule; and he isn't the only one [packing]. *He had*

ksəxʷkʕacqáx̌aʔm tk̓asʔasíl iʔ sck̓aʕʷmísts 215 ixíʔ {iʔ sə} iʔ
k+sxʷ=k+ʕac=qáx̌aʔ+m tk=ʔas•ʔasíl iʔ sc -k̓aʕʷ+míst -s ixíʔ iʔ
have_packer two_persons art pftv -hire -3i that art
packers, he had hired two, *they are*

səxʷk̓ʷúl̓əms iʔ səxʷkʕacqáx̌aʔm 216 uɬ kɬk̓ʷəlcəncútən uɬ axáʔ cniɬc
sxʷ=k̓ʷul̓+m -s iʔ sxʷ=k+ʕac=qáx̌aʔ+m uɬ kɬ+k̓ʷl̓=cn+cut+n uɬ axáʔ cniɬ+c
worker -3in art packer and have_cook and this (s)he
his hired hands, the packers. *And he has a cook, and he is just*

t̓i ilmíxʷəm 217 ixíʔ məɬ {k ə} kməqʷqʷí··naʔ mqʷaqʷ ixíʔ məɬ wiʔíkst
t̓iʔ yl=mixʷ+m ixíʔ mɬ k+mqʷ•qʷ=ínaʔ mqʷ•aqʷ ixíʔ mɬ wẏ=ikst
evid chief then and snowed_in snow_fall then and get_done
the boss. *Then they got snowed in, it's winter, and my father*

axáʔ inlʔíw 218 uɬ aɬíʔ kʷa nak̓ʷá uɬá pnicíʔ uɬ aɬiʔá
axáʔ in -lʔiw uɬ aɬíʔ kʷa nak̓ʷá uɬ+á pn+icíʔ uɬ aɬi+á
this 1in -m's_father and so intj not and_not at_that_time and not
quits working, *because at that time they don't*

cənʔáx̌ʷqstsəlx iʔ xəwíɬ 219 swit_aɬíʔ kmix iʔ l
c -n+ʔax̌ʷ=qs -t -s -lx iʔ xwiɬ swit_aɬíʔ kmix iʔ l
cust^ -plow_road -st -3erg -pl art road in_fact only art for
plow the roads. (24:05) *Because at that time*

sənkɬc̓aʔsqáx̌aʔ t̓i_kmix nqəqəlxʷáqaʔs iʔ xəwíɬ pnicíʔ 220 lut t̓a
sn+kɬ+c̓aʔ=sqáx̌aʔ t̓iʔ_kmix n+q•qlxʷ=áqaʔs iʔ xwiɬ pn+icíʔ lut t̓
horse only trail art road at_that_time not negfac
there are only trails for horses. *They*

kɬəncəkʷmnáqs {kʷ} uɬ aɬíʔ lut t̓a ksənckʷmínəlx pnicíʔ kiʔ ixíʔ
kɬ+n+ckʷ+mn=aqs uɬ aɬíʔ lut t̓ k+sn+ckʷ+min -lx pn+icíʔ kiʔ ixíʔ
there_be_wagon_road and because not negfac have_buggy -pl at_that_time rel then
didn't have wagon roads, they didn't have wagons at that time, that's how it was.

221 waẏ uɬ aɬíʔ ʕapnáʔ {kʷu ɬ} waẏ uɬ kɬəncəkʷmnáqs kʷa uɬ
waẏ uɬ aɬíʔ ʕapnáʔ waẏ uɬ kɬ+n+ckʷ+mn=aqs kʷa uɬ
well and so now yes and have_wagon_road intj and
Now there are wagon roads and

kɬtqəcəlxálqʷ {kɬ} 222 uɬ axáʔ kɬt̓əxʷtəlwís {uɬ} 223 waẏ uɬ ixíʔ k̓əɬc̓sáp
kɬ+t+qc+lx=alqʷ uɬ axáʔ kɬ+t̓xʷt+lwis waẏ uɬ ixíʔ k̓ɬ+c̓sa+p
have_rail and this have_fly_around well and that finished
railroads *and airplanes.* *Horse packing is*

ʕapnáʔ ia nq̓ʷaɬtsqáx̌aʔtən {uɬ i} 224 uɬ ixíʔ kʷa {l is} l isck̓ʷúl̓l̓
ʕapnáʔ iʔ n+q̓ʷaɬ+t=sqáx̌aʔ+tn uɬ ixíʔ kʷa l i -sc+k̓ʷúl̓•l̓
now art horse_packing and then intj at 1in -being_born
all gone now. *When I was born*

225 kiʔ ixíʔ kmix ia nxʷilwístəns iʔ sqilxʷ iʔ l {iʔ} sənkɬc̓aʔsqáx̌aʔ {inaud}
kiʔ ixíʔ kmix iʔ n+xʷy+lwis+tn iʔ s+qilxʷ iʔ l sn+kɬ+c̓aʔ=sqáx̌aʔ
rel then only art vehicle art Indian art on horse
the only way Indians travel is on horses. (25:00)

226 ixíʔ uɬ_iʔ kʷu taʔxʷsuyápix xʷəxʷ waẏ axáʔ ta cpəx̌pəx̌twílx
ixíʔ uɬ_iʔ kʷu taʔxʷ+s+wyápy=x xʷəxʷ waẏ axáʔ ? c -px̌•px̌+t+wilx
then and_then 4kn get_white_people intj yes this hab -get_senses
Now that's when we got white people, and lot of sense.

227 ixíʔ uɬ taʔxʷɬx̌ʷíc̓laʔxʷtən ixíʔ iʔ l sənkɬc̓aʔsqáx̌aʔ iʔ t
ixíʔ uɬ taʔxʷ+ɬ+x̌ʷíc̓=laʔxʷ+tn ixíʔ iʔ l sn+kɬ+c̓aʔ=sqáx̌aʔ iʔ t
then and get_mowers that art for horse art obl
Then they got cutting machinery for horses, machinery

x̌ʷíc̓laʔxʷtən 228 uɬ axáʔ iʔ t k̓ʷúl̓mən nixʷ {i l} i la cəlk̓íw̓s̓
x̌ʷíc̓=laʔxʷ+tn uɬ axáʔ iʔ t k̓ʷul̓+mn nixʷ iʔ l c -lk̓=iw̓s
mower and this art obl tool also art for hab -bundle
to cut, and machinery to bundle.

229 ixíʔ uɬ nixʷ taʔxʷɬx̌ʷíc̓laʔxʷtnəlx uɬ taʔxʷsəp̓qíntnəlx 230 uɬ axáʔ
ixíʔ uɬ nixʷ taʔxʷ+ɬ+x̌ʷíc̓=laʔxʷ+tn -lx uɬ taʔxʷ+sp̓=qín+tn -lx uɬ axáʔ
then and also get_mowers -pl and get_threshers -pl and this
They also got hay mowers, and they got threshers. And

incá ixíʔ la_cxʔítiʔ kən ɬ k̓ʷúl̓əm 231 uɬ kʷaʕtá i l naqs sx̌əlx̌ʕált
in+cá ixíʔ la_c+xʔít+iʔ kn ɬ k̓ʷul̓+m uɬ kʷaʕtá iʔ l naqs s+x̌l•x̌aʕl+t
I then at_first 1kn when work and quarter art for one day
when I first worked I got paid two bits a day,

isqláw i[xíʔ] mat ʔupənkst x̌əx̌y̓áɬnəxʷ 232 kən kaxmútyaʔ kaʔ
i -s+qlaw ixíʔ mat ʔupn=kst x̌•x̌yaɬ=nxʷ kn kax+m=útyaʔ kiʔ
1in -money then maybe ten hour 1kn on_foot rel
maybe ten hours. I was on foot

ckskəmqíʔstən axáʔ {iʔ} iʔ l stqam axáʔ iʔ t 233 aɬíʔ uɬ
c -kskm=qiʔ -st -n axáʔ iʔ l s+tqa+m axáʔ iʔ t aɬíʔ uɬ
cust^ -? -^cust -1erg this art for stacking this art obl so and
whey I was driving the team to stack... (26:07) I can't

lut iksʔamnúnəm iʔ ta nqílxʷcən {ca} axáʔ iʔ t
lut i -ks -ʔam -nun -m iʔ t n+qilxʷ=cn axáʔ iʔ t
not 1i -futt^ -name -manage -apsv art agInst Indian_language this art obl
say "derrick fork"

derrick fork 234 way̓ uɬ {katə} kən nstils taʔlíʔ ixíʔ {xʷit} xʷʔit
way̓ uɬ kn n+st=ils taʔlíʔ ixíʔ xʷʔi+t
yes and 1kn think very_much that much
in Indian. And I thought that what I earned

isƛ̓xʷúp 235 uɬ axáʔm iʔ ƛ̓ax̌əx̌ƛ̓x̌áp naqs sqlaw {iʔ iʔ} iʔ
i -s+ƛ̓xʷu+p uɬ axáʔ+m iʔ ƛ̓ax̌•x̌•ƛ̓x̌á+p naqs s+qlaw iʔ
1in -earning and this art elders one money art
is a lot. The older ones get paid

sx̌áq̓əq̓səlx 236 uɬ aɬíʔ pnicí uɬ kʷaʔ yaʕyáʕt_stim̓
s+x̌aq̓•q̓ -s -lx uɬ aɬíʔ pn+icíʔ uɬ kʷaʔ yaʕ•yáʕ+t_stim̓
payment -3in -pl and so at_that_time and intj everything
one dollar. At that time everything was

nk̓ʷək̓ʷim̓áqsəm {iʔ s} 237 iʔ sʔíɬən iʔ q̓aʔxán {iʔ stət} t̓əxʷ iʔ stətəm̓tím̓
n+k̓ʷ•k̓ʷy=m=aqs+m iʔ s+ʔiɬn iʔ q̓aʔ=xán t̓xʷ iʔ s+t•tm̓•tim̓
small_wages art food art shoes emph art clothes
cheap, food, shoes, clothes;

238 uɬ taʔlíʔ kʷu cx̌ast 239 ʕapnáʔ uɬ ʕapnáʔ uɬ náx̌əmɬ
uɬ taʔlíʔ kʷu c -x̌as+t ʕapnáʔ uɬ ʕapnáʔ uɬ nax̌mɬ
and very_much 4kn hab -good now and now and but
and we sure had a good time. But now we have

talí? uɬ kstx̌áq̓əq̓pla? i? sk̓ʷúl̓əm
ta?lí? uɬ k+s+t+x̌áq̓•q̓=pla? i? s+k̓ʷul̓+m
very_much and have_high_wages art work
high wages

240 t̓i_kmix timɬ x̌əx̌yáɬnəxʷ way̓
t̓i?_kmix timɬ x̌•x̌yaɬ=nxʷ way̓
only eight hour yes
and you only work

akɬtk̓ʷúl̓mən {ayəm}
a -kɬ -t+k̓ʷul̓+mn
2i -to_be -work
eight hours.

241 mat k̓əl ?upənkstɬcílkst kəm̓ ?asl?úpənkst {i kɬ}
mat k̓l ?upn=kst+ɬ+cíl=kst km̓ ?asl+?úpn=kst
maybe about fifteen or twenty
15 or 20 [dollars] is the lowest

i? ksk̓ʷək̓ʷína?s {aksɬ aks} aksx̌áq̓əq̓ {k̓ʷam axá? i?}
i? k -s+k̓ʷ•k̓ʷy=ína? -s a -k -s+x̌aq̓•q̓
art to_be -little -3i 2i -to_be -payment
you can pay. (27:10)

242 ʕapná? i? smaňxʷ {uɬ a}
ʕapná? i? s+maňxʷ
now art tobacco
Now tobacco is

ka?ɬəl?upənksɬsísp̓əlk̓ *cents* axá? {i? i··} i? k̓əl nəqsíc̓a?
ka?ɬl+?upn=ks+ɬ+sí•sp̓lk̓ axá? i? k̓l nqs=íc̓a?
thirty_seven this art for one_package
37 cents a package.

243 uɬ axá?
uɬ axá?
and this
And

pnicí? i? l kʷaʕtá kən ɬa? ck̓ʷúl̓əm
pn+icí? i? l kʷaʕtá kn ɬa? c -k̓ʷul̓+m
at_that_time art for quarter 1kn the_one_that hab -work
at that time, when I was working for a quarter,

244 uɬ ixí?
uɬ ixí?
and then
it was

k̓apənkstíc̓a? naqs sqlaw
k+?apn=kst=íc̓a? naqs s+qlaw
ten_packages one dollar
ten packages for one dollar.

245 uɬ talí? {kʷu?} kʷu cx̌ast pnicí
uɬ ta?lí? kʷu c -x̌as+t pn+icí?
and very_much 4kn hab -good at_that_time
At that time we were satisfied,

iwá sk̓ʷək̓ʷín{y}[a]?s {i? s} i? sx̌áq̓əq̓t[t] i? l sk̓ʷúl̓əm
iwá s -k̓ʷ•k̓ʷy=ína? -s i? s+x̌aq̓•q̓ -tt i? l s+k̓ʷul̓+m
even nom -small -3i art payment -4in art for work
no matter how small our pay for work was.

246 ʕapná? uɬ
ʕapná? uɬ
now and
Now

nsilxʷa?áqsəm uɬ ta?lí? uɬ lut {t̓a c} mat t̓a ckɬcəqqítkʷəlx
n+silxʷa?=áqs+m uɬ ta?lí? uɬ lut mat t̓ c -kɬ+cq•q=itkʷ -lx
high_wages and very_much and not maybe negfac hab -top_of_water -pl
wages are very high and those who are working never come

i? sck̓ʷúl̓xəlx
i? sc -k̓ʷul̓ -x -lx
art ipftvp^ -work -^ipftvp -pl
to the top of the water,

247 sícəm_put axá? i? txʷa?xʷ?ílt
sic+m_put axá? i? t=xʷa?•xʷ?=ílt
especially this art many_offspring
especially those with lots of children. (28:00)

248 uɬ axá? aɬí? axá? q̓sapi? a ixí?, ixí? wi?sksupúla?xʷməlx
uɬ axá? aɬí? axá? q̓sápi? a ixí? ixí? wy̓+s+k+s+wp=úla?xʷ+m -lx
and this so this long_ago intj then then finish_haying -pl
Long ago they got done haying,

249 wi?stqəntí··səlx i? supúla?xʷ
wy̓+s+tq -nt -is -lx i? s+wp=úla?xʷ
finish_stacking -nt -3erg -pl art hay
they got done stacking the hay,

250 məɬ ixí? k̓á?ilx məɬ ixí?
mɬ ixí? k̓ay̓•y+lx mɬ ixí?
and then turn_fall and then
and then in the late fall

ckəlk̓íc̓aʔms[ts]əlx axáʔ iʔ t sənkɬc̓aʔsqáx̌aʔ {iʔ way̓}
c -k+lk̓=íc̓aʔ+m -st -s -lx axáʔ iʔ t sn+kɬ+c̓aʔ=sqáx̌aʔ
cust^ -bale -^cust -3erg -pl this art agInst horse
they bale it with horses.

251 uɬ ilíʔ kən ɬ ck̓ʷúləm kən ɬ cksqəmqínəm iʔ l
uɬ ilíʔ kn ɬ c -k̓ʷul̓+m kn ɬ c -ksqm=qin+m iʔ l
and there 1kn when hab -work 1kn when hab -drive_team art in
That's when I worked driving the team

skəlk̓íc̓aʔm 252 məɬ put {əl} i l *Christmas* xi‥ʔ mi kʷu uʔíkst 253 uɬ
s+k+lk̓=íc̓aʔ+m mɬ put iʔ l ixíʔ mi kʷu wy̓=ikst uɬ
baling and just art at then fut 4kn get_done and
to bale hay. *Christmas is when we finish.* *And*

axáʔ iʔ nixʷá iʔ kɬsəp̓qíntən 254 məɬ ixíʔ səp̓qínməlx iʔ l sk̓ʔay
axáʔ iʔ nixʷ+á iʔ kɬ+sp̓=qin+tn mɬ ixíʔ sp̓=qin+m -lx iʔ l s+k̓[ʔ]ay
this art also_not art have_thresher and then thresh -pl art in autumn
they also didn't have threshing machines. *They thresh in the fall when*

wiʔsx̌ʷíc̓laʔxʷməlx 255 uɬ aɬíʔ way̓ cun way̓ axáʔ ɬ
wy̓+s+x̌ʷíc̓=laʔxʷ+m -lx uɬ aɬíʔ way̓ cu -n way̓ axáʔ ɬ
finish_mowing -pl and so yes tell -1erg yes this when
they get done cutting. *And like I said, when they got*

taʔxʷɬsənkɬc̓aʔsqáx̌aʔ iʔ ta lk̓íw̓stən 256 ixíʔ wiʔsəlk̓íw̓sməlx
taʔxʷ+ɬ+sn+kɬ+c̓aʔ=sqáx̌aʔ iʔ t lk̓=iw̓s+tn ixíʔ wy̓+s+lk̓=iw̓s+m -lx
get_horses art obl baler then finish_bundling -pl
horse-powered balers (29:00) *then they get done with*

məɬ {nay kʷiɬ ta ilí}
mɬ
and
the baling.[7] *(29:08)*

7 A couple of words I cannot decipher follow, and the tape ends. We recorded no continuation tape.

Racing horses

1 a·· kən ctaʔxʷspəx̌páx̌t uɫ axáʔ inqíck iʔ sxʔitx
a kn c -taʔxʷ+s+px̌•páx̌+t uɫ axáʔ in -qick iʔ s+xʔit=x
intj 1kn hab -get_senses and this 1in -older_brother art oldest_one
I got my senses. My oldest brother,

2 scústsəlx nyas iʔ skʷists 3 ixíʔ uɫ mat {kʷu} kʷu
s -cu -st -s -lx nyas iʔ s+kʷist -s ixíʔ uɫ mat kʷu
custˆ -tell -ˆcust -3erg -pl Eneas art name -3in then and maybe 1obj
they call him Eneas, *he pitied*

nqʷən̓mís {uɫ kʷu} 4 caʔkʷ cus i ta nqílxʷcən kʷu
n+qʷn̓+mi -s caʔkʷ cu -s iʔ t n+qilxʷ=cn kʷu
feel_sorry_for -3erg as tell -3erg art agInst Indian_language 1obj
me. *Like they say in Indian,*

qʷaʔqʷaʔmstís i l sk̓amtíw̓s 5 uɫ aɫíʔ way̓
qʷaʔ•qʷaʔm -st -is iʔ l s+k+ʔam=t=íw̓s uɫ aɫíʔ way̓
train -st -3erg art in horseback_riding and so well
he trained me in riding. *As you*

cmistíxʷ iʔ sccm̓ilt x̌mínksəlx iʔ sk̓amtíw̓s
c -my -st -ixʷ iʔ s+c•cm̓=il̓t x̌m=ink -s -lx iʔ s+k+ʔam=t=íw̓s
custˆ -know -ˆcust -2erg art children like -3erg -pl art horseback_riding
know youngsters like to ride horseback,

6 uɫ lut t̓a cmistín iʔ sk̓amtíw̓s 7 way̓ uɫ ixíʔ
uɫ lut t̓ c -my -st -in iʔ s+k+ʔam=t=íw̓s way̓ uɫ ixíʔ
and not negfac custˆ -know -ˆcust -1erg art horseback_riding well and then
and I didn't know how to ride. *We got*

kʷu nyaʕsqáx̌aʔməlx axáʔ {naʔɫ} naʔɫ knaqs nixʷ inqíck
kʷu n+yaʕ=sqáx̌aʔ+m -lx axáʔ naʔɫ k=naqs nixʷ in -qick
4kn corral_horses -pl this with one_person also 1in -older_brother
the horses corralled with another older brother of mine,1:04

8 ixíʔ nixʷ pyarís iʔ skʷists, axáʔm iʔ sxʔitx {ini} inkɫʔám ixíʔ
ixíʔ nixʷ pyarís iʔ s+kʷist -s axáʔ+m iʔ s+xʔit=x in -k+ɫʔa+m ixíʔ
that also m's_name art name -3in this art oldest_one 1in -close_to that
his name is Peter Pichette, and the oldest one is my close

inqíck 9 uɫ axáʔm {iʔ} iʔ knaqs caʔkʷ cus a nuyápixcən
in -qick uɫ axáʔ+m iʔ k=naqs caʔkʷ cu -s a n+wyap=x=cn
1in -older_bro and this art one_person as tell -3erg art say_in_English
older brother. *The other one is, as they say in English,*

in *-first_cousin* 10 uɫ aɫíʔ ta nqílxʷcən {uɫ in} c̓x̌iɫt inqíck
in uɫ aɫíʔ t n+qilxʷ=cn c+ʔx̌iɫ+t in -qick
1in and so agInst Indian_language like 1in -older_brother
my "first cousin," *and in Indian also*

nixʷ 11 waẏ nyaʕsq̓áx̌aʔməlx uɬ ixíʔ ɬəxʷpússəlx iʔ
nixʷ waẏ n+yaʕ=sq̓áx̌aʔ+m -lx uɬ ixíʔ ɬxʷ+p=us -s -lx iʔ
also well corral_horses -pl and then rope -3erg -pl art
"qick." They put the horses in the corral and they roped

q̓əq̓ʔík {uɬ aɬíʔ mat kən} 12 waẏ uɬ t̓əxʷ kən cpəx̌pəx̌twílaʔx uɬ waẏ
q̓•q̓ẏik waẏ uɬ t̓xʷ kn c -px̌•px̌+t+wílaʔx uɬ waẏ
colt well and evidently 1kn hab -gain_senses_dim and yes
a colt. And I had just come to my senses,

cmistín 13 uɬ náx̌əmɬ lut t̓a
c -my -st -in uɬ nax̌mɬ lut t̓
cust^ -know -^cust -1erg and but not negfac
and I remember. But I didn't know

cmistín iʔ sk̓amtíẇs 14 waẏ ixíʔ kʷu
c -my -st -in iʔ s+k+ʔam=t=íẇs waẏ ixíʔ kʷu
cust^ -know -^cust -1erg art horseback_riding well then 1obj
how to ride horses. My brother Eneas

kt̓k̓ʷíẇsəs axáʔ inqíck, nyas, {uɬ axáʔ iʔ t} axáʔ i l q̓əq̓ʔík
k+t̓k̓ʷ=iẇs -s axáʔ in -qick nyas axáʔ iʔ l q̓•q̓ẏik
place_on_horse -3erg this 1in -older_brother Eneas this art on colt
put me on the horse, on the colt,

15 uɬ axáʔ iʔ t knaqs iʔ t inqíck
uɬ axáʔ iʔ t k=naqs iʔ t in -qick
and this art agInst one_person art agInst 1in -older_brother
and my other brother

ckskʷənkʷánksts 16 məɬ ixíʔ kʷu ɬuníkstmsəlx
c -ks -kʷn•kʷan=k -st -s mɬ ixíʔ kʷu ɬwn=ikst+m -s -lx
cust^ -? -hold -^cust -3erg and then 1obj let_go_of -3erg -pl
is holding it. 2:02 And then they turned me loose.

17 aɬíʔ yaʔx̌í t̓i {n} npnuʔscút iʔ q̓əq̓ʔík məɬ kən yaxʷt 18 waẏ məɬ
aɬíʔ yaʔx̌í t̓iʔ n+pn=ẇs+cut iʔ q̓•q̓ẏik mɬ kn yaxʷ+t waẏ mɬ
so yonder evid buck art colt and 1kn fall well and
Then the colt would just buck, and I'd fall off. Sometimes

mat kən lxʷap məɬ ixíʔ kən c̓qʷaqʷ 19 məɬ kʷu cus axáʔ
mat kn lxʷa+p mɬ ixíʔ kn c̓qʷ•aqʷ mɬ kʷu cu -s axáʔ
maybe 1kn get_hurt and then 1kn cry and 1obj tell -3erg this
I'd get hurt, and I'd cry. My older brother said to me,

inqíck lut {aks} aksc̓qʷáqʷ 20 ńíńẇiʔ kʷ c̓qʷaqʷ mi
in -qick lut a -ks -c̓qʷ•aqʷ ńíńẇiʔ kʷ c̓qʷ•aqʷ mi
1in -older_brother not 2i -futi -cry a_while 2kn cry fut
"Don't cry. If you cry

ksp̓íc̓aʔntsən 21 sc̓kinx anx̌əmínk kʷ
k+sp̓=íc̓aʔ -nt -s -n sc+ʔkin+x an -x̌m=ink kʷ
whip -nt -2obj -1erg why_is_it 2in -like 2kn
I'll whip you. Why is it, you'd like

[s]k̓amtíw̓saʔx   22 uł lut kʷ t̓ x̌ənnúmt uł_i kʷ {ał}
s -k+ʔam=t=íw̓s -aʔx   uł lut kʷ t̓ x̌n̓+numt uł_iʔ kʷ
incp^ -sg_ride_horseback -^incp   and not 2kn negfac get_hurt and_then 2kn
to ride   *and you don't get hurt, and still*

c̓qʷaqʷ   23 way̓ uł ałíʔ {is} isənx̌əlx̌əlsnúxʷ axáʔ inqíck iʔ
c̓qʷ•aqʷ   way̓ uł ałíʔ i -s+n+x̌l•x̌l+s=nuxʷ axáʔ in s+xʔit=x iʔ
cry   yes and so 1in -fear this 1in oldest_one art
you cry."   *And I am dead scared of my brother*

sxʔitx   24 uł ałíʔ uníxʷ taʔlí {u} yuyəʕʷákst {ła} kʷu łaʔ
s+xʔit=x   uł ałíʔ wnixʷ taʔlíʔ yw•yw=ʕakst kʷu łaʔ
oldest_one   and because true very_much strong_hand 1obj when
the oldest one   *because it's strong when*

ckspíc̓aʔsts   25 way̓ məł {kən ł kən ł} kən łk̓amtíw̓s kʷu
c -k+sp̓=íc̓aʔ -st -s   way̓ mł kn ł+k+ʔam=t=íw̓s kʷu
cust^ -whip -^cust -3erg   well and 1kn ride_again 1obj
he whips me.   *And then I ride again,*

łkt̓k̓ʷíw̓səs {way̓ mat}   26 a uł t̓i mat ʔasíl ksnpnuʔscúts məł
ł+k+t̓k̓ʷ=iw̓s -s   a uł t̓iʔ mat ʔasíl ks -n+pn=w̓s+cut -s mł
put_on_horse_again -3erg   intj and evid maybe two futi -buck -3i and
he puts me back on.   *He'll just buck a couple of times, and I fall off*

kən łyaxʷt   27 uł lut t̓a cənt̓k̓ʷíkən̓ kəm̓ lut {t̓a c} t̓a
kn ł+yaxʷ+t   uł lut t̓ c -n+t̓k̓ʷ=ikn̓ km̓ lut t̓
1kn fall_again   and not negfac hab -saddle or not negfac
again. 3:05   *And there is no saddle and*

cənlk̓íkən̓   28 way̓ t̓i{kmix}_kmix {iʔ l} iʔ l skc̓iwlpsc mi
c -n+lk̓=ikn̓   way̓ t̓iʔ_kmix iʔ l s+k+c̓iw=lps -c mi
hab -strap   well only art on mane -3in fut
no strap,   *the only hold I have*

kən {ctkʷnim} ctkʷənkʷním   29 way̓ uł mat ʔúpənkst iksyáxʷt
kn c -t+kʷn•kʷnim   way̓ uł mat ʔupn=kst i -ks -yaxʷ+t
1kn hab -hold_on   well and maybe ten 1i -futi -fall
is the mane.   *I'd fall off maybe ten times*

i l naqs sx̌əlx̌áʕlt   30 hoy uł kən tqʷaʔmíw̓s, way̓ uł siʔsiʔtwílx i
i l naqs s+x̌l•x̌aʕl+t   hoy uł kn t+qʷaʔm=iw̓s way̓ uł sy̓•sy̓+twilx iʔ
art in one day   finish and 1kn be_accustomed yes and smart_dim art
in one day.   *Then I got used to it, got smarter*

l sk̓amtíw̓s   31 ixíʔ uł k̓ʷəl̓laʔxʷílpəms {t ksən} t
l s+k+ʔam=t=íw̓s   ixíʔ uł s -k̓ʷl̓=laʔxʷ=ilp+m -s t
at horseback_riding   then and nom -fix_a_surface -3i obl
at riding.   *Then he fixed a bed to*

ksənqíxʷməns   32 i[xíʔ] caʔkʷ cus {i} ia nqílxʷcən {t axáʔ l} i l
k -s+n+qixʷ+mn -s   ixíʔ caʔkʷ cu -s iʔ n+qilxʷ=cn iʔ l
to_be -training -3i   that as tell -3erg art Indian_language art for
train horses;   *as they say in Indian,*

sq̓ʷq̓ʷúƛ̓aʔxnəm k̓ʷəl̓sqáx̌aʔm 33 məɬ ixíʔ uɬ qixʷs ilíʔ 34 way̓
s+q̓ʷ•q̓ʷúƛ̓+aʔ=xn+m k̓ʷl̓=sqáx̌aʔ+m mɬ ixíʔ uɬ qixʷ -s ilíʔ way̓
race horse_training and then and drive -3erg there well
they train horses for races, and they train there. Then

ixíʔ wiʔstís {iʔ} iʔ sck̓ʷəl̓laʔxʷílps i ksənqíxʷmən 35 uɬ
ixíʔ wy̓ -st -is iʔ sc -k̓ʷl̓=laʔxʷ=ílp -s i k -s+n+qixʷ+mn uɬ
then finish -st -3erg art pftv -prepare_surface -3i art to_be -training and
he finished the bed to train horses, 4:03 and

ixíʔ {kʷu} kʷu kt̓k̓ʷíw̓səs {iʔ} iʔ l naqs 36 uɬ axáʔ mat
ixíʔ kʷu k+t̓k̓ʷ=iw̓s -s iʔ l naqs uɬ axáʔ mat
then 1obj place_on_horse -3erg art on one and this maybe
then he put me on one. And there were maybe

tkaʔkaʔɬís way̓ ixíʔ sqʷʔamsəlx {is} iʔ sk̓amtíw̓s axáʔ iʔ
t=kaʔ•kaʔɬís way̓ ixíʔ s -qʷʔa+m -s -lx iʔ s+k+ʔam=t=íw̓s axáʔ iʔ
three_persons yes then nom -get_used_to -3i -pl art horseback_riding these art
two or three who were trained to ride,

snk̓ʷɬtutwít 37 way̓ məɬ {kʷu} kʷu xítmiʔst, kʷu qíxʷəm 38 way̓ {inaud}
s+nk̓ʷ+ɬ+tw̓•tw̓it way̓ mɬ kʷu xít+miʔst kʷu qixʷ+m way̓
fellow_boys well and 4kn run_pl 4kn ride well
boys like me. Then we run, we train. From where

atláʔ kʷu ɬət̓pmíst uɬ axáʔ isləx̌láx̌t súxʷxʷəlx 39 k̓əm incá
atláʔ kʷu ɬt̓+p+mist uɬ axáʔ i -s+l̓x̌•l̓ax̌+t suxʷ•xʷ -lx k̓m in+cá
from_here 4kn jump and this 1in -friends leave_pl -pl except I
we jump to start my friends are gone; just me,

way̓ uɬ qá··qcəlx inkəwáp mi_sic nux̌ʷəx̌ʷtíʔst 40 way̓ məɬ yaʔx̌í súxʷəxʷ
way̓ uɬ qa•qc+lx in -kwap mi_sic n+wx̌ʷ•x̌ʷ+t=iʔst way̓ mɬ yaʔx̌í suxʷ•xʷ
yes and trot 1in -horse then gallop well and that_one leave_pl
my horse trots for a while before it starts to gallop, and my friends

isl̓əx̌l̓áx̌t 41 way̓ mi_sic {qəl} qacəcxí[ʔst] inkəwáp way̓ məɬ {kən} kʷu
i -s+l̓x̌•l̓ax̌+t way̓ mi_sic qac•c=íʔst in -kwap way̓ mɬ kʷu
1in -friends well then run 1in -horse well and 1obj
are gone. Then my horse starts to run, and

xəƛ̓pnúsəlx 42 way̓ mat ksʔasíls ki way̓ kən tqʷaʔmíw̓s
xƛ̓+p -nu -s -lx way̓ mat ks -ʔasíl -s kiʔ way̓ kn t+qʷaʔm=iw̓s
beat -manage -3erg -pl well maybe futi -two -3i rel yes 1kn be_accustomed
they beat me. Maybe twice, then I got used to it,

43 way̓ məɬ ixíʔ xəƛ̓pnúnəlx 44 hoy {uɬ} uɬ aɬíʔ pnicí uɬ
way̓ mɬ ixíʔ xƛ̓+p -nu -n -lx hoy uɬ aɬíʔ pn+icíʔ uɬ
well and then beat -manage -1erg -pl finish and so at_that_time and
and then I beat them. 5:02 At that time

taʔlí kʷu ciyáʕ̓ 45 way̓ {t̓i ə} t̓i pəllúlaʔxʷ {ə·· wis··} t̓əxʷ {t̓iʔ way}
taʔlíʔ kʷu c -yaʕ way̓ t̓iʔ pl•l=úlaʔxʷ t̓xʷ
much 4kn hab -gather well evid grass_sprouts evidently
we gathered a lot. When the grass starts to sprout,

wiʔsláqʷnaʔm iʔ sənkłc̓aʔsqáx̌aʔ 46 kłx̌səlxʷílx ixíʔ məł
wy̓+s+láqʷ=naʔ+m iʔ s+n+kł+c̓aʔ=sqáx̌aʔ kł+x̌s=lxʷ+ilx ixíʔ mł
shed_hair art horse coat_turn_sleek then and
the horses get done shedding hair, *they turn sleek,*

q̓ʷəq̓ʷúƛ̓aʔxnəməlx aláʔ la ncaʔlím i l naqs skaʕcíw̓s 47 ilíʔ iʕyáʕ
q̓ʷ•q̓ʷúƛ̓+aʔ=xn+m -lx aláʔ l n+caʔlím iʔ l naqs s+k+ʕac=íw̓s ilíʔ y•yaʕ
race -pl here at Inchelium art for one week there gather
then they race here at Inchelium for one week. *The Indians*

iʔ sqilxʷ 48 way̓ məł ilíʔ q̓ʷaʔq̓ʷúƛ̓aʔxnəməlx ksk̓laxʷ 49 uł {ə}
iʔ s+qilxʷ way̓ mł ilíʔ q̓ʷaʔ•q̓ʷúƛ̓+aʔ=xn+m -lx k+s+k̓laxʷ uł
art person well and there race_rep -pl all_day and
gather there *and they race there until dark.* *I ride*

niʕíp ilíʔ kən c̓kamtíw̓s hoy məł {k̓əl} k̓a nxʷəxʷʔítaʔkʷ
nyʕip ilíʔ kn c -k+ʔam=t=íw̓s hoy mł k̓ n+xʷ•xʷʔ=ítaʔkʷ
always there 1kn hab -sg_ride_horseback finish and to Meteor
all day long, and when that finishes, then [they go] to Meteor,

50 ik̓líʔ łiyáʕ̓lx i l naqs skaʕcíw̓s 51 ilíʔ la_cxʔítiʔ kiʔ kən
ik̓líʔ ł+y•yaʕ̓+lx iʔ l naqs s+k+ʕac=íw̓s ilíʔ la_c+xʔít+iʔ kiʔ kn
there gather_again art for one week there at_first rel 1kn
and they gather there another week. *There is where I rode [raced]*

k̓amtíw̓s 52 uł ixíʔ {in} inqíck təxʷłqəxʷsqáx̌aʔ[tn]əm
k+ʔam=t=íw̓s uł ixíʔ in -qick txʷ+ł+qxʷ=sqáx̌aʔ+tn+m
sg_ride_horseback and then 1in -older_brother get_whip
the first time. 6:00 *My brother got horse whips,*

ʔaslálqʷ {i s} i stəxʷłqəxʷsqáx̌aʔtəns 53 ixíʔ kʷu xʷíc̓əłts iʔ
ʔasl=álqʷ iʔ s -txʷ+ł+qxʷ=sqáx̌aʔ+tn -s ixíʔ kʷu xʷic̓ -łt -s iʔ
two_rd_obj art nom -get_whip -3i then 1obj give -łt -3erg art
two horse whips. *He gave me one,*

naqs, uł {i} k̓im iʔ naqs ctxət̓stís 54 cun uł {kʷ}
naqs uł k̓im iʔ naqs c -txt̓ -st -is cu -n uł
one and but art one cust^ -watch_so -^cust -3erg tell -1erg and
and he kept the other. *I said to him, “What are*

aksəxkínəm ixíʔ iʔ naqs 55 lut kʷu {kʷu t̓ aks} t̓
a -ks -x+kin+m ixíʔ iʔ naqs lut kʷu t̓
2i -futi -do_what that art one not 1obj negfac
you going to do with the other one? *I don’t want you to whip my horse,*

aksənqíxʷp[łt]əm {a} ʕapnáʔ way̓ uł kʷu ʔawtmaʔsqílxʷ 56 ixíʔm iʔ
a -ks -n+qixʷ+p -łt -m ʕapnáʔ way̓ uł kʷu ʔawt=maʔ+s+qílxʷ ixíʔ+m iʔ
2i -futi -whip -łt -apsv now yes and 4kn contemporaries that art
we are up to date now.” *(It used to*

xatmaʔsqílxʷ {ła} łaʔ kłənk̓ʷúl̓mən a cənqəxʷpənwíxʷ
xat=maʔ+s+qílxʷ łaʔ kł -n+k̓ʷul̓+mn a c -n+qxʷ+p+nwixʷ
first_people the_one_that łaʔ_pos -custom art hab -whip_rec
be the old timers’ custom to whip each other’s horses.)

57 kʷu cus lut, way̓ uníxʷ lut k̓im kʷu t̓a cənqəxʷpənwíxʷ
kʷu cu -s lut way̓ wnixʷ lut k̓im kʷu t̓ c -n+qxʷ+p+nwixʷ
1obj tell -3erg not yes true not but 4kn negfac hab -whip_rec
He said to me, "No, it's true that now we don't whip one another's horse;

58 axáʔ x̌əl anwí kiʔ axáʔ k̓im iʔ txət̓əntín iʔ naqs qəxʷsqáx̌aʔtən
axáʔ x̌l anwí kiʔ axáʔ k̓im iʔ txt̓ -nt -in iʔ naqs qxʷ=sqáx̌aʔ+tn
this for you rel this but art watch_so -nt -1erg art one horse_whip
I am keeping the other whip for you.

59 ṅíṅw̓iʔ laʔkín mi nckʷúsəntxʷ iʔ sənkɬċaʔsqáx̌aʔ kʷ ʕaláp
ṅíṅw̓iʔ la+ʔkíṅ mi n+ckʷ=us -nt -xʷ iʔ s+n+kɬ+ċaʔ=sqáx̌aʔ kʷ ʕalá+p
a_while when fut pull_rein -nt -2erg art horse 2kn lose_gambling
If you pull the reins on the horse and get beat, if you

kʷ qʷíləm 60 uɬ ixíʔ {kʷ iks} kʷ iksksṗíċaʔm {axáʔ} ixíʔ iʔ t
kʷ qʷil+m uɬ ixíʔ kʷ i -ks -k+sṗ=íċaʔ+m ixíʔ iʔ t
2kn cheat and then 2kʷu 1i -futi -whip that art agInst
cheat, 7:02 *then I will whip you with*

qəxʷsqáx̌aʔtən 61 sċx̌ilx ki ixíʔ txət̓əntín 62 uɬ axáʔ iʔ
qxʷ=sqáx̌aʔ+tn sc+ʔx̌il+x kiʔ ixíʔ txt̓ -nt -in uɬ axáʔ iʔ
horse_whip reason_why rel that watch_so -nt -1erg and this art
the whip. *That's why I kept it,* *and I*

xʷíċəɬtsən iʔ naqs 63 ixíʔm iʔ x̌əl sənkɬċaʔsqáx̌aʔ {i}
xʷiċ -ɬt -s -n iʔ naqs ixíʔ+m iʔ x̌l s+n+kɬ+ċaʔ=sqáx̌aʔ
give -ɬt -2obj -1erg art one that art for horse
gave you one. *That's for you to*

aksqəxʷsqáx̌aʔtən 64 axáʔ iʔ l anq̓ʷəq̓ʷúƛ̓aʔxən[tən] 65 kʷu
a -k -s+qxʷ=sqáx̌aʔ+tn axáʔ iʔ l an -q̓ʷ•q̓ʷúƛ̓+aʔ=xn+tn kʷu
2i -to_be -whip this art for 2in -race_horse 1obj
whip the horse, *for your race horse."* *He*

cus aláʔ sċx̌ilx {ki} ki ixíʔ cúntsən, ṁáyaʔɬtsən
cu -s aláʔ sc+ʔx̌il+x kiʔ ixíʔ cu -nt -s -n ṁáyaʔ -ɬt -s -n
tell -3erg here reason_why rel that tell -nt -2obj -1erg tell -ɬt -2obj -1erg
said to me, "That's why I told you, I taught you,

66 ṅíṅw̓iʔ {kʷɬ} kʷ ɬ sisyús, ṅíṅw̓iʔ ixíʔ k̓aʕʷmístməntsəlx iʔ t
ṅíṅw̓iʔ kʷ ɬ sy•sy=us ṅíṅw̓iʔ ixíʔ k̓aʕʷ+míst+m -nt -s -lx iʔ t
a_while 2kn if smart a_while then hire -nt -2obj -pl art agInst
that if you are smart, your friends will hire

asl̓əx̌l̓áx̌t 67 kʷ k̓amtíw̓s iʔ ta kɬkəw̓wáp ta kɬƛ̓əx̌ƛ̓əx̌sqáx̌aʔ
a -s+l̓x̌•l̓ax̌+t kʷ k+ʔam=t=íw̓s iʔ t kɬ+kw̓•w•ap t kɬ+ƛ̓x̌•ƛ̓x̌=sqáx̌aʔ
2in -friends 2kn sg_ride_horseback art obl have_horses obl have_race_horses
you [to ride]. *If you ride for someone who has horses, race horses, it's because*

aɬíʔ {kʷ} kʷ sisyús 68 uɬ ṅíṅw̓iʔ lut kʷ qʷíləm uɬ taʔlí··
aɬíʔ kʷ sy•sy=us uɬ ṅíṅw̓iʔ lut kʷ qʷil+m uɬ taʔlíʔ
because 2kn smart and a_while not 2kn cheat and very_much
you are good. *And if you don't cheat you'll have*

txʷaxʷʔít aksləx̌láx̌t
t=xʷaʔ•xʷʔí+t a -k -s+lʼx̌•lʼax̌+t
many 2i -to_be -friends
lots of friends, 8:03

69 cəm̓ yaʕyáʕt_swit akslʼáx̌t
cm̓ yaʕ•yáʕ+t_swit a -k -s+lʼax̌+t
maybe everybody 2i -to_be -friend
everybody will be your friend.

70 náx̌əmɬ cəm̓ kʷ qʷíləm nckʷúsəntxʷ {ə} uɬ lut_swit {aks} tʼ
naxmɬ cm̓ kʷ qʷil+m n+ckʷ=us -nt -xʷ uɬ lut_swit tʼ
but maybe 2kn cheat pull_rein -nt -2erg and nobody negfac
But if you cheat and pull the reins, nobody will be

akslʼáx̌t
a -k -s+lʼax̌+t
2i -to_be -friend
your friend,

71 tʼi iwá axáʔ i {kʷu anƛ̓} kʷu askʼʷíƛ̓təm kəm̓
tʼiʔ iwá axáʔ iʔ kʷu a -s+kʼʷiƛ̓t+m km̓
evid even this art 4kn 2in -brothers or
even we who are your brothers, or

anƛ̓ax̌əx̌ƛ̓x̌áp
an -ƛ̓ax̌•x̌•ƛ̓x̌á+p
2in -elders
your parents,

72 lut_swit tʼə ksx̌əcámsəlx l anwí
lut_swit tʼ ks -x̌ca+m -s -lx l anwí
nobody negfac futi -bet -3i -pl on you
nobody will bet on you."

73 a··
a
intj
I said

cun way̓ {ixíʔ uɬ} ixíʔ uɬ lut {kən tʼa c} tʼa cənckʷústən {uɬ} uɬ
cu -n way̓ ixíʔ uɬ lut tʼ c -n+ckʷ=us -t -n uɬ
tell -1erg OK then and not negfac cust^ -pull_rein -st -1erg and
"Ok," and I never did pull the reins, and

niʕíp kən cxəƛ̓páɬq {kən·}
nyʕip kn c -xƛ̓+p=aɬq
always 1kn hab -win
I always came ahead.

74 kən sisyús aɬíʔ i l sk̓amtíw̓s
kn sy•sy=us aɬíʔ iʔ l s+k+ʔam=t=íw̓s
1kn smart so art at horseback_riding
I am good at jockeying.

75 uɬ axáʔ ixíʔ {ək} suyápix ilíʔ a ksntumístən la nxʷəxʷʔítaʔkʷ
uɬ axáʔ ixíʔ s+wyapy=x ilíʔ a k+s+n+tw+mist+n l n+xʷ•xʷʔ=ítaʔkʷ
and this that white_person there art have_store in Meteor
And the white man who owns a store in Meteor,

76 ixíʔ sc̓umstsəlx t *Coleman* uɬ axáʔ ta simupyár
ixíʔ c[1] -ʔum -st -s -lx t uɬ axáʔ t simupyár
that cust^ -call -^cust -3erg -pl obl and this obl m's_name
they call him "Coleman," and Pete Noyes,

səkʼʷtəmsqíltk
s+kʼʷt+m+s+qil=tk
half_blood
a half-breed,

77 uɬ ixíʔ {ac} iʔ ʔawtsíw̓səlx
uɬ ixíʔ iʔ ʔaw+t+s=iw̓s -lx
and that art compete -pl
they are against one another. 9:02

78 way̓
way̓
well
They

nqʷəlqʷəlcənwíxʷəlx kʷa məɬ ixíʔ {s} sq̓ʷəq̓ʷúƛ̓aʔxnəmsəlx {ks}
n+qʷl•qʷl=cn+wixʷ -lx kʷa mɬ ixíʔ s -q̓ʷ•q̓ʷúƛ̓+aʔ=xn+m -s -lx
argue -pl intj and then nom -race -3i -pl
argue and then they race,

1 This is the expected form. The s- is unexplained.

79 nx̌əltcənwíxʷəlx ksq̓ʷəq̓ʷúƛ̓aʔxnaʔxəlx 80 waẏ məɬ axáʔ {i}
n+x̌lt=cn+wixʷ -lx ks -q̓ʷ•q̓ʷúƛ̓+aʔ=xn -aʔx -lx waẏ mɬ axáʔ
ask_recip -pl incp^ -race -^incp -pl well and this
they ask [challenge] one another to race. *I got to be*

taʔxʷsl̓áx̌tmən axáʔ iʔ suyápix iʔ *Coleman* 81 məɬ ixíʔ kʷu
taʔxʷ+s+l̓áx̌+t+m -n axáʔ iʔ s+wyapy=x iʔ mɬ ixíʔ kʷu
get_friend -1erg this art white_person art and then 1kʷu
friends with the white man Coleman, *and he*

cus waẏ kʷu k̓amtíẇxtxʷ 82 waẏ məɬ ixíʔ
cu -s waẏ kʷu k+ʔam=t=íẇ -xt -xʷ waẏ mɬ ixíʔ
tell -3erg well 1obj ride -xit -2erg well and then
said to me, "Come jockey for me." *And then*

isk̓amtíẇs, waẏ məɬ {kən} kən xəƛ̓páɬq 83 waẏ məɬ t̓i ilíʔ {ɬ}
i -s -k+ʔam=t=íẇs waẏ mɬ kn xƛ̓+p=aɬq waẏ mɬ t̓iʔ ilíʔ
1i -intt -sg_ride_horseback well and 1kn win well and evid there
I rode, and I won. *As soon as we run,*

kʷu ɬ t̓uwísəst məɬ t̓i ilíʔ ɬənqʷəlqʷəlcənwíxʷəlx 84 axáʔ {l} simupiyár
kʷu ɬ t̓wis•s•t mɬ t̓iʔ ilíʔ ɬ+n+qʷl•qʷl=cn+wixʷ -lx axáʔ simupyár
4kn when in_line and evid there argue_again -pl this m's_name
they'll have an argument *Pete Noyes*

axáʔ naʔɬ *Coleman* {waẏ} 85 waẏ məɬ {ɬ} ɬənx̌əltcənwíxʷəlx 86 cútəlx
axáʔ naʔɬ waẏ mɬ ɬ+n+x̌lt=cn+wixʷ -lx cut -lx
this and well and ask_recip_again -pl say -pl
and Coleman. *They'll challenge one another,* *they'd say,*

waẏ {waẏ k̓ə t̓i} k̓əɬʔayxʷíẇsəntəm iʔ kəẇwáptət 87 anwí kʷintxʷ
waẏ k̓ɬ+ʔayxʷ=íẇs -nt -m iʔ kw•w•ap -tt anwí kʷin -t -xʷ
well exchange -nt -4erg art horses -4in you take -nt -2erg
"Let's exchange horses. 10:03 *You take the one*

axáʔ iʔ naqs iʔ xƛ̓ap məɬ incá {i ixtəpəm} iʔ ƛ̓xʷup 88 məɬ waẏ kʷu
axáʔ iʔ naqs iʔ xƛ̓a+p mɬ in+cá iʔ ƛ̓xʷu+p mɬ waẏ kʷu
this art one art lose and I art win and yes 4kn
that got beat and I the one that won, *and we'll race again,"*

ɬq̓ʷəq̓ʷúƛ̓aʔxnəm, nʕíc̓pəm 89 cúntəm t simupyár *Coleman*,
ɬ+q̓ʷ•q̓ʷúƛ̓+aʔ=xn+m n+ʕic̓p+m cu -nt -m t simupyár
race_again argue_over tell -nt -psv agInst m's_name
he [Pete Noyes] won't give up [arguing]. *Pete Noyes said to Coleman,*

hah waẏ, waẏ məɬ ixíʔ ɬəɬx̌cənwíxʷsəlx 90 waẏ məɬ axáʔ kʷu
hah waẏ waẏ mɬ ixíʔ ɬ -ɬ+x̌c+nwixʷ -s -lx waẏ mɬ axáʔ kʷu
intj yes yes and then nom -bet_again_recip -3i -pl well and this 1obj
"Ok," and they make bets again. *Then Coleman*

ɬkt̓k̓ʷíẇsəs *Coleman* {i l} i l kəwáps {waẏ məɬ} 91 məɬ waẏ kən
ɬ+k+t̓k̓ʷ=iẇs -s iʔ l kwap -s mɬ waẏ kn
put_on_horse_again -3erg art on horse -3in and yes 1kn
put me on his horse *and I won*

ɬxəƛ̓páɬq uɬ aɬíʔ uɬ qʷaʔmíkstmən iʔ sənkɬc̓aʔsqáx̌aʔ
ɬ+xƛ̓+p=aɬq uɬ aɬíʔ uɬ qʷaʔm=íkst+m -n iʔ s+n+kɬ+c̓aʔ=sqáx̌aʔ
win_again and because and get_used_to -1erg art horse
again, because I got used to horses,

92 qʷaʔm·ín iʔ sq̓ʷəq̓ʷúƛ̓aʔxnəm {uɬ} 93 way̓ ilíʔ x̌í··lməlx məɬ_iʔ[2]
qʷaʔm+mí -n iʔ s+q̓ʷ•q̓ʷúƛ̓+aʔ=xn+m way̓ ilíʔ x̌il+m -lx mɬ_iʔ
get_used_to -1erg art race well there do_like -pl until
I got used to running races. *They'll do that until the*

culáy 94 ixíʔ məɬ sic {i} iʕyáʕlx aláʔ la ncaʔlím 95 l
culáy ixíʔ mɬ sic y̓•yaʕ -lx aláʔ l n+caʔlím l
4th_of_July then and then gather -pl here at Inchelium for
4th of July. *That's when they gather here at Inchelium.* *For*

t̓əq̓əmkstásq̓ət ksq̓ʷaʔq̓ʷúƛ̓aʔxəmsəlx ksculáymsəlx 96 xʷʔit
t̓q̓m=kst=asq̓t ks -q̓ʷ•q̓ʷúƛ̓+aʔ=xn+m -s -lx ks -culáy+m -s -lx xʷʔi+t
six_days futi -race -3i -pl futi -celebrate -3i -pl many
six days they race and they celebrate, 11:05 *lots of*

sqilxʷ, təl tqəltká··lqʷ, təl skícuʔ,[3] təl sənyál̓mən {ə··} xʷaʔɬcwílxʷtən
s+qilxʷ tl t+qlt=k=alqʷ tl s+kic+w tl s+n+yal̓+mn xʷaʔ+ɬ+cw=ilxʷ+tn
person from Canada from Idaho from Montana many_tribes
people, from Canada, from Idaho, from Montana, lots of tribes.

97 ilíʔ ciyáʕ yaʕpqín sqilxʷ 98 way̓ {məɬ ixíʔ} ʔax̌əlásq̓ət ilíʔ
ilíʔ c -yaʕ yaʕ+p=qín s+qilxʷ way̓ ʔax̌l=ásq̓t ilíʔ
there hab -gather lots person well every_day there
They gather there, lots of people. *Every day*

sq̓ʷaʔq̓ʷúƛ̓aʔxnəmsəlx 99 ixíʔ uɬ axáʔ {kʷukɬ} kʷu kɬqick
s -q̓ʷ•q̓ʷúƛ̓+aʔ=xn+m -s -lx ixíʔ uɬ axáʔ kʷu kɬ+qick
nom -race -3i -pl then and this 4kn have_older_brother
they have races. *We have an older brother,*

caʔkʷ cus iʔ t suyápix *cousin*tət 100 uɬ aɬíʔ ta
caʔkʷ cu -s iʔ t s+wyapy=x -tt uɬ aɬíʔ t
as tell -3erg art agInst white_person cousin -4in and so agInst
as they say in English our "cousin," *and in Indian*

nqílxʷcən uɬ ixíʔ {s} qícktət 101 a[xáʔ] təl kɬyípuʔs
n+qilxʷ=cn uɬ ixíʔ qick -tt axáʔ tl kɬ+yip=ẁs
Indian_language and that older_brother -4in this from Republic
our "qick," *from Republic,*

ixíʔ uɬ smisqílxʷ aɬíʔ ilmíxʷəm 102 sc̓úmstsəlx
ixíʔ uɬ s+my+s+qilxʷ aɬíʔ yl=mixʷ+m c -ʔum -st -s -lx
that and important_people because chief cust^ -call -^cust -3erg -pl
and he's an important person, a boss, *they call him*

2 This form parallels uɬ iʔ.
3 Variant (?) of s+kic+wx.

tə" pacís tunásq̓ət 103 ixíʔ uɬ tumíst mat mus iʔ
t pacís twn=asq̓t ixíʔ uɬ tw+mist mat mus iʔ
agInst Baptiste Tonasket then and sell maybe four art
Baptiste Tonasket. 12:00 He bought maybe four

sƛ̓əx̌ƛ̓əx̌sqáx̌aʔs {iʔ} 104 a[xáʔ] iʔ swipsqáx̌aʔ iʔ ƛ̓əx̌ƛ̓áx̌t 105 ixíʔ
s+ƛ̓x̌•ƛ̓x̌=sqáx̌aʔ -s axáʔ iʔ s+wyp=sqáx̌aʔ iʔ ƛ̓x̌•ƛ̓ax̌+t ixíʔ
race_horses -3in this art white_man's_horse art fast then
race horses, white people's race horses, and

məɬ ck̓əwsqílxʷ cxʷuy ak̓láʔ la ncaʔlím 106 way̓ uɬ lut t̓a
mɬ c+k+ʔaw+s+qilxʷ c+xʷuy ak̓láʔ l n+caʔlím way̓ uɬ lut t̓
and come_to_Indians come here at Inchelium well and not negfac
then he came to the Indians, came to Inchelium. And he never

cxəƛ̓páɬ̓q 107 uɬ talí nx̌síw̓s iʔ kəw̓wáps sknxʷaʔtús[4] iʔ
c -xƛ̓+p=aɬq uɬ taʔlíʔ n+x̌s=iw̓s iʔ kw•w•ap -s s+k+n+xʷaʔ+t=ús iʔ
hab -win and very_much good art horses -3in big_money art
won. His horses are good looking, he paid big money

l naqs 108 ixíʔ uɬ cúntəm axáʔ iʔ t inqíck axáʔ iʔ
l naqs ixíʔ uɬ cu -nt -m axáʔ iʔ t in -qick axáʔ iʔ
for one then and tell -nt -psv this art agInst 1in -older_brother this art
for one. And my brother asked his friend,

sl̓áx̌ts, cus 109 uɬ sc̓kinx ankəw̓wáp, 110 way̓ x̌əsx̌ást
s+l̓ax̌+t -s cu -s uɬ sc+ʔkin+x an -kw•w•ap way̓ x̌s•x̌as+t
friend -3in tell -3erg and why_is_it 2in -horses well good_pl
he said: "What is the matter with your horses? They are good

asckənxʷaʔtús uɬ way̓ cx̌síkstəmstxʷ 111 uɬ lúti
a -sc -kn+xʷaʔ+t=ús uɬ way̓ c -x̌s=ikst+m -st -xʷ uɬ lút+i
2i -pftv -high_price and yes cust^ -do_well -^cust -2erg and not_yet
looking, and you paid a good price for them, and you are a good trainer, and you

kʷ aɬ cxəƛ̓páɬ̓q 112 cut axáʔ tunásq̓ət, way̓ uníxʷ, way̓ ixíʔ incá
kʷ aɬ c -xƛ̓+p=aɬq cut axáʔ twn=asq̓t way̓ wnixʷ way̓ ixíʔ in+cá
2kn compl hab -win say this Tonasket well true yes that I
haven't won yet." Tonasket said, "That's true, I am

cənwaʔlílsmstən 113 uɬ laʔkín_sc̓kinx uɬ lúti kən əɬ
c -n+waʔl=íls+m -st -n uɬ la+ʔkin_sc+ʔkin+x uɬ lút+i kn ɬ
cust^ -puzzle -^cust -1erg and how_come and not_yet 1kn compl
puzzled by it too. Why is it that I don't

cxəƛ̓páɬ̓q 114 talí cx̌əsk̓ʷúl̓ən axáʔ inkəw̓wáp {uɬ} 115 uɬ
c -xƛ̓+p=aɬq taʔlíʔ c -x̌s+k̓ʷul̓ -n axáʔ in -kw̓•w•ap uɬ
hab -win much act -train_well -1erg this 1in -horses and
win? I give good training to my horses, 13:00 and

4 n+xʷaʔ is attested. The function of k+ is not clear.

lúti kən əɬ cxəƛ̓páɬq 116 cúntəm axáʔ iʔ t
lút+i kn ɬ c -xƛ̓+p=aɬq cu -nt -m axáʔ iʔ t
not_yet 1kn compl hab -win tell -nt -psv this art agInst
I haven't won." *My brother said to him,*

inqíck {uɬ uc k} ck̓əɬʔayxʷíw̓stxʷ asəxʷk̓amtíw̓s 117 cut
in -qick c -k̓ɬ+ʔayxʷ=íw̓s -t -xʷ a -sxʷ=k+ʔam=t=íw̓s cut
1in -older_brother cust^ -exchange -st -2erg 2in -jockey say
"Have you changed your jockey?" *He said,*

lut, {cu} cut aɬíʔ lut kən t̓a csəxʷsqílxʷ 118 uɬ way̓ t̓iʔ_kmix
lut cut aɬíʔ lut kn t̓ c -sxʷ+s+qilxʷ uɬ way̓ t̓iʔ_kmix
not say because not 1kn negfac hab -be_acqainted and well only
"No," he said, "I am not acqainted with the people, *I only know*

axáʔ {csuxʷ} csúxʷstən axáʔ iʔ cxʷúystən axáʔ i {s}
axáʔ c -suxʷ -st -n axáʔ iʔ c+xʷuy+st -n axáʔ iʔ
this cust^ -recognize -^cust -1erg this art bring_st -1erg this art
the white man

suyápix 119 axáʔ isəxʷk̓amtíw̓s, ixíʔ niʕíp iʔ kʷu a
s+wyapy=x axáʔ i -sxʷ=k+ʔam=t=íw̓s ixíʔ nyʕip iʔ kʷu a
white_person this 1in -jockey that always art 1obj art
I brought, *my jockey, he's the one that rides for me*

ck̓amtíw̓xts 120 cúntəm a[xáʔ] t inqíck uɬ
c -k+ʔam=t=íw̓ -xt -s cu -nt -m axáʔ t in -qick uɬ
cust^ -ride -xit -3erg tell -nt -psv this agInst 1in -older_brother and
all the time." *My brother said to him,*

way̓ x̌ast {akʷɬ} k̓əɬʔíysəntxʷ 121 ixíʔ mi mipnúntxʷ
way̓ x̌as+t k̓ɬ+ʔiys -nt -xʷ ixíʔ mi my+p -nu -nt -xʷ
well good change -nt -2erg then fut learn -manage -nt -2erg
"It's best you change him; *then you'll find out what*

laʔkín_sc̓kinx {pna kʷ} 122 pna asəxʷk̓amtíw̓s kʷ sqʷíləms
la+ʔkin_sc+ʔkin+x pnaʔ a -sxʷ=k+ʔam=t=íw̓s kʷ s -qʷil+m -s
how_come maybe 2in -jockey 2kʷu nom -cheat -3i
the matter is. *Maybe your jockey is cheating you."*

123 cut way̓ k aɬíʔ uɬ lut t̓a cmistín swit {i k}
cut way̓ k aɬíʔ uɬ lut t̓ c -my -st -in swit
say well intj because and not negfac cust^ -know -^cust -1erg who
He said, "Well, I don't know who to hire,

iksck̓aʕʷmíst iksck̓əɬʔíys 124 cut uɬ kʷa swit, cúntəm
i -ksc -k̓aʕʷ+míst i -ksc -k̓ɬ+ʔiys cut uɬ kʷa swit cu -nt -m
1i -futPerfi -hire 1i -futPerfi -change say and intj who tell -nt -psv
who to change." 14:00 *He said, "And who?" and he said*

way̓ axáʔ t̓əxʷ iʔ sƛ̓áx̌tət isíncaʔ 125 way̓ ixíʔ caʔkʷ {iʔ}
way̓ axáʔ t̓xʷ iʔ s+ƛ̓ax̌+t -t i -síncaʔ way̓ ixíʔ caʔkʷ
well this emph art friend -4in 1in -younger_brother yes that should
"Our partner, my little brother. *He should be*

k̓amtíw̓xtəms 126 cúntəm way̓ uɬ aɬíʔ lut t̓a
k+ʔam=t=íw̓ -xt -m -s cu -nt -m way̓ uɬ aɬíʔ lut t̓
ride -xit -2obj -3erg tell -nt -psv well and because not negfac
jockeying for you.” *He said, “I'm not acquainted*

csúxʷstən iʔ síncaʔtət {t̓əxʷ tis} 127 way̓ t̓iʔ_kmix anwí a
c -suxʷ -st -n iʔ síncaʔ -tt way̓ t̓iʔ_kmix anwí a
cust^ -recognize -^cust -1erg art younger_brother -4in well only you art
with our young brother; *it's only*

csúxʷstmən {i} 128 way̓ t̓əxʷ cunt 129 ixíʔ kʷu
c -suxʷ -st -m -n way̓ t̓xʷ cu -nt ixíʔ kʷu
cust^ -recognize -^cust -2obj -1erg well emph tell -nt then 1obj
you I know. *Ask him.”* *Then*

txʷúyms axáʔ inqíck, kʷu cus way̓ 130 uc caʔkʷ iʔ
t+xʷuy+m -s axáʔ in -qick kʷu cu -s way̓ uc caʔkʷ iʔ
go_towards -3erg this 1in -older_brother 1obj tell -3erg OK dub would art
my brother came to me, he said, “Well, *would you*

k̓amtíw̓xtxʷ iʔ sl̓áx̌tət i l sq̓ʷəq̓ʷúƛ̓aʔxnəm {aɬíʔ l axáʔ l}
k+ʔam=t=íw̓ -xt -xʷ iʔ s+l̓ax̌+t -t iʔ l s+q̓ʷ•q̓ʷúƛ̓+aʔ=xn+m
ride -xit -2erg art friend -4in art in race
ride for our friend in the race,

131 iʔ l kʷáʕta, kʷáʕta səxʷmʔúlaʔxʷtən 132 uɬ aɬ ixíʔ ta
iʔ l kʷáʕta kʷáʕta sxʷ=mʔ=úlaʔxʷ+tn uɬ aɬ ixíʔ t
art in quarter quarter mile and compl that agInst
in the quarter mile?” *(Quarter of a mile*

nuyápixcən uɬ *it's it's 400 yards, quarter of a mile* 133 a·· cun way̓ {ə}
n+wyap=x=cn uɬ a cu -n way̓
say_in_English and intj tell -1erg well
and in English that's 400 yards.) 15:00 *I said, “If that's*

spuʔúsəmp 134 way̓ ixíʔ {i} isk̓amtíw̓s kʷu
s+puʔ=ús -mp way̓ ixíʔ i -s -k+ʔam=t=íw̓s kʷu
heart -5in well then 1i -intt -sg_ride_horseback 1obj
what you want.” *So I rode, they put me*

kt̓k̓ʷíw̓ssəlx 135 t̓i kɬkʷilxʷ iʔ kəwáps {i l} i l k̓ík̓aʔt
k+t̓k̓ʷ=iw̓s -s -lx t̓iʔ kɬ+kʷil=lxʷ iʔ kwap -s iʔ l k̓í•k̓aʔt
place_on_horse -3erg -pl evid dark_sorrel art horse -3in art for near
on the horse. *It was a chestnut horse for short distances.*

136 i way̓ x̌əsʕáč̓əč̓ {iʔ} iʔ kɬkʷilxʷ swit_aɬíʔ sƛ̓əx̌sqáx̌aʔ 137 uɬ
i way̓ x̌s+ʕač̓•č̓ iʔ kɬ+kʷil=lxʷ swit_aɬíʔ s+ƛ̓x̌=sqáx̌aʔ uɬ
intj yes good_to_look_at art dark_sorrel in_fact race_horse and
He is sure a good looking horse, no wonder he's a race horse. *And*

aɬíʔ pintk cnaʔnaʔx̌ʷtstən məɬ mipnún č̓kin iʔ
aɬíʔ pin=tk c -naʔ•naʔx̌ʷ+t -st -n mɬ my+p -nu -n c+ʔkin iʔ
because always cust^ - -^cust -1erg and learn -manage -1erg how art
I always lope it [a horse] around, and I find out what

sisyúsc 138 kəm̓ ha nyəʕʷyʕʷús kəm̓ ha {c} cłc̓ac̓ {ac}
sy•sy=us -c km̓ haʔ n+yʕʷ•yʕʷ=us km̓ haʔ c -łc̓•ac̓
power -3in or inter stiff_neck or inter gpat -hit
strength he has, or if he is stiff necked, or if he can stand a whipping.

139 uł ixíʔ ixíʔ ilíʔ cnaʔnaʔx̌ʷtstən 140 uł axáʔ t
uł ixíʔ ixíʔ ilíʔ c -naʔ•naʔx̌ʷ+t -st -n uł axáʔ t
and then then there cust^ -lope -^cust -1erg and this agInst
And I loped him around. And a white man

suyápix {kʷu kʷu} kʷu łəmmníw̓sts uł ixíʔ kʷu k̓aʕʷmístəms
s+wyapy=x kʷu łm•m•n=iw̓s -t -s uł ixíʔ kʷu k̓aʕʷ+míst+m -s
white_person 1obj side_by_side -st -3erg and then 1obj hire -3erg
got side by side with me, and he engaged me. 16:03

141 kʷu cus way̓ way̓ axáʔ {ka cəl} kaʔłəlʔupənkstłcílkst mi
kʷu cu -s way̓ way̓ axáʔ kaʔłl+ʔupn=kst+ł+cil=kst mi
1obj tell -3erg well well this thirty_five fut
He said to me, "35 if you

nckʷúsəntxʷ 142 ixíʔ kʷ iksx̌áq̓əm {al} 143 uł lut t̓a
n+ckʷ=us -nt -xʷ ixíʔ kʷ i -ks -x̌aq̓+m uł lut t̓
pull_rein -nt -2erg that and not negfac
hold him back, That's what I'll pay you." I wasn't

csúxʷstən axáʔ iʔ suyápix uł t̓i_kmix kəʕʷincútmən
c -suxʷ -st -n axáʔ iʔ s+wyapy=x uł t̓iʔ_kmix k+ʕʷy+ncut+m -n
cust^ -recognize -^cust -1erg this art white_man and only laugh_at -1erg
acquainted with the white man, and I just laughed at him.

144 way̓ kʷu xítmiʔst 145 way̓ t̓iʔ cəncəkʷckʷú··stən uł kʷu
way̓ kʷu xít+miʔst way̓ t̓iʔ c -n+ckʷ•ckʷ=us -t -n uł kʷu
well 4kn run_pl well evid cust^ -hold_back -st -1erg and 4kn
We ran. I held him back,[5] and we ran to the finish

nłix̌ʷpt 146 niʕíp lut̓ łəc̓əntín axáʔ ink̓amtíw̓stən
n+łix̌ʷ+p+t nyʕip lut_t̓ łc̓ -nt -in axáʔ in -k+ʔam=t=íw̓s+tn
finish always neg_emph whip -nt -1erg this 1in -horse
[and won]. I never whipped my horse.

147 way̓, way̓ {kʷu} kʷu nq̓ʔíksəs axáʔ inqíck t
way̓ way̓ kʷu n+q̓ʔ=iks -s axáʔ in -qick t
well well 1obj put_in_the_hand -3erg this 1in -older_brother obj_tr
My brother put three dollars

kaʔłís sqəláw 148 kʷu cus way̓ axáʔ límtməntsən l
kaʔłís s+qlaw kʷu cu -s way̓ axáʔ lim+t+m -nt -s -n l
three dollar 1obj tell -3erg well this be_glad_for -nt -2obj -1erg on
in my hand. He said to me, "I thank you for riding

5 "I didn't have to push him."

ask̓amtíw̓s {uł axáʔ i} 149 uł lut t̓a cmistín c̓kin
a -s -k+ʔam=t=íw̓s uł lut t̓ c -my -st -in c+ʔkin
2i -intt -sg_ride_horseback and not negfac cust^ -know -^cust -1erg how
the horse.” 17:00 *And I don’t know how much he won,*

cniłc iʔ sƛ̓xʷups i sx̌acs {uł axáʔ} 150 ixíʔ ʕác̓ənt uł {ca} caʔkʷ ła
cnił+c iʔ s+ƛ̓xʷup -s iʔ s+x̌ac -s ixíʔ ʕac̓ -nt uł caʔkʷ łaʔ
(s)he art earning -3in art bet -3in then look -nt and if if
what he bet. *And, look, if I had pulled*

nckʷúłtən 151 uł kaʔłəlʔupənkstłcílkst {iks} iksx̌áq̓əq̓ 152 uł
n+ckʷ=u -łt -n uł kaʔłl+ʔupn=kst+ł+cil=kst i -ks -x̌aq̓•q̓ uł
pull_back -łt -1erg and thirty_five 1i -futi -pay and
the reins *my pay would have been 35.* *And*

axáʔ lut t̓a nckʷúsən, kən xəƛ̓páłq 153 uł t̓i_kmix kaʔłís sqlaw {is}
axáʔ lut t̓ n+ckʷ=us -n kn xƛ̓+p=ałq uł t̓iʔ_kmix kaʔłís s+qlaw
this not negfac pull_rein -1erg 1kn win and only three dollar
I didn’t pull the rains, I won the race, *and I only got three dollars*

isx̌áq̓əq̓ iʔ tl a kłkwap 154 way̓ náx̌əmł i tl isl̓ax̌l̓áx̌t
i -s+x̌aq̓•q̓ iʔ tl̓ a kł+kwap way̓ nax̌mł iʔ tl̓ i -s+l̓x̌•l̓ax̌+t
1in -payment art from art have_horse well but art from 1in -friends
from the one that owns the horse. *But from my friends*

uł ałíʔ yaʕyáʕt_swit isl̓áx̌t 155 məł ixíʔ way̓ kən k̓amtíw̓s məł
uł ałíʔ yaʕ•yáʕ+t_swit i -s+l̓ax̌t mł ixíʔ way̓ kn k+ʔam=t=íw̓s mł
and so everybody 1in -friend and then yes 1kn sg_ride_horseback and
(and everybody is my friend), *when I ride they bet*

x̌cáməlx l incá 156 məł c̓kin iʔ ksx̌ácsəlx {məł} məł ixíʔ kən xəƛ̓páłq
x̌ca+m -lx l in+cá mł c+ʔkin iʔ ks -x̌ac -s -lx mł ixíʔ kn xƛ̓+p=ałq
bet -pl on I and how art futi -bet -3i -pl and then 1kn win
on me. *And they bet whatever, and when I win*

157 məł kʷu nq̓ʔíkssəlx iʔ knaqs sk̓ʷut, kəm̓ iʔ naqs naqs
mł kʷu n+q̓ʔ=iks -s -lx iʔ k=naqs s+k̓ʷut km̓ iʔ naqs naqs
and 1obj put_in_the_hand -3erg -pl art one_person half or art one one
they put [money] in my hand, one puts half, or one

sqlaw {kəm̓ i k} 158 təl knaqs iʔ xʷʔit iʔ sx̌acs uł ʔúpənkst
s+qlaw tl k=naqs iʔ xʷʔi+t iʔ s+x̌ac -s uł ʔupn=kst
dollar from one_person art much art bet -3in and ten
dollar, 18:00 *from one who bets lots ten;*

159 uł ixíʔ {i} nək̓ʷsq̓ʷq̓ʷúƛ̓aʔxnəm məł ksx̌an təl x̌əccíkst isƛ̓xʷúp
uł ixíʔ nk̓ʷ+s+q̓ʷ•q̓ʷúƛ̓+aʔ=xn+m mł k+sx̌a+n tl x̌c•c=ikst i -s+ƛ̓xʷup
and then one_race and past than hundred 1in -earning
and from one race I won more that one hundred.

160 ixíʔ t̓iʔ i tl isl̓əx̌l̓áx̌t iʔ kʷu xʷíc̓xtsəlx 161 ixíʔ
ixíʔ t̓iʔ iʔ tl̓ i -s+l̓x̌•l̓ax̌+t iʔ kʷu xʷic̓ -xt -s -lx ixíʔ
that evid art from 1in -friends art 1obj give -xit -3erg -pl that
That’s from what my friends gave me. *That’s*

incáwt uɬ waẏ uníxʷ nak̓ʷm axáʔ inqíck {i} iʔ kʷu
in -caw+t uɬ waẏ wnixʷ nak̓ʷ+m axáʔ in -qick iʔ kʷu
1in -doing and yes true evid this 1in -older_brother art 1obj
what happened to me, and what my brother told me

c̓x̌ʷntis {uɬ} 162 ɬ istəɬtáɬt uɬ talí xʷʔit
c̓x̌ʷ -nt is ɬ i -s -tɬ•taɬ+t uɬ taʔlíʔ xʷʔi+t
lecture -nt -3erg if 1in -intt -straight and very_much many
is true: *If I am honest I'll have lots*

iksl̓əx̌l̓áx̌t 163 náx̌əmɬ kən ck̓ʷarr {ts} uɬ lut_swit
i -k -s+l̓x̌•l̓ax̌+t naxmɬ kn c -k̓ʷar•r uɬ lut_swit
1in -to_be -friends but 1kn hab -crooked and nobody
of friends; *but if I am crooked I won't*

iksl̓áx̌t 164 ixíʔ uɬ ilíʔ kʷu ɬ kícəs {ta}
i -k -s+l̓ax̌+t ixíʔ uɬ ilíʔ kʷu ɬ kic -s
1i -to_be -friend then and there 1obj ? reach_st/sb -3erg
have any friends. *Then a man came to me,*

c̓úmstsəlx t kcəwáʕkstxən 165 suyápix uɬ aɬíʔ mat
c -ʔum -st -s -lx t k+cw=ʕakst=xn s+wyapy=x uɬ aɬíʔ mat
cust^ -call -^cust -3erg -pl obj_tr chaps white_person and so maybe
they call him "Chaps," *white man, must be a*

káwpoy 166 uɬ aɬíʔ mat {ə" sc} niʕíp sckcəwcwáʕkstxənx
káwpoy uɬ aɬíʔ mat nyʕip sc -k+cw•cw=ʕakst=xn -x
cowboy and because maybe always ipftvp^ -wear_chaps -^ipftvp
cowboy, *he always wears chaps 19:00*

167 uɬ itlíʔ uɬ ixíʔ a ksʔamtúɬtsəlx t
uɬ itlíʔ uɬ ixíʔ a ks -ʔam -tuɬt -s -lx t
and from_there and then art futt^ -name -tuɬt -3erg -pl obj_tr
and that's why they call him

kcəwcəwʕákstxən 168 ixíʔ cpusqílxʷ 169 ixíʔ kʷu ckics
k+cw•cw=ʕakst=xn ixíʔ c -pu=s+qílxʷ ixíʔ kʷu c+kic -s
wear_chaps that hab -Indian_wife then 1obj arrive_cisl -3erg
"Chaps." *He's got an Indian wife.* *My friend came to me,*

axáʔ isl̓áx̌t uɬ kʷu cus waẏ 170 waẏ kʷ ikscúnəm axáʔ
axáʔ i -s+l̓ax̌+t uɬ kʷu cu -s waẏ waẏ kʷ i -ks -cun+m axáʔ
this 1in -friend and 1obj tell -3erg well well 2kʷu 1i -futi -tell this
and he said to me: *"I am going to tell you this,*

iʔ kʷ isl̓áx̌t 171 ṅíṅwiʔ kʷu ɬ aksk̓amtíẁxtəm mi waẏ
iʔ kʷ i -s+l̓ax̌+t ṅíṅwiʔ kʷu ɬ a -ks -k+ʔam=t=íẁ -xt -m mi waẏ
art 2kʷu 1in -friend a_while 1obj if 2i -futi -ride -xit -apsv fut yes
my partner: *If you ride for me, I am going to*

kən nx̌əltcənwíxʷ {kʷu} k̓əl q̓ʷəq̓ʷúƛ̓aʔxə 172 kʷu k̓amtíwxtxʷ
kn n+x̌lt=cn+wixʷ k̓l q̓ʷ•q̓ʷúƛ̓+aʔ=xn kʷu k+ʔam=t=íẃ -xt -xʷ
1kn ask_recip to race 1obj ride -xit -2erg
challenge a race at the race track.[6] *If you ride for me."*

173 waẏ k̓aɬáʔ k̓ɬirmnílsən, cun sc̓kinx {s} kʷ cut kʷ
waẏ k̓a+ɬáʔ k̓ɬ+yr+mn=ils -n cu -n sc+ʔkin+x kʷ cut kʷ
well on_that_side turn_down -1erg tell -1erg why_is_it 2kn say 2kn
I turned him down, I said to him, "Why did you say 'you are

isl̓áx̌t 174 uɬ kiʔ kʷu əɬ kákaʔməntxʷ 175 kʷu cus
i -s+l̓ax̌+t uɬ kiʔ kʷu ɬ ká•kaʔ+m -nt -xʷ kʷu cu -s
1in -friend and rel 1obj compl make_fun_of -nt -2erg 1obj tell -3erg
my partner?' Are you making fun of me?" He said to me,

uɬ sc̓kinx uɬ ilíʔ kʷ əɬ nʔax̌líls, iʔ kʷu əɬ cuntxʷ
uɬ sc+ʔkin+x uɬ ilíʔ kʷ ɬ n+ʔax̌l=íls iʔ kʷu ɬ cu -nt -xʷ
and why_is_it and there 2kn compl think_so art 1obj compl tell -nt -2erg
"What makes you think that, that you say that to me?"

176 cun waẏ, cun tkaʔkaʔɬís aɬəɬsqʷsíʔ a uc ixíʔ
cu -n waẏ cu -n t=kaʔ•kaʔɬís a -ɬɬ -s+qʷsiʔ a uc ixíʔ
tell -1erg well tell -1erg three_persons 2in -pl -son intj dub that
I said, "Well, you have three sons, is that right?"

177 kʷu cus waẏ, cun uɬ ixíʔ ʔamʔúmɬtnəlx Iʔ
kʷu cu -s waẏ cu -n uɬ ixíʔ ʔam•ʔúm -ɬt -n -lx Iʔ
1obj tell -3erg well tell -1erg and then announce -ɬt -1erg -pl Art
He said "Yes," and I said,

skʷskʷístsəlx 178 cúnəlx uɬ miɬsisyúsəlx təl incá {i l} i l
s+kʷs•kʷist -s -lx cu -n -lx uɬ my+ɬ+sy•sy=us -lx tl in+cá iʔ l
name_pl -3in -pl tell -1erg -pl and smart_comptv -pl than I art at
I named them. 20:04 I said to him, "And they are smarter than I at

sk̓amtíẃs 179 uɬ incá iʔ {kʷuəɬ} kʷu əɬ k̓aʕʷmístməntxʷ
s+k+ʔam=t=íẃs uɬ in+cá iʔ kʷu ɬ k̓aʕʷ+míst+m -nt -xʷ
horseback_riding and I art 1obj compl hire -nt -2erg
riding and then it's me you hire

kʷ iksk̓amtíẃxtəm 180 kʷu cus waẏ, waẏ uníxʷ
kʷ i -ks -k+ʔam=t=íẃ -xt -m kʷu cu -s waẏ waẏ wnixʷ
2kʷu 1i -futi -ride -xit -apsv 1obj tell -3erg yes yes true
to ride for you?" He said to me, "Yes, it's true."

181 kʷu cus uɬ náx̌əmɬ ixíʔ ʔamʔúməntxʷ iɬəɬsqʷsíʔ waẏ
kʷu cu -s uɬ nax̌mɬ ixíʔ ʔam•ʔúm -nt -xʷ i -ɬɬ -s+qʷsiʔ waẏ
1obj tell -3erg and but then announce -nt -2erg 1i -pl -son well
He said to me, "The boys you named are only in it

6 Not clear. Probably "I am going to bet on you to win."

kmix x̌əl sqlaw 182 lut x̌əl stmáliʔscəlx 183 waẏ {i} iwá kʷu
kmix x̌l s+qlaw lut x̌l s+tm=áliʔs -c -lx waẏ iwá kʷu
only for money not for relatives -3in -pl well even 1kʷu
for the money; *they are not for their relatives.* *Even if I am*

lʔíwsəlx, uɬ waẏ t'iʔ kʷu ksənckʷúɬtsəlx inkəwáp {uɬ}
lʔiw -s -lx uɬ waẏ t'iʔ kʷu ks -n+ckʷ=u -ɬt -s -lx in -kwap
m's_father -3in -pl and yes evid 1obj futt^ -pull_back -ɬt -3erg -pl 1in -horse
their father, they'll pull the reins on my horse." End of tape. 20:35

A hunting trip

1 púti? kən ɬa? ilí? i? l sənx̌ʷúċəċtən 2 waẏ uɬ axá? {ta?xʷ}
pút+i? kn ɬa? ilí? i? l sn+x̌ʷuċ•ċ+tn waẏ uɬ axá?
still 1kn when there art at cut_something yes and this
When I used to live at sənx̌ʷúċəċtən, *there was snow*

ta?xʷsmík̓ʷt 3 ca?kʷ cus ia nqílxʷcən ?ístkəm waẏ uɬ
ta?xʷ+s+mík̓ʷt ca?kʷ cu -s i? n+qilxʷ=cn ?is=tk+m cu waẏ uɬ
get_snow as tell -3erg art Indian_language winter tell yes and
on the ground, *as they say in Indian, it was winter, and there was*

xʷ?it i? smik̓ʷt 4 waẏ kʷṁiɬ ilí? {kʷu kə c} kʷu
xʷ?i+t i? s+mik̓ʷt waẏ kʷṁiɬ ilí? kʷu
much art snow_on_ground well suddenly there 1obj
lots of snow. *All at once some friends*

kícsəlx isľəx̌ľáx̌t 5 axá? inqíck uɬ axá?
kic -s -lx i -s+ľx̌•ľax̌+t axá? in -qick uɬ axá?
reach_st/sb -3erg -pl 1in -friends this 1in -older_brother and this
came to me, *my oldest brother and Cricket*

sẏalẃánk 6 ixí? uɬ {kə?} kʷu cúsəlx waẏ kʷu kspíx̌a?x kʷu
s+ẏalẃ=ánk ixí? uɬ kʷu cu -s -lx waẏ kʷu ks -pix̌ -a?x kʷu
Cricket then and 1obj tell -3erg -pl well 4kn incp^ -hunt -^incp 4kn
[Idaho Fry]. *And they said to me, "Let's go*

kspíx̌a?x 7 cúnəlx waẏ uɬ {l kʷu} kʷu k̓ʷəɬxəntíp uɬ lut
ks -pix̌ -a?x cu -n -lx waẏ uɬ kʷu k̓ʷɬx -nt -ip uɬ lut
incp^ -hunt -^incp tell -1erg -pl well and 1obj startle -nt -5erg and not
hunting." 1:00 *I told them, "You got me on surprise and*

kən t̓a kscx̌əcməncút 8 waẏ t̓əxʷ kʷu xʷíċxətp
kn t̓ ksc -x̌c+mncut waẏ t̓xʷ kʷu xʷiċ -xt -p
1kn negfac pperf -get_ready well emph 1obj give -xit -5erg
I have nothing ready. *Give me this one day*

ʕapná?_i?_sx̌əlx̌áʕlt kən x̌əcməncút 9 kən táwnəm, [kən] təxʷst̓ík̓ləm, mi uɬ
ʕapná?_i?_s+x̌l•x̌aʕl+t kn x̌c+mncut kn tawn+m kn txʷ+s+t̓ik̓l+m mi uɬ
today 1kn get_ready 1kn go_to_town 1kn get_grub fut and
to get ready. *I'll go to town, get me some groceries, and then*

kʷu xʷuy 10 waẏ, waẏ ixí? {kik} istáwnəm, kən təxʷst̓ík̓ləm, uɬ
kʷu xʷuy waẏ waẏ ixí? i -s -tawn+m kn txʷ+s+t̓ik̓l+m uɬ
4kn go well well then 1i -intt -go_to_town 1kn get_grub and
we'll go. *I go to the store, I get some grub, and I'll have*

ixí? {kn} kən k̓ɬwina?scút 11 waẏ kʷu ksk̓əlxʷína?, kʷu ksx̌əlpína?, waẏ
ixí? kn k̓ɬ+wẏ=na?+scút waẏ kʷu k+s+k̓lxʷ=ína? kʷu k+s+x̌l+p=ína? waẏ
then 1kn be_ready well 4kn have_evening 4kn have_daylight well
everything ready." *Night came, daylight came,*

ixíʔ {kʷu s} kʷu sʔimxs 12 ah, axáʔ kʷu cúntəm t
ixíʔ kʷu s -ʔim+x -s ah axáʔ kʷu cu -nt -m t
then 4kn nom4^ -move -^nom4 intj this 3e4obj tell -nt -3e4obj agInst
then we started to move. Ah, Cricket said

sẏaľẇánk 13 waẏ {caʔkʷ} caʔkʷ kxɬúlmən, uɬ lut kən t̓a
s+ẏaľẇ=ánk waẏ caʔkʷ kx -ɬulm -n uɬ lut kn t̓
Cricket yes would follow -5obj -1erg and not 1kn negfac
to us: "I'd like to go with you, but I haven't got

ksululmínk {cúnəlx} 14 cun sẏalẇánk 15 waẏ incá kən ʔasəlínk uɬ
k+s+wl•wl+m=ink cu -n s+ẏaľẇ=ánk waẏ in+cá kn ʔasl=ínk uɬ
have_gun tell -1erg Cricket well I 1kn two_guns and
a gun." I said to Cricket: "I have two guns

xʷʔit incq̓ílən itlíʔ [mi] kʷ nk̓ʷaʔk̓ʷínəm {əy} 16 iʔ naqs caʔkʷ
xʷʔi+t in -cq̓=iln itlíʔ mi kʷ n+k̓ʷaʔ+k̓ʷin+m iʔ naqs caʔkʷ
much 1in -arrow from_there fut 2kn pick art one as
and lots of cartridges, pick one." 2:03 One gun they

cus iʔ ta nuyápəxcən *Winchester* 17 uɬ axáʔ iʔ naqs iʔ
cu -s iʔ t n+wyap+x=cn uɬ axáʔ iʔ naqs iʔ
tell -3erg art agInst say_in_English and this art one art
call "Winchester" in English; and the other gun

sululmínk ixíʔ ta nuyápəxcən uɬ {ay} *Marlin* 18 kʷu cus waẏ axáʔ
s+wl•wl+m=ink ixíʔ t n+wyapy+x=cn uɬ kʷu cu -s waẏ axáʔ
gun that obl say_in_English and 1obj tell -3erg well this
they call "Marlin" in English. He said to me, "I'll take

iʔ *Winchester* mi kʷin 19 ah cun, waẏ, a cxəƛ̓uʔsús
iʔ mi kʷi -n ah cu -n waẏ a c -xƛ̓+ẇs=us
art fut take -1erg intj tell -1erg Ok art hab -full
the Winchester." I said "Ok." My belt is full of

incəq̓ílən axáʔ iʔ l iniq̓íp, iṅíṅk̓mən 20 waẏ uɬ axáʔ kʷin iʔ
in -cq̓=iln axáʔ iʔ l in -yq̓=ip i -ṅi•ṅk̓+mn waẏ uɬ axáʔ kʷi -n iʔ
1in -bullet this art in 1in -belt 1in -knife well and this take -1erg art
cartridges, my hunting knife. And I took

naqs iʔ sululmínk {iʔ} iʔ Marlin 21 waẏ kʷu sx̌əƛ̓x̌íƛ̓əm[s]
naqs iʔ s + wl•wl + m=ink iʔ waẏ kʷu s -x̌ƛ̓•x̌iƛ̓ + m -s
one art gun art well 4kn nom4^ -climb -^nom4
the other gun, the Marlin. We went up in the mountains.

22 waẏ ik̓líʔ {kʷu} kʷu t̓qəlímx k̓əl kyríptən 23 waẏ {kʷu} kʷu ksx̌əlpínaʔ
waẏ ik̓líʔ kʷu t̓ql=imx[1] k̓l k+yr=ip+tn waẏ kʷu k+s+x̌l+p=ínaʔ
well there 4kn stop at Push_Pack well 4kn have_daylight
We went and stopped at Push Pack. It got daylight.

1 The relationship of -imx to ʔimx, if any, is unclear.

24 waẏ ixíʔ {kʷu s} kʷu wiʔwiʔcín 25 uɬ axáʔ inqíck inqíck
waẏ ixíʔ kʷu wẏ•wẏ=cin uɬ axáʔ in -qick in
well then 4kn finish_eating_pl and this 1in -older_brother 1in
We got done eating. 3:01 *And my brother knows*

ixíʔ aɬíʔ cminúlaʔxʷsts, x̌əlínaʔs {uɬ i} 26 kʷu
ixíʔ aɬíʔ c -my+n=úlaʔxʷ -st -s x̌l=ínaʔ -s kʷu
that so cust^ -know_the_country -^cust -3erg cache -3in 3e4obj
the country, it's his cache. *He said*

cúntəm waẏ axáʔ t̓i t̓íxəlx uɬ iʔ sƛ̓aʔcínəm
cu -nt -m waẏ axáʔ t̓iʔ t̓ix+lx -lx uɬ iʔ s+ƛ̓aʔ=cín+m
tell -nt -3e4obj yes this evid come_to_shore -pl and art deer
to us, "Just after you cross, there are deer all over.

27 ixíʔ {c ə c} cənlwlʕ̓ʷútəm, waẏ ixíʔ mi píx̌əntəm {uɬ} 28 uɬ axáʔ naʔɬ
ixíʔ c -n+lw•lʕ̓ʷ=ut+m waẏ ixíʔ mi pix̌ -nt -m uɬ axáʔ naʔɬ
there hab -gulches yes there fut hunt -nt -4erg and this and
There are gulches, and that's where we'll hunt." *And my*

inqíck kʷu ksyríwaʔxən 29 uɬ axáʔ iʔ sl̓áx̌tət sẏal̓ẃánk
in -qick kʷu k+s+yr=íwaʔ=xn uɬ axáʔ iʔ s+l̓ax̌+t -t s+ẏal̓ẃ=ánk
1in -older_brother 4kn have_snowshoes and this art partner -4in Cricket
brother and I had snowshoes, *but our friend Cricket*

lut t̓a ksyríwaʔxən 30 waẏ kʷu t̓íxəlx uɬ ixíʔ axáʔ iʔ
lut t̓ k+s+yr=íwaʔ=xn waẏ kʷu t̓ix+lx uɬ ixíʔ axáʔ iʔ
not negfac have_snowshoes well 4kn come_to_shore and there this art
didn't have snowshoes. *We crossed the*

cəcẃíxaʔ 31 uɬ ixíʔ cúntəm, kʷu c̓x̌ʷúlaʔxʷxtəm axáʔ
c•cẃíxaʔ uɬ ixíʔ cu -nt -m kʷu c̓x̌ʷ=úlaʔxʷ -xt -m axáʔ
little_creek and then tell -nt -3e4obj 3e4obj show_country -xit -3e4obj this
little creek, *and then my brother told us*

t inqíck 32 cúntəm, waẏ uɬ axáʔ píx̌əntəm axáʔ
t in -qick cu -nt -m waẏ uɬ axáʔ pix̌ -nt -m axáʔ
agInst 1in -older_brother tell -nt -3e4obj well and this hunt -nt -4erg this
where to go. *He said, "We'll hunt*

cəlʕ̓ʷútəm 33 k̓liʔ kiʔ cp̓əp̓sʕáwaʔs k̓əl sp̓áp̓ƛ̓əmqən 34 ixíʔ iʔ
c+lʕ̓ʷ=ut+m ik̓líʔ kiʔ c -p̓•p̓s=áwaʔs k̓l s+p̓a•p̓ƛ̓+m=qn ixíʔ iʔ
valley there rel hab -low_place to head_of_gulch that art
this gulch." *There is a low place, the head of the gulch;* *that's*

sənk̓əɬcahmín, ixíʔ iʔ sxʷaʔxʷúytəns iʔ sƛ̓aʔcínəm {əɬ}
sn+k̓ɬ+cah+mín ixíʔ iʔ s+xʷaʔ•xʷúy+tn -s iʔ s+ƛ̓aʔ=cín+m
place_to_sit_and_watch that art place_of_repeated_walking -3in art deer
where to sit and watch, that's the deer's trail. 4:02

35 waẏ k̓laʔ naqs ɬ nsaʕməncútəlx {kəm̓ k̓laʔ k̓əl kəm̓ ta ck̓əl k̓əl} kəm̓
waẏ ak̓láʔ naqs ɬ n+saʕ+mncút -lx km̓
well here one compl go_down -pl or
They go down to another gulch, or to

ta ck̓əl 36 ik̓líʔ ł nsaʕməncútəlx 37 way̓ cun axáʔ
ta+c+k̓l ik̓líʔ ł n+saʕ+mncút -lx way̓ cu -n axáʔ
in_direction_of there compl go_down -pl well tell -1erg this
[Wilmont Creek]. *They'll go down there.* *I said to*

inqíck, {way̓} way̓ anwí mi {k^{w}} k^{w} ʔawsk̓əłchám 38 caʔk^{w} cus a
in -qick way̓ anwí mi k^{w} ʔaw+s+k̓ł+chá+m caʔk^{w} cu -s a
1in -older_brother yes you fut 2kn go_set_watch as tell -3erg art
my brother, "You go sit and watch" *(as they say in*

nqílx^{w}cən, anwí k^{w} lx^{w}úsəm 39 way̓ ix̌íxtəmt 40 k^{w}u
n+qilx^{w}=cn anwí k^{w} lx^{w}=us+m way̓ yx̌=iʔ -xt -m -t k^{w}u
Indian_language you 2kn be_on_watch yes drive -xit -2obj -4erg 1obj
Indian), you be the one to "sit and watch." *"We'll do the driving."* *He*

cúntəm way̓, way̓ ixíʔ sx^{w}uys 41 uł axáʔ {t} cun
cu -nt -m way̓ way̓ ixíʔ s -x^{w}uy -s uł axáʔ cu -n
tell -nt -3e4obj yes yes then nom -go -3i and this tell -1erg
told us "Ok," and he went. *And I said*

sy̓alw̓ánk way̓ anwí lut k^{w} t̓a cyríwaʔxən 42 incám kən
s+y̓al̓w̓=ánk way̓ anwí lut k^{w} t̓ c -yr=íwaʔ=xn incá+m kn
Cricket well you not 2kn negfac hab -snow_shoe I 1kn
to Cricket: "You haven't got showshoes. *I have*

cyríwaʔxən, way̓ incá iʔ kən k̓əłkyx^{w}út 43 uł ałíʔ lut t̓a
c -y=ríwaʔ=xn way̓ in+cá iʔ kn k̓ł+k+yx^{w}=ut uł ałíʔ lut t̓
hab -snow_shoe well I art 1kn go_below and so not negfac
showshoes and I'll go the lower route. 5:02 *There is*

csúləm iʔ smik̓^{w}t 44 axáʔm axáʔ iʔ k̓əl [k̓əł]x̌sínk uł
c -sul+m iʔ s+mik̓^{w}t axáʔ+m axáʔ iʔ k̓l k̓ł+x̌s=ink uł
hab -frozen_crust art snow_on_ground this this art to side_hill and
no crust on the snow. *But there is a crust*

csúləm uł {a} lut {aks} akscəpcípx̌^{w}t 45 way̓, way̓ ixíʔ
c -sul+m uł lut a -ks -cp•cipx̌^{w}+t way̓ way̓ ixíʔ
hab -frozen_crust and not 2i -futi -break_through yes well then
in the upper place, and you won't break through the snow." *He*

sx^{w}uys {cun uł} 46 way̓ {ałi ay} k̓əłʔímən x̌əl ʔayxáxaʔ, uł sic kən x^{w}uy
s -x^{w}uy -s way̓ k̓ł+ʔim -n x̌l ʔayxáxaʔ uł sic kn x^{w}uy
nom -go -3i well wait_for -1erg for a_while and then 1kn go
went. *I waited for him a little while, then I went.*

47 way̓ kən k̓əłk̓^{w}ƛ̓áp ałíʔ uł sx̌əsúlaʔx^{w}əx^{w} [iʔ]
way̓ kn k̓ł+k̓^{w}ƛ̓a+p ałíʔ uł s -x̌s=úlaʔx^{w} -x^{w} iʔ
well 1kn come_in_sight because and ipftv^ -open_country -^ipftv art
I came in sight; where we were headed was

ksx^{w}úytəntət {inaud} 48 k̓łənxəlpín̓kən axáʔ iʔ sl̓áx̌tət 49 way̓ kən
k -sx^{w}uy+tn -tt k̓ł+nxl+p=ink -n axáʔ iʔ s+l̓ax̌+t -t way̓ kn
to_be -travel -4i hear_shot -1erg this art friend -4in well 1kn
open country. *I heard our partner's shot.* *I came*

k̓əɬk̓ʷƛ̓áp way̓ k̓ iksxʷúytən
k̓ɬ+k̓ʷƛ̓a+p way̓ k̓ i -k -s+xʷuy+tn
come_in_sight well to 1i -to_be -travel
in sight to where I was going.

50 ih kiʔ sťíqʷkstəms, {a ɬa}
ih kiʔ s -ťiqʷ=kst+m -s
intj rel nom -shoot_around -3i
He was shooting around,

cnusməlxús cťíqʷkstəm
c -n+ws+m+lx=us c -ťiqʷ=kst+m
hab -point_upward hab -shoot_around
shooting with his gun pointed up.

51 məɬ wíkən a[xáʔ] iʔ sƛ̓aʔcínəm,
mɬ wik -n axáʔ iʔ s+ƛ̓aʔ=cín+m
and see -1erg this art deer
And I saw the deer,

nťa yaʕ̓pqín atáʔ iʔ xítmiʔst
nťa yaʕ̓+p=qín atáʔ iʔ xít+miʔst
intj many_gathered here art run_pl
a whole bunch, running. 6:00

52 way̓ ixíʔ sťaʕpsqílxʷs, way̓
way̓ ixíʔ s -ťaʕp+s+qílxʷ -s way̓
yes that nom -fire_gun -3i yes
He was shooting, and I got

kən picxʷt
kn picxʷ+t
1kn disgusted
disgusted.

53 way̓ uɬ axáʔ [kən] ʔax̌əlməncút {uɬ axáʔ} ta cniɬc iʔ k̓əl
way̓ uɬ axáʔ kn ʔax̌l+mncút t cniɬ+c iʔ k̓l
well and this 1kn turn_around from (s)he art to
I turned away to where he was

ksxʷúytəns
k -s+xʷuy+tn -s
to_be -travel -3i
supposed to go,

54 ik̓líʔ kən ɬ xʷuy
ik̓líʔ kn ɬ xʷuy
there 1kn compl go
that's where I went.

55 way̓ ik̓líʔ k̓əɬwíkxən {i··}
way̓ ik̓líʔ k̓ɬ+wik=xn -n
yes there see_tracks -1erg
There I saw tracks.

56 pəx̌ʷməncút yaʔx̌í iʔ sƛ̓aʔcínəm, uɬ sísp̓əlk̓ ta ck̓əl k̓əɬxənxn̓ínk {ɬə}
px̌ʷ+mncut yaʔx̌í iʔ s+ƛ̓aʔ=cín+m uɬ si•sp̓lk̓ ta+c+k̓l k̓ɬ+xn•xn=ink
scatter yonder art deer and seven in_direction_of side_hill
The deer had scattered, seven had gone towards the side hill.

57 k̓əɬxətmiʔstínkəlx {way̓ ixíʔ}
k̓ɬ+xt+miʔst=ínk -lx
run_on_side_hill -pl
They ran on the side hill.

58 ixíʔ kílnəlx, ik̓líʔ
ixíʔ kil -n -lx ik̓líʔ
then chase -1erg -pl there
I started to run after them,

nkəcníkiʔnəlx
n+kc+n==íkiʔ -n -lx
catch_up_with -1erg -pl
I overtook them.

59 way̓ kən ƛ̓xʷam t ʔasíl
way̓ kn ƛ̓xʷa+m t ʔasíl
yes 1kn kill_many obj_itr two
I killed two.

60 way̓ sta way̓
way̓ sta way̓
well intj yes
That's

ixíʔ xʷʔit
ixíʔ xʷʔi+t
that enough
enough.

61 way̓ {iɬɬ} iɬəɬcxʷúy, [kən] ɬcxʷuy nkʷəkʷʔác kən
way̓ i -ɬ -ɬ+c+xʷuy kn ɬ+c+xʷuy n+kʷ•kʷʔac kn
well 1i -nom -come_again 1kn come_again dark 1kn
Then I came back, I came back and I got back

ɬckicx
ɬ+c+kic+x
arrive_cisl_again
after dark. 7:07

62 way̓ ɬkʷlíwtəlx isl̓əx̌l̓áx̌t way̓ ixíʔ
way̓ ɬ+kʷl=iwt -lx i -s+l̓x̌•l̓ax̌+t way̓ ixíʔ
well sit_pl_again -pl 1in -friends yes then
My partners were back at camp, and they

smay̓ncútsəlx {a}
s -m̓ay+ncút -s -lx
nom -tell_story -3i -pl
started telling stories.

63 cut axáʔ inqíck, way̓ kʷu ƛ̓músəs
cut axáʔ in -qick way̓ kʷu ƛ̓m=us -s
say this 1in -older_brother yes 1obj left_behind -3erg
My brother said, "The deer went

iʔ t sƛ̓aʔcínəm {waẏ kə lut i} 64 waẏ kən kicx, waẏ itíʔ iʔ
iʔ t s+ƛ̓aʔ=cín+m waẏ kn kic+x waẏ itíʔ iʔ
art agInst deer well 1kn arrive finish from_that art
ahead of me. *When I got back they are already gone,*

sxʷúyʔytəns uɬ lut isuksqílxʷ 65 waẏ axáʔ cut t sẏalẇánk,
s+xʷuy•y+tn -s uɬ lut i -s -wk+sqilxʷ waẏ axáʔ cut t s+ẏaľẇ=ánk
tracks -3in and not 1i -nom -see well this say agInst Cricket
and I saw nothing.” *Cricket said, he started his story,*

maẏncút, cut 66 waẏ incá uɬ ťəxʷ kən c̓əspqníʔ waẏ kən c̓əxəmscút
m̓ay+ncút cut waẏ in+cá uɬ ťxʷ kn c̓s+p=qn=iʔ waẏ kn c̓x+mscut
tell_story say well I and emph 1kn bullets_finish yes help embarrassed
he said: *“I used every one of my shells, I am embarrassed [to say].*

67 kən ťaʕpsqí··lxʷ uɬ kən c̓əspqníʔ 68 uɬ lut kən ťa ílpiʔst uɬ
kn ťaʕp+s+qílxʷ uɬ kn c̓s+p=qn=iʔ uɬ lut kn ť yíl+p=iʔst uɬ
1kn fire_gun and 1kn bullets_finish and not 1kn negfac hit_target and
I shot and shot and ran out of ammunition. *I never hit one, and they’re*

súxʷəxʷ 69 waẏ mat isululmínk lut ť sx̌əstmíx 70 uɬ
suxʷ•xʷ waẏ mat i -s+wl•wl+m=ink lut ť s -x̌s+t -mix uɬ
leave_pl well must 1in -gun not negfac ipftv^ -good -^ipftv and
gone. *I guess my gun must be no good.”* *And*

aɬíʔ cyaʔyáx̌aʔstən {a} 71 ta ck̓a cnusməlxús {ɬa} iʔ
aɬíʔ c -yaʔ•yáx̌aʔ -st -n ta c+k̓ c -n+ws+m+lx=us iʔ
because cust^ -watch -^cust -1erg toward hab -point_upward art
I had been watching him. *He was shooting at the sky,*

sululmínks ɬaʔ ckťaʔťaʔpásq̇təm 72 uɬ ixíʔ caʔkʷ cus
s+wl•wl+m=ink -s ɬaʔ c -k+ťaʔ•ťaʔp=ásq̇t+m c uɬ ixíʔ caʔkʷ cu -s
gun -3in when hab -shoot_skyward hab and that as tell -3erg
his gun pointed upward. 8:00 *He must have had the*

ya nuyápəxcən ixíʔ *buck fever* 73 waẏ, waẏ {kʷu ks} kʷu pulx, kʷu
ya n+wyap+x=cn ixíʔ waẏ waẏ kʷu pul+x kʷu
art say_in_English that well yes 4kn camp 4kn
buck fever, as they say in English. *We went to bed,*

ksx̌əlpínaʔ 74 ah, ixíʔ iʔ k̓laxʷ naɬcəcám, waẏ kʷu
k+s+x̌l+p=ínaʔ ah ixíʔ iʔ k̓laxʷ naɬc•c•ám waẏ kʷu
have_daylight intj then art evening forget yes 3e4obj
daylight came. *Oh, I forgot, in the evening two others*

nkəcníkiʔntəm t k̓əsʔasíl 75 axáʔ t sqəmqəm·ín {naʔɬ}
n+kc+n=íkiʔ -nt -m t k+ʔs•ʔasíl axáʔ t s+qm•qm+min
catch_up_with -nt -3e4obj agInst two_persons this agInst m’s_name
overtook us. *Albert Toulou*

iʔ naʔɬ skləkʷtílts 76 waẏ nák̓ʷəm sc̓əx̌ʷxtwíxʷs axáʔ
iʔ naʔɬ s+k+lkʷ=t=ilt -s waẏ nak̓ʷ+m s+c̓x̌ʷ+xtwixʷ -s axáʔ
art and distant_child -3in well evid arrangement -3in this
and his distant son, *that was my brother*

inqíck nyas 77 uɬ ixíʔ nixʷ kʷu sənʔúcxnəm[s]
in -qick nyas uɬ ixíʔ nixʷ kʷu s -n+ʔuc=xn+m -s
1in -older_brother Eneas and that also 3e4obj nom4^ -follow -^nom4
Eneas's date. *And they followed us*

uɬ spíx̌əxəlx {waẏ} 78 waẏ uɬ kl̓əl̓lkʷút uɬ ur̓ísəlp̓məlx uɬ
uɬ s -pix̌ -x -lx waẏ uɬ k+l̓•l̓kʷ=ut uɬ wr̓=islp̓+m -lx uɬ
and ipftv^ -hunt -^ipftv -pl well and far_dim and build_fire -pl and
hunting. *Little ways from there they made a fire, and we*

cúntməlx 79 sc̓kinx axáʔ qʷámqʷəmt axáʔ iʔ snur̓ísəlp̓təntət
cun -nt -m -lx sc+ʔkin+x axáʔ qʷam•qʷm+t axáʔ iʔ sn+wr̓=islp̓+tn -tt
tell -nt -4erg -pl why_is_it this excellent this art fireplace -4in
said to them: 9:03 *"What's the matter, there is a good fireplace here!*

80 waẏ taʔmúlaʔxʷ, cʔáx̌ʷlaʔxʷ, lut, waẏ axáʔ x̌ast 81 uɬ aláʔ {u}
waẏ taʔm=úlaʔxʷ c -ʔáx̌ʷ=laʔxʷ lut waẏ axáʔ x̌as+t uɬ aláʔ
yes snow_melt hab -cleared_land not yes this good and here
We got the snow cleared away, heck, this is good. *We should*

caʔkʷ kʷu yaʕ̓məncút kʷu ʔaɬʔíɬən 82 lut, waẏ kʷu kst̓ík̓əl 83 waẏ
caʔkʷ kʷu yaʕ+mncút kʷu ʔaɬ•ʔíɬn lut waẏ kʷu k+s+t̓ik̓l waẏ
should 4kn all 4kn eat_pl not yes 4kn have_grub well
eat all together here." *No, we got our lunch.* *They*

k̓əɬxʷípməlx axáʔ kɬcqəntísəlx axáʔ {iʔ} iʔ sənq̓ʷúctən iʔ ɬkap
k̓ɬ+xʷip+m -lx axáʔ kɬ+cq -nt -is -lx axáʔ iʔ sn+q̓ʷuc+tn iʔ ɬkap
spread_down -pl this put_st_on -nt -3erg -pl this art lard art bucket
spread a tablecloth, and they put a lard bucket on it.

84 waẏ ilíʔ nák̓ʷəm a cənq̓əq̓əʔq̓ʔíwaʔs {i} 85 caʔkʷ cus a
waẏ ilíʔ nak̓ʷ+m a c -n+q̓•q̓ʔ=íw̓aʔs caʔkʷ cu -s a
well there evid art hab -sandwich_dim as tell -3erg art
It was nothing but a little sandwich. *Like they say*

nuyápixcən iʔ *sandwiches,* ixíʔ st̓ík̓əls 86 uɬ cúntməlx axáʔ iʔ
n+wyap+x=cn iʔ ixíʔ s+t̓ik̓l -s uɬ cun -t -m -lx axáʔ iʔ
say_in_English art that grub -3in and tell -nt -psv -pl this art
in English, "sandwiches," that was their lunch. *And my brother said*

t inqíck 87 {uy} ixíʔ scuts sqəmqəmmín, waẏ lut
t in -qick ixíʔ s -cut -s s+qm•qm+min waẏ lut
agInst 1in -older_brother then nom -say -3i m's_name well not
to them...[tape ends] 9:37 *sqəmqmmín said*

t̓a csíwstəm[2] a lkapí 88 náx̌əmɬ uc p kɬəncíx
t̓ c -siw -st -m a lkapí naxmɬ uc p kɬ+n=cix
negfac cust^ -drink -st -4erg art coffee but dub 5kn have+warm_water
"We never drink coffee. *But do you have warm water?"*

2 This verb has two stems: siw and siw+st, where +st may go back to an earlier +sut *reflexive*.

89 cúntəm a t inqíck, way̓ xʷʔit ia ncix 90 cut
cu -nt -m a t in -qick way̓ xʷʔi+t iʔ n=cix cut
tell -nt -psv art agInst 1in -older_brother yes much art warm_water say
My brother told him, "We have lots of warm water." *He*

kmix iʔ {ə} pústəm a csiwstəm 91 way̓ ixíʔ {sk̓ʷəlɬ}
kmix iʔ pustm a c -siw -st -m way̓ ixíʔ
only art postum art cust^ -drink -st -4erg well then
said "We just drink Postum." *They made*

sk̓ʷəlɬlkapímsəlx iʔ t pústəm {way əy} 92 t̓i kʷu
s -k̓ʷl̓+ɬ+lkapí+m -s -lx iʔ t pustm t̓iʔ kʷu
nom -make_coffee -3i -pl art agInst Postum evid 4kn
coffee with Postum. *It got*

ksx̌əlpínaʔ uɬ c̓əspəst̓ík̓əllx 93 way̓ ixíʔ nk̓ʷəɬʔaɬʔíɬnməntməlx
k+s+x̌l+p=ínaʔ uɬ c̓s+p+s+t̓íkl -lx way̓ ixíʔ nk̓ʷ+ɬ+ʔaɬ•ʔíɬn+m -nt -m -lx
have_daylight and finish_grub -pl well then eat_with -nt -mdl -pl
daylight and they ran out of grub. *We ate with them. 1:01*

94 way̓ uɬ axáʔ {i i} síwstsəlx i ta lkapí 95 way̓ uɬ kʷu
way̓ uɬ axáʔ siw -st -s -lx iʔ t lkapí way̓ uɬ kʷu
well and this drink -st -3erg -pl art prttv coffee well and 4kn
They drank the coffee. *Daylight*

ksx̌əlpínaʔ, uɬ ixíʔ kʷu spíx̌əms 96 way̓ {kʷu} kʷu
k+s+x̌l+p=ínaʔ uɬ ixíʔ kʷu s -pix̌+m -s way̓ kʷu
have_daylight and then 4kn nom4^ -hunt -^nom4 well 4kn
came and we went hunting. *We came*

k̓əɬʔíq̓ʷ iʔ k̓əl sənʔístktəns iʔ sƛ̓aʔcínəm 97 ixíʔ
k̓+ɬ[ʔ]iq̓ʷ iʔ k̓l sn+ʔis=tk+tn -s iʔ s+ƛ̓aʔ=cín+m ixíʔ
come_in_sight art at wintering_place -3in art deer there
in sight of the place where the deer winter. *It's*

cənqʷʔúlaʔxʷ, səlxʷaʔúlaʔxʷ {way cúntəm} 98 kʷu cúntəm axáʔ
c -n+qʷʔ=úlaʔxʷ slxʷaʔ=úlaʔxʷ kʷu cu -nt -m axáʔ
hab -ground_pocket big_place 3e4obj tell -nt -3e4obj this
a big pocket, a big place. *My brother told us,*

iʔ t inqíck, ixíʔ aɬíʔ iʔ səxʷc̓x̌ʷúlaʔxʷəm 99 way̓ {əɬ}
iʔ t in -qick ixíʔ aɬíʔ iʔ sxʷ=c̓x̌ʷ=úlaʔxʷ+m way̓
art agInst 1in -older_brother that because art guide well
because he is the guide, *"We are*

atláʔ məɬ kʷu px̌ʷməncút 100 uɬ swit iʔ ksxʷúyaʔx iʔ k̓əl, caʔkʷ
atláʔ mɬ kʷu px̌ʷ+mncut uɬ swit iʔ ks -xʷuy -aʔx iʔ k̓l caʔkʷ
from_here and 4kn scatter and who art incp^ -go -^incp art to as
going to scatter. *And who is going to be,*

cus iʔ ta nqílxʷcən iʔ səlxʷúsəm 101 iʔ k̓əl sxʷúytəns
cu -s iʔ t n+qilxʷ=cn iʔ s+lxʷ=us+m iʔ k̓l s+xʷuy+tn -s
tell -3erg art agInst Indian_language art watch art to step -3in
like they say in Indian, those that sit up and watch *to where the deer are going,*

i? sƛ̓a?cínəm, ?awsk̓əɬchám
i? s+ƛ̓a?=cín+m ?aw+s+k̓ɬ+chá+m
art deer go_set_watch
[who is going to] go to sit and watch?”

102 cun axá? inqíck, {way̓} way̓
cu -n axá? in -qick way̓
tell -1erg this 1in -older_brother well
I said to my brother,

anwí mi k^w x^{w}uy
anwí mi k^w x^{w}uy
you fut 2kn go
“You go.

103 anwím cminúla?x^{w}stx^w, way̓ n̓ín̓wi?
anwí+m c -myn=úla?x^w -st -x^w way̓ n̓ín̓wi?
you cust^ -know_the_country -^cust -2erg yes a_while
You know the country well. We'll drive

yx̌í?səntst
yx̌=i?s -nt -s -t
drive -nt -2obj -4erg
the deer to you.”

104 ah, way̓ {way̓ ixí?s} k^{w}u cúntəm way̓ axá?
ah way̓ k^{w}u cu -nt -m way̓ axá?
intj well 3e4obj tell -nt -3e4obj well this
He said to us, “I and my partner

na?ɬ isl̓áx̌t na?ɬ sqəmqəmmín
na?ɬ i -s+l̓ax̌+t na?ɬ s+qm•qm+min
with 1in -partner with m's_name
sqəmqmmín, 2:11

105 k^{w}u tk̓as?asíl k^{w}u x^{w}uy k^{w}u
k^{w}u tk=?as•?asíl k^{w}u x^{w}uy k^{w}u
4kn two_persons 4kn go 4kn
the two of us will go

?awsk̓əɬchám
?aw+s+k̓ɬ+chá+m
go_set_watch
set up watch.

106 uɬ axá? anwí na?ɬ asl̓áx̌t ixí? p yx̌í?səm
uɬ axá? anwí na?ɬ a -s+l̓ax̌+t ixí? p yx̌=i?s+m
and this you with 2in -partner then 5kn drive
You and your friend will drive them.

107 ik̓lí? mi p kɬəwscút
ik̓lí? mi p k+ɬw+scut
there fut 5kn part_ways
Then you will split up.

108 n̓ín̓wi? k^{w}u k̓əɬ?íməntp {q̓əq̓əs} t̓əx^w
n̓ín̓wi? k^{w}u k̓ɬ+?im -nt -p t̓x^w
a_while 1obj wait_for -nt -5erg evidently
Wait for us because it will take us

put q̓əq̓sápi? i? ksx^{w}úytət
put q̓•q̓sápi? i? ks -x^{w}uy -tt
just little_while art futi -go -4i
a little while for us to go,

109 aɬí? k^{w}u kscxa?tmíxa?x, mi_sic
aɬí? k^{w}u ksc -xa?t -míx+a?x mi_sic
so 4kn futPerfkn^ -first -^futPerfkn then
for us to get in the lead.

p x^{w}uy {p ha}
p x^{w}uy
5kn go
Then you go,

110 uɬ ixí? uɬ way̓ put {k^{w}u} pənhíw̓səntəm i?
uɬ ixí? uɬ way̓ put pnh=iw̓s -nt -m i?
and then and yes just meet_with -nt -4erg art
and we will get the deer,

sƛ̓a?cínəm i? kscqíx^{w}əmp
s+ƛ̓a?=cín+m i? ksc -qix^w -mp
deer art futPerfi -drive -5in
the ones you drive.”

111 cun way̓, way̓ ilí··? uɬ k^{w}u
cu -n way̓ way̓ ilí? uɬ k^{w}u
tell 1erg OK yes there and 4kn
I said “Ok.” We were there

q̓əq̓sápi?
q̓•q̓sápi?
little_while
a while,

112 uɬ cun axá? isl̓áx̌t
uɬ cu -n axá? i -s+l̓ax̌+t
and tell -1erg this 1i -friend
and I said to my partner:

113 way̓ q̓sápi? ca?k^w iwá
way̓ q̓sápi? ca?k^w iwá
well long_time if even
“It's been long enough, even

?ak^{w}tlílxəlx uɬ way̓, way̓ put yáʕpəlx
?ak^{w}t+lílx -lx uɬ way̓ way̓ put yaʕ+p -lx
crawl_pl -pl and yes yes just arrive_pl -pl
if they were crawling, they'd be there by now. 3:00

114 huhúy k^{w}u
hu+húy k^{w}u
OK 4kn
Now

skłuscútx
s -k+łw+scut -x
ipftv^ -part_ways -^ipftv
we'll part."

115 cun way̓ anwí lut kʷ t̓a
cu -n way̓ anwí lut kʷ t̓
tell -1erg well you not 2kn negfac
I told him, "You have no

cyríwaʔxnəm
c -yr=íwaʔ=xn+m
hab -snowshoes
snowshoes.

116 way̓ axáʔ t k̓əłx̌sínk kʷ ł nq̓aʔq̓ʔíw̓s mi kʷ xʷuy
way̓ axáʔ t k̓ł+x̌s=ink kʷ ł n+q̓aʔ•q̓ʔ=íw̓s mi kʷ xʷuy
well this obl side_hill 2kn ? go_between fut 2kn go
You go on the open side hill, you'll be between, you go [there].

117 way̓ incá axáʔ iʔ {t} ta ntx̌ʷúlaʔxʷ
way̓ in+cá axáʔ iʔ t n+tx̌ʷ=úlaʔxʷ
yes I this art obl center
And I'll go in the center.

118 uł ixíʔ lut {ac} put
uł ixíʔ lut put
and there not just
[There] the snow doesn't

acsúlt iʔ smik̓ʷt uł incám kən ksyyríwaʔxən
c -sul+t iʔ s+mik̓ʷt uł incá+m kn k+s+yr=íwaʔ=xn
hab -snow_crust art snow_on_ground and I 1kn have_snowshoes
have a crust, and I have snowshoes."

119 ah
ah
intj
And

uł cun {uł} uł ńíńw̓iʔ swit ł t̓aʕpsqílxʷ axá tla mnímłtət
uł cu -n uł ńíńw̓iʔ swit ł t̓aʕp+s+qílxʷ axáʔ tla mnimł+tt
and tell -1erg and a_while who if fire_gun this from us
I said, "If any of us shoots,

120 uł
uł
and
do

ha cmistíxʷ ha kʷ ksxkínaʔx
haʔ c -my -st -ixʷ haʔ kʷ ks -x+kin -aʔx
inter cust^ -know -st -2erg inter 2kn incp^ -how -^incp
you know what to do?"

121 ah cut way̓, cut
ah cut way̓ cut
intj say yes say
He said, "Yes,"

way̓ uł kən ƛ̓lap t̓əxʷ ilíʔ kən ƛ̓aʔƛ̓ʔúsəm
way̓ uł kn ƛ̓la+p t̓xʷ ilíʔ kn ƛ̓aʔ•ƛ̓ʔ=ús+m
well and 1kn stop emph there 1kn look_for
he said, "I stop and then I look for it."

122 cun lut, cun
cu -n lut cu -n
tell -1erg not tell -1erg
I said "No," I said,

ʕác̓ənt {a} nƛ̓x̌cin axáʔ iʔ smik̓ʷt
ʕac̓ -nt n+ƛ̓x̌=cin axáʔ iʔ s+mik̓ʷt
look -nt loud this art snow_on_ground
"Look, [walking on] snow makes lots of noise.

123 uł ńíńw̓iʔ kʷ ƛ̓aʔƛ̓ʔúsəm
uł ńíńw̓iʔ kʷ ƛ̓aʔ•ƛ̓ʔ=ús+m
and a_while 2kn look_for
Look for

kin iʔ t k̓ík̓aʔt a ciyíp {ixíʔ}
kiń iʔ t k̓í•k̓aʔt a c+yip
where art obl near art tree
the closest tree.

124 ik̓líʔ kʷ xʷuy mi kʷ
ik̓líʔ kʷ xʷuy mi kʷ
there 2kn go fut 2kn
Go there and stand

k̓əłtłxálqʷ
k̓ł+tł+x=alqʷ
stand_next_to_tree
next to it." 4:02

125 cun uł cəm̓ axáʔ iʔ sƛ̓aʔcínəm ta ck̓əl
cu -n uł cm̓ axáʔ iʔ s+ƛ̓aʔ=cín+m ta+c+k̓l
tell -1erg and maybe this art deer in_direction_of
And I said, "And if the deer comes

anwí ł cxʷuy {uł}
anwí ł c+xʷuy
you if come
towards you

126 uł lut kswíkənts, cəm̓ put
uł lut ks -wik -nt -s cm̓ put
and not futt^ -see -nt -3e2obj maybe just
he won't see you, it'll get right up

kícənts mi wíkənts 127 uɬ náx̌əmɬ iʔ l x̌súlaʔxʷ {kʷ}
kic -nt -s mi wik -nt -s uɬ nax̌mɬ iʔ l x̌s=úlaʔxʷ
reach_st/sb -nt -3e2obj fut see -nt -3e2obj and but art in open_country
to you before it sees you. But if you stand

kʷ ɬ tiɬx 128 uɬ {k} t̓i waẏ ck̓əɬkʷƛ̓áp uɬ waẏ wíkənts
kʷ ɬ tiɬ+x uɬ t̓iʔ waẏ c -k̓ɬ+kʷƛ̓a+p uɬ waẏ wik -nt -s
2kn if stand_sg and evid yes hab -come_in_sight and yes see -nt -3e2obj
in the open as soon as he comes in sight he'll see you and run

uɬ kmaʔmənciút 129 uɬ lut {aks} aksť̓aʕpsqílxʷ 130 ah waẏ, waẏ
uɬ k+maʔ+mncút uɬ lut a -ks -t̓aʕp+s+qílxʷ ah waẏ waẏ
and run_away and not 2i -futi -fire_gun intj yes well
the other way. And you won't [get to] shoot." "Ok." Then

kʷu skɬəwscúts 131 waẏ kən xʷu¨y uɬ, waẏ uɬ axáʔ ta
kʷu s -k+ɬw+scut -s waẏ kn xʷuy uɬ waẏ uɬ axáʔ t
4kn nom4^ -part_ways -^nom4 well 1kn go and well and this obl
we parted. I went, and I was in the center of

ntx̌ʷúlaʔxʷ uɬ ixíʔ uɬ isənx̌əƛ̓múlaʔxʷ 132 uɬ wíkən iʔ
n+tx̌ʷ=úlaʔxʷ uɬ ixíʔ uɬ i -s -n+x̌ƛ̓+m=úlaʔxʷ uɬ wik -n iʔ
center and then and 1i -nom -incline and see -1erg art
that pocket, and then I started to go up the hill, and I saw

sƛ̓aʔcínəm ɬəq̓ʷlút[3] mus 133 uɬ lut kʷu t̓ wíksəlx 134 uɬ ixíʔ
s+ƛ̓aʔ=cín+m ɬq̓ʷ=lut mus uɬ lut kʷu t̓ wik -s -lx uɬ ixíʔ
deer lie_down four and not 1obj negfac see -3erg -pl and then
the deer lying there, four. And they didn't see me. And I

ilíʔ k̓əɬʔímnəlx axáʔ isl̓əx̌l̓áx̌t, i¨ uɬ {q̓a} q̓asəspílsmən
ilíʔ k̓ɬ+ʔim -n -lx axáʔ i -s+l̓x̌•l̓ax̌+t i¨ uɬ q̓as•s•p+ils+m -n
there wait_for -1erg -pl this 1in -friends intj and think_long_time -1erg
waited for my partners, and I thought it had been long enough.

135 waẏ put, waẏ ik̓líʔ k̓əl ksənk̓əɬcahmínsəlx 136 waẏ ixíʔ
waẏ put waẏ ik̓líʔ k̓l k -sn+k̓ɬ+cah+mín -s -lx waẏ ixíʔ
well just well there to to_be -place_to_sit_and_watch -3i -pl well then
They would just run to where they're watching. 5:01 I

ist̓aʕpsqílxʷ 137 oy uɬ xʷət̓xʷət̓ət̓pnúmt axáʔ iʔ sƛ̓aʔcínəm
i -s -t̓aʕp+sqílxʷ oy uɬ xʷt̓•xʷt̓+p+numt axáʔ iʔ s+ƛ̓aʔ=cín+m
1i -nom -fire_gun intj and jump_up_pl this art deer
shot. The deer jumped up.

138 waẏ axáʔ {i s} iʔ t̓aʕpəntín waẏ x̌ʷc̓íksən 139 waẏ uɬ
waẏ axáʔ iʔ t̓aʕp -nt -in waẏ x̌ʷc̓=iks -n waẏ uɬ
well this art shoot -nt -1erg well break_front_leg -1erg well and
I shot and I broke the front leg off one. They

3 Is this an error for ɬq̓ʷ=ut?

ixíʔ stxírrptsəlx 140 oy uɬ itlíʔ kən xʷuy {kən ɬ} kən
ixíʔ s -t+xir•r+pt -s -lx oy uɬ itlíʔ kn xʷuy kn
then nom -run_up -3i -pl intj and from_there 1kn go 1kn
ran up the hill. *Then I went and*

ɬxʷuy kən ɬk̓əɬk̓ʷƛ̓áp {uɬ ixíʔ} 141 uɬ lut {t̓a} t̓ wíkən iʔ
ɬ+xʷuy kn ɬ+k̓ɬ+k̓ʷƛ̓a+p uɬ lut t̓ wik -n iʔ
go_back 1kn come_in_sight_again and not negfac see -1erg art
I came in sight, *and I didn't*

sƛ̓aʔcínəm náx̌əmɬ 142 waẏ k̓əɬk̓íl̓lxʷtəlx 143 uɬ axáʔ {i}
s+ƛ̓aʔ=cín+m nax̌mɬ waẏ k̓ɬ+k̓il+l+xʷt -lx uɬ axáʔ
deer but yes out_of_sight -pl and this
see the deer. *They were already out of sight.* *And I started*

isl̓áx̌t iʔ ƛ̓aʔƛ̓aʔúsmən 144 waẏ wíkən waẏ k̓əɬʔaksuxálqʷ
i -s+l̓ax̌+t iʔ ƛ̓aʔ•ƛ̓aʔ=ús+m -n waẏ wik -n waẏ k̓ɬ+ʔaks+wx=álqʷ
1in -friend art look_for -1erg yes see -1erg yes stand_under_tree
looking for my partner. *I saw him standing right next*

iʔ {l} la ciyíp 145 waẏ {c} wíkən axáʔ {iʔ} isct̓aʕp ck̓əɬqcəlxínk
iʔ l c+yip waẏ wik -n axáʔ i -sc -t̓aʕp c -k̓ɬ+qclx=ink
art at tree well see -1erg this 1i -pftv -shoot hab -run_on_hill
to a tree. *I saw the crippled deer running on the side hill.*

146 uɬ aɬíʔ {kʷ} kʷa ixíʔ cus iʔ xatmaʔsqílxʷ 147 ṅíṅẇiʔ
uɬ aɬíʔ kʷa ixíʔ cu -s iʔ xat=maʔ+s+qílxʷ ṅíṅẇiʔ
and because intj that tell -3erg art first_people a_while
And the old timers say *when*

t̓aʕpəntíxʷ iʔ sƛ̓aʔcínəm 148 ṅíṅẇiʔ x̌əṅnúmt iwá kils iʔ
t̓aʕp -nt -ixʷ iʔ s+ƛ̓aʔ=cín+m ṅíṅẇiʔ x̌ṅ+numt iwá kil -s iʔ
shoot -nt -2erg art deer a_while hurt try_to chase -3erg art
you shoot a deer 6:00 *if he is hurt he will try to follow*

sk̓ʷíƛ̓təms 149 uɬ náx̌əmɬ lut t̓ qəɬnús ɬ
s+k̓ʷiƛ̓tm -s uɬ nax̌mɬ lut t̓ qɬ -nu -s ɬ
others -3in and but not negfac accomplish -manage -3erg subord
the others, *but can't go up*

ksx̌íƛ̓əms {uɬ waẏ ɬ} 150 uɬ waẏ cpəlk̓úsəm {ta c} ta cixʷməlxús cxʷuy
ks -x̌iƛ̓+m -s uɬ waẏ c+p̓lk̓=us+m t c+yxʷ+m+lx=us c+xʷuy
futi -climb -3i and yes turn_around_cisl obl below come
the hill. *He'll turn around to go down.*

151 uɬ waẏ ixíʔ axáʔ ist̓aʕp uɬ ck̓əɬqcəlxínk 152 waẏ
uɬ waẏ ixíʔ axáʔ i -s -t̓aʕp uɬ c -k̓ɬ+qclx=ink waẏ
and yes that this 1i -nom -shoot and hab -run_on_hill well
That's the one I shot and it's running on the side hill. *It*

txʷú··ymantəm axáʔ isl̓ax̌t iʔ k̓ɬʔaksuxálqʷ 153 waẏ
t+xʷuy+m -nt -m axáʔ i -s+l̓ax̌+t iʔ k̓ɬ+ʔaks+wx=álqʷ waẏ
go_towards -nt -psv this 1in -partner art stand_under_tree well
went straight for my partner who was standing behind a tree. *It*

kícəntəm, kiʔ wíkəntəm 154 way̓ ƛ̓lap iʔ sƛ̓aʔcínəm 155 way̓
kic -nt -m kiʔ wik -nt -m way̓ ƛ̓la+p iʔ s+ƛ̓aʔ=cín+m way̓
reach_st/sb -nt -psv rel see -nt -psv well stop art deer well
got right to him, then he saw him. The deer stopped. My

ixíʔ isl̓áx̌t {c··} t̓aʕpəntís, way̓ nməsqníʔ 156 way̓ uł lut t̓
ixíʔ i -s+l̓ax̌+t t̓aʕp -nt -is way̓ n+ms=qn=iʔ way̓ uł lut t̓
then 1in -partner shoot -nt -3erg yes four_shots well and not negfac
partner shot him, four times. He didn't

ksəlxʷəntís 157 ʔakswí··x a[xáʔ] iʔ sƛ̓aʔcínəm, uł ixíʔ
k+slxʷ -nt -is ʔaks+wíx axáʔ iʔ s+ƛ̓aʔ=cín+m uł ixíʔ
hit -nt -3erg stand this art deer and then
hit him. The deer was standing there,

łənt̓aʕpəntís iʔ sululmínks 158 uł t̓i_kmix
ł+n+t̓aʕp -nt -is iʔ s+wl•wl+m=ink -s uł t̓iʔ_kmix
load_again -nt -3erg art gun -3in and only
and he started loading his gun. He kept

cʕác̓əsts 159 way̓ uł kən nstils staʔ way̓ cəm̓ lkʷakʷ
c -ʕac̓ -st -s way̓ uł kn n+st=ils staʔ way̓ cm̓ lkʷ•akʷ
cust^ -look_at -^cust -3erg well and 1kn think intj well maybe far
watching him. I thought the deer I crippled

axáʔ isnáx̌ʷaʔst 160 way̓ ist̓aʕpám, ih tla ixʷút
axáʔ i -s -náx̌ʷ=aʔst way̓ i -s -t̓aʕpá+m ih tla yxʷ=ut
this 1i -? -wounded_game_get_away well 1i -intt -shoot intj from below
might go far. 7:00 I shot, I shot it

ixíʔ t̓aʕpəntín, ixíʔ st̓k̓ʷakʷs {iʔ txʷu··y} 161 [kən] xʷu··y, ik̓líʔ
ixíʔ t̓aʕp -nt -in ixíʔ s -t̓k̓ʷ•akʷ -s kn xʷuy ik̓líʔ
that shoot -nt -1erg that nom -fall -3i 1kn go there
from down below, it fell. I went and

kícən 162 cun way̓ uł kʷ nməsqníʔ {uł lut ał} uł k̓ʷinx
kic -n cu -n way̓ uł kʷ n+ms=qn=iʔ uł k̓ʷin+x
reach_st/sb -1erg tell -1erg well and 2kn four_shots and how_many
I got there. I said, "You shot four times, how many

uł asct̓áʕp 163 kʷu kʕʷəyncútəms, kʷu cus way̓ uł
uł a -sc -t̓aʕp kʷu k+ʕʷy+ncut+m -s kʷu cu -s way̓ uł
and 2i -pftv -shoot 1obj laugh_at -3erg 1obj tell -3erg yes and
did you hit?" He laughed at me, and he said,

t̓əxʷ ixíʔ axáʔ {is} a ct̓aʕt̓aʕpstín 164 uł cut axáʔ uł
t̓xʷ ixíʔ axáʔ a c -t̓aʕ•t̓aʕp -st -in uł cut axáʔ uł
evidently that this art cust^ -shoot -^cust -1erg and say this and
"That's the one I was shooting at." He said, "He

kʷu kics 165 nməsqmíʔxtən uł lut̓ ksəlxʷəntín
kʷu kic -s n+ms=qniʔ -xt -n uł lut_t̓ k+slxʷ -nt -in
1obj reach_st/sb -3erg four_shots -xit -1erg and neg_emph hit -nt -1erg
got right up to me. I shot him four times, and I never hit it.

166 uł t ispícxʷt t̓i kən ał wiʔsənt̓pínkəm {uł i} ik̓líʔ kən ł
uł t i -s -picxʷt t̓iʔ kn ał wẏ+s+n+t̓p=ink+m ik̓líʔ kn ł
and ? 1i -nom -disgusted evid 1kn compl finish_loading there 1kn ?
I got disgusted, and after I got done loading I just stood

ʔakswíx 167 iʔ tla ixʷút iʔ ct̓aʕpəntíxʷ 168 uł iʔ l
ʔaks+wíx iʔ tla yxʷ=ut iʔ c -t̓aʕp -nt -ixʷ uł iʔ l
stand art from below art act -shoot -nt -2erg and art in
there. *And then you shot it from below.* *And it fell*

isk̓əłk̓míls iʔ t̓k̓ʷak̓ʷ 169 uł ixíʔ cun ah {uł stim̓} taʔkín {ki}
i -s+k̓ł+k̓m=ils iʔ t̓k̓ʷ•ak̓ʷ uł ixíʔ cu -n ah ta+ʔkíṅ
1in -front art fall and then tell -1erg intj how_far
right in front of me." *And I said to him, "Where did you*

kiʔ ksxət̓ntíxʷ 170 cut waẏ axáʔ iʔ t k̓aʔk̓aʔqínxəns
kiʔ ks -xt̓ -nt -ixʷ cut waẏ axáʔ iʔ t k̓aʔ•k̓aʔ=qín=xn
rel ? aim -nt -2erg say well this art obl knees
point the gun?" *He said "Right at the knees." 8:02*

171 scutx ałíʔ isckʷłnínk uł axáʔ iʔ kʷu cus
s -cut -x ałíʔ i -sc -kʷłn=ink uł axáʔ iʔ kʷu cu -s
ipftv^ -say -^ipftv because 1i -pftv -borrow_gun and this art 1obj tell -3erg
He said, "I borrowed a gun, and that's what the owner

iʔ t a ksululmínk 172 taʔlí ctqiltkm axáʔ
iʔ t a k+s+wl•wl+m=ink taʔlíʔ c -t+qilt=k+m axáʔ
art agInst art have_gun very_much hab -be_high this
of the gun told me. *'My gun shoots high,*

isululmínk, uł t̓áq̓əmkst *inch* 173 sk̓ʷut sċuʔxán {i aks}
i -s+wl•wl+m=ink uł t̓aq̓m=kst s+k̓ʷut s+ċẁ=xan
1in -gun and six inches half animal_hind_leg
six inches. *You have to shoot*

aksk̓əłmáʕm iʔ sk̓əłixʷúts 174 uł ixíʔ waẏ put
a -ks -k̓ł+maʕ+m iʔ s+k̓ł+yxʷ=ut -s uł ixíʔ waẏ put
2i -futi -line_up art below -3in and then yes exact
half a foot below, *and then*

ilpnúntxʷ {cun} 175 cun waẏ kiʔ ixíʔ mat iʔ la lkʷut
yl+p -nu -nt -xʷ cu -n waẏ kiʔ ixíʔ mat iʔ l lkʷ=ut
hit -manage -nt -2erg tell -1erg well rel that maybe art at far
you'll hit it.'" *I said to him, "Maybe from a distance,*

176 uł axáʔ iʔ l k̓ík̓aʔt lut ċx̌ił itíʔ {ks} ksnwists iʔ kstqiltks
uł axáʔ iʔ l k̓í•k̓aʔt lut c+ʔx̌ił itíʔ ks -nwist -s iʔ ks -t+qilt=k -s
and this art at near not like that futi -high -3i art futi -height -3i
but from close it won't shoot that high.

177 uł caʔkʷ ł ilpnúntxʷ uł axáʔ iʔ t stk̓əmmáqstxəns
uł caʔkʷ ł yl+p -nu -nt -xʷ uł axáʔ iʔ t s+t+k̓m•m=aqst=xn -s
and if if hit -manage -nt -2erg and this art obl legs -3in
And if you hit it [it will be] on the legs,

caʔkʷ x̌ʷəƛ̓x̌ʷíƛ̓xən 178 way̓ iʔ cun, way̓ ixíʔ uɬ itlíʔ
caʔkʷ x̌ʷƛ̓•x̌ʷiƛ̓=xn way̓ iʔ cu -n way̓ ixíʔ uɬ itlíʔ
if broken_legs well art tell -1erg well then and from_there
break his legs.” I said to him, “You follow

nʔúcxəntxʷ {a} asxʷúy 179 ńíńw̓iʔ yaʔx̌í {ks} i
n+ʔuc=xn -t -xʷ a -s -xʷuy ńíńw̓iʔ yaʔx̌í iʔ
track -nt -2erg 2i -intt -go a_while yonder art
the rest, go. The ones that are watching

ksk̓əɬcahmíxaʔx st̓aʕpsqílxʷəxʷ məɬ cəm̓
ks -k̓ɬ+cah -míx+aʔx s -t̓aʕp+s+qílxʷ -xʷ mɬ cm̓
incp^ -face_to_face -^incp ipftv^ -fire_gun -^ipftv and maybe
will shoot and they [the deer]

ɬctqʷayʔilx 180 way̓ uɬ ctkʷʔínaʔntsəlx,
ɬ+c+t+qʷay+y -lx way̓ uɬ c -tkʷʔ=ínaʔ -nt -s -lx
come_back_down -pl well and act -run_into -nt -2obj -pl
will run back down. 9:02 They'll run into you, they'll follow

cənʔacxəncútəlx 181 way̓ ixíʔ itlíʔ sxʷuys 182 way̓
c -n+ʔac=xn+cút -lx way̓ ixíʔ itlíʔ s -xʷuy -s way̓
hab -follow_own_tracks -pl well then from_there nom -go -3i well
their own tracks.” Then he went. And

uɬ axáʔ incá ptk̓ínkən, uɬ ixíʔ ntəlkʷíɬc̓aʔn 183 ah uɬ
uɬ axáʔ in+cá ptk̓=ink[4] -n uɬ ixíʔ n+tlkʷ=íɬc̓aʔ -n ah uɬ
and this I gut -1erg and then disembowel -1erg intj and
I gutted the deer, took out the insides. Oh, I

nɬíptmən {isər isərə} isyríwaʔxən 184 uɬ ixíʔ ik̓líʔ ɬƛ̓aʔntín
n+ɬiptm -n i -s+yr=íwaʔ=xn uɬ ixíʔ ik̓líʔ ɬ+ƛ̓aʔ -nt -in
forget -1erg 1in -snowshoes and then to_there fetch_again -nt -1erg
forgot my snowshoes. And I had to go after them.

185 ixíʔ uɬ sic kən xʷuy, [kən] xʷu··y, ik̓líʔ kícnəlx
ixíʔ uɬ sic kn xʷuy kn xʷuy ik̓líʔ kic -n -lx
then and then 1kn go 1kn go there reach_st/sb -1erg -pl
Then I went, I went and overtook them.

186 kʷlí··wtəlx {uɬ lut aɬ} lut t̓ st̓aʕpsqílxʷsəlx 187 way̓
kʷl=iwt -lx lut t̓ s -t̓aʕp+s+qílxʷ -s -lx way̓
sit -pl not negfac nom -fire_gun -3i -pl well
They were sitting there, they never even got a shot. I

cúnəlx, way̓ uɬ {ha uɬ tət} ha p kɬcaq̓əlnútyaʔ 188 uɬ ha t̓i
cu -n -lx way̓ uɬ haʔ p kɬ+caq̓=ln=útyaʔ uɬ haʔ t̓iʔ
tell -1erg -pl well and inter 5kn have_arrow and inter evid
asked them, “Have you got a bow and arrow, have you

4 Analysis uncertain.

p caq̓əlnútyaʔ uɬ a[xáʔ] ƛ̓əxʷəntíp iʔ sƛ̓aʔcínəm iscqíxʷ
p caq̓=ln=útyaʔ uɬ axáʔ ƛ̓xʷ -nt -ip iʔ s+ƛ̓aʔ=cín+m i -sc -qixʷ
5kn arrow and this kill_many -nt -5erg art deer 1i -pftv -drive
a bow and arrow to kill the deer I drove?"

189 way̓ kʷu cúsəlx sta way̓ nc̓əspúlaʔxʷstxʷ 190 lut atáʔ
way̓ kʷu cu -s -lx sta way̓ n+c̓s+p=úlaʔxʷ -st -xʷ lut atáʔ
well 1obj tell -3erg -pl intj well kill -st -2erg not here
They said to me, "You killed them, *they*

kʷu t̓ə txəwíləntəm 191 cúnəlx lut, uɬ axáʔ iʔ
kʷu t̓ t+xwil -nt -m cu -n -lx lut uɬ axáʔ iʔ
3e4obj negfac pass_by -nt -3e4obj tell -1erg -pl not and this art
never went by here." 10:00 *I told them "No, here are*

sxʷúytənsəlx ist̓əcənʔúcxnəm 192 uɬ axáʔ atáʔ iʔ
s+xʷuy+tn -s -lx i -s -t̓c -n+ʔuc=xn+m uɬ axáʔ atáʔ iʔ
track -3in -pl 1i -nom -habCisl - follow_tracks and this this art
the tracks I have been following, *and these are*

sxʷúytənsəlx uɬ lut̓ ɬpəlk̓úsməlx 193 i·· spicxʷts axáʔ
s+xʷuy+tn -s -lx uɬ lut_t̓ ɬ+p̓lk̓=us+m -lx i·· s -picxʷ+t -s axáʔ
track -3in -pl and neg_emph turn_back -pl intj nom -disgusted -3i this
their tracks, and they never turned back." *My brother was disgusted,*

inqíck, cut way̓, way̓ {kə} kən pəcxʷmscút 194 cut aɬíʔ ixíʔ
in -qick cut way̓ way̓ kn pcxʷ+mscut cut aɬíʔ ixíʔ
1in -older_brother say well yes 1kn disgusted_with_self say so then
he said, "I'm disgusted with myself." *He said,*

kʷu cxʷuy axáʔ naʔɬ isl̓áx̌t 195 uɬ aɬíʔ {kʷu asəs asə}
kʷu c+xʷuy axáʔ naʔɬ i -s+l̓ax̌+t uɬ aɬíʔ
4kn come this and 1in -partner and because
"My partner and I got here. *And my partner*

səsəlxʷaʔálqʷx uɬ way̓ t̓iʔ kʷu ʔaslípuʔstxən 196 məɬ tkʷap {its}
s -slxʷaʔ=álqʷ -x uɬ way̓ t̓iʔ kʷu ʔasl=íp=w̓stxn mɬ tkʷa+p
ipftv^ -large -^ipftv and well evid 4kn two_steps and choked
is so fat, we take two steps *and he gets*

iʔ t sʔayx̌ʷt məɬ ilíʔ ɬ k̓əɬʔímən {i ki} 197 uɬ iʔ ki kən
iʔ t s+ʔayx̌ʷ+t mɬ ilíʔ ɬ k̓ɬ+ʔim -n uɬ iʔ kiʔ kn
art agInst tiredness and there subord wait_for -1erg and art rel 1kn
so tired, he gets choked, and I have to wait for him. *And I got to thinking*

xat̓əlsmíst 198 t̓a {kʷu s} kʷu səlxʷúsx a uɬ aɬ
xat̓=ls+míst nt̓a kʷu s -lxʷ=us -x a uɬ aɬ
be_fooled intj 4kn ipftv^ -set_watch -^ipftv intj and compl
I am a fool. *We are here to watch for deer, and [instead]*

ck̓əɬʔamlwístən 199 way̓ cəm̓ kʷu ƛ̓músəntəm
c -k̓ɬ+ʔam+lwís -t -n way̓ cm̓ kʷu ƛ̓m=us -nt -m
cust^ -sit_around -st -1erg well maybe 3e4obj go_ahead_of -nt -3e4obj
I'm waiting for him. *I think the deer will go*

iʔ t sƛ̓aʔcínəm 200 ixíʔ sic isckswítmiʔst 201 cut
iʔ t s+ƛ̓aʔ=cín+m ixíʔ sic i -sc -k+s+wít+miʔst cut
art agInst deer then then 1i -pftv -do_one's_best say
ahead of us. *And I did my best.* *I hadn't*

way̓ {kən} lúti iskícx kiʔ kʷ t̓ət̓aʕpsqílxʷ 202 uɬ nák̓ʷəm way̓
way̓ lút+i i -s -kic+x kiʔ kʷ t̓•t̓aʕp+s+qílxʷ uɬ nak̓ʷ+m way̓
well not_yet 1i -nom -arrive rel 2kn shoot and evid yes
gotten here, and you started shooting. *And they*

kʷu ƛ̓músəntəm kʷu ƛ̓músəs ixíʔ uɬ sic aláʔ i
kʷu ƛ̓m=us -nt -m kʷu ƛ̓m=us -s ixíʔ uɬ sic aláʔ iʔ
3e4obj go_ahead_of -nt -3e4obj 3e4obj go_ahead_of -3erg then and then here art
went ahead of us, they got ahead of me before I got

kən ckicx 203 way̓ {way̓ cuntə} [s]cuts sqəmqmmín, cus
kn c+kic+x way̓ s -cut -s s+qm•qm+min cu -s
1kn arrive_cisl well nom -say -3i m's_name tell -3erg
here." 11:05 *sqəmqmmín said to his*

axáʔ iʔ sƛ̓əx̌pílts 204 way̓ uɬ anwí xʷuy may̓ncútaʔx 205 way̓
axáʔ iʔ s+ƛ̓x̌+p=ilt -s way̓ uɬ anwí xʷuy m̓ay+ncút -aʔx[5] way̓
this art grown_child -3in well and you go tell_story -? well
grown child: *"Tell about yourself.* *You*

kʷ nməsqníʔ, uɬ k̓ʷinx 206 way̓ cut way̓ lut̓
kʷ n+ms=qn=iʔ uɬ k̓ʷin+x way̓ cut way̓ lut_t̓
2kn four_shots and how_many well say well neg_emph
shot four times, how many [did you get]?" *He said, "I never*

ksəlxʷəntín {ay} 207 snáx̌ʷaʔsts axáʔ isl̓áx̌t, ixíʔ
k+slxʷ -nt -in s -náx̌ʷ=aʔst -s axáʔ i -s+l̓ax̌+t ixíʔ
hit -nt -1erg nom -wounded_game_get_away -3i this 1in -partner then
even hit it. *My partner crippled him, I was going to shoot it*

iwá isənt̓aʕpáx̌nəm 208 cut uɬ kʷu kics uɬ mat
iwá i -s -n+t̓aʕp=áx̌n+m cut uɬ kʷu kic -s uɬ mat
try_to 1i -intt -shoot_under_arm say and 1obj reach_st/sb -3erg and maybe
under the arm." *He said, "He got right up to me and*

k̓ʷsəntín i {ta} ta npq̓ʷmín {i} 209 nməsqníʔxtən, uɬ
k̓ʷs -nt -in iʔ t n+pq̓ʷ+min n+ms=qn=iʔ -xt -n uɬ
singe -nt -1erg art agInst black_powder four_shots -xit -1erg and
I singed him with black powder.[6] *I shot him four times,*

lut̓ ksləxʷəntín 210 ixíʔ uɬ itíʔ ispícxʷt, uɬ lut
lut_t̓ k+slxʷ -nt -in ixíʔ uɬ itíʔ i -s -picxʷt uɬ lut
neg_emph hit -nt -1erg then and from_that 1i -nom -disgusted and not
and I never hit it. *I got so disgusted, I didn't try to*

5 The expected prefix ks- *inceptive* is missing.
6 "I was so close that ..."

nixʷ itlíʔ isťaʕpsqílxʷ 211 waỷ isľáx̌t tla ixʷút ki
nixʷ itlíʔ i -s -ťaʕp+sqílxʷ waỷ i -s+ľax̌+t tla yxʷ=ut kiʔ
more from_there 1i -nom -fire_gun yes 1in -partner from below rel
shoot any more. *It was my partner that shot it*

ťaʕpəntís, ixíʔ ťk̓ʷak̓ʷ 212 ixíʔ ilíʔ kʷu ckics uł i kʷu
ťaʕp -nt -is ixíʔ ťk̓ʷ•ak̓ʷ ixíʔ ilíʔ kʷu c+kic -s uł iʔ kʷu
shoot -nt -3erg then fall then there 1obj arrive_cisl -3erg and art 1obj
from below; then it fell. *He got to me and he said*

cus 213 waỷ xʷuyx, itlíʔ {cəm̓} cəm̓ yaʔx̌í {łta}
cu -s waỷ xʷuy -x itlíʔ cm̓ yaʔx̌í
tell -3erg well go -isimptv from_there maybe that_one
to me: *'Go ahead, if they shoot one*

nťaʕpíw̓ssəlx, 214 uł waỷ łctqʷaylx
n+ťaʕp=íw̓s -s -lx uł waỷ ł+c+t+qʷay -lx
shoot_one_of -3erg -pl and yes come_back_down -pl
of the bunch 12:02 *they'll run back down, they'll follow*

łcənʔacxəncútəlx 215 waỷ, waỷ itlíʔ kʷu
ł+c+n+ʔac=xn+cút -lx waỷ waỷ itlíʔ kʷu
follow_own_tracks_cisl_again -pl well well from_there 4kn
their own tracks.'" *Then we went to*

sxʷuys, waỷ itlíʔ k̓la nəqsúlaʔxʷ 216 waỷ ixíʔ itlíʔ
s -xʷuy -s waỷ itlíʔ k̓l nqs=úlaʔxʷ waỷ ixíʔ itlíʔ
nom4^ -go -^nom4 well from_there to place well then from_there
another gulch. *My brother*

kʷu cúntəm axáʔ iʔ t inqíck {waỷ a} 217 waỷ axáʔ
kʷu cu -nt -m axáʔ iʔ t in -qick waỷ axáʔ
3e4obj tell -nt -3e4obj this art agInst 1in -older_brother yes this
told us: *"The deer*

nixʷ {sənʔəłkíłxʷts} sənʔístktəns iʔ sƛ̓aʔcínəm 218 uł axáʔ iʔ
nixʷ sn+ʔis=tk+tn -s iʔ s+ƛ̓aʔ=cín+m uł axáʔ iʔ
also wintering_place -3in art deer and this art
winter here too. *And the ones*

cqíxʷəntəm mat aláʔ łƛ̓lap waỷ axáʔ łpíx̌əntəm
c -qixʷ -nt -m mat aláʔ ł+ƛ̓la+p waỷ axáʔ ł+pix̌ -nt -m
act -drive -nt -4erg maybe here stop_again well this hunt_again -nt -4erg
we drove, I guess they settled here, we'll hunt this ground."

219 waỷ ixíʔ kʷu łc̓x̌ʷxítəm iʔ t ksxʷúytəntət
waỷ ixíʔ kʷu ł+c̓x̌ʷ -xit -m iʔ t k -sxʷuy+tn -tt
well then 3e4obj instruct_again -xit -3e4obj art obj_tr to_be -travel -4i
They instructed us to where we should go.

220 uł ixíʔ kʷu cúntəm swit uł iʔ ksəlxʷúsaʔx
uł ixíʔ kʷu cu -nt -m swit uł iʔ ks -lxʷ=us -aʔx
and then 3e4obj tell -nt -3e4obj who and art incp -set_watch -^incp
He asked us, "Who is going to do the watching?"

221 cun axáʔ inqíck, waẏ anwím kʷ cminúlaʔxʷəm
cu -n axáʔ in -qick waẏ anwí+m kʷ c -my+n=úlaʔxʷ+m
tell -1erg this 1in -older_brother well you 2kn hab -know_country
I said to my brother, "You know the country;

222 waẏ ṅ[íṅẇiʔ] kʷu ix̌ísəm 223 ah, waẏ, waẏ ixíʔ sxʷuys
waẏ ṅíṅẇiʔ kʷu yx̌=iʔs+m ah waẏ waẏ ixíʔ s -xʷuy -s
well a_while 4kn drive_stock intj OK well then nom -go -3i
we will drive the deer." "Ok;" he went.

224 cut waẏ náx̌əmɬ t̓i kən knánaq[s] 225 uɬ axáʔ kʷu cúntəm
cut waẏ nax̌mɬ t̓iʔ kn k=ná•naqs uɬ axáʔ kʷu cu -nt -m
say well but evid 1kn alone and this 3e4obj tell -nt -3e4obj
He said "I'll go alone." sqəmqmmín said to us,

t sqəmqmmín, waẏ waẏ p ikscúnəm 226 lut
t s+qm•qm+min waẏ waẏ p i -ks -cun+m lut
agInst m's_name well well 5kʷu 1i -futi -tell not
"I'm going to tell you, 13:01 don't

kscíxʷaʔmp {kən ɬ} kən ɬ t̓ət̓aʕpsqílxʷ kən ɬaʔ nməsqníʔ 227 ixíʔ
ks -cíxʷaʔ -mp kn ɬ t̓+t̓aʕp+s+qílxʷ kn ɬaʔ n+ms=qn=iʔ ixíʔ
futi -be_fooled -5in 1kn if shoot 1kn the_one_that four_shots that
get fooled if I shoot four times. I'm

uɬ p iscúnəm waẏ, ixíʔ waẏ kən ɬxʷuy 228 waẏ kən
uɬ p i -s -cun+m waẏ ixíʔ waẏ kn ɬ+xʷuy waẏ kn
and 5kʷu 1i -nom -tell yes then yes 1kn go_back yes 1kn
letting you know I'm going home. I am tired

sʔayx̌ʷtx uɬ aɬíʔ kən scəpcípx̌ʷxənx iʔ t
s -ʔayx̌ʷ+t -x uɬ aɬíʔ kn s -cp•cipx̌ʷ=xn -x iʔ t
ipftv^ -tired -^ipftv and so 1kn ipftv^ -foot_breaks_through -^ipftv art obl
from breaking through the crust of the snow too many

smik̓ʷt 229 waẏ kən ɬxʷuy 230 cúntəm waẏ, uɬ t̓iʔ
s+mik̓ʷt waẏ kn ɬ+xʷuy cu -nt -m waẏ uɬ t̓iʔ
snow_on_ground yes 1kn go_back tell -nt -4erg OK and evid
times. I'll go back." We said "Ok,"

kʷu nstils mat skʷsəscínx 231 waẏ kʷu pəx̌ʷməncút uɬ ixíʔ
kʷu n+st=ils mat s -kʷs+s=cin -x waẏ kʷu px̌ʷ+mncut uɬ ixíʔ
4kn think maybe ipftv^ -joke -^ipftv well 4kn scatter and then
and we just thought he was joking. We scattered,

kʷu xʷuy 232 lut kʷu swíkɬc̓aʔs, waẏ kʷu ɬkcənwíxʷ waẏ
kʷu xʷuy lut kʷu s -wík=ɬc̓aʔ -s waẏ kʷu ɬ+kc+nwixʷ waẏ
4kn go not 4kn nom4^ -see_game -^nom4 well 4kn get_together_again well
we went. We didn't see a deer, and we got back all together,

t̓iʔ kʷu tkaʔkaʔɬís 233 waẏ k̓aw sqəmqəmmín {uɬ ixíʔ} waẏ uɬ ixíʔ
t̓iʔ kʷu t=kaʔ•kaʔɬís waẏ k̓aw s+qm•qm+min waẏ uɬ ixíʔ
evid 4kn three_persons well gone m's_name well and then
the three of us. sqəmqmmín was gone, and we waited and

k̓əɬʔí··məntəm 234 uɬ {i·· s i} kʷu sťaʔqʷcíns, waẏ lut {kʷu k̓əɬ}
k̓ɬ+ʔim -nt -m uɬ kʷu s -ťaʔqʷ=cín -s waẏ lut
wait_for -nt -4erg and 4kn nom4^ -holler -^nom4 well not
waited for him. *We started hollering, he never gave*

kʷu k̓əɬkʷínxʷcəntəm 235 naɬcəcám ixíʔ iʔ {kə} k̓əɬnxəlpíňkəntəm
kʷu k̓ɬ+kʷinxʷ=cn -t -m naɬc•c•ám ixíʔ iʔ k̓ɬ+n+xlp=ink -nt -m
3e4obj answer -nt -3e4obj forget that art hear_shot -nt -4erg
an answer. *I forgot, we heard him shoot four*

nməsqníʔ 236 waẏ cun axáʔ inqíck, waẏ {k} ixíʔ ƛ̓əm iʔ
n+ms=qn=iʔ waẏ cu -n axáʔ in -qick waẏ ixíʔ ƛ̓m iʔ
four_shots well tell -1erg this 1in -older_brother well that past art
times. 14:06 *I said to my brother, "sqəmqmmín*

kʷu cúntəm t sqəmqəmmín
kʷu cu -nt -m t s+qm•qm+min
3e4obj tell -nt -3e4obj agInst m's_name
told us

237 ňíňw̓iʔ nʔayx̌ʷtíls məɬ ixíʔ sťaʕpsqílxʷs nməsqníʔ {məɬ ixíʔ s}
ňíňw̓iʔ n+ʔayx̌ʷ+t=íls mɬ ixíʔ s -ťaʕp+s+qílxʷ -s n+ms=qn=iʔ
a_while get_tired and then nom -fire_gun -3i four_shots
if he gets tired he'll shoot four times.

238 ixíʔ uɬ waẏ scutx waẏ uɬ kən ɬəɬxʷúyx kən
ixíʔ uɬ waẏ s -cut -x waẏ uɬ kn ɬ -ɬ+xʷuy -x kn
then and yes ipftv^ -say -^ipftv well and 1kn ipftv^ -go_back -^ipftv 1kn
He said, 'That's when I am going home, I am

sʔayx̌ʷtx 239 uɬ waẏ uɬ ɬxʷuy, waẏ kʷu cus, waẏ uníxʷ
s -ʔayx̌ʷ+t -x uɬ waẏ uɬ ɬ+xʷuy waẏ kʷu cu -s waẏ wnixʷ
ipftv^ -tired -^ipftv and yes and go_back well 1obj tell -3erg yes true
tired.' *And he went back, he told me, that's true."*

240 waẏ itlíʔ kʷu ɬəɬcxʷúys ixíʔ uɬ aɬíʔ waẏ uɬ
waẏ itlíʔ kʷu ɬ -ɬ+c+xʷuy -s ixíʔ uɬ aɬíʔ waẏ uɬ
well from_there 4kn nom4^ -come_again -^nom4 then and so yes and
We came back, and the snow

cʔix {i} iʔ smik̓ʷt 241 uɬ cəpcípx̌ʷxən axáʔ iʔ sľáx̌tət, lut
c[ʔ]ix iʔ s+mik̓ʷt uɬ cp•cipx̌ʷ=xn axáʔ iʔ s+ľax̌+t -t lut
get_warm art snow and foot_breaks_through this art partner -4in not
got warm, *and our friend breaks through the crust, he doesn't*

ťa {c} cyríwaʔxən 242 waẏ kʷu ɬəɬxʷúys {taʔc} kʷu
ť c -yr=íwaʔ=xn waẏ kʷu ɬ -ɬ+xʷuy -s kʷu
negfac hab -snow_shoe well 4kn nom4^ -go_back -^nom4 4kn
have snowshoes. *"Let's go back,*

ɬəɬpíx̌əms [kʷu ɬəɬʔippíx̌əms] ta ck̓əl
ɬ -ɬ+pix̌+m -s kʷu ɬ -ɬ+ʔip=píx̌+m -s ta+c+k̓l
nom4^ hunt_again -^nom4 4kn nom4^ -hunt_on_way_again -^nom4 in_direction_of
we'll hunt on the way back

cítxʷtət 243 ah, axáʔ nɬíptmən axáʔ isl'áx̌t iʔ sỷal'wánk,
citxʷ -tt ah axáʔ n+ɬiptm -n axáʔ i -s+l'ax̌+t iʔ s+ỷal'ẁ=ánk
house -4in intj this forget -1erg this 1in -partner art cricket
to the camp." *Oh, I forgot about my partner Cricket, I forgot*

ixíʔ naɬcəcám 244 kʷu ksx̌əlpínaʔ uɬ {i} iʔ cut waỷ kən c̓əspqníʔ {i t s}
ixíʔ naɬc•c•ám kʷu k+s+x̌l+p=ínaʔ uɬ iʔ cut waỷ kn c̓s+p=qn=iʔ
that forget 4kn have_daylight and art say well 1kn bullets_finish
that. 15:07 *The morning after he said: "I'm all out of cartridges,"*

245 cun kwaỷ axáʔ kən kɬcq̓ílən, ilíʔ t'iʔ paʔpút iʔ sənt'pínktət
cu -n k+waỷ axáʔ kn kɬ+cq̓=iln ilíʔ t'iʔ paʔ•pút iʔ sn+t'p=ink -tt
tell -1erg well this 1kn have_bullet there evid match art gun -4in
I said to him, "I have more cartridges, our guns are the same."

246 kʷu cus lut, {waỷ uɬ} waỷ myaɬ kən picxʷt 247 waỷ
kʷu cu -s lut waỷ myaɬ kn picxʷ+t waỷ
1kʷu tell -3erg not yes too_much help disgusted yes
He said "No, I am too disgusted. *I*

myaɬ kən xʷaʔqníʔ uɬ lut {is} isilpíʔst 248 anwí məɬ kʷ
myaɬ kn xʷaʔ=qn=íʔ uɬ lut i -s -ylp=iʔst anwí mɬ kʷ
too_much 1kn many_shots and not 1i -nom -hit you and 2kn
shot too many times, and I hit nothing. *But you*

[sc]tx̌əsəsmíkstx, {waỷ} waỷ t'iʔ kən míc̓aʔm 249 k̓aʔkín i
sc -t+x̌s•s+m=ikst -x waỷ t'iʔ kn míc̓aʔ+m k̓a+ʔkín iʔ
ipftvp^ -lucky -^ipftvp well evid 1kn fetch_killed_game to_where art
are lucky, I'll just go after the deer that's killed. *Where did you*

asct'áp 250 cun waỷ ixíʔ taʔck̓əl k̓ɬxənxəń́ínk {ɬ} k̓əl
a -sc -t'ap cu -n waỷ ixíʔ ta c+k̓l k̓ɬ+xn•xn=ink k̓l
2i -pftv -object_lies tell -1erg well that in_direction_of place_name to
kill it?" *I told him it was over at "big slabs of rock,"*

nixʔúlaʔxʷəms k̓ɬxənxəń́ínk 251 ilíʔ kiʔ a nkəcníkənn, waỷ ilíʔ
n+yxʔ=úlaʔxʷ+m[7] -s k̓ɬ+xn•xn=ink ilíʔ kiʔ a n+kc+n=ikn -n waỷ ilíʔ
across 3i place_name there rel art overtake -1erg yes there
across from k̓ɬxənxəń́ínk. *"That's where I overtook them, that's*

kən t'aʕpám 252 uɬ ilíʔ waỷ c̓íqʷən uɬ ilíʔ {ə} ɬwin
kn t'aʕpá+m uɬ ilíʔ waỷ c̓iqʷ -n uɬ ilíʔ ɬwi -n
1kn shoot and there finish skin -1erg and there leave -1erg
where I shot. *I already skinned it, and I left it there." 16:03*

253 cun, uɬ t'i waỷ kʷu nt'ək̓ʷk̓ʷmíɬtxʷ {uɬ} isxʷúytən iʔ
cu -n uɬ t'iʔ waỷ kʷu n+t'k̓ʷ•k̓ʷ+mi -ɬt -xʷ i -s+xʷuy+tn iʔ
tell -1erg and evid well 1obj get_in_someone's_X -ɬt -2erg 1in -track art
I said to him, "When you get

7 The analysis of this form is not clear to me.

l isyríwaʔxən 254 uł ixíʔ kʷu nʔúcxəłtxʷ {uł waẏ} 255 kʷu
l i -s+yr=íwaʔ=xn uł ixíʔ kʷu n+ʔuc=x -łt -xʷ kʷu
on 1in -snowshoes and then 1obj follow -łt -2erg 1obj
on my snoeshoe tracks, follow them." He

cus {waẏ ʔkin uł} uc kʷ ksp̓íc̓ən 256 waẏ ałíʔ ńíńẃiʔ kən ł
cu -s uc kʷ k+s+p̓ic̓n waẏ ałíʔ ńíńẃiʔ kn ł
tell -3erg dub 2kn have_rope well so a_while 1kn when
asked me, "Do you have rope for when I tie it onto

kʕacqáx̌aʔm iʔ kłlk̓íkən 257 cun waẏ, cun waẏ ixíʔ
k+ʕac+qáx̌aʔ+m iʔ kł+lk̓=ikn cu -n waẏ cu -n waẏ ixíʔ
tie_to_horse art tie_on_back tell -1erg yes tell -1erg yes that
the back of the horse?" I said "Yes, be sure and

inq̓ʷəłtsqáx̌aʔtən mi xʷuyst 258 waẏ ixíʔ sxʷuys 259 waẏ kʷu
in -q̓ʷł+t=sqáx̌aʔ+tn mi xʷuy+st waẏ ixíʔ s -xʷuy -s waẏ kʷu
1in -pack_horse fut take_st well then nom -go -3i well 4kn
take my pack horse." Then he went. We

łyaʕp, waẏ k̓aw iʔ sl̓áx̌tət yal̓wánk 260 axáʔ sqəmqəmmín waẏ
ł+yaʕ+p waẏ k̓aw iʔ s+l̓ax̌+t -t ẏal̓ẃ=ánk axáʔ s+qm•qm+min waẏ
arrive_again well gone art friend -4in Cricket this m's_name yes
got back, our friend Cricket is gone. sqəmqmmín was back

łmut {waẏ} 261 waẏ iʔ sk̓ʷəl̓cəncúts ałíʔ axáʔ inqíck
ł+mut waẏ iʔ s -k̓ʷl̓=cn+cut -s ałíʔ axáʔ in -qick
back_home_sg well art nom -cook -3i because this 1in -older_brother
at camp. Then my brother started to cook because

sisyús iʔ l sk̓ʷəl̓cəncút {ay} 262 ck̓ʷəl̓cəncút waẏ {ł} kipúlaʔxʷ
sy•sy=us iʔ l s+k̓ʷl̓=cn+cut c -k̓ʷl̓=cn+cut waẏ ky+p=úlaʔxʷ
smart art at cooking hab -cook yes dusk
he is good at cooking. He cooked and it was getting dark. 17:03

263 waẏ {łta} ck̓əłníxlməntəm t syal̓ẃánk ł t̓əcxʷúy
waẏ c -k̓ł+nixl+m -nt -m t s+ẏal̓ẃ=ánk ł t̓c -xʷuy
well act -hear_noise -nt -4erg obl Cricket when habCisl -go
We heard a noise, it's Cricket coming.

264 waẏ łckicx waẏ lut {aks} t̓a ksq̓ʷəłtsqáx̌aʔ 265 waẏ
waẏ ł+c+kic+x waẏ lut t̓ k+s+q̓ʷł+t=sqáx̌aʔ waẏ
well arrive_cisl_again well not negfac have_horse_pack well
He got back, he had no pack on the horse. He

nk̓ʷəxʷkiʔsqáx̌aʔm uł {ʕaʕac} ʕacʕacntís 266 ʔamtís iʔ
n+k̓ʷxʷ+kiʔ=sqáx̌aʔ+m uł ʕac•ʕac -nt -is ʔam -t -is iʔ
take_saddle_off and tie -nt -3erg feed -nt -3erg art
took the saddle off, he tied it up. He fed

sənkłc̓aʔsqáx̌aʔ, ixíʔ uł_iʔ cúntəm 267 waẏ uł ʔkin uł {as}
sn+kł+c̓aʔ=sqáx̌aʔ ixíʔ uł_iʔ cu -nt -m waẏ uł ʔkin uł
horse then and_then tell -nt -4erg well and indef and
the horse, and we asked him: "What happened to

ascmíc̓a? 268 wa-y̓ ixí? kʷu cus way̓ {kʷuɬ} put c̓x̌iɬ {tə}
a -sc -míc̓a? way̓ ixí? kʷu cu -s way̓ put c+?x̌iɬ
2i -pftv -dead_game well then 1obj tell -3erg well just like
your dead deer?" *He said to me, "Your tracks are just*

t sənk̓líp asxʷúytən 269 way̓ uɬ k̓əɬsəl̓xnún{xən}tsən
t sn+k̓l̓=ip a -s+xʷuy+tn way̓ uɬ k̓ɬ+sl̓=x -nu -nt -s -n
obj_c̓x̌iɬ Coyote 2in -track well and lose_tracks -manage -nt -2obj -1erg
like a coyote's, *and I lost your tracks,*

270 uɬ lut {a t̓ək} t̓ wíkən i? sƛ̓a?cínəm 271 cun uɬ ha
uɬ lut t̓ wik -n i? s+ƛ̓a?=cín+m cu -n uɬ ha?
and not negfac see -1erg art deer tell -1erg and inter
and I didn't find the deer." *I said to him,*

sc̓kinx, uɬ lut̓ k̓ʷíƛ̓ən isyríwa?xən 272 way̓ niʕ̓íp {inaud}
sc+?kin+x uɬ lut_t̓ k̓ʷiƛ̓ -n i -s+yr=íwa?=xn way̓ nyʕ̓ip
why_is_it and neg_emph take_off -1erg 1in -snowshoes yes always
"What's the matter, I never took my snowshoes off, *I kept them*

kən a yríwa?xnəm {uɬ inaud} uɬ niʕ̓íp kən scyríwa?xənx uɬ
kn a yr=íwa?=xn+m uɬ nyʕ̓ip kn sc -yr=íwa?=xn -x uɬ
1kn art wear_snowshoes and always 1kn ipftvp^ -snow_shoe -^ipftvp and
on all the time until

put kʷu ɬcyaʕ̓p 273 uɬ {a} i? sxʷ?its i? smík̓ʷts
put kʷu ɬ+c+yaʕ̓+p uɬ i? s -xʷ?i+t -s i? s+mik̓ʷt -s
just 4kn arrive_cisl_again and art nom -much -3i art snow_on_ground -3in
we got back." 18:03 *And there is plenty of snow*

ɬa {uɬ a kən kən ɬca} ck̓ʷíƛ̓stən isyríwa?xən 274 way̓ ixí?
ɬa? c -k̓ʷiƛ̓ -st -n i -s+yr=íwa?=xn way̓ ixí?
when cust^ -take_off -^cust -1erg 1in -snowshoes well then
for me to be taking my snowshoes off.[8] *The next*

kʷu ksx̌əlpína? uɬ ixí? cun axá? inqíck 275 way̓ uɬ
kʷu k+s+x̌l+p=ína? uɬ ixí? cu -n axá? in -qick way̓ uɬ
4kn have_daylight and then tell -1erg this 1in -older_brother well and
day I said to my brother *Coyotes*

cmay t sənk̓líp kʷu 276 ah ixí? kʷu ksk̓əlxʷína? uɬ ixí? kʷu
cmay t sn+k̓l̓=ip kʷu ah ixí? kʷu k+s+k̓lxʷ=ína? uɬ ixí? kʷu
maybe agInst Coyote 1obj intj then 4kn have_evening and then 1obj
might... [unfinished]. *That evening my brother*

cus axá? inqíck 277 way̓ uɬ sɬíqʷtət kʷu
cu -s axá? in -qick way̓ uɬ s+ɬiqʷ -tt kʷu
tell -3erg this 1in -older_brother well and meat -4in 4kn
said to me: *"We are running*

8 The import of this utterance is unclear.

kscʼəspsɬíqʷaʔx t kʷukʷús [kʷu kscʼəspɬkʷukúsaʔx][9] {uɬ aɬíʔ}
ks -cʼs+p+s+ɬiqʷ -aʔx t kʷu•kʷús kʷu ks -cʼs+p+ɬ+kʷu•kʷús -aʔx
incp^ -run_out_of_meat -^incp obj_itr pig 4kn incp^ -run_out_of_bacon -^incp
out of bacon.

278 kən nstíls tʼi kʷu tkʼa·síl uɬ kmix tʼiʔ kʷu tkʼəsʔasíl {i}
kn n+st=ils tʼiʔ kʷu tk=ʔas•ʔasíl uɬ kmix tʼiʔ kʷu tk=ʔas•ʔasíl
1kn think evid 4kn two_persons and only evid 4kn two_persons
I thought it's just two of us, and I got food enough

istxʷstʼíkʼəl 279 uɬ axáʔ iʔ kʷu taʔxʷlʼəx̌lʼáx̌t axáʔ iʔ tkaʔkaʔɬís
i -s+txʷ+s+tʼikʼl uɬ axáʔ iʔ kʷu taʔxʷ+lʼx̌•lʼáx̌+t axáʔ iʔ t=kaʔ•kaʔɬís
1in -gathered_food and this art 4kn have_friends this art three_persons
for two; *and now we got partners, three of them. 19:00*

280 uɬ aɬíʔ tʼi nkʼʷʔíɬəntəm {ti} iʔ stʼíkʼəltət 281 kʷu cus, uɬ
uɬ aɬíʔ tʼiʔ nkʼʷ+ʔiɬn -t -m iʔ s+tʼikʼl -tt kʷu cu -s uɬ
and because evid one_meal -nt -4erg art grub -4in 1obj tell -3erg and
And we ate our grub in one meal." *He asked me,*

uc lkʷut axáʔ akʼláʔ asctʼáʕp 282 cun lut, kʷu cus wayʼ {tʼiʔ}
uc lkʷ=ut axáʔ akʼláʔ a -sc -tʼaʕp cu -n lut kʷu cu -s wayʼ
dub far this here 2i -pftv -shoot tell -1erg not 1obj tell -3erg well
"Is it far where you shot the deer?" *I said "No," and he said to me,*

tʼiʔ x̌ast kʷu ɬ mícʼaʔm 283 cun uɬ axáʔ iʔ l
tʼiʔ x̌as+t kʷu ɬ mícʼaʔ+m cu -n uɬ axáʔ iʔ l
evid good 4kn subord fetch_killed_game tell -1erg and this art in
"It's better we get some meat." *I said "In the*

sənkʷkʷʔác 284 kʷu cus wayʼ kʷu ɬaʔ cuʔqʼím 285 cun
sn+kʷ•kʷʔac kʷu cu -s wayʼ kʷu ɬaʔ c -wqʼim cu -n
night 1obj tell -3erg well 4kn when hab -moonlight tell -1erg
dark?" *He said to me, "We have moonlight."* *I said,*

uɬ lutʼ kskʼəɬkícəntəm iʔ t sənkɬcʼaʔsqáx̌aʔ 286 uɬ aɬíʔ
uɬ lut_tʼ ks -kʼɬ+kic -nt -m iʔ t sn+kɬ+cʼaʔ=sqáx̌aʔ uɬ aɬíʔ
and neg_emph futt^ -reach -nt -psv art agInst horse and because
"The horse will not reach it, *the snow*

sult iʔ smikʼʷt 287 kʷu cus wayʼ, nʼ[ínʼwiʔ] kʷu
sul+t iʔ s+mikʼʷt kʷu cu -s wayʼ nʼínʼwiʔ kʷu
snow_crust art snow_on_ground 1obj tell -3erg well a_while 4kn
is crusted." *He said to me, "We'll use*

yríwaʔxnəm 288 nʼ[ínʼwiʔ] xʷúystəm iʔ kəwʼwáptət {kʷu kʼa} kʼa
yr=íwaʔ=xn+m nʼínʼwiʔ xʷuy+st -m iʔ kw+wap -tt kʼ
wear_snowshoes a_while take_st -4erg art horses -4in to
snowshoes. *We'll take our horses as far as*

9 MD suggests this form.

ntx̌ʷitkʷ k̓əl kyríptən 289 ilíʔ mi ʕacʕacəntím məɬ itlíʔ kʷu
n+tx̌ʷ=itkʷ k̓l k+yr=ip+tn ilíʔ mi ʕac•ʕac -nt -im mɬ itlíʔ kʷu
river to Push_Pack there fut tie -nt -4erg and from_there 4kn
the river to kyríptən, we'll tie them up there,

k̓əɬtkʷaʔtínk iʔ l syríwaʔxən 290 uɬ ńíńw̓iʔ t̓iʔ sckʷəntím {ti} iʔ l
k̓ɬ+tkʷaʔ=t=ínk iʔ l s+yr=íwaʔ=xn uɬ ńíńw̓iʔ t̓iʔ ckʷ -nt -im iʔ l
walk_side_hill art on snowshoes and a_while evid pull -nt -4erg art at
and from there we'll go on the side hill. We'll drag it

kəw̓wáptət ckícəntəm 291 ixíʔ uɬ {c} cq̓ʷəɬtsqáx̌aʔməntəm
kw•w•ap -tt c+kic -nt -m ixíʔ uɬ c -q̓ʷɬ+t=sqáx̌aʔ+m -nt -m
horses -4in arrive_cisl -nt -4erg then and act -horse_pack -nt -4erg
as far as our horses, then we'll pack it

iʔ la nq̓ʷəɬtsqáx̌aʔtən 292 məɬ kʷu ɬcx̌əƛ̓x̌íƛ̓əm 293 cun
iʔ l n+q̓ʷɬ+t=sqáx̌aʔ+tn mɬ kʷu ɬ+c+x̌ƛ̓•x̌iƛ̓+m cu -n
art on pack_horse and 4kn climb_cisl_again tell -1erg
on the horse. 20:02 And then we'll come back up the hill." I said

way̓, way̓ kʷu sxʷuyx, xʷu··y, {kʷu} kʷu ntkɬlilx 294 way̓ ilíʔ
way̓ way̓ kʷu s -xʷuy -x xʷuy kʷu n+tkɬ+lilx way̓ ilíʔ
OK well 4kn ipftv^ -go -^ipftv time_go_by 4kn get_to_bottom well there
"Ok." We went, we went and got to the bottom; we tied

ʕacʕacəntím iʔ kəw̓wáptət 295 way̓ itlíʔ kʷu
ʕac•ʕac -nt -im iʔ kw+wap -tt way̓ itlíʔ kʷu
tie -nt -4erg art horses -4in well from_there 4kn
our horses there; from there we

syríwaʔxnəms 296 ixíʔ uɬ {kʷu} kʷu sx̌əƛ̓x̌íƛ̓əms,
s -yr=íwaʔ=xn+m -s ixíʔ uɬ kʷu s -x̌ƛ̓•x̌iƛ̓+m -s
nom4^ -wear_snowshoes -^nom4 then and 4kn nom4^ -climb -^nom4
went on snowshoes; then we went up the hill, then we walked

kʷu k̓əɬtkʷaʔtínk 297 [kʷu] xʷu··y, uɬ kícəntəm ist̓áʕp
kʷu k̓ɬ+tkʷaʔt=ínk kʷu xʷuy uɬ kic -nt -m i -s+t̓aʕp
4kn walk_side_hill 4kn go and reach_st/sb -nt -4erg 1in -shooting
on the side hill. We went, and we got to the deer I shot.

298 way̓ way̓ ixíʔ {c ə·· c} cʕacʕacxəntís, uɬ axáʔ {i}
way̓ way̓ ixíʔ c -ʕac•ʕac+xn -nt -is uɬ axáʔ
well well then act -tie_feet -nt -3erg and this
He tied up his feet and he tied

ckəɬʕacəcís 299 kʷu cus, way̓, way̓ incá iʔ kən
c -kɬ+ʕac•cí -s kʷu cu -s way̓ way̓ in+cá iʔ kn
act -tie_around_neck -3erg 1obj tell -3erg well yes I art 1kn
around the neck. He said to me, "I'll go

ksxaʔtmíxaʔx aɬíʔ kən ksk̓əɬk̓ʷínstaʔx 300 uɬ anwí
ks -xaʔt -míx+aʔx aɬíʔ kn ks -k̓ɬ+k̓ʷin+st -aʔx uɬ anwí
incp^ -first -^incp because 1kn incp^ -pick_way -^incp and you
first, because I got to pick our way out. You

ckʷískʷəstxʷ lut kskəʕʷáps ta cixʷməl̓xús 301 ixíʔ uɬ
c -kʷis•kʷs -t -xʷ lut ks -kʕʷa+p[10] -s t c+yxʷ+m+lx=us ixíʔ uɬ
cust^ -hold_on_to -st -2erg not futi -slide -3i obl below then and
hold it so it won't slide down the hill. *And then*

t̓i kʷu k̓əɬtkʷaʔtínk 302 ah cun way̓, way̓ ixíʔ {c}
t̓iʔ kʷu k̓ɬ+tkʷaʔt=ínk ah cu -n way̓ way̓ ixíʔ
evid 4kn walk_side_hill intj tell -1erg OK well then
we'll just walk on the side hill." *I said "Ok," and then*

scəkʷəntís kʷu scəkʷkʷíɬc̓aʔms uɬ aɬíʔ sílxʷaʔ
s -ckʷ -nt -is kʷu s -ckʷ•kʷ=íɬc̓aʔ+m -s uɬ aɬíʔ sílxʷaʔ
act -drag -nt -3erg 4kn nom4^ -drag_game -^nom4 and because big
we dragged it, because it's big. 21:03

303 uɬ incá ckʷískʷəstən lut sckəʕʷaps axáʔ iʔ t
uɬ in+cá c -kʷis•kʷs -st -n lut sc -kʕʷa+p -s axáʔ iʔ t
and I cust^ -hold_on_to -^cust -1erg not pftv -slide -3i this art agInst
And I held it with the rope so it won't slide

sp̓íc̓ən 304 kʷu ɬcsəx̌ʷtlí··lx kʷu ɬcyʕáp̓ iʔ l kəw̓wáptət
s+p̓ic̓n kʷu ɬ+c+sx̌ʷ+t+lilx kʷu ɬ+c+yaʕ+p iʔ l kw+wap -tt
rope 4kn come_downhill_again 4kn arrive_cisl_again art at horses -4in
down. *We came down the hill and then we got back to our horses.*

305 uɬ ixíʔ {ɬ} ckt̓k̓ʷiw̓səntəm ɬckʕacəntím uɬ ixíʔ
uɬ ixíʔ c -k+t̓k̓ʷ=iw̓s -nt -m ɬ+c+k+ʕac -nt -im uɬ ixíʔ
and then act -put_on_horse -nt -4erg tie_again_to_cisl -nt -4erg and then
Then we put it on the horse, we tied it to it again, and we came

kʷu ɬcx̌əƛ̓x̌íƛ̓əm 306 way̓ ixíʔ kʷu ksx̌əlpínaʔ uɬ ixíʔ {i} cun
kʷu ɬ+c+x̌ƛ̓•x̌iƛ̓+m way̓ ixíʔ kʷu k+s+x̌l+p=ínaʔ uɬ ixíʔ cu -n
4kn climb_cisl_again well then 4kn have_daylight and then tell -1erg
back up the hill. *The next morning I said to*

axáʔ inqíck {way̓} 307 way̓ uɬ t̓i ixíʔ ismíc̓aʔm
axáʔ in -qick way̓ uɬ t̓iʔ ixíʔ i -s -míc̓aʔ+m
this 1in -older_brother well and evid then 1i -intt -fetch_killed_game
my brother: *"I'll go after my deer.*

308 way̓ cəm̓ {i t} iʔ t sənk̓líp {kʷu} kʷu náq̓ʷəmɬts axáʔ {iɬ} uɬ
way̓ cm̓ iʔ t sn+k̓l̓=ip kʷu naq̓ʷ+m -ɬt -s axáʔ uɬ
well maybe art agInst Coyote 1obj steal_from -ɬt -3erg this and
Coyotes might steal it from us, it's been overnight

way̓ pulx uɬ ksk̓laxʷ 309 kʷu cus, way̓ kəxəntsín,
way̓ pul+x uɬ k+s+k̓laxʷ kʷu cu -s way̓ kxn -t -s -in
well overnight and all_day 1obj tell -3erg well follow -nt -2obj -1erg
and all day." *He said "I'll go with you,"*

10 This analysis is unclear.

cun ah way̓ 310 cut axáʔ sy̓al'w̓ánk, way̓ incá k̓əm kən
cu -n ah way̓ cut axáʔ s+y̓al'w̓=ánk way̓ in+cá k̓m kn
tell -1erg intj OK say this Cricket well I except 1kn
and I said "Ok." *Cricket said, "I'm going to*

smutx {uł axáʔ} 311 way̓ ixíʔ {kʷu s} kʷu sxʷuys, kʷu xʷu··y
s -mut -x way̓ ixíʔ kʷu s -xʷuy -s kʷu xʷuy
ipftv^ -be_home -^ipftv well then 4kn nom4^ -go -^nom4 4kn go
stay here." *Then we went, we went*

uł ik̓líʔ iʔ t xəwíł, iʔ ta nqəqəlxʷáqaʔs 312 caʔkʷ {ł} iʔ l
uł ik̓líʔ iʔ t xwił iʔ t n+q•qlxʷ+áqaʔs caʔkʷ iʔ l
and there art agInst road art agInst trail if art in
and we hit a road, a trail. 22:08 *If it were*

scʔaqʷ way̓ itíʔ {i} łəx̌ʷmíw̓s iʔ sƛ̓aʔcínəm 313 itíʔ uł kʷu
s+cʔaqʷ way̓ itíʔ łx̌ʷ+m=iw̓s iʔ s+ƛ̓aʔ=cín+m itíʔ uł kʷu
summer yes from_that go_through art deer from_that and 4kn
summer the deer would go there. *We got*

nt̓k̓ʷak̓ʷ iʔ t syríwaʔxən iʔ t isxʷúytən uł axáʔ iʔ
n+t̓k̓ʷ•ak̓ʷ iʔ t s+yr=íwaʔ=xn iʔ t i -s+xʷuy+tn uł axáʔ iʔ
enter_from_side_road art obl snowshoes art obl 1in -track and this art
on the trail where I and the deer

sƛ̓aʔcínəm 314 kʷu xʷu··y uł kícəntəm 315 cun
s+ƛ̓aʔ=cín+m kʷu xʷuy uł kic -nt -m cu -n
deer 4kn go and reach_st/sb -nt -4erg tell -1erg
had been. *We went and we got there.* *I said*

inqíck aláʔ i ki uł isənc̓íqʷmən 316 aláʔ kiʔ tx̌ʷáyqən
in -qick aláʔ iʔ kiʔ uł i -sn+c̓iqʷ+mn aláʔ kiʔ t+x̌ʷay=qn
1in -older_brother here art rel and 1in -skinning_place here rel pile
to my brother, "It's right here that I was skinning, *and that I piled*

iʔ słiqʷ 317 way̓ t̓iʔ k̓aw 318 uł ixíʔ uł kən ƛ̓aʔƛ̓aʔúsəm 319 mʕan
iʔ s+łiqʷ way̓ t̓iʔ k̓aw uł ixíʔ uł kn ƛ̓aʔ•ƛ̓aʔ=ús+m mʕan
art meat well evid gone and then and 1kn look_for intj
the meat." *It's gone.* *I looked around,* *and*

ilíʔ ksənw̓rm̓íń 320 way̓ ilíʔ k̓əłwíkxən axáʔ isl'áx̌t
ilíʔ k+sn+w̓r+m̓iń way̓ ilíʔ k̓ł+wik=xn -n axáʔ i -s+l'ax̌+t
there have_small_fire well there see_tracks -1erg this 1in -friend
there was a fire built there. *I saw my partner's tracks.*

321 ałíʔ lut t̓a cyriwáxən iʔ sqəlqəlwítəm[s] 322 ay cun
ałíʔ lut t̓ c -yr=íwaʔ=xn iʔ s+ql•ql=wit+m -s ay cu -n
because not negfac hab -snow_shoe art steps -3in intj tell -1erg
His tracks didn't have snowshoes. *I told*

axáʔ isl'áx̌t 323 way̓ axáʔ aláʔ iʔ sl'áx̌tət iʔ sxʷúytəns
axáʔ i -s+l'ax̌+t way̓ axáʔ aláʔ iʔ s+l'ax̌+t -t iʔ s+xʷuy+tn -s
this 1in -friend well this here art partner -4in art track -3in
my partner: 23:00 *"Here are our partner's tracks."*

324 way̓ ilíʔ ƛ̓aʔƛ̓aʔúsəmən k̓əl w̓íw̓aʔst ki {c} əcmkʷíwt 325 uɬ
way̓ ilíʔ ƛ̓aʔ•ƛ̓aʔ=ús+m -n k̓l w̓í•w̓aʔs+t kiʔ c -mkʷ=iwt uɬ
well there look_for -1erg to high_dim rel hab -mound and
I looked around and up on the side of the hill there was a lump. *It*

aɬíʔ mqʷaqʷ ixíʔ i l sənkʷkʷʔác uɬ ckəmqʷína? 326 ik̓líʔ
aɬíʔ mqʷ•aqʷ ixíʔ i l sn+kʷ•kʷʔac uɬ c -k+mqʷ=ínaʔ ik̓líʔ
because snow_fall then art at night and hab -snow_cover there
had snowed that night and it had covered everything. *I went*

ʔawsʕ̓ác̓ən 327 sta ixíʔ iʔ sƛ̓aʔcínəm 328 way̓ i[xíʔ] mat
ʔaw+s+ʕ̓ác̓+m sta ixíʔ iʔ s+ƛ̓aʔ=cín+m way̓ ixíʔ mat
go_look intj that art deer well that must
to look. *That was the deer.* *He must have*

kʕacíkiʔs uɬ ixíʔ ksq̓ʷíɬtmiʔs 329 uɬ aɬíʔ {a t k̓əl} k̓əl w̓íw̓aʔst
k+ʕac==íkiʔ -s uɬ ixíʔ ks -q̓ʷíɬt+mi -s uɬ aɬíʔ k̓l w̓í•w̓aʔs+t
tie_bundle -3erg and then futi -pack -3i and because to high_dim
prepared it for packing, *because he had left*

kiʔ kəw̓wáps iʔ ɬwis 330 way̓ way̓ uɬ ilíʔ uɬ
kiʔ kw+w+ap -s iʔ ɬwi -s way̓ way̓ uɬ ilíʔ uɬ
rel horses -3in art leave -3erg well yes and there and
his horses a little above on the hill. *It was too*

təlxʷkíń {uɬ aɬíʔ a axáʔ} 331 way̓ ixíʔ k̓ʷíxʷən axáʔ iʔ {ks i}
tlxʷ+kin[11] way̓ ixíʔ k̓ʷixʷ -n axáʔ iʔ
difficult well then untie -1erg this art
heavy. *I started to untie it,*

kskɬíw̓səntəm iʔ kskʕacqáx̌aʔtət 332 way̓ kmix sc̓əwc̓uxán
ks -kɬ=iw̓s -nt -m iʔ k -s+k+ʕac+qáx̌aʔ -tt way̓ kmix s+c̓w̓•c̓w̓=xan
futt^ -divide -nt -4erg art to_be -tie_on_horse -4in well only legs
we were going to divide it up to put it on our horses. *There was only the legs,*

uɬ ʔásx̌əm uɬ k̓əspán 333 way̓ lut t̓a kɬcək̓ck̓íɬp 334 hi
uɬ ʔasx̌m uɬ k̓span way̓ lut t̓ kɬ+ck̓•ck̓•iɬp hi
and back and nape_of_neck well not negfac have_ribs intj
the back and the neck. *It didn't have ribs.* *I*

kʕ̓ʷəyncútmən, uɬ cun axáʔ islʼáx̌t 335 way̓ way̓
k+ʕ̓ʷy+ncut+m -n uɬ cu -n axáʔ i -s+lʼax̌+t way̓ way̓
laugh_at -1erg and tell -1erg this 1in -friend well yes
laughed and I said to my partner: 24:01 *"Our*

skcʔíɬəɬnx axáʔ iʔ slʼáx̌tət nák̓ʷəm 336 uɬ iʔ
s -kc -ʔiɬ•ɬ•n -x axáʔ iʔ s+lʼax̌+t -t nak̓ʷ+m uɬ iʔ
ipftv^ -? -eat -^ipftvp this art partner -4in evid and art
partner must have eaten it. *That's*

11 This suffix is unfamiliar to me.

təlxʷkíṅ {i təs} iwá mat ksq̓ʷíłtmiʔs 337 uł ałíʔ axáʔ {iwáł}
tlxʷ+kin iwá mat ks -q̓ʷíłt+mi -s uł ałíʔ axáʔ
difficult try_to maybe futi -pack -3i and so this
why he couldn't pack it. *He must have*

uləntís iʔ cḱcḱiłp {uł} 338 uł lut ťa uláp iʔ sċiṁ, ilíʔ
wl -nt -is iʔ cḱ•cḱ=iłp uł lut ť wla+p iʔ s+ċim ilíʔ
burn -nt -3erg art ribs and not negfac burn art bone there
burned the ribs." *The bones wouldn't burn, they were*

cənp̓nús 339 waẏ kʷu {ł} kʕacqáx̌aʔm uł waẏ kʷu
c -n+p̓n=us waẏ kʷu k+ʕac+qáx̌aʔ+m uł waẏ kʷu
hab -lay_long_objects_on_fire well 4kn tie_to_horse and well 4kn
lying in the fireplace. *We tied them on the horse and*

łcxʷuy kʷu łciyáʕp 340 waẏ kʷu 341 kʷu
ł+c+xʷuy kʷu ł+c+y•yáʕ+p waẏ kʷu ł -ł+c+ʔimx kʷu
come_again 4kn get_back_cisl well 4kn nom4ˆ -move_back_cisl 4kn
we went and we got back. *We went back home.* *We*

łcxʷuy kʷu łciyáʕp k̓əl sənx̌ʷúċəc̓tən 342 waẏ
ł+c+xʷuy kʷu ł+c+y•yáʕ+p k̓l sn+x̌ʷuċ•c̓+tn waẏ
come_again 4kn get_back_cisl to cut_something well
went back and we got back there to sənx̌ʷúċəc̓tən. *I*

px̌ʷmxítnəlx axáʔ isľəx̌ľáx̌t t słiqʷ 343 uł ixíʔ {i}
px̌ʷ+m -xit -n -lx axáʔ i -s+ľx̌•ľax̌+t t s+łiqʷ uł ixíʔ
distribute -xit -1erg -pl this 1in -friends obj_tr meat and then
passed the meat around to my partners. *Then*

łəłcxʷúyʔsəlx 344 ixíʔ nċayxʷápəlqs
ł -ł+c+xʷuy•y -s -lx ixíʔ n+ċayxʷ=áp=lqs
nom -come_back_pl -3i -pl that end_of_story
they came back. *That's the end. 24:54*

Marriage customs

1 way̓ kʷ ikscaptíkʷɬtəm q̓sápiʔ axáʔ inxaʔcín {iʔ} iʔ
way̓ kʷ i -ks -captíkʷ -ɬt -m q̓sápiʔ axáʔ in -xaʔ=cín[1] iʔ
well 2kʷu 1i -futi -legend -ɬt -apsv long_ago this 1in -ancestor art
I am going to tell a story about my ancestors'

cáwtsəlx 2 axáʔ {ils ils} iʔ l scmrim, {ilak} ɬaʔ ctaʔxʷɬtkəɬmílxʷ
cawt -s -lx axáʔ iʔ l sc+mrim ɬaʔ c -taʔxʷ+ɬ+tkɬ+m=ilxʷ
doing -3in -pl this art at marriage when hab -get_wife
ways, *about marriage, when a man gets*

t̓əxʷ axáʔ iʔ sqəltmíxʷ 3 kəm̓ axáʔ iʔ tkəɬmilxʷ məɬ {taʔxʷɬ}
t̓xʷ axáʔ iʔ s+qlt=mixʷ km̓ axáʔ iʔ tkɬ+m=ilxʷ mɬ
evidently this art man or this art woman and
a woman, *or a woman gets*

taʔxʷsqəltmíxʷ 4 kəm̓ axáʔ {it i··} iʔ sqəl̓tmíxʷ taʔxʷɬtkəɬmílxʷ {i·t} 5 uɬ
taʔxʷ+s+qlt=mixʷ km̓ axáʔ iʔ s+qlt=mixʷ taʔxʷ+ɬ+tkɬ+m=ilxʷ uɬ
get_husband or this art man get_wife and
a man, *or a man gets a woman.* *At*

aɬíʔ nak̓ʷáʔ pnicí uɬ ɬaʔ ksuyápix ksnkc̓x̌ʷíplaʔtən 6 uɬ aɬíʔ
aɬíʔ nak̓ʷ+á pn+icíʔ uɬ ɬaʔ k+s+wyapy=x k+s+n+k+c̓x̌ʷ=íplaʔ+tn uɬ aɬíʔ
so not at_that_time and when have+white have+law and so
that time there were no white people, no laws. *That's*

xatmaʔsqílxʷ 7 uɬ nak̓ʷáʔ ckʷənɬq̓əy̓mínməlx a kaʔ cmríməlx, lut
xat=maʔ+s+qílxʷ uɬ nak̓ʷ+á c -kʷn+ɬ+q̓y̓+min+m a kiʔ c -mrim -lx lut
first and not hab -take_papers intj rel hab -marry -pl not
real old timers. *They don't take papers when they get married, no. (1:00)*

8 way̓ t̓i_kmix cənkʷən·wíxʷəlx {i··ʔ} 9 iʔ ƛ̓ax̌əx̌ƛ̓x̌áp {i ac} ia ilmíxʷəm
way̓ t̓iʔ_kmix c -n+kʷn+nwixʷ -lx iʔ ƛ̓ax̌•x̌•ƛ̓x̌á+p iʔ yl=mixʷ+m
yes only hab -take_one_another -pl art elders art chief
They pick one another. *The parents are the bosses*

a[xáʔ] i l sqʷəsqʷasíaʔsəlx 10 uɬ caʔkʷ iwá xəƛ̓pspíntk uɬ niʕíp
axáʔ iʔ l s+qʷs•qʷasíʔa -s -lx uɬ caʔkʷ iwá xƛ̓+p+s+pintk uɬ nyʕip
this art for children -3in -pl and if even mature_age and always
of their children. *And even if they are of age,*

əck̓əɬpaʔx̌xítsəlx iʔ sqʷəsqʷasíaʔsəlx 11 uɬ ʕapnáʔ uɬ aɬíʔ
c -k̓ɬ+paʔx̌ -xit -s -lx iʔ s+qʷs•qʷasíʔa -s -lx uɬ ʕapnáʔ uɬ aɬíʔ
custˆ -think_about -xit -3erg -pl art children -3in -pl and now and so
they still have to think for their children. *But now*

1 xaʔ with loss of t before c.

iʔ suyápix, náx̌əmɬ iʔ kʷu wipwílx 12 way̓ t̓iʔ kʷu xƛ̓pspintk
iʔ s+wyapy=x nax̌mɬ iʔ kʷu wyp+wilx way̓ t̓iʔ kʷu xƛ̓+p+s+pin=tk
art white_person but art 4kn become_white yes evid 4kn mature_age
we are all turning white: *when we are 21*

kʷu ʔasəlʔupənksɬnk̓ʷəspíntk ixíʔ uɬ way̓ kʷu *of age* 13 uɬ q̓sápiʔ lut,
kʷu ʔasl+ʔupn=ks+ɬ+nk̓ʷ+s+pin=tk ixíʔ uɬ way̓ kʷu uɬ q̓sápiʔ lut
4kn twenty_one then and yes 4kn and long_ago not
we are of age. *Not so a long time*

way̓ niʕ̓íp iʔ ƛ̓ax̌əx̌ƛ̓x̌áp ia ilmíxʷəm {iʔ} 14 axáʔ {iʔ} iʔ sisyús {il} iʔ l
way̓ nyʕ̓ip iʔ ƛ̓ax̌•x̌•ƛ̓x̌á+p iʔ yl=mixʷ+m axáʔ iʔ sy•sy=us iʔ l
yes always art elders art chief this art smart art at
ago, the parents are the boss all the time. *Those smart at getting*

stəxʷcəncút, way̓ iʔ l qáqxʷəlx kəm̓ axáʔ {il} iʔ l sƛ̓aʔcínəm 15 ixíʔ iʔ
s+txʷ=cn+cut way̓ iʔ l qa•qxʷ+lx km̓ axáʔ iʔ l s+ƛ̓aʔ=cín+m ixíʔ iʔ
food yes art at fish or this art at deer that art
things to eat, getting fish, or deer, (2:09) *the smart*

sisyús ixíʔ iʔ l stəxʷcəncút ixíʔ {iˑʔ} ia cilmíxʷəmstsəlx iʔ
sy•sy=us ixíʔ iʔ l s+txʷ=cn+cut ixíʔ iʔ c -yl=mixʷ+m -st -s -lx iʔ
smart that art at food that art cust^ -chief -^cust -3erg -pl art
ones are those they

sisyús {aɬíʔ} 16 ixíʔ məɬ cúsəlx axáʔ aláʔ {it itkəɬ} iʔ st̓əmkʔíltsəlx
sy•sy=us ixíʔ mɬ cu -s -lx axáʔ aláʔ iʔ s+t̓mkʔ=ilt -s -lx
smart then and tell -3erg -pl this here art daughter -3in -pl
make boss. *And they tell their daughter:*

17 way̓ ixíʔ {aks} aksqəltmíxʷ, ixíʔ akɬənx̌stán 18 lut caʔkʷ
way̓ ixíʔ a -k -s+qlt=mixʷ ixíʔ a -kɬ -n+x̌s+tan lut caʔkʷ
yes that 2i -to_be -man then 2i -to_be -good not if
“That will be your man, then you’ll be satisfied. *Whether*

iwá lut cx̌susc, kəm̓ swiʔnúmtxs 19 uɬ aɬíʔ náx̌əmɬ lut
iwá lut s+x̌s=us -c km̓ s+wy̓+numt=x -s uɬ aɬíʔ nax̌mɬ lut
even not good_looks -3in or handsome -3in and so but not
he is not good looking, or he’s handsome, *you’ll never*

akscəksq̓míltən, ʕ̓ác̓ənt sisyús iʔ l stəxʷcəncút 20 uɬ axáʔ nixʷ
a -ksc -k+s+q̓m=ilt+n ʕ̓ac̓ -nt sy•sy=us iʔ l s+txʷ=cn+cut uɬ axáʔ nixʷ
2i -futPerfi -hunger look -nt smart art at food and this also
get hungry. Look, he is smart in getting things to eat. *And another*

iʔ kʷu ƛ̓ax̌əx̌ƛ̓x̌áp uɬ kʷu cthim i {tl} tl aksqəltmíxʷ {kʷu}
iʔ kʷu ƛ̓ax̌•x̌•ƛ̓x̌á+p uɬ kʷu c -thim[2] i tl̓ a -k -s+qlt=mixʷ
art 4kn elders and 4kn hab -benefit art from 2i -to_be -man
thing, we old people will get benefit too from your man.

2 Uncertain form.

21 kʷu c̓amstíxʷ t qáqxʷəlx kəm̓ t sƛ̓aʔcínəm 22 uɬ
kʷu c -ʔam -st -ixʷ t qa•qxʷ+lx km̓ t s+ƛ̓aʔ=cín+m uɬ
1obj cust^ -feed -^cust -2erg obj_tr fish or obj_tr deer and
You will feed us fish or deer meat." (3:03) *At*

aɬíʔ nak̓ʷáʔ pnicíʔ uɬ way̓ uɬ a ksqľaw, {i way̓} kəm ksəntumístən
aɬíʔ nak̓ʷ+á pn+icíʔ uɬ way̓ uɬ a k+s+qlaw km̓ k+s+n+tw+mist+n
because not at_that_time and yes and intj have_money or have_store
that time there was no money, or stores,

kəm stim̓, lut 23 way̓ t̓i_kmix {s} sqəlxʷúlaʔxʷ, kʷu taɬt kʷu sqilxʷ
km̓ stim̓ lut way̓ t̓iʔ_kmix s+qlxʷ=úlaʔxʷ kʷu taɬ+t kʷu s+qilxʷ
or thing not yes only reserve 4kn surely 4kn Indian
or anything, *only Indian things, just us Indians*

pnicíʔ 24 way̓ axáʔ {i} kmix síp̓iʔ iʔ {təm} təm̓tm̓útəntət 25 axáʔ iʔ
pn+icíʔ way̓ axáʔ kmix síp̓iʔ iʔ tm̓•tm̓=ut+n -tt axáʔ iʔ
at_that_time yes this only hide art clothes -4in this art
at that time. *Our clothes are just buckskin,* *buckskin*

sƛ̓aʔcnmíc̓aʔ ixíʔ xʷí··kʷsəlx {məɬ} 26 məɬ ixíʔ uɬ k̓ʷúľsəlx
s+ƛ̓aʔ=cn+m=íc̓aʔ ixíʔ xʷikʷ -s -lx mɬ ixíʔ uɬ k̓ʷuľ -s -lx
deer_hide that tan_hides -3erg -pl and then and make -3erg -pl
that they tan. *And the women fix*

ksip̓iʔálqs axáʔ iʔ smamʔím 27 ixíʔ uɬ ɬəɬáxʷsəlx {i} iʔ
k+sip̓iʔ=álqs axáʔ iʔ s+ma•mʔím ixíʔ uɬ ɬ•ɬaxʷ -s -lx iʔ
buckskin_clothes this art women that and dress -3in -pl art
bukskin clothes, *their dresses are*

sip̓iʔálqs 28 uɬ axáʔ iʔ sqəlqəltmíxʷ uɬ c̓x̌iɬ 29 uɬ ixíʔ
sip̓iʔ=álq -s uɬ axáʔ iʔ s+ql•qlt=mixʷ uɬ c+ʔx̌iɬ uɬ ixíʔ
buckskin_clothes -3in and this art men and like then then
buckskin clothes. *And the men the same:* *the women*

ck̓ʷúľɬtəm iʔ t tkəɬmílxʷ ixíʔ uɬ t sp̓iʔálqs 30 uɬ
c -k̓ʷuľ -ɬt -m iʔ t tkɬmilxʷ ixíʔ uɬ t sp̓iʔ=alqs uɬ
cust^ -make -ɬt -psv art agInst woman that and obj_tr buckskin_dress and
fix their buckskin clothes. *And*

axáʔ {i} kskʕacʕacqínxən, ixíʔ síp̓iʔ {ixíʔ uɬ c} 31 ixíʔ uɬ {aʔ}
axáʔ k+s+k+ʕac•ʕac=qín=xn ixíʔ síp̓iʔ ixíʔ uɬ
this have+leggings that hide that and
they have leggings and that's buckskin. *That's what*

scústsəlx axáʔ iʔ sx̌íƛ̓xən, ixíʔ uɬ skʕacʕacqínxən 32 uɬ
s -cu -st -s -lx axáʔ iʔ s+x̌iƛ̓=xn ixíʔ uɬ s+k+ʕac•ʕac=qín=xn uɬ
cust^ -tell -^cust -3erg -pl this art trousers that and leggings and
they call pants now, that's leggings. (4:00) *But*

ʕapnáʔ aɬíʔ uɬ náx̌əmɬ way̓ uɬ axáʔ iʔ {kʷu xatmaʔ} kʷu ʔawtmaʔsqílxʷ
ʕapnáʔ aɬíʔ uɬ nax̌mɬ way̓ uɬ axáʔ iʔ kʷu ʔawt=maʔ+s+qílxʷ
now so and but yes and this art 4kn people
now we are the now people,

33 waẏ uł ałíʔ kʷu wipwílx
waẏ uł ałíʔ kʷu wyp+wilx
yes and so 4kn become_white
we are turning white people,

34 uł waẏ uł k̓ʷúl̓ntəm {iʔ} iʔ
uł waẏ uł k̓ʷul̓ -nt -m iʔ
and yes and do -nt -4erg art
and we follow

suyápix a nk̓ʷúl̓məns
s+wyapy=x a n+k̓ʷul̓+mn -s
white_person art custom -3in
the white people's ways.

35 a·· təl suyápix kiʔ uł
a tl s+wyapy=x kiʔ uł
intj from white_person rel and
From the white people

mipnúntəm iʔ sql̓aw
my+p -nu -nt -m iʔ s+qlaw
learn -manage -nt -4erg art money
we learn money,

36 uł ixíʔ {təl} kʷu ksəntumístən
uł ixíʔ kʷu k+s+n+tw+mist+n
and then 4kn have_store
and we have stores,

cənʔístəm iʔ sc̓íłən kəṁ axáʔ {iʔ} iʔ təṁtṁútəntət {ixíʔ uł}
c -n+ʔiys -t -m iʔ sc+ʔiłn kṁ axáʔ iʔ tṁ•tṁ=ut+n -tt
cust^ -trade ^-cust -psv art food or this art clothes -4in
we buy groceries or our clothes.

37 ixíʔ uł k̓əłc̓sáp axáʔ {iʔis} iʔ síp̓iʔ iʔ təṁtṁútən
ixíʔ uł k̓ł+c̓sa+p axáʔ iʔ síp̓iʔ iʔ tṁ•tṁ=ut+n
then and finished this art hide art clothes
And buckskin clothes are out of date,

38 uł waẏ kmix i
uł waẏ kmix i
and yes only art
[we wear them] only

l siyáʕ̓
l s+yaʕ
at gathering
at gatherings.

39 swit iʔ q̓ʷíłq̓ʷəłt məł i[xíʔ] {i ac} i
swit iʔ q̓ʷił•q̓ʷł+t mł ixíʔ iʔ
somebody art strong and that art
If anybody is ambitious enough

acsip̓iʔálqsəm kəṁ síp̓iʔ t̓əxʷ iʔ kstətəṁtíṁs
c -sip̓iʔ=álqs+m kṁ síp̓iʔ t̓xʷ iʔ k -s+t•tṁ•tiṁ -s
hab -make_buckskin_clothes or hide evidently art to_be -clothes -3in
to make buckskin clothes, or skin clothes,

40 uł ixíʔ {ils} iʔ l swanx kmi[x] {uł t̓i} t̓i sc̓aʕc̓ {il} iʔ l siyáʕ̓
uł ixíʔ iʔ l s+wanx kmix t̓iʔ sc+ʕac̓ iʔ l s+yaʕ
and then art at war_dance only evid looks art at gathering
for the war dance, it's only for show at a gathering. (5:07)

41 ixíʔm ałíʔ q̓sápiʔ kʷa ixíʔ t̓iʔ iʔ təṁtṁútənsəlx
ixíʔ+m ałíʔ q̓sápiʔ kʷa ixíʔ t̓iʔ iʔ tṁ•tṁ=ut+n -s -lx
that so long_ago intj that evid art clothes -3in -pl
Long time ago that's all they had to wear.

42 uł ixíʔ iʔ
uł ixíʔ iʔ
and then art
Like

t cun,[3] lut {t̓ak} t̓a ksəntumístən, lut ałíʔ t̓a ksuyápix {t̓ak}
t cu -n lut t̓ k+sn+tw+mist+n lut ałíʔ t̓ k+s+wyapy=x
obl tell -1erg not negfac have_store not so negfac have_white
I said, there was no store, there were no white people.

3 Note the idiomatic use of iʔ t cun here, in 44 and elsewhere, also with other person markers.

43 uɬ way̓ t̓i [yaʕ]yáʕt sqəlxʷəlscút iʔ təm̓tm̓útənsəlx 44 ixíʔ iʔ
uɬ way̓ t̓iʔ yaʕ•yáʕ+t s+qlxʷ=lscut iʔ tm̓•tm̓=ut+n -s -lx ixíʔ iʔ
and yes evid all Indian_clothes art clothes -3in -pl then art
{Well that's about all.} Their clothes were all Indian clothes. *Like*

t cun, ixíʔ {uɬ} uɬ aɬíʔ cənk̓ʷənnwíxʷ 45 uɬ sc̓x̌ilx uɬ
t cu -n ixíʔ uɬ aɬíʔ c -n+k̓ʷn+nwixʷ uɬ sc+ʔx̌il+x uɬ
obl tell -1erg then and so hab -pick_one_another and reason_why and
I said, they pick out one another, *and that's why some of*

iʔ acpuʔtxʷaʔxʷʔít axáʔ iʔ sisyús i l stəxʷcəncút 46 axáʔ mʕ̓an
iʔ c -pu=t=xʷaʔ•xʷʔí+t axáʔ iʔ sy•sy=us i l s+txʷ=cn+cut axáʔ mʕ̓an
art hab -many_wives this art smart art at food this intj
them got more than one wife, those that are smart at getting things to eat. *They*

ixíʔ kʷu scústsəlx axá{i} int̓at̓úpaʔ təl
ixíʔ kʷu s -cu -st -s -lx axáʔ in -t̓aʔ•t̓úpaʔ tl
that 1obj cust^ -tell -^cust -3erg -pl this 1in -great_grandfather from
told me about it, my great-grandfather from

inlʔíw 47 inlʔíw mat {ɬaʔ kɬ ɬaʔ kɬ stim̓} sx̌áx̌paʔs kəm̓
in -lʔiw in -lʔiw mat s+x̌á•x̌paʔ -s km̓
1in -m's_father 1in -m's_father maybe grandfather -3in or
my father, *maybe his paternal grandfather or maybe*

mat k̓ík̓əwaʔs 48 ixíʔ k̓úpənkst iʔ smaʔmʔíms
mat k̓í•k̓waʔ -s ixíʔ k+ʔupn=kst iʔ s+maʔ•mʔím -s
maybe mother's_father -3in that ten_persons art women -3in
his maternal grandfather. (6:06) *He had ten wives.*

49 sc̓x̌ilx uɬ axáʔ incá mʕ̓an uɬ kʷu scusts axáʔ
sc+ʔx̌il+x uɬ axáʔ in+cá mʕ̓an uɬ kʷu s -cu -st -s axáʔ
reason_why and this I intj and 1obj cust^ -tell -^cust -3erg this
That's why, and my parents

inƛ̓ax̌əx̌ƛ̓áp 50 púti ɬaʔ cxʷəlxʷált way̓ {k} kʷu ksnəqsílxʷ {k̓əl}
in -ƛ̓ax̌•x̌•ƛ̓x̌á+p pút+iʔ ɬaʔ c -xʷl•xʷal+t way̓ kʷu k+s+nqs=ilxʷ
1in -elders still when hab -alive yes 4kn have_relative
told me *when they were alive, that we got relatives*

k̓əl sənyál̓mən uɬ axáʔ k̓əl skícux 51 ik̓líʔ kʷu ksnəqsílxʷ uɬ axáʔ {k̓əl}
k̓l s+n+yal̓+mn uɬ axáʔ k̓l s+kic+wx ik̓líʔ kʷu k+s+nqs=ilxʷ uɬ axáʔ
at Montana and this at Idaho there 4kn have_relative and this
in Montana and in Idaho. *We have relatives there,*

k̓əl tqəltqálqʷ 52 ik̓líʔ nixʷ iʔ kʷu ksnəqsílxʷ 53 uɬ aɬíʔ ixíʔ
k̓l t+qlt=k=alqʷ ik̓líʔ nixʷ iʔ kʷu k+s+nqs=ilxʷ uɬ aɬíʔ ixíʔ
at across_line there also art 4kn have_relative and because that
and in Canada, *there too we have relatives.* *My*

spuʔtxʷaʔxʷʔítx {in} int̓at̓úpaʔ 54 uɬ ixíʔ úɬi
s -pu=t+xʷaʔ•xʷʔí+t -x in -t̓aʔ•t̓úpaʔ uɬ ixíʔ uɬ iʔ
ipftv^ -many_wives -^ipftv 1in -great_grandfather and there and_then
great great grandfather had many wives. *Then they scattered*

px̌ʷməncútəlx uɬ iʔ taʔxʷs{s· s}maʔmʔím axáʔ iʔ sqʷəsqʷasíʔasəlx
px̌ʷ+mncut -lx uɬ iʔ taʔxʷ+s+maʔ•mʔím axáʔ iʔ s+qʷs•qʷasíʔa -s -lx
scatter -pl and art get_wives this art children -3in -pl
and their children had wives, and children

uɬ_iʔ itlíʔ k̓ʷul̓l̓ 55 uɬ_i sc̓x̌ilx uɬ ik̓líʔ iʔ {kʷu} kʷu
uɬ_iʔ itlíʔ k̓ʷul̓•l̓ uɬ_iʔ sc+ʔx̌il+x uɬ ik̓líʔ iʔ kʷu
and_then from_there born and_then reason_why and there art 4kn
were born, *and that's why we got relations*

aʔksnəqsílxʷ axáʔ ixíʔ iʔ k̓əl ʔamʔúmlaʔxʷən 56 uɬ {axáʔ iʔ} axáʔ
k+s+nqs=ilxʷ axáʔ ixíʔ iʔ k̓l ʔam•ʔúm=laʔxʷ -n uɬ axáʔ
have_relative this that art at name_place -1erg and this
in all the places I mentioned. (7:05) *But the*

náx̌əmɬ {iʔ} iʔ x̌ʷupt lut i kʷis a nc̓x̌ʷíltən 57 itíʔ kmix
nax̌mɬ iʔ x̌ʷup+t lut i kʷi -s a n+c̓x̌ʷ=ilt+n itíʔ kmix
but art weak not art take -3erg art child_training that only
good for nothing didn't take what they were taught, *they only*

c̓itx {uɬ} uɬ c̓íɬən uɬ way̓ 58 t swit c̓amstím
c -ʔitx uɬ c -ʔiɬn uɬ way̓ t swit c -ʔam -st -im
hab -sleep and hab -eat and all agInst somebody custˆ -feed -ˆcust -psv
sleep and eat, and that's all. *Somebody just feeds them.*

59 uɬ ixíʔ{lut} lut ixíʔ{t̓act̓ac} t̓a cənk̓ʷínkstəm {ɬ k} ɬ
uɬ ixíʔ lut ixíʔ t̓ c -n+k̓ʷin=ks -t -m ɬ
and then not that negfac custˆ -pick -st -psv subord
Them kind don't get picked out to be,

ksník̓əɬxʷməntəm 60 t̓a cmutxtm t
k -s+nik̓=ɬxʷ+m -nt -m t̓ c -mut -xt -m t
fut -be_son_in_law -nt -psv negfac custˆ -sit_sg -xit -psv obj_tr
a son-in-law *or put down for them*

kɬtkɬmilxʷs 61 aɬíʔ myaɬ x̌ʷupt 62 uɬ aɬíʔ ixíʔ t
kɬ -tkɬ+m=ilxʷ -s aɬíʔ myaɬ x̌ʷup+t uɬ aɬíʔ ixíʔ t
to_be -wife -3in because too_much weak and so that obl
somebody to be his wife, *because they are too lazy.* *Like I said,*

cun aɬíʔ way̓ kmix sʔíɬən {i txʷc} 63 iʔ sisyús i l stəxʷcəncút axáʔ
cu -n aɬíʔ way̓ kmix s+ʔiɬn iʔ sy•sy=us iʔ l s+txʷ=cn+cut axáʔ
tell -1erg so yes only food art smart art at food this
it's just for eats, *those smart at getting*

i l qáqxʷəlx kəm̓ {i l} i l sƛ̓aʔcínəm 64 uɬ aɬíʔ nak̓ʷá
iʔ l qa•qxʷ+lx km̓ iʔ l s+ƛ̓aʔ=cín+m uɬ aɬíʔ nak̓ʷá
art at fish or art at deer and because indeed_not
things to eat, fish, or deer. *At that time*

pnicí uɬ a way̓ {ac} cq̓ʷánɬqməlx t patáq t liplí kəm
pn+icíʔ uɬ a way̓ c -k̓ʷan=ɬq+m -lx t patáq t liplí km̓
at_that_time and intj yes hab -grow_crop -pl obj_itr potato obj_itr corn or
they didn't cultivate potatoes or corn,

t limnó, lut, 65 axáʔ sic ki ixíʔ {i} ckicx aláʔ iʔ
t limnó lut axáʔ sic kiʔ ixíʔ c+kic+x aláʔ iʔ
obj_itr watermelon not this new rel that arrive_cisl here art
or watermelon, no. (8:08) It's not long ago that the

ċumstsəlx t i *H.B. people* 66 ixíʔ ki
c -ʔum -st -s -lx t iʔ ixíʔ kiʔ
cust^ -call -^cust -3erg -pl obj_tr art then rel
Hudson's Bay people, as they call them,

cxʷuysts aláʔ {i} ixíʔ iʔ liplí uɬ iʔ patáq 67 ixíʔ úɬi {i}
c -xʷuy -st -s aláʔ ixíʔ iʔ liplí uɬ iʔ patáq ixíʔ uɬ iʔ
cust^ -go -caus -3erg here that art corn and art potato then and_then
brought here corn and potatoes. That's when

mipnús iʔ sqilxʷ {uɬ_i ac iʔ} ɬə ksk̓ʷáṅɬqiʔslx
my+p -nu -s iʔ s+qilxʷ ɬ ks -k̓ʷan=ɬq y̓ -s -lx
learn -manage -3erg art Indian subord futt^ -plant_garden -nt -3erg -pl
the Indians learned how to plant

iʔ liplí uɬ iʔ patáq uɬ axáʔ iʔ lawán iʔ səsp̓qín 68 ixíʔ {x̌əl s} x̌əl
iʔ liplí uɬ iʔ patáq uɬ axáʔ iʔ lawán iʔ s•sp̓=qin ixíʔ x̌l
art corn and art potato and this art oats art wheat that for
corn and potatoes and oats, wheat. That's for

sənkɬċaʔsqáx̌aʔ, uɬ ixíʔ nixʷ iʔ cxʷúystsəlx iʔ sənkɬċaʔsqáx̌aʔ
sn+kɬ+ċaʔ=sqáx̌aʔ uɬ ixíʔ nixʷ iʔ c+xʷuy+st -s -lx iʔ sn+kɬ+ċaʔ=sqáx̌aʔ
horse and that also art bring_st -3erg -pl art horse
the horses, and they also brought the horses.

69 qʷəṅqʷáṅt axáʔ iʔ {kʷu} kʷu sqilxʷ laʔcxʔít 70 way̓ t̓i_kmix {kʷu} kʷu
qʷṅ•qʷaṅ+t axáʔ iʔ kʷu s+qilxʷ la_c+xʔít+iʔ way̓ t̓iʔ_kmix kʷu
pitiful this art 4kn Indian first, yes only 4kn
We Indians were pitiful at first. We only went

nkaʔxmútyaʔ 71 kəm̓ axáʔ {i l} i l siwɬkʷ uɬ ck̓ʷúl̓məlx t
n+kaʔx+m=útyaʔ km̓ axáʔ i l siwɬ=kʷ uɬ c -k̓ʷul̓+m -lx t
go_on_foot or this intj on water and hab -build -pl obj_itr
afoot or by water. They made

ƛ̓ʔiʔ 72 uɬ ixíʔ t̓i a nxʷilwístəns 73 lut {t̓a k t̓a kɬ} t̓a
ƛ̓ʔiʔ uɬ ixíʔ t̓iʔ a n+xʷy+lwis+tn lut t̓
canoe and that evid art vehicle not negfac
bark boats and that's their transportation; (9:00) they didn't have

ksənkɬċaʔsqáx̌aʔ pṅicíʔ, {t̓a kɬ} t̓a kst̓máʕlt 74 uɬ ixíʔ caʔkʷ cus
k+sn+kɬ+ċaʔ=sqáx̌aʔ pn+icíʔ t̓ k+s+t̓maʕlt uɬ ixíʔ caʔkʷ cu -s
have_horse at_that_time negfac have_cow and then as tell -3erg
horses at the time, or cows. And like they say

a nqílxʷcən ixíʔ {iʔ} iʔ sámaʔ ixíʔ *H.B. people* 75 ixíʔ kiʔ
a n+qilxʷ=cn ixíʔ iʔ sámaʔ ixíʔ ixíʔ kiʔ
art Indian_language that art white_person that that rel
in the Indian language, the Hudson's Bay people are white people, they

cxʷuysts iʔ sənkłċaʔsqáx̌a iʔ sťmʕált aláʔ 76 uł ixíʔ i liplí,
c+xʷuy+st -s iʔ sn+kł+ċaʔ=sqáx̌aʔ iʔ s+ťmaʕlt aláʔ uł ixíʔ i liplí
bring_st -3erg art horse art cow here and that intj corn
are the ones that brought horses and cows here, and corn,

patáq uł axáʔ i lawán uł ixíʔ yayáʕt ixíʔ cxʷúystsəlx
patáq uł axáʔ i lawán uł ixíʔ yaʕ•yáʕ+t ixíʔ c+xʷuy+st -s -lx
potato and this intj oats and that all that bring_st -3erg -pl
potatoes, and oats. They brought all that,

77 uł_iʔ {iʔ} máyaʔłtməlx iʔ sqilxʷ ł ksk̓ʷanłqmsəlx kəm̓
uł_iʔ m̓áyaʔ -łt -m -lx iʔ s+qilxʷ ł ks -k̓ʷan=łq+m -s -lx km̓
and_then tell -łt -psv -pl art Indian subord futi -grow_crop -3i -pl or
and they taught the Indians how to put in gardens

ł kstaʔxʷłqms 78 way̓ uł ałíʔ ʕapnáʔ uł way̓ ixíʔ kʷu
ł ks -taʔxʷ=łq+m -s way̓ uł ałíʔ ʕapnáʔ uł way̓ ixíʔ kʷu
one_that futi -get_crop -3i yes and so now and yes then 4kn
and how to harvest. And now we turned

wipwílx 79 ťəxʷ axáʔ {iʔ} iʔ kʷu taʔxʷłnunxʷínaʔtən ta
wyp+wilx ťxʷ axáʔ iʔ kʷu taʔxʷ+ł+n+wnxʷ=ínaʔ+tn t
become_white evidently this art 4kn get_belief obj_itr
white people. And another thing, we got to believing

nk̓ʕáwmən 80 uł ʕapnáʔ way̓ put kʷu ckʷənłq̇əy̓mínəm mi kʷu
n+k̓aʕʷ+mn uł ʕapnáʔ way̓ put kʷu c -kʷn+ł+q̇y̓+min+m mi kʷu
prayer and now yes just 4kn hab -take_papers fut 4kn
in prayers. And now we take papers when

cmrim 81 uł lut kʷu kskłəwscút mi put {ƛ̓l} kʷu nƛ̓əlsíw̓s[4]
c -mrim uł lut kʷu ks -k+łw+scut mi put kʷu n+ƛ̓l+s=iw̓s
hab -marry and not 1kʷu futi -divorce fut just 1kʷu die
we marry. (10:03) And there is no divorce until one dies,

82 ƛ̓lal iʔ sqəltmíxʷ kəm̓ iʔ tkłmilxʷ 83 ixíʔ məł itlíʔ {ł} xʷuy {ła}
ƛ̓l•al iʔ s+qlt=mixʷ km̓ iʔ tkł+m=ilxʷ ixíʔ mł itlíʔ xʷuy
dead art man or art woman then and from_there time_go_by
the man or the woman dies. Then for a year one gets to

nk̓ʷəspíntk məł nťaʔlíls məł itlíʔ ł taʔxʷsənq̇ʷíċtənn
nk̓ʷ+s+pin=tk mł n+ťaʔl=íls mł itlíʔ ł taʔxʷ+s+n+q̇ʷiċ+tn
one_year and satisfied and from_there subord get_new_mate
feeling better and get somebody in their place,

84 itlíʔ łk̓ʷəl̓łtkłmílxʷəm kəm̓ łk̓ʷəl̓sqəltmíxʷəm 85 ixíʔ way̓
itlíʔ ł+k̓ʷl̓+ł+tkł+m=ilxʷ+m km̓ ł+k̓ʷl̓+s+qlt=mixʷ+m ixíʔ way̓
from_there get_second_wife or get_second_husband that all
take another woman, or take another man. That's all. (10:32)

4 +s suffixed to ƛ̓l is not clear.

After the birth of a child

1 way̓ q̓sápiʔ iʔ sqilxʷ t̓əxʷ {ia} a nk̓ʷúl̓məns 2 way̓ kən
way̓ q̓sápiʔ iʔ s+qilxʷ t̓xʷ a n+k̓ʷul̓+mn -s way̓ kn
well long_ago art Indian evidently art custom -3in well 1kn
The customs of the Indians long ago. *I gained*

cpəx̌pəx̌twílx {ixíʔ uɬ a c} ixíʔ uɬ {ə¨} taʔxʷsqʷəsqʷsíʔlx 3 məɬ ixíʔ {c put}
c -px̌•px̌+t+wilx ixíʔ uɬ taʔxʷ+s+qʷs•qʷsíʔ -lx mɬ ixíʔ
hab -get_senses then and get_baby -pl and then
knowledge, and when they have a baby *they*

púta?səlx iʔ uʔx̌tílaʔt 4 tk̓asəlmístəlx t̓əxʷ axáʔ iʔ sqəltmíxʷ uɬ
púta? -s -lx iʔ w̓x̌t=ílaʔt tk=ʔasl+míst -lx t̓xʷ axáʔ iʔ s+qlt=mixʷ uɬ
respect -3erg -pl art newborn two_persons -pl emph this art man and
respect the baby, *both of them, the man,*

iʔ tkəɬmílxʷ 5 lut axáʔ iʔ sqəltmíxʷ {ks piʔ ə} kspíx̌əms t̓əxʷ
iʔ tkɬmilxʷ lut axáʔ iʔ s+qlt=mixʷ ks -pix̌+m -s t̓xʷ
art woman not this art man futi -hunt -3i emph
and the woman. *The man does not hunt,*

kst̓aʕpəntís iʔ sƛ̓aʔcínəm kəm stim̓ kspulsts
ks -t̓aʕp -nt -is iʔ s+ƛ̓aʔ=cín+m km̓ s+tim̓ ks -pul -st -s
futt^ -shoot -nt -3erg art deer or whatever futt^ -kill_one -st -3erg
shoot a deer, or kill anything;

6 kəm̓ iwá nixʷ caʔkʷ ɬ nk̓amtíw̓səms iʔ sənkɬc̓aʔsqáx̌aʔ 7 nixʷ ɬ
km̓ iwá nixʷ caʔkʷ ɬ n+k+ʔam=t=iw̓s+m -s iʔ s+n+kɬ+c̓aʔ=sqáx̌aʔ nixʷ ɬ
or even also if if ride -3erg art horse also if
or even if he rides a horse, *if*

kskʷalt uɬ ixíʔ nixʷ lut, k̓ast {ə¨} 8 kəm̓ axáʔ iʔ sɬɬt̓am, sxiʔmíx stim̓
k+s+kʷal̓+t uɬ ixíʔ nixʷ lut k̓as+t km̓ axáʔ iʔ s+ɬ•ɬt̓a+m s+xiʔ+míx s+tim̓
have_sweat and then also not bad or this art fishing whatever thing
it sweats, that's not [good], it's bad. 1:01 *Or fishing, anything*

t̓əxʷ pulsts, ƛ̓lal {uɬ uɬ ilíʔ} 9 uɬ aɬíʔ cəm̓ tríwyaʔm iʔ uʔx̌tílaʔt
t̓xʷ pul -st -s ƛ̓l•al uɬ aɬíʔ cm̓ tríwyaʔ+m iʔ w̓x̌t=ílaʔt
emph kill_one -st -3erg dead and so maybe react art newborn
that he kills, dead, *the child might react [negatively].*

10 sc̓úmstsəlx t̓əxʷ ksyúmcən 11 uɬ axáʔ way̓ kən
c -ʔum -st -s -lx t̓xʷ k+s+yum=cn uɬ axáʔ way̓ kn
cust^ -call -^cust -3erg -pl emph have_curse and this yes 1kn
They say "it has a curse." *I had gained*

cpəx̌pəx̌twílx k axáʔ inqíck 12 ixíʔ tkəɬmílxʷs {taʔxʷs}
c -px̌•px̌+t+wilx kiʔ axáʔ in -qick ixíʔ tkɬ+m=ilxʷ -s
hab -get_senses rel this 1in -older_brother then wife -3in
some smarts when my oldest brother's *wife*

taʔxʷsqʷəsqʷsíʔ 13 uɬ ixíʔ cúntəm axáʔ iʔ {t is} t isk̓ʷúy
taʔxʷ+s+qʷs•qʷsíʔ uɬ ixíʔ cu -nt -m axáʔ iʔ t i -s+k̓ʷuy
get_baby and then tell -nt -psv this art agInst 1in -mother
had a child. *And my mother said to him,*

14 x̌aʔntím, cúntəm lut_stim̓ aksk̓ʷúl̓əm 15 mi put xəƛ̓pásq̓ət
x̌aʔn -t -im cu -nt -m lut_s+tim̓ a -ks -k̓ʷul̓ -m mi put xƛ̓+p=asq̓t
stop -nt -psv tell -nt -psv nothing 2i -futi -do -apsv fut just duration
she stopped him and said to him, "Don't do anything *for the duration,*

ixíʔ ʔapənkstásq̓ət 16 cəm̓ ksyúmcən asqʷəsqʷsíʔ {way̓ uɬ} 17 way̓ uɬ
ixíʔ ʔapn=kst=ásq̓t cm̓ k+s+yum=cn a -s+qʷs•qʷsiʔ way̓ uɬ
that ten_days maybe have_curse 2in -child well and
that's ten days. *Your child might get the curse."* *He didn't*

lut_stim̓ t̓a ck̓ʷúl̓sts {uɬ} ixíʔ uɬ {mə} mat k̓ʷənxásq̓ət lut iʔ
lut_s+tim̓ t̓ c -k̓ʷul̓ -st -s ixíʔ uɬ mat k̓ʷn+x=asq̓t lut iʔ
nothing negfac cust^ -do -^cust -3erg that and maybe a_few_days not art
do anything for several days, [but] not the

sxəƛ̓pásq̓əts 18 uɬ mat t̓əxʷ t̓iyám aɬíʔ {ɬaʔ} t̓i_kmix ɬaʔ
s -xƛ̓+p=asq̓t -s uɬ mat t̓xʷ t̓ya+m aɬíʔ t̓iʔ_kmix ɬaʔ
nom -duration -3i and maybe evidently be_lazy because only when
complete period. 3:02 *Maybe he got bored*

c̓amtəlwís, lut_stim̓ t̓a ck̓ʷulsts {uɬ} 19 uɬ ixíʔ mat nixʷ
c -ʔam=t+lwís lut_s+tim̓ t̓ c -k̓ʷul̓ -st -s uɬ ixíʔ mat nixʷ
hab -sit_around nothing negfac cust^ -do -^cust -3erg and then maybe also
just sitting around, doing nothing, *maybe also*

sənɬíptəms, way̓ ixíʔ staʔɬululíms 20 axáʔ mat stim̓ {a}
s -n+ɬipt+m -s way̓ ixíʔ s -taʔ+ɬ+wl•wlím -s axáʔ mat s+tim̓
nom -forget -3i well then nom -blacksmithing -3i this maybe something
he forgot, he did some blacksmithing *maybe for the point*

t̓lúlaʔxʷtəns sənk̓máqs 21 mat ixíʔ {ks ə··} ksəncq̓áqsiʔs
t̓l=úlaʔxʷ+tn -s s+n+k̓m=aqs mat ixíʔ ks -n+cq̓=aqs y̓ -s
plow -3in point maybe that futt^ -hit_tip -nt -3erg
of his plow. *Maybe he was going to hammer it.*

22 uɬ ixíʔ ia ur̓ísəlp̓əm uɬ ixíʔ iʔ l səntaʔɬululímtən 23 ixíʔ uɬ {iʔ}
uɬ ixíʔ iʔ wr̓=islp̓+m uɬ ixíʔ iʔ l s+n+taʔ+ɬ+wl•wlím+tn ixíʔ uɬ
and then ? build_fire and that art in forge then and
So he made a fire in the forge; *he placed*

iʔ kmáʕuʔsəs axáʔ {iʔ ks} iʔ kstaʔɬululíms {uɬ i} 24 ixíʔ ńíńwiʔ
iʔ k+maʕ=w̓s -s axáʔ iʔ ks -taʔ+ɬ+wl•wlím -s ixíʔ ńíńwiʔ
art lay_across -3erg this art futi -blacksmithing -3i that a_while
what he was going to work across the fire, *and when*

tx̌alʕásxən məɬ ixíʔ cəq̓əntís 25 t̓əxʷ {ə} ncq̓áqsəs
t+x̌al=ʕásxn mɬ ixíʔ cq̓ -nt -is t̓xʷ n+cq̓=aqs -s
red_hot and then hit -nt -3erg evidently hammer_on_the_point -3erg
it became red hot he hit it. *He hammered*

ixíʔ {ə} a nk̓maqs iʔ t̓l̓úlaʔxʷtən 26 uɬ axáʔ t̓iʔ_kʷmiɬ kiʔ isk̓ʷúy
ixíʔ a n+k̓m=aqs iʔ t̓l=úlaʔxʷ+tn uɬ axáʔ t̓iʔ_kʷm̓iɬ kiʔ i -s+k̓ʷuy
that art point art plow and this at_once rel 1in -mother
the plow on the point. *Suddenly my mother*

sɬəx̌ʷp̓ám 27 uɬ ilíʔ {kən sic} kən iʔ l tk̓əmkn̓iɬxʷ uɬ iʔ kʷu cus
c+ɬx̌ʷp̓a+m uɬ ilíʔ kn iʔ l t+k̓m=kn̓=iɬxʷ uɬ iʔ kʷu cu -s
run_out_cisl and there 1kn art in outside and art 1obj tell -3erg
dashed out, *and I was there outside, and she said to me: 3:03*

28 xkínəm aɬqáqcaʔ 29 a cun ik̓líʔ k̓əl səntaʔɬululímtən {iə}
x+kin+m a -ɬqáqcaʔ a cu -n ik̓líʔ k̓l s+n+taʔ+ɬ+wl•wlím+tn
do_what 2in -older_brother intj tell -1erg there at forge
"What did your brother do?" *I said, "He was messing around*

c̓x̌əl·wís 30 kʷu cus xʷuyx {txə txʷət̓pmi ə·} xʷət̓pəncútx
c -ʔax̌l+lwis kʷu cu -s xʷuy -x xʷt̓p+ncut -x
hab -mill_about 1obj tell -3erg go -isimptv run -isimptv
in the shop." *She said to me, "Go, run,*

mi cuntxʷ 31 mi cxʷuyx xʷəsxʷúslx 32 a ixíʔ
mi cu -nt -xʷ mi c+xʷuy -x xʷs•xʷus+lx a ixíʔ
fut tell -nt -2erg fut come -isimptv hurry intj then
tell him, *'Come, hurry.'"* *I rushed*

isxʷət̓pəncút {a i} cun a[xáʔ] inqíck 33 way̓ kʷ
i -s -xʷt̓p+ncut cu -n axáʔ in -qick way̓ kʷ
1i -nom -run tell -1erg this 1in -older_brother well 2kn
and I said to my older brother: *"They*

scx̌əlítəmsəlx, xʷəsxʷúsəlx kʷ sxʷúyaʔx {a} 34 mat stim̓
sc -x̌lit+m -s -lx xʷs•xʷus+lx kʷ s -xʷuy -aʔx mat s+tim̓
pftv -summon -3i -pl hurry 2kn incp^ -go -^incp maybe something
are calling you, hurry, go. *They are*

sənq̓aʔílsxəlx 35 uɬ ixíʔ {ɬ} ɬckəxəntín {uɬ} uɬ
s -n+q̓aʔ=íls -x -lx uɬ ixíʔ ɬ+c+kx -nt -in uɬ
ipftv^ -concerned -^ipftv -pl and then follow_cisl_again -nt -1erg and
worried about something." *I followed him back,*

wíkən {iʔ iʔ t a} 36 kʷu ɬcənppílx {k} naʔɬ {iɬ} inqíck 37 uɬ ixíʔ
wik -n kʷu ɬ+c+n+p•pilx naʔɬ in -qick uɬ ixíʔ
see -1erg 4kn enter_cisl_again with 1in -older_brother and then
and I saw. *We went back in, I and my brother,* *and*

cúntəm t isk̓ʷúy 38 huy mʕan anwí ʕác̓ənt {a} kʷ ɬaʔ {s}
cu -nt -m t i -s+k̓ʷuy hoy mʕan anwí ʕac̓ -nt kʷ ɬaʔ
tell -nt -psv agInst 1in -mother well intj you look -nt 2kn when
my mother said to him: *"Now look, for your*

cənt̓it̓ínaʔ 39 uɬ axáʔ asqʷəsqʷsíʔ uɬ iʔ ksyum 40 uɬ cəm̓
c -n+t̓y•t̓í=naʔ uɬ axáʔ a -sqʷ+sqʷsiʔ uɬ iʔ k+s+yum uɬ cm̓
hab -disobedient and this 2in -son and art have_curse and maybe
stubborness *your son has the curse; 4:02* *and if*

anwí asck̓ʷúl̓ mi ɬ ƛ̓lal 41 {ay} uɬ axáʔ wíkən iʔ sk̓ʷək̓ʷíməlt
anwí a -sc -k̓ʷul̓ mi ɬ ƛ̓l•al uɬ axáʔ wik -n iʔ s+k̓ʷ•k̓ʷiy=m=lt
you 2i -pftv -do fut if dead and this see -1erg art baby
it dies, it's your doing." *And I saw the baby*

x̌íləm axáʔ iʔ ta ululím 42 kʷa ɬaʔ cxʔítiʔ ɬ kmáʕuʔsəs {i l} i
x̌il+m axáʔ iʔ t wl•wlim kʷa ɬaʔ c+xʔít+iʔ ɬ k+maʕ=w̓s -s i
do_like this art obl iron intj when at_first subord lay_across -3erg art
act like the iron *when he first lay it*

l sur̓ísəlp̓ 43 uɬ cʔix uɬ t̓əxʷ t̓iʔ q̓ʷaʕy, q̓ʷaʕy t̓əxʷ c̓kin̓
l s+wr̓=islp̓ uɬ c[ʔ]ix uɬ t̓xʷ t̓iʔ q̓ʷaʕy q̓ʷaʕy t̓xʷ c+ʔkin
on fire and get_warm and emph evid black black emph indef
on the fire. *It warms, and it's black,*

44 kʷaʔ c̓kin̓ {yay} t̓əxʷ {ɬ} ululím {lut̓a c} lut ɬaʔ {c} cʔix kcaʔxísxən
kʷaʔ c+ʔkin t̓xʷ wl•wlim lut ɬaʔ c[ʔ]ix k+caʔx=ísxn
intj indef evidently iron not when get_warm hot_iron
it's like the iron, it doesn't glow[1] *when it heats.*

45 uɬ {t̓iʔ} t̓iʔ_c̓x̌iɬ iʔ sʕác̓əc̓əs 46 way̓ uɬ axáʔ niʕíp {sc} c̓qʷaqʷ axáʔ
uɬ t̓iʔ_c+ʔx̌iɬ iʔ s+ʕac̓•c̓ -s way̓ uɬ axáʔ nyʕip c̓qʷ•aqʷ axáʔ
and just_like art looks -3in well and this always cry this
It looked just like it. *The child was crying*

iʔ sk̓ʷk̓ʷíməlt {oy u} 47 ixíʔ itlíʔ {ɬ} k̓ɬʔaysəncút axáʔ {iʔ} iʔ sk̓ʷək̓ʷíməlt
iʔ s+k̓ʷ•k̓ʷiy=m̓+l̓t ixíʔ itlíʔ k̓ɬ+ʔays+ncút axáʔ iʔ s+k̓ʷ•k̓ʷiy=m=lt
art child then from_there change this art baby
steadily. *The baby's looks*

iʔ sʕác̓əc̓əs 48 t̓iʔ kʷill··xʷ {a} aɬíʔ ilíʔ x̌íləm {kʷa i} axáʔ ululím ɬ
iʔ s+ʕac̓•c̓ -s t̓iʔ kʷil=lxʷ aɬíʔ ilíʔ x̌il+m axáʔ wl•wlim ɬ
art looks -3in evid red so there do_like this iron when
changed. *It turned red, acted like the iron when*

kcaʔxísxəns 49 uɬ t̓iʔ kʷill·· {iʔ skcaʔ} iʔ stx̌aláʕsxəns 50 ixíʔ uɬ
k+caʔx=ísxn -s uɬ t̓iʔ kʷil•l iʔ s+t+x̌al=ʕásxn -s ixíʔ uɬ
glow -3in and evid red art brightness -3in then and
it glows. 5:00 *It turned red, [with] its brightness.* *The*

ʔácqaʔ axáʔ iʔ sɬxʷəncúts iʔ sk̓ʷk̓ʷíməlt 51 uɬ ixíʔ cúntəm axáʔ
ʔácqaʔ axáʔ iʔ s+ɬxʷ+ncut -s iʔ s+k̓ʷ•k̓ʷiy=m̓=l̓t uɬ ixíʔ cu -nt -m axáʔ
go_out this art breath -3in art child and then tell -nt -psv this
baby's breath went out. *She said to*

inqíck 52 huhúy mʕan {kʷ ɬaʔ səc kʷ ɬayq} kʷ ɬaʔ cq̓iwɬtíɬən
in -qick hu+húy mʕan kʷ ɬaʔ c -q̓y=w̓=ɬtiɬn
1in -older_brother OK intj 2kn when hab -doubt
my brother: *"Now, see, you doubted.*

1 The *glow* notion is not in the Cv.

53 uɬ caʔkʷ kʷu níxlməntxʷ lut ksx̌íləms ksƛ̓lals axáʔ {asa}
uɬ caʔkʷ kʷu nixl+m -nt -xʷ lut ks -x̌il+m -s k+s -ƛ̓l•al -s axáʔ
and if 1obj listen_to -nt -2erg not futi -do_like -3i futi -dead -3i this
If you had listened to me this wouldn't have happened, your son wouldn't

sqʷəsqʷsíʔmp 54 uɬ anwí c̓x̌iɬ asck̓ʷúl̓ uɬ ƛ̓lal {iʔ} axáʔ iʔ
s+qʷs•qʷsiʔ -mp uɬ anwí c+ʔx̌iɬ a -sc -k̓ʷul̓ uɬ ƛ̓l•al axáʔ iʔ
son -5in and you like 2i -pftv -do and dead this art
be dead. *And it's like your fault that the baby*

sk̓ʷək̓ʷíməlt 55 uɬ lut aɬíʔ t̓ pútʔantxʷ uɬ ixíʔ ksyúmcnəm
s+k̓ʷ•k̓ʷiy=m=lt uɬ lut aɬíʔ t̓ pútaʔ -nt -xʷ uɬ ixíʔ k+s+yum=cn
baby and not because negfac respect -nt -2erg and then have_curse
is dead. *You didn't show respect for it and he got the curse."*

56 cúntəm uɬ ixíʔ {kɬ} aʔ kɬmrímstən 57 {s}cútəlx ixíʔ t̓xʷ sqilxʷ
cu -nt -m uɬ ixíʔ aʔ kɬ+mrim+st+n cut -lx ixíʔ t̓xʷ s+qilxʷ
tell -nt -psv and then art have_medicine say -pl that emph Indian
She said, "There is a remedy, *They call it the "Indian*

nc̓xʷíntəns 58 cut ixíʔ ńíńw̓iʔ lut ɬ qəɬnúntxʷ {ɬ aks} ɬ
n+c̓xʷi+n+tn[2] -s cut ixíʔ ńíńw̓iʔ lut ɬ qɬ -nu -nt -xʷ ɬ
enema -3in say then a_while not if able -manage -nt -2erg if
enema." *But if you cannot succeed in respecting*

akspútʔam iʔ l ʔapənkstásq̓ət 59 uɬ waẏ kʷ ksmrímstaʔx
a -ks -pútaʔ+m iʔ l ʔapn=kst=ásq̓t uɬ waẏ kʷ ks -mrim+st -aʔx
2i -futi -respect art for ten_days and yes 2kn incp^ -doctor -^incp
the ten days *you have to doctor yourself. 6:00*

60 axáʔ ńíńw̓iʔ {ɬ} iʔ l spíx̌əm 61 uɬ {axáʔ} axáʔ nc̓əxʷəntíxʷ {iʔ} iʔ l
axáʔ ńíńw̓iʔ iʔ l s+pix̌+m uɬ axáʔ n+c̓xʷ -nt -ixʷ iʔ l
this a_while art at hunting and this fill -nt -2erg art in
If in hunting, *pour water in a lard bucket,*

sənq̓ʷúc̓tən t̓əxʷ axáʔ iʔ l ɬəɬkápaʔ 62 uɬ ixíʔ kʷ klkʷínaʔ ixíʔ
s+n+q̓ʷuc+tn t̓xʷ axáʔ iʔ l ɬ•ɬkáp+aʔ uɬ ixíʔ kʷ k+lkʷ=ínaʔ ixíʔ
lard_bucket evidently this art in bucket_dim and then 2kn ste_back that
a little bucket. *Move back and*

t̓aʕpəntíxʷ kɬəx̌ʷm̓úsaʔ uɬ iʔ siwɬkʷ itíʔ c̓xʷaxʷ 63 uɬ ixíʔ
t̓aʕp -nt -ixʷ k+ɬx̌ʷ+m=úsaʔ uɬ iʔ siwɬ=kʷ itíʔ c̓xʷ•axʷ uɬ ixíʔ
shoot -nt -2erg hole_through and art water from_that spill and then
shoot a hole through it [so] the water will drain out, *and*

lut {ks} ksksyúmcəns asqʷəsqʷsíʔ 64 caʔkʷ iwáʔ ɬ t̓aʕpəntíxʷ
lut ks -k+s+yum=cn -s a -sqʷ+sqʷsiʔ caʔkʷ iwá ɬ t̓aʕp -nt -ixʷ
not futi have_curse -3i 2in -son if even if shoot -nt -2erg
your child won't have the curse. *Even if you shoot*

2 I cannot identify the n of c̓xʷin.

iʔ sƛ̓aʔcínəm {iʔ sƛ̓aʔ} 65 ia məɬk̓íyaʔs ɬ wíkəntxʷ ɬ c̓xʷaxʷ
iʔ s+ƛ̓aʔ=cín+m iʔ mɬk̓íyaʔ -s ɬ wik -nt -xʷ ɬ c̓xʷ•axʷ
art deer art blood -3in if see -nt -2erg subord spill
a deer *and see its blood spill,*

66 uɬ lut {əks} t̓ə kstríwyaʔms t̓ ksksyúmcən[s] 67 kəm̓
uɬ lut t̓ ks -tríwyaʔ+m -s t̓ ks -k+s+yum=cn -s km̓
and not negfac futi -react -3i negfac futi -curse -3i or
he won't react, won't fall under the curse. *Or*

axáʔ iʔ sənkɬc̓aʔsqáx̌aʔ ixíʔ nk̓amtíw̓sməntxʷ {uɬ} 68 uɬ ixíʔ
axáʔ iʔ s+n+kɬ+c̓aʔ=sqáx̌aʔ ixíʔ n+k+ʔam=t=íw̓s+m -nt -xʷ uɬ ixíʔ
this art horse that ride -nt -2erg and then
when you ride a horse *and*

qí··xʷəntxʷ uɬ ks{kʷal̓}tx̌ʷúsəsaʔx 69 uɬ ixíʔ skʷalt {uɬ ixíʔ} ixíʔ
qixʷ -nt -xʷ uɬ ks -t+x̌ʷus•s -aʔx uɬ ixíʔ s+kʷal̓+t ixíʔ
drive -nt -2erg and incpˆ -foam -ˆincp and then sweat that
you push him hard and he sweats til he foams, *scoop the sweat*

utəntíxʷ iʔ t ankílx 70 uɬ ixíʔ míƛ̓əntxʷ axáʔ
wt -nt -ixʷ iʔ t an -kilx uɬ ixíʔ miƛ̓ -nt -xʷ axáʔ
put_down -nt -2erg art agInst 2in -hand and then paint -nt -2erg this
with your hand 7:08 *and rub it*

ask̓əɬk̓mílt t̓əxʷ astk̓ʷəƛ̓k̓ʷƛ̓ús ask̓ʷƛ̓ús 71 uɬ ixíʔ nixʷ lut
a -s+k̓ɬ+k̓m=ilt t̓xʷ a -s+t+k̓ʷƛ̓•k̓ʷƛ̓=us a -s+k̓ʷƛ̓=us uɬ ixíʔ nixʷ lut
2in -chest emph 2in -eyes 2in -face and then also not
on your chest, on your eyes, on your face, *and this way too*

ksksyúmcəns asqʷəsqʷsíʔ 72 ixíʔ {isc} naʔnaʔq̓nwísən[3] axáʔ la
ks k+s+yum=cn -s a -sqʷ+sqʷsiʔ ixíʔ naʔ•naʔq̓+nwís -n axáʔ l
futi have_curse -3i 2in -son that witness -1erg this in
your child won't have the curse." *That's what I saw*

cxʔítiʔ l isk̓ʷək̓ʷíməlt kiʔ ixíʔ cwík̓ən 73 uɬ aɬíʔ pnicíʔ iʔ
c+xʔít+iʔ l i -s+k̓ʷ•k̓ʷiy=m=lt kiʔ ixíʔ c -wik -n uɬ aɬíʔ pn+icíʔ iʔ
at_first in 1in -baby rel that act -see -1erg and so at_that_time art
in my early childhood, that's what I saw. *At that time*

sqilxʷ uɬ way̓ cnun·xʷínaʔmsts {iʔ} ixíʔ a nk̓ʷúl̓mən {ixíʔ s}
s+qilxʷ uɬ way̓ c -n+wn•n•xʷ=ínaʔ+m -st -s ixíʔ a n+k̓ʷul̓+mn
Indian and yes custˆ -believe -ˆcust -3erg that art custom
the Indians believed in these ways.

74 uɬ náx̌əmɬ ʕapnáʔ sic iʔ kʷu sck̓ʷul̓l̓ 75 lut_swit t̓a
uɬ nax̌mɬ ʕapnáʔ sic iʔ kʷu sc -k̓ʷul̓•l̓ lut_swit t̓
and but now new art 4kn pftv -born nobody negfac
But now this generation, *nobody*

3 Unclear form.

cnun·xʷína?msts ixí? uɬ{lut} lut t'a cksyúmcən
c -n+wn•n•xʷ=ína?+m -st -s ixí? uɬ lut t' c-+k+syum=cn
cust^ -believe -^cust -3erg then and not negfac hab -curse
believes it, there is no curse.

76 {ɬa?ks ɬa··} ɬa? ck'ʷəl'l'ílt lut t'a cpət?ásq'ət
ɬa? c -k'ʷl'•l'=ilt lut t' c-pt?=asq't
when hab -have_baby not negfac hab -respect_days
When they have a child they don't respect the days.
{That's about just the end of that.} 8:00

Partnership butchering

1 way̓ ixíʔ axáʔ iʔ caʔkʷ cus [t]a nqílxʷcən t̓aʕpám t
way̓ ixíʔ axáʔ iʔ caʔkʷ cu -s t n+qilxʷ=cn t̓aʕpá+m t
well that this art as tell -3erg agInst Indian_language shoot obj_itr
Well, this, as they say in Indian, shooting

sƛ̓aʔcínəm 2 uɬ ixíʔ c̓iqʷs 3 ixíʔ uɬ nək̓ní··k̓s a k̓əɬník̓əs {iʔ}
s+ƛ̓aʔ=cín+m uɬ ixíʔ c̓iqʷ -s ixíʔ uɬ nk̓•nik̓ -s a k̓ɬ+nik̓
deer and then butcher -3erg then and cut -3erg art cut_out
deer... *They skin it,* *then they cut it.*

4 iʔ sciʔíkst uɬ iʔ sc̓uʔxán 5 uɬ axáʔ{iʔ} iʔ ck̓iɬp k̓la stxmníw̓s
iʔ s+cʔ=ikst uɬ iʔ s+c̓w̓=xan uɬ axáʔ iʔ ck̓=iɬp k̓l s+t+xmn=iw̓s
art front_leg and art animal_hind_leg and this art rib to both_sides
They cut off the front foot, and the feet, *and the ribs on both sides,*

6 ixíʔ uɬ kmix_k̓əm iʔ ʔásx̌əm {ixíʔ a} 7 uɬ axáʔ iʔ k̓əspán 8 uɬ
ixíʔ uɬ kmix_k̓m iʔ ʔasx̌m uɬ axáʔ iʔ k̓span uɬ
that and only art back and this art nape_of_neck and
and only the backbone, *and the nape of the neck.* *And*

ixíʔ uɬ kʷ ɬaʔ ksl̓əx̌l̓áx̌t ixíʔ uɬ pəx̌ʷmɬtíxʷəlx 9 kəm̓ t̓iʔ
ixíʔ uɬ kʷ ɬaʔ k+s+l̓x̌•l̓ax̌+t ixíʔ uɬ px̌ʷm -ɬt -ixʷ -lx km̓ t̓iʔ
that and 2kn if have_friends that and distribute -ɬt -2erg -pl or evid
when you have friends you pass it around to them; *or if you*

knaqs asl̓áx̌t 10 uɬ ixíʔ xʷíc̓əɬtxʷ {iʔ} iʔ ʔásx̌əm uɬ axáʔ iʔ
k=naqs a -s+l̓ax̌+t uɬ ixíʔ xʷic̓ -ɬt -xʷ iʔ ʔasx̌m uɬ axáʔ iʔ
one_person 2in -partner and then give -ɬt -2erg art back and this art
have only one partner, *you give him the backbone and*

sc̓uʔxán 11 uɬ nsək̓ʷtínk ck̓iɬp uɬ axáʔ sc̓ʔikst
s+c̓w̓=xan uɬ n+s+k̓ʷt=ink ck̓=iɬp uɬ axáʔ s+cʔ=ikst
animal_hind_leg and half rib and this front_leg
one foot, *and half the ribs and the hind quarter, 1:05*

12 ixíʔ uɬ ixíʔ sənq̓ʷɬtáqs asl̓áx̌t {i uɬ náx̌əm} 13 uɬ ʔasíl
ixíʔ uɬ ixíʔ s+n+q̓ʷɬ+t=aqs a -s+l̓ax̌+t uɬ ʔasíl
then and that share_one_carries 2in -partner and two
and that's your partner's share. *And if*

aksct̓áʕp uɬ t̓k̓ʷɬtíxʷ naqs sƛ̓aʔcínəm asl̓áx̌t 14 uɬ
a -ksc -t̓aʕp uɬ t̓k̓ʷ -ɬt -ixʷ naqs s+ƛ̓aʔ=cín+m a -s+l̓ax̌+t uɬ
2i -pperf -shoot and put_down -ɬt -2erg one deer 2in -partner and
you shoot two, you put down one deer for your partner, *and*

t̓iʔ naqs kʷintxʷ, ixíʔ uɬ {ps} p ɬxʷuy
t̓iʔ naqs kʷin -t -xʷ ixíʔ uɬ p ɬ+xʷuy
evid one take -nt -2erg then and 5kn go_back
you take one, and then you both go back. 1:25

Pete concluded with this summary, in English:

"See, what I say, in the early days, well, when you kill a deer, and you are hunting and you got a partner, well, if you kill only one deer, well you butcher it, cut [the] front shoulder, and the ham, that is [the] hind quarter, and then the ribs, a whole one side {indec} the back bone, same with the other side. Well, here the neck and the head, that's separate. But here the back bone, that's separate, it's got more meat on the back bone. Well, you give that to your partner, the back bone, and the shoulder, and one side of the ribs, and the ham. So, well, then you take the neck and the rib and the shoulder and the ham. So you give your partner the biggest, the best part of the meat. But if you kill two, well, you give your partner one whole deer, and then you keep one whole deer, 'cause that's partnership when you're hunting, that's the Indian ways, how they hunt, that's the way I was told, so, well, I do the same. So that's all."

The attainment of provisions

1[1] waẏ q̓sápiʔ iʔ sqilxʷ ixíʔ iʔ sʔíɬəns iʔ sƛ̓aʔcínəm iʔ stəxʷcəncút,
waẏ q̓sápiʔ iʔ s+qilxʷ ixíʔ iʔ s+ʔiɬn -s iʔ s+ƛ̓aʔ=cín+m iʔ s+txʷ=cn+cut
well long_ago art Indian that art food -3in art deer art food
Long ago the Indians' food was deer, things they hunt,

iʔ skəkáʕkaʔ 2 uɬ ixíʔ {kən c kən c} kən cƛ̓x̌ap kən
iʔ s+k•kʕá•kaʔ uɬ ixíʔ kn c -ƛ̓x̌a+p kn
art animal and then 1kn hab -grow_sg 1kn
fowl. *Then I grew up and gained*

ctaʔxʷspəx̌páx̌t 3 uɬ ixíʔ kən ckəxstín axáʔ
c -taʔxʷ+s+px̌•páx̌+t uɬ ixíʔ kn c -kx -st -in axáʔ
hab -get_senses and then 1kn custˆ -follow -ˆcust -1erg this
some knowledge, *and I followed my oldest brother when*

inqíck kʷu ɬaʔ cpíx̌əm 4 mat tk̓ʷínk̓ʷənx iʔ t
in -qick kʷu ɬaʔ c -pix̌+m mat t+k̓ʷin•k̓ʷn+x iʔ t
1in -older_brother 4kn when hab -hunt maybe indef_number art obl
we went hunting. *A group at*

sk̓aʔyám {indec} 5 k̓aʔyám uɬ ixíʔ x̌əw̓əntísəlx {iʔ} iʔ sɬiqʷ[2] 6 ixíʔ uɬ {tə}
s+k̓aʔẏá+m k̓aʔẏá+m uɬ ixíʔ x̌w̓ -nt -is -lx iʔ s+ɬiqʷ ixíʔ uɬ
fall_hunt fall_hunt and then dry -nt -3erg -pl art meat then and
fall time, *they fall hunt and they dry the meat; (1:00)* *and when*

qʷayílsəlx {iʔ} iʔ t sɬiqʷ put waẏ kstaʔmínaʔlx {məɬ} 7 məɬ ixíʔ
qʷay=íls -lx iʔ t s+ɬiqʷ put waẏ k+s+taʔm=ínaʔ -lx mɬ ixíʔ
enough -pl art prttv meat just all have_spring -pl and then
they have enough meat to last them the winter, *then*

ɬc̓imx iʔ sqilxʷ ɬciyáʕpəlx 8 məɬ ixíʔ kʷúmsəlx aɬíʔ
ɬ+c+ʔimx iʔ s+qilxʷ ɬ+c+yaʕ+p -lx mɬ ixíʔ kʷum -s -lx aɬíʔ
move_back_cisl art person arrive_cisl_again -pl and then store -3erg -pl because
they move back home, they get back. *And they store it, they have*

ksənkʷúmcəntən iʔ t x̌əw̓áw̓ 9 məɬ {k̓ə} k̓a nwist iʔ la c̓əlc̓ál məɬ
k+s+n+kʷum=cn+tn iʔ t x̌w̓•aw̓ mɬ k̓ n+wis+t iʔ l c̓l•c̓al mɬ
have_a_storage_place art obl dried and to high art in trees and
a storing place for dry stuff. *They make a platform up high*

tx̌əlíw̓sməlx 10 məɬ ilíʔ kcwínaʔsəlx {məɬ kc} kʷúmsəlx ilíʔ iʔ
t+x̌l=iw̓s+m -lx mɬ ilíʔ k+cw=ínaʔ -s -lx kʷum -s -lx ilíʔ iʔ
make_platform -pl and there cover -3erg -pl store -3erg -pl there art
in the trees, *then they cover it, and they store the*

1 Pete says: "I don't know how to start it. Don't make no difference any time of the year?" "No."

2 Pete interjects: "Well, I'm telling now what they're doing. They dry the meat when they go fall hunting. See, them days they didn't have no freezer storage. Well, they dry it and that way it keeps for the winter. So, that's what I'm telling."

sɬiqʷ 11 uɬ lut {s} iʔ t skəkáʕkaʔ
s+ɬiqʷ uɬ lut iʔ t s+k•kʕá•kaʔ km̓ iʔ t stim̓
meat and not art agInst animal or art agInst whatever
meat. (2:02) And no birds or anything can steal it

ksnáq̓ʷəmɬtməlx 12 ixíʔ iʔ cawts q̓sápiʔ iʔ sqilxʷ 13 uɬ
ks -naq̓ʷ+m -ɬt -m -lx ixíʔ iʔ cawt -s q̓sápiʔ iʔ s+qilxʷ uɬ
futt^ -steal_from -ɬt -psv -pl that art doing -3in long_ago art Indian and
from them. That's the way the Indians did it long ago. As

axáʔm incá way̓ kən {c} ƛ̓x̌ap 14 uɬ way̓ mipnúsəlx {i i¨}
axáʔ+m in+cá way̓ kn ƛ̓x̌a+p uɬ way̓ my+p -nu -s -lx
this I yes 1kn grow_sg and yes learn -manage -3erg -pl
for myself, I have grown. Then they found out, they got

taʔxʷsənkʷúmcəntən 15 axáʔ iʔ t suʔw̓íkiʔst iʔ t suyápix {i} iʔ
taʔxʷ+s+n+kʷum=cn+tn axáʔ iʔ t s+ʔw̓=íkiʔ+st iʔ t s+wyapy+x iʔ
get_storage_device this art agInst electricity art agInst white_person art
a storage device, a white people's storage device

sənkʷúmcəntəns 16 caʔkʷ cus iʔ ta nuyápixcən *iʔ[3] deep freeze*
s+n+kʷum=cn+tn -s caʔkʷ cu -s iʔ t n+wyap+x=cn iʔ
storage_place -3in as tell -3erg art agInst say_in_English art
with electricity, what they call in English "deep freezer."

17 ixíʔ {uɬ} uɬ niʕ̓íp kən {kən c} cpíx̌əm 18 aɬíʔ ck̓ɬənk̓ahk̓ʷíp
ixíʔ uɬ nyʕ̓ip kn c -pix̌+m aɬíʔ c -k̓ɬ+n+k̓ahk̓ʷ=íp
then and always 1kn hab -hunt because hab -open
I have always hunted: (3:01) deer and bird [hunting]

iʔ sƛ̓aʔcínəm iʔ skəkáʕkaʔ axáʔ iʔ l sqəlxʷúlaʔxʷ iʔ kʷu x̌əl sqilxʷ
iʔ s+ƛ̓aʔ=cín+m iʔ s+k•kʕá•kaʔ axáʔ iʔ l s+qlxʷ=úlaʔxʷ iʔ kʷu x̌l s+qilxʷ
art deer art bird this art on s+qlxʷ=úlaʔxʷ iʔ kʷu for Indian
is open on the Reservation to us Indians.

19 uɬ niʕ̓íp kən cpíx̌əm {lani} kən ksɬiqʷ iʔ t sƛ̓aʔcínəm {i la}
uɬ nyʕ̓ip kn c -pix̌+m kn k+s+ɬiqʷ iʔ t s+ƛ̓aʔ=cín+m
and always 1kn hab -hunt 1kn have_meat art prttv deer
I have always hunted, and I have deer meat.

20 xiʔmíx kən c̓əspcín məɬ kən píx̌əm məɬ ixíʔ kən
xiʔ+míx kn c̓s+p=cin mɬ kn pix̌+m mɬ ixíʔ kn
whatever 1kn run_out_of_food and 1kn hunt and then 1kn
Anytime I run out I hunt and I get

ɬtaʔxʷɬqlíɬc̓aʔ 21 uɬ ʕapnáʔ náx̌əmɬ way̓ uɬ kn {kən} knmqin
ɬ+taʔxʷ+ɬ+ql=íɬc̓aʔ uɬ ʕapnáʔ nax̌mɬ way̓ uɬ kn knm=qin
get_fresh_meat_again and now however yes and 1kn blind
fresh meat again. And now I am going blind,

3 Pete continues in English: "deep freeze, ain't it? That's what you all put the meat away."

22 waẏ uɬ lut {ťa c} ťa cwíkstən inktk̓ústən 23 uɬ lut
waẏ uɬ lut ť c -wik -st -n in -k+tk̓=us+tn uɬ lut
well and not negfac custˆ -see -ˆcust -1erg 1in -gun_sights and not
and I can't see my sights, *and*

xkínəm mi kən cpíx̌əm 24 uɬ taʔlí·· x̌əx̌əstmámən
x+kin+m mi kn c -pix̌+m uɬ taʔlíʔ x̌•x̌s+t+m+amn
do_what fut 1kn hab -hunt and much talk_funny
I can't hunt. *Hunting is*

cx̌əstmístən {iʔ} iʔ spíx̌əm iʔ l istətwít 25 iwá ťəxʷ
c -x̌s+t+mi -st -n iʔ s+pix̌+m iʔ l i -s+t•tẇit iwá ťxʷ
custˆ -like -ˆcust -1erg art hunting art in 1in -boyhood even evidently
very enjoyable, I enjoyed it in my youth, *even if*

sʔayʔáyx̌ʷts[4] kʷu cənkxám 26 kəṁ iʔ l sənkɬċaʔsqáx̌aʔ kʷu
s -ʔay•ʔáyx̌ʷt -s kʷu c -n+kxa+m kṁ iʔ l s+n+kɬ+ċaʔ=sqáx̌aʔ kʷu
nom -tired_pl -3i 4kn hab -go_on_foot or art on horse 4kn
it was tiring and we had to walk. *Or we rode on*

stkʷəllíẇ[s] 27 kəṁ axáʔ iʔ l sʔistk {i l} xʷʔit iʔ l smik̓ʷt
s -t+kʷl•l=iẇs kṁ axáʔ iʔ l s+ʔis=tk xʷʔi+t iʔ l s+mik̓ʷt
hab -pl_on_horseback or this art in winter much art in snow_on_ground
horses, (4:00) *or in the winter when there is lots of snow*

kʷu cyríwaʔxnəm 28 uɬ náx̌əmɬ axáʔ iʔ l sɬəɬťám axáʔ {isc}
kʷu c -yr=íwaʔ+xn+m uɬ nax̌mɬ axáʔ iʔ l s+ɬ•ɬťa+m axáʔ
4kn hab -wear_snowshoes and but this art about fishing this
we snowshoed. *But about fishing,*

inqíck taʔlí ctəxʷcəncút iʔ t qáqxʷəlx 29 uɬ incá
in -qick taʔlíʔ c -txʷ=cn+cut iʔ t qa•qxʷ+lx uɬ in+cá
1in -older_brother very_much hab -get_food art obj_itr fish and I
my oldest brother he got a lot of fish, *but I*

náx̌əmɬ lut ťa cmistín iʔ sɬəɬťám, waẏ kmix iʔ spíx̌əm
nax̌mɬ lut ť c -my -st -in iʔ s+ɬ•ɬťa+m waẏ kmix iʔ s+pix̌+m
but not negfac custˆ -know -ˆcust -1erg art fishing yes only art hunting
don't know fishing—only hunting.

30 uɬ nixʷ q̇sápiʔ ixíʔ nixʷ iʔ caʔkʷ cúsəlx {iʔ} iʔ sqəlwíċaʔ
uɬ nixʷ q̇sápiʔ ixíʔ nixʷ iʔ caʔkʷ cu -s -lx iʔ s+qlw=íċaʔ
and also long_ago that also art as tell -3erg -pl art raw_hide
Also long ago, as they call it, "raw hides,"

31 ixíʔ {nʕac} nʕacúsməlx məɬ tumístmsəlx iʔ síṗiʔ 32 uɬ ixíʔ a
ixíʔ n+ʕac=ús+m -lx mɬ tw+mist+m -s -lx iʔ síṗiʔ uɬ ixíʔ a
then trap -pl and sell -3erg -pl art hide and that art
they trapped and they sold the hides. *That's*

4 This construction is not understood.

scústsəlx sqəl'wíc̓aʔ 33 uɬ ixíʔ incá náx̌əmɬ lut ixíʔ t̓ə {t̓ə}
s -cu -st -s -lx s+qlw=íc̓aʔ uɬ ixíʔ in+cá nax̌mɬ lut ixíʔ t̓
cust^ -tell -^cust -3erg -pl raw_hide and that I but not that negfac
what they call "raw hides." *I did not practice*

ck̓ʷúl'[st]ən ixíʔ iʔ snʕacúsəm iʔ {iʔ iʔ} t sqəl'wíc̓aʔ
c -k̓ʷul' -st -n ixíʔ iʔ s+n+ʕac=ús+m iʔ t s+qlw=íc̓aʔ
cust^ -practice -^cust -1erg that art trapping art obl raw_hide
trapping [for] raw hides, (5:05)

34 axáʔ {i} a scústsəlx {i} iʔ stunx {ixíʔ i} ixíʔ iʔ stənxíc̓aʔ
axáʔ a s -cu -st -s -lx iʔ s+tunx ixíʔ iʔ s+tnx=íc̓aʔ
this art cust^ -tell -^cust -3erg -pl art beaver that art beaver_hide
what they call "beaver," "beaver hides."

35 ixíʔ kʷa iʔ sípiʔs a ctumístəmstsəlx kəm̓ axáʔ iʔ
ixíʔ kʷa iʔ sípiʔ -s a c -tw+mist+m -st -s -lx km̓ axáʔ iʔ
that intj art hide -3in art cust^ -sell -^cust -3erg -pl or this art
These are the skins they sell, or the weasel,

p̓íp̓q̓əs ixíʔ sqláw 36 uɬ axáʔ {i} iʔ skəmxíst, iʔ səmx̌íkən lut put aʔ
p̓i•p̓q̓s ixíʔ s+qlaw uɬ axáʔ iʔ s+kmxist iʔ s+mx̌=ikn lut put aʔ
weasel that money and this art bear art grizzly not just art
that's money. *Brown bear, grizzly, their hides don't have*

ksənʔíys iʔ sípiʔ[s] 37 way̓ kmix axáʔ iʔ p̓íp̓q̓əs uɬ {iʔ i} iʔ stunx iʔ
k+s+n+ʔiys iʔ sípiʔ -s way̓ kmix axáʔ iʔ p̓i•p̓q̓s uɬ iʔ s+tunx iʔ
have_price art hide -3in yes only this art weasel and art beaver art
a good price, *only the skins of the weasel and*

sípiʔs 38 uɬ axáʔ t̓əxʷ xʷʔúsəm t̓əxʷ nixʷ itíʔ {is is} iʔ
sípiʔ -s uɬ axáʔ t̓xʷ xʷʔ=us+m t̓xʷ nixʷ itíʔ iʔ
hide -3in and this emph many_kinds emph more from_that art
the beaver [do]. *There are more animals,*

skəkáʕkaʔ iʔ tmixʷ 39 uɬ aɬíʔ lut way̓ t cun t̓a
s+k•kʕá•kaʔ iʔ tmixʷ uɬ aɬíʔ lut way̓ t cu -n t̓
animal art creature and so not yes obl tell -1erg negfac
creatures, *and, like I said, I don't*

cmistín iʔ sənʕacúsəm 40 uɬ lut t̓a
c -my -st -in iʔ s+n+ʕac=ús+m uɬ lut t̓
cust^ -know -^cust -1erg art trapping and not negfac
know trapping, (6:00) *I don't*

cmimistín 41 way̓ kmix ixíʔ iʔ skəmxíst uɬ iʔ səmx̌íkən ixíʔ
c -my•my -st -in way̓ kmix ixíʔ iʔ s+kmxist uɬ iʔ s+mx̌=ikn ixíʔ
cust^ -know_pl -^cust -1erg well only that art bear and art grizzly that
know them, *I have seen only the bear,*

aʔ cwíkstən uɬ axáʔ iʔ sƛ̓aʔcínəm
aʔ c -wik -st -n uɬ iʔ s+ƛ̓aʔ=cín+m
intj cust^ -see -^cust -1erg and art deer
and the grizzly, and the deer. (6:23) {That's about all I can remember.}

The rainy hunting trip

1 waẏ {ʔəxʷ kʷiks tixʷ} itlíʔ kən kscaptíkʷlaʔx axáʔ iʔ sqilxʷ iʔ
waẏ itlíʔ kn ks -captíkʷl -aʔx axáʔ iʔ s+qilxʷ iʔ
well from_there 1kn incp^ -tell_stories -^incp this art Indian art
I'm going to tell an Indian

cawts 2 axáʔ caʔkʷ cus ya nqílxʷcən axáʔ {kʷus} kʷu
cawt -s axáʔ caʔkʷ cu -s ya n+qilxʷ=cn axáʔ kʷu
doing -3in this as tell -3erg art Indian_language this 4kn
story. *Like they say in Indian, we North Halfs,*

sənʕíckstx, kʷu sx̌ʷʔiɬpx 3 i iḱlíʔ isənḱʷúl̓l̓tən {i} 4 ixíʔ uɬ {ḱaʔ}
s+n+ʕic=kst+x kʷu s+x̌ʷʔ=iɬp=x i iḱlíʔ i -s+n+ḱʷul̓•l̓+tn ixíʔ uɬ
Lakes 4kn Colville intj there 1in -birthplace then and
we Colvilles, *that's where I was born.* *When fall*

ḱáẏilx waẏ ixíʔ sḱaẏámsəlx 5 uɬ mat tḱʷínkʷənx {iʔ iə}
ḱaẏ•y+lx waẏ ixíʔ s -ḱaẏá+m -s -lx uɬ mat t+ḱʷin•kʷn+x
fall_comes yes then nom -fall_hunt -3i -pl and maybe indef_number
came they went fall hunting, *I don't know how many.*

6 uɬ ksmamʔíməlx, uɬ axáʔ knaqs lut {t̓a kɬ} t̓a kɬtkɬmilxʷ
uɬ k+s+ma•mʔím -lx uɬ axáʔ k=naqs lut t̓ kɬ+tkɬ+m=ílxʷ
and have_women -pl and this one_person not negfac have_woman
They had their wives along, and there's one that doesn't have a woman.

7 ixíʔ ċúmstsəlx t q̓əẏpyáwt 8 waẏ t̓qlímxəlx, axáʔ
ixíʔ c -ʔum -st -s -lx t q̓ẏpyawt waẏ t̓ql=imx -lx axáʔ
that cust^ -call -^cust -3erg -pl obj_tr m's_name well settle -pl this
They call him "Freckled." *They settled down, they*

nḱəwílxəlx {t s·} t sənʔaw·tíɬxʷtən 9 iḱlí··ʔ uɬ {ka} t̓qlímxəlx 10 ixíʔ
n=ḱw+ilx -lx t s+n+ʔaw·t=iɬxʷ+tn iḱlíʔ uɬ t̓ql=imx -lx ixíʔ
go_upstream -pl obl river to_there and settle -pl that
went up the sənʔaw·tíɬxʷtən river. (1:04) *They went up and settled down.* *That*

iʔ sənḱaʔytán ixíʔ iʔ cwix 11 waẏ t̓qlímxəlx 12 waẏ
iʔ s+n+ḱaẏ+tán ixíʔ iʔ cwix waẏ t̓ql=imx -lx waẏ
art fall_hunting_place that art creek yes settle -pl well
creek is the fall hunting place. *They settled down,* *they*

wiʔsḱʷəl̓ḱʷúl̓ɬxʷməlx, wiʔsxʷúɬxʷməlx {waẏ} 13 waẏ kícəntməlx
wẏ+s+ḱʷl̓•ḱʷul̓=ɬxʷ+m -lx wẏ+sxʷ=ɬxʷ+m -lx waẏ kic -nt -m -lx
finish_fixing_house -pl set_tipi -pl well reach_st/sb -nt -psv -pl
got done fixing their lodges, their tipis. *The rain got there,*

iʔ t sq̓it tq̓tínaʔlx 14 waẏ mat uɬ ḱʷənxásq̓ət sq̓its {uɬ uɬ ixíʔ}
iʔ t s+q̓it t+q̓t=ínaʔ -lx waẏ mat uɬ ḱʷn+x=asq̓t s -q̓it -s
art agInst rain caught_in_rain -pl well maybe and a_few_days nom -rain -3i
it poured on them. *I don't know how many days it rained.*

15 uɬ aɬíʔ lut xkínməlx mi píx̌{l}məlx 16 cəm̓ ɬáʕtʼəlx {kəm̓} kəm̓
uɬ aɬíʔ lut x+kin+m -lx mi pix̌+m -lx cm̓ ɬaʕtʼ -lx km̓
and so not do_what -pl fut hunt -pl maybe wet -pl or
They can't do anything about hunting; they'll either get wet

nsľípəlx axáʔ i l sq̓it 17 uɬ way̓ tʼiʔ ƛ̓ílmiʔstəlx 18 way̓ ixíʔ
n+sľi+p -lx axáʔ i l s+q̓it uɬ way̓ tʼiʔ ƛ̓íl+miʔst -lx way̓ ixíʔ
lost -pl this art in rain and yes evid stay_put -pl well then
or get lost in the rain. They stayed put, and they

sənʔawqənwíxʷsəlx 19 scútsəlx huhúy, huhúy swit mi
s -n+ʔaw=qn+wíxʷ -s -lx s -cut -s -lx hu+húy hu+húy swit mi
nom -challenge_recipr -3i -pl nom -say -3i -pl OK OK who fut
started challenging one another. They said, "Now who is going to stop

x̌aʔnúxʷəm 20 pna cmiscút {i l} i l sx̌aʔnúxʷəm i
x̌aʔn=úxʷ+m pnaʔ c -my+scut i l s+x̌aʔn=úxʷ+m iʔ
stop_weather maybe hab -know_how art about stop_weather art
the weather? (2:01) Maybe somebody knows how to stop the weather,

cmiscút {i l} l ksuy̓ásq̓əts 21 way̓ {cúsəlx a} cútəlx axáʔ ya
c l ks -wy̓=ásq̓t -s way̓ cut -lx axáʔ ya
hab in futi -stop_rain -3i well say -pl this art
to end the rain." The ones that had wives

ksmamʔím 22 way̓ kʷ qʷəňcənmíst 23 way̓ lut kʷu tʼa
k+s+ma•mʔím way̓ kʷ qʷň=cn+mist way̓ lut kʷu tʼ
have_women well 2kn pitiful_thing well not 4kn negfac
said, "You are talking pitifully. We don't know

cmiscút kʷu ɬ ksx̌aʔnúxʷəms 24 way̓ cúsəlx
c -my+scut kʷu ɬ ks -x̌aʔ=núxʷ+m -s way̓ cu -s -lx
hab -know_how 4kn subord futi^4 -stop_weather -futi^4 well tell -3erg -pl
anything about stopping the weather." They said to the one

axáʔ lut ya kɬtkəɬmílxʷ 25 huhúy anwí, q̓əy̓pyáwt, ixíʔ aɬíʔ iʔ skʷists
axáʔ lut ya kɬ+tkɬ+m=ílxʷ hu+húy anwí q̓y̓pyawt ixíʔ aɬíʔ iʔ s+kʷist -s
this not art have_woman OK you m's_name that so art name -3in
that didn't have a woman: "You do it, q̓y̓pyawt," (because that's his name).

26 ə cut, way̓, way̓ ňíňw̓iʔ kən x̌aʔnúxʷəm 27 uɬ náx̌əmɬ lut kʷu
ə cut way̓ way̓ ňíňw̓iʔ kn x̌aʔn=úxʷ+m uɬ nax̌mɬ lut kʷu
intj say OK OK a_while 1kn stop_weather and but not 1obj
He said, "Ok, I'll stop the rain. But don't let me

ksc̓əľpmíntp 28 uɬ {ňiňw̓i kʷu} ňíňw̓iʔ nluʕ̓ʷúsəntp iʔ p
ks -c̓l+p+mi -nt -p uɬ ňíňw̓iʔ n+lʕ̓ʷ=us -nt -p iʔ p
futt^ -let_spook -nt -5erg and a_while match -nt -5erg art 5kʷu
spook you; if you do what I'm telling you,

ikscúnəm, {i kʷu ks} iʔ kʷu kstx̌ilstp {iʔ i kʷu ks} 29 uł waẏ
i -ks -cun+m iʔ kʷu ks -t+x̌il[1] -st -p uł waẏ
1i -futi -tell art 1obj futt^ -do_a_certain_way -st -5erg and yes
what [I'll ask] you to do to me, *if it fits,*

ńíńẇiʔ cənluʕ̓ʷús wiʔásq̓ət 30 uł náx̌əmł {kʷu} lut kʷu nluʕ̓ʷúłtp
ńíńẇiʔ c -n+lʕ̓ʷ=us wẏ=ásq̓t uł nax̌mł lut kʷu n+lʕ̓ʷ=u -łt -p
a_while hab -match stop_rain and but not 1obj match -łt -5erg
it will stop raining. *But if you don't do what I'm telling you,*

iʔ cúłmən {i} iʔ kʷu ksk̓ʷúl̓əntp 31 uł ałíʔ lut t̓ xkínəm
iʔ cu -łm -n iʔ kʷu ks -k̓ʷul̓ -nt -p uł ałíʔ lut t̓ x+kin+m
art tell -5obj -1erg art 1obj futt^ -do -nt -5erg and so not negfac do_what
what you have to do to me, (3:03) *then it won't*

mi {kən} wiʔásq̓ət 32 a, cúsəlx waẏ {cut waẏ} 33 cut waẏ
mi wẏ=ásq̓t a cu -s -lx waẏ cut waẏ
fut stop_rain intj tell -3erg -pl OK say well
stop raining." *They said "Ok."* *He said:*

inx̌mínk iʔ tkəłmílxʷ {ixíʔiks} itíʔ mi {kʷu} kʷu ʔacʔackńíkstəmiʔs
in -x̌m=ink iʔ tkłmilxʷ itíʔ mi kʷu ʔac+ʔac=kn=íkst+mi -s
1in -want art woman from_that fut 1obj play -3erg
"Ok, but I'll have to have a woman that plays with me.

34 uł axáʔ ńíńẇiʔ kən txʷəlscút 35 axáʔ c̓úmstsəlx {t s} t
uł axáʔ ńíńẇiʔ kn txʷ=lscut axáʔ c -ʔum -st -s -lx t
and this a_while 1kn get_ready this cust^ -call -^cust -3erg -pl obj_tr
I'll be getting things ready. *They call those "Oregon Grape"*

sc̓ərsíłməlx {i} 36 ixíʔ uł ałíʔ {kłə} t̓əxʷ ksx̌ʷəyx̌ʷáyt c̓x̌iłt
s+c̓rs=iłmlx ixíʔ uł ałíʔ t̓xʷ k+s+x̌ʷy•x̌ʷay+t c+ʔx̌ił+t
Oregon_grape that and so evidently have_sharpness like
bushes, *those that have thorns just like rose bushes*

skʷkʷʔíłp kłƛ̓qʷúmən 37 uł ixíʔ ńíńẇiʔ tixʷn 38 məł
s+kʷ•kʷʔ=iłp kł+ƛ̓qʷu+mn uł ixíʔ ńíńẇiʔ tixʷ -n mł
rose_bush have_thorns and that a_while obtain -1erg and
have thorns. *I'll get them* *and*

ńíńẇiʔ {kʕacʕac} kʕacʕacíc̓aʔn {məł} 39 uł ńíńẇiʔ ixíʔ cixs axáʔ i
ńíńẇiʔ k+ʕac•ʕac=íc̓aʔ -n uł ńíńẇiʔ ixíʔ cix -s axáʔ iʔ
a_while tie_in_bundle -1erg and a_while that warm -3erg this art
I'll tie them in a bundle, *and she will heat them up*

l surísəlp̓ 40 uł ałíʔ ckurkńíłxʷəlx scx̌əẇəncútxəlx
l s+wr̓+islp̓ uł ałíʔ c -k+wr̓=kń=iłxʷ -lx sc -x̌ẇ+ncut -x -lx
on fire and so hab -fire_outside_house -pl ipftvp^ -dry_self -^ipftvp -pl
in the fire." *(Their fire is outside the tipi, they're drying themselves.)*

1 I have posited a root √ʔx̌l. The ʔ is not present in this stem.

41 uɬ n̓ín̓w̓iʔ axáʔ kən wiʔs{k}ktməlxʷəncút 42 n̓ín̓w̓iʔ mi kʷu
uɬ n̓ín̓w̓iʔ axáʔ kn wy̓+s+k+tm=lxʷ+ncut n̓ín̓w̓iʔ mi kʷu
and a_while this 1kn finish_stripping a_while fut 1obj
"And I'll take all my clothes off, *and she will whip me [with the*

ksp̓íc̓aʔs 43 uɬ n̓ín̓w̓iʔ {kən} swit_aɬíʔ axáʔ ta stʔikʷ uɬ sic
k+sp̓=íc̓aʔ -s uɬ n̓ín̓w̓iʔ swit_aɬíʔ axáʔ t s+t[ʔ]ikʷ uɬ sic
whip -3erg and a_while in_fact this obl spark and then
bundle] (4:04) *when it has sparks, then*

axáʔ {iʔ təs} iʔ t ƛ̓əqʷƛ̓qʷúmən 44 uɬ aɬíʔ cəm̓ axáʔ aɬíʔ
axáʔ iʔ t ƛ̓qʷ•ƛ̓qʷu+mn uɬ aɬíʔ cm̓ axáʔ aɬíʔ
this art agInst thorns and because maybe this because
with the thorns. *And I'll be naked,*

cəm̓ kən ktmalxʷ uɬ cəm̓ q̓íltmən 45 way̓ uɬ cəm̓ t̓iʔ {kən}
cm̓ kn k+tma=lxʷ uɬ cm̓ q̓il+t+m -n way̓ uɬ cm̓ t̓iʔ
maybe 1kn naked and maybe hurt -1erg well and maybe evid
and I'll be hurting. *I'll jump from one side*

kɬənusəlxílsmən 46 kɬnusəlxíw̓sən axáʔ iʔ
kɬ+n+ws+lx=ils+m -n kɬ+n+ws+lx=iw̓s -n axáʔ iʔ
jump_from_one_side_to_another -1erg jump_back_and_forth -1erg this art
of the fire to the other, *I'll jump over*

sur̓ísəlp̓ 47 uɬ n̓ín̓w̓iʔ kən txlak niʕ̓íp kʷu ksp̓íc̓aʔs 48 way̓
s+wr̓=islp̓ uɬ n̓ín̓w̓iʔ kn t+xlak n+yʕ=ip kʷu k+sp̓=íc̓aʔ -s way̓
fire and a_while 1kn turn_around always 1obj whip -3erg yes
the fire. *And if I go around she always has to whip me.* *That's*

n̓ín̓w̓iʔ ixíʔ uɬ wiʔásq̓ət 49 lut {kʷu ks} kʷu ksənqʷən̓mí[ntp]
n̓ín̓w̓iʔ ixíʔ uɬ wy̓=ásq̓t lut kʷu ks -n+qʷn̓+mi -nt -p
a_while then and stop_rain not 1obj futtˆ -feel_sorry_for -nt -5erg
when it'll stop raining. *Don't pity me."*

50 a· cúsəlx way̓ 51 way̓ nʔawqənwíxʷ axáʔ iʔ smamʔím 52 axáʔ
a cu -s -lx way̓ way̓ n+ʔaw=qn+wíxʷ axáʔ iʔ s+ma•mʔím axáʔ
intj tell -3erg -pl OK well challenge_recipr this art women this
They said "Ok." *The women started challenging one another.* *Then*

knaqs tkɬmilxʷ cut way̓ way̓ n̓ t incá 53 way̓ scúts way̓
k=naqs tkɬ+m=ilxʷ cut way̓ way̓ n̓ t in+cá way̓ s -cut -s way̓
one_person woman say OK OK now agInst I well nom -say -3i OK
one woman said, "Ok, I'll do it." *She said, "Ok, ok,*

way̓ n̓ t incá 54 cúsəlx way̓ way̓ {way̓ axáʔ ixíʔ skic} c̓səlxʷəncúts
way̓ n̓ t in+cá cu -s -lx way̓ way̓ c̓s=lxʷ+ncut
OK now agInst I tell -3erg -pl OK well strip
I'll do it." *[Tape ends] They said "Ok." q̓y̓pyawt took his*

axáʔ q̓iʔpyáwt 55 uɬ aɬíʔ way ilíʔ wiʔstqəntís axáʔ {i i} iʔ
axáʔ q̓y̓pyawt uɬ aɬíʔ way̓ ilíʔ wy̓+s+tq -nt -is axáʔ iʔ
this m's_name and so finish there finish_place -nt -3erg this art
clothes off. (5:00) *She already had put the oregon grape there*

sċərsíɬməlx 56 waẏ {kʷus} wiʔskċsəlxʷəncút 57 uɬ axáʔ iʔ təkɬmílxʷ
s+ċrs=iɬmlx waẏ wẏ+s+k+ċs=lxʷ+ncut uɬ axáʔ iʔ tkɬmilxʷ
Oregon_grape yes finish_stripping and this art woman
[on the fire], *he already had his clothes off,* and the woman had

waẏ wiʔsktqúsəs axáʔ 58 uɬ ixíʔ tʔikʷ
waẏ wẏ+s+k+tq=us -s axáʔ uɬ ixíʔ t[ʔ]ikʷ
finish finish_putting_on_fire -3erg this and then spark
already put [the Oregon Grapes] on the fire. *It's sparking,*

ksulpmíxaʔx ixíʔ 59 ɬċíẇsəntəm axáʔ q̓iʔpyáwt iʔ
ks -wl+p -míx+aʔx ixíʔ ɬċ=iẇs -nt -m axáʔ q̓ẏpyawt iʔ
incp^ -burn -^incp that whip_back -nt -psv this m's_name art
ready to burn. *She hit q̓ẏpyawt on the back, ih,*

niq̓ísk̓itəm nwísəlx 60 a ɬt̓it̓íʔstəm {wa} kɬnusəlxílx axáʔ
n+yq̓==ísk̓iʔt+m n+wis+lx a ɬt̓•ít̓=iʔst+m kɬ+n+ws+lx+ilx axáʔ
grunt jump intj jump jump_over this
he groaned, jumped up. *She followed him right up, and he jumped back and forth*

iʔ t curísəlp̓ 61 uɬ t̓i_niʕíp̓ ɬt̓it̓íʔstəm
iʔ t s+wr̓=islp̓ uɬ t̓iʔ_n+yʕ=ip ɬt̓•ít̓=iʔst+m
art obl fire and continuously jump
over the fire. (1:00 – Tape Part 2) *She kept following him and whipping*

ksp̓íċaʔntəm 62 níkxna nyq̓iq̓ísk̓itəms 63 waẏ ah, {axáʔ} axáʔ
k+sp̓=íċaʔ -nt -m níkxnaʔ n+yq̓•yq̓=ísk̓it+m -s waẏ ah axáʔ
whip -nt -psv goodness groan -3erg well intj this
him on the back. *He just groaned.* *They all laughed,*

yaʕyáʕt ʕʷəyʕʷəyncútəlx aɬíʔ uɬ x̌əx̌stmámən {x̌ílməlx} 64 x̌íləm uɬ t
yaʕ•yáʕ+t ʕʷy•ʕʷy+ncut -lx aɬíʔ uɬ x̌•x̌s+t+m+amn x̌il+m uɬ t
all laugh -pl because and talk_funny do_like and obl
because they looked funny, *they went on*

sccmíltəlx iʔ cáwtsəlx 65 waẏ uẏásq̓ət, waẏ ixíʔ
s -c•cm̓=il't -lx iʔ caw+t -s -lx waẏ wẏ=asq̓t waẏ ixíʔ
hab -children -pl art doing -3in -pl well stop_rain well then
like little kids. *Well, it quit raining, and*

səcpíx̌əmsəlx[2] 66 axáʔ iʔ sk̓aẏámsəlx x̌əsx̌əsnúxʷəlx
s c+pix̌+m -s -lx axáʔ iʔ s -k̓aẏá+m -s -lx x̌s•x̌s=nuxʷ -lx
nom -hunt -3i -pl this art nom -fall_hunt -3i -pl good_weather -pl
they went hunting. *They had good days and they fall hunted.*

67 ah, ixíʔ naqs a nɬíptmən 68 naɬcəcám axáʔ t̓iʔ q̓ypyawt {tis}
ah ixíʔ naqs a n+ɬiptm -n naɬc•c•ám axáʔ t̓iʔ q̓ẏpyawt
intj that one art forget -1erg forget this evid m's_name
Ah, I forgot one thing: *I forgot that q̓ẏpyawt*

2 The form səcpíx̌əmsəlx requires an analysis of c+pix̌ *cisl+hunt.*

ťiʔ_kmix x̌minks {axáʔ} knaqs iʔ tkɬmilxʷ ixíʔ puilmíxʷəm 69 ixíʔ lut
ťiʔ_kmix x̌m=ink -s k=naqs iʔ tkɬ+m=ilxʷ ixíʔ pu=yl=mixʷ+m ixíʔ lut
only like -3in one_person art woman that chief's_wife that not
liked only one woman, the chief's wife. *She*

ťa cqʷəlqʷílt {a} c̓x̌iɬt a cnaʕm 70 lut ťa cʕʷəyncút kəm̓
ť c -qʷl•qʷil+t c+ʔx̌iɬ+t a c -naʕm lut ť c -ʕʷy+ncut km̓
negfac hab -talk like art hab deaf_mute not negfac hab -laugh or
never talks, she's like deaf and dumb, *she never laughs or talks*

ťa cqʷəlqʷəltíɬən 71 uɬ ixíʔ ksmipnúys a mat
ť c -qʷl•qʷl+t=iɬn uɬ ixíʔ ks -my+p -nu -y̓ -s a mat
negfac hab -talk and then futtˆ -learn -manage -nt -3erg intj maybe
to anybody. *He wanted to find out if she could*

ha lut qɬnus aɬ ksqʷəlqʷílts {inaud} 72 kiʔ ixíʔ ilíʔ
haʔ lut qɬ -nu -s aɬ ks -qʷl•qʷil+t -s kiʔ ixíʔ ilíʔ
inter not able -manage -3erg compl futi -talk -3i rel that there
talk or not. *That's why he got*

yx̌aʔnúxʷəxʷ 73 way̓ ʕʷəyncút ixíʔ iʔ tkəɬmílxʷ {uɬ} 74 a·· nák̓ʷəm
? way̓ ʕʷy+ncut ixíʔ iʔ tkɬmilxʷ a nak̓ʷ+m
? well laugh that art woman intj evid
himself whipped. (2:06) *Well, the woman laughed.* *She wasn't*

way̓ {c} lut {ətət} ťa cənáʕmt 75 way̓ kʷu kʕʷəyncútəms
way̓ lut ť c -naʕm+t way̓ kʷu k+ʕʷy+ncut+m -s
yes not negfac hab -deaf_mute yes 1obj laugh_at -3erg
deaf and dumb. *"She laughed at me."*

76 way̓ ixíʔ wiʔásq̓ət, way̓ ixíʔ nc̓ayxʷápəlqs
way̓ ixíʔ wy̓=asq̓t way̓ ixíʔ n+c̓ayxʷ=áp=lqs
well then stop_rain well that end_of_story
Well, it quit raining. It's the end of the story, that's all.(2:28)

Black Pig

1 {a} kʷlíˑˑwt aʔ nx̌ʷənx̌ʷíẇs, miʔsqílxʷəlx 2 ksqʷəsqʷsíʔlx, t̓i
kʷl=iwt aʔ nx̌ʷ•nx̌ʷ=iẇs s+my+s+qilxʷ -lx k+s+qʷs•qʷsiʔ -lx t̓iʔ
live art married_couple important_people -pl have_son -pl evid
A couple lived there, important people. *They had a son,*

knəqsəltílaʔt 3 ixíʔ i skʷəstíltsəlx q̓ʷʕay kʷukʷús 4 ilmíxʷəm uł
k=nqs=lt=ílaʔt ixíʔ iʔ s+kʷst=ilt -s -lx q̓ʷʕay kʷu•kʷús yl=mixʷ+m uł
only_child that art child's_name -3in -pl black pig chief and
an only child. *They had named that child "Black Pig."* *He was a chief.*

lut_itíʔ x̌əẇáp iʔ smaʔmʔím 5 itíʔ sənsucənmístx
lut_itíʔ x̌ẇa+p iʔ s+maʔ•mʔím itíʔ s -n+sw=cn+mist -x
good_about_one dry_mouth art women from_that ipftvˆ -propose -ˆipftv
And the women are just about dry mouthed. *They propose to*

k̓əl q̓ʷʕay kʷukʷús, ʔax̌lásq̓ət 6 huˑˑy, knaqs tkəłmílxʷ uł ixíʔ
k̓l q̓ʷʕay kʷu•kʷús ʔax̌l=ásq̓t huy k=naqs tkɬ+m=ilxʷ uł ixíʔ
to black pig every_day intj one_person woman and then
Black Pig every day. *His parents consented to*

xʔínaʔmsəlx iʔ t ƛ̓ax̌əx̌ƛ̓x̌áp[s] 7 cúsəlx "way̓"
xʔ=ínaʔ+m -s -lx iʔ t ƛ̓ax̌•x̌•ƛ̓x̌á+p -s cu -s -lx way̓
consent -3erg -pl art agInst elders -3in tell -3erg -pl OK
this one woman. *They told her "Ok." 1:01*

8 cúntəm axáʔ iʔ {təs} t q̓ʷʕay kʷukʷús axáʔ iʔ tkəłmílxʷ, 9 "way̓
cu -nt -m axáʔ iʔ t q̓ʷʕay kʷu•kʷús axáʔ iʔ tkɬ+m=ilxʷ way̓
tell -nt -psv this art agInst black pig this art woman OK
Black Pig said to this woman: *"Well,*

mat aspuʔús kʷu kscm̓ríma?x 10 way̓ kʷu
mat a -s+puʔ=ús kʷu ksc -mrim -aʔx way̓ kʷu
maybe 2in -heart 4kn futPerfknˆ -marry -ˆfurPerfkn well 1obj
I guess it's your wish that we marry. *You see me,*

wíkəntxʷ axáʔ kən q̓ʷʕay kʷukʷús 11 way̓ kʷu aksənk̓ʷəłmərˑím
wik -nt -xʷ axáʔ kn q̓ʷʕay kʷu•kʷús way̓ kʷu a -k -s+nk̓ʷ+ɬ+mr•r•im
see -nt -2erg this 1kn black pig well 1kʷu 2i -to_be -spouse
I'm just a black pig, *and then you want to marry me.*

12 uł lut haʔ kʷu aksċaʔxmínəm" 13 uł cut a[xáʔ] iʔ tkəłmílxʷ
uł lut haʔ kʷu a -k+s -ċaʔx+mín -m uł cut axáʔ iʔ tkɬ+m=ilxʷ
and not inter 1kʷu 2i- futi -ashamed -apsv and say this art woman
Aren't you going to be ashamed of me?" *And the woman said:*

14 "lut, lut {iksċaˑ} kʷ t̓ iksċaʔxmínəm, kʷ inx̌mínk"
lut lut kʷ t̓ i -ks -ċaʔx+mín -m kʷ in -x̌m=ink
not not 2kʷu negfac 1i -futtˆ -ashamed -apsv 2kʷu 1in -like
"No, I'm not going to be ashamed of you, I like you."

15 waẏ, cúntəm, “waẏ, kʷaʔ lut aksxʷúsəskaʔ 16 ṅíṅẇiʔ pulx,
waẏ cu -nt -m waẏ kʷaʔ lut a -ks -xʷús•s+kaʔ ṅíṅẇiʔ pul+x
well tell -nt -psv well intj not 2i -futi -be_in_hurry a_while camp
“Well,” he told her, “Don’t get in a hurry. At bed time

akskˀəłnəqsáċaʔ 17 ixíʔ mi_sic kʷu cmərím, kʷu asx̌ílwiʔ”
a -ks -kˀł+nqs=áċaʔ ixíʔ mi_sic kʷu c -mrim kʷu a -s+x̌ílwiʔ
2i -futi -sleep_alone then then 4kn hab -marry 4kn 2in -husband
you’ll sleep by yourself. Then we’ll get married, and you’ll have a husband.”

18 “a··, waẏ 19 waẏ t̓i_lut, uł ixíʔ sxʷərrápəps axáʔ iʔ
a waẏ waẏ t̓iʔ_lut uł ixíʔ s -xʷr•ra+p -s axáʔ iʔ
intj OK well in_no_time and then nom -nervous -3i this art
“Ah, ok.” 2:00 It wasn’t long, the woman got

tkəłmílxʷ 20 “uł haʔ sċkinx a[xáʔ] iksqəlˀtmíxʷ {a} ki
tkł+m=ilxʷ uł haʔ sc -ʔkin -x axáʔ i -k -s+qlˀt+mixʷ kiʔ
woman and inter ipftvp^ -indef -^ipftvp this 1i -to_be -husband rel
anxious. “What’s wrong with my husband-to-be, the one I am

a ckˀəłq̓əmstín” 21 uł ałíʔ ckˀəłtáp axáʔ iʔ
a c -kˀł+q̓m -st -in uł ałíʔ c -kˀł+tap axáʔ iʔ
art cust^ -wish_for -^cust -1erg and so hab -behind_curtain this art
wishing for.” The man was staying behind

sqəlˀtmíxʷ 22 [n]t̓a i[xíʔ] kˀəłckʷəntís, 23 axáʔ t̓i kˀaw axáʔ {iʔ iʔ}
s+qlˀt=mixʷ nt̓a ixíʔ kˀł+ckʷ -nt -is axáʔ t̓iʔ kˀaw axáʔ
man intj then pull_away -nt -3erg this evid gone this
a curtain. She pulled it open. Her husband-to-be

iʔ ksqəlˀtmíxʷs q̓ʷʕay kʷukʷús 24 waẏ t̓i iʔ l qʷúłlaʔxʷ
iʔ k -s+qltmixʷ -s q̓ʷʕay kʷu•kʷús waẏ t̓iʔ iʔ l qʷúł=laʔxʷ
art to_be -man -3i black pig well evid art in dust
Black Pig was gone. The woman was left

ki {łc k łtə} ʔakswíx axáʔ iʔ tkəłmílxʷ 25 aláʔ ʔímxəlx axáʔ {iʔ} ia
kiʔ ʔaks+wíx axáʔ iʔ tkł+m=ilxʷ aláʔ ʔim+x -lx axáʔ iʔ
rel stand this art woman here move -pl this art
standing in the dust. The couple had moved away

nəx̌ʷnx̌ʷíẇs naʔł sqʷsíʔsəlx, naʔł q̓ʷʕay kʷukʷús sqʷsíʔsəlx,
nx̌ʷ•nx̌ʷ=iẇs naʔł s+qʷsiʔ -s -lx naʔł q̓ʷʕay kʷu•kʷús s+qʷsiʔ -s -lx
married_couple with son -3in -pl with black pig son -3in -pl
with their son Black Pig.

26 waẏ ixíʔ sċqʷaqʷs axáʔ iʔ tkəłmílxʷ 27 ċqʷa··qʷ, ċqʷa··qʷ
waẏ ixíʔ s -ċqʷ•aqʷ -s axáʔ iʔ tkł+m=ilxʷ ċqʷ•aqʷ ċqʷ•aqʷ
yes that nom -cry -3i this art woman cry cry
That woman started to cry. She cried and cried.

28 waẏ uł ixíʔ sxʷists iʔ t təmxʷúlaʔxʷ 29 ƛ̓aʔƛ̓aʔntís iʔ
waẏ uł ixíʔ s -xʷist -s iʔ t tmxʷ=úlaʔxʷ ƛ̓aʔ•ƛ̓aʔ -nt -is iʔ
well and then nom -walk -3i art obl country look_for -nt -3erg art
She started to walk the country. 3:03 She looked for

ksqəl̓tmíxʷs 30 ki·· uɬ kicx {iʔl} iʔ l scwíxəx, t̓əxʷ
k -s+qltmixʷ -s ki uɬ kic+x iʔ l sc -wix -x t̓xʷ
to_be -man -3i intj and arrive art in ipftvp^ -live -^ipftvp evidently
her man. *She went, and she got to where some people live,*

iʔ l tawn, sílxʷaʔ tawn, 31 uɬ náx̌əmɬ lut {t̓a cmiɬ t̓ aks} t̓a
iʔ l tawn sílxʷaʔ tawn uɬ nax̌mɬ lut t̓
art in town big town and so not negfac
it's a town, a big town, *but I don't know*

cmiɬtín iʔ skʷəstúlaʔxʷ[s] 32 waẏ ilíʔ iʔ l
c -my -ɬt -in iʔ s+kʷst=úlaʔxʷ -s waẏ ilíʔ iʔ l
cust^ -know -ɬt -1erg art name_of_place -3in well there art in
the name of the town. *There was*

tk̓k̓əmqsíɬaʔxʷ, ilíʔ {k} cẇíẇaʔx, pəptwínaʔxʷ 33 waẏ ilíʔ ƛ̓lap
t+k̓•k̓m=qs=íɬaʔxʷ ilíʔ c -ẇi•ẇaʔx p•ptwínaʔxʷ waẏ ilíʔ ƛ̓la+p
small_house_by_itself there hab -live_dim old_woman well there stop
a little house all by itself, a little building, an old lady['s]. *She stopped there.*

34 waẏ uɬ aɬíʔ xʷʔásq̓ət 35 waẏ uɬ iʔ skt̓əɬɬíċaʔs iʔ
waẏ uɬ aɬíʔ xʷʔ=asq̓t waẏ uɬ iʔ s+k+t̓ɬ•ɬ=iċaʔ -s iʔ
well and because many_days yes and art dirty_body -3in art
And because it had been quite a few days *her body was dirty and the clothes*

stk̓síċaʔs axáʔ {iʔ} iʔ l sck̓ʷəl̓kstmísts {uɬ a iɬ} 36 waẏ ixíʔ
s+t+k̓s=iċaʔ -s l iʔ l sc -k̓ʷl̓+kst+mist -s waẏ ixíʔ
bad_appearance -3in in art in pftv -doll_up -3i well then
she had outfitted herself with looked bad. *Then*

cúntəm axáʔ iʔ t xaʔxʔíts 37 ixíʔ uɬ aɬíʔ
cu -nt -m axáʔ iʔ t xaʔ•xʔít -s ixíʔ uɬ aɬíʔ
tell -nt -psv this art agInst older_relative -3in then and so
her grandmother[1] said to her, *(because she had started*

k̓ampla?ncútməntəm sənʔímaʔt, 38 {t} "waẏ kʷu kícəntxʷ,
k+ʔam=plaʔ+ncút+m -nt -m s+n+ʔím+aʔ+t waẏ kʷu kic -nt -xʷ
call_by_a_name -nt -psv grandchild yes 1obj reach_st/sb -nt -2erg
calling her granddaughter): *"Well, you have come to see me,*

sənʔímaʔt, 39 waẏ aláʔ {kʷu} kʷu ntkʷílsəntxʷ 40 waẏ
s+n+ʔím+aʔ+t waẏ aláʔ kʷu n+t+kʷil=s -nt -xʷ waẏ
grandchild yes here 1obj keep_company -nt -2erg well
granddaughter. *Keep company here with me. 4:01* *In*

ʔayxáxaʔ kscmərímaʔx yaʔ ilmíxʷəmtət q̓ʷʕay kʷukʷús
ʔayxáxaʔ ksc -mrim -aʔx iʔ yl=mixʷ+m -tt q̓ʷʕay kʷu•kʷús
a_while futPerfkn^ -marry -^furPerfkn art chief -4in black pig
a while our head boss Black Pig is going to get married.

1 "Grandomther" is generic reference (and address) term for an elderly woman.

41 uɬ ixíʔ scx̌lítəmsəlx iʔ sqílxʷ 42 t̓əxʷ aɬíʔ axáʔ
uɬ ixíʔ sc -x̌lit+m -s -lx iʔ s+qilxʷ t̓xʷ aɬíʔ axáʔ
and then pftv -summon -3i -pl art person evidently because this
They are summoning the people, *because he's*

ilmíxʷəm 43 uɬ aɬíʔ ilmíxʷəm təl̓ yaʕɬcwílxʷtən 44 aláʔ
yl=mixʷ+m uɬ aɬíʔ yl=mixʷ+m tl̓ yaʕ+ɬ+cw=ílxʷ+tn aláʔ
chief and because chief from entire_world here
a boss, *he's the boss of all the world.* *They'll*

kscyaʕ̓míxaʔx 45 ixíʔ {ks} ksc̓awsq̓ʷəy̓məncútaʔxəlx
ksc -yaʕ̓ -míx+aʔx ixíʔ ks -c+ʔaw+s+q̓ʷy̓+mncút -aʔx -lx
futPerfkn^ -gather ^futPerfkn then incp^ -come_to_dance -^incp -pl
gather here; *they are going to come and dance*

iʔ l kscmríms" 46 a··, cut "way̓ {t̓xʷ}" 47 way̓ ixíʔ
iʔ l ksc -mrim -s a cut way̓ way̓ ixíʔ
art in futPerfi -marry -3i intj say OK well then
at his wedding." *"Ah," she said "Ok."* *Then*

cáʕʷlxstəm iʔ t xaʔxʔíts 48 way̓ x̌əcmstím
caʕʷ+lx -st -m iʔ t xaʔ•xʔít -s way̓ x̌c+m -st -im
bathe -caus -psv art agInst older_relative -3in yes get_so_ready -caus -psv
the grandmother bathed her, *she got her ready*

t kstətəm̓tím̓s, k̓ʷúl̓kstməntəm 49 way̓ əct̓íxʷləm tkɬmílxʷ,
t k -s+t•tm̓•tim̓ -s k̓ʷul̓=kst+m -nt -m way̓ c -t̓ixʷl+m tkɬ+m=ílxʷ
obj_tr to_be -clothes -3i doll_up -nt -psv yes hab -different woman
with nice clothes, she dolled her up. *And the girl looked different,*

swiʔnúmtx 50 {ə uɬ cúntəm axáʔ iʔt} ixíʔ uɬ sxʷúysəlx iʔ k̓əl
s+wy̓+numt=x ixíʔ uɬ s -xʷuy -s -lx iʔ k̓l
handsome then and nom -go -3i -pl art to
good looking. 5:00 *So they went to the boss's*

silmxʷíɬxʷ 51 cúntəm iʔ t xaʔxʔíts, "way̓ axáʔ kʷu
s+yl=mxʷ=iɬxʷ cu -nt -m iʔ t xaʔ•xʔít -s way̓ axáʔ kʷu
chief's_house tell -nt -psv art agInst older_relative -3in OK this 4kn
house. *Her grandmother said to her, "Now we*

nppilx 52 n̓ín̓w̓iʔ wíkənts t q̓ʷʕay kʷukʷús, ixíʔ
n+p•pilx n̓ín̓w̓iʔ wik -nt -s t q̓ʷʕay kʷu•kʷús ixíʔ
enter_pl a_while see -nt -3e2obj agInst black pig then
go in. *Black Pig will see you. He's the one*

kscmərímaʔx 53 uɬ way̓ aɬíʔ k̓ʷul̓l̓ t sqilxʷ 54 uɬ
ksc -marim -aʔx uɬ way̓ aɬíʔ k̓ʷul̓•l̓ t s+qilxʷ uɬ
futPerfkn^ -marry -^furPerfkn and yes so turn_into obl person and
who's getting married, *he has turned into a human.*[2] *He'll*

2 Probably to be interpreted as a parenthetical remark.

ṅíṅẇiʔ x̌lítənts p q̓ʷəy̓məncút 55 uɬ ṅíṅẇiʔ uɬ cəṁ
ṅíṅẇiʔ x̌lit -nt -s p q̓ʷy̓+mncut uɬ ṅíṅẇiʔ uɬ cṁ
a_while summon -nt -3e2obj 5kn dance and a_while and maybe
ask you to dance and you'll dance, *and you'll be*

aksx̌əsx̌síkst {aks} 56 uɬ aɬíʔ axáʔ wíkənts taʔlíʔ kʷ swiʔnúmtx
a -ks -x̌s•x̌s=ikst uɬ aɬíʔ axáʔ wik -nt -s taʔlíʔ kʷ s+wy̓+numt=x
2i -futi -good_at and so this see -nt -3e2obj very_much 2kn handsome
a good dancer. *He'll see that you are very beautiful.*

57 kʷ miɬswiʔnúmtx kiʔ təl̓ ksənk̓ʷəɬmərríms 58 uɬ axáʔ kʷ
kʷ my+ɬ+s+wy̓+numt=x kiʔ tl̓ k -s+nk̓ʷ+ɬ+mr•r•im -s uɬ axáʔ kʷ
2kn more_beautiful rel from to_be -spouse -3i and this 2kn
You are more beautiful than the one he's about to marry. *And if when*

ɬ q̓ʷəy̓məncút kʷ x̌əsx̌síkst 59 uɬ lútiʔ ksənp̓əƛ̓músc iʔ
ɬ q̓ʷy̓+mncut kʷ x̌s•x̌s=ikst uɬ lút+i ks -n+p̓ƛ̓+m=us -c iʔ
if dance 2kn be_good_at and before futi -end -3i art
you dance you dance well, *before the dance is over,*

sq̓ʷəy̓məncút, {mi kʷ} mi kʷ məlx̌aʔstq̓əlq̓əlxʷúsxən 60 mi cuntxʷ, húmaʔ
s+q̓ʷy̓+mncut mi kʷ mlx̌aʔ+s+t+q̓l•q̓lxʷ=us=xn mi cu -nt -xʷ húmaʔ
dance fut 2kn pretend_to_trip fut tell -nt -2erg exhort
pretend you trip. 6:03 *Say to him,*

ilíʔ kʷu ɬuníkstmənt[xʷ], kʷu ƛ̓lap, kʷu ɬuníkstməntp,
ilíʔ kʷu ɬwn=ikst+m -nt -xʷ kʷu ƛ̓la+p kʷu ɬwn=ikst+m -nt -p
there 1obj let_go_of -nt -2erg 1obj stop 1obj let_go_of -nt -5erg
"Stop, let me go.

61 {xa isks} kən s]kləxʷpxənmíx"[3] 62 ixíʔ ṅíṅẇiʔ
kn s -k+lxʷ+p=xn -mix ixíʔ ṅíṅẇiʔ
1kn ipftv^ -hurt_foot -^ipftv then a_while
I have hurt my foot." *Then*

ɬuníkstməntəm, 63 məɬ ixíʔ {s} asɬəx̌ʷp̓ám 64 uɬ {a} kʷ tk̓ʷəƛ̓pxán
ɬwn=ikst+m -nt -m mɬ ixíʔ a -s -ɬx̌ʷp̓a+m uɬ kʷ t+k̓ʷƛ̓+p=xan
let_go_of -nt -psv and then 2i -intt -run_out and 2kn shoe_off
he'll let you go, *and you'll run out.* *Your shoe'll come off.*

65 uɬ náx̌əmɬ lut i akskƛ̓əlpmínəm, məɬ ixíʔ uɬ kʷ ɬcxʷuy
uɬ nax̌mɬ lut iʔ a -ks -k+ƛ̓l+p+min+m mɬ ixíʔ uɬ kʷ ɬ+c+xʷuy
and but not art 2i -futi -stop and then and 2kn come_again
But don't stop for that, come back home.

66 uɬ ixíʔ ṅíṅẇiʔ k̓əɬʔíysəs q̓ʷʕay kʷukʷús iʔ spuʔúsc 67 cəṁ
uɬ ixíʔ ṅíṅẇiʔ k̓ɬ+ʔiys -s q̓ʷʕay kʷu•kʷús iʔ s+puʔ=ús -c cṁ
and then a_while change -3erg black pig art heart -3in maybe
And that's when Black Pig will change his mind. *His*

3 The expected root here is √ɬxʷ

iʔ nx̌mínktəns uɬ k̓əl anwí, anwí ɬənq̓əmscínmənts 68 anwí
iʔ n+x̌m=ink+tn -s uɬ k̓l anwí anwí ɬ+n+q̓m=s=cin+m -nt -s anwí
art love -3in and to you you get_stuck_on_again -nt -3e2obj you
love'll go to you, he'll get stuck on you again, *you'll*

kʷ kɬtkəɬmílxʷs 69 uɬ ixíʔ ṅíṅw̓iʔ cəṁ cut 70 cus iʔ sqilxʷ
kʷ kɬ -tkɬ+m=ilxʷ -s uɬ ixíʔ ṅíṅw̓iʔ cṁ cut cu -s iʔ s+qilxʷ
2kn to_be-woman -3i and then a_while maybe say tell -3erg art person
be his woman. *And he'll say,* *he'll tell*

axáʔ iʔ syaʕ̓ʕ̓míx təl̓ yaʕ̓ɬcwílxʷtən 71 "way̓
axáʔ iʔ s -yaʕ̓•ʕ̓ -míx tl̓ yaʕ+ɬ+cw=ílxʷ+tn way̓
this art ipftv^ -be_gathered -^ipftv from whole_world yes
the people gathered here from all over: *"I've*

ɬk̓əɬʔíysən, way̓ lut ʕapnáʔ ikscmərím 72 {a} pna {i}
ɬ+k̓ɬ+ʔiys -n way̓ lut ʕapnáʔ i -ksc -mrim pnaʔ
change_mind_again -1erg yes not now 1i -futPerfi -marry maybe
changed my mind, I'm not going to get married now. *Maybe*

ṅíṅw̓iʔ x̌lap nkʷəkʷʔác, pútiʔ kən səck̓əɬpaʔx̌míx" 73 uɬ ixíʔ
ṅíṅw̓iʔ x̌la+p n+kʷ•kʷʔac pút+iʔ kn sc -k̓ɬ+paʔx̌ -mix uɬ ixíʔ
a_while tomorrow dark still 1kn ipftvp^ -think_about -^ipftvp and then
tomorrow night, I'm still studying it." 7:04 *Because*

ṅíṅw̓iʔ aɬíʔ ckʷískʷəsts ixíʔ iʔ q̓aʔxán 74 uɬ ixíʔ t̓i
ṅíṅw̓iʔ aɬíʔ c -kʷis•kʷs -t -s ixíʔ iʔ q̓aʔ=xán uɬ ixíʔ t̓iʔ
a_while because cust^ -hold_on_to -st -3erg that art shoe and then evid
he would still be holding the shoe. *And just as soon as*

ṅíṅw̓iʔ np̓əƛ̓mús 75 məɬ ixíʔ sx̌əltsqílxʷs q̓ʷʕay kʷukʷús 76 məɬ
ṅíṅw̓iʔ n+p̓ƛ̓+m=us mɬ ixíʔ s -x̌lt+s+qilxʷ -s q̓ʷʕay kʷu•kʷús mɬ
a_while end and then nom -ask_people -3i black pig and
[the dance] is over, *Black Pig will start asking the people.* *He'll*

ixíʔ cúntməlx axáʔ iʔ smamʔím, 77 "way̓ ṅíṅw̓iʔ swit mi ləʕ̓ʷəntís
ixíʔ cu -nt -m -lx axáʔ iʔ s+ma•mʔím way̓ ṅíṅw̓iʔ swit mi lʕ̓ʷ -nt -is
then tell -nt -psv -pl this art women yes a_while who fut fit -nt -3erg
tell the women: *"Whoever this fits, whoever*

axáʔ iʔ q̓aʔxán, ləʕ̓ʷpnús 78 way̓ ixíʔ iksənk̓ʷəɬmərrím"
axáʔ iʔ q̓aʔ=xán lʕ̓ʷ+p -nu -s way̓ ixíʔ i -k -s+nk̓ʷ+ɬ+mr•r•im
this art shoe fit -manage -3erg yes that 1i -to_be -spouse
can put this shoe on, *that's the one I'm going to marry."*

79 {neʔk} way̓ uɬ axáʔ iʔ ksənk̓ʷəɬmərríms, ixíʔ iʔ sxaʔtəmscút
way̓ uɬ axáʔ iʔ k -s+nk̓ʷ+ɬ+mr•r•im -s ixíʔ iʔ s+xaʔt+mscút
well and this art to_be -spouse -3i that art put_oneself_first
The one he was going to marry is the first one [to try it].

80 ixíʔ iwá ləʕ̓ʷəntís, uɬ aɬíʔ {s} sp̓ísƛ̓aʔxənx, uɬ lut
ixíʔ iwá lʕ̓ʷ -nt -is uɬ aɬíʔ s -p̓ísƛ̓aʔ=xn -x uɬ lut
that to_no_avail fit -nt -3erg and because ipftv^ -big_footed -^ipftv and not
She tried to fit it, but she has big feet, and it won't [fit].

81 wim̓ ʔiyls, uł {i c} cúntəm t q̓ʷʕay kʷukʷús 82 "way̓ lut,
wim̓ yil[4] -s uł cu -nt -m t q̓ʷʕay kʷu•kʷús way̓ lut
in_vain force_st -3erg and tell -nt -psv agInst black pig well not
She tried to force it, and Black Pig said to her: *"No,*

way̓ myał kʷ p̓ísƛ̓aʔxən, cəm̓ kt̓líw̓səntxʷ iʔ q̓aʔ[xán]"
way̓ myał kʷ p̓ísƛ̓aʔ=xn cm̓ k+t̓l=iw̓s -nt -xʷ iʔ q̓aʔ=xán
yes too_much 2kn big_footed maybe split_lengthwise -nt -2erg art shoe
your feet are too big, you might bust the shoe."

83 {a˙˙y uł} huy uł k̓laxʷ {xiʔ} 84 uł way̓ txƛ̓ap iʔ sqilxʷ
hoy uł k̓laxʷ uł way̓ t+xƛ̓a+p iʔ s+qilxʷ
well and evening and yes complete art person
It got late. 8:03 *All the people had tried [the shoe] on.*

85 sułtíłən axáʔ q̓ʷʕay {l} kʷukʷús 86 "ha way̓ yaʕyáʕt ha p txƛ̓ap
sw=łtiłn axáʔ q̓ʷʕay kʷu•kʷús haʔ way̓ yaʕ•yáʕ+t haʔ p t+xƛ̓a+p
ask_info this black pig inter yes all inter 5kn complete
Black Pig asked: *"Have all of you tried putting*

iʔ p scsúxʷmaʔx {il q̓aʔ} iʔ l q̓aʔxán" 87 cútəlx, "way̓"
iʔ p sc -súxʷ=maʔ -x iʔ l q̓aʔ=xán cut -lx way̓
art 5kn ipftvp^ -measure -^ipftvp Art in shoe say -pl yes
the shoe on?" *They said, "yes."*

88 cúntməlx, "ha miystp" "staʔ way̓" 89 cut axáʔ iʔ
cun -nt -m -lx haʔ miy -st -p staʔ way̓ cut axáʔ iʔ
tell -nt -psv -pl inter be_sure_of -st -5erg Intj yes say this art
He said to them, "Mm, yes." *The old*

pəptwínaʔxʷ 90 "aʔ, nałccám, kən ksənʔímaʔt 91 ixíʔ mut, lut t̓ə
p•ptwínaʔxʷ aʔ nałc+cám kn k+s+n+ʔím+aʔ+t ixíʔ mut lut t̓
old_woman intj forget 1kn have_grandchild that be_home not negfac
woman said: *"Oh, I forgot, I have a grandchild.* *She stayed home, she didn't*

cxʷuy" 92 cútəlx, "xʷuyx ƛ̓ʔant" 93 way̓ ixíʔ ƛ̓aʔntís
c+xʷuy cut -lx xʷuy -x ƛ̓ʔa -nt way̓ ixíʔ ƛ̓aʔ -nt -is
come say -pl go –isimptv fetch -nt well that fetch -nt -3erg
come." *They said to her, "Go get her."* *She went and got her.*

94 way̓ k̓əxʷkʷú˙˙nəms iʔ sənʔímaʔts way̓ cxʷuy 95 way̓ {ł}
way̓ k+ʔxʷ+kʷun+m -s iʔ s+nʔ=ím+aʔ+t -s way̓ c+xʷuy way
yes coax -3erg art grandchild -3in yes come yes
She talked to her granddaughter, and she came. *She*

cənʔúłxʷ {xʷi} xʷíc̓əłtsəlx iʔ q̓aʔxán 96 uł ałíʔ iʔ q̓aʔxáns,
c+n+ʔułxʷ xʷic̓ -łt -s -lx iʔ q̓aʔ=xán uł ałíʔ iʔ q̓aʔ=xán -s
enter_cisl give -łt -2obj -pl art shoe and because art shoe -3in
came in, and they gave her the shoe. *And because it's her shoe,*

4 The root is not certain.

ťi ckʷis, ləʕ̓ʷəntís, ťi ləʕ̓ʷúp 97 nstils axáʔ q̓ʷʕay kʷukʷús, way̓,
ťiʔ c+kʷi -s lʕ̓ʷ -nt -is ťiʔ lʕ̓ʷu+p n+st=ils axáʔ q̓ʷʕay kʷu•kʷús way̓
evid take -2obj fit -nt -3erg evid fit think this black pig yes
she took it, slipped it on, and it fit. 9:04 Black Pig thought, "Yes, that's

kʷaʔ aɬíʔ way̓ kən nstils 98 ixíʔ, swit ləʕ̓ʷpnús, ixíʔ ɬaʔ
kʷaʔ aɬíʔ way̓ kn n+st=ils ixíʔ swit lʕ̓ʷ+p -nu -s ixíʔ ɬaʔ
intj so yes 1kn think then who fit -manage -3erg that the_one_that
just what I thought. The one who can make it fit, that's her shoe,

kɬq̓aʔxán iʔ səl̓mís, 99 uɬ ixíʔ iksənk̓ʷəɬmərrím" 100 way̓ ixíʔ
kɬ+q̓aʔ=xán iʔ sl̓+mi -s uɬ ixíʔ i -k -s+nk̓ʷ+ɬ+mr•r•im way̓ ixíʔ
have+shoe art lose -3erg and that 1i -to_be -spouse well then
that's the one who lost it. That's the one I'm going to marry." He said

cus iʔ sqilxʷ 101 "way ixíʔ iscqʷəlqʷílt 102 swit
cu -s iʔ s+qilxʷ way̓ ixíʔ i -s+c -qʷl•qʷil+t swit
tell -3erg art person yes that 1i -pftv -talk who
to the people: "This is why I said that

ləʕ̓ʷpnús axáʔ iʔ q̓aʔxán, uɬ ixíʔ iksənk̓ʷəɬmər·ím"
lʕ̓ʷ+p -nu -s axáʔ iʔ q̓aʔ=xán uɬ ixíʔ i -k -s+nk̓ʷ+ɬ+mr•r•im
fit -manage -3erg this arts hoe and that 1i -to_be -spouse
whoever this shoe fits,[5] that's the one I'm going to marry."

103 way̓ ixíʔ [s]q̓ʷəy̓məncútsəlx {way̓ t} 104 məríməntməlx, way̓ uɬ ixíʔ
way̓ ixíʔ s -q̓ʷy̓+mncut -s –lx mrim -nt -m -lx way̓ uɬ ixíʔ
well then nom -dance -3i -pl marry -nt -psv -pl yes and then
They started to dance. They got married, and then they

sq̓ʷəy̓məncútsəlx 105 q̓ʷəy̓məncú··təlx, uɬ ksx̌əlpínaʔlx{uɬ} 106 ixíʔ
s -q̓ʷy̓+mncut -s -lx q̓ʷy̓+mncut -lx uɬ k+s+x̌l+p=ínaʔ -lx ixíʔ
nom -dance -3i -pl dance -pl until have_daylight -pl then
started to dance. They danced until daylight. And

uɬ iʔ cúnəlx, "way̓ aɬíʔ kən səcm̓aʔ•m̓áyaʔx 107 way̓
uɬ iʔ cu -n -lx way aɬíʔ kn sc -m̓aʔ•m̓áyaʔ -x way̓
and art tell -1erg -pl well because 1kn ipftvp^ -teach -^ipftvp well
I told them, "I'm going to school.[6] 10:00 My

cəm̓ {k̓əɬ kʷu ck̓əɬ k̓i} kʷu ck̓əɬʔímsts {i} iscəm̓aʔ•m̓áyaʔ 108 way̓
cm̓ kʷu c -k̓ɬ+ʔim-st i -sc+m̓aʔ•m̓áyaʔ way̓
Maybe 1obj cust^ -wait_for 1in -pupil yes
school boy is waiting for me. I'm

ɬwíɬmən, ixíʔ úɬiʔ kən ɬcxʷuy" 109 nc̓əyxʷápəlqs
ɬwi -ɬm -n ixíʔ uɬ iʔ kn ɬ+c+xʷuy n+c̓ayxʷ=áplqs
leave -5obj -1erg then and_then 1kn come_again end_of_story
leaving you, but then I'll come back home." That's the end of it. 10:12

5 Lit. "who can make the shoe fit."
6 Pete is referring to the fact that he is teaching (telling stories to) his school boy (Mattina).

The grateful dead version 1 (unfinished)

1 cwí··xəlx axáʔ a ilmíxʷəm
c -wix -lx axáʔ a yl=mixʷ+m
hab live -pl this art chief
There lived a king.

2 way̓ aɬíʔ əxʷ incaptíkʷɬ way̓
way̓ aɬíʔ əxʷ in -captíkʷɬ way̓
well because again 1in -legends yes
Because my fairy tales [have]

ilmíxʷəm kəm̓ sənk̓líp
yl=mixʷ+m km̓ s+n+k̓l̓=ip
chief or Coyote
a boss, or Coyote.

3 ixíʔ kən kscaptíkʷlaʔx
ixíʔ kn ks -captíkʷl -aʔx
that 1kn incp^ -tell_stories -^incp
This is what I am going to tell,

4 wa··y̓ uɬ
way̓ uɬ
well and
[about]

ƛ̓x̌ap axáʔ {unfinished}
ƛ̓x̌a+p axáʔ
grow_sg this
a grown [young man].

5 knəqsəltílaʔt axáʔ ilmíxʷəm ksqʷsiʔ naɬcəcám
k=nqs=lt=ílaʔt axáʔ yl=mixʷ+m k+s+qʷsiʔ naɬc•c•ám
only_child this chief have_son forget
This chief had a son, I had forgotten,

6 way̓ uɬ ƛ̓x̌ap iʔ sqʷsíʔsəlx
way̓ uɬ ƛ̓x̌a+p iʔ s+qʷsiʔ -s -lx
yes and grow_sg art son -3in -pl
and their son was grown.

7 ixíʔ uɬ cus {i} ia lʔiws,
ixíʔ uɬ cu -s iʔ lʔiw -s
then and tell -3erg art m's_father -3in
And he told his father,

way̓ kən ƛ̓x̌ap
way̓ kn ƛ̓x̌a+p
well 1kn grow_sg
"I am grown,

8 uɬ way̓ kən t̓saq̓ʷ aláʔ kən ɬaʔ cmut
uɬ way̓ kn t̓saq̓ʷ aláʔ kn ɬaʔ c -mut
and well 1kn bored here 1kn when hab -be_home
and I am bored of staying here,

9 uɬ
uɬ
and
and

way̓ caʔkʷ iksxʷəstlwísəm iʔ təmxʷúlaʔxʷ
way̓ caʔkʷ i -ks -xʷst+lwis+m iʔ tmxʷ=úlaʔxʷ
yes should 1i -futi -travel art land
I want to travel the world,

10 kən
kn
1kn
I

kswí··klaʔxʷaʔx
ks -wík=laʔxʷ -aʔx
incp^ -see_country -^incp
want to see places.

11 uɬ aláʔ n̓in̓ kalá··məntsən
uɬ aláʔ n̓ín̓w̓iʔ k+alá+m -nt -s -n
and here a_while stay_with -nt -2obj -1erg
And if I stay here with you,

12 uɬ
uɬ
and
then

lut ikswíklaʔxʷm iʔ təmxʷúlaʔxʷ
lut i -ks -wík=laʔxʷ+m iʔ tmxʷ=úlaʔxʷ
not 1i -futi -see_country art land
I won't see the world,

13 kəm̓ nixʷ lut
km̓ nixʷ lut
or also not
and I won't

iksukuksqílxʷ iʔ t kʷúkʷaʔ
i -ks -wk•wk+s+qilxʷ iʔ t kʷú•kʷaʔ
1i -futi -see_people art obj_itr strange
get acquainted with different people. 1:04

14 náx̌əmɬ t̓iʔ kən xʷstlwis,
nax̌mɬ t̓iʔ kn xʷst+lwis
but evid 1kn travel_around
But if I travel around

uɬ ixíʔ kən wíklaʔxʷəm t təmxʷúlaʔxʷ
uɬ ixíʔ kn wík=laʔxʷ+m t tmxʷ=úlaʔxʷ
and then 1kn see_country obj_itr country
I'll see the world,

15 uɬ kən ukuksqílxʷ t {tə}
uɬ kn wk•wk+s+qilxʷ t
and 1kn see_people obj_itr
I will see

t̓əxʷləmsqílxʷ 16 cúntəm iʔ ta lʔiws, way̓ way̓ mat
t̓xʷl+m+s+qilxʷ cu -nt -m iʔ t lʔiw -s way̓ way̓ mat
different_people tell -nt -psv art agInst m's_father -3in well well maybe
different tribes." *His father said to him, "Ok, if it's*

aspuʔús 17 way̓ uníxʷ kʷ ƛ̓x̌ap uɬ lut kʷ smaʔmínəm
a -s+puʔ=ús way̓ wnixʷ kʷ ƛ̓x̌a+p uɬ lut kʷ s+maʔ+mín+m
2in -heart yes true 2kn grow_sg and not 2kn sent_away
your wish. *It's true you are old enough, and we're not tired of you;*

18 t̓i tx̌ast mi kʷ xʷist aɬíʔ anwí aspuʔús 19 way̓ iwá
t̓iʔ t+x̌as+t mi kʷ xʷist aɬíʔ anwí a -s+puʔ=ús way̓ iwá
evid good fut 2kn walk because you 2in -heart well to_no_avail
it's all right if you go, it's your wish. *I hate*

q̓íx̌əx̌məntsən {ɬa ks} 20 pna itíʔ {kʷ} kʷ kstaʔttímaʔx, kʷ
q̓ix̌•x̌+m -nt -s -n pnaʔ itíʔ kʷ k -s+ta•t•tím̓ -aʔx kʷ
keep_close -nt -2obj -1erg maybe from_that 2kn incp^ -something -^incp 2kn
to see you go. *Something might happen to you, you might die,*

ƛ̓lal, uɬ lut t̓ sx̌asts 21 talí {kʷ} kʷu paʔpaʔsínk
ƛ̓l•al uɬ lut t̓ s -x̌as+t -s taʔlíʔ kʷu paʔ•paʔs=ínk
dead and not negfac nom -good -3i very_much 4kn sad
and that's no good. *We feel bad, because you are*

aɬíʔ kʷ skn̓əqsl̓tílaʔt 22 cúntəm iʔ t sqʷsiʔs, way̓ way̓
aɬíʔ kʷ s+k+n̓qs=l̓t=ílaʔt cu -nt -m iʔ t s+qʷsiʔ -s way̓ way̓
because 2kn only_child_dim tell -nt -psv art agInst son -3in yes yes
the only child we have." *His son said, "Yes, that's*

uníxʷ 23 uɬ aɬíʔ náx̌əmɬ ixíʔ cúntsən, uɬ aɬíʔ way̓ kən t̓saq̓ʷ
wnixʷ uɬ aɬíʔ nax̌mɬ ixíʔ cu -nt -s -n uɬ aɬíʔ way̓ kn t̓saq̓ʷ
true and so but that tell -nt -2obj -1erg and because well 1kn bored
true. *As I said, I am bored staying here*

aláʔ ɬaʔ ckaláʔməstmən {uɬ} 24 uɬ way̓
aláʔ ɬaʔ c -k+aláʔ+m -st -m -n uɬ way̓
here when cust^ -stay_with -^cust -2obj -1erg and yes
with you. 2:04 *And*

cmistíxʷ way̓ cníxlmstmən 25 uɬ way̓ t̓i
c -my -st -ixʷ way̓ c -nixl+m -st -m -n uɬ way̓ t̓iʔ
cust^ -know -^cust -2erg yes cust^ -listen_to -^cust -2obj -1erg and yes evid
you know that I always listen to you. *Be at ease,*

kʷ nqmílsəm, lut {t̓ iks} t̓ isqʷqʷáʕʷqʷut 26 uɬ lut
kʷ n+qm=ils+m lut t̓ i -s -qʷ•qʷaʕʷ•qʷw+t uɬ lut
2kn at_ease not negfac 1i -nom -crazy and not
I am not wild, *and I won't do*

iksqʷəʕʷmscút 27 cúntəm way̓ 28 way̓ ixíʔ utxí··təm {t}
i -ks -qʷʕʷ+mscut cu -nt -m way̓ way̓ ixíʔ wt -xit -m
1i -futi -act_crazy tell -nt -psv Ok well then put_down -xit -psv
anything wrong." *He said, "Ok."* *The chief put something [down]*

k̓ahkʷqís {ałí} iʔ sənqľáwtəns ya ilmíxʷəm 29 uł ałíʔ {na} i la lkasát
k̓ahk̓ʷ=qí -s iʔ s+n+qlaw+tn -s ya yl=mixʷ+m uł ałíʔ iʔ l lkasát
open -3erg art money_bank -3in art chief and so art in box
for him. He opened his money bank, in a trunk.

30 way̓ ixíʔ utxí··təm t ksqľaws, uł put way̓ xʷʔit
way̓ ixíʔ wt -xit -m t k -s+qlaw -s uł put way̓ xʷʔi+t
well then put_down -xit -psv obj_tr to_be -money -3i and just yes much
He put down money for him, lots.

31 cúntəm way̓ axáʔ t̓ík̓ləntsən 32 cúntəm uł ałíʔa lut_a[1]
cu -nt -m way̓ axáʔ t̓ik̓l -nt -s -n cu -nt -m uł ałi+á lut+á
tell -nt -psv well this grub -nt -2obj -1erg tell -nt -psv and so_not not
He said, "This is for your grub," he said, "because you can't go

aksksqľáw 33 uł {t} ixíʔ axáʔ akłk̓íłntən 34 kəm̓ kʷ
a -ks -k -s+qlaw uł ixíʔ axáʔ a -kł -k+ʔiłn+tn km̓ kʷ
2i -? -to_be -money and then this 2i -to_be -food or 2kn
without money. This is what you'll have for food. Or you might

yaʕ̓pcín akłx̌áq̓mən kʷ k̓aʕʷmíst {kəm̓} 35 kəm̓ {a k k} kʷ
yaʕ+p=cín a -kł -x̌aq̓+mn kʷ k̓aʕʷ+míst km̓ kʷ
need 2i -to_be -reward 2kn hire or 2kn
get hard up for your wages if you hire somebody. 3:00 Or you might

ktəmxʷíc̓aʔ, uł ixíʔ akłktuc̓aʔncútən 36 kəm̓ kʷ k̓aʕʷmíst
k+tmxʷ=íc̓aʔ uł ixíʔ a -kł -k+tw=c̓aʔ+ncút+n km̓ kʷ k̓aʕʷ+míst
clothes_wear_out and then 2i -to_be -buy_clothes or 2kn hire
wear your clothes out and this is to buy clothes. Or you will hire

nq̓ʷaʔtkʷəlscútənsəlx 37 cúntəm way̓ 38 way̓ kʷínksəs {i}
n+q̓ʷaʔ=tkʷ=lscut -nt -s -lx cu -nt -m way̓ way̓ kʷin=ks -s
wash_clothes -nt -3e2obj -pl tell -nt -psv OK well shake_hands -3erg
to get your clothes washed." He said, "Ok." He shook hands

ia lʔíws uł iʔ sk̓ʷuys 39 way̓, way̓ ixíʔ sʔácqaʔs
iʔ lʔiw -s uł iʔ s+k̓ʷuy -s way̓ way̓ ixíʔ s -ʔácqaʔ -s
art m̓s_father -3in and art mother -3in well well then nom -go_out -3i
with his father and his mother, then he walked out.

40 uł lut t̓a cmistís k̓aʔkín ł ksxʷúyaʔx uł
uł lut t̓ c -my -st -is k̓a+ʔkín ł ks -xʷuy -aʔx uł
and not negfac cust^ -know -^cust -3erg to_where compl incp^ -go -^incp and
And he didn't kow just where he was going, he just

way̓ t̓iʔ ʔácqaʔ 41 uł t̓əxʷ mat kicx iʔ təmxʷúlaʔxʷ {way̓ t̓i}
way̓ t̓iʔ ʔácqaʔ uł t̓xʷ mat kic+x iʔ tmxʷ=úlaʔxʷ
well evid go_out and evidently maybe arrive art country
went out. And he arrived at a place.

1 The post-clitic a is parallel to km̓+a, ałíʔ+a, etc.

42 kʷm̓iɬ uɬ xʷist ik̓lí? a cəncahchús uɬ ta ck̓lí? ɬ xʷuy
kʷm̓iɬ uɬ xʷist ik̓lí? a c -n+cah•ch=ús uɬ ta c+k̓lí? ɬ xʷuy
suddenly and walk to_there art hab -be_facing and in_that_direction and go
He started walking and where he was facing, he just went.

43 xʷu··y̓ uɬ k̓əɬk̓ʷƛ̓áp axá? i? l kɬx̌siw̓s 44 nt̓a? {stim̓ ə} stim̓
xʷuy uɬ k̓ɬ+k̓ʷƛ̓a+p axá? i? l kɬ+x̌s=iw̓s nt̓a s+tim̓
go and come_in_sight this art in level_country intj what
He went and he came in sight in level country. 4:05 *Gee, what did he see,*

i? kscwiks, way̓ c̓x̌iɬt sqilxʷ t scyaʕ̓míx 45 uɬ aɬí?
i? ksc -wik -s way̓ c+?x̌iɬ+t s+qilxʷ t sc+yaʕ̓+míx uɬ aɬí?
art futPerfi -see -3i well like person obj_c̓x̌iɬ gathering and because
like people gathered. *And because*

ik̓lí? {s} k̓əl ksxʷúytəns uɬ t̓i ktɬməncútəms 46 uɬ aɬí?
ik̓lí? k̓l k -s+xʷuy+tn -s uɬ t̓i? k+tɬ+mncut+m -s uɬ aɬí?
there to to_be -path -3i and evid go_straight -3erg and because
it's right in his path, he just went straight for it. *And because*

ik̓lí? scxʷuyx way̓ {tk̓} tk̓a?túsəms 47 way̓ sqilxʷ way̓
ik̓lí? sc -xʷuy -x way̓ t+k̓a?t=ús+m -s way̓ s+qilxʷ way̓
there ipftvp^ -go -^ipftvp well get_close -3erg well person yes
that's where he is going, he got close. *It's people*

əcxtxí?tmistəlx {a c} 48 t̓i sc̓íckna?xəlx uɬ t̓i
c -xt•xít+mi?st -lx t̓i? sc -?íckn+a? -x -lx uɬ t̓i?
hab -run_around -pl evid ipftvp^ -play -^ipftvp -pl and evid
running around, *they are playing, and*

scyaʕ̓míxəlx {sts} sc̓íckna?xəlx 49 uɬ stim̓ a
sc -yaʕ̓ -mix -lx sc -?íckn+a? -x -lx uɬ s+tim̓ a
ipftvp^ -gather -^ipftvp -pl ipftvp^ -play -^ipftvp and what art
they gather, *and what*

ctərqstísəlx 50 lut c̓x̌iɬ t stk̓ək̓xʷúm̓ a
c -trq -st -is -lx lut c+?x̌iɬ t s+t+k̓•k̓xʷum a
cust^ -kick -^cust -3erg -pl not like obj_c̓x̌iɬ ball art
is it they are kicking? *What they are kicking is not like*

ctər̓qstísəlx 51 məɬ ixí? kʷísəlx uɬ
c -trq -st -is -lx mɬ ixí? kʷi -s -lx uɬ
cust^ -kick -^cust -3erg -pl and that take -3erg -pl and
a football. *They take it, and they*

n?alksnwíxʷmsəlx 52 t knaqs kʷənnús məɬ ixí?
n+?al=ks+nwíxʷ+m -s -lx t k=naqs kʷn -nu -s mɬ ixí?
fight_over -3erg -pl agInst one_person take -manage -3erg and then
fight over it. 5:00 *One gets hold of it and runs with it,*

ɬxʷt̓púsəs {məɬ ixí? ɬ} t̓əxʷ ɬckʷáqsəs 53 məɬ ixí? {a··} təl s?iwt
ɬ+xʷt̓+p=us -s t̓xʷ ɬ+ckʷ=aqs -s mɬ ixí? tl s+?iwt
run_back -3erg emph drag_back -3erg and then from one_behind
and he drags it. *And they kick what they are*

ɬtər̓qəntísəlx axáʔ a sckʷaqsc 54 xʷu··y uɬ k̓aʔítət,
ɬ+trq -nt -is -lx axáʔ a s+ckʷ=aqs -c xʷuy uɬ k̓aʔít•t
kick_back -nt -3erg -pl this art dragged -3in go and get_near
dragging from behind. *He went, got close,*

kmimipúsəms 55 a way̓ sqilxʷ axáʔ a
k+my•my+p=us+m -s a way̓ s+qilxʷ axáʔ a
realize -3erg intj yes person this art
made out what it was. *It's a human what*

ck̓x̌íləmstsəlx, ixíʔ a cktər̓qíc̓aʔstsəlx 56 way̓
c -k+ʔx̌il+m -st -s -lx ixíʔ a c -k+trq=íc̓aʔ -st -s -lx way̓
cust^ -do_so -^cust -3erg -pl that art cust^ -kick_body -^cust -3erg -pl well
they are doing that to, it's a body that they are kicking. *He*

xʷuy uɬ kics kmimipúsəms 57 way̓ lut {ə} t̓a
xʷuy uɬ kic -s k+my•my+p=us+m -s way̓ lut t̓
go and reach_st/sb -3erg realize -3erg well not evid
went, got there, and made out what it was. *This person*

cxʷəlxʷált axáʔ iʔ sqilxʷ 58 way̓ təmtəmníʔ axáʔ a
c -xʷl•xʷal+t axáʔ iʔ s+qilxʷ way̓ tm•tmniʔ axáʔ a
hab -alive this art person yes corpse this art
is not alive. *What they are doing*

ck̓x̌ílmstsəlx nak̓ʷm 59 way̓ {ixíʔ} ixíʔ x̌aʔntíməlx
c -k+ʔx̌il+m -st -s -lx nak̓ʷ+m way̓ ixíʔ x̌aʔn -t -im -lx
cust^ -do_so -^cust -3erg -pl evid well then stop -nt -psv -pl
that to is a corpse, is what it is. *Then the boy stopped*

axáʔ iʔ t tətw̓ít 60 cúntməlx, húmaʔ ilíʔ ƛ̓lápwi 61 way̓
axáʔ iʔ t t•tw̓it cu -nt -m -lx húmaʔ ilíʔ ƛ̓l+ap -wy way̓
this art agInst boy tell -nt -psv -pl exhort there stop -ipimptv well
them. 6:00 *He said to them, "Wait a minute, stop!"* *The*

ƛ̓lápəlx axáʔ iʔ sqilxʷ 62 cúntməlx p iksíwm,
ƛ̓la+p -lx axáʔ iʔ s+qilxʷ cu -nt -m -lx p i -ks -siw+m
stop -pl this art person tell -nt -psv -pl 5kn 1i -futi -ask
people stopped. *He said, "I want to ask you.*

63 cúntməlx uɬ sc̓kinx təmtəmníʔ {a səm} mat {snək̓ʷpsqi}
cu -nt -m -lx uɬ sc+ʔkin+x tm•tmniʔ mat
tell -nt -psv -pl and why_is_it corpse maybe
And why is it, it's a corpse, a human being, one

snək̓ʷsqílxʷəmp 64 uɬ ilíʔ aɬ c̓x̌ilstp 65 kʷa
s+nk̓ʷ+s+qilxʷ -mp uɬ ilíʔ aɬ c -ʔx̌il -st -p kʷa
fellow_Indian -5in and there compl cust^ -do_like -^cust -5erg intj
of you. *And you are doing what you are doing to it.* *A corpse*

npútaʔtən iʔ təmtəmníʔ təl incá iʔ təl intəmxʷúlaʔxʷ itlíʔ kən
n+pútaʔ+tn iʔ tm•tmniʔ tl in+cá iʔ tl in -tmxʷ=úlaʔxʷ itlíʔ kn
respected art corpse from I art from 1in -country from_there 1kn
is respected in the country where I come

cxʷuy 66 waỷ kʷu ṅ λ̓lal, uɬ cpútaʔstəm, mi_sic
c+xʷuy waỷ kʷu ṅ λ̓l•al uɬ c -pútaʔ -st -m mi_sic
come well 4kn now dead and cust^ -respect -^cust -4erg then
from. *When we have dead ones we respect them, we put them away,*

kʷúməntəm, líq̓ntəm 67 uɬ mnímɬəmp waỷ
kʷum -nt -m liq̓ -nt -m uɬ mnimɬ+mp waỷ
store -nt -4erg bury -nt -4erg and you well
we bury them. *But you folks*

cqʷṅíkstəmstp axáʔ iʔ təmtəmníʔ 68 cúsəlx waỷ ha
c -qʷṅ=ikst+m -st -p axáʔ iʔ tm•tmniʔ cu -s -lx waỷ haʔ
cust^ -do_st_pitiful -^cust -5erg this art corpse tell -3erg -pl well inter
treat this corpse pitifully." *They said, "Are you done*

kʷ k̓wap, waỷ {cúntməlx} 69 cúsəlx axáʔ iʔ tətwít 70 aɬíʔ ɬaʔ
kʷ k̓wa+p waỷ cu -s -lx axáʔ iʔ t•tẁit aɬíʔ ɬaʔ
2kn quiet yes tell -3erg -pl this art boy because when
talking?" "Yes." *They told the boy: 7:00* *"When he*

cxʷəlxʷált uɬ cx̌litsts iʔ xʷəlxʷílt uɬ axáʔ təl
c -xʷl•xʷal+t uɬ c -x̌lit -st -s iʔ xʷl•xʷilt uɬ axáʔ tl
hab -alive and cust^ -call -^cust -3erg art debt and this from
was alive he asked for credit from

səntumístən 71 kəṁ {tlia} təl̓ yaʕyáʕt_swit, k̓əl yaʕyáʕt_swit
s+n+tw+mist+n kṁ tl̓ yaʕ•yáʕ+t_swit k̓l yaʕ•yáʕ+t_swit
store or from everybody to everybody
the store, *he has debts with*

səkɬxʷəlxʷíltx[2] 72 lut t̓a cx̌aq̓sts iʔ xʷəlxʷílts
s kɬ+xʷl•xʷilt -x lut t̓ c -x̌aq̓ -st -s iʔ xʷl•xʷilt -s
ipftv^ have+debt -^ipftv not negfac cust^ -pay -^cust -3erg art debt -3in
everybody; *and he didn't pay his debts.*

73 uɬ ixíʔ λ̓lal, waỷ uɬ səl̓míntəm 74 aɬíʔ lut t̓a ksnəqsílxʷ,
uɬ ixíʔ λ̓l•al waỷ uɬ sl̓+mi -nt -m aɬíʔ lut t̓ k+s+nqs=ilxʷ
and then dead well and lose -nt -4erg because not negfac have_relative
And when he died we lost all of that. *He hasn't got relatives,*

uɬ səl̓míntəm iʔ sql̓áwtət 75 lut t̓a kɬswit t̓a ksnəqsílxʷ
uɬ sl̓+mi -nt -m iʔ s+qlaw -tt lut t̓ kɬ+swit t̓ k+s+nqs=ilxʷ
and lose -nt -4erg art money -4in not evid have_someone evid have_relative
and we lost all our money. *He's got no living relatives*

kʷu ɬə ksənsíwpəms iʔ k̓la cxʷəlxʷált 76 uɬ nixʷ put {ks}
kʷu ɬ ks -n+siw+p+m -s iʔ k̓l c -xʷl•xʷal+t uɬ nixʷ put
4kn comp futi -ask_for ? art to hab -alive and also just
for us to ask money of. *And one has to*

2 This form shows the *have* stem inflected.

kɬx̌áq̓mən ksqlaw mi ktíwčaʔsəlx kəm̓ t kɬəntək̓ʷmíns
kɬ+x̌aq̓+mn k+s+qlaw mi k+tíw=č̓aʔ -s -lx km̓ t kɬ -n+t̓k̓ʷ+min -s
have_reward have_money fut buy_clothes -3erg -pl or obj_tr to_be -coffin -3i
have money to buy clothes and a coffin,

77 k̓ʷúl̓xtsəlx t kɬntək̓ʷmíns 78 kəm̓ nixʷ x̌áq̓məlx mi
k̓ʷul̓ -xt -s -lx t kɬ -n+t̓k̓ʷ+min -s km̓ nixʷ x̌aq̓+m -lx mi
make -xit -3erg -pl obj_tr to_be -coffin -3i or also pay -pl fut
to make a coffin. 8:00 *And one has to pay*

ksk̓əɬcíqaʔx mi líq̓səlx 79 uɬ axáʔ lut t̓a ksql̓aw
ks -k̓ɬ+ciq -aʔx mi liq̓ -s -lx uɬ axáʔ lut t̓ k+s+qlaw
incpˆ -dig -ˆincp fut bury -3erg -pl and this not evid have_money
to have diggers to bury him. *And he doesn't have any money.*

80 uɬ {ixíʔ uɬiac} ixíʔ uɬ a cənčkmúɬtəm axáʔ {iʔ} iʔ xʷəlxʷílts
uɬ ixíʔ uɬ a c -n+č̓k+m -uɬt -m axáʔ iʔ xʷl•xʷilt -s
and then and art custˆ -figure -tuɬt -4erg this art debt -3in
So we are figuring his debts,

81 ia {c cktər̓qi} cktər̓qíčaʔstəm axáʔ t knaqs 82 ixíʔ məɬ
iʔ c -k+trq=íčaʔ -st -m axáʔ t k=naqs ixíʔ mɬ
art custˆ -kick_body -ˆcust -4erg this agInst one_person then and
and that's why each is kicking him. *When*

axáʔ ʔayx̌ʷt {axáʔ ia i səc i səc} itíʔ a cktər̓qíčaʔstm
axáʔ ʔayx̌ʷ+t itíʔ a c -k+trq=íčaʔ -st -m
this tired from_that art custˆ -kick_body -ˆcust -4erg
he gets tired of kicking him,

83 məɬ nstils way̓ way̓ staʔ kʷ nxƛ̓pús, huy itlíʔ anwí 84 məɬ
mɬ n+st=ils way̓ way̓ staʔ kʷ n+xƛ̓p=us hoy itlíʔ anwí mɬ
and think well yes intj 2kn break_even finish from_there you and
he thinks, 'You are paid up, now it's your turn.' *And*

itlíʔ iʔ t knaqs {kʷist} kʷíntəm məɬ ixíʔ itlíʔ
itlíʔ iʔ t k=naqs kʷi -nt -m mɬ ixíʔ itlíʔ
from_there art agInst one_person take -nt -psv and then grom_there
then the next takes him, and he kicks him more. And then the next takes him,

ɬktər̓qíčaʔntəm 85 i··ʔ məɬ axáʔ nixʷ npútəls 86 iʔ t
ɬ+k+trq=íčaʔ -nt -m ih mɬ axáʔ nixʷ n+put=ls iʔ t
kick_body_again -nt -psv intj and this also satisfied art prttv
and he kicks him more. *He does that, until he too is satisfied* *that*

xʷəlxʷílts way̓ nxəƛ̓púsəs iʔ xʷəlxʷílts 87 məɬ ixíʔ itlíʔ
xʷl•xʷilt -s way̓ n+xƛ̓p=us -s iʔ xʷl•xʷilt -s mɬ ixíʔ itlíʔ
debt -3in well be_even -3erg art debt -3in and then from_there
his debt is paid. *Then he gives him*

xʷíčəɬts {k̓əl} k̓əl knaqs 88 hoy uɬ way̓ txƛ̓ap {i··} ia kɬxʷəlxʷílt
xʷič -ɬt -s k̓l k=naqs hoy uɬ way̓ t+xƛ̓a+p iʔ kɬ+xʷl•xʷilt
give -ɬt -3erg to one_person finish and all complete art have_debt
to another one, 9:00 *until those he owes to all take their turn.*

89 kiʔ axáʔ iʔ kʷ ckicx 90 uɬ náx̌əmɬ {i} k̓im {il} iʔ l
kiʔ axáʔ iʔ kʷ c+kic+x uɬ nax̌mɬ k̓im iʔ l
rel this art 2kn arrive_cisl and but only art for
And then you got here. *But this is only for his clothes,*

kstətəm̓tím̓s iʔ l kɬəntˀk̓ʷmíns uɬ iʔ l ksk̓əɬcíq̣aʔx
k -s+t•tm̓•tim̓ -s iʔ l kɬ -n+tˀk̓ʷ+min -s uɬ iʔ l ks -k̓ɬ+ciq -aʔx
to_be -clothes -3i art for to_be -coffin -3in and art for incp^ -dig -^incp
for his coffin, and for the grave diggers.

91 k̓əm ixíʔ {k k} ksksqlˀáwaʔx {ki ixíʔ} 92 itlíʔ ixíʔ
k̓m ixíʔ ks k+s+qlaw -aʔx itlíʔ ixíʔ
except that incp^ have_money -^incp from_there that
He is going to have to pay for that. *We were*

ksənc̓kmúɬtəm {ixíʔ uɬ} ixíʔ uɬ_iʔ {iʔ} kʷu x̌aʔntíxʷ 93 a, cúntəm
ks -n+c̓k+m -uɬt -m ixíʔ uɬ_iʔ kʷu x̌aʔn -t -ixʷ a cu -nt -m
futt^ -figure -tuɬt -4erg then and_then 1obj stop -nt -2erg intj tell -nt -psv
going to figure all that out, and then you stopped us." *He said to them,*

way̓, huy tˀəxʷ xƛ̓məncútwi, tˀwístwi 94 way̓ ixíʔ
way̓ huy tˀxʷ xƛ̓+mncut -wy tˀwist -wy way̓ ixíʔ
well intj emph all -ipimptv stand_pl -ipimptv well then
"All of you, stand in a row." *They all*

sxəƛ̓məncútsəlx, tˀwístəlx 95 way̓ a[xáʔ] cənk̓ʷəƛ̓ntís iʔ
s -xƛ̓+mncut -s -lx tˀwist -lx way̓ axáʔ c -n+k̓ʷƛ̓ -nt -is iʔ
nom -all -3i -pl stand_pl -pl well this act pull_out -nt -3erg art
stood in a row. *The boy took out*

sənqlˀáwtəns axáʔ iʔ tətw̓ít {uɬ xi c} 96 ixíʔ cúntəm axáʔ
s+n+qlaw+tn -s axáʔ iʔ t•tw̓it ixíʔ cu -nt -m axáʔ
money_bank -3in this art boy then tell -nt -psv this
his purse. *He said to the one*

ckcəhám 97 cúntəm uɬ c̓kin a {a} cxʷəlxʷíltstms
c -k+cha+m cu -nt -m uɬ c+ʔkin a c -xʷl•xʷilt -st -m -s
hab -facing tell -nt -psv and how art cust^ -debt -^cust -2obj -3erg
in front of him, *he asked him, "How much did he owe you?" 10:04*

98 cus way̓, ixíʔ {c} m̓áyaʔɬts c̓kin, way̓ ixíʔ
cu -s way̓ ixíʔ m̓áyaʔ -ɬt -s c+ʔkin way̓ ixíʔ
tell -3erg well that tell -ɬt -3erg how well what
He told him how much, and he

nxʷəc̓xúɬts 99 uɬ itlíʔ iʔ knaqs, way̓ uɬ ixíʔ nixʷ
n+xʷc̓+x -uɬt -s uɬ itlíʔ iʔ k=naqs way̓ uɬ ixíʔ nixʷ
give_equivalent -tuɬt -3erg and from_there art one_person well and that also
gave it to him. *And then another one,*

m̓áyaʔɬtəm, uɬ ixíʔ nxʷəc̓xúsəs 100 way̓ nxʷəc̓xú··səs {uɬ}
m̓áyaʔ -ɬt -m uɬ ixíʔ n+xʷc̓+x=us -s way̓ n+xʷc̓+x=us -s
tell -ɬt -psv and that give_equivalent -3erg well give_equivalent -3erg
and he told him, and he gave it to him. *He paid all the ones*

uɫ txƛ̓ap axáʔ ia cxʷəlxʷíltstəm 101 cúntməlx, way {u}
uɫ t+xƛ̓a+p axáʔ iʔ c -xʷl•xʷilt -st -m cu -nt -m -lx way̓
and complete this art cust^ -debt -^cust -psv tell -nt -psv -pl well
he owed. *He asked them,*

uɫ c̓kin {i kɫ} t iʔ kɫəntʼək̓ʷmíns 102 ixíʔ m̓ áyaʔɫtsəlx axáʔ
uɫ c+ʔkin t iʔ kɫ -n+tʼk̓ʷ+min -s ixíʔ m̓ áyaʔ -ɫt -s -lx axáʔ
and how obl art to_be -coffin -3in then tell -ɫt -3erg -pl this
"And how much is his coffin?" *The coffin-makers*

iʔ t səxʷk̓ʷúl̓əm i la ntʼək̓ʷmín 103 cut way̓ c̓x̌iɫ itíʔ kən ɫaʔ
iʔ t sxʷ=k̓ʷul̓+m iʔ l n+tʼk̓ʷ+min cut way̓ c+ʔx̌iɫ itíʔ kn ɫaʔ
art agInst worker art with coffin say well like that 1kn when
told him. *One [of them] said "This is how much*

cx̌əq̓ncút 104 way̓ ixíʔ x̌áq̓ɫtəm {i} x̌áq̓əntəm ixíʔ 105 cúntəm
c -x̌q̓+ncut way̓ ixíʔ x̌aq̓ -ɫt -m x̌aq̓ -nt -m ixíʔ cu -nt -m
hab -get_paid well then pay -ɫt -psv pay -nt -psv that tell -nt -psv
I get for it." *He paid him that.* *He told him,*

way̓ k̓ʷul̓xtxʷ t kɫəntʼək̓ʷmíns 106 cúntəm itlíʔ a
way̓ k̓ʷul̓ -xt -xʷ t kɫ -n+tʼk̓ʷ+min -s cu -nt -m itlíʔ a
well make -xit -2erg obj_tr to_be -coffin -3in tell -nt -psv from_there art
"Now make him a coffin." *He said to the store*

ksəntumístən 107 cúntəm uɫ anwí c̓kin iʔ stətəm̓tím̓ {ɫə c}
k+s+n+tw+mist+n cu -nt -m uɫ anwí c+ʔkin iʔ s+t•tm̓•tim̓
have_store tell -nt -psv and you how art clothes
keeper, 11:00 *he said, "And you, how much*

ck̓əɫc̓kstíxʷ 108 iʔ l scƛ̓əl·míx iʔ
c -k̓ɫ+c̓k -st -ixʷ iʔ l sc -ƛ̓l•l -mix iʔ
cust^ -charge -^cust -2erg art for ipftvp^ -dead -^ipftvp art
do you charge *for clothes*

kstətəm̓tím̓s {kɫ} 109 kɫyaʕyáʕilxʷs, {a ks} kɫnəqsílxʷs,
k -s+t•tm̓•tim̓ -s kɫ -yaʕ•yáʕ=ilxʷ -s kɫ -nqs=ilxʷ -s
to_be -clothes -3i to_be -complete_outfit -3i to_be -neighbor -3i
for dead people? *A complete outfit, a suit,*

110 q̓aʔx̌áns, ksnsísuʔxəns, kɫlasmísc, uɫ axáʔ {i t s}
q̓aʔ=xán -s k -s+n+si•sw̓=xn -s kɫ -lasmís -c uɫ axáʔ
shoes -3in to_be -socks -3i to_be -shirt -3i and this
shoes, socks, shirts, and a handkerchief for

kɫk̓ɫir̓cíns 111 uɫ ixíʔ aɫíʔ {m} t suyápix uɫ cúsəlx
kɫ -k̓ɫ+yr̓=cin -s uɫ ixíʔ aɫíʔ t s+wyapy=x uɫ cu -s -lx
to_be -kerchief -3i and that so agInst white_person and tell -3erg -pl
his neck." *In English they call this*

necktie 112 uɫ axáʔm iʔ t sqilxʷ uɫ aɫíʔ way̓ k̓ɫir̓cín 113 way̓
uɫ axáʔ+m iʔ t s+qilxʷ uɫ aɫíʔ way̓ k̓ɫ+yr̓=cin way̓
and this art agInst Indian and so well kerchief well
"necktie" *and in Indian "k̓ɫir̓cín."* *"Every*

ixíʔ xƛ̓ap 114 way̓ ʔúmɬtəm i ta ksəntumístən, way̓ ixíʔ
ixíʔ xƛ̓a+p way̓ ʔum -ɬt -m iʔ t k+s+n+tw+mist+n way̓ ixíʔ
that everything well name -ɬt -psv art agInst have_store well that
thing." *The store keeper told him,*

x̌áq̓ɬtəm {cúntəm axáʔ ia c cunt} 115 cúntməlx uɬ swit ya ck̓əɬcíqəm
x̌aq̓ -ɬt -m cu -nt -m -lx uɬ swit ya c -k̓ɬ+ciq+m
pay -ɬt -psv tell -nt -psv -pl and who art hab -dig
and he paid. 12:00 *He asked, "Who is the digger?"*

116 way̓ ixíʔ {scútsəlx a} ʔaməncútəlx axáʔ ia ck̓əɬcíqəm 117 mat
way̓ ixíʔ ʔam+ncút -lx axáʔ iʔ c -k̓ɬ+ciq+m mat
well then call_self -pl this art hab -dig maybe
They named the grave digger, *or maybe*

tk̓ʷínk̓ʷənxəlx, mat tk̓asʔasíl, kəm̓ tkaʔkaʔɬís, kəm̓ kmúsəms
t+k̓ʷin•k̓ʷn+x -lx mat tk=ʔas•ʔasíl km̓ t=kaʔ•kaʔɬís km̓ k=mus•ms
indef_number -pl maybe two_persons or three_persons or four_persons
three or four.

118 i[xíʔ] cútəlx, ixíʔ uɬ aɬíʔ kʷu ck̓ɬʔaysnwíxʷ lut kʷu
ixíʔ cut -lx ixíʔ uɬ aɬíʔ kʷu c -k̓ɬ+ʔays+nwíxʷ lut kʷu
then say -pl then and so 4kn hab -change_place not 4kn
They told him, "We take turns, *we don't*

scƛ̓laps 119 way̓ knaqs c̓əspísk̓it məɬ itlíʔ
s c+ƛ̓la+p -s way̓ k=naqs c̓s+p=ísk̓it mɬ itlíʔ
nom4ˆ -stop -ˆnom4 well one_person out_of_breath and from_there
stop. *When one is out of breath,*

knaqs nxtʼsíw̓səm 120 huy məɬ kʷu txƛ̓ap məɬ itlíʔ ia cxʔit {ɬ}
k=naqs n+xtʼ+s=iw̓s+m huy mɬ kʷu t+xƛ̓a+p mɬ itlíʔ iʔ c+xʔit
one_person join_in intj and 4kn complete and from_there art first
then another joins in. *We all take our turn, and then the first one again,*

121 uɬ way̓ aɬíʔ skɬaʔxʷísk̓its məɬ itlíʔ {ɬ} nxətʼsíw̓səm,
uɬ way̓ aɬíʔ s -k+ɬaʔxʷ=ísk̓it -s mɬ itlíʔ n+xtʼ+s=iw̓s+m
and yes because nom -rested -3i and from_there join_in
because he is rested, and then he'll join in

itlíʔ cíqəm. 122 lut kʷu tʼa cƛ̓lap, tʼiʔ ixíxiʔ məɬ kʷu
itlíʔ ciq+m lut kʷu tʼ c -ƛ̓la+p tʼiʔ ix•íxiʔ mɬ kʷu
from_there dig not 4kn negfac hab -stop evid in_a_while and 4kn
and dig. *We never stop, and in just a little while we have*

wiʔsk̓əɬcíqəm 123 uɬ ixíʔ kʷu ɬaʔ ckpq̓ʷínaʔm, ilíʔ kʷu
wy̓+s+k̓ɬ+ciq+m uɬ ixíʔ kʷu ɬaʔ c -k+pq̓ʷ=ínaʔ+m ilíʔ kʷu
finish_dig and then 4kn when hab -fill_hole there 4kn
our grave dug. *And when we fill the grave we do*

c̓x̌íləm 124 axáʔ iʔ tk̓asʔasíl kəpq̓ʷínaʔm i·· uɬ
c -ʔx̌il+m axáʔ iʔ tk=ʔas•ʔasíl k+pq̓ʷ=ínaʔ+m i·· uɬ
hab -do_same this art two_persons fill_hole intj and
the same thing. *Two will start filling it,*

ck̓əɬʔaw̓stím iʔ t sl̓əx̌l̓áx̌ts 125 way̓ mat nʔayx̌ʷtíls
c -k̓ɬ+ʔaw̓ -st -im iʔ t s+l̓x̌•l̓ax̌+t -s way̓ mat n+ʔayx̌ʷ+t=íls
cust^ -wait -^cust -psv art agInst friends -3in well maybe get_tired
and their partners wait. 13:04 *When they figure*

məɬ ixíʔ yirəntísəlx iʔ sl̓áx̌tsəlx axáʔ iʔ tk̓əsʔasíl
mɬ ixíʔ yir -nt -is -lx iʔ s+l̓ax̌+t -s -lx axáʔ iʔ tk=ʔs•ʔasíl
and then push -nt -3erg -pl art friend -3in -pl this art two_persons
they must be tired, the two will push their partners aside

126 məɬ itlíʔ ixíʔ ɬkchamәncútəlx ɬkpq̓ʷínaʔm 127 ixíʔ məɬ
mɬ itlíʔ ixíʔ ɬ+k+cah+mncut -lx ɬ+k+pq̓ʷ=ínaʔ+m ixíʔ mɬ
and from_there then take_turn_again -pl fill_hole_again then and
and they will take their turns filling in the grave. *When*

wiʔsklíq̓naʔsəlx uɬ tk̓ʷúl̓naʔsəlx 128 cúntməlx way̓ uɬ
wy̓+s+líq̓=naʔ -s -lx uɬ t+k̓ʷúl̓=naʔ -s -lx cu -nt -m -lx way̓ uɬ
finish_burying -3erg -pl and fix_surface -3erg -pl tell -nt -psv -pl well and
they finish burying they fix the grave." *And he asked them,*

k̓ʷinx iʔ mnímɬəmp {iʔ} iʔ sql̓áwəmp ɬaʔ cx̌əq̓ncút 129 way̓
k̓ʷin+x iʔ mnimɬ+mp iʔ s+qlaw -mp ɬaʔ c -x̌q̓+ncut way̓
how_much art you art money -5in when gpat -get_paid well
"How much do you charge?" *They*

ʔúmsəlx, ixíʔ x̌əl kmúsəms 130 i·· uɬ c̓əspsql̓áw a[xáʔ] iʔ tətw̓ít,
ʔum -s -lx ixíʔ x̌l k=mus•ms i·· uɬ c̓s+p+s+qlaw axáʔ iʔ t•tw̓it
name -3erg -pl that for four_persons intj and money_finish this art boy
told him, for the four of them. *And the boy is flat broke when they*

ixiʔ náx̌əmɬ put cwiʔslíq̓ 131 way̓, way̓ ixíʔ yaʔx̌í yaʕyáʕt
ixíʔ nax̌mɬ put c -wy̓+s+liq̓ way̓ way̓ ixíʔ yaʔx̌í yaʕ•yáʕ+t
then but just hab -finish_bury well well then that_one all
are done with the burying. *They all put their money in*

npkʷsql̓áwməlx 132 way̓ uɬ kʷənkʷənksnwíxʷmsəlx {axáʔ iʔ}
n+pkʷ+s+qlaw+m -lx way̓ uɬ kʷn•kʷn=ks+nwixʷ+m -s -lx
pour_money_in -pl well and hold_two_sides -3erg -pl
their pockets. *They picked him up on both sides. 14:00*

133 cúsəlx uɬ aɬíʔ mat way̓ ksəntəmtmníʔtən 134 cúntməlx
cu -s -lx uɬ aɬíʔ mat way̓ k+s+n+tm•tmniʔ+tn cu -nt -m -lx
tell -3erg -pl and because must yes have+graveyard tell -nt -psv -pl
They told him (there must be a graveyard)... *He said to them,*

way̓ náx̌əmɬ ta mnímɬəmp k̓ʷúl̓əntp axáʔ iʔ ta ksntəmtəmníʔtən
way̓ nax̌mɬ t mnimɬ+mp k̓ʷul̓ -nt -p axáʔ iʔ t k+s+n+tm•tmniʔ+tn
well but agInst you fix -nt -5erg this art obl have_graveyard
"Now you fix him for the grave,

135 t̓əxʷ iʔ ta kstətəm̓tím̓, ta kɬənt̓ək̓ʷmín 136 way̓ kʷísəlx
t̓xʷ iʔ t k+s+t•tm̓•tim̓ t kɬ+n+t̓k̓ʷ+min way̓ kʷi -s -lx
emph art obl have_clothes obl have_coffin well take -3erg -pl
with clothes, with a coffin." *They took him,*

uɬ_iʔ nʔúɬxʷstsəlx i? k̓əl səntəmtəmníʔtən 137 way̓ ixíʔ
uɬ_iʔ n+ʔuɬxʷ -st -s -lx iʔ k̓l s+n+tm•tmniʔ+tn way̓ ixíʔ
and_then enter -caus -3erg -pl art to graveyard well then
and they took him to the cemetery. They

cʕáwlxstsəlx, kc̓í·wc̓aʔsəlx way̓ 138 way̓ cyaʕp iʔ təl
caʕʷ+lx -st -s -lx k+c̓íw̓=c̓aʔ -s -lx way̓ way̓ c+yaʕ+p iʔ tl
bathe -caus -3erg -pl wash_body -3erg -pl yes well arrive_here art from
bathed him, washed his body well. They got clothes from

səntumístən iʔ kstətəm̓tím̓s, yaʕyáʕt sic {ə}
s+n+tw+mist+n iʔ k -s+t•tm̓•tim̓ -s yaʕ•yáʕ+t sic
store art to_be -clothes -3i all new
the store, everything new.

139 x̌əcmstísəlx iʔ t kɬk̓ɬixʷtəlscúts, t
x̌c+m -st -is -lx iʔ t kɬ -k̓ɬ+yxʷ=t=lscut -s t
get_so_ready -caus -3erg -pl art obl to_be -underwear -3i obl
They got him ready with underwear,

ksənsísuʔxəns 140 way̓ x̌əcmstísəlx axáʔ iʔ
k -s+n+si•sw̓=xn -s way̓ x̌c+m -st -is -lx axáʔ iʔ
to_be -socks -3i well get_so_ready -caus -3erg -pl this art
stockings. They got him ready, they put

ksx̌íƛ̓xəns ləʕ̓ʷɬtísəlx {uɬ} 141 uɬ axáʔ iʔ kɬlascmísc, uɬ
k -s+x̌iƛ̓=xn -s lʕ̓ʷ -ɬt -is -lx uɬ axáʔ iʔ kɬ -lasmíst -s uɬ
to_be -trousers -3i fit -ɬt -3erg -pl and this art to_be -shirt -3i and
pants on him, a shirt,

ixíʔ {iʔ t} iʔ t kɬk̓ɬir̓cíns 142 way̓ uɬ lkapúsəlx nt̓a uɬ
ixíʔ iʔ t kɬ -k̓ɬ+yr̓=cin -s way̓ uɬ lkapú -s -lx nt̓a uɬ
then art obl to_be -kerchief -3i well and coat -3erg -pl intj and
a tie, 15:00 and they put a coat on him,

kɬnəqsílxʷ[s] 143 qʷámqʷəmt iʔ kɬnəqsílxʷ iʔ stətəm̓tím̓s 144 uɬ
kɬ -nqs=ilxʷ -s qʷam•qʷm+t iʔ kɬ+nqs=ilxʷ iʔ s+t•tm̓•tim̓ -s uɬ
to_be -suit -3i excellent art have_suit art clothes -3in and
a suit. He had on a beautiful outfit. And

a[xáʔ] iʔ q̓aʔxáns, yaʕyáʕt sic 145 way̓ wiʔsənt̓ək̓ʷəntísəlx i
axáʔ iʔ q̓aʔ=xán -s yaʕ•yáʕ+t sic way̓ wy̓+s+n+t̓k̓ʷ -nt -is -lx iʔ
this art shoes -3in all new well finish_put_in -nt -3erg -pl art
his shoes, everything new. They finished putting him

la nt̓ək̓ʷmín 146 way̓ wiʔstís axáʔ iʔ səxʷk̓ʷəl̓ɬt̓k̓ʷmínəm, {uɬ iʔ kic i}
l n+t̓k̓ʷ+min way̓ wy̓ -st -is axáʔ iʔ sxʷ=k̓ʷl̓+ɬ+t̓k̓ʷ+min+m
in coffin well finish -st -3erg this art coffin_maker
in the coffin. He finished the coffin, and

a[xáʔ] nt̓ək̓ʷəntísəlx 147 way̓ ʕalqísəlx, way ixíʔ
axáʔ n+t̓k̓ʷ -nt -is -lx way̓ ʕal̓=qí -s -lx way̓ ixíʔ
this put_in -nt -3erg -pl well cover -3erg -pl well then
they put him in it. They closed the cover.

s?akʷɬtmní?msəlx 148 aɬí? axá? {i?} i? sck̓əɬcíq[x]
s -?akʷ+ɬ+tmní?+m -s -lx aɬí? axá? i? sc -kɬ+ciq -x
nom -funeral -3i -pl so this art ipftvp^ -dig -^ipftvp
They were having a funeral now. *There were four*

kmúsəms 149 uɬ ixí? ʕapná? i? suyápix ia ncucw̓íksəs
k=mus•ms uɬ ixí? ʕapná? i? s+wyapy=x i? n+cw•cw=iks -s
four_persons and that now art white_person art do_same -3erg
grave diggers. *The white people now do the same thing.*

150 ixí? ʕapná? {i s} i? səstkʷníx i? l təmtəmní? 151 uɬ
ixí? ʕapná? i? s -s+t+kʷni -x i? l tm•tmni? uɬ
then now art ipftv^ -holder -^ipftv art for corpse and
Now they have poll bearers, *four*

kmúsəms kəm̓ kt̓áq̓t̓əq̓mkst, ixí? c̓umstəm i? t suyápix
k=mus•ms km̓ k=t̓aq̓•t̓q̓m=kst ixí? c -?um -st -m i? t s+wyapy=x
four_persons or six_persons that cust^ -call -^cust -psv art agInst white_person
or six, the white people call these

pall bearers 152 xʷú··ystsəlx kɬt̓k̓ʷússəlx i? k̓əl
xʷuy+st -s -lx kɬ+t̓k̓ʷ=us -s -lx i? k̓l
take_st -3erg -pl put_down_at_edge -3erg -pl art at
"pall bearers." 16:00 *They took him and they put him down on the edge of*

səntəmtəmní?tən 153 way̓ ɬa?ɬa?xʷísk̓it way̓ nt̓k̓ʷúla?xʷsəlx 154 way̓
s+n+tm•tmni?+tn way̓ ɬa?•ɬa?xʷ=ísk̓it way̓ n+t̓k̓ʷ=úla?xʷ -s -lx way̓
graveyard well rested_pl yes put_in_ground -3erg -pl well
the grave. *They rested, and then they put him in the ground.* *Then*

ixí? kmám̓na?s[əlx] 155 way̓ wi?skmám̓na?səlx, way̓ ixí?
ixí? k+mám̓=na? -s -lx way̓ wy̓+s+k+mám̓=na? -s -lx way̓ ixí?
then fill_hole -3erg -pl well finish_fill_hole -3erg -pl well then
they filled in the grave. *They got done filling in the grave,*

itlí? sxʷuys axá? i? tətwít 156 ah na?ɬcəcám, ixí? naqs
itlí? s -xʷuy -s axá? i? t•tw̓it ah naɬc•c•ám ixí? naqs
from_there nom -go -3i this art boy intj forget that one
and then the boy left. *Oh, I just thought of something,*

isənɬipt {axá? la} 157 axá? ɬa? cʕac̓x̌ɬq̓əy̓mínəm axá? i? tətw̓ít
i -s+n+ɬip+t axá? ɬa? c -ʕac̓x̌+ɬ+q̓y̓+mín+m axá? i? t•tw̓it
1in -forgot_thing this when hab -read_books this art boy
I forgot one thing. *When the boy was reading books,*

púti {ɬ} ɬ mut i? l ƛ̓ax̌əx̌ƛ̓x̌áps 158 way̓ wíkəm t
pút+i? ɬ mut i? l ƛ̓x̌•x̌•ƛ̓x̌a+p -s way̓ wik+m t
still when be_home art at parents -3in well see obj_itr
when he was at his parents, *he had seen a picture,*

sk̓əɬq̓əy̓ncút, tkəɬmílxʷ, st̓a?k̓míx 159 nt̓a·· way̓ swi?númtx 160 way̓
s+k̓ɬ+q̓y̓+ncut tkɬmilxʷ s+t̓a?k̓+míx nt̓a way̓ s+wy̓+numt=x way̓
picture woman virgin intj yes handsome well
a woman, a maiden. *Gee, she's good looking. 17:01* *He*

t'i wiks uł ixíʔ nq̓əmscínəms 161 uł ałíʔ way̓ ƛ̓x̌ap way̓
t'iʔ wik -s uł ixíʔ n+q̓m=s=cin+m -s uł ałíʔ way̓ ƛ̓x̌a+p way̓
evid see -3erg and then pine_for -3erg and so yes grow_sg yes
had only seen it, and he got stuck on her. *He is growing up, and he has*

pəx̌pəx̌twílx, way̓ uł {n} nnəx̌ʷnəxʷíls 162 uł cut way̓ ixíʔ
px̌•px̌+t+wilx way̓ uł n+nx̌ʷ•nx̌ʷ=ils uł cut way̓ ixíʔ
get_senses yes and want_wife and say well that
already lots of sense, and a desire for women. *And he said, "I am*

iksƛ̓aʔƛ̓ʔám axáʔ iʔ sk̓əłq̓əyncút 163 ṅíṅẁiʔ kaʔkícən məł ixíʔ {ikł}
i -ks -ƛ̓aʔ•ƛ̓ʔá+m axáʔ iʔ s+k̓ł+q̓y̓+ncut ṅíṅẁiʔ kaʔ•kíc -n mł ixíʔ
1i -futi -look_for this art picture a_while find -1erg and that
going to look for [the one in] this picture. *If I find her, she's going to be*

ikłnáx̌ʷnəx̌ʷ 164 i· kən xʷilwís iʔ t təmxʷúlaʔxʷ put kaʔkícən
i -kł -nax̌ʷ•nx̌ʷ i· kn xʷy+lwis iʔ t tmxʷ=úlaʔxʷ put kaʔ•kíc -n
1i -to_be -wife intj 1kn wander art obl country just find -1erg
my wife. *I am going to travel the world until I find her before*

mi kən cpəlk̓úsəm 165 ixíʔ naʔłcəcám, ixíʔ ia nłíptmən {ixiʔ uł i}
mi kn c+p̓lk̓=us+m ixíʔ nałc•c•ám ixíʔ iʔ n+łip+t+m -n
fut 1kn turn_around_cisl that forget that art forget -1erg
I turn back." *That's what I thought of, that's what I forgot.*

166 uł lut ixíʔ ukʷtúłts iʔ ƛ̓ax̌əx̌ƛ̓x̌áps 167 lut ixíʔ {t'ə} t'ə
uł lut ixíʔ wkʷ -tułt -s iʔ ƛ̓x̌•x̌•ƛ̓x̌a+p -s lut ixíʔ t'
and not that hide -tułt -3erg art parents -3in not then negfac
He hid this from his parents, *he didn't tell them*

m̓áyaʔłts ixíʔ iʔ l sk̓əłq̓əy̓ncút 168 uł way̓ t'iʔ_kmix st'imíx łaʔ
m̓áyaʔ -łt -s ixíʔ iʔ l s+k̓ł+q̓y̓+ncut uł way̓ t'iʔ_kmix s+t'y+mix łaʔ
tell -łt -3erg that art in picture and yes only lazy when
about the one in the picture, 18:03 *only how tired he was of staying*

cmut {ks ks ə··} 169 kshaháʕʷmistaʔx kswíklaʔxʷaʔx
c -mut ks -ha•háʕʷ+mist -aʔx ks -wík=laʔxʷ -aʔx
hab -be_home incp^ -loosen_up -^incp incp^ -see_world -^incp
at home. *He is going to loosen up and see the world,*

170 ksxʷstlwísmiʔs iʔ təmxʷúlaʔxʷ 171 uł cəm̓ ixíʔ
ks -xʷst+lwís+miʔ -s iʔ tmxʷ=úlaʔxʷ uł cm̓ ixíʔ
futi -travel_around -3i art country and maybe that
he is going to walk the world over. *But it's that*

ksƛ̓aʔƛ̓aʔntís ixíʔ iʔ tkəłmílxʷ 172 ixíʔ iʔ l sk̓əłq̓əyncút i l
ks -ƛ̓aʔ•ƛ̓aʔ -nt -is ixíʔ iʔ tkłmilxʷ ixíʔ iʔ l s+k̓ł+q̓y̓+ncut iʔ l
futt^ -look_for -nt -3erg that art woman that art in picture art in
he is going to look for *the woman in the picture*

q̓əy̓mín 173 ixíʔ naʔłcəcám, ixíʔ ia nłíptmən 174 ałíʔ yaʔx̌í
q̓y̓+min ixíʔ nałc•c•ám ixíʔ iʔ n+łip+t+m -n ałíʔ yaʔx̌í
paper that forget that art forget -1erg because that_one
in the book. *This is what I thought of, what I forgot.* *Because*

inqáqna? waẏ mat t'aq̇əmkɬ?apnkspíntk ki? ixí? kʷu a
in -qá•qna? waẏ mat t'aq̇m=k+ɬ+?apn=ks+pin=tk ki? ixí? kʷu a
1in -fa's_mother well maybe sixty_years rel that 1obj art
my grandma maybe sixty years ago

ccaptíkʷɬts 175 uɬ {ixí? uɬ} ixí? uɬ waẏ i? kna nɬəpɬípt
c -captíkʷ -ɬt -s uɬ ixí? uɬ waẏ i? kn n+ɬp•ɬip+t
act -legend -ɬt -3erg and that and yes art 1kn forget
told me this story. *And that's why I forget.*

176 xi? waẏ axá? u?ípunlx,[3] itlí? kən nċṗq̇síẇs[m]
ixí? waẏ axá? wẏ+ipwn -lx itlí? kn n+ċṗq̇+s=iẇs+m
then yes this finish_bury -pl from_there 1kn splice
They got done with the funeral, and now I'm going to continue.

177 u?ípunlx waẏ itlí? sxʷuys 178 xʷu··y uɬ
wẏ+ipwn -lx waẏ itlí? s -xʷuy -s xʷuy uɬ
finish_bury -pl well from_there nom -go -3i go and
They got done with the funeral, and he started on. 19:00 *He went,*

cxʷuy uɬ miná lut aɬí? waẏ sic ta?xʷɬxəwíɬ 179 waẏ ?ilxʷt, uɬ
c -xʷuy uɬ miná lut aɬí? waẏ sic ta?xʷ+ɬ+xwíɬ waẏ ?ilxʷ+t uɬ
hab -go and futNeg not because yes then have_road well hungry and
and I guess there is a road now. *He got hungry,*

kʷa aɬí? waẏ sqilxʷ ?ilxʷt məɬ {ac} a cksq̇míltən {kəm̓ a t'əxʷ kiw}
kʷa aɬí? waẏ s+qilxʷ ?ilxʷ+t mɬ a c -k+s+q̇m=ilt+n
intj so yes person hungry and art hab -hunger
and when people get hungry that's when they want food.

180 uɬ ixí? {s} sksq̇míltən i? s?ilxʷt 181 məɬ ixí? məɬ n?ayx̌ʷtíls
uɬ ixí? s+k+s+q̇m=ilt+n i? s+?ilxʷ+t mɬ ixí? mɬ n+?ayx̌ʷ+t=íls
and that hunger art hunger and then and get_tired
I guess wishing for food is being hungry. *People also get tired*

nixʷ {i s} i? sqilxʷ kʷa ?ilxʷt, uɬ n?ayx̌ʷtíls 182 waẏ axá? ?ilxʷt uɬ
nixʷ i? s+qilxʷ kʷa ?ilxʷ+t uɬ n+?ayx̌ʷ+t=íls waẏ axá? ?ilxʷ+t uɬ
also art person intj hungry and get_tired well this hungry and
when they are hungry, and he got tired. *This boy*

n?ayx̌ʷtíls axá? i? tətẇit 183 waẏ uɬ nstils, way {lut kən t'a uɬ} ca?kʷ iwá
n+?ayx̌ʷ+t=íls axá? i? t•tẇit waẏ uɬ n+st=ils waẏ ca?kʷ iwá
get_tired this art boy well and think well if even
got hungry and tired. *And he thought, "Even if*

kən ɬuksqílxʷ 184 uɬ waẏ lut kən t'a ksqlaw ɬ
kn ɬ+wk+s+qilxʷ uɬ waẏ lut kn t' k+s+qlaw ɬ
1kn see_again and yes not 1kn negfac have_money subord
I do see people *I don't have money to buy food,*

3 Form not clear.

ikstíwcən waỷ c̓əspnún isqláw 185 ilíʔ nʔax̌əlíls
i -ks -tiw=cn waỷ c̓s+p -nu -n i -s+qlaw ilíʔ n+ʔax̌l=íls
1i -futi -get_groceries yes rid -manage -1erg 1in -money there think_so
I spent all my money." 20:04 *That's his thought.*

186 waỷ k̓əɬk̓ʷƛ̓áp, sta səstipmíx siwɬkʷ 187 uɬ
waỷ k̓ɬ+k̓ʷƛ̓a+p sta sc -ty+p -mix siwɬ=kʷ uɬ
well come_in_sight intj ipftvp^ -water_flow -^ipftvp water and
He came in sight of flowing water. *There*

cənx̌líẁs axáʔ iʔ t ksxʷúytəns {əɬ aɬ itiʔ ixiʔ} 188 iʔ cxʷist
c -n+x̌l=iẁs axáʔ iʔ t k -s+xʷuy+tn -s iʔ c -xʷist
hab -bridge this art obl futi -travel -3i art hab -walk
is a bridge right where he is going. *From the time*

tlaʔx̌íʔ {u} iʔ {təl} təl ƛ̓ax̌əx̌ƛ̓x̌áps 189 uɬ a ncháqsəms uɬ
ʔx̌íʔ iʔ tl ƛ̓x̌•x̌•ƛ̓x̌a+p -s uɬ a n+ch=aqs+m -s uɬ
from_there art from parents -3in and art facing -3in and
he walked from over there from his parents, *the way he was facing*

niʕíp̓ ta ck̓líʔ təɬməncút 190 uɬ aɬíʔ lut t̓a
n+yʕ=ip ta c+k̓líʔ tɬ+mncut uɬ aɬíʔ lut t̓
always in_that_direction go_straight_(up) and so not negfac
he continued straight in the same direction. *He doesn't recognize*

csúxʷlaʔxʷəm, cminúlaʔxʷəm 191 lut t̓a cmistís
c -súxʷ=laʔxʷ+m c -my+n=úlaʔxʷ+m lut t̓ c -my -st -is
hab -know_country hab -know_country not hab hab -know -^cust -3erg
the country, he doesn't know the country. *He doesn't know*

k̓aʔkín səcxʷúy[x] 192 itíʔ tanm̓ús t̓i səcxʷúyx
k̓a+ʔkín sc -xʷuy -x itíʔ tanm̓=ús t̓iʔ sc -xʷuy -x
to_where ipftvp^ -go -^ipftvp from_that nothing evid ipftvp^ -go -^ipftvp
where he is going. *He is just going for nothing [end of tape]. 20:48*

193 waỷ itlíʔ kən nc̓əp̓q̓síẁsəm a[xáʔ] iʔ l incaptíkʷɬ
waỷ itlíʔ kn n+c̓p̓q̓+s=iẁs+m axáʔ iʔ l in -captíkʷɬ
well from_there 1kn splice this art with 1in -legends
Now I am going to splice my story.

194 aɬíʔ kən ksmáʔmən̓xʷaʔx, caʔkʷ cus iʔ ta nuyápixcən
aɬíʔ kn ks -maʔ•m•n̓xʷ -aʔx caʔkʷ cu -s iʔ t n+wyap=x=cn
because 1kn incp^ -smoke_dim -^incp as tell -3erg art agInst speak_English
I am smoking, as they say in the white people language,

195 uɬ aɬíʔ kulúsən inpíspayp 196 ixíʔ kən
uɬ aɬíʔ k+wl=us -n in -píspayp ixíʔ kn
and so light -1erg 1in -peace_pipe then 1kn
I lit my "peace pipe." *I just*

swiʔsmán̓xʷəxʷ, uɬ itlíʔ kən nc̓əp̓q̓síẁsəm 197 waỷ
s -wy̓+s+man̓xʷ -xʷ uɬ itlíʔ kn n+c̓p̓q̓+s=iẁs+m waỷ
ipftv^ -finish_smoking -^ipftv and from_there 1kn splice well
got done smoking, and now I'll splice. *The*

k̓əɬʔál·qʷaʔ a[xáʔ] iʔ tətw̓ít 198 ixíʔ uɬ ʔanwís way̓ kən ʔayx̌ʷt
k̓+ɬʔ=álqʷ+aʔ axáʔ iʔ t•tw̓it ixíʔ uɬ ʔanwí -s way̓ kn ʔayx̌ʷ+t
next_to_shore this art boy then and feel -3erg well 1kn tired
boy got next to the river, *and he felt, "I am really tired."*

199 kʷa iʔ sqilxʷ aɬíʔ ʔayx̌ʷt uɬ {uɬ ac} a cksq̓míltən 200 way̓
kʷa iʔ s+qilxʷ aɬíʔ ʔayx̌ʷ+t uɬ a c -k+s+q̓m=ilt+n way̓
intj art person because tired and art hab -hunger well
When a person gets tired he wishes for food. *But*

uɬ aɬíʔ x̌áq̓əms yaʕyáʕt iʔ sqľaws 201 uɬ nstils way̓ t̓əxʷ
uɬ aɬíʔ x̌aq̓+m -s yaʕ•yáʕ+t iʔ s+qlaw -s uɬ n+st=ils way̓ t̓xʷ
and so pay -3erg all art money -3in and think well emph
he paid all his money out, *and he thought,*

qʷńcin, uɬ t̓xʷ kən xkínəm {mi k} 202 caʔkʷ iwá kən ɬ kicx iʔ l tawn
qʷń=cin uɬ t̓xʷ kn x+kin+m caʔkʷ iwá kn ɬ kic+x iʔ l tawn
pity and emph 1kn do_what if even 1kn if arrive art at town
"That's pitiful, and what can I do? *Even if I get to a town I can't get*

mi kən ʔaɬəɬníʔst 203 way̓ xiʔ sənʔax̌lílsc uɬ i[xíʔ] skɬxʷists
mi kn ʔaɬ•ɬ•n=íʔst way̓ ixíʔ s+n+ʔax̌l=íls -c uɬ ixíʔ s -kɬ+xʷist -s
fut 1kn get_food well that want_to_do -3in and then nom -walk_on_st -3i
anything to eat." *That's just what he thought when he walked on the bridge*

axáʔ iʔ ta nx̌liw̓s axáʔ a ctyap 204 way̓ put a l nmiw̓síkń
axáʔ iʔ t n+x̌l=iw̓s axáʔ a c -tya+p way̓ put a l n+miw̓s=íkń
this art obl bridge this art hab -water_runs well just art in middle
over running water. 1:04 *Just as he got to the middle*

a iwá staʔx̌ílx {a kəm ɬiwt} 205 ilí··ʔ k̓amtíwaʔs a[xáʔ] tətw̓ít
a iwá s -ta+ʔx̌íl -x ilíʔ k+ʔam=t=íwaʔs axáʔ t•tw̓it
intj even ipftv^ -do_a_certain_way -^ipftvp there sit_on_dim this boy
of the bridge, he did like that,[4] *and there was a boy sitting there,*

206 k̓ʷək̓ʷyúmaʔ iʔ tətw̓ít, t̓əxʷ púti {uɬ c} cqəcqícəlx náx̌əmɬ
k̓ʷ•k̓ʷy=úmaʔ iʔ t•tw̓it t̓xʷ pút+iʔ c -qc•qic+lx nax̌mɬ
small art boy evidently still hab -run but
a boy, small, but able to run around,

207 ck̓ʷəck̓ʷáct uɬ taʔlí náx̌əmɬ sk̓ʷk̓ʷíməlt 208 cúntəm axáʔ
c -k̓ʷc•k̓ʷac+t uɬ taʔlíʔ nax̌mɬ s+k̓ʷ•k̓ʷiy=ṁ=ľt cu -nt -m axáʔ
hab -strong and very_much but child_dim tell -nt -psv this
strong, but very young. *The little one*

ixíʔ t k̓amtíwaʔs, way̓ atáʔ kʷ {cxʷil} cxʷilwís kʷ sqilxʷ
ixíʔ t k+ʔam=t=íwaʔs way̓ atáʔ kʷ c -xʷy+lwis kʷ s+qilxʷ
that agInst sit_on_dim well here 2kn hab -wander 2kn person
sitting there said to him, "So you are traveling around, pilgrim."

4 A head motion probably accompanied this utterance.

209 cus way̓ 210 k̓aʔkín kʷ səcxʷuyx 211 way̓ {k}
cu -s way̓ k̓a+ʔkín kʷ sc -xʷuy -x way̓
tell -3erg yes to_where 2kn ipftvpˆ -go -ˆipftvp well
He said to him, "Yes." *"Where are you going?"* *"I don't*

t̓əxʷ lut t̓a cmistín k̓aʔkín kən səcxʷúyx
t̓xʷ lut t̓ c -my -st -in k̓a+ʔkín kn sc -xʷuy -x
emph not evid custˆ -know -ˆcust -1erg to_where 1kn ipftvpˆ -go -ˆipftvp
know where I am going,

212 way̓ t̓i {t̓i k} isəcxʷəstlwísəm iʔ [t] təmxʷúlaʔxʷ 213 a··, cúntəm
way̓ t̓iʔ i -sc -xʷst+lwis+m iʔ t tmxʷ=úlaʔxʷ a cu -nt -m
well evid 1i -pftv -travel art obl country intj tell -nt -psv
I am just traveling around the world." *"Ah," he said,*

way̓ caʔkʷ uc iʔ kxəntsín 214 nstils axáʔ iʔ tətw̓ít, way̓ lut
way̓ caʔkʷ uc iʔ kx+n -t -s -in n+st=ils axáʔ iʔ t•tw̓it way̓ lut
well could dub art follow -nt -2obj -1erg think this art boy well not
"Can I go with you?" 2:01 *The boy thought, "Heck no.*

215 uɬ axáʔ lut kən t̓a ksql̓aw, uɬ way̓ myaɬ k̓ʷək̓ʷyúmaʔ
uɬ axáʔ lut kn t̓ k+s+qlaw uɬ way̓ myaɬ k̓ʷ•k̓ʷy=úmaʔ
and this not 1kn negfac have_money and yes too_much small
I haven't got any money, and he is too small.

216 uɬ laʔkín m[i] kʷu ʔaxkínəm mi kʷu {kʷu} ʔaɬəɬníʔst, iwá caʔkʷ kʷu ɬ
uɬ la+ʔkíń mi kʷu ʔax+kín+m mi kʷu ʔaɬ•ɬ•n=íʔst iwá caʔkʷ kʷu ɬ
and how fut 4kn do_how fut 4kn get_food even if 4kn if
How can we get food, even if we

kicx i l tawn 217 uɬ nixʷ pna cmay nixʷ kʷu xárkstəms
kic+x iʔ l tawn uɬ nixʷ pnaʔ cmay nixʷ kʷu xar=kst+m -s
arrive art at town and also maybe maybe also 1obj take_time -3erg
get to a town? *And besides, he might slow me down.*

218 way̓ myaɬ k̓ʷk̓ʷyúmaʔ 219 lut t̓ qəɬnús {ə} ɬə
way̓ myaɬ k̓ʷ•k̓ʷy=úmaʔ lut t̓ qɬ -nu -s ɬ
well too_much small not negfac accomplish -manage -3erg compl
He is too small, *he could never walk*

ksxʷists iʔ l ksk̓laxʷ kəm̓ i l ksx̌lap 220 uɬ lut kən t̓a
ks -xʷist -s iʔ l k+s+k̓laxʷ km̓ iʔ l k+s+x̌la+p uɬ lut kn t̓
futi -walk -3i art for all_day or art for all_night and not 1kn negfac
the whole day and night. *And I haven't got*

ksnilíʔtən, lut {k t̓əxʷ} kən t̓a ksql̓aw {qiɬc} 221 cakʷ iwá kʷu ɬ
k+s+n+ilíʔ+tn lut kn t̓ k+s+qlaw caʔkʷ iwá kʷu ɬ
have_dwelling_place not 1kn negfac have_money if even 4kn if
a place to stop, we haven't got any money, *even if*

yaʕp iʔ l tawn 222 kʷu ɬə {ks} sxʷuys k̓əl sənʔíɬəntən kəm̓
yaʕ+p iʔ l tawn kʷu ɬ s -xʷuy -s k̓l s+n+ʔiɬn+tn km̓
arrive_pl art at town 4kn if nom4ˆ -go -ˆnom4 to restaurant or
we get to a town, *if we go to an eating place, or*

k̓əl sənpúlxtən 223 cus lut, way̓ kʷ k̓ʷək̓ʷyúmaʔ, kʷ {inaud}
k̓l s+n+pul+x+tn cu -s lut way̓ myał kʷ k̓ʷ•k̓ʷy=úmaʔ kʷ
to camping_place tell -3erg not well too_much 2kn small 2kn
to a hotel.” He said to him “No, you are too small, you are

x̌ʷupt 224 cəm̓ kʷu xárkstməntxʷ, lkʷut {is} iksxʷúytən
x̌ʷup+t cm̓ kʷu xar=kst+m -nt -xʷ lkʷ=ut i -k -s+xʷuy+tn
weak maybe 1obj take_time -nt -2erg far 1i -to_be -travel
helpless, you might slow me down, I am going far.” 3:05

225 cúntəm lut, way̓ kən k̓ʷəck̓ʷáct, way̓ kən sisyús 226 way̓ t̓iʔ_niʕíp
cu -nt -m lut way̓ kn k̓ʷc•k̓ʷac+t way̓ kn sy•sy=us way̓ t̓iʔ_n+iʕ=íp
tell -nt -psv not yes 1kn strong yes 1kn smart well always
He said to him “No, I am strong, I am smart. I always

inx̌mínk {p iksxʷuy} kʷ ikskxnám 227 {ə wim̓} uʔw̓im̓
in -x̌m=ink kʷ i -ks -kx+na+m w̓•w̓im̓
1in -want 2kʷu 1i -futi -go_along in_vain_dim
wanted to go with you.” He tried to

m̓aʔm̓ís uł {ns} 228 nstils kway̓ t̓əxʷ isənqʷn̓mínəm, mat
maʔ+mí -s uł n+st=ils k+way̓ t̓xʷ i -s -n+qʷn̓+min+m mat
send away -3erg and think well emph 1i -intt -pity maybe
discourage him. He thought, "Well, I pity him, he might be

pna cmay ktəl̓típlaʔ 229 uł sic siws, cus uł sc̓kinx lut
pnaʔ cmay k+tl̓t=íplaʔ uł sic siw -s cu -s uł sc+ʔkin+x lut
maybe maybe orphan and then ask -3erg tell -3erg and why_is_it not
an orphan.” Then he asked him, “What’s the matter, don’t you

askłƛ̓ax̌əx̌ƛ̓x̌áp 230 lut, lut aláʔ kən t̓a kłƛ̓ax̌əx̌ƛ̓x̌áp 231 kən
a -s -kł+ƛ̓ax̌•x̌•ƛ̓x̌á+p lut lut aláʔ kn t̓ kł+ƛ̓ax̌•x̌•ƛ̓x̌á+p kn
2i -nom -have_parents not not here 1kn negfac have_parents 1kn
have any parents?” “No, I haven’t got any parents, I

t̓a ksniliʔtən, uł {aláʔ} aláʔ iʔ {kən sc i} kən taʔ kən kłxʷist
t̓ k+s+n+ilíʔ+tn uł aláʔ iʔ kn atáʔ kn kł+xʷist
negfac have_dwelling_place and here art 1kn here 1kn walk_on_st
don’t have a place to stay.

232 úłi {kən} iʔ kən kƛ̓aʔƛ̓aʔús t iksnkxəntán 233 uł
uł iʔ iʔ kn k+ƛ̓aʔ•ƛ̓ʔ=ús t i -k -s+n+kx+n+tan uł
and_then art 1kn look_for obj_itr 1i -to_be -travel_companion and
And I walked here, and then I looked for someone to go with. Then

anwí wíkəntsən, səc̓x̌ílx ka nkxnílsməntsən 234 uł
anwí wik -nt -s -n sc+ʔx̌il+x ka n+kx+n=ils+m -nt -s -n uł
you see -nt -2obj -1erg reason_why rel want_to_follow -nt -2obj -1erg and
I saw you, and I want to go with you.” The

nstils axáʔ iʔ tətwít 235 way̓ nák̓ʷəm mat ha sck̓əłnəq̓ʷmístx
n+st=ils axáʔ iʔ t•tw̓it way̓ nak̓ʷ+m mat haʔ sc -k̓ł+nq̓ʷ+mist -x
think this art boy well evid must inter ipftvp^ -run_away -^ipftvp
boy thought 4:00 he must be running away.

236 cúntəm lut ha kʷ sck̓əłnəq̓ʷmistx 237 lut 238 ahá·
cu -nt -m lut haʔ kʷ sc -k̓ł+nq̓ʷ+mist -x lut ahá
tell -nt -psv not inter 2kn ipftvp^ -run_away -^ipftvp not intj
He said, "Aren't you running away?" "No." "Or

kəm̓ ha kʷ scənsl̓ípx 239 lut, way̓ wim̓ uł nstils {k way̓ t̓}
km̓ haʔ kʷ sc -n+sl̓i+p -x lut way̓ wim̓ uł n+st=ils
or inter 2kn ipftvp^ -lost -^ipftvp not well in_vain and think
are you lost?" "No," and he thought, "Maybe

way̓ lut iksnk̓əstmínəm {may lwi} 240 cus way, way̓ ałíʔ x̌əl naqs iʔ
way̓ lut i -ks -n+k̓st+min+m cu -s way̓ way̓ ałíʔ x̌l naqs iʔ
well not 1i -futi -fall_ill tell -3erg well well because for one art
he wouldn't bother me." He told him, "Just for one thing I don't

maʔmíntsən 241 uł k̓ʷam incá kən ƛ̓əx̌ƛ̓x̌áp, {uł} uł way̓ kən
maʔ+mín -t -s -n uł k̓ʷam in+cá kn ƛ̓x̌•ƛ̓x̌a+p uł way̓ kn
turn_away -nt -2obj -1erg and evid I 1kn elder and yes 1kn
want you with me. Even if I am a grown man, I get tired

ʔayx̌ʷt kən ksq̓míltən 242 uł lut kən t̓a ksql̓aw 243 uł axáʔ
ʔayx̌ʷ+t kn k+s+q̓m=ilt+n uł lut kn t̓ k+s+qlaw uł axáʔ
tired 1kn have_hunger and not 1kn evid have_money and this
and I get hungry, and I don't have money. And you

anwí kʷ sk̓ʷk̓ʷíməlt, uł way̓ cəm̓ kʷ ʔayx̌ʷt uł kʷ ksq̓míltən
anwí kʷ s+k̓ʷ•k̓ʷy=im̓=l̓t uł way̓ cm̓ kʷ ʔayx̌ʷ+t uł kʷ k+s+q̓m=ilt+n
you 2kn child_dim and yes maybe 2kn tired and 2kn have_hunger
are little, and you will get tired, and you will get hungry.

244 uł cəm̓ way̓ mał kʷu nq̓aʔílsəntxʷ 245 cúntəm
uł cm̓ way̓ myał kʷu n+q̓aʔ=íls -nt -xʷ cu -nt -m
and maybe well too_much 1obj concerned -nt -2erg tell -nt -psv
And then you will bother me." The little boy

a[xáʔ] iʔ t tətw̓ít lut, lut ilíʔ aksnʔax̌líls 246 way̓
axáʔ iʔ t t•tw̓it lut lut ilíʔ a -ks -n+ʔax̌l=íls way̓
this art agInst boy not not there 2i -futi -think_so yes
said, "Don't think that way. I am

isqʷʔám isksq̓míltən nixʷ, way̓ t̓i kʷu x̌əctwíxʷ
i -s -qʷʔam i -s -k+s+q̓m=ilt+n nixʷ way̓ t̓iʔ kʷu x̌c+twixʷ
1i -intt -get_used_to 1i -intt -hunger also yes evid 4kn be_companions
used to getting hungry, we'll just go partners." 5:04

247 a, way̓, cúntəm way̓, way̓ ixíʔ sxʷúys[əlx] 248 cúntəm
a way̓ cu -nt -m way̓ way̓ ixíʔ s -xʷuy -s -lx cu -nt -m
intj OK tell -nt -psv well well then nom -go -3i -pl tell -nt -psv
He said "Ok," and so they went. The boy,

ałíʔ axáʔ iʔ t tətw̓ít t qaʔłilmíxʷəm 249 cuntəm uł ałíʔ
ałíʔ axáʔ iʔ t t•tw̓it t qaʔł=yl=míxʷ+m cu -nt -m uł ałíʔ
so this art agInst boy agInst chief's_children tell -nt -psv and so
the king's son said to him: "I am tired

waẏ kən ʔayx̌ʷt kən ksq̓míltən 250 uł lut t̓ qəłnún
waẏ kn ʔayx̌ʷ+t kn k+s+q̓m=ilt+n uł lut t̓ qł -nu -n
yes 1kn tired 1kn hunger and not negfac able -manage -1erg
and hungry. *I won't be able to pack you*

cəm̓ kʷ ł ksʔayx̌ʷtáyn kʷ t̓ iksq̓ʷíłtəm 251 ah, cus
cm̓ kʷ ł k+s+ʔayx̌ʷ+t+áyn kʷ t̓ i -ks -q̓ʷił+t+m ah cu -s
maybe 2kn if have_tiredness 2kn negfac 1i -futi -carry intj tell -3erg
if you get tired." *He said to him,*

lut, lut ilíʔ aksnʔax̌líls 252 waẏ put kən sisyús, lut kʷu t̓
lut lut ilíʔ a -ks -n+ʔax̌l=íls waẏ put kn sy•sy=us lut kʷu t̓
not not there 2i -futi -think_so yes just 1kn smart not 1obj negfac
"No, don't think that way. *I am smart, you won't have*

aksq̓ʷíłtəm 253 lut t̓ iksksʔayx̌ʷtáyn, waẏ t̓i kʷ
a -ks -q̓ʷił+t+m lut t̓ i -ks -k+s+ʔayx̌ʷ+t+áyn waẏ t̓iʔ kʷ
2i -futi -carry not negfac 1i -futi -have_tiredness yes evid 2kʷu
to pack me. *I won't get tired, I just want to*

isənkxnílsəm 254 cúntəm waẏ, waẏ ixíʔ sic
i -s -n+kx+n=ils+m cu -nt -m waẏ waẏ ixíʔ sic
1i -intt -want_to_follow tell -nt -psv OK well then then
go with you." *He said "Ok," then they joined hands*

kʷənksnwíxʷsəlx, waẏ uł skłtəkʷʔútsəlx 255 waẏ
kʷn=ks+nwixʷ -s -lx waẏ uł s -kł+tkʷʔ=ut -s -lx waẏ
shake_hands -3erg -pl well and nom -walk_on -3i -pl well
and they walked. 6:02 *They*

tkʷənksnwáxʷəlx {ə} naʔł tətw̓ít, {ə} sm̓ayxtwíxʷsəlx 256 waẏ nstils
t+kʷn=ks+nwaxʷ -lx naʔł t•twit s -m̓ay+xt+wíxʷ -s -lx waẏ n+st=ils
hold_hands -pl with boy nom -tell_stories_rec -3i -pl well think
joined hands, he and the little boy, and they started telling stories. *Then he*

t̓əxʷ waẏ {indec} kən taʔxʷłəntkʷíl{s} 257 uł {ma} ixíʔ t̓əxʷ kən
t̓xʷ waẏ kn taʔxʷ+ł+n+t+kʷil uł ixíʔ t̓xʷ kn
emph yes 1kn have_company and then emph 1kn
thought, "Now I got company. *I am worried, I think*

k̓əłpaʔsəncút, kən nstils pna cəm̓ kʷu kƛ̓ʔíplaʔs 258 pnaʔ
k̓ł+paʔs+ncút kn n+st=ils pnaʔ cm̓ kʷu k+ƛ̓ʔ=íplaʔ -s pnaʔ
worried 1kn think maybe maybe 1obj make_trouble -3erg maybe
maybe he'll get me in trouble. *Maybe*

sk̓əłnəq̓ʷmístx, kəm̓ pnaʔ kłƛ̓ax̌əx̌ƛ̓x̌áp 259 ń̓íń̓w̓iʔ {xəƛ̓'}
s -k̓ł+nq̓ʷ+mist -x km̓ pnaʔ kł+ƛ̓ax̌•x̌•ƛ̓x̌á+p ń̓íń̓w̓iʔ
ipftv^ -run_away -^ipftv or maybe have_parents a_while
he ran away, maybe he has parents. *They might*

xsnúsəlx cəm̓ ƛ̓aʔƛ̓aʔntísəlx 260 uł {kʷu}
xs -nu -s -lx cm̓ ƛ̓aʔ•ƛ̓aʔ -nt -is -lx uł
miss -manage -3erg -pl maybe look_for -nt -3erg -pl and
miss him and look for him, *and they'll*

ka?kíci?səlx l incá {c} ckxan 261 uɬ la?kín {k} kən
ka?•kíc ẏ -s -lx l in+cá c -kxa+n uɬ la+?kíṅ kn
find -nt -3erg -pl with I hab -follow and how 1kn
find him following me. *And what will I do,*

xkínəm, {kən} kən ċint 262 uɬ cəṁ t̓i kʷu ləḱəntísəlx
x+kin+m kn ċint uɬ cṁ t̓i? kʷu lḱ -nt -is -lx
do_what 1kn say_what and maybe evid 1obj tie -nt -3erg -pl
what will I say? *They might arrest me,*

263 uɬ aɬí? lut kən xkínəm mi kən tx̌əq̓pla?míst 264 uɬ náx̌əmɬ waẏ
uɬ aɬí? lut kn x+kin+m mi kn t+x̌q̓=pla?+míst uɬ nax̌mɬ waẏ
and so not 1kn do_what fut 1kn pay_fine and but yes
and what can I do to pay my fine?" *But he [also]*

scutx lut t̓a kɬƛ̓ax̌əx̌ƛ̓x̌áp, uɬ lut t̓ə ksnilí?tən
s -cut -x lut t̓ kɬ+ƛ̓ax̌•x̌•ƛ̓x̌á+p uɬ lut t̓ k+s+n+ilí?+tn
ipftv^ -say -^ipftv not evid have_parents and not negfac have_place_to_stay
thought, "He has no parents, and no place to stay,

265 uɬ lut t̓ scḱəɬnəq̓ʷmístx, uɬ t̓əxʷ pna? sċkinx
uɬ lut t̓ sc -ḱɬ+nq̓ʷ+mist -x uɬ t̓xʷ pna? sc+?kin+x
and not negfac ipftvp^ -run_away -^ipftvp and emph maybe why_is_it
and he is not running away, and I wonder why.

266 mat mat cktəltípla?, mat sċkinx la?kín sċkinx 267 ixí?
mat mat c -k+tlt=ípla? mat sc+?kin+x la+?kíṅ sc+?kin+x ixí?
maybe maybe hab -orphan maybe why_is_it how why_is_it that
Maybe he is orphaned, I wonder what can be." 7:04 *That's*

i? scḱəɬpá?x̌s axá? i? tətẃit 268 waẏ xʷu··ẏilx waẏ lut
i? sc -ḱɬ+pa?x̌ -s axá? i? t•tẃit waẏ xʷuy•ay -lx waẏ lut
art pftv -think_about -3i this art boy well go -pl well not
what the boy has been thinking. *They went, they*

səlkʷúts i? scxʷúysəlx 269 waẏ wíkməlx {i? t} i? t citxʷ
s -lkʷ=ut -s i? sc -xʷuy -s -lx waẏ wik+m -lx i? t citxʷ
nom -far -3i art pftv -go -3i -pl well see -pl art obj_itr house
hadn't gone far *and they saw a house.*

270 nt̓a·· waẏ sílxʷa? i? citxʷ, nt̓a qʷámqʷəmt i? citxʷ {waẏ t̓i uɬt}
nt̓a waẏ sílxʷa? i? citxʷ nt̓a qʷam•qʷm+t i? citxʷ
intj yes big art house intj excellent art house
My, that's a big house, a beautiful house.

271 aɬí? ḱəl skənxa?cínəmsəlx {ki} ta cḱlí?
aɬí? ḱl s -k+n+xa?=cín+m -s -lx ta c+ḱlí?
because to nom -on_way -3i -pl in_that_direction
It's right in their path to where

səcxʷúyxəlx 272 waẏ xʷuylx uɬ ktáɬɬəlx
sc -xʷuy -x -lx waẏ xʷuy -lx uɬ k+taɬ•ɬ -lx
ipftvp^ -go -^ipftvp -pl well go -pl and in_front_of -pl
they are going. *They went and they got right*

sənk̓ək̓tá?qa?s 273 uɬ nstils axá? t̓əxʷ i? {c} tətwít 274 way̓
c -n+k̓•k̓t=áqa?s uɬ n+st=ils axá? t̓xʷ i? t•tw̓it way̓
hab -close_to_road and think this evidently art boy yes
opposite to it. *And the boy thought:* *"I am*

myaɬ t̓əxʷ kən ?ayx̌ʷt, kən ksq̓mílt[ən] 275 pna cmay nqʷəń qʷń íls
myaɬ t̓xʷ kn ?ayx̌ʷ+t kn k+s+q̓m=ilt+n pna? cmay n+qʷń•qʷń=ils
too_much emph 1kn tired 1kn have_hunger maybe maybe have_pity
really tired, and I am hungry. *Maybe the people will*

axá? a? kɬcitxʷ 276 ńíńw̓i? nx̌əlcín· t̓əxʷ t skmaʕ̓ʷáqs
axá? a? kɬ+citxʷ ńíńw̓i? n+x̌l=cin[5] -n t̓xʷ t s+k+maʕʷ=áqs
this art have_house a_while ask_for_food -1erg emph obj_tr left_overs
feel sorry. 8:04 *I'll ask for left overs or for garbage,*

kəm̓ i? t sx̌ʷalqs uɬ way̓ ixí? 277 uɬ pna? {t̓ i?} i? l
km̓ i? t s+x̌ʷal=qs uɬ way̓ ixí? uɬ pna? i? l
or art obj_tr food_thrown_away and yes that and maybe art in
and that'll be all right. *And maybe*

sənt̓əwscqáx̌a?tən 278 t̓əxʷ sxi?míx {i? l t̓ik̓ʷlx} i? l t̓ik̓ʷlx t
s+n+t̓wst+s=qáx̌a?+tn t̓xʷ s+xi?+míx i? l t̓ik̓ʷ+lx t
barn emph whatever art in bed obl
in the barn, *or whatever it is they'll give us*

ksənpúlxtəntət 279 [na]k̓ʷá? i? l citxʷ {indec} iksənpúlx
k -s+n+pul+x+tn -tt nak̓ʷá i? l citxʷ i -ks -n+pul+x
to_be -camping_place -4i indeed_not art in house 1i -futi -camp_in
to sleep. *They don't have to put us up in the house."*

280 ay̓ ixí? scən?ax̌líls[c] 281 way̓ xʷuylx uɬ ixí? i? l
ay̓ ixí? sc -n+?ax̌l=íls -c way̓ xʷuy -lx uɬ ixí? i? l
intj that pftv -think_so -3i well go -pl and then art at
That's what he was thinking. *They went and they got to*

scənsíq̓əms la nɬa?máqs 282 uɬ nstils axá? i? qa?ɬilmíxʷəm
sc -n+siq̓+m -s l n+ɬa?+m=aqs uɬ n+st=ils axá? i? qa?ɬ=yl=míxʷ+m
cust^ -split -3i in close_to_road and think this art chief's_children
where the road forks, *and the chief's son thought:*

283 way̓ t̓əxʷ ixí? isck̓əɬpá?x̌, way̓ myaɬ kən ?ayx̌ʷt 284 way̓ lut
way̓ t̓xʷ ixí? i -sc -k̓ɬ+pa?x̌ way̓ myaɬ kn ?ayx̌ʷ+t way̓ lut
well emph that 1i -pftv -figure_out yes too_much 1kn tired well not
"This is what I figured: I am too tired. *I am not*

iksk̓əɬpa?səncút, way̓ t̓əxʷ cawts i? sqilxʷ {uɬ} uɬ cmúskstəm
i -ks -k̓ɬ+pa?s+ncút way̓ t̓xʷ cawt -s i? s+qilxʷ uɬ c -mus=kst+m
1i -futi -worried yes emph doing -3in art person and hab -try
going to be particular, people take chances. 9:00

5 Probably n+x̌l(t)=cin, with unexplained loss of t.

285 kən cmúskst[əm], pna? cmay nqʷənqʷńíls 286 way̓ ik̓lí?
kn c -mus=kst+m pna? cmay n+qʷń•qʷń=ils way̓ ik̓lí?
1kn hab -try maybe maybe have_pity well there
I'll take a chance, maybe they are merciful." *They went*

sənsəq̓síq̓msəlx 287 cus i? slax̌ts way̓ ak̓lá? kʷu
s -n+sq̓•siq̓+m -s -lx cu -s i? s+l̓ax̌+t -s way̓ ak̓lá? kʷu
hab -cut_across -hab -pl tell -hab art friend -hab well here 4kʷu
there. *He said to his friend, "Let's turn to*

nsəq̓síq̓əm axá? i? k̓a cwix 288 ah cúntəm way̓, anwí ałí? kʷ
n+sq̓•siq̓+m axá? i? k̓ c -wix ah cu -nt -m way̓ anwí ałí? kʷ
cut_across this art to hab -live intj tell -nt -psv well you because 2kn
where that house is." *He [the little one] said to him, "You are*

ilmíxʷəm, kʷ isckxnám 289 xi?míx kʷ xkínəm uł way̓ ilí? kən
yl=mixʷ+m kʷ i -sc -kx+na+m xi?+míx kʷ x+kin+m uł way̓ ilí? kn
chief 2kn 1i -pftv -go_along whatever 2kn do_what and yes there 1kn
the boss, I am following you. *Whatever you do*

ksx̌íla?x 290 ah way, way̓ ilí? nsəq̓síq̓məlx 291 way̓
ks -x̌il -a?x ah way̓ way̓ ilí? n+sq̓•siq̓+m -lx way̓
incp^ -act_so -^incp intj OK well there cut_across -pl well
I'll do." *They turned off the road.* *They*

k̓łənc?ípəm, way̓ {c} c{k̓ł}k̓łənk̓ahk̓ʷípłtməlx 292 ní··kxna way̓ qʷámqʷəmt
k̓ł+n+c?=ip+m way̓ c -k̓ł+n+k̓ahk̓ʷ=íp -łt -m níkxna? way̓ qʷam•qʷm+t
knock_on_door yes act -open -łt -psv goodness yes excellent
knocked on the door, they opened the door for them. *Goodness, she's*

swi?númtx 293 cúntməlx way̓ kʷu kícəntp p tu?twít
s+wy̓+numt=x cu -nt -m -lx way̓ kʷu kic -nt -p p tw̓•tw̓it
handsome tell -nt -psv -pl well 1obj reach_st/sb -nt -5erg 5kn boys
beautiful. *She said to them, "You got here, boys."*

294 cúsəlx way̓ 295 cúntməlx way̓ mat tla?kín tla
cu -s -lx way̓ cu -nt -m -lx way̓ mat tla+?kín tla
tell -3erg -pl yes tell -nt -psv -pl yes maybe from_there from
They said, "Yes". *She said to them, "Maybe it's from*

lkʷut {p} ki? p st'əcxʷúyx[6] 296 lut_pəńkíń t'a
lkʷ=ut ki? p s -t'c+xʷuy -x lut_pn+?kiń t'
far rel 5kn ipftv^ -come -^ipftv never negfac
somewhere far that you come. *I haven't*

cwíkłmən 297 axá? alá? yaʕyáʕt csúxʷstən
c -wik -łm -n axá? alá? yaʕ•yáʕ+t c -suxʷ -st -n
cust^ -see -5obj -1erg this here all cust^ -recognize -^cust -1erg
seen you before. *I know everybody*

6 Here t'c- is derivational: the stem t'c+xʷuy receives the inflectional affixation. The form is in the third person, so perhaps in indirect discourse or otherwise unclear.

i? sqilxʷ 298 uɬ i? scəcm̓ílt t̓əxʷ i? ƛ̓ax̌əx̌ƛ̓x̌áp i? na?ɬ scəcm̓íl̓t
i? s+qilxʷ uɬ i? s+c•cm̓=il̓t t̓xʷ i? ƛ̓ax̌•x̌•ƛ̓x̌á+p i? na?ɬ s+c•cm̓=il̓t
art person and art children emph art elders art and children
here, 10:02 *the children, and the old people,*

299 uɬ axá? mnímɬəmp lut t̓a cwíkɬmən 300 cúntəm
uɬ axá? mnimɬ+mp lut t̓ c -wik -ɬm -n cu -nt -m
and this you not negfac cust^ -see -5obj -1erg tell -nt -psv
and I have never seen you." *The boss's*

axá? i? t qa?ɬilmíxʷəm 301 way̓, way̓ uníxʷ, tla lkʷut {kas} ka
axá? i? t qa?ɬ=yl=míxʷ+m way̓ way̓ wnixʷ tla lkʷ=ut ka
this art agInst chief's_children yes yes true from far rel
son said: *"Yes, that's right, I come from*

st̓əcxʷúyx 302 cúntməlx cənppílxwi, mat way̓ p
s -t̓c+xʷuy -x cu -nt -m -lx c+n+p•pilx -wy mat way̓ p
ipftv^ -come -^ipftv tell -nt -psv -pl enter_pl_cisl -ipimptv must yes 5kn
very far." *She said to them, "Come in, you must be*

ksq̓mmíltən p ?ay?áyx̌ʷt 303 ńíńwi? k̓ʷúl̓cɬmən, way̓ uɬ k̓a?ítət
k+s+q̓m•m=ilt+n p ?ay•?áyx̌ʷ+t ńíńwi? k̓ʷul̓=c -ɬm -n way̓ uɬ k̓a?ít•t
have_hunger 5kn tired_pl a_while cook -5obj -1erg yes and get_near
hungry and tired. *I'll cook for you, it's close to*

inwi?wáy̓ t̓əxʷ ikɬtk̓ʷəl̓cəncútən 304 uɬ aɬí? {kən k} kən
in -wy̓•way̓ t̓xʷ i -kɬ -t+k̓ʷl̓=cn+cut+n uɬ aɬí? kn
1in -finish evidently 1i -to_be -cooking_time and so 1kn
my cooking time. *Then I am going*

ksk̓áwa?x {cunt xa i c} 305 nstils axá? i? tətwít 306 kway̓ uɬ kʷu
ks -k̓aw -a?x n+st=ils axá? i? t•twit k+way̓ uɬ kʷu
incp^ -gone -^incp think this art boy well and 4kn
to be gone." *And the boy thought:* *"We're lucky*

kukscút[7] kʷu ksənqʷńán 307 way̓ nc̓q̓mnílsntəm uɬ axá? i? {kʷu}
kʷkʷ+scut kʷu k+s+n+qʷń•ań way̓ n+c̓q̓+mn=ils -nt -m uɬ axá? i?
lucky 4kn have_so's_pity well throw_thought -nt -psv and this art
to get pitied. *We are being given a good thought, and we are*

kʷu kstim 308 uɬ ca?kʷ kən k̓əɬtuńlsmíst kʷu ɬa ntx̌ʷáqsəm
kʷu k+s+tiṁ uɬ ca?kʷ kn k̓ɬ+twn=ls+mist kʷu ɬa? n+tx̌ʷ=aqs+m
4kn have_something and would 1kn think_one_falls_short 4kn if go_straight
not worth it. 11:00 *We would have come up short if we'd gone straight,*

309 uɬ way {kʷu} kʷu ƛ̓axʷt t sq̓míltən 310 way̓ mat nqʷńqʷńíls,
uɬ way̓ kʷu ƛ̓axʷ+t t s+q̓m=ilt+n way̓ mat n+qʷń•qʷń=ils
and yes 1kʷu dead_pl agInst hunger yes must kind
and we would have starved. *She must be merciful*

7 √kʷkʷ or √kʷk?

úłi? kʷu a nqʷn̓míntəm 311 way̓ kʷu nppílx naʔł
uł iʔ kʷu a n+qʷn̓+min -t -m way̓ kʷu n+p•pilx naʔł
and_then 3e4obj art pity -nt -3e4obj well 4kn enter_pl with
that she took pity on us.” *We went in, my partner*

isl̓ax̌t 312 cun way̓ {kʷist} kʷu nppilx 313 way̓ kʷu
i -s+l̓ax̌+t cu -n way̓ kʷu n+p•pilx way̓ kʷu
1in -partner tell -1erg yes 4kn enter_pl well 4kn
and I.[8] *I said to him, “We'll go in the house.”* *We went in*

nppilx way̓ kʷu ʔawtípəntəm axáʔ iʔ t tkłmilxʷ 314 uł
n+p•pilx way̓ kʷu ʔaw+t=íp -nt -m axáʔ iʔ t tkł+m=ilxʷ uł
enter_pl well 3e4obj follow -nt -3e4obj this art agInst woman and
and the woman followed us. *Then*

ixíʔ ilíʔ kʷu kłsəlxítəm iʔ t ksənkłmútəntət {uł ixíʔ}
ixíʔ ilíʔ kʷu kł+sl -xit -m iʔ t k -s+n+kł+mut+n -tt
then there 3e4obj set_table -xit -3e4obj art obj_tr to_be -chair -4in
she gave us

[ksənkłkʷíl·təntət] 315 kʷu cúntəm way̓, way̓ ixíʔ ik̓líʔ k̓la
k -s+n+kł+kʷil•l+tn -tt kʷu cu -nt -m way̓ way̓ ixíʔ ik̓líʔ k̓l
to_be -chairs -4in 3e4obj tell -nt -3e4obj well well that there to
chairs. *She told us, “In the other room*

nqsíłc̓aʔ iʔ k̓łənk̓míp 316 ixíʔ ilíʔ iʔ ksənkc̓əw̓íw̓stən iʔ səncáʕʷlxtən
nqs=íłc̓aʔ iʔ k̓ł+n+k̓m=ip ixíʔ ilíʔ iʔ k+s+n+k+c̓aw̓=íw̓s+tn iʔ s+n+caʕʷ+lx+tn
one_room art door that there art have+wash_basin art bath_tub
(there is a door) *there is a wash basin there, a bath tub.*

317 way̓ ik̓líʔ p ʔawskc̓əw̓íw̓səm 318 way̓ uł ixíʔ k̓ʷúl̓cłmən,
way̓ ik̓líʔ p ʔaw+s+k+c̓aw̓=íw̓s+m way̓ uł ixíʔ k̓ʷul̓=c -łm -n
well there 5kn go_wash well and then cook -5obj -1erg
Go there and wash your face. *Then I'll cook for you,*

uł t spuʔúsəmp t̓əxʷ p caʕʷlx {t̓əxʷm ixiw} 319 way̓ ik̓líʔ
uł t s+puʔ=ús -mp t̓xʷ p caʕʷ+lx way̓ ik̓líʔ
and obl heart -5in emph 5kn bathe well there
do whatever, bathe.” *They*

sənppílxsəlx {way̓ uł ilíʔ} 320 cúntməlx uł ilíʔ nixʷ kən ksənʔácqaʔtən
s -n+p•pilx -s -lx cu -nt -m -lx uł ilíʔ nixʷ kn k+s+n+ʔácqaʔ+tn
nom -enter_pl -3i -pl tell -nt -psv -pl and there also 1kn have_bathroom
went in.[9] *12:01* *She told them, “I also got an outhouse.”*

321 way̓ ixíʔ k̓ʷúl̓msəlx, uł lut scáʕwlxsəlx {kəm̓ mat} 322 way̓
way̓ ixíʔ k̓ʷul̓+m -s -lx uł lut s -caʕʷ+lx -s -lx way̓
well then use -3erg -pl and not nom -bathe -3i -pl well
They used it, but they didn't bathe. *They*

8 For a few lines it's the boss's son who is telling the story.
9 Pete resumes the story in the third person.

kc̓aw̓í·w̓smǝlx, uł síwstǝlx iʔ t siwłkʷ 323 níkxna way̓
k+c̓aw̓=íw̓s+m -lx uł siw+st -lx iʔ t siwł=kʷ níkxnaʔ way̓
wash -pl and drink -pl art obj_itr water goodness yes
washed and they drank some water. *Goodness,*

nqʷámqʷǝmkʷ iʔ siwłkʷ, nc̓ałt 324 way̓ wiʔskc̓aw̓íw̓sǝmǝlx,
n-qʷam•qʷm=kʷ iʔ siwł=kʷ n=c̓ał+t way̓ wy̓+s+k+c̓aw̓=íw̓s+m -lx
excellent_water art water cold_water well finish_washing -pl
it's real nice water, cold. *They washed,*

wiʔsíwstǝlx 325 wiʔsʔíp̓smǝlx iʔ t stxmin txámǝlx
wy̓+siw+st -lx wy̓+s+ʔip̓=s+m -lx iʔ t s+tx+min txa+m -lx
finish_drinking -pl finish_wiping_face -pl art agInst comb comb -pl
they drank, *they wiped their faces, they combed with a comb.*

326 way̓ {ł} łǝnpǝpílxǝlx k̓la nǝqsíłc̓aʔ 327 way̓ ilíʔ skłkʷil·x
way̓ ł+n+p•pilx -lx k̓l nqs=íłc̓aʔ way̓ ilíʔ s -kł+kʷil•l -x
well enter_again -pl to one_room well there ipftv^ -sit_pl -^ipftv
They went into another room, *they sat down in*

i l {s sǝn} sǝnkłkʷíl·tǝn 328 way̓ t̓i ixíʔ put ƛ̓lápǝlx iʔ l
iʔ l s+n+kł+kʷil•l+tn way̓ t̓iʔ ixíʔ put ƛ̓la+p -lx iʔ l
art in chairs well evid then just stop -pl art in
a sitting place. *They just got settled in the chairs,*

sǝnkłkʷíl·tǝn, way̓ cknʔúłxʷmǝntmǝlx iʔ t 329 a··
s+n+kł+kʷil•l+tn way̓ c -k+n+ʔułxʷ+m -nt -m -lx iʔ t a
chairs well act -take_so_in -nt -psv -pl art agInst intj
and she brought them in {unfinished}. *He*

nłǝk̓ʷk̓ʷmís {a ł} lut, lúti nłǝk̓ʷk̓ʷmís iʔ {a} sk̓ǝłq̓ǝy̓ncút 330 t̓iʔ
n+łk̓ʷ•k̓ʷ+mi -s lut lút+i n+łk̓ʷ•k̓ʷ+mi -s iʔ s+k̓ł+q̓y̓+ncut t̓iʔ
think_about -3erg not not_yet think_about -3erg art picture evid
thought of..., no, he hadn't thought of the picture yet. 13:12 *Because*

púti sʔáyx̌ʷtx, uł itíʔ sal̓ms 331 way̓
pút+iʔ s -ʔayx̌ʷ+t -x uł itíʔ sal̓+m -s way̓
still ipftv^ -tired -^ipftv and from_that distracted -3erg well
he is still tired, and he didn't think about anything. *She*

ckǝnʔúłxʷmǝntmǝlx, cúntmǝlx way̓ way̓ iʔsk̓ʷúl̓cłmǝn, 332 ha
c -k+n+ʔułxʷ+m -nt -m -lx cu -nt -m -lx way̓ way̓ y̓+s+k̓ʷul̓=cn+m haʔ
act -take_so_in -nt -psv -pl tell -nt -psv -pl well well inish_cooking inter
came in to them, and said to them, "I'm done with cooking for you, come in. *Have*

way̓ p wiʔskc̓aw̓íw̓sǝm 333 way̓ 334 way̓ {c cǝnʔułxʷǝxʷ}
way̓ p wy̓+s+k+c̓aw̓=íw̓s+m way̓ way̓
yes 5kn finish_washing yes well
you washed?" *"Yes."* *They*

cǝnpǝpílxǝlx 335 ní[kxna] way̓ cxʷʔul iʔ ksc̓iłǝnsǝlx
c+n+p•pilx -lx níkxnaʔ way̓ c -xʷ[ʔ]ul iʔ k -sc+ʔiłn -s -lx
enter_pl_cisl -pl goodness well hab -steam_inch art to_be -food -3i -pl
went in. *My, their food is steaming.*

336 uł ałíʔ mat axáʔ iʔ l suʔwíkiʔst iʔ snur̓ísəlp̓təns 337 uł
uł ałíʔ mat axáʔ iʔ l s+w̓•w̓ík=iʔst iʔ s+n+wr̓=islp̓+tn -s uł
and so maybe this art with electricity art stove -3in and
I suppose her cooking stove is electric, *it's*

mał xʷúsxʷəst łə ksur̓ísəlp̓əms 338 xʷus ł
mał xʷus•xʷs+t ł ks -wr̓=islp̓+m -s xʷus ł
too_much hurry subord futi -start_fire -3i hurry subord
too quick [for her] to have started the fire, *to get it*

kskcaʔxísxəns ł ksp̓iʔqíltəns 339 axáʔ mnímłcəlx t̓i
ks k+caʔx=ísxn -s ł ks -p̓y̓q=iltn -s axáʔ mnimł+c+lx t̓iʔ
futi -warm_st -3i subord futi -cooked -3i this they evid
hot, to get things cooked. *They had just*

wiʔskc̓aw̓íw̓səm úłiʔ t̓i cx̌lítntməlx 340 way̓, way̓ kłkʷil·lx,
wy̓+s+k+c̓aw̓=íw̓s+m uł iʔ t̓iʔ c -x̌lit -nt -m -lx way̓ way̓ kł+kʷil•l -lx
finish_washing and_then evid act -call -nt -psv -pl well well sit_pl -pl
finished washing when they were called. 14:03 *They sat down,*

nt̓a·· nwíl̓uʔs iʔ ksc̓íłəns 341 kmax k̓l inƛ̓ax̌əx̌ƛ̓x̌áp k axáʔ
nt̓a n+wil=w̓s iʔ k -sc+ʔiłn -s kmax k̓l in -ƛ̓ax̌•x̌•ƛ̓x̌á+p kiʔ axáʔ
intj lots art to_be -food -3i only at 1in -elders rel this
there are all kinds of things to eat. *"Gee, it's only at my father's*

əcwíkstən iksc̓íłən 342 ʕapnáʔ{ka} aláʔ ka łwíkən
c -wik -st -n i -k -sc+ʔiłn ʕapnáʔ aláʔ ka ł+wik -n
cust^ -see -^cust -1erg art -to_be -food now here rel see_again -1erg
that I have seen this kind of food. *Now I see it here."*

343 mat nstílsəlx mat uníxʷ smyłtkłmílxʷ 344 uł lut {c} nixʷ
mat n+st=ils -lx mat wnixʷ s+my+ł+tkł+m=ilxʷ uł lut nixʷ
maybe think -pl must true important_woman and not also
They thought she was a really important woman. *And they*

t̓ swíkmsəlx kəm̓ {t} t̓a ck̓əłníxləms[ts] ta
t̓ s -wik+m -s -lx km̓ t̓ c -k̓ł+nixl+m -st -s t
negfac nom -see -3i -pl or negfac cust^ -hear -^cust -3erg obl
didn't see or hear any [other]

ksqilxʷ {t} 345 xiʔ sílxʷaʔ citxʷ 346 uł ixíʔ ʔí··łnəlx uł taʔkín iʔ
k+s+qilxʷ ixíʔ sílxʷaʔ citxʷ uł ixíʔ ʔiłn -lx uł ta+ʔkín̓ iʔ
have_person that big house and then eat -pl and how_far art
people, *it's a big house.* *They ate and*

sc̓íłənsəlx t̓əxʷ məq̓məq̓ínkəlx a nt̓qcínəlx 347 {c cuntə·}
sc+ʔiłn -s -lx t̓xʷ mq̓•mq̓=ink -lx a n+t̓q=cin -lx
food -3in -pl evidently full_stomach -pl art full -pl
they got filled up. *They,*

cúsəlx axáʔ iʔ tkłmílxʷ, t̓əxʷ iʔ t qaʔłilmíxʷəm 348 way̓
cu -s -lx axáʔ iʔ tkł+m=ilxʷ t̓xʷ iʔ t qaʔł=yl=míxʷ+m way̓
tell -3erg -pl this art woman evidently art agInst chief's_children well
the king's son, said to the woman: 15:00 *"Well,*

way̓ kʷu wiʔwiʔcín {way̓} 349 cúntəm way̓, way̓ haʔ p put
way̓ kʷu wy̓•wy̓=cin cu -nt -m way̓ way̓ haʔ p put
yes 4kn finish_eating_pl tell -nt -psv well well inter 5kn just
we are done eating." *She asked them, "Did you really get enough,*

350 kəm̓{p} pna p sc̓aʔc̓aʔxmíx, mat lut smisʔíłnəmp
km̓ pnaʔ p sc -c̓aʔ•c̓aʔx -mix mat lut s -my+s+ʔiłn -mp
or maybe 5kn ipftvp^ -bashful_pl -^ipftvp maybe not nom -eat_more -5i
or maybe you are bashful, maybe you didn't eat enough."

351 cut lut, way̓ taʔlíʔ kʷu txʷʔaqs way̓ kʷu məq̓mq̓ínk 352 way̓
cut lut way̓ taʔlíʔ kʷu t+xʷʔ=aqs way̓ kʷu mq̓•mq̓=ink way̓
say not well very_much 4kn much_food yes 4kn full_stomach well
He said, "No, we got plenty, we got filled up. *We*

t̓əxʷ i kʷu ʔalʔílxʷt uł way̓ xʷʔit iʔ sc̓íłəntət 353 uł way̓ kʷu
t̓xʷ iʔ kʷu ʔal•ʔílxʷ+t uł way̓ xʷʔi+t iʔ sc+ʔiłn -tt uł way̓ kʷu
emph art 4kn hungry and yes much art food -4in and yes 4kn
were plenty hungry and we got lots to eat. *We are*

məq̓mq̓ínk 354 lut ilíʔ nixʷ qəłnúntəm {łkł} itlíʔ nixʷ {iks ks}
mq̓•mq̓=ink lut ilíʔ nixʷ qł -nu -nt -m itlíʔ nixʷ
full_stomach not there more able -manage -nt -4erg from_there more
filled up. *We can't eat*

kʷu ksʔíłəns 355 uł lut k̓ík̓tstəm axáʔ iʔ sk̓ʷəl̓cəncút
kʷu ks -ʔiłn -s uł lut k̓i•k̓t -st -m axáʔ iʔ s+k̓ʷl̓=cn+cut
4kʷu futi4^4 -eat -^futi4 and not near -st -4erg this art cooking
any more. *We didn't even get most of the food."*

356 cúntməlx way̓ way̓ kʷa p ism̓áyaʔłtəm iʔ
cu -nt -m -lx way̓ way̓ kʷa p i -s -m̓áyaʔ -łt -m iʔ
tell -nt -psv -pl well yes intj 5kʷu 1i -intt -tell -łt -apsv art
She said to them, "Now I am going to show you where you

ksnilíʔtnəmp 357 ałíʔ way̓ t cúłmən kən
k -s+n+iliʔ+tn -mp ałíʔ way̓ t cu -łm -n kn
to_be -dwelling_place -5i because yes as tell -5obj -1erg 1kn
are going to stay. *Because, as I told you, I am going*

ksk̓áwaʔx {əł} 358 caʔkʷ ń̓íń̓aʔxʷ uł kʷu ƛ̓mípstəp uł ałíʔ
ks -k̓aw -aʔx caʔkʷ ń̓í•ń̓aʔxʷ uł kʷu ƛ̓mi+p -st -p uł ałíʔ
incp^ -gone -^incp if more_dim and 1obj be_late -st -5erg and because
to be gone. *A little bit more and you would have missed me,*

kən {sc} sc̓əx̌ʷtwíxʷəxʷ 359 uł way̓ ń̓íń̓wiʔ m̓áyaʔłmən iʔ
kn s -c̓x̌ʷ+twixʷ -xʷ uł way̓ ń̓íń̓wiʔ m̓áyaʔ -łm -n iʔ
1kn ipftv^ -appointment -^ipftv and yes a_while tell -5obj -1erg art
because I have a date. 16:03 *And now I'll show you where you*

ksnilíʔtnəmp 360 uł way̓ ik̓líʔ {p} p ilíʔ 361 ixíʔ uł
k -s+n+iliʔ+tn -mp uł way̓ ik̓líʔ p ilíʔ ixíʔ uł
to_be -dwelling_place -5i and yes there 5kn there then and
are going to stay. *And you'll be there.* *Whatever*

xiʔmíx spuʔúsəmp, p pulx t̓əxʷ p łáʔxʷsk̓itəm 362 way̓ ixíʔ
xiʔ+míx s+puʔ=ús -mp p pul+x t̓xʷ p łáʔxʷ=sk̓it+m way̓ ixíʔ
whatever heart -5in 5kn overnight emph 5kn rest well then
you want, you can go to bed, or rest." *She took*

xʷúystməlx, ʔácəcqaʔlx 363 ilíʔ ckəwxkn̓íłxʷ {k̓ʷək̓ʷik̓ʷək̓ʷimu}
xʷuy+st -m -lx ʔác•c•qaʔ -lx ilíʔ c -k+wx=kn̓=iłxʷ
take_st -psv -pl go_out_pl -pl there hab -annex
them there, they went out. *And there is another building,*

k̓ʷk̓ʷim̓íłaʔxʷ 364 t̓əxʷ lut sílxʷaʔ st̓i_put 365 way̓ npəpílxəlx,
k̓ʷ•k̓ʷy=m=íłaʔxʷ[10] t̓xʷ lut sílxʷaʔ s+t̓iʔ_put way̓ n+p•pilx -lx
small_house evidently not big just_enough well enter_pl -pl
a little house, *not big, just enough.* *They went in,*

k̓łənk̓ahk̓ʷíps, {łak} claklí {ałíʔ uł} 366 k̓łənk̓ahk̓ʷíps ixíʔ nppilx
k̓ł+n+k̓ahk̓ʷ=íp -s c -laklí k̓ł+n+k̓ahk̓ʷ=íp -s ixíʔ n+p•pilx
open -3erg hab -lock open -3erg then enter_pl
they opened the door. It's locked. *They opened the door, they went in.*

367 ih qʷámqʷəmt iʔ sk̓ʷul̓s axáʔ 368 uł c̓x̌ił təl̓ tk̓əmkn̓íłxʷ
ih qʷam•qʷm+t iʔ s+k̓ʷul̓ -s axáʔ uł c+ʔx̌ił tl̓ t+k̓m=kn=iłxʷ
intj excellent art how_made -3in this and like from outside
It's fixed beautifully, *and it's the same on the outside.*

369 x̌ast iʔ sk̓ʷul̓s iʔ smiƛ̓ts 370 uł i[xíʔ]
x̌as+t iʔ s+k̓ʷul̓ -s iʔ s+miƛ̓+t -s uł ixíʔ
good art how_made -3in art how_painted -3in and then
It's made well and the paint is good. *There are*

ksənkłmútən{s}, ʔasíl iʔ sənkłmútən, i[xíʔ] kłlatáp 371 uł i[xíʔ]
k+s+n+kł+mut+n ʔasíl iʔ s+n+kł+mut+n ixíʔ kł+latáp uł ixíʔ
have_chair two art chair that have+table and then
chairs, two chairs, and there is a table, 17:01 *and*

ksənłq̓ʷútən, t̓əxʷ ʔasíl iʔ sənłq̓ʷútən nixʷ 372 cúntməlx way̓
k+s+n+łq̓ʷ=ut+n t̓xʷ ʔasíl iʔ s+n+łq̓ʷ=ut+n nixʷ cu -nt -m -lx way̓
have+bed evidently two art bed also tell -nt -psv -pl well
there is a bed, two beds. *She told them,*

axáʔ k̓la nəqsíłc̓aʔ ixíʔ iʔ sənʔácqaʔtən uł ixíʔ sncáʕʷlxtən
axáʔ k̓l nqs=íłc̓aʔ ixíʔ iʔ s+n+ʔácqaʔ+tn uł ixíʔ s+n+caʕʷ+lx+tn
this to one_room that art bathroom and that bath_tub
"Next door there is a bathroom and a bathtub.

373 cúntməlx uł ilíʔ p caʕʷlx 374 wiʔscáʕʷlx {uł} uł ilíʔ
cu -nt -m -lx uł ilíʔ p caʕʷ+lx wy̓+s+caʕʷ+lx uł ilíʔ
tell -nt -psv -pl and there 5kn bathe finish_bathe and there
And there you can bathe. *When you are done*

10 =m is probably a variant of =umaʔ.

cután {i ks} iʔ ksɬəq̓əlxálqsəmp 375 uɬ ixíʔ uɬ {t ip ɬ uɬ ax uɬ} uɬ axáʔ
c -wt+an iʔ k -s+ɬq̓+lx=alqs -mp uɬ ixíʔ uɬ uɬ axáʔ
hab -placed art to_be -pajamas -5i and then and and this
bathing, your night clothes are there. *And here is also*

ilíʔ nixʷ iʔ kɬk̓əɬʔaysəlscútnəmp 376 uɬ aláʔ k̓ʷíƛ̓əntp
ilíʔ nixʷ iʔ kɬ -k̓ɬ+ʔays=lscút+n -mp uɬ aláʔ k̓ʷiƛ̓ -nt -p
there also art to_be -change_of_clothes -5i and here take_off -nt -5erg
a change of top clothes. *And when you take off*

axáʔ iʔ stətəm̓tím̓p 377 iʔ sk̓ʷəƛ̓lscútəmp ixíʔ ilíʔ
axáʔ iʔ s+t•tm̓•tim̓ -mp iʔ s+k̓ʷƛ̓=lscut -mp ixíʔ ilíʔ
this art clothes -5in art clothes_taken_off -5in that there
your clothes, *throw what you take off*

nt̓əqmíntp ilíʔ iʔ l lkasát 378 uɬ axáʔ {iʔ t} ixíʔ t
n+t̓q+min -t -p ilíʔ iʔ l lkasát uɬ axáʔ ixíʔ t
throw_sheet_like_obj -nt -5erg there art in box and this then agInst
in the box, *and get dressed with*

kɬk̓əɬʔaysəlscútəmp itíʔ p x̌əcməncút 379 ixíʔ uɬ ləʕ̓ʷəntíp
kɬ -k̓ɬ+ʔays=lscút -mp itíʔ p x̌c+mncut ixíʔ uɬ lʕ̓ʷ -nt -ip
to_be -change_clothes -5i from_that 5kn get_dressed then and fit -nt -5erg
your change of clothes. 18:00 *Put your sleeping*

iʔ ksɬəq̓əlxálqsəmp {uɬ ixíʔ uɬ} 380 ixíʔ iʔ kɬcáwtəmp, uɬ lut
iʔ k -s+ɬq̓+lx=alqs -mp ixíʔ iʔ kɬ -cawt -mp uɬ lut
art to_be -pajamas -5i that art to_be -doing -5i and not
clothes on. *That's what you are going to do,*

ksk̓əɬpaʔsəncútəmp 381 ixíʔ sic {p c} p cənppílx k̓laʔ uɬ {wi} p
ks -k̓ɬ+paʔs+ncút -mp ixíʔ sic p c+n+p•pil+x ak̓láʔ uɬ p
futi -worried -5i then then 5kn enter_pl_cisl here and 5kn
and don't be backwards. *Then go in there when you are done*

wiʔscáʕʷlx p wiʔsk̓əɬʔaysəlscút 382 ixíʔ uɬ lut ksyaʕmíntp
wy̓+s+caʕʷ+lx p wy̓+s+k̓ɬ+ʔays=lscút ixíʔ uɬ lut ks -yaʕ̓+mín -t -p
finish_bathe 5kn finish_changing then and not futtˆ -fear -nt -5erg
bathing and changing your clothes, *don't be bashful about using*

a[xáʔ] iʔ sənɬq̓ʷútnəmp 383 lut ksənstílsəmp cəm̓ q̓ʷʕayɬtám {i s}
axáʔ iʔ s+n+ɬq̓ʷ=ut+n -mp lut ks -n+st=ils -mp cm̓ q̓ʷʕay -ɬt -am
this art bed -5in not futi -think -5i maybe black -ɬt -psv
the beds. *Don't think that you'll get them dirty,*

aɬíʔ way̓ p wiʔscáʕʷlx 384 i[xíʔ] cúntəm lut ksk̓əɬpaʔsəncútəmp,
aɬíʔ way̓ p wy̓+s+caʕʷ+lx ixíʔ cu -nt -m lut ks -k̓ɬ+paʔs+ncút -mp
because yes 5kn finish_bathe then tell -nt -psv not futi -worried -5i
because you've already bathed. *Don't be backward,*

way̓ p ʔayʔáyx̌ʷt 385 ilíʔ p kɬqmínmiʔst i l sənɬq̓ʷútnəmp, p
way̓ p ʔay•ʔáyx̌ʷ+t ilíʔ p kɬ+qm+ín+miʔst iʔ l s+n+ɬq̓ʷ=ut+n -mp p
yes 5kn tired_pl there 5kn lie_on art on bed -5in 5kn
you are tired. *Just lay around on the bed,*

łáʔxʷsk̓itəm 386 i·· p ksʔatxílx {hi ł·} p pulx
łáʔxʷ=sk̓it+m i·· p k+s+ʔatx+ílx p pul+x
rest intj 5kn sleepy 5kn camp
rest. 19:03 *When you get sleepy go to bed.*

387 i[xíʔ] x̌lap uł ńíńẇiʔ {c} cx̌lítłmən p ksʔałʔíłnaʔx,
ixíʔ x̌la+p uł ńíńẇiʔ c -x̌lit -łm -n p ks -ʔał•ʔíłn -aʔx
then tomorrow and a_while act -call -5obj -1erg 5kn incp^ -eat_pl -^incp
Tomorrow I'll call you to eat,

ixíʔ uł p xʷt̓lilx 388 kəm̓ ł waẏ łə sqíłłtəmp
ixíʔ uł p xʷt̓+lilx km̓ ł waẏ ł s -qił•ł+t -mp
then and 5kn get_up_pl or if already if nom -wake_up_pl -5i
and you can get up. *Or, if you are already awake,*

389 uł ilíʔ t̓əxʷ {p kʷl} p wiʔskc̓aẇíẇsəm p wiʔsx̌əcməncút iʔ t
uł ilíʔ t̓xʷ p wẏ+s+k+c̓aẇ=íẇs+m p wẏ+s+x̌c+mncut iʔ t
and there emph 5kn finish_washing 5kn finish_dressing art obl
and already washed,

kstim̓mp 390 uł {kʷu} kʷu k̓əłʔíməntp ixíʔ mi
k -s+tim̓ -mp uł kʷu k̓ł+ʔim -nt -p ixíʔ mi
to_be -thing -5i and 1obj wait_for -nt -5erg then fut
and dressed, *wait for me to*

x̌lítłmən 391 ixíʔ uł sic {p} p c̓ácəcqaʔ p cxʷuy iʔ k̓əl citxʷ
x̌lit -łm -n ixíʔ uł sic p c+ʔác•c•qaʔ p c+xʷuy iʔ k̓l citxʷ
call -5obj -1erg then and then 5kn enter_cisl_pl 5kn come art to house
call you. *Then you come out and come to the house.*

392 p ʔałʔíłən{t} kʷu ʔałʔíłən 393 waẏ ixíʔ{iʔ} iʔ cúntməlx axáʔ iʔ
p ʔał•ʔíłn kʷu ʔał•ʔíłn waẏ ixíʔ iʔ cu -nt -m -lx axáʔ iʔ
5kn eat_pl 4kn eat_pl well that art tell -nt -psv -pl this art
You will eat, we will eat." *That's what the woman told*

t təkłmílxʷ 394 i[xíʔ] łʔácqaʔ axáʔ iʔ tkəłmílxʷ {t} 395 waẏ kən
t tkłmilxʷ ixíʔ ł+ʔácqaʔ axáʔ iʔ tkłmilxʷ waẏ kn
agInst woman then go_out_again this art woman well 1kn
them. *Then the woman went out.* *"I have*

łʔawsənc̓íẇm mi_sic {kən} kən xʷist 396 əłʔácqaʔ 397 waẏ ixíʔ {a}
ł+ʔaw+s+n+c̓íẇ+m mi_sic kn xʷist ł+ʔácqaʔ waẏ ixíʔ
go_back_wash_dishes then 1kn walk go_out_again well then
to go wash dishes before I go." 20:02 *She went out.* *He*

sənʔúłxʷs 398 cus {iʔ} iʔ łsísəncaʔs waẏ caʔkʷ {kʷa·} kʷ
s -n+ʔułxʷ -s cu -s iʔ ł+sí•sncaʔ -s waẏ caʔkʷ kʷ
nom -enter -3i tell -3erg art younger_bro -3in well should 2kn
went in, *and said to his little brother, "You better*

ʔawscáʕʷlx 399 cúntəm axáʔ iʔ t tətẇít, cúntəm tah k anwí
ʔaw+s+cáʕʷ+lx cu -nt -m axáʔ iʔ t t•tẇit cu -nt -m tah kiʔ anwí
go_bathe tell -nt -psv this art agInst boy tell -nt -psv intj rel you
go bathe." *The little boy said to him, he said, "You are*

kʷ sxʔitx 400 incá kən stətʔíwtaʔx, incá uɬ kən c̓iwt 401 anwí
kʷ s+xʔit=x in+cá kn s+t•tʔíw+t=aʔx in+cá uɬ kn c+ʔiwt anwí
2kn oldest_one I 1kn youngest I and 1kn last you
the oldest, and I am the little one; I'll

la_cxʔítiʔ kʷ caʕʷlx {kʷ iscaʕʷlx mi} 402 kʷ isckxnám ʕ̓ác̓ənt,
la_c+xʔit+iʔ kʷ caʕʷ+lx kʷ i -sc -kx+na+m ʕac̓ -nt
first 2kn bathe 2kʷu 1i -pftv -go_along look_at -nt
be last, you bathe first. I'm following you,

sc̓x̌ilx uɬ way̓ kʷ iksxaʔtəmstím aɬíʔ kən stətʔíwtaʔx
sc+ʔx̌il+x uɬ way̓ kʷ i -ks -xaʔt+m -st -im aɬíʔ kn s+t•tʔíw+t+aʔx
reason_why and yes 2kʷu 1i -futt^ -first -st -apsv because 1kn youngest
that's why I let you do things first, because I am the youngest."

403 way̓ ixíʔ sənʔúɬxʷs iʔ k̓l {yaʔ a ixi} ilíʔ iʔ səncáʕʷlxtən
way̓ ixíʔ s -n+ʔuɬxʷ -s iʔ k̓l ilíʔ iʔ s+n+caʕʷ+lx+tn
well then hab -enter -3i art to there art bath_tub
He went into the bath.

404 ixíʔ nc̓əxʷəntí··s aɬíʔ ncix uɬ nc̓aɬt uɬ way̓ put
ixíʔ n=c̓xʷ -nt -is aɬíʔ n=cix uɬ n=c̓aɬ+t uɬ way̓ put
then fill_w_liquid -nt -3erg so warm_water and cold_water and yes exact
He poured water in, it's warm, and it's just right.

405 uɬ way̓ ilíʔ ckɬt̓aq {ikɬ} iʔ kɬxƛ̓aps, iʔ kɬʔip̓stn,
uɬ way̓ ilíʔ c -kɬ+t̓aq iʔ kɬ+xƛ̓ap -s iʔ kɬ+ʔip̓=s+tn
and yes there hab -lie_on art have_everything ? art have_face_wiper
There is everything there, a towel, soap,

ksc̓əw̓íw̓s[tən], stxmin 406 way̓ scaʕʷlxs, ca··ʕʷlx, wiʔscáʕʷlx, way̓
k+s+c̓w̓=iw̓s+tn s+tx+min way̓ s -caʕʷ+lx -s caʕʷ+lx wy̓+s+caʕʷ+lx way̓
have_towel comb well nom -bathe -3i bathe finish_bathe well
a comb. 21:02 He bathed and bathed, got done bathing and

k̓ap̓c̓aʔncút 407 ntah ƛ̓aʔƛ̓aʔúsəm way̓ ilíʔ iʔ kɬk̓əɬʔaysəlscútəns,
k+ʔap̓=c̓aʔ+ncút ntah ƛ̓aʔ•ƛ̓aʔ=ús+m way̓ ilíʔ iʔ kɬ -k̓ɬ+ʔays=lscút+n -s
dry_body intj look_for well there art to_be -change_of_clothes -3i
dried himself. He looked around and also a change of clothes was

nixʷ ckɬt̓aq 408 way̓ ixíʔ ckʷis luləʕʷəntís nt̓a t̓iʔ pu··t
nixʷ c -kɬ+t̓aq way̓ ixíʔ c+kʷi -s lw̓•lʕ̓ʷ -nt -is nt̓a t̓iʔ put
also hab -lie_on well then take -3erg put_on_pl -nt -3erg intj evid exact
put there. He took them and put them on, they fit perfectly,

409 nt̓a uníxʷ xʷəm t̓i scsúxʷmaʔ 410 way̓ kɬlasmísts
nt̓a wnixʷ xʷm t̓iʔ sc -súxʷ=maʔ way̓ kɬ -lasmíst -s
intj true intj evid pftv -measure yes to_be -shirt -3i
like measured. His shirt, his trousers,

ksx̌íƛ̓xəns, kɬq̓aʔxáns, yáʕt sic 411 ixíʔ uɬ ilíʔ
k -s+x̌iƛ̓=xn -s kɬ -q̓aʔ=xán -s yaʕ•yáʕ+t sic ixíʔ uɬ ilíʔ
to_be -trousers -3i to_be -shoes -3i all new then and there
his shoes, everything new. There is also

kɬlkapús, t̓əxʷ axáʔ {iʔ l} iʔ l citxʷ a lkapú 412 kʷa ʕác̓ənt,
kɬ -lkapú -s t̓xʷ axáʔ iʔ l citxʷ a lkapú kʷa ʕac̓ -nt
to_be -coat -3i evidently this art for house art coat intj look_at -nt
a coat, a house coat. *Look,*

i l sənq̓əltíɬxʷtən uɬ ixíʔ kɬlkapúlx 413 ixíʔ uɬ aɬíʔ c̓x̌iɬt
iʔ l s+n+q̓l+t=iɬxʷ+tn uɬ ixíʔ kɬ+lkapú -lx ixíʔ uɬ aɬíʔ c+ʔx̌iɬ+t
art at hospital and that have_coat -pl that and so like
at the hospital they have those, *they are like*

sq̓əlxálqsəlx iʔ l citxʷ iʔ ta lkapú {waẏ} 414 waẏ ɬənʔúɬxʷ,
s+q̓l+x=alq -s -lx iʔ l citxʷ iʔ t lkapú waẏ ɬ+n+ʔuɬxʷ
sleeping_coat -3in -pl art for house art obl coat well enter_again
a sleeping coat. 22:00 *He went back in,*

cus axáʔ iʔ síncaʔs 415 huy ɬ t anwí waẏ kən
cu -s axáʔ iʔ síncaʔ -s huy ɬ t anwí waẏ kn
tell -3erg this art younger_brother -3in intj and obl you yes 1kn
said to his little brother: *"It's your turn, I'm done*

wiʔscáʕʷlx 416 waẏ nʔuɬxʷ axáʔ iʔ stʔiwtx, {ikaw} ʔayxáxaʔ ɬc̓ácqaʔ
wẏ+s+caʕʷ+lx waẏ n+ʔuɬxʷ axáʔ iʔ s+tʔiw+t=x ʔayxáxaʔ ɬ+c+ʔácqaʔ
finish_bathe well enter this art young_one a_while come_out_again
bathing." *The little one went in, in a little while he came out.*

417 waẏ cwiʔscáʕʷlx nixʷ, waẏ nixʷ st̓íxʷləm iʔ stətəm̓tím̓s
waẏ c -wẏ+s+caʕʷ+lx nixʷ waẏ nixʷ s -t̓ixʷl+m iʔ s+t•tm̓•tim̓ -s
well hab -finish_bathe also yes also hab -different art clothes -3in
He is done bathing too, he too had different clothes on,

418 waẏ nixʷ {k ɬ} iʔ l citxʷ kɬlkapú, 419 axáʔ {i t} iʔ t wísxən iʔ t
waẏ nixʷ iʔ l citxʷ kɬ+lkapú axáʔ iʔ t wis=xn iʔ t
well also art for house have_coat this art obl long art obl
he also had a house coat, *a long*

pəpíqəlxʷ ta lkapú {kəm̓ t̓əxʷ caqniɬ} 420 waẏ put {txi} ƛ̓lap axáʔ iʔ tətw̓ít
p•piq=lxʷ t lkapú waẏ put ƛ̓la+p axáʔ iʔ t•tw̓it
white_coat obl coat well just stop this art boy
white coat. *The boy had just settled down*

421 t̓i_kʷm̓iɬ kiʔ cənʔúɬxʷ {iʔ} iʔ tkɬmilxʷ {a kɬ} ia kɬcitxʷ 422 i·
t̓iʔ_kʷm̓iɬ kiʔ c+n+ʔuɬxʷ iʔ tkɬ+m=ilxʷ iʔ kɬ+citxʷ i·
at_once rel enter_cisl art woman art have_house intj
when the woman that owned the house came in. 23:02 She's

sk̓ʷəl̓kstmísts nt̓a waẏ kɬcawt 423 qʷámqʷəmt iʔ ɬəɬáxʷs
s -k̓ʷl̓=kst+mist -s nt̓a waẏ kɬ+cawt qʷam•qʷm+t iʔ ɬ•ɬaxʷ -s
nom -doll_up -3i intj yes quite_something excellent art dress -3in
fixed up to the max. *Her dress is beautiful,*

424 uɬ x̌ast a[xáʔ] yaʕyáʕt {iʔ} t̓əxʷ iʔ sk̓ʷəl̓kstmísts iʔ
uɬ x̌as+t axáʔ yaʕ•yáʕ+t t̓xʷ iʔ s -k̓ʷl̓=kst+mist -s iʔ
and good this all emph art nom -doll_up -3i art
and everything how she was fixed was beautiful, her

qəpqíntəns 425 nt’a uɬ iʔ k̓ənk̓ənpqínkstəns uɬ np̓aʔp̓aʔxʷús iʔ
qp=qin+tn -s nt’a uɬ iʔ k̓n•k̓np̓=qin=kst+n -s uɬ n+p̓aʔ•p̓aʔxʷ=ús iʔ
hair -3in intj and art rings -3in and bright art
hair... *Gee, her rings were blinding*

t sp̓aʔáxʷs 426 way̓ ixíʔ cúntəm axáʔ iʔ sxʔítx
t s+p̓aʔxʷ -s way̓ ixíʔ cu -nt -m axáʔ iʔ s+xʔit=x
agInst shine -3in well then tell -nt -psv this art oldest_one
with shine. *The woman said to the oldest boy,*

qaʔɬilmíxʷəm axáʔ {iʔ t} iʔ t tkɬmílxʷ 427 cúntəm way̓ uɬ
qaʔɬ=yl=míxʷ+m axáʔ iʔ t tkɬ+m=ilxʷ cu -nt -m way̓ uɬ
chief's_children this art agInst woman tell -nt -psv well and
the king's son, *she said to him,*

k̓ʷəƛ̓əntís iʔ k̓ənpqínkstəns uɬ cúntəm 428 way̓ axáʔ {kʷu}
k̓ʷƛ̓ -nt -is iʔ k̓np̓=qin=kst+n -s uɬ cu -nt -m way̓ axáʔ
take_off -nt -3erg art ring -3in and tell -nt -psv well this
she took off her ring and said to him: *"Take care of*

kʷu txət’ɬtíxʷ axáʔ ink̓ənpqínkstən 429 aɬíʔ kʷa xʷaʔsənʔís
kʷu t+xt’ -ɬt -ixʷ axáʔ in -k̓np̓=qin=kst+n aɬíʔ kʷa xʷaʔ+s+n+ʔíys
1obj watch_so -ɬt -2erg this 1in -ring because intj expensive
my ring for me, *because it's expensive and*

cəm̓ səl’mín 430 n̓ín̓w̓iʔ x̌lap kʷ xʷt’ilx mi kʷu
cm̓ sl’+mi -n n̓ín̓w̓iʔ x̌la+p kʷ xʷt’+ilx mi kʷu
maybe lose -1erg a_while tomorrow 2kn get_up fut 1obj
I might lose it. *Tomorrow morning when you get up you*

ɬxʷíc̓əɬtxʷ ɬ x̌lítɬtsən {t’əxʷ mi} 431 [kʷu] ʔaɬʔíɬən mi kʷu
ɬ+xʷic̓ -ɬt -xʷ ɬ x̌lit -ɬt -s -n kʷu ʔaɬ•ʔíɬn mi kʷu
give_again -ɬt -2erg when call -ɬt -2obj -1erg 4kn eat_pl fut 1obj
give it back to me, when I ask for it. 24:07 *When we eat you give it*

ɬxʷíc̓əɬtxʷ {s} 432 t’əxʷ cƛ̓aʔɬúlmən p ksʔaɬʔíɬnaʔx
ɬ+xʷic̓ -ɬt -xʷ t’xʷ c -ƛ̓aʔ -ɬulm -n p ks -ʔaɬ•ʔíɬn -aʔx
give_again -ɬt -2erg emph act -fetch -5obj -1erg 5kn incp^ -eat_pl -^ipftv
back to me. *When I come after you for breakfast*

ixíʔ mi kʷu ɬxʷíc̓əɬtxʷ 433 a·· way̓, {a nu t’xʷ liʔ} ilíʔ uɬ aɬíʔ
ixíʔ mi kʷu ɬ+xʷic̓ -ɬt -xʷ a way̓ ilíʔ uɬ aɬíʔ
then fut 1obj give_again -ɬt -2erg intj well there and so
you give it to me." *There is a*

kɬl’aʔtáp iʔ l sənɬq̓ʷútən 434 cúntəm t’əxʷ ilíʔ kɬt’k̓ʷant
kɬ+l’aʔtáp iʔ l s+n+ɬq̓ʷ=ut+n cu -nt -m t’xʷ ilíʔ kɬ+t’k̓ʷa -nt
have_table_dim art at bed tell -nt -psv emph there put_down -nt
small table there by the bed. *He said to her, "Lay it down there."*

435 way̓ axáʔ {ɬ} ɬʔácqaʔ axáʔ iʔ tkɬmilxʷ 436 ixíʔ uɬ axáʔ
way̓ axáʔ ɬ+ʔácqaʔ axáʔ iʔ tkɬ+m=ilxʷ ixíʔ uɬ axáʔ
well this go_out_again this art woman then and this
Then the woman went out, *the woman*

snisc axáʔ iʔ tkɬmílxʷ 437 waẏ ʔayxáxaʔ {ɬ} ɬʕáċəs
s -nis -c axáʔ iʔ tkɬ+m=ilxʷ waẏ ʔayxáxaʔ ɬ+ʕaċ -s
nom -sg_gone -3i this art woman well a_while look_again -3erg
left. *In a little while, just before*

axáʔ {t t} iʔ tʼəxʷ kspúlxsəlx 438 ʕáċəs axáʔ {iʔ} iʔ
axáʔ iʔ tʼxʷ ks -pul+x -s -lx ʕaċ -s axáʔ iʔ
this art evidently futi -overnight -3i -pl look_at -3erg this art
he went to bed he glanced at it, 25:00 *the boy*

tətẇít axáʔ iʔ ḱənpqínkstən 439 ƛ̓əm ilíʔ iʔ kɬtʼəḱʷəntís iʔ l
t•tẇit axáʔ iʔ ḱnṗ=qin=kst+n ƛ̓m ilíʔ iʔ kɬ+tʼḱʷ -nt -is iʔ l
boy this art ring past there art put_st_down -nt -3erg art on
looked at the ring, *where she had put it*

latáp, waẏ tʼi ḱaw 440 uɬ axáʔ lut tʼ yúm̓miʔstəlx naʔɬ
latáp waẏ tʼiʔ ḱaw uɬ axáʔ lut tʼ yúm+miʔst -lx naʔɬ
table well evid gone and this not negfac move -pl with
on the table. Gee, it's gone. *And he and his partner hadn'd*

slʼax̌ts (tʼ syúmmiʔstsəlx) 441 tʼi ḱaʔx̌í la nsəḱʷtílp {l}
s+lʼax̌+t -s tʼ s -yúm+miʔst -s -lx tʼiʔ ḱa+ʔx̌íʔ l n+s+ḱʷt=ilp
partner -3in negfac nom -move -3i -pl evid there at across_bed
made a move. *His partner was*

ilíʔ {c} iʔ slʼax̌t[s] ɬq̓ʷut 442 uɬ cniɬc aláʔ {iʔ} ɬq̓ʷut 443 uɬ {cniɬc}
ilíʔ iʔ s+lʼax̌+t -s ɬq̓ʷ=ut uɬ cniɬ+c aláʔ ɬq̓ʷ=ut uɬ
there art partner -3in lie_down and (s)he here lie and
across the room lying down, *and he is lying on this side.* *And she*

ḱəl cniɬc {iʔ} iʔ ḱaʕʷmístməntəm kstxətʼɬtís iʔ
ḱl cniɬ+c iʔ ḱaʕʷ+míst+m -nt -m ks -txtʼ -ɬt -is iʔ
to (s)he art hire -nt -psv futt^ -watch_so -ɬt -3erg art
had hired him to take care of

ḱənpqínkstəns {si} 444 cus waẏ ilíʔ tʼəxʷ kəɬtʼəḱʷánt iʔ l latáp
ḱnṗ=qin=kst+n -s cu -s waẏ ilíʔ tʼxʷ kɬ+tʼḱʷa -nt iʔ l latáp
ring -3in tell -3erg well there emph put_down -nt art on table
the ring. *He had told her, "Put it on the table."*

445 waẏ, waẏ walʼəmscút, walʼíkstməntəm 446 waẏ lut tʼa
waẏ waẏ walʼ+mscút walʼ=íkst+m -nt -m waẏ lut tʼ
well well puzzle trick -nt -psv well not evid
Something queer is going on, she played a trick on him. 26:01 *He doesn't*

ksćḱəɬpáʔx̌ 447 ixíʔ cus iʔ slʼax̌ts, síncaʔs waẏ
ksc -ḱɬ+paʔx̌ ixíʔ cu -s iʔ s+lʼax̌+t -s síncaʔ -s waẏ
futPerfi -figure_out then tell -3erg art partner -3in younger_brother -3in well
know what to think. *So he says to his partner, his younger*

ƛ̓əm aláʔ 448 ah lut waẏ kən ḱəɬḱʷíƛ̓ət 449 ixíʔ naʔɬcám iʔ púlxəlx,
ƛ̓m aláʔ ah lut waẏ kn ḱɬ+ḱʷitʼ•tʼ ixíʔ naɬc•c•ám iʔ pul+x -lx
past here intj not well 1kn that forget art camp -pl
brother... *Oh, no, I took a shortcut.* *I forgot. They went to bed.*

ixíʔ {l} ksx̌əlpínaʔlx xʷt̓lílxəlx 450 ixíʔ uɬ wiʔskc̓aw̓íw̓smәlx
ixíʔ k+s+x̌lp=ínaʔ -lx xʷt̓+lilx -lx ixíʔ uɬ wy̓+s+k+c̓aw̓=íw̓s+m -lx
then have_daylight -pl get_up_pl -pl then and finish_wash -pl
Daytime came and they got up. *They got done washing, and they*

k̓ɬyaʔwámәlx 451 ixíʔ naʔɬcәcám kiʔ nɬәk̓ʷk̓ʷmís iʔ k̓әnpqínkst
k̓ɬ+yaʔwá+m -lx ixíʔ naɬc•c•ám kiʔ n+ɬk̓ʷ•k̓ʷ+mi -s iʔ k̓np̓=qin=kst
wait -pl that forget rel think_about -3erg art ring
are waiting. *That's the time he thought of the ring.*

452 uɬ aɬíʔ laklís axáʔ iʔ laklíʔstәlx 453 uɬәm lut t̓a
uɬ aɬíʔ laklí -s axáʔ iʔ lakl=íʔst -lx uɬ+m lut t̓
and because lock -3erg this art lock -pl and not evid
They had locked the door. *They don't have*

ksql̓awlx uɬ a claklístәlx k̓ʷna náq̓ʷq̓ʷәlx 454 uɬ
k+s+qlaw -lx uɬ a c -laklí -st -lx k̓ʷnaʔ naq̓ʷ•q̓ʷ -lx uɬ
have_money -pl and art cust^ -lock -^cust -pl intj be_robbed -pl and
any money that might be stolen for them to lock; *it's*

aɬí axáʔ iʔ k̓әnpqínkst[әn], nstils uɬ nak̓ʷáʔ k̓ʷәk̓ʷínaʔ iʔ sәnʔíysc
aɬíʔ axáʔ iʔ k̓np̓=qin=kst+n n+st=ils uɬ nak̓ʷ+á k̓ʷ•k̓ʷy=ínaʔ iʔ s+n+ʔiys -c
because this art ring think and not small art price 3in
on account of the ring, it doesn't cost just a little.

455 cәm̓ way̓ ixíʔ pnaʔ kɬqʷáʕʷqʷut {axa} aláʔ ckicx {kʷu} 456 kʷu
cm̓ way̓ ixíʔ pnaʔ kɬ+qʷaʕʷ•qʷw+t aláʔ c+kic+x kʷu
maybe yes that maybe have_crazy here arrive_cisl 3e4obj
"There might be some no good people get here, 27:02 *they*

ʔatxaʔíntәm ixíʔ kʷu náq̓ʷmәntәm 457 ixíʔ uɬ
ʔatx+aʔ=í[11] -nt -m ixíʔ kʷu naq̓ʷ+m -nt -m ixíʔ uɬ
catch_asleep -nt -3e4obj then 3e4obj steal_from -nt -3e4obj that and
might catch us asleep, and steal from us." *That's*

laklís, ilíʔ {t ks} ckәɬt̓ak̓ʷ iʔ {t} laklí 458 way̓ ixíʔ
laklí -s ilíʔ c -kɬ+t̓ak̓ʷ iʔ laklí way̓ ixíʔ
lock -3erg there hab -lie_on art lock well then
why they locked, and the key was on the table. *They*

wiʔskc̓aw̓íw̓smәlx {i} wiʔstxtxámәlx {ixiɬ} 459 k̓ɬәnk̓ahk̓ʷíps {iʔ} iʔ
wy̓+s+k+c̓aw̓=íw̓s+m -lx wy̓+s+tx•txa+m -lx k̓ɬ+n+k̓ahk̓ʷ=íp -s iʔ
finish_wash -pl finish_comb -pl open -3erg art
got done washing and combing. *He opened the door of*

citxʷ {s txʷ ɬ} 460 ixíʔ uɬ ilíʔ ɬkɬәxʷpntís iʔ laklí 461 way̓
citxʷ ixíʔ uɬ ilíʔ ɬ+k+ɬxʷ+p -nt -is iʔ laklí way̓
house then and there hang_again -nt -3erg art lock well
the house, *and he hung the key there.* *He*

11 This analysis is tentative. I don't recognize +aʔí.

ʕáċəs {i li·} iʔ l latáp iʔ cus iʔ kskɬt̓ək̓ʷəntís axáʔ iʔ
ʕaċ -s iʔ l latáp iʔ cu -s iʔ ks -kɬ+t̓k̓ʷ -nt -is axáʔ iʔ
look_at -3erg art at table art tell -3erg art futt^ -put_st_down -nt -3erg this art
looked at the table (he had told the woman to put it down

tkəɬmílxʷ 462 swinúmtx iʔ tkəɬmílxʷ 463 way̓ t̓i k̓aw, a
tkɬmilxʷ s+wy̓+numt=x iʔ tkɬmilxʷ way̓ t̓iʔ k̓aw a
woman handsome art woman well evid gone art
there, the good looking woman). It's gone.

nwaʔlílsəms 464 uɬ ha sċkinx axáʔ kʷu claklíst
n+waʔl=íls+m -s uɬ haʔ sc+ʔkin+x axáʔ kʷu c -lakl=íʔst
puzzle -3erg and inter why_is_it this 4kn gpat -locked
He got puzzled. "What is the matter?" We were locked in,

465 uɬ kʷu tk̓asəlmíst acʕáċstəm kiʔ ilíʔ kɬt̓ək̓ʷəntís
uɬ kʷu tk=ʔasl+míst c -ʕaċ -st -m kiʔ ilíʔ kɬ+t̓k̓ʷ -nt -is
and 4kn two_persons cust^ -look -^cust -4erg rel there put_st_down -nt -3erg
and two of us watched when she put it down there

t cniɬc 466 uɬ ɬʔácqaʔ uɬ ixíʔ laklíntəm iʔ citxʷ uɬ a
t cniɬ+c uɬ ɬ+ʔácqaʔ uɬ ixíʔ laklí -nt -m iʔ citxʷ uɬ a
agInst (s)he and go_out_again and then lock -nt -4erg art house and art
herself." 28:00 Then she went out and they locked the house, and it's

ɬk̓aw 467 lut_swit kʷu t̓ kícəntəm 468 ámaʔ
ɬ+k̓aw lut_swit kʷu t̓ kic -nt -m ámaʔ
gone_again nobody 3e4obj negfac reach_st/sb -nt -3e4obj intj
gone. "Nobody has got here to us. I am

isíwm isíncaʔ, pnaʔ {cmiɬc} cniɬc cmistís
i-siw+m i -síncaʔ pnaʔ cniɬ+c c -my -st -is
1i -ask 1in -younger_brother maybe (s)he cust^ -know -^cust -3erg
going to ask my little brother, maybe he knows."

469 cúntəm a lut, way̓ kən málx̌aʔ {kə} 470 la_cxʔit iʔ x̌əx̌yáɬnəxʷs,
cu -nt -m a lut way̓ kn málx̌aʔ la_c+xʔit iʔ x̌•x̌yaɬ=nxʷ -s
tell -nt -psv intj not well 1kn lie at_first art clock -3in
He said ... No, I am lying.[12] *I forgot, first it was her watch,*

lut t̓ k̓ənpqínkst 471 ixíʔ iʔ x̌əx̌yáɬxnəxʷs a ck̓əɬyrk̓ʷcníkst
lut t̓ knp̓=qin=kst ixíʔ iʔ x̌•x̌yaɬ=nxʷ -s a c -k̓ɬ+yrk̓ʷ=cn=ikst
not negfac ring that art clock -3in art hab -wrist_band
not her ring, her watch that goes around the wrist.

472 uɬ aɬíʔ way̓ myaɬ xʷaʔspíntk ki kʷu ccaptíkʷɬtsəlx
uɬ aɬíʔ way̓ myaɬ xʷaʔ+s+pín=tk kiʔ kʷu c -captíkʷ -ɬt -s -lx
and because yes too_much many_years rel 1obj cust^ -legend -ɬt -3erg -pl
Because it's been too many years that my old relatives told me

12 Here it's Pete talking, making a correction to the story.

inxaʔxʔít 473 uɬ way̓ {n} nɬəpɬíptm[ən] 474 k̓əɬʔayxʷíw̓stən {iʔ}
in -xaʔ•xʔít uɬ way̓ n+ɬp•ɬip+t+m -n k̓ɬ+ʔayxʷ=íw̓s -t -n
1in -ancestor and yes forget_pl -1erg mix_up -caus -1erg
the stories. *I forget them,* *I get the stories*

iʔ captíkʷɬ, t̓əxʷ nɬíptmən 475 ixíʔ uɬ nɬək̓ʷk̓ʷmín naʔɬccám
iʔ captíkʷɬ t̓xʷ n+ɬip+t+m -n ixíʔ uɬ n+ɬk̓ʷ•k̓ʷ+mi -n naɬc•c•ám
art legends emph forget -1erg then and think_about -1erg forget
mixed up, I forget. *Then I thought of it, I remembered it was*

x̌əx̌y̓áɬnəxʷs 476 way̓ i[xíʔ] cus iʔ sƛ̓ax̌ts, cus
x̌•x̌yaɬ=nxʷ -s way̓ ixíʔ cu -s iʔ s+ƛ̓ax̌+t -s cu -s
watch -3in well then tell -3erg art partner -3in tell -3erg
a watch. 29:03 *Then he asked his partner, he said:*

477 uɬ uc cʕac̓stxʷ axáʔ iʔ tkɬmilxʷ kiʔ kʷu
uɬ uc c -ʕac̓ -st -xʷ axáʔ iʔ tkɬ+m=ilxʷ kiʔ kʷu
and dub cust^ -look -^cust -2erg this art woman rel 1obj
"Were you watching the woman when she

ktəlməntúɬts ixíʔ iʔ x̌əx̌yáɬnəxʷs 478 uɬ_i cun
k+tl+mn -tuɬt -s ixíʔ iʔ x̌•x̌yaɬ=nxʷ -s uɬ_iʔ cu -n
put_in_custody_of -tuɬt -3erg that art clock -3in and_then tell -1erg
put me in charge of her watch, *and I told her*

ilíʔ kskəɬt̓ək̓ʷəntís 479 uɬ aɬíʔ k̓ʷəƛ̓ntís iʔ təl
ilíʔ ks -kɬ+t̓k̓ʷ -nt -is uɬ aɬíʔ k̓ʷƛ̓ -nt -is iʔ tl
there futt^ -put_st_down -nt -3erg and so take_off -nt -3erg art from
to put it down? *And she took it off*

k̓ɬk̓əmcníksts 480 cúntəm way̓, way̓ cʕác̓[stən]
k̓ɬ+k̓m=cn=ikst cu -nt -m way̓ way̓ c -ʕac̓ -st -n
wrist tell -nt -psv yes yes cust^ -look -^cust -1erg
her wrist?" *He said to him, "Yes, I was watching."*

481 cúntəm uɬ kʷaʔ t̓i ʔácqaʔ uɬ {aɬ la} laklín iʔ cítxʷtət
cu -nt -m uɬ kʷaʔ t̓iʔ ʔácqaʔ uɬ laklí -n iʔ citxʷ -tt
tell -nt -psv and intj evid go_out and lock -1erg art house -4in
He said, "And she went out, and I locked our house.

482 uɬ aɬíʔ kʷu c̓ayʔáyx̌ʷt cəm̓ kʷu k̓əɬʔatətxnúmt 483 mi kʷu
uɬ aɬíʔ kʷu c -ʔay•ʔáyx̌ʷt cm̓ kʷu k̓ɬ+ʔat•t•x+númt mi kʷu
and because 4kn hab -tired_pl maybe 4kn fall_asleep fut 3e4obj
And we are tired, and we might fall asleep, *and*

ckícstəm t swit, kʷu
c -kic -st -m t swit kʷu
cust^ -reach_st/sb -^cust -3e4obj agInst somebody 3e4obj
somebody might get to us,

cnaq̓ʷmstəm 484 nak̓ʷáʔ kʷu kstim̓ mnímɬtət, məɬ
c -naq̓ʷ+m -st -m nak̓ʷ+á kʷu k+s+tim̓ mnimɬ+tt mɬ
cust^ -steal_from -^cust -3e4obj not 4kn have_something we and
and steal from us. *We have nothing like money for them*

stim̓ sql̓áwtət kʷu náq̓ʷmłtəm 485 uł t̓əxʷ kʷu
s+tim̓ s+qlaw -tt kʷu naq̓ʷ+m -łt -m uł t̓xʷ kʷu
something money -4in 3e4obj steal_from -łt -3e4obj and emph 4kn
to steal from us. *We are just*

nstilsm ixíʔ iʔ x̌əx̌yáłnəxʷ kʷu náq̓ʷəmłtəm 486 sc̓x̌ilx
nst=ils+m ixíʔ iʔ x̌•x̌yał=nxʷ kʷu naq̓ʷ+m -łt -m sc+ʔx̌il+x
think that art clock 3e4obj steal_from -łt -3e4obj reason_why
thinking they might steal the watch from us. *That's why we*

kiʔ kʷu laklíʔst 487 uł lut t̓ k̓əłʔanwínəm, uc anwí 488 lut, uł
kiʔ kʷu lakl=íʔst uł lut t̓ k̓ł+ʔanwín+m uc anwí lut uł
rel 4kn lock and not negfac notice dub you not and
locked ourselves in. *And we didn't notice anyone. Did you?" 30:03* *"No,*

ałíʔ nixʷ kən ʔitx 489 cúntəm way̓, way̓ cənləʕʷíkstəm a t̓əxʷ
ałíʔ nixʷ kn ʔitx cu -nt -m way̓ way̓ c -n+lʕʷ=ikst+m a t̓xʷ
because also 1kn sleep tell -nt -psv yes well hab -stick_hand_in intj emph
I was asleep too." *He [the little one] said "Yes," he stuck his hand,*

lut [ck̓ʷəƛ̓əntís ilíʔ x̌əx̌yáłnəxʷ 490 ilqəntís {iʔ} iʔ
lut c -k̓ʷƛ̓ -nt -is ilíʔ x̌•x̌yał=nxʷ ylq -nt -is iʔ
not act -pull_out -nt -3erg there clock uncover -nt -3erg art
pulled it out, there is the watch. *The boy uncovered*

k̓əłk̓əmcníksts axáʔ iʔ tətwít 491 ilíʔ ck̓ʷəƛ̓ntís ixíʔ
k̓ł+k̓m=cn=ikst -s axáʔ iʔ t•tw̓it ilíʔ c+k̓ʷƛ̓ -nt -is ixíʔ
wrist -3in this art boy there pull_out -nt -3erg that
his wrist. *He took it off and gave it*

xʷíc̓əłts iʔ sl̓ax̌ts 492 cus ixíʔ axáʔ i x̌əx̌yáłnəxʷ 493 a··
xʷic̓ -łt -s iʔ s+l̓ax̌+t -s cu -s ixíʔ axáʔ iʔ x̌•x̌yał=nxʷ a
give -łt -3erg art partner -3in tell -3erg that this art clock intj
to his partner. *He said, "Here is the watch."* *"Oh,*

t anwí {askʷín} askʷním 494 kíwa ałíʔ isk̓íntəm k̓ʷnaʔ
t anwí a -s+kʷni+m kíw+a ałíʔ i -s+k̓int+m k̓ʷnaʔ
agInst you 2in -taking yes because 1in -fear intj
you took it!" *"Yes, because I was afraid*

səl̓míntəm 495 ki kʷin iʔ txət̓ntín 496 uł səc̓x̌ílx
sl̓+mi -nt -m kiʔ kʷi -n iʔ txt̓ -nt -in uł sc+ʔx̌il+x
lose -nt -4erg rel take -1erg art watch_so -nt -1erg and reason_why
we might lose it. *That's why I kept it.* *That's why*

kiʔ k̓əłləʕʷcníkstmən 497 uł ałíʔ {lut} lut_ksluts {iks}
kiʔ k̓ł+lʕʷ=cn=ikst+m -n uł ałíʔ lut_k+s+lut+s
rel put_on_wrist -1erg and because there_is_no_no_about_it
I put it around my wrist. *And there is no two ways about it,*

498 iksqíłt {iksqíłt} mi kʷu ł kʷiłts kʷu ł k̓əłk̓ʷəƛ̓cníksəs
i -ks -qiłt mi kʷu ł kʷi -łt -s kʷu ł k̓ł+k̓ʷƛ̓=cn=iks -s
1i -futi -awaken fut 1obj if take -łt -3erg 1obj if pull_off_of_wrist -3erg
I'll wake up if they [try to] take it off my wrist." 31:04

499 waẏ kʷint a[xáʔ] waẏ put {put a¨} ckʷis {k̓əɬi} ɬkəɬt̓ək̓ʷəntís iʔ
waẏ kʷin -t axáʔ waẏ put c+kʷi -s ɬ+kɬ+t̓k̓ʷ -nt -is iʔ
well take -nt this well just take -3erg put_back_on_st -nt -3erg art
He just took it and put it on

l latáp 500 waẏ cənʔúɬxʷ iʔ tkɬmilxʷ {ixíʔ cut} 501 cúntəm ha kiṅ
l latáp waẏ c+n+ʔuɬxʷ iʔ tkɬ+m=ilxʷ cu -nt -m haʔ ʔkin
on table well enter_cisl art woman tell -nt -psv inter indef
the table. *The woman came in.* *She asked "Where is*

iʔ ktílməntsən iʔ x̌əx̌yáɬnəxʷ 502 naʔɬccám, axáʔ iʔ tkɬmilxʷ
iʔ k+tilm -nt -s -n iʔ x̌•x̌yaɬ=nxʷ naɬc•c•ám axáʔ iʔ tkɬ+m=ilxʷ
art entrust -nt -2obj -1erg art clock forget this art woman
the watch I gave you to keep for me?" *I thought of something.*[13]

nák̓ʷəm aɬíʔ c̓x̌iɬ ta nʔaɬnaʔsqílxʷtən 503 waẏ t̓i ixíʔ {ɬ}
nak̓ʷ+m aɬíʔ c+ʔx̌iɬ t n+ʔaɬn+aʔ+s+qílxʷ+tn waẏ t̓iʔ ixíʔ
evid because like obj_c̓x̌iɬ man_eater well evid then
This woman is like a cannibal. *She went back*

ɬʔácqaʔ uɬ paʔsmís iʔ x̌əx̌yáɬnəxʷs 504 uɬ
ɬ+ʔácqaʔ uɬ paʔs+mí -s iʔ x̌•x̌yaɬ=nxʷ -s uɬ
go_out_again and think_about -3erg art clock -3in and
out and wished her watch back to herself. *Her*

cənkəcníkəntəm iʔ t x̌əx̌yáɬnəxʷs 505 ixíʔ uɬ cənʔúɬxʷ
c -n+kc+n=ikn -t -m iʔ t x̌•x̌yaɬ=nxʷ -s ixíʔ uɬ c+n+ʔuɬxʷ
act -reach -nt -psv art agInst clock -3in then and enter_cisl
watch went to her. *She went*

uɬ tk̓iwlx c̓kiṅ {n n} 506 nkaʔɬəlmíẇs {kʷa} t ksənmsmíẇsc iʔ
uɬ t+k̓iw+lx c+ʔkin n+kaʔɬl+m=íẇs t k -s+n+ms+m=iẇs -c iʔ
and climb indef three_stories obl to_be -fourth_floor -3i art
upstairs, *three stories, the fourth floor of*

citxʷs 507 ik̓líʔ kiʔ sənkʷúməns, yaʕyáʕt əclklaklí
citxʷ -s ik̓líʔ kiʔ s+n+kʷum+n -s yaʕ•yáʕ+t c -lk•laklí
house -3in there rel storage_place -3in all gpat -lock_pl
the house. 32:00 *That's where she stores her things, all locked.*

508 ixíʔ tk̓i¨wlx, uɬ kɬqilt iʔ k̓əl sənkʷúməns 509 k̓ahk̓ʷqís
ixíʔ t+k̓iw+lx uɬ kɬ+qilt iʔ k̓l s+n+kʷum+n -s k̓ahk̓ʷ=qí -s
then climb and on_top art to storage_place -3in open -3erg
She went up and got to the top where she stores her things. *She opened*

ia lkasáts iʔ səntətəm̓tím̓təns ilíʔ nt̓ək̓ʷəntís 510 ixíʔ
iʔ lkasát -s iʔ s+n+t•tm̓•tim̓+tn -s ilíʔ n+t̓k̓ʷ -nt -is ixíʔ
art box -3in art wardrobe -3in there put_in -nt -3erg then
the trunk where her clothes are, and she put it there. *She*

13 The import of this utterance is "I should have mentioned this before."

ɬlaklís uɬ t̓əxʷ ixíʔ ulqís uɬ laklís 511 ɬʔácqaʔ
ɬ+laklí -s uɬ t̓xʷ ixíʔ wl=qi -s uɬ laklí -s ɬ+ʔácqaʔ
lock_again -3erg and emph then cover -3erg and lock -3erg go_out_again
covered it and locked it. *Then she*

uɬ ixíʔ laklís iʔ k̓ɬənk̓míp 512 itlíʔ csax̌ʷt uɬ i k̓əl
uɬ ixíʔ laklí -s iʔ k̓ɬ+n+k̓m=ip itlíʔ c+sax̌ʷ+t uɬ iʔ k̓l
and then lock -3erg art door from_there come_downhill and art to
went out and locked the door. *She came down to another door,*

k̓ɬənəqsíp uɬ {ləklə} 513 ləklaklí··s uɬ {cənɬ} cəntíkɬ 514 ixíʔ uɬ sic
k̓ɬ+nqs=ip uɬ lk•laklí -s uɬ c -n+tikɬ ixíʔ uɬ sic
one_door and lock_pl -3erg and hab -bottom then and then
and [locked it]. *She locked them all to the bottom.* *And then*

iʔ xʷist 515 hoy, ixíʔ uɬ {x̌lítɬtəm iʔ} x̌lítɬtəm, cúntəm, 516 uɬ
iʔ xʷist hoy ixíʔ uɬ x̌lit -ɬt -m cu -nt -m uɬ
art walk finish then and call -ɬt -psv tell -nt -psv and
she left. *Then she asked, she said:* *"Where*

kiń iʔ ktílməntsən inx̌əx̌yáɬnəxʷ 517 waẏ kən ɬckicx,
ʔkin iʔ k+tilm -nt -s -n in -x̌•x̌yaɬ=nxʷ waẏ kn ɬ+c+kic+x
indef art entrust -nt -2obj -1erg 1in -clock well 1kn arrive_cisl_again
is the watch I gave you to take care of? *I am back,*

waẏ uɬ inx̌mínk 518 a·· uɬ laʔkín kiʔ {iʔ} cúntsən mi
waẏ uɬ in -x̌m=ink a uɬ la+ʔkíń kiʔ cu -nt -s -n mi
well and 1in -want intj and wherever rel tell -nt -2obj -1erg fut
I want it." *"Ah, and where did I tell you*

utəntíxʷ 519 uɬ ixíʔ t̓əxʷ mat ckt̓k̓ʷiẇs laʔkín iʔ
wt -nt -ixʷ uɬ ixíʔ t̓xʷ mat c -k+t̓k̓ʷ=iẇs la+ʔkíń iʔ
put_down -nt -2erg and then evidently must hab -place_on_st wherever art
to put it? 33:04 *I guess it's there, wherever you*

kt̓ək̓ʷíẇsənt[xʷ] 520 waẏ ik̓líʔ ʕáċəm axáʔ iʔ tkɬmilxʷ 521 uɬ ixíʔ
k+t̓k̓ʷ=iẇs -nt -xʷ waẏ ik̓líʔ ʕaċ+m axáʔ iʔ tkɬ+m=ilxʷ uɬ ixíʔ
place_on_st -nt -2erg well there look this art woman and there
put it." *The woman looked there,* *and*

a ckt̓k̓ʷiẇs a[xáʔ] iʔ x̌əx̌yáɬnəxʷs 522 waẏ ckʷis iʔ
a c -k+t̓k̓ʷ=iẇs axáʔ iʔ x̌•x̌yaɬ=nxʷ -s waẏ c+kʷi -s iʔ
art hab -place_on_st this art clock -3in well take -3erg art
there was the watch. *The woman took it.*

tkɬmilxʷ t̓əxʷ t̓i paʕs 523 axáʔ aláʔ tl isckícx axáʔ i l
tkɬ+m=ilxʷ t̓xʷ t̓iʔ paʕs axáʔ aláʔ tl̓ i -sc -kic+x axáʔ iʔ l
woman emph evid surprise this here from 1i -pftv -arrive this art on
My, she was surprised. *"Since I got here to this*

təmxʷúlaʔxʷ 524 lut_swit ilíʔ kʷu t̓a ċx̌ilsts
tmxʷ=úlaʔxʷ lut_swit ilíʔ kʷu t̓ c -ʔx̌il -st -s
world nobody there 1obj evid custˆ -do_like -ˆcust -3erg
world *nobody has ever done this to me.*

525 kʷu t'a ɬcka?kícɬts kʷu t'a ɬəcxʷíc̓əɬts i?
kʷu t' ɬ+c+ka?•kíc -ɬt -s kʷu t' ɬ+c+xʷic̓ -ɬt -s i?
1obj evid find_again_cisl -ɬt -3erg 1obj evid give_back_cisl -ɬt -3erg art
Nobody has found, or given back what I have given them to

ktílmən 526 nt'a mat waẏ yawpyáʕʷt 527 waẏ ?ácqa?,
k+til+m -n nt'a mat waẏ yaw+p+yáʕʷ+t waẏ ?ácqa?
entrust -1erg intj must yes powerful well go_out
look after. He must be real smart." She stepped outside,

cúntməlx {waẏ} ha waẏ p wi?skc̓aw̓íw̓s 528 cútəlx waẏ
cu -nt -m -lx ha? waẏ p wẏ+s+k+c̓aw̓=íw̓s cut -lx waẏ
tell -nt -psv -pl inter finish 5kn finish_wash say -pl yes
she asked them, "Are you freshened up?" They told her "Yes."

529 waẏ t'əxʷ kʷu ɬkxəntíp uɬ kʷu ?aɬ?íɬən 530 waẏ {əɬ əc}
waẏ t'xʷ kʷu ɬ+kx+n -t -ip uɬ kʷu ?aɬ•?íɬn waẏ
well emph 1obj follow_back -nt -5erg and 4kn eat_pl well
"Well, come back with me, we are going to eat." They

kxəntísəlx ?awtípi?səlx 531 npəpílxəlx {k̓i} i? k̓əl {smi}
kx+n -t -is -lx ?aw+t=íp ẏ -s -lx n+p•pilx -lx i? k̓l
follow -nt -3erg -pl follow -nt -3erg -pl enter_pl -pl art to
went with her, they followed her. 34:03 They went into

citxʷ[s] axá? i? tkɬmilxʷ {ta kwaẏ i ti cxʷ} 532 ckɬsal i?
citxʷ -s axá? i? tkɬ+m=ilxʷ c -kɬ+sal i?
house -3in this art woman hab -laid_out art
the woman's house. The food is

ksc̓íɬənsəlx, nt'a waẏ cxʷ?ul {kmix axá? i?} 533 kmix náx̌əmɬ i?
ksc -?iɬn -s -lx nt'a waẏ c -xʷ[?]ul kmix nax̌mɬ i?
futPerfi -eat -3i -pl intj yes hab -steam_inch only but art
already laid out, it's steaming. It wasn't just

síryəl {a kʷa i?} i lawán {kəm̓ i? stim̓ a hwit ta nqílxʷcən i? sáma?} 534 a t'əxʷ
síryəl i? lawán a t'xʷ
cereal art oats intj emph
ceral, rolled oats, white

i? swyps?íɬən, uɬ aɬí? ixí?m lut t'a ck̓ʷúl̓cstsəlx {uɬ a}
i? s+wyp+s+?iɬn uɬ aɬí? ixí?+m lut t' c -k̓ʷul̓=c -st -s -lx
art white_food and so that not evid cust^ -cook -^cust -3erg -pl
man's food, [the kind] that they don't cook,

535 t'i_kmix i? t sq?im 536 məɬ k̓əɬc̓xʷípsəlx uɬ ixí? {ɬ?uc} məɬ
t'i?_kmix i? t s+q?im mɬ k̓ɬ+c̓xʷ=ip -s -lx uɬ ixí? mɬ
only art agInst milk and pour_on -3erg -pl and then and
the kind with milk, the kind they pour [milk] on

?íɬsəlx {am} 537 náx̌əmɬ i? sənc̓a?xʷíɬc̓a? i? kʷukʷús i? ?a?úsa? {ixí?} ixí?
?iɬ -s -lx nax̌mɬ i? s+n+c̓a?xʷ=íɬc̓a? i? kʷu•kʷús i? ?a?=úsa? ixí?
eat -3erg -pl but art pancake art bacon art egg that
and eat. But hot cakes, bacon, eggs, cooked

scṗayq 538 waẏ ʔí··ɬnəlx, uɬ lut t̓a ksċíɬnəlx 539 uɬ
sc+ṗaẏq waẏ ʔiɬn -lx uɬ lut t̓ ksc -ʔiɬn -lx uɬ
cooked_food well eat -pl and not evid futPerfi -eat -pl and
food. 35:00 *They ate, and not much,* *because*

aɬíʔ {waẏ} waẏ nkəcníkiʔsəlx iʔ sq̇əm·íltənsəlx 540 waẏ
aɬíʔ waẏ n+kc+n=íkiʔ -s -lx iʔ s+q̇m•m=ilt+n -s -lx waẏ
because yes catch_up_with -3erg -pl art hunger_pl -3in -pl yes
they had overtaken their hunger, *they*

taʔlíʔ txʷʔáqsəlx t spisċíɬt 541 waẏ wiʔwiʔcínəlx, waẏ
taʔlíʔ t+xʷʔ=aqs -lx t s+piʔ+s+ċíɬt[14] waẏ wẏ•wẏ=cin -lx waẏ
very_much much_food -pl obl yesterday well finish_eating_pl -pl well
ate lots already the day before. *They got done eating*

uɬ cúntməlx axáʔ {iʔ t} iʔ t tkɬmilxʷ 542 waẏ mat ixíʔ iʔ
uɬ cu -nt -m -lx axáʔ iʔ t tkɬ+m=ilxʷ waẏ mat ixíʔ iʔ
and tell -nt -psv -pl this art agInst woman well maybe that art
and the woman said to them: *"Just like I said*

t cúɬmən, mat taʔlíʔ p ʔayʔáyx̌ʷt 543 uɬ waẏ aláʔ p
t cu -ɬm -n mat taʔlíʔ p ʔay•ʔáyx̌ʷ+t uɬ waẏ aláʔ p
obl tell -5obj -1erg maybe very_much 5kn tired_pl and yes here 5kn
to you, you must be very tired. *Stay here and rest as*

ɬáʔxʷsk̓itəm l k̓ʷənxásq̇ət 544 spuʔúsəmp l másq̇ət məɬ l ʔaslásq̇ət ixíʔ
ɬáʔxʷ=sk̓it+m l k̓ʷn+x=asq̇t s+puʔ=ús -mp l m=asq̇t mɬ l ʔasl=ásq̇t ixíʔ
rest for a_few_days heart -5in in four_days and in two_days then
many days as you wish. *If you wish four days or two days, whenever*

p ɬaʔɬaʔxʷísk̓it 545 mi itlíʔ p xʷuy k̓aʔkín mat p ɬ
p ɬaʔ•ɬaʔxʷ=ísk̓it mi itlíʔ p xʷuy k̓a+ʔkín mat p ɬ
5kn rested fut from_there 5kn go to_where maybe 5kn compl
you are rested *then you go wherever*

stəkʷʔtəkʷʔútx 546 uɬ axáʔ aɬíʔ nstils iʔ tkəɬmílxʷ uɬ aɬíʔ
s -tkʷʔ+tkʷʔ=ut -x uɬ axáʔ aɬíʔ n+st=ils iʔ tkɬmilxʷ uɬ aɬíʔ
ipftv^ -travel -^ipftv and this so think art woman and because
you are going." *And the woman thought,*

mat_stim̓ nʔaɬnaʔsqílxʷtən 547 uɬ nstils waẏ ń̓iń̓w̓iʔ ayxáxaʔ ɬk̓laxʷ
mat_s+tim̓ n+ʔaɬn+aʔ+s+qílxʷ+tn uɬ n+st=ils waẏ ń̓iń̓w̓iʔ ʔayxá•xaʔ ɬ+k̓laxʷ
must_be man_eater and think well a_while a_while dark_again
(she is a man-eater), 36:02 *she thought, "Later this evening*

mi ɬkícən inilmíxʷəm 548 t̓əxʷ ʔayxáxaʔ ɬkícən ɬkícən
mi ɬ+kic -n in -yl=mixʷ+m t̓xʷ ʔayxáxaʔ ɬ+kic -n
fut arrive_back -1erg 1in -chief emph a_while arrive_back -1erg
I'll go to my boss, *in a while I'll get to*

14 This analysis is unconfirmed. But see Sp s-piʔ-s-ċeʔ; also Th s/piʔh=éwt.

inilmíxʷəm {n} 549 x̌lítən mi tqʷəlqʷəltíwxtən kʷu ɬkics
in -yl=mixʷ+m x̌lit -n mi t+qʷl•qʷl+t=iw̓ -xt -n kʷu ɬ+kic -s
1in -chief call -1erg fut phone -xit -1erg 1obj arrive_back -3erg
my boss. *I'll call him on the phone and my boss'll get back*

inilmíxʷəm 550 i[xíʔ] mi {ɬc} siwn uɬ aɬíʔ nak̓ʷá tanm̓ús {a} kiʔ
in -yl=mixʷ+m ixíʔ mi siw -n uɬ aɬíʔ nak̓ʷá tanm̓=ús kiʔ
1in -chiefa then fut ask -1erg and because not nothing rel
to me. *Then I'll ask him, it's not for nothing that he is my boss,*

inilmíxʷəm taʔlíʔ pəx̌páx̌t 551 sc̓x̌ilx uɬ incá {iʔ kʷu s} iʔ kʷu
in -yl=mixʷ+m taʔlíʔ px̌•pax̌+t sc+ʔx̌il+x uɬ in+cá iʔ kʷu
1in -chief much smart reason_why and I art 1obj
he is smart, *that's why*

mílaʔs uɬ a cƛ̓əxʷstím iʔ st̓əlsqílxʷ 552 way̓
mílaʔ -s uɬ a c -ƛ̓xʷ -st -im iʔ s+t̓l+s+qilxʷ way̓
bait -3erg and art cust^ -kill_many -^cust -4erg art earth_people well
I am his bait to kill humans. *He'll*

n̓ín̓w̓iʔ k̓əɬpax̌x̌íʔst mi ƛ̓əxʷəntíməlx axáʔ iʔ tuʔtw̓ít 553 way̓
n̓ín̓w̓iʔ k̓ɬ+paʔx̌•x̌=íʔst mi ƛ̓xʷ -nt -im -lx axáʔ iʔ tw̓•tw̓it way̓
a_while think_of_something fut kill_many -nt -4erg -pl this art boys well
thing of something and we'll kill these boys." *They*

ixíʔ wiʔwiʔcínəlx uɬ cúntməlx axáʔ iʔ t tkɬmilxʷ 554 way̓
ixíʔ wy̓•wy̓=cin -lx uɬ cu -nt -m -lx axáʔ iʔ t tkɬ+m=ilxʷ way̓
then finish_eating_pl -pl and tell -nt -psv -pl this art agInst woman well
got done eating, and the woman said to them: 37:08 *"You*

aláʔ p ɬáʔxʷsk̓itəm {a} 555 uɬ iʔ cúɬmən mat lkʷut {is} tla
aláʔ p ɬáʔxʷ=sk̓it+m uɬ iʔ cu -ɬm -n mat lkʷ=ut tla
here 5kn rest and art tell -5obj -1erg maybe far from
stay here and rest. *Like I said to you, far,*

lkʷut p sqilxʷ p scutx 556 uɬ taʔlí··ʔ mat p
lkʷ=ut p s+qilxʷ p s -cut -x uɬ taʔlíʔ mat p
far 5kn person 5kn ipftv^ -say -^ipftv and very_much must 5kn
you must come from far. *You must be tired,*

ʔayʔáyx̌ʷt, p kaʔkaʔnxán 557 kəm̓ mat pupíwt iʔ {c̓u} sc̓uʔc̓uʔxánəmp
ʔay•ʔáyx̌ʷ+t p kaʔ•kaʔn=xán km̓ mat pw•piw+t iʔ s+c̓w̓•c̓w̓=xan -mp
tired_pl 5kn sore_feet or maybe blisters art feet -5in
and foot-sore; *or maybe your feet are full of blisters (and you*

uɬ p ukʷmíst {aláʔ ta} 558 t̓əxʷ p ɬáʔxʷsk̓it̓əm spuʔúsəmp mnímɬəmp
uɬ p wkʷ+mist t̓xʷ p ɬáʔxʷ=sk̓it+m s+puʔ=ús -mp mnimɬ+mp
and 5kn keep_secret emph 5kn rest heart -5in you
would hide that). *Get rested, just as you like,*

559 ʔaslásq̓ət, kəm̓ másq̓ət, way̓ t̓əxʷ t̓iʔ sxiʔmíx p ɬaʔxʷísk̓it 560 mi
ʔasl=ásq̓t km̓ m=asq̓t way̓ t̓xʷ t̓iʔ s+xiʔ+míx p ɬaʔxʷ=ísk̓it mi
two_days or four_days well emph evid whatever 5kn rest fut
two days, four days, whatever, for you to get rested. *Then*

itlíʔ p tk^{w}ʔut k̓aʔkín p səcx^{w}úy[x] 561 cútəlx way̓
itlíʔ p tk^{w}ʔ=ut k̓a+ʔkín p sc -x^{w}uy -x cut -lx way̓
from_there 5kn walk_pl to_where 5kn ipftvp^ -go ^ipftvp say -pl yes
you can go wherever you are going." *They said "Yes."*

562 cúntməlx uɬ t̓iʔ spuʔúsəmp 563 ɬ spuʔúsəmp t̓i ɬ
cu -nt -m -lx uɬ t̓iʔ s+puʔ=ús -mp ɬ s+puʔ=ús -mp t̓iʔ ɬ
tell -nt -psv -pl and evid heart -5in if heart -5in evid if
She said, "As you wish, *you can lay around,*

ksqmínəmp aláʔ p ʔatxílx ixíʔ p m̓ayxtwíx^{w} 564 kəm̓
ks -qm+in -mp aláʔ p ʔatx+ílx ixíʔ p m̓ay+xt+wix^{w} km̓
futi -rest -5i here 5kn sleep_pl then 5kn tell_stories_rec or
sleep, or talk. 38:03 *Or*

[s]puʔúsəmp axáʔ ilíʔ l tk̓əmkn̓íɬx^{w} p tək^{w}tək^{w}ʔút 565 p taʔk^{w}ʔút,
s+puʔ=ús -mp axáʔ ilíʔ l t+k̓m=kn̓=iɬx^{w} p tk^{w}+tk^{w}ʔ=ut p taʔk^{w}ʔ=ut
heart -5in this there on outside 5kn walk 5kn walk_pl
you can walk outside, *walk around,*

t̓iʔ p ʔícəckən p ʔaxkínəm 566 məɬ lut náx̌əmɬ ksəlk^{w}ák^{w}əmp, aɬíʔ
t̓iʔ p ʔic•c•kn p ʔax+kín+m mɬ lut nax̌mɬ ks -lk^{w}•ak^{w} -mp aɬíʔ
evid 5kn play 5kn do_how and not but futi -far -5i because
or play. *But don't go far, because you are tired,*

p cʔayʔáyx̌^{w}t, kəm̓ p nsəl̓sl̓íp 567 lut p t̓a
p c -ʔay•ʔáyx̌^{w}+t km̓ p n+sl̓•l̓i+p lut p t̓
5kn hab -tired_pl or 5kn get_lost not 5kn negfac
or you might get lost, *you don't*

cminúlaʔx^{w}əm 568 uɬ ʕác̓ənt p scutx lut p t̓a
c -my+n=úlaʔx^{w}+m uɬ ʕac̓ -nt p s -cut -x lut p t̓
hab -know_country and look -nt 5kn ipftv^ -say -^ipftv not 5kn negfac
know the country. *Look, you were saying you don't*

cminúlaʔx^{w}əm 569 uɬ t̓i tanm̓ús {p səs} p səstək^{w}tək^{w}ʔútx
c -my+n=úlaʔx^{w}+m uɬ t̓iʔ tanm̓=ús p sc -tk^{w}+tk^{w}ʔ=ut -x
hab -know_country and evid nothing 5kn ipftvp^ -walk -^ipftvp
know the country, *you are just going for nothing, just looking*

p səcwíklaʔx^{w}x^{w} 570 uɬ lut kskəlk^{w}ák^{w}əmp {cəm̓} k^{w}aʔ p
p sc -wík=laʔx^{w} -x^{w} uɬ lut ks -k+lk^{w}•ak^{w} -mp k^{w}aʔ p
5kn ipftvp^ -see_world -^ipftvp and not futi -far -5i intj 5kn
the country over. *Don't go far, and when you*

ɬaʔɬaʔx^{w}ísk̓it 571 mi_sic itlíʔ p x^{w}uy, uɬ ixíʔ lut k^{w}u
ɬaʔ•ɬaʔx^{w}=ísk̓it mi_sic itlíʔ p x^{w}uy uɬ ixíʔ lut k^{w}u
rested then from_there 5kn go and then not 1obj
are rested *then you can go, you won't bother*

ksənq̓aʔílsəntp 572 a·· cúsəlx way̓, way̓ límləmtx
ks -n+q̓aʔ=íls -nt -p a cu -s -lx way̓ way̓ lim•lm+t+x
futt^ -concerned -nt -5erg intj tell -3erg -pl yes yes thank_you
my mind." *They told her, "Yes, thank you."*

573 waẏ ilíʔ kʷlutlwí··səlx, waẏ axáʔ {tiɬəɬ} ɬkicx {axáʔ} ɬʔácəcqaʔlx
waẏ ilíʔ kʷl=wt+lwis -lx waẏ axáʔ ɬ+kic+x ɬ+ʔác•c•qaʔ -lx
well there sit_around -pl well this arrive_again exit_again_pl -pl
They sat around, then they went back out. 39:01

574 waẏ uɬ ixíʔ {ɬ} sənċíẇms {ixiɬ} tqʷəlqʷəltíwx̣ts {a} ia
waẏ uɬ ixíʔ s -n=ċiẇ+m -s t+qʷl•qʷl+t=iẇ -xt -s iʔ
well and then nom -wash_dishes -3i phone -xit -3erg art
She washed the dishes, she called

ilmíxʷəms 575 cus waẏ waẏ kʷ inilmíxʷəm 576 waẏ
yl=mixʷ+m -s cu -s waẏ waẏ kʷ in -yl=mixʷ+m waẏ
chief -3in tell -3erg well well 2kn 1in -chief well
her boss. *She said, "Boss,* *I*

cúntsən ƛ̓əm sənkʷkʷʔác ilíʔ tuʔtẇít isənppúl·x 577 mat
cu -nt -s -n ƛ̓m s+n+kʷ•kʷʔac ilíʔ tẇ•tẇit i -s+n+p•pul=x mat
tell -nt -2obj -1erg past night there boys 1in -guest maybe
told you last night two boys were my guests. *They*

sənc?íẇs, ƛ̓x̌ap waẏ {iʔ} iʔ knaqs 578 uɬ náx̌əmɬ iʔ knaqs
sncʔ=iẇs ƛ̓x̌a+p waẏ iʔ k=naqs uɬ nax̌mɬ iʔ k=naqs
brothers grow_sg well art one_person and but art one_person
may be brothers; one of them is grown, *but the other is*

k̓ʷək̓ʷyúmaʔ 579 náx̌əmɬ waẏ mat pəx̌páx̌t, uɬ mʕan lkʷut {iʔs} iʔ
k̓ʷ•k̓ʷy=úmaʔ nax̌mɬ waẏ mat px̌•pax̌+t uɬ mʕan lkʷ=ut iʔ
small but yes maybe smart and intj far art
small. *But he must be smart, and they come from*

scxʷúẏitənsəlx 580 təl naqs təmxʷúlaʔxʷ, qaʔɬilmíxʷəm a
sc+xʷuy•y+tn -s -lx tl naqs tmxʷ=úlaʔxʷ qaʔɬ=yl=míxʷ+m a
travels -3in -pl from one country chief's_children art
a long ways, *from another country, he's a king's son, his lineage*

nk̓ʷúl̓təns 581 [s]təkʷtəkʷʔútxəlx axáʔ iʔ t təmxʷúlaʔxʷ
n+k̓ʷul̓+tn -s s -tkʷ•tkʷʔ=ut -x -lx axáʔ iʔ t tmxʷ=úlaʔxʷ
origin -3in ipftv^ -walk -^ipftv -pl this art obj_itr country
is king. *They are traveling the country over."*

582 cut uɬ {ƛ̓'əm kʷs} ƛ̓əm kʷ scutx, ixíʔ {iks} ikɬmílaʔ
cut uɬ ƛ̓m kʷ s -cut -x ixíʔ i -kɬ -mílaʔ
say and past 2kn ipftv^ -say -^ipftv that 1i -to_be -bait
And she said, "And you said that I was to use as bait

inx̌əx̌ẏáɬnəxʷ 583 {ktəlməntúɬtxʷ} iksktəlməntúɬtəm
in -x̌•x̌yaɬ=nxʷ i -ks -k+tl+mn -tuɬt -m
1in -watch 1i -futi -put_in_custody_of -tuɬt -apsv
my watch 40:02 *for them to keep.*

584 uɬ ixíʔ ṅíṅẇwiʔ {mi} mi ƛ̓əxʷəntím 585 ṅíṅẇiʔ {lut ɬ·} ɬə
uɬ ixíʔ ṅiṅẇ•ẇiʔ mi ƛ̓xʷ -nt -im ṅíṅẇiʔ ɬ
and then a_while fut kill_many -nt -4erg a_while if
Then we will kill them *if*

sk̓aws iʔ x̌əx̌yáɬnəxʷ 586 uɬ ixíʔ ktəlməntúɬtnəlx
s -k̓aw -s iʔ x̌•x̌yaɬ=nxʷ uɬ ixíʔ k+tl+mn -tuɬt -n -lx
nom -gone -3i art clock and that put_in_custody_of -tuɬt -1erg -pl
the watch is gone. *I gave it to them to keep,*

lúti iscxʷúy {ɬ} ctxʷúyməntsən 587 uɬ ixíʔ ṅíṅẁiʔ xiʔ
lút+i i -s+c+xʷuy c+t+xʷuy+m -nt -s -n uɬ ixíʔ ṅíṅẁiʔ ixíʔ
before 1i -coming come_toward -nt -2obj -1erg and then a_while that
and I came over to see you. *I gave it to*

ktəlməntúɬtən axáʔ {iʔ t} iʔ sxʔitx 588 uɬ kʷu cus
k+tl+mn -tuɬt -n axáʔ iʔ s+xʔit=x uɬ kʷu cu -s
put_in_custody_of -tuɬt -1erg this art oldest_one and 1obj tell -3erg
the oldest one to keep, *and he said to me,*

ixíʔ {iʔ l} t̓əxʷ i l latáp ilíʔ kɬt̓ək̓ʷánt {tu} 589 uɬ t incá ilíʔ
ixíʔ t̓xʷ iʔ l latáp ilíʔ kɬ+t̓k̓ʷa -nt uɬ t in+cá ilíʔ
that evidently art on table there put_down -nt and agInst I there
'Put it on the table,' *and I put it*

kɬt̓ək̓ʷəntín 590 uɬ i[xíʔ] kən ɬʔácqaʔ uɬ ɬpaʔsmín
kɬ+t̓k̓ʷ -nt -in uɬ ixíʔ kn ɬ+ʔácqaʔ uɬ ɬ+paʔs+mí -n
put_st_down -nt -1erg and then 1kn go_out_again and wish_back -1erg
on the table. *Then I went back out, and I wished*

inx̌əx̌yáɬnəxʷ 591 uɬ waẏ ck̓əɬləʕʷcníkstmən 592 waẏ kən tk̓iwlx
in -x̌•x̌yaɬ=nxʷ uɬ waẏ c -k̓ɬ+lʕ̓ʷ=cn=ikst+m -n waẏ kn t+k̓iw+lx
1in -clock and yes act -fit_on_wrist -1erg well 1kn climb
my watch back, *and I had it come to my wrist.* *I went*

k̓la nwist uɬ kən k̓lənɬaʔíp 593 uɬ aɬíʔ ctxət̓stín
k̓l n+wis+t uɬ kn k̓ɬ+n+ɬaʔ=íp uɬ aɬíʔ c -txt̓ -st -in
to high and 1kn be_next_to and because cust^ -watch_so -^cust -1erg
upstairs and went to the door. *I had the key with me (it was locked),*

inlaklí, claklí k̓ɬənk̓ahk̓ʷípən 594 uɬ itlíʔ kən xʷuy, i[xíʔ] t
in -laklí c -laklí k̓ɬ+n+k̓ahk̓ʷ=íp -n uɬ itlíʔ kn xʷuy ixíʔ t
1in -lock hab -lock open -1erg and from_there 1kn go then obl
and I unlocked it. 41:03 *I continued for*

ksənməsmíẁs 595 yaʕyáʕt cləklaklí iʔ k̓ɬənk̓əṁmíp 596 ki
k -s+n+ms+m=iẁs yaʕ•yáʕ+t c -lk•laklí iʔ k̓ɬ+n+k̓m•m=ip kiʔ
? -fourth_floor all hab -lock_pl art doors rel
four floors, *the doors were all locked.* *There*

isənkʷúm·ən i {st} lkasát{n} iʔ l səntətəṁtíṁtən 597 waẏ ilíʔ {nt̓}
i -s+n+kʷum+n iʔ lkasát iʔ l s+n+t+tṁ•tiṁ+tn waẏ ilíʔ
1in -storage_place art box art for wardrobe well there
is my storage place, the trunk for clothes, *and I*

nt̓ək̓ʷəntín inx̌əx̌yáɬnəxʷ 598 ixíʔ ɬənʕalqín uɬ ɬlaklín
n+t̓k̓ʷ -nt -in in -x̌•x̌yaɬ=nxʷ ixíʔ ɬ+n+ʕal̓=qí -n uɬ ɬ+laklí -n
put_in -nt -1erg 1in -clock then cover_again -1erg and lock_again -1erg
put my watch there. *I closed it and I locked it.*

599 i[xíʔ] uɬ kən ɬċácqaʔ uɬ laklín, yaʕyáʕt claklí··n
ixíʔ uɬ kn ɬ+c+ʔácqaʔ uɬ laklí -n yaʕ•yáʕ+t c -laklí -n
then and 1kn come_out_again and lock -1erg all act -lock -1erg
Then I went out and I locked, I locked everything;

600 uɬ kən ntikɬ uɬ {iʔ kən} iʔ kən cxʷuy, txʷúyməntsən
uɬ kn n+tikɬ uɬ iʔ kn c+xʷuy t+xʷuy+mn -t -s -n
and 1kn bottom and art 1kn come go_towards -nt -2obj -1erg
I got to the bottom and then I came, I went to you.

601 uɬ kʷa aláʔ ksx̌lap isaláʔ, uɬ kaláʔməntsən uɬ
uɬ kʷa aláʔ k+s+x̌la+p i -s -aláʔ uɬ k+aláʔ+m -nt -s -n uɬ
and intj here all_night 1i -nom -here and stay_with -nt -2obj -1erg and
And I was here all night, I was here with you.

602 way̓ kən ɬkicx ixíʔ {ɬ} ɬx̌lítɬtən axáʔ iʔ ktílmən
way̓ kn ɬ+kic+x ixíʔ ɬ+x̌lit -ɬt -n axáʔ iʔ k+til+m -n
well 1kn arrive_again then summon_again -ɬt -1erg this art entrust -1erg
Then I went back and I asked the boy for what

axáʔ iʔ tətw̓ít 603 uɬ kʷu cus, a·· {kʷə} laʔkín kiʔ a
axáʔ iʔ t•tw̓it uɬ kʷu cu -s a la+ʔkín̓ kiʔ a
this art boy and 1obj tell -3erg intj wherever rel art
I gave him. *And he said to me, ‘Oh, wherever you put it,*

utəntíxʷ, uɬ mat ilíʔ cután {lut ixkəɬ} 604 sta kən ʕác̓əm ik̓líʔ l
wt -nt -ixʷ uɬ mat ilíʔ c -wt+an sta kn ʕac̓+m ik̓líʔ l
put_down -nt -2erg and must there hab -placed intj 1kn look there on
it must still be there.’ 42:07 *I looked*

latáp ilíʔ kɬtʼək̓ʷəntín 605 uɬ aɬíʔ way̓ m̓ístən
latáp ilíʔ kɬ+tʼk̓ʷ -nt -in uɬ aɬíʔ way̓ miy -st -n
table there put_st_down -nt -1erg and because yes be_sure_of -st -1erg
on the table where I had put it, *and I was sure I had locked it in the trunk*

way̓ {l} laklín l inlkasát, tʼi tanm̓ús iscsíwm 606 uɬ aɬíʔ
way̓ laklí -n l in -lkasát tʼiʔ tanm̓=ús i -sc -siw+m uɬ aɬíʔ
well lock -1erg in 1in -box evid nothing 1i -pftv -ask and so
and I just asked for nothing. *And if*

n̓ín̓wiʔ {l} lut, uɬ ixíʔ ƛ̓əxʷəntíməlx 607 oyə kən ʕác̓əm iʔ k̓l {stə}
n̓ín̓wiʔ lut uɬ ixíʔ ƛ̓xʷ -nt -im -lx oyə kn ʕac̓+m iʔ k̓l
a_while not and then kill_many -nt -4erg -pl intj 1kn look art to
it’s not there we kill them. *I looked there,*

[i]líʔ ckɬtʼak̓ʷ {in} inx̌əx̌yáɬnəxʷ 608 ntʼa·· tʼi kən paʕs 609 uɬ axáʔ
ilíʔ c -kɬ+tʼak̓ʷ in -x̌•x̌yaɬ=nxʷ ntʼa tʼiʔ kn paʕs uɬ axáʔ
there hab -lie_on 1in -clock intj evid 1kn surprised and this
and my watch was there! *Gee, was I puzzled.* *And*

nxʷaʔmíw̓s tʼəxʷ nməsmíw̓s axáʔ iʔ citxʷ 610 yaʕyáʕt {kɬən}
n+xʷaʔ+m=íw̓s tʼxʷ n+ms+m=iw̓s axáʔ iʔ citxʷ yaʕ•yáʕ+t
many_between evidently four_between this art house all
are lots of doors, four levels in the house, *they all*

kɬk̓ɬənk̓m̓míp, uɬ yaʕyáʕt ixíʔ {ɬəɬ} claklí 611 uɬ axáʔ
kɬ+k̓ɬ+n+k̓m•m=ip uɬ yaʕ•yáʕ+t ixíʔ c -laklí uɬ axáʔ
have_doors and all that hab -lock and this
have a door, and they were all locked. *And*

intətəm̓tím̓tən ixíʔ nixʷ laklín 612 ilíʔ kiʔ kʷúmən uɬ {xi} yaʕyáʕt
in -t•tm̓•tim̓+tn ixíʔ nixʷ laklí -n ilíʔ kiʔ kʷum -n uɬ yaʕ•yáʕ+t
1in -clothes that also lock -1erg there rel store -1erg and all
my clothes, I had locked that too. *That's where I store things.*

ɬclaklín, uɬ kən ɬcəntíkɬ 613 uɬ laʔkín xkínəm kiʔ uɬ
ɬ+c+laklí[15] -n uɬ kn ɬ+c+n+tikɬ uɬ la+ʔkíń x+kin+m kiʔ uɬ
lock_cisl_again -1erg and 1kn come_back_down and how do_what rel and
And I locked all back, and I came back down. 43:03 *And how*

iʔ ɬckʷən·ús 614 way̓ mat yaʕʷpyáwt, x̌áʔx̌aʔ ixíʔ iʔ
iʔ ɬ+c+kʷn -nu -s way̓ mat yaw+p+yáʕʷ+t x̌aʔ•x̌áʔ ixíʔ iʔ
art take_back_cisl -manage -3erg well must powerful great that art
did he get it back? *The boy, the oldest one, must be*

tətw̓ít iʔ sxʔitx {cúntəm way̓} 615 cúntəm way̓ way̓ ʕapnáʔ {nixʷ}
t•tw̓it iʔ s+xʔit+x cu -nt -m way̓ way̓ ʕapnáʔ
boy art oldest_one tell -nt -psv well well now
powerful, great." *He said to her, "Now your ring is*

ank̓ənp̓qínkst aksktəlməntúɬt[əm] 616 lut axáʔ caʔkʷ iwá
an -k̓np̓=qin=kst a -ks -k+tl+mn -tuɬt -m lut axáʔ caʔkʷ iwá
2in -ring 2i -futt^ -put_in_custody_of -tuɬt -apsv not this if even
what you are going to have him keep. *Even if this boy*

ɬ x̌aʔ•x̌áʔ axáʔ iʔ tətw̓ít 617 lut kɬkʷənnús iʔ k̓ənp̓qín
ɬ x̌aʔ•x̌áʔ axáʔ iʔ t•tw̓it lut k -ɬ+kʷn -nu -s iʔ k̓np̓=qin
if great this art boy not futt^ -keep_again -manage -3erg art ring
is powerful *he can't hang on to the ring.*

618 way̓ way̓ kʷ nqmílsəm lut akspaʔpaʔsínk lut təl
way̓ way̓ kʷ n+qm=ils+m lut a -ks -paʔ•paʔs=ínk lut tl
well yes 2kn at_ease not 2i -futi -sad not from
Put your mind at ease, don't feel bad because we didn't

ƛ̓əxʷəntím 619 way̓ ixíʔ t̓əxʷ {ks} ksmysɬaʔɬaʔxʷísk̓itaʔx
ƛ̓xʷ -nt -im way̓ ixíʔ t̓xʷ ks -my+s+ɬaʔ•ɬaʔxʷ=ísk̓it -aʔx
kill_many -nt -4erg well then evidently incp^ -rest_more_pl -^incp
kill them. *They'll be more rested now. 44:00*

620 ixíʔ uɬ cúntəm way̓ xʷuyx, ʔítxəx, cəm̓ kʷ cʔaxʷ
ixíʔ uɬ cu -nt -m way̓ xʷuy -x ʔitx -x cm̓ kʷ c[ʔ]axʷ
then and tell -nt -psv well go -isimptv sleep -isimptv maybe 2kn tired
Go, sleep, you might get tired.

15 This form invites an analysis of ɬ+ *again*, c- *hab*, laklí *lock*, with the inflectional c- inside the stem. This analysis is rejected.

621 ṅ k̓laxʷ mi {kʷ ɬ} kʷ ɬcxʷuy, kʷu ɬctxʷúymənt {cut cúntəm ə}
ṅ k̓laxʷ mi kʷ ɬ+c+xʷuy kʷu ɬ+c+t+xʷuy+m -nt
a_while evening fut 2kn come_again 1obj come_back_to -nt
This evening you come back, come back to me."

622 cus axáʔ iʔ t stʔiwtx, cus iʔ {s} qicks
cu -s axáʔ iʔ t s+tʔiw+t=x cu -s iʔ qick -s
tell -3erg this art agInst young_one tell -3erg art older_brother -3in
The youngest one said to him, said to his older brother:

623 cus way̓ qick, way̓ uc kʷ t̓saq̓ʷ, incá way̓ kən t̓saq̓ʷ
cu -s way̓ qick way̓ uc kʷ t̓saq̓ʷ in+cá way̓ kn t̓saq̓ʷ
tell -3erg well older_brother well dub 2kn bored I yes 1kn bored
"Brother, are you tired of sitting around? I am bored.

624 nt̓a way̓ ixíʔ kʷu cúntəm spuʔústət {ɬi} t̓i kʷu taʔkʷʔút
nt̓a way̓ ixíʔ kʷu cu -nt -m s+puʔ=ús -tt t̓iʔ kʷu taʔkʷʔ=ut
intj well then 3e4obj tell -nt -3e4obj heart -4in evid 4kn walk_pl
She told us if we want to we can walk around,

625 axáʔ iʔ t tk̓əmkṅíɬxʷ ixíʔ uɬ lut mat kʷu kst̓saq̓ʷ
axáʔ iʔ t t+k̓m=kn=iɬxʷ ixíʔ uɬ lut mat kʷu ks -t̓saq̓ʷ
this art obl outside then and not maybe 4kn futi -bored
we can walk around outside so we won't get bored."

626 cúntəm a⋅⋅, way̓
cu -nt -m a way̓
tell -nt -psv intj OK
He said "Yes."

627 way̓ ixíʔ sʔácəcqaʔs
way̓ ixíʔ s -ʔác•c•qaʔ -s
well then nom -go_out_pl -3i
So they went out.

628 cúntəm axáʔ iʔ t stʔiwtx
cu -nt -m axáʔ iʔ t s+tʔiw+t=x
tell -nt -psv this art agInst young_one
The young one said to him, 45:00

629 cus iʔ qicks haʔ kʷ kɬṅíṅk̓mən
cu -s iʔ qick -s haʔ kʷ kɬ+ṅi•ṅk+m̓ṅ
tell -3erg art older_brother -3in inter 2kn have_knife
he asked his older brother, "Do you have a knife?"

630 way̓, kən kɬṅíṅk̓mən
way̓ kn kɬ+ṅi•ṅk+m̓ṅ
yes 1kn have_knife
He said, "Yes, I got a knife."

631 a⋅⋅ way̓ x̌ast ixíʔ kɬx̌mínktət
a way̓ x̌as+t ixíʔ kɬ -x̌m=ink -tt
intj well good that to_be -want -4i
"Good, this is what we want."

632 uɬ akstím̓
uɬ a -k -s+tim̓
and 2i -to_be -thing
"And what are you going to do with it?"

633 cus {i s} e⋅ t̓əxʷ {kʷu ks} kʷu ksx̌ʷəƛ̓x̌ʷíƛ̓aʔstaʔx
cu -s e⋅ t̓xʷ kʷu ks -x̌ʷƛ̓•x̌ʷíƛ̓=aʔst -aʔx
tell -3erg intj emph 4kn incp^ -whittle_a_weapon -^incp
He said, "We are going to get a weapon.

634 {kʷu ksk̓əɬ} kʷu kstxʷəlscútaʔx
kʷu ks -t+xʷl=scut -aʔx
4kn incp^ -get_ready -^incp
We are going to do something important."

635 way̓
way̓
OK
He said "Ok."

636 way̓ i[xíʔ] sxʷúysəlx way̓
way̓ ixíʔ s -xʷuy -s -lx way̓
well then nom -go -3i -pl well
They came, they saw that

wíkməlx ilíʔ cłəłák lut sk̓s̓úlaʔxʷ {łi} 637 wíksəlx {aʔ} lut iʔ k̓əl
wik+m -lx ilíʔ c -ł•łak lut s+k̓s=úlaʔxʷ wik -s -lx lut iʔ k̓l
see -pl there hab -brush not bad_land see -3erg -pl not art to
there was brush, not bad brush. *They saw it, they weren't going*

kscənsəl̓sl̓ípstaʔx sənx̌əłx̌íłtsəlx 638 way̓ ik̓líʔ
ksc -n+sl̓•sl̓i+p+st -aʔx s -n+x̌ł•x̌ił+t -s -lx way̓ ik̓líʔ
futPerfkn^ -get_lost -^furPerfkn nom -be_afraid -3i -pl well there
to get lost or be afraid of it. *They*

sənłəxʷtəlílxsəlx 639 way̓ t̓a nak̓ʷm{s} sənxʷaʔxʷaʔnkíłptən {i}
s -n+łxʷ+t+lilx -s -lx way̓ nt̓a nak̓ʷ+m s+n+xʷaʔ•xʷaʔnk=íłp+tn
nom -go_in_bush_pl -3i -pl well intj evid thorn_bush
went in there. 46:00 *What grows there is thorn bush,*

640 ixíʔ a cłak {sxʷaxʷ} kmix sxʷaʔxʷaʔnkíłp 641 nt̓a·· iʔ sənppəl̓úlaʔxʷ
ixíʔ a c+łak kmix s+xʷaʔ•xʷaʔ+nk=íłp nt̓a iʔ s+n+p•pl̓=úlaʔxʷ
that art swamp only thornbush intj art sprouts
only thorn bush. *Gee, the young shoots,*

642 way̓ {x̌əsx̌sala} x̌əx̌sx̌sálaʔqʷ t̓i put {i s} iʔ siʔl̓yúl̓aʔts 643 c̓x̌ił
way̓ x̌•x̌s•x̌s=álaʔqʷ t̓iʔ put iʔ s+yl̓•yúl̓+aʔt[16] -s c+ʔx̌ił
yes good_sprouts evid just art circumference -3in like
nice shoots, just the right size, *just*

axáʔ iʔ t istawnqínaʔkst 644 way̓ ixíʔ stk̓ít̓kssəlx axáʔ
axáʔ iʔ t i -s+tawn=qínaʔ=kst way̓ ixíʔ s -t+k̓it̓=ks -s -lx axáʔ
this art obj_c̓x̌ił 1in -little_finger well then nom -cut -3i -pl this
like my little finger. *They started cutting because*

tk̓əsəlmístəlx ałíʔ uł kłn̓ín̓k̓mən 645 cus iʔ qicks
tk=ʔasl+míst -lx ałíʔ uł kł+n̓i•n̓k̓+m̓n̓ cu -s iʔ qick -s
two_people -pl because and have_knife tell -3erg art older_brother -3in
both had knives. *He said to his big brother:*

646 way uł {kʷ t} kʷ txʷəlscút sxiʔmíx put kʷíntəm {i ks i ks} iʔ
way̓ uł kʷ txʷ=lscut s+xiʔ+míx put kʷi -nt -m iʔ
well and 2kn get_ready whatever just take -nt -4erg art
"Get enough, get

ksílxʷaʔs 647 put kʷintxʷ iʔ {ta· kskʷintxʷ i tan} t ankílx
k -sílxʷaʔ -s put kʷi -nt -xʷ iʔ t an -kilx
to_be -big -3i just take -nt -2erg art obl 2in -hand
so much, *enough to hold in your hand.*

648 ixíʔ uł way̓ {kən ək} kəlk̓íc̓aʔntxʷ, ixíʔ way̓ knəqsíc̓aʔ
ixíʔ uł way̓ k+lk̓=íc̓aʔ -nt -xʷ ixíʔ way̓ k+nqs=íc̓aʔ
that and yes wrap -nt -2erg that yes one_bundle
Wrap it, and that's one bundle.

16 A diminutive form based on yul+t.

649 cúntəm put kmúsc̓a? {i ks} i? ksctíxʷtət
cu -nt -m put k+mús=c̓a? i? ksc -tixʷ -tt
tell -nt -psv just four_packages art futPerfi -obtain -4i
We will get four packages." 47:03

650 a·· uɬ
a uɬ
intj and
"And what are we

kstímtət
k -s+tim̓ -tt
to_be -what -4i
going to do with it?"

651 cúntəm axá? i? t sínca?s,
cu -nt -m axá? i? t sínca? -s
tell -nt -psv this art agInst younger_brother -3in
His little brother said to him,

ṅíṅw̓i? ixí? wi?stíxʷəntəm
ṅíṅw̓i? ixí? wy̓+s+tixʷ -nt -m
a_while that finish_gather -nt -4erg
"When we finish getting them

652 ixí? mi máya?ɬtsən
ixí? mi m̓áya? -ɬt -s -n
then fut tell -ɬt -2obj -1erg
then I will tell you what

kstímtət
k -s+tim̓ -tt
to_be -thing -4i
we'll use it for."

653 cúntəm way̓ kʷ xʷəsxʷúslx
cu -nt -m way̓ kʷ xʷs•xʷus+lx
tell -nt -psv OK 2kn hurry
He said to him, "Hurry up."[17] 47:35

17 The recording ends here.

The grateful dead version 2

1 way̓ t’əxʷ kən kscaptíkʷlaʔx
way̓ t’xʷ kn ks -captíkʷl -aʔx
well evidently 1kn incp^ -tell_stories -^incp
I’m going to tell a fairy tale.

2 way̓ t’əxʷ ilmíxʷəm a
way̓ t’xʷ yl=mixʷ+m a
well evidently chief art
The boss had

ksqʷsiʔ
k+s+qʷsiʔ
have+son
a son.

3 i[xíʔ] uɬ mat ɬa cx̌əl·wís t’i {uɬ} uɬ wíkəm {təs}
ixíʔ uɬ mat ɬaʔ c -ʔx̌al+lwís t’iʔ uɬ wik+m
then and maybe when hab -fool_around evid and see
Maybe he [the son] was doing something, and he saw

t sk̓əɬq̓əy̓ncút
t s+k̓ɬ+q̓y̓+ncut
obj_itr picture
a picture.

4 way̓ swiʔnúmtx {iʔ} iʔ st’ak̓míx
way̓ s+wy̓+numt=x iʔ s+t’aʔk̓+míx
yes handsome art virgin
It was a good looking maiden,

5 stim̓
s+tim̓
something
a young

t’əxʷ st’ak̓míx kəm̓ tkəɬmílxʷ {inaud}
t’xʷ s+t’aʔk̓+míx km̓ tkɬmilxʷ
evidently virgin or woman
virgin or a woman.

6 way̓ ixíʔ {i} nq̓əmscínəms
way̓ ixíʔ n+q̓m=s=cin+m -s
well then pine_for -3erg
He got stuck on her.

7 way̓ t’iʔ wiks uɬ nq̓əmscínəms
way̓ t’iʔ wik -s uɬ n+q̓m=s=cin+m -s
well evid see -3erg and pine_for -3erg
He saw her and got stuck on her.

8 a way̓ iksƛ̓aƛ̓ʔám̓ {way̓ iks ə}
a way̓ i -ks -ƛ̓aʔ•ƛ̓ʔá+m
intj yes 1i -futi -look_for
“I’m going to look for her.

9 ńíńw̓iʔ kaʔkícən məɬ ixíʔ insucənmístmən
ńíńw̓iʔ kaʔ•kíc -n mɬ ixíʔ in -sw=cn+mist+mn
a_while find -1erg and then 1in -proposal
If I find her I’m going to propose. 1:03

10 ixíʔ
ixíʔ
that
She’s

ikɬtkəɬmílxʷ, way̓ swiʔnúmtx
i -kɬ -tkɬ+m=ilxʷ way̓ s+wy̓+numt=x
1i -to_be -wife yes handsome
going to be my wife, she’s beautiful."

11 uɬ aɬíʔ milsmíst aɬíʔ
uɬ aɬíʔ mils+míst aɬíʔ
and so confident because
He thinks he can do it, because

qaʔɬilmíxʷəm {inaud}
qaʔɬ=yl=míxʷ+m
chief’s_children
he’s the chief’s son.

12 ixíʔ cus iʔ ƛ̓ax̌əx̌ƛ̓x̌áps
ixíʔ cu -s iʔ ƛ̓x̌•x̌•ƛ̓x̌a+p -s
then tell -3erg art parents -3in
So he told his parents:

13 way̓ p
way̓ p
well 5kʷu
“I’m going

iksɬwínəm
i -ks -ɬwin+m
1i -futi -leave
to leave you.”

14 cúsəlx uɬ sc̓kinx, {ta} taʔlí
cu -s -lx uɬ sc+ʔkin+x taʔlíʔ
tell -3erg -pl and why_is_it very_much
They said, “And why?

stuʔtíwaʔstəmt
s -tw̓•tíw̓+aʔ -st -m -t
cust^ -baby -^cust -2obj -4erg
We baby you a lot;

15 ʕác̓ənt kʷ sknəqsəltílaʔt[ət] uɬ iʔ
ʕac̓ -nt kʷ s+k=nqs=lt=ílaʔt -t uɬ iʔ
look_at -nt 2kn only_child -4in and art
you are our only son, and you are

kʷu aksłwínəm 16 uł mat stim̓ kʷ snac̓əntíls 17 lut
kʷu a -ks -łwin+m uł mat s+tim̓ kʷ s -nac̓nt=íls lut
1kʷu 2i -futi -leave and maybe something 2kn hab -think not
going to leave us? *Maybe something is bothering you;* *you*

cx̌əstmíntxʷ a ctxət̓stúmt uł 18 cut lut, cut
c -x̌s+t+mi -nt -xʷ a c -t+xt̓ -st -um -t uł cut lut cut
act -like -nt -2erg art cust^ -watch_so -^cust -2obj -4erg and say not say
don't like the way we take care of you and..." *He said "No,"*

uł ałí? alá? {kən} kən alá··?, kalá?młmən 19 uł way̓ kən
uł ałí? alá? kn alá? k+alá?+m -łm -n uł way̓ kn
and because here 1kn here stay_with -5obj -1erg and yes 1kn
he said "I've been here with you 2:05 *and now*

ƛ̓x̌ap kən sqəl̓tmíxʷ {uł} 20 uł lut ikswíkla?xʷəm i? təmxʷúla?xʷ
ƛ̓x̌a+p kn s+qlt=mixʷ uł lut i -ks -wík=la?xʷ+m i? tmxʷ=úla?xʷ
grow_sg 1kn man and not 1i -futi -see_country art country
I've grown, I'm a man; *and I won't see the world.*

21 uł t̓i_kmix kən ksxʷilwísa?x ikswíkla?xʷəm i? təmxʷúla?xʷ
uł t̓i?_kmix kn ks -xʷy+lwis -a?x i -ks -wík=la?xʷ+m i? tmxʷ=úla?xʷ
and only 1kn incp^ -wander -^incp 1i -futi -see_country art world
I only want to travel around and see the world.

22 sc̓x̌ilx ki? kən ksxʷúya?x 23 uł ixí? p
sc+?x̌il+x ki? kn ks -xʷuy -a?x uł ixí? p
reason_why rel 1kn incp^ -go -^incp and that 5kʷu
That's why I am leaving. *And I am going*

iksc̓əx̌ʷxítəm 24 ńíńw̓i? ł iscxʷəlxʷált 25 uł ńíńw̓i?
i -ks -c̓x̌ʷ -xit -m ńíńw̓i? ł i -sc -xʷl•xʷal+t uł ńíńw̓i?
1i -futi -promise -xit -apsv a_while if 1i -pftv -alive and a_while
to tell you that, *if I am alive,* *I'll come back*

t̓x̌iw̓twílx put x̌íləm atá? mi kən łckicx 26 a· {cus} cúntəm
t̓x̌=iwt+wilx put x̌il+m atá? mi kn ł+c+kic+x a cu -nt -m
next_year just do_like this fut 1kn arrive_cisl_again intj tell -nt -psv
in one year just about this time." *His father*

i ta l?iws 27 way̓ ałí? aspu?ús, [nak̓ʷá?]
i? t l?iw -s way̓ ałí? a -s+pu?=ús nak̓ʷ+á
art agInst m's_father -3in well because 2in -heart indeed_not
said to him: *"If that's what you want, I'm not*

q̓íx̌məntsən 28 uł cut ńíńw̓i? kʷu nk̓aw?awpíls 29 ałí?
q̓ix̌+m -nt -s -n uł cut ńíńw̓i? kʷu n+k̓aw•aw+p=íls ałí?
drive_away -nt -2obj -1erg and say a_while 4kn lonesome_pl so
sending you away." *He said "We will get lonesome.* *Just*

way̓ {a} ixí? t cuntxʷ 30 way̓ kʷ xəƛ̓pspíntk uł way̓ kʷ
way̓ ixí? t cu -nt -xʷ way̓ kʷ xƛ̓+p+s+pin=tk uł way̓ kʷ
well that obl tell -nt -2erg yes 2kn mature_age and yes 2kn
as you said, *you are of age, and you can decide what you're*

k̓əɬpaʔx̌cút 31 uɬ aɬíʔ waẏ aɬíʔ mat aspuʔús {cuntəm wa}
k̓ɬ+paʔx̌+cút uɬ aɬíʔ waẏ aɬíʔ mat a -s+puʔ=ús
decide and because well because maybe 2in -heart
going to do, 3:03 *if that's what you want."*

32 cus ya lʔiws waẏ waẏ ixíʔ isck̓əɬpáʔx̌ 33 uɬ
cu -s ya lʔiw -s waẏ waẏ ixíʔ i -sc -k̓ɬ+paʔx̌ uɬ
tell -3erg art m's_father -3in yes yes that 1i -pftv -deliberate and
He told his father, "Yes, yes, that's what I've decided. *I want*

aɬíʔ kən kswíklaʔxʷaʔx axáʔ iʔ t təmxʷúlaʔxʷ 34 waẏ ixíʔ {c}
aɬíʔ kn ks -wík=laʔxʷ -aʔx axáʔ iʔ t tmxʷ=úlaʔxʷ waẏ ixíʔ
because 1kn incp^ -see_world -^incp this art obj_itr country well then
to see the country." *So*

kʷis iʔ sənqláw̓tən, {a} iʔ sənqláwtəns axáʔ ilmíxʷəm 35 waẏ ixíʔ
kʷi -s iʔ s+n+qlaw̓+tn iʔ s+n+qlaw̓+tn -s axáʔ yl=mixʷ+m waẏ ixíʔ
take -3erg art wallet art wallet -3in this chief well then
the chief took his money box *and*

c̓kxí··təm mat 36 lut náx̌əmɬ t̓a cmistín mat
c̓k -xit -m mat lut nax̌mɬ t̓ c -my -st -in mat
count -xit -psv maybe not but negfac cust^ -know -^cust -1erg maybe
maybe he counted, *but I don't know*

k̓ʷinx iʔ sqlaw 37 ixíʔ xʷíc̓xtəm, cúntəm waẏ axáʔ, axáʔ
k̓ʷin+x iʔ s+qlaw ixíʔ xʷic̓ -xt -m cu -nt -m waẏ axáʔ axáʔ
how_much art money that give -xit -psv tell -nt -psv well this this
how much money. *He gave it to him, he said "I give you this*

t̓ík̓ləntsən 38 pna cmay ńíńw̓iʔ kʷ syaʕpcínx kʷ
t̓ik̓l -nt -s -n pnaʔ cmay ńíńw̓iʔ kʷ s -yaʕ+p=cín -x kʷ
grub -nt -2obj -1erg maybe maybe a_while 2kn ipftv^ -need -^ipftv 2kn
for your lunch. *You might be hard up or*

t̓i ksq̇míltən {kəm̓ kʷ} 39 kəm̓ kʷ ktəmxʷíc̓aʔ 40 uɬ ixíʔ l
t̓iʔ k+s+q̇m=ilt+n km̓ kʷ k+tmxʷ=íc̓aʔ uɬ ixíʔ l
evid have_hunger or 2kn clothes_wear_out and that for
get hungry, 4:02 *or your clothes might wear out.* *And this is*

aksttəm̓tím̓ uɬ axáʔ aksk̓íɬəntən 41 kiʔ ixíʔ axáʔ iʔ
a -k -s+t+tm̓•tim̓ uɬ axáʔ a -k -s+k+ʔiɬn+tn kiʔ ixíʔ axáʔ iʔ
2i -to_be -clothes and this 2i -to_be -food rel that this art
for your clothes and for your food, *that's why*

xʷíc̓əɬtsən iʔ sqlaw 42 cus waẏ 43 waẏ ixíʔ kʷis,
xʷic̓ -ɬt -s -n iʔ s+qlaw cu -s waẏ waẏ ixíʔ kʷi -s
give -ɬt -2obj -1erg art money tell -3erg OK well that take -3erg
I'm giving you money." *He said "Ok."* *He took it,*

waẏ {i··} kʷums t̓əxʷ i l sənqláwtəns uɬ {nt̓ək̓ʷ} 44 waẏ ixíʔ
waẏ kʷum -s t̓xʷ iʔ l s+n+qlaw̓+tn -s uɬ waẏ ixíʔ
well store -3erg evidently art in wallet -3in and well then
he saved it in his money pouch. *He*

kʷənkʷínksəs i? ƛ̓ax̌əx̌ƛ̓x̌áps 45 waẏ ixí? sxʷists 46 uɬ lut
kʷn•kʷin=ks -s i? ƛ̓x̌•x̌•ƛ̓x̌a+p -s waẏ ixí? s -xʷist -s uɬ lut
shake_hands -3erg art parents -3in well then nom -go -3i and not
shook hands with his elders, *he left.* *And*

t'a cmistís ḱa?kíń {ɬ} ɬə ksxʷúya?x 47 uɬ t'i?
t' c -my -st -is ḱa+?kíń ɬ ks -xʷuy -a?x uɬ t'i?
evid cust^ -know -^cust -3erg where_to compl incp^ -go -^incp and evid
he didn't know where he was going; *wherever*

axá? t'i? iḱlí? ncahahúsəs ɬ ?ácqa? i? t citxʷ 48 ixí? uɬ
axá? t'i? iḱlí? n+cah•ah=ús -s ɬ ?ácqa? i? t citxʷ ixí? uɬ
this evid there face -3erg when go_out art obl house then and
he was facing when he walked out of the house, *no trail or*

tanm̓súla?xʷ uɬ xʷist 49 aɬí? mat x̌súla?xʷ, mat spíləm,
tanm̓=s=úla?xʷ uɬ xʷist aɬí? mat x̌s=úla?xʷ mat s+pil+m
walk_aimlessly and walk because maybe open_country maybe flat_land
nothing, he just walked. 5:02 *Maybe it's level ground, open and level,*

lut {t} t'a kɬxəwíɬ 50 waẏ xʷu··y {ḱəɬə·} ḱəɬḱʷƛ̓áp 51 waẏ i? sqilxʷ
lut t' kɬ+xwiɬ waẏ xʷuy ḱɬ+ḱʷƛ̓a+p waẏ i? s+qilxʷ
not negfac have_road well go come_in_sight yes art person
there's no road. *He went and came in sight.* *There are people*

i l kɬx̌siẇs 52 yaʕpqín sqilxʷ i? scwiks uɬ
i? l kɬ+x̌s=iẇs yaʕ+p=qín s+qilxʷ i? sc -wik -s uɬ
art on level_country many_gathered person art pftv -see -3i and
there on the level. *He saw lots of people, and what*

sc̓a?xkínxəlx 53 mat {sc̓a·s} sc̓íccckna?xəlx kəm̓ {sc}
sc -?ax+kín -x -lx mat sc -?ic•c•kn -a?x -lx km̓
ipftvp^ -do_what -^ipftvp -pl maybe ipftv^ -play -^ipftvDim -pl or
are they doing? *They are playing, or running around,*

alá? cxtxítmi?stəlx uɬ stim̓ {aɬ} 54 lut t'a cmistís,
alá? c -xt•xít+mi?st -lx uɬ s+tim̓ lut t' c -my -st -is
here hab -run_around -pl and what not negfac cust^ -know -^cust -3erg
or something. *He doesn't know, because*

uɬ aɬí? lkʷut 55 sta waẏ ixí? ikstxʷúym {i kən kən ksuxʷs} kən
uɬ aɬí? lkʷ=ut sta waẏ ixí? i -ks -t+xʷuy+m kn
and because far intj yes that 1i -futi -go_towards 1kn
it's far. 6:00 *"I am going to go*

ksuksqílxʷa?x 56 ixí? sic iksuksqílxʷ uɬ ixí? {kən} kən
ks -wk+sqilxʷ -a?x ixí? sic i -ks -wk+sqilxʷ uɬ ixí? kn
incp^ -see -^incp then then 1i -futi -see and then 1kn
and see. *I'm going*

ksuksqílxʷa?x 57 waẏ ktəɬməncú··təms 58 waẏ ḱa?ítət {ki c k ə}
ks -wk+sqilxʷ -a?x waẏ k+tɬ+mncut+m -s waẏ ḱa?ít•t
incp^ -see -^incp well go_straight -3erg well get_near
to go see." *He went straight for them;* *he got close,*

t̓əxʷ {na} nʔaɬxʷíw̓s axáʔ i l yapqín i l sqilxʷ 59 stim̓ a
t̓xʷ n+ʔaɬxʷ=íw̓s axáʔ iʔ l yaʕ+p=qín iʔ l s+qilxʷ s+tim̓ a
emph one_enters this art in lots art with person what art
then he was right in the crowd of people. *What are*

ctəřqstísəlx {a yac} a ckʷənxtwíxʷmstsəlx ixíʔ {mɬ i} 60 məɬ
c -trq -st -is -lx a c -kʷn+xtwixʷ+m -st -lx ixíʔ mɬ
cust^ -kick -^cust -3erg -pl art cust^ -take_from_recip -^cust -pl that and
they kicking and taking away from each other? *And*

ixíʔ {ɬ} knaqs {ɬə} ɬ kcahahám məɬ ixíʔ {ɬ} təřqəntís 61 lut t̓
ixíʔ k=naqs ɬ k+cah•ah+ám mɬ ixíʔ trq -nt -is lut t̓
then one_person ? match and then kick -nt -3erg not negfac
when it's one's turn he kicks it. *It's not a*

stk̓ək̓xʷúm̓ 62 way̓ uɬ {mis} ik̓líʔ k̓ítəlx 63 way̓ k̓aʔítət {ə·}
s+t+k̓•k̓xʷum way̓ uɬ ik̓líʔ k̓it+lx way̓ k̓aʔít•t
ball well and there near well get_near
baseball. 7:00 *He came closer,* *he got close and*

kmimipúsəms 64 k̓aʔtmís uɬ kmimipúsəms, 65 way̓
k+my•my+p=us+m -s k̓aʔt+mí -s uɬ k+my•my+p=us+m -s way̓
make_out -3erg get_close -3erg and make_out -3erg well
recognized what it was. *He got close and recognized it:* *it's*

sútən, nák̓ʷəm sqilxʷ, {tə·} way̓ ƛ̓lal, 66 təmtəmníʔ axáʔ {iac} ia
sutn nak̓ʷ+m s+qilxʷ way̓ ƛ̓l•al tm•tmniʔ axáʔ iʔ
thing evid person yes dead corpse this art
something, a person, dead. *What they're grabbing*

ckʷənxtwíxʷmstsəlx 67 uɬ ixíʔ {acacktə} a cktəřqíc̓aʔsəlx
c -kʷn+xtwixʷ+m -st -lx uɬ ixíʔ a c -k+trq=íc̓aʔ -s -lx
cust^ -take_from_recip -^cust -pl and then art act -kick_body -3erg -pl
from one another is a corpse. *Each takes his turn*

i t knaqs ɬa ckcahahám {is} 68 uɬ ha sc̓kinx {a} təmtəmníʔ
iʔ t k=naqs ɬaʔ c k+cah•ahá+m uɬ haʔ sc+ʔkin+x tm•tmniʔ
art agInst one_person when hab face and inter why_is_it corpse
at kicking. *It's a corpse*

uɬ {aɬc} aɬ ckʷəl̓tk̓ək̓əxʷúmstsəlx aɬ ckcahahám {is}
uɬ aɬ c -k̓ʷl̓+t+k̓•k̓xʷum -st -s -lx aɬ c -k+cah•ah+ám
and compl cust^ -make_ball -^cust -cust^ -pl compl hab -face
and they are making a ball out of it

cʔackníkstmstsəlx 69 way̓ ixíʔ {cusəlx ia} cus axáʔ iʔ
c -ʔackn=íkst+m -st -s -lx way̓ ixíʔ cu -s axáʔ iʔ
cust^ -play -^cust -3erg -pl well then tell -3erg this art
and playing with it. *He said to*

sqilxʷ 70 húma ilíʔ ƛ̓lápwi, p iksíwm 71 way̓
s+qilxʷ húmaʔ ilíʔ ƛ̓l+ap -wy p i -ks -siw+m way̓
person exhort there stop -ipimptv 5kʷu 1i -futi -ask well
the people: 8:06 *"Wait, stop for a minute, I want to ask you something."* *They*

ixíʔ sƛ̓lápsəlx uɬ ƛ̓əlpstísəlx axáʔ iʔ təmtəmníʔ {cu}
ixíʔ s -ƛ̓la+p -s -lx uɬ ƛ̓l+p -st -is -lx axáʔ iʔ tm•tmniʔ
then nom -stop -3i -pl and stop -st -3erg -pl this art corpse
stopped and stopped playing with the corpse.

72 cúsəlx uɬ sc̓kinx 73 sc̓kinx axáʔ təmtəmníʔ kaʔ {ɬc ə} ɬ
cu -s -lx uɬ sc+ʔkin+x sc+ʔkin+x axáʔ tm•tmniʔ kiʔ ɬ
tell -3erg -pl and why_is_it why_is_it this corpse rel ?
He said to them "What's the matter? What's the matter with the corpse

c̓ackníkstəmstp {aɬ} 74 t̓əxʷ {aɬc} aɬ cpulstp
c -ʔackn=íkst+m -st -p t̓xʷ aɬ c -pul -st -p
cust^ -play -^cust -5erg evidently compl cust^ -kill_one -^cust -5erg
that you are playing with it? That you are killing it,

c̓x̌iɬ 75 lut, lut t̓ sc̓ackníkstmp, uɬ a
c+ʔx̌iɬ lut lut t̓ sc -ʔackn=íkst+m -p uɬ a
like not not negfac pftv -play -5i and art
like? No, you're not playing,

cktər̓qíc̓aʔstp 76 way̓ cut axáʔ iʔ knaqs way̓ 77 cut
c -k+trq=íc̓aʔ -st -p way̓ cut axáʔ iʔ k=naqs way̓ cut
cust^ -kick_body -^cust -5erg well say this art one_person well say
you are kicking it." One of them said, he said

aɬíʔ ɬaʔ cxʷəlxʷált 78 uɬ talí {c·} kʷu ckʷús·təm[1] t
aɬíʔ ɬaʔ c -xʷl•xʷal+t uɬ taʔlíʔ kʷu c -kʷus·s·t+m t
because when hab -alive and very_much 3e4obj hab -lend obj_tr
"When he was alive 9:00 we lent him money

sqlaw {kəm̓ t} kəm̓ t xʷəlxʷílt 79 uɬ lut t̓a cx̌áq̓əsts {iʔ} iʔ
s+qlaw km̓ t xʷl•xʷilt uɬ lut t̓ c -x̌aq̓ -st -s iʔ
money or obj_tr debt and not negfac cust^ -pay -^cust -3erg art
and paid his debts, and he didn't pay

scxʷəlxʷílsts 80 kəm̓ iʔ sckʷúɬəns iʔ sqlaw 81 uɬ ixíʔ uɬ_iʔ {iʔ}
sc -xʷl•xʷilt -s km̓ iʔ sc -kʷuɬn -s iʔ s+qlaw uɬ ixíʔ uɬ_iʔ
pftv -debt -3i or art pftv -borrow -3i art money and then and_then
his debts or the money he borrowed. And when he died

ƛ̓lal uɬ aɬíʔ {laʔkín} lut t̓a kstim̓ 82 uɬ aɬíʔ laʔkín̓ mi kʷu
ƛ̓l•al uɬ aɬíʔ lut t̓ k+s+tim̓ uɬ aɬíʔ la+ʔkín̓ mi kʷu
dead and because not evid have_thing and so how fut 3e4obj
he didn't have anything. And how are we going to get

ɬkʷən·úntəm iʔ sqláwtət 83 iʔ kʷu a
ɬ+kʷn -nu -nt -m iʔ sqlaw -tt iʔ kʷu a
keep_again -manage -nt -3e4obj art money -4in art 3e4obj art
our money back, what he

1 Uncertain form.

cxʷəlxʷíltstəm 84 uɬ sc̓x̌ilx uɬ ixíʔ {ac} ia
c -xʷl•xʷilt -st -m uɬ sc+ʔx̌il+x uɬ ixíʔ iʔ
custˆ -debt -ˆcust -3e4obj and reason_why and then art
owes us? *And that's why we are*

c̓ackníkstəmstəm 85 uɬ ixíʔ ṅíṅẃiʔ nxəƛ̓púsəs iʔ
c -ʔackn=íkst+m -st -m uɬ ixíʔ ṅíṅẃiʔ n+xƛ̓p=us -s iʔ
custˆ -play -ˆcust -4erg and then a_while be_even -3erg art
playing with him. *So when he pays all*

xʷəlxʷílts 86 ixíʔ mi uɬ sic {ɬuə} ɬəwníkstməntəm {t̓əxʷ} 87 ṅu
xʷl•xʷilt -s ixíʔ mi uɬ sic ɬwn=ikst+m -nt -m ṅu
debt -3in then fut and then let_go_of -nt -4erg a_while
his debts *then we'll let him go. 10:00* *We'll*

kʷu ʔaluʔsíkstəm mi líq̓əntəm t̓əxʷ 88 x̌əcmstím t
kʷu ʔal=ẃs=íkst+m mi liq̓ -nt -m t̓xʷ x̌c+m -st -im t
4kn collect fut bury -nt -4erg emph get_so_ready -st -4erg obj_tr
take a collection and we'll bury him, *we'll get him*

kɬənt̓ək̓ʷmíns 89 a, cúntməlx waẏ, cúntməlx waẏ
kɬ -n+t̓k̓ʷ+min -s a cu -nt -m -lx waẏ cu -nt -m -lx waẏ
to_be -coffin -3i intj tell -nt -psv -pl well tell -nt -psv -pl well
a coffin." *He said "Well,*

90 huhúy xəƛ̓məncútwi ya cxʷəlxʷíltɬəms 91 p t̓wist
hu+húy xƛ̓+mncut -wy ya c -xʷl•xʷilt -ɬm -s p t̓wist
OK all -ipimptv art custˆ -debt -5obj -3erg 5kn stand_pl
all of you that he owes get in a row. *Stand up and*

p tər̓məncút 92 p t̓wist p tər̓məncút 93 uɬ ṅíṅẃiʔ axáʔ {təl} təl̓
p tr̓+mncut p t̓wist p tr̓+mncut uɬ ṅíṅẃiʔ axáʔ tl̓
5kn form_line 5kn stand_pl 5kn form_line and a_while this from
get in a line, *Stand up and get in a line,* *and from one end I'll start*

sk̓əmáqs {mi mi} mi síwən 94 k̓ʷinx ya cxʷəlxʷíltəm 95 ṅíṅẃiʔ
s+k̓m=aqs mi siw -n k̓ʷin+x ya c -xʷl•xʷilt+m ṅíṅẃiʔ
end fut ask -1erg how_much art hab -owe a_while
a-questioning you. *However much he owes you* *I'll*

uɬ t incá {x̌aq̓n} tx̌áq̓plaʔn 96 a, cútəlx waẏ 97 waẏ ixíʔ
uɬ t in+cá t+x̌áq̓=plaʔ -n a cut -lx waẏ waẏ ixíʔ
and agInst I reward -1erg intj say -pl OK well then
pay it." *They said "Ok."* *They*

sxəƛ̓məncútsəlx, t̓wístəlx {uɬ t̓i tx̌iw xi uɬ axáʔ təl} 98 xʷuy təl̓ sk̓maqs
s -xƛ̓+mncut -s -lx t̓wist -lx xʷuy tl̓ s+k̓m=aqs
nom -all -3i -pl stand_pl -pl go from end
got in a line, they stood. 11:00 *He went from*

itlíʔ 99 uɬ siws {i} ya cxʔit, cus 100 uɬ c̓kin anwí a
itlíʔ uɬ siw -s ya c+xʔit cu -s uɬ c+ʔkin anwí a
from_there and ask -3erg art first tell -3erg and how you art
one end *and asked the first one, he said:* *"How much*

cxʷəlxʷíltstəms 101 cut waẏ, ʔums k̓ʷinx 102 waẏ
c -xʷl•xʷilt -st -m -s cut waẏ ʔum -s k̓ʷin+x waẏ
cust^ -debt -^cust -2obj -3erg say well name -3erg how_much well
does he owe you?" He said, well, he named how much. He

ixíʔ, ixíʔ x̌aq̓s 103 waẏ uɬ ixíʔ itlíʔ sxʷuys 104 uɬ {itlí}
ixíʔ ixíʔ x̌aq̓ -s waẏ uɬ ixíʔ itlíʔ s -xʷuy -s uɬ
that that pay -3erg well and then from_there nom -go -3i and
paid him. Then he went on, and

itlíʔ iʔ knaqs síwəntəm itlíʔ tk̓ík̓aʔt 105 cúntəm uɬ
itlíʔ iʔ k=naqs siw -nt -m itlíʔ t+k̓í•k̓aʔt cu -nt -m uɬ
from_there art one_person ask -nt -psv from_there get_near tell -nt -psv and
he asked the one next to him. He said,

anwí čkin a cxʷəlxʷíltstəms 106 ixíʔ m̓áyaʔɬtəm čkin,
anwí c+ʔkin a c -xʷl•xʷilt -st -m -s ixíʔ m̓áyaʔ -ɬt -m c+ʔkin
you how art cust^ -debt -^cust -2obj -3i then teach -ɬt -psv how
"How much does he owe you?" He told him how much,

uɬ ixíʔ x̌aq̓s 107 way ixíʔ x̌a¨q̓s {uɬ} uɬ txƛ̓ap 108 waẏ
uɬ ixíʔ x̌aq̓ -s waẏ ixíʔ x̌aq̓ -s uɬ t+xƛ̓a+p waẏ
and that pay -3erg well that pay -3erg and complete well
and he paid him. He paid everybody. He

cúntməlx, uɬ, waẏ ksəntumístən {t̓əxʷ iʔ} 109 cúntəm waẏ n̓ín̓w̓iʔ
cu -nt -m -lx uɬ waẏ k+s+n+tw+mist+n cu -nt -m waẏ n̓ín̓w̓iʔ
tell -nt -psv -pl and yes have+store tell -nt -psv well a_while
said to them (and there is a store), 12:03 he said to them

xʷiċxtp t ksttəm̓tím̓s t kɬk̓əɬʔaysəlscútəns t
xʷiċ -xt -p t k -s+t•tm̓•tim̓ -s t kɬ -k̓ɬ+ʔays=lscút+n -s t
give -xit -5erg obj_tr to_be -clothes -3i obj_tr to_be -change_of_clothes -3i obj_tr
"Give him clothes, a new change of

sic 110 uɬ ixíʔ n̓ín̓w̓iʔ x̌áq̓ən, k̓əɬċəkntíxʷ čkin iʔ {ks}
sic uɬ ixíʔ n̓ín̓w̓iʔ x̌aq̓ -n k̓ɬ+ċk -nt -ixʷ c+ʔkin iʔ
new and that a_while pay -1erg name_price -nt -2erg how art
clothes. I'll pay for it, you name the price."

111 waẏ ixíʔ k̓əɬq̓əẏntís uɬ cut waẏ itíʔ čx̌iɬ {iʔ} 112 waẏ ixíʔ
waẏ ixíʔ k̓ɬ+q̓ẏ -nt -is uɬ cut waẏ itíʔ c+ʔx̌iɬ waẏ ixíʔ
well that write_down -nt -3erg and say well that like well that
He took it down, and said what it was; he paid

x̌aq̓s 113 cus {uɬ i} uɬ aɬiá pnicí uɬ a waẏ {kɬə}
x̌aq̓ -s cu -s uɬ aɬi+á pn+icíʔ uɬ a waẏ
pay -3erg tell -3erg and because_not at_that_time and intj yes
for it. He said (and at that time there was

kɬ*undertaker* {kɬ} 114 uɬ ixíʔ cúntəm, waẏ uɬ t swit n̓ín̓w̓iʔ {mi}
uɬ ixíʔ cu -nt -m waẏ uɬ t swit n̓ín̓w̓iʔ
have_undertaker and then tell -nt -psv well and agInst who a_while
no undertaker), he said, "Whoever will bury him can

mi líq̓əs, k̓əłcíqəm 115 kʷis t̓əxʷ xʷuysts k̓əl səntəmtəmníʔtən
mi liq̓ -s k̓ł+ciq+m kʷi -s t̓xʷ xʷuy+st -s k̓l s+n+tm•tmniʔ+tn
fut bury -3erg dig take -3erg emph take_st -3erg to graveyard
dig the grave 13:00 *and take him to the graveyard."*

116 mat ksəntəmtəmníʔtən, 117 məł ik̓líʔ k̓əłcíqəm 118 məł ixíʔ {ł}
mat k+s+n+tm•tmniʔ+tn mł ik̓líʔ k̓ł+ciq+m mł ixíʔ
maybe have_graveyard and there dig and then
I guess there is a graveyard, *and there they dug a grave,* *and they*

wiʔsx̌əcmstísəlx {əł· twi ł} ta nt̓k̓ʷmin naʔłcəcám, uł nt̓k̓ʷəntísəlx
wy̓+s+x̌c+m -st -is -lx t n+t̓k̓ʷ+min nałc•c•ám uł n+t̓k̓ʷ -nt -is -lx
finish_ready -st -3erg -pl obj_tr coffin forget and put_in -nt -3erg -pl
got a coffin ready, I forgot, they put him there.

119 məł ixíʔ {xʷ} xʷuystp məł líq̓əntp 120 uł ixíʔ {i} kʷu
mł ixíʔ xʷuy+st -p mł liq̓ -nt -p uł ixíʔ kʷu
and then take_st -5erg and bury -nt -5erg and then 1obj
"You take him there and bury him. *Tell me*

m̓áyaʔłtp iʔ ksx̌əq̓əncútəmp 121 way̓ ixíʔ m̓áyaʔłtsəlx {uł}
m̓áyaʔ -łt -p iʔ k -s+x̌q̓+ncut -mp way̓ ixíʔ m̓áyaʔ -łt -s -lx
teach -łt -5erg art to_be -pay -5i well that tell -łt -3erg -pl
your price." *They told him.*

122 ixíʔ uł c̓əspsql̓áw 123 uł, way̓, way̓ ixíʔ itlíʔ sxʷuys
ixíʔ uł c̓s+p+s+qlaw uł way̓ way̓ ixíʔ itlíʔ s -xʷuy -s
then and money_finish and well well then from_there nom -go -3i
And he ran out of money. *He went on.*

124 ixíʔ uł mat náx̌əmł taʔxʷłxəwíł 125 uł ta_ck̓líʔ t̓əxʷ ta {cłs}
ixíʔ uł mat nax̌mł taʔxʷ+ł+xwíł uł ta_c+k̓líʔ t̓xʷ t
then and maybe but have_road and that_way evidently obl
Then there were roads, *and he went*

cahcháqs ik̓líʔ {is} iʔ scxʷuys 126 uł ta_ck̓líʔ ła
cah•ch=aqs ik̓líʔ iʔ sc -xʷuy -s uł ta_c+k̓líʔ łaʔ
face_direction there art pftv -go -3i and that_way the_one_that
in the same direction, 14:03 *he walked*

nkxám 127 xʷu··y k̓əłʔál·qʷaʔ 128 k̓əłk̓ʷƛ̓áp, k̓əłʔál·qʷaʔ
n+kxa+m xʷuy k̓+łʔ=álqʷ+aʔ k̓ł+k̓ʷƛ̓a+p k̓+łʔ=álqʷ+aʔ
go_on_foot go close_to_shore come_in_sight shore
there. *He went and got to a shore,* *he came in sight to a shore, it's*

ctyap 129 t̓əxʷ púti? sənsəlxʷʔítkʷs, uł a kłənx̌líw̓s
c -tya+p t̓xʷ pút+iʔ s -n+slxʷʔ=itkʷ -s uł a kł+n+x̌l=iw̓s
hab -water_runs evidently still nom -big_water -3i and art have_bridge
running water, *it's not a big river, and it has a bridge.*

130 axáʔ iʔ xəwíł ya cənkxənmísts ałíʔ nkaʔxm̓útyaʔ
axáʔ iʔ xwił ya c -n+kx+n+mi -st -s ałíʔ n+kaʔx+m=útyaʔ
this art road art cust^ -follow -^cust -3erg because go_on_foot
That's the road he's been walking on, because he's on foot.

131 xʷu··y, k̓əłkícx iʔ k̓la nx̌əlíw̓s 132 ixíʔ sk̓əłxʷísts put iʔ l
xʷuy k̓ł+kic+x iʔ k̓l n+x̌l=iw̓s ixíʔ s -k̓ł+xʷist -s put iʔ l
go get_to_arrive art to bridge then nom -walk -3i just art at
He went and got to the bridge, *and he walked on it to half*

k̓łtx̌ʷiw̓s 133 kʷm̓ił kiʔ qʷəlqʷíltstəm axáʔ t sk̓ʷək̓ʷíməlt 134 a
k̓ł+tx̌ʷ=iw̓s kʷm̓ił kiʔ qʷl•qʷil -st -m axáʔ t s+k̓ʷ•k̓ʷiy=m=lt a
half_way suddenly rel talk -st -psv this agInst baby intj
way. *Suddenly a child spoke to him.* *He*

ƛ̓aʔƛ̓ʔúsəms {a i} la nk̓əmłníw̓ts ya nx̌əlíw̓s 135 a· ik̓líʔ kiʔ tətw̓ít {ə·}
ƛ̓aʔ•ƛ̓ʔ=ús+m -s l n+k̓m=łniwt -s ya n+x̌l=iw̓s a ik̓líʔ kiʔ t•tw̓it
look_for -3erg on side -3in art bridge intj there rel boy
looked around and on the side of the bridge *a boy was sitting there*

k̓amtíw̓s k̓amtálqʷ t̓əxʷ {i l} la nx̌əłłníw̓tən 136 cúntəm waẏ
k+ʔam=t=íw̓s k+ʔam=t=álqʷ t̓xʷ l n+x̌l=łniwt+n cu -nt -m waẏ
sg_ride_horseback sit_on_log evidently on side_rail tell -nt -mdl well
on the rail of the bridge. 15:03 *He asked him,*

uł lut t̓ asck̓ínt {ta ła} 137 cus axáʔ iʔ tətw̓ít lut t̓
uł lut t̓ a -sc -k̓in+t cu -s axáʔ iʔ t•tw̓it lut t̓
and not negfac 2i -pftv -afraid tell -3erg this art boy not negfac
"Aren't you scared?" *He said to the boy, "Aren't*

asck̓ínt 138 cəm̓ {kʷ} kʷ nsəl̓pqín kəm̓ {kʷ} mi kʷ nixʷtítkʷ
a -sc -k̓in+t cm̓ kʷ n+sl̓+p=qin km̓ mi kʷ n+yxʷ=itkʷ
2i -pftv -afraid maybe 2kn dizzy or fut 2kn fall_in_water
you scared? *You might get dizzy and fall in the water."*

139 lut, cut axáʔ iʔ tətw̓ít 140 lut, lut [kən] t̓a ck̓int {ay} lut kən
lut cut axáʔ iʔ t•tw̓it lut lut kn t̓ c -k̓in+t lut kn
not say this art boy not not 1kn negfac hab -afraid not 1kn
The boy said "No. *No, I'm not scared,*

t̓a cən{səlsəl}səl̓səl̓pús {uł waył} 141 a· cus waẏ t̓əxʷ
t̓ c -n+sl̓•sl̓+p=us a cu -s waẏ t̓xʷ
negfac hab -dizzy intj tell -3erg well emph
I don't get dizzy." *He said "All right then,*

csax̌ʷt[x] {kʷu kʷu sa·} 142 kʷu sqʷəlqʷəlstwíxʷəxʷ t̓əxʷ {kʷum}
c+sax̌ʷ+t -x kʷu s -qʷl•qʷl+st+nwixʷ -xʷ t̓xʷ
come_downhill -isimptv 4kn ipftv^ -talk_rec -^ipftv emph
get off. *Let's talk and understand*

mi kʷu nsxʷnaʔmənwíxʷ 143 uł ałíʔ ik̓líʔ {kʷ} kʷ kəlkʷút 144 uł lut
mi kʷu n+sxʷ=naʔ+mnwíxʷ uł ałíʔ ik̓líʔ kʷ k+lkʷ=ut uł lut
fut 4kn acquaint_rec and because there 2kn far and not
one another. *You are too far* *and I*

put txƛ̓ínaʔməntsən, níxəlməntsən 145 waẏ ixíʔ
put t+xƛ̓=ínaʔ+m -nt -s -n nixl+m -nt -s -n waẏ ixíʔ
just hear_all -nt -2obj -1erg hear -nt -2obj -1erg well then
can't make out every word you say, I can't hear you." 16:00 *Then*

scsax̌ʷts axáʔ iʔ tətw̓ít 146 uɬ ixíʔ {c} kícəntəm ilíʔ
s -c+sax̌ʷt -s axáʔ iʔ t•tw̓it uɬ ixíʔ kic -nt -m ilíʔ
nom -come_downhill -3i this art boy and then reach -nt -psv there
the boy climbed down *and got there*

uɬ 147 cúntəm uɬ k̓aʔkín kʷ scxʷuyx 148 cut t̓əxʷ
uɬ cu -nt -m uɬ k̓a+ʔkín kʷ sc -xʷuy -x cut t̓xʷ
and tell -nt -psv and to_where 2kn ipftvp^ -go -^ipftvp say emph
and *he asked him, "Where are you going?"* *He said*

lut t̓a cmistín k̓aʔkín kən səcxʷúyx 149 way̓
lut t̓ c -my -st -in k̓a+ʔkín kn sc -xʷuy -x way̓
not negfac cust^ -know -^cust -1erg to_where 1kn ipftvp^ -go -^ipftvp well
"I don't know where I am going. *I'm*

t̓iʔ kiʔ iscxʷəstlwísəm iʔ təmxʷúlaʔxʷ, ikscwíklaʔxʷəm iʔ
t̓iʔ kiʔ i -sc -xʷst+lwis+m iʔ tmxʷ=úlaʔxʷ i -ksc -wík=laʔxʷ+m iʔ
evid rel 1i -pftv -travel art country 1i -futPerfi -see_country art
just walking the country, I want to see

təmxʷúlaʔxʷ 150 uɬ t̓i way̓ kən cəncháqs 151 uɬ t̓iʔ ta_ck̓líʔ k̓la
tmxʷ=úlaʔxʷ uɬ t̓iʔ way̓ kn c -n+ch=aqs uɬ t̓iʔ ta_c+k̓líʔ k̓l
country and evid well 1kn hab -be_facing and evid that_way to
the country. *Whatever direction I face,* *wherever it goes,*

cxʷuy iʔ kən cənt̓k̓ʷák̓ʷ iʔ t xəwíɬ {uɬ} 152 uɬ
c -xʷuy iʔ kn c -n+t̓k̓ʷ•ak̓ʷ iʔ t xwiɬ uɬ
hab -go art 1kn hab -enter_from_side_road art obl road and
I follow the road there; *and*

ta_ck̓líʔ {k̓lacəl} ki ksxʷúytən ya cq̓ax̌ 153 uɬ ixíʔ
ta_c+k̓líʔ kiʔ k+s+xʷuy+tn ya c -q̓ax̌ uɬ ixíʔ
that_way rel have_track art hab -clear and that
where there is a clear road *that's*

əctkəxstín 154 uɬ axáʔ aláʔ kən ck̓əɬʔál·qʷ way̓
c -t+kx -st -in uɬ axáʔ aláʔ kn c -k̓+ɬʔ=al·qʷ way̓
cust^ -follow -^cust -1erg and this here 1kn hab -next_to_shore yes
what I follow. *And here I have come to this shore*

wíkəntsən 155 cúntəm axáʔ iʔ t tətw̓ít, way̓ {kʷu ə}
wik -nt -s -n cu -nt -m axáʔ iʔ t t•tw̓it way̓
see -nt -2obj -1erg tell -nt -psv this art agInst boy well
and I saw you." *The little boy said,*

kxəntsín 156 cúntəm lut, uɬ sc̓kinx pnaʔ
kx+n -t -s -in cu -nt -m lut uɬ sc+ʔkin+x pnaʔ
follow -nt -2obj -1erg tell -nt -psv not and why_is_it maybe
"I'll follow you." 17:00 *He said to him, "And what's the matter, maybe,*

157 pnaʔ kʷ kɬƛ̓ax̌əx̌ƛ̓x̌áp, cəm̓ xsnúntsəlx 158 cut lut,
pnaʔ kʷ kɬ+ƛ̓ax̌•x̌•ƛ̓x̌á+p cm̓ xs -nu -nt -s -lx cut lut
maybe 2kn have_parents maybe miss -manage -nt -3e2obj -pl say not
maybe you have parents, and they'll miss you." *He said,*

lut kən t̓a kɬƛ̓ax̌əx̌ƛ̓x̌áp 159 waỷ, waỷ t̓iʔ_x̌ast ɬ kxəntsín
lut kn t̓ kɬ+ƛ̓ax̌•x̌•ƛ̓x̌á+p waỷ waỷ t̓iʔ_x̌as+t ɬ kx+n -t -s -in
not 1kn negfac have_parents yes yes as_well if follow -nt -2obj -1erg
"No, I don't have parents. *It's best I follow you."*

160 cúntəm lut, lut t̓a cmistín k̓aʔkíṅ kən
cu -nt -m lut lut t̓ c -my -st -in k̓a+ʔkíṅ kn
tell -nt -psv not not evid cust^ -know -^cust -1erg where_to 1kn
He said "No, I don't know where

səcxʷúyx {pnaʔ kən ksq̓milt} 161 pnaʔ kʷ ksq̓míltən kəṁ kʷ ʔayx̌ʷt
sc -xʷuy -x pnaʔ kʷ k+s+q̓m=ilt+n kṁ kʷ ʔayx̌ʷ+t
ipftvp^ -go -^ipftvp maybe 2kn have_hunger or 2kn tired
I am going; *maybe you'll get hungry or tired,*

162 uɬ nixʷ lut kən t̓a ksqlaw, {uɬ iks} 163 iwá kʷu ɬ kicx {k̓əl} iʔ l
uɬ nixʷ lut kn t̓ k+s+qlaw iwá kʷu ɬ kic+x iʔ l
and also not 1kn negfac have_money even 4kn if arrive art at
and I don't have any money. *And if we get to a town,*

tawn kʷu ɬ ksʔíɬəns iʔ k̓əl sənʔíɬəntən 164 kəṁ k̓əl sənpúlxtən
tawn kʷu ɬ ks -ʔiɬn -s iʔ k̓l s+n+ʔiɬn+tn kṁ k̓l s+n+pul+x+tn
town 4kn if futi4^ -eat -^futi4 art to restaurant or to camping_place
how can we eat at a restaurant 18:00 *or stay at a*

kʷu ɬ kspulx[s] 165 uɬ waỷ myaɬ cəṁ kʷ
kʷu ɬ ks -pul+x -s uɬ waỷ myaɬ cṁ kʷ
4kn if futi4^ -overnight -^futi4 and well too_much maybe 2kn
sleeping place? *You are too*

qʷəṅqʷṅəmscút 166 cus lut, waỷ, waỷ t̓iʔ kxəntsín {waỷ isqʷam}
qʷṅ•qʷṅ+m+scut cu -s lut waỷ waỷ t̓iʔ kx+n -t -s -in
hard_time tell -3erg not yes well evid follow -nt -2obj -1erg
pitiful." *He told him "No, I'll follow you."*

167 waỷ waỷ aspuʔús 168 waỷ ixíʔ {s} kxəntím 169 waỷ
waỷ waỷ a -s+puʔ=ús waỷ ixíʔ kx+n -t -im waỷ
well well 2in -heart well then follow -nt -psv well
"Well, if that's how you feel." *So he followed him.* *They*

xʷú··ỷilx, lut {mat s} mat spúlxsəlx, waỷ k̓əɬk̓ʷƛ̓áp {əlxa}
xʷuỷ•y -lx lut mat s -pul+x -s -lx waỷ k̓ɬ+k̓ʷƛ̓a+p
go_pl -pl not maybe nom -overnight -3i -pl yes come_in_sight
went, I don't think they overnighted, they came in sight.

170 waỷ qʷá··mqʷəmt iʔ citxʷ a cwix 171 sílxʷaʔ iʔ citxʷ 172 uɬ
waỷ qʷam•qʷm+t iʔ citxʷ a c -wix sílxʷaʔ iʔ citxʷ uɬ
well excellent art house art hab -live big art house and
A beautiful house stood there, *a big house.* *It*

púti, púti kəɬx̌ỷáɬnəxʷ, lútiʔ sk̓laxʷs 173 ixíʔ uɬ axáʔ, axáʔm
pút+iʔ pút+iʔ kɬ+x̌yaɬ=nxʷ lút+i s -k̓laxʷ -s ixíʔ uɬ axáʔ axáʔ+m
still still have_sun not_yet nom -evening -3i then and this this
wasn't sundown yet, wasn't evening yet. 19:03 *And this traveling person*

iʔ sǝcxʷǝstlwísx uɬ way̓ nʔayx̌ʷtíls 174 uɬ aɬíʔ way̓
iʔ sc -xʷst+lwis -x uɬ way̓ n+ʔayx̌ʷ+t=íls uɬ aɬíʔ way̓
art ipftvp^ -travel_around -^ipftvp and yes get_tired and because well
commenced to get tired, *and he hadn't*

yaʔx̌í iʔ l siɬkʷkʷáʕst kaʔ c̓íɬǝn 175 uɬ lut t̓a kst̓ík̓ǝl uɬ
yaʔx̌í iʔ l siɬ+kʷ•kʷ=ʕast[2] kiʔ c -ʔiɬn uɬ lut t̓ k+s+t̓ik̓l uɬ
that_one art in early_morning rel hab -eat and not negfac have_grub and
eaten since morning, *he hadn't had any lunch,*

axáʔ c̓ǝspsqláw 176 uɬ nstils way̓ t̓ǝxʷ pnaʔ nqʷǝn̓qʷn̓íls
axáʔ c̓s+p+s+qlaw uɬ n+st=ils way̓ t̓xʷ pnaʔ n+qʷn̓•qʷn̓=ils
this money_finish and think well emph maybe have_pity
and he's got no money. *And he thought, "Well, maybe they'll have pity.*

177 way̓ kʷu ksƛ̓lpmíxaʔx iʔ la cwix 178 t̓ǝxʷ kʷu
way̓ kʷu ks -ƛ̓l+p -míx+aʔx iʔ l cwix t̓xʷ kʷu
well 4kn incp^ -stop -^incp art at live emph 4kn
We'll stop at that house; *we are going*

ksuɬtíɬnaʔx 179 n̓ín̓w̓iʔ pnaʔ {kʷu} kʷu xʷíc̓xtǝm t
k -sw=ɬtiɬn -aʔx n̓ín̓w̓iʔ pnaʔ kʷu xʷic̓ -xt -m t
incp^ -ask_info -^incp a_while maybe 3e4obj give -xit -3e4obj obj_tr
to inquire. *Maybe they'll give us*

ksck̓ʷúl̓tǝt 180 ɬaʔ kʷu ʔamtím, t ksnilítǝntǝt
ksc -k̓ʷul̓ -tt ɬaʔ kʷu ʔam -t -im t k -s+n+ilíʔ+tn -tt
futPerfi -work -4i if 3e4obj feed -nt -3e4obj obj_tr to_be -dwelling_place -4i
a job, *maybe they'll feed us, give us a place to stay."*

181 uɬ axáʔ siws {i s} iʔ sl̓ax̌ts axáʔ iʔ tǝtwít 182 axáʔ iʔ
uɬ axáʔ siw -s iʔ s+l̓ax̌+t -s axáʔ iʔ t•tw̓it axáʔ iʔ
and this ask -3erg art friend -3in this art boy this art
And he asked his partner, the little boy, *his*

ɬsísǝncaʔs, uɬ aɬíʔ ɬsísǝncaʔs 183 cniɬc aɬíʔ uɬ way̓
ɬ+sí•sncaʔ -s uɬ aɬíʔ ɬ+sí•sncaʔ -s cniɬ+c aɬíʔ uɬ way̓
younger_bro -3in and because younger_bro -3in (s)he because and yes
little brother (he claims him as his little brother 20:02 *because he is*

sqǝl̓tmíxʷ, uɬ axáʔ k̓ʷǝk̓ʷy̓úmaʔ axáʔ iʔ tǝtwít 184 cus, uɬ uc kʷ
s+qlt=mixʷ uɬ axáʔ k̓ʷ•k̓ʷy=úmaʔ axáʔ iʔ t•tw̓it cu -s uɬ uc kʷ
man and this small this art boy tell -3erg and dub 2kn
a man, and the boy is little), *he asked him, "Are you*

ʔayx̌ʷt 185 cus lut, lut t̓ sǝlkʷúts kʷaʔ {i} iscxʷúy mǝɬ
ʔayx̌ʷ+t cu -s lut lut t̓ s+lkʷ=ut -s kʷaʔ i -sc -xʷuy mɬ
tired tell -3erg not not negfac distance -3in intj 1i -pftv -go and
tired?" *He said "No, I haven't come very far for me*

2 siɬ+ is not understood.

kən ɬ ċayx̌ʷt
kn ɬ c -ʔayx̌ʷ+t
1kn subord hab -tired
to be tired."

186 cúntəm uɬ lut ha asksq̓míltən
cu -nt -m uɬ lut haʔ a -s -k+s+q̓m=ilt+n
tell -nt -psv and not inter 2i -nom -have_hunger
He asked, "Ain't you hungry?"

187 lut, nixʷ lut isksq̓míltən
lut nixʷ lut i -s -k+s+q̓m=ilt+n
not also not 1i -nom -have_hunger
"No, I'm not hungry, either."

188 cus, náx̌əmɬ incá way̓, way̓
cu -s nax̌mɬ in+cá way̓ way̓
tell -3erg but I yes yes
He said to him,

kən ʔayx̌ʷt, uɬ way̓ kən ksq̓míltən
kn ʔayx̌ʷ+t uɬ way̓ kn k+s+q̓m=ilt+n
1kn tired and yes 1kn have_hunger
"But I am tired, and I'm hungry.

189 uɬ aɬíʔ lkʷut iscxʷúy
uɬ aɬíʔ lkʷ=ut i -sc -xʷuy
and because far 1i -pftv -go
I have come far,

190 uɬ t siɬkʷkʷáʕst ki kən ċíɬən
uɬ t syɬ+kʷ•kʷ=ʕast kiʔ kn c -ʔiɬn
and from early_morning rel 1kn hab -eat
and it's morning since I've eaten.

191 way̓ k̓laʔ {ks}
way̓ ak̓láʔ
well here
We are going

kstxʷúymәntəm axáʔ aʔ cwix
ks -t+xʷuy+m -nt -m axáʔ aʔ cwix
futt^ -go_towards -nt -4erg this art dwelling
to go over to this house.

192 pnaʔ nqʷəňqʷəňníls, kʷu
pnaʔ n+qʷň•qʷň=ils kʷu
maybe have_pity 3e4obj
Maybe they'll have pity,

nqʷəňmíntəm, kʷu ʔamtím
n+qʷň+mi -nt -m kʷu ʔam -t -im
feel_sorry_for -nt -3e4obj 3e4obj feed -nt -3e4obj
have pity on us, feed us."

193 cut way̓ aspuʔús
cut way̓ a -s+puʔ=ús
say well 2in -heart
He said, "If that's your wish."

194 way̓ xʷú··y̓ilx, yáʕpəlx, way̓ k̓ɬancʔíp[məlx]
way̓ xʷuy̓•y -lx yaʕ+p -lx way̓ k̓ɬ+n+cʔ=ip+m -lx
well go_pl -pl arrive_pl -pl yes knock_on_door -pl
They went, got there, knocked on the door. 21:03

195 way̓ {c}
way̓
well
A woman

ck̓ɬənk̓ahk̓ʷípɬtməlx iʔ t tkəɬmílxʷ
c -k̓ɬ+n+k̓ahk̓ʷ=íp -ɬt -m iʔ t tkɬmilxʷ
act -open_door -ɬt -psv art agInst woman
opened the door for them,

196 nťa·· way̓ swiʔnúmt iʔ
nťa way̓ s+wy̓+numt iʔ
intj yes handsome art
a good looking

tkəɬmílxʷ
tkɬmilxʷ
woman
woman.

197 cúntməlx, way̓ atáʔ p ctəkʷtəkʷʔút
cu -nt -m -lx way̓ atáʔ p c -tkʷ+tkʷʔ=ut
tell -nt -psv -pl well here 5kn hab -walk
She said to them, "You folks are traveling around.

198 lut
lut
not
It's

[s]qʷays kʷu ťa ckícəc iʔ sqílxʷ, mnímɬəmp kiʔ kʷu aɬ
s -qʷay -s kʷu ť c -kic•c iʔ s+qilxʷ mnimɬ+mp kiʔ kʷu aɬ
nom -often -3i 4kn negfac hab -be_visited art person you rel 1obj compl
not often that people visit here, and then you folks

kícəntp
kic -nt -p
reach_st/sb -nt -5erg
got here.

199 uɬ k̓aʔkíń p ɬ səcxʷúyx
uɬ k̓a+ʔkíń p ɬ sc -xʷuy -x
and where_to 5kn compl ipftvp^ -go -^ipftvp
And where are you folks going?"

200 cut axáʔ {iʔ} iʔ sxʔitx, t̓əxʷ, lut t̓a cmistím k̓aʔkín kʷu
cut axáʔ iʔ s+xʔit=x t̓xʷ lut t̓ c -my+st -im k̓a+ʔkín kʷu
say this art oldest_one emph not negfac cust^ -know -4erg to_where 4kn
The older one said, "We don't know where

ɬ səc[xʷuyx] 201 way̓ t̓iʔ kʷu səctəkʷtəkʷʔútx axáʔ
ɬ sc -xʷuy -x way̓ t̓iʔ kʷu sc -tkʷ+tkʷʔ=ut -x axáʔ
compl ipftvp^ -go -^ipftvp well evid 4kn ipftvp^ -walk -^ipftvp this
we are going, we are just traveling

iʔ t təmxʷúlaʔxʷ, kʷu səcwíklaʔxʷxʷ {uɬ uɬ cakʷ} 202 uɬ way̓ kʷu
iʔ t tmxʷ=úlaʔxʷ kʷu sc -wík=laʔxʷ -xʷ uɬ way̓ kʷu
art obl country 4kn ipftvp^ -see_world -^ipftvp and well 4kn
around the country, sightseeing. We are

ʔayʔáyx̌ʷt 203 cúntməlx mat way̓ aɬíʔ p ʔayʔáyx̌ʷt 204 cut
ʔay•ʔáyx̌ʷ+t cu -nt -m -lx mat way̓ aɬíʔ p ʔay•ʔáyx̌ʷ+t cut
tired_pl tell -nt -psv -pl maybe yes so 5kn tired_pl say
tired." 22:03 She said to them, "You must be tired." He

way̓, way̓, kʷu ʔayʔáyx̌ʷt uɬ {kʷu} kʷu ksq̓míltən 205 t̓əxʷ kən ksq̓míltən
way̓ way̓ kʷu ʔay•ʔáyx̌ʷ+t uɬ kʷu k+s+q̓m=ilt+n t̓xʷ kn k+s+q̓m=ilt+n
yes yes 4kn tired_pl and 4kn have_hunger emph 1kn have_hunger
told her, "Yes we are tired and hungry. I am

axáʔ incá 206 uɬ axáʔ {is} iskəxnílt nixʷ mat way̓, nixʷ ʔilxʷt,
axáʔ in+cá uɬ axáʔ i -s+kx+n=ilt nixʷ mat way̓ nixʷ ʔilxʷ+t
this I and this 1in -young_follower also must yes also hungry
hungry, and my child follower must really be hungry,

ʔayx̌ʷt 207 uɬ uc caʔkʷ aláʔ iʔ kʷu pulx 208 a, cúntməlx way̓,
ʔayx̌ʷ+t uɬ uc caʔkʷ aláʔ iʔ kʷu pul+x a cu -nt -m -lx way̓
tired and dub could here art 4kn camp intj tell -nt -psv -pl yes
tired. Can we camp here?" She told them "Yes, yes,

way̓ ṅíṅẁiʔ náx̌əmɬ, {l} p wiʔwiʔcín mi 209 ixíʔ k̓ʷúl̓cɬmən mi
way̓ ṅíṅẁiʔ nax̌mɬ p wy̓•wy̓=cin mi ixíʔ k̓ʷul̓=c -ɬm -n mi
yes a_while but 5kn finish_eating_pl fut then cook -5obj -1erg fut
when you are done eating ... I'll cook for you

xʷíc̓ɬmən iʔ {t ks} t ksnilíʔtnəmp iʔ t
xʷic̓ -ɬm -n iʔ t k -s+n+ilíʔ+tn -mp iʔ t
give -5obj -1erg art obj_tr to_be -dwelling_place -5i art obj_tr
and I'll give you a place to stay,

ksənɬq̓ʷútnəmp 210 way̓, way̓ ixíʔ {s} cúntməlx, way̓ {cən}
k -s+n+ɬq̓ʷ=ut+n -mp way̓ way̓ ixíʔ cu -nt -m -lx way̓
to_be -bed -5i well well then tell -nt -psv -pl yes
a bed." She said to them,

cənppílxwy 211 a, lut, naɬccám {u} 212 xʷúystməlx {i}
c+n+p•pilx -wy a lut naɬc•c•ám xʷuy+st -m -lx
enter_pl_cisl -ipimptv intj not forget take_st -psv -pl
"Come in." Oh, no, wait a minute. 23:01 She took them

iḱlíʔ iʔ ḱəl l̓kʷut, t̓əxʷ lut_səlkʷú[ts] 213 iʔ ḱəl tḱəmkn̓íɬxʷ ilíʔ {c}
iḱlíʔ iʔ ḱl l̓kʷ=ut t̓xʷ lut_s+lkʷ=ut+s iʔ ḱl t+ḱm=kn=iɬxʷ ilíʔ
there art to little_way evidently not_far art to outside there
a way away, not too far; *just outside there was*

cwix ḱʷəḱʷy̓úmaʔ iʔ citxʷ 214 xʷúystməlx ixíʔ
c -wix ḱʷ•ḱʷy=úmaʔ iʔ citxʷ xʷuy+st -m -lx ixíʔ
hab -dwell small art house take_st -psv -pl then
a small building there. *She took them there,*

ḱɬənḱahḱʷípɬtməlx 215 ixíʔ ilíʔ {kɬ} kɬyayáʕt {iʔ} ixíʔ iʔ citxʷ {p səl}
ḱɬ+n+ḱahḱʷ=íp -ɬt -m -lx ixíʔ ilíʔ kɬ+yaʕ•yáʕ+t ixíʔ iʔ citxʷ
open -ɬt -psv -pl then there have+all that art house
she opened the door. *She said to them: "That house has everything."*

216 cúntməlx ixíʔ ksəncáʕwlxtən ilíʔ {unint} 217 kɬkc̓awʔíw̓stən
cu -nt -m -lx ixíʔ k+s+n+caʕʷ+lx+tn ilíʔ kɬ+k+c̓aw̓=íw̓s+tn
tell -nt -psv -pl that have_bathtub there have_soap
She told them, "There is a bath there, *there is soap*

ilíʔ {p} spuʔúsəmp p caʕwlx uɬ p kc̓aʔwʔíw̓səm 218 way̓ uɬ ixíʔ
ilíʔ s+puʔ=ús -mp p caʕʷ+lx uɬ p k+c̓aw̓=íw̓s+m way̓ uɬ ixíʔ
there heart -5in 5kn bathe and 5kn wash_face well and then
there; if you want to, you can bathe and wash. *I am going to*

ʔawsḱʷúl̓cɬmən uɬ ixíʔ kɬcítxʷəmp uɬ ixíʔ
ʔaw+s+ḱʷúl̓=c -ɬm -n uɬ ixíʔ kɬ -citxʷ -mp uɬ ixíʔ
go_cook_for -5obj -1erg and that to_be -house -5i and that
go cook for you; and that'll be your house and that'll be

ksənɬq̓ʷútnəmp 219 uɬ ilíʔ p pulx, way̓ mat p ʔayʔáyx̌ʷt
k -s+n+ɬq̓ʷ=ut+n -mp uɬ ilíʔ p pul+x way̓ mat p ʔay•ʔáyx̌ʷ+t
to_be -bed -5i and there 5kn camp yes must 5kn tired_pl
your beds. *You can camp there, you must be tired. 24:00*

220 way̓ ixíʔ {ɬəɬ} iɬəɬxʷúy ɬʔawsḱʷúl̓cɬmən
way̓ ixíʔ i -ɬ -ɬ+xʷuy ɬ+ʔaw+s+ḱʷul̓=c -ɬm -n
well then 1i -nom -go_back go_back_to_cook_for -5obj -1erg
I'm going back to cook for you.

221 ńíńw̓iʔ {p̓iʔq p̓iʔqíltən} kən p̓iʔqíltən məɬ c̓úkʷɬmən iʔ
ńíńw̓iʔ kn p̓y̓q=ilt+(t)n mɬ c+ʔukʷ -ɬm -n iʔ
a_while 1kn cook and bring -5obj -1erg art
When my cooking is done I'll bring you what

ksc̓íɬnəmp ksc̓íɬnəmp ksc̓íɬnəmp 222 way̓ way̓ [ɬ]ɬʔácqaʔs axáʔ iʔ
k -sc+ʔiɬn -mp way̓ way̓ ɬ -ɬ+ʔácqaʔ -s axáʔ iʔ
to_be -food -5i well well nom -go_out_again -3i this art
you are going to eat." *Then the woman went*

tkəɬmílxʷ 223 uɬ axáʔ ɬaʔ cwikʷm ixíʔ ɬaʔ ckmənkíń axáʔ iʔ
tkɬ+m=ilxʷ uɬ axáʔ ɬaʔ c -wikʷ+m ixíʔ ɬaʔ c -kmn=kiń axáʔ iʔ
woman and this when hab -hide that when hab -turn_back this art
back out. *And secretely, when the good looking woman*

tkəɬmílxʷ, iʔ swiʔnúmt axáʔ iʔ tkəɬmílxʷ 224 ixíʔ
tkɬ+m=ilxʷ iʔ s+wẏ+numt axáʔ iʔ tkɬ+m=ilxʷ ixíʔ
woman art handsome this art woman then
turns her back, *he*

cḱəɬḱʷəƛ̓álqsəms uɬ axáʔ iʔ sḱəɬq̓əẏncút {a c} 225 taɬt_uɬ,
c -ḱɬ+ḱʷƛ̓=alqs+m -s uɬ axáʔ iʔ s+ḱɬ+q̓ẏ+ncut taɬ+t_uɬ
act -take_from_under_clothes -3erg and this art picture goodness
takes the picture out of his clothes. *Goodness,*

c̓x̌iɬt ixíʔ iʔ tkəɬmílxʷ iʔ sḱəɬq̓əẏncúts[3] 226 waẏ, waẏ {ɬ c nia}
c+ʔx̌iɬ+t ixíʔ iʔ tkɬ+m=ilxʷ iʔ s+ḱɬ+q̓ẏ+ncut -s waẏ waẏ
like that art woman art picture -3in well well
it's just like that woman's picture. 25:00 *When*

cḱɬ[n]ḱahḱʷípɬtməlx, waẏ wiʔskc̓awʔíw̓sməlx, uɬ ixíʔ
c -ḱɬ+n+ḱahḱʷ=íp -ɬt -m -lx waẏ wẏ+s+k+c̓aw̓=íw̓s+m -lx uɬ ixíʔ wẏ+s+tx•txam
act -open_door -ɬt -psv -pl well finish_wash -pl and then finish_comb
she opened the door they are all washed up and combed.

227 waẏ ḱɬənḱahḱʷípɬtməlx {iʔ cət} iʔ ḱɬənḱmíp, waẏ {e c eh} cxʷʔul
waẏ ḱɬ+n+ḱahḱʷ=íp -ɬt -m -lx iʔ ḱɬ+n+ḱm=ip waẏ c -xʷ[ʔ]ul
well open -ɬt -psv -pl art door yes hab -steam_inch
She opened the door, their food

iʔ ksc̓íɬənsəlx {a} 228 uɬ ilíʔ kɬlatápəlx 229 waẏ ixíʔ ilíʔ
iʔ ksc -ʔiɬn -s -lx uɬ ilíʔ kɬ+latáp -lx waẏ ixíʔ ilíʔ
art futPerfi -eat -3i -pl and there have_table -pl well then there
is steaming. *There is a table there.* *She put it down*

kɬcəqɬtíməlx {iʔ} 230 ixíʔ utxítməlx {t kɬ kɬənʔiɬ} ilíʔ kɬənʔíɬəntən
kɬ+cq -ɬt -im -lx ixíʔ wt -xit -m -lx ilíʔ kɬ+n+ʔiɬn+tn
put_st_on -ɬt -psv -pl then put_down -xit -psv -pl there have_dish
on the table. *She went got ...; there were dishes there.*

231 cúntəm waẏ uɬ p ʔaɬʔíɬən 232 waẏ ʔaɬʔíɬnəlx, wiʔwiʔcínəlx
cu -nt -m waẏ uɬ p ʔaɬ•ʔíɬn waẏ ʔaɬ•ʔíɬn -lx wẏ•wẏ=cin -lx
tell -nt -psv well and 5kn eat_pl well eat_pl -pl finish_eating_pl -pl
She said to them, "Eat." *They ate, they got done eating.*

233 waẏ {ɬ} ɬkəm̓ntís axáʔ {i} ya nʔíɬəntənsəlx 234 waẏ {inaud}
waẏ ɬ+km̓ -nt -is axáʔ ya n+ʔiɬn+tn -s -lx waẏ
well take_back -nt -3erg this art dish -3in -pl well
She took back their plates [tape ends]. 25:52 *She*

ḱɬəncʔípntməlx 235 waẏ cúsəlx waẏ cənʔúɬxʷəxʷ
ḱɬ+n+cʔ=ip -nt -m -lx waẏ cu -s -lx waẏ c+n+ʔuɬxʷ -xʷ
knock_on_door -nt -psv -pl well tell -3erg -pl well enter_cisl -isimptv
knocked on the door. *They told her, "Come in."*

3 Pete interjects, in English: "That means he looked at his picture and I guess that girl, or woman, young woman, looks the picture, looks like it's her picture, that's who he was looking for."

236 waẏ {cən?úɬxʷ} cən?úɬxʷməntməlx axá? i? t tkəɬmílxʷ
waẏ c+n+?uɬxʷ+m -nt -m -lx axá? i? t tkɬ+m=ilxʷ
well enter_st -nt -psv -pl this art agInst woman
The woman came in to them.

237 cúntməlx waẏ {ki ?ax̌i} kən ksxʷúya?x i?
cu -nt -m -lx waẏ kn ks -xʷuy -a?x i?
tell -nt -psv -pl well 1kn incp^ -go -^incp art
She said "I am going there

k̓əl kscyaʕmíxa?x k̓əl ksq̓ʷəẏməncúta?x 238 ik̓lí? kʷu
k̓l ksc -yaʕ -míx+a?x k̓l ks -q̓ʷẏ+mncut -a?x ik̓lí? kʷu
to futPerfkn^ -gather -^futPerfkn to incp^ -dance -^incp there 1kʷu
to the gathering, to the dance. *They*

sx̌lítəmsəlx 239 uɬ aɬí? t̓i? kən sknaqsx uɬ
s -x̌lit+m -s -lx uɬ aɬí? t̓i? kn s -k=naqs -x uɬ
intt -summon -3i -pl and because evid 1kn ipftv^ -one_person -^ipftv and
invite me to go there; *and I am alone and then I might*

axá? cəm̓ səl̓mín inlaklí 240 uɬ waẏ axá? {kʷi} kʷu
axá? cm̓ sl̓+mi -n in -laklí uɬ waẏ axá? kʷu
this maybe lose -1erg 1in -lock and well this 1kʷu
lose my key. *And I want you*

akstxət̓ɬtím inlaklí axá? {il} i? l citxʷ 241 cəm̓
a -ks -t+xt̓ -ɬt -im in -laklí axá? i? l citxʷ cm̓
2i -futi -watch_so -ɬt -apsv 1in -lock this art in house maybe
to take care of my key to the house, *I might*

səl̓mín uɬ aɬí? {kən c̓xʷnxkistəl} 242 cəm̓ t̓əxʷ pútəm {k}
sl̓+mi -n uɬ aɬí? cm̓ t̓xʷ put+m
lose -1erg and so maybe emph just
lose it, *and I might have*

k̓ɬənmáʕwpən ink̓ɬənk̓míp mi kən n?aɬxʷíɬxʷ {cus} 243 cus waẏ
k̓ɬ+n+maʕʷ=p -n in -k̓ɬ+n+k̓m=ip mi kn n+?aɬxʷ=íɬxʷ cu -s waẏ
break_door -1erg 1in -door fut 1kn enter_house tell -3erg well
to break my door before I can get in the house." 1:05 *He said to her,*

t̓əxʷ ixí? ik̓lí? i? k̓əl {səl} i? l latáp ilí? t̓əxʷ kɬt̓k̓ʷntíxʷ
t̓xʷ ixí? ik̓lí? i? k̓l i? l latáp ilí? t̓xʷ kɬ+t̓k̓ʷ -nt -ikʷ
evidently that there art to art on table there emph put_st_down -nt -imptv
"There, put it there on the table."

244 nstils axá? i? tkəɬmílxʷ uɬ ha sc̓kinx ha, {a kʷuks} 245 kʷu
n+st=ils axá? i? tkɬ+m=ilxʷ uɬ ha? sc+?kin+x ha? kʷu
think this art woman and inter why_is_it inter 1obj
The woman thought, "What's the matter? *When*

kskʷumɬts ki? ktəlməntúɬtən 246 náx̌əmɬ {a} ilí? i?
ks -kʷum -ɬt -s ki? k+tl+mn -tuɬt -n nax̌mɬ ilí? i?
futt^ -store -ɬt -3erg rel put_in_custody_of -tuɬt -1erg but there art
I ask him to take care of it for me he should put it away. *And it's*

l latáp məɬ ckɬťáƙʷ {ɬťəƙʷ} 247 waẏ ilíʔ kɬťƙʷəntís, waẏ
l latáp mɬ c -kɬ+ťaƙʷ waẏ ilíʔ kɬ+ťƙʷ -nt -is waẏ
on table and hab -lie_on well there put_st_down -nt -3erg well
there on the table." *She put it down there,*

sʔácqaʔs 248 cut waẏ ṅíṅẇiʔ cəṁ ƙəl {unfin} 249 x̌lap
s -ʔácqaʔ -s cut waẏ ṅíṅẇiʔ cṁ ƙl x̌la+p
nom -go_out -3i say well a_while maybe to tomorrow
and she went out. *She said: 2:03* *"Tomorrow*

siɬkʷkʷáʕst mi kən ɬckicx mi ɬx̌lítɬtsən inlaklí
syɬ+kʷ•kʷ=ʕast mi kn ɬ+c+kic+x mi ɬ+x̌lit -ɬt -s -n in -laklí
early_morning fut 1kn arrive_cisl_again fut summon_again -ɬt -2obj -1erg 1in -key
morning I'll come back and ask you for the key."

250 waẏ xiʔmíx 251 waẏ sʔácqaʔs 252 ixíʔ sic cúntəm
waẏ xiʔ+míx waẏ s -ʔácqaʔ -s ixíʔ sic cu -nt -m
yes whayever well nom -go_out -3i then then tell -nt -psv
"Any time." *She went out.* *Then his little brother said*

axáʔ iʔ t ɬsísəncaʔs 253 cúntəm waẏ ixíʔ
axáʔ iʔ t ɬ+sí•sncaʔ -s cu -nt -m waẏ ixíʔ
this art agInst younger_bro -3in tell -nt -psv well that
to him, *he said to him,*

nʔaɬnaʔsqílxʷtən {ixíʔ} ixíʔ iʔ tkəɬmílxʷ 254 ixíʔ ʕ̓áċənt {a} 255 cəṁ
n+ʔaɬn+aʔ+s+qílxʷ+tn ixíʔ iʔ tkɬ+m=ilxʷ ixíʔ ʕaċ -nt cṁ
man_eater that art woman that look_at -nt maybe
"That woman is a man-eater. *Look here.* *When*

ixíʔ {ɬ··} ɬpaʔsəsmís uɬ ťiʔ ɬƙaw ixíʔ laklíʔ 256 ʕáċənt waẏ
ixíʔ ɬ+paʔs•s+mí -s uɬ ťiʔ ɬ+ƙaw ixíʔ laklí ʕaċ -nt waẏ
then wish_back -3erg and evid gone_again that key look_at -nt yes
she'll have wished it back, the key'll be gone. *Look,*

uníxʷ ťiʔ ɬƙaw 257 uɬ ʕáċəs iʔ l[aklí], waẏ uníxʷ ťiʔ ƙaw
wnixʷ ťiʔ ɬ+ƙaw uɬ ʕaċ -s iʔ laklí waẏ wnixʷ ťiʔ ƙaw
true evid gone_again and look_at -3erg art key yes true evid gone
it's really gone." *He looked at the [key], and sure enough,*

iʔ lak[lí] 258 cus waẏ, waẏ ƙaw, waẏ {ɬ} səľmín 259 waẏ
iʔ laklí cu -s waẏ waẏ ƙaw waẏ sľ+mi -n waẏ
art key tell -3erg well well gone yes lose -1erg well
it's gone. *He told him "Yes, yes, it's gone, I lost it."* *His*

cúntəm axáʔ iʔ t síncaʔs 260 waẏ {ki} ixíʔ
cu -nt -m axáʔ iʔ t síncaʔ -s waẏ ixíʔ
tell -nt -psv this art agInst younger_brother -3in well that
little brother told him: 3:03 *"We'll*

nʔúcxən ɬƛ̓aʔntín, mat lútiʔ {s} sxʷists
n+ʔuc=xn -n ɬ+ƛ̓aʔ -nt -in mat lút+i s -xʷist -s
track -1erg fetch_again -nt -1erg maybe not_yet nom -go -3i
follow her, we'll get it, maybe she hasn't gone yet.

261 ṅíṅẇi? kʷums 262 waẏ ixíxi? ki łckicx axá? i?
ṅíṅẇi? kʷum -s waẏ ix•íxi? ki? ł+c+kic+x axá? i?
a_while store -3erg well in_a_while rel arrive_cisl_again this art
She'll put it away." *In a little while his little brother came back.*

263 cúntəm, cus i? łsísənca?s łsísənca?s, cúntəm
cu -nt -m cu -s i? ł+sí•snca? -s ł+sí•snca? -s cu -nt -m
tell -nt -psv tell -3erg art younger_bro -3in younger_bro -3in tell -nt -psv
He told him, he told his little brother,

i? t łsísənca?s 264 waẏ axá? kʷənnún i? laklí,
i? t ł+sí•snca? -s waẏ axá? kʷn -nu -n i? laklí
art agInst younger_bro -3in well this take -manage -1erg art key
his little brother told him: *"I got the key,*

łkʷənnúłtən 265 waẏ {ł} kʷums {i l} i? l sənkʷúm·əns
ł+kʷn -nu -łt -n waẏ kʷum -s i? l sn+kʷum+n -s
keep_again -manage -łt -1erg well store -3erg art in storage -3in
I got it back. *She put it away where she puts things away.*

266 uł ṅíṅẇi? t incá txəť'ntín 267 ṅíṅẇi?
uł ṅíṅẇi? t in+cá txť -nt -in ṅíṅẇi?
and a_while agInst I watch_so -nt -1erg a_while
I'll take care of it. *Tomorrow*

x̌lap {tk̓əl ə ṅiṅẇí łcə} tk̓əlk̓ələntím waẏ kłəłckícxa?x
x̌la+p t+k̓l•k̓l -nt -im waẏ kł -ł+c+kic+x -a?x
tomorrow expect_so -nt -4erg well incp^ -arrive_cisl_again -^incp
we'll wait for her to come back, 4:05

268 mi {mi ilí? l ilí? kłťk̓ʷəntíxʷ i?} ilí? łkłťk̓ʷəntíxʷ
mi ilí? ł+kł+ťk̓ʷ -nt -ixʷ
fut there put_back_on_st -nt -2erg
and you'll put it back there.

269 ṅíṅẇi? łcən?úłxʷ síwənts, cunts, waẏ inlaklí
ṅíṅẇi? ł+c+n+?ułxʷ siw -nt -s cu -nt -s waẏ in -laklí
a_while come_back_in ask -nt -3e2obj tell -nt -3e2obj well 1in -key
She'll come back in and ask you, 'I'm after

iłəłcƛ̓?ám 270 mi cuntxʷ a, {ťəxʷ la?ki} ƛ̓əm waẏ
i -ł -ł+c+ƛ̓?a+m mi cu -nt -xʷ a ƛ̓m waẏ
1i -intt -cisl_again_fetch fut tell -nt -2erg intj past well
my key.' *You'll tell her, 'Ah, I told you*

cúncən ilí? mi kłťək̓ʷəntíxʷ 271 ťəxʷ ilí? xʷuyx,
cu -nt -s -n ilí? mi kł+ťk̓ʷ -nt -ixʷ ťxʷ ilí? xʷuy -x
tell -nt -2obj -1erg there fut put_st_down -nt -2erg emph there go -isimptv
to put it down there. *Go there,*

ilí? mat ckłťak̓ʷ 272 uł ṅíṅẇi? k̓li? ł wiks i? laklís
ilí? mat c -kł+ťak̓ʷ uł ṅíṅẇi? ik̓lí? ł wik -s i? laklí -s
there must hab -lie_on and a_while there when see -3erg art key -3in
and it must be there.' *When she sees the key*

ilíʔ ckɬt'ak̓ʷ 273 uɬ cəm̓, cəm̓ məɬ t'iʔ paʕs 274 lut_pəňkíň aɬíʔ
ilíʔ c uɬ cm̓ cm̓ mɬ t'iʔ paʕs lut_pn+ʔkiň aɬíʔ
there hab and maybe maybe and evid surprised never so
lying there *she'll be surprised;* *never has*

swit {t'a c} t'a ɬckʷíɬtəm ɬaʔ ɬckʷumsts {ɬaʔ ɬc}
swit t' ɬ+c+kʷi -ɬt -m ɬaʔ ɬ+c+kʷum -st -s
anybody evid take_back_cisl -ɬt -psv then store_again_cisl -st -3erg
anyone taken it back when she puts it away."

275 way̓ {k̓a··w ah} ixíʔ púlxəlx 276 cáʕʷlxəlx, wiʔscáʕʷlxəlx way̓
way̓ ixíʔ pul+x -lx caʕʷ+lx -lx wy̓+s+caʕʷ+lx -lx way̓
well then camp -pl bathe -pl finish_bathing -pl well
They went to bed. 5:01 *Ah, they took a bath, finished,*

púlxəlx 277 uɬ aɬíʔ sʔayʔáyx̌ʷtxəlx, ʔatxílxəlx
pul+x -lx uɬ aɬíʔ s -ʔay•ʔáyx̌ʷt -x -lx ʔatx+ílx -lx
camp -pl and because ipftv^ -tired_pl -^ipftv -pl sleep_pl -pl
went to bed. *They are tired, they went to sleep.*

278 way̓ t'iʔ {k̓əl ks} k̓əl ksx̌lap, way̓ k̓əl ksxəƛ̓púlaʔxʷs
way̓ t'iʔ k̓l k+s+x̌la+p way̓ k̓l k -s+xƛ̓+p=úlaʔxʷ -s
well evid about towards_daylight well about to_be -full_daylight -3i
Towards daylight, when it's daylight all over

279 ixíʔ ncaʔlqsíkstməntəm aɬíʔ ɬəq̓lílxəlx iʔ naʔɬ ɬsísəncaʔs
ixíʔ n+caʔ=lqs=íkst+m -nt -m aɬíʔ ɬq̓+lilx -lx iʔ naʔɬ ɬ+sí•sncaʔ -s
then elbow_so -nt -psv because in_bed_pl -pl art with younger_bro -3in
he elbowed him, because he went to bed with his little brother.

280 ncaʔlqsíkstməntəm iʔ t ɬsísəncaʔs 281 cúntəm, a,
n+caʔ=lqs=íkst+m -nt -m iʔ t ɬ+sí•sncaʔ -s cu -nt -m a
elbow_so -nt -psv art agInst younger_bro -3in tell -nt -psv intj
His little brother elbowed him; *he said to him,*

qiɬtx {iʔ} way̓, kʷintxʷ axáʔ iʔ laklí 282 mi k̓liʔ
qiɬt -x way̓ kʷi -nt -xʷ axáʔ iʔ laklí mi ik̓líʔ
awaken -isimptv well take -nt -2erg this art key fut there
"Ah, wake up, take the key; *put it back*

ɬkɬt'ək̓ʷntíxʷ ilíʔ 283 way̓ kʷu k̓əɬx̌əlx̌láp {inaud} way̓
ɬ+kɬ+t'k̓ʷ -nt -ixʷ ilíʔ way̓ kʷu k̓ɬ+x̌l•x̌la+p way̓
put_back_on_st -nt -2erg there well 4kn daylight well
down there. *It's daylight, she's about*

cxʔal 284 way̓ ilíʔ ɬkɬt'ək̓ʷntís iʔ laklí 285 i·
c -x[ʔ]al way̓ ilíʔ ɬ+kɬ+t'k̓ʷ -nt -is iʔ laklí i·
hab -appear_inch well there put_back_on_st -nt -3erg art key intj
to show up." *He put the key there;* *they*

skc̓awʔíw̓səmsəlx {uɬ way̓ kəl kslapay} kc̓awʔíw̓sməlx, 286 way̓
s -k+c̓aw̓=íw̓s+m -s -lx k+c̓aw̓=íw̓s+m -lx way̓
nom -wash_face -3i -pl wash_face -pl well
started washing their faces, 6:01 *they*

wiʔskc̓awʔíw̓smǝlx, txtxámǝlx 287 way̓ uɬ kʷm̓iɬ kiʔ
wy̓+s+k+c̓aw̓=íw̓s+m -lx tx•txa+m -lx way̓ uɬ kʷm̓iɬ kiʔ
finish_wash -pl comb_pl -pl well and suddenly rel
washed, they combed their hair. *All of a sudden*

ɬk̓ɬǝnciʔípǝntmǝlx iʔ la ɬxǝƛ̓púlaʔxʷ 288 way̓
ɬ+k̓ɬ+n+ciʔ=íp -nt -m -lx iʔ l ɬ+xƛ̓+p=úlaʔxʷ way̓
knock_on_door_again -nt -psv -pl art at daylight_again well
somebody knocked in the daylight. *They*

k̓ɬǝnk̓ahk̓ʷípɬtsǝlx, way̓ {cǝn} cǝnʔúɬxʷ 289 cut way̓ i laklí
k̓ɬ+n+k̓ahk̓ʷ=íp -ɬt -s -lx way̓ c+n+ʔuɬxʷ cut way̓ iʔ laklí
open -ɬt -3erg -pl well enter_cisl say well art key
opened the door for her, she came in. *She said,*

iɬǝɬƛ̓ʔám, way̓ kǝn ɬckicx 290 cúntǝm axáʔ {iʔ t} iʔ
i -ɬ -ɬ+ƛ̓ʔa+m way̓ kn ɬ+c+kic+x cu -nt -m axáʔ iʔ
1i -intt -fetch_again yes 1kn arrive_cisl_again tell -nt -psv this art
"I am after the key, I came back." *The grown boy*

t ƛ̓x̌ap, axáʔ t̓ǝxʷ iʔ t tǝtwít, a, kway̓
t ƛ̓x̌a+p axáʔ t̓xʷ iʔ t t•tw̓it a k+way̓
agInst grow_sg this evidently art agInst boy intj yes
said to her, "Ah,

291 cúntsǝn ilíʔ mi kɬt̓ǝk̓ʷntíxʷ, ilíʔ t̓ǝxʷ mat
cu -nt -s -n ilíʔ mi kɬ+t̓k̓ʷ -nt -ixʷ ilíʔ t̓xʷ mat
tell -nt -2obj -1erg there fut put_st_down -nt -2erg there evidently must
I told you to put it there, I guess it's

ckɬt̓ak̓ʷ 292 xʷuyx ik̓líʔ, ƛ̓aʔƛ̓ʔúsmǝntxʷ 293 way̓ cǝnʔúɬxʷ,
c -kɬ+t̓ak̓ʷ xʷuy -x ik̓líʔ ƛ̓aʔ•ƛ̓ʔ=ús+m -nt -xʷ way̓ c+n+ʔuɬxʷ
hab -lie_on go -isimptv there look_for -nt -2erg well enter_cisl
there. *Go there, go look for it."* *She went*

ik̓líʔ xʷuy 294 ilíʔ kɬt̓k̓ʷǝntís, way̓ ilíʔ ckɬt̓ák̓ʷ a[xáʔ] iʔ
ik̓líʔ xʷuy ilíʔ kɬ+t̓k̓ʷ -nt -is way̓ ilíʔ c -kɬ+t̓ak̓ʷ axáʔ iʔ
there go there put_st_down -nt -3erg yes there hab -lie_on this art
in there. *Where she had put it down, the key was lying*

laklí 295 nt̓a·· t̓iʔ paʕs axáʔ iʔ tkǝɬmílxʷ 296 ckʷis iʔ
laklí nt̓a t̓iʔ paʕs axáʔ iʔ tkɬ+m=ilxʷ c+kʷi -s iʔ laklí
key intj evid surprised this art woman take -3erg art key
there. *The woman was sure surprised.* *She took the key.*

297 t̓a lut_xʷuy_pǝnkíń iʔ t sqilxʷ ilíʔ t̓a c̓x̌ílstǝm,
nt̓a lut_xʷuy_pn+ʔkiń iʔ t s+qilxʷ ilíʔ t̓ c -ʔx̌il -st -m
intj never art agInst person there evid cust^ -do_like -^cust -psv
Nobody ever had done that to her,

way̓ lut 298 uɬ aɬíʔ kʷums, ɬpaʔsmís uɬ {ɬ əɬkʷ} ɬkʷis
way̓ lut uɬ aɬíʔ kʷum -s ɬ+paʔs+mí -s uɬ ɬ+kʷi -s
yes not and so store -3erg wish_back -3erg and take_again -3erg
no. 7:01 *She had put it away, she had got it back with a wish,*[4] *she had taken*

iʔ laklís uɬ iʔ txʷəm̓qəncút 299 way̓ {ɬkəl} ɬkʷis iʔ laklís,
iʔ laklí -s uɬ iʔ t+xʷm̓=qn+cut way̓ ɬ+kʷi -s iʔ laklí -s
art key -3in and art forget well take_again -3erg art key -3in
the key and forgotten about it. *She took her key back and*

way̓ ɬəɬʔácqaʔs {cus} 300 cúntəm way̓ uɬ ixíʔ k̓ʷúl̓cɬmən
way̓ ɬ -ɬ+ʔácqaʔ -s cu -nt -m way̓ uɬ ixíʔ k̓ʷul̓=c -ɬm -n
well nom -go_out_again -3i tell -nt -psv well and then cook -5obj -1erg
went back out. *She said to them, "I'm going to cook for you*

n̓ín̓w̓iʔ 301 kʷ wiʔwiʔcín məɬ sic, {a''} mi_sic incá {kən} kən ʔitx
n̓ín̓w̓iʔ kʷ wy̓•wy̓=cin mɬ sic mi_sic in+cá kn ʔitx
a_while 2kn finish_eating_pl and then then I 1kn sleep
in a while. *When you are done with your eating then I'll take my nap*

302 way̓ aɬíʔ uɬ kən {sc} scx̌əlpmíx iʔ k̓əl
way̓ aɬíʔ uɬ kn sc -x̌l+p -mix iʔ k̓l
well because and 1kn ipftvp^ -daylight -^ipftvp art at
because I was out at the dance all night,

scq̓ʷəy̓məncútx, lut isʔítx 303 cúsəlx {uɬ uɬ ə}
sc -q̓ʷy̓+mncut -x lut i -s -ʔitx cu -s -lx
ipftvp^ -dance -^ipftvp not 1i -nom -sleep tell -3erg -pl
I haven't slept yet." *She said to them,*

cúntməlx, lut ksk̓əɬpaʔsəncútəmp pna p ʔayʔáyx̌ʷt
cu -nt -m -lx lut ks -k̓ɬ+paʔs+ncút -mp pnaʔ p ʔay•ʔáyx̌ʷ+t
tell -nt -psv -pl not futi -worried -5i maybe 5kn tired_pl
"Don't be backwards; you are tired. 8:01

304 {way̓ t̓əxʷ} way̓ p pulx l ʔaslásq̓ət 305 p ɬaʔɬaʔxʷísk̓it mi
way̓ p pul+x l ʔasl=ásq̓t p ɬaʔ•ɬaʔxʷ=ísk̓it mi
well 5kn overnight for two_days 5kn rested fut
Stay here two nights; *get rested and then*

tliʔ p xʷuy k̓aʔkín̓ p scxʷuyx 306 lut
itlíʔ p xʷuy k̓a+ʔkín̓ p sc -xʷuy -x lut
from_there 5kn go where_to 5kn ipftvp^ -go -^ipftvp not
continue your trip. *Don't*

ksk̓əɬpaʔsəncútəmp, way̓ ixíʔ axáʔ cítxʷəmp, aláʔ p aláʔ 307 way̓ aláʔ
ks -k̓ɬ+paʔs+ncút -mp way̓ ixíʔ axáʔ citxʷ -mp aláʔ p aláʔ way̓ aláʔ
futi -worried -5i yes that this house -5in here 5kn here well here
be backwards, this is your house, you can stay here. *You can*

4 The key had magically returned to her.

ta p takʷʔút {unint isnilíʔtn} 308 uɬ aɬíʔ incá waẏ kən ksʔítxaʔx
ʔ p takʷʔ=út uɬ aɬíʔ in+cá waẏ kn ks -ʔitx -aʔx
ʔ 5kn walk_pl and so I yes 1kn incp^ -sleep -^incp
walk around. *I am going to bed, I'm going to*

kən ksɬáxʷsk̓ita?x 309 uɬ lut {p t̓ iks} kʷu t̓ ksx̌áq̓əntp
kn ks -ɬáʔxʷ=sk̓it -aʔx uɬ lut kʷu t̓ ks -x̌aq̓ -nt -p
1kn incp^ -rest -^incp and not 1obj negfac futt^ -pay -nt -5erg
take a rest. *You don't have to pay me.*

310 uɬ waẏ ixíʔ {kʷu kʷu} kʷu x̌áq̓əntp úɬiʔ {kʷu c lu} kʷu
uɬ waẏ ixíʔ kʷu x̌aq̓ -nt -p uɬ iʔ kʷu
and yes that 1obj pay -nt -5erg and_then 1obj
You have already paid me, you took care

txət̓ɬtíp inlaklí 311 uɬ ṅíṅẉiʔ pnaʔ nixʷ {t k} ixíʔ waẏ put
t+xt̓ -ɬt -ip in -laklí uɬ ṅíṅẉiʔ pnaʔ nixʷ ixíʔ waẏ put
watch_so -ɬt -5erg 1in -key and a_while maybe also that yes just
of my key. 9:08 *It's just like you are working for*

ċx̌iɬ {p s} p sck̓ʷúl̓x [s]cənk̓ʷúl̓səmp aláʔ iʔ scaláʔmp
c+ʔx̌iɬ p sc -k̓ʷul̓ -x sc -n+k̓ʷul̓=s -mp aláʔ iʔ sc -aláʔ -mp
like 5kn ipftvp^ -work -^ipftvp *pftv* -work -5i here art pftv -here -5i
your board and room."

312 cut waẏ, waẏ ɬʔácqaʔ, ayxáxaʔ {ɬc} ɬcənʔúɬxʷ 313 nt̓a paʕs
cut waẏ waẏ ɬ+ʔácqaʔ ʔayxá+xaʔ ɬ+c+n+ʔuɬxʷ nt̓a paʕs
say yes well go_out_again a_while come_back_in intj surprised
She said, she went back out, a little while she came back in. *The woman*

axáʔ iʔ tkəɬmílxʷ 314 nt̓a·· nstils, nt̓a waẏ waẏ waẏ mat yaʕʷpyáẉt
axáʔ iʔ tkɬ+m=ilxʷ nt̓a n+st=ils nt̓a waẏ waẏ waẏ mat yaw+p+yáʕʷ+t
this art woman intj think intj yes yes yes must powerful
was surprised. *She thought, "Gee, that man must be*

axáʔ iʔ sqəltmíxʷ {uɬ aɬ} 315 lut̓_xʷu··y, kʷaʔ swit {iʔ kʷu t̓aɬc} kʷu t̓a
axáʔ iʔ s+qlt=mixʷ lut_t̓_xʷuy kʷaʔ swit kʷu t̓
this art man never intj anybody 1obj negfac
really smart. *It never happened that anybody could take care of*

ɬctxət̓t̓núɬts inlaklí inlaklí 316 uɬ cniɬc
ɬ+c+t+xt̓•t̓[5] -nu -ɬt -s in -laklí in uɬ cniɬ+c
take_care_of_again -manage -ɬt -3erg 1in -key 1in and (s)he
my key. *And*

waẏ {kʷu aɬ unfin} 317 ilíʔ kɬt̓ək̓ʷəntín uɬ ƛ̓əm paʔsmín
waẏ ilíʔ kɬ+t̓k̓ʷ -nt -in uɬ ƛ̓m paʔs+mí -n
yes there put_st_down -nt -1erg and past think_about -1erg
he... *I put it down there, and I got it back with my wishing,*

5 This form forces the analysis of c- as *cisl*, or ?.

uɬ {ɬ ɬ} kʷu ɬcənkcníki?[ɬt]s inlaklí 318 úɬi? kʷúmən i
uɬ kʷu ɬ+c+n+kcn=íki? -ɬt -s in -laklí uɬ i? kʷum -n i?
and 1obj overtake_cisl_again -ɬt -3erg 1in -key and_then store -1erg art
and he overtook the key. *And I had put it away*

l inlkasát i? kʷúmən 319 nstils axá? ia n?aɬna?sqílxʷtən i?
l in -lkasát i? kʷum -n n+st=ils axá? i? n+?aɬn+a?+s+qílxʷ+tn i?
in 1in -box art store -1erg think this art man_eater art
in my box." 10:02 *The man-eater, the woman,*

tkəɬmílxʷ 320 waỷ nixʷá ʕapná?, axá? i l k̓laxʷ ṅíṅẇi? 321 ixí? {mi}
tkɬ+m=ilxʷ waỷ nixʷ+á ʕapná? axá? i? l k̓laxʷ ṅíṅẇi? ixí?
woman well also_not now this art in evening a_while that
thought, *"Well, not this time, this evening.* *I'm*

mi ƛ̓xʷupən lut kʷu t̓ kska?kícɬtsəlx {il} iksktíləm
mi ƛ̓xʷu+p -n lut kʷu t̓ ks -ka?•kíc -ɬt -s -lx i -ks -k+til+m
fut win -1erg not 1obj negfac futt^ -find -ɬt -3erg -pl 1i -futi -entrust
going to win, they're not going to find what I'll give them to keep."

322 waỷ k̓ʷúl̓cəntməlx 323 waỷ p̓i?qíltən, ṅíṅẇi?
waỷ k̓ʷul̓=cn -t -m -lx waỷ p̓ỷq=ilt+n ṅíṅẇi?
well cook -nt -psv -pl well cook a_while
She cooked for them. *She cooked, she took*

ɬən?akʷcíntəm 324 uɬ lut t̓a cx̌lítɬtməlx i? k̓əl
ɬ+n+?akʷ=cín -t -m uɬ lut t̓ c -x̌lit -ɬt -m -lx i? k̓l
bring_in_food_again -nt -psv and not negfac act -call -ɬt -psv -pl art to
the food back. *She didn't ask them to*

citxʷs, {t̓a c} t̓a cwíkɬts ixí? i? citxʷs {ta} 325 waỷ ixí?
citxʷ -s t̓ c -wik -ɬt -s ixí? i? citxʷ -s waỷ ixí?
house -3in negfac act -see -ɬt -3erg that art house -3in well that
the house, they hadn't seen her house. *She*

utxítməlx kɬsəlxítməlx 326 waỷ uɬ ?aɬ?íɬn,
wt -xit -m -lx kɬ+sl -xit -m -lx waỷ uɬ ?aɬ•?íɬn
put_down -xit -psv -pl set_table -xit -psv -pl well and eat_pl
put it down, set the table for them. *They ate, they*

wi?wi?cínəlx {waỷ} 327 waỷ ɬxʷúỷɬtməlx ia n?íɬəntənsəlx {əy uɬ}
wỷ•wỷ=cin -lx waỷ ɬ+xʷuy -ɬt -m -lx i? n+?iɬn+tn -s -lx
finish_eating_pl -pl well take_back -ɬt -psv -pl art dish -3in -pl
got done eating. 11:02 *She took the dishes back.*

328 ayxáxa? uɬ cnu?ís 329 cúntəm axá? i? t
?ayxá•xa? uɬ c -n+w[?]is cu -nt -m axá? i? t
a_while and hab -rise tell -nt -psv this art agInst
In a while the sun came up. *His little brother said,*

ɬsísənca?s, hahúy, hoy q̓ʷíɬmi?stx 330 hahúy {kʷu s} kʷu
ɬ+sí•snca? -s hu+húy hoy q̓ʷíɬ+mi?st -x hu+húy kʷu
younger_bro -3in OK well do_prowess -isimptv OK 4kn
"Ok, do something smart. *Let's get*

stxʷəlscútx {ay} 331 ha kʷ kɬṅíṅk̓mən 332 cut axáʔ {iʔ} iʔ
s -txʷ=lscut -x haʔ kʷ kɬ+ṅi•ṅk̓+m̓ṅ cut axáʔ iʔ
ipftv^ -get_ready -^ipftv inter 2kn have_knife say this art
something to fight with. *Do you have a knife?"* The old one

sxʔitx, waẏ kən kɬṅíṅk̓mən 333 cut waẏ ha x̌ʷəyx̌ʷáyt 334 ki, t̓əxʷ
s+xʔit=x waẏ kn kɬ+ṅi•ṅk̓+m̓ṅ cut waẏ haʔ x̌ʷy•x̌ʷay+t kiw t̓xʷ
oldest_one well 1kn have_knife say well inter sharp yes emph
said, "Yes, I have a knife." *He asked, "Is it sharp?"* *"Yes,*

waẏ put x̌ʷəyx̌ʷáyt 335 ha kʷu ksc̓íqʷaʔx ha kʷu
waẏ put x̌ʷy•x̌ʷay+t haʔ kʷu ks -c̓iqʷ -aʔx haʔ kʷu
yes just sharp inter 4kn incp^ -butcher -^incp inter 4kn
sharp enough. *Are we going to butcher, or what*

ksx[kínaʔx] 336 lut, t̓əxʷ kʷu kstxʷəlscútaʔx 337 cúntəm
ks -x+kin -aʔx lut t̓xʷ kʷu ks -t+xʷl=scut -aʔx cu -nt -m
incp^ -do -^incp not emph 4kn incp^ -get_ready -^incp tell -nt -psv
are we going to do?" *"No, we are going to get something." 12:00* *He said*

pna lkʷut iʔ ksxʷúytəntət 338 waẏ stəkʷʔútsəls 339 t̓iʔ
pnaʔ lkʷ=ut iʔ k -sxʷuy+tn -tt waẏ s -tkʷʔ=ut -s -lx t̓iʔ
maybe far art futi -travel -4i well nom -walk_pl -3i -pl evid
to him, "We are going quite a ways." *They started to walk,* *they*

itíʔ uɬ tkʷʔútəlx 340 t̓iʔ_lut səlkʷútsəlx {k̓ɬ} t̓əxʷ
itíʔ uɬ tkʷʔ=ut -lx t̓iʔ_lut s -lkʷ=ut -s -lx t̓xʷ
from_that and walk_pl -pl in_no_time nom -far -3i -pl evidently
walked. *They didn't go far, they got out of sight,*

k̓əlxʷúlaʔxʷəlx uɬ k̓əɬʔíq̓ʷəlx axáʔ iʔ t cɬak 341 lut
k̓lxʷ=úlaʔxʷ -lx uɬ k̓+ɬ[ʔ]iq̓ʷ -lx axáʔ iʔ t c+ɬak lut
disappear -pl and come_in_sight -pl this art obl swamp not
and they came in sight of a swamp. *Not*

səlxʷʔúlaʔxʷs t̓əxʷ {ya} a cɬak 342 waẏ, waẏ ik̓líʔ sxʷúẏsəlx,
slxʷʔ=úlaʔxʷ -s t̓xʷ a c+ɬak waẏ waẏ ik̓líʔ s -xʷuy -s -lx
big_place -3in evidently art swamp well well there nom -go -3i -pl
a big swamp. *They went and got*

waẏ ɬaʔíysləx 343 waẏ {n ə} nɬəxʷtlílxəlx 344 ta¨ {i s} iʔ
waẏ ɬaʔ=íys -lx waẏ n+ɬxʷ+t+lilx -lx nta iʔ
well near_edge -pl well go_in_bush_pl -pl intj art
to the edge. *They walked in the swamp.* *My,*

sxʷaʔxʷʔankíɬp put iʔ sp̓əp̓aʕc̓álqʷəms 345 cúntəm waẏ hoy
s+xʷaʔ•xʷaʔ=nk=íɬp put iʔ s -p̓•p̓aʕc̓=álqʷ+m -s cu -nt -m waẏ hoy
thornbush just art nom -plant_shoots -3i tell -nt -psv well well
the thornbushes, they are just grown. *He said, "Now*

anṅínk̓mən 346 ixíʔ uł {asc nik̓ nik̓} asənx̌cípəm axáʔ iʔ t
an -ṅi•ṅk̓+mn ixíʔ uł a -s -n+x̌c=ip+m axáʔ iʔ t
2in -knife then and 2i -nom -cut_low this art obj_itr
your knife, *start cutting these*

sṗəṗaʕc̓álaʔqʷ iʔ t sxʷaxʷʔankíłp 347 cus uł kstíṁtət
s+ṗ•ṗaʕc̓=álaʔqʷ iʔ t s+xʷaʔ•xʷaʔ=nk=íłp cu -s uł k -s+tiṁ -tt
plant_shoots art obj_itr thorn_bushes tell -3erg and futi -what -4i
thornbush shoots.” 13:03 *He said, “And what are we*

uł ha 348 lut ixíʔ t̓a ck̓ʷúľəms[6] náx̌əmł ha kʷu
uł haʔ lut ixíʔ t̓ ? nax̌mł haʔ kʷu
and inter not that negfac ? but inter 4kn
going to do with them? *Are we going to*

ksk̓ʷəľłcq̓ílnaʔx 349 cúntəm lut, ixíʔ ṅíṅw̓iʔ kłk̓ʷúľməntət
ks -k̓ʷľ+ł+cq̓=iln -aʔx cu -nt -m lut ixíʔ ṅíṅw̓iʔ kł -k̓ʷuľ+mn -tt
incp^ -make_arrows -^incp tell -nt -psv not that a_while to_be -tool -4i
make arrows?” *He told him “No, we got a use for it,*

350 ṅíṅw̓iʔ ṁáyaʔłtsən 351 cúntəm mus, mus kʕacíc̓aʔtən {aks}
ṅíṅw̓iʔ ṁáyaʔ -łt -s -n cu -nt -m mus mus k+ʕac=íc̓aʔ+tn
a_while tell -łt -2obj -1erg tell -nt -psv four four tied_bunches
I'll tell you. *You have to get*

akstxʷəlscút 352 put, put kʷənnúnt[xʷ] {ay} məł lk̓íw̓səntxʷ
a -ks -txʷ=lscut put put kʷn -nu -nt -xʷ mł lk̓=iw̓s -nt -xʷ
2i -futi -get_ready just just take -manage -nt -2erg and bundle -nt -2erg
four bundles, *just as much as you can hold,*

axáʔ iʔ sxʷaʔxʷʔankíłp 353 axáʔ {iʔ aks iʔ aks i} [a]kłtk̓míplaʔt[n] way̓
axáʔ iʔ s+xʷaʔ•xʷaʔ=nk=íłp axáʔ a -kł -t+k̓m=íplaʔ+tn way̓
this art thornbush this 2i -to_be -handle yes
tie these thornbushes. *And where you are going to hold it*

354 ixíʔ náx̌əmł {ə} k̓əłləq̓ləq̓ntíxʷ {i s} iʔ ƛ̓qʷƛ̓qʷúmən 355 uł ałíʔ
ixíʔ nax̌mł k̓ł+lq̓•lq̓ -nt -ixʷ iʔ ƛ̓qʷ•ƛ̓qʷu+mn uł ałíʔ
that but peel_off -nt -2erg art thorns and because
cut the thorns off, *because*

cəṁ anwí kʷ łuʔłuʔwíkst 356 k̓im axáʔ {i s} iʔ smiw̓sálqʷs, 357 ixíʔ
cṁ anwí kʷ łw̓•łw̓=ikst k̓im axáʔ iʔ s+miw̓s=alqʷ -s ixíʔ
maybe you 2kn prick_hands but this art midway -3in then
that will prick your hands. *Halfway the stem.[7]* *Don't*

náx̌əmł ilíʔ kłƛ̓qʷƛ̓qʷúmən lut {aks} iʔ aksk̓əłlq̓lq̓ám
nax̌mł ilíʔ kł+ƛ̓qʷ•ƛ̓qʷu+mn lut iʔ a -ks -kł+lq̓•lq̓a+m
but there have_thorns not art 2i -futi -peel_off
cut the thorns off, leave the thorns on.” 14:05

6 Unclear what Pete meant, or if this is a false start.
7 “Peel the thorns off the bases of the stem where you will be holding them.”

358 łəłənwaʔlílsəms axáʔ {iʔ} iʔ sxʔitx 359 wa𝑦̓, wa𝑦̓ ixíʔ {s··} ixíʔ
ł -ł+n+waʔl=íls+m -s axáʔ iʔ s+xʔit=x wa𝑦̓ wa𝑦̓ ixíʔ ixíʔ
nom -puzzle_again -3i this art oldest_one well well then that
The big one got puzzled again. *He started*

skt̓ípəms 360 kt̓í··pəm uł wa𝑦̓ put, put {kʷə·} kʷənnús məł
s -kt̓=ip+m -s kt̓=ip+m uł wa𝑦̓ put put kʷn -nu -s mł
nom -cut_low -3i cut_low and yes just just take -manage -3erg and
cutting. *He cut until he was holding*

ixíʔ 361 uł ałíʔ axáʔ {łc ck̓əł} ck̓əłləq̓ləq̓stís iʔ tk̓míplaʔ
ixíʔ uł ałíʔ axáʔ c -kł+lq̓•lq̓ -st -is iʔ t+k̓m=íplaʔ
that and so this cust^ -peel_off -^cust -3erg art handle
enough; *and he had been cutting the [thorns off the]*

ckłic̓ksts 362 ih, {k̓əł} wa𝑦̓ txəƛ̓xəƛ̓pnús
c -łic̓=k -st -s ih wa𝑦̓ t+xƛ̓•xƛ̓+p -nu -s
cust^ -cut_off -^cust -3erg intj well complete -manage -3erg
handle. *He got his four*

kmúsc̓aʔ 363 cut wa𝑦̓, wa𝑦̓ uc axáʔ 364 ixíʔ wa𝑦̓ 365 huhúy
k+mús=c̓aʔ cut wa𝑦̓ wa𝑦̓ uc axáʔ ixíʔ wa𝑦̓ hu+húy
four_packages say well well dub this that all OK
bundles. 15:03 *He said, "Is this enough?"* *"Yes, enough.* *Our*

pna kʷu łxʷuy, wa𝑦̓ pna xaʔlsqíłt a ilmíxʷəmtət[8]
pnaʔ kʷu ł+xʷuy wa𝑦̓ pnaʔ xaʔl+s+qíł+t a yl=mixʷ+m -tt
maybe 4kn go_back well maybe near_awake art chief -4in
boss will soon wake up." 16:00

366 wa𝑦̓ łxʷu··ylx łyáʕp̓əlx 367 cúntəm {ə} kʷúməntxʷ, lut
wa𝑦̓ ł+xʷuy -lx ł+yaʕ+p -lx cu -nt -m kʷum -nt -xʷ lut
well go_back -pl arrive_again -pl tell -nt -psv store -nt -2erg not
They went and got back. *He said, "Put it away,*

ksłíq̓ʷts, lut kswíkiʔs axáʔ {iʔ} a ilmíxʷmtət 368 pna
ks -łiq̓ʷ+t -s lut ks -wík 𝑦̓ -s axáʔ a yl=mixʷ+m -tt pnaʔ
futi -appear -3i not fut -see -nt -3erg this art chief -4in maybe
don't let it show, don't let our boss see it. *Maybe*

cəm̓ k̓əłpaʔsəncút {st̓i} 369 cənwaʔlílsəmsts axáʔ iʔ sxʔitx
cm̓ k̓ł+paʔs+ncút c -n+waʔl=íls+m -st -s axáʔ iʔ s+xʔit=x
maybe worried cust^ -puzzle -^cust -3erg this art oldest_one
she'll get wise." *The oldest one keeps getting puzzled.*

370 wa𝑦̓ łyáʕp̓əlx, wa𝑦̓ i[xíʔ] kʷums {skəs} 371 mat t stim̓
wa𝑦̓ ł+yaʕ+p -lx wa𝑦̓ ixíʔ kʷum -s mat t s+tim̓
well arrive_again -pl well then store -3erg maybe agInst something
They got back, and he covered it *with something*

8 Here begins a long pause, with some speaking noises barely audible.

ktpínaʔs lut sɬiq̓ʷts {inaud} k̓a n·qsíɬc̓aʔ 372 way̓ k̓laxʷ {ɬ} way̓
k+tp=ínaʔ -s lut s -ɬiq̓ʷ+t -s k̓ n+nqs=íɬc̓aʔ way̓ k̓laxʷ way̓
cover -3erg not nom -appear -3i to in_other_room well evening well
so it would't show in another room. *In the evening*

ɬʔamtíməlx[9] 373 wiʔwiʔcínəlx uɬ {ə} nc̓íwɬtməlx a
ɬ+ʔam -t -im -lx wy̓•wy̓=cin -lx uɬ n+c̓iw̓ -ɬt -m -lx a
feed_again -nt -psv -pl finish_eating_pl -pl and wash_dishes -ɬt -psv -pl art
she fed them again. 17:01 *They finished eating and she washed*

nʔíɬəntənsəlx 374 way̓ {ɬ} ʔayxáxaʔ ɬckicx
n+ʔiɬn+tn -s -lx way̓ ʔayxáxaʔ ɬ+c+kic+x
dish -a3in -pl well a_while arrive_cisl_again
their dishes. *In a little while*

ɬckícəntməlx 375 cúntəm axáʔ iʔ sxʔitx way̓, way̓ kən
ɬ+c+kic -nt -m -lx cu -nt -m axáʔ iʔ s+xʔit=x way̓ way̓ kn
arrive_cisl_back -nt -psv -pl tell -nt -psv this art oldest_one well well 1kn
she came back. *She told the oldest one,*

kɬəɬk̓áwaʔx 376 way̓ kʷ iksktəlməntúɬtəm axáʔ
kɬ -ɬ+k̓aw -aʔx way̓ kʷ i -ks -k+tl+mn -tuɬt -m axáʔ
incp^ -gone_again -^incp well 2kʷu 1i -futi -put_in_custody_of -tuɬt -apsv this
"I'll be gone again. *I want you to keep this ring*

ink̓np̓qínkst[ən] 377 ixíʔ k̓ʷƛ̓əntís 378 i aɬíʔ axáʔ iʔ kʷkʷr̓íʔt
in -k̓np̓=qin=kst+n ixíʔ k̓ʷƛ̓ -nt -is i aɬíʔ axáʔ iʔ kʷ•kʷr̓iʔ+t
1in -ring then take_off -nt -3erg intj so this art yellow
for me." *She took it off.* *Her ring is*

iʔ k̓ənp̓qínkstəns 379 uɬ ixíʔ mat {a c ə} t̓əxʷ a cp̓ʔaxʷ iʔ
iʔ k̓np̓=qin=kst+n -s uɬ ixíʔ mat t̓xʷ a c -p̓[ʔ]axʷ iʔ
art ring -3in and that maybe evidently art hab -shine art
gold, *and it shines,*

stim̓ mat ɬaʔ c̓úmstsəlx 380 a, *diamond ring*
s+tim̓ mat ɬaʔ c -ʔum -st -s -lx a
whatever maybe the_one_that cust^ -call -^cust -3erg -pl intj
what do they call it, 18:00 *"diamond ring."*

381 ixíʔ a cp̓ʔaxʷ, xʷaʔsənʔíys 382 ńíńw̓iʔ {cəm̓ iʔ} cəm̓ səl̓mín
ixíʔ a c -p̓[ʔ]axʷ xʷaʔ+s+n+ʔíys ńíńw̓iʔ cm̓ sl̓+mi -n
that art hab -shine expensive a_while maybe lose -1erg
It shines, it's valuable. *"I might lose*

axáʔ ink̓ənp̓qínkst[ən] 383 uɬ axáʔ {ik} aláʔ iʔ
axáʔ in -k̓np̓=qin=kst+n uɬ axáʔ aláʔ iʔ
this 1in -ring and this here art
my ring; *I'll have you*

9 The root √ʔmn loses its n before -(n)t in the entire transitive paradigm.

ktəl'məntúłtsən 384 way̓ ṅíṅẇiʔ x̌lap kən
k+tl+mn -tułt -s -n way̓ ṅíṅẇiʔ x̌la+p kn
put_in_custody_of -tułt -2obj -1erg well a_while tomorrow 1kn
keep it. *And tomorrow when I get back*

łckicx {mi ł} mi kʷu łxʷíċəłtxʷ 385 a, t'əxʷ ilíʔ
ł+c+kic+x mi kʷu ł+xʷiċ -łt -xʷ a t'xʷ ilíʔ
arrive_cisl_again fut 1obj give_again -łt -2erg intj evidently there
you'll give it back to me." *"Put it there*

kt'k̓ʷíẇsənt {iʔ} iʔ l latáp {kł} 386 kəṁ axáʔ {ils} iʔ l sənqpíłċaʔtən {iʔ}
k+t'k̓ʷ=iẇs -nt iʔ l latáp kṁ axáʔ iʔ l s+n+qp=íłċaʔ+tn
place_on_st -nt art on table or this art on cupboard
on the table, *or in the cupboard."*

387 way̓ ixíʔ ilíʔ kt'k̓ʷíẇsəs axáʔ iʔ tkəłmílxʷ 388 k̓ʷƛ̓əntís
way̓ ixíʔ ilíʔ k+t'k̓ʷ=iẇs -s axáʔ iʔ tkł+m=ilxʷ k̓ʷƛ̓ -nt -is
well then there place_on_st -3erg this art woman take_off -nt -3erg
The woman put it down there. *She took it off*

uł ilíʔ kt'k̓ʷíẇsəs 389 i ʔácqaʔ, {əm} t'iʔ ʔácqaʔ łpaʔsmís
uł ilíʔ k+t'k̓ʷ=iẇs -s i ʔácqaʔ t'iʔ ʔácqaʔ ł+paʔs+mí -s
and there place_on_st -3erg intj go_out evid go_out wish_back -3erg
and put it there. *She went out, went out*

iʔ k̓ənṗqínkst[əns] {way̓ ł} 390 way̓ łclaʕʷqínkst 391 ixíʔ
iʔ k̓nṗ=qin=kst+n -s way̓ ł+c+laʕʷ=qín=kst ixíʔ
art ring -3in well fit_back_on_finger then
and wished back her ring. *It was back on her finger. 19:00* *She*

łxʷu··y {łən} łənʔúłxʷ {cus} 392 cúntəm axáʔ, cus iʔ
ł+xʷuy ł+n+ʔułxʷ cu -nt -m axáʔ cu -s iʔ
go_back enter_again tell -nt -psv this tell -3erg art
went back, went back in. *He told his older brother,*

qicks axáʔ iʔ stʔiwtx 393 way̓ ʕapnáʔ mi {kʷu kʷu} kʷu ƛ̓axʷt
qick -s axáʔ iʔ s+tʔiw+t=x way̓ ʕapnáʔ mi kʷu ƛ̓axʷ+t
older_brother -3in this art young_one well now fut 4kn dead_pl
the older one: *"Now we'll be dead if we*

ṅíṅẇiʔ lut łaʔ nk̓ək̓típəntəm 394 way̓ uł ixíʔ nʔúcxn·
ṅíṅẇiʔ lut łaʔ n+k̓•k̓t=ip -nt -m way̓ uł ixíʔ n+ʔuc=xn -n
a_while not if catch_up_with -nt -4erg well and then track -1erg
don't catch up with it. *I'm going to follow her [and see]*

395 ṅíṅẇiʔ łə łckʷíłtən[10] ilíʔ {ili ili iks} iʔ kskʷúmiʔs
ṅíṅẇiʔ ł ł+c+kʷi -łt -n ilíʔ iʔ ks -kʷum y̓ -s
a_while if take_back_cisl -łt -1erg there art fut -store -nt -3erg
if I can get it back from where she's going to store it."

10 MD suggests it should be ł ikscкʷíłtəm.

396 a, waẏ, cúntəm waẏ t̓əxʷ aɬíʔ anwí kʷ sq̓ʷíɬq̓ʷəɬtx
a waẏ cu -nt -m waẏ t̓xʷ aɬíʔ anwí kʷ s -q̓ʷiɬ•q̓ʷɬ+t -x
intj well tell -nt -psv yes emph because you 2kn ipftv^ -strong -^ipftv
He said to him, "Well, you are smart,"

397 cus axáʔ iʔ stʔiwtx
cu -s axáʔ iʔ s+tʔiw+t=x
tell -3erg this art young_one
he told the young one,

398 waẏ cúntəm iʔ t sxʔitx,
waẏ cu -nt -m iʔ t s+xʔit=x
well tell -nt -psv art agInst oldest_one
the oldest one told him,

cus axáʔ iʔ síncaʔs
cu -s axáʔ iʔ síncaʔ -s
tell -3erg this art younger_brother -3in
he told his little brother.

399 waẏ, waẏ ɬʔácqaʔ axáʔ iʔ
waẏ waẏ ɬ+ʔácqaʔ axáʔ iʔ
well well go_out_again this art
The boy, the little fellow,

tətwít iʔ stʔiwtx
t•tẇit iʔ s+tʔiw+t=x
boy art young_one
went out.

400 ʔayxáxaʔ q̓sápiʔ {i ɬci} iʔ ɬcənʔúɬxʷ
ʔayxáxaʔ q̓sápiʔ iʔ ɬ+c+n+ʔuɬxʷ
a_while long_time art come_back_in
In a while after he'd been gone he came back in; 20:03

401 waẏ ɬ t̓əckʷískʷəsts iʔ k̓ənp̓qínk[stən]
waẏ ɬ t̓c -kʷis•kʷs -t -s iʔ k̓np̓=qin=kst+n
well ? habCisl -hold_on_to -st -3erg art ring
he was holding the ring.

402 cut waẏ, cut
cut waẏ cut
say well say
He said,

waẏ iwá miskʷúms, cut a[xáʔ] iʔ l məsmíẇs aɬíʔ mat iʔ citxʷ
waẏ iwá my+s+kʷum -s cut axáʔ iʔ l ms+m=iẇs aɬíʔ mat iʔ citxʷ
well even store_well -3erg say this art in fourth_layer so maybe art house
"She really hid it," he said "in the four(th) floor of the house."

403 uɬ yaʕyáʕt ixíʔ {c ə} nəqsmíẇs uɬ ixíʔ {kɬ} kɬlaklíʔ
uɬ yaʕ•yáʕ+t ixíʔ nqs+m=iẇs uɬ ixíʔ kɬ+laklí
and all that one_layer and that have_key
All of them, the first floor has a key;

404 yaʕyáʕt ixíʔ
yaʕ•yáʕ+t ixíʔ
all that
they are all

cləklaklíʔ uɬ iʔ {k̓la i k̓əl} k̓a nk̓əmkníɬxʷ
c -lk•laklí uɬ iʔ k̓ n+k̓m=kń=iɬxʷ
hab -lock_pl and art to top_of_house
locked to the top of the house.

405 uɬ ilíʔ {ks ksəntəm}
uɬ ilíʔ
and there
And there is a thing

ksəntətəm̓tím̓tən
k+s+n+t•tm̓•tim̓+tn
have_wardrobe
to store things in,

406 axáʔ {iʔ} iʔ *trunk*
axáʔ iʔ
this art
a trunk,

407 uɬ ixíʔ ilíʔ kiʔ
uɬ ixíʔ ilíʔ kiʔ
and that there rel
and that's where

nt̓k̓ʷəntís {iʔ l} axáʔ iʔ k̓ənp̓qínksts
n+t̓k̓ʷ -nt -is axáʔ iʔ k̓np̓=qin=kst -s
put_in -nt -3erg this art ring -3in
she puts her ring.

408 uɬ ixíʔ ɬlaklís {iʔ} iʔ *trunk*
uɬ ixíʔ ɬ+laklí -s iʔ
and then lock_again -3erg art
And she locks the trunk back. 21:01

409 uɬ axáʔ yaʕyáʕt iʔ k̓ɬənk̓m·íp {ɬc} laklís uɬ ɬcəntíkɬ
uɬ axáʔ yaʕ•yáʕ+t iʔ k̓ɬ+n+k̓m•m=ip laklí -s uɬ ɬ+c+n+tikɬ
and this all art doors lock -3erg and come_back_down
She locked all the doors and she went back down.

410 ixíʔ uɬ sic iʔ ʔácqaʔ,
ixíʔ uɬ sic iʔ ʔácqaʔ
then and then art go_out
And then she went back out.

411 ixíʔ {cks} kɬnmusp mat
ixíʔ kɬ+n+mus=p mat
that have_four_doors maybe
That makes four doors, maybe her house

nkaʔɬəlmíẁs iʔ cit[xʷs]
n+kaʔɬl+m=íẁs iʔ citxʷ -s
three_stories art house -3in
has three thicknesses [stories].[11]

412 ixíʔ úɬiʔ nis
ixíʔ uɬ iʔ nis
then and_then sg_gone
And she left.

413 cúntəm waẏ
cu -nt -m waẏ
tell -nt -psv well
She said to him,

axáʔ
axáʔ
this
"Here it is."

414 a cus t'əxʷ ilíʔ, {iʔ l} ilíʔ {ikt} iʔ kt'k̓ʷíẁsəs
a cu -s t'xʷ ilíʔ ilíʔ iʔ k+t'k̓ʷ=iẁs -s
intj tell -3erg evidently there there art place_on_st -3erg
He said to her, "There," and she put it

iʔ l sənqpíɬc̓[aʔtən]
iʔ l s+n+qp=íɬc̓aʔ+tn
art on cupboard
in the cupboard.

415 ilíʔ mi ɬkt'k̓ʷíẁsən[txʷ]
ilíʔ mi ɬ+k+t'k̓ʷ=iẁs -nt -xʷ
there fut put_on_horse_again -nt -2erg
"Put it there."

416 waẏ, waẏ ɬpulx
waẏ waẏ ɬ+pul+x
well well camp_again
They went back to bed.

417 waẏ ksx̌əlpínaʔlx t'əcxʷuẏ sx̌lap waẏ
waẏ k+s+x̌lp=ínaʔ -lx t'c -xʷuy s+x̌la+p waẏ
well have_daylight -pl habCisl -go morning well
When daylight comes, daylight came,

ɬqiɬs {iʔ} iʔ qicks
ɬ+qiɬ -s iʔ qick -s
wake_again -3erg art older_brother -3in
and his older brother woke back up.

418 a··, cúntəm, waẏ
a cu -nt -m waẏ
intj tell -nt -psv well
He said to him,

qiɬtx, waẏ cəm̓ kʷ pənpən·íẁs
qiɬt -x waẏ cm̓ kʷ pn•pnh=iẁs
awaken -isimptv well maybe 2kn get_caught
"Wake up, you might get caught.

419 waẏ cxʔal {iʔ} a ilmíxʷmtət
waẏ c -x[ʔ]al a yl=mixʷ+m -tt
yes hab -appear_cisl art chief -4in
Our boss is coming back." 22:01

420 cúntəm ṅíṅẇiʔ síwənts axáʔ iʔ l k̓ənp̓qínkst[ən]s
cu -nt -m ṅíṅẇiʔ siw -nt -s axáʔ iʔ l k̓np̓=qin=kst+n -s
tell -nt -psv a_while ask -nt -3e2obj this art for ring -3in
He said to him, "When she asks you for her ring

421 mi cuntxʷ waẏ t'əxʷ laʔkíṅ kiʔ waẏ
mi cu -nt -xʷ waẏ t'xʷ la+ʔkíṅ kiʔ waẏ
fut tell -nt -2erg well emph wherever rel well
you'll tell her,

cúntsən, ilíʔ kt'k̓ʷíẁsəntxʷ
cu -nt -s -n ilíʔ k+t'k̓ʷ=iẁs -nt -xʷ
tell -nt -2obj -1erg there place_on_st -nt -2erg
'wherever I said to you to put it,

422 mat ilíʔ ckt'k̓ʷíẁs
mat ilíʔ c -k+t'k̓ʷ=iẁs
must there hab -place_on_st
it must be there.

11 The reference is not clear.

423 lut_swit kʷu t'a ckícstəm 424 uɬ aɬí?
lut_swit kʷu t' c -kic -st -m uɬ aɬí?
nobody 1obj negfac cust^ -reach_st/sb -^cust -psv and so
Nobody gets here to us; *and we*

claklístəm i? citxʷ i? k̓ɬənk̓míp 425 a ik̓lí? axá? {i?} a
c -laklí -st -m i? citxʷ i? k̓ɬ+n+k̓m=ip a ik̓lí? axá? a
cust^ -lock -^cust -4erg art house art door intj there this art
locked the house, the door.'" *The man-eater*

n?aɬna?sqílxʷtən ik̓lí? ɬxʷuy k̓əl snəqpíɬc̓a? ʕác̓əm, ilí··?
n+?aɬn+a?+s+qílxʷ+tn ik̓lí? ɬ+xʷuy k̓l s+n+qp=íɬc̓a? ʕac̓+m ilí?
man_eater there go_back to cupboard look there
went back to the cupboard, she looked,

cktk̓ʷíw̓s {ai} i? k̓ənp̓qínk[stən] 426 nt'a·· t'i? paʕs axá? i? tkəɬmílxʷ
c -k+t'k̓ʷ=iw̓s i? k̓np̓=qin=kst+n nt'a t'i? paʕs axá? i? tkɬ+m=ilxʷ
hab -place_on_st art ring intj evid surprised this art woman
the ring is there. *Gee, the woman is real surprised.*

427 a nstils uɬ nt'a·· way̓ way̓ way̓ mat yaw̓pyáʕʷt 428 way̓
a n+st=ils uɬ nt'a way̓ way̓ way̓ mat yaw+p+yáʕʷ+t way̓
intj think and intj yes yes yes must powerful yes
She thought, "My, he is smart; *he is*

miɬsisyús tl incá 429 way̓ uɬ {kʷu} kʷu ƛ̓xʷups 430 way̓, ixí?
my+ɬ+sy•sy=us tl' in+cá way̓ uɬ kʷu ƛ̓xʷu+p -s way̓ ixí?
smart_comptv than I well and 1obj beat -3erg well that
smarter than I am. 23:00 *He has beaten me."* *She*

ɬloʕ̓ʷəntís {a iɬ} 431 cúntməlx, way̓ ixí? uɬ {əl} p
ɬ+lʕ̓ʷ -nt -is cu -nt -m -lx way̓ ixí? uɬ p
fit_again -nt -3erg tell -nt -psv -pl well then and 5kʷu
put it back on, *she said to them, "I'll*

iɬəɬk̓ʷúl'cnəm 432 ṅíṅwi? p wi?wi?cín {s} mi_sic incá {kən ɬ} kən
i -ɬ -ɬ+k̓ʷul'=cn+m ṅíṅwi? p wy̓•wy̓=cin mi_sic in+cá kn
1i -intt -cook_again a_while 5kn finish_eating_pl then I 1kn
cook for you. *When you are done eating then I will*

pulx {wiskʷ} 433 aɬí? uɬ kən scksx̌əlpmíx 434 way̓ xʷuy̓,
pul+x aɬí? uɬ kn sc -k+s+x̌l+p -mix way̓ xʷuy
overnight because and 1kn ipftvp^ -all_night -^ipftvp well go
go to bed. *I was up all night."* *She*

way̓, way̓ ixí? ɬ?ácqa? 435 ?ayxáxa? {st} aɬí? lut sq̓əq̓sápi?[s], way̓
way̓ way̓ ixí? ɬ+?ácqa? ?ayxáxa? aɬí? lut s -q̓•q̓sápi? -s way̓
well well then go_out_again a_while so not nom -little_while -3i well
went, she went back out. *In a little while, it wasn't very long, it was just a little*

t'i?_?ayxáxa? uɬ {ɬ} ɬckic 436 məɬ way̓ cxʷ?ul i?
t'i?_?ayxáxa? uɬ ɬ+c+kic+x mɬ way̓ c -xʷ[?]ul i?
little_while and arrive_cisl_again and yes hab -steam_inch art
while, she came back. *Their food was all steaming,*

ksc̓íłənsəlx {iʔ} iʔ sənc̓aʔxʷíłc̓aʔ {iʔ iʔ} 437 iʔ *oatmeal* kəm̓ iʔ ʔaʔúsaʔ
ksc -ʔiłn -s -lx iʔ s+n+c̓aʔxʷ=íłc̓aʔ iʔ km̓ iʔ ʔa•ʔús=aʔ
futPerfi -eat -3i -pl art pancake art or art egg
the hot cakes, 24:01 *the oatmeal, or the eggs.*

438 uł ałíʔ mat kł{lektrik}*electricstove* pnicíʔ uł way̓ 439 ałíʔ
uł ałíʔ mat kł pn+icíʔ uł way̓ ałíʔ
and because maybe have_electric_stove at_that_time and well so
I suppose she had electric stove at the time, *she is*

nʔałnaʔsqílxʷ[tən] 440 way̓ cənpəpílxłtməlx iʔ ksc̓íłənsəlx,
n+ʔałn+aʔ+s+qílxʷ+tn way̓ c+n+p•pilx -łt -m -lx iʔ ksc -ʔiłn -s -lx
man_eater well enter_pl_cisl -łt -psv -pl art futPerfi -eat -3i -pl
a man-eater. *She brought their food in,*

way̓ cxʷʔul 441 way̓ ʔałʔí··łnəlx, wiʔwiʔcínəlx 442 way̓
way̓ c -xʷ[ʔ]ul way̓ ʔał•ʔíłn -lx wy̓•wy̓=cin -lx way̓
yes hab -steam_inch well eat_pl -pl finish_eating_pl -pl well
it's steaming. *They ate, they got done eating.* *She*

cúntməlx,a ha way̓ {ha p} pa nqils {unint} iʔ l sc̓ałʔíłnəmp
cu -nt -m -lx haʔ way̓ p nq=ils iʔ l sc -ʔał•ʔíłn -mp
tell -nt -psv -pl inter well 5kn satisfied art with pftv -eat_pl -5i
asked them, "Are you satisfied with what I cooked for you?

443 pna, pna, pnaʔ lut sxʷʔits {ka} ła
pnaʔ pnaʔ pnaʔ lut s -xʷʔi+t -s łaʔ
maybe maybe maybe not nom -enough -3i the_one_who
Maybe I don't cook enough for you,

ck̓ʷúl̓cłmən łaʔ c̓amłúlmən {unint} 444 cútəlx lut, way̓
c -k̓ʷul̓=c -łm -n łaʔ c -ʔam -łulm -n cut -lx lut way̓
act -cook -5obj -1erg the_one_that act -feed -5obj -1erg say -pl not well
don't feed you enough." *They said*

talí {kʷu} kʷu nanaʕnqcín[12] 445 t̓iʔ kʷ scənłmílsəm uł yaʕyáʕt a
taʔlíʔ kʷu na+naʕ•nq=cín t̓iʔ kʷ sc -n+łm=ils+m uł yaʕ•yáʕ+t a
very_much 4kn filled_up evid 2kn ? -be_nice_to and all art
"No, we are plenty filled up. *We don't want to hurt your feelings*

c̓íłstəm uł ałíʔ {łi} 446 kiʔ uł {kłəł k} łkəm̓ntísəlx {iʔ iʔ}
c -ʔił -st -m uł ałíʔ kiʔ uł ł+km̓ -nt -is -lx
cust^ -eat -^cust -4erg and so rel and take_back -nt -3erg -pl
and we eat everything." 25:00 *They picked up*

ia nʔíłəntən[səlx] 447 nwísəlx axáʔ iʔ stʔiwtx kʷniʔútyaʔsts
iʔ n+ʔiłn+tn -s -lx n+wis+lx axáʔ iʔ s+tʔiw+t=x kʷniʔ=útyaʔ -st -s
art dish -3in -pl jump this art young_one grab -st -3erg
their dishes. *The little one jumped up, grabbed*

12 Analysis unclear.

axáʔ {iʔ} iʔ tkəɬmílxʷ 448 cus axáʔ iʔ qick[s] kiṅ {as as}
axáʔ iʔ tkɬ+m=ilxʷ cu -s axáʔ iʔ qick -s ʔkin
this art woman tell -3erg this art older_brother -3in indef
the woman. *He asked his big brother, "Where is the whip*[13]

asyílwiʔ {as} akɬc̓íltən 449 cənppílxstxʷ mi kʷintxʷ
a -s+yílwiʔ a -k -ɬc̓=ilt+n c -n+p•pilx -st -xʷ mi kʷi -nt -xʷ
2in -whip 2i -to_be -whip act -enter_pl -caus -2erg fut take -nt -2erg
you are going to whip with? *Bring them in, and take one, and start*

iʔ naqs məɬ ixíʔ ńíńẃiʔ ixíʔ uɬ ksp̓íc̓aʔntxʷ 450 ńíńẃiʔ put
iʔ naqs mɬ ixíʔ ńíńẃiʔ ixíʔ uɬ k+sp̓=íc̓aʔ -nt -xʷ ńíńẃiʔ put
art one and then a_while then and whip -nt -2erg a_while just
whipping her. *She will say*

tx̌ʔancənmíst 451 ńíńẃiʔ {ńíńẃiʔ t̓əxʷ} ʔanwís nckʷísk̓itəm 452 uɬ
t+x̌ʔan=cn+míst ńíńẃiʔ ʔanwí -s n+ckʷ=ísk̓it+m uɬ
stop_with_words a_while feel -3erg groan and
it's enough; 26:99 *she'll feel it and she'll groan;* *and*

ńíńẃiʔ tx̌ʔancənmíst, ixíʔ mi ciʔstxʷ 453 t̓əxʷ cúntsən
ńíńẃiʔ t+x̌ʔan=cn+míst ixíʔ mi ciʔ -st -xʷ t̓xʷ cu -nt -s -n
a_while stop_with_words then fut stop -st -2erg emph tell -nt -2obj -1erg
she'll say 'enough,' that's when you stop. *I'll tell you*

waẏ ciʔskʷ 454 kʷənmútyaʔsts axáʔ ya nʔaɬnaʔsqílxʷtən axáʔ
waẏ ciʔ -skʷ kʷn+m=útyaʔ -st -s axáʔ ya n+ʔaɬn+aʔ+s+qílxʷ+tn axáʔ
yes stop -tsimptv grab -st -3erg this art man_eater this
'quit.'" *The young fellow grabbed*

iʔ t stʔiwtx {ixíʔ cənpláʔs} 455 waẏ ixí ckʷis axáʔ iʔ,
iʔ t s+tʔiw+t=x waẏ ixíʔ c+kʷi -s axáʔ iʔ
art agInst young_one well then take -3erg this art
the man-eater. *He took*

ckəm̓ntís axáʔ iʔ kmúsc̓aʔs 456 nák̓ʷəm ixíʔ iʔ
c -km̓ -nt -is axáʔ iʔ k+mús=c̓aʔ -s nak̓ʷ+m ixíʔ iʔ
act -take_pl -nt -3rg this art four_packages -3in evid that art
the four bundles, *that's*

kɬc̓íltəns talí {unfin} 457 cúntəm lut {aks} aksənqʷńmínəm
k -ɬc̓=ilt+n -s taʔlíʔ cu -nt -m lut a -ks -n+qʷń+min+m
to_be -whip -3i very_much tell -nt -psv not 2i -futi -pity
his whip. *He told him "Don't take pity on her."*

458 cúntəm nʔaɬnaʔsqílxʷtən 459 ńíńẃiʔ lut ƛ̓xʷúpəntəm, waẏ t̓iʔ
cu -nt -m n+ʔaɬn+aʔ+s+qílxʷ+tn ńíńẃiʔ lut ƛ̓xʷu+p -nt -m waẏ t̓iʔ
tell -nt -psv man_eater a_while not beat -nt -4erg yes evid
He told him, "That's a man-eater. *If we don't defeat her*

13 The thornbush bundles. Lit. "twisted twig(s)."

kʷu λ̓xʷəntím 460 ixíʔ kʷu ksλ̓xʷəntím iʔ
kʷu λ̓xʷ -nt -im ixíʔ kʷu ks -λ̓xʷ -nt -im iʔ
3e4obj kill_many -nt -3e4obj then 3e4obj futtˆ -kill_many -nt -3e4obj art
she'll kill us. *She'll kill us, she's trying*

kʷu a ckswítstəm axáʔ iʔ l k̓ənp̓qínksts
kʷu a c -k+swit -st -m axáʔ iʔ l k̓np̓=qin=kst -s
3e4obj art custˆ -do_one's_best -ˆcust -3e4obj this art with ring -3in
her best to get us with her ring, 27:02

461 uɬ {a} axáʔ iʔ l laklís uɬ axáʔ iʔ l k̓ənp̓qínk[sts] 462 way̓
uɬ axáʔ iʔ l laklí -s uɬ axáʔ iʔ l k̓np̓=qin=kst -s way̓
and this art with key -3in and this art with ring -3in well
with her key and her ring." *He*

ɬc̓əntí··s uɬ axáʔ kɬʔaʔ, axáʔ iʔ knəqsíc̓aʔ 463 uɬ ixíʔ itlíʔ
ɬc̓ -nt -is uɬ axáʔ k+ɬʔ•aʔ axáʔ iʔ k+nqs=íc̓aʔ uɬ ixíʔ itlíʔ
whip -nt -3erg and this next_to this art one_bundle and then from_there
whipped her, and the first bundle got to the end; *and he took*

ckʷis iʔ knəqsíc̓aʔ {uɬ iɬ} 464 way̓ uɬ axáʔ lut {t̓a c} t̓a
c+kʷi -s iʔ k+nqs=íc̓aʔ way̓ uɬ axáʔ lut t̓
take -3erg art one_bundle well and this not negfac
another bundle. *She doesn't*

cənckʷísk̓itəm axáʔ {t} 465 t̓i ckəʕʷyncútmstəm axáʔ {iʔ} iʔ
c -n+ckʷ=ísk̓it+m axáʔ t̓iʔ c -k+ʕʷy+ncut+m -st -m axáʔ iʔ
hab -groan this evid custˆ -laugh_at -ˆcust -psv this art
even groan. *That woman is laughing at them.*

t tkəɬmílxʷ 466 way̓[14] ɬəc̓əntí··s {uɬ uɬ axáʔ kɬa inaud} xíʔ uɬ k̓əslíc̓aʔ {a}
t tkɬ+m=ilxʷ way̓ ɬc̓ -nt -is ixíʔ uɬ k+ʔsl=íc̓aʔ[15]
agInst woman well whip -nt -3erg that and two_bundles
[tape ends] 27:37 *He beat her, and that's the second bundle.*

467 itlíʔ ɬəc̓ntí··s, kʷis {iʔ inaud} iʔ tkaʔɬlíc̓aʔ, ɬəc̓ntí··s
itlíʔ ɬc̓ -nt -is kʷi -s iʔ t+kaʔɬl=íc̓aʔ[16] ɬc̓ -nt -is
from_there whip -nt -3erg take -3erg art three_bundles whip -nt -3erg
He beat her; he took the third bundle, he beat her;

468 uɬ ixíʔ nixʷ c̓sap, way̓ uɬ lut 469 t̓iʔ_kmix
uɬ ixíʔ nixʷ c̓sa+p way̓ uɬ lut t̓iʔ_kmix
and that also gone well and not only
and that's gone too, and no, *she just*

ckʕʷəyncútmstməlx 470 lut t̓a cənckʷísk̓itəm a[xáʔ
c -k+ʕʷy+ncut+m -st -m -lx lut t̓ c -n+ckʷ=ísk̓it+m axáʔ
custˆ -laugh_at -ˆcust -psv -pl not negfac hab -groan this
laughs at them. *The woman doesn't even*

14 Pete starts without ricapitulating or announcing that he is continuing. I did not notice that the microphone was not properly connected, and the tape is of poor quality.
15 k+ is probably a lexical prefix. See also t- in 466.
16 t+ is probably a lexical prefix.

i?] tkəɬmílxʷ 471 waẏ ixí? i? kskmúsċa?s {xi} 472 ixí? uɬ ċsap waẏ
i? tkɬ+m=ilxʷ waẏ ixí? i? k -s+k+mús=ċa? -s ixí? uɬ ċsa+p waẏ
art woman well that art to_be -four_bundles -3i that and gone yes
groan. *That's his fourth one,* *and that's all*

put 473 mat k̓ʷənxíkxtəm {i? t kmus} i? t kmúsċa?s {i? s} i?
put mat k̓ʷn+x=ik -xt -m i? t k+mús=a? -s i?
just maybe do_several_times -xit -psv art agInst four_packages -hab art
gone. *I don't know how many times with*

t ɬċíltəns 474 ixí? ki? nckʷísk̓itəm axá? i? tkəɬmílxʷ 475 waẏ
t ɬċ=ilt+n -s ixí? ki? n+ckʷ=ísk̓it+m axá? i? tkɬ+m=ilxʷ waẏ
agInst whip -hab that rel groan this art woman well
the fourth whip, *and that's when the woman groaned.* *He*

itlí? {lu li} ɬəċəntís, waẏ tx̌a?ncənmíst 476 waẏ ixí? úɬi wíkəm,
itlí? ɬċ -nt -is waẏ t+x̌a?n=cn+míst waẏ ixí? uɬ i? wik+m
from_there whip -nt -3erg well stop_orally well then and_then see
still whipped her; then she tried to stop him. 1:03 *He saw something but*

lut t' kmimipúsəms stim̓ t 477 axá? {təl s} i? tla
lut t' k+my•my+p=us+m -s s+tim̓ t axá? i? tla
not negfac make_out -3erg what obl this art from
he couldn't make out what it was. *It came out from where*

cəɬċstís itlí? {k} ?ácqa? t'i xəp[17] [ɬup] 478 lut t'
c -ɬċ -st -is itlí? ?ácqa? t'i? xp ɬup lut t'
cust^ -whip -^cust -3erg from_there go_out evid suck_in suck_in not negfac
he was hitting, and it was sucked in.[18] *He*

kmimipúsəms stim̓, [ix]í? t'uxʷt[19] 479 waẏ ixí?
k+my•my+p=us+m -s s+tim̓ ixí? t'uxʷt waẏ ixí?
make_out -3erg what then fly well then
couldn't make out what it was, it flew. *The woman*

tx̌a?ncənmístməntəm axá? i? t tkəɬmílxʷ 480 cut {waẏ kʷu} waẏ
t+x̌a?n=cn+míst+m -nt -m axá? i? t tkɬ+m=ilxʷ cut waẏ
stop_orally -nt -psv this art agInst woman say well
tried to stop them. *She said,*

talí kən tkcxils, waẏ {kʷu} kʷu ƛ̓xʷúpəntxʷ 481 a·· ixí?
ta?lí? kn t+kcx=ils waẏ kʷu ƛ̓xʷu+p -nt -xʷ a ixí?
very_much 1kn be_in_pain yes 1obj beat -nt -2erg intj then
"I'm really hurt, you win me." *So*

ci?sts {cus} 482 ixí? uɬ x̌lítəntəm {i? k̓əl} sic i? k̓əl citxʷs,
ci? -st -s ixí? uɬ x̌lit -nt -m sic i? k̓l citxʷ -s
stop -st -3erg then and call -nt -psv then art to house -3in
he stopped. *She asked them to her house,*

17 This form is unclear.
18 Whatever spirit possessed her is now sucked out of her body.
19 The tape recording from here on is of extremely poor quality.

x̌lítəntməlx 483 waẏ ixíʔ s[ic] sxʷúẏysəls, waẏ npəpílxəlx,
x̌lit -nt -m -lx waẏ ixíʔ sic s -xʷuẏ•y -s -lx waẏ n+p•pilx -lx
call -nt -psv -pl well then then nom -go_pl -3i -pl well enter_pl -pl
she asked them. *They went, went in, went*

i·· {s} spúlxsəlx 484 aɬíʔ {m} axáʔm cʕawlx axáʔ iʔ
i·· s -pul+x -s -lx aɬíʔ axáʔ+m caʕʷ+lx axáʔ iʔ
intj nom -overnight -3i -pl so this bathe this art
to bed. *The woman took*

tkəɬmílxʷ {uɬ iɬ} 485 k̓əɬʔaysəlscút, waẏ púlxəlx 486 ixíʔ ɬq̓lílxəlx
tkɬ+m=ilxʷ k̓ɬ+ʔays=lscút waẏ pul+x -lx ixíʔ ɬq̓+lilx -lx
woman change_clothes well camp -pl then in_bed_pl -pl
a bath. *She changed, they went to bed.* *They went to bed,*

axáʔ {i naʔ} iʔ naʔɬ tkəɬmílxʷ {indec} 487 k̓əɬnəqsáċaʔ axáʔm {iʔ} iʔ stʔiwtx
axáʔ iʔ naʔɬ tkɬ+m=ilxʷ k̓ɬ+nqs=áċaʔ axáʔ+m iʔ s+tʔiw+t=x
this art and woman sleep_alone this art young_one
he and the woman. *The little one was under another blanket.*

488 waẏ ixíʔ {ks} ksx̌əlpínaʔlx ixíʔ uɬ aɬíʔ cmrim
waẏ ixíʔ k+s+x̌l+p=ínaʔ -lx ixíʔ uɬ aɬíʔ c -mrim
well then have_daylight -pl then and so hab -marry
The next morning they got married.

489 mrímәntməlx axáʔ iʔ t stʔiwtx 490 cúntəm axáʔ iʔ
mrim -nt -m -lx axáʔ iʔ t s+tʔiw+t=x cu -nt -m axáʔ iʔ
marry -nt -psv -pl this art agInst young_one tell -nt -psv this art
The young one married them. *The little one said,*

t stʔiwtx, {waẏ uɬ} waẏ kaʔkícəntxʷ {iʔ} 491 cúntəm uɬ
t s+tʔiw+t=x waẏ kaʔ•kíc -nt -xʷ cu -nt -m uɬ
agInst young_one well find -nt -2erg tell -nt -psv and
"Well, now you found her." *He asked*

xkistxʷ ask̓əɬq̓əẏncút 492 uɬ lut t̓a cmistís
x+ki -st -xʷ a -s+k̓ɬ+q̓ẏ+ncut uɬ lut t̓ c -my -st -is
do_what -st -2erg 2in -picture and not negfac cust^ -know -^cust -3erg
"What did you do with your picture?" *The young one didn't*

axáʔ iʔ stʔiwtx 493 nstils axáʔ iʔ sxʔitx 494 uɬ lut t̓a
axáʔ iʔ s+tʔiw+t=x n+st=ils axáʔ iʔ s+xʔit=x uɬ lut t̓
this art young_one think this art oldest_one and not negfac
know. *The older one thought:* *"He doesn't know*

cmistís kən ksk̓əɬq̓əẏncút 495 uɬ kiʔ kʷu aɬ
c -my -st -is kn k+s+k̓ɬ+q̓ẏ+ncut uɬ kiʔ kʷu aɬ
cust^ -know -^cust -3erg 1kn have_picture and rel 1obj compl
I have a picture *for him to*

csíwsts 496 uɬ t̓iʔ_kmix incá cmistín a
c -siw -st -s uɬ t̓iʔ_kmix in+cá c -my -st -in a
cust^ -ask -^cust -3erg and only I cust^ -know -^cust -1erg art
ask me about. *Only I know it, and I've been*

cwíkʷstən {uɬ cət} 497 waẏ uɬ axá? i? kʷu aɬ x̌əlítɬts
c -wikʷ -st -n waẏ uɬ axá? i? kʷu aɬ x̌lit -ɬt -s
cust^ -hide -^cust -1erg well and this art 1obj compl call -ɬt -3erg
hiding it. *And for him to ask me..."*

498 waẏ ixí? xʷíċəɬts {i s cus a} 499 waẏ axá? i? cḱəɬḱʷƛ̓álqsəm {waẏ a}
waẏ ixí? xʷiċ -ɬt -s waẏ axá? i? c+ḱɬ+ḱʷƛ̓=alqs+m
well that give -ɬt -3erg well this art take_from_under_clothes_cisl
He gave it to him. *He pulled it from under his clothes.*

500 cúntəm uc ixí? axá? {i?} i? kɬmut axá? {ia} antkəɬmílxʷ 501 uc
cu -nt -m uc ixí? axá? i? kɬ+mut axá? an -tkɬ+m=ilxʷ uc
tell -nt -psv dub that this art sit_on this 2in -woman dub
He asked, "Is this, the one sitting here, your woman? 4:03 *Is*

ixí? axá? i? sḱəɬq̓əẏncúts, uc sċx̌ilx i? sʕaċ[ċəs] 502 cut waẏ
ixí? axá? i? s+ḱɬ+q̓ẏ+ncut -s uc sc+?x̌il+x i? s+ʕaċ•ċ -s cut waẏ
that this art picture -3in dub reason_why art looks -3in say yes
this her picture that looks like her?" *He said yes.*

503 cut uc ixí? a cƛa?ƛa?stíxʷ 504 waẏ, ixí? a
cut uc ixí? a c -ƛa?•ƛa? -st -ixʷ waẏ ixí? a
say dub that art cust^ -look_for -^cust -2erg yes that art
"Is this the one you've been looking for?" *He said, "Yes,*

cƛa?ƛa?stín 505 uɬ lut_pəńkíń t̓a cwikstxʷ
c -ƛa?•ƛa? -st -in uɬ lut_pn+?kiń t̓ c -wik -st -xʷ
cust^ -look_for -^cust -1erg and never negfac cust^ -see -^cust -2erg
that's the one I'm looking for." *"And you hadn't seen this woman*

axá? i? tkəɬmílxʷ 506 waẏ uɬ t̓i?_kmix wíkəntxʷ axá? i? sḱəɬq̓əẏncút
axá? i? tkɬ+m=ilxʷ waẏ uɬ t̓i?_kmix wik -nt -xʷ axá? i? s+ḱɬ+q̓ẏ+ncut
this art woman well and only see -nt -2erg this art picture
before, *you had only seen this picture.*

507 lut t̓a cmistíxʷ swit ɬa? ksḱəɬq̓əẏncút
lut t̓ c -my -st -ixʷ swit ɬa? k+s+ḱɬ+q̓ẏ+ncut
not negfac cust^ -know -^cust -2erg who the_one_that have_picture
You didn't know whose picture it was.

508 uɬ t̓i tańmús uɬ a cƛa?ƛa?stíxʷ 509 cúntəm kʷ
uɬ t̓i? tanḿ=ús uɬ a c -ƛa?•ƛa? -st -ixʷ cu -nt -m kʷ
and evid nothing and art cust^ -look_for -^cust -2erg tell -nt -psv 2kʷu
And you looked for her for nothing." *He told him,*

isənqʷəńmínəm 510 ca?kʷ waẏ kʷ ƛ̓lal, n?aɬna?sqílxʷtən axá? i?
i -s -n+qʷń+min+m ca?kʷ waẏ kʷ ƛ̓l•al n+?aɬn+a?+s+qílxʷ+tn axá? i?
1i -intt -pity should yes 2kn dead man_eater this art
"I pitied you. *You would have been dead, the woman is*

tkəɬmílxʷ 511 uɬ ixí? i? t̓íkḷənts anl?íw i?
tkɬ+m=ilxʷ uɬ ixí? i? t̓ikḷ -nt -s an -l?iw i?
woman and that art grub -nt -3e2obj 2in -m's_father art
a man-eater. *And your father gave you*

sqlaw̓ {iʔ xʷíc̓əɬtxʷ} xʷíc̓xtəms 512 akɬk̓íɬəntən
s+qlaw xʷic̓ -xt -m -s a -kɬ -k+ʔiɬn+tn
money give -xit -2obj -3erg 2i -to_be -food
money *for your eats and*

uɬ {a a la stətəm a··} l akstətəm̓tím̓ kʷ ɬ təmxʷəlscút 513 uɬ
uɬ l a -k -s+t•tm̓•tim̓ kʷ ɬ tmxʷ=lscut uɬ
and for 2i -to_be -clothes 2kn if clothes_wear_out and
for your clothes if you wear them out; *and*

ixíʔ a nqʷən̓míntxʷ iʔ təmtəmníʔ iʔ tx̌áq̓plaʔntxʷ 514 i uɬ
ixíʔ a n+qʷn̓+min -nt -xʷ iʔ tm•tmniʔ iʔ t+x̌áq̓=plaʔ -nt -xʷ i uɬ
then art pity -nt -2erg art corpse art reward -nt -2erg intj and
you pitied the corpse, you paid his bills. 5:07 *And*

iʔ kʷ *broke* 515 sc̓x̌il[x] ka nqʷən̓míntsən, incá kən
iʔ kʷ sc+ʔx̌il+x ka n+qʷn̓+mi -nt -s -n in+cá kn
art 2kn reason_why rel be_sorry_for -nt -2obj -1erg I 1kn
then you were broke. *That's why I pitied you, I am*

k̓ʷəl̓əncútən 516 [s]c̓x̌ilx kiʔ kənxítmən {iʔ} iʔ kaʔkícəntxʷ a
k̓ʷl̓+ncut+n sc+ʔx̌il+x kiʔ kn+xit -m -n iʔ kaʔ•kíc -nt -xʷ a
god reason_why rel help -2obj -1erg art find -nt -2erg art
god. *That's why I helped you, and you found what you are*

sƛ̓aʔƛ̓aʔstíxʷ 517 way̓ ʕapnáʔ k̓ʷul̓l̓_t sqilxʷ
c -ƛ̓aʔ•ƛ̓aʔ -st -ixʷ way̓ ʕapnáʔ k̓ʷul̓•l̓_t s+qilxʷ
cust^ -look_for -^cust -2erg well now turn_into person
looking for. *Now she's turned into a human.”*

518 cúntəm {lut lut ə} lut axáʔ iʔ k̓əl tx̌ʷmut axáʔ iʔ k̓əl sqilxʷ
cu -nt -m lut axáʔ iʔ k̓l tx̌ʷ+m=ut axáʔ iʔ k̓l s+qilxʷ
tell -nt -psv not this art to normal this art to person
He[20] said, “No, she doesn't go to the straight people

519 ka {c ia} cxʷuy̓ k̓əl scq̓ʷəy̓məncút {tas·} 520 iʔ k̓əl sx̌əmənkʕáwaʔsc
ka c -xʷuy k̓l sc+q̓ʷy̓+mncut iʔ k̓l s+x̌m=nk=áwaʔ -s
rel hab -go to dance art to lover -3in
when she goes to the dance. *She goes to her lover,*

aɬíʔ ƛ̓xʷúpəntəm axáʔ {yax̌í unint} iʔ t sx̌ʷílmən 521 uɬ ik̓líʔ
aɬíʔ ƛ̓xʷu+p -nt -m axáʔ iʔ t s+x̌ʷil+mn uɬ ik̓líʔ
because win -nt -psv this art agInst devil and there
because the devil had won her. 6:00 *That's*

aɬ txʷúyəmsts uɬ a[xáʔ] iʔ l sənkʷkʷʔác 522 uɬ ixíʔ {unint}
aɬ t+xʷuy+m -st -s uɬ axáʔ iʔ l s+n+kʷ•kʷʔac uɬ ixíʔ
compl go_towards -st -3erg and this art at night and then
where she goes every night. *She goes*

20 The little fellow continues his account.

iʔ k̓əl scq̓ʷəy̓məncút scxʷuys 523 uɬ ixíʔ ktəlməntúɬts
iʔ k̓l sc+q̓ʷy̓+mncut sc -xʷuy -s uɬ ixíʔ k+tl+mn -tuɬt -s
art to dance pftv -go -3i and then put_in_custody_of -tuɬt -3erg
to the dance. *And then the first time she let*

iʔ laklís la_cxʔítiʔ {uɬ uɬ aɬíʔ} 524 uɬ aɬíʔ incá kən k̓ʷl̓əncútən uɬ
iʔ laklí -s la_c+xʔít+iʔ uɬ aɬíʔ in+cá kn k̓ʷl̓+ncut+n uɬ
art key -3in at_first and because I 1kn god and
you take care of her key. *Because I am god,*

aɬíʔ cmistín 525 uɬ sc̓x̌ilx ka {cústsən uɬ aɬ} iʔ
aɬíʔ c -my -st -in uɬ sc+ʔx̌il+x ka iʔ
so cust^ -know -^cust -1erg and reason_why rel art
I know. *And that's why*

cúntsən, 526 way̓ uɬ lut kʷúməntxʷ axáʔ iʔ laklí 527 uɬ
cu -nt -s -n way̓ uɬ lut kʷum -nt -xʷ axáʔ iʔ laklí uɬ
tell -nt -2obj -1erg well and not store -nt -2erg this art key and
I told you; *and you don't put the key away,* *and*

way̓ ɬpaʔsmís, 528 uɬ way̓ t̓iʔ ɬk̓aw ia laklí 529 kiń ɬ
way̓ ɬ+paʔs+mí -s uɬ way̓ t̓iʔ ɬ+k̓aw iʔ laklí ʔkin ɬ
yes wish_back -3erg and yes evid gone_again art key indef if
she thinks it back; *and the key is gone again.* *When*

ʕáċəntxʷ uɬ way̓ t̓iʔ ɬk̓aw 530 cun way̓ uɬ ixíʔ
ʕaċ -nt -xʷ uɬ way̓ t̓iʔ ɬ+k̓aw cu -n way̓ uɬ ixíʔ
look -nt -2erg and yes evid gone_again tell -1erg yes and that
you look the key is gone again. *And I said "I'm going to*

ɬənʔúcxən 531 uɬ ixíʔ {la k} iʔ lkasát kiʔ la nixʷút kiʔ
ɬ+n+ʔuc=xn -n uɬ ixíʔ iʔ lkasát kiʔ l n+yxʷ=ut kiʔ
follow_again -1erg and that art box rel in inside rel
follow her." *She locks the key*

laklís {iʔ laklís} 532 ilíʔ laklís iʔ laklí {xi} 533 uɬ axáʔ iʔ
laklí -s ilíʔ laklí -s iʔ laklí uɬ axáʔ iʔ
lock -3erg there lock -3erg art key and this art
in the trunk, *she locks the key there.* *And she did*

k̓ənpqínkstəns ilíʔ x̌ilsts 534 axáʔ iʔ k̓la nkaʔɬlmíw̓s {ki}
k̓np̓=qin=kst+n -s ilíʔ ʔx̌il -st -s axáʔ iʔ k̓l n+kaʔɬl+m=íw̓s
ring -3in there do_like -st -3erg this art to three_stories
the same with her ring, 7:03 *to the three rooms.*

535 ixíʔ əcləklaklí uɬ sic iʔ la lkasát əcləklaklísts 536 uɬ
ixíʔ c -lk•laklí uɬ sic iʔ l lkasát c -lk•laklí -st -s uɬ
that hab -lock_pl and then art in box cust^ -lock_pl -^cust -3erg and
They are locked, she locks all of them. *I got*

itlíʔ ɬckʷíɬtən uɬ aɬíʔ kʷ isənqʷəńmínəm
itlíʔ ɬ+c+kʷi -ɬt -n uɬ aɬíʔ kʷ i -s -n+qʷń+min+m
from_there take_back_cisl -ɬt -1erg and because 2kʷu 1i -intt -pity
them from there because I pitied you;

537 tla nqʷən̓míntxʷ {iʔ} iʔ təmtəmníʔ iʔ {iʔ} tx̌áq̓plaʔntxʷ
tla n+qʷn̓+min -nt -xʷ iʔ tm•tmniʔ iʔ t+x̌áq̓=plaʔ -nt -xʷ
from pity -nt -2erg art corpse art reward -nt -2erg
you pitied the corpse and paid his debts.”

538 cúntəm way̓, ixíʔ axáʔ {iʔ} iʔ kʷ iksc̓x̌ʷxítəm
cu -nt -m way̓ ixíʔ axáʔ iʔ kʷ i -ks -c̓x̌ʷ -xit -m
tell -nt -psv well then this art 2kʷu 1i -futi -lecture -xit -apsv
He said, “Now I am going to instruct you.

539 way̓ ixíʔ nqʷən̓míntsən, way̓ kʷənnúntxʷ a
way̓ ixíʔ n+qʷn̓+mi -nt -s -n way̓ kʷn -nu -nt -xʷ a
well then feel_sorry_for -nt -2obj -1erg yes take -manage -nt -2erg art
I pitied you, and now you got what you

cƛ̓aʔƛ̓aʔstíxʷ 540 ixíʔ uɬ ɬwíntsən, ixíʔ uɬ
c -ƛ̓aʔ•ƛ̓aʔ -st -ixʷ ixíʔ uɬ ɬwi -nt -s -n ixíʔ uɬ
cust^ -look_for -^cust -2erg then and leave -nt -2obj -1erg then and
were looking for. *And now I'm leaving you, I am going*

iɬəɬxʷúy {k̓əl} k̓əl stk̓másq̓ət 541 uɬ n̓ín̓w̓iʔ {kʷ ɬ taʔxʷs} kʷ ɬ
i -ɬ -ɬ+xʷuy k̓l s+t+k̓m=asq̓t uɬ n̓ín̓w̓iʔ kʷ ɬ
1i -intt -go_back to sky and a_while 2kn when
back to the sky. *When you get your child,*

k̓ʷəl̓l̓ilt cmay n̓ín̓w̓iʔ kʷ k̓ʷəl̓l̓ílt 542 cəm̓ tətwít iʔ {ks ia ksqəs}
k̓ʷl̓•l̓=ilt cmay n̓ín̓w̓iʔ kʷ k̓ʷl̓•l̓=ilt cm̓ t•tw̓it iʔ
have_baby maybe a_while 2kn have_baby maybe boy art
I think you'll get a child, 8:02 *the woman's child*

[ks]qʷəsqʷsíʔs axáʔ iʔ tkəɬmílxʷ 543 cúntəm uɬ ixíʔ {kʷu aks}
k -s+qʷs•qʷsiʔ -s axáʔ iʔ tkɬ+m=ilxʷ cu -nt -m uɬ ixíʔ
to_be -son -3i this art woman tell -nt -psv and that
will be a boy. *That's what you'll*

náx̌əmɬ ixíʔ kʷu aksx̌áq̓əm iʔ l kənxítmən 544 ixíʔ kʷu
nax̌mɬ ixíʔ kʷu a -ks -x̌aq̓+m iʔ l kn+xit -m -n ixíʔ kʷu
but that 1kʷu 2i -futi -pay art for help -2obj -1erg then 1obj
pay me for helping you. *You'll*

xʷíc̓əɬtxʷ {as asqʷs} asqʷsíʔ, ya cxʔit iʔ ksqʷəsqʷsíʔ[s] 545 ixíʔ
xʷic̓ -ɬt -xʷ a -s+qʷsiʔ ya c+xʔit iʔ k -s+qʷs•qʷsiʔ -s ixíʔ
give -ɬt -2erg 2in -son art first art to_be -son -3in then
give me your son, her first son. *From*

uɬ təl̓ k̓aɬáʔ uɬ ixíʔ {inaud} yayáʕt mnímɬəmp iʔ sqʷəsqʷsíʔmp
uɬ tl̓ k̓a+ɬáʔ uɬ ixíʔ yaʕ•yáʕ+t mnimɬ+mp iʔ s+qʷs•qʷsiʔ -mp
and from that_point and then all all_of_you art child -5in
then on they'll be all your children.”

546 cúntəm way̓, ixíʔ uɬ ɬwíntsən [k̓əɬm̓cín] 547 uɬ ixíʔ
cu -nt -m way̓ ixíʔ uɬ ɬwi -nt -s -n k̓ɬ+ʔm=cin uɬ ixíʔ
tell -nt -psv OK then and leave -nt -2obj -1erg agree and then
He said “Ok.” “Now I'm leaving you.” He agreed. *“And when*

ṅíṅẇiʔ put nləʕ̓ʷpús t̓x̌iwtwíl̓x {əl} mat {al} mi aláʔ
ṅíṅẇiʔ put n+lʕ̓ʷ+p=us t̓x̌=iwt+wilx mat mi aláʔ
a_while just fit next_year maybe fut here
it comes to the same day next year I'll

ɬckícəntsən {ixi}
ɬ+c+kic -nt -s -n
arrive_cisl_back -nt -2obj -1erg
come back here,

548 uɬ waẏ ṅíṅẇiʔ kʷ ksqʷəsqʷsíʔ uɬ ilíʔ
uɬ waẏ ṅíṅẇiʔ kʷ k+s+qʷs•qʷsiʔ uɬ ilíʔ
and yes a_while 2kn have_child and there
and you'll have a child,

uɬ iscƛ̓ʔám {iks} iksx̌áq̇əq̇
uɬ i -sc -ƛ̓ʔa+m i -k -s+x̌aq̇•q̇
and 1i -pftv -look_for 1i -to_be -payment
and I'll collect my pay."

549 a, waẏ aɬíʔ aspuʔús
a waẏ aɬíʔ a -s+puʔ=ús
intj OK because 2in -heart
"If that's how you feel.

550 waẏ iwá talí q̇íx̌əx̌məntsən
waẏ iwá taʔlíʔ q̇ix̌•x̌+m -nt -s -n
well to_no_avail very_much keep_close -nt -2obj -1erg
I'm sure going to miss you.

551 cəṁ waẏ kən
cṁ waẏ kn
maybe yes 1kn
I'm going

nk̓əwpíls kʷu ɬwintxʷ
n+k̓w+p=ils kʷu ɬwi -nt -xʷ
lonesome 1obj leave -nt -2erg
to miss you when you leave me.

552 uɬ aɬíʔ aspuʔús
uɬ aɬíʔ a -s+puʔ=ús
and so 2in -heart
[If] that's what you want to do."

553 cúntəm waẏ, aɬíʔ {kən} kən k̓ʷl̓əncútən {uɬ}
cu -nt -m waẏ aɬíʔ kn k̓ʷl̓+ncut+n
tell -nt -psv yes because 1kn god
He said, "Yes, because I am god.

554 uɬ lut, ṅíṅẇiʔ
uɬ lut ṅíṅẇiʔ
and not a_while
But no,

niʕíp {cə} c̓x̌iɬ ckaláʔmstmən
n+yʕ=ip c+ʔx̌iɬ c -k+aláʔ+m -st -m -n
always like cust^ -stay_with -^cust -2obj -1erg
I'll be with you all the time.

555 ctxət̓stúmən uɬ aɬíʔ náx̌əmɬ lut kʷu
c -t+xt̓ -st -um -n uɬ aɬíʔ nax̌mɬ lut kʷu
cust^ -watch_so -^cust -2obj -1erg and so but not 1kʷu
I'll lok after you, and you

akscwíkəm aɬíʔ {kən unint}
a -ksc -wik+m aɬíʔ
2i -futPerfi -see so
can't see me."

556 waẏ waẏ ixíʔ sʔácqaʔs {way ɬa ik}
waẏ waẏ ixíʔ s -ʔácqaʔ -s
well well then nom -go_out -3i
He went out.

557 k̓ácəcqaʔmsəlx t̓əxʷ ʔawtípiʔsəlx uɬ ʔácqaʔ
k+ʔác•c•qaʔ+m t̓xʷ ʔaw+t=íp ẏ -s -lx uɬ ʔácqaʔ
go_out_with evidently follow -nt -3erg -pl and go_out
They followed him and he went out.

558 uɬ aɬíʔ axáʔ
uɬ aɬíʔ axáʔ
and so this
This

iʔ tkəɬmílxʷ uɬ aɬíʔ k̓ʷul̓l̓_t tkəɬmílxʷ, lut k̓əm t̓a nʔaɬnaʔsqíl[xʷtən]
iʔ tkɬ+m=ilxʷ uɬ aɬíʔ k̓ʷul̓•l̓_t tkɬ+m=ilxʷ lut k̓m t̓ n+ʔaɬn+aʔ+sqílxʷ+tn
art woman and so turn_into woman not except negfac man_eater
woman turned into a real woman, she's not a man-eater any more.

559 uɬ t̓iʔ_niʕíp̓ x̌minks axáʔ iʔ staʔxʷsqəltmíxʷs {uɬ} 560 way̓
uɬ t̓iʔ_n+yʕ=ip x̌m=ink -s axáʔ iʔ s+taʔxʷ+s+qlt=míxʷ way̓
and always like -3erg this art new_husband well
She likes the man she got. *They*

ʔác[əc]qaʔlx, uɬ t̓iʔ ʔácqaʔ axáʔ iʔ təl̓ {tk} k̓ɬənk̓míp uɬ i l
ʔác•c•qaʔ -lx uɬ t̓iʔ ʔácqaʔ axáʔ iʔ tl̓ k̓ɬ+n+k̓m=ip uɬ iʔ l
go_out_pl -pl and evid go_out this art than door and art on
went out, and as soon as he went out the door and on

k̓ɬənx̌əlpəncútən 561 uɬ nwaʔwaʔsxáns axáʔ iʔ tətw̓ít 562 uɬ
k̓ɬ+n+x̌l+p+ncut+n uɬ n+waʔ•waʔs=xán -s axáʔ iʔ t•tw̓it uɬ
porch and feet_off_ground -3in this art boy and
the porch *the boy's feet left the ground;* *he*

t̓íxʷəxʷləm, k̓ʷul̓l̓_t yasukrí {i ɬəl} 563 cʕá··c̓stsəlx, uɬ nis {i t}
t̓ixʷ•xʷ•l+m k̓ʷul̓•l̓_t yasukrí c -ʕac̓ -st -s -lx uɬ nis
different turn_into JC cust^ -look -^cust -3erg -pl and sg_gone
changed, he turned into JC.[21] *They looked, and he was gone*

k̓əl stk̓másq̓ət 564 cp̓a··xʷ, {uɬ ni k̓əɬ} k̓əɬk̓əlxʷúsəms 565 nt̓a way̓ uɬ
k̓l s+t+k̓m=asq̓t c -p̓[ʔ]axʷ k̓ɬ+k̓lxʷ=us+m -s nt̓a way̓ uɬ
to sky hab -shine disappear -3erg intj well and
to the sky. *It was shiny, and then it got out of sight.* *They were*

x̌ast {i sc} iʔ sckʷlíwtsəlx axáʔ 566 x̌mink[s] axáʔ {iʔ c} iʔ [t]
x̌as+t iʔ sc -kʷl=iwt -s -lx axáʔ x̌m=ink -s axáʔ iʔ t
good art pftv -be_home -3i -pl this like -3erg this art agInst
getting along well. *His wife started to love him,*

tkəɬmílxʷs uɬ x̌minks 567 lut x̌əl̓ stim̓ t̓a
t+kɬm=ilxʷ -s uɬ x̌m=ink -s lut x̌l s+tim̓ t̓
wife -3in and like -3erg not for whatever negfac
and he her. *They don't have any trouble*

ck̓əsəsmílxəlx 568 uɬ t̓əxʷ lut t̓a ckícstməlx
c -k̓s•s+m+ilx -lx uɬ t̓xʷ lut t̓ c -kic -st -m -lx
hab -quarrel -pl and evidently not evid cust^ -reach_st/sb -^cust -psv -pl
of any kind. *They don't get any*

iʔ t sqilxʷ 569 way̓ uɬ {a taʔxʷsqʷəs} taʔxʷsqʷəsqʷsíʔ axáʔ iʔ
iʔ t s+qilxʷ way̓ uɬ taʔxʷ+s+qʷs•qʷsíʔ axáʔ iʔ
art agInst person well and get_baby this art
company. *Then the woman got*

tkəɬmílxʷ, way̓ tətw̓ít 570 way̓ {uɬ} uɬ aɬíʔ captíkʷɬ 571 uɬ {t̓iʔ} t̓iʔ
tkɬ+m=ilxʷ way̓ t•tw̓it way̓ uɬ aɬíʔ captíkʷɬ uɬ t̓iʔ
woman yes boy well and because legends and evid
a baby, a boy. *And because it's a fairy tale* *he was born and*

21 The character is best viewed as a generic Western supernatural being.

k̓ʷuľľ lut_sq̓sápiʔs uɬ ƛ̓x̌ap, 572 uɬ waẏ {c} a cxʷilwís, ċíckən
k̓ʷuľ•ľ lut_s+q̓sápiʔ+s uɬ ƛ̓x̌a+p uɬ waẏ a c -xʷy+lwis c -ʔickn
born not_long_after and grow_sg and yes art hab -wander hab -play
it wasn't long after that, he grew up, *and was running around and playing,*

waẏ {c} cqəcqícəlx 573 ixíʔ uɬ nlaʕ̓ʷpús {iʔkɬəɬ} nɬək̓ʷk̓ʷmís iʔ {s}
waẏ c -qc•qic+lx ixíʔ uɬ n+lʕ̓ʷ+p=us n+ɬk̓ʷ•k̓ʷ+mi -s iʔ
yes gpat -run then and time_fit think_about -3erg art
running around. *Then it came to that time, he thought of it,*

sľáx̌ts ɬə kɬəɬkícəntəm 574 waẏ cus {iʔ} iʔ
s+ľax̌+t -s ɬ kɬ -ɬ+kic -nt -m waẏ cu -s iʔ
partner -3in compl futtˆ -arrive_back -nt -psv well tell -3erg art
that his friend is going to get back. *He said to*

tkəɬmílxʷs 575 waẏ {ə kʷə} kən ɬwiʔnaʔscút 576 waẏ naɬcəcám,
t+kɬm=ilxʷ -s waẏ kn ɬ+wẏ=naʔ+scút waẏ naɬc•c•ám
wife -3in well 1kn prepared_again well forget
his wife: *"I am all prepared.* *That's right,*

isľáx̌t kʷu kɬəɬckíciʔs ixíʔ kʷu ċəx̌ʷxíts
i -s+ľax̌+t kʷu kɬ -ɬ+c+kíc ẏ -s ixíʔ kʷu ċx̌ʷ -xit -s
1in -partner 1kʷu fut -get_here_again -nt -3erg then 1obj promise -xit -3erg
my partner is going to get here, that's our date.

577 waẏ kʷ k̓ʷəľcəncút iʔ {t} t x̌ast {iʔ t} iʔ t sʔíɬən 578 uɬ axáʔ
waẏ kʷ k̓ʷľ=cn+cut iʔ t x̌as+t iʔ t s+ʔiɬn uɬ axáʔ
well 2kn cook art obj_itr good art obj_itr food and this
I want you to cook the best things to eat, *and*

iʔ {t i} kʷ xʷk̓ʷíɬxʷəm 579 xʷk̓ʷəntíxʷ iʔ citxʷ, iʔ {k} latáp iʔ
iʔ kʷ xʷk̓ʷ=iɬxʷ+m xʷk̓ʷ -nt -ixʷ iʔ citxʷ iʔ latáp iʔ
art 2kn clean_house clean -nt -2erg art house art table art
clean the house; *clean the house and*

ksənʔíɬəntəntət 580 waẏ axáʔ iʔ tkəɬmílxʷ waẏ ixíʔ ilíʔ
k -s+n+ʔiɬn+tn -tt waẏ axáʔ iʔ tkɬ+m=ilxʷ waẏ ixíʔ ilíʔ
to_be -table -4i well this art woman well that there
the table." *The woman*

sx̌íləms 581 uɬ aɬíʔ x̌minks {iʔ s} iʔ sqəľtmíxʷs 582 waẏ
s -x̌il+m -s uɬ aɬíʔ x̌m=ink -s iʔ s+qlt=mixʷ -s waẏ
nom -do_like -3i and because like -3erg art husband -3in well
did just that, *because she likes her husband.* *She*

xʷk̓ʷí··ɬxʷəm, wiʔsxʷk̓ʷíɬxʷəm 583 waẏ uɬ k̓ʷəľcəncú··t {i t} iʔ t
xʷk̓ʷ=iɬxʷ+m wẏ+s+xʷk̓ʷ=iɬxʷ+m waẏ uɬ k̓ʷľ=cn+cut iʔ t
clean_house finish_clean_house well and cook art obj_itr
cleaned house and got done cleaning house. *She cooked*

pie iʔ t *cake* 584 uɬ aɬíʔ waẏ {kɬ} kɬululqín iʔ t
iʔ t uɬ aɬíʔ waẏ kɬ+wl•wl=qin iʔ t
art obj_itr and because yes have_canned_goods art obl
pie and cake, *because she had*

spi̓ʔqáɬq {uɬ ixí} 585 way̓ put wiʔskɬclám, ixíʔ uɬ axáʔ iʔ x̌əx̌y̓áɬnəxʷ {t}
s+p̓y̓q=aɬq way̓ put wy̓+s+kɬ+sla+m ixíʔ uɬ axáʔ iʔ x̌•x̌yaɬ=ṅxʷ
fruit well just finish_set_table then and this art clock
canned fruit. *She just got done setting the table, and the clock*

lu·wíw̓s la ntəx̌ʷəx̌ʷqín 586 ixíʔ ck̓əɬncʔípəntməlx 587 way̓
lw=iw̓s l n+tx̌ʷ•x̌ʷ=qin ixíʔ c -k̓ɬ+n+cʔ=ip -nt -m -lx way̓
ring at noon then act -knock_on_door -nt -psv -pl well
rang twelve o'clock. *Somebody knocked on the door.* *They*

k̓ɬənk̓ahk̓ʷípɬtsəlx 588 way̓ ixíʔ iʔ slax̌ts, axáʔ iʔ tətw̓ít
k̓ɬ+n+k̓ahk̓ʷ=íp -ɬt -s -lx way̓ ixíʔ iʔ s+l̓ax̌+t -s axáʔ iʔ t•tw̓it
open -ɬt -3erg -pl well that art friend -3in this art boy
opened the door. *That's his friend, the boy;*

589 way̓ ɬk̓ʷul̓l̓_t tətw̓ít 590 way {t limt uɬ t} límtəmsəlx
way̓ ɬ+k̓ʷul̓•l̓_t t•tw̓it way̓ lim+t+m -s -lx
well turn_back_into boy well be_glad_for -3erg -pl
he had turned back into a boy. *They were glad to see him again,*

ɬkʷínksəs {i s} iʔ síncaʔs, xʷaʔntís t̓əxʷ aɬíʔ
ɬ+kʷin=ks -s iʔ sincaʔ -s xʷaʔ -nt -is t̓xʷ aɬíʔ
shake_hands_again -3erg art younger_brother -3in pick_up -nt -3erg emph so
he shook hands with his brother, took him on his lap.

591 way̓ uɬ axáʔ iʔ t tkəɬmílxʷ {iɬ} nixʷ x̌ílstəm,
way̓ uɬ axáʔ iʔ t tkɬ+m=ilxʷ nixʷ x̌il -st -m
well and this art agInst woman also act_so -st -psv
The woman did the same, she shook hands

kʷínksəntəm 592 uɬ k̓əɬt̓máʕsəntəm, límtməntəm 593 way̓
kʷin=ks -nt -m uɬ k̓ɬ+t̓m=ʕas -nt -m lim+t+m -nt -m way̓
shake_hands -nt -psv and kiss -nt -psv be_glad_for -nt -psv well
with him, *she kissed him, was tickled.* *He*

uɬ cúntəm way̓ uɬ ixíʔ way̓ cwiʔskɬsál 594 c̓x̌əɬ ta
uɬ cu -nt -m way̓ uɬ ixíʔ way̓ c -wy̓+s+kɬ+sal c+ʔx̌iɬ t
and tell -nt -psv yes and then yes gpat -finish_setting like obj_c̓x̌iɬ
said to him, "The table is already set. *We know you,*

cmistúmt uɬ ixíʔ t̓əxʷ iʔ scáxʷtət
c -my -st -um -t uɬ ixíʔ t̓xʷ iʔ s+caxʷ -tt
cust^ -know -^cust -2obj -4erg and then evidently art affection -4in
and this is what we do.

595 way̓ {kʷu ʔa} kʷu ʔíɬən, uɬ axáʔ iʔ sk̓ʷk̓ʷíməlt uɬ ixíʔ
way̓ kʷu ʔiɬn uɬ axáʔ iʔ s+k̓ʷ•k̓ʷiy=m̓=l̓t uɬ ixíʔ
well 4kn eat and this art child_dim and that
We'll eat." And the child[22] is sitting right

22 The couple's son.

k̓amɬníwtəntəm 596 eˑ way̓ ʔaɬʔíɬnəlx, wiʔwiʔcín[əlx]
k+ʔam=ɬniwt -nt -m eˑ way̓ ʔaɬ•ʔíɬn -lx wy̓•wy̓=cin -lx
sit_beside -nt -psv intj well eat_pl -pl finish_eating_pl -pl
by his side. *They got done eating.*

597 cúntəm axáʔ {i ts} iʔ t síncaʔs 598 way̓,
cu -nt -m axáʔ iʔ t sínca? -s way̓
tell -nt -psv this art agInst younger_brother -3in well
His little brother said to him: *"I'm*

way̓ {uɬ ə lut lut kʷu aks} lut {kʷ t̓ isən} kʷ t̓ iksənpúlxəm
way̓ lut kʷ t̓ i -ks -n+pul+x+m
well not 2kʷu negfac 1i -futi -camp_with_so
not going to camp with you.[23]

599 uɬ way̓ ixíʔ nk̓ʷɬʔíɬənməntsən 600 uɬ way̓ ixíʔ, uɬ way̓
uɬ way̓ ixíʔ nk̓ʷ+ɬ+ʔiɬn+m -nt -s -n uɬ way̓ ixíʔ uɬ way̓
and well that eat_with -nt -2obj -1erg and well that and well
I just ate with you. *And*

t̓iʔ_kmix ixíʔ {kʷu as} iʔ sc̓əx̌ʷxtwíxʷtət {ixíʔ i} 601 ixíʔ iscƛ̓ʔám {is}
t̓iʔ_kmix ixíʔ iʔ s+c̓x̌ʷ+xtwixʷ -tt ixíʔ i -sc -ƛ̓ʔa+m
only that art arrangement -4in that 1i -pftv -look_for
our bargain, *I'm after*

isx̌áq̓əq̓ 602 t̓əxʷ way̓ iʔ kʷu x̌áq̓əntxʷ, ixíʔ
i -s+x̌aq̓•q̓ t̓xʷ way̓ iʔ kʷu x̌aq̓ -nt -xʷ ixíʔ
1i -payment emph yes art 1obj pay -nt -2erg that
my pay. *That's what you pay me, what I*

x̌əq̓əncútməntsən 603 ixíʔ kʷa {i} asxaʔtmíxəlt, kʷa tətw̓ít
x̌q̓+ncut+m -nt -s -n ixíʔ kʷa a -s+xaʔt+míx=lt kʷa t•tw̓it
ask_to_pay -nt -2obj -1erg that intj 2in -first_child intj boy
asked you to pay, *your first born child, a little boy.*

604 uɬ ixíʔ axáʔ uɬ way̓ ixíʔ cƛ̓aʔntín {uɬ a ixí} 605 [way̓] ixíʔ
uɬ ixíʔ axáʔ uɬ way̓ ixíʔ c -ƛ̓aʔ -nt -in way̓ ixíʔ
and then this and yes that act -fetch -nt -1erg well that
Now I'm after it. *That's the deal*

sc̓əx̌ʷxtwíxʷtət, ha cənɬək̓ʷək̓ʷtmístxʷ 606 cut axáʔ {i s} iʔ
s+c̓x̌ʷ+xtwixʷ -tt haʔ c -n+ɬk̓ʷ•k̓ʷ+t+mi -st -xʷ cut axáʔ iʔ
arrangement -4in inter cust^ -remember -^cust -2erg say this art
we made, do you remember?" (maybe cənt'ək̓ʷəɬk̓ʷtmístxʷ)a *The oldest one said*

sxʔitx way̓ cənɬək̓ʷɬk̓ʷtmístən ixíʔ uɬ nax̌əmɬ q̓íx̌əx̌əms {iʔ}
s+xʔit=x way̓ c -n+ɬk̓ʷ•ɬk̓ʷ+t+mi -st -n ixíʔ uɬ nax̌mɬ q̓ix̌•x̌+m -s
oldest_one yes cust^ -remember -^cust -1erg that and but keep_close -3erg
"I remember." But he got stingy

23 "Spend the night."

iʔ sqʷsiʔs 607 uɬ aɬíʔ qʷəńcín uɬ ixíʔ waẏ x̌áq̓əmənts
iʔ s+qʷsiʔ -s uɬ aɬíʔ qʷń=cin uɬ ixíʔ waẏ x̌aq̓+m -nt -s
art son -3in and so pity and that yes pay -nt -3e2obj
of his son. "It's a pity, and it's what you pay me."

608 ixíʔ uɬ waẏ cmistím axáʔ iʔ t k̓ʷəl̓əncútən
ixíʔ uɬ waẏ c -my+st -im axáʔ iʔ t k̓ʷl̓+ncut+n
then and yes cust^ -know -psv this art agInst god
And god knew all his thoughts;

609 cúntəm waẏ, waẏ q̓íx̌əx̌məntxʷ asqʷsíʔ 610 uɬ t̓iʔ kʷ
cu -nt -m waẏ waẏ q̓ix̌•x̌+m -nt -xʷ a -s+qʷsiʔ uɬ t̓iʔ kʷ
tell -nt -psv well yes keep_close -nt -2erg 2in -son and evid 2kn
he said to him, "Well, you are stingy of your son, and you are

sukʷmístx 611 uɬ cut kwaẏ, waẏ unixʷ q̓íx̌əx̌mən
s -wkʷ+mist -x uɬ cut k+waẏ waẏ wnixʷ q̓ix̌•x̌+m -n
ipftv^ -keep_secret -^ipftv and say yes yes true keep_close -1erg
keeping[24] it to yourself." He said, "It's true, I am stingy of him.

612 uɬ aɬíʔ qʷəńcín ixíʔ sqʷaʔqʷʔáltət 613 a, cúntəm uɬ kiń kʷa
uɬ aɬíʔ qʷń=cin ixíʔ s+qʷaʔ•qʷʔál -tt a cu -nt -m uɬ ʔkin kʷa
and so pity that agreement -4in intj tell -nt -psv and indef intj
It's a pity, but that's our bargain." He asked, "Where is

ansp̓ústən 614 ha kʷ kɬənsp̓ústən 615 cut waẏ, waẏ ixíʔ
a -n+sp̓=us+tn haʔ kʷ kɬ+n+sp̓=us+tn cut waẏ waẏ ixíʔ
2in -sword inter 2kn have_sword say yes well that
your sword? Have you got a sword?" He said "Yes," and

xʷíc̓xəts {a n} 616 cúntəm ha x̌ast {i a} aspuʔús {ɬa n} ɬa
xʷic̓ -xt -s cu -nt -m haʔ x̌as+t a -s+puʔ=ús ɬaʔ
give -xit -3erg tell -nt -psv inter good 2in -heart if
gave it to him. He asked "Will your feelings be good if I hit him

nxl̓áẃsqən' 617 uɬ ńíńwiʔ {t} tx̌ʷíẃsəntəm 618 kʷintxʷ anwí
n+xl=aẃs=qn -n uɬ ńíńwiʔ tx̌ʷ=iẃs -nt -m kʷi -nt -xʷ anwí
chop_head -1erg and a_while divide -nt -4erg take -nt -2erg you
on the head and then we divide him? You take

ansək̓ʷtsiẃs {kʷintxʷ aɬíʔyasq̓ax̌əm} 619 məɬ incá ya nsk̓ʷtsiẃs kʷin {tə}
a -n+s+k̓ʷt=s=iẃs mɬ in+cá ya n+s+k̓ʷt=s=iẃs kʷi -n
2in -half and I art half take -1erg
one half and I take the other half?"

620 cúntəm uɬ caʔkʷ {mɬ tk} ɬ sənʔassíl uɬ t̓iʔ waẏ {k} cxʷəlxʷált
cu -nt -m uɬ caʔkʷ ɬ s+n+ʔas•s•íl uɬ t̓iʔ waẏ c -xʷl•xʷal+t
tell -nt -psv and should if two and evid yes hab -alive
He said "If they were two, and alive,

24 The gist is "you want to keep it."

621 waẏ knaqs incá kʷin, uɬ anwí {i} iʔ knaqs 622 nstils
waẏ k=naqs in+cá kʷi -n uɬ anwí iʔ k=naqs n+st=ils
yes one_person I take -1erg and you art one_person think
I'd take one, and you the other." *The oldest*

axáʔ {iʔ} iʔ sxʔitx 623 uɬ ha sċkinx uɬ {məɬ} cənsq̇íẇs
axáʔ iʔ s+xʔit=x uɬ haʔ sc+ʔkin+x uɬ c -n+sq̇=iẇs
this art oldest_one and inter why_is_it and hab -split
one thought: *"And what's the matter, split in two,*

624 uɬ lut t' ksxʷəlxʷálts {axáʔ iʔ} axáʔ ia cənsq̇íẇs {tla ki} 625 t'əxʷ
uɬ lut t' ks -xʷl•xʷal+t -s axáʔ iʔ c -n+sq̇=iẇs t'xʷ
and not hab futi -alive -3i this art hab -split emph
it can't be alive split in two. *But*

aɬíʔ ixíʔ scqʷəlqʷílts 626 uɬ waẏ miná taṅmús{kiu} kiʔ ixíʔ qʷəlqʷílt
aɬíʔ ixíʔ sc+qʷl•qʷil+t -s uɬ waẏ miná tanṁ=ús kiʔ ixíʔ qʷl•qʷil+t
so that word -3in and yes futNeg nothing rel that talk
that's what he said. *I guess it's not for nothing that he said that,*

627 ilíʔ {t} tixʷkʷúnəm 628 cus waẏ, kwaẏ aspuʔús
ilíʔ tixʷ+kʷún+m cu -s waẏ k+waẏ a -s+puʔ=ús
there talk tell -3erg well yes 2in -heart
that he talked like that." *He said "Go ahead, if that's what you think.*

629 waẏ cúntsən uɬ ixíʔ sqʷaʔqʷʔál[tət] 630 k anwí
waẏ cu -nt -s -n uɬ ixíʔ s+qʷaʔ•qʷʔál -tt kiʔ anwí
well tell -nt -2obj -1erg and that agreement -4in rel you
I told you that's the bargain we made. *I agreed*

k̇ɬəmcíntsən ixíʔ kʷu x̌əq̇ncútməntəm 631 uɬ waẏ t'əxʷ,
k̇ɬ+ʔm=cin -t -s -n ixíʔ kʷu x̌q̇+ncut+m -nt -m uɬ waẏ t'xʷ
agree -nt -2obj -1erg that 3e4obj ask_to_pay -nt -3e4obj and well emph
with you with what you asked for pay. *Go ahead,*

waẏ anwí aspuʔús 632 a· waẏ 633 taʔx̌íləm {ckʷis} kʷis a
waẏ anwí a -s+puʔ=ús a waẏ ta+ʔx̌íl+m kʷi -s a
well you 2in -heart intj OK do_a_certain_way take -3erg art
do what you think best." *"Ok."* *He took*

nsṗústən 634 nixláẇsqs axáʔ {iʔ iʔ s} 635 ih ɬt'ap ak̓láʔ a
n+sṗ=us+tn ny+xl=aẇs=q[25] -s axáʔ ih ɬt'a+p ak̓láʔ a
sword chop_head -3erg this intj fly_off here art
the sword, *he hit him on top of the head.* *The half*

nsək̓ʷtsíẇs 636 k̓aʔx̌í iʔ kɬtíɬəx {iʔ t a} iʔ tətẇít 637 ak̓láʔ iʔ naqs
n+s+k̓ʷt=s=iẇs k̓a+ʔx̌íʔ iʔ kɬ+tiɬ•ɬ+x iʔ t•tẇit ak̓láʔ iʔ naqs
half there art stand_on art boy 638 ak̓láʔ iʔ naqs
flew off *and a boy stood there;* *another*

25 The prefix ny+ is unknown to me.

ɬƛ̓ap k̓la·· nixʷ kɬtíɬəɬx 639 ƛ̓iʔ put c̓ax̌ʔax̌lús uɬ
ɬƛ̓a+p k̓laʔ nixʷ kɬ+tiɬ•ɬ+x ƛ̓iʔ put c -ʔax̌•ʔax̌l=ús uɬ
here art one fly_off to also stand_on evid just hab -same_face and
flew and it stood there too. *Their faces are alike,*

put c̓ax̌ʔax̌lálqʷəlx ƛ̓iʔ 640 put iʔ stə{tim̓}təm̓tím̓səlx
put c -ʔax̌•ʔax̌l=álqʷ -lx ƛ̓iʔ put iʔ s+t•tm̓•tim̓ -s -lx
exact hab -same_height -pl evid just art clothes -3in -pl
and their heights too; *their clothes are the same.*

641 cúntəm way̓, nƛ̓a way̓ yuyáʕʷt aspuʔús 642 way̓ uníxʷ kʷ
cu -nt -m way̓ nƛ̓a way̓ yw•yaʕʷ+t a -s+puʔ=ús way̓ wnixʷ kʷ
tell -nt -psv yes intj yes strong 2in -heart yes true 2kn
He said to him, "Your thoughts are very strong; *you really*

kɬnunxʷínaʔtən 643 lut_swit {ƛ̓ə ks ə} ƛ̓ə ksxʷíc̓xəms iʔ
kɬ+n+wnxʷ=ínaʔ+tn lut_swit ƛ̓ ks -xʷic̓+x+m -s iʔ
have_religion nobody negfac futi -give_to -3i art
believed. *Nobody'd give away*

sqʷəsqʷsíʔs {ili ɬ iks} ƛ̓ iksənsq̓íw̓ɬ[təm] 644 uɬ anwí {uɬ a}
s+qʷs•qʷsiʔ -s ƛ̓ i -ks -n+sq̓=iw̓ -ɬt -m uɬ anwí
son -3in negfac 1i -futi -split_in_half -ɬt -apsv and you
his son to have him split in two, *but you [did]."*

645 cúntəm way̓, {xiʔ axáʔ ixí aik} ixíʔ way̓ kɬíw̓səntəm 646 way̓
cu -nt -m way̓ ixíʔ way̓ kɬ=iw̓s -nt -m way̓
tell -nt -psv well then yes divide -nt -4erg well
He said "Yes," "and then we split it. *You*

kʷintxʷ axáʔ iʔ knaqs 647 məɬ incá kʷin 648 ixíʔ ṅíṅw̓iʔ
kʷi -nt -xʷ axáʔ iʔ k=naqs mɬ in+cá kʷi -n ixíʔ ṅíṅw̓iʔ
take -nt -2erg this art one_person and I take -1erg then a_while
take one; *and I'll take one.* *And when*

ɬ ƛ̓alaʔxwílx iʔ sƛ̓əlsqílxʷ 649 lut ƛ̓iʔ_kmix kskṅáṅaqs iʔ
ɬ ƛ̓alaʔ+x+wílx iʔ s+ƛ̓l+s+qilxʷ lut ƛ̓iʔ_kmix k+s+k=ṅá•ṅaqs iʔ
when next_generation art earth_people not only have_person_dim art
the next generation comes *it won't always be one*

sk̓ʷk̓ʷíməlt 650 məɬ laʔkíṅ {uɬ} məɬ {c} cənʔaʔssíl 651 cúntəm
s+k̓ʷ•k̓ʷiy=m̓=l̓t mɬ la+ʔkíṅ mɬ c -n+ʔa•ʔs•s•íl cu -nt -m
child_dim and whenever and hab -twins_dim tell -nt -psv
child born. *There will be twins."* *He said,*

way̓, way̓ ixíʔ {ɬwi} ɬwíntsən 652 way̓, cúntəm way̓ ilíʔ {as}
way̓ way̓ ixíʔ ɬwi -nt -s -n way̓ cu -nt -m way̓ ilíʔ
well well then leave -nt -2obj -1erg well tell -nt -psv well there
"I'm going to leave you." He said "They are

asqʷəsqʷasíʔa 653 way̓ ixíʔ {ɬ} ɬənwísəlx axáʔ iʔ k̓ʷl̓əncútən 654 ƛ̓i
a -s+qʷs•qʷasíʔa way̓ ixíʔ ɬ+n+wis+lx axáʔ iʔ k̓ʷl̓+ncut+n ƛ̓iʔ
2in -children well then rise_again this art god evid
your children." *And god rose up.* *It*

[k]lkʷakʷ uɬ p̓ʔaxʷ 655 uɬ t̓iʔ c̓ʕá··c̓stsəlx uɬ
k+lkʷ•akʷ uɬ p̓[ʔ]axʷ uɬ t̓iʔ c -ʕac̓ -st -s -lx uɬ
far and shine and evid cust^ -look -^cust -3erg -pl and
went a little way and it shone; *they looked, and*

k̓əɬk̓əlxʷúsəmsəlx iʔ k̓əl stk̓másq̓ət 656 way̓, way̓ kʷlíwtəlx mat
k̓ɬ+k̓lxʷ=us+m -s -lx iʔ k̓l s+t+k̓m=asq̓t way̓ way̓ kʷl=iwt -lx mat
disappear -3erg -pl art to sky well well be_home -pl maybe
he got out of sight in the sky. *They were sitting around I don't*

k̓ʷənxásq̓ət 657 way̓ {ɬ} nt̓a t̓iʔ paʕs axáʔ iʔ tkəɬmílxʷ {t̓əxʷ}
k̓ʷn+x=asq̓t way̓ nt̓a t̓iʔ paʕs axáʔ iʔ tkɬ+m=ilxʷ
a_few_days well intj evid surprised this art woman
know how many days, *and the woman felt surprised.*

658 uɬ nixʷ axáʔ iʔ sqəltmíxʷ nixʷ t̓i paʕs 659 way̓ cus
uɬ nixʷ axáʔ iʔ s+qlt=mixʷ nixʷ t̓iʔ paʕs way̓ cu -s
and also this art man also evid surprised well tell -3erg
And the man felt surprised too. *He said*

axáʔ {iʔ} iʔ tkəɬmílxʷs 660 way̓, {way̓ kʷu} way̓ nk̓əw̓pílsmən
axáʔ iʔ t+kɬm=ilxʷ -s way̓ way̓ n+k̓w+p=ils+m -n
this art wife -3in well well be_lonesome_for -1erg
to his woman: *"I am lonesome for*

inƛ̓axəx̌ƛ̓x̌áp̓ 661 way̓ {xi n} nlaʕ̓ʷpús {i kɬ} iʔ c̓əx̌ʷxítnəlx
in -ƛ̓ax̌•x̌•ƛ̓x̌á+p way̓ n+lʕ̓ʷ+p=us iʔ c̓x̌ʷ -xit -n -lx
1in -elders well time_fit art promise -xit -1erg -pl
my folks. *The day has come that I told them*

662 n̓ ɬ iscxʷəlxʷált, {uɬ ʕapn} ixíʔ mi ɬkícnəlx {uɬ} 663 uɬ way̓
n̓ ɬ i -sc -xʷl•xʷal+t ixíʔ mi ɬ+kic -n -lx uɬ way̓
a_while if 1i -pftv -alive then fut arrive_back -1erg -pl and yes
if I am alive I'm supposed to get back, *I am*

nk̓əw̓pílsmnəlx inƛ̓axəx̌ƛ̓x̌áp̓ 664 uɬ way̓ mat {kʷu} nixʷ kʷu
n+k̓w+p=ils+m -n -lx in -ƛ̓ax̌•x̌•ƛ̓x̌á+p uɬ way̓ mat nixʷ kʷu
be_lonesome_for -1erg -pl 1in -elders and well must also 1obj
lonesome for my elders, *and they'll be lonesome*

nk̓əw̓pílsmsəlx 665 way̓ mat kʷu ctk̓əlk̓əlstísəlx
n+k̓w+p=ils+m -s -lx way̓ mat kʷu c -t+k̓l•k̓l -st -is -lx
be_lonesome_for -3erg -pl well maybe 1obj cust^ -expect_so -^cust -3erg -pl
for me too. *I guess they are looking for me.*

666 uɬ way̓ {kʷu ks} kʷu ksxʷúyaʔx 667 uɬ aɬíʔ nixʷ {ks}
uɬ way̓ kʷu ks -xʷuy -aʔx uɬ aɬíʔ nixʷ
and well 4kn incp^ -go -^incp and because also
Let's go. *And I want them*

kswíkiʔsəlx axáʔ iʔ sənʔamʔímaʔtsəlx 668 uɬ axáʔ {iʔ} anwí
ks -wík y̓ -s -lx axáʔ iʔ s+n+ʔam•ʔímaʔt -s -lx uɬ axáʔ anwí
futi -see -nt -3erg -pl this art grand_children -3in -pl and this you
to see their grandchildren, *and to*

kswíkəntsəlx 669 aksúxʷmaʔm asx̌aʔ•x̌áʔ uɬ
ks -wik -nt -s -lx a -k -súxʷ=maʔ+m a -s+x̌áʔ•x̌aʔ uɬ
futtˆ -see -nt -3erg -pl 2i -futi -acquaint 2in -father_in_law and
see you. You can get acquainted with your father-in-law and

aɬcíck 670 cut waẏ, cut axáʔ iʔ tkəɬmílxʷ waẏ 671 uɬ aɬíʔ
a -ɬ+ci•ck cut waẏ cut axáʔ iʔ tkɬ+m=ilxʷ waẏ uɬ aɬíʔ
2in -mother_in_law say OK say this art woman OK and because
mother-in-law." The woman said "All right. You are

anwí {kʷ i kʷi s} kʷ isqəltmíxʷ, kʷ isənk̓ʷəɬmərím {uɬ} 672 uɬ waẏ
anwí kʷ i -s+qlt=mixʷ kʷ i -s+nk̓ʷ+ɬ+mrim uɬ waẏ
you 2kʷu 1i -husband 2kʷu 1i -spouse and yes
my man, I'm married to you. That'll

t̓iʔ_x̌ast {uɬ kʷ} waẏ ṅíṅẇiʔ kxəntsín 673 lut iksťiʔám
t̓iʔ_x̌as+t waẏ ṅíṅẇiʔ kx+n -t -s -in lut i -ks -ťyá+m
as_well yes a_while follow -nt -2obj -1erg not 1i -futi -refuse
be fine, I'll go with you. I won't refuse.

674 sc̓kinx ha, kən limt {a} ikswíkəm {is} isənɬx̌əmtán {is} 675 waẏ
sc+ʔkin+x haʔ kn lim+t i -ks -wik+m i -s+n+ɬx̌m+tan waẏ
why_is_it inter 1kn glad 1i -futi -see 1in -in_law well
Sure, I'm glad to see my relatives." Daylight

ksx̌əlpínaʔlx {waẏ ixíʔ} 676 uɬ aɬíʔ axáʔ smisqílxʷ axáʔ iʔ
k+s+x̌l+p=ínaʔ -lx uɬ aɬíʔ axáʔ s+my+s+qilxʷ axáʔ iʔ
have_daylight -pl and because this important_people this art
come, and because

tkəɬmílxʷ iʔ sƛ̓xʷups iʔ staʔxʷɬtkəɬmilxʷs 677 waẏ
tkɬ+m=ilxʷ iʔ s+ƛ̓xʷup -s iʔ s+taʔxʷ+ɬ+tkɬ+m=ílxʷ -s waẏ
woman art earning -3in art acquired_wife -3in well
the woman he won is important, he

ckəṁntís iʔ qʷámqʷəmt iʔ kəẇwáps {iʔ} 678 axáʔ iʔ t
c -kṁ -nt -is iʔ qʷam•qʷm+t iʔ kw+w+ap -s axáʔ iʔ t
act -take_pl -nt -3erg art excellent art horses -3in this art prttv
got the best horses and the

sənccəkʷṁíṅ 679 uɬ aɬíʔ pṅicíʔ uɬ nak̓ʷá kɬənʔakʷtáqs {a} kəṁ
s+n+c•ckʷ+ṁiṅ uɬ aɬíʔ pn+icíʔ uɬ nak̓ʷá kɬ+n+ʔakʷ=t=áqs kṁ
buggy_dim and because at_that_time and not have_car or
little buggy. Because at that time they didn't have cars or

kɬt̓əxʷtlwís 680 waẏ skəɬkʷílsəlx 681 waẏ ixíʔ
kɬ+t̓xʷt+lwis waẏ s -kɬ+kʷil -s -lx waẏ ixíʔ
have_fly_around well nom -sit_in -3i -pl well then
airplanes. They got in the rig, they

sxʷúẏisəlx 682 hi·, iʔ kəẇwápsəls qʷəṁqʷíṁ kɬʔax̌əx̌luʔsílxʷ
s -xʷuẏ•y -s -lx hi iʔ kw+wap -s -lx qʷṁ•qʷiṁ kɬ+ʔax̌•x̌•l=ẇs=ílxʷ
nom -go_pl -3i -pl intj art horses -3in -pl prance have_matched_coats
went. Their horses prance and they're well matched,

683 uɬ aɬíʔ waẏ {c axáʔ iʔ} ckəw·l̓ína? axáʔ {iʔ} iʔ səncəcəkʷm̓ín̓
uɬ aɬíʔ waẏ c -k+w•wl=ínaʔ axáʔ iʔ s+n+c•ckʷ+m̓in̓
and so well hab -cover this art buggy_dim
and the buggy has a top,

684 uɬ ʔasíl iʔ sənkɬkʷíltən
uɬ ʔasíl iʔ s+n+kɬ+kʷil+tn
and two art seats
and it's a two-seater.

685 uɬ axáʔ iʔ tuʔtwít k̓əl sʔiwt
uɬ axáʔ iʔ tw̓•tw̓it k̓l s+ʔiwt
and this art boys to one_behind
The boys are in the back

686 uɬ axáʔ iʔ ƛ̓ax̌əx̌ƛ̓x̌áp {k̓əl sxaʔ} k̓əl sxʔit {k s} kɬkʷlíwtəlx
uɬ axáʔ iʔ ƛ̓ax̌•x̌•ƛ̓x̌á+p k̓l s+xʔit kɬ+kʷl=iwt -lx
and this art elders to front sit_in -pl
and the parents sit in front.

687 uɬ aɬíʔ waẏ tk̓əlk̓əlám axáʔ iʔ ƛ̓ax̌əx̌ƛ̓x̌áp uɬ waẏ nk̓əwpílsəlx iʔ k̓əl sqʷsíʔsəlx
uɬ aɬíʔ waẏ t+k̓l•k̓la+m axáʔ iʔ ƛ̓ax̌•x̌•ƛ̓x̌á+p uɬ waẏ n+k̓w+p=ils -lx iʔ k̓l s+qʷsiʔ -s -lx
and because yes expect_so this art elders and yes lonesome -pl art for son -3in -pl
The elders have been searching and they are lonesome for their son,

688 aɬíʔ sk̓n̓əqsəl̓tílaʔtsəlx
aɬíʔ s+k=nqs=lt=íla?t -s -lx
because only_child -3in -pl
because he's their only son;

689 niʕíp̓ ckƛ̓aʔƛ̓ʔúsəms[tsəlx]
n+yʕ=ip̓ c -k+ƛ̓aʔ•ƛ̓ʔ=ús+m -st -s -lx
always cust^ -watch -^cust -3erg -pl
they are always looking for him.

690 waẏ t̓iʔ_kʷmiɬ ki cwíkməlx ck̓əɬkʷƛ̓áp {t} iʔ sənckʷmín {ay}
waẏ t̓iʔ_kʷm̓iɬ kiʔ c -wik+m -lx c -k̓ɬ+kʷƛ̓a+p iʔ s+n+ckʷ+min
well at_once rel hab -see -pl hab come_in_sight art buggy
All of a sudden they saw the wagon come in sight.

691 cútəlx waẏ, waẏ mat ixíʔ iʔ sqʷsíʔtət
cut -lx waẏ waẏ mat ixíʔ iʔ s+qʷsiʔ -tt
say -pl well yes maybe that art son -4in
They said "Maybe that's our son,

692 a ckƛ̓aʔƛ̓ʔús[mstəm]
a c -k+ƛ̓aʔ•ƛ̓ʔ=us+m -st -m
art cust^ -look_for -^cust -4erg
the one we've been looking for."

693 waẏ ck̓aʔítət náx̌əmɬ {ckɬ} kmimipúsəms
waẏ c -k̓aʔít•t nax̌mɬ k+my•my+p=us+m -s
well hab -get_near so make_out -3erg
He got closer and they recognized him.

694 cútəlx waẏ lut, waẏ mat kʷu scxík̓ək̓x
cut -lx waẏ lut waẏ mat kʷu sc -xik̓•k̓ -x
say -pl well not well maybe 4kn ipftvp^ -mistake -^ipftvp
They said "No, maybe we are mistaken."

695 waẏ yaʔx̌í mat cut axáʔ {i} ia lʔiw
waẏ yaʔx̌í mat cut axáʔ iʔ lʔiw
well that_one maybe say this art m's_father
Maybe the father [said]:

696 waẏ mat isənk̓ʷɬilmíxʷəm {maɬ}
waẏ mat i -s+nk̓ʷ+ɬ+yl=mixʷ+m
well maybe 1in -fellow_chief
"Maybe that's a fellow chief,

697 maɬ x̌ast {iʔ} ia
maɬ x̌as+t iʔ
too_much good art
he's got too much

nxʷilwístəns i? kəw̓wáps {iʔ} uɬ iʔ {iʔ} sənckʷmíns 698 uɬ
n+xʷy+lwis+tn -s iʔ kw+w+ap -s uɬ iʔ s+n+ckʷ+min -s uɬ
vehicle -3in art horses -3in and art buggy -3in and
of a good outfit, horses, wagon. *And*

ksəx̌cút nixʷ t tkəɬmílxʷ uɬ tuʔtẇit 699 waẏ mat
k+s+x̌c+ut nixʷ ? tkɬ+m=ilxʷ uɬ tẇ•tẇit waẏ mat
have_companion also ? woman and boys well must
he has a companion, a woman, and boys. *It must be*

isək̓ʷɬilmíxʷəm 700 waẏ ck̓ɬəncaʔqqípəlx, waẏ
i -s+nk̓ʷ+ɬ+yl=mixʷ+m waẏ c -k̓ɬ+n+caʔq•q=íp -lx waẏ
1in -fellow_chief well hab -come_close_to_door -pl well
a boss like me." *They[26] got close to the door,*

csʕaməncútəlx 701 uɬ k̓liʔ ʔawstkícsəlx, ṅta ixíʔ iʔ
c -saʕ+mncút -lx uɬ ik̓líʔ ʔaw+s+t+kíc -s -lx ṅta ixíʔ iʔ
hab -dismount -pl and there go_meet -3erg -pl intj that art
they got off. *They went to meet them, that's*

sqʷsíʔsəlx 702 níkxna límtmsəlx iʔ t
s+qʷsiʔ -s -lx níkxnaʔ lim+t+m -s -lx iʔ t
son -3in -pl goodness be_glad_for -3erg -pl art agInst
their son. *Gee, his parents are tickled*

ƛ̓ax̌əx̌ƛ̓x̌ápsəlx 703 uɬ kʷinkssəlx, k̓əɬt̓máʕssəlx {uɬ ɬi·}
ƛ̓ax̌•x̌•ƛ̓x̌á+p -s -lx uɬ kʷin=ks -s -lx k̓ɬ+t̓m=ʕas -s -lx
elders -3in -pl and shake_hands -3erg -pl kiss -3erg -pl
to see him! *They shook his hand and kissed him.*

704 cus a lʔiws uɬ iʔ sk̓ʷuys 705 waẏ ixíʔ axáʔ {iʔ}
cu -s a lʔiw -s uɬ iʔ s+k̓ʷuy -s waẏ ixíʔ axáʔ
tell -3erg art m's_father -3in and art mother -3in well that this
He said to his father and mother: *"This is your*

iʔ sípnəmp 706 ixíʔ axáʔ istaʔxʷɬtkəɬmílxʷ 707 ixíʔ iʔ
iʔ sipn -mp ixíʔ axáʔ i -s+taʔxʷ+ɬ+tkɬmílxʷ ixíʔ iʔ
art daughter_in_law -5in that this 1in -acquired_wife that art
daughter-in-law, *that's the one I got for a woman,* *she's the one*

ƛ̓aʔƛ̓aʔntín 708 kiʔ uɬ iʔ cúɬmən iʔ kən ksxʷilwísaʔx
ƛ̓aʔ•ƛ̓aʔ -nt -in kiʔ uɬ iʔ cu -ɬm -n iʔ kn ks -xʷy+lwis -aʔx
look_for -nt -1erg rel and art tell -5obj -1erg art 1kn incp^ -wander -^incp
I was looking for. *I told you I am going to travel*

iʔ l təmxʷúlaʔxʷ 709 ikswíklaʔxʷ[əm] 710 uɬ ixíʔ axáʔ
iʔ l tmxʷ=úlaʔxʷ i -ks -wík=laʔxʷ+m uɬ ixíʔ axáʔ
art in world 1i -futi -see_country and that this
the country, *I'm going to see the country over.* *And these are*

26 The visitors.

isqʷəsqʷasíʔa {cutx is} 711 sənʔaʔssíl paʔpút 712 níkxna ixíʔ
i -s+qʷs•qʷasíʔa s+n+ʔa•s•síl paʔ•pút níkxnaʔ ixíʔ
1in -children two match goodness then
my children, they're twins, they're alike." Gee,

slímtəmsəlx 713 kʷínkssəlx iʔ sípənsəlx
s -lim+t+m -s -lx kʷin=ks -s -lx iʔ sipn -s -lx
nom -be_glad_for -3i -pl shake_hands -3erg -pl art daughter_in_law -3in -pl
they're glad. They shook hands with their daughter-in-law,

714 waẏ uł axáʔ iʔ tuʔtẃít {iʔ} kʷinkssəlx
waẏ uł axáʔ iʔ tẃ•tẃit kʷin=ks -s -lx
well and this art boys shake_hands -3erg -pl
they shook hands with the boys,

715 xʷaʔntísəlx 716 axáʔ iʔ t tkəłmílxʷ iʔ knaqs
xʷaʔ -nt -is -lx axáʔ iʔ t tkł+m=ilxʷ iʔ k=naqs
pick_up -nt -3erg -pl this art agInst woman art one_person
took them on their lap. The woman took one boy

xʷaʔntís iʔ tətẃít 717 uł axáʔ {iʔ} iʔ t sqəltmíxʷ kʷis
xʷaʔ -nt -is iʔ t•tẃit uł axáʔ iʔ t s+qlt=mixʷ kʷi -s
pick_up -nt -3erg art boy and this art agInst man take -3erg
in her lap, and the man took the

iʔ knaqs 718 xʷaʔntísəlx, waẏ uł cxʷíltməlx 719 waẏ
iʔ k=naqs xʷaʔ -nt -is -lx waẏ uł cxʷ=ilt+m -lx waẏ
art one_person pick_up -nt -3erg -pl well and hold_child -pl well
other boy. They picked them up and petted them. They

wiʔslímtməlx 720 waẏ {x̌əlítsəlx iʔ} x̌lítəntməlx iʔ k̓əl citxʷ
wẏ+s+lim+t+m -s -lx waẏ x̌lit -nt -m -lx iʔ k̓l citxʷ
be_glad -3erg -pl well call -nt -psv -pl art to house
were glad. They asked them to the house.

721 uł axáʔ cus {iʔ} iʔ səxʷk̓ʷúl̓əms axáʔ a ilmíxʷəm 722 waẏ
uł axáʔ cu -s iʔ sxʷ=k̓ʷul̓+m -s axáʔ a yl=mixʷ+m waẏ
and this tell -3erg art worker -3in this art chief well
And the boss told his working man: "Fix

k̓ʷul̓łtp axaʔ iʔ kəẃwáps iʔ k̓əl sənt̓əwscqáx̌aʔtən
k̓ʷul̓ -łt -p axáʔ iʔ kw+w+ap -s iʔ k̓l s+n+t̓wst+s=qáx̌aʔ+tn
fix -łt -5erg this art horses -3in art to barn
his horses, take them

nppilxstp {waẏ} 723 waẏ ʔamtíməlx, wiʔwiʔcínəlx
n+p•pil+x -st -p waẏ ʔam -t -im -lx wẏ•wẏ=cin -lx
enter_pl -caus -5erg well feed -nt -psv -pl finish_eating_pl -pl
to the barn." They fed them and they got done eating.

724 [cún]tməlx, waẏ ixíʔ tqʷəlqʷəltíẃsts axáʔ {iʔ} ia ilmíxʷəm ya
cu -nt -m -lx waẏ ixíʔ t+qʷl•qʷl+t=iẃ -st -s axáʔ iʔ yl=mixʷ+m ya
tell -nt -psv -pl well then phone -st -3erg this art chief art
The boss, the father is going to call on the

lʔiw 725 waẏ ixíʔ {s} la cmalk̓ʷ i l *neighborhood* 726 cut waẏ
lʔiw waẏ ixíʔ l cut waẏ
m's_father well that in say well
telephone *the whole neighborhood.* *He said*

ɬckicx {is} isqʷsíʔ {uɬ} 727 uɬ waẏ ʕapnáʔ p
ɬ+c+kic+x i -s+qʷsiʔ uɬ waẏ ʕapnáʔ p
arrive_cisl_again 1in -son and yes now 5kn
"My son is back. *You are going*

kscyaʕ̓míxaʔx, kʷu ksʔíckaʔx 728 waẏ {taʔxʷs}
ksc -yaʕ̓ -míx+aʔx kʷu ks -ʔickn -aʔx waẏ
futPerfkn^ -gather -^futPerfkn 4kn incp^ -play -^incp well
to gather, we are going to play. *He has*

taʔxʷsqʷəsqʷasíʔa, ixíʔ {p ks} p kswíkltaʔx {i c} 729 uɬ aɬíʔ_swit kʷa
taʔxʷ+s+qʷs•qʷasíʔa ixíʔ p ks -wik=lt -aʔx uɬ aɬíʔ_swit kʷa
have_children that 5kn incp^ -see_child -^incp and in_fact intj
children and you are going to get acquainted with them." *At that time*

iʔ sx̌əẁx̌əẁúscəlx {iʔ} iʔ sqilxʷ {iʔ} pnicíʔ 730 kʷa iʔ sq̓ʷəẏməncút
iʔ s -x̌ẁ•x̌ẁ=us -c -lx iʔ s+qilxʷ pn+icíʔ kʷa iʔ s+q̓ʷẏ+mncut
art nom -eager -3i -pl art person at_that_time intj art dance
the people are always looking for an excuse to gather *and to dance.*

731 nákna waẏ waẏ {əc} cyaʕ̓lx yaʕyáʕt {iʔ s} iʔ sqʷəsqʷasíʔas
níkxnaʔ waẏ waẏ c -yaʕ̓ -lx yaʕ•yáʕ+t iʔ s+qʷs•qʷasíʔa -s
goodness well well hab -gather -pl all art children -3in
Gee, all the boss's children

axáʔ a ilmíxʷəm 732 ixíʔ kyaʕ̓mísəlx 733 waẏ ixíʔ {c t} q̓ʷiċt
axáʔ a yl=mixʷ+m ixíʔ k+yaʕ̓+mí -s -lx waẏ ixíʔ q̓ʷiċ+t
this art chief then gather -3erg -pl well then full
gathered, *they all gathered.* *The boss's house,*

axáʔ {iʔ s} iʔ siləmxʷíɬxʷ iʔ sənq̓ʷəyməncútən 734 níkna waẏ
axáʔ iʔ s+yl=mxʷ=iɬxʷ iʔ s+n+q̓ʷẏ+mncut+n níkxnaʔ waẏ
this art chief's_house art dance_hall goodness yes
the dance hall, filled up. *Gee*

ɬlímtməntməlx 735 ixíʔ ɬkʷínksəntməlx {axáʔ iʔ} axáʔ iʔ sqʷsiʔ
ɬ+lim+t+m -nt -m -lx ixíʔ ɬ+kʷin=ks -nt -m -lx axáʔ iʔ s+qʷsiʔ
glad_again -nt -psv -pl then shake_hands_again -nt -psv -pl this art son
they are happy. *They shook hands with the son*

736 uɬ axáʔ {iʔ s} iʔ skɬəx̌əx̌ámsəlx axáʔ t̓əxʷ iʔ {s} tkəɬmílxʷs
uɬ axáʔ iʔ s+k+ɬx̌•x̌•am -s -lx axáʔ t̓xʷ iʔ t+kɬm=ilxʷ -s
and this art in_laws -3in -pl this emph art wife -3in
and his wife's in-laws;

737 uɬ axáʔ iʔ{s} tuʔtẁít iʔ sqʷəsqʷasíʔas 738 waẏ q̓ʷəẏməncú··təlx {waẏ}
uɬ axáʔ iʔ tẁ•tẁit iʔ s+qʷs•qʷasíʔa -s waẏ q̓ʷẏ+mncut -lx
and this art boys art children -3in well dance -pl
and with the boys, his children. *They danced.*

739 uɬ aɬíʔ t̓i ilíʔ ilíʔ kən cənxaʔyáwaʔ
uɬ aɬíʔ t̓iʔ ilíʔ ilíʔ kn c -n+xaʔy=áwaʔ
and because evid there there 1kn hab -in_midst
And I was right there with them.

740 way̓ t̓iʔ_lut sxəƛ̓púlaʔxʷs
way̓ t̓iʔ_lut s -xƛ̓+p=úlaʔxʷ -s
well in_no_time nom -daylight -3i
It's not quite daylight.

741 ixíʔ t̓əxʷ t̓íxʷxʷləm mi {u} ksxəƛ̓púlaʔxʷs
ixíʔ t̓xʷ t̓ixʷ•xʷ•l+m mi k -s+xƛ̓+p=úlaʔxʷ -s
then emph different fut futi -full_daylight -3i
Things commence to be different and then daylight comes,

742 mat cənpaʔqcín
mat c -n+paʔq=cín
maybe hab -dawn
the first light comes on.

743 ixíʔ {kən} kən ksʔayx̌ʷtáyn
ixíʔ kn k+s+ʔayx̌ʷ+t+áyn
then 1kn have_tiredness
I am tired.

744 ixíʔ uɬ cúnəlx way̓ way̓ kən scənlqíw̓sx
ixíʔ uɬ cu -n -lx way̓ way̓ kn sc -n+lq=iw̓s -x
then and tell -1erg -pl well yes 1kn ipftvp^ -weed -^ipftvp
Then I tell them, "I am weeding,

745 way̓ staʔ kən ɬxʷuy
way̓ staʔ kn ɬ+xʷuy
yes intj 1kn go_back
I should go back home.

746 way̓ kən ksʔayx̌ʷtáyn
way̓ kn k+s+ʔayx̌ʷ+t+áyn
yes 1kn have_tiredness
I am tired.

747 way̓, way̓, way̓ nxixayápəlqs
way̓ way̓ way̓ n+xy•xay=áplqs
yes yes yes end_of_story
It's the end of the story.

Pete continues: "That means 'that's the end of the story." Then he tells the story in English. The quality of the recording is intermittently poor until the end of the tape. Here I transcribe the clearest parts to give the reader a flavor of Pete's English diction.

... "Let me ask you a word or two before you continue your doing." They said "All right," they stopped. Then he says "What's the idea of you folks abusing the dead body like that? I thought they respect a dead body." He says "That's what they do where I come from," And they said "Well," he says, "When he was alive," he says "He owed. Borrowed money, or gets stuff on credit, and he didn't have no people, and then he didn't have any worth, that is, saved money, didn't have any money. And when he died, well, he owed all us, and he didn't have nothing, no people. We didn't know how could ... to collect it. So that's what we are collecting by abusing him, hitting him, and kicking him, and when we get done, well, then the next one that he owes takes turns til, til they all get their share kicking him and abusing him. Why, then we're there." So, well, then he told them, he says, "Well," he says, "You know, where I come from they respect a corpse... I'll tell you what I'll do," he says, "You fellows line up, you get those that's got a bill again[st] him and after you're lined up, well, then you tell me and I ... [tape ends].

The Devil and the Black Man

1 uɬ cus i? sl̓ax̌ts 2 way̓, way̓, uɬ t̓i x̌ast kʷu ɬ
uɬ cu -s i? s+l̓ax̌+t -s way̓ way̓ uɬ t̓i? x̌as+t kʷu ɬ
and tell -3erg art friend -3in well yes and evid good 4kn compl
And he said to his friend: *“Might as well we go*

l̓əx̌tíw̓səm 3 way̓ lut mat t̓a ksqilxʷ t ḱíḱa?t 4 uɬ t̓i la?ɬ
l̓x̌+t=iw̓s+m way̓ lut mat t̓ k+s+qilxʷ t ḱí•ḱa?t uɬ t̓i? na?ɬ
go_partners well not maybe negfac have_person obl near and evid and
partners. *I don’t think there are people around here,* *and it’s*

anwí kʷu {k} kcnwixʷ 5 uɬ way̓ t̓i_x̌ast kʷu ɬ l̓əx̌tíw̓səm
anwí kʷu kc+nwixʷ uɬ way̓ t̓i?_x̌ast kʷu ɬ l̓x̌+t=iw̓s+m
you 4kn be_with_one_another and well as_well 4kn compl go_partners
just you (and) I here. *It’s just as well we go partners.”*

6 a·· way̓ aspu?ús,” cuntəm i? t q̓ʷəyʕas axá? i? sx̌ʷílmən
a way̓ a -s+pu?=ús cu -nt -m i? t q̓ʷy=ʕas axá? i? s+x̌ʷil+mn
intj well 2in -heart tell -nt -psv art agInst black_face this art devil
“Ah, if that’s how you feel,” said the Black Face to the Devil.

7 a i? sx̌ʷílmən {i?} i? scxa?tɬqʷəlqʷíltx 8 ixí? uɬ
a i? s+x̌ʷil+mn i? sc -xa?t+qʷl•qʷíl+t -x ixí? uɬ
intj art devil art ipftvp^ -talk_first -^ipftvp then and
The Devil is the one that does the talking. *Spring*

ks[t]a?mína?lx mat t̓əxʷ t stim̓ {i? k} ki? ksta?mína?lx
k+s+ta?m=ína? -lx mat t̓xʷ t s+tim̓ ki? k+s+ta?m=ína? -lx
have_spring -pl maybe evidently agInst something rel have_spring -pl
came, somehow they made it through winter,

9 mat t sqʷl̓ip {i?} kʷa {i?} i? s?íɬəns i? q̓sápi? {skənwi} i?
mat t s+qʷl̓=ip kʷa i? s+?iɬn -s i? q̓sápi? i?
maybe agInst moss intj art food -3in art long_ago art
maybe with moss (long ago moss was

sqʷl̓ip {uɬ} 10 way̓ ksta?mína?lx ixí? uɬ c̓sap i? smíḱʷət uɬ
s+qʷl̓=ip way̓ k+s+ta?m=ína? -lx ixí? uɬ c̓sa+p i? s+miḱʷ+t uɬ
moss well have_spring -pl then and gone art snow_on_ground and
food). (1:00) *Spring came, and the snow was gone,*

axá? i? súl̓la?xʷ ixí? waʕ̓múla?xʷ {uɬ} 11 uɬ way̓ ḱəl
axá? i? sul=la?xʷ ixí? waʕ+m=úla?xʷ uɬ way̓ ḱl
this art frozen_ground then thaw and yes about
and the frozen earth thawed *and it’s*

kspəl̓l̓úla?xʷs uɬ ixí? {c c} scuts axá? {i? s} i? sx̌ʷílmən
ks -pl̓•l̓=úla?xʷ -s uɬ ixí? s -cut -s axá? i? s+x̌ʷil+mn
futi -sprout -3i and then nom -say -3i this art devil
getting time for the grass to sprout, and the devil said,

12 cus i? q̓ʷəyʕás waẏ uɬ aɬí? mat kʷu sləx̌tíẇs uɬ waẏ kʷu
cu -s i? q̓ʷy=ʕas waẏ uɬ aɬí? mat kʷu c -l̓x̌+t=iẇs uɬ waẏ kʷu
tell -3erg art black_face well and so maybe 4kn hab -friends and yes 4kn
he said to the Black Man, "Well, being that we are partners, and now there is no more

ksta?mína? 13 uɬ aɬí? t'i nəqsíɬxʷəlx, uɬ t'i {nəqsiɬnə··t'i} naqs{i?} ya
k+s+ta?m=ína? uɬ aɬí? t'i? nqs=iɬxʷ -lx uɬ t'i? naqs ya
have_spring and so evid next_door -pl and evid one art
snow..." *And they live in one house, and just it's one inside,*

nyxʷut lut t'a cənʕalíẇs, 14 kmix {i?} i? sur̓ísəlp̓ la nq̓a?q̓?íẇs
n+yxʷ=ut lut t' c n+ʕal̓=íẇs kmix i? s+wr̓=islp̓ l n+q̓a?•q̓?=íẇs
inside not negfac hab -partition only art fire in go_between
it's not partitioned; *there's only the fireplace that burns*

ki? cwár̓ {uɬ i··} 15 uɬ k̓la nsək̓ʷtslíp̓ {i s} i? q̓ʷəyʕás
ki? c -war̓ uɬ k̓l n+s+k̓ʷt+slip̓ i? q̓ʷy=ʕas
rel hab -burn and to across_fire art black_face
between them. *And on one side of the room is the Black Face. (2:07)*

16 ixí? cniɬc i? təmxʷúla?xʷs, uɬ ixí? cniɬc ck̓ʷəl̓cəncút 17 uɬ axá?
ixí? cniɬ+c i? tmxʷ=úla?xʷ -s uɬ ixí? cniɬ+c c -k̓ʷl̓=cn+cut uɬ axá?
that (s)he art ground -3in and there (s)he hab -cook and this
That's where he stays, and that's where he cooks. *And*

i? sx̌ʷílmən, axá? {i} k̓la nsək̓ʷtslíp̓, uɬ ixí?{c} ck̓ʷəl̓cəncút {xi uɬ} 18 ixí?
i? s+x̌ʷil+mn axá? k̓l n+s+k̓ʷt+slip̓ uɬ ixí? c -k̓ʷl̓=cn+cut ixí?
art devil this to across_fire and that hab -cook then
the Devil is on the other side, and that's where he cooks.

uɬ ɬa? cp̓i?qíltnəlx, {uɬ ctkams} ctkɬáməlx ɬa? {c} c̓aɬ?íɬnəlx
uɬ ɬa? c -p̓y̓q=ilt+n -lx c -t+kɬa+m -lx ɬa? c -?aɬ•?íɬn -lx
and when hab -cook -pl hab -separate -pl when hab -eat_pl -pl
And when they cook, they eat separately.

19 ixí? waẏ k̓la nsək̓ʷtslíp̓ i? sənilí?tns axá? i? knáqs, uɬ axá?
ixí? waẏ k̓l n+s+k̓ʷt+slip̓ i? s+n+ilí?+tn -s axá? i? k=naqs uɬ axá?
that yes to across_fire art dwelling_place -3in this art one_person and this
One stays on one side, and the other

i? knaqs k̓la nsək̓ʷtílp 20 waẏ ksta?mína?lx, a uɬ
i? k=naqs k̓l n+s+k̓ʷt=ilp waẏ k+s+ta?m=ína? -lx a uɬ
art one_person to across_bed well have_spring -pl intj and
on the other side. *The snow came off the ground, the frost is out of*

waʕmúla?xʷ 21 ixí? uɬ waẏ {i·} i? sk̓ʷanɬqəm {ə} nləʕʷpús 22 uɬ
waʕ+m=úla?xʷ ixí? uɬ waẏ i? s+k̓ʷan=ɬq+m n+lʕʷ+p=us uɬ
thaw then and well art planting fit and
the ground, (3:00) *and then garden time came.* *And*

ixí? cúntəm i? t sx̌ʷílmən axá? i? q̓ʷəyʕás 23 waẏ uɬ
ixí? cu -nt -m i? t s+x̌ʷil+mn axá? i? q̓ʷy=ʕas waẏ uɬ
then tell -nt -psv art agInst devil this art black_face well and
the Devil said to the Black Face: *"Well,*

aɬíʔ {mat kʷu slə} kʷu sl̓əx̌tíw̓sx, uɬ way̓ kʷu kstaʔmínaʔ,
aɬíʔ kʷu s -l̓x̌+t=iw̓s -x uɬ way̓ kʷu k+s+taʔm=ínaʔ
because 4kn ipftv^ -be_partners -^ipftv and yes 4kn have_spring
since we are partners, and the snow is all gone,

24 uɬ way̓ t̓i_x̌ast kʷu ɬ k̓ʷánɬqəm 25 ńíńw̓iʔ pnaʔ_cmay kʷu
uɬ way̓ t̓iʔ_x̌ast kʷu ɬ k̓ʷan=ɬq+m ńíńw̓iʔ pnaʔ_cmay kʷu
and well as_well 4kn compl grow_crop a_while maybe 4kn
just as well we put in a garden. *We might reach winter*

ɬk̓astkínaʔ, kʷu cxʷəl·xʷált mi ɬʔístkəm 26 uɬ way̓ kʷu
ɬ+k+ʔas=tk=ínaʔ kʷu c -xʷl·•xʷal+t mi ɬ+ʔis=tk+m uɬ way̓ kʷu
reach_winter_again 4kn hab -alive_pl fut winter_again and yes 4kn
again, we might stay alive until winter. *Let's*

ksk̓ʷánɬqaʔx {i·} t kɬk̓astkínaʔtət 27 cúntəm iʔ
ks -k̓ʷan=ɬq -aʔx t kɬ -k+ʔas=tk=ínaʔ -tt cu -nt -m iʔ
incp^ -plant_garden -^incp obj_itr to_be -winter_supply -4in tell -nt -psv art
put in a garden for our winter supply." *The Black Face*

t q̓ʷəyʕás, way̓, way̓ anwí kʷ sxəxʔítaʔx, 28 way̓ anwí
t q̓ʷy=ʕas way̓ way̓ anwí kʷ s+x•xʔít=aʔx way̓ anwí
agInst black_face yes well you 2kn oldest_dim well you
said, "All right. You are the oldest, *you*

k̓əɬpaʔx̌əntíxʷ {uɬ} uɬ way̓ x̌ast asck̓əɬpáʔx̌. 29 uɬ way̓ t anwí
k̓ɬ+paʔx̌ -nt -ixʷ uɬ way̓ x̌as+t a -sc -k̓ɬ+paʔx̌ uɬ way̓ t anwí
figure_out -nt -2erg and yes good 2i -pftv -figure_out and yes agInst you
do the thinking, your thinking is good. (4:04) *And you*

mi ʔúməntxʷ iʔ ksk̓ʷánɬqtət 30 uɬ axáʔ iʔ sx̌ʷílmən cut, way̓,
mi ʔum -nt -xʷ iʔ k -s+k̓ʷan=ɬq -tt uɬ axáʔ iʔ s+x̌ʷil+mn cut way̓
fut name -nt -2erg art to_be -garden -4i and this art devil say well
name what we're going to plant." *And the Devil said,*

way̓ t̓əxʷ {kʷu ah} patáq iʔ ksk̓ʷánɬqtət 31 a··, way̓, way̓ aspuʔús
way̓ t̓xʷ patáq iʔ k -s+k̓ʷan=ɬq -tt a way̓ way̓ a -s+puʔ=ús
yes emph potato art to_be -garden -4i intj well yes 2in -heart
"Well, let's plant potatoes." *"Ah, if that's how you feel.*

32 uɬ laʔkín mi {kʷu ks kʷu kɬ} kʷu kɬpatáq {i t ks} iʔ t ksk̓ʷánɬqtət
uɬ la+ʔkíń mi kʷu kɬ+patáq iʔ t k -s+k̓ʷan=ɬq -tt
and how fut 4kn have_potato art obl to_be -garden -4i
And from where will we get potatoes for our garden?" (5:00)

33 a··, cut iʔ sx̌ʷílmən, way̓ ixíʔ ńíńw̓iʔ incá kən yaʔyaʕncút 34 ah, way̓,
a cut iʔ s+x̌ʷil+mn way̓ ixíʔ ńíńw̓iʔ in+cá kn yaʕ•yaʕ+ncút ah way̓
intj say art devil well that a_while I 1kn rustle intj well
"Ah, said the Devil, I will rustle them." *"Ok,*

way̓ incá uɬ ixíʔ {ist} ist̓lúlaʔxʷəm, isk̓ʷəl̓laʔxʷílpəm i l
way̓ in+cá uɬ ixíʔ i -s -t̓l=úlaʔxʷ+m i -s -k̓ʷl̓=laʔxʷ=ílp+m iʔ l
well I and that 1i -intt -plow 1i -intt -fix_a_surface art for
and I will do the plowing, and fix the surface

ksənk̓ʷánɬqtəntət
k -s+n+k̓ʷan=ɬq+tn -tt
to_be -garden -4i
in our garden.

35 uɬ ixíʔ put ɬ ikswiʔstƛ̓úlaʔxʷəm {mi k}
uɬ ixíʔ put ɬ i -ks -wy̓+s+tƛ̓=úlaʔxʷ+m
and then just when 1i -futi -finish_plowing
And just when I'll be done plowing you will be

mi way̓ aksk̓ʷánɬq {inaud}
mi way̓ a -ks -k̓ʷan=ɬq
fut yes 2i -futi -plant_garden
ready for planting.

36 way̓ t̓i ixíʔ uɬ kʷu
way̓ t̓iʔ ixíʔ uɬ kʷu
well evid then and 4kn
Just then we will

sk̓ʷánɬqəms
s -k̓ʷan=ɬq+m -s
nom4ˆ -grow_crop -ˆnom4
put in a garden."

37 way̓ {way̓ axáʔ i s} iʔ q̓ʷəyʕás ixíʔ
way̓ iʔ q̓ʷy=ʕas ixíʔ
well art black_face then

stƛ̓úlaʔxʷəms, uɬ ixíʔ náx̌əmɬ lut t̓a cmystin stim̓,
s -tƛ̓=úlaʔxʷ+m -s uɬ ixíʔ nax̌mɬ lut t̓ c -my -st -in s+tim̓
nom -plow -3i and that but not negfac custˆ -know -ˆcust -1erg what
Well, the Black Face plowed, but I don't know what it is, (6:04)

38 [s]t̓əlt̓últ̓ċaʔ, kəm̓ axáʔ iʔ áksəs a ntƛ̓úlaʔxʷtən {inaud}
s+tƛ̓•t̓úl=ċaʔ km̓ axáʔ iʔ akss a n+tƛ̓=úlaʔxʷ+tn
mules or this art oxen art plow
mules, or oxen, that they use for plowing.

39 huy uɬ plal
hoy uɬ pl•al
finish and grow
It grew.

hoy uɬ əcnəlqí··w̓səlx, uɬ aɬíʔ náx̌əmɬ nsíclaʔxʷ
hoy uɬ c -n+lq=iw̓s -lx uɬ aɬíʔ nax̌mɬ n+síc=laʔxʷ
finish and hab -weed -pl and because but new_ground
They weeded, and because it's new ground

40 lut {t̓a k} put
lut put
not just
there are

t̓a ksənpəllíw̓s
t̓ k+s+n+pl•l=iw̓s
negfac have_weeds
hardly any weeds.

41 way̓ uɬ ixíʔ klíq̓naʔsəlx,
way̓ uɬ ixíʔ k+líq̓=naʔ -s -lx
well and then hill_ground -3erg -pl
They hilled the garden; after they

wiʔsklíq̓naʔsəlx, hoy cplal
wy̓+s+líq̓=naʔ -s -lx hoy c -pl•al
finish_hilling -3erg -pl well hab -grow
got done hilling the garden it started to grow.

42 a· ċʔák̓ʷəm axáʔ iʔ patáq, ixíʔ
a ċʔak̓ʷ+m axáʔ iʔ patáq ixíʔ
intj flower this art potato then
The potatoes flowered,

uɬ klíq̓naʔsəlx, níkxnaʔ, qʷámqʷəmt {i s} iʔ sċaʔk̓ʷáɬqsəlx
uɬ k+líq̓=naʔ -s -lx níkxnaʔ qʷam•qʷm+t iʔ s+ċaʔk̓ʷ=áɬq -s -lx
and hill_ground -3erg -pl goodness excellent art blossoms -3in -pl
then they hilled it, the blooms are beautiful. (7:00)

43 i·· {uɬ} uɬ k̓áy̓ilx {ay ɬ}
i·· uɬ k̓ay̓•y+lx
intj and become_fall
Then fall came.

44 cútəlx way̓, way̓ t̓əxʷ kʷu táxʷɬqəm {cúntəm ə}
cut -lx way̓ way̓ t̓xʷ kʷu taxʷ=ɬq+m
say -pl well well emph 4kn harvest
They said, "Now we will harvest our crop."

45 cut axáʔ iʔ q̓ʷəyʕás way̓ {cut cus iʔ q̓ʷəy} cúntəm iʔ t q̓ʷəyáʕs
cut axáʔ iʔ q̓ʷy=ʕas way̓ cu -nt -m iʔ t q̓ʷy=ʕas
say this art black_face well tell -nt -psv art agInst black_face
The Black Face said to

axáʔ {iʔ} iʔ sx̌ʷílmən 46 waỷ t̓əxʷ anwí kʷ sxəxʔítaʔx, anwí kʷ pəx̌páx̌t,
axáʔ iʔ s+x̌ʷil+mn waỷ t̓xʷ anwí kʷ s+x•xʔít=aʔx anwí kʷ px̌•pax̌+t
this art devil well emph you 2kn oldest_dim you 2kn smart
the Devil: *"You are the oldest, you are smart.*

47 hu•húy, huy stx̌ʷíw̓sənt[əm] iʔ sk̓ʷánɬqtət, kin anx̌mínk 48 cut
hu+húy hoy s -tx̌ʷ=iw̓s -nt -m iʔ s+k̓ʷan=ɬq -tt ʔkin an -x̌m=ink cut
OK well ? -divide -nt -4erg art harvest -4in indef 2in -want say
Ok, let's divide in half our crop, which do you like?" *The*

iʔ sx̌ʷílmən, waỷ, ksxʔkístəm mi ctx̌ʷíw̓stəm 49 mat
iʔ s+x̌ʷil+mn waỷ ks -x+ʔki -st -m mi c -tx̌ʷ=iw̓s -t -m mat
art devil well futt^ -do_what -st -4erg fut cust^ -divide -st -4erg maybe
Devil said, "Yeah, how are we going to divide it? (8:00) *Maybe*

waỷ kʷ ksck̓əɬpáʔx̌ cúntəm axáʔ iʔ q̓ʷəyʕás 50 cúntəm iʔ
waỷ kʷ ksc -k̓ɬ+paʔx̌ cu -nt -m axáʔ iʔ q̓ʷy=ʕas cu -nt -m iʔ
yes 2kn pperf -figure_out tell -nt -psv this art black_face tell -nt -psv art
you have figured it out," he said to the Black Face. *The Black Face*

t q̓ʷəyʕás, waỷ km̓aʔ_stím̓ 51 waỷ ṅíṅw̓iʔ t̓ít̓im ɬ
t q̓ʷy=ʕas waỷ km̓a_s+tim̓ waỷ ṅíṅw̓iʔ t̓i•t̓ym ɬ
agInst black_face well nothing_to_it well a_while easy compl
said, "There's nothing to it. *It'll be easy to figure it out,*

ksk̓əɬpaʔx̌əntím, ɬ iksk̓əɬpaʔx̌ám 52 axáʔ iʔ knaqs
ks -k̓ɬ+paʔx̌ -nt -im ɬ i -ks -k̓ɬ+paʔx̌á+m axáʔ iʔ k=naqs
futt^ -figure_out -nt -4erg compl 1i -futi -figure_out this art one_person
for me to figure it out. *One will take*

kʷis {i s"} iʔ siyúps, uɬ ixíʔ cniɬc {i kskʷ} iʔ kskʷiʔs 53 uɬ ṅíṅw̓iʔ
kʷi -s iʔ sy=ups uɬ ixíʔ cniɬ+c iʔ ks -kʷiʔ -s uɬ ṅíṅw̓iʔ
take -3erg art tail and that (s)he art futi -take -3i and a_while
the tails, and that will be his share. *And then*

axáʔ {kəm iʔ} k̓əm iʔ sʕ̓ʷx̌ʷip, ixíʔ iʔ knaqs {i kskʷ} iʔ kskʷiʔs
axáʔ k̓m iʔ s+ʕ̓ʷx̌ʷ=ip ixíʔ iʔ k=naqs iʔ ks -kʷiʔ -s
this except art roots that art one_person art futi -take -3i
just the roots, that will be the other one's share."

54 cut, waỷ, waỷ x̌ast ixíʔ asck̓əɬpáʔx̌ {cúntəm uɬ ə"} 55 t q̓ʷəyʕás
cut waỷ waỷ x̌as+t ixíʔ a -sc -k̓ɬ+paʔx̌ t q̓ʷy=ʕas
say yes yes good that 2i -pftv -figure_out agInst black_face
He said, "Yeah, that's good thinking." (9:00) *The Black Face*

cúntəm axáʔ iʔ sx̌ʷílmən 56 waỷ anwí kʷ sxəxʔítaʔx, uɬ anwí mi kʷ
cu -nt -m axáʔ iʔ s+x̌ʷil+mn waỷ anwí kʷ s+x•xʔít=aʔx uɬ anwí mi kʷ
tell -nt -psv this art devil well you 2kn oldest_dim and you fut 2kn
said to the Devil: *"You are the oldest, and you will be the first*

cxʔit, 57 ʔúməntxʷ {ə"} y akstáxʷɬq, uɬ incá k̓əm {iʔ} iʔ snʕáyu {iʔ}
c+xʔit ʔum -nt -xʷ iʔ a -ks -taxʷ=ɬq uɬ in+cá k̓m iʔ s+n+ʕáyu
first name -nt -2erg art 2i -futi -harvest and I except art remainder
one. *You name what you want to harvest, and I will take*

iʔ tíxʷən 58 waẏ {i uɬ ixíʔ} ɬ wiks {i s} iʔ sx̌ʷílmən {ɬaʔ} ɬaʔ
iʔ tixʷ -n waẏ ɬ wik -s iʔ s+x̌ʷil+mn ɬaʔ
art obtain -1erg well when see -3erg art devil when
what's left." *When the Devil saw from the time*

cplál, 59 ɬə ƛ̓əksúpsəm a[xáʔ iʔ patáq, nt̓aʔ uɬ iʔ sc̓əʔák̓ʷ
c -pl•al ɬ ƛ̓k=s=ups+m axáʔ iʔ patáq nt̓a uɬ iʔ s+c̓ʔak̓ʷ
hab -grow when sprout this art potato intj and art flower
they grew, *the potatoes sprouted, my the blooms!*

60 wni··xʷ qʷámqʷəmt {i səc̓} iʔ sc̓əʔák̓ʷ 61 i·· cus iʔ sl̓ax̌ts:
wnixʷ qʷam•qʷm+t iʔ s+c̓ʔak̓ʷ i·· cu -s iʔ s+l̓ax̌+t -s
true excellent art flower intj tell -3erg art partner -3in
Truly beautiful blooms. (10:00) *He said to his partner:*

62 waẏ, ixíʔ waẏ wnixʷ asck̓əɬpáʔx̌ 63 "waẏ, uɬ aɬíʔa {ɬik} ɬ
waẏ ixíʔ waẏ wnixʷ a -sc -k̓ɬ+paʔx̌ waẏ uɬ aɬi_a ɬ
well that yes true 2i -pftv -figure_out yes and so_not compl
"Is it true that you want it that way?" *"Yes, I am not going to change*

ikɬəɬlútəm 64 waẏ cúntsən anwí kʷ sxəxʔítaʔx 65 anwí
i -kɬ -ɬ+lut+m waẏ cu -nt -s -n anwí kʷ s+x•xʔít=aʔx anwí
1i -futi -no_again well tell -nt -2obj -1erg you 2kn oldest_dim you
my mind. *I told you, you are the oldest one,* *you*

mi {ɬ} nk̓ʷintxʷ, ʔkin y akɬx̌mínk, ixíʔ uɬ tx̌ʷíẇsəntəm
mi n+k̓ʷin -t -xʷ ʔkin iʔ a -kɬ -x̌m=ink ixíʔ uɬ tx̌ʷ=iẇs -nt -m
fut pick -nt -2erg indef art 2i -to_be -want then and divide -nt -4erg
will have your pick, whatever you want, and we'll divide it up."

66 cut iʔ sx̌ʷílmən, waẏ, waẏ incá ikskʷním {i sc̓aʔ i s} iʔ siyúps, məɬ anwí,
cut iʔ s+x̌ʷil+mn waẏ waẏ in+cá i -ks -kʷni+m iʔ sy=ups mɬ anwí
say art devil OK well I 1i -futi -take art tail and you
The Devil said, "All right, I will take the tops, and you

anwí iʔ sʕ̓ʷx̌ʷip 67 haʔ x̌ast aspuʔús 68 cúntəm iʔ t
anwí iʔ s+ʕ̓ʷx̌ʷ=ip haʔ x̌as+t a -s+puʔ=ús cu -nt -m iʔ t
you art roots inter good 2in -heart tell -nt -psv art agInst
the roots. *Are you well satisfied?"* *The Black Face said,*

q̓ʷəyʕás, waẏ, uɬ scʔkínx {aʔ} a kʷ sxʔitx a, scʔx̌ilx {kiʔ xaʔtmscus} kiʔ
q̓ʷy=ʕas waẏ uɬ sc+ʔkin+x a kʷ s+xʔit=x a sc+ʔx̌il+x kiʔ
black_face yes and why_is_it art 2kn oldest_one intj reason_why rel
"Of course, you are the oldest, that's why I told you

xaʔtəms[túmən] 69 waẏ, huhúy, kʷu staxʷɬqx
xaʔt+m -st -um -n waẏ hu•húy kʷu s -taxʷ=ɬq -x
first -caus -2obj -1erg OK OK 4kn ipftv^ -harvest -^ipftv
to go first. (11:10) *Ok, now let's take our crop in."*

70 cúntəm {a t} iʔ t sx̌ʷílmən cúntəm iʔ q̓ʷəyáʕs 71 waẏ, {t̓əxʷ}
cu -nt -m iʔ t s+x̌ʷil+mn cu -nt -m iʔ q̓ʷy=ʕas waẏ
tell -nt -psv art agInst devil tell -nt -psv art black_face well
The Devil said to the Black Face [The Black Face said to the Devil: *"Well,*

t’əx^{w} k^{w}u k̓əɬʔíməntx^{w}, 72 incá {iʔ kən ksxaʔtms} iʔ kən
t’x^{w} k^{w}u k̓ɬ+ʔim -nt -x^{w} in+cá iʔ kn
emph 1obj wait_for -nt -2erg I art 1kn
you wait for me. *I’ll do my work*

ksxaʔtəmscútaʔx 73 uɬ aɬíʔ cəm̓ t’i k^{w}intx^{w} {iʔ} iʔ
ks -xaʔt+m+scút -aʔx uɬ aɬíʔ cm̓ t’iʔ k^{w}in -t -x^{w} iʔ
incp^ -be_first -^incp and because maybe evid take -nt -2erg art
first, *since you take the tops of*

siyúpsc {i} axáʔ iʔ sk̓^{w}ánɬqtət, 74 uɬ axáʔ incá {lut iks} aɬíʔ la
sy=ups -c axáʔ iʔ s+k̓^{w}an=ɬq -tt uɬ axáʔ in+cá aɬíʔ l
tail -3in this art harvest -4in and this I because in
our garden *and I what’s*

nyx^{w}túlaʔx^{w} 75 uɬ aɬíʔ axáʔ iʔ siyúps {ə} i l tqiltk, 76 uɬ
n+yx^{w}=t=úlaʔx^{w} uɬ aɬíʔ axáʔ iʔ sy=ups iʔ l t+qilt=k uɬ
underground and because this art tail art on top and
underground. *Since the tails are on top* *it’s*

t’it’im {ɬ ak} ɬ akstáx^{w}ɬqəm; 77 uɬ axáʔ incá uɬ lut t’
t’i•t’ym ɬ a -ks -tax^{w}=ɬq+m uɬ axáʔ in+cá uɬ lut t’
easy compl 2i -futi -harvest and this I and not negfac
easy for you to take your crop, (12:00) *but I can’t see where they*

ikswíkəm {kə} 78 sc̓x̌ilx uɬ incá iʔ kən ksxaʔtəmscútaʔx
i -ks -wik+m sc+ʔx̌il+x uɬ in+cá iʔ kn ks -xaʔt+m+scút -aʔx
1i -futi -see reason_why and I art 1kn incp^ -be_first -^incp
[the roots] are. *That’s why I wanted to go first.*

79 incá ṅíṅẇiʔ kən ƛəqáɬqəm, ƛəqəntín axáʔ iʔ sʕ̓^{w}x̌^{w}ip, 80 ṅíṅẇiʔ
in+cá ṅíṅẇiʔ kn ƛq=aɬq+m ƛq -nt -in axáʔ iʔ s+ʕ^{w}x̌^{w}=ip ṅíṅẇiʔ
I a_while 1kn dig_crop dig -nt -1erg this art roots a_while
I will dig my crop [first], I will dig the roots. *When*

ixíʔ {i} wiʔsƛəqəntín, 81 məɬ ṅíṅẇiʔ mi miymstín axáʔ iʔ
ixíʔ wẏ+s+ƛq -nt -in mɬ ṅíṅẇiʔ mi my+m -st -in axáʔ iʔ
then finish_digging -nt -1erg and a_while fut pile -st -1erg this art
I get done taking them *then I will pile together the tops*

siyúpsc axáʔ iʔ patáq 82 [il]í··ʔ tx̌^{w}əyx̌^{w}áyqən, uɬ t’ít’im anwí {ɬ aks}
sy=ups -c axáʔ iʔ patáq ilíʔ t+x̌^{w}y•x̌^{w}ay=q -n uɬ t’i•t’ym anwí
tail -3in this art potato there pile -1erg and easy you
of the potatoes. *I’ll pile them there, and it’ll be easy for you*

ɬ aksk^{w}úmcən 83 uɬ incá {iʔ} iʔ tíltəlx^{w}t 84 uɬ aɬíʔ {put}
ɬ a -ks -k^{w}um=cn uɬ in+cá iʔ til•tlx^{w}+t uɬ aɬíʔ
comp 2i -futi -save_for_food and I art difficult and because
to put away your share. *Mine is the hardest* *because*

put ksiyúps aɬíʔ mi cmistín laʔkín iʔ kən
put k+sy=ups aɬíʔ mi c -my -st -in la+ʔkíṅ iʔ kn
just have_tail so fut cust^ -know -^cust -1erg wherever art 1kn
it just has to have its tail before I know

ksƛ̓əqmíxaʔx 85 way̓, {way̓} cúntəm, xʷuyx {əy} 86 way̓ ixíʔ
ks -ƛ̓q -míxaʔx way̓ cu -nt -m xʷuy -x way̓ ixíʔ
incpˆ -dig -ˆincp OK tell -nt -psv go -isimptv well then
where to dig." "Ok," he said, "Go." (13:00) The

sƛ̓qáɬqəms iʔ sx̌ʷílmən [iʔ q̓ʷəyʕás] 87 ƛ̓əqəntí··s {iʔ} iʔ patáq, way̓
s -ƛ̓q=aɬq+m -s iʔ s+x̌ʷil+mn iʔ q̓ʷy=ʕas ƛ̓q -nt -is iʔ patáq way̓
nom -dig_crop -3i art devil art black_face dig -nt -3erg art potato well
Black Face went, he started to dig. He dug the potatoes,

uɬ tx̌ʷəyx̌ʷáyqs, 88 wiʔstx̌ʷix̌ʷáyqs uɬ axáʔ {iʔ} iʔ sƛ̓aqs
uɬ t+x̌ʷy•x̌ʷay=q -s wy̓+s+t+x̌ʷy•x̌ʷay=q -s uɬ axáʔ iʔ s+ƛ̓aq -s
and pile -3erg finish_piling -3erg and this art digging -3in
and piled them up. He got done piling what he dug

89 uɬ axáʔ {iʔ} iʔ syupsc ixíʔ tkəɬəmstís k̓əl sk̓ʷut ilíʔ
uɬ axáʔ iʔ sy=ups -c ixíʔ t+kɬ+m -st -is k̓l s+k̓ʷut ilíʔ
and this art tail -3in then one_side -st -3erg to other_side there
and then he put the tails to one side,

tx̌ʷəyx̌ʷáyqs 90 ixíʔ uɬ wiʔsƛ̓qáɬqəm[s] 91 uɬ ixíʔ cus
t+x̌ʷy•x̌ʷay=q -s ixíʔ uɬ wy̓+s+ƛ̓q=aɬq+m -s uɬ ixíʔ cu -s
pile -3erg then and finish_digging -3erg and then tell -3erg
he piled them. He finished digging and then he said

iʔ sl̓ax̌ts, way̓, way̓ kən uʔíkst 92 way̓ uɬ xiʔmíx anwí
iʔ s+l̓ax̌+t -s way̓ way̓ kn wy̓=ikst way̓ uɬ xiʔ+míx anwí
art partner -3in well yes 1kn get_done well and whatever you
to his partner, "Well, I am done; do whatever

akskcəwtíkxtəm {an akɬciw} akɬtx̌ʷíw̓s 93 uɬ incá nixʷ iliʔ
a -ks -k+cwt=ik -xt -m a -kɬ -tx̌ʷ=iw̓s uɬ in+cá nixʷ ilíʔ
2i -futi -do_st_unpleasant -xit -apsv 2i -to_be -half and I also there
you want to do with your share, and I too will do

kən ʔx̌íləm 94 ixíʔ uɬ x̌əl sʔistk 95 way̓, way̓ uɬ axáʔ {iʔ} iʔ
kn ʔx̌il+m ixíʔ uɬ x̌l s+ʔis=tk way̓ way̓ uɬ axáʔ iʔ
1kn do_same that and for winter well well and this art
the same. That's for the winter." And this Black Man,

q̓ʷəyʕás {mat} mat laʔkín, uɬ mat q̓y̓am, uɬ {təkɬ} t kɬƛ̓áqnaʔs
q̓ʷy=ʕas mat la+ʔkín̓ uɬ mat q̓y̓a+m uɬ t kɬ -ƛ̓áq=naʔ -s
black_face maybe wherever and maybe write and obl to_be -bag -3i
I guess he wrote somewhere, and sent for sacks. (14:14)

96 way̓ ixíʔ {npn} npkʷəntí··s iʔ l ƛ̓áqnaʔ, 97 uɬ ixíʔ q̓ʷəc̓q̓ʷíc̓əs
way̓ ixíʔ n+pkʷ -nt -is iʔ l ƛ̓áq+naʔ uɬ ixíʔ q̓ʷc̓•q̓ʷic̓ -s
well then pour -nt -3erg art in bag and then fill -3erg
He filled the sacks. He filled the sacks,

iʔ ƛ̓əqƛ̓áqnaʔs uɬ t̓i_put {iʔ s} iʔ ƛ̓áqnaʔs 98 way̓ ixíʔ {s}
iʔ ƛ̓q•ƛ̓áq=naʔ -s uɬ t̓iʔ_put iʔ ƛ̓áq=naʔ -s way̓ ixíʔ
art bags -3in and just_enough art bag -3in well then
he had just enough sacks. He brought

ʔukʷs iʔ k̓əl cítxʷsəlx 99 way̓ uɬ aɬíʔ k̓la nsək̓ʷtílp {q̓ʷay}
ʔukʷ -s iʔ k̓l citxʷ -s -lx way̓ uɬ aɬíʔ k̓l n+s+k̓ʷt=ilp
take_around -3erg art to house -3in -pl well and so to across_bed
them to their house. *And the Black Man had his place*

q̓ʷəyʕás {iʔ} iʔ sənilíʔtəns 100 uɬ axáʔ iʔ sx̌ʷílmən k̓la nsək̓ʷtílp
q̓ʷy=ʕas iʔ s+n+ilíʔ+tn -s uɬ axáʔ iʔ s+x̌ʷil+mn k̓l n+s+k̓ʷt=ilp
black_face art dwelling_place -3in and this art devil to across_bed
to one side of the house, *and the Devil to the other.*

101 uɬ axáʔ {k̓la nsək̓ʷt k̓əl} q̓ʷəyʕás iʔ k̓la nsək̓ʷtílps {ik̓líʔ} 102 ik̓líʔ kiʔ
uɬ axáʔ q̓ʷy=ʕas iʔ k̓l n+s+k̓ʷt=ilp -s ik̓líʔ kiʔ
and this black_face art to across_bed -3in there rel
And the Devil brought the potatoes to his side. *He*

pkʷəntís iʔ patáq way̓ uɬ yaʕpqín patáq 103 way̓ uɬ
pkʷ -nt -is iʔ patáq way̓ uɬ yaʕ+p=qín patáq way̓ uɬ
pour_solids -nt -3erg art potato yes and lots potato well and
put them there, lots of potatoes. (15:04) *And*

axáʔ {i s} iʔ sx̌ʷílmən iʔ ʔaʔúkʷiʔs iʔ siyúpsc 104 uɬ ixíʔ
axáʔ iʔ s+x̌ʷil+mn iʔ ʔa+ʔúkʷ y̓ -s iʔ sy=ups -c uɬ ixíʔ
this art devil art bring_pl -m -3erg art tail -3in and then
the Devil took his tops, *and*

t̓əqəntís {ə} nixʷ k̓la nsək̓ʷtílp 105 ixíʔ uɬ nixʷ yaʕpqín siyúps, {i s} iʔ
t̓q -nt -is nixʷ k̓l n+s+k̓ʷt=ilp ixíʔ uɬ nixʷ yaʕ+p=qín sy=ups iʔ
stack -nt -3erg also to across_bed that and also lots tail art
he put them also to one side. *That too was lots of tails, his crop,*

sctaxʷɬqs nx̌ʷəx̌ʷíckʷiʔs 106 way̓ ixíʔ uɬ ksʔastkín[aʔ], ixíʔ
sc -taxʷ=ɬq -s n+x̌ʷ•x̌ʷíckʷ y̓ -s way̓ ixíʔ uɬ k+s+ʔas=tk=ínaʔ ixíʔ
pftv -harvest -3i slice -nt -3erg well then and have_winter then
he slices them.[1] *Then winter time came. The ground froze,*

uɬ {m} súl̓laʔxʷ, uɬ mqʷaqʷ 107 a uɬ axáʔ q̓ʷəyʕás məɬ ixíʔ {s i}
uɬ sul=laʔxʷ uɬ mqʷ•aqʷ a uɬ axáʔ q̓ʷy=ʕas mɬ ixíʔ
and frozen_ground and snow_fall intj and this black_face and then
and the snow fell. *And the Black Face started*

sk̓ʷəl̓cəncúts 108 kc̓í·w̓sxiʔs iʔ patáq, məɬ ixíʔ nɬxʷpúsəs
s -k̓ʷl̓=cn+cut -s k+c̓íw̓=sxiʔ -s iʔ patáq mɬ ixíʔ n+ɬxʷ+p=us -s
nom -cook -3i wash_rd_obj -3erg art potato and then boil -3erg
to cook. *He washes the potatoes, and then he boils them. (16:00)*

109 t̓i uɬ lut ckəm̓íkxts {məɬ əɬ} kəlq̓ísxiʔs məɬ ixíʔ
t̓iʔ uɬ lut c -km̓=ik -xt -s k+lq̓=ísxiʔ -s mɬ ixíʔ
evid and not cust^ -do_so -xit -3erg peel -3erg and then
He doesn't have a particular way; he peels them and he

1 Not clear what Pete had in mind.

sənx̌ʷəx̌ʷí··ckʷəm {məɬ} 110 ťəxʷ mat laʔkín {uɬ i əks i} a ksɬiqʷ, uɬ
c -n+x̌ʷ•x̌ʷickʷ+m ťxʷ mat la+ʔkíń a k+s+ɬiqʷ uɬ
hab -slice evidently maybe wherever art have_meat and
slices them. *I don't know where he gets his meat,*

ixíʔ [iʔ] sɬíqʷ nx̌ʷəx̌ʷíckʷs 111 ixíʔ uɬ qʷámqʷəmt ixíʔ iʔ capsúyaʔ
ixíʔ iʔ s+ɬiqʷ n+x̌ʷ•x̌ʷickʷ -s ixíʔ uɬ qʷam•qʷm+t ixíʔ iʔ capsúya
then art meat slice -3erg that and excellent that art chop_suey
and he slices the meat. *And it's excellent chop suey.*

112 waẏ uɬ axáʔ iʔ sx̌ʷílmən waẏ waẏ lut iwá {kmə} kmix {i k} axáʔ iʔ
waẏ uɬ axáʔ iʔ s+x̌ʷil+mn waẏ waẏ lut iwá kmix axáʔ iʔ
well and this art devil yes yes not even only this art
And all the Devil has from

sk̓ʷanɬqs, 113 waẏ lút, lut, lut ʔaɬəɬnútəm {iʔ s} iʔ siyúpsc [iʔ] patáq
s+k̓ʷan=ɬq -s waẏ lut lut lut ʔaɬ•ɬ•n+út+m iʔ sy=ups -c iʔ patáq
garden -3in well not not not edible art tail -3in art potato
his garden *is nothing: the tails of the potatoes are not edible.*

114 waẏ ťa_uníxʷ iʔ kstaʔmínaʔ{lx} 115 waẏ taʔlíʔ uɬ {s} axáʔ
waẏ ťa_wnixʷ iʔ k+s+taʔm=ínaʔ waẏ taʔlíʔ uɬ axáʔ
well for_sure art have_spring well very_much and this
He sure had a hard time to pull through winter. *The Devil lost lots*

ckəẃtwílx iʔ sx̌ʷílmən 116 nťaʔ uɬ axáʔ {iʔ} iʔ q̓ʷəyʕás nťa uɬ
c -kẃ+t+wilx iʔ s+x̌ʷil+mn nťa uɬ axáʔ iʔ q̓ʷy=ʕas nťa uɬ
hab -lose_weight art devil intj and this art black_face intj and
of weight. (17:02) *Gee, but the Black Man got*

silxʷaʔəlqʷwílx {alaʔ} 117 uɬ tx̌saqs axáʔ {iʔ t} iʔ t patáq, iʔ t
silxʷaʔ=lqʷ+wílx uɬ t+x̌s=aqs axáʔ iʔ t patáq iʔ t
get_big and good_food this art prttv potato art prttv
big and fat. *He had good things to eat, potatoes,*

sʕʷx̌ʷips 118 waẏ ixíʔ {sɬ lə·· ɬ} kstaʔmínaʔ, 119 ťa_uní··xʷ kiʔ
s+ʕʷx̌ʷ=ip -s waẏ ixíʔ k+s+taʔm=ínaʔ ťa_wnixʷ kiʔ
roots -3in well then have_spring for_sure rel
roots. *Spring time came.* *The Devil sure*

kstaʔmínaʔ axáʔ iʔ sx̌ʷílmən 120 uɬ axáʔ məɬ iʔ q̓ʷəyáʕs uɬ
k+s+taʔm=ínaʔ axáʔ iʔ s+x̌ʷil+mn uɬ axáʔ mɬ iʔ q̓ʷy=ʕas uɬ
have_spring this art devil and this and art black_face and
had a hard time pulling through winter, *and the Black Face*

səlxʷaʔalqʷwílx, q̓ʷuc̓t 121 waẏ uɬ cús iʔ sľax̌ts waẏ uɬ
slxʷaʔ=alqʷ+wílx q̓ʷuc̓+t waẏ uɬ cu -s iʔ s+ľax̌+t -s waẏ uɬ
get_big fat well and tell -3erg art partner -3in well and
got big and fat. *"Now we will put in*

ťəxʷ {kʷu ɬ} kʷu ɬk̓ʷánɬqəm, 122 waẏ aɬíʔ {kʷu} kʷu ľəx̌tíẃs kʷaʔ kʷu
ťxʷ kʷu ɬ+k̓ʷan=ɬq+m waẏ aɬíʔ kʷu ľx̌+t=iẃs kʷaʔ kʷu
emph 4kn plant_again yes because 4kn be_partners intj 4kn
a garden again, *because we are partners, we are*

səxʷnwíxʷ, 123 uł way̓ talí {kʷu l̓əx} kʷu l̓əx̌tíw̓s kʷu
sxʷ+nwixʷ uł way̓ taʔlíʔ kʷu l̓x̌+t=iw̓s kʷu
acquaintances and yes very_much 4kn be_partners 4kn
acquaintances. *We are good friends, we have*

x̌ástəm {way̓ itlíʔ kʷu} 124 way̓ itlíʔ kʷu łk̓ʷánłqəm, 125 a náx̌əmł
x̌ast+m way̓ itlíʔ kʷu ł+k̓ʷan=łq+m a nax̌mł
do_well well from_there 4kn plant_again intj but
done good. (18:06) *We will put in a garden again.* *But*

ʕapnáʔ {k̓əl} k̓əłʔíysəntəm iʔ sk̓ʷánłqtət {cəm̓} 126 cəm̓ k̓əstwílx axáʔ iʔ
ʕapnáʔ k̓ł+ʔiys -nt -m iʔ s+k̓ʷan=łq -tt cm̓ k̓s+t+wilx axáʔ iʔ
now change -nt -4erg art garden -4in might spoil this art
this time we'll change what we're going to plant, *because the weeds*

sənk̓ʷánłqtən iʔ cənpəllíw̓s t̓əxʷ 127 cúntəm way̓, stim̓ uł iʔ
s+n+k̓ʷan=łq+tn iʔ c -n+pl•l=iw̓s t̓xʷ cu -nt -m way̓ s+tim̓ uł iʔ
garden art hab weeds emph tell -nt -psv OK what and art
will spoil the ground." *He said, "All right, but what are*

ksənk̓ʷánłqtət 128 cut axáʔ iʔ q̓ʷəyʕás, way̓ t̓əxʷ səsp̓qín, səsp̓qín
k -s+n+k̓ʷan=łq -tt cut axáʔ iʔ q̓ʷy=ʕas way̓ t̓xʷ s•sp̓=qin s•sp̓=qin
to_be -garden -4in say this art black_face well emph wheat wheat
we going to plant?" *The Black Face said, "Wheat,*

iʔ ksk̓ʷánłqtət 129 way̓ kʷu ł k̓əłʔaysáqsəm {iʔ ktx̌iwt} ʕác̓ənt, kʷa
iʔ k -s+k̓ʷan=łq -tt way̓ kʷu ł k̓ł+ʔays=áqs+m ʕac̓ -nt kʷa
art to_be -harvest -4in well 4kn ? change_grub look -nt intj
we'll plant wheat. *We will change grub. Look, we've had potatoes, now let's*

patáq, ʕapnáʔ səsp̓qín 130 way̓ {a əxəł} lut t̓a łt̓lúlaʔxʷsəlx, uł
patáq ʕapnáʔ s•sp̓=qin way̓ lut t̓ ł+t̓l=úlaʔxʷ -s -lx uł
potato now wheat well not negfac plow_again -3erg -pl and
have wheat." (19:02) *They didn't have to plow, because they kept*

ałíʔ nyʕ̓íp way̓ cnəlqíw̓stsəlx 131 xʷúk̓ʷlaʔxʷ, náx̌əmł t̓i
ałíʔ nyʕ̓ip way̓ c -n+lq=iw̓s -t -s -lx xʷúk̓ʷ=laʔxʷ nax̌mł t̓iʔ
because always yes cust^ -weed ^cust -3erg -pl deserted but evid
pulling the weeds, *it's clean soil, but they*

cʕá··x̌laʔxʷsəlx uł way̓ pkʷúlaʔxʷməlx 132 way̓ ixíʔ {s}
c -ʕáx̌=laʔxʷ -st -s -lx uł way̓ pkʷ=úlaʔxʷ+m -lx way̓ ixíʔ
cust^ -harrow -^cust -3erg -pl and yes sow -pl well then
just harrowed it, and they sowed the wheat. *It grew,*

cplal ałíʔ swit_ałíʔ nx̌súlaʔxʷ iʔ təmxʷúlaʔxʷ 133 nt̓a t̓i
c -pl•al ałíʔ swit_ałíʔ n+x̌s=úlaʔxʷ iʔ tmxʷ=úlaʔxʷ nt̓a t̓iʔ
hab -grow because in_fact good_soil art ground intj evid
because that land is good land. *Goodness*

nxʷúk̓ʷuʔs, lut t̓a ksənpəllíw̓s {ay uy} 134 uł ałíʔ kʷaʔ
n+xʷuk̓ʷ=w̓s lut t̓ k+s+n+pl•l=iw̓s uł ałíʔ kʷaʔ
clean not negfac have_weeds and because intj
there are no weeds, or anything *because*

nk̓ʷəsc̓ʔák̓ʷəm {a c} a cnəlqíw̓st[səlx]
nk̓ʷ+s+c̓ʔak̓ʷ+m a c -n+lq=iw̓s -t -s -lx
all_summer art cust^ -weed -^cust -3erg -pl
all summer long they pulled weeds.

135 uɬ ɬk̓ay̓ílx
uɬ ɬ+k̓ay̓•y+lx
and autumn_again
And it's fall again,

uɬ q̓ʷəyʕás cus iʔ sl̓ax̌ts
uɬ q̓ʷy=ʕas cu -s iʔ s+l̓ax̌+t -s
and black_face tell -3erg art partner -3in
and the Black Man said to his partner: (20:06)

136 way̓, way̓ uɬ k̓ay̓ílx, way̓
way̓ way̓ uɬ k̓ay̓•y+lx way̓
well well and become_fall yes
"It's fall, soon it will snow,

xʔal̓ ksmqʷáqʷs, ksʔístkəms
x[ʔ]al ks -mqʷ•aqʷ -s ks -ʔis=tk+m -s
soon futi -snow_fall -3i futi -winter -3i
winter starts.

137 way̓ cəm̓ kʷu kməqʷqʷínaʔ,
way̓ cm̓ kʷu k+mqʷ•qʷ=ínaʔ
well maybe 4kn snowed_in
We might get caught in the snow,

way̓ t̓i kʷu ksxʷəsxʷúsəlxaʔx
way̓ t̓iʔ kʷu ks -xʷs•xʷus+lx -aʔx
well evid 4kn incp^ -hurry -^incp
we better hurry.

138 hu•húy, {o} aɬíʔ qʷən̓cín aɬíʔ
hu+húy aɬíʔ qʷn̓=cin aɬíʔ
OK so pity because
Well, it's a pity that

anwí kʷ sxəxʔítaʔx
anwí kʷ s+x•xʔít=aʔx
you 2kn oldest_dim
you are the oldest."

139 cúntəm iʔ t q̓ʷəyáʕs axáʔ iʔ sx̌ʷílmən
cu -nt -m iʔ t q̓ʷy=ʕas axáʔ iʔ s+x̌ʷil+mn
tell -nt -psv art agInst black_face this art devil
The Black Face said to the devil:

140 way̓ anwí kʷ sxəxʔítaʔx
way̓ anwí kʷ s+x•xʔít=aʔx
well you 2kn oldest_dim
"You are the older one,

141 way̓ anwí nk̓ʷaʔk̓ʷíntxʷ {a k} kin̓ {ank}
way̓ anwí n+k̓ʷaʔ•k̓ʷín -t -xʷ ʔkin̓
well you pick -nt -2erg indef
you pick out what you want,

akɬx̌mínk, iʔ sʕ̓ʷx̌ʷíp, kəm̓ {i s} iʔ tqíltk {is}
a -kɬ -x̌m=ink iʔ s+ʕ̓ʷx̌ʷ=ip km̓ iʔ t+qilt=k
2i -to_be -want art roots or art top
the roots, or the tops."

142 nstíls iʔ sx̌ʷílmən,
n+st=ils iʔ s+x̌ʷil+mn
think art devil
The Devil thought,

way̓, way̓ lut haʔ {i} iskʷním iʔ tqíltk {i s} iʔ sx̌əx̌c̓iʔmálqʷ {is}
way̓ way̓ lut haʔ i -s -kʷni+m iʔ t+qilt=k iʔ s+x̌•x̌c̓iʔ+m=álqʷ
well well not inter 1i -intt -take art top art stalk
"Haven't I taken the tops before, the stalks? (21:12)

143 qʷámqʷəmt kʷa iʔ sc̓ʔak̓ʷ {uɬ}
qʷam•qʷm+t kʷa iʔ s+c̓ʔak̓ʷ
excellent intj art flower
And the flowers were beautiful,

144 cut kʷa talí·· kiʔ kən
cut kʷa taʔlíʔ kiʔ kn
say intj very_much rel 1kn
and sure enough I had a hard time

kstaʔmínaʔ, way̓ uɬ kən ʕalpəncút
k+s+taʔm=ínaʔ way̓ uɬ kn ʕal+p+ncút
have_spring yes and 1kn loser
to pull through winter, I was the loser all the way.

145 uɬ axáʔ {iʔ} iʔ q̓ʷəyʕás
uɬ axáʔ iʔ q̓ʷy=ʕas
and this art black_face
But the Black Face

náx̌əmɬ nq̓ʷaʔcmís ixíʔ {i s} iʔ səʕ̓ʷx̌ʷíp
nax̌mɬ n+q̓ʷaʔc̓+mi -s ixíʔ iʔ s+ʕ̓ʷx̌ʷ=ip
but get_fat_on -3erg that art roots
got fat on the roots.

146 way̓ ʕapnáʔ iʔ saʕ̓ʷx̌ʷíp
way̓ ʕapnáʔ iʔ s+ʕ̓ʷx̌ʷ=ip
well now art roots
This time I will take

mi kʷin {inaud} 147 lut nixʷ ikɬ{əkɬ}əɬʕalpəncút 148 cus iʔ
mi kʷi -n lut nixʷ i -kɬ -ɬ+ʕal+p+ncút cu -s iʔ
fut take -1erg not again 1i -futi -lose_again tell -3erg art
the roots. *I am not going to be the loser this time."* *He told*

sľax̌ts, way̓, way̓ ťəxʷ incá iʔ səʕ̓ʷx̌ʷíp mi kʷín, 149 məɬ anwí
s+ľax̌+t -s way̓ way̓ ťxʷ in+cá iʔ s+ʕ̓ʷx̌ʷ=ip mi kʷi -n mɬ anwí
partner -3in well well emph I art roots fut take -1erg and you
his partner, "This time I will take the roots (22:00) *and you*

iʔ tqiltk {i s} iʔ səsp̓qín 150 a·· way̓, way̓ ixíʔ ha uníxʷ ixíʔ
iʔ t+qilt=k iʔ s•sp̓=qin a way̓ way̓ ixíʔ haʔ wnixʷ ixíʔ
art top art wheat intj OK OK that inter true that
the tops of the wheat." *"Ah, are you sure that you want it*

asck̓əɬpáʔx̌, a kʷ isľáx̌t 151 way̓ way̓ kən npútəls, 152 a··,
a -sc -k̓ɬ+paʔx̌ a kʷ i -s+ľax̌+t way̓ way̓ kn n+put=ls a
2i -pftv -deliberate intj 2kʷu 1in -friend yes yes 1kn satisfied intj
that way, my partner?" *"Yes, yes, I am satisfied."* *"Ah,*

way̓ way̓ ťi {x̌ast} x̌ast aspuʔús, uɬ x̌ast aɬíʔ kʷu ľəx̌tíw̓s, anwí
way̓ way̓ ťiʔ x̌as+t a -s+puʔ=ús uɬ x̌as+t aɬíʔ kʷu ľx̌+t=iw̓s anwí
well well evid good 2in -heart and good because 4kn be_partners you
you are well satisfied, and we are good partners;

kʷ sxəxʔítaʔx 153 cúntəm iʔ t q̓ʷəyʕas axáʔ iʔ sx̌ʷílmən
kʷ s+x•xʔít=aʔx cu -nt -m iʔ t q̓ʷy=ʕas axáʔ iʔ s+x̌ʷil+mn
2kn oldest_dim tell -nt -psv art agInst black_face this art devil
you are the oldest." *The Black Face said to the Devil:*

154 náx̌əmɬ naqs iʔ kʷ ikscúnəm 155 way̓ lut kʷu əxkínəm {mi} mi
nax̌mɬ naqs iʔ kʷ i -ks -cun+m way̓ lut kʷu xkin+m mi
but one art 2kʷu 1i -futi -say well not 4kn do_what fut
"But I'm going to say to you one thing: *I don't know what to do*

kʷu {ks} k̓səlmíst kʷu táxʷɬqəm 156 way̓ ťi kʷu k̓əɬʔamnwíxʷ 157 uɬ
kʷu k+ʔsl+mist kʷu taxʷ=ɬq+m way̓ ťiʔ kʷu k̓ɬ+ʔam+nwíxʷ uɬ
4kn two 4kn harvest well evid 4kn wait_rec and
for us two to harvest together. (23:02) *We will wait for one another.* *I*

way̓ cəm̓ ťi incá mi kən k̓əɬxaʔtxnáʔm, 158 aɬíʔ incá iʔ
way̓ cm̓ ťiʔ in+cá mi kn k̓ɬ+xaʔt=xnáʔ+m aɬíʔ in+cá iʔ
yes maybe evid I fut 1kn go_ahead because I art
will go ahead *because I have*

sx̌əx̌c̓iʔmálqʷ, {i s} iʔ sɬiqʷ, ťəxʷ cʔx̌íɬ 159 ixíʔ incá ikstíxʷəm, uɬ
s+x̌•x̌c̓iʔm=álqʷ iʔ s+ɬiqʷ ťxʷ c+ʔx̌iɬ ixíʔ in+cá i -ks -tixʷ+m uɬ
stalk art meat emph like then I 1i -futi -gather and
the stalks, the meat of it, like. *I am the one who is going to*

anwí {i} iʔ k̓ɬixʷút iʔ t ɬúkʷlaʔxʷ, iʔ səʕ̓ʷx̌ʷíp 160 ixíʔ {anwi aks aks}
anwí iʔ k̓ɬ+yxʷ=ut iʔ t ɬúkʷ=laʔxʷ iʔ s+ʕ̓ʷx̌ʷ=ip ixíʔ
you art underneath art obl dirt art roots that
take that, and you the things under ground, the roots. *You*

anwí akstíxʷəm aksútən 161 uɬ {a} anwí kʷ sk̓əɬxátxnaʔm
anwí a -ks -tixʷ+m a -k -sutn uɬ anwí kʷ s -k̓ɬ+xát=xna+m
you 2i -futi -gather 2i -to_be -thing and you 2kn ? -go_first
will take that for your own. *You'll be the first to*

ɬ x̌ʷíc̓laʔxʷəntxʷ 162 ixíʔ ɬ kʷúməntxʷ {aks ʔastkin}
ɬ x̌ʷíc̓=laʔxʷ -nt -xʷ ixíʔ ɬ kʷum -nt -xʷ
subord mow -nt -2erg then ? store -nt -2erg
cut the grain[2] *and put away*

aksʔastkínaʔ {uɬ} 163 uɬ way̓ lut ikskaʔkícəm a, lut {ixíʔ way̓}
a -k -s+ʔas=tk=ínaʔ uɬ way̓ lut i -ks -kaʔ•kíc+m a lut
2i -to_be -winter_supply and well not 1i -futi -find intj not
your winter supply. *And I can't find..." Oh, no!*[3] *(24:05)*

164 cut iʔ sx̌ʷílmən, way̓, way̓ ixíʔ {s} kʷís {i} iʔ x̌ʷíc̓laʔxʷtəns,
cut iʔ s+x̌ʷil+mn way̓ way̓ ixíʔ kʷi -s iʔ x̌ʷíc̓=laʔxʷ+tn -s
say art devil OK well then take -3erg art mower -3in
The Devil said, "Ok," and he took the cutter...

165 uɬ ixíʔ náx̌əmɬ a nɬíptmən 166 ƛ̓əm kskʷist ixíʔ iʔ
uɬ ixíʔ nax̌mɬ a n+ɬiptm -n ƛ̓m k+s+kʷist ixíʔ iʔ
and that but art forget -1erg past have_name that art
But I forget. *The mower has*

x̌ʷíc̓laʔxʷtən, 167 a kc̓lalqʷ, kc̓lalqʷ, ixíʔ iʔ skʷists
x̌ʷíc̓=laʔxʷ+tn a k+c̓l=alqʷ k+c̓l=alqʷ ixíʔ iʔ s+kʷist -s
mower intj bundling_scythe bundling_scythe that art name -3in
a name, *cradle scythe, cradle scythe, that's the name.*

168 ixíʔ x̌ʷíc̓əntxʷ sp̓úlaʔxʷəntxʷ, {uɬ w} məɬ t̓i axáʔ iʔ ník̓ək̓ {məɬ t̓ic"}
ixíʔ x̌ʷic̓ -nt -xʷ sp̓=úlaʔxʷ -nt -xʷ mɬ t̓iʔ axáʔ iʔ nik̓•k̓
then cut -nt -2erg hit_on_ground -nt -2erg and evid this art cut
You cut it and it hits the ground; and when it cuts, (25:00)

169 uɬ aɬíʔ ckc̓lalqʷ uɬ ilíʔ ƛ̓áp, k̓aʔx̌íʔ
uɬ aɬíʔ c -k+c̓l=alqʷ uɬ ilíʔ ƛ̓a+p k̓a+ʔx̌íʔ
and because hab -bundling_scythe and there stop over_there
because it has finger-like things, it stops right there.

ɬwníkstməntxʷ 170 məɬ put way̓ cəlk̓íw̓s 171 a x̌ʷí··c̓laʔxʷ
ɬwn=ikst+m -nt -xʷ mɬ put way̓ c -lk̓=iw̓s a x̌ʷíc̓=laʔxʷ
let_go_of -nt -2erg and just yes hab -bundle intj mow
You let go there, *and it's just enough for a bundle.* *He cut it*

wiʔsx̌ʷíc̓laʔxʷəm məɬ ixíʔ səlk̓íw̓səs 172 uɬ ixíʔ cus {iʔ} iʔ
wy̓+s+x̌ʷíc̓=laʔxʷ+m mɬ ixíʔ s -lk̓=iw̓s -s uɬ ixíʔ cu -s iʔ
finish_mowing and then nom -bundle -3i and then tell -3erg art
and got done cutting, and he was bundling. *And then he said to*

2 This is backwards: the Black Face goes first and cuts the wheat.
3 Pete realizes he has said it backwards.

sl̓ax̌ts, way̓ way̓ incá kən wiʔstáxʷɬqəm 173 hu•húy [u]ɬ t anwí
s+l̓ax̌+t -s way̓ way̓ in+cá kn wy̓+s+taxʷ=ɬq+m hu+húy uɬ t anwí
partner -3in well well I 1kn finish_harvest OK and obl you
his partner, "I am done harvesting; now it's your turn."

174 way̓ {ə} ckʷis {iʔ} mat iwá k̓ʷins i lapál {iʔ} nɬək̓ʷk̓ʷmís
way̓ c+kʷi -s mat iwá k̓ʷin -s iʔ lapál n+ɬk̓ʷ•k̓ʷ+mi -s
well take -3erg maybe try_to try -3erg art shovel think_about -3erg
He took the shovel, and he tried, he remembered what

[nyxʷxʷmis] iʔ sl̓ax̌ts 175 kəm̓ axáʔ {i ə} i l patáq {i} iʔ
n+yxʷ•xʷ+mi -s iʔ s+l̓ax̌+t -s km̓ axáʔ iʔ l patáq iʔ
imitate -3erg art partner -3in or this art for potato art
his partner did-- or the potato

ƛ̓əqmín 176 iwá uɬ t̓ləntís uɬ way̓ lut lut ixíʔ t̓a
ƛ̓q+min iwá uɬ t̓l -nt -is uɬ way̓ lut lut ixíʔ t̓
digger to_no_avail and tear -nt -3erg and well not not that negfac
digger. He dug, but it didn't do any good, it didn't

kskcahəhám 177 way̓ uɬ t̓iʔ t̓əxʷ səlqúlaʔxʷs, ixíʔ uɬ
ks -k+cah•há+m way̓ uɬ t̓iʔ t̓xʷ s -lq=úlaʔxʷ -s ixíʔ uɬ
? -match well and evid evidently nom -pull -3i then and
work. (26:03) He pulled them by hand, then he

uʔíksts 178 way̓ uɬ {nt̓a••} nt̓əqəntís paʔsíxəms {ə•• uɬ} 179 nt̓a
wy̓=ikst way̓ uɬ n+t̓q -nt -is paʔsíx+m -s nt̓a
get_done well and fill -nt -3erg pack -3erg intj
got done. He packed them and stored them. Lots

yaʕpqín səʕ̓ʷx̌ʷíp iʔ l sək̓ʷtílp {i s} x̌əl sʔistk 180 way̓ uɬ axáʔ ta
yaʕ+p=qín s+ʕ̓ʷx̌ʷ=ip iʔ l s+k̓ʷt=ilp x̌l s+ʔis=tk way̓ uɬ axáʔ ?
lots roots art on one_side_of_room for winter well and this ?
of roots on one side of the room for winter. And the Black Face

q̓ʷəyʕás way̓ uɬ ixíʔ syaʕyaʕ̓ncúts t kɬk̓əɬxʷípməns
q̓ʷy=ʕas way̓ uɬ ixíʔ s -yaʕ̓•yaʕ̓+ncút -s t kɬ -k̓ɬ+xʷip+mn -s
black_face well and then nom -rustle -3i obj_itr to_be -spread -3i
started looking for something to put under [the wheat].

181 way̓ taʔxʷɬk̓əɬxʷípmən, way̓ uɬ ixíʔ ksəp̓əntís {iʔ i ə ək}[4] 182 nt̓a
way̓ taʔxʷ+ɬ+k̓ɬ+xʷip+mn way̓ uɬ ixíʔ k+sp̓ -nt -is nt̓a
well get_liner well and then thrash -nt -3erg intj
He got something to spread down, and started threshing the wheat. (27:06) He

4 Pete can't think of the word and says: "Getting forgetful, forgetting what they call wheat in Indian oh." I whisper "səsp̓qín səsp̓qín." Pete: "həʔ" "səsp̓qín, wheat, wheat". Pete: "What is it?" "you are saying wheat." Pete: "Yeah." "səsp̓qín. Pete: "Oh yeah yeah. I am getting forgetting my own language əy s ..."

ɬ[5] npəkʷpəkʷntís wa y̓ ɬ qmis {indec} yaʕpqín staʔxʷsəsṗqíns
ɬ n+pkʷ•pkʷ -nt -is way̓ ɬ qmi -s yaʕ+p=qín s -taʔxʷ+s•sṗ=qín -s
? pour_solids_pl -nt -3erg well ? put_down -3erg lots nom -get_wheat -3i
filled the sacks, he lay them down. He had lots of wheat. (28:00

183 hoy ixíʔ k̓ʷəlcəncútəlx 184 way̓ axáʔ {tən} ċiẇs axáʔ iʔ səsṗqín
hoy ixíʔ k̓ʷl̓=cn+cut -lx way̓ axáʔ ċiẇ -s axáʔ iʔ s•sṗ=qin
well then cook -pl well this wash -3erg this art wheat
Then they cooked. *The Black Face*

axáʔ iʔ sx̌ʷílmən [iʔ q̇ʷəyʕás] 185 way̓ məɬ ixíʔ {t} máṙwiʔs t
axáʔ iʔ s+x̌ʷil+mn iʔ q̇ʷy=ʕas way̓ mɬ ixíʔ máṙwiʔ -s t
this art devil art black_face well and then season -3erg obl
washes the wheat, *then he mixes it*

kʷukʷús məɬ ixíʔ wiʔsənċíws nt̓a məɬ ʔíɬən 186 kəṁ axáʔ {ɬ} i l
kʷu•kʷús mɬ ixíʔ wy̓+s+n+ċiẇ -s nt̓a mɬ ʔiɬn kṁ axáʔ iʔ l
pig and then finish_washing -3erg intj and eat or this art in
with bacon, then he eats. *Or [he grinds it]*

sənəlkapítən {iʔ} iʔ x̌ʷaq̇ʷməns {i l} 187 ixíʔ {ixíʔ} wiʔsx̌ʷáq̇ʷəs məɬ
s+n+lkapí+tn iʔ x̌ʷaq̇ʷ+mn -s ixíʔ wy̓+s+x̌ʷaq̇ʷ -s mɬ
coffee_mill art grinder -3in then finish_grinding -3erg and
in the coffee mill. *He gets it ground and then*

ixíʔ sk̓ʷəl̓ɬlkalátəms, 188 kəṁ {ɬ ki} k̓ʷúl̓əm t sənqʷl̓ús
ixíʔ s -k̓ʷl̓+ɬ+lkalát+m -s kṁ k̓ʷul̓+m t s+n+qʷl̓=us
then nom -make_biscuits -3i or work obj_itr bannock
he makes biscuits; *or he'll make bannock.*

189 níkxnaʔ {uɬ i ɬ} tqʷámqʷəmqs axáʔ iʔ q̇ʷəyʕás 190 k̓əm axáʔ iʔ
níkxnaʔ t+qʷam•qʷm=qs axáʔ iʔ q̇ʷy=ʕas k̓m axáʔ iʔ
goodness good_food this art black_face except this art
Goodness, the Black Face has good things to eat. *But the Devil,*

sx̌ʷílmən way̓ iwá kcahcahmtís axáʔ iʔ saʕ̓ʷx̌ʷíp 191 way̓ lut
s+x̌ʷil+mn way̓ iwá k+cah•cah+m -t -is axáʔ iʔ s+ʕ̓ʷx̌ʷ=ip way̓ lut
devil well try_to make_fit -? -3erg this art roots well not
he tries to work the roots. (29:00) *It doesn't*

t̓a kskcahhəhám, way̓ uɬ t̓i nƛ̓əl·íls iʔ t sq̇míltən
t̓ ks -k+cah•h•há+m way̓ uɬ t̓iʔ n+ƛ̓l=ils iʔ t s+q̇m=ilt+tn
negfac ? -match well and evid feel_like_dying art agInst hunger
work. He's going to die of starvation.

192 way̓ uɬ talíʔ uɬ ʕʷəċáp, ixíʔ uɬ way̓ k̓əl syaʔk̓ʷáqs 193 ixíʔ
way̓ uɬ taʔlíʔ uɬ ʕʷċa+p ixíʔ uɬ way̓ k̓l s+y̓aʔk̓ʷ=áqs ixíʔ
well and very_much and waste then and well to mid_winter then
He's going very much to nothing. And it was past mid winter. *Then*

5 Here and elsewhere ɬ may be a variant of uɬ.

cúntəm {t} t q̓ʷəyáʕs, lut, t sx̌ʷílmən, cúntəm axáʔ q̓ʷəyʕás
cu -nt -m t q̓ʷy=ʕas lut t s+x̌ʷil+mn cu -nt -m axáʔ q̓ʷy=ʕas
tell -nt -psv agInst black_face not agInst devil tell -nt -psv this black_face
the Black Face said... no, the Devil said to the Black Man:

194 way̓ sl̓ax̌t, way̓ {kʷu ks kʷu ksƛ̓u} kʷu ksx̌ʷəlstwíxʷaʔx 195 a··
way̓ s+l̓ax̌+t way̓ kʷu ks -x̌ʷl+stwixʷ -aʔx a
well friend well 4kn incp^ -discard_rec -^incp intj
"Well, partner, we are going to quit one another." The

cúntəm iʔ t q̓ʷəyʕás, uɬ scʔkínx, 196 talíʔ kʷu l̓əx̌tíw̓s,
cu -nt -m iʔ t q̓ʷy=ʕas uɬ sc+ʔkin+x taʔlíʔ kʷu l̓x̌+t=iw̓s
tell -nt -psv art agInst black_face and why_is_it very_much 4kn be_partners
Black Face said to him, "And what's the matter? We are real partners,

uɬ_iʔ {kʷu as} kʷu aksx̌ʷíləm 197 cúntəm, lút, way̓ ʔasíl sʔístk
uɬ_iʔ kʷu a -ks -x̌ʷil+m cu -nt -m lut way̓ ʔasíl s+ʔis=tk
and_then 1kʷu 2i -futi -throw_away tell -nt -psv not well two winter
and then you're going to throw me away?" He answered, "No, it's two winters

way̓ kʷu ƛ̓xʷúpəntxʷ i l sk̓ʷánɬqtət {waɬki} 198 t̓a_uní··xʷ ʕapnáʔ kiʔ
way̓ kʷu ƛ̓xʷup -nt -xʷ iʔ l s+k̓ʷan=ɬq -tt t̓a_wnixʷ ʕapnáʔ kiʔ
yes 1obj beat -nt -2erg art in garden -4in for_sure now rel
you get the best of me in our crops. This time I sure

kən kstaʔmínaʔ mat uc c̓kin kən kstaʔmínaʔ 199 way̓ t̓əxʷ
kn k+s+taʔm=ínaʔ mat uc c+ʔkin kn k+s+taʔm=ínaʔ way̓ t̓xʷ
1kn have_spring maybe dub how 1kn have_spring well evident
had a hard time pulling through winter." (30:00) It's past

yaʔk̓ʷáqsəm uɬ aɬíʔ púti way̓ k̓əm ksxʷúyənt yaʕpqín sxʷúyənt {əy}
y̓aʔk̓ʷ=áqs+m uɬ aɬíʔ pút+i way̓ k̓m k+s+xʷuy+nt yaʕ+p=qín s+xʷuy+nt
mid_winter and so still yes except have_ice lots ice
mid-winter, and there is still ice, lots of ice.

200 cúntəm t sx̌ʷílmən q̓ʷəyáʕs, cúntəm way̓ sl̓ax̌t 201 way̓
cu -nt -m t s+x̌ʷil+mn q̓ʷy=ʕas cu -nt -m way̓ s+l̓ax̌+t way̓
tell -nt -psv agInst devil black_face tell -nt -psv well friend well
The Devil said to the Black Face, he said, "Well, partner, now

ʕapnáʔ iʔ kʷu ɬunwíxʷ 202 uc kən cxʷəlxʷált kəm̓ kən
ʕapnáʔ iʔ kʷu ɬwn+wixʷ uc kn c -xʷl•xʷal+t km̓ kn
now art 4kn part dub 1kn hab -alive or 1kn
we're going to leave one another. If I live, or if I don't make it to

k̓əɬtwín mi uɬ kʷu ksqʷaʔcínaʔ 203 way̓ ʔasíl sʔistk kʷu təl
k̓ɬ+twi -n mi uɬ kʷu k+s+qʷaʔc=ínaʔ way̓ ʔasíl s+ʔis=tk kʷu tl
fall_short -1erg fut and 4kn have_warm_weather well two winter 4kn from
when the warm weather arrives, (31:01) we have been partners two

sl̓əx̌tíw̓səms ʔax̌əlspíntk kʷu ƛ̓xʷúpəntxʷ 204 uɬ way̓
s -l̓x̌+t=iw̓s+m -s ʔax̌l+s+pin=tk kʷu ƛ̓xʷup -nt -xʷ uɬ way̓
nom4^ -go_partners -^nom4 every_year 1obj beat -nt -2erg and yes
years, and every year you get the best of me. And now

ʕapnáʔ uɬ waẏ lut ikskstaʔmínaʔ {waẏ kʷu ks} 205 ná[x̌əmɬ] uɬ waẏ
ʕapnáʔ uɬ waẏ lut i -ks k+s+taʔm=ínaʔ nax̌mɬ uɬ waẏ
now and yes not 1i -futi have_spring but and yes
I can't make it to spring. *I'm telling you,*

cúntsən, waẏ lut k̓im kʷu ksləx̌tíw̓s 206 caʔkʷ iwá kʷ ɬ ƛ̓lal,
cu -nt -s -n waẏ lut k̓im kʷu ks -l̓x̌+t=iw̓s caʔkʷ iwá kʷ ɬ ƛ̓l•al
tell -nt -2obj -1erg well not but 4kn futi -friends if even 2kn if dead
we are quitting our friendship. *Even if you were to die,*

uɬ waẏ lut kʷ t̓ ikskʷním 207 cúntəm iʔ t q̓ʷəyáʕs
uɬ waẏ lut kʷ t̓ i -ks -kʷni+m cu -nt -m iʔ t q̓ʷy=ʕas
and yes not 2kn negfac 1i -futi -take tell -nt -psv art agInst black_face
I would't take you." *The Black Face said*

a[xáʔ iʔ] sx̌ʷílmən 208 cúntəm lut, lut ilíʔ aksnʔax̌líls 209 lut
axáʔ iʔ s+x̌ʷil+mn cu -nt -m lut lut ilíʔ a -ks -n+ʔax̌l+íls lut
this art devil tell -nt -psv not not there 2i -futi -think_so not
to the Devil, *he said, "No, don't feel that way.* *I*

[t̓]a sƛ̓xʷúpstmən, niʕ̓íp anwí, 210 waẏ
t̓a c -ƛ̓xʷup -st -m -n nyʕ̓ip anwí waẏ
emph_neg cust^ -beat -^cust -2obj -1erg always you well
didn't get the best of you. It's always you [who did]. *I*

cúntsən anwí kʷ sxəxʔítaʔx 211 uɬ anwí a
cu -nt -s -n anwí kʷ s+x•xʔít=aʔx uɬ anwí a
tell -nt -2obj -1erg you 2kn oldest_dim and you art
told you, you are the oldest one. *I always*

ctxaʔtmstúmən ki {kʷu acia} ctx̌ʷíw̓stəm iʔ
c -t+xaʔt+m -st -um -n kiʔ c -tx̌ʷ=iw̓s -t -m iʔ
cust^ -go_first -^cust -2obj -1erg rel cust^ -divide -^cust -4erg art
had you go first when we divided

sk̓ʷanɬq 212 uɬ ixíʔ anwí iʔ kʷ acxʔít, uɬ anwí kʷ acʕalpəncút
s+k̓ʷan=ɬq uɬ ixíʔ anwí iʔ kʷ c+xʔit uɬ anwí kʷ c -ʕal+p+ncút
harvest and then you art 2kn first and you 2kn hab -loser
the garden. *You go first, and it's you that makes yourself lose." (32:03)*

213 cut iʔ sx̌ʷílmən {l} kʷa ixíʔ isqʷəlqʷílt 214 waẏ ńíńw̓iʔ kʷ ɬ
cut iʔ s+x̌ʷil+mn kʷa ixíʔ i -s -qʷl•qʷil+t waẏ ńíńw̓iʔ kʷ ɬ
say art devil intj that 1i -intt -talk well a_while 2kn if
The Devil said, "What I said goes. *Even if you*

ƛ̓lal lut kʷ t̓ ikskʷním 215 cúntəm {ta} waẏ, waẏ aspuʔús
ƛ̓l•al lut kʷ t̓ i -ks -kʷni+m cu -nt -m waẏ waẏ a -s+puʔ=ús
dead not 2kʷu negfac 1i -futi -take tell -nt -psv well OK 2in -heart
were to die, I wouldn't take you." *He said, "Well, if that's how you feel."*

216 waẏ cúntəm t sx̌ʷílmən cúntəm axáʔ q̓ʷəyáʕs
waẏ cu -nt -m t s+x̌ʷil+mn cu -nt -m axáʔ q̓ʷy=ʕas
well tell -nt -psv agInst devil tell -nt -psv this black_face
The Devil said, he said to the Black Face,

217 cúntəm, axáʔ naqs iʔ kʷ ikscúnəm, 218 ʕapnáʔ kʷu
cu -nt -m axáʔ naqs iʔ kʷ i -ks -cun+m ʕapnáʔ kʷu
tell -nt -psv this one art 2kʷu 1i -futi -say now 1obj
he said, "I'm going to say one thing to you. Now

aksk̓ʷúl̓xtəm t ikɬcítxʷ, ixíʔ uɬ kʷu kɬuscút 219 uɬ
a -ks -k̓ʷul̓ -xt -m t i -kɬ -citxʷ ixíʔ uɬ kʷu k+ɬw+scut uɬ
2i -futi -fix -xit -apsv obj_itr 1i -to_be -house then and 4kn part_ways and
I want you to fix me a house, then we will part." And

ixíʔ uɬ cúntəm iʔ t q̓ʷəyʕás, cus iʔ sx̌ʷílmən, 220 way̓,
ixíʔ uɬ cu -nt -m iʔ t q̓ʷy=ʕas cu -s iʔ s+x̌ʷil+mn way̓
then and tell -nt -psv art agInst black_face tell -3erg art devil OK
the Black Face said to the Devil: (33:01) "OK,

way̓ aɬíʔ ixíʔ mat anwí aspuʔús 221 nak̓ʷá kʷ
way̓ aɬíʔ ixíʔ mat anwí a -s+puʔ=ús nak̓ʷá kʷ
yes because that maybe you 2in -heart indeed_not 2kʷu
if you want it that way. I don't want

iksmaʔmínəm {a kʷu} kəm̓aʔ kʷu k̓əsk̓ásəs {kʷu kinm} 222 way̓ t̓əxʷ t̓i anwí
i -ks -maʔ+mín+m km̓+a kʷu k̓s•kas•s way̓ t̓xʷ t̓iʔ anwí
1i -futi -send_away not 4kn quarrel well emph evid you
to get rid of you, nor did we quarrel. Do as

aspuʔús 223 uɬ hu•húy {kʷ iks} kʷ iksíwm, c̓kin anx̌mínk
a -s+puʔ=ús uɬ hu+húy kʷ i -ks -siw+m c+ʔkin an -x̌m=ink
2in -heart and OK 2kʷu 1i -futi -ask how 2in -like
you please. And now I'm going to ask you, what kind of house

i akɬcítxʷ 224 cúntəm iʔ t sx̌ʷílmən, 225 way̓ inx̌mínk
iʔ a -kɬʷ -citx cu -nt -m iʔ t s+x̌ʷil+mn way̓ in -x̌m=ink
art 2i -to_be -house tell -nt -psv art agInst devil well 1in -like
would you like?" The Devil told him: "I want

ikɬcítxʷ {k} kmix nx̌əlsʕáɬxʷc̓aʔm, uɬ xl·ákək 226 k̓aʔkín k[ən] ʕác̓əm
i -kɬ -citxʷ kmix n+x̌l=s=ʕáɬxʷ=c̓aʔ+m uɬ xl•l•ak•k k̓a+ʔkín kn ʕac̓+m
1i -to_be -house only glass_house and round to_where 1kn look
my house to be all glass, all around. Wherever I look

məɬ way̓ ik̓líʔ wíkən k̓əl tk̓əmkn̓íɬxʷ 227 uɬ axáʔ ia nwist ilíʔ c̓x̌iɬ,
mɬ way̓ ik̓líʔ wik -n k̓l t+k̓m+kn̓=iɬxʷ uɬ axáʔ iʔ n+wis+t ilíʔ c+ʔx̌iɬ
and yes there see -1erg to outside and this art high there like
I'll see the outside, and up above there the same,

uɬ k̓a ixʷút 228 ixíʔ uɬ ixíʔ kʷu xʷíc̓ɬtsən yaʕyʕát
uɬ k̓ yxʷ=ut ixíʔ uɬ ixíʔ kʷu xʷic̓ -ɬt -s -n yaʕ•yáʕ+t
and to below then and then 1kʷu give -ɬt -2obj -1erg all
and down below. And I'll give you all

isqláw̓ 229 way̓, cúntəm iʔ t sx̌ʷílmən [q̓ʷəyʕás],
i -s+qlaw way̓ cu -nt -m iʔ t s+x̌ʷil+mn q̓ʷy=ʕas
1in -money well tell -nt -psv art agInst devil black_face
my money." (34:00) The Black Face said to him:

230 waẏ t̓əxʷ lut kʷ t̓ ikscíxʷaʔm kʷ t̓ ikscúnəm
waẏ t̓xʷ lut kʷ t̓ i -ks -cíxʷaʔ+m kʷ t̓ i -ks -cun+m
well emph not 2kʷu negfac 1i -futi -fool 2kʷu negfac 1i -futi -tell
"Certainly not I'm going to fool you and tell you [right away].

231 waẏ ṅíṅẇiʔ ilíʔ {kən} kən k̓ʷúl̓əm 232 way ṅíṅẇiʔ k̓əɬpaʔx̌əntín
waẏ ṅíṅẇiʔ ilíʔ kn k̓ʷul̓+m waẏ ṅíṅẇiʔ k̓ɬ+paʔx̌ -nt -in
well a_while there 1kn work yes a_while think_about -nt -1in
I will stay with the job. *I will think about it,*

pnaʔ_cmay k̓əɬpaʔx̌əx̌nún 233 mi ixíʔ k̓ʷúl̓ɬtsən {as}
pnaʔ_cmay k̓ɬ+paʔx̌•x̌ -nu -n mi ixíʔ k̓ʷul̓ -ɬt -s -n
maybe have_figured -manage -1erg fut then make -ɬt -2obj -1erg
maybe I'll get the right idea *and I'll fulfill*

ask̓əɬq̓ám {i ə} 234 waẏ ixíʔ qʷəlqʷílstmən 235 aɬíʔ nƛ̓ʕámcən axáʔ
a -s+k̓ɬ+q̓am waẏ ixíʔ qʷl•qʷil -st -m -n aɬíʔ n+ƛ̓ʕam+cn axáʔ
2in -wish well that talk_to -st -2obj -1erg so thirsty this
your wish. *That's what I'm going to tell you."* *The Black Face*

iʔ q̓ʷəyʕás, uɬ mat ta nc̓aɬt ksíwstaʔx 236 waẏ xʷúy k̓əl
iʔ q̓ʷy=ʕas uɬ mat t n+c̓aɬ+t k -siw+st -aʔx waẏ xʷuy k̓l
art black_face and maybe prttv cold_water incp^ -drink -^incp well go to
got thirsty, maybe he wants to drink cold water, *he went to*

síwɬkʷ, ik̓líʔ kicx {ə··} nt̓əpqsám ksíwstaʔx 237 a stiṁ a[xáʔ] iʔ
siwɬ=kʷ ik̓líʔ kic+x n+t̓p=qsa+m k -siw+st -aʔx a s+tiṁ axáʔ iʔ
water there arrive tip_head incp^ -drink -^incp intj what this art
the water, he got there, he tipped his head to drink. (35:03) *Ah, what did he see*

kscwíks k̓la nyxʷtitkʷ 238 sta iʔ sqáqlaʔxʷs wiks {inaud}
ksc -wik -s k̓l n+yxʷ=t=itkʷ sta iʔ s+qá+qlaʔxʷ -s wik -s
futPerfi -see -3i to in_water intj art reflection -3in see -3erg
there down in the water? *Gee, he saw his image.*

239 ixíʔ k̓əɬpaʔx̌əx̌nús {hoy hoy xi} 240 waẏ ixíʔ mi k̓ʷúl̓ɬxʷən c̓x̌iɬ
ixíʔ k̓ɬ+paʔx̌•x̌ -nu -s waẏ ixíʔ mi k̓ʷul̓=ɬxʷ -n c+ʔx̌iɬ
then have_figured -manage -3erg yes that fut build_house -1erg like
It was then that he got the idea: *"I will build a house*

itíʔ mi k̓ʷúl̓ɬxʷxtən axáʔ {i} isl̓áx̌t 241 waẏ ixíʔ {ə}
itíʔ mi k̓ʷul̓=ɬxʷ -xt -n axáʔ i -s+l̓ax̌+t waẏ ixíʔ
that fut build_house -xit -1erg this 1in -partner well then
just like that for my friend." *The Black Face*

ʔalk̓ʷsíʔstəms axáʔ iʔ q̓ʷəyʕás {i i} axáʔ iʔ sas iʔ áys·as {xʷmi}
ʔalk̓ʷ=s=íʔst+m -s axáʔ iʔ q̓ʷy=ʕas axáʔ iʔ sa -s iʔ áysa -s
sharpen -3erg this art black_face this art saw -3in art ice_saw -3erg
started sharpening the ice saw, (36:00)

242 t sqilxʷ cus sxúyənt naʔník̓mən 243 waẏ ixíʔ
t s+qilxʷ cu -s sxʷuynt naʔ+ník̓+mn waẏ ixíʔ
agInst Indian tell -3erg ice saw well then
one could call it sxʷúyənt naʔník̓mən in Indian. *He got done*

wiʔsʔalk̓ʷúsəs, way̓ nis ník̓əmsts tə·· sxʷúyənt 244 a·· nt'a
wy̓+s+ʔalk̓ʷ=ús -s way̓ nis nik̓+m -st -s t s+xʷuy+nt a nt'a
finish_sharpening -3erg well sg_gone cut -st -3erg obj_tr ice intj intj
sharpening it, he went, he cut the ice. *He*

way̓ {ə} uɬ aɬíʔ {səxʷʔmu} səxʷmʔúlaʔxʷs iʔ ksniliʔtəns {uɬ siwən}
way̓ uɬ aɬíʔ sxʷ=mʔ=úlaʔxʷ -s iʔ k -s+n+ilíʔ+tn -s
well and so measure -3erg art to_be -dwelling_place -3i
measured the ground where the house was going to be. (37:03)

245 siws iʔ sl̓ax̌ts, cus laʔkín y anx̌mínk y
siw -s iʔ s+l̓ax̌+t -s cu -s la+ʔkín̓ iʔ an -x̌m=ink iʔ
ask -3erg art partner -3in tell -3erg wherever art 2in -want art
He asked his friend, "Where would you like

akɬcítxʷ 246 cut iliʔ, ixíʔ uɬ q̓y̓úlaʔxʷs 247 i
a -kɬ -citxʷ cut ilíʔ ixíʔ uɬ q̓y̓=úlaʔxʷ -s i
2i -to_be -house say there then and mark_ground -3erg intj
your house?" *He said "Here," and so he marked the ground.* *He*

qmí··s iʔ sxʷúyənt {uɬ ii uɬ hi uɬ} uɬ k̓la nk̓əmqníɬxʷ, way̓, way̓
qmi -s iʔ s+xʷuy+nt uɬ k̓l n+k̓m=qn=iɬxʷ way̓ way̓
put_down -3erg art ice and to ceiling well well
laid the ice up to the ceiling,

wiʔstís 248 way̓ ƛ̓aʔƛ̓ʔúsəm, way̓ t'i_put c̓x̌iɬ ta
wy̓ -st -is way̓ ƛ̓aʔ•ƛ̓ʔ=ús+m way̓ t'iʔ_put c+ʔx̌iɬ t
finish -st -3erg well look_for yes just_enough like obj_c̓x̌iɬ
he got done. *He looked around, it's just*

nx̌əlsʕáɬc̓aʔtn {indec} 249 k̓aʔkín ʕác̓əm uɬ way̓ t'i_c̓x̌i··ɬ {k̓əl} k̓əl tk̓əmkn̓íɬxʷ
n+x̌l=s=ʕáɬc̓aʔ+tn k̓a+ʔkín ʕac̓+m uɬ way̓ t'iʔ_c+ʔx̌iɬ k̓l t+k̓m+kn̓=iɬxʷ
window to_where look and yes just_like to outside
like window: *wherever he looks it's like outside.*

250 way̓ ixíʔ {ɬ} ɬƛ̓aʔntís iʔ sl̓ax̌ts, 251 way̓ uɬ
way̓ ixíʔ ɬ+ƛ̓aʔ -nt -is iʔ s+l̓ax̌+t -s way̓ uɬ
well then fetch_again -nt -3erg art partner -3in well and
He went after his partner, (38:00) *and*

kənʔúɬxʷməntəm iʔ sx̌ʷílmən t q̓ʷəyʕás 252 cúntəm, way̓, way̓
k+n+ʔuɬxʷ+m -nt -m iʔ s+x̌ʷil+mn t q̓ʷy=ʕas cu -nt -m way̓ way̓
take_so_in -nt -psv art devil agInst black_face tell -nt -psv well yes
the Black Face brought the Devil into the house. *He said,*

wiɬtsín {a} akɬcítxʷ, uɬ lut {kʷ is} kʷ isənlk̓əmníksəm
wy̓ -ɬt -s -in a -kɬ -citxʷ uɬ lut kʷ i -s -n+lk̓+mn=iks+m
finish -ɬt -2obj -1erg 2i -to_be -house and not 2kʷu 1i -intt -force
"Well, I finished your house, and I am not forcing you.

253 t'i way̓ anwí [a]spuʔús ixíʔ kʷu k̓ʕawmístməntxʷ 254 uɬ
t'iʔ way̓ anwí a -s+puʔ=ús ixíʔ kʷu k̓aʕʷ+míst+m -nt -xʷ uɬ
evid yes you 2in -heart then 1obj hire -nt -2erg and
It was you who wanted to hire me. *And*

sc̓x̌ilx ʔkiʔ cúntsən, 255 ṅíṅẇiʔ ʕác̓əntxʷ kʷ npútəls, uɬ
sc+ʔx̌il+x kiʔ cu -nt -s -n ṅíṅẇiʔ ʕac̓ -nt -xʷ kʷ n+put=ls uɬ
reason_why rel tell -nt -2obj -1erg a_while look -nt -2erg 2kn satisfied and
that's why I told you. *If you go look and you are satisfied,*

waẏ sic kʷu x̌áq̓əntxʷ, 256 náx̌əmɬ lut kʷ npútəls, uɬ lut kʷu
waẏ sic kʷu x̌aq̓ -nt -xʷ nax̌mɬ lut kʷ n+put=ls uɬ lut kʷu
yes then 1obj pay -nt -2erg but not 2kn satisfied and not 1kʷu
then you can pay me. *But if you are not satisfied, then*

aksx̌áq̓əm 257 waẏ cxʷuyx, waẏ ik̓líʔ c̓ácəcqaʔlx 258 huy
a -ks -x̌aq̓+m waẏ c+xʷuy -x waẏ ik̓líʔ c -ʔác•c•qaʔ -lx hoy
2i -futi -pay well come -isimptv well there hab -enter_pl -pl well
don't pay me. *Come!" And they went out there.* *And*

uɬ nppílxəlx, uɬ aɬíʔ kɬk̓ɬənk̓míp {uɬ ɬəl} 259 uɬ aɬíʔ náx̌əmɬ {nyʕíp}
uɬ n+p•pilx -lx uɬ aɬíʔ kɬ+k̓ɬ+n+k̓m=ip uɬ aɬíʔ nax̌mɬ
and enter_pl -pl and so have_door and so but
they went in, and it has a door *and windows*

yaʕyʕátəlx nxənsíɬxʷtn uɬ xl·ákək 260 waẏ kɬxʷaʔxʷí··st iʔ sx̌ʷílmən
yaʕ•yáʕ+t -lx n+xn=s=iɬxʷ+tn uɬ xl•l•ak•k waẏ kɬ+xʷaʔ+xʷíst iʔ s+x̌ʷil+mn
all -pl window and round well walk_all_over art devil
all around. (39:03) *The Devil walked all around.*

261 waẏ, {waẏ kən an put} waẏ kən npútəls, waẏ límləmtx {inaud} 262 waẏ
waẏ waẏ kn n+put=ls waẏ lim•lm+t+x waẏ
yes yes 1kn satisfied yes thank_you well
"Yes, yes, I am satisfied, thank you." *He*

xʷíc̓əɬtəm yaʕyʕát iʔ sqláẇs {ə} 263 q̓ʷəyʕás taʔxʷsqláẇ, uɬ
xʷic̓ -ɬt -m yaʕ•yáʕ+t iʔ s+qlaw -s q̓ʷy=ʕas taʔxʷ+s+qlaẇ uɬ
give -ɬt -psv all art money -3in black_face get_money and
gave him all his money. *The Black Man got the money,*

taʔxʷɬcítxʷ iʔ sx̌ʷílmən {ntəm waẏ waẏ kʷən} 264 kʷənksnwíxʷəlx
taʔxʷ+ɬ+cítxʷ iʔ s+x̌ʷil+mn kʷn=ks+nwixʷ -lx
get_house art devil shake_hands -pl
and the Devil got the house. *They shook hands.*

265 cúntəm iʔ t sx̌ʷílmən {t} 266 waẏ ʔasəlspíntk waẏ {kʷu kʷu}
cu -nt -m iʔ t s+x̌ʷil+mn waẏ ʔasl+s+pin=tk waẏ
tell -nt -psv art agInst devil well two_years yes
The Devil said: *"Two years*

kʷu ksq̓míltstxʷ i l sk̓ʷánɬqtət 267 t̓a_uníxʷ kiʔ kən
kʷu k+s+q̓m=ilt -st -xʷ i l s+k̓ʷan=ɬq -tt t̓a_wnixʷ kiʔ kn
1obj starve -caus -2erg art in garden -4in for_sure rel 1kn
you starved me with our garden. *I had a hard time*

kstaʔmínaʔ uɬ sc̓x̌ilx kiʔ cúntsən 268 kʷu k̓ʷúl̓ɬxʷxt
k+s+taʔm=ínaʔ uɬ sc+ʔx̌il+x kiʔ cu -nt -s -n kʷu k̓ʷul̓=ɬxʷ -xt
have_spring and reason_why rel tell -nt -2obj -1erg 1obj build_house -xit
pulling through winter, and that's why I said to you *build me*

t ikłcítkʷ ixíʔ kʷu wiʔłtíxʷ ixíʔ uł kʷu kłuscút
t i -kł -citxʷ ixíʔ kʷu wẏ -łt -ixʷ ixíʔ uł kʷu k+łw+scut
obj_tr 1i -to_be -house then 1obj finish -łt -2erg then and 4kn part_ways
a house, and when you finish it we will part,

269 uł lut_k̓im kʷu iʔ sl̓ax̌t 270 cúntəm iʔ t q̓ʷəyʕás
uł lut_k̓im kʷu iʔ s+l̓ax̌+t cu -nt -m iʔ t q̓ʷy=ʕas
and no_more 4kn art partner tell -nt -psv art agInst black_face
we won't be partners any more." (40:05) *The Black Face said to him,*

lut, lut ilíʔ aksənʔax̌líls 271 anwí anwí niʕ̓íp {ast̓k̓ʷəmstu} anwí iʔ
lut lut ilíʔ a -ks -n+ʔax̌l+íls anwí anwí nyʕip anwí iʔ
not not there 2i -futi -think_so you you always you art
"No, don't think that way. *You are the one*

kʷ {ac} a ckʷístxʷ {i} axáʔ iʔ sk̓ʷánłqtət 272 iʔ l liplí uł
kʷ a c -kʷi -st -xʷ axáʔ iʔ s+k̓ʷan=łq -tt iʔ l liplí uł
2kn art cust^ -take -^cust -2erg this art garden -4in art with corn and
who always picked our crop, *corn or potato,*

i l patáq, uł anwí iʔ kʷ scƛ̓xʷpəncútx 273 ə·· cut waẏ
iʔ l patáq uł anwí iʔ kʷ sc -ƛ̓xʷ+p+ncut -x ə cut waẏ
art with potato and you art 2kn ipftvp^ -beat_self -^ipftvp intj say yes
and you that beat yourself." *He said,*

ixíʔ ispuʔús {waẏ waẏ} 274 waẏ kłwscútəlx 275 waẏ knánəqs q̓ʷəyʕás,
ixíʔ i -s+puʔ=ús waẏ k+łw+scut -lx waẏ k+ná•naqs q̓ʷy=ʕas
that 1in -heart well part_ways -pl well alone black_face
"That's what I think." *They parted. (41:01)* *The Black Face*

k̓im {i l s} i l cítxʷs 276 uł axáʔ nt̓əqəlmxíłc̓aʔ sx̌ʷílmən 277 waẏ
k̓im iʔ l citxʷ -s uł axáʔ n+t̓ql=mx=íłc̓aʔ s+x̌ʷil+mn waẏ
only art at house -3erg and this settle devil well
was all alone at his house *and the Devil got settled.* *When*

t̓iʔ scʔixs {iʔ s} 278 i ałíʔ usəncút uł {sx̌ʷ} sx̌ʷílmən, qʷámqʷəmt iʔ
t̓iʔ s -cʔix -s i ałíʔ ws+ncut uł s+x̌ʷil+mn qʷam•qʷm+t iʔ
evid nom -get_warm -3i intj so brag and devil excellent art
it gets warm... *The Devil is bragging how beautiful*

staʔxʷłcítxʷs 279 k̓aʔkín ʕác̓əm, uł waẏ t̓i ik̓líʔ kʷəkʷl̓ál̓
s -taʔxʷ+ł+cítxʷ -s k̓a+ʔkín ʕac̓+m uł waẏ t̓iʔ ik̓líʔ kʷ•kʷl̓•al̓
nom -get_house -3i to_where look and yes evid there sun_shine
the house he got is. *Wherever he looks, there it's bright*

t̓i_c̓x̌ił, 280 uł axáʔ nixʷ iʔ k̓łənk̓míp uł nixʷ ixíʔ {c} cʔx̌íł nixʷ,
t̓iʔ_c̓x̌ił uł axáʔ nixʷ iʔ k̓ł+n+km=ip uł nixʷ ixíʔ c+ʔx̌ił nixʷ
like and this also art door and also that like also
like; *and the doors are also like that,*

281 uł axáʔ a nk̓əmqníłxʷ, kəm̓ axáʔ iʔ sx̌lilp 282 npútəls iʔ
uł axáʔ a n+k̓m=qn=iłxʷ km̓ axáʔ iʔ s+x̌l=ilp n+put=ls iʔ
and this art ceiling or this art floor satisfied art
and the ceiling, and the floor. *The Devil was well*

sx̌ʷílmən 283 waẏ t̓i_kʷṁił {uł i} kiʔ ciʔíx iʔ skʷal̓t, {ə} 284 ałí
s+x̌ʷil+mn waẏ t̓iʔ_kʷṁił kiʔ c[ʔ]íx iʔ s+kʷal̓+t ałíʔ
devil well at_once rel get_warm art sun so
satisfied. (42:00) At once it got warm from the sun; the

ʕamáp {iʔ s} iʔ smík̓ʷət uł axáʔ iʔ sxʷúyənt, 285 waẏ uł axáʔ
ʕamá+p iʔ s+mik̓ʷ+t uł axáʔ iʔ s+xʷuy+nt waẏ uł axáʔ
melt art snow_on_ground and this art ice well and this
snow and the ice melted, and the house

ʕamáp iʔ citxʷ, waẏ uł ksəx̌ʷpínaʔ 286 a t̓i_wiṁ uł {nx̌əl} nx̌l̓áwəlx
ʕamá+p iʔ citxʷ waẏ uł k+sx̌ʷ+p=ínaʔ a t̓iʔ_wiṁ uł n+x̌la+wlx
melt art house well and have_runoff intj powerless and get_scared
melted and the water started running. And the Devil got

sx̌ʷílmən 287 waẏ pna cəṁ itíʔ mi kən ckəmłłínaʔ 288 waẏ
s+x̌ʷil+mn waẏ pnaʔ cṁ itíʔ mi kn c+k+mł•ł=ínaʔ waẏ
devil well maybe maybe from_that fut 1kn cave_in_cisl well
scared. "Now it's going to fall on me." He

ixíʔ sʔácqaʔs łx̌ʷṗám 289 put ʔácqaʔ {kł} uł axáʔ nmłəłúlaʔxʷ iʔ
ixíʔ s -ʔácqaʔ -s łx̌ʷṗa+m put ʔácqaʔ uł axáʔ n+mł•ł=úlaʔxʷ iʔ
then nom -go_out -3i run_out just go_out and this cave_in art
went out fast, he just got out when the house

cítxʷ 290 a··, nstíls sx̌ʷílmən, waẏ, waẏ nixʷ a kʷu ƛ̓xʷups
citxʷ a n+st=ils s+x̌ʷil+mn waẏ waẏ nixʷ a kʷu ƛ̓xʷu+p -s
house intj think devil yes yes again intj 1obj beat -3erg
caved in. "Ah," thought the Devil, "Again my partner

isl̓áx̌t 291 ṅíṅẇiʔ iwá ł ƛ̓lal, ilíʔ {kn} lut t̓ ikskʷním
i -s+l̓ax̌+t ṅíṅẇiʔ iwá ł ƛ̓l•al ilíʔ lut t̓ i -ks -kʷni+m
1in -partner a_while even if dead there not negfac 1i -futi -take
beat me. When he dies I am not going to take him, (43:00)

292 waẏ myał kʷu łaʔ cƛ̓xʷúpsts 293 waẏ ixíʔ uł
waẏ myał kʷu łaʔ c -ƛ̓xʷu+p -st -s waẏ ixíʔ uł
yes too_much 1obj comp cust^ -beat -^cust -3erg well then and
he gets the best of me too much." Then

mat sic {łʔukʷ łə··} łʔimx iʔ k̓əl snilíʔtns 294 waẏ axáʔ
mat sic ł+ʔimx iʔ k̓l s+n+ilíʔ+tn -s waẏ axáʔ
maybe then move_back art to dwelling_place -3in well this
he moved to where he belongs. When

ksx̌əlpínaʔ q̓ʷəyʕás, uł ʕác̓əs iʔ sl̓áx̌ts 295 k̓aw iʔ
k+s+x̌l+p=ínaʔ q̓ʷy=ʕas uł ʕac̓ -s iʔ s+l̓ax̌+t -s k̓aw iʔ
have_daylight black_face and look_at -3erg art partner -3in gone art
daylight came to the Black Face, he looked over to his partner's. His house

cítxʷs, waẏ k̓aw iʔ sl̓ax̌ts 296 uł haʔ sc̓kinx, mat t̓i t
citxʷ -s waẏ k̓aw iʔ s+l̓ax̌+t -s uł haʔ s+c+ʔkin+x mat t̓iʔ t
house -3in well gone art partner -3in and inter why_is_it must evid obl
is gone, his partner is gone. "And what's the matter,

sənkʷəkʷʔác uɬ_iʔ {iʔ} ʔímx uɬ 297 lut kʷu tʼ cus, waẏ ixíʔ
s+n+kʷ+kʷʔac uɬ_iʔ ʔimx uɬ lut kʷu tʼ cu -s waẏ ixíʔ
night and_then move and not 1obj negfac tell -3erg well then
he must have moved in the night. *He didn't even say,*

ɬwíntsən {uɬ i} 298 pnaʔ uɬ k̓aʔkín ɬ xʷúy 299 huy {i} aláʔ
ɬwi -nt -s -n pnaʔ uɬ k̓a+ʔkín ɬ xʷuy hoy aláʔ
leave -nt -2obj -1erg maybe and to_where compl go well here
'I'm leaving you.' *I wonder where he went." (44:00)* *After*

ck̓əɬpaʔx̌əmlwís, waẏ, waẏ q̓ilt uɬ aɬíʔ mat sənk̓əwpílsx,
c -k̓ɬ+paʔx̌+m+lwís waẏ waẏ q̓il+t uɬ aɬíʔ mat s -n+k̓w+p+ils -x
hab -be_thinking well well sick and because maybe ipftv^ -lonesome -^ipftv
he was figuring around, he got sick maybe because he got lonesome,

300 uɬ aɬíʔ_swit tʼi knánəqs 301 waẏ tʼi_lut, uɬ ƛ̓lal axáʔ q̓ʷəyʕás
uɬ aɬíʔ_swit tʼiʔ k+ná•naqs waẏ tʼiʔ_lut uɬ ƛ̓l•al axáʔ q̓ʷy=ʕas
and in_fact evid alone well in_no_time and dead this black_face
because he's all alone. *It was no time, and the Black Face died.*

302 waẏ xʷu··y axáʔ {i s} iʔ sənkaʔkəʔíw̓sc caʔkʷ {cus that's} cus
waẏ xʷuy axáʔ iʔ s+n+kaʔ•kʔ=íw̓s -c caʔkʷ cu -s
well go this art soul -3in as tell -3erg
His life went out of his body. His soul went, like they say in English, 'his soul went out

ta nuyápixcən {i} 303 waẏ wiks waẏ ʔasíl iʔ xəw̓wíɬ 304 axáʔ
t n+wyap=x=cn waẏ wik -s waẏ ʔasíl iʔ xw̓•w•iɬ axáʔ
agInst English well see -3erg yes two art roads this
of his body'. *He saw two roads.* *One*

cx̌əƛ̓mús iʔ xəwíɬ k̓əl skcəhíksts 305 waẏ mat tʼəxʷ
c -x̌ƛ̓+m=us iʔ xwiɬ k̓l s+k+ch=ikst -s waẏ mat tʼxʷ
hab -uphill art road to right_hand -3in well maybe evidently
is steep uphill, the road to his right. (45:00) *It's dim,*

cq̓əq̓áx̌, uɬ ilíʔ náx̌əmɬ lut {tʼaks} tʼa ksxʷuytn put 306 uɬ axáʔ
c -q̓•q̓ax̌ uɬ ilíʔ nax̌mɬ lut tʼ k+s+xʷuy+tn put uɬ axáʔ
hab -clearing and there but not negfac have_track just and this
and there aren't many tracks on it. *And*

k̓əl skc̓íkʷaʔ talí náx̌əmɬ ə·· a csəx̌ʷstús k̓əl skc̓íkʷaʔ
k̓l s+k+c̓íkʷaʔ taʔlíʔ nax̌mɬ ə a c -sx̌ʷ+st=us k̓l s+k+c̓íkʷaʔ
to left_hand very_much but intj art hab -downhill to left_hand
the one to the left is downhill.

307 níkxna·· tʼi nqʷúɬqən ik̓líʔ xwiɬ, qʷámqʷəmt t xəwíɬ 308 waẏ
níkxnaʔ tʼiʔ n+qʷuɬ=qn ik̓líʔ xwiɬ qʷam•qʷm+t t xwiɬ waẏ
goodness evid dust there road excellent prttv road well
Goodness, it's nothing but dust[6] there, it's a beautiful road. *The*

6 The sense is "well-traveled."

nstíls q̓ʷəyʕás, way̓ t̓əxʷ axáʔ iʔ {k̓əl} k̓la nx̌saqs mi kən xʷúy
n+st=ils q̓ʷy=ʕas way̓ t̓xʷ axáʔ iʔ k̓l n+x̌s=aqs mi kn xʷuy
think black_face well emph this art to good_road fut 1kn go
Black Face thought, "I am going to the good road.

309 mat ak̓láʔ iʔ k̓əl skcəhíkst mat lut t̓a qʷay iʔ sqílxʷ ik̓líʔ
mat ak̓láʔ iʔ k̓l s+k+ch=ikst mat lut t̓ qʷay iʔ s+qilxʷ ik̓líʔ
maybe here art to right_hand maybe not negfac often art person there
It doesn't look like people go to the right

cxʷuy 310 way̓ sxʷuys axáʔ iʔ k̓əl skc̓íkʷaʔ, {iʔ} a csix̌ʷt
c -xʷuy way̓ s -xʷuy -s axáʔ iʔ k̓l s+k+c̓íkʷaʔ a c+six̌ʷ+t
hab -go well nom -go -3i this art to left_hand art downhill
often." (46:00) He went to the left, downhill.

311 xʷu··y, nt̓aʔ k̓əɬk̓ʷƛ̓áp, níkxnaʔ qʷámqʷəmt iʔ k̓ɬənk̓míp, t̓i x̌al··
xʷuy nt̓a k̓ɬ+k̓ʷƛ̓a+p níkxnaʔ qʷam•qʷm+t iʔ k̓ɬ+n+k̓m=ip t̓iʔ x̌al
go intj come_in_sight goodness excellent art door evid glitter
He went, he came in sight, gee, there is a beautiful gate, it glitters.

312 náx̌əmɬ k̓aʔítət, uɬ way̓ t̓i ʔanwís {i s i s} iʔ sciʔíxs 313 way̓
nax̌mɬ k̓aʔít•t uɬ way̓ t̓iʔ ʔanwí -s iʔ s+c[ʔ]íx -s way̓
but get_near and yes evid feel -3erg art heat -3in well
He got closer, and he started feeling the heat. He got

k̓ɬənɬaʔíp, way̓ kcaʔcaʔálqʷəm, wəypáyam 314 way̓
k̓ɬ+n+ɬaʔ+íp way̓ k+caʔ+caʔ=álqʷ+m wyp=áya+m way̓
be_next_to yes knock_on_pole play_white_man well
right to the door, he knocked on it, he played white man. He

k̓ɬənk̓ahk̓ʷípɬtəm, ckʷənɬənq̓ʔíw̓s 315 a suxʷs ixíʔ a
k̓ɬ+n+k̓ahk̓ʷ=íp -ɬt -m c -kʷn+ɬ+n+q̓ʔ=iw̓s a suxʷ -s ixíʔ a
open -ɬt -psv hab -hold_fork intj recognize -3erg that intj
opened the door, he had a fork in his hand. He recognized him, "That's my

isl̓áx̌t 316 cus, way̓ sl̓ax̌t, way̓ kícəntsən
i -s+l̓ax̌+t cu -s way̓ s+l̓ax̌+t way̓ kic -nt -s -n
1in -partner tell -3erg well partner well reach_st/sb -nt -2obj -1erg
partner." He said, "Well, partner, here I am."

317 cúntəm axáʔ t sl̓ax̌ts, way̓ lut, lut k̓im kʷu t̓a sl̓ax̌t
cu -nt -m axáʔ t s+l̓ax̌+t -s way̓ lut lut k̓im kʷu t̓ s+l̓ax̌+t
tell -nt -psv this agInst partner -3in well not not but 4kn negfac partner
He said, "No, we're not partners. (47:01)

318 way̓ cúntsən {ə·ɬ} púti kʷu ɬaʔ cxʷəl·xʷált axáʔ i l
way̓ cu -nt -s -n pút+i kʷu ɬaʔ c -xʷl••xʷal+t axáʔ iʔ l
yes tell -nt -2obj -instr still 4kn when hab -alive_pl this art on
I told you while we were living

təmxʷúlaʔxʷ {ə kʷu} 319 kʷu ƛ̓xʷúpəntxʷ {al} ʔaslúsəm i l sk̓ʷanɬq
tmxʷ=úlaʔxʷ kʷu ƛ̓xʷu+p -nt -xʷ ʔasl=ús+m iʔ l s+k̓ʷan=ɬq
earth 1obj beat -nt -2erg two art in garden
on earth, you got the best of me twice in the garden,

320 uɬ axáʔ i l cítxʷ, nixʷ ilíʔ kʷu ƛ̓xʷúpəntxʷ {indec} 321 kən
uɬ axáʔ iʔ l citxʷ nixʷ ilíʔ kʷu ƛ̓xʷu+p -nt -xʷ kn
and this art in house also there 1obj beat -nt -2erg 1kn
and in the house, there too you got the best of me. *And*

cx̌ʷlúlaʔxʷəm məɬ ʕapnáʔ aláʔ kən aɬ k̓ʷəl̓ɬtəmxʷúlaʔxʷəm
c -x̌ʷl=úlaʔxʷ+m mɬ ʕapnáʔ aláʔ kn aɬ k̓ʷl̓+ɬ+tmxʷ=úlaʔxʷ+m
hab -leave_country and now here 1kn compl make_home
then I left that country and now I have made my home here."

322 cúntəm {u cutk uɬ aɬíʔ} way̓ sl̓ax̌t uɬ aɬíʔ way̓ kən ƛ̓lal, 323 lut uɬ
cu -nt -m way̓ s+l̓ax̌+t uɬ aɬíʔ way̓ kn ƛ̓l•al lut uɬ
tell -nt -psv well partner and so yes 1kn dead not and
He said, "Partner, I am dead. *I don't*

k̓aʔkín t̓ iksənxʷúy {tn} kmix aláʔ {indec} 324 cúntəm, lut,
k̓a+ʔkín t̓ i -ks -n+xʷuy kmix aláʔ cu -nt -m lut
to_where negfac 1i -futi -go_in only here tell -nt -psv not
have where to go, only here." *He said,*

way̓ cúntsən lut kʷ t̓ isl̓áx̌t, ixíʔ aɬ k̓ɬənʕalíps
way̓ cu -nt -s -n lut kʷ t̓ i -s+l̓ax̌+t ixíʔ aɬ k̓ɬ+n+ʕal̓=íp -s
yes tell -nt -2obj -1erg not 2kʷu negfac 1in -friend then compl close_gate -3erg
"You're not my friend," and he shut the door.

325 way̓ ilí··ʔ ʔakswíx, uɬ nstíls, 326 way̓ t̓əxʷ aɬíʔ qʷəńcín aɬíʔ kən
way̓ ilíʔ ʔaks+wíx uɬ n+st=ils way̓ t̓xʷ aɬíʔ qʷń=cin aɬíʔ kn
well there stand and think well emph so pity because 1kn
He stood there, and he thought, *"Well, it's a pity*

xkínəm mi kən ɬxʷəlxʷált 327 uɬ way̓ kən ƛ̓lál 328 way̓ ixíʔ
x+ʔkin+m mi kn ɬ+xʷl•xʷal+t uɬ way̓ kn ƛ̓l•al way̓ ixíʔ
do_what fut 1kn alive_again and yes 1kn dead well then
I can't go back to life, (48:05) *I am dead."* *Then*

ɬəɬṗəlk̓úsəms, ixíʔ ɬəɬx̌íƛ̓əms axáʔ la nwapáqs 329 lut
ɬ -ɬ+ṗlk̓=us+m -s ixíʔ ɬ -ɬ+x̌iƛ̓+m -s axáʔ l n+wap=áqs lut
nom -turn_back_again -3i then nom -climb_back -3i this in grassy_road not
he turned around, went up the hill in the road where all kinds of things grow. *It's*

t̓a cqʷay itíʔ t̓a cxʷuy 330 x̌í··ƛ̓əm, kɬqilt, i·ʔ nt̓aʔ {i s}
t̓ c -qʷay itíʔ t̓ c -xʷuy x̌iƛ̓+m kɬ+qilt i nt̓a
negfac hab -often from_that negfac hab -go climb on_top intj intj
not often that they travel there. *He went up the hill, got to*

iʔ sṗəʔáxʷs {iʔ} iʔ k̓ɬənk̓míp, uɬ kəlkʷákʷ 331 xʷu··y, kicx, {ə}
iʔ s+ṗʔaxʷ -s iʔ k̓ɬ+n+k̓m=ip uɬ k+lkʷ•akʷ xʷuy kic+x
art shine -3in art door and far go arrive
the top, gee there's a shining door, and it's far. *He went, he got there, he*

k̓ɬənciʔípəm 332 way̓ ck̓ɬənk̓ahk̓ʷípɬtəm, ixíʔ {t s t s} t
k̓ɬ+n+cʔ=ip+m way̓ c -k̓ɬ+n+k̓ahk̓ʷ=íp -ɬt -m ixíʔ t
knock_on_door well act -open_door -ɬt -psv that agInst
knocked on the door. *Saint Peter opened the door, pyar*

Saint_Peter pyar t'əxʷ i? skʷists sqilxʷ 333 pyar, ití?
pyar t'xʷ i? s+kʷist -s s+qilxʷ pyar ití?
Peter emph art name -3in Indian Peter that
in Indian. *Peter, he's the one who*

ck̓łənk̓ahk̓ʷípłtəm 334 cúntəm, way̓ stim̓ uł aspu?ús
c -k̓ł+n+k̓ahk̓ʷ=íp -łt -m cu -nt -m way̓ s+tim̓ uł a -s+pu?=ús
act -open_door -łt -psv tell -nt -psv well what and 2in -heart
opened the door. (49:04) *He asked, "What do you want?"*

335 cúntəm, way̓, way̓ ałí? kən ƛ̓lal, uł kən
cu -nt -m way̓ way̓ ałí? kn ƛ̓l•al uł kn
tell -nt -psv well well because 1kn dead and 1kn
He said, "I am dead, and I am hard up for a place

sənyaʕpcənlúpx, 336 uł_i? {kən c} kən cxʷuy alá?, way̓ kən
s -n+yaʕ+p=cn=lúp -x uł_i? kn c+xʷuy alá? way̓ kn
ipftv^ -need_a_place -^ipftv and_then 1kn come here yes 1kn
to stay. *That's why I came here.*

ksən?úłxʷa?x 337 cúntəm t *Saint Peter,* lu⋅⋅t, kən
ks -n+?ułxʷ -a?x cu -nt -m t lut kn
incp^ -enter -^incp tell -nt -psv agInst not 1kn
Let me in." *Saint Peter said, "I just*

sk̓ʷúk̓ʷl̓a?x 338 cúntəm uł lut{a}_swit t'a cənppílx alá?,
s -k̓ʷú•k̓ʷl̓a? -x cu -nt -m uł lut_swit t' c+n+p•pil+x alá?
ipftv^ -work_dim -^ipftv tell -nt -psv and nobody negfac enter_pl_cisl here
work here. *And it's not anybody who can get in here,*

kmix i? x̌ast 339 ʕác̓ənt anwí púti? kʷ cxʷəlxʷált uł
kmix i? x̌as+t ʕac̓ -nt anwí pút+i? kʷ c -xʷl•xʷal+t uł
only art good look -nt you still 2kn hab -alive and
only the good. *Look, when you were still alive*

l̓áx̌tməntxʷ i? sx̌ʷílmən 340 uł lut t'a
l̓ax̌+t+m -nt -xʷ i? s+x̌ʷil+mn uł lut t'
be_friends_with -nt -2erg art devil and not negfac
you were partners with the Devil. *And you never*

cpa?smístxʷ ank̓ʕáwmən 341 łxʷuyx i? k̓
c -pa?s+mí -st -xʷ an -k̓aʕʷ+mn ł+xʷuy -x i? k̓
cust^ -think_about -^cust -2erg 2in -prayers go_back -isimptv art to
thought about your prayers. *Go to your partner,*

asl̓ax̌t, k̓əl sx̌ʷílmən {indec} 342 ksk̓łənʕalípi?s uł_i?
a -s+l̓ax̌+t k̓l s+x̌ʷil+mn ks -k̓ł+n+ʕal̓=íp -ẏ -s uł_i?
2in -partner to devil futt^ -close_door -nt -3erg and_then
to the Devil." (50:03) *He was going to close the door*

cúntəm {t'i put i k̓am} 343 kʷa púti? kʷ cxʷəlxʷált uł_i? kʷ
cu -nt -m kʷa pút+i? kʷ c -xʷl•xʷal+t uł_i? kʷ
tell -nt -psv intj still 2kn hab -alive and_then 2kn
and he said: *"When you were still alive you were partners*

l̓aẍtəm i k̓əl sẍʷílmən {ut} 344 lu··t, ałíʔ {l} way̓ lut nixʷ kʷu t̓
l̓aẍ+t+m iʔ k̓l s+ẍʷil+mn lut ałíʔ way̓ lut nixʷ kʷu t̓
be_friends_with art to devil not because well not also 1obj negfac
with the Devil." *"No, my friend doesn't want me either,*

ẍminks iʔ t isl̓áẍt uł lut kən xkínəm mi kən łxʷəlxʷált,
ẍm=ink -s iʔ t i -s+l̓aẍ+t uł lut kn x+ʔkin+m mi kn ł+xʷl•xʷal+t
want -3erg art agInst 1in -friend and not 1kn do_what fut 1kn alive_again
and I can do nothing to go back to life.

345 way̓ kən {ksən} ksəniliʔtnaʔx 346 way̓ {indec} t̓əxʷ
way̓ kn k -s+n+iliʔ+tn -aʔx way̓ t̓xʷ
well 1kn incp^ -dwelling_place -^incp well emph
I have got to have a place to stay. *Come on*

k̓łənk̓ahk̓ʷípəntxʷ, kmix nwík̓łc̓aʔn {k̓a n} k̓a nyxʷut, 347 ixíʔ kmix mi
k̓ł+n+k̓ahk̓ʷ=íp -nt -xʷ kmix n+wík=łc̓aʔ -n k̓ n+yxʷ=ut ixíʔ kmix mi
open -nt -2erg only see_inside -1erg to inside then only fut
and open the door, I only want to see inside there, *and then*

uł kən nẍstəlsmíst 348 cúntəm, way̓, way̓ k̓łənk̓ahk̓ʷípłtəm
uł kn n+ẍs+t=ls+mist cu -nt -m way̓ way̓ k̓ł+n+k̓ahk̓ʷ=íp -łt -m
and 1kn satisfy_self tell -nt -psv OK well open -łt -psv
I will be satisfied." *He said, "Ok," and he opened the door. (51:00)*

349 axáʔ nłət̓pməncút i l spiksts a q̓ʷəyʕás 350 c̓əq̓mís iʔ
axáʔ n+łt̓+p+mncut i l sp=ikst -s a q̓ʷy=ʕas c̓q̓+mi -s iʔ
this jump_inside art in glove -3in art black_face throw -3erg art
The Black Face jumped in his glove, *he threw*

spiksts k̓la nixʷút 351 ik̓líʔ {k̓la} k̓a nixʷút t̓k̓ʷak̓ʷ iʔ spikst, ilíʔ
sp=ikst -s k̓l n+yxʷ=ut ik̓líʔ k̓ n+yxʷ=ut t̓k̓ʷ•ak̓ʷ iʔ sp=ikst ilíʔ
glove -3in to inside there to inside land_flat art glove there
his glove in there. *The glove landed inside there, and there*

namút 352 uł yaʔẍíʔ k̓łənʕalíp[s] *Saint_Peter,* sanpyár {cúntəm}
n+ʔam=út uł yaʔẍíʔ k̓ł+n+ʕal̓=íp -s sanpyár
sit_inside and yonder close_gate -3erg St_Peter
it sat. *Saint Peter closed the door, and he looked behind himself,*

353 uł nʕac̓əẍkən̓cút wíkəntəm ilíʔ naʔmút i l spikst
uł n+ʕac̓ẍ=kn̓+cút wik -nt -m ilíʔ n+ʔam=út iʔ l sp=ikst
and look_behind see -nt -psv there sit_inside art in glove
and he saw him there sitting in the glove.

354 cúntəm way̓ cúntsən way̓ lut akscənʔúłxʷ uł_iʔ
cu -nt -m way̓ cu -nt -s -n way̓ lut a -ksc -n+ʔułxʷ uł_iʔ
tell -nt -psv well tell -nt -2obj -1erg yes not 2i -futPerfi -enter and_then
He said, "I told you not to come in,

kʷ ał cənʔúłxʷ 355 cus {saint pər} *Saint_Peter,* uł way̓ t̓əxʷ kən
kʷ ał c+n+ʔułxʷ cu -s uł way̓ t̓xʷ kn
2kn compl enter_cisl tell -3erg and well emph 1kn
and you came in!" *He said to Saint Peter, "Now*

cənʔúɬxʷ 356 uɬ way̓ lut {kʷu t̓a a kʷu t̓ akɬ} kʷ xkínəm mi kʷu
c+n+ʔuɬxʷ uɬ way̓ lut kʷ x+ʔkin+m mi kʷu
enter_cisl and yes not 2kn do_what fut 1obj
I am in, and you can't do anything to throw me

ɬkcəq̓mənkn̓íɬxʷəntxʷ 357 put ilíʔ tixʷkʷúnəm {ə} kiʔ
ɬ+k+c̓q̓+mn=kn̓=iɬxʷ -nt -xʷ put ilíʔ tixʷ+kʷún+m kiʔ
throw_outside_again -nt -2erg just there talk rel
back out.” He had just said that when

ktíɬxməntməlx t yasukrí 358 cúntəm {ta} sanpyár, xʷúyx
k+tiɬ+x+m -nt -m -lx t yasukrí cu -nt -m sanpyár xʷuy -x
stand_by -nt -psv -pl agInst JC tell -nt -psv St_Peter go -isimptv
JC was standing there. (52:05) He said to St Peter, “Go,

anwí {t aks'} way̓ t incá cqʷəlqʷílstən 359 xʷuyx anwí
anwí way̓ t in+cá c -qʷl•qʷil -st -n xʷuy -x anwí
you yes agInst I cust^ -talk_to -^cust -1erg go -isimptv you
I'll talk to him. You go to

k̓l asck̓ʷúl̓ 360 hoy sxʷists {ta} sanpyár {uɬ k̓im} 361 i nák̓ʷəm{a}
k̓l a -sc -k̓ʷul̓ hoy s -xʷist -s sanpyár i nak̓ʷm
to 2i -pftv -work well nom -walk -3i St_Peter intj evid
your work.” St Peter went. And that's

iʔ k̓ʷəl̓əncútn cúntəm iʔ t k̓ʷəl̓əncútn 362 way̓, cúntəm, way̓
iʔ k̓ʷl̓+ncut+n cu -nt -m iʔ t k̓ʷl̓+ncut+n way̓ cu -nt -m way̓
art god tell -nt -psv art agInst god well tell -nt -psv well
God himself, God said: “Well Black Man,

q̓ʷəyʕás, incá iʔ kən k̓ʷəl̓əncútn {uɬ ə··} 363 uɬ aslək̓məncút, ki
q̓ʷy=ʕas in+cá iʔ kn k̓ʷl̓+ncut+n uɬ a -s -lk̓+mncut kiʔ
black_face I art 1kn god and 2i -intt -force_oneself rel
I am God. And you forced yourself here.

ilí k cunts ɬ aksənʔúɬxʷ 364 uɬ_iʔ kʷ cənʔúɬxʷ
ilíʔ kiʔ cu -nt -s ɬ a -ks -n+ʔuɬxʷ uɬ_iʔ kʷ c+n+ʔuɬxʷ
there rel tell -nt -3e2obj subord 2i -futi -enter and_then 2kn enter_cisl
He didn't tell you to come here (53:03) and then you came here.

365 uɬ {i} way̓ ixíʔ kʷ ikskc̓x̌ʷíplaʔm 366 t aspíkst kiʔ
uɬ way̓ ixíʔ kʷ i -ks -k+c̓x̌ʷ=íplaʔ+m t a -sp=ikst kiʔ
and yes then 2kʷu 1i -futi -sentence agInst 2in -glove rel
And now I'm going to give you a sentence. You got in with your glove.

cənʔúɬxʷstəms, ilíʔ kʷ nʔuɬxʷ iʔ l aspíkst uɬ_iʔ
c -n+ʔuɬxʷ -st -m -s ilíʔ kʷ n+ʔuɬxʷ iʔ l a -sp=ikst uɬ_iʔ
act -enter -caus -2obj -3erg there 2kn enter art in 2in -glove and_then
You went in your glove and

ncq̓mintxʷ 367 uɬ ilíʔ nyʕ̓íp kʷ snaʔmútaʔx iʔ l
n+c̓q̓+min -t -xʷ uɬ ilíʔ nyʕ̓ip kʷ s -n+ʔam=út -aʔx iʔ l
throw_in -nt -2erg and there always 2kn incp^ -sit_inside -^incp art in
you threw it in. So you are going to stay in your glove

aspíkst mi put la ċíwt sx̌əlx̌ʕált
a -sp=ikst mi put l c+ʔiwt s+x̌l•x̌aʕl+t
2in -glove fut exact on last day
until the last day." (53:32)

How Coyote got his powers

1 way̓ t’əxʷ kən kscaptíkʷlaʔx axáʔ la cxʔit {iʔ l} ɬ kʷúl̓l̓ yasukrí
way̓ t’xʷ kn ks -captíkʷl -aʔx axáʔ l c+xʔit ɬ kʷul̓•l̓ yasukrí
well emph 1kn incp^ -tell_stories -^incp this at first when born JC
I am going to tell a story. When Christ was first born

2 uɬ ixíʔ {ɬ} ckicx axáʔ iʔ l təmxʷúlaʔxʷ 3 uɬ ixíʔ x̌lits
uɬ ixíʔ c+kic+x axáʔ iʔ l tmxʷ=úlaʔxʷ uɬ ixíʔ x̌lit -s
and then arrive_cisl this art on land and then summon -3erg
and he got here on earth, he called

yaʕyá··ʕt iʔ skəkáʕkaʔ uɬ axáʔ {i s iʔ} ia ctəkʷtəkʷʔút 4 həɬsənk̓líp,
yaʕ•yáʕ+t iʔ s+k•kʕá•kaʔ uɬ axáʔ iʔ c -tkʷ+tkʷʔ=ut hɬ=s+n+k̓l̓=ip
all art bird and this art hab -walk coyote_group
all the birds, and the ones that walk on the ground, coyotes,

həɬwápupxən, {həɬ} həɬnc̓íʔcən 5 t’əxʷ yaʕyáʕt ia [c]təkʷtəkʷʔút {i s i s}
hɬ=wap•wp+xn hɬ=nc̓iʔ+cn t’xʷ yaʕ•yáʕ+t iʔ c -tkʷ+tkʷʔ=ut
lynx_group wolf_group emph all art hab -walk
lynxes, wolves, all those that walk on the ground.

6 ixíʔ x̌lítəntməlx, lut iʔ sqilxʷ 7 t’iʔ_kmix axáʔ iʔ caʔkʷ us
ixíʔ x̌lit -nt -m -lx lut iʔ s+qilxʷ t’iʔ_kmix axáʔ iʔ caʔkʷ cu -s
then summon -nt -psv -pl not art person only this art as tell -3erg
He asked all of them to come, not the human beings, only what they call in English

iʔ ta nuyápixcən iʔ *animals* 8 uɬ axáʔ iʔ skəkáʕkaʔ {iʔ} iʔ *birds* 9 ixíʔ
iʔ t n+wyap=x=cn iʔ uɬ axáʔ iʔ s+k•kʕá•kaʔ iʔ ixíʔ
art agInst say_in_English art and this art bird art then
“animals,” 1:02 and the fowl, the birds. He

cúntməlx, {ixíʔ p iks} ʕapnáʔ kʷu ksyaʕ̓míxaʔx 10 ixíʔ way̓
cu -nt -m -lx ʕapnáʔ kʷu ks -yaʕ̓ -míx+aʔx ixíʔ way̓
tell -nt -psv -pl now 4kn incp^ -gather -^incp then yes
said to them, “Now we are going to gather. Just now

t’alaʔxwílx axáʔ iʔ təmxʷúlaʔxʷ 11 uɬ way̓ p iksk̓əɬʔíysəm 12 axáʔ
t’alaʔ+x+wílx axáʔ iʔ tmxʷ=úlaʔxʷ uɬ way̓ p i -ks -k̓ɬ+ʔiys+m axáʔ
next_generation this art land and yes 5kʷu 1i -futi -change this
this world is going to come to life and I am going to change you. You

iʔ p skəkáʕkaʔ ixíʔ p kskəkáʕkaʔ 13 uɬ ixíʔ p
iʔ p s+k•kʕá•kaʔ ixíʔ p k -s+k+káʕ+kaʔ uɬ ixíʔ p
art 5kn bird then 5kn to_be -chicken and then 5kn
birds that fly in the air, you are going to be birds, and you are

kst’əxʷt’əxʷtlílxaʔx k̓la nwist 14 uɬ axáʔ {iʔ p iʔ} iʔ p kmúsxən, lut
ks -t’xʷ•t’xʷt+lilx -aʔx k̓l n+wis+t uɬ axáʔ iʔ p k=mus=xn lut
incp^ -fly_pl -^incp to high and this art 5kn quadruped not
going to be those that fly in the air. And you that stand on four legs,

iʔ p aʔkstqtqpíʔstən 15 ixíʔ uɬ həɬsənk̓líp, {uɬ} uɬ axáʔ həɬsəmx̌íʔkən,
iʔ p k+s+tq•tqp=íʔst+n ixíʔ uɬ hɬ=s+n+k̓l̓=ip uɬ axáʔ hɬ=s+mx̌=ikn
art 5kn have_wings then and Coyote_group and this Grizzly_group
you that don't have wings, the coyotes, and the grizzlies,

həɬskəmxíst uɬ iʔ sƛ̓aʔcínəm 16 t̓əxʷ yaʕyáʕt {ixíʔ ixíʔ} ixíʔ axáʔ iʔ l
hɬ=s+kmxist uɬ iʔ s+ƛ̓aʔ=cín+m t̓xʷ yaʕ•yáʕ+t ixíʔ axáʔ iʔ l
Bear_group and art deer emph all that this art on
and the black bears, and the deer, everything that is on this earth,

təmxʷúlaʔxʷ uɬ náx̌əmɬ k̓əl wist {ks} 17 lut nixʷ iʔ l sqilxʷ {kscənmíƛ̓əm}
tmxʷ=úlaʔxʷ uɬ nax̌mɬ k̓l wis+t lut nixʷ iʔ l s+qilxʷ
country and but to mountains not more art with person
but high [in the mountains], 2:06 you are not going to be

kcənmíƛ̓əmp 18 uɬ way̓ ixíʔ k̓ɬəm̓cínlx 19 uɬ cúntməlx
kc -n+miƛ̓ -mp uɬ way̓ ixíʔ k̓ɬ+ʔm=cin-lx uɬ cu -nt -m -lx
futImp -mixed -5in and yes then agree-pl and tell -nt -psv -pl
mixed up with the people." They all agreed. He said to them

x̌lap put ixíʔ sxəlákəks {i as} iʔ x̌yáɬnəxʷ 20 i[xíʔ] kʷu ɬiyáʕ aláʔ
x̌la+p put ixíʔ s -xl•l•ak•k -s iʔ x̌yaɬ=nxʷ ixíʔ kʷu ɬ+yaʕ aláʔ
tomorrow just then nom -round -3i art sun then 4kn gather_again here
"Tomorrow, just when the sun is turning, we'll gather back here.

21 aláʔ ixíʔ mi ɬxʷíc̓ɬmən iʔ kɬcq̓ílnəmp 22 ixíʔ uɬ p
aláʔ ixíʔ mi ɬ+xʷic̓ -ɬm -n iʔ kɬ -cq̓=iln -mp ixíʔ uɬ p
here then fut give_again -5obj -1erg art to_be -arrow -5i then and 5kn
That's when I'll give you what's going to be your arrows. That's when

pəx̌ʷmancút iʔ k̓la cməq̓ʷmáq̓ʷ 23 lut kɬəɬc̓úluʔsəmp iʔ naʔɬ
px̌ʷ+mncut iʔ k̓l c -mq̓ʷ•maq̓ʷ lut kɬ -ɬ+c+ʔul=w̓s -mp iʔ naʔɬ
scatter art to hab -mountains not futi -gather_cisl_again -5i art with
you'll scatter to the mountains. You won't be mixed up with

sqilxʷ 24 way̓ k̓ɬəmcínəlx, way̓ ixíʔ cúntməlx way̓ uɬ p pəx̌ʷməncút
s+qilxʷ way̓ k̓ɬ+ʔm=cin -lx way̓ ixíʔ cu -nt -m -lx way̓ uɬ p px̌ʷ+mncut
person well agree -pl yes then tell -nt -psv -pl well and 5kn scatter
the people." They all agreed. He said to them, "You can scatter,

p ʔawspúlx 25 ixíʔ {m} p ksx̌əlpínaʔ uɬ ixíʔ ɬcənlaʕ̓ʷús ixíʔ iʔ l
p ʔaw+s+púl+x ixíʔ p k+s+x̌l+p=ínaʔ uɬ ixíʔ ɬ+c+n+lʕ̓ʷ=us ixíʔ iʔ l
5kn go_to_bed then 5kn have_daylight and then fit_cisl_again then art in
go to bed. When daylight comes on you, and the turning

sxəl̓lákək[s] {uɬ i} 26 mi aláʔ p ɬciyáʕ ixíʔ məɬ xʷíc̓ɬmən iʔ
s -xl•l•ak•k -s mi aláʔ p ɬ+c+yaʕ ixíʔ mɬ xʷic̓ -ɬm -n iʔ
nom -round -3i fut here 5kn gather_cisl_again then and give -5obj -1erg art
fits again[1] 3:03 you will all gather here again, and I'll give you

1 "At this same time."

cq̓ílən̓ 27 waẏ cútəlx waẏ, waẏ ixíʔ {s} pəx̌ʷməncútəlx {ixíʔ uł} iʔ k̓əl
cq̓=iln waẏ cut -lx waẏ waẏ ixíʔ px̌ʷ+mncut -lx iʔ k̓l
arrow well say -pl OK well then scatter -pl art to
the arrows."[2] *They said "Ok," and they scattered to where they are going*

ksənpúlxtənsəlx 28 uł ałíʔ mat ilíʔ cyaʕ̓mílx iʔ l
k -s+n+pul+x+tn -s -lx uł ałíʔ mat ilíʔ c -yaʕ̓+m+ílx iʔ l
to_be -camping_place -3i -pl and so maybe there hab -together art at
to camp. *I guess their camping place is*

ksənpúlxtənsəlx {uł ixíʔ ł} 29 axáʔ atáʔ sənk̓líp ixíʔ uł ałíʔ kʷaʔ sənk̓líp
k -s+n+pul+x+tn -s -lx axáʔ atáʔ s+n+k̓l̓=ip ixíʔ uł ałíʔ kʷaʔ s+n+k̓l̓=ip
to_be -camping_place -3i -pl this here Coyote then and because intj Coyote
all together. *And then Coyote, because he is Coyote,*

30 uł ixíʔ sk̓əłpaʔx̌áms 31 ntils waẏ incá iksƛ̓xʷúpəm ia
uł ixíʔ s -k̓ł+paʔx̌á+m -s nt=ils[3] waẏ in+cá i -ks -ƛ̓xʷu+p+m iʔ
and then nom -figure_out -3i think well I 1i -futi -win art
he started thinking up things. *He thought, "I am going to win the first arrow,*

cxʔit {iʔ} iʔ cq̓ilən iʔ wísxən 32 waẏ lut iksʔítx 33 waẏ, waẏ uł ixíʔ
c+xʔit iʔ cq̓=iln iʔ wis=xn waẏ lut i -ks -ʔitx waẏ waẏ uł ixíʔ
first art arrow art long well not 1i -futi -sleep well well and then
the longest. *I am not going to sleep."* *Well, Coyote started*

sxʷaʔxʷísts sənk̓líp 34 t̓iʔ_lu··t uł ʔayx̌ʷt iʔ t
s -xʷaʔ•xʷíst -s s+n+k̓l̓=ip t̓iʔ_lut uł ʔayx̌ʷ+t iʔ t
nom -walk_back_and_forth -3i Coyote in_no_time and tired art agInst
walking back and forth. *In no time he got tired from*

sxʷaʔxʷísts 35 uł axáʔ iʔ k̓ʷiƛ̓t púlxəlx, kmix_k̓əm
s -xʷaʔ•xʷíst -s uł axáʔ iʔ k̓ʷiƛ̓+t pul+x -lx kmix_k̓m
nom -walk_back_and_forth -3i and this art others overnight -pl only
walking back and forth. *And the others all went to bed, it's only Coyote*

sənk̓líp a c̓x̌əl·wís 36 waẏ uł [t̓iʔ_]lut uł ʔayx̌ʷt iʔ t
s+n+k̓l̓=ip a c -ʔax̌l+lwis waẏ uł t̓iʔ_lut uł ʔayx̌ʷ+t iʔ t
Coyote art hab -mill_about well and in_no_time and tired art agInst
fooling around. 4:00 *In no time he got tired from*

scxʷaʔxʷísts 37 waẏ ixíʔ smuts {indec} t̓iʔ mut uł ixíʔ
sc -xʷaʔ•xʷíst -s waẏ ixíʔ s -mut -s t̓iʔ uł ixíʔ
pftv -walk_back_and_forth -3i well then nom -sit_sg -3i evid and then
his walking back and forth; *then he sat down, he sat down and*

sksʔitxs 38 uł waẏ lut, uł waẏ ʔayx̌ʷt łaʔ cxʷaʔxʷíst
s -k+s+ʔitx -s uł waẏ lut uł waẏ ʔayx̌ʷ+t łaʔ c -xʷaʔ•xʷíst
nom -sleepy -3i and well not and yes tired when hab -walk_back_and_forth
he got sleepy. *Heck no, he got tired walking.*

2 Arrows vary in length is direct proportion to the importance of the recipient.
3 ntils is a variant of nstils, with root √st. The reanalysis of ntils gives us √nt.

39 way̓ uɫ {m} iwá ɫ ktqínaʔs {i s} ɫ stkʷƛ̓ústəns stim̓ csək̓ʷtús
way̓ uɫ iwá ɫ k+tq=ínaʔ -s ɫ s+t+k̓ʷƛ̓=us+tn -s s+tim̓ c -s+k̓ʷt=us
well and try_to ? hold_down -3erg ? eye -3in what hab -one_eye
He holds one eye down, just one eye,

40 uɫ lut, way̓ nixʷ lut 41 way̓ uɫ ixíʔ ksʔitx {iʔiac} a
uɫ lut way̓ nixʷ lut way̓ uɫ ixíʔ k+s+ʔitx a
and not well again not well and then sleepy art
but no, still no; he is still sleepy.

cƛ̓aʔƛ̓ʔúsəmsts uɫ axáʔ cktqqínaʔsts 42 məɫ
c -ƛ̓aʔ•ƛ̓aʔ=ús+m -st -s uɫ axáʔ c -k+tq•q=ínaʔ -st -s mɫ
cust^ -look_for -^cust -3erg and this cust^ -hold_down -^cust -3erg and
He presses one down, even

iwá {ɫ} ɫpəlk̓məncút k̓əl sksək̓ʷtúsc ktəqsəncút məɫ axáʔ iʔ naqs uɫ way̓
iwá ɫ+p̓lk̓+mncut k̓l s -k+s+k̓ʷt=us -c k+tq=s+ncut mɫ axáʔ iʔ naqs uɫ way̓
try_to turn_again to ? -one_eye -3in press_eye and this art one and well
when he turns to the other eye and he presses the other down, it still

lut nixʷ 43 way̓ wi··m̓ sx̌əlwísts 44 uɫ axáʔ {iʔ l} iʔ
lut nixʷ way̓ wim̓ s -ʔax̌l+wís -c uɫ axáʔ iʔ
not again well in_vain nom -fool_around -3i and this art
doesn't work. Whatever he does is to no avail. And his partners,

sl̓əx̌l̓áx̌ts axáʔ iʔ k̓ʷiƛ̓t uɫ c̓atxílxəlx tx̌ʷáq̓ʷəlqsəlx 45 way̓ ixíʔ
s+l̓x̌•l̓ax̌+t -s axáʔ iʔ k̓ʷiƛ̓+t uɫ c -ʔatx+ílx -lx t+x̌ʷaq̓ʷ=lqs -lx way̓ ixíʔ
friends -3in this art others and hab -sleep_pl -pl snore -pl well then
the rest of them, are asleep, snoring. Then he thought

k̓əɫpaʔx̌x̌íʔst 46 way̓ ixíʔ sx̌ʷc̓ams t sx̌əx̌c̓íʔ, way̓ ixíʔ put a
k̓ɫ+paʔx̌•x̌=íʔst way̓ ixíʔ s -x̌ʷc̓a+m -s t s+x̌•x̌c̓iʔ way̓ ixíʔ put a
think_of_something well then nom -break -3i obj_itr stick well then just intj
of something. 5:00 He broke a stick, he propped

kt̓əkt̓əksəncút 47 way̓ t̓iʔ_c̓x̌iɫ a way̓ ixíʔ iʔ ksck̓ʷul̓ 48 way̓ ixíʔ
k+t̓k•t̓k=s+ncut way̓ t̓iʔ_c+ʔx̌iɫ a way̓ ixíʔ iʔ ksc -k̓ʷul̓ way̓ ixíʔ
prop_open well just_like intj well then art pperf -fix well then
his eyes open. What he fixed is still the same. He

st̓ək̓ʷəncúts way̓ kʷm̓aɫ ʔitx 49 ʔi··tx, ʔi··tx uɫ aɫíʔ mat k̓əɫʔatətxnúmt
s -t̓k̓ʷ+ncut -s way̓ kʷm̓aɫ ʔitx ʔitx ʔitx uɫ aɫíʔ mat k̓ɫ+ʔat•t•x+númt
nom -lie_down -3i well at_once sleep sleep sleep and so must fall_asleep
lay down, and he fell asleep. He slept and slept, and he must have overslept.

50 uɫ mat cənʔuʔís kiʔ qiɫt 51 way̓, way̓ uɫ t̓iʔ_lut uɫ t̓a
uɫ mat c -n+w[ʔ]is kiʔ qiɫ+t way̓ way̓ uɫ t̓iʔ_lut uɫ t̓
and maybe hab -early_morn rel awaken well well and in_no_time and negfac
The sun must have been high when he woke up. Heck, he could not see,

cuksqílxʷ, uɫ aɫíʔ tx̌uʔx̌uʔús 52 uɫ way̓ iwá k̓náyaʔqən, way̓ k̓aw,
c -wk+s+qilxʷ uɫ aɫíʔ t+x̌ẇ•x̌ẇ=us uɫ way̓ iwá k̓náyaʔ=qn way̓ k̓aw
hab -see and because dry_eyes and well try_to try_to_listen well gone
because his eyes went dry. He tried to listen. They are gone,

lut t̓a ck̓əłníx̣əl[msts] 53 way̓ uł t̓iʔ ilíʔ ƛ̓ílmiʔst, ilíʔ
lut t̓ c -k̓ł+nixl+m -st -s way̓ uł t̓iʔ ilíʔ ƛ̓íl+miʔst ilíʔ
not evid cust^ -hear -^cust -3erg well and evid there stay_put there
he can't hear anything. He lay there still,

t̓əkʷəncút 54 sta kʷaʔ ilíʔ uł{t} cqíłqəłt, way̓ qiłt {kʷʔax} 55 ixíʔ uł axáʔ
t̓k̓ʷ+ncut sta kʷaʔ ilíʔ uł c -qił+qł+t way̓ qił+t ixíʔ uł axáʔ
lie_down intj intj there and hab -awake well awaken then and this
lying down. He stayed there, he was awake, awake. 6:04 They

iʔʕáʔ̣ ik̓líʔ iʔ k̓əl ksniyaʕ̓tánsəlx 56 ilíʔ yasukrí {łə} iʔ
y•yaʕ ik̓líʔ iʔ k̓l k -s+n+yaʕ̓+tán -s -lx ilíʔ yasukrí iʔ
gather there art at to_be -gathering_place -3i -pl there JC art
gathered there at the gathering place. JC was there

ksxʷíc̓łtməlx iʔ t cq̓ílənsəlx 57 way̓ ilíʔ iʔʕ̓áʔ̣lx, way̓ ƛ̓laplx
ks -xʷic̓ -łt -m -lx iʔ t cq̓=iln -s -lx way̓ ilíʔ y•yaʕ -lx way̓ ƛ̓la+p -lx
futt^ -give -łt -psv -pl art obj_tr arrow -3in -pl well there gather -pl well stop -pl
to give them their arrows. They gathered there,

iʔ t siʔʕ̓áʔ̣lx txƛ̓ápəlx {uł} 58 ixíʔ uł kicx yasukrí, ixíʔ {nla}
iʔ t s+y•yaʕ -s -lx t+xƛ̓ap -lx ixíʔ uł kic+x yasukrí ixíʔ
art obl gathering_place -3in -pl complete -pl then and arrive JC then
they got there, all got there. Then JC got there, then

nlaʕʷpús 59 cúntməlx way̓, way̓ aláʔ p yaʕyáʕt 60 cútəlx way̓, way̓
n+lʕ̓ʷ+p=us cu -nt -m -lx way̓ way̓ aláʔ p yaʕ•yáʕ+t cut -lx way̓ way̓
fit tell -nt -psv -pl well well here 5kn all say -pl yes yes
it was time. He asked them, "Are you all here?" They said, "Yes,

aláʔ {kʷu yaʕya} kʷu yaʕyáʕt 61 cúntməlx way̓, xʷíc̓łtəm axáʔ iʔ
aláʔ kʷu yaʕ•yáʕ+t cu -nt -m -lx way̓ xʷic̓ -łt -m axáʔ iʔ
here 4kn all tell -nt -psv -pl well give -łt -psv this art
we are all here." He said to them "Ok." He would give one

wísxən {ə} yasukrí ckəm̓kəm̓stís iʔ cq̓ílən {i nək̓ʷnkáwstən} 62 ixíʔ iʔ
wis=xn yasukrí c -km̓•km̓ -st -is iʔ cq̓=iln ixíʔ iʔ
long JC cust^ -hold -^cust -3erg art arrow that art
the longest [arrow]. JC was holding the arrows. He

sxʔimłwísxən xʷíc̓łtəm {ta} səmx̌íkən 63 cúntəm way̓ anwí iʔ kʷ
s+xʔim+ł+wís=xn xʷic̓ -łt -m s+mx̌=ikn cu -nt -m way̓ anwí iʔ kʷ
longest give -łt -psv grizzly tell -nt -psv well you art 2kn
gave the longest one to Grizzly. He said to him, "You'll be

[k]łilmíxʷəm axáʔ {il} iʔ l təmxʷúlaʔxʷ {il} p həłtəkʷtəkʷʔút {anwí p kłilmi}
kł -yl=mixʷ+m axáʔ iʔ l tmxʷ=úlaʔxʷ p hł=tkʷ+tkʷʔ=ut
to_be -chief this art on land 5kn quadruped_group
the head boss on earth of you that walk; 7:09

64 anwí kʷ kłilmíxʷəm 65 way̓ ixíʔ xʷíc̓əłtəm, uł ixíʔ kʷis
anwí kʷ kł -yl=mixʷ+m way̓ ixíʔ xʷic̓ -łt -m uł ixíʔ kʷi -s
you 2kn to_be -chief well that give -łt -psv and that take -3erg
you will be the boss." He was given it, and he took it.

66 way̓ uɬ axáʔ {i} itlíʔ naqs, ixíʔ nq̓aʔkstúɬtəm axáʔ məlqnúps
way̓ uɬ axáʔ itlíʔ naqs ixíʔ n+q̓aʔ=kst -uɬt -m axáʔ ml=qn=ups
well and this from_there one that put_in_hand -tuɬt -psv this golden_eagle
And then another. He put it in Eagle's hand.

67 cúntəm anwí kʷ kɬilmíxʷəm iʔ l skəkáʕkaʔ a la
cu -nt -m anwí kʷ kɬ -yl=mixʷ+m iʔ l s+k•kʕá•kaʔ a l
tell -nt -psv you 2kn to_be -chief art for bird intj for
He was told, "You will be the chief of the birds, those

ct̓əxʷt̓əxʷtlílx 68 ixíʔ anwí kʷ kɬilmíxʷəm, uɬ kʷintxʷ axáʔ, ixíʔ
c -t̓xʷ•t̓xʷt+lilx ixíʔ anwí kʷ kɬ -yl=mixʷ+m uɬ kʷin -t -xʷ axáʔ ixíʔ
hab -fly_pl that you 2kn to_be -chief and take -nt -2erg this then
that fly, *you will be their boss, take this*

uɬ kʷ xʷuy 69 uɬ ixíʔ akɬtəmxʷúlaʔxʷ {k̓əl} k̓əl wist 70 lut iʔ k̓əl
uɬ kʷ xʷuy uɬ ixíʔ a -kɬ -tmxʷ=úlaʔxʷ k̓l wis+t lut iʔ k̓l
and 2kn go and that 2i -to_be -country to mountain not art to
and go. *That will be your home, up high.* *You won't be*

sqilxʷ kɬəɬcənxíʔmp 71 way̓ nxƛ̓í··ksəntməlx yaʕyáʕt {uɬ t}
s+qilxʷ kɬ -ɬ+c+n+xy̓ -mp way̓ n+xƛ̓=iks -nt -m -lx yaʕ•yáʕ+t
person futi -be_mixed_with_again -5i well do_to_all -nt -psv -pl all
mixed up with people." *He gave them*

uɬ txƛ̓ápəlx 72 ixíʔ uɬ {k̓əm} k̓im {naqs} naqs iʔ cq̓ílən, k̓im
uɬ t+xƛ̓ap -lx ixíʔ uɬ k̓im naqs iʔ cq̓=iln k̓im
and complete -pl then and only one art arrow only
all out, *except one arrow, the shortest one*

sxʔimɬt̓ət̓áq̓aʔt 73 uɬ ixíʔ cúntməlx t yasukrí, way̓ ha p
s+xʔim+ɬ+t̓•t̓áq̓aʔt uɬ ixíʔ cu -nt -m -lx t yasukrí way̓ haʔ p
shortest and then tell -nt -psv -pl agInst JC well inter 5kn
[that was left]. 8:05 *So JC asked them, "Is it*

txƛ̓ap 74 cútəlx way̓ kʷu txƛ̓ap 75 cúntməlx uɬ sc̓kinx, kʷa aláʔ
t+xƛ̓a+p cut -lx way̓ kʷu t+xƛ̓a+p cu -nt -m -lx uɬ sc+ʔkin+x kʷa aláʔ
complete say -pl yes 4kn complete tell -nt -psv -pl and why_is_it intj here
all of you?" *They said, "It's all of us."* *He said to them, "And what's the matter, you*

p txƛ̓ap 76 uɬ k̓im axáʔ nəqsíʔst, k̓im axáʔ, way̓ mat knaqs lut
p t+xƛ̓a+p uɬ k̓im axáʔ nqs=iʔst k̓im axáʔ way̓ mat k=naqs lut
5kn complete and left this one_arrow left this yes maybe one_person not
are all here *and there is one arrow left? One person must not be here."*

77 way̓ ixíʔ kiʔ ɬ nɬək̓ʷk̓ʷmísəlx sənk̓líp 78 cútəlx way̓, way̓ k̓əm
way̓ ixíʔ kiʔ ɬ n+ɬk̓ʷ•k̓ʷ+mi -s -lx s+n+k̓l̓=ip cut -lx way̓ way̓ k̓m
well then rel ? think_about -3erg -pl Coyote say -pl yes yes except
Then they thought of Coyote. *They said,*

sənk̓líp lut aláʔ iʔ scənxíʔs 79 uɬ sc̓kinx {t̓əxʷ ya} 80 cútəlx ʕan
s+n+k̓l̓=ip lut aláʔ iʔ sc -n+xy̓ -s uɬ sc+ʔkin+x cut -lx ʕan
Coyote not here art pftv -amidst -3i and why_is_it say -pl onom
"Coyote is not here." *"And why?"* *They said,*

sk̓əɬʔatətxnúmtx mat 81 scutx aɬíʔ a
s -k̓ɬ+ʔat•t•x+númt -x mat s -cut -x aɬíʔ a
ipftv^ -fall_asleep -^ipftv maybe ipftv^ -say -^ipftv because intj
"He must have overslept. He was walking up and down

cxʷaxʷí··st uɬ iʔ kʷu ʔatxílx 82 uɬ mat ixíʔ ɬq̓ilx uɬ iʔ
c -xʷaʔ•xʷíst uɬ iʔ kʷu ʔatx+ílx uɬ mat ixíʔ ɬq̓+ilx uɬ iʔ
hab -walk_back_and_forth and art 4kn sleep_pl and maybe then lie and art
when we went to sleep. Then he must have gone to bed and

k̓əɬʔatətxnúmt 83 uɬ t̓iʔ {xi} way̓ t̓iʔ kʷu qíɬəɬt uɬ way̓ i kʷu cxʷuy
k̓ɬ+ʔat•t•x+númt uɬ t̓iʔ way̓ t̓iʔ kʷu qiɬ•ɬ+t uɬ way̓ i kʷu c+xʷuy
fall_asleep and evid well evid 4kn wake_up_pl and yes art 4kn come
overslept. When we woke up we came,

84 aɬíʔ k̓ʷnaʔ {kʷu} kʷu ʔiywt {uɬ i} 85 kʷa aɬíʔ cq̓ay̓ put {pi}
aɬíʔ k̓ʷnaʔ kʷu ʔiwt kʷa aɬíʔ c -q̓ay̓ put
because intj 4kn behind intj because gpat -write just
because [otherwise] we might get behind. 9:03 It's written down just

pənkíń x̌əx̌y̓áɬnəxʷ iʔ l sx̌lap 86 mi aláʔ kʷu iʔyʕąʔ {inaud} 87 ixíʔ uɬ
pn+ʔkin x̌•x̌yaɬ=nxʷ iʔ l s+x̌la+p mi aláʔ kʷu y•yaʕ ixíʔ uɬ
when watch art in morning fut here 4kn gather then and
what time in the morning we gather here. We

aɬíʔ way̓ put kʷu ƛ̓lap kiʔ uɬ iʔ kʷ ckicx {uɬ} 88 cut axáʔ yasukrí, way̓
aɬíʔ way̓ put kʷu ƛ̓la+p kiʔ uɬ iʔ kʷ c+kic+x cut axáʔ yasukrí way̓
so yes just 4kn stop rel and art 2kn arrive_cisl say this JC well
just got settled here, and then you came." JC said,

xʷúywi kʷa ƛ̓aʔánti 89 ńíńw̓iʔ iwá t̓iyám uɬ
xʷuy -wy kʷa ƛ̓ʔa -nt -y ńíńw̓iʔ iwá t̓ya+m uɬ
go -ipimptv intj fetch -nt -tpimptv a_while even be_lazy and
"Go and get him.

ɬcq̓ʷíɬtməntp lut_ksluts aláʔ kscənxíʔs
ɬ+c+q̓ʷiɬ+t+m -nt -p lut_k+s+lut+s aláʔ ksc -n+xy̓ -s
pack_cisl_again -nt -5erg there_is_no_no_about_it here futPerfi -amidst -3i
Even if he gets lazy, pack him! There is no no about it, he has to be here."

90 cúntməlx axáʔ iʔ splal 91 way̓ ixíʔ sxiʔtmístsəlx axáʔ
cu -nt -m -lx axáʔ iʔ s+pl•al way̓ ixíʔ s -xít+miʔst -s -lx axáʔ
tell -nt -psv -pl this art young_growth well then nom -run_pl -3i -pl this
He told the young folks. The young people

iʔ splal 92 xʷu··ylx ik̓líʔ iʔʕáp̨əlx {indec} 93 sənk̓líp {a} a
iʔ s+pl•al xʷuy -lx ik̓líʔ y̓•yaʕ+p -lx s+n+k̓l̓=ip a
art young_growth go -pl there arrive -pl Coyote art
ran. They went and they got there. Coyote was

ck̓ʷəlk̓ʷəlkílx 94 wiḿ {sxc} sckswitmísts {sksa} ksuksqílxʷaʔx
c -k̓ʷl•k̓ʷlk̓+ilx wiḿ sc -k+swít+miʔst -s ks -wk+sqilxʷ -aʔx
hab -roll_around in_vain pftv -do_one's_best -pftv incp^ -see -^incp
rolling around. He is trying his best to see,

95 waẏ uɬ lut t̓a cuksqílxʷ uɬ aɬíʔ tx̌əw̓x̌əw̓ús 96 waẏ ixíʔ
waẏ uɬ lut t̓ c -wk+s+qilxʷ uɬ aɬíʔ t+x̌w̓•x̌w̓=us waẏ ixíʔ
well and not evid hab -see and because dry_eyes well then
but he can't see, because his eyes have dried out. 10:00 *They went,*

cq̓ʷíɬtmsəlx {t̓əxʷ ckníkstsəlx mat} xʷu¨ylx waẏ ckícstsəlx [ckícxstsəlx]
c -q̓ʷiɬ+t+m -s -lx xʷuy -lx waẏ c+kic+st -s -lx c+kic+x+st -s -lx
act -pack -3erg -pl go -pl yes bring -3erg -pl bring -3erg -pl
got him there,

ixíʔ uɬ ilíʔ mútstsəlx 97 k̓əɬʔamtílstsəlx iʔ k̓ʷəl̓əncútən
ixíʔ uɬ ilíʔ mut+st -s -lx k̓ɬ+ʔam=t=ils+st -s -lx iʔ k̓ʷl̓+ncut+n
then and there set_down -3erg -pl set_before -3erg -pl art god
they sat him down there, *they sat him in front of the creator.*

98 cúntməlx, waẏ xʷúywi, px̌ʷməncútwi 99 waẏ kʷintp
cu -nt -m -lx waẏ xʷuy -wy px̌ʷ+mncut -wy waẏ kʷi -nt -p
tell -nt -psv -pl well go -ipimptv scatter -ipimptv yes take -nt -5erg
They were told, "Go, scatter. *Take*

iʔ cq̓ílən iʔ xʷíc̓xəɬmən 100 uɬ axáʔ k̓əm nəqsíʔst uɬ waẏ ṅíṅw̓iʔ
iʔ cq̓=iln iʔ xʷic̓+x -ɬm -n uɬ axáʔ k̓m nqs=iʔst uɬ waẏ ṅíṅw̓iʔ
art arrow art give_away -5obj -1erg and this except one_arrow and yes a_while
the arrows I gave you. *And I will give the arrow that's left*

xʷíc̓ɬtən sənk̓líp {məɬ} 101 uɬ ixíʔ uɬ waẏ xʷúywi 102 waẏ ixíʔ
xʷic̓ -ɬt -n s+n+k̓l̓=ip uɬ ixíʔ uɬ waẏ xʷuy -wy waẏ ixíʔ
give -ɬt -1erg Coyote and then and yes go -ipimptv well then
to Coyote. *Now go."* *Then*

uɬ spəx̌ʷməncútsəlx 103 waẏ, waẏ ixíʔ nq̓aʔkstúɬtəm sənk̓líp
uɬ s -px̌ʷ+mncut -s -lx waẏ waẏ ixíʔ n+q̓aʔ=kst -uɬt -m s+n+k̓l̓=ip
and nom -scatter -3i -pl well yes then put_in_hand -tuɬt -psv Coyote
they scattered. *He put it right in Coyote's hand,*

104 cúntəm waẏ, sənk̓líp axáʔ {ɬi} qʷəncín kʷ sʔiwtx 105 uɬ
cu -nt -m waẏ s+n+k̓l̓=ip axáʔ qʷṅ=cin kʷ s -ʔiwt -x uɬ
tell -nt -psv well Coyote this pity 2kn ipftv^ -behind -^ipftv and
he said, "Coyote, it's a pity you got behind. *This*

waẏ t̓əxʷ t̓i k̓əm axáʔ iʔ sxiʔmíx axáʔ a cq̓ílən 106 ixíʔ axáʔ {aɬ}
waẏ t̓xʷ t̓iʔ k̓m axáʔ iʔ s+xiʔ+míx axáʔ a cq̓=iln ixíʔ axáʔ
yes emph evid except this art whatever this art arrow then this
is the only arrow left. 11:00 *Take it,*

kʷintxʷ ixíʔ akɬcq̓ílən, uɬ ixíʔ akskʷíst sənk̓líp 107 ixíʔ
kʷin -t -xʷ ixíʔ a -kɬ -cq̓=iln uɬ ixíʔ a -k -s+kʷist s+n+k̓l̓=ip ixíʔ
take -nt -2erg that 2i -to_be -arrow and that 2i -to_be -name Coyote then
this will be your arrow, and Coyote will be your name. *Now*

uɬ {k} kʷ xʷuy, ixíʔ uɬ aɬíʔ waẏ txƛ̓aplx ixíʔ uɬ waẏ 108 waẏ {i}
uɬ kʷ xʷuy ixíʔ uɬ aɬíʔ waẏ t+xƛ̓ap -lx ixíʔ uɬ waẏ waẏ
and 2kn go that and so yes complete -pl that and finish well
you can go, that's all of them." *Coyote*

kʷis sənk̓líp 109 waẏ t̓iʔ kʷis uɬ {tkliw} kəl̓l̓kʷákʷ uɬ ixíʔ {s sə··}
kʷi -s s+n+k̓l̓=ip waẏ t̓iʔ kʷi -s uɬ k+l̓•l̓kʷ•akʷ uɬ ixíʔ
take -3erg Coyote well evid take -3erg and far_dim and then
took it. He took it and went a little ways, and Coyote

sənk̓lípəps sənk̓líp 110 waẏ nstils waẏ lut 111 sċkinx ha kən
s -n+k̓l=ip•p -s s+n+k̓l̓=ip waẏ n+st=ils waẏ lut sc+ʔkin+x haʔ kn
nom -buffoon -3i Coyote well think well not why_is_it inter 1kn
started being a coyote. He thought, "Heck no. What's up with that,

smisqílxʷ ha kə axáʔ iʔ sxʔimɬt̓ət̓áq̓aʔt cq̓ílən uɬ aɬ kʷin
s+my+s+qilxʷ haʔ kiʔ axáʔ iʔ s+xʔim+ɬ+t̓•t̓áq̓aʔt cq̓=iln uɬ aɬ kʷi -n
important_people inter rel this art shortest arrow and compl take -1erg
I'm way up in class, and I took the shortest arrow?

112 kʷu aɬ xʷíċəɬts 113 waẏ {indec} iksənʔúcxnəm axáʔ səmx̌íkən
kʷu aɬ xʷiċ -ɬt -s waẏ i -ks -n+ʔuc=xn+m axáʔ s+mx̌=ikn
1obj compl give -ɬt -3erg well 1i -futi -follow this grizzly
He gave it to me. I am going to follow Grizzly."

114 uɬ aɬíʔ mat waẏ mipnús səmx̌íkən iʔ kʷis iʔ wísxən iʔ
uɬ aɬíʔ mat waẏ my+p -nu -s s+mx̌=ikn iʔ kʷi -s iʔ wis=xn iʔ
and so maybe yes learn -manage -3erg grizzly art take -3erg art long art
I guess he found out Grizzly is the one who took the longest

cq̓ílən 115 waẏ nkí··lkiʔs uɬ aɬíʔ ċx̌iɬ iʔ sxʷúytəns {uɬ} 116 waẏ uɬ
cq̓=iln waẏ n+kíl=kiʔ -s uɬ aɬíʔ c+ʔx̌iɬ iʔ s+xʷuy+tn -s waẏ uɬ
arrow well follow -3erg and because plain art track -3in well and
arrow. He followed him, his tracks are plain. 12:02 He

naqs sənt̓áq̓əms iʔ ta cəlʕ̓ʷútəm i kiʔ nkəcníkiʔs 117 waẏ ixíʔ
naqs s -n+t̓aq̓+m -s iʔ t c+lʕ̓ʷ=ut+m i kiʔ n+kc+n=íkiʔ -s waẏ ixíʔ
one nom -cross -3i art obl valley intj rel catch_up_with -3erg well then
crossed a big valley and he overtook him. He

k̓əɬʔaxʷʔaxʷúksts səmx̌íkən 118 cus waẏ a {kʷu} kʷu
k̓ɬ+ʔaxʷ•ʔaxʷ+kʷú=kst[4] -s s+mx̌=ikn cu -s waẏ a kʷu
coax -3erg grizzly tell -3erg well intj 4kn
started coaxing Grizzly. He said to him,

sənʔayxʷíw̓sa?x iʔ t cq̓íləntət 119 ƛ̓əlpstís aɬíʔ səmx̌íkən
s -n+ʔayxʷ=íw̓s -aʔx iʔ t cq̓=iln -tt ƛ̓l+p+st -is aɬíʔ s+mx̌=ikn
incp^ -exchange -^incp art obj_itr arrow -4in stop_so -3erg so grizzly
"Let's trade our arrows." He stopped Grizzly.

120 cúntəm lut, cúntəm waẏ t yasukrí kʷu xʷíċəɬts axáʔ iʔ cq̓ílən
cu -nt -m lut cu -nt -m waẏ t yasukrí kʷu xʷiċ -ɬt -s axáʔ iʔ cq̓=iln
tell -nt -psv not tell -nt -psv yes agInst JC 1obj give -ɬt -3erg this art arrow
He [Grizzly] said to him "No," he said, "JC gave me this arrow,

4 This analysis is tentative.

121 uɬ kʷu cus ixíʔ n̓iʕíp ikstxt̓ám 122 uɬ lut kʷu t̓
uɬ kʷu cu -s ixíʔ ny̓ʕip i -ks -t+xt̓a+m uɬ lut kʷu t̓
and 1obj tell -3erg that always 1i -futi -care_for and not 1obj negfac
and he told me always to take care of it. *He didn't*

cus iksənʔayxʷíw̓səm {iʔ t} 123 uɬ aɬíʔ lut t̓ iksənʔayxʷíw̓səm
cu -s i -ks -n+ʔayxʷ=íw̓s+m uɬ aɬíʔ lut t̓ i -ks -n+ʔayxʷ=íw̓s+m
tell -3erg 1i -futi -trade and so not negfac 1i -futi -trade
tell me to trade it. *I am not going to trade it off,*

124 lut̓ iksənx̌ʷílcnəm yasukrí {i uɬ} 125 cut {l} sənk̓líp {ɬki} uɬ
lut_t̓ i -ks -n+x̌ʷil=cn+m yasukrí cut s+n+k̓l̓=ip uɬ
neg_emph 1i -futi -discard_word JC say Coyote and
I am not going to throw away my word to JC." *Coyote said,*

k̓əɬʔaxʷ•ʔaxʷkʷúksts 126 cus way̓ {kʷu a kʷu} t̓i kʷu kʷúɬəntxʷ
k̓ɬ+ʔaxʷ•ʔaxʷ+kʷú=kst -s cu -s way̓ t̓iʔ kʷu kʷuɬn -t -xʷ
coax -3erg tell -3erg well evid 1obj borrow -nt -2erg
(he started coaxing him), *he said to him, "Just lend me*

ixíʔ t ancq̓ílən {uɬ n̓ín̓w̓iʔ ə} 127 n̓ín̓w̓iʔ ɬxʷíc̓ɬtsən
ixíʔ t an -cq̓=iln n̓ín̓w̓iʔ ɬ+xʷic̓ -ɬt -s -n
that obj_tr 2in -arrow a_while give_again -ɬt -2obj -1erg
your arrow. 13:03 *I'll give it back to you."*

128 cúntəm t səmx̌íkən, lut 129 kway̓ nixʷ lut t̓ə qəɬnún
cu -nt -m t s+mx̌=ikn lut k+way̓ nixʷ lut t̓ qɬ -nu -n
tell -nt -psv agInst grizzly not well also not negfac able -manage -1erg
Grizzly said to him, "No. *I can never make myself*

kʷ ikskʷúɬnəm 130 aɬíʔ kʷu cus yasukrí ikstxt̓ám, n̓iʕíp
kʷ i -ks -kʷuɬn+m aɬíʔ kʷu cu -s yasukrí i -ks -t+xt̓a+m ny̓ʕip
2kʷu 1i -futi -lend because 1obj tell -3erg JC 1i -futi -care_for always
lend it to you *because JC told me to keep it, to keep it*

ikstxt̓ám {lut} 131 lut kʷu t̓ cus n̓ín̓w̓iʔ ckʷɬnxíxəmstxʷ {kəm̓}
i -ks -t+xt̓a+m lut kʷu t̓ cu -s n̓ín̓w̓iʔ c -kʷɬn+xixm -st -xʷ
1i -futi -care_for not 1obj negfac tell -3erg a_while cust^ -lend -^cust -2erg
forever. *He didn't tell me to lend it out.*

132 uɬ aɬíʔ way̓ ixíʔ kʷu kc̓x̌ʷíplaʔɬts {uɬ ixíʔ ckəxʷkə} 133 ixíʔ uɬ
uɬ aɬíʔ way̓ ixíʔ kʷu k+c̓x̌ʷ=íplaʔ -ɬt -s ixíʔ uɬ
and because yes that 1obj judge -ɬt -3erg then and
He gave it to me as judgment." *Then*

ktíɬxməntməlx t yasukrí 134 uɬ ixíʔ cúntəm səmx̌íkən uɬ kʷ
k+tiɬ+x+m -nt -m -lx t yasukrí uɬ ixíʔ cu -nt -m s+mx̌=ikn uɬ kʷ
stand_by -nt -psv -pl agInst JC and then tell -nt -psv grizzly and 2kn
JC stood over them *and he said to Grizzly,*

səsc̓ínəms axáʔ t sənk̓líp 135 cut way̓ t̓əxʷ kʷu
sc -c̓in+m -s axáʔ t s+n+k̓l̓=ip cut way̓ t̓xʷ kʷu
pftv -say_what -3i this agInst Coyote say well evidently 1kʷu
"What is Coyote saying to you?" *He said "He has been*

sck̓łʔaxʷ•ʔaxʷkʷúnəms 136 ikskʷúłnəm axáʔ iʔ t incq̓ílən, iʔ
sc -k̓ł+ʔaxʷ•ʔaxʷ+kʷún+m -s i -ks -kʷułn+m axáʔ iʔ t in -cq̓=iln iʔ
pftv -coax -3i 1i -futi -lend this art obj_itr 1in -arrow art
coaxing me *to lend him my arrow,*

kʷu t xʷic̓xtxʷ 137 uł_iʔ cun lut, {uł} uł itlíʔ kʷu
kʷu t xʷic̓ -xt -xʷ uł_iʔ cu -n lut uł itlíʔ kʷu
1obj ? give -xit -2erg and_then tell -1erg not and from_there 1obj
the one you gave me. *And I told him no,*

łk̓əłʔaxʷ•ʔaxʷkʷúksts t̓i kʷu kskʷłəntúłts [iʔs] 138 uł_iʔ cun
ł+k̓ł+ʔaxʷ•ʔaxʷ+kʷú=kst -s t̓iʔ kʷu ks -kʷłn -tułt -s uł_iʔ cu -n
coax_again -3erg evid 1obj futt^ -lend -tułt -3erg and_then tell -1erg
and he coaxed me more for me to lend it to him. 14:04 *And I said to him,*

ałíʔ lut t̓ qəłnún kʷ t̓ ikskʷłəntúłtəm 139 uł
ałíʔ lut t̓ qł -nu -n kʷ t̓ i -ks -kʷłn -tułt -m uł
so not negfac able -manage -1erg 2kʷu negfac 1i -futi -lend -tułt -apsv and
'I can't make myself loan it to you, *the*

ałíʔ way̓ kʷu cus {t} iʔ t k̓ʷəl̓ncútən ikstxt̓ám ixíʔ cq̓ílən
ałíʔ way̓ kʷu cu -s iʔ t k̓ʷl̓+ncut+n i -ks -t+xt̓a+m ixíʔ cq̓=iln
because yes 1obj tell -3erg art agInst god 1i -futi -care_for that arrow
creator told me to keep this arrow,

140 lut {iks} ikskʷáłənxix 141 a, cúntəm way̓, xʷuyx,
lut i -ks -kʷáłn+xix a cu -nt -m way̓ xʷuy -x
not 1i -futi -lend_out intj tell -nt -psv well go -isimptv
not to lend it out.'" *He said to him, "Go, go,*

xʷuyx {lut} lut aksəntq̓aʔlsínaʔm {a} sənk̓líp 142 way̓ n̓ t incá
xʷuy -x lut i -ks -n+tq̓aʔls=ínaʔ+m s+n+k̓l̓=ip way̓ n̓ t in+cá
go -isimptv not 1i -futi -pay_attention Coyote well now agInst I
don't pay attention to Coyote. *I'll talk*

qʷəlqʷílstən 143 way̓ ixíʔ sxʷuys səmx̌íkən, itlíʔ xʷuy 144 way̓
qʷl•qʷil+st -n way̓ ixíʔ s -xʷuy -s s+mx̌=ikn itlíʔ xʷuy way̓
talk_to -1erg well then nom -go -3i grizzly from_there go well
to him." *Grizzly went on, he went.* *There*

k̓əm sənk̓líp ilíʔ 145 cúntəm ilíʔ mutx kʷ
k̓m s+n+k̓l̓=ip ilíʔ cu -nt -m ilíʔ mut -x kʷ
except Coyote there tell -nt -psv there sit_sg -isimptv 2kʷu
is only Coyote there. *He said to him, "Sit down, I am going to*

iksqʷəlqʷílstəm 146 way̓ axáʔ k̓əłk̓láxʷ{s} səmx̌íkən 147 uł ixíʔ
i -ks -qʷl•qʷil+st -m way̓ axáʔ k̓ł+k̓laxʷ s+mx̌=ikn uł ixíʔ
1i -futi -talk_to -apsv well this disappear grizzly and then
talk with you." *Then Grizzly got out of sight* *and*

cúntəm iʔ t k̓ʷəl̓ncútən sənk̓líp 148 way̓, way̓ kʷ qʷən̓qʷán̓t sənk̓líp
cu -nt -m iʔ t k̓ʷl̓+ncut+n s+n+k̓l̓=ip way̓ way̓ kʷ qʷn̓•qʷan̓+t s+n+k̓l̓=ip
tell -nt -psv art agInst god Coyote well yes 2kn pitiful Coyote
the creator said to Coyote: *"You are pitiful, Coyote. 15:00*

149 waẏ aɬíʔ nak̓ʷá {tə} t ank̓əɬcútən   150 t̓əxʷ ixíʔ uɬ aɬíʔ {kʷ snk} kʷ
waẏ aɬíʔ nak̓ʷá t an -k̓ɬ+cut+n   t̓xʷ ixíʔ uɬ aɬíʔ kʷ
well so indeed_not ? 2in -training   evidently then and so 2kn
You haven't got any training.   *You keep putting yourself*

sənkxaʔcnməscútx   151 caʔkʷ ixíʔ t̓i_kʷm̓iɬ kʷ ʔitx   152 uɬ lut
s -n+k+xaʔ=cn+mscút[5] -x   caʔkʷ ixíʔ t̓iʔ_kʷm̓iɬ kʷ ʔitx   uɬ lut
ipftv^ -deem_self_superior -^ipftv   if then at_once 2kn sleep   and not
higher than others.   *If you had gone to sleep right away*   *it wouldn't*

ilíʔ ksc̓x̌iɬts[6]   153 ixíʔ uɬ aɬíʔ kʷ k̓əɬpaʔpaʔx̌ám   154 uɬ
ilíʔ ks -c+ʔx̌iɬ+t -s   ixíʔ uɬ aɬíʔ kʷ k̓ɬ+paʔ•paʔx̌á+m   uɬ
there futi -like -3i   then and so 2kn think_up_things   and
have gone this way.   *Then you thought all kinds of things.*   *I am*

aɬíʔ incá kən k̓ʷəl̓əncútən, lut kʷu t̓ aksƛ̓xʷúp   155 ixíʔ uɬ_iʔ
aɬíʔ in+cá kn k̓ʷl̓+ncut+n lut kʷu t̓ a -ks -ƛ̓xʷup   ixíʔ uɬ_iʔ
because I 1kn god not 1kʷu negfac 2i -futi -beat   then and_then
the creator, you can't outwit me.   *Then*

kʷ k̓əɬpaʔpaʔx̌ám uɬ kʷu aksƛ̓xʷúpəm iʔ {ti} t isck̓əɬpáʔx̌
kʷ k̓ɬ+paʔ•paʔx̌á+m uɬ kʷu a -ks -ƛ̓xʷu+p+m iʔ t i -sc -k̓ɬ+paʔx̌
2kn think_up_things and 1kʷu 2i -futi -win art obj_itr 1i -pftv -figure_out
you did all kinds of figuring to get the best of my decisions.

156 uɬ aɬíʔ anwí kʷ kscxaʔtmíxaʔx   157 ixíʔ uɬ_iʔ kʷ
uɬ aɬíʔ anwí kʷ ksc -xaʔt -míx+aʔx   ixíʔ uɬ_iʔ kʷ
and so you 2kn futPerfkn^ -first -^futPerfkn   then and_then 2kn
And you wanted to be first   *and you*

kt̓əkt̓əksəncút iʔ t sx̌əx̌c̓íʔ   158 uɬ_iʔ kʷ tx̌əẇx̌əẇús
k+t̓k•t̓k=s+ncut iʔ t s+x̌•x̌c̓iʔ   uɬ_iʔ kʷ t+x̌ẇ•x̌ẇ=us
prop_open art agInst stick   and_then 2kn dry_eyes
propped your eyes with sticks   *and that's how your eyes got dried up."*

159 cúntəm waẏ, uɬ waẏ ʕapnáʔ [lkʷilxstxʷ] ixíʔ [iʔ] sx̌əx̌c̓í {ta} iʔ kʷ
cu -nt -m waẏ uɬ waẏ ʕapnáʔ lkʷ+ilx+st -xʷ ixíʔ iʔ s+x̌•x̌c̓iʔ iʔ kʷ
tell -nt -psv well and yes now remove -2erg that art stick art 2kn
He said to him, "Now take those sticks out of

cktək̓tk̓ús   160 waẏ sənk̓líp ixíʔ lkʷilxsts axáʔ ia
c -k+t̓k•t̓k=us   waẏ s+n+k̓l̓=ip ixíʔ lkʷ+ilx+st -s axáʔ iʔ
hab -prop_eyelids   well Coyote then remove -3erg this art
your eyes."   *Coyote took out the sticks that he had propped*

cktək̓tək̓úsmsts {ixíʔ}   161 taʔx̌íləm {uɬ} uɬ mat ilíʔ ksiwɬkʷ
c -k+t̓k•t̓k=us+m -st -s   ta+ʔx̌íl+m uɬ mat ilíʔ k+siwɬ=kʷ
cust^ -prop_eyelids -^cust -3erg   do_a_certain_way and maybe there have_water
his eyes with. 16:01   *He went like that, (there must have been water there),*

5 xaʔ with loss of t before c.
6 This construction is unclear to me.

162 taʔx̌íləm təl siwłkʷ t kilxs ck̓əłmúləm 163 uł ixíʔ
ta+ʔx̌íl+m tl siwł=kʷ t kilx -s c -k̓ł+mul+m uł ixíʔ
do_a_certain_way from water agInst hand -3in hab -dip and then
he did like that, he dipped from the water with his hand. *Coyote*

skc̓əw̓c̓íw̓səntəm sənk̓líp way̓ c̓x̌ił atáʔ łuksqílxʷ 164 cúntəm
k+c̓w̓•c̓iw̓=s -nt -m sn+k̓l̓=ip way̓ c̓x̌ił atáʔ ł+wk+s+qilxʷ cu -nt -m
wash_eyes -nt -psv Coyote yes like this see_again tell -nt -psv
washed his eys, just like that he could see. *He said to him,*

way̓, {i way i} ixíʔ łkʷintxʷ {an} anƛ̓aʔƛ̓aʔústən 165 uł axáʔ iʔ kʷ
way̓ ixíʔ ł+kʷi -nt -xʷ an -ƛ̓aʔ•ƛ̓aʔ=ús+tn uł axáʔ iʔ kʷ
well then take_again -nt -2erg 2in -eyesight and this art 2kn
"Now you got back your eyesight. *I am telling you,*

ikscúnəm lut nixʷ akłələmʔíkstəm kiṅ {itlí} iʔ təl tmixʷ 166 iʔ təl
i -ks -cun+m lut nixʷ a -kł -ł+mʔ=ikst+m ʔkin iʔ tl tmixʷ iʔ tl
1i -futi -tell not again 2i -futi -bother_again indef art of creature art of
don't bother any of the animals *or of*

skəkáʕkaʔ kəm̓ t̓əxʷ iʔ tla ctəkʷtəkʷʔút iʔ l təmxʷúlaʔxʷ 167 lut
s+k•kʕá•kaʔ km̓ t̓xʷ iʔ tla c -tkʷ+tkʷʔ=ut iʔ l tmxʷ=úlaʔxʷ lut
bird or emph art from hab -walk art on land not
the birds, or the animals that walk the earth. *Don't*

akłəłmaʔcínəm, uł way̓ t̓əxʷ nqʷəṅmíntsən 168 ixíʔ uł_iʔ
a -kł -ł+maʔ=cín+m uł way̓ t̓xʷ n+qʷṅ+mi -nt -s -n ixíʔ uł_iʔ
2i -futi -bother_again and yes emph feel_sorry_for -nt -2obj -1erg then and_then
bother them; I pity you." *That's when*

kəlk̓əlk̓íc̓aʔxtəm {i t} iʔ t kłksisyústəns, kmúsc̓aʔ 169 cúntəm
k+lk̓•lk̓=íc̓aʔ -xt -m iʔ t kł -k+sy•sy=ús+tn -nt k+mús=c̓aʔ cu -nt -m
bundles -xit -psv art obl to_be -powers -nt four_packages tell -nt -psv
he gave him wrapped up things for his powers, four packages. *He said to him,*

axáʔ kʷintxʷ, kmúsc̓aʔ axáʔ ia nqʷəṅmíntsən
axáʔ kʷin -t -xʷ k+mús=c̓aʔ axáʔ iʔ n+qʷṅ+mi -nt -s -n
this take -nt -2erg four_packages this art feel_sorry_for -nt -2obj -1erg
"Take these four packages for my pitying you." 17:06

170 cúntəm lut x̌əl tanm̓ús kʷ isənqʷṅmínəm 171 i[xíʔ] kʷ
cu -nt -m lut x̌l tanm̓=ús kʷ i -s -n+qʷṅ+min+m ixíʔ kʷ
tell -nt -psv not for nothing 2kʷu 1i -intt -pity then 2kʷu
He said to him, "It's not for nothing that I pity you: *I want*

isk̓aʕʷmístəm 172 i[xíʔ] q̓əmq̓əməntíxʷ axáʔ iʔ kmúsc̓aʔ
i -s -k̓aʕʷ+míst+m ixíʔ q̓m•q̓m -nt -ixʷ axáʔ iʔ k+mús=c̓aʔ
1i -intt -hire that swallow -nt -2erg this art four_packages
to hire you. *Swallow these four packages.*

173 laʔkín kʷ yaʕpcín iʔ la nʔałnaʔsqílxʷtən 174 məł ixíʔ
la+ʔkiṅ kʷ yaʕ̓+p=cín iʔ l n+ʔałn+aʔ+s+qílxʷ+tn mł ixíʔ
whenever 2kn scared art with man_eater and then
Whenever you get crowded with man-eaters *you*

x̌əlítənxʷəlx axáʔ iʔ kmúsċaʔ 175 uł ixíʔ ṅíṅẁiʔ
x̌lit -nt -xʷ -lx axáʔ iʔ k+mús=ċaʔ uł ixíʔ ṅíṅẁiʔ
summon -nt -2erg -pl this art four_packages and then a_while
summon these four packages *and they*

kənxítəmsəlx {cun} 176 cúłtxʷəlx asyaʕ̓pcín 177 məł ixíʔ ṅíṅẁiʔ
kn -xit -m -s -lx cu -łt -xʷ -lx a -s+yaʕ̓+p=cín mł ixíʔ ṅíṅẁiʔ
help -xit -2obj -3erg -pl tell -łt -2erg -pl 2in -need and then a_while
will help you. *Tell them your troubles* *and they*

cúntsəlx waẏ laʔkín kʷ xkínəm 178 uł ixíʔ akłksisyústən
cu -nt -s -lx waẏ la+ʔkíṅ kʷ x+kin+m uł ixíʔ a -kł -k+sy•sy=ús+tn
tell -nt -3e2obj -pl yes how 2kn do_what and that 2in -to_be -powers
will tell you what to do. *They are going to be your powers,*

məł pəlstnúntxʷ ia nʔałnaʔsqílxʷtən 179 uł ixíʔ ṅíṅẁiʔ yaʕyáʕt
mł pl+st -nu -nt -xʷ iʔ n+ʔałn+aʔ+s+qílxʷ+tn uł ixíʔ ṅíṅẁiʔ yaʕ•yáʕ+t
and kill -manage -nt -2erg art man_eater and then a_while all
and you will be able to kill man-eaters. *And all over*

axáʔ iʔ l təmxʷúlaʔxʷ 180 ƛ̓əxʷəxʷnúntxʷ {aʔ n} a nʔałnaʔsqílxʷtən
axáʔ iʔ l tmxʷ=úlaʔxʷ ƛ̓xʷ•xʷ -nu -nt -xʷ a n+ʔałn+aʔ+s+qílxʷ+tn
this art in land kill_pl -manage -nt -2erg 2in man_eater
the world *you will kill man-eaters.*

181 ixíʔ mi kʷ uʔíkst, i kʷ ikscúnəm {i t k̓ʷəl} t yasukrí cúntəm waẏ
ixíʔ mi kʷ wẏ=ikst i kʷ i -ks -cun+m t yasukrí cu -nt -m waẏ
then fut 2kn get_done art 2kn 1i -futi -tell agInst JC tell -nt -psv OK
That's when you are done,[7] this is what I am telling you." JC said.18:06

182 waẏ i[xíʔ] xʷíċəłtəm a[xáʔ] iʔ kmúsċaʔ 183 waẏ ixíʔ q̓əmq̓əm̓əntís
waẏ ixíʔ xʷiċ -łt -m axáʔ iʔ k+mús=ċaʔ waẏ ixíʔ q̓m•q̓m -nt -is
well then give -łt -psv this art four_packages well that swallow -nt -3erg
He gave him the four packages. *Coyote swallowed them,*

sənk̓líp, cúntəm q̓əmq̓mánt 184 waẏ ixíʔ q̓əmq̓əmntís 185 uł
s+n+k̓l̓=ip cu -nt -m q̓m•q̓ma -nt waẏ ixíʔ q̓m•q̓m -nt -is uł
Coyote tell -nt -psv swallow -nt well then swallow -nt -3erg and
he had said "Swallow them." *He swallowed them.* *He*

cúntəm waẏ xʷuyx lut nixʷ tl aksmaʔcənmłtíłən axáʔ {iʔ t}
cu -nt -m waẏ xʷuy -x lut nixʷ tl̓ a -ks -maʔ=cn+m=łtíłn axáʔ
tell -nt -psv well go -isimptv not more from 2i -futi -bother_w_talk this
was told, "Go, don't bother with talk the bears

hałckəm̓xíst hałsuʔsẁít 186 uł ałíʔ waẏ ixíʔ iscwiʔskċx̌ʷípla?
hł=c+km̓xist hł=sẁ•sẁit uł ałíʔ waẏ ixíʔ i -sc -wẏ+s+k+ċx̌ʷ=ípla?
Bear_*group* whoever_group and because yes that 1i -pftv -finish_ordering
or anybody. *I have already settled all that.*

7 "When you kill all the man-eaters."

187 ilíʔ lut {ak} t̓a kskʷúłənsəlx iʔ təl cq̓íln̓ 188 way̓ ixíʔ
ilíʔ lut t̓ ks -kʷułn -s -lx iʔ tl cq̓=iln way̓ ixíʔ
there not evid futi -borrow -3i -pl art from arrow well then
They will never lend the arrows." *Then*

xʷíc̓əłtəm ixíʔ iʔ cq̓íln̓ 189 way̓, way̓ ixíʔ {c} [s]xʷuys, cúntəm way̓
xʷic̓ -łt -m ixíʔ iʔ cq̓=iln way̓ way̓ ixíʔ s -xʷuy -s cu -nt -m way̓
give -łt -psv that art arrow well well then nom -go -3i tell -nt -psv yes
he gave him the arrow. 18:44 *He went, he said to him*

xʷuyx 190 ixíʔ uł way̓ {nwísləx} nwísəlx {a} yasukrí k̓əl stk̓ṃásq̓ət
xʷuy -x ixíʔ uł way̓ n+wis+lx yasukrí k̓l s+t+k̓m=asq̓t
go -isimptv then and yes raise JC to sky
"Go." *Then JC rose to the sky.*

191 way̓ cxʷuʼʼy sənk̓líp way̓ uł q̓íwsəs axáʔ yasukrí 192 way̓ mat
way̓ c -xʷuy s+n+k̓l̓=ip way̓ uł q̓iy=ẃs -s axáʔ yasukrí way̓ mat
well hab -go Coyote well and doubt -3erg this JC well maybe
Coyote went, he wouldn't believe JC. *"Maybe*

kʷu səstqəqnúnəms, way̓ ikskṁiʔṁáym[8] [ikskṁiʔṁáyam] 193 ixíʔ
kʷu sc -tq•q+nun+m -s way̓ i -ks -ṁy•ṁáy+m i -ks -ṁy•ṁáya+m ixíʔ
1kʷu pftv -fool -3i well 1i -futi -find_out 1i -futi -find_out then
he is fooling me. I'm going to get to the truth of it." *He*

sƛ̓laps smuts 194 way̓ ixíʔ x̌lits axáʔ {iʔ i s} iʔ
s -ƛ̓lap -s s -mut -s way̓ ixíʔ x̌lit -s axáʔ iʔ
nom -stop -3i nom -sit_sg -3i well then summon -3erg this art
stopped and sat down. *He summoned what was given*

sxʷíc̓əc̓xs a c{kəlk̓}kəlk̓əlk̓íc̓aʔ 195 way̓ ixíʔ {scuts} cus way̓ p̓əs
s+xʷic̓•c̓+x -s a c -k+lk̓•lk̓=íc̓aʔ way̓ ixíʔ cu -s way̓ p̓s
what_is_given -3in art hab -bundles well then tell -3erg well onom
to him, the bundles. *He said*

p̓əs p̓əs p̓əs kʷƛ̓up 196 way̓ a t̓i_kʷṁił aláʔ kłt̓k̓ʷak̓ʷ stiṁ 197 way̓,
p̓s p̓s p̓s kʷƛ̓up way̓ a t̓iʔ_kʷṁił aláʔ kł+t̓k̓ʷ•ak̓ʷ s+tiṁ way̓
onom onom onom come well intj at_once here fall_down what well
"p̓s p̓s p̓s p̓s Come out!" *All at once it fell, what is it? 1:01* *Then*

ixíʔ {itlíʔ} itlíʔ x̌lits iʔ knaqs p̓əs p̓əs p̓əs kʷƛ̓up
ixíʔ itlíʔ x̌lit -s iʔ k=naqs p̓s p̓s p̓s kʷƛ̓up
then from_there summon -3erg art one_person onom onom onom come_out
he called another one: "p̓s p̓s p̓s p̓s Come out!"

198 way̓ ixíʔ nixʷ kłt̓k̓ʷak̓ʷ, nixʷ sqilxʷ 199 way̓ kmúsəms iʔ
way̓ ixíʔ nixʷ kł+t̓k̓ʷ•ak̓ʷ nixʷ s+qilxʷ way̓ k=mus•ms iʔ
well that also fall_down also person well four_persons art
He also fell out, another person. *He called four of them,*

8 This form was corrected by MD as noted here.

scx̌lits, way̓ yaʕyáʕt k̓ʷulꞋ t sqilxʷ {cuntə} 200 cúsəlx way̓
sc -x̌lit -s way̓ yaʕ•yáʕ+t k̓ʷulꞋ•lꞋ t s+qilxʷ cu -s -lx way̓
pftv -summon -3i well all turn_into obl person tell -3erg -pl well
all turned into humans. *They said to him,*

kʷu cma?cínmənt[xʷ] sənk̓líp 201 stim̓ aɬí? asyaʕpcín 202 cut
kʷu c -ma?=cín+m -nt -xʷ s+n+k̓lꞋ=ip s+tim̓ aɬí? a -s+yaʕ̓+p=cín cut
1obj habnt -bother -nt -2erg Coyote what so 2in -hardship say
"Why are you bothering us, Coyote? *What is your trouble?"* *And*

sənk̓líp lut, lut kən t̓a ksyaʕpcín {way̓ way̓ t̓i kə} 203 cútəlx way̓ t̓i? kʷu
s+n+k̓lꞋ=ip lut lut kn t̓ k+s+yaʕ̓+p=cín cut -lx way̓ t̓i? kʷu
Coyote not not 1kn negfac have_hardship say -pl well evid 1obj
Coyote said, "No, I have no trouble." *They said,*

xʷúskstmənt kʷa uɬ kʷu si?súy̓t kʷu k̓ay̓it 204 way̓ ixí?
xʷus=kst+m -nt kʷa uɬ kʷu sy•suy̓+t kʷu k̓ay̓•y+t way̓ ixí?
do_quickly -nt intj and 4kn cold 4kn cold well then
"Hurry up with us, we are chilled, we are cold." *Coyote*

ɬq̓əmq̓əmntís sənk̓líp, way̓ itlí? sxʷuys 205 ixí? uɬ
ɬ+q̓m•q̓m -nt -is s+n+k̓lꞋ=ip way̓ itlí? s -xʷuy -s ixí? uɬ
swallow_again -nt -3erg Coyote well from_there nom -go -3i then and
swallowed them back, then he went on. *Then*

nun·xʷína? a way̓ 206 hoy, ixí? xʷilwísəs i? təmxʷúla?xʷ sənk̓líp
n+wnxʷ=ína? a way̓ hoy ixí? xʷy+lwis -s i? tmxʷ=úla?xʷ s+n+k̓lꞋ=ip
believe intj yes finish then wander -? art country Coyote
he believed. *Then Coyote started traveling the world.*

207 ixí? uɬ ƛ̓əxʷəntís {a n?a} a n?aɬna?sqílxʷtən 208 aɬí? uɬ axá?
ixí? uɬ ƛ̓xʷ -nt -is a n+?aɬn+a?+s+qílxʷ+tn aɬí? uɬ axá?
then and kill_many -nt -3erg art man_eater because and this
Then he started killing man-eaters. 2:03 *His friends*[9]

i? {təs} t sl̓əx̌l̓áx̌ts i? t xʷíc̓xtəm i? kɬksisyústəns
i? t s+l̓x̌•l̓ax̌+t -s i? t xʷic̓ -xt -m i? kɬ -k+sy•sy=us+tn -s
art agInst friends -3in art ? give -xit -psv art to_be -powers -3i
had given him something to be powerful with.

209 ʕ̓an t̓i? yaʕ̓pcín məɬ ixí? x̌əlíts məɬ kícsəlx 210 məɬ
ʕan t̓i? yaʕ̓+p=cín mɬ ixí? x̌lit -s mɬ kic -s -lx mɬ
onom evid need and then summon -3erg and reach_st/sb -3erg -pl and
See, when he gets in a corner he calls them, and they get to him, *and*

ixí? {si?} siws məɬ ixí? cus i? syaʕ̓pcíns i? cəcám̓a?t i? sqilxʷ
ixí? siw -s mɬ ixí? cu -s i? s+yaʕ̓+p=cín -s i? c•cám̓+a?t i? s+qilxʷ
then ask -3erg and then tell -3erg art needa -3in art small art person
they ask, and he tells the little people what his trouble is.

9 His four powers.

211 a ƛ̓əxʷəntí··s a n?ałna?sqílxʷtən uł ixí? nc̓əspúla?xʷsts
a ƛ̓xʷ -nt -is a n+?ałn+a?+s+qílxʷ+tn uł ixí? n+c̓s+p=úla?xʷ -st -s
intj kill_many -nt -3erg art man_eater and that kill -st -3erg
He killed and killed man-eaters until he cleaned them up.

212 i·· cxʷu··y sənk̓líp way̓ tkics tətw̓ít 213 way̓ ƛ̓lap, ixí? uł {t}
i·· c -xʷuy s+n+k̓l̓=ip way̓ t+kic -s t•tw̓it way̓ ƛ̓la+p ixí? uł
intj hab -go Coyote well meet -3erg boy well stop then and
Coyote went, he ran into a boy. *He stopped,*

t̓əxʷ tk̓asəlmístəlx ƛ̓lápəlx 214 ixí? uł sənk̓líp cus axá? i? tətw̓ít,
t̓xʷ tk=?asl+míst -lx ƛ̓la+p -lx ixí? uł s+n+k̓l̓=ip cu -s axá? i? t•tw̓it
evidently two_persons -pl stop -pl then and Coyote tell -3erg this art boy
they both stopped. *Coyote said to the boy:*

215 way̓ uł łsísənca? atá? kʷ cxʷuy, tla?kín kʷ t̓əcxʷúy
way̓ uł ł+sí•snca? atá? kʷ c -xʷuy tla+?kín kʷ t̓c -xʷuy
well and younger_bro here 2kn hab -go from_there 2kn habCisl -go
"Well, young brother, you are traveling around, where do you come from?" 3:03

216 cúntəm axá? i? t tətw̓ít, lut, lut kʷu t̓ ałsísənca?
cu -nt -m axá? i? t t•tw̓it lut lut kʷu t̓ a -ł+sí•sn•ca?
tell -nt -psv this art agInst boy not not 1kʷu negfac 2in -younger_bro
The little boy said to him, "No, I'm not your younger brother.

217 anwí {i kʷ} i? kʷ stət?íw̓ta?x, incá i? kən sx?itx 218 ah, cut sənk̓líp,
anwí i? kʷ s+t•t?íw+t=a?x in+cá i? kn s+x?it=x ah cut s+n+k̓l̓=ip
you art 2kn youngest I art 1kn oldest_one intj say Coyote
You are the younger one, I am the older." *"Ah," Coyote said,*

pəpkʷúsəm cut ah lut, 219 kʷa lut ha cmistíxʷ ha ƛ̓əm
p•pkʷ=us+m cut ah lut kʷa lut ha? c -my -st -ixʷ ha? ƛ̓m
shake_head say intj not intj not inter cust^ -know -^cust -2erg inter past
he shook his head and said "No. *Don't you know that when*

ha kʷ u?x̌tíl̓a?t 220 uł cq̓ʷa?q̓ʷíłtəmstmən,
ha? kʷ w̓x̌t=íla?t uł c -q̓ʷa•q̓ʷíł+t+m -st -m -n
inter 2kn newborn and cust^ -pack_rep -^cust -2obj -1erg
you were a baby *I used to pack you around,*

cxʷəsxʷa?stústmən 221 mʕ̓an ł isx?ítx uł anwí kʷ
c -xʷs•xʷa?st=ú -st -m -n mʕ̓an ł i -s+x?it=x uł anwí kʷ
cust^ -walk_floor -^cust -2obj -1erg intj ? 1in -oldest_one and you 2kn
I walked the floor with you? *I am the oldest, and you are the*

stət?íw̓ta?x 222 cúntəm {a} i? t tətw̓ít, a way̓ xʷuy ṅ ła? uníxʷ
s+t•t?íw+t+a?x cu -nt -m i? t t•tw̓it a way̓ xʷuy ṅ ła? wnixʷ
youngest tell -nt -psv art agInst boy intj well go now if true
youngest one." *The boy said to him, "All right, if that is true,*

sənk̓líp 223 mi ixí? axá? a cmaq̓ʷ mi síx̌əlxstxʷ {indec} 224 ak̓lá? mi
s+n+k̓l̓=ip mi ixí? axá? a c+maq̓ʷ mi six̌+lx -st -xʷ ak̓lá? mi
Coyote fut then this art mountain fut move -st -2erg here fut
Coyote, *move this mountain, 4:00* *put it*

ɬt̓k̓ʷəntíxʷ 225 cut sənk̓líp a· uɬ tanm̓ús ixíʔ, way̓
ɬ+t̓k̓ʷ -nt -ixʷ cut s+n+k̓l̓=ip a uɬ tanm̓=ús ixíʔ way̓
put_down_again -nt -2erg say Coyote intj and nothing that yes
down over here." Coyote said, "That's nothing.

cúntsən incá kən sxʔitx 226 ixíʔ síx̌əlxsts ak̓láʔ c̓aq̓ʷs
cu -nt -s -n in+cá kn s+xʔit=x ixíʔ six̌+lx -st -s ak̓láʔ c̓aq̓ʷ -s
tell -nt -2obj -1erg I 1kn oldest_one that move -st -3erg here point_to -3erg
I told you I am the oldest." He moved it over. Coyote

sənk̓líp 227 ak̓laʔ ɬʔax̌líkstəms ik̓líʔ mi kɬəɬct̓k̓ʷmíx[aʔx]
s+n+k̓l̓=ip ak̓láʔ ɬ+ʔax̌l=íkst+m -s ik̓líʔ mi kɬ -ɬ+c+t̓k̓ʷ -míx+aʔx
Coyote here turn_st_again -3erg there fut incp^ -put_down_cisl_again -^incp
pointed, he turned it around and was going to put it down.

228 uɬ itíʔ tkxan ia cmaq̓ʷ {ik̓liɬ} ik̓líʔ ɬt̓k̓ʷak̓ʷ 229 cus ʕác̓ənt,
uɬ itíʔ t+kxa+n iʔ c+maq̓ʷ ik̓líʔ ɬ+t̓k̓ʷ•ak̓ʷ cu -s ʕac̓ -nt
and from_that follow art mountain there settle_again tell -3erg look -nt
And the mountain followed and settled there. He said to him,

incá iʔ kən sxəxʔítaʔx 230 cúntəm axáʔ {it} iʔ ta cqʷəlqʷílstəm
in+cá iʔ kn s+x•xʔít=aʔx cu -nt -m axáʔ iʔ t c -qʷl•qʷil+st -m
I art 1kn oldest_dim tell -nt -psv this art agInst cust^ -talk_to -psv
"See, I am the oldest one." His interlocutor said to him:

231 way̓, huhúy kʷa ɬcíx̌əlxskʷ, ik̓lí k̓əl sənt̓ək̓ʷtáns 232 a· kʷa
way̓ hu+húy kʷa ɬ+cix̌+lx -skʷ ik̓líʔ k̓l s+n+t̓k̓ʷ+tan -s a kʷa
well OK intj move_back -tsimptv there to resting_place -3in intj intj
"Ok, move it back now to where it was down before." "Ah,

tanm̓ús, nt̓a wi··m sənk̓líp sc̓áq̓ʷəms way̓ lut 233 iwá mi {t} t
tanm̓=ús nt̓a wim̓ s+n+k̓l̓=ip s -c̓aq̓ʷ+m -s way̓ lut iwá mi t
nothing intj in_vain Coyote nom -point -3i well not even fut agInst
that's nothing." Coyote pointed for nothing, heck no. 5:01 He even

kilxs iwá {məɬ i} sc̓əlc̓əlx̌ʷúlaʔxʷms {kəlɬ a la} 234 lut, swit_aɬíʔ cmaq̓ʷ, way̓
kilx -s iwá s -c̓l•c̓lx̌ʷ=úlaʔxʷ+m -s lut swit_aɬíʔ c+maq̓ʷ way̓
hand -3in even nom -scratch_earth -3i not in_fact mountain well
scratched it with his hand. No, it's a mountain, no,

uɬ lut, lut t̓a kɬcawt 235 ixíʔ cúntəm axáʔ t yasukrí
uɬ lut lut t̓ kɬ+cawt ixíʔ cu -nt -m axáʔ t yasukrí
and not not negfac effort then tell -nt -psv this agInst JC
he had no show. Then JC told him,

236 cúntəm way̓, incá iʔ kən yasukrí 237 t incá kiʔ xʷíc̓əɬtsən
cu -nt -m way̓ in+cá iʔ kn yasukrí t in+cá kiʔ xʷic̓ -ɬt -s -n
tell -nt -psv well I art 1kn JC agInst I rel give -ɬt -2obj -1erg
he said to him, "I am JC. It was I who gave you

ixíʔ {as} aksysyús akɬksisyústən 238 ixíʔ a ckəlk̓əlk̓íc̓aʔ {inaud}
ixíʔ a -k -sy•sy=us a -kɬ -k+sy•sy=ús+tn ixíʔ a c -k+lk̓•lk̓=íc̓aʔ
that 2i -to_be -power 2i -to_be -powers that art hab -bundles
your smarts, your powers, the bundles, the four

kmúsc̓aʔ 239 ixíʔ uɬ_iʔ k̓aʕʷmístməntsən aksƛ̓xʷám
k+mús=c̓aʔ ixíʔ uɬ_iʔ k̓aʕʷ+míst+m -nt -s -n a -ks -ƛ̓xʷa+m
four_packages then and_then hire -nt -2obj -1erg 2i -futi -kill_many
packages. *Then I hired you to kill all*

yaʕyáʕt {anx̌əɬ} a nʔaɬnaʔsqílxʷtən 240 uɬ way̓ yaʕyáʕt
yaʕ•yáʕ+t a n+ʔaɬn+aʔ+s+qílxʷ+tn uɬ way̓ yaʕ•yáʕ+t
all art man_eater and yes all
the man-eaters. *And you killed*

c̓əspnúntxʷ 241 uɬ nixʷ incá uɬ kʷu aksməlpúlstəm
c̓s+p -nu -nt -xʷ uɬ nixʷ in+cá uɬ kʷu a -ks -ml+pul+st -m
rid -manage -nt -2erg and also I and 1obj 2i -futi -want_to_beat -apsv
them all.[10] *And now you want to beat me too.*

242 t incá i kʷu anilmíxʷəm, incá kən yasukrí 243 uɬ lut̓
t in+cá iʔ kʷu an -yl=mixʷ+m in+cá kn yasukrí uɬ lut_t̓
? I art 1kʷu 2in -chief I 1kn JC and neg_emph
It is I who is your boss, I am JC, 6:00 *and you*

qəɬnúntxʷ kʷu ɬ akspúlstəm 244 uɬ laʔcxʔít
qɬ -nu -nt -xʷ kʷu ɬ a -ks -pul+st -m uɬ la_c+xʔít+iʔ
able -manage -nt -2erg 1kʷu comp 2i -futi -kill_one -apsv and first,
can't beat me. *The first time*

iʔ {kʷ is} kʷ isənqʷən̓mínəm 245 kiʔ ixíʔ síx̌əlxstxʷ a cmaq̓ʷ
iʔ kʷ i -s -n+qʷn̓+min+m kiʔ ixíʔ six̌+lx -st -xʷ a c+maq̓ʷ
art 2kʷu 1i -intt -pity rel then move -st -2erg art mountain
I pitied you *and you moved the mountain.*

246 uɬ ixíʔ aksmipnúnəm kʷa iʔ cúntsən
uɬ ixíʔ a -ks -my+p -nun -m kʷa iʔ cu -nt -s -n
and then 2i -futt̂ -learn -manage -apsv intj art tell -nt -2obj -1erg
And you are going to learn. I told you to put

ɬsíx̌əlxstxʷ iʔ k̓əl [s]t̓ək̓ʷtán[s] 247 uɬ way̓ wi··m̓ asx̌əl·wís
ɬ+six̌+lx -st -xʷ iʔ k̓l s+t̓k̓ʷ+tan -s uɬ way̓ wim̓ a -sx̌+lwis
move_back -st -2erg art to resting_place -3in and yes in_vain 2i -move_st
the mountain where it belongs *and you tried and couldn't move it.*

248 uɬ aɬíʔ kʷ xkínəm, incá iʔ kna ilmíxʷəm, 249 incá kən ɬa
uɬ aɬíʔ kʷ x+kin+m in+cá iʔ kn yl=mixʷ+m in+cá kn ɬaʔ
and so 2kn do_what I art 1kn chief I 1kn the_one_that
And what can you do, I am the boss. *I am the one*

kɬksisyústən, kən ɬa ksysyús 250 cúntəm ʕapná kʷu
kɬ+k+sy•sy=us+tn kn ɬaʔ k+sy•sy=us cu -nt -m ʕapnáʔ kʷu
have_powers 1kn the_one_that have_power tell -nt -psv now 1obj
who has smarts." *He said to him,*

10 These feats are recounted in the various man-eater narratives.

nx̌ʷílcəntxʷ, ixíʔ kc̓əx̌ʷíplaʔntsən 251 ixíʔ uł asclák̓
n+x̌ʷil=cn -t -xʷ ixíʔ k+c̓x̌ʷ=íplaʔ -nt -s -n ixíʔ uł a -sc -lak̓
disregard_order -nt -2erg then judge -nt -2obj -1erg then and 2i -pftv -jail
"Now you didn't listen to me. I am going to judge you. You will be in prison

put la c̓iwt sx̌əlx̌áʕlt 252 mi kʷ łənkcxíw̓s iʔ k̓əl ksqilxʷ {t kmi} iʔ k̓əl
put l c+ʔiwt s+x̌l•x̌aʕl+t mi kʷ ł+n+kc+x=iw̓s iʔ k̓l k+s+qilxʷ iʔ k̓l
just on last day fut 2kn in_midst_again art to have_person art on
until the last day.[11] *That's when you will get back where there are people*

təmxʷúlaʔxʷ 253 ixíʔ uł_iʔ kʷíntəm {k̓əl} k̓aʔkín mat {at̓əxʷ} k̓əl siwłkʷ
tmxʷ=úlaʔxʷ ixíʔ uł_iʔ kʷi -nt -m k̓a+ʔkín mat k̓l siwł=kʷ
country then and_then take -nt -psv to_where maybe to water
on earth." Then he took him somewhere, maybe to the water, 7:06

254 sílxʷaʔ iʔ k̓əl siwłkʷ iʔ *ocean* 255 ik̓líʔ {k} mat {kə} kłksunkʷ, ik̓líʔ kiʔ
sílxʷaʔ iʔ k̓l siwł=kʷ iʔ ik̓líʔ mat kł+k+sun=kʷ ik̓líʔ kiʔ
big art to water art there maybe have_island there rel
to the big water, the ocean. Maybe there is an island there, that's where

t̓ək̓ʷəntím 256 cúntəm ixíʔ akłtəmxʷúlaʔxʷ {kʷ łlak} put laʔc̓íwt
t̓k̓ʷ -nt -im cu -nt -m ixíʔ a -kł -tmxʷ=úlaʔxʷ put la_c+ʔiwt
set_in_place -nt -psv tell -nt -psv that 2i -to_be -country just last
he put him. He told him, "That's your place until judgment

sx̌əlx̌áʕlt 257 uł scútxəlx uł axáʔ iʔ t suyápix iʔ t
s+x̌l•x̌aʕl+t uł s -cut -x -lx uł axáʔ iʔ t s+wyapy=x iʔ t
day and ipftv^ -say -^ipftv -pl and this art agInst white_person art agInst
day." And they say that with the white people's

ʕác̓mən 258 uł cwíkstəm ilíʔ sənk̓líp cxʷaʔxʷíst
ʕac̓+mn uł c -wik -st -m ilíʔ s+n+k̓l̓=ip c -xʷaʔ•xʷíst
binoculars and cust^ -see -^cust -psv there Coyote hab -walk_back_and_forth
binoculars one can see Coyote walk around there

iʔ l *island* 259 məł iwá ik̓líʔ xʷuylx iʔ l stáłəm uł lut t̓a
iʔ l mł iwá ik̓líʔ xʷuy -lx iʔ l s+tałm uł lut t̓
art on and even there go -pl art in boat and not negfac
on the island. And even if they go there in a boat, they can never

ck̓əłkícstəm 260 uł t̓iʔ k̓li··ʔ məł səlʔúsəmsəlx
c -k̓ł+kic -st -m uł t̓iʔ ik̓líʔ mł sl̓=us+m -s -lx
cust^ -reach -^cust -psv and evid there and lose_sight_of -3erg -pl
reach him. They get close and their eyes lose it.

261 iʔ nc̓ayxʷápəlqs
iʔ n+c̓ayxʷ=áplqs
art end_of_story
That's the end of it. 7:51

11 An allusion to purgatory.

Coyote and Whale

1 way̓ kən c̓əpq̓síwsəm i l incaptíkʷɬ {ə} axáʔ iʔ l sənk̓líp 2 ixíʔ
way̓ kn c̓pq̓+s=iw̓s+m iʔ l in -captíkʷɬ axáʔ iʔ l s+n+k̓l̓=ip ixíʔ
well 1kn splice art with 1in -legends this art with Coyote then
I am continuing with my Coyote story.[1] *He*

taʔxʷɬcq̓ílən iʔ t t̓ət̓áq̓aʔt iʔ t cq̓ílən 3 uɬ_i
taʔxʷ+ɬ+cq̓=íln iʔ t t̓•t̓áʔq̓aʔ+t iʔ t cq̓=iln uɬ_iʔ
get art obj_itr short art obj_itr arrow and_then
[Coyote] had got an arrow, a short arrow; *and*

nqʷən̓míntəm iʔ t k̓ʷəl̓əncútən {təl s} təl̓ stx̌əw̓x̌əw̓úsc
n+qʷn̓+mi -nt -m iʔ t k̓ʷl̓+ncut+n tl̓ s+t+x̌w̓•x̌w̓=us -c
feel_sorry_for -nt -psv art agInst god from dry_eyes -3in
the Creator pitied him because his eyes went dry.

4 uɬ {i} ixíʔ iʔ kəlk̓əlk̓íc̓aʔxtəm a lqúlaʔxʷəm {təs} t st̓ʔíʔ 5 [ix]íʔ
uɬ ixíʔ iʔ k+lk̓•lk̓=íc̓aʔ -xt -m a lq=úlaʔxʷ+m t s+t̓ʔiʔ ixíʔ
and then art bundles -xit -psv art uproot obj_itr grass then
And he wrapped it up for him, he pulled it from the grass, *he*

kəlk̓əlk̓íc̓aʔɬtəm uɬ kmúsc̓aʔ 6 cúntəm {u} sənk̓líp, way̓ axáʔ iʔ
k+lk̓•lk̓=íc̓aʔ -ɬt -m uɬ k+mús=c̓aʔ cu -nt -m s+n+k̓l̓=ip way̓ axáʔ iʔ
bundles -ɬt -psv and four_packages tell -nt -psv Coyote well this art
wrapped that, four bundles. *He told Coyote, “Because*

kʷ iksənqʷən̓mínəm 7 axáʔ akɬkənxcútən, aksl̓əx̌l̓áx̌t
kʷ i -ks -n+qʷn̓+min+m axáʔ a -kɬ -kn+x+cut+n a -k -s+l̓x̌•l̓ax̌+t
2kʷu 1i -futi -pity this 2i -to_be -help 2i -to_be -friends
I pity you *these are what is going to help you, your partners,*

kmúsəms axáʔ 8 uɬ kʷ ksk̓ʷúlaʔx ki axáʔ iʔ xʷíc̓əɬtsən
k=mus•ms axáʔ uɬ kʷ ks -k̓ʷul̓ -aʔx kiʔ axáʔ iʔ xʷic̓ -ɬt -s -n
four_persons this and 2kn incpˆ -work -ˆincp rel this art give -ɬt -2obj -1erg
four of them. 1:00 *Now you are going to work, this is what I give to you.*

9 aksk̓əɬx̌ʷíləm yaʕyáʕt {iʔ} ia nʔaɬnaʔsqílxʷtən 10 ia
a -ks -k̓ɬ+x̌ʷil+m yaʕ•yáʕ+t iʔ n+ʔaɬn+aʔ+s+qílxʷ+tn iʔ
2i -futi -get_rid_of all art man_eater art
You are going to destroy all the man-eaters, *those*

cƛ̓əxʷstís iʔ sqilxʷ 11 yaʕyáʕt ixíʔ aksƛ̓əxʷám
c -ƛ̓xʷ -st -is iʔ s+qilxʷ yaʕ•yáʕ+t ixíʔ a -ks -ƛ̓xʷa+m
custˆ -kill_many -ˆcust -3erg art person all that 2i -futi -kill_many
that kill people, *you are going to kill all of them.*

1 cəpcaptíkʷɬ represent the cosmology and mythology of the Cv-Ok. In that body of knowledge one can isolate components that can stand as individual texts. The narrator says that he is “splicing” his story, a logical continuation of what he had narrated five days earlier, thus making the point that there is a sort of Cv-Ok macro-captíkʷɬ.

12 ki axáʔ iʔ k̓aʕʷmístməntsən 13 axáʔ iʔ xʷíc̓xtmən
kiʔ axáʔ iʔ k̓aʕʷ+míst+m -nt -s -n axáʔ iʔ xʷic̓ -xt -m -n
rel this art hire -nt -2obj -1erg this art give -xit -2obj -1erg
That's why I'm hiring you *and I gave you these for*

axáʔ akɬksisyústən 14 ṅíṅẇiʔ laʔkín kʷ yaʕpcín uɬ ixíʔ
axáʔ a -kɬ -k+sy•sy=ús+tn ṅíṅẇiʔ la+ʔkíṅ kʷ yaʕ+p=cín uɬ ixíʔ
this 2i -to_be -powers a_while whenever 2kn scared and then
your powers. *When you get cornered*

x̌lítəntxʷəlx 15 uɬ ixíʔ ṅíṅẇiʔ cúntsəlx stiṁ uɬ i
x̌lit -nt -xʷ -lx uɬ ixíʔ ṅíṅẇiʔ cu -nt -s -lx s+tiṁ uɬ iʔ
summon -nt -2erg -pl and then a_while tell -nt -2obj -pl what and art
you call them *and then they'll say to you*

anx̌mínk uɬ_iʔ kʷu x̌əlítəntxʷ 16 məɬ cúntxʷəlx waẏ ixíʔ
an -x̌m=ink uɬ_iʔ kʷu x̌lit -nt -xʷ mɬ cu -nt -xʷ -lx waẏ ixíʔ
2in -want and_then 1obj summon -nt -2erg and tell -nt -2erg -pl yes that
'What is it you want that you called us?' *and you tell them, 'Yes,*

kən syaʕpcínx̧ 17 ixíʔ a nʔaɬnaʔsqílxʷtən {i iks}
kn s -yaʕ+p=cín -x ixíʔ a n+ʔaɬn+aʔ+s+qílxʷ+tn
1kn ipftv^ -scared -^ipftv that art man_eater
I am cornered. *I am going to beat the man-eater,*

iksƛ̓xʷúpəm, {hu} ikspúlstəm {uɬ} 18 məɬ cúsəlx waẏ məɬ ixíʔ
i -ks -ƛ̓xʷu+p+m i -ks -pul -st -m mɬ cu -s -lx waẏ mɬ ixíʔ
1i -futi -win 1i -futi -kill_one -st apsv and tell -3erg -pl OK and then
I'm going to kill him.' *And they'll say 'Ok,' and they'll*

ṁáyaʔɬtsəlx laʔkín xkínəm 19 ṅíṅẇiʔ kənxítsəlx {uɬ ixíʔ} 20 məɬ
ṁáyaʔ -ɬt -s -lx la+ʔkíṅ x+kin+m ṅíṅẇiʔ kn+xit -s -lx mɬ
tell -ɬt -2obj -pl whenever do_what a_while help -3e2obj -pl and
show you what to do, 2:03 *and they'll help you."*

ixíʔ pəlstnús ia nʔaɬnaʔsqílxʷtən 21 waẏ {ay cúntəm sənk̓líp}
ixíʔ pl+st -nu -s iʔ n+ʔaɬn+aʔ+s+qílxʷ+tn waẏ
then kill -manage -3erg art man_eater well
And then he can kill the man-eater. *Then*

cúntəm axáʔ iʔ t yasukrí sənk̓líp 22 xʷuyx waẏ, lut
cu -nt -m axáʔ iʔ t yasukrí s+n+k̓lʼ=ip xʷuy -x waẏ lut
tell -nt -psv this art agInst Jesus_Christ Coyote go -isimptv well not
JC said to Coyote: *"Go, and don't*

nixʷ akɬəlṁṁaʔcínməlx axáʔ iʔ həlsəmx̌íkən, kəṁ swit 23 waẏ
nixʷ a -k -ɬ+ṁ•ṁaʔ=cín+m -lx axáʔ iʔ hɬ=s+mx̌=ikn kṁ swit waẏ
more 2i -futi -bother_again -pl this art grizzly_group or anyone well
bother the Grizzly Bear or anybody. *You*

yaʕyáʕt anwí kʷ xaʔítət {iʔ} 24 kʷ miɬsisyús ixíʔ {təl} təl
yaʕ•yáʕ+t anwí kʷ xaʔít•t kʷ my+ɬ+sy•sy=us ixíʔ tl
all you 2kn be_first 2kn smart_comptv that than
are first. *You are more powerful*

yaʕyáʕt {ixíʔ təl} iʔ təl̓ iʔ tla k{ɬs}wísxən {i t cq̓} iʔ t cqílən̓ 25 way̓,
yaʕ•yáʕ+t iʔ tl̓ iʔ tla k+wis=xn iʔ t cq̓=iln way̓
all art from art from longer art from arrow well
than anybody that has a longer arrow." Then

way̓ i[xíʔ] ɬwíntəm 26 way̓ i[xíʔ itlíʔ] sxʷuy[s] 27 way̓ xʷuy
way̓ ixíʔ ɬwin -t -m way̓ ixíʔ itlíʔ s -xʷuy -s way̓ xʷuy
well then leave -nt -psv well then from_there nom -go -3i well go
he left him. Then he went. He went

kəl·kʷákʷ 28 uɬ axáʔ aɬíʔ nwísəlx yasukrí k̓əl stk̓m̓ásq̓ət{ay}
k+lkʷ•akʷ uɬ axáʔ aɬíʔ n+wis+lx yasukrí k̓l s+t+k̓m=asq̓t
far and this so raise JC to sky
and got a ways away. 3:00 And JC went up to the sky.

29 way̓ nstils sənk̓líp, way̓ mat ha kʷu stqəqnúnəms {a} iʔ t
way̓ n+st=ils s+n+k̓l̓=ip way̓ mat haʔ kʷu s -tq•q+nun+m -s iʔ t
well think Coyote yes maybe inter 1kʷu intt -fool -3i art agInst
Coyote thought, "I think god's just

k̓ʷləncútən 30 way mat ha uɬ t̓i {l} lut, lut mat ha cənləʕ̓ʷús {iʔ}
k̓ʷl̓+ncut+n way̓ mat haʔ uɬ t̓iʔ lut lut mat haʔ c -n+lʕ̓ʷ=us
creator well maybe inter and evid not not maybe inter hab -fit
fooling me. No, it doesn't make sense.

31 way̓ sta iksksmaʔmáyəm 32 way̓ ixíʔ sƛ̓aps sənk̓líp
way̓ sta i -ks -k+s+m̓aʔ•m̓áy+m way̓ ixíʔ s -ƛ̓ap -s s+n+k̓l̓=ip
well intj 1i -futi -get_story well then nom -stop -3i Coyote
I'm going to get the story of this." Coyote stopped.

33 way̓ ixíʔ scuts p̓əs p̓əs p̓əs p̓əs k̓ʷƛ̓up {ay̓ k way̓ {tk}
way̓ ixíʔ s -cut -s p̓s p̓s p̓s p̓s k̓ʷƛ̓up
well then nom -say -3i onom onom onom onom come_out
He said "p̓s p̓s p̓s p̓s Come out!"

34 t̓k̓ʷk̓ʷúlaʔxʷ 35 cúntəm way̓ stim̓ {a} anx̌mínk 36 a,
t̓k̓ʷ•k̓ʷ=úlaʔxʷ cu -nt -m way̓ s+tim̓ an -x̌m=ink a
fall_to_ground tell -nt -psv well what 2in -want intj
They fell to the ground. They asked him, "What do you want?" "Ah,

lut, t̓əxʷ {t̓i} t̓iʔ_kmix iksmipnúnəm 37 itlíʔ nixʷ
lut t̓xʷ t̓iʔ_kmix i -ks -my+p -nun -m itlíʔ nixʷ
not emph only 1i -futi -learn -manage -apsv from_there again
nothing, I just want to find out." Again he said

ɬcut p̓əs p̓əs p̓əs k̓ʷƛ̓up 38 way̓ nixʷ knaqs nixʷ
ɬ+cut p̓s p̓s p̓s k̓ʷƛ̓up way̓ nixʷ k=naqs nixʷ
say_again onom onom onom come_out well again one_person again
"p̓s p̓s p̓s p̓s Come out!" And again one dropped

t̓k̓ʷk̓ʷúlaʔxʷ {qilxʷt} 39 cúntəm way̓ sənk̓líp, stim̓ uɬ anx̌mínk
t̓k̓ʷ•k̓ʷ=úlaʔxʷ cu -nt -m way̓ s+n+k̓l̓=ip s+tim̓ uɬ an -x̌m=ink
fall_to_ground tell -nt -psv well Coyote what and 2in -want
to the ground. 4:00 He asked him, "Coyote, what do you want?"

40 a, lut, t̓əxʷ t̓i {kʷu} iksksmaʔmáy̓əm 41 way̓ itlíʔ nixʷ
a lut t̓xʷ t̓iʔ i -ks -k+s+m̓aʔ•m̓áy+m way̓ itlíʔ nixʷ
intj not emph evid 1i -futi -get_story well from_there again
"Oh, nothing, I just want to get the story out of you." *Again*

p̓əs p̓əs p̓əs kʷƛ̓up 42 way̓ nixʷ itlíʔ knaqs 43 way̓ ixíʔ
p̓s p̓s p̓s kʷƛ̓up way̓ nixʷ itlíʔ k=naqs way̓ ixíʔ
onom onom onom come_out yes again from_there one_person well then
"p̓s p̓s p̓s p̓s Come out!" *Then another one;* *he*

nixʷ síwəntəm 44 cut lut, way̓ t̓i_kmix kʷ isksm̓aʔm̓áyəm {kʷ iks}
nixʷ siw -nt -m cut lut way̓ t̓iʔ_kmix kʷ i -s -k+s+m̓aʔ•m̓áy+m
again ask -nt -psv say not well only 2kʷu 1i -intt -get_story
asked him too. *He said, "No, I just want to get the story from you.*

45 ha uníxʷ 46 way̓ itlíʔ nixʷ p̓əs p̓əs p̓əs kʷƛ̓up 47 ixíʔ
ha? wnixʷ way̓ itlíʔ nixʷ p̓s p̓s p̓s kʷƛ̓up ixíʔ
inter true well from_there again onom onom onom come_out then
Is it true?" *Again "p̓s p̓s p̓s [p̓s] Come out!"* *The*

uɬ kmúsəms 48 cúntəm stim̓ uɬ anx̌mínk sənk̓líp 49 uɬ
uɬ k=mus•ms cu -nt -m s+tim̓ uɬ an -x̌m=ink s+n+k̓l̓=ip uɬ
and four_persons tell -nt -psv what and 2in -want Coyote and
fourth one. *He said "What did you want, Coyote,* *and*

kʷu {t} siʔsúy̓kstməntxʷ 50 cut lut, way̓ t̓i_kmix p
kʷu sy•suy̓=kst+m -nt -xʷ cut lut way̓ t̓iʔ_kmix p
1obj get_chilled -nt -2erg say not well only 5kʷu
you are getting us chilled?" *He said, "No, I just want to find*

isksm̓aʔm̓áyəm 51 ha uníxʷ 52 cúsəlx way̓ uníxʷ
i -s -k+s+m̓aʔ•m̓áy+m ha? wnixʷ cu -s -lx way̓ wnixʷ
1i -intt -get_story inter true tell -3erg -pl well true
the story out from you. *Is it true?"* *They told him, "Sure it's true.*

53 i[xíʔ] cunts iʔ t k̓ʷəl̓əncútən uɬ way̓ uníxʷ ixíʔ 54 a
ixíʔ cu -nt -s iʔ t k̓ʷl̓+ncut+n uɬ way̓ wnixʷ ixíʔ a
that tell -nt -3e2obj art agInst god and yes true that intj
That's what god told you and it's true." *"Oh,*

way̓ 55 way̓ i[xíʔ] ɬq̓əmq̓əmntís axáʔ ckəlk̓əlk̓íc̓aʔ i[2] itlíʔ
way̓ way̓ ixíʔ ɬ+q̓m•q̓m -nt -is axáʔ c -k+lk̓•lk̓=íc̓aʔ itlíʔ
OK well then swallow_again -nt -3erg this hab -bundles ? from_there
Ok." *Then he swallowed the bundles back,*

sxʷuys 56 xʷu··y {əy} kicx {ə k̓əl} k̓əl sənʕíckstx 57 ik̓líʔ ki {uɬ}
s -xʷuy -s xʷuy kic+x k̓l s+n+ʕic=kst=x ik̓líʔ kiʔ
nom -go -3i go arrive to Lakes there rel
then he went on. *He went, and he got to the Lakes tribe. 5:12* *He got*

2 Possibly a false start.

kicx {a} 58 axáʔ {níxləm} níxəls sənk̓líp knaqs {a} st̓aʔk̓míx təl̓ {s}
kic+x axáʔ nixl -s s+n+k̓l̓=ip k=naqs s+t̓aʔk̓+míx tl̓
arrive this hear -3erg Coyote one_person virgin from
there. *He heard that there was a maiden from*

sənyál̓mənx {ki} 59 itlíʔ ki əcksl̓íplaʔ 60 uł lut t̓a
s+n+yal̓+mn=x itlíʔ kiʔ c -k+sl̓=íplaʔ uł lut t̓
Montana_person from_there rel hab -be_gone and not evid
Montana. *She had disappeared from there.* *They don't*

cmistísəlx k̓aʔkín łə xʷuy 61 uł lut t̓ ƛ̓lal
c -my -st -is -lx k̓a+ʔkín ł xʷuy uł lut t̓ ƛ̓l•al
cust^ -know -^cust -3erg -pl to_where compl go and not negfac dead
know where she went. *She is not dead.*

62 uł ałíʔ iʔ stətəm̓tím̓s ilíʔ {iʔ l} iʔ l łaʔmcnítkʷ 63 a
uł ałíʔ iʔ s+t•tm̓•tim̓ -s ilíʔ iʔ l łʔa+m=cn=ítkʷ a
and so art clothes -3in there art on close_to_shore art
Her clothes were right close to the shore, *a*

ct̓əqcnítkʷ axáʔ {iʔ l sil} iʔ l siwłkʷ i la ctyap 64 ilíʔ
c -t̓q=cn=itkʷ axáʔ iʔ l siwł=kʷ iʔ l c -tya+p ilíʔ
hab -lie_on_shore this art in water art in hab -water_runs there
bundle right close to the water where the water runs. 6:05 *Her*

st̓əqcnítkʷ iʔ stətəm̓tím̓s uł axáʔ {i} iʔ tkłmilxʷ k̓aw 65 uł
c -t̓q=cn=itkʷ iʔ s+t•tm̓•tim̓ -s uł axáʔ iʔ tkł+m=ilxʷ k̓aw uł
hab -lie_on_shore art clothes -3in and this art woman gone and
clothes are close to the water, and the woman is gone. *And*

ilmíxʷəm łaʔ kst̓amkʔílt ixíʔ {a} a cksl̓íplaʔ
yl=mixʷ+m łaʔ k+s+t̓mkʔ=ilt ixíʔ a c -k+sl̓=íplaʔ
chief the_one_that have_daughter that art hab -be_gone
it's the chief''s daughter that disappeared.

66 sənmúlx ixíʔ uł_i {əc} əcksl̓íplaʔ 67 uł ixíʔ łə
s -n+mul -x ixíʔ uł_iʔ c -k+sl̓=íplaʔ uł ixíʔ
ipftv^ -dip_water -^ipftv then and_then hab -be_gone and then ?
She went after water and then she disappeared. *Morning*

ksx̌əlpínaʔ 68 uł ixíʔ {łə} ƛ̓aʔƛ̓aʔntísəlx, kiʔ wíkłtsəlx iʔ
k+s+x̌l+p=ínaʔ uł ixíʔ ƛ̓aʔ•ƛ̓aʔ -nt -is -lx kiʔ wik -łt -s -lx iʔ
have_daylight and then look_for -nt -3erg -pl rel see -łt -3erg -pl art
came. *They looked for her, and that's when they saw*

stətəm̓tím̓s 69 ilíʔ iʔ l yaʕcín t̓əqcnítkʷ 70 uł iʔ łkaps {ixíʔ uł}
s+t•tm̓•tim̓ -s ilíʔ iʔ l yaʕ=cín t̓q=cn=itkʷ uł iʔ łkap -s
clothes -3in there art on the_shore lie_on_shore and art bucket -3in
her clothes: *they were lying close to the shore.* *And her bucket.*

71 uł ixíʔ {s ə··} scuts, sw̓aw̓áʔms axáʔ ilmíxʷəm, {a} iʔ l
uł ixíʔ s -cut -s s -waʔ•wáʔ+m -s axáʔ yl=mixʷ+m iʔ l
and then nom -say -3i nom -announce -3i this chief art at
Then he said, the boss from Montana hollered,

sənyáľmən axáʔ ilmíxʷəm 72 ixíʔ uɬ waʔwáʔm uɬ ixíʔ scuts
s+n+yaľ+mn axáʔ yl=mixʷ+m ixíʔ uɬ waʔ•wáʔ+m uɬ ixíʔ s -cut -s
Montana this chief then and announce and then nom -say -3i
the chief, he hollered and said: 7:00

73 waẏ axáʔ cksľípla? isťəmkʔílt 74 uɬ kʷu kɬƛ̓aʔƛ̓aʔɬtíp
waẏ axáʔ c -k+sľ=ípla? i -s+ťmkʔ=ilt uɬ kʷu ks -ƛ̓aʔ•ƛ̓aʔ -ɬt -ip
well this hab -be_gone 1in -daughter and 1obj futt^ -look_for -ɬt -5erg
"My daughter has disappeared. You will search for

isťəmkʔílt 75 luť ƛ̓lal, lut ť wíkɬtəm iʔ sqiltks {kəṁ iʔ}
i -s+ťmkʔ=ilt lut_ť ƛ̓l•al lut ť wik -ɬt -m iʔ s+qilt=k -s
1in -daughter neg_emph dead not negfac see -ɬt -4erg art body -3in
my daughter. She is not dead, we didn't see her body that

ɬə ksƛ̓lals 76 waẏ kmix iʔ stətəṁtíṁs ilíʔ wíkɬtəm
ɬ ks -ƛ̓l•al -s waẏ kmix iʔ s+t•tṁ•tiṁ -s ilíʔ wik -ɬt -m
compl futi -dead -3i well only art clothes -3in there see -ɬt -psv
she is dead, we saw only her clothes bundled

əcťəqcnítkʷ 77 sənmúlx uɬ ixíʔ əcksľípla? 78 uɬ
c -ťq=cn=itkʷ s -n+mul -x uɬ ixíʔ c -k+sľ=ípla? uɬ
hab -lie_on_shore ipftv^ -dip_water -^ipftv and then hab -be_gone and
by the water. She was dipping water, and she disappeared. Maybe

waẏ mat cxʷəlxʷált 79 uɬ ixíʔ p iksx̌áq̓əm 80 uɬ
waẏ mat c -xʷl•xʷal+t uɬ ixíʔ p i -ks -x̌aq̓+m uɬ
yes maybe hab -alive and that 5kʷu 1i -futi -pay and
she is alive. And this is what I am offering to pay"

aɬíʔ swiʔnúmtx iʔ sťəmkʔílts 81 cut ṅíṅẇiʔ swit kaʔkíciʔs
aɬíʔ s+wẏ+numt=x iʔ s+ťmkʔ=ilt -s cut ṅíṅẇiʔ swit kaʔ•kíc ẏ -s
because handsome art daughter -3in say a_while who find -nt -3erg
(because his daughter is good looking). He said, "Whoever finds her, he

uɬ ixíʔ kɬnáx̌ʷnəx̌ʷs 82 níkxnaʔ uɬ axáʔ iʔ splal aɬíʔ
uɬ ixíʔ kɬ -nax̌ʷ•nx̌ʷ -s níkxnaʔ uɬ axáʔ iʔ s+pl•al aɬíʔ
and then to_be -wife -3i goodness and this art young_growth so
can have her for his wife." Gee, these young fellows

sq̓əwxʷmíxəlx {ixíʔ iʔ k̓əl stə} iʔ k̓əl sťaʔk̓míx 83 uɬ aɬíʔ swiʔnúmtx {uɬ}
s -q̓xʷ -mix -lx iʔ k̓l s+ťaʔk̓+míx uɬ aɬíʔ s+wẏ+numt=x
ipftv^ -wish_for -^ipftv -pl art for virgin and because handsome
were horny for the girl, because she is good looking,

uɬ waẏ {əc} əck̓əɬtunəlsmístəlx 84 uɬ aɬíʔ lut {ť ks} ť
uɬ waẏ c -k̓ɬ+twn=ls+mist -lx uɬ aɬíʔ lut ť
and yes hab -think_one_falls_short -pl and because not negfac
and they don't think they are good enough 8:00 and she wouldn't

ksxʔínaʔməntməlx ɬə ksənsucənmístsəlx axáʔ {i ta} k̓la ilmíxʷəm
ks -xʔ=ínaʔ+m -nt -m -lx ɬ ks -n+sw=cn+mist -s -lx axáʔ k̓l yl=mixʷ+m
futt^ -consent -nt -psv -pl if futi -propose -3i -pl this to chief
consent if they proposed for her to the chief.

85 waẏ ixíʔ {ta xi} tkʷúpxənsəlx ixíʔ sƛ̓ʔámsəlx {li}
waẏ ixíʔ t+kʷup=xn -s -lx ixíʔ s -ƛ̓ʔa+m -s -lx
well then rush_to -3erg -pl that nom -look_for -3i -pl
They all rushed and looked for her.

86 nxməníw̓ssəlx ixíʔ a ctyap {iʔ} a nsilxʷʔítkʷ {i·· uɬ oɬ} 87 lut
n+xmn=iw̓s -s -lx ixíʔ a c -tya+p a n+silxʷʔ=ítkʷ lut
both_sides -3erg -pl that art hab -water_runs art big_water not
They looked on both sides of the running water by the big water, but

uɬ t̓a ckaʔkícsəlx 88 kəm̓ lut t̓a
uɬ t̓ c -kaʔ•kíc -st -s -lx km̓ lut t̓
and negfac cust^ -find -^cust -3erg -pl or not negfac
they didn't find her. And they didn't

cníxəlmsəlx k̓aʔkín 89 ixíʔ {uɬ} uɬ p̓áʕʷəlx, uɬ
c -nixl+m -s -lx k̓a+ʔkín ixíʔ uɬ p̓aʕw -lx uɬ
act -hear_about -3erg -pl to_where then and tire -pl and
hear where she went. And they got tired, and

qmápəlx {ixíʔ uɬ} 90 axáʔ t {a} sənk̓líp uɬ ixíʔ níxləms 91 waẏ
qma+p -lx axáʔ t s+n+k̓l̓=ip uɬ ixíʔ nixl+m -s waẏ
give_up -pl this agInst Coyote and then hear_about -3erg well
they gave up. Coyote heard about it. And

uɬ ixíʔ, aɬíʔ sənk̓líp 92 uɬ ixíʔ {s} x̌əmínks ixíʔ {kc} iwá lut
uɬ ixíʔ aɬíʔ s+n+k̓l̓=ip uɬ ixíʔ x̌m=ink -s ixíʔ iwá lut
and that because Coyote and that like -3in that even not
because, because he's Coyote he wants her, even if had never

cwiksts ixíʔ iʔ st̓aʔk̓míx 93 uɬ aɬíʔ x̌minks {kskt̓aʔk̓əmxla}
c -wik -st -s ixíʔ iʔ s+t̓aʔk̓+míx uɬ aɬíʔ x̌m=ink -s
cust^ -see -^cust -3erg that art virgin and so want -3in
seen the girl; he wants to get a taste

kskt̓aʔk̓əmxáqsaʔx 94 waẏ uɬ ixíʔ sƛ̓ʔams 95 əy xʷu··y,
ks -k+t̓aʔk̓+mx=áqs -aʔx waẏ uɬ ixíʔ s -ƛ̓ʔa+m -s əy xʷuy
incp^ -taste_of_maiden -^incp well and then nom -look_for -3i intj go
of the maiden. 9:05 So he looked for her. He went,

sənk̓lip ənk̓wí··lx {uɬ a} mat i l ƛ̓ʔiʔs 96 uɬ k̓aʔx̌í nqilt
s+n+k̓l̓=ip n+k̓w+ilx mat iʔ l ƛ̓ʔiʔ -s uɬ k̓a+ʔx̌íʔ n+qilt
Coyote go_upstream maybe art in canoe -3in and there waterfall
Coyote went upstream, maybe in his bark canoe. He got over a falls,

k̓əl·· sc̓úmstsəlx {ə c} iʔ t sqilxʷ k̓əl st̓iltx iʔ cwix
k̓l c -ʔum -st -s -lx iʔ t s+qilxʷ k̓l s+t̓ilt=x iʔ cwix
to cust^ -call -^cust -3erg -pl art agInst Indian to Kutenai art creek
in Indian they call it "Kutenai River."

97 itlíʔ {t aɬ ixíʔ} t̓ikʷt, itlíʔ kiʔ {c} sp̓áƛ̓əmqən axáʔ a ntx̌ʷitkʷ
itlíʔ t̓ikʷt itlíʔ kiʔ s+p̓aƛ̓+m=qn axáʔ a n+tx̌ʷ=itkʷ
from_there lake from_there rel head_of_river this art river
It's from the lake, the head of this big river is from there.

98 a[xáʔ] scústsəlx iʔ *Roosevelt Lake* {təm} ta nwyapxcən
axáʔ s -cu -st -s -lx iʔ t n+wyap=x=cn
this cust^ -tell -^cust -3erg -pl art agInst say_in_English
They call it "Roosevelt Lake" in English,

99 uɬ aɬí t sqílxʷ uɬ {n} nx̌ʷəntkʷítkʷ
uɬ aɬíʔ t s+qilxʷ uɬ n+x̌ʷn=tkʷ=itkʷ
and so agInst Indian and Columbia_River
and in Indian "nx̌ʷəntkʷítkʷ."

100 itlíʔ iʔ
itlíʔ iʔ
from_there art
The head of the river is

sp̓áƛ̓mqən
s+p̓aƛ̓+m=qn
head_of_river
from there. 10:01

101 a·· itlíʔ ixíʔ ɬəɬcənʔáx̌ʷts
a itlíʔ ixíʔ ɬ -ɬ+c+n+ʔax̌ʷ+t -s
intj from_there then nom -come_downstream_again -3i
From there he came back downriver.

102 ɬcxʷu··y uɬ {a} aláʔ {l} i l sx̌ʷnitkʷ {ə ɬ} ɬck̓əɬʔiq̓ʷ
ɬ+c+xʷuy uɬ aláʔ iʔ l s+x̌ʷn=itkʷ ɬ+c+k+ɬ[ʔ]iq̓ʷ
come_again and here art at Colville come_in_sight_again
He came back, and at Kettle Falls he came back in sight.

103 a··
a
intj
He

ɬcxʷu··y uɬ cənyáxʷt sx̌ʷnitkʷ
ɬ+c+xʷuy uɬ c -n+yaxʷ+t s+x̌ʷn=itkʷ
come_again and hab -downstream Colville
came back, downriver, at Kettle Falls.

104 [w]aẏ q̓əməntím i
waẏ q̓m -nt -im iʔ
well swallow -nt -psv art
He was swallowed

ta nx̌aʔx̌ʔítkʷ
t n+x̌aʔ•x̌ʔ=ítkʷ
agInst water_monster
by the whale.

105 aɬíʔ uɬ mat {ə ksɬ} kɬƛ̓ʔiʔ axáʔ sənk̓líp {l kʷ}
aɬíʔ uɬ mat kɬ+ƛ̓ʔiʔ axáʔ s+n+k̓l̓=ip
because and maybe have_canoe this Coyote
Maybe Coyote had a bark canoe,

106 i[xíʔ] uɬ q̓məntím
ixíʔ uɬ q̓m -nt -im
then and swallow -nt -psv
and she swallowed him.

107 waẏ ixíʔ {s··} wiks axáʔ i {la} la
waẏ ixíʔ wik -s axáʔ iʔ l
well then see -3erg this art in
He saw in the insides, the insides

nyxʷut {i} i snixʷtíɬc̓aʔs a nx̌aʔx̌ʔítkʷ
n+yxʷ=ut iʔ s+n+yxʷ=t=íɬc̓aʔ -s a n+x̌aʔ•x̌ʔ=ítkʷ
inside art insides -3in art water_monster
of the sea monster, 11:01

108 way uɬ xʷʔit sqilxʷ
waẏ uɬ xʷʔi+t s+qilxʷ
yes and many person
that there were lots

ilíʔ a ilíʔ {axáʔ iʔ}
ilíʔ a ilíʔ
there art there
of people there.

109 axáʔ {iʔ s} iʔ sqilxʷ a ilíʔ waẏ púti a
axáʔ iʔ s+qilxʷ a ilíʔ waẏ pút+iʔ a
this art person art there yes still art
The people there are still

cxʷəl·xʷált
c -xʷl·•xʷal+t
hab -alive_pl
alive,

110 mat sic iʔ sq̓mam,
mat sic iʔ s+q̓m•am
maybe new art what's_swallowed
maybe the newly swallowed,

111 uɬ ixíʔ {c}
uɬ ixíʔ
and that
and these

cxʷəl·xʷált {ia sx̌ís}
c -xʷl·•xʷal+t
hab -alive_pl
are alive.

112 uɬ axáʔ {i} náx̌əmɬ mat waẏ i q̓əsəspwílx uɬ
uɬ axáʔ nax̌mɬ mat waẏ iʔ q̓s•s•p+wilx uɬ
and this but maybe yes art be_long_time and
But the ones that have been there a long time,

way̓ uł nƛ̓xʷtílsəlx i? t sq̓míltən 113 uł axá? i? k̓ʷiƛ̓t uł
way̓ uł n+ƛ̓xʷ+t=ils -lx i? t s+q̓m=ilt+n uł axá? i? k̓ʷiƛ̓+t uł
yes and start_to_die_pl -pl art agInst hunger and this art rest and
they have died of starvation. *And some of them*

way̓ ƛ̓axʷt 114 uł púti t̓əxʷ {k} ksłiqʷ {ł yə} 115 uł axá? náx̌əmł i?
way̓ ƛ̓axʷ+t uł pút+i? t̓xʷ k+s+łiqʷ uł axá? nax̌mł i?
yes dead_pl and still evidently have_meat and this but art
are dead. *They still have some meat on.* *But the ones*

k̓ʷiƛ̓t itlí? a nxa?tmíw̓s way̓ uł kmix [s]c̓im k̓əm 116 way̓
k̓ʷiƛ̓+t itlí? a n+xa?t+m=íw̓s way̓ uł kmix s+c̓im k̓m way̓
others from_there art first_ones yes and only bone except well
before that, they are just bones. *The*

uł ixí? ƛ̓axʷt, mat ixí? {la} l nxa?tmíw̓s 117 ixí? nák̓ʷəm
uł ixí? ƛ̓axʷ+t mat ixí? l n+xa?t+m=íw̓s ixí? nak̓ʷ+m
and that dead_pl maybe that in first_ones that evid
first ones are dead. *The sea monster*

n?ałna?sqílxʷtən ixí? a nx̌a?x̌?ítkʷ 118 a mipnús
n+?ałn+a?+s+qílxʷ+tn ixí? a n+x̌a?•x̌?=ítkʷ a my+p -nu -s
man_eater that art water_monster intj learn -manage -3erg
is a man-eater. *Coyote found*

sənk̓líp {way̓} 119 way̓ ixí? {s} sxʷilwísc ilí? {uł i··} 120 uł
s+n+k̓l̓=ip way̓ ixí? s -xʷy+lwis -c ilí? uł
Coyote well then nom -wander -3i there and
out. 12:00 *He started traveling around there*

axá? {i? təl i? təl a} [i l] snixʷtíłc̓a?s ałí? {a n} a nx̌a?x̌?ítkʷ {ta uł i s}
axá? i? l s+n+yxʷ=t=íłc̓a? -s ałí? a n+x̌a?•x̌?=ítkʷ
this art in insides -3in so art water_monster
in the insides of the sea monster,

i? sq̓ʷísəsc 121 ixí? uł cənk̓ʷəƛ̓ntís i? ma?qʷálən sənk̓líp
i? s+q̓ʷis•s -c ixí? uł c -n+k̓ʷƛ̓ -nt -is i? ma?qʷ=áln s+n+k̓l̓=ip
art fat -3in then and act -pull_out -nt -3erg art knife Coyote
[he saw] its fat. *Coyote took out the knife.*

122 i·· xi? uł {s··} ckník̓əms i? təl sq̓ʷísəs ixí? uł s?íłəns
i·· ixí? uł c -k+nik̓+m -s i? tl s+q̓ʷis•s ixí? uł s -?iłn -s
intj then and act -cut_off -3erg art from fat then and nom -eat -3i
He started cutting the fat off, and he ate it.

123 a uł axá? nq̓əmq̓əmcísəlx axá? k̓əm i? ta cxʷəl·xʷált i?
a uł axá? n+q̓m•q̓m=ci -s -lx axá? k̓m i? t c -xʷl··xʷal+t i?
intj and this wish_for -3erg -pl this except art agInst hab -alive_pl art
The people who are still alive wished

t sqilxʷ 124 {way̓} way̓ ixí? nxƛ̓íksntməlx 125 way̓ uł ixí?
t s+qilxʷ {way̓} way̓ ixí? n+xƛ̓=iks -nt -m -lx way̓ uł ixí?
agInst person {way̓} well then do_to_all -nt -psv -pl well and then
for it. *He gave each some* *and they*

sʔíɬənsəlx uɬ aɬíʔ xʷʔásq̓ət lut t̓a c̓aɬʔíɬn {ay} 126 waẏ uɬ axáʔ
s+ʔiɬn -s -lx uɬ aɬíʔ xʷʔ=asq̓t lut t̓ c -ʔaɬ•ʔíɬn waẏ uɬ axáʔ
food -3i -pl and because many_days not evid hab -eat_pl well and this
started to eat, because it's been many days since they ate. *The sea monster*

tk̓sils a nx̌aʔx̌ʔítkʷ 127 xiʔ uɬ {tkʷcəncút} cúntəm uɬ kʷ
t+k̓s=ils a n+x̌aʔ•x̌ʔ=ítkʷ ixíʔ uɬ cu -nt -m uɬ kʷ
bad_stomach art water_monster then and tell -nt -psv and 2kn
got sick to the stomach. 13:04 *He said, "What's the matter*

sc̓kinx əxʷ sənk̓líp 128 uɬ lut kən t̓a ck̓sils,
sc -ʔkin -x əxʷ s+n+k̓l̓=ip uɬ lut kn t̓ c -k̓s=ils
ipftvp^ -indef -^ipftvp intj Coyote and not 1kn negfac hab -sick_stomach
Coyote? *I don't get sick,*

kən t̓a c̓x̌íləm itíʔ put {a} anwí ik̓lí kʷ kicx 129 uɬ
kn t̓ c -ʔx̌il+m itíʔ put anwí ik̓líʔ kʷ kic+x uɬ
1kn evid hab -do_same from_that just you there 2kn arrive and
I never felt like that until you got here. *I*

q̓məntsín uɬ waẏ kən tk̓sils 130 a·· sənk̓líp lut
q̓m -nt -s -in uɬ waẏ kn t+k̓s=ils a s+n+k̓l̓=ip lut
swallow -nt -2obj -1erg and yes 1kn bad_stomach intj Coyote not
swallowed you and I am sick to the stomach." *Coyote [said],*

a {t̓i kən s} i·· kən cmaẏxtwíxʷaʔx axáʔ aláʔ 131 uɬ_i kʷu {aɬ kʷu aɬ}
a i·· kn c -m̓ay+xt+wíxʷ -aʔx axáʔ aláʔ uɬ_iʔ kʷu
intj intj 1kn ? -have_meeting -? this here and_then 1obj
"No, we are just telling stories here. *And then*

nsʕáycəntxʷ 132 i [u]ɬ ɬqmap nx̌aʔx̌ʔítkʷ 133 waẏ məɬ
n+saʕy=cn -t -xʷ i uɬ ɬ+qma+p n+x̌aʔ•x̌ʔ=ítkʷ waẏ mɬ
interrupt -nt -2erg intj and calm_again water_monster well and
you interrupt me!" *Then the sea monster quieted down.* *Then*

itlíʔ ɬkəlk̓ám (?) i təl sq̓ʷísəs 134 níkxnaʔ ilíʔ
itlíʔ ɬ+k+l̓ka+m i tl s+q̓ʷis•s níkxnaʔ ilíʔ
from_there take_again art from fat goodness there
he'd take another slab from the fat. *Gee, it's hanging*

sənuxʷuxʷínks {uɬ i uɬ i} 135 swit_aɬíʔ yaʕpqín axáʔ iʔ sc̓íɬəns 136 cut
s -n+wxʷ•xʷ=ink -s swit_aɬíʔ yaʕ+p=qín axáʔ iʔ sc -ʔiɬn -s cut
nom -hang_uneven -3i in_fact lots this art pftv -eat -3i say
down uneven. *Because he ate lots.* *The*

nx̌aʔx̌ʔit[kʷ] anwí məɬ lut_nixʷ ksíwəntəm nx̌aʔx̌ʔítkʷ 137 waẏ kʷ
n+x̌aʔ•x̌ʔ=ítkʷ anwí mɬ lut_nixʷ k -siw -nt -m n+x̌aʔ•x̌ʔ=ítkʷ waẏ kʷ
water_monster you and no_more futt^ -ask -nt -psv water_monster yes 2kn
sea-monster said:[3] *"You*

3 The sense is not clear, and the utterance seems ill-formed: anwí should govern a second person verb form, not third.

sənk̓lípəp sənk̓líp {axáʔ cut} 138 nstils axáʔ a nx̌aʔx̌ʔítkʷ way̓ {awa}
c -n+k̓l=ip•p s+n+k̓l̓=ip n+st=ils axáʔ a n+x̌aʔ•x̌ʔ=ítkʷ way̓
hab -buffoon Coyote think this art water_monster well
are coyoteing, Coyote." *The sea monster thought,*

sənk̓líp i kʷu ack̓x̌íləm[4] [kʷu ck̓x̌ílmsts] 139 way̓ sta i··
s+n+k̓l̓=ip iʔ kʷu kʷu c -k+ʔx̌il+m -st -s way̓ sta i··
Coyote art 1obj 1obj cust^ -do_so -^cust -3erg well intj intj
"It must be Coyote that is doing this to me." *So he*

p̓c̓mʕántəm sənk̓líp 140 way̓ k̓əl tətʔí··wltk ki t̓ək̓ʷək̓ʷcnítkʷ ki
p̓c̓+am -aʕnt -m s+n+k̓l̓=ip way̓ k̓l t•tʔ=iwl=tk kiʔ t̓k̓ʷ•k̓ʷ=cn=itkʷ kiʔ
squirt -nt -psv Coyote well to up_on_shore rel fall_on_shore rel
squirted Coyote out. *He fell way up on the shore,*

t̓k̓ʷak̓ʷ {a ntil} 141 way̓ nstils way̓, way̓ {a} 142 way̓ {i t} uɬ aɬí wiks
t̓k̓ʷ•ak̓ʷ way̓ n+st=ils way̓ way̓ way̓ uɬ aɬíʔ wik -s
land_flat well think well well well and so see -3erg
he fell. *He thought "Ok."* *He had seen*[5]

ilíʔ {c} a ck̓əɬxár ixíʔ i l snyxʷtíɬc̓aʔ 143 uɬ axáʔ {t} ck̓əɬxár
ilíʔ a c -k̓ɬ+xar ixíʔ iʔ l s+n+yxʷt=íɬc̓aʔ uɬ axáʔ c -k̓ɬ+xar
there art hab -curtain there art in insides and this hab -curtain
a curtain there in the inside. 15:00 *There was a curtain,*

lut {t̓a kɬ} t̓a kɬk̓ɬənk̓míp kəm̓ t̓a kɬənxənsíɬxʷtən {uɬ} 144 uɬ
lut t̓ kɬ+k̓ɬ+n+k̓m=ip km̓ t̓ kɬ+n+xn=s=iɬxʷ+tn uɬ
not evid have_door or negfac have_window and
but there was no door, or window. *And*

iwá {suɬt} siws axáʔ ilíʔ k̓əm a cxʷəl·xʷált {i} iʔ sck̓máx̌ən
iwá siw -s axáʔ ilíʔ k̓m a c -xʷl•xʷal+t iʔ sc+km̓=ax̌n
to_no_avail ask -3erg this there except art hab -alive_pl art kidnapped
he had asked the kidnapped ones that were still alive:

145 uɬ stim̓ axáʔ a ck̓əɬxár 146 cútəlx aɬíʔ uɬ lut t̓a
uɬ s+tim̓ axáʔ a c -k̓ɬ+xar cut -lx aɬíʔ uɬ lut t̓
and what this art hab -curtain say -pl so and not evid
"What is that curtain?" *They had said "We don't*

cmistím 147 uɬ aɬíʔ way̓ t̓i aláʔ kʷu iyáʕp uɬ way̓
c -my+st -im uɬ aɬíʔ way̓ t̓iʔ aláʔ kʷu y•yáʕ+p uɬ way̓
act -know -4erg and so well evid here 4kn arrive_pl and yes
know. *We got here and we saw*

wíkəntəm ilíʔ a ck̓əɬxár 148 uɬ lut t̓a cmistím stim̓
wik -nt -m ilíʔ a c -k̓ɬ+xar uɬ lut t̓ c -my+st -im s+tim̓
see -nt -4erg there art hab -curtain and not negfac act -know -4erg what
the curtain there. *We don't know*

4 Form rejected by MD.

5 In the narrative Coyote is still inside the Whale, and the best English translations are with past perfect forms.

səntím̓tən ixíʔ 149 way̓, way̓ nstils sənk̓líp 150 way̓ {tał} tałt mat
s+n+tim̓+tn ixíʔ way̓ way̓ n+st=ils s+n+k̓l̓=ip way̓ tał+t mat
storage that well well think Coyote well surely maybe
what is in there." *Coyote thought:* *"I bet that's*

ixíʔ i sckʷánx̌ən axáʔ {i} iʔ sťaʔk̓míx təl sənẏálmən 151 uł lut ť
ixíʔ iʔ sc+kʷan=x̌n axáʔ iʔ s+ťaʔk̓+míx tl s+n+yal+mn uł lut ť
that art kidnapped this art virgin from Montana and not negfac
the kidnapped one, the girl from Montana." *"I hadn't*

mipnún uł_i {kʷu i} kʷu ckəcq̓mənk{i}níłxʷs 152 [s]ta
my+p -nu -n uł_iʔ kʷu c -k+c̓q̓+mn=kn=iłxʷ -s sta
learn -manage -1erg and_then 1obj act -throw_out_of_house -3erg intj
found out and he threw me out. *I'm*

way̓ {i kc} iksksm̓aʔm̓áyəm 153 way̓ ń̓ín̓w̓iʔ x̌lítən {i}
way̓ i -ks k+s+m̓aʔ•m̓áy+m way̓ ń̓ín̓w̓iʔ x̌lit -n
well 1i -futi have_news well a_while summon -1erg
going to have to find out. 16:00 *I'll ask*

isl̓əx̌l̓áx̌t {ət xʷə} 154 way̓ ixíʔ sənk̓əwí··lxs 155 xʷu··y uł {ł}
i -s+l̓x̌•l̓ax̌+t way̓ ixíʔ s -n+k̓w+ilx -s xʷuy uł
1in -friends well then nom -go_upstream -3i go and
my partners." *He started to go up the river.* *He went and*

łənqílt t sx̌ʷnitkʷ 156 way̓ k̓li·· k̓la nʔiƛ̓tk {kʷa ixí ł} 157 ixíʔ
ł+n+qilt t s+x̌ʷn=itkʷ way̓ k̓liʔ k̓l n+ʔiƛ̓=tk ixíʔ
back_to_top obl Colville yes there to north then
got back above Kettle Falls, *way up North.* *Then*

x̌lits axáʔ iʔ sl̓əx̌l̓áx̌ts 158 way̓ cus axáʔ iʔ
x̌lit -s axáʔ iʔ s+l̓x̌•l̓ax̌+t -s way̓ cu -s axáʔ iʔ
summon -3erg this art friends -3in well tell -3erg this art
he called his partners. *He said to the*

knaqs {way̓ p xi} 159 ixíʔ ałíʔ {ə} łə ksx̌lítiʔs way̓ ixíʔ
k=naqs ixíʔ ałíʔ ł ks -x̌lít y̓ -s way̓ ixíʔ
one_person then because when fut -summon -nt -3erg well that
first one, *he was getting ready to ask,*

scuts 160 p̓əs p̓əs p̓əs p̓əs k̓ʷƛ̓up {ə k} 161 way̓ uł axáʔ
s -cut -s p̓s p̓s p̓s p̓s k̓ʷƛ̓up way̓ uł axáʔ
nom -say -3i onom onom onom onom come_out well and this
then he said: *"p̓s p̓s p̓s p̓s Come out!"* *He fell*

ťək̓ʷk̓ʷúlaʔxʷ {axáʔ iʔ} ixíʔ iʔ sxʔitx 162 uł lut səkskʷístsəlx
ťk̓ʷ•k̓ʷ=úlaʔxʷ ixíʔ iʔ s+xʔit=x uł lut s -k+s+kʷist -s -lx
fall_to_ground that art oldest_one and not nom -have_name -3i -pl
to the ground, that's the first one. *They don't have names.*

163 cúntəm [s]tim uł_iʔ kʷu ał x̌lítəntxʷ 164 lut, {ťəxʷ i}
cu -nt -m stim̓ uł_iʔ kʷu ał x̌lit -nt -xʷ lut
tell -nt -psv what and_then 1obj compl call -nt -2erg not
He said, "Why is you called me?" *"No, I am*

way̓ talí kən yaʕpcín 165 way̓ axáʔ ia nx̌aʔx̌ʔítkʷ nák̓ʷəm {axáʔ n}
way̓ taʔlíʔ kn yaʕ+p=cín way̓ axáʔ iʔ n+x̌aʔ•x̌ʔ=ítkʷ nak̓ʷ+m
yes very_much 1kn scared well this art water_monster evid
in a heap of trouble. 17:02 *This sea monster*

a nx̌aʔx̌ʔítkʷ nák̓ʷəm ixíʔ {ixíʔ ə··} nʔaɬnaʔsqílxʷtən 166 uɬ itlíʔ
a n+x̌aʔ•x̌ʔ=ítkʷ nak̓ʷ+m ixíʔ n+ʔaɬn+aʔ+s+qílxʷ+tn uɬ itlíʔ
art water_monster evid that man_eater and from_there
is a man-eater, *And*

kʷu ckəcq̓mənkńíɬxʷs 167 uɬ xʷʔi··t iʔ sckḿáx̌əns way̓ aɬíʔ
kʷu c -k+c̓q̓+mn=kn=iɬxʷ -s uɬ xʷʔi+t iʔ sc+kḿ=ax̌n -s way̓ aɬíʔ
1obj act -throw_out_of_house -3erg and many art kidnapped -3in yes so
and it threw me out of there. *There are lots he kidnapped, and some are*

ƛ̓a··xʷt 168 uɬ {k̓əm iʔ} k̓əm a xʷəl·xʷált uɬ way̓ nƛ̓xʷtílsəlx {i t} iʔ
ƛ̓axʷ+t uɬ k̓m a c -xʷl·•xʷal+t uɬ way̓ n+ƛ̓xʷ+t=ils -lx iʔ
dead_pl and except art hab -alive_pl and yes start_to_die_pl -pl art
dead; *and those that are alive are starving*

t sq̓míltən 169 uɬ ixíʔ kʷu kskənxítp kiʔ x̌lítəntəm
t s+q̓m=ilt+n uɬ ixíʔ kʷu ks -kn -xit -p kiʔ x̌lit -nt -m
agInst hunger and then 1obj futtˆ -help -xit -5erg rel call -nt -psv
to death. *And I want you to help me, that's why*

[x̌lítɬmən x̌lítntsən] 170 aɬíʔ itlíʔ kʷu
x̌lit -ɬm -n x̌lit -nt -s -n aɬíʔ itlíʔ kʷu
call -5obj -1erg call -nt -2obj -1erg because from_there 1obj
I called you. *The sea-monster*

skcq̓mənkńíɬxʷ{t}s iʔ ta nx̌aʔx̌ʔítkʷ 171 a, cúntəm way̓,
c -k+c̓q̓+mn=kn=iɬxʷ -s iʔ t n+x̌aʔ•x̌ʔ=ítkʷ a cu -nt -m way̓
act -throw_out_of_house -3erg art agInst water_monster intj tell -nt -psv well
threw me out of there." *"Ah," he said,*

way̓ ńíńw̓iʔ kənxít[mən] {s} 172 incá iʔ kʷu akɬƛ̓ʔíʔ {n w ay} 173 kən
way̓ ńíńw̓iʔ kn -xit -m -n in+cá iʔ kʷu a -kɬ -ƛ̓ʔiʔ kn
well a_while help -xit -2obj -1erg I art 1kʷu 2i -to_be -canoe 1kn
"I'll help you. 18:03 *I'll be your bark boat.* *I*

cənməlk̓ʷqín kən cənməlk̓ʷqín {axáʔ iʔ kən iʔ} axáʔ iʔ kən kɬqáqulp̓
c -n+mlk̓ʷ=qin kn c -n+mlk̓ʷ=qin axáʔ iʔ kn kɬ -qa•qw=lp̓
hab -whole_head 1kn hab -whole_head this art 1kn to_be -driftwood
will be a whole, a whole driftwood.

174 ixíʔ məɬ ilíʔ {xi akɬ} [kən] kɬmaʕítkʷ ixíʔ məɬ ixíʔ akɬənxʷúytən
ixíʔ mɬ ilíʔ kn kɬ+maʕ=ítkʷ ixíʔ mɬ ixíʔ a -kɬ -n+xʷuy+tn
that and there 1kn float then and that 2i -to_be -vehicle
It'll stay on top of the water, and I'll be your transportation."

175 cúntəm way̓ 176 way̓ itlíʔ knaqs x̌lits p̓əs p̓əs
cu -nt -m way̓ way̓ itlíʔ k=naqs x̌lit -s p̓s p̓s
tell -nt -psv OK well from_there one_person summon -3erg onom onom
He said "Ok." *"p̓s p̓s p̓s p̓s*

ṗəs ṗəs k̓ʷƛ̓up 177 waẏ t̓ək̓ʷk̓ʷúlaʔxʷ nixʷ knaqs
ṗs ṗs k̓ʷƛ̓up waẏ t̓k̓ʷ•k̓ʷ=úlaʔxʷ nixʷ k=naqs
onom onom come_out yes fall_to_ground more one_person
Come out!" *Another one fell on the ground.*

178 cúntəm waẏ uɬ {kʷu csisúykstmənct} kʷu csisúẏkstəmstxʷ
cu -nt -m waẏ uɬ kʷu c -sy•suẏ=kst+m -st -xʷ
tell -nt -psv well and 1obj cust^ -get_chilled -^cust -2erg
He said, "You are getting me chilled.

179 stiṁ uɬ anx̌mínk 180 a, cus, waẏ uɬ aɬíʔ{kən} kən
s+tiṁ uɬ an -x̌m=ink a cu -s waẏ uɬ aɬíʔ kn
what and 2in -want intj tell -3erg well and because 1kn
What is it you want?" *He said, "I am*

scyṁəṁscútx 181 waẏ axáʔ iʔ {t} ta nx̌aʔx̌ʔítkʷ kʷu
sc -yṁ•ṁ+scut -x waẏ axáʔ iʔ t n+x̌aʔ•x̌ʔ=ítkʷ kʷu
ipftvp^ -helpless -^ipftvp yes this art agInst water_monster 1obj
cornered. 19:00 *The sea-monster is going*

kspulsts. {ixíʔ uɬ i} 182 itlíʔ uɬ_i {x̌əl} x̌lítəntsən {i}
ks -pul -st -s itlíʔ uɬ_iʔ x̌lit -nt -s -n
futt^ -kill_one -st -3erg from_there and_then summon -nt -2obj -1erg
to kill me. *That's why I am calling you.*

183 kʷu kskənxítp, kspúlstəm a nx̌aʔx̌ʔítkʷ
kʷu ks -kn -xit -p ks -pul -st -m a n+x̌aʔ•x̌ʔ=ítkʷ
1obj futt^ -help -xit -5erg futt^ -kill_one -st -4erg art water_monster
I want you to help me, we will kill the sea-monster."

184 a·· waẏ, waẏ t̓əxʷ incá kən kɬn̓ínkmən uɬ ixíʔ ṅíṅwiʔ {i} kʷ
a waẏ waẏ t̓xʷ in+cá kn kɬ -ni•nk̓+mn uɬ ixíʔ ṅíṅwiʔ kʷ
intj OK OK emph I 1kn to_be -knife and that a_while 2kʷu
"I am going to be a big knife, that's the help I'm going

ikskənxítəm 185 waẏ, waẏ itlíʔ x̌lits nixʷ {iʔ} iʔ
i -ks -kn -xit -m waẏ waẏ itlíʔ x̌lit -s nixʷ iʔ
1i -futt^ -help -xit -apsv well well from_there summon -3erg more art
to give you." *The he called another*

knaqs 186 i· ṗəs ṗəs ṗəs k̓ʷƛ̓up 187 waẏ nixʷ [ix]íʔ
k=naqs i· ṗs ṗs ṗs k̓ʷƛ̓up waẏ nixʷ ixíʔ
one_person intj onom onom onom come_out well also that
one: *"ṗs ṗs ṗs [ṗs] Come out!"* *He too fell*

t̓ək̓ʷək̓ʷúlaʔxʷ 188 waẏ kʷu csisúẏkstməstxʷ stiṁ uɬ anx̌mínk
t̓k̓ʷ•k̓ʷ=úlaʔxʷ waẏ kʷu c -sy•suẏ=kst+m -nt -xʷ s+tiṁ uɬ an -x̌m=ink
fall_to_ground well 1obj cust^ -get_chilled -nt -2erg what and 2in -want
to the ground. *"You call me? What do you want,*

sənk̓líp 189 cus waẏ, waẏ t̓i k̓áwcənx 190 waẏ t̓i kʷu
s+n+k̓l̓=ip cu -s waẏ waẏ t̓iʔ k̓aw=cn -x waẏ t̓iʔ kʷu
Coyote tell -3erg well well evid quiet -isimptv yes evid 1kʷu
Coyote?" *He said to him, "Keep quiet!* *You are going*

akskənxítəm, way̓ kən ym̓mscut 191 way̓ kən
a -ks -kn -xit -m way̓ kn ym̓•m̓+scut way̓ kn
2i -futt^ -help -xit -apsv yes 1kn helpless well 1kn
to help me, I am cornered. 20:00 *I am going*

sʕacəcqənmənwíxʷxʷ iʔ k̓la nx̌aʔx̌ʔítkʷ 192 xʷʔi··t nák̓ʷəm iʔ
s -ʕac•c=qn+mnwíxʷ -xʷ iʔ k̓l n+x̌aʔ•x̌ʔ=ítkʷ xʷʔi+t nak̓ʷ+m iʔ
ipftv^ -go_head_to_head -^ipftv art at water_monster many evid art
head to head with the sea-monster. *He has lots*

sqilxʷ iʔ sckm̓áx̌əns 193 uɬ way̓ iʔ k̓ʷíƛ̓ət way̓ ɬə npaʕíw̓s iʔ
s+qilxʷ iʔ sc+km̓=ax̌n -s uɬ way̓ iʔ k̓ʷiƛ̓+t way̓ ɬ n+paʕ=íw̓s iʔ
person art kidnapped -3in and yes art rest yes ? bleached art
of people kidnapped. *The others, the bones of the dead ones*

sc̓ímsəlx iʔ ƛ̓axʷt 194 uɬ k̓im a cxʷəl·xʷált way̓ uɬ nixʷ
s+c̓im -s -lx iʔ ƛ̓axʷ+t uɬ k̓im a c -xʷl·•xʷal+t way̓ uɬ nixʷ
bone -3in -pl art dead_pl and but art hab -alive_pl yes and also
are bleached. *And the ones who are alive*

nƛ̓əxʷtíls[əlx] 195 a·· way̓, way̓ n̓ín̓w̓iʔ kənxítmən 196 way̓ nixʷ
n+ƛ̓xʷt=ils -lx a way̓ way̓ n̓ín̓w̓iʔ kn+xit -m -n way̓ nixʷ
start_to_die_pl -pl intj OK OK a_while help -2obj -1erg OK also
are dying too." *"Ok, I am going to help you.* *I'll*

incá {kənkɬ} kən kɬn̓ínk̓mən 197 cúntəm {axáʔ iʔ aɬíʔ} kʷa aɬíʔ
in+cá kn kɬ -ni•nk̓+mn cu -nt -m kʷa aɬíʔ
I 1kn to_be -knife tell -nt -psv intj because
also be a knife." *He said to him, "The sea-monster*

nx̌aʔx̌ʔítkʷ kʷa nʔaɬnaʔsqílxʷtən 198 cəm̓ n̓ín̓w̓iʔ axáʔ
n+x̌aʔ•x̌ʔ=ítkʷ kʷa n+ʔaɬn+aʔ+s+qílxʷ+tn cm̓ n̓ín̓w̓iʔ axáʔ
water_monster intj man_eater maybe a_while this
is a man-eater." *"My brother*

kpaʔsəntsís axáʔ inqíck 199 cəm̓ ixíʔ təllútət uɬ
k+paʔs -nt -s -is axáʔ in -qick cm̓ ixíʔ tl•l•ut•t uɬ
think_about -nt -2obj -3erg this 1in -older_brother maybe that fail and
will think about you. *If that doesn't work*

maʕʷt iʔ n̓ín̓k̓mən, uɬ itlíʔ incá kən kcahhám 200 cúntəm
maʕʷ+t iʔ ni•nk̓+mn uɬ itlíʔ in+cá kn k+cah•há+m cu -nt -m
break art knife and from_there I 1kn have_turn tell -nt -psv
and the [first] knife breaks, then I'll go next." 21:00 *He said*

ixíʔ way̓, a way̓ 201 way̓ itlíʔ x̌lits {iʔ} iʔ knaqs 202 way̓
ixíʔ way̓ a way̓ way̓ itlíʔ x̌lit -s iʔ k=naqs way̓
that OK intj OK well from_there summon -3erg art one_person well
"Ok." *Then he called the other one,* *he*

nixʷ ilíʔ tixʷkʷúkstəm 203 cúntəm way̓ nixʷ incá kən kɬn̓ín̓k̓əmən
nixʷ ilíʔ tixʷ+kʷú=kst+m cu -nt -m way̓ nixʷ in+cá kn kɬ -ni•nk̓+mn
also there repeat tell -nt -psv well also I 1kn to_be -knife
told him the same thing. *He said, "I'll be a knife too."*

204 ixíʔ uɬ mus, mus iʔ staʔxʷɬńíńk̓mәns iʔ {iʔ kɬ iʔ kɬ}
ixíʔ uɬ mus mus iʔ s -taʔxʷ+ɬ+ní•nk̓+mn -s iʔ
then and four four art nom -have_knives -3i art
So he's going to have

kɬkәnxcútәns 205 aɬíʔ kmúsc̓aʔ {a ixíʔ} 206 uɬ aɬíʔ
kɬ -kn+x+cut+n -s aɬíʔ k+mús=c̓aʔ uɬ aɬíʔ
to_be -help -3i because four_packages and so
four knives *because there were four bundles.*[6] *It went*

k̓әɬxiʔúsә[s] sәnk̓líp iʔ {t} t scúnmaʔs 207 a kʷmiɬ {a} wiks axáʔ
k̓ɬ+xy̓=us•s s+n+k̓l̓=ip iʔ t s+cún=maʔ -s a kʷm̓iɬ wik -s axáʔ
conform Coyote art obl account -3in intj suddenly see -3erg this
just the way they told Coyote. *He saw the driftwood,*

ia cmaʕcnítkʷ {t̓i ilíʔ cma} ilíʔ {iʔnaɬ iʔnaʔɬ} naʔɬ[7] sәʕ̓ʷx̌ʷíps 208 [ix]íʔ uɬ
iʔ c -maʕ=cn=ítkʷ ilíʔ naʔɬ s+ʕʷx̌ʷ=ip -s ixíʔ uɬ
art hab -come_to_shore there with roots -3in that and
a whole thing with its roots. 22:07 *The whole*

mat ilíʔ ntәlkʷíp uɬ {a n} a nmaʕítkʷ 209 ilíʔ cәnmәlk̓ʷqín {i ti}
mat ilíʔ n+tlkʷ=ip uɬ a n+maʕ=ítkʷ ilíʔ c -n+mlk̓ʷ=qin
maybe there uproot and art fall_in_water there hab -whole_head
thing uprooted and fell in the water, *the whole tree*

ckɬmaʕítkʷ {ilíʔ t̓i sәnq̓ʷuy} 210 wáy̓ {cut cu} cúsәlx ixíʔ {akɬ}
c -kɬ+maʕ=ítkʷ way̓ cu -s -lx ixíʔ
hab -float well tell -3erg -pl that
is in the water. *His friends said,*

akɬƛ̓ʔíʔ sәnk̓líp axá {iʔ tәs} iʔ t sl̓әx̌l̓áx̌ts 211 cuslx
a -kɬ -ƛ̓ʔiʔ s+n+k̓l̓=ip axáʔ iʔ t s+l̓x̌•l̓ax̌+t -s cu -s -lx
2i -to_be -canoe Coyote this art agInst friends -3in tell -3erg -pl
"This is your canoe, Coyote. *They told him,*

ixíʔ mɬ ilíʔ kʷ k̓amtálqʷ 212 a mәɬ ixíʔ uɬ asxәƛ̓cәnmíst
ixíʔ mɬ ilíʔ kʷ k+ʔam=t=álqʷ a mɬ ixíʔ uɬ a -s -xƛ̓=cn+mist
then and there 2kn sit_on_log intj and then and 2i -intt -say_things
"Sit on that log; *then you can say whatever you want.*

213 kswálnaʔntxʷ {nx̌aɬ} nx̌aʔx̌ʔítkʷ 214 ńíńw̓iʔ cәm̓ t̓iʔ wi··m̓ mi
ks -wál̓=naʔ -nt -xʷ n+x̌aʔ•x̌ʔ=ítkʷ ńíńw̓iʔ cm̓ t̓iʔ wim̓ mi
futt^ -talk_smart -nt -2erg water_monster a_while maybe evid in_vain fut
Talk smart to the whale. *Then the sea-monster*

nk̓sínaʔmәnts {ta n} ta nx̌aʔx̌ʔítkʷ 215 uɬ way̓ ńíńw̓iʔ
n+ks=ínaʔ+m -nt -s t n+x̌aʔ•x̌ʔ=ítkʷ uɬ way̓ ńíńw̓iʔ
angry_at -nt -3e2obj agInst water_monster and yes a_while
will get mad at you 23:01 *and then*

6 Actually three knives, because the first helper is a driftwood boat.
7 Pete pauses and says "I can't think of the roots in Indian, ah..."

ɬq̓məntsís {uɬ ixíʔ} 216 ixíʔ uɬ way̓ axáʔ {i kʷ ɬ} way̓ kʷ
ɬ+q̓m -nt -s -is ixíʔ uɬ way̓ axáʔ way̓ kʷ
swallow_again -nt -2obj -3erg then and yes this yes 2kn
he will swallow you. *And you will have*

[k]ɬnəx̌cílstən {axáʔ i l} 217 t̓əxʷ aɬíʔ t yaʕyáʕt cúsəlx {way̓ uɬ axáʔ} ixíʔ
kɬ+n+x̌c=ilst+n t̓xʷ aɬíʔ t yaʕ•yáʕ+t cu -s -lx ixíʔ
have_ready_weapon emph so agInst all tell -3erg -pl then
weapons." *They all told him,*

uɬ kənxítməmt axáʔ iʔ kʷu ṅíṅk̓mən 218 uɬ_iʔ kʷu
uɬ kn -xit -m -t axáʔ iʔ kʷu ni•nk̓+mn uɬ_iʔ kʷu
and help -xit -2obj -4erg this art 4kn knife and_then 4kʷu
"We will help you, us knives. *We are going to be*

akɬksisyústən 219 uɬ aɬíʔ lut {t̓aks} t̓a
a -kɬ -k+sy•sy=us+tn uɬ aɬíʔ lut t̓
2i -to_be -power and because not negfac
your help. *You wouldn't be capable*

aksyəʕʷpyáwt t̓i_kmix [ɬ] náṅaqs an·ínk̓mən 220 talí··
a -k -s+yaw+p•yaʕʷ+t t̓iʔ_kmix ɬ ṅá•ṅaqs an -ni•nk̓+mn taʔlíʔ
2i -to_be -power only if one_dim 2in -knife very_much
if you have just one knife. *The sea-monster*

sysyús {a} axáʔ a nx̌aʔx̌ʔítkʷ {i} 221 sc̓x̌ilx ka nʔaɬnaʔsqílxʷtən
sy•sy=us axáʔ a n+x̌aʔ•x̌ʔ=ítkʷ sc+ʔx̌il+x ka n+ʔaɬn+aʔ+s+qílxʷ+tn
smart this art water_monster reason_why rel man_eater
is very smart. *That's why he is a man-eater."*

222 way̓ ixíʔ k̓əwpmín[təm] 223 way̓ {i} yirmnúsəs sənk̓líp
way̓ ixíʔ k̓w+p+mi -nt -m way̓ yr+mn=us -s s+n+k̓l̓=ip
well then stop_asking -nt -psv well push_away -3erg Coyote
Then they quit preaching to him. *Then Coyote pushed away from shore. 24:01*

224 way̓ sk̓amtálqʷs 225 way̓ {ixíʔ s} ixíʔ skləmxqínəms,
way̓ s -k+ʔam=t=álqʷ -s way̓ ixíʔ s -k+lmx=qin+m -s
well nom -sit_on_log -3i well then nom -love_song -3i
He was sitting on the driftwood. *He started to sing a love song,*

nkʷnims 226 ixíʔ uɬ tqʷəlqʷəltínaʔs nx̌aʔx̌ʔítkʷ 227 way̓
n+kʷni+m -s ixíʔ uɬ t+qʷl•qʷl+t=ínaʔ -s n+x̌aʔ•x̌ʔ=ítkʷ way̓
sing -3erg then and insult -3erg water_monster well
and he sang. *He started to insult the sea-monster.* *He*

t̓i wi··m uɬ way̓ k̓aʔítət k̓əl sx̌ʷnítkʷ, {i s} k̓əl scixʷítkʷs 228 wi··m̓
t̓iʔ wim̓ uɬ way̓ k̓aʔít•t k̓l s+x̌ʷn=itkʷ k̓l sc+yxʷ=itkʷ -s wim̓
evid in_vain and yes get_near to Colville to water_fall -pftv in_vain
got close to the falls, Kettle Falls. *The*

sənyuʕ̓ʷlscúts nx̌aʔx̌ʔítkʷ 229 way̓ uɬ nk̓sínaʔməntəm
s -n+yʕʷ=lscut -s n+x̌aʔ•x̌ʔ=ítkʷ way̓ uɬ n+k̓s=ínaʔ+m -nt -m
pftv -control_temper -3i water_monster well and angry_at -nt -psv
sea-monster tried to control its temper. *He didn't like what Coyote*

sənk̓líp 230 aɬí? uɬ ctqʷəlqʷəltína?m 231 wa{y̓} {q̓məntím}
s+n+k̓l̓=ip aɬí? uɬ c -t+qʷl•qʷl+t=ína?+m way̓
Coyote because and hab -insult well
said, because he was giving him bad hints. He swallowed

ɬq̓məntím sənk̓líp 232 cut ʕapná? nixʷ lut t̓
ɬ+q̓m -nt -im s+n+k̓l̓=ip cut ʕapná? nixʷ lut t̓
swallow_again -nt -psv Coyote say now again not negfac
Coyote back. He said, "Now I am not going

ikɬəɬuníkstəm 233 ilí? t̓əxʷ məɬ nixʷ nƛ̓lal x̌íləm i? t k̓ʷiƛ̓t
i -kɬ -ɬwn=ikst+m ilí? t̓xʷ mɬ nixʷ n+ƛ̓l•al x̌il+m i? t k̓ʷiƛ̓+t
1i -futi -let_go_of there evidently and also drown do_like art obl rest
to let him loose again. He'll be there and die like the rest." 25:00

234 [w]ay̓ q̓məntím uɬ axá? náx̌əmɬ {i? i··ə} i? ƛ̓?i?s a
way̓ q̓m -nt -im uɬ axá? nax̌mɬ i? ƛ̓?i? -s a
yes swallow -nt -psv and this but art canoe -3in art
He didn't swallow it, the canoe,

cənməlk̓ʷqín ixí? lut náx̌əmɬ t̓ məlq̓məntím[8] 235 ixí? {ka} ak̓lá?
c -n+mlk̓ʷ=qin ixí? lut nax̌mɬ t̓ ml+q̓m -nt -im ixí? ak̓lá?
hab -whole_head that not but negfac swallow -nt -psv then here
the whole thing. He pushed it

?ax̌láqsəms 236 way̓ t̓i?_kmix sənk̓líp {i?} i? q̓məntím 237 way̓
?ax̌l=áqs+m -s way̓ t̓i?_kmix s+n+k̓l̓=ip i? q̓m -nt -im way̓
push_aside -3erg well only Coyote art swallow -nt -psv well
to one side and swallowed only Coyote. And

nt̓k̓ʷak̓ʷ sənk̓líp 238 way̓ {k̓əl} i? k̓əl sl̓əx̌l̓áx̌ts
n+t̓k̓ʷ•ak̓ʷ s+n+k̓l̓=ip way̓ i? k̓l s+l̓x̌•l̓ax̌+t -s
enter_from_side_road Coyote well art to friends -3in
Coyote fell in there, he fell back in with

nkcxiw̓s {axá? i? k̓əl s} 239 way̓ uɬ aɬí? nxʷa?xʷa?ƛ̓íɬc̓a? 240 way̓
n+k+cx=iw̓s way̓ uɬ aɬí? n+xʷa?•xʷa?ƛ̓=íɬc̓a? way̓
fall_back_in well and so have_enough_to_eat yes
his partners. They had started to pick up.[9] They

límtmsəlx tla {ɬc} ɬckícəntməlx uɬ cútəlx 241 way̓
lim+t+m -s -lx tla ɬ+c+kic -nt -m -lx uɬ cut -lx way̓
be_glad_for -3erg -pl from arrive_cisl_back -nt -psv -pl and say -pl well
were glad that he got back, and they said: "We

uɬ {kʷu ɬ} kʷu ɬ?ilxʷt 242 uɬ aɬí? t̓i {kʷu} kʷu nxʷa?xʷa?ƛ̓íɬc̓a?
uɬ kʷu ɬ+?ilxʷ+t uɬ aɬí? t̓i? kʷu n+xʷa?•xʷa?ƛ̓=íɬc̓a?
and 4kn hungry_again and so evid 4kn have_enough_to_eat
are hungry again. We were just picking up

8 ml+ of this form is indeterminate. See also ml+pul+st+m (Nams 241).
9 Because Coyote had fed them the monster's fat.

uɬ_i kʷ nis 243 uɬ way̓ uɬ kʷu ɬʔilxʷt 244 a·· way̓ {a eɬk}
uɬ_iʔ kʷ nis uɬ way̓ uɬ kʷu ɬ+ʔilxʷ+t a way̓
and_then 2kn sg_gone and yes and 4kn hungry_again intj well
when you left. *We are hungry again."* *He started*

ɬkník̓əms iʔ təl̓ sq̓ʷísəsc 245 e·· uɬ nxəƛ̓í··ksəntməlx {axáʔ uɬ e a}
ɬ+nik̓+m -s iʔ tl̓ s+q̓ʷis•s -c e uɬ n+xƛ̓=iks -nt -m -lx
cut_again -3erg art from fat -3in intj and do_to_all -nt -psv -pl
cutting some of its fat again. 26:01 *He passed it around,*

axáʔ ɬəɬtkʷúpxənsəlx ɬəɬʔaɬʔíɬnsəlx 246 way̓ [ixíʔ] txƛ̓apəlx
axáʔ ɬ -ɬ+t+kʷup=xn -s -lx ɬ -ʔaɬ•ʔíɬn -s -lx way̓ ixíʔ t+xƛ̓ap -lx
this nom -rush_again -3i -pl nom -eat_pl -3i -pl well then complete -pl
they all rushed again, and they ate again. *He passed that around,*

way̓ sənk̓líp ixíʔ uɬ {iʔ k̓əl k̓əla} iʔ k̓əl spuʔúsc {iʔ knal iʔ spuʔusc} a
way̓ s+n+k̓l̓=ip ixíʔ uɬ iʔ k̓l s+puʔ=ús -c a
well Coyote then and art to heart -3in art
and then Coyote [got] to the heart

nʔaɬnaʔsqílxʷtən iʔ t sílxʷaʔs 247 swit_aɬíʔ nʔaɬnaʔ[sqílxʷtən]
n+ʔaɬn+aʔ+s+qílxʷ+tn iʔ t sílxʷaʔ -s swit_aɬíʔ n+ʔaɬn+aʔ+s+qílxʷ+tn
man_eater art ? big -3in in_fact man_eater
of the sea-monster; it's big, *because cannibals have*

səlxʷaʔspuʔús 248 way̓ uɬ ixíʔ {uɬ s a ɬ} ck̓əɬník̓əɬts iʔ spuʔúsc
slxʷaʔ+s+puʔ=ús way̓ uɬ ixíʔ c -k̓ɬ+nik̓ -ɬt -s iʔ s+puʔ=ús -c
generous well and then act -cut_out -ɬt -3erg art heart -3in
big hearts. *He cut its heart out.*

249 way̓ uɬ t̓i ixíʔ sník̓əms iʔ t ńíńk̓mən 250 way̓ t̓i_lut {uɬ}
way̓ uɬ t̓iʔ ixíʔ s -nik̓+m -s iʔ t ni•nk̓+mn way̓ t̓iʔ_lut
well and evid then nom -cut -3i art agInst knife well in_no_time
He cut it with a knife. *Before long*

uɬ lq̓ʷəlq̓ʷíw̓s iʔ ńíńk̓mən 251 way̓, way̓ itlíʔ naqs, e itlíʔ
uɬ lq̓ʷ•lq̓ʷ=iw̓s iʔ ni•nk̓+mn way̓ way̓ itlíʔ naqs e itlíʔ
and break_in_two art knife well well from_there one intj from_there
the knife broke in two. 27:00 *Then another one, and*

məɬ k̓əɬník̓əm[s] {t̓i way̓} 252 way̓ t̓i_lu··t uɬ kɬcawts 253 lut
mɬ k̓ɬ+nik̓+m -s way̓ t̓iʔ_lut uɬ kɬ+cawt -s lut
and cut_off -3erg well in_no_time and effort -3i not
he starts cutting again. *Before he gets anything done,* *it*

stx̌uʔsúlaʔxʷs uɬ nixʷ lq̓ʷəlq̓ʷíw̓s iʔ ńíńk̓mən {way̓} 254 way̓
s -tx̌ʷ=w̓s=úlaʔxʷ -s uɬ nixʷ lq̓ʷ•lq̓ʷ=iw̓s iʔ ni•nk̓+mn way̓
nom -half_way_around -3i and also break_in_two art knife well
wasn't quite half, and the knife breaks in two again. *He*

itlíʔ naqs {ɬs} k̓ʷəƛ̓əntís {iʔ t is} 255 way̓ ixíʔ nixʷ ɬəɬník̓əms
itlíʔ naqs k̓ʷƛ̓ -nt -is way̓ ixíʔ nixʷ ɬ -ɬ+nik̓+m -s
from_there one take_off -nt -3erg well then again nom -cut_again -3i
took another from where it was fastened *and he started cutting again.*

256 way̓ t̓i? cxʷuy i? scniks̓ uɬ ixí? {s} nixʷ lq̓ʷəlq̓ʷíw̓s 257 a
way̓ t̓i? c+xʷuy i? sc -nik̓ -s uɬ ixí? nixʷ lq̓ʷ•lq̓ʷ=iw̓s a
well evid come art pftv -cut -3i and then also break_in_two intj
He kept cutting and it also broke in two. *That*

ixí? t̓əxʷ ksləq̓ʷləq̓ʷíw̓s 258 uɬ ixí? niq̓ísk̓itəm a
ixí? t̓xʷ ks -lq̓ʷ•lq̓ʷ=iw̓s -a?x uɬ ixí? n+yq̓=ísk̓it+m a
that emph incp^ -break_in_two -^incp and then grunt art
also broke in two. *The sea-monster*

nx̌a?x̌?ítkʷ 259 cúntəm uɬ a kʷ sc̓kinx ha kʷ
n+x̌a?•x̌?=ítkʷ cu -nt -m uɬ a kʷ sc -?kin -x ha? kʷ
water_monster tell -nt -psv and intj 2kn ipftvp^ -indef -^ipftvp inter 2kn
groaned. *"What is the matter with you,*

sənk̓líp 260 a i? təl kʷu kícəntxʷ {a ɬ} uɬ way̓ kən
s+n+k̓l̓=ip a i? tl kʷu kic -nt -xʷ uɬ way̓ kn
Coyote intj art from 1obj reach_st/sb -nt -2erg and yes 1kn
Coyote? *Since you got here I have been sick*

səctk̓síls 261 cúntəm t sənk̓líp lut, a t̓i kən
sc -t+k̓s=ils -x cu -nt -m t s+n+k̓l̓=ip lut a t̓i? kn
ipftvp^ -bad_stomach -^ipftvp tell -nt -psv agInst Coyote not intj evid 1kn
to my stomach." 28:04 *Coyote said, "No,*

səcɬínəmtx {uɬ a} 262 a t̓i kən scənc̓a?ř̓ínkx uɬ
sc -ɬin+mt -x a t̓i? kn sc -n+c̓a?r=ínk -x uɬ
ipftvp^ -deny -^ipftvp intj evid 1kn ipftvp^ -diarrhea -^ipftvp and
I am denying it. *I got diarrhea, and maybe that makes you*

itlí? uɬ mat {i? tk̓sil} i? kʷ tk̓sils 263 huy ixí? uɬ a? c̓iwt
itlí? uɬ mat i? kʷ t+k̓s=ils hoy ixí? uɬ a? c+?iwt
from_there and maybe art 2kn bad_stomach finish then and art last
sick to the stomach." *That's the last*

i? ṅínk̓mən {way̓ t̓i wiṁ uɬ} 264 nx̌a?x̌?ítkʷ nstils {way̓ way̓ kən} 265 way̓
i? ni•nk̓+mn n+x̌a?•x̌?=ítkʷ n+st=ils way̓
art knife water_monster think well
knife. *The sea-monster thought:* *"This*

way̓ t̓i iksənk̓əstmínəm 266 way̓ t̓i? {kən ks} kən ksƛ̓llmíxa?x
way̓ t̓i? i -ks -n+k̓s+t+min+m way̓ t̓i? kn ks -ƛ̓l•l -míx+a?x
well evid 1i -futi -fall_ill well evid 1kn incp^ -dead -^incp
is not good for me, *I am going to die.*

267 way̓ kən kɬəɬxʷúya?x {k̓l is} k̓ intəmxʷúla?xʷ 268 ik̓lí? mi kən
way̓ kn k -ɬɬ+xʷuy -a?x k̓ in -tmxʷ=úla?xʷ ik̓lí? mi kn
well 1kn incp^ -go_home -^incp to 1in -country there fut 1kn
I am going back to my country. *There I'll doctor*

mrimst a mi kən ɬx̌əstwílx 269 uɬ axá {i? k̓əl} i? k̓əl sílxʷa? i? k̓əl
mrim+st a mi kn ɬ+x̌s+t+wilx uɬ axá? i? k̓l sílxʷa? i? k̓l
doctor intj fut 1kn get_well_again and this art to big art to
myself, and then I'll get well, 29:00 *there at the*

siwłkʷ 270 i caʔkʷ cus i ta nuyápəxcən *ocean*
siwł=kʷ i caʔkʷ cu -s i t n+wyap=x=cn
water intj as tell -3erg intj agInst say_in_English
big water." *They call it "ocean" in the white man's language.*

271 i ik̓líʔ {kən ł kən ł} kən łkicx i·· kən łx̌əstwílx, kən mrimst
i ik̓líʔ kn ł+kic+x i·· kn ł+x̌s+t+wilx kn mrim+st
intj there 1kn arrive_again intj 1kn get_well_again 1kn doctor
"I'm going back there, there I'll get well, I'll doctor myself."

272 way̓ ixíʔ uł sənʔáx̌ʷts, xʷuy, 273 uł axáʔ ałíʔ nałcəcám
way̓ ixíʔ uł s -n+ʔax̌ʷ+t -s xʷuy uł axáʔ ałíʔ nałc•c•ám
well then and nom -downriver -3i go and this because forget
Then he went downstream. *He went... I thought of something.*

274 sənk̓líp {ki t} təl sl̓əx̌l̓áx̌ts uł ixíʔ xʷíc̓xtsəlx t {kł}
s+n+k̓l̓=ip tl s+l̓x̌•l̓ax̌+t -s uł ixíʔ xʷic̓ -xt -s -lx t
Coyote from friends -3in and then give -xit -3erg -pl obj_tr
His friends gave Coyote something to make

kłnirk̓ʷíptəns 275 aʔ sílxʷaʔ {iʔ s} iʔ scyark̓ʷs iʔ sx̌əx̌c̓íʔ
kł -n+yrk̓ʷ=ip+tn -s aʔ sílxʷaʔ iʔ sc -yark̓ʷ -s iʔ s+x̌•x̌c̓iʔ
to_be -hoop -3i intj big art pftv -crooked -3i art stick
a hoop with, *a stick's big hoop.*

276 cúntəm ńíńw̓iʔ ł kswílqəntxʷ ł pulstxʷ a
cu -nt -m ńíńw̓iʔ ł ks -wil=qn -t -xʷ ł pul -st -xʷ a
tell -nt -psv a_while if futtˆ -have_chance -nt -2erg if kill -st -2erg art
They said to him, "If you get a chance to kill

nʔałnaʔsqílxʷtən 277 ł ƛ̓əllnúntxʷ, uł {lut} lúti ksƛ̓lals
n+ʔałn+aʔ+s+qílxʷ+tn ł ƛ̓l•l -nu -nt -xʷ uł lút+i ks -ƛ̓l•al -s
man_eater if dead -manage -nt -2erg and before futi -dead -3i
the man-eater, *to kill him, before he dies*

278 uł ixíʔ k̓əl ʔawtíłc̓aʔs ńíńw̓iʔ ilíʔ mi kłnirk̓ʷípəntxʷ
uł ixíʔ k̓l s+ʔawt=íłc̓aʔ -s ńíńw̓iʔ ilíʔ mi k̓ł+n+yrk̓ʷ=ip -nt -xʷ
and then to back_side -3in a_while there fut put_hoop -nt -2erg
put the hoop to his hind part. 30:03

279 ixíʔ uł_iʔ {iʔ} kłxəwíłəmp itíʔ məł p ʔácəcqaʔ {iʔ} 280 way̓
ixíʔ uł_iʔ kł -xwił -mp itíʔ mł p ʔác•c•qaʔ way̓
that and_then to_be -road -5i from_that and 5kn go_out_pl well
That will be your way to get out, and you will get out." *Then*

t̓i_wim̓ axáʔ nʔałnaʔsqílxʷtən uł axáʔ {t} xiʔwílx t *Coulee Dam* [ntqiw̓s]
t̓iʔ_wim̓ axáʔ n+ʔałn+aʔ+s+qílxʷ+tn uł axáʔ xy̓+wílx t n+tq=iw̓s
powerless this man_eater and this pass_by obl dam
the man-eater went by Coulee Dam.

281 uł ałíʔ mat cnuyápxcn[əm] t sənk̓líp 282 uł way̓
uł ałíʔ mat c -n+wyap=x=cn+m t s+n+k̓l̓=ip uł way̓
and so maybe hab -speak_English agInst Coyote and yes
I suppose Coyote can talk English *and he*

cmistís Coulee Dam {ut}
c -my -st -is
cust^ -know -^cust -3erg
knew Coulee Dam.

283 ixí? ití? uɬ axá?
ixí? ití? uɬ axá?
that from_that and this
There is a dam

cəntqíw̓s,
c -n+tq=iw̓s
hab -dam
there, 31:24

284 ití? uɬ way̓ lut ksk̓əɬkícxs i? k̓əl {si}
ití? uɬ way̓ lut ks -k̓ɬ+kic+x -s i? k̓l
from_that and well not futi -manage_to_arrive -3i art to
he'll never reach

sílxʷa? i? siwɬkʷ
sílxʷa? i? siwɬ=kʷ
big art water
the ocean,

285 ixí? {k̓əl s} i? k̓əl háspitəls [sənq̓əltíɬxʷtəns]
ixí? i? k̓l háspitl -s s+n+q̓l+t=iɬxʷ+tn -s
then art to hospital -3in hospital -3in
his hospital.

286 a uɬ atá? mi kstɬúla?xʷa?x
a uɬ atá? mi ks -tɬ=úla?xʷ -a?x
intj and here fut incp^ -shortcut -^incp
He is going to take a shortcut

287 way̓ ixí? mi k̓əɬkícx
way̓ ixí? mi k̓ɬ+kic+x
well then fut manage_to_arrive
to make it.

288 way̓ ití? tɬúla?xʷəm uɬ aɬí? ití? siwɬkʷ tyap
way̓ ití? tɬ=úla?xʷ+m uɬ aɬí? ití? siwɬ=kʷ tya+p
well from_that take_shortcut and so from_that water water_runs
He went straight and the water ran through.

289 way̓,
way̓
well
He

way̓ put miw̓súla?xʷ ixí? uɬ k̓əɬk̓ət̓pnúɬtəm t sənk̓líp {i?s}
way̓ put miw̓s=úla?xʷ ixí? uɬ k̓ɬ+k̓t̓+p -nu -ɬt -m t s+n+k̓l̓=ip
well just half_way then and manage_to_cut -manage -ɬt -psv agInst Coyote
was just half way when Coyote cut off

i? spu?úsc
i? s+pu?=ús -c
art heart -3in
his heart. 32:00

290 way̓ uɬ ilí? uɬ ƛ̓lal a n?aɬna?sqílxʷtən
way̓ uɬ ilí? uɬ ƛ̓l•al a n+?aɬn+a?+s+qílxʷ+tn
well and there and dead art man_eater
The man-eater died there.

291 way̓ {uɬ axá? ixí?} ixí? aɬí? ksƛ̓əlmíxa?x
way̓ ixí? aɬí? ks -ƛ̓l -míx+a?x
well then so incp^ -dead -^incp
And just before he died

292 ixí? {uɬ ə}
ixí?
then
Coyote

k̓əɬnirk̓ʷíps sənk̓líp axá? {i? i? s} i? sən?ácqa?təns
k̓ɬ+n+yrk̓ʷ=ip -s s+n+k̓l̓=ip axá? i? s+n+?ácqa?+tn -s
place_hoop -3erg Coyote this art anus -3in
put that hoop there in the sea-monster's

n?aɬna?sqílxʷtən {ixí? uɬ}
n+?aɬn+a?+s+qílxʷ+tn
man_eater
back side.

293 ixí? uɬ ƛ̓lal
ixí? uɬ ƛ̓l•al
then and dead
And then he died.

294 uɬ aɬí? t̓i ƛ̓lal uɬ
uɬ aɬí? t̓i? ƛ̓l•al uɬ
and so evid dead and
And as soon as he died

axá? {i?} i? siwɬkʷ {ɬc ɬc} ɬcənwíwpəm
axá? i? siwɬ=kʷ ɬ+c+n+wi•wp+m
this art water back_up_again
the water backed up

295 uɬ ɬxʷuy i? t
uɬ ɬ+xʷuy i? t
and go_back art obl
and went back to where

sxʷúytəns 296 ixí? uɬ axá? ɬx̌əw̓úla?xʷ {axá? i? ixí? uɬ way̓ cúntməlx ax cən}
s+xʷuy+tn -s ixí? uɬ axá? ɬ+x̌w̓=úla?xʷ
track -3in then and this dry_land_again
it was running *and the river went dry. [end of tape] 32:48*

297 way̓ ixí? u[ɬ] t̓əxʷ itlí? iscnc̓əpq̓síw̓səm axá? i? t
way̓ ixí? uɬ t̓xʷ itlí? i -sc -n+c̓pq̓+s=iw̓s+m axá? i? t
well then and emph from_there 1i -pftv -splice this art obj_itr
I continue

incaptíkʷɬ 298 ixí? t cun, axá? ƛ̓lal a nx̌a?x̌?ítkʷ 299 uɬ
in -captíkʷɬ ixí? t cu -n axá? ƛ̓l•al a n+x̌a?•x̌?=ítkʷ uɬ
1in -legends that obl tell -1erg this dead art water_monster and
my story. *Like I said, the monster from the ocean is dead* *and*

axá? {s¨} sənk̓líp way̓ wi?sk̓ɬirk̓ʷíps i? k̓əl {s¨} s?awtíɬc̓a?s
axá? s+n+k̓l̓=ip way̓ wy̓+s+k̓ɬ+yrk̓ʷ=ip -s i? k̓l s+?awt=íɬc̓a? -s
this Coyote yes finish_putting_hoop -3erg art to back_side -3in
Coyote already put a hoop around the

axá? a nx̌a?x̌?ítkʷ 300 ixí? uɬ cus axá? {i?} i? sqilxʷ,
axá? a n+x̌a?•x̌?=ítkʷ ixí? uɬ cu -s axá? i? s+qilxʷ
this art water_monster then and tell -3erg this art person
whale's back-end. *He said to the people,*

xʷúywi, ?ácəcqa?wi 301 p xʷəsxʷúsəlx, pna {kʷu} kʷu pən̓n̓híw̓s
xʷuy -wy ?ác+cqa? -wy p xʷs•xʷus+lx pna? kʷu pn•n•h=iw̓s
go -ipimptv go_out_pl -ipimptv 5kn hurry maybe 4kn be_caught
"Go on, get out. *We might get caught."*

302 way̓ ixí? s?ácəcqa?səlx axá? 303 ?á¨cəcqa?lx {uɬ} uɬ
way̓ ixí? s -?ác•c•qa? -s -lx axá? ?ác•c•qa? -lx uɬ
well then nom -go_out_pl -3i -pl this go_out_pl -pl and
They all got out. *They all went out,*

təxƛ̓ápəlx 304 ixí? way̓ kstxəƛ̓pmíxa?x uɬ c̓iwt axá?
t+xƛ̓a+p -lx ixí? way̓ ks -t+xƛ̓+p -míx+a?x uɬ c+?iwt axá?
complete -pl then well incp^ -complete -^incp and last this
the whole bunch. *It was going to be all of them, and Woodtick is the last*

kək̓c̓ílxkən 305 put miw̓s kək̓c̓ílxkən ki? {ya?x̌í} x̌ʷc̓ap {i?} i?
k+k̓c̓+ilx=kn put miw̓s k+k̓c̓+ilx=kn ki? x̌ʷc̓a+p i?
woodtick just middle woodtick rel break_in_two art
of them. 1:11 *Woodtick was half-way out when that hoop*

k̓ɬnirk̓ʷíptən 306 way̓, way̓ kíp̓u?səntəm k̓c̓ílxkən {na} 307 way̓
k̓ɬ+n+yrk̓ʷ=ip+tn way̓ way̓ kip̓=w̓s -nt -m k̓c̓+ilx=kn way̓
hoop well well pinch_middle -nt -psv woodtick yes
broke. *It pinched Woodtick right in the center.* *He*

kɬcawt {ki?} ki ?ácəcqa?i?st ixí? uɬ aɬí? txƛ̓ápəlx 308 aɬí?m
kɬ+cawt ki? ?ác•c•qa?=i?st ixí? uɬ aɬí? t+xƛ̓ap -lx aɬí?+m
effort rel manage_to_get_out then and because complete -pl because
had a hard time before he got out because he was the last one. *First*

axáʔ la_cxʔítiʔ {ta} sənkl̓íp 309 ixíʔ axáʔ ksíwplaʔs ixíʔ {ac} a
axáʔ la_c+xʔít+iʔ s+n+kl̓=ip ixíʔ axáʔ k+síw=plaʔ -s ixíʔ a
this at_first Coyote then this ask_about -3erg that art
Coyote *inquired about another part,*

nəqsíɬc̓aʔ ixíʔ {a c} a cənxáȓuʔs axáʔ la nx̌aʔx̌ʔítkʷ 310 uɬ t̓i
nqs=íɬc̓aʔ ixíʔ a c -n+xar=ẁs axáʔ l n+x̌aʔ•x̌ʔ=ítkʷ uɬ t̓iʔ
one_room that art hab -curtain this in water_monster and evid
the curtain, in the whale.[10] *It's*

iʔ {s··} nəqsíɬc̓aʔ ixíʔ 311 uɬ ixíʔ ksíwplaʔs axáʔ iʔ l sqilxʷ iʔ
iʔ nqs=íɬc̓aʔ ixíʔ uɬ ixíʔ k+síw=plaʔ -s axáʔ iʔ l s+qilxʷ iʔ
art one_room that and then ask_about -3erg this art with person art
another part, 2:02 *and he inquired about it of those people*

l sckṁáx̌ən 312 uɬ xiʔ cútəlx mat aɬíʔ uɬ lut t̓a
l sc+kṁ=ax̌n uɬ ixíʔ cut -lx mat aɬíʔ uɬ lut t̓
with kidnapped and then say -pl maybe so and not evid
kidnapped. *And they told him, "We haven't*

cwíkstəm 313 waẏ t̓i aláʔ kʷu yaʕp ixíʔ uɬ waẏ ilíʔ
c -wik -st -m waẏ t̓iʔ aláʔ kʷu yaʕ+p ixíʔ uɬ waẏ ilíʔ
cust^ -see -^cust -4erg well evid here 4kn arrive_pl then and yes there
seen anything; *we've been here, what we saw is*

scwíkəmtət 314 waẏ mat ixíʔ snəqsíɬc̓aʔ 315 ixíʔ uɬ_iʔ ckʷis
sc -wik+m -tt waẏ mat ixíʔ s+nqs=íɬc̓aʔ ixíʔ uɬ_iʔ c+kʷi -s
pftv -see -4i well maybe that room then and_then take -3erg
here." *I guess that's another part.* *That's when he took*

iʔ ṅíṅk̓ṁəṅs 316 ixíʔ {c} [s]ənk̓ríẁsəs {iʔ axáʔ iʔ} ixíʔ a nəqsíɬc̓aʔ
iʔ ṅi•ṅk̓+ṁṅ -s ixíʔ s -n+k̓r=iẁs -s ixíʔ a nqs=íɬc̓aʔ
art knife -3in then nom -cut_open -3i that irt one_room
his knife, *and cut wide open that part.*

317 uɬ aɬíʔ mat {s··} sútən, síp̓iʔ kəṁ mat stiṁ 318 lut t̓
uɬ aɬíʔ mat sutn síp̓iʔ kṁ mat s+tiṁ lut t̓
and because maybe thing hide or maybe something not negfac
I guess it's just skin, or something, *that curtain*

spapík axáʔ {i} ia nxáȓuʔs 319 waẏ nt̓a qʷámqʷəmt iʔ st̓aʔk̓míx ilíʔ a
s+pa•pík axáʔ iʔ n+xar=ẁs waẏ nt̓a qʷam•qʷm+t iʔ s+t̓aʔk̓+míx ilíʔ a
board this art curtain well intj excellent art virgin there art
is not board. *A beautiful girl was sitting*

naʔmút 320 ik̓líʔ k̓əɬnʔaɬxʷíps uɬ ixíʔ siws 321 cus
n+ʔam=út ik̓líʔ k̓ɬ+n+ʔaɬxʷ=íp -s uɬ ixíʔ siw -s cu -s
sit_inside there go_in -3erg and then ask -3erg tell -3erg
there. *He went in there and asked her:* *"Why is it*

10 Pete is backtracking and fills in.

sc̓kinx uɬ aláʔ iʔ kʷ əɬ mut 322 cúntəm way, waẏ kʷ
sc+ʔkin+x uɬ aláʔ iʔ kʷ ɬ mut cu -nt -m waẏ waẏ kʷ
why_is_it and here art 2kn subord sit_sg tell -nt -psv well yes 2kn
that you are sitting here?" 3:00 *She said, "You talk*

nqʷəṅqʷəṅcín 323 tla lkʷu··t intəmxʷúlaʔxʷ 324 itlíʔ ki kʷu
n+qʷṅ•qʷṅ=cin tla lkʷ=ut in -tmxʷ=úlaʔxʷ itlíʔ kiʔ kʷu
talk_pitifully from far 1in -country from_there rel 1obj
pitiful. *I come from long ways away.* *It's from there that*

ckʷanx̌s {sic} axáʔ iʔ ta nx̌aʔx̌ʔítkʷ 325 aláʔ uɬ aláʔ iʔ kʷu
c -kʷan=x̌ -s axáʔ iʔ t n+x̌aʔ•x̌ʔ=ítkʷ aláʔ uɬ aláʔ iʔ kʷu
act -kidnap -3erg this art agInst water_monster here and here art 1obj
this here whale kidnapped me, *he got me prisoner*

alk̓əntís {aha··} 326 cúntəm waẏ waẏ cmistín yaʕyáʕt axáʔ
lk̓ -nt -is cu -nt -m waẏ waẏ c -my -st -in yaʕ•yáʕ+t axáʔ
tie -nt -3erg tell -nt -psv yes yes cust^ -know -^cust -1in all this
in here." *He said, "I know everything*

cmalk̓ʷ axáʔ iʔ təmxʷúlaʔxʷ 327 huhúy t̓əxʷ ʔúmlaʔxʷənt
c -malk̓ʷ axáʔ iʔ tmxʷ=úlaʔxʷ hu+húy t̓xʷ ʔúm=laʔxʷ -nt
hab -entire this art land Ok emph call_a_place -nt
in the world. *Name*

antəmxʷúlaʔxʷ 328 uɬ waẏ ṅíṅẉiʔ {mip} mipnún 329 cut
an -tmxʷ=úlaʔxʷ uɬ waẏ ṅíṅẉiʔ my+p -nu -n iʔ cut
2in -country and yes a_while learn -manage -1erg art say
your country. *I will know the name."* *She*

waẏ, təl̓ sənẏál̓mənx, itlíʔ {kən ɬ} kən ɬ sqilxʷ 330 itlíʔ ki
waẏ tl̓ s+n+yal̓+mn=x itlíʔ kn ɬ s+qilxʷ itlíʔ kiʔ
well from Montana from_there 1kn one_that Indian from_there rel
said "From Montana, I am an Indian from there. *That's where*

kʷu ckʷanx̌s axáʔ iʔ ta nʔaɬnaʔsqílxʷtən, a[xáʔ] iʔ ta
kʷu c -kʷan=x̌ -s axáʔ iʔ t n+ʔaɬn+aʔ+s+qílxʷ+tn axáʔ iʔ t
1obj act -kidnap -3erg this art agInst man_eater this art agInst
he kidnapped me, this here cannibal,

nx̌aʔx̌ʔítkʷ. 331 a·· cúntəm waẏ waẏ ixíʔ
n+x̌aʔ•x̌ʔ=ítkʷ a cu -nt -m waẏ waẏ ixíʔ
water_monster intj tell -nt -psv yes yes that
the Whale." *He said, "Well, yes, I know*

cminúlaʔxʷstən 332 ixíʔ itíʔ kən cxʷilwís
c -my+n=úlaʔxʷ -st -n ixíʔ itíʔ kn c -xʷy+lwis
cust^ -know_the_country -^cust -1erg that from_that 1kn hab -wander
that country. 4:03 *I've been through there*

uɬ {cmiɬ} cmistín asnəqsílxʷ ixíʔ antəmxʷúlaʔxʷ
uɬ c -my -st -in a -s+nqs=ilxʷ ixíʔ an -tmxʷ=úlaʔxʷ
and cust^ -know -^cust -1erg 2in -relative that 2in -country
and I know your people and your country."

333 ixíʔ uɬ {iʔ} cúntəm {xʷuy kʷa} cxʷuyx ixíʔ uɬ {kʷu} kʷu ʔácəcqaʔ
ixíʔ uɬ cu -nt -m c+xʷuy -x ixíʔ uɬ kʷu ʔác•c•qaʔ
then and tell -nt -psv come -isimptv then and 4kn go_out_pl
So he said, “Come on, let's get out

334 ixíʔ uɬ ɬʔúkʷəntsən k̓əl antəmxʷúlaʔxʷ 335 way̓ ixíʔ
ixíʔ uɬ ɬ+ʔukʷ -nt -s -n k̓l an -tmxʷ=úlaʔxʷ way̓ ixíʔ
then and take_back -nt -2obj -1erg to 2in -country well then
and then I'll take you back to your country.” He

ctkʷínksəs {uɬ iʔ} uɬ_iʔ {cu} cúntəm axáʔ iʔ t tkəɬmílxʷ iʔ t
c -t+kʷin=ks -s uɬ_iʔ cu -nt -m axáʔ iʔ t tkɬmilxʷ iʔ t
act -take_by_hand -3erg and_then tell -nt -psv this art agInst woman art agInst
took her by the hand, and the woman, the virgin

st̓aʔk̓míx 336 cúntəm {uɬ} uɬ axáʔ {in} nʔaɬnaʔsqílxʷtən axáʔ uɬ lut
s+t̓aʔk̓+míx cu -nt -m uɬ axáʔ n+ʔaɬn+aʔ+s+qílxʷ+tn axáʔ uɬ lut
virgin tell -nt -psv and this man_eater this and not
said to him, she said, “And this here monster, don't you think

ha kʷu ksƛ̓əxʷəntím {stut} 337 staʔ, lut, staʔk way̓ ƛ̓lal,
haʔ kʷu ks -ƛ̓xʷ -nt -im staʔ lut staʔk way̓ ƛ̓l•al
inter 3e4obj futt^ -kill_many -nt -3e4obj intj not intj yes dead
he'll kill us?” “Why no, he's already dead,

cqʷəńcínməstxʷ ɬ kɬxʷəlxʷálts 338 huy xʷustx
c -qʷń=cin+m -st -xʷ ɬ k -ɬ+xʷl•xʷal+t -s hoy xʷus+t -x
cust^ -pity -^cust -2erg subord futi -alive_again -3i well hurry -isimptv
pity him, he'll not come to life. Hurry.”

339 way̓ ixíʔ sic stkxənməncúts 340 way̓ [u]ɬ xʷəsxʷúsəlx, aɬíʔ
way̓ ixíʔ sic s -t+kx+n+mncut -s way̓ uɬ xʷs•xʷus+lx aɬíʔ
well then then nom -follow -3i well and hurry so
And then she followed him. They hurried, and they

ʔácəcqaʔləx 341 aɬí ʔá··cəcqaʔləx, {uɬ naɬ} ixíʔ uɬ_iʔ {i} ʔiwt kək̓ċílxkən
ʔác•c•qaʔ -lx aɬíʔ ʔác•c•qaʔ -lx ixíʔ uɬ_iʔ ʔiwt k+k̓ċ+ilx=kn
go_out_pl -pl so go_out_pl -pl then and_then behind woodtick
went out. 5:00 They went out and that's when Woodtick got behind,

342 uɬ axáʔ {iʔ} iʔ maʕʷt axáʔ {iʔ} iʔ k̓ɬnirk̓ʷíptən 343 way̓ uɬ_iʔ
uɬ axáʔ iʔ maʕʷ+t axáʔ iʔ k̓ɬ+n+yrk̓ʷ=ip+tn way̓ uɬ_iʔ
and this art break this art hoop yes and_then
and that's when that hoop broke. Then he got

k̓íp̓əp 344 way̓ kɬcawt {ki} ki {ʔácəcqaʔ} ʔacəcqaʔíʔst {kək̓ċilx} kək̓ċílxkən
k̓ip̓•p̓ way̓ kɬ+cawt kiʔ ʔac•c•qaʔ=íʔst k+k̓ċ+ilx=kn
pinched well effort rel struggle_to_exit woodtick
pinched. Woodtick had an awful time before he got out.

345 sċx̌ilx uɬ_iʔ ʕapnáʔ iʔ wíkəntp iʔ kək̓ċílxkən uɬ t̓iʔ pəpí··l̓
sc+ʔx̌il+x uɬ_iʔ ʕapnáʔ iʔ wik -nt -p iʔ k+k̓ċ+ilx=kn uɬ t̓iʔ p•pil̓
that's_why and_then now art see -nt -5erg art woodtick and evid flat
That's why if you see Woodtick today he is flat.

346 uɬ aɬ[íʔ] ixíʔ sk̓íp̓əp̓x ixíʔ ki ilíʔ, ilíʔ x̌íləm
uɬ aɬíʔ ixíʔ s -k̓ip̓•p̓ -x ixíʔ kiʔ ilíʔ ilíʔ x̌il+m
and because there ipftv^ -pinched -^ipftv that rel there there do_like
Because he got pinched there, that's how it happened.

347 hoy axáʔ {s} kəlkʷákʷəlx uɬ ixíʔ {s"} cúntəm t sənk̓líp axáʔ iʔ
hoy axáʔ k+lkʷ•akʷ -lx uɬ ixíʔ cu -nt -m t s+n+k̓l̓=ip axáʔ iʔ
well this far -pl and then tell -nt -psv agInst Coyote this art
After they went a ways, Coyote said to

st̓aʔk̓míx 348 cúntəm way̓ t̓əxʷ anwí {m}
s+t̓aʔk̓+míx cu -nt -m way̓ t̓xʷ anwí
virgin tell -nt -psv well evidently you
the girl, *he said, "Well, you know*

cminúlaʔxʷstxʷ antəmxʷúlaʔxʷ 349 uɬ {i} t̓i
c -myn=úlaʔxʷ -st -xʷ an -tmxʷ=úlaʔxʷ uɬ t̓iʔ
cust^ -know_the_country -^cust -2erg 2in -country and evid
the way to your country. 6:00 *As long as*

kstəɬtáɬts iʔ kscxʷúytət 350 lut {kʷu ks} kʷu kstxəlxa·lkáqs
ks -tɬ•taɬ+t -s iʔ ksc -xʷuy -tt lut kʷu ks -t+xl•xa·lk=áqs
futi -straight -3i art futPerfi -go -4i not 4kn ? -go_around_curves
we go the right way, *we won't go around curves,*

t̓i way̓ t̓i kʷ tɬúlaʔxʷəm 351 cúntəm axáʔ iʔ t st̓aʔk̓míx
t̓iʔ way̓ t̓iʔ kʷ tɬ=úlaʔxʷ+m cu -nt -m axáʔ iʔ t s+t̓aʔk̓+míx
evid well evid 2kn take_shortcut tell -nt -psv this art agInst virgin
you go straight." *The virgin said to him:*

352 wáy̓, way̓ cminúlaʔxʷstən, səwít_aɬíʔ intəmxʷúlaʔxʷ {uɬ}
way̓ way̓ c -my+n=úlaʔxʷ -st -n swit_aɬíʔ in -tmxʷ=úlaʔxʷ
yes yes cust^ -know_the_country -^cust -1erg in_fact 1in -country
"Yes, yes, I know the way, because it's my country.

353 uɬ náx̌əmɬ {maʔ} kʷ iscúnəm, way̓ pna cəm̓ kʷ ʔayx̌ʷt
uɬ nax̌mɬ kʷ i -s -cun+m way̓ pnaʔ cm̓ kʷ ʔayx̌ʷ+t
and but 2kʷu 1in -intt -tell well maybe maybe 2kn tired
But let me tell you, if you get tired

354 way̓ t̓i x̌ast ɬ q̓ʷíɬtməntsən 355 cúntəm axáʔ iʔ t
way̓ t̓iʔ x̌as+t ɬ q̓ʷiɬ+t+m -nt -s -n cu -nt -m axáʔ iʔ t
yes evid good if carry -nt -2obj -1erg tell -nt -psv this art agInst
it's better if I pack you on my back." *That's what the girl*

st̓aʔk̓míx sənk̓líp 356 kʕʷəyncútəms axáʔ {iʔ} iʔ st̓aʔk̓míx t
s+t̓aʔk̓+míx s+n+k̓l̓=ip k+ʕʷy+ncut+m -s axáʔ iʔ s+t̓aʔk̓+míx t
virgin Coyote laugh_at -3erg this art virgin agInst
said to Coyote. *Coyote laughed at the girl,*

sənk̓líp, kʕʷəyncútməntəm 357 cúntəm uɬ ha kʷ
s+n+k̓l̓=ip k+ʕʷy+ncut+m -nt -m cu -nt -m uɬ haʔ kʷ
Coyote laugh_at -nt -psv tell -nt -psv and inter 2kn
he laughed at her. *He said "What are*

səsc̓íntx 358 a kən sqəltmíxʷ a 359 ʕapná {a kʷ} kʷ
ss -c̓int -x a kn s+qlt=mixʷ a ʕapnáʔ kʷ
pftv -say_what -^ipftvp intj 1kn man intj now 2kn
you saying? I am a man. You are

ctəkłmílxʷ {unint} kʷu ł cq̓ʷíłtməstxʷ 360 mátəm {kən}
c -tkł+m=ilxʷ kʷu ł c -q̓ʷił+t+m -st -xʷ mat+m
hab -woman 1obj subord cust^ -carry -^cust -2erg maybe
the woman, and you'd be packing me! It's because

t isisyús {ki} kiʔ kaʔkícəntsən 361 incá iʔ kʷu
t i -sy•sy=us kiʔ kaʔ•kíc -nt -s -n in+cá iʔ kʷu
agInst 1in -smart rel find -nt -2obj -1erg I art 1obj
I am smart that I found you. 7:02 It's your parents

ckʷulsts[11] [t] anƛ̓ax̌əx̌ƛ̓x̌áp {ikə} ki sƛ̓aʔƛ̓aʔntsín
c -kʷulst -s t an -ƛ̓ax̌•x̌•ƛ̓x̌á+p kiʔ c -ƛ̓aʔ•ƛ̓aʔ -nt -s -in
act -send -3erg agInst 2in -elders rel act -look_for -nt -2obj -1erg
that sent me over here and that's why I looked for you.

362 uł ha kʷu ł q̓ʷəłtəlwístxʷ 363 t incá iʔ kʷ
uł haʔ kʷu ł q̓ʷł+t+lwis -t -xʷ t in+cá iʔ kʷ
and inter 1obj subord pack_around -st -2erg agInst I art 2kʷu
And then you'd pack me around? I should be

ikscq̓ʷíłtəm 364 a·· cúntəm wa̓y, huhúy, kʷa huhúy
i -ksc -q̓ʷił+t -m a cu -nt -m wa̓y hu+húy kʷa hu+húy
1i -futPerfi -pack_on_back -apsv intj tell -nt -psv well OK intj OK
packing you." He said, "Let's go,

kʷu təkʷʔút {xi a s·· i sc} 365 xʷət̓t̓pnúmt axáʔ iʔ tkəłmílxʷ iʔ st̓aʔk̓míx
kʷu tkʷʔ=ut xʷt̓•t̓+p+numt axáʔ iʔ tkłmilxʷ iʔ s+t̓aʔk̓+míx
4kn walk_pl get_up this art woman art virgin
let's walk." The woman jumped up.

366 a k̓ʷull̓ t st̓mʕált, q̓ʷəyq̓ʷʕáy t st̓mʕált {e} 367 nwísəlxsts
a k̓ʷul•l̓ t s+t̓m=ʕalt q̓ʷy•q̓ʷaʕy t s+t̓m=ʕalt n+wis+lx -st -s
intj turn_into obl cow black obl cow raise -st -3erg
She turned into a cow, a Buffalo cow. She raised

iʔ siyúpsc, uł [ix]íʔ sqáqcəlxs 368 eh sənk̓líp atáʔ
iʔ sy=ups -c uł ixíʔ s -qa•qc+lx -s eh s+n+k̓l̓=ip atáʔ
art tail -3in and then nom -trot -3i intj Coyote here
her tail up, and she trotted. Coyote was running

tqcəlxníwts {unint} 369 tqcxəlxłníw̓ts {a} məł axáʔ nxílsəməlx iʔ ta
t+qc+lx=łniwt -s t+qc+lx=łniwt -s mł axáʔ n+xil=s+m -lx iʔ t
trot_alongside -3erg trot_alongside -3erg and this edge_of -pl art obl
alongside her. He was running alongside her, and they got to the top over

11 The sequence st of the root functions as the transitivizer.

cənlʕʷútəm {a uɬ i} 370 niʕíp̓ axáʔ lut {t̓a c} t̓a ck̓ək̓aʔlíʔst axáʔ {iʔ s}
c -n+lʕʷ=ut+m n+yʕ=ip axáʔ lut t̓ c -k̓•k̓aʔl=íʔst axáʔ
hab -valley always this not negfac hab -go_slow this
a valley. 8:06 *The cow never did*

iʔ st̓əm̓ʕált 371 way̓ t̓i ntíkɬ məɬ x̌íƛ̓əm, məɬ t̓i_niʕíp̓ {cqa} cqáqcəlx
iʔ s+t̓m=ʕalt way̓ t̓iʔ n+tikɬ mɬ x̌iƛ̓+m mɬ t̓iʔ_n+yʕ=ip c -qa•qc+lx
art cow well evid bottom and climb and continuously hab -trot
slack up; *she got down to the bottom, then up the hill, and she's always trotting.*

372 uɬ t̓i_niʕíp̓ {iʔ} iʔ sƛ̓ax̌ts 373 i[xíʔ] {c} cxʷuy 374 ha··y məɬ
uɬ t̓iʔ_n+yʕ=ip iʔ s+ƛ̓ax̌+t -s ixíʔ c -xʷuy hay mɬ
and continuously art speed -3in then hab -go intj and
She's always fast. *They went.* *Then*

qíllltəlx {əm} uɬ itlíʔ xʷuylx məɬ itlíʔ nsʕaməncútəlx
qil•l•t -lx uɬ itlíʔ xʷuy -lx mɬ itlíʔ n+saʕ+mncút -lx
get_to_top -pl and from_there go -pl and from_there go_down -pl
they got to the top, they kept on going, then they went down again.

375 mat k̓ʷinx, mat kaʔɬís sənsaʕməncútsəlx [ax]áʔ iʔ ta
mat k̓ʷin+x mat kaʔɬís s -n+saʕ+mncút -s -lx axáʔ iʔ t
maybe a_few maybe three nom -go_down -3i -pl this art obl
I don't know how many times, maybe three times

nixʷixʷút iʔ ta cənlʕʷútəm 376 way̓ nʔayx̌ʷtíls sənk̓líp 377 wa··y̓
n+yxʷ•yxʷ=ut iʔ t c -n+lʕʷ=ut+m way̓ n+ʔayx̌ʷ+t=íls s+n+k̓l̓=ip way̓
deep art obl hab -valley well get_tired Coyote well
they went down deep gulches. *Coyote is getting tired.* *And*

c̓əwqəmstím sənk̓líp 378 ho··y pu··t uɬ {ksqil} ksqílltaʔxəlx {uɬ}
c̓wq+m -st -im s+n+k̓l̓=ip hoy put uɬ ks -qil•l•t -aʔx -lx
behind -caus -psv Coyote well just and incp^ -get_to_top -^incp -pl
Coyote is falling behind. *They were about to get to the top and*

ixíʔ uɬ hoy sənk̓líp iʔ t sʔayx̌ʷt 379 ixíʔ uɬ sʔammútət
ixíʔ uɬ hoy s+n+k̓l̓=ip iʔ t s+ʔayx̌ʷ+t ixíʔ uɬ s -ʔam•m=út•t -s
then and finish Coyote art agInst tiredness then and nom -sit_down -3i
Coyote gave out with tiredness. 9:01 *And Coyote sat*

sənk̓líp 380 way̓, way̓ ɬəx̌ʷpnún isckʷánx̌ən 381 way̓,
s+n+k̓l̓=ip way̓ way̓ ɬx̌ʷ+p -nu -n i -sc -kʷan=x̌n way̓
Coyote well yes escape -manage -1erg 1i -pftv -kidnapped well
right down. *"Heck, I am going to lose what I kidnapped."* *He*

way̓ ilí··ʔ mut x̌əɬ ʔayxáxaʔ ɬaʔxʷísk̓it 382 way̓ t̓əxʷ mat tanmús
way̓ ilíʔ mut x̌ɬ ʔayxáxaʔ ɬaʔxʷ=ísk̓it way̓ t̓xʷ mat tanm̓=ús
well there sit_sg stop a_while rest well evidently maybe nothing
sat there a little while until he got rested. *He is going to follow*

ilíʔ sənʔúcxən[s] 383 way̓ itlíʔ sxʷuys 384 xʷu··y {t̓i}
ilíʔ s -n+ʔuc=xn -s way̓ itlíʔ s -xʷuy -s xʷuy
there nom -track -3i well from_there nom -go -3i go
for nothing. *Then he went.* *He went*

t̓iʔ qammscút, xʷu¨y qáqəlt
t̓iʔ qam•m+scút xʷuy qa•qlt
evid slow go top_dim
and took his time, went and got on top of the hill.

385 mu¨t axáʔ iʔ sƛ̓aʔk̓míx
mut axáʔ iʔ s+ƛ̓aʔk̓+míx
sit_sg this art virgin
The woman was sitting there.

386 a cúntəm way̓ uɬ q̓asəspílsməntsən
a cu -nt -m way̓ uɬ q̓as•s•p=ils+m -nt -s -n
intj tell -nt -psv yes and think_long_time -nt -2obj -1erg
She said, "You are taking too long on me.

387 uɬ way̓ kən
uɬ way̓ kn
and yes 1kn
And I thought

nstils mat kʷ səxkínx kʷ sx̌ənnúmt[x] lúti
n+st=ils mat kʷ s -x+kin -x kʷ s -x̌n̓+numt -x lút+i
think maybe 2kn ipftv^ -do_what -^ipftv 2kn ipftv^ -get_hurt -^ipftv not_yet
maybe something happened to you, you got hurt and that's why you didn't

ascqílt
a -sc -qilt
2i -pftv -top
get to the top."

388 cut lut, way̓ t̓əxʷ t̓iʔ kən x̌ast
cut lut way̓ t̓xʷ t̓iʔ kn x̌as+t
say not well emph evid 1kn good
He said "No, I'm Ok."

389 cúntəm way,
cu -nt -m way̓
tell -nt -psv well
She said

way kʷ sʔayx̌ʷtx
way̓ kʷ s -ʔayx̌ʷ+t -x
yes 2kn ipftv^ -tired -^ipftv
"You are tired."

390 way̓, way̓ cut sənk̓líp, lut t̓a
way̓ way̓ cut s+n+k̓l̓=ip lut t̓
yes yes say Coyote not negfac
"Yes, yes," Coyote said;

ksukʷmísts
ks -wkʷ+mist -s
futi -keep_secret -3i
he didn't deny it.

391 cut way̓ way̓ kən ʔayx̌ʷt
cut way̓ way̓ kn ʔayx̌ʷ+t
say well yes 1kn tired
He said, "Yes, yes, I got tired."

392 cúntəm way̓
cu -nt -m way̓
tell -nt -psv yes
She said,

cúntsən
cu -nt -s -n
tell -nt -2obj -1erg
"I told you.

393 huhúy, {ck̓am¨ kʷu} kʷu cənk̓əmtíw̓smәntxʷ,
hu+húy kʷu c -n+k+ʔam=t=íw̓s+m -nt -xʷ
OK 1obj act -ride -nt -2erg
Go ahead and ride on me,

kʷu cənɬq̓əlxíkənt
kʷu c -n+ɬq̓+lx=ikn̓ -t
1obj act -lie_on_one's_back -nt
lie flat on my back.

394 [a]xáʔ məɬ kʷu cənkəlxúsəntxʷ
axáʔ mɬ kʷu c -n+klx=us -nt -xʷ
this and 4kʷu act -arms_around -nt -2erg
Put your arms around me and

məɬ lut t̓ aksƛ̓aʔƛ̓ʔúsəm
mɬ lut t̓ a -ks -ƛ̓aʔ•ƛ̓aʔ=ús+m
and not negfac 2i -futi -look_for
don't look around.

395 cəm̓ kʷ ƛ̓aʔƛ̓ʔúsəm mi {kʷ} kʷ
cm̓ kʷ ƛ̓aʔ•ƛ̓ʔ=ús+m mi kʷ
maybe 2kn look_for fut 2kn
If you look around you'll get dizzy,

nsəl̓pqín mi kʷ yaxʷt
n+sl̓+p=qin mi kʷ yaxʷ+t
dizzy fut 2kn fall
and you'll fall off.

396 ixíʔ uɬ scuts cəm̓ {ta} ta_niʕ̓íp
ixíʔ uɬ s -cut -s cm̓ ta_n+yʕ=ip
then and nom -say -3i maybe forever
And then I'll leave you for ever,

x̌ʷílstmən, lut kʷ ikɬəɬk̓əɬʔím
x̌ʷil -st -m -n lut kʷ i -kɬ -ɬ+k̓ɬ+ʔim
discard -st -2obj -1erg not 2kʷu 1i -futi -wait_again
I won't wait for you.

397 uɬ náx̌əmɬ kʷu
uɬ nax̌mɬ kʷu
and but 1obj
But if you listen to

níxəlməntxʷ axáʔ iʔ t cúntsən {uɬ} 398 uɬ waẏ t̓iʔ kʷu {ɬ}
nixl+m -nt -xʷ axáʔ iʔ t cu -nt -s -n uɬ waẏ t̓iʔ kʷu
listen_to -nt -2erg this art obl tell -nt -2obj -1erg and yes evid 4kn
what I am telling you *then we'll both*

tk̓səlmíst mi kʷu ɬyaʕp {k̓ is} k̓ isnəqsílxʷ 399 cúntəm
tk=ʔasl+míst mi kʷu ɬ+yaʕ+p k̓ i -s+nqs=ilxʷ cu -nt -m
two_people fut 4kn arrive_again to 1in -relatives tell -nt -psv
get back to my people." *He said*

waẏ, {sənk̓líp waẏ i s} 400 i[xíʔ n]k̓amtíẇsəms axáʔ iʔ tkɬmilxʷ {uɬ}
waẏ ixíʔ n+k+ʔam=t=iẇs+m -s axáʔ iʔ tkɬ+m=ilxʷ
Ok then ride -3erg this art woman
"Ok." 11:00 *Then he climbed on the woman,*

iʔ st̓aʔk̓míx 401 uɬ nɬəq̓əlxíkiʔs uɬ {uɬ i} nxəlkúsəs
iʔ s+t̓aʔk̓+míx uɬ n+ɬq̓+lx=íkiʔ -s uɬ n+xlk=us -s
art virgin and lie_on_back -3erg and around_neck -3erg
on the maiden. *He lay flat on her back and put his arms around her neck.*

402 waẏ {i} axáʔ [i]tlíʔ sqícəlxs axáʔ {i s} iʔ sq̓ʷəyq̓ʷáʕy{t} iʔ
waẏ axáʔ itlíʔ s -qic+lx -s axáʔ iʔ s+q̓ʷy•q̓ʷaʕy iʔ
well this from_there nom -run_sg -3i this art black art
Then the Black Cow continued

st̓m̓ʕalt 403 xʷu··y məɬ itlíʔ nxílsəm məɬ ixíʔ nʔucklípəm {a lut}
s+t̓m=ʕalt xʷuy mɬ itlíʔ n+xil=s+m mɬ ixíʔ n+ʔuckl=íp+m
cow go and from_there edge_of and then go_down_slope
to run. *She started to go down, and she kept her speed,*

t̓i_niʕ̓íp t̓i [i]xíʔ sƛ̓axts uɬ niʕ̓íp t̓i ixíʔ lut t̓a
t̓iʔ_n+yʕ=ip t̓iʔ ixíʔ s+ƛ̓ax̌+t -s uɬ n+yʕ=ip t̓iʔ ixíʔ lut t̓
continuously evid then speed -3in and always evid then not negfac
she won't go

ck̓əkaʔlíʔ {t̓a c} 404 iwá ɬaʔ cx̌íƛ̓əm kəm̓ iwá t̓aʔt̓ʔúlaʔxʷ 405 waẏ
c -k̓•kaʔlíʔ iwá ɬaʔ c -x̌iƛ̓+m km̓ iwá t̓aʔ•t̓ʔ=úlaʔxʷ waẏ
hab -slow even if hab -climb or even level_ground yes
slow *even if she goes uphill or on the level.* *She*

t̓i_niʕ̓íp {i} put i sƛ̓axts 406 i·· {lak} kínəm {i s} sənk̓líp ɬ
t̓iʔ_n+yʕ=ip put iʔ s+ƛ̓ax̌+t -s i·· kin̓+m s+n+k̓l̓=ip ɬ
continuously exact art speed -3in intj indef Coyote ?
is always fast. *My, the trees,*

kc̓íc̓x̌ʷsəm nt̓a·· ya sc̓əlc̓ál t̓i ɬ taqí·· t sƛ̓ax̌ts {a məɬ} 407 məɬ {ɬ an}
k+c̓i•c̓x̌ʷ=s+m nt̓a ya s+c̓l•c̓al t̓iʔ ɬ taqí t s+ƛ̓ax̌+t -s mɬ
peek intj art trees evid when ? obl speed -3in and
the shadows are running by fast. *He closed*

ɬnc̓íp̓c̓əp̓səm {waẏ ixí··ʔ ɬ··} 408 waẏ ɬlʕ̓ʷútəm {ɬ ɬa··} ɬəncahməncútəlx
ɬ+n+c̓ip̓•c̓p̓=s+m waẏ ɬ+lʕ̓ʷ=ut+m ɬ+n+cah+mncút -lx
close_eyes_tight_again well valley_again straight_for -pl
his eyes tight again. 12:01 *They go through a valley, they go straight for it.*

409 hu··y səntkɬílxəlx, way̓ uɬ ɬtxí··rəptəlx uɬ ɬqilt 410 way̓
huy c -n+tkɬ+ilx -lx way̓ uɬ ɬ+t+xir+p+t -lx uɬ ɬ+qilt way̓
intj hab -bottom -pl yes and climb_again -pl and top_again well
They go to the bottom, and back up, to the top. *The*

ixíʔ sƛ̓laps axáʔ {iʔ} iʔ q̇ʷəyq̇ʷáʕy iʔ sťəm̓ʕált 411 uɬ ixíʔ
ixíʔ s -ƛ̓lap -s axáʔ iʔ q̇ʷy•q̇ʷaʕy iʔ s+ťm=ʕalt uɬ ixíʔ
then nom -stop -3i this art black art cow and then
Black Cow stopped. *She said,*

cúntəm way̓ {cunt t tk̓ʷənt} cúntəm huy ixʷməncútx 412 aɬíʔ
cu -nt -m way̓ cu -nt -m hoy yxʷ+mncut -x aɬíʔ
tell -nt -psv well tell -nt -psv well get_off -isimptv so
"Now get off." *The*

uɬ ɬq̇ilx axáʔ {iʔ} iʔ sťaʔk̓míx 413 way̓ sixʷməncúts sənk̓líp {t}
uɬ ɬq̇+ilx axáʔ iʔ s+ťaʔk̓+míx way̓ s -yxʷ+mncut -s s+n+k̓l̓=ip
and lie this art virgin well nom -get_off -3i Coyote
woman lay down. *Coyote got down.*

414 huy ƛ̓aʔƛ̓ʔúsmənt 415 ʕ̓ant yaʔx̌í k̓əl iʔ sťmʕált
hoy ƛ̓aʔ•ƛ̓aʔ=ús+m -nt ʕaċ -nt yaʔx̌í kl kɬ+kiw iʔ s+ťm̓=ʕalt
well look_for -nt look_at -nt that_one to open_area art cow
"Look around. *The Cows, the Black Buffaloes,*

iʔ qʷəspíċaʔ {iʔ i s} iʔ q̇ʷəyq̇ʷáʕy 416 ixíʔ uɬ aɬíʔ a
iʔ qʷsp=íċaʔ iʔ q̇ʷy•q̇ʷaʕy ixíʔ uɬ aɬíʔ a
art buffalo art black that and so art
are over there in the open. *They call them*

scústsəlx q̇ʷəyq̇ʷʕáy sťmʕalt 417 aɬíʔ {m} qʷəspíċaʔ iʔ {s}
s -cu -st -s -lx q̇ʷy•q̇ʷaʕy s+ťm=ʕalt aɬíʔ qʷsp=íċaʔ iʔ
custˆ -tell -ˆcust -3erg -pl black cow so buffalo art
"Black Cows," 13:02 *they call those*

ʔúms {iʔ} [ix]í··ʔ isnəqsílxʷ {cúntəm} 418 cut sənk̓líp way̓ way̓ aláʔ kʷa mi
ʔum -s ixíʔ i -s+nqs=ilxʷ cut s+n+k̓l̓=ip way̓ way̓ aláʔ kʷa mi
call -3erg that 1in -relatives say Coyote well well here intj fut
"Buffalo Robes," they are my people." *Coyote said,*

kʷu ɬwintxʷ 419 way̓ ťi anwí kʷ knánaqs {mi kʷ} mi kʷ xʷuy k̓l
kʷu ɬwi -nt -xʷ way̓ ťiʔ anwí kʷ k=ná•naqs mi kʷ xʷuy k̓l
1obj leave -nt -2erg yes evid you 2kn alone fut 2kn go to
"Leave me here. *Go by yourself to*

asnəqsílxʷ 420 cúntəm sċki··nx 421 cus ťəxʷ
a -s+nqs=ilxʷ cu -nt -m sc -ʔkin -x cu -s ťxʷ
2in -relative tell -nt -psv ipftvpˆ -indef -ˆipftvp tell -3erg emph
your people." *She asked him "Why?"* *He said,*

lut {aɬi ka ks} kən ksɬáʔxʷsk̓itaʔxʷ {ɬa·· he} 422 uɬ ikɬaʔxʷísk̓it {wa i kʷɬ} sic
lut kn ks -ɬáʔxʷ=sk̓it -aʔx uɬ i -k -ɬaʔxʷ=ísk̓it sic
not 1kn incpˆ -rest -ˆincp and 1i -incpˆ -rest then
"No; I'm going to rest. *When I get rested you can come back*

kʷu ɬckícən[txʷ] kʷu ɬckƛ̓aʔntísəlx 423 waẏ,
kʷu ɬ+c+kic -nt -xʷ kʷu ɬ+c+ƛ̓aʔ -nt -is -lx waẏ
1obj arrive_cisl_back -nt -2erg 1obj fetch_again_cisl -nt -3erg -pl well
and get me, they can come back after me." *She*

cúntəm waẏ aspuʔús 424 eh nwísəlxsts iʔ siyúpsc, [ix]íʔ
cu -nt -m waẏ a -s+puʔ=ús eh n+wis+lx -st -s iʔ sy=ups -c ixíʔ
tell -nt -psv yes 2in -heart intj raise -st -3erg art tail -3in then
said, "If this is how you feel." 14:03 *The Black Cow raised her tail,*

sʔucklípəms axáʔ iʔ q̓ʷəyq̓ʷʕáy iʔ sťm̓áʕlt 425 ixíʔ {i s·· ə s··}
s -ʔuckl+íp+m -s axáʔ iʔ q̓ʷy•q̓ʷaʕy iʔ s+ťm=ʕalt ixíʔ
nom -run_down_canyon -3i this art black art cow then
she ran down the hill. *She*

sťəqʷcínəms {i s··} iʔ snəqsílxʷs 426 waẏ t mnímɬcəlx {i t} i ta
s -ťqʷ=cin+m -s iʔ s+nqs=ilxʷ -s waẏ t mnimɬ+c+lx iʔ t
nom -yell_at -3i art relative -3in yes obl they art obl
hollered at her people. *It was their*

nťəqʷcíntənsəlx 427 nťa yaʔx̌í iʔ tuʔ iʔ sťəmʕ̓ált 428 ixíʔ {aɬ··}
n+ťqʷ=cin+tn -s -lx nťa yaʔx̌í iʔ tw̓ iʔ s+ťm=ʕalt ixíʔ
holler -3in -pl intj that_one art herd art cow then
holler, *a herd of cows.* *They*

[s]xəlkmənċútsəlx {nťa uní} 429 wíks {lp} nťa sənk̓líp nťa iʔ
s -xlk+mncut -s -lx wik -s nťa s+n+k̓lˀ=ip nťa iʔ
nom -turn -3i -pl see -3erg intj Coyote intj art
turned around. *My, the dust*

sənw̓áʔsts {i s} iʔ ɬúkʷlaʔxʷ {i··ʔ aẏ} 430 x̌lap waẏ put x̌lap uɬ {n}
s -n+w̓aʔs+t -s iʔ ɬúkʷ=laʔxʷ x̌la+p waẏ put x̌la+p uɬ
nom -raise_rep -3i art dirt morning yes just morning and
just rose. *Next day, just at daylight,*

nʔaɬxʷíw̓s axáʔ {iʔ} iʔ sťaʔk̓míx yaʔx̌í iʔ k̓əl tuʔ 431 waẏ níkxna
n+ʔaɬxʷ=íw̓s axáʔ iʔ s+ťaʔk̓+míx yaʔx̌í iʔ k̓l tw̓ waẏ níkxnaʔ
one_enters this art virgin that_one art at herd well goodness
the virgin was back in the herd. 15:10 *Boy,*

ɬ límtmsəlx axáʔ {iʔ} iʔ t sťm̓ʕalt {it t} 432 waẏ
ɬ lim+t+m -s -lx axáʔ iʔ t s+ťm=ʕalt waẏ
subord be_glad_for -3erg -pl this art agInst cow well
were the Cows tickled! *They*

lí··mtmsəlx, waẏ cxʷəntí··səlx {iʔ} iʔ t xaʔxʔíts ťəxʷ iʔ
lim+t+m -s -lx waẏ cxʷ -nt -is -lx iʔ t xaʔ•xʔít -s ťxʷ iʔ
be_glad_for -3erg -pl yes pat -nt -3erg -pl art agInst older_relative -3in emph art
were glad, her grandparents and her parents;

t ƛ̓ax̌əx̌ƛ̓x̌á··psəlx iʔ t snəqsílxʷs {waẏ uɬ} 433 ixíʔ uɬ
t ƛ̓ax̌•x̌•ƛ̓x̌á+p -s -lx iʔ t s+nqs=ilxʷ -s ixíʔ uɬ
agInst elders -3in -pl art agInst relative -3in then and
her relatives licked her. *They*

[s]tkʷʔútsəlx uɬ k̓əɬk̓íl·xʷtəlx, {ck̓əɬxʷ} ck̓əɬk̓əlxʷmúlaʔxʷ 434 e··
s -tkʷʔ=ut -s -lx uɬ k̓ɬ+k̓ilxʷ+t -lx c -k̓ɬ+k̓lxʷ+m=úlaʔxʷ e
nom -walk_pl -3i -pl and get_out_of_sight -pl hab -hidden_place intj
started to walk and they got out of sight; they went to a hidden place. *And*

ilíʔ uɬ q̓sápiʔ uɬ sənk̓líp uɬ nstils 435 way̓ uɬ ixíʔ uɬ
ilíʔ uɬ q̓sápiʔ uɬ s+n+k̓l̓=ip uɬ n+st=ils way̓ uɬ ixíʔ uɬ
there and long_time and Coyote and think well and then and
Coyote was there, and it was a long time, and he thought: *"Well, I guess that's it.*

mat ɬəx̌ʷpnún axáʔ {is} lúti uɬ iskəm̓sqláwm
mat ɬx̌ʷ+p -nu -n axáʔ lút+i uɬ i -s -km̓+s+qlaw+m
maybe let_get_away -manage -1erg this not_yet and 1i -intt -get_paid
She got away from me, I didn't get rewarded. 16:02

436 uɬ way̓ kʷu nq̓ʷimps {i} ya ilmíxʷəm 437 kʷm̓iɬ {i c a cwik}
uɬ way̓ kʷu n+q̓ʷim+p -s ya yl=mixʷ+m kʷm̓iɬ
and yes 1obj take_from -3erg art chief suddenly
The chief stole it from me." *All at once*

ck̓əɬkʷíƛ̓pt, a kʷkʷəl̓kʷl̓ála?xʷ, 438 axáʔ q̓ʷəyq̓ʷáʕy iʔ kʷəl̓kʷəl̓álxʷs
c -k̓ɬ+kʷiƛ̓+p+t a kʷ•kʷl̓•kʷl̓=álaʔxʷ axáʔ q̓ʷy•q̓ʷaʕy iʔ kʷl̓•kʷl̓=alxʷ -s
hab -come_in_sight art calves this black art calf -3in
little calves came back in sight. *They were little Black Calves,*

ixíʔ {t'} ʔasíl 439 way̓ cxʷú··ylx cx̌í··ƛ̓m[əlx] ckícsəlx sənk̓líp
ixíʔ ʔasíl way̓ c+xʷuy -lx c+x̌iƛ̓+m -lx c+kic -s -lx s+n+k̓l̓=ip
that two well come -pl climb_cisl -pl arrive_cisl -3erg -pl Coyote
two of them. *They are coming, they came up the hill, they got to Coyote.*

440 cúsəlx way̓ sənk̓líp, kʷu sckʷúlstəm[12] iʔ t
cu -s -lx way̓ s+n+k̓l̓=ip kʷu s -c+kʷulst -m iʔ t
tell -3erg -pl well Coyote 3e4obj cust^ -send_cisc -3e4obj art agInst
They said to Coyote,

ƛ̓ax̌əx̌ƛ̓x̌áptət {uɬ iʔ} iʔ t ƛ̓ax̌əx̌ƛ̓x̌áptət uɬ iʔ kʷ sckƛ̓ʔám
ƛ̓ax̌•x̌•ƛ̓x̌á+p -tt iʔ t ƛ̓ax̌•x̌•ƛ̓x̌a+p -tt uɬ iʔ kʷ sc -k+ƛ̓ʔa+m
elders -4in art agInst elders -4in and art 2kn ? -fetch
"Our elders sent us, and we came after you."

441 cúntməlx xʷúywi, cəm̓ a nsp̓íliʔɬmən {a km̓a} 442 km̓a
cu -nt -m -lx xʷuy -wy cm̓ a n+sp̓=íliʔ -ɬm -n km̓+a
tell -nt -psv -pl go -ipimptv maybe intj club -5obj -1erg not
He said to them, "Go on, or I'll club you. *It's not*

[a]xáʔ ʔux̌ʔux̌x̌tílaʔt atáʔ i p ikɬkƛ̓aʔncútən 443 sta kʷa kən
axáʔ w̓x̌•w̓x̌•x̌•t=ílaʔt atáʔ iʔ p i -kɬ -k+ƛ̓aʔ+ncút+n sta kʷa kn
this babies this art 5kʷu 1i -to_be -fetcher intj intj 1kn
babies I want to come after me. 17:01 *Why, I am*

12 The sequence st of the root functions as the transitivizer.

sílxʷaʔ kən ilmíxʷəm 444 ixíʔ uɬ aɬíʔ waẏ ɬq̓ʷaʔstíṅkəm sənk̓líp
sílxʷaʔ kn yl=mixʷ+m ixíʔ uɬ aɬíʔ waẏ ɬ+q̓ʷaʔs+t=ínk+m s+n+k̓l̓=ip
big 1kn chief then and so yes do_magic_again Coyote
a big boss." *So Coyote started his powers.*

445 uɬ waẏ ɬkícsəlx iʔ t syúmcənsəlx 446 uɬ
uɬ waẏ ɬ+kic -s -lx iʔ t s+yum=cn -s -lx uɬ
and yes arrive_back -3erg -pl art obj_itr curse -3in -pl and
His friends already got to him. *They*

cúsəlx waẏ uɬ stim̓ uɬ {kʷu} kʷu csisúẏkstəms[txʷ]
cu -s -lx waẏ uɬ s+tim̓ uɬ kʷu c -sy•suẏ=kst+m -st -xʷ
tell -3erg -pl well and what and 1obj cust^ -get_chilled -^cust -2erg
said to him, "Why it is you are getting us chilled?"

447 cúntməlx xʷúscənwi, xʷúscənwi 448 waẏ kən kicx {iʔ k̓əl}
cu -nt -m -lx xʷus=cn -wy xʷus=cn -wy waẏ kn kic+x
tell -nt -psv -pl hurry -ipimptv hurry -ipimptv well 1kn arrive
He said to them, "Hurry, hurry! *I got to*

iʔ k̓əl t̓xʷəlmílxʷ, waẏ k̓əl q̓ʷəyq̓ʷáʕy k̓əl st̓mʕ̓ált {waẏ cəm̓ kən ks kə¨}
iʔ k̓l t̓xʷl+m=ilxʷ waẏ k̓l q̓ʷy•q̓ʷaʕy k̓l s+t̓m=aʕlt
art to different_tribe yes to black to cow
a different tribe, the Black Cows.

449 t ikstətəm̓tím̓, kʷu ksxʷíc̓xtəp {t iks} t
t i -k -s+t•tm̓•tim̓ kʷu ks -xʷic̓ -xt -p t
agInst 1i -to_be -clothes 1obj futt^ -give -xit -5erg agInst
Give me something to wear, something

iks{ə¨}nyáʕʷt 450 ixíʔ uɬ ikɬt̓kíkstən uɬ ikɬcq̓ílən
i -k -s+n+yaʕʷ+t ixíʔ uɬ i -kɬ -t̓k=ikst+n uɬ i -kɬ -cq̓=iln
1i -to_be -strength that and 1i -to_be -cane and 1i -to_be -arrow
to be strong. *A cane and some arrows."*

451 way, cúsəlx way, way ixíʔ kɬṅíṅk̓m̓əṅ 452 waẏ ixíʔ xəƛ̓pəlscút
waẏ cu -s -lx waẏ waẏ ixíʔ kɬ+ṅi•ṅk̓+m̓ṅ waẏ ixíʔ xƛ̓+p=lscut
well tell -3erg -pl yes yes that have_knife well then complete_outfit
They said, "Here is a knife." 18:03 *He got everything.*

453 cúsəlx huhúy uɬ ixíʔ waẏ x̌əcməncútwi, a,
cu -s -lx hu+húy uɬ ixíʔ waẏ x̌c+mncut -wy a
tell -3erg -pl OK and then well get_dressed -ipimptv intj
They told him, "Go ahead, put your things on,

x̌əcməncútx, ixí məɬ kʷ xʷuy 454 waẏ kʷ xəƛ̓pəlscút 455 way
x̌c+mncut -x ixíʔ mɬ kʷ xʷuy waẏ kʷ xƛ̓+p=lscut waẏ
get_ready -isimptv then and 2kn go yes 2kn complete_outfit well
and then go. *You are fully outfitted."* *Then*

ixíʔ sx̌əcməncúts sənk̓líp 456 waẏ wiʔsx̌əcməncút {ay əɬ} kiʔ ixíʔ
ixíʔ s -x̌c+mncut -s s+n+k̓l̓=ip waẏ wẏ+s+x̌c+mncut kiʔ ixíʔ
then nom -get_ready -3i Coyote well finish_dressing rel then
Coyote got ready. *He got ready. Where are the people*

i {həɬ} həɬckícsəlx 457 waẏ axáʔ ɬckícsəlx ixíʔ iʔ
i hɬ=c+kic -s -lx waẏ axáʔ ɬ+c+kic -s -lx ixíʔ iʔ
intj group_comes -3erg -pl well this arrive_cisl_back -3erg -pl that art
that came to him? *Some yearlings came to him,*

t nək̓ʷənk̓ʷspínaʔtk i t kʷəl̓kʷl̓ál̓xʷ, {t} waẏ st̓mʕ̓alt 458 waẏ ixíʔ
t nk̓ʷ•nk̓ʷ+s+pín=aʔtk iʔ t kʷl̓•kʷl̓=alxʷ waẏ s+t̓m=ʕalt waẏ ixíʔ
agInst yearlings_dim art agInst calf yes cow well that
calves, cow calves. *Again*

nixʷ ɬʔamasənsp̓íliʔsəs 459 sta cus {ta i} a i t
nixʷ ɬ+ʔama+s+n+sp̓=íliʔs -s sta cu -s a iʔ t
also threaten_to_beat_again -3erg intj tell -3erg intj art agInst
he threatened to lick them. *And he said to them,*

isənk̓ʷəɬililmíxʷəm mi ikɬkƛ̓aʔncútn {s suk̓ʷs} 460 smisqílxʷ,
i -s+nk̓ʷ+ɬ+yl•yl=mixʷ+m mi i -kɬ -k+ƛ̓aʔ+ncút+n s+my+s+qilxʷ
1in -fellow_chiefs fut 1i -to_be -fetch important_people
"My own kind is to come after me, 19:02 *important people,*

nak̓ʷa axáʔ {iʔ t} iʔ p t həɬm̓əqʷm̓áqʷ 461 waẏ
nak̓ʷ+á axáʔ iʔ p t hɬ=m̓q̓ʷ•m̓aq̓ʷ waẏ
not this art 5kn agInst group_mounds_dim well
not you little nothings." *And*

ɬəɬtqʷáysəlx yaʔx̌í nx̌əɬx̌íɬəlx, waẏ ɬtqʷaẏlx,
ɬ -ɬ+t+qʷay -s -lx yaʔx̌í n+x̌ɬ•x̌iɬ -lx waẏ ɬ+t+qʷay -lx
nom -discend_again -3i -pl that_one scare -pl yes discend_again -pl
they ran back down. They got scared, and they ran down,

462 way {ɬən} ɬənppəlxíw̓s iʔ k̓əl snəqʷsílxʷsəlx 463 uɬ cúsəlx uɬ
waẏ ɬ+n+p•plx=iw̓s iʔ k̓l s+nqs=ilxʷ -s -lx uɬ cu -s -lx uɬ
well enter_again art to relative -3in -pl and tell -3erg -pl and
got back to the herd, to their relatives. *And they asked,*

sc̓kinx uɬ kin̓ {a} iʔ skƛ̓ʔamp 464 cútəlx {kəm̓ ɬa} waẏ kʷu
sc+ʔkin+x uɬ ʔkin iʔ s+k+ƛ̓ʔa -mp cut -lx waẏ kʷu
why_is_it and indef art fetched_one -5in say -pl well 3e4obj
"What's the matter, where is the one you went to get?" *They said "He*

ʔamasənsp̓íliʔsəntəm 465 iʔ kʷu əɬckʷúlstəm {cúntəm ə} uɬ iʔ
ʔama+s+n+sp̓=íliʔs -nt -m iʔ kʷu ɬ+c+kʷulst[13] -m uɬ iʔ
threaten_to_club -nt -3e4obj art 3e4obj send_back_cisl -3e4obj and art
threatened to club us. *He sent us back here,*

kʷu cúntəm 466 sta i t isənk̓ʷɬəlililmíxʷəm
kʷu cu -nt -m sta iʔ t i -s+nk̓ʷ+ɬ+yl•yl=mixʷ+m
3e4obj tell -nt -3e4obj intj art agInst 1in -fellow_chiefs
and he told us: *'I want my kind to come*

13 The sequence st of the root functions as the transitivizer.

ikɬkƛ̓aʔncútən 467 lut axáʔ {xa i p s} iʔ t p scəcm̓ílt
i -kɬ -k+ƛ̓aʔ+ncút+n lut axáʔ iʔ t p s+c+cm̓=il̓t
1i -to_be -fetch not this art agInst 5kn children
and get me, not you kids.'

468 ixíʔ uɬ_i kʷu {əɬ ca} ɬcililtmíntəm 469 way̓ ixíʔ
ixíʔ uɬ_iʔ kʷu ɬ+c+yl•yl+min -t -m way̓ ixíʔ
then and_then 3e4obj drive_back_cisl -nt -3e4obj well then
And that's how we were run back."20:01 Then

kʷúlstməlx itlíʔ {a} iʔ sʔasʔasəlspíntk 470 way̓ ixíʔ
kʷulst+m -lx itlíʔ iʔ s+ʔas•ʔasl+s+pin=tk way̓ ixíʔ
send -pl from_there art two_year_old well then
they sent the two year olds. Then

ɬəɬxʷúy̓iʔsəlx 471 way̓ ik̓líʔ kícsəlx sənk̓líp 472 way̓
ɬ -ɬ+xʷuy̓•y -s -lx way̓ ik̓líʔ kic -s -lx s+n+k̓l̓=ip way̓
nom -go_back_pl -3i -pl yes there reach_st/sb -3erg -pl Coyote well
they went. They got to Coyote. And

nixʷ tixʷkʷúkstməlx uɬ ʔamasənsp̓íliʔsəntəm 473 i[xíʔ]
nixʷ tixʷkʷu=kst+m -lx uɬ ʔama+s+n+sp̓=íliʔs -nt -m ixíʔ
again tell_same_thing -pl and threaten_to_club -nt -psv then
the same happened to them, he threatened to club them. They

ɬəɬctqʷáysəlx, way̓ ɬciʕápəlx 474 way̓ nixʷ
ɬ -ɬ+c+t+qʷay -s -lx way̓ ɬ+c+yaʕ+p -lx way̓ nixʷ
nom -come_back_down -3i -pl yes arrive_cisl_again -pl well again
ran down the hill, they got back. They said

ɬmincútəlx cútəlx way̓ 475 way̓ itlíʔ iʔ skaʔkaʔɬəlspíntk, way̓
ɬ+my+ncut -lx cut -lx way̓ way̓ itlíʔ iʔ s+kaʔ•kaʔ+l+s+pín=tk way̓
repeat_again -pl say -pl yes well from_there art three_year_olds well
the same thing. The boss sent

ɬkʷúlstməlx iʔ ta ilmíxʷəm 476 way̓ ixíʔ ɬəɬxʷúysəlx axáʔ
ɬ+kʷulst+m -lx iʔ t yl=mixʷ+m way̓ ixíʔ ɬ -ɬ+xʷuy -s -lx axáʔ
send_back -pl art agInst chief well then nom -go_back -3i -pl this
the three year olds. The three year olds

iʔ {s} kaʔkaʔɬəlspíntk 477 way̓ ik̓líʔ nixʷ {ɬ} yáʕpəlx 478 nixʷ ilíʔ
iʔ kaʔ•kaʔɬl+s+pín=tk way̓ ik̓líʔ nixʷ yaʕ+p -lx nixʷ ilíʔ
art three_year_old well there also arrive_pl -pl again there
went. They got there too. Coyote

tixʷkʷúkstməlx sənk̓líp way̓ nixʷ {c} cmaʔmaʔmíntməlx
tixʷkʷu=kst+m -lx s+n+k̓l̓=ip way̓ nixʷ c -maʔ•maʔ+mín -t -m -lx
tell_same_thing -pl Coyote yes also act -send_away_pl -nt -psv -pl
told them the same thing, he sent them away. 21:08

479 way̓ i[xíʔ] ɬəɬctqʷáy̓səlx 480 way̓ ixíʔ scuts {i} a
way̓ ixíʔ ɬ -ɬ+c+t+qʷay -s -lx way̓ ixíʔ s -cut -s a
well then nom -come_back_down -3i -pl well then nom -say -3i art
They went back down the hill. The chief told them,

ilmíxʷəm waẏ waẏ axáʔ t̓əxʷ a[xáʔ] iʔ p sməsməspíntk 481 itlíʔ
yl=mixʷ+m waẏ waẏ axáʔ t̓xʷ axáʔ iʔ p s+ms•ms+pin=tk itlíʔ
chief well well this emph this art 5kn four_year_olds from_there
"You four year olds, *now*

p ɬkcahahám 482 cútəlx waẏ[14] 483 waẏ itlíʔ {kən cəq} kən
p ɬ+k+cah•há+m cut -lx waẏ waẏ itlíʔ kn
5kn turn_again say -pl Ok well from_there 1kn
it's your turn." *They said "Ok."* *I am going*

ɬənc̓əpq̓síw̓səm aɬíʔ uɬ kən sɬaʔxʷsk̓ítx 484 waẏ kən
ɬ+n+c̓pq̓+s=iw̓s+m aɬíʔ uɬ kn s -ɬáʔxʷ=sk̓it -x waẏ kn
splice_again because and 1kn ipftv^ -be_rested -^ipftv yes 1kn
to continue, I am going to rest, *and I am*

ɬaʔxʷísk̓it 485 waẏ axáʔ {iʔ ts k} iʔ t sməsməspíntk iʔ t q̓ʷəyq̓ʷáʕy
ɬaʔxʷ=ísk̓it waẏ axáʔ iʔ t s+ms•ms+pin=tk iʔ t q̓ʷy•q̓ʷaʕy
rest well this art agInst four_year_olds art agInst black
rested. *Then the four year old*

iʔ t scəɬcúɬəm 486 ixíʔ ɬkʷúlstməlx i ta ilmíxʷəm
iʔ t s+cɬ•cuɬm ixíʔ ɬ+kʷulst+m -lx iʔ t yl=mixʷ+m
art agInst bulls then send_back -pl art agInst chief
bulls. *The boss sent them.*

487 cúntməlx huhúy, mnímɬəmp 488 ixíʔ mat mi xəʔína? ya
cu -nt -m -lx hu+húy mnimɬ+mp ixíʔ mat mi xʔ=ínaʔ ya
tell -nt -psv -pl OK you then maybe fut consent art
He told them, "Now you. *I guess that's when that boss*

ilmíxʷəm ɬ cxʷuy kswíkəntəm 489 waẏ ixíʔ {s stxírrpts axáʔ}
yl=mixʷ+m ɬ c+xʷuy ks -wik -nt -m waẏ ixíʔ
chief subord come futt^ -see -nt -? well then
will consent and come to see." 22:07 *So the four year olds*

txirrp axáʔ iʔ scəɬcúɬəm iʔ sməsməspíntk 490 xʷu··y kícsəlx
t+xir•r+p axáʔ iʔ s+cɬ•cuɬm iʔ s+ms•ms+pin=tk xʷuy kic -s -lx
run_uphill this art bulls art four_year_olds go reach_st/sb -3erg -pl
ran up the hill. *They went and got to*

sənk̓líp 491 mu··t {əc cs əc əc} scw̓áw̓nəxs 492 cúsəlx,
s+n+k̓l̓=ip mut sc -w̓a•w̓n̓x -s cu -s -lx
Coyote sit_sg ipftvp^ -war_dance_dim -3i tell -3erg -pl
Coyote. *He was sitting there singing a war song.* *They said*

waẏ {kʷ sc} kʷ scƛ̓ʔam, axáʔ iʔ kʷ a ilmíxʷəm 493 waẏ lut nixʷ
waẏ kʷ sc+ƛ̓ʔa+m axáʔ iʔ kʷ a yl=mixʷ+m waẏ lut nixʷ
well 2kn fetched this art 2kn intj chief well not again
to him, "We've come after you, boss. *Now don't you*

14 Pete said "I'm going to take a breath."

itlíʔ akswal̓cənm̓íst 494 way̓ ʕá··c̓əntməlx t sənk̓líp
itlíʔ a -ks -wal̓=cn+míst way̓ ʕac̓ -nt -m -lx t s+n+k̓l̓=ip
from_there 2i -futi -talk_funny well look -nt -psv -pl agInst Coyote
get talking funny again." *Coyote looked them over.*

495 way̓ ixíʔ cut way̓ sənk̓əlíp way̓ ixíʔ x̌ast ispuʔús way̓ itíʔ
way̓ ixíʔ cut way̓ s+n+k̓l̓=ip way̓ ixíʔ x̌as+t i -s+puʔ=ús way̓ itíʔ
well then say yes Coyote yes then good 1in -heart yes from_that
Then Coyote said "Now I'm satisfied, they're

isənk̓ʷsplál {i tl} 496 uɬ ixíʔ x̌ast ispuʔús 497 ixíʔ la_cxʔítiʔ uɬ
i -s+nk̓ʷ+s+pl•al uɬ ixíʔ x̌as+t i -s+puʔ=ús ixíʔ la_c+xʔít+iʔ uɬ
1in -fellow_young and then good 1in -heart then at_first and
my kind 23:04 *and I am satisfied.* *The first times*

aɬ[íʔ] ixíʔ i {s} scəcm̓íl̓t uɬ axáʔ {cps} cpəspsáʕyaʔ 498 uɬ ixíʔ
aɬíʔ ixíʔ iʔ s+c+cm̓=il̓t uɬ axáʔ c -ps+ps=áʕyaʔ uɬ ixíʔ
so that art children and this hab -feeble_minded and that
it was kids, and they haven't got sense. *And I*

lut {t̓ inxi} t̓ inx̌mínk uɬ lut_i kəxəntín 499 nak̓ʷáʔ kən
lut t̓ in -x̌m=ink uɬ lút+i kx+n -t -in nak̓ʷ+á kn
not negfac 1in -like and not_yet follow -nt -1erg not 1kn
don't like that, and I didn't go with them. *I wasn't*

st̓imíx, [nak̓ʷ]á kən scakʷm̓scútaʔx 500 cúsəlx way̓
s+t̓y+mix nak̓ʷá kn s -caʔkʷ+mscút -aʔx cu -s -lx way̓
lazy not 1kn ipftv^ -hard_to_get -^ipftvDim tell -3erg -pl yes
lazy to go or I wasn't trying to be hard to get." *They said "Ok."*

501 way̓ ixíʔ uɬ txəmnuʔsɬníw̓tsəlx 502 xʷu··ylx, {ɬ} npəpəlxíw̓səlx
way̓ ixíʔ uɬ t+xmn=w̓s=ɬniwt -s -lx xʷuy -lx n+p•plx=iw̓s -lx
well then and both_sides -3erg -pl go -pl several_enter -pl
They were on each side of him. *They went right in the herd,*

ixí aɬíʔ {ck̓ʷɬ} ck̓əɬqʷáʔ {i} cənɬx̌ʷúlaʔxʷ 503 nt̓a·· {ti} yaʕpqín
ixíʔ aɬíʔ c -k̓ɬ+qʷaʔ c -n+ɬx̌ʷ=úlaʔxʷ nt̓a yaʕ+p=qín
that so hab -ground_pocket hab -hole intj lots
it's a big ground pocket, a hollow in the ground. *There are lots*

sxʷulɬxʷ 504 way̓ uɬ wiks iʔ sqilxʷ {i s} a ctəkʷtəkʷʔút way̓ uɬ
s+xʷul=ɬxʷ way̓ uɬ wik -s iʔ s+qilxʷ a c -tkʷ+tkʷʔ=ut way̓ uɬ
tipi well and see -3erg art person art hab -walk yes and
of tipis. *Then he saw lots of people walking*

sqílxʷ 505 uɬ axáʔ {əɬ ʕac̓} ʕác̓əs axáʔ iʔ k̓əl sq̓ʷut axáʔ {iʔ} iʔ
s+qilxʷ uɬ axáʔ ʕac̓ -s axáʔ iʔ k̓l s+q̓ʷut axáʔ iʔ
person and this look_at -3erg this art to across this art
around. *He looked on one side, and those that had come after him,*

kƛ̓aʔncútəns uɬ sqilxʷ 506 uɬ {ak} ʕác̓əm k̓əl sq̓ʷut uɬ nixʷ sqilxʷ {a}
k+ƛ̓aʔ+ncút+n -s uɬ s+qilxʷ uɬ ʕac̓+m k̓l s+q̓ʷut uɬ nixʷ s+qilxʷ
fetcher -3in and person and look to across and also person
they are people. 24:07 *He looked on the other side, they are also people.*

507 [u]ɬ ha sc̓kinx, {a} ƛ̓əm {a} q̓ʷəyq̓ʷáʕy sťmáʕlt a[xáʔ] inkƛ̓aʔncútən
uɬ haʔ sc+ʔkin+x ƛ̓m q̓ʷy•q̓ʷaʕy s+ťm=ʕalt axáʔ in -k+ƛ̓aʔ+ncút+n
and inter why_is_it past black cow this 1in -fetcher
"What's the matter, they were Black Cows that came after me.

508 uɬ sqilxʷ, k̓ʷuľlx uɬ t sqilxʷ
uɬ s+qilxʷ k̓ʷuľ•ľ -lx uɬ t s+qilxʷ
and person turn_into -pl and obl person
They turned into people.

509 way̓ mat iʔ yaʕ̓ʷpyáwtəlx
way̓ mat iʔ yaw+p•yáʕʷ+t -lx
well must art powerful -pl
They must be powerful."

510 way̓ xʷú··ystsəlx {a i} iʔ la nq̓aʔq̓ʔíw̓s {i}
way̓ xʷuy+st -s -lx iʔ l n+q̓aʔ•q̓ʔ=íw̓s
well take_st -3erg -pl art in go_between
They took him, and right in the center

511 ilíʔ kiʔ {c} cwix iʔ
ilíʔ kiʔ c -wix iʔ
there rel hab -live art
there was a tipi there,

sxʷulɬxʷ {i} iʔ nmásqən iʔ sxʷulɬxʷ a cɬəmníw̓s {xi s}
s+xʷul=ɬxʷ iʔ n+mas=qn iʔ s+xʷul=ɬxʷ a c -ɬmn=iw̓s
tipi art four_head art tipi art hab -tied_together
four tipis put together.

512 way̓ npəpílxəlx {way̓ n}
way̓ n+p•pilx -lx
well enter_pl -pl
They went in there.

513 uɬ aɬíʔ way̓ wiʔsk̓əɬx̌əqəntísəlx
uɬ aɬíʔ way̓ wy̓+s+k̓ɬ+x̌q -nt -is -lx
and so yes finish_clear_place -nt -3erg -pl
They already have a place for him.

514 wiʔsk̓ʷlaʔxʷílpsəlx axáʔ a ilmíxʷəm, sənk̓líp, myaw
wy̓+s+k̓ʷľ=laʔxʷ=ílp -s -lx axáʔ a yl=mixʷ+m s+n+k̓ľ=ip myaw
finish_fix_bed -3erg -pl this art chief Coyote Coyote
They had fixed a bed because Coyote is a boss, a great man. 25:03

515 cúsəlx way̓ kʷ ilmíxʷəm, way̓ {axáʔ iʔ} axáʔ {iʔ aks}
cu -s -lx way̓ kʷ yl=mixʷ+m way̓ axáʔ
tell -3erg -pl well 2kn chief well this
They said to him, "You are the boss. Here is a place for you

aksmútən
a -k -s+mut+n
2i -to_be -place_to_sit
to sit down,

516 way̓ axáʔ {iʔ kɬ} wiʔsk̓ʷəlaʔxʷílps[əlx]
way̓ axáʔ wy̓+s+k̓ʷľ=laʔxʷ=ílp -s -lx
yes this finish_fix_bed -3erg -pl
for you to

[aksk̓ʷlaʔxʷílps]
a -k -s+k̓ʷľ=laʔxʷ=ilp
2i -to_be -bed
lay down on."

517 hi sxʷəpxʷípəplaʔxʷs {iʔ a} iʔ q̓ʷəyq̓ʷáʕy iʔ
hi s -xʷp•xʷp=íp•p=laʔxʷ -s iʔ q̓ʷy•q̓ʷaʕy iʔ
intj nom -spread_on_floor -3i art black art
They had spread around black hides

síp̓iʔs {iʔ way̓ ac i ac} ia cxʷikʷ
síp̓iʔ -s iʔ c -xʷikʷ
hide -3in art hab -tan_hides
that are tanned,

518 ixíʔ uɬ a
ixíʔ uɬ a
that and art
the ones

scústsəlx qʷəspíc̓aʔ
s -cu -st -s -lx qʷsp=íc̓aʔ
cust^ -tell -^cust -3erg -pl buffalo
they call "qʷəspíc̓aʔ."

519 cúsəlx way̓ ilíʔ mi uɬ kʷ mut
cu -s -lx way̓ ilíʔ mi uɬ kʷ
tell -3erg -pl well there fut and 2kn
They said to him, "You'll sit down here."

520 waẏ {ixíʔ} ixíʔ uɬ kcwílsəlx
waẏ ixíʔ uɬ k+cwil -s -lx
well then and give_to_eat -3erg -pl
Then they gave him something to eat.

521 waẏ sʔíɬənsəlx,
waẏ s -ʔiɬn -s -lx
yes nom -eat -3i -pl
They ate and

ʔí··ɬənəlx wiʔwiʔcínəlx
ʔiɬn -lx wẏ•wẏ=cin -lx
eat -pl finish_eating_pl -pl
they got done eating. 26:02

522 uɬ cúntəm {aɬí} ta ilmíxʷəm
uɬ cu -nt -m t yl=mixʷ+m
and tell -nt -psv agInst chief
And the chief said to him:

523 waẏ
waẏ
well
"I

waẏ mat t̓əxʷ kʷ ɬaʔxʷísk̓it
waẏ mat t̓xʷ kʷ ɬaʔxʷ=ísk̓it
well maybe evidently 2kn rest
suppose you are rested now."

524 ixíʔ uɬ cus, aɬíʔ kʷ spútaʔm
ixíʔ uɬ cu -s aɬíʔ kʷ s+pútaʔ+m
then and tell -3erg so 2kn respected
He said, "We respect you

uɬ lúti iʔ síwəntst
uɬ lút+i iʔ siw -nt -s -t
and not_yet art ask -nt -2obj -4erg
and we didn't ask you yet.

525 uɬ ʕapnáʔ waẏ kʷ ɬaʔxʷísk̓it
uɬ ʕapnáʔ waẏ kʷ ɬaʔxʷ=ísk̓it
and now yes 2kn rest
But now you are rested

526 uɬ waẏ ixíʔ uɬ səwsíwəntst laʔkíṅ úɬiʔ {iʔ}
uɬ waẏ ixíʔ uɬ sw•siw -nt -s -t la+ʔkíṅ uɬ iʔ
and yes then and ask_rep -nt -2obj -4erg wherever and_then
and now we are going to ask you

ckaʔkícəntxʷ axáʔ ist̓əmkʔílt
c -kaʔ•kíc -nt -xʷ axáʔ i -s+t̓mkʔ=ilt
act -find -nt -2erg this 1in -daughter
where you found my daughter."

527 uɬ aɬíʔ ixíʔ
uɬ aɬíʔ ixíʔ
and so then
And his daughter

qʷaʔmənwíxʷstməlx axáʔ iʔ t st̓əmkʔílts
qʷaʔm+nwíxʷ -st -m -lx axáʔ iʔ t s+t̓mkʔ=ilt -s
introduce_rec -caus -psv -pl this art agInst daughter -3in
introduced him.

528 cúntəm
cu -nt -m
tell -nt -psv
She said,

axáʔ ixíʔ axáʔ inṁístəm, ixíʔ ya ilmíxʷəm
axáʔ ixíʔ axáʔ in -ṁist+m ixíʔ ya yl=mixʷ+m
this that this 1in -w's_father that art chief
"This is my father, that's the boss;

529 uɬ ixíʔ axáʔ
uɬ ixíʔ axáʔ
and that this
and this is

intúṁ, ixíʔ puʔilmíxʷəm
in -tuṁ ixíʔ pu=yl=míxʷ+m
1in -w's_mother that chief's_spouse
my mother, she's the boss's wife.

530 uɬ axáʔ iʔ sk̓ʷiƛ̓təm, axáʔ ixíʔ
uɬ axáʔ iʔ s+k̓ʷiƛ̓t+m axáʔ ixíʔ
and this art others this that
And these are the

t̓əxʷ {i s}
t̓xʷ
evidently
others." 27:00

531 waẏ cut smiyáw
waẏ cut s+myaw
well say Coyote
Then the great one said:

532 waẏ {xəlkm} ixíʔ
waẏ ixíʔ
well then
"I had heard

níxəlmən axáʔ iʔ ɬ ast̓amkʔílt {i ɬ} i ɬ saƛ̓ts
nixl+m -n axáʔ iʔ ɬ a -s+t̓mkʔ=ilt iʔ ɬ saƛ̓+t -s
hear_about -1erg this art about 2in -daughter art about lost -3in
about your daughter getting lost;

533 uɬ
uɬ
and
and

ixíʔ {iʔ} iʔ níxəlmən {əɬ} tx̌áq̓plaʔntxʷ səwít kaʔkíciʔs
ixíʔ iʔ nixl+m -n t+x̌áq̓=plaʔ -nt -xʷ swit kaʔ•kíc y̓ -s
then art hear_about -1erg reward -nt -2erg who find -nt -3erg
then I heard that you'd give a reward to whoever finds her,

534 uɬ ixíʔ ksƛ̓xʷúpaʔx t sqlaw̓ 535 cut a ilmíxʷm way̓,
uɬ ixíʔ ks -ƛ̓xʷu+p -aʔx t s+qlaw cut a yl=mixʷ+m way̓
and then incp^ -win -^incp obj_itr money say art chief yes
and he is going to get money." *The chief said,*

way̓ ixíʔ iscqʷəlqʷílt 536 cúntəm axáʔ i ta ilmíxʷəm
way̓ ixíʔ i -sc -qʷl•qʷil+t cu -nt -m axáʔ iʔ t yl=mixʷ+m
yes that 1i -pftv -talk tell -nt -psv this art agInst chief
"Yes, that's what I said." *The chief said to him:*

537 lut, lut kmix sqlaw̓, ixíʔ sqlaw̓ tanm̓ús 538 uɬ ixíʔ axáʔ inx̌áq̓mən
lut lut kmix s+qlaw ixíʔ s+qlaw tanm̓=ús uɬ ixíʔ axáʔ in -x̌aq̓+mn
not not only money that money nothing and that this 1in -reward
"Not only money; money is nothing. *This is my reward,*

ixíʔ t islímt 539 uɬ aɬíʔ way̓ t̓i sənƛ̓əláltət {uɬ n} 540 uɬ ixíʔ
ixíʔ t i -s+lim+t uɬ aɬíʔ way̓ t̓iʔ s+n+ƛ̓l•al -tt uɬ ixíʔ
that from 1in -gladness and so yes evid loss -4in and that
I am so glad. *We had her for dead. 28:03* *This is*

nixʷ inktáxʷ, ixíʔ iscút 541 n̓ín̓w̓iʔ səwít kaʔkícəntəm
nixʷ in -k+taxʷ ixíʔ i -s -cut n̓ín̓w̓iʔ swit kaʔ•kíc -nt -m
also 1in -addition that 1in -nom -what_said a_while who find -nt -psv
what I give to boot, this is what I said: *whoever finds her,*

uɬ ixíʔ kɬtkəlmílxʷs 542 uɬ ixíʔ ikslímt {təl} təl
uɬ ixíʔ kɬ -tkɬ+m=ilxʷ -s uɬ ixíʔ i -ks -lim+t tl
and that to_be -wife -3i and then 1i -futi -glad from
she'll be his wife. *I would be so glad*

ksxʷəlxʷálts axáʔ ist̓əmkʔílt 543 cúntəm way̓, uɬ ixíʔ {u}
ks -xʷl•xʷal+t -s axáʔ i -s+t̓mkʔ=ilt cu -nt -m way̓ uɬ ixíʔ
futi -alive -3i this 1in -daughter tell -nt -psv OK and then
that my daughter is alive." *He said "Ok." And then*

cus iʔ st̓əmkʔílts 544 xʷuyx uɬ k̓amtɬníw̓təntxʷ ixíʔ
cu -s iʔ s+t̓mkʔ=ilt -s xʷuy -x uɬ k+ʔam=t=ɬníwt -nt -xʷ ixíʔ
tell -3erg art daughter -3in go -isimptv and sit_next_to -nt -2erg that
he said to his daughter: *"Go sit by his side, and he becomes*

uɬ way̓ astaʔxʷsqəltmíxʷ 545 uɬ aɬíʔ t cniɬc kiʔ {xʷ}
uɬ way̓ a -s+taʔxʷ+s+qlt=míxʷ uɬ aɬíʔ t cniɬ+c kiʔ
and yes 2in -new_husband and because agInst (s)he rel
your man. *He's the one that brought you back alive,*

xʷəlxʷəltstúms uɬ a ɬwíkəntst {e} 546 t̓i cxʷt̓up
xʷl•xʷl+t -st -um -s uɬ a ɬ+wik -nt -s -t t̓iʔ c+xʷ̓u+p
alive -caus -2obj -3erg and intj see_again -nt -2obj -4erg evid jump_up
and then we saw you again." *And the woman*

axáʔ iʔ tkəɬmílxʷ uɬ ixíʔ k̓amtɬníw̓təntəm [s]miyáw 547 [ix]íʔ uɬ
axáʔ iʔ tkɬmilxʷ uɬ ixíʔ k+ʔam=t=ɬníwt -nt -m s+myaw ixíʔ uɬ
this art woman and then sit_next_to -nt -psv Coyote that and
jumped up, and sat down by the great man's side. And he is

aɬíʔ swiʔnúmtx xʷaʔ aɬíʔ uɬ sic {iʔ s iʔ s} iʔ stətəm̓tím̓s iʔ
aɬíʔ s+wy̓+numt=x xʷaʔ aɬíʔ uɬ sic iʔ s+t•tm̓•tim̓ -s iʔ
because handsome intj because and new art clothes -3in art
handsome with his clothes, good things

sx̌əsəlscút[s] 548 iʔ sk̓ʷəl̓scúts iʔ {s} sx̌əcməncúts 549 way̓, way̓
s+x̌s=lscut -s iʔ s+k̓ʷl̓+scut -s iʔ s+x̌c+mncut -s way̓ way̓
good_clothes -3in art dolling_up -3in art attire -3in well well
to wear, 29:00 how he was fixed, the way he was dressed. Coyote

taʔxʷsənɬx̌əmtán {s} sənk̓líp 550 i·· məɬ {k} ksx̌əlpínaʔ məɬ k̓əɬk̓awílxəlx
taʔxʷ+s+n+ɬx̌m+tán s+n+k̓l̓=ip i·· mɬ k+s+x̌l+p=ínaʔ mɬ k̓ɬ+k̓aw+ílx -lx
get_in_laws Coyote intj and have_daylight and go_on_prairie -pl
got law relation. Then at daylight they go out on the prairie.

551 t̓i kəl̓əl̓kʷákʷəlx məɬ ɬk̓ʷul̓lx axáʔ {t} t st̓mʕált axáʔ {iʔ}
t̓iʔ k+l̓•l̓kʷ•akʷ -lx mɬ ɬ+k̓ʷul̓•l̓ -lx axáʔ t s+t̓m=ʕalt axáʔ
evid far_dim -pl and turn_into_again -pl this obl cow this
They go a little ways and the people turn into Cows

iʔ sqilxʷ ia ckəlkʷákʷ {məɬ} 552 i·· k̓əláxʷ məɬ ɬcyʕap 553 ho··y
iʔ s+qilxʷ iʔ c -k+lkʷ•akʷ i·· k̓laxʷ mɬ ɬ+c+yaʕ+p hoy
art person art hab -far intj evening and arrive_cisl_again well
when they go away. In the evening they go back. One

uɬ nk̓ʷəspíntk 554 way̓ {taʔxʷ} taʔxʷsqʷəsqʷsíʔ axáʔ iʔ tkəɬmílxʷ
uɬ nk̓ʷ+s+pin=tk way̓ taʔxʷ+s+qʷs•qʷsíʔ axáʔ iʔ tkɬmilxʷ
and one_year well get_baby this art woman
year went by and the woman got a baby. 30:00

555 níkxnaʔ ɬ límtəlx axáʔ iʔ xaʔxʔít {ɬ} ɬə cxʷíltməlx 556 wa··y̓ uɬ
níkxnaʔ ɬ lim+t -lx axáʔ iʔ xaʔ•xʔít ɬ cxʷ=ilt+m -lx way̓ uɬ
goodness ? glad -pl this art older_relative ? hold_child -pl well and
Goodness, the elders, their elders, are glad, they make over the baby. Then

itlíʔ ɬtx̌iwtwílx itlíʔ nixʷ taʔxʷsqʷəsqʷəsíʔ 557 way̓ nixʷ ixíʔ
itlíʔ ɬ+t̓x̌=iwt+wílx itlíʔ nixʷ taʔxʷ+s+qʷs•qʷsíʔ way̓ nixʷ ixíʔ
from_there year_again from_there again get_baby well again then
the next year she got another baby. They were tickled

ɬlímtəmsəlx, i·· uɬ{ɬ} way̓ uɬ ʔamtlwís axáʔ {is} iʔ stʔiwtx
ɬ+lim+t+m -s -lx i·· uɬ way̓ uɬ ʔam=t+lwís axáʔ iʔ s+tʔiw+t=x
glad_again -3erg -pl intj and yes and sit_around this art young_one
to death again, and the first one got to be sitting around.

558 ixíʔ uɬ {cus} cus t sənk̓líp iʔ sənɬx̌əmtáns 559 way̓ axáʔ
ixíʔ uɬ cu -s t s+n+k̓l̓=ip iʔ s+n+ɬx̌m+tan -s way̓ axáʔ
then and tell -3erg agInst Coyote art in_law -3in well this
And Coyote said to his law relations: "You are

iʔ kʷ isənɬx̌əmtán 560 waẏ uɬ ʔasəlspíntk waẏ {təl} təl̓ ɬwin
iʔ kʷ i -s+n+ɬx̌m+tan waẏ uɬ ʔasl+s+pin=tk waẏ tl̓ ɬwi -n
art 2kʷu 1i -in_law yes and two_years well from leave -1erg
my law relation. It's two years since I left my folks,

isnəqsílxʷ intəmxʷúlaʔxʷ 561 waẏ kən nk̓əwpəlsúlaʔxʷ,
i -s+nqs=ilxʷ in -tmxʷ=úlaʔxʷ waẏ kn n+k̓w+p=ls=úlaʔxʷ
1in -relative 1in -country well 1kn miss_country
my country. 31:03 I am lonesome for my country,

nk̓awpílsmən isnəqsílxʷ
n+k̓aw+p=íls+m -n i -s+nqs=ilxʷ
miss -1erg 1in -relative
I am lonesome for my people.

562 uɬ waẏ ṅíṅẇiʔ x̌əláp, x̌əláp mi uɬ ɬwíntsən
uɬ waẏ ṅíṅẇiʔ x̌la+p x̌la+p mi uɬ ɬwi -nt -s -n
and yes a_while tomorrow tomorrow fut and leave -nt -2obj -1erg
And tomorrow morning I am leaving you.

563 ixíʔ kʷ iksc̓x̌ʷxítəm axáʔ iʔ kʷ isx̌aʔ•x̌áʔ
ixíʔ kʷ i -ks -c̓x̌ʷ -xit -m axáʔ iʔ kʷ i -s+x̌aʔ•x̌áʔ
then 2kʷu 1i -futi -promise -xit -apsv this art 2kʷu 1in -father_in_law
This is what I telling you, my father-in-law."

564 a·· cúntəm waẏ, waẏ, waẏ aspuʔús 565 nak̓ʷá kʷ smaʔmínəm,
a cu -nt -m waẏ waẏ waẏ a -s+puʔ=ús nak̓ʷá kʷ s+maʔ+mín+m
intj tell -nt -psv Ok Ok Ok 2in -heart not 2kn sent_away
He told him, "Ok, if that's how you feel. We didn't send you away,

anwí aspuʔús 566 ʕác̓ənt axáʔ pna axáʔ anwí {kʷ} iʔ_t cuntxʷ,
anwí a -s+puʔ=ús ʕac̓ -nt axáʔ pnaʔ axáʔ anwí iʔ_t cu -nt -xʷ
you 2in -heart look -nt this maybe this you as tell -nt -2erg
it's your wish. Look, as you said, you have

kʷ [k]snəqsílxʷ 567 uɬ mat k̓əɬtəqpí··lsmənsəlx mat i t
kʷ k+s+nqs=ilxʷ uɬ mat k̓ɬ+tqp=ils+m -nt -s -lx mat i t
2kn have_relative and maybe worry_about -nt -3e2obj -pl maybe art agInst
relatives. I suppose your relatives are worrying

asnəqsílxʷ 568 mat taʔlí mat xʷaʔɬk̓əɬpaʔx̌áməlx 569 mat
a -s+nqs=ilxʷ mat taʔlíʔ mat xʷaʔ+ɬ+k̓ɬ+paʔx̌á+m -lx mat
2in -relative maybe very_much maybe think_much -pl maybe
about you. They must be thinking lots of things; they

nstílsəlx mat ha kʷ cxʷəlxʷá··lt {kṁ ha} km mat waẏ kʷ ƛ̓lal
n+st=ils -lx mat haʔ kʷ c -xʷl•xʷal+t kṁ mat waẏ kʷ ƛ̓l•al
think -pl maybe inter 2kn hab -alive or maybe yes 2kn dead
must wonder whether you are alive, or maybe you are dead.

570 uɬ q̓sápiʔ uɬ lut t̓ə cwíkstəmsəlx 571 uɬ
uɬ q̓sápiʔ uɬ lut t̓ c -wik -st -m -s -lx uɬ
and long_time and not negfac custˆ -see -ˆcust -2obj -3erg -pl and
It's been a long time since they have seen you. And

ʕáċənt ilíʔ mʕan kʷu x̌íləm mnímɬtət axáʔ iʔ l sťəmkʔíltət
ʕaċ -nt ilíʔ mʕan kʷu x̌il+m mnimɬ+tt axáʔ iʔ l s+ť mkʔ=ilt -t
look_at -nt there intj 4kn do_like we this art about daughter -4in
look, that's just the way we figured about our daughter. 32:05

572 uɬ talí·· {kʷu} kʷu xʷaʔɬk̓əɬpaʔx̌ám kʷu paʔpaʔsínk 573 ɬ
uɬ taʔlíʔ kʷu xʷaʔ+ɬ+k̓ɬ+paʔx̌á+m kʷu paʔ•paʔs=ínk ɬ
and very_much 4kn think_much 4kn sad if
We wondered about lots of things, we felt bad if

ksmipnúntəm ɬ kscxʷəlxʷálts kəm̓ ƛ̓lal 574 uɬ
ks -my+p -nu -nt -m ɬ ksc -xʷl•xʷal+t -s km̓ ƛ̓l•al uɬ
futt^ -learn -manage -nt -4erg if futPerfi -alive -3i or dead and
we would find out if she was alive or dead. And

ʕapnáʔ iʔ {kʷu əɬ} kʷu əɬckícəntəm, [t] anwí xʷəlxʷəltstíxʷ
ʕapnáʔ iʔ kʷu ɬ+c+kic -nt -m t anwí xʷl•xʷl+t -st -ixʷ
now art 3e4obj arrive_cisl_back -nt -psv agInst you alive -caus -2erg
now we got her back, you brought her back alive.

575 uɬ ixíʔ {kʷ iks} kʷ ikscúnəm axáʔ {iʔ kʷ is} iʔ kʷ
uɬ ixíʔ kʷ i -ks -cun+m axáʔ iʔ kʷ
and that 2kʷu 1i -futi -say this art 2kn
And now this is what I am going to say to you, my son-in-law.

isník̓əɬxʷ {uɬ lut xí i} 576 {i··ksx̌əlpínaʔlx} i·· ksx̌əlpínaʔlx 577 cúntəm
i -s+nik̓=ɬxʷ i·· k+s+x̌lp=ínaʔ -lx cu -nt -m
1in -son_in_law intj have_daylight -pl tell -nt -psv
[end of tape] 32:38 *Daylight came.* *His*

i t sx̌aʔ•x̌áʔs sənk̓líp 578 axáʔ tx̌ʷiws a tl
iʔ t s+x̌áʔ•x̌aʔ -s s+n+k̓lʼ=ip axáʔ tx̌ʷ=iw̓s a tľ
art agInst father_in_law -3in Coyote this half intj from
father-in-law said to Coyote: *"Half of*

isqʷəsqʷasíʔa 579 [a]ɬíʔ incá iʔ kən a ilmíxʷəm 580 uɬ
i -s+qʷs•qʷasíʔa aɬíʔ in+cá iʔ kn a yl=mixʷ+m uɬ
1in -children because I art 1kn art chief and
my children... *I am the one who is boss,* *and*

ixíʔ {i s laʔkín̓} ċinstn axáʔ {isqʷsqʷs} isqʷəsqʷasíʔa 581 uɬ ixíʔ
ixíʔ ċin -st -n axáʔ i -s+qʷs•qʷasíʔa uɬ ixíʔ
that say_what -st -1erg this 1in -children and then
whatever I say to my children *they*

x̌ast iʔ spuʔúscəlx {uɬ huym} 582 tx̌ʷiw̓s axáʔ iʔ tl isqʷəsqʷasíʔa
x̌as+t iʔ s+puʔ=ús -c -lx tx̌ʷ=iw̓s axáʔ iʔ tľ i -s+qʷs•qʷasíʔa
good art heart -3in -pl half this art from 1in -children
consent to it. *Half of my children is*

ixíʔ inktxʷmín 583 ixíʔ kɬəntkʷílsc axáʔ {iʔ}
ixíʔ in -k+txʷ+min ixíʔ kɬ -n+t+kʷil=s -c axáʔ
that 1in -contribution that to_be -keep_company -3i this
my bonus to you. *My grandchildren are going to be*

isən?am?íma?t 584 ałí? qʷəňcín 585 talí x̌mínkən
i -s+n+?am•?íma?t ałí? qʷň=cin ta?lí? x̌m=ink -n
1in -grand_children so pity very_much like -1erg
their companions. *It's a pity; 1:00* *I love*

isən?am?íma?t 586 uł {ałí} ałí? asqʷəsqʷasí?a uł ałí? waẏ {t ł}
i -s+n+?am•?íma?t uł ałí? a -s+qʷs•qʷasí?a uł ałí? waẏ
1in -grand_children and because 2in -children and so yes
my grandchildren. *Because they are your children you'll take them*

łxʷúystxʷəlx 587 uł cəm̓ nk̓aw?awpílsəlx 588 uł {ałí} mnímłtət
ł+xʷuy+st -xʷ -lx uł cm̓ n+k̓aw•aw+p=íls -lx uł mnimł+tt
take_st_back -2erg -pl and maybe lonesome_pl -pl and we
back with you. *They might get lonesome* *because*

kʷu ťíxʷləm kʷu sqilxʷ 589 kʷu q̓ʷəyq̓ʷáy kʷu sťmʕált 590 uł axá?
kʷu ťixʷl+m kʷu s+qilxʷ kʷu q̓ʷy•q̓ʷaʕy kʷu s+ťm=ʕalt uł axá?
4kn different 4kn person 4kn black 4kn cow and this
we are different people. *We are Black Buffaloes* *and you*

mnímłəmp {p s s} p sqilxʷ 591 uł lut xʷus {ťəks ťəksa··} ťə
mnimł+mp p s+qilxʷ uł lut xʷus ť
you 5kn person and not in_a_hurry negfac
are people. *And they won't get acquainted*

ksúxʷi?səlx i t xa?x?ítsəlx 592 sc̓x̌ilx uł
k -súxʷ ẏ -s -lx i? t xa?•x?ít -s -lx sc+?x̌il+x uł
futt^ -know -nt -3erg -pl art agInst older_relative -3in -pl reason_why and
[quickly] with their relatives; *that's why*

cəm̓ {nk̓əw} nk̓əw?awpíls 593 uł waẏ tx̌ʷiws axá? i tl
cm̓ n+k̓aw•aw+p=íls uł waẏ tx̌ʷ=iẃs axá? i? tl̓
maybe lonesome_pl and yes half this art from
they might get lonesome. *Half of my children*

isqʷəsqʷasí?a ia kłəłxʷúym[əlx] 594 i[xí?] kłəntkʷílscəlx axá?
i -s+qʷs•qʷasí?a i? kł -ł+xʷuy+m ixí? kł -n+t+kʷil=s -c -lx axá?
1in -children art futi -go_back that to_be -keep_company -3i -pl this
will be going back; 2:06 *they are going to be companions to*

isən?am?íma?t 595 ixí? kʷ iksc̓əx̌ʷxítəm {s} [ax]á? i kʷ
i -s+n+?am•?íma?t ixí? kʷ i -ks -c̓x̌ʷ -xit -m axá? i? kʷ
1in -grand_children that 2kʷu 1i -futi -promise -xit -apsv this art 2kʷu
my grandchildren. *This is what I am telling you, you are*

ilmíxʷəm 596 cut sənk̓líp waẏ, waẏ lut, lut ixí? asck̓əłpáx̌ 597 waẏ
yl=mixʷ+m cut s+n+k̓l̓=ip waẏ waẏ lut lut ixí? a -sc -k̓ł+pax̌ waẏ
chief say Coyote well well not not that 2i -pftv -thinking well
the chief." *Coyote said, "What you are thinking is not right.* *It's*

ilí? alá? asnəqsílxʷ {uł} 598 uł axá? {as} asqʷəsqʷasí?a waẏ ilí?lx
ilí? alá? a -s+nqs=ilxʷ uł axá? a -s+qʷs•qʷasí?a waẏ ilí? -lx
there here 2in -relative and this 2in -children yes there -pl
your people, they'll stay here. *And your children*

alá? salá?xəlx
alá? s -alá? -x -lx
here ipftv^ -here -^ipftv -pl
will stay here.

599 uɬ ixí? asən?am?íma?t alá? nixʷ
uɬ ixí? a -s+n+?am•?íma?t alá? nixʷ
and then 2in -grand_children here also
And your grandchildren will also

salá?xəlx
s -alá? -x -lx
ipftv^ -here -^ipftv -pl
stay here.

600 uɬ axá? intkɬmílxʷ nixʷ alá? salá?x
uɬ axá? in -tkɬ+m=ilxʷ nixʷ alá? s -alá? -x
and this 1in -wife also here ipftv^ -here -^ipftv
And even my wife stays here. 3:01

601 waẏ t'i kən kṅáṅaqs mi kən ɬxʷuy
waẏ t'i? kn k=ṅá•ṅaqs mi kn ɬ+xʷuy
well evid 1kn alone_dim fut 1kn go_back
I'll go back alone."

602 cúntəm axá? i ta
cu -nt -m axá? i? t
tell -nt -psv this art agInst
The chief said to him,

ilmíxʷəm uɬ sċkinx
yl=mixʷ+m uɬ sc+?kin+x
chief and why_is_it
"And why?

603 sċkinx {as} asənk̓ʷəɬmrrím antkəɬmílxʷ
sc+?kin+x a -s+nk̓ʷ+ɬ+mr•r•im an -tkɬ+m=ilxʷ
why_is_it 2in -spouse 2in -wife
Why, it's your wife, your woman,

uɬ asqʷəsqʷasí?a məɬ alá kʷu ɬ cəɬwíɬtxʷ
uɬ a -s+qʷs•qʷasí?a mɬ alá? kʷu ɬ c -ɬwi -ɬt -xʷ
and 2in -children and here 1obj subord act -leave -ɬt -2erg
and your children, that you leave here with me."

604 cúntəm
cu -nt -m
tell -nt -psv
Coyote

t sənk̓líp, lut, t'əxʷ ixí? aɬí? isck̓əɬpáx̌
t s+n+k̓l'=ip lut t'xʷ ixí? aɬí? i -sc -k̓ɬ+pax̌
agInst Coyote not emph that so 1i -pftv -thinking
said, "Well, no, this is what I have figured.

605 waẏ ixí? lut ʕáċənt
waẏ ixí? lut ʕaċ -nt
well then not look -nt
Look,

anwí {t} t' isənt'ina?scút kʷu ɬa cqʷəlqʷílstxʷ {uɬ}
anwí t' i -s -n+t'y=na?+scút kʷu ɬa? c -qʷl•qʷil -st -xʷ
you negfac 1i -intt -dispute 1obj when cust^ -talk -caus -2erg
I didn't dispute what you were telling me.

606 uɬ lut incá {kʷuaks} kʷu aksənt'ina?cútxtəm
uɬ lut in+cá kʷu a -ks -n+t'y=na?+cút -xt -m
and not I 1kʷu 2i -futi -dispute -xit -apsv
Don't you dispute my word.

607 ixí? waẏ
ixí? waẏ
that yes
This is

isck̓əɬpáx̌
i -sc -k̓ɬ+pax̌
1i -pftv -thinking
what I figured."

608 cúntəm axá? i? t q̓ʷəyq̓ʷáʕy {i ts} ta
cu -nt -m axá? i? t q̓ʷy•q̓ʷaʕy t
tell -nt -psv this art agInst black agInst
The Black boss said

ilmíxʷəm
yl=mixʷ+m
chief
to him, 4:01

609 cúntəm waẏ, waẏ mat t'əxʷ ixí? aspu?ús
cu -nt -m waẏ waẏ mat t'xʷ ixí? a -s+pu?=ús
tell -nt -psv well well maybe evidently that 2in -heart
he said to him, "Well, if that's how you feel.

610 waẏ límləmtx, {lut} lut {k} t' isənstíls t' aksɬwínəm
waẏ lim•lm+t+x lut t' i -s -n+stils t' a -ks -ɬwin+m
well thank_you not negfac 1i -intt -think negfac 2i -futi -leave
Thank you. I didn't think you'd leave your

asənk̓ʷəɬmrrím {uɬ} 611 aɬ[í?] ixí? asƛ̓xʷúp {astaxʷ} uɬ way̓ anwí
a -s+nk̓ʷ+ɬ+mr•r•im aɬí? ixí? a -s+ƛ̓xʷup uɬ way̓ anwí
2in -spouse so that 2in -earning and well you
married woman. *Look, you earned her, and if it's the way*

aspu?ús 612 cúntəm way̓ náx̌əmɬ lut {aks} ta_niʕíp aksənɬíptəm
a -s+pu?=ús cu -nt -m way̓ nax̌mɬ lut ta_n+yʕ=ip a -ks -n+ɬipt+m
2in -heart tell -nt -psv well but not forever 2i -futi -forget
you want it..." *He said "Yes," "But don't ever forget*

antkɬmílxʷ 613 la?kín uɬ {kʷ kʷɬ t̓əstxʷúymstxʷ}
an -tkɬ+m=ilxʷ la+?kín uɬ
2in -wife whenever and
your woman. *Come over and see*

t̓əstxʷúymstxʷ asqʷəsqʷasí?a 614 cut sənk̓líp way̓ way̓
t̓s -t+xʷuy+m -st -xʷ a -s+qʷs•qʷasí?a cut s+n+k̓l̓=ip way̓ way̓
habCisl -go_towards -st -2erg 2in -children say Coyote well well
your children whenever." *Coyote said,*

ṅíṅw̓i? ixí? ɬ t̓əckícɬmən 615 way̓ t̓i_kmix incá kən {s}
ṅíṅw̓i? ixí? ɬ t̓c -kic -ɬm -n way̓ t̓i?_kmix in+cá kn
a_while then ? habCisl -reach_st/sb -5obj -1erg well only I 1kn
"Ok, I'll be over to see you all. *It's only that I got lonesome*

nk̓awpíls k̓ isnəqsílxʷ {məɬ} 616 uɬ {aɬ lut} lut scuts {sən} sənk̓líp uɬ
n+k̓aw+p=íls k̓ i -s+nqs=ilxʷ uɬ lut s -cut -s s+n+k̓l̓=ip uɬ
lonesome to 1in -relative and not nom -say -3i Coyote and
for my people." 5:04 *Coyote didn't tell him that*

aɬí? way̓ alá? kɬtkɬmilxʷ 617 ixí? t cúsəlx pul̓, púl̓la?xʷ
aɬí? way̓ alá? kɬ+tkɬ+m=ilxʷ ixí? cu -s -lx pul̓ púl̓=la?xʷ
because yes here have_wife then ? tell -3erg -pl Gopher Gopher
he already has a wife, *that's the one they call Gopher, "blow the dirt."*

618 ixí? uɬ aɬí? cniɬc uɬ scusts alapúl̓ 619 way̓ ixí?
ixí? uɬ aɬí? cniɬ+c uɬ s -cu -st -s ʕalapúl way̓ ixí?
that and so (s)he and cust^ -tell -^cust -3erg Gopher well that
And he calls her "alapúl." *That's*

nxixayápəlqs, kəṁ nc̓ayxʷápəlqs
n+xy•xay=áplqs kṁ n+c̓ayxʷ=áplqs
end_of_story take end_of_story
the end of the story. 5:32

Coyote and Grizzly

1 axáʔ sənk̓líp [iʔ] captíkʷłc {iksc} ikscaptíkʷl[əm] 2 kʷlí··wtəlx
axáʔ s+n+k̓l̓=ip iʔ captíkʷł -c i -ks -captíkʷl+m kʷl=iwt -lx
this Coyote art legends -3in 1i -futi -tell_stories live -pl
This is Coyote's fairy tale story I'm going to tell. *Coyote*

həłsənk̓líp naʔł sqʷəsqʷasíʔas 3 uł ałíʔ {is} isʔamʔúmłtəm
hł=s+n+k̓l̓=ip naʔł s+qʷs•qʷasíʔa -s uł ałíʔ i -s -ʔam•ʔúm -łt -m
Coyote_group with children -3in and so 1i -intt -announce -łt -apsv
and his family were sitting around, *and I am going to announce*

iʔ skʷíst[s] 4 t̓əxʷm t̓i sənk̓əlíp iʔ tkəłmílxʷs t̓i kmix a
iʔ s+kʷist -s t̓xʷ+m t̓iʔ s+n+k̓l̓=ip iʔ tkł+m=ilxʷ -s t̓iʔ kmix a
art name -3in emph evid Coyote art wife -3in evid only art
their names. *All I know is Coyote's*

cmiłtín 5 a·· xiʔ a[xáʔ] sənk̓líp iʔ skʷists, ixíʔ sənk̓əlíp
c -my -łt -in a ixíʔ axáʔ s+n+k̓l̓=ip iʔ s+kʷist -s ixíʔ s+n+k̓l̓=ip
cust^ -know -łt -1in intj that this Coyote art name -3in that Coyote
wife's [name]. *Coyote's name is "Coyote."*

6 uł axáʔ iʔ tkəłmílxʷ pul̓, púl̓laʔxʷ, uł t̓i tx̌ʷəmstís uł pul̓
uł axáʔ iʔ tkł+m=ilxʷ pul̓ púl̓=laʔxʷ uł t̓iʔ tx̌ʷm -st -is uł pul̓
and this art woman Gopher Gopher and evid straight -st -3erg and Gopher
And the woman is "Pul," "Gopher," and for short "Pul."

7 uł kmúsəms iʔ {łəł}, kcílcəlkst iʔ łəłsqʷsíʔs 8 axáʔ iʔ sxʔitx
uł k=mus•ms iʔ k+cil•cl=kst iʔ łł -sqʷsiʔ -s axáʔ iʔ s+xʔit=x
and four_persons art five art pl -son -3in this art oldest_one
And he has four, [no,] five sons. *The oldest one is*

ixíʔ sʕ̓aʔníxʷ, ixíʔ skəlkʷtílts 9 uł axáʔ {m} iʔ kmúsəms,
ixíʔ s+ʕan̓íxʷ ixíʔ s+k+lkʷ=t=ilt -s uł axáʔ iʔ k=mus•ms
that Muskrat that distant_child -3in and this art four_persons
Muskrat, his son from another woman; 1:00 *and these four here,*

ixíʔ {təl} təl̓ pul̓, púl̓laʔxʷ iʔ łəłsqʷsíʔs 10 xi··ʔ uł xƛ̓áƛ̓əlx
ixíʔ tl̓ pul̓ púl̓=laʔxʷ iʔ łł -sqʷsiʔ -s ixíʔ uł xƛ̓•aƛ̓ -lx
that from Gopher Gopher art pl -son -3in then and be_grown_pl -pl
from Gophie, they are Gopher's sons. *And the brothers*

axáʔ iʔ səncaʔcʔíliʔs 11 uł axáʔ səmx̌íkən, təkłmílxʷ ł səmx̌íkən,
axáʔ iʔ s+ncaʔ•cʔ=íliʔs uł axáʔ s+mx̌=ikn tkł+m=ilxʷ ł s+mx̌=ikn
this art brothers and this grizzly woman one_that grizzly
are grown up. *And Grizzly, Grizzly is a woman,*

nʔałnaʔsqílxʷt[ən] 12 uł kst̓əmkʔílt səmx̌íkən 13 way̓ swiʔnúmtx, ixíʔ
n+ʔałn+aʔ+s+qílxʷ+tn uł k+s+t̓mkʔ=ilt s+mx̌=ikn way̓ s+wy̓+numt=x ixíʔ
man_eater and have_daughter grizzly yes handsome that
a man-eater. *And Grizzly has a daughter.* *She is good looking, and*

iʔ mílaʔs 14 ixíʔ uɬ a cƛ̓əxʷstís {iʔ} iʔ sqilxʷ aɬíʔ
iʔ mílaʔ -s ixíʔ uɬ a c -ƛ̓xʷ -st -is iʔ s+qilxʷ aɬíʔ
art bait -3in that and art cust^ -kill_many -^cust -3erg art person because
she is her bait. *That's how she kills people, because she is*

nʔaɬnaʔsqílxʷtən 15 uɬ axáʔ matlán tla nx̌ʷyaʔɬpítkʷ kiʔ
n+ʔaɬn+aʔ+s+qílxʷ+tn uɬ axáʔ matlán tla n+x̌ʷyaʔ=ɬp=ítkʷ kiʔ
man_eater and this Madeline from Kettle rel
a cannibal. *Madeline[1] from Kettle River was living*

scwíxəx i l ɬʔamcnítkʷ 16 axáʔ ta səmx̌íkən 17 uɬ náx̌əmɬ
sc -wix -x iʔ l ɬʔa+m=cn=ítkʷ axáʔ t s+mx̌=ikn uɬ nax̌mɬ
ipftvp^ -live -^ipftvp art in close_to_shore this obl grizzly and but
right close to the river, 2:04 *this here Grizzly.* *But*

lut cmistín laʔkín put sənk̓líp 18 ixíʔ uɬ ksx̌əlpínaʔlx
lut c -my -st -in la+ʔkíń put s+n+k̓l̓=ip ixíʔ uɬ k+s+x̌l+p=ínaʔ -lx
not cust^ -know -^cust -1in wherever just Coyote then and have_daylight -pl
I don't know just where Coyote was. *His children are all grown up,*

uɬ aɬíʔ waẏ xƛ̓aƛ̓ axáʔ iʔ sqʷəsqʷasíʔas 19 uɬ axáʔ iʔ
uɬ aɬíʔ waẏ xƛ̓•aƛ̓ axáʔ iʔ s+qʷs•qʷasíʔa -s uɬ axáʔ iʔ
and so finish be_grown_pl this art children -3in and this art
and then one morning, *the oldest one*

sxʔitx way nnəx̌ʷnəx̌ʷíls 20 niʕíp q̓x̌ʷax̌ʷ k̓əl səmx̌íkən iʔ
s+xʔit=x waẏ n+nx̌ʷ•nx̌ʷ=ils n+yʕ=ip q̓x̌ʷ•ax̌ʷ k̓l s+mx̌=ikn iʔ
oldest_one yes want_wife always be_smitten for grizzly art
is thinking about a mate. *He started flirting with Grizzly's*

st̓əmkʔílts 21 uɬ cus iʔ ƛ̓ax̌əx̌ƛ̓x̌áps 22 waẏ ixíʔ
s+t̓mkʔ=ilt -s uɬ cu -s iʔ ƛ̓x̌•x̌•ƛ̓x̌a+p -s waẏ ixíʔ
daughter -3in and tell -3erg art parents -3in well then
daughter. *And he said to his parents:* *"I am*

ɬwíɬmən, waẏ kən ksʔawsənsucənmístaʔx k̓əl səmx̌íkən [iʔ
ɬwi -ɬm -n waẏ kn ks -ʔaw+s+n+sw=cn+míst -aʔx k̓l s+mx̌=ikn iʔ
leave -5obj -1erg yes 1kn incp^ -go_propose -^incp to grizzly art
going to leave you now, I am going to propose to Grizzly for

st̓əmkʔílts] 23 a··, cúsəlx waẏ, xʷuyx 24 waẏ ixíʔ
s+t̓mkʔ=ilt -s a cu -s -lx waẏ xʷuy -x waẏ ixíʔ
daughter -3in intj tell -3erg -pl OK go -isimptv well then
her daughter." *They said to him, "OK, go."* *He started*

sk̓ʷəlkstmísts, ca··ʕʷlx, uɬ k̓əɬʔaysəlscú··t 25 mat ʔá··q̓ʷsəm, {nixʷ mə}
s -k̓ʷl̓=kst+mist -s caʕʷ+lx uɬ k̓ɬ+ʔays=lscút mat ʔaq̓ʷ=s+m
nom -doll_up -3i bathe and change_clothes maybe shave
to doll himself up. He changed his clothes, 3:00 *I suppose he shaved,*

1 Apparently the man-eater's name.

mat nixʷ kaʕílsxnəm[2] 26 way̓ ixíʔ sxʷuys {i l} iʔ l stáɬəm 27 way̓
mat nixʷ kaʕ=ilsxn+m way̓ ixíʔ s -xʷuy -s iʔ l s+taɬm way̓
maybe also cut_hair well then nom -go -3i art in boat well
maybe cut his hair too. *Then he went in the boat.* *He*

ixíʔ sʔúcləms t̓əxʷ mat {k̓lak̓awtki} k̓awtímtk iʔ
ixíʔ s -ʔucl+m -s t̓xʷ mat k+ʔawtím=tk iʔ
then nom -paddle -3i evident maybe south art
paddled. And I guess he was going

silíʔxləx 28 uɬ mʕan ɬə ksənk̓wílxs a
s -ilíʔ -x -lx[3] uɬ mʕan ɬ ks -n+k̓w+ilx -s a
ipftv^ -there -^ipftv -pl and intj subord futi -go_upstream -3i art
south, *that's why he had to go up the*

nx̌ʷəyaʔɬpítkʷ 29 xʷu··y cəqəqcnítkʷ iʔ l skiyaʕcínəms səmx̌íkən
n+x̌ʷyaʔ=ɬp=ítkʷ xʷuy cq•q=cn=itkʷ iʔ l s+k+yaʕ=cin+m -s s+mx̌=ikn
Kettle go come_on_shore art at shore -3in grizzly
Kettle River.[4] *He went and landed in front of Grizzly's.*

30 way̓ ʕacəntís iʔ stáɬəms uɬ ixíʔ, kʷis {iʔ i a·} iʔ cq̓íləns
way̓ ʕac -nt -is iʔ s+taɬm -s uɬ ixíʔ kʷi -s iʔ cq̓=iln -s
yes tie -nt -3erg art boat -3in and then take -3erg art arrow -3in
He tied his boat, and he took his bow and arrows.

31 kʷis iʔ cq̓íləns uɬ ixíʔ nɬəxʷpápqnəms 32 uɬ ixíʔ
kʷi -s iʔ cq̓=iln -s uɬ ixíʔ n+ɬxʷ+p=ap=qn+m -s uɬ ixíʔ
take -3erg art arrow -3in and then loop_over_head -3erg and then
He took his bow and arrow and he looped it over his shoulder. *He went up*

sx̌ʔíƛ̓əms kɬqəltús 33 ilíʔ ckɬwix səmx̌íkən 34 way̓
s -x̌iƛ̓+m -s kɬ+qlt=us ilíʔ c -kɬ+wix s+mx̌=ikn way̓
nom -climb -3i hill_top there hab -live grizzly well
the bank, got up there. 4:00 *That's where Grizzly's house is.* *He*

k̓ɬənciʔípəm {ə t̓əxʷ} uɬ ixíʔ ksmiʔmáyts 35 iwá t̓əxʷ
k̓ɬ+n+cʔ=ip+m uɬ ixíʔ ks+my̓•may+t[5] -s iwá t̓xʷ
knock_on_door and that proper_way -3in even evidently
knocked on the door, because that's the proper way,[6] *even though it's just*

nx̌ʷáyqən 36 uɬ t̓əxʷ {i·} i l məlkʷút uɬ k̓əɬnciʔípəm 37 way̓
n+x̌ʷay=qn uɬ t̓xʷ iʔ l mlkʷ=ut uɬ k̓ɬ+n+cʔ=ip+m way̓
poles_tied_together and evidently art in pole and knock_on_door well
a tipi. *He knocked on the pole.* *And*

2 I have recorded this stem also as qaʕ=ílsxn.
3 This use of -lx is unclear.
4 The geography is not clear. The Kettle river runs north to south.
5 The laryngealization of the y in this form is not clear; the analysis is uncertain.
6 Actually, this is not the proper Colville way, but it is the proper way for a white audience.

cúntəm t səmx̌íkən cən?úɬxʷəxʷ 38 uɬ ilí? kɬa?qís {i?}
cu -nt -m t s+mx̌=ikn c+n+?uɬxʷ -xʷ uɬ ilí? k+ɬa?=qí -s
tell -nt -psv agInst grizzly enter_cisl -ˆimptv and there lean_st_against -3erg
Grizzly said, "Come in!" *He leaned his weapons there,*

a nx̌əcílstəns, i cq̓íləns uɬ i? ckʷinks 39 {uɬ} uɬ aɬí?
a n+x̌c=ils+tn -s i? cq̓=iln -s uɬ i? ckʷ=ink s uɬ aɬí?
art bow_and_arrow -3in art arrow -3in and art bow 3in and because
his arrow and his bow, *because*

kʷa i? sqilxʷ uɬ {ksəˑ} ksənq̓ʷəɬtí?stən 40 uɬ {c?x̌iɬ t} c?x̌iɬt suyápix
kʷa i? s+qilxʷ uɬ k+s+n+q̓ʷɬ+t=i?st+n uɬ c+?x̌iɬ+t s+wyapy=x
intj art Indian and have_scabbard and like white_person
Indians have scabbards, *just like white people.*

41 kʷa ʕaċənt i? suyápix {uɬksya} nixʷ ksənq̓ʷəɬtí?stən i? l sululmínk
kʷa ʕaċ -nt i? s+wyapy=x nixʷ k+s+n+q̓ʷɬ+t=i?st+n i? l s+wl•wlm=ink
intj look_at -nt art white_person also have_scabbard art for gun
And look, white people, too, have scabbards for their guns,

42 uɬ axá? nixʷ c?x̌iɬ axá? i l cq̓ílən 43 uɬ sċx̌ilx aɬí? ṫi
uɬ axá? nixʷ c+?x̌iɬ axá? i? l cq̓=iln uɬ sc+?x̌il+x aɬí? ṫi?
and this also like this art for arrow and reason_why because evid
just like for arrows. *That's how the arrows*

ilí? ctxam {i?} i? cq̓íləns {uɬ} na?ɬ ckʷinks 44 ṫi kʷm̓iɬ məɬ
ilí? c -txa+m i? cq̓=iln -s na?ɬ ckʷ=ink -s ṫi? kʷm̓iɬ mɬ
there hab -insert art arrow -3in with bow -3in evid suddenly and
and the bow are stuck in [the scabbard]. 5:05 *Promptly*

ɬəxʷpúsəms məɬ ?uckláx̌nəms {a} 45 lut ṫa
ɬxʷ+p=us+m -s mɬ ?uckl=áx̌n+m -s lut ṫ
loop_over_head -3erg and loop_over_shoulder -3erg not negfac
he looped it over his shoulder and over his head. *He doesn't*

ckəm̓km̓stís 46 way̓ cúntəm t səmx̌íkən
c -km̓•km̓ -st -is way̓ cu -nt -m t s+mx̌=ikn
custˆ -hold -ˆcust -3erg well tell -nt -psv agInst grizzly
hold them in his hand. *Grizzly said,*

cən?úɬxʷəxʷ 47 way̓ n?uɬxʷ 48 cúntəm t səmx̌íkən, way̓ kʷu
c+n+?uɬxʷ -xʷ way̓ n+?uɬxʷ cu -nt -m t s+mx̌=ikn way̓ kʷu
enter_cisl -isimptv yes enter tell -nt -psv agInst grizzly well 1obj
"Come in!" *He went in.* *Grizzly said, "You arrived here to me,*

kícəntxʷ, way̓ kʷu x̌ċíkstməntxʷ 49 aˑˑ cus
kic -nt -xʷ way̓ kʷu x̌ċ=ikst+m -nt -xʷ a cu -s
reach_st/sb -nt -2erg well 1obj surprise -nt -2erg intj tell -3erg
you surprise me." *He said,*

way̓, {lut kʷ ṫə} ṫəxʷ lut x̌əċx̌áċt {ṫəxʷ} 50 way̓ kʷ
way̓ ṫxʷ lut x̌ċ•x̌aċ+t way̓ kʷ
yes emph not important well 2kʷu
"It's not important. *I have*

isċawsənsucənmístəm {xa} l astʼəmkʔílt 51 uɬ aɬíʔ ilíʔ mut iʔ
i -s -c+ʔaw+s+n+sw=cn+míst+m l a -s+tʼmkʔ=ilt uɬ aɬíʔ ilíʔ mut iʔ
1i -intt -come_propose for 2in -daughter and so there sit_sg art
come to propose to you for your daughter." And she was sitting right

stʼəmkʔílts k̓la nsək̓ʷtílp 52 eh waẏ swiʔnúmtx 53 cus, a··
s+tʼmkʔ=ilt -s k̓l n+s+k̓ʷt=ilp eh waẏ s+wẏ+numt=x cu -s a
daughter -3in to across intj yes handsome tell -3erg intj
there on the other side of the room. My, she's good looking. She [the mother]

waẏ, cus uɬ naqs náx̌əmɬ {m} iʔ kʷ ikscúnəm 54 ixíʔ uɬ
waẏ cu -s uɬ naqs nax̌mɬ iʔ kʷ i -ks -cun -m ixíʔ uɬ
OK tell -3erg and one but art 2kʷu 1i -futi -tell -apsv then and
said to him, "All right. But I am going to tell you one thing." 6:00 She

cársəms iʔ stʼəmkʔílts ɬə ksʔácqaʔx 55 waẏ ixíʔ
cars+m -s iʔ s+tʼmkʔ=ilt -s ɬ ks -ʔácqaʔ -x waẏ ixíʔ
motion -3erg art daughter -3in subord incp^ -go_out -^incp yes then
made a motion to her daughter to go out. And the woman

sʔácqaʔs axáʔ iʔ təkɬmílxʷ 56 ixíʔ ʔácqaʔ uɬ ixíʔ mat axáʔ
s -ʔácqaʔ -s axáʔ iʔ tkɬ+m=ilxʷ ixíʔ ʔácqaʔ uɬ ixíʔ mat axáʔ
nom -go_out -3i this art woman that go_out and then maybe this
[the daughter] went out. She went out and she stepped

nqəlʼqəlʼutípɬtəm axáʔ {iʔ} iʔ cq̓íləns 57 uɬ aɬíʔ kʷa iʔ
n+ql•ql=ut=íp -ɬt -m axáʔ iʔ cq̓=iln -s uɬ aɬíʔ kʷa iʔ
step_on -ɬt -apsv this art arrow -3in and because intj art
on his arrows. Hard points

sənululmúsaʔst[ən] uɬ {c} cəncəqʷcáqʷqən {i l} i l sənk̓ámqən
s+n+wl•wlm=ús=aʔst+n uɬ c -n+cqʷ•caqʷ=qn iʔ l s+n+k̓m=qn
arrow_points and hab -stuck_on_end art in tip
are stuck on the ends.

58 {uɬ aɬíʔ tə· iʔ t sútən iʔ t} a kləʕʷəntís iʔ snululmúsaʔstən
a k+lʕʷ -nt -is iʔ s+n+wl•wlm=ús=aʔst+n
intj fasten -nt -3erg art arrow_points
He fastens the hard points with sinew,

59 məɬ {its} iʔ t tinx nlk̓ips 60 məɬ iʔ t tʼiċ
mɬ iʔ t tinx n+lk̓=ip -s mɬ iʔ t tʼiċ
and art agInst sinew tie_tip -3erg and art agInst pitch
he wraps it around [the points]. Then he melts

ʕaməntís 61 məɬ ixíʔ kmíƛ̓ċaʔs məɬ yaʔx̌í {x̌ə} x̌əẇáẇ uɬ ixíʔ
ʕam -nt -is mɬ ixíʔ k+míƛ̓=ċaʔ -s mɬ yaʔx̌í x̌ẇ•aẇ uɬ ixíʔ
melt -nt -3erg and then smear -3erg and that_one dried and then
pitch, and he smears it around, and when it gets dry, it's glued

ilíʔ ki cṗaq̓ 62 {uɬ put cʔx̌iɬ t t a ɬtʼaʕpmíst} put cʔx̌iɬ t sululmín{k}
ilíʔ kiʔ ċpaq̓ put c+ʔx̌iɬ t s+wl•wl+min
there rel glued just like obj_cʔx̌iɬ gun
strong. 7:01 It's just like a gun,

ki? stəɬtáɬts 63 uɬ axá? aɬí? {cnululmast} cənululmúsa?st
ki? s -tɬ•taɬ+t -s uɬ axá? aɬí? c -n+wl•wlm=ús=a?st
rel nom -be_right -3i and this so hab -hard_points
straight. *And it has the hard points,*

64 uɬ ixí? lut {t̓a} t̓a cx̌ʷc̓ap 65 put c?x̌iɬ i? t
uɬ ixí? lut t̓ c -x̌ʷc̓a+p put c+?x̌iɬ i? t
and that not negfac hab -break_in_two just like art obj_c+?x̌iɬ
that's the kind that don't break. *They are sharp*

nínk̓mən i? sx̌ʷy̓x̌ʷáy̓c 66 ɬa? ciláp i? stim̓ məɬ txi?xán
ni•nk̓+mn i? s+x̌ʷy•x̌ʷay+t -s ɬa? c -yla+p i? stim̓ mɬ t+xy̓=xán
knife art sharpness -3in when hab -be_hit art something and through
as a knife. *One with strong arms, whatever it hits*

n?úɬxʷ, kəm̓ i? k̓ʷəck̓ʷcáx̌ən 67 uɬ ksɬəx̌ʷm̓úsa? axá? i? t
n+?uɬxʷ km̓ i? k̓ʷc•k̓ʷc=ax̌n uɬ ks -ɬx̌ʷ+m=úsa? axá? i? t
enter or art strong_arm and futi -go_through this art obj_itr
it goes right through, *it goes right through*

sƛ̓a?cínəm, i? t stim̓ 68 a uɬ ixí? cúntəm t səmx̌íkən
s+ƛ̓a?=cín+m i? t stim̓ a uɬ ixí? cu -nt -m t s+mx̌=ikn
deer art obj_itr something intj and then tell -nt -psv agInst grizzly
deer or anything. *Grizzly said to him:*

69 a·· way̓, way̓ {i} mat aspu?ús, uɬ axá? naqs i? kʷ
a way̓ way̓ mat a -s+pu?=ús uɬ axá? naqs i? kʷ
intj yes yes maybe 2in -heart and this one art 2kʷu
"Ah, your heart is in a good place. I am going to tell you

ikscúnəm 70 way̓ ixí? {k̓la ɬ?a} k̓əl naɬ?úla?xʷ ixí? i? l
i -ks -cun -m way̓ ixí? k̓l na+ɬ?=úla?xʷ ixí? i? l
1i -futi -tell -apv well there to other_side_of_mountain there art at
one thing. *Over at that open place on the other side of*

k̓əɬx̌sínk 71 ilí? ki? k̓əɬ?aksuxínk i? səmx̌íkən 72 way̓ ixí? kʷu
k̓ɬ+x̌s=ink ilí? ki? k̓ɬ+?aks+wx=ínk i? s+mx̌=ikn way̓ ixí? kʷu
side_hill there rel stand_on_side_hill art grizzly well that 1obj
the hill, *that is where a grizzly stays.* *I want you to get it for*

ƛ̓a?ɬtíkʷ iksənqəqpáqstxən 73 axá? {i s} t̓əxʷ i? síp̓i?s
ƛ̓a? -ɬt -ikʷ i -k -s+n+q•qp=aqst=xn axá? t̓xʷ i? síp̓i? -s
fetch -ɬt -imptv 1i -to_be -under_hip_mat this emph art hide -3in
me to put [its hide] under my hip to lay on. 8:04 *Go after*

ixí? ƛ̓a?ntíxʷ 74 ixí? uɬ kʷu kʷiɬtxʷ ist̓əmk?ílt alá? kʷu
ixí? ƛ̓a? -nt -ixʷ ixí? uɬ kʷu kʷi -ɬt -xʷ i -s+t̓mk?=ilt alá? kʷu
that fetch -nt -2erg then and 1obj take -ɬt -2erg 1i -daughter here 1obj
her hide. *Then after you bring it to me you can take*

ckicxɬtxʷ 75 uɬ kʷu kʷiɬtxʷ axá? ist̓əmk?ílt 76 a··
c+kic+x -ɬt -xʷ uɬ kʷu kʷi -ɬt -xʷ axá? i -s+t̓mk?=ilt a
arrive_cisl -ɬt -2erg then 1obj take -ɬt -2erg this 1i -daughter intj
my daughter, *you can have my daughter."* *He*

cus waẏ, ixíʔ ɬa kɬcucín 77 a uɬ aɬíʔ miʔílsəms
cu -s waẏ ixíʔ ɬaʔ kɬ+cw=cin a uɬ aɬíʔ my=ils+m -s
tell -3erg OK that the_one_that good_word intj and so deem -3erg
said, "All right, that's what I like to hear." *And he thought the arrows*

qʷámqʷəmt iʔ sk̓ʷúl̓aʔsts iʔ cq̓íləns uɬ iʔ ckʷinks 78 uɬ
qʷam•qʷm+t iʔ s+k̓ʷúl̓=aʔst -s iʔ cq̓=iln -s uɬ iʔ ckʷ=ink -s uɬ
excellent art handywork -3in art arrow -3in and art bow -3in and
and the bow he had fixed are good. *And*

sisyús iʔ l spíx̌əm {i s} 79 lut t̓a cənx̌íləmsts iʔ səmx̌íkən
sy•sy=us iʔ l s+pix̌+m lut t̓ c -n+x̌il+m -st -s iʔ s+mx̌=ikn
smart art at hunting not negfac cust^ -fear -^cust -3erg art grizzly
that he is good at hunting. *He isn't afraid of grizzlies or of*

iʔ stim̓ 80 waẏ ixíʔ sxʷuys uɬ iʔ k̓əl stáɬəms 81 axáʔ
iʔ stim̓ waẏ ixíʔ s -xʷuy -s uɬ iʔ k̓l s+taɬm -s axáʔ
art whatever well then nom -go -3i up_to art to boat -3in this
anything. *He went to his boat.* *He*

ɬəxʷpúsəms, t̓i ʔácqaʔ uɬ ɬəxʷpúsəms {i} iʔ cq̓íləns,
ɬxʷ+p=us+m -s t̓iʔ ʔácqaʔ uɬ ɬxʷ+p=us+m -s iʔ cq̓=iln -s
loop_over_head -3erg evid go_out and loop_over_head -3erg art arrow -3in
went out and put his weapon over his neck, looped it under

nʔucqláx̌nəms 82 ixíʔ naʔɬcəcám 83 ixíʔ sic naʔmút iʔ l
n+ʔuckl=áx̌n+m -s ixíʔ naɬc•c•ám ixíʔ sic n+ʔam=út iʔ l
loop_over_arm -3erg that forget that then sit_inside art in
his arm. 9:02 *I forgot.* *He sat in his boat and*

stáɬəms uɬ ixíʔ {sk̓əwílxs} 84 a· st̓áq̓əms k̓la nsq̓ʷut
s+taɬm -s uɬ ixíʔ a s -t̓aq̓m -s k̓l n+s+q̓ʷut
boat -3in and then intj nom -cross_stream -3i to other_side
{went upstream}; *He crossed to the other side;*

85 waẏ k̓la nsq̓ʷut cqaq 86 aʔ ixíʔ nɬíptmən 87 cúntəm t
waẏ k̓l n+s+q̓ʷut cq•aq aʔ ixíʔ n+ɬiptm -n cu -nt -m t
yes to other_side land intj that forget -1erg tell -nt -psv agInst
he landed on the other side. *Oh, I forgot.*[7] *Grizzly had*

səmx̌íkən, cúntəm 88 lut {təl} təl ẇíẇaʔst mi {ts} st̓aʕpəntíxʷ
s+mx̌=ikn cu -nt -m lut tl ẇí•ẇaʔs+t mi c -t̓aʕp -nt -ixʷ
grizzly tell -nt -psv not from high_dim fut act -shoot -nt -2erg
told him: *"Don't try to shoot it [the grizzly] from above.*

89 {cəm} cəm̓ ləxʷpnúnts t̓əxʷ wíkənts aɬíʔ 90 lúti
cm̓ lxʷ+p -nun -t -s t̓xʷ wik -nt -s aɬíʔ lút+i
maybe hurt -manage -nt -3e2obj emph see -nt -3e2obj so before
She [the grizzly] might hurt you if she sees you.[8] *Before*

7 "I forgot to mention what I am about to relate."
8 While person markers are sex-independent in Colville, we can't avoid a choice in English.

aksk̓ətmínəm məɬ waẏ k̓əɬníxəlmənts 91 atlá? tla ixʷút, tla
a -ks -k̓t+min+m mɬ waẏ k̓ɬ+nixl+m -nt -s atlá? tla yxʷ=ut tla
2i -futi -get_close and yes hear -nt -3e2obj from_here from below from
you get close to her she'll hear you. *Go towards her*

ixʷút mi txʷúyməntxʷ 92 {uɬ ixí? mi lut} ixí? mi k̓a?tmíntxʷ,
yxʷ=ut mi t+xʷuy+m -nt -xʷ ixí? mi k̓a?t+min -t -xʷ
below fut go_towards -nt -2erg then fut go_near -nt -2erg
from below. *That's how you can get close to her,*

ixí? lut ksləxʷpnúnts 93 a· waẏ, 94 ixí? naɬcəcám, i?
ixí? lut ks -lxʷ+p -nun -t -s a waẏ ixí? naɬc•c•ám i?
that not futt^ -hurt -manage -nt -3e2obj intj Ok that forget art
she won't hurt you." *"Oh, Ok."* *That's what I just*

cúntəm t səmx̌íkən 95 waẏ ixí? cqəqcnítkʷ 96 waẏ
cu -nt -m t s+mx̌=ikn waẏ ixí? cq•q=cn=itkʷ waẏ
tell -nt -psv agInst grizzly well then come_on_shore yes
thought of, what Grizzly had said. *Then he landed. 10:03* *He*

ʕacəntís i? stáɬəms, ixí? sx̌íƛ̓əms 97 i·· cəm̓ k̓əɬkʷƛ̓áp
ʕac -nt -is i? s+taɬm -s ixí? s -x̌iƛ̓+m -s i·· cm̓ k̓ɬ+kʷƛ̓a+p
tie -nt -3erg art boat -3in then nom -climb -3i intj maybe come_in_sight
tied his boat, and went up the hill. *Maybe he'll get her in sight*

i l k̓əɬx̌sínk 98 i··, c̓x̌əl·wís a? t səmx̌íkən
i? l k̓ɬ+x̌s=ink i·· c -?ax̌l+lwís a? t s+mx̌=ikn
art in side_hill intj hab -mill_about art obl grizzly
in the open ground. *Grizzly was fooling around there,*

99 səccíqx axá? {t s} t səʕʷx̌ʷíp {xʷat} 100 aɬiá
sc -ciq -x axá? t s+ʕʷx̌ʷ=ip aɬi+á
ipftvp^ -dig -^ipftvp this obj_itr roots because_not
digging for roots. *I don't know*

cmiɬtín axá? i? s?íɬəns i? səmx̌íkən 101 ixí? a
c -my -ɬt -in axá? i? s+?iɬn -s i? s+mx̌=ikn ixí? a
cust^ -know -ɬt -1erg this art food -3in art grizzly that art
what grizzlies eat, *but*

cciqsts uɬ ixí? s?íɬənsəlx 102 ?ax̌əl·wís, waẏ ixí? axá?
c -ciq -st -s uɬ ixí? s+?iɬn -s -lx ?ax̌l+wís waẏ ixí? axá?
cust^ -dig -^cust -3erg and that food -3in -pl fool_around yes then this
what she was digging is what they eat. *He fooled around from below,*

tla yxʷut, uɬ {?aw?awtíw̓s} 103 ?aw?awcís, xʷu··y uɬ k̓a?tmís
tla yxʷ=ut uɬ ?aw•?aw=cí -s xʷuy uɬ k̓a?t+mí -s
from below and be_watching -3erg go and get_close -3erg
and {sneaked up to it}. *He was watchful. He went and got close to it.*

ki ixí? ƛ̓lap 104 uɬ ixí? xʷiws axá? c̓x̌al·wís
ki? ixí? ƛ̓la+p uɬ ixí? xʷiw -s axá? c -?x̌al+lwís
rel that stop and then whistle_at -3erg this hab -fool_around
Then he stopped. *He whistled at the one that's fooling around [at the grizzly].*

105 taʔx̌íləm ixíʔ c̓ʕác̓əntəm {i}
ta+ʔx̌íl+m ixíʔ c -ʕac̓ -nt -m
do_a_certain_way that act -look -nt -psv
She turned around and looked at him.

106 x̌aʔsí··kstmiʔs
x̌aʔs=íkst+miʔ -s
aim -3erg
He aimed, and he shot her

k̓əɬxət̓xt̓áx̌s
k̓ɬ+xt̓•xt̓=ax̌ -s
hit_under_arm -3erg
under the arm.

107 uɬ aɬíʔ_swit axáʔ {c} cmuʔmáʕʷ iʔ
uɬ aɬíʔ_swit axáʔ c -mʕʷ•maʕʷ iʔ
and in_fact this hab -broken art
But the hard points are

snululmúsaʔstəns
s+n+wl•wlm=ús=aʔst+n -s
arrow_points -3in
broken, 11:05

108 cənsq̓əsq̓íws uɬ ixíʔ ilíʔ cktt̓əɬt̓áɬ
c -n+sq̓•sq̓=iw̓s uɬ ixíʔ ilíʔ c -k+t̓•t̓ɬ•t̓aɬ
hab -split and that there hab -stick_dim
they are split, barely stuck there.

109 a xʷuy axáʔ iʔ cq̓íləna k̓əɬcq̓áx̌əntəm
a xʷuy axáʔ iʔ cq̓=iln k̓ɬ+cq̓=ax̌n -t -m
intj go this art arrow hit_under_arm -nt -psv
The arrow went and hit her under the arm,

110 uɬ lut t̓
uɬ lut t̓
and not negfac
but it didn't even

sənʔúɬxʷs t̓əxʷ iʔ t síp̓iʔ
s -n+ʔuɬxʷ -s t̓xʷ iʔ t síp̓iʔ
nom -enter -3i evidently art obl hide
go through the hide.

111 uɬ k̓əɬyáxʷt iʔ təl cq̓íllən
uɬ k̓ɬ+yaxʷ+t iʔ tl cq̓=iln
and fall_off art from arrow
It fell off of the arrow.

112 uɬ axáʔ aɬíʔ iʔ slip̓ lut ksnʔuɬxʷs axáʔ i t síp̓iʔ
uɬ axáʔ aɬíʔ iʔ slip̓ lut ks -n+ʔuɬxʷ -s axáʔ iʔ t síp̓iʔ
and this so art fire_wood not futi -enter -3i this art as hide
The arrow won't go through the skin.

113 way̓
way̓
yes
And

txʷət̓pmíntəm iʔ t səmx̌íkən
t+xʷt̓+p+min -t -m iʔ t s+mx̌=ikn
grab -nt -psv art agInst grizzly
Grizzly jumped towards him.

114 way̓ ilíʔ ɬckʷnim iʔ t
way̓ ilíʔ ɬ+c+kʷni+m iʔ t
well there take_cisl_again art obj_itr
He took another arrow,

cq̓íləns məɬ itlíʔ ɬt̓aʕpəntís
cq̓=iln -s mɬ itlíʔ ɬ+t̓aʕp -nt -is
arrow -3in and from_there shoot_again -nt -3erg
and then he shot again.

115 st̓aʕpstí··m
c -t̓aʕp -st -im
cust^ -shoot -^cust -psv
He was shooting,

uɬ {kcəlmik} kc̓əlmíntəm {i m} púlstəm
uɬ k+c̓l+min -t -m pul -st -m
and reach -nt -psv beat -st -psv
she got to him, and started to kill him.

116 way̓ a k̓aw uɬ
way̓ a k̓aw uɬ
well intj gone and
It's late in the evening,

ksk̓əlxʷínaʔ səmx̌íkən {uɬ}
k+s+k̓lxʷ=ínaʔ s+mx̌=ikn
have_evening grizzly
and he [Coyote's son] is still gone [from Coyote's place].

117 nkʷkʷʔac, way̓ ixíʔ
n+kʷ•kʷʔac way̓ ixíʔ
dark yes then
It's dark,

spaʔpaʔsínks səmx̌íkən
s -paʔ•paʔs=ínk -s s+mx̌=ikn
nom -sad -3i grizzly
and Grizzly [Coyote] started to feed bad. 12:06

118 cut way̓ way̓ ƛ̓lal {i}
cut way̓ way̓ ƛ̓l•al
say well yes dead
He said, "Well, my son

isqʷsíʔ 119 caʔkʷ sxʷəlxʷəltmíx púti kɬx̌əyáɬnəxʷ uɬ
i -s+qʷsiʔ caʔkʷ s -xʷl•xʷl+t -mix pút+iʔ kɬ+x̌yaɬ=nxʷ uɬ
1in -son if ipftv^ -alive -^ipftv still have+sun and
is dead. *If he were alive he would have been back*

ɬckicx 120 way̓ iʔ sƛ̓əl·míx uɬ iʔ k̓aw 121 ixíʔ
ɬ+c+kic+x way̓ iʔ s -ƛ̓l•l -mix uɬ iʔ k̓aw ixíʔ
arrive_cisl_again yes art ipftv^ -dead -^ipftv and art gone then
by sundown. *He's dead, that's why he is gone."* *Then*

ksx̌əlpínaʔlx uɬ ixíʔ scuts axáʔ iʔ t k̓ík̓aʔt i [l] sxʔitx
k+s+x̌l+p=ínaʔ -lx uɬ ixíʔ s -cut -s axáʔ iʔ t k̓í•k̓aʔt iʔ l s+xʔit=x
have_daylight -pl and then nom -say -3i this art agInst near art at oldest_one
it got to be the next day, and [the son] next to the oldest one said:

122 way̓ way̓ incá {i} ɬəwíntsən 123 way̓ t̓əxʷ iksƛ̓aʔƛ̓ʔám
way̓ way̓ in+cá ɬwi -nt -s -n way̓ t̓xʷ i -ks -ƛ̓aʔ•ƛ̓ʔá+m
well yes I leave -nt -2obj -1erg yes emph 1i -futi -look_for
"Well, I am going to leave you, *I am going to look for my*

inqíck 124 t̓əxʷ ṅíṅwiʔ cxʷəlxʷált uɬ way̓ kən
in -qick t̓xʷ ṅíṅwiʔ c -xʷl•xʷal+t uɬ way̓ kn
1in -older_brother emph a_while hab -alive and yes 1kn
older brother. *If he is still alive, then I'll*

ɬckicx 125 uɬ t̓əxʷ {ni kəṁ} kəṁ kən nq̓ʷíc̓tnəm
ɬ+c+kic+x uɬ t̓xʷ kṁ kn n+q̓ʷic̓+tn+m
arrive_cisl_again and emph or 1kn be_replacement_husband
come back. *[Or] I might be his replacement husband.*

126 uɬ way̓ {m} t̓i kən ɬckicx ɬ iscxʷəlxʷált 127 náx̌əmɬ
uɬ way̓ t̓iʔ kn ɬ+c+kic+x ɬ i -sc -xʷl•xʷal+t nax̌mɬ
and yes evid 1kn arrive_cisl_again if 1i -pftv -alive but
I'll still get back if I am alive. *But*

lut kən ɬckicx uɬ way̓ kən sƛ̓əl·míx 128 cúntəm i
lut kn ɬ+c+kic+x uɬ way̓ kn s -ƛ̓l•l -mix cu -nt -m iʔ
not 1kn arrive_cisl_again and yes 1kn ipftv^ -dead -^ipftv tell -nt -psv art
I won't come back if I am dead." 13:02 *His father*

ta lʔiws naʔɬ sk̓ʷuys 129 way̓ way̓ aspuʔús
t lʔiw -s naʔɬ s+k̓ʷuy -s way̓ way̓ a -s+puʔ=ús
agInst m's_father -3in and mother -3in well yes 2in -heart
and mother said to him: *"Well, all right, if that's how you feel.*

130 way̓ x̌ast ksṁaʔṁáʔyaʔməntxʷ anqíck 131 ixíʔ uɬ
way̓ x̌as+t ks -ṁaʔ•ṁáyaʔ+m -nt -xʷ an -qick ixíʔ uɬ
yes good futt^ -find_out -nt -2erg 2in -older_brother then and
It's good that you find out about your brother, *then*

kʷu kmiypínaʔ {ɬ} ɬə sƛ̓lals 132 {uɬ} uɬ way̓ kʷu kmahqənmíst[9]
kʷu k+my+p=ínaʔ ɬ s -ƛ̓l•al -s uɬ way̓ kʷu k+mah=qn+míst
4kn find_out_truth if ipftv^ -dead -3i and yes 4kn give_up
we'll know if he is dead, *and we can give up.*

133 uɬ púti t̓əxʷ kʷu cmúsəls 134 ay xʷuy, xʷu··y kicx waẏ iʔ l
uɬ pút+iʔ t̓xʷ kʷu c -mus=ls ay xʷuy xʷuy kic+x waẏ iʔ l
and still emph 4kn hab -hope intj go go arrive yes art at
[But] we still have hopes." *He [the second oldest] went and got to*

stáɬəm 135 waẏ xʷu··y, kicx k̓əl səmx̌íkən, waẏ cqaq 136 a ilíʔ
s+taɬm waẏ xʷuy kic+x k̓l s+mx̌=ikn waẏ cq•aq a ilíʔ
boat yes go arrive at grizzly yes land intj there
the boat. *He went and got to Grizzly. He landed.* *He tied*

ʕacəntís iʔ stáɬəms, kʷis i cq̓íləns uɬ ixíʔ
ʕac -nt -is iʔ s+taɬm -s kʷi -s iʔ cq̓=iln -s uɬ ixíʔ
tie -nt -3erg art boat -3in take -3erg art arrow 3in and then
his boat, took his weapon and slung it

nʔuckláx̌nəms 137 x̌íƛ̓əm kɬqəltús 138 ilíʔ
n+ʔuckl=áx̌n+m -s x̌iƛ̓+m kɬ+qlt=us ilíʔ
loop_over_arm -3erg climb hill_top there
over his shoulder. *He went up the hill, and got on the bank.* *There*

ckɬwix səmx̌íkən 139 ay xʷuy k̓ɬənɬaʔíp iʔ t sxʷuɬxʷ
c -kɬ+wix s+mx̌=ikn ay xʷuy k̓ɬ+n+ɬaʔ=íp iʔ t s+xʷul=ɬxʷ
hab -live grizzly intj go be_next_to art obl tipi
was Grizzly's place. *He went and got next to the door of the tipi. 14:00*

140 waẏ t̓iʔ kcaʔcaʔálqʷəm iʔ l sq̓íʔmən 141 waẏ cúntəm t
waẏ t̓iʔ k+caʔ•caʔ=álqʷ+m iʔ l s+q̓iy+mn waẏ cu -nt -m t
yes evid knock_on_pole art at tipi_poles well tell -nt -psv agInst
He knocked on the poles. *Grizzly said,*

səmx̌íkən, waẏ cənʔúɬxʷəxʷ 142 waẏ sənʔúɬxʷs, cúntəm t
s+mx̌=ikn waẏ c+n+ʔuɬxʷ -xʷ waẏ s -n+ʔuɬxʷ -s cu -nt -m t
grizzly well enter_cisl -isimptv yes nom -enter -3i tell -nt -psv agInst
"Come in!" *He went in. Grizzly*

səmx̌íkən 143 wa··ẏ kʷu kícəntxʷ st̓əlsqílxʷ 144 lut
s+mx̌=ikn waẏ kʷu kic -nt -xʷ s+t̓l+s+qilxʷ lut
grizzly well 1obj reach_st/sb -nt -2erg earth_people not
said: *"Well, you got to me, human.* *It's*

sqʷays {iʔ sqilxʷs} iʔ sqilxʷ kiʔ kʷu aɬ kícəntxʷ 145 cus
s+qʷay+s iʔ s+qilxʷ kiʔ kʷu aɬ kic -nt -xʷ cu -s
often art person rel 1obj compl reach_st/sb -nt -2erg tell -3erg
not often that people get here to me." *She said,*

waẏ, a, waẏ stim̓ ascənq̓aʔíls 146 waẏ t̓əxʷ axáʔ ast̓əmkʔílt axáʔ
waẏ a waẏ stim̓ a -s+c+n+q̓aʔ=íls waẏ t̓xʷ axáʔ a -s+t̓mkʔ=ilt axáʔ
well intj well what 2in -problem well emph this 2in -daughter this
"Well, what is on your mind?" *"Well, it's your daughter, the one*

9 I have recorded this stem as k+max̌=qn+míst. Cf. Sp č=mš=qn-mist *he gave up. He was discouraged.*

iʔ mut 147 waẏ kən sc̓awsənsucənmístx 148 cus
iʔ mut waẏ kn sc -ʔaw+s+n+sw=cn+míst -x cu -s
art sit_sg well 1kn ipftvp^ -go_propose -^ipftvp tell -3erg
sitting here. *I came over to propose."* *She said,*

waẏ, waẏ mat aspuʔús 149 waẏ t̓əxʷ ixíʔ mut 150 {ixíʔ uɬ waẏ}
waẏ waẏ mat a -s+puʔ=ús waẏ t̓xʷ ixíʔ mut
well well maybe 2in -heart yes evidently that sit_sg
"Well, if that's what you want." *She was sitting there.* *She*

cársəms iʔ st̓əmkʔílts ksʔácqaʔx 151 waẏ uɬ ixíʔ
cars+m -s iʔ s+t̓mkʔ=ilt -s ks -ʔácqaʔ -x waẏ uɬ ixíʔ
motion -3erg art daughter -3in incp^ -go_out -^incp yes and then
motioned to her daughter to go out, *and the woman*

sxʷət̓ílxs axáʔ iʔ tkəɬmílxʷ {uɬ} uɬ ʔácqaʔ 152 uɬ aɬíʔ ilíʔ iʔ l
s -xʷt̓+ilx -s axáʔ iʔ tkɬ+m=ilxʷ uɬ ʔácqaʔ uɬ aɬíʔ ilíʔ iʔ l
nom -get_up -3i this art woman and go_out and so there art at
got up and went out. 15:01 *And right there where*

qicks {iʔ} iʔ kɬaʔqís iʔ sənq̓ʷəɬtíʔstəns 153 ilíʔ
qick -s iʔ k+ɬaʔ=qí -s iʔ s+n+q̓ʷɬ+t=iʔst+n -s ilíʔ
older_brother -3in art lean_st_against -3erg art scabbard -3in there
his older brother had leaned his scabbard, *he also*

nixʷ kɬaʔqís iʔ sənq̓ʷəɬtíʔstəns 154 uɬ aɬíʔ miná {lu}
nixʷ k+ɬaʔ=qí -s iʔ s+n+q̓ʷɬ+t=iʔst+n -s uɬ aɬíʔ miná
also lean_st_against -3erg art scabbard -3in and because maybe_not
leaned his scabbard there. *It's not like*

lut t̓a ck̓əɬkʷúl̓ {ilíʔ} ilíʔ iʔ l sənkʷúmən 155 uɬ mat t̓i ilíʔ {a}
lut t̓ c -k̓ɬ+kʷul̓ ilíʔ iʔ l s+n+kʷum+n uɬ mat t̓iʔ ilíʔ
not negfac hab -fix there art in storage_place and maybe evid there
there is a place there for storing things, *that's where*

a ckʷəməlscútəlx 156 waẏ cúntəm t səmx̌íkən 157 waẏ
a c -kʷm=lscut -lx waẏ cu -nt -m t s+mx̌=ikn waẏ
art hab -store_clothes -pl well tell -nt -psv agInst grizzly well
they store things. *Grizzly said to him:* *"But*

náx̌əmɬ naqs iʔ kʷ ikscúnəm 158 {t} kʷ ikskaʕʷmístəm
nax̌mɬ naqs iʔ kʷ i -ks -cun -m kʷ i -ks -k̓aʕʷ+míst -m
but one art 2kʷu 1i -futi -tell -apsv 2kʷu 1i -futi -hire -apsv
I am going to tell you one thing. *I am going to hire you.*

159 waẏ mat aɬíʔ kʷ iksník̓əɬxʷ 160 sc̓x̌ilx uɬ iʔ kʷ
waẏ mat aɬíʔ kʷ i -k -s+nik̓=ɬxʷ sc+ʔx̌il+x uɬ iʔ kʷ
well maybe so 2kʷu 1i -to_be -son_in_law reason+why and art 2kʷu
I suppose you are going to be my son-in-law, *that's why I'm going to*

ikskʷúlstəm 161 cúntəm ixíʔ {k̓laɬ} k̓əl naɬáʔ ixíʔ iʔ l
i -ks kʷulst+m cu -nt -m ixíʔ k̓l naɬáʔ ixíʔ iʔ l
1i -futt^ send tell -nt -psv there to other_side there art in
send you on an errand." *She said, "Right across there in that*

k̓əɬx̌sínk 162 ilíʔ ki k̓əɬʔaksuxínk iʔ səmx̌íkən 163 ixíʔ kʷu
k̓ɬ+x̌s=ink ilíʔ kiʔ k̓ɬ+ʔaks+wx=ínk iʔ s+mx̌=ikn ixíʔ kʷu
side_hill there rel stand_on_side_hill art grizzly that 1obj
open place, *that's where a grizzly dwells.* *Get it*

aksƛ̓aʔɬtím iklənqəqpáqstxən 164 way̓ ma··ɬ kən
a -ks -ƛ̓aʔ -ɬt -im i -kɬ -n+q•qp=aqst=xn way̓ maɬ kn
2i -futt^ -fetch -ɬt -apsv 1i -to_be -mat yes too_much 1kn
for me to put under my hip. 16:00 *Where I lay is*

ck̓əɬk̓ak̓ʔáʔ 165 uɬ ixíʔ ksxʷípəlps ixíʔ iʔ x̌minks iʔ síp̓iʔ
c -k̓ɬ+k̓aʔ•k̓ʔáʔ uɬ ixíʔ k -s+xʷip=lp -s ixíʔ iʔ x̌m=ink -s iʔ síp̓iʔ
hab -lumpy and that to_be -mat -3in that art want -3i art hide
too hard." *She wants the hide to put under her.*

166 a·· cus, way̓, way̓ mat aspuʔús 167 way̓ n̓ín̓w̓iʔ
a cu -s way̓ way̓ mat a -s+puʔ=ús way̓ n̓ín̓w̓iʔ
intj tell -3erg OK yes maybe 2in -heart yes a_while
He said to her, "Ok, if that's your wish, *I'll go after it*

ƛ̓aʔɬtsín 168 ixíʔ uɬ sʔácqaʔs {a ckʷis i} lut aɬíʔ uɬ
ƛ̓aʔ -ɬt -s -in ixíʔ uɬ s -ʔácqaʔ -s lut aɬíʔ uɬ
fetch -ɬt -2obj -1erg then and nom -go_out -3i not because and
for you." *He went out, and it never entered his mind*

sk̓ək̓tílsc ilíʔ {inaud} kɬaʔqíntn 169 ckʷis iʔ {a}
s -k̓•k̓t=ils -c ilíʔ k+ɬaʔ=qín+tn c+kʷi -s iʔ
nom -close_to_mind -3i there place_to_lean take -3erg art
that where he had leaned it [might not be good]. *He took his*

sənq̓ʷəɬtíʔstəns, ixíʔ nʔucqláx̌[n]əms 170 ixíʔ ssax̌ʷts
s+n+q̓ʷɬ+t=iʔst+n -s ixíʔ n+ʔuckl=ax̌n+m -s ixíʔ s -sax̌ʷ+t -s
scabbard -3in that loop_over_shoulder -3erg then nom -go_downhill -3i
scabbard, looped it over his shoulder; *he went down to his boat,*

iʔ k̓əl stáɬəm, {kəwxplaʔ} sənʔamút[s] 171 ixíʔ st̓áq̓əms
iʔ k̓l s+taɬm s -n+ʔam=út -s ixíʔ s -t̓aq̓+m -s
art to boat nom -sit_inside -3i then nom -cross_stream -3i
he sat in his boat. *He crossed,*

uɬ t̓íxəlx 172 way̓ ʕacəntís, ixíʔ sx̌íƛ̓əms 173 naʔɬccám,
uɬ t̓ix+lx way̓ ʕac -nt -is ixíʔ s -x̌iƛ̓+m -s naɬc•c•ám
and come_to_shore yes tie -nt -3erg then nom -climb -3i forget
and landed. *He tied [the boat], then went up the hill.* *I forgot.*

nixʷ ilíʔ tixʷkʷúkstəm {a} qəɬsənk̓líp 174 cúntəm lut təl
nixʷ ilíʔ tixʷ+kʷú=kst+m qɬ=s+n+k̓l̓=ip cu -nt -m lut tl
also there repeat Coyote's_children tell -nt -psv not from
She said the same thing to Coyote's son. *She said, "Don't go*

w̓íw̓aʔst akstxəlkmínəm 175 cəm̓ lúti akskícx mi uɬ
w̓í•w̓aʔs+t a -ks -t+xlk+min+m cm̓ lút+i a -ks -kic+x mi uɬ
high_dim 2i -futi -go_around maybe before 2i -futi -arrive fut and
around from above. 17:01 *Before you get there*

k̓əɬʔanwínts 176 pna cmay ləxʷpnúnts 177 way̓
k̓ɬ+ʔanwí -nt -s pnaʔ cmay lxʷ+p -nun -t -s way̓
hear_st -nt -3e2obj maybe maybe hurt -manage -nt -3e2obj yes
she will notice you. *She might hurt you.* *Go*

atláʔ tla ixʷút mi txʷúyməntxʷ 178 ixíʔ uɬ lut
atláʔ tla yxʷ=ut mi t+xʷuy+m -nt -xʷ ixíʔ uɬ lut
from_here from below fut go_towards -nt -2erg then and not
towards it from below, *and she*

ksk̓əɬʔanwínts 179 a·, way̓ 180. ixíʔ ṅ[íṅw̓iʔ] atláʔ tla
ks -k̓ɬ+ʔanwí -nt -s a way̓ ixíʔ ṅíṅw̓iʔ atláʔ tla
futt^ -hear_st -nt -3e2obj intj Ok then a_while from_here from
will not notice you." *"Ah, ok."* *So he was going from below*

ixʷút ixíʔ k̓əɬk̓ʷƛ̓áp uɬ wiks 181 way̓ uɬ t̓i niʕíp tla ixʷút
yxʷ=ut ixíʔ k̓ɬ+k̓ʷƛ̓a+p uɬ wik -s way̓ uɬ t̓iʔ n+yʕ=ip tla yxʷ=ut
below that come_in_sight and see -3erg well and evid always from below
and he came in sight and saw her. *He climbed from*

sx̌íƛ̓əms 182 way̓ k̓k̓aʔlí··ʔst uɬ k̓aʔtmís 183 way̓ staʔ ixíʔ
s -x̌iƛ̓+m -s way̓ k̓•k̓aʔl=íʔst uɬ k̓aʔt+mí -s way̓ staʔ ixíʔ
nom -climb -3i well go_slow and get_close -3erg yes intj then
below, *he went slowly and got pretty close.* *Then he wistled*

xʷiws yaʔx̌í a cíqlaʔxʷəm 184 way̓ cʕáċəntəm 185 ƛ̓lap
xʷiw -s yaʔx̌í a cíq=laʔxʷ+m way̓ c -ʕaċ -nt -m ƛ̓la+p
whistle_at -3erg that_one art dig yes act -look -nt -psv stop
to the one that was digging. *She looked at him.* *He*

aɬíʔ uɬ cʕáċəntəm {ay} t̓aʕpəntís 186 swit_aɬíʔ way̓ cmaʕʷ iʔ
aɬíʔ uɬ c -ʕaċ -nt -m t̓aʕp -nt -is swit_aɬíʔ way̓ c -maʕʷ iʔ
so and act -look -nt -psv shoot -nt -3erg in_fact yes hab -break art
stopped there. She looked at him, he shot her. *But his hard points*

snululmúsaʔstəns 187 cacáʕypəm uɬ kstxʷət̓pmíntəm
s+n+wl•wlm=ús=aʔst+n -s ca•cáʕy+p+m uɬ ks -t+xʷt̓+p+min -t -m
arrow_points -3in cry and futt^ -chase -nt -psv
are broken. *She gave a yell, and jumped after him.*

188 way̓ st̓áʕpstí··s uɬ kícəntəm 189 way̓
way̓ s -t̓aʕp -st -is uɬ kic -nt -m way̓
well cust^ -shoot -^cust -3erg and reach_st/sb -nt -psv yes
He kept shooting, and she got to him. 18:00 *She*

t̓qʷápqəntəm, {i·} púlstəm, ƛ̓lənúntəm 190 ay, ixíʔ uɬ
t̓qʷ=ap=qn -t -m pul -st -m ƛ̓l•l -nun -t -m ay ixíʔ uɬ
slap_on_head -nt -psv beat -st -psv dead -manage -nt -psv intj that and
slapped him on top of the head, fought him, and killed him. *That's two*

tk̓əsʔasíl iʔ ƛ̓əxʷəntím, sənk̓líp [iʔ] ɬəɬsqʷsíʔs 191 way̓ uɬ
tk=ʔas•ʔasíl iʔ ƛ̓xʷ -nt -im s+n+k̓l̓=ip iʔ ɬɬ -sqʷsiʔ -s way̓ uɬ
two_persons art kill_many -nt -psv Coyote art pl -son -3in well and
of them she killed, Coyote's sons. *Then*

ya?xí cni?ák̓ʷ i? tkəłmílxʷ qəłsəmx̌íkən 192 waẏ k̓aw axá? {i?} i?
ya?xí c -n=ẏák̓ʷ i? tkł+m=ilxʷ qł=smx̌=ikn waẏ k̓aw axá? i?
that_one hab -swim art woman grizzly's_child yes gone this art
the woman, Grizzly's child, swam across. *Coyote's son*

sqʷsi?s sənk̓líp 193 {k̓əlxʷ} k̓laxʷ, nkʷəkʷ?ác 194 waẏ nstílsəlx, cut
s+qʷsi? -s s+n+k̓l̓=ip k̓laxʷ n+kʷ•kʷ?ac waẏ n+st=ils -lx cut
son -3in Coyote evening dark well think -pl say
is gone. *It got late, got dark.* *They thought, Coyote*

waẏ ƛ̓lal isqʷsí? 195 ca?kʷ scxʷəlxʷəltmíx púti
waẏ ƛ̓l•al i -s+qʷsi? ca?kʷ sc -xʷl•xʷl+t -mix pút+i?
yes dead 1in -son if ipftvp^ -alive -^ipftvp still
said, "Well, my son is dead. *If he were living, he'd been back*

kłx̌yáłnəxʷ uł łckicx 196 waẏ púlxəlx 197 waẏ
kł -x̌yał=nxʷ uł ł+c+kic+x waẏ pul+x -lx waẏ
there_is -sun and arrive_cisl_again yes camp -pl yes
before sundown." *They went to bed.* *It got*

ksx̌əlpína?lx, uł ałí? kʷáʕctməlx, kʷəctáʕmnəlx sənk̓líp
k -s+x̌l+p=ína? -lx uł ałí? kʷaʕc+t+m -lx kʷc+t+ʕamn -lx s+n+k̓l̓=ip
there_be -daylight -pl and because early_morning -pl rise_early -pl Coyote
daylight, they got up early—the Coyotes are early risers. 19:02

198 waẏ wi?wi?cínəlx, uł ixí? cúntəm axá? i? t q̓a?íws
waẏ wẏ•wẏ=cin -lx uł ixí? cu -nt -m axá? i? t q̓a?=íẇs
yes finish_eating_pl -pl and then tell -nt -psv this art agInst middle_one
They got done breakfasting, and the middle one said:

199 waẏ, waẏ n?úcxən iłəłqíck 200 waẏ uł
waẏ waẏ n+?uc=xn -n i -łł -qick waẏ uł
well yes track -1erg 1in -pl -older_brother well and
"Well, I'll just track down my brothers. *How is it*

sc̓kinx uł tk̓a?səlmíst uł a cksəl̓sl̓ípla? 201 uł waẏ
sc -?kin -x uł tk=?asl+míst uł a c -k+sl̓•sl̓=ípla? uł waẏ
ipftvp^ -indef -^ipftvp and two_persons and art hab -be_lost and yes
that both of them are lost? *I am*

ƛ̓a?ƛ̓a?ntínəlx, iksmipnúnəm 202 uł ńíńẇi? kən k̓aw
ƛ̓a?•ƛ̓a? -nt -in -lx i -ks -my+p -nun -m uł ńíńẇi? kn k̓aw
look_for -nt -1erg -pl 1i -futt^ -learn -manage -apsv and a_while 1kn gone
going to look for them, I want to find out. *And if I'm gone*

mi nkʷkʷ?ac məł waẏ kən sƛ̓l·míx 203 uł náx̌əmł ł
mi n+kʷ•kʷ?ac mł waẏ kn s -ƛ̓l•l -mix uł nax̌mł ł
fut dark and yes 1kn ipftv^ -dead -^ipftv and but if
until dark, then I'm dead. *But if I*

iscxʷəlxʷált uł púti kłx̌yáłnəxʷ mi kən łckicx
i -sc -xʷl•xʷal+t uł pút+i? kł -x̌yał=nxʷ mi kn ł+c+kic+x
1i -pftv -alive and still there_is -sun fut 1kn arrive_cisl_again
am alive, I'll be back before sundown."

204 cúntəm t sənk̓líp, way̓ way̓ xʷuyx 205 way̓ taʔlí
cu -nt -m t s+n+k̓l̓=ip way̓ way̓ xʷuy -x way̓ taʔlíʔ
tell -nt -psv agInst Coyote yes yes go -isimptv yes very_much
Coyote said, "Well, yes, go. *We are very*

kʷu nq̓aʔíls 206 uɬ kʷu cmúsəls nixʷ, ixíʔ iwá spulxs
kʷu n+q̓aʔ=íls uɬ kʷu c -mus=ls nixʷ ixíʔ iwá s -pul+x -s
4kn concerned and 4kn hab -hope also that even nom -camp -3i
worried. 20:02 *We have hopes. Even though he's gone overnight,*

sk̓aws uɬ t̓əxʷ kʷu cmúsəls 207 uɬ x̌ast kʷu ɬa
s -k̓aw -s uɬ t̓xʷ kʷu c -mus=ls uɬ x̌as+t kʷu ɬaʔ
nom -gone -3i and emph 4kn hab -hope and good 4kn when
we still have hopes. *It'll be good and our feelings*

nx̌əstəlsmíst kʷu ɬ níxəl cxʷəlxʷált kəm̓ ƛ̓lal 208 ɬ ƛ̓lal uɬ kʷu
n+x̌s+t=ls+mist kʷu ɬ nixl c -xʷl•xʷal+t km̓ ƛ̓l•al ɬ ƛ̓l•al uɬ kʷu
satisfy_self 4kn if hear hab -alive or dead if dead and 4kn
will be settled when we hear if he is still alive or dead. *If he is dead, we'll*

kmahqənmíst 209 way̓ xʷuy, way̓ ixíʔ sxʷuys, xʷu··y {i l} ʔəxʷ i l
k+mah=qn+míst way̓ xʷuy way̓ ixíʔ s -xʷuy -s xʷuy ʔəxʷ iʔ l
give_up well go well that nom -go -3i go intj art in
give up." *Then he went. He went in the boat*

stáɬəm 210 ʔú··cləm, cəqəqcnítkʷ i l skaʕcínəms səmx̌íkən
s+taɬm ʔucl+m cq•q=cn=itkʷ iʔ l s+kaʕ=cín+m -s s+mx̌=ikn
boat paddle come_on_shore art in landing_place -3in grizzly
again.[10] *He paddled, and he landed right below Grizzly's house.*

211 way̓ ʕacəntís iʔ stáɬəms uɬ kʷis iʔ sənq̓ʷəɬtíʔstəns, ixíʔ
way̓ ʕac -nt -is iʔ s+taɬm -s uɬ kʷi -s iʔ s+n+q̓ʷɬ+t=iʔst+n -s ixíʔ
yes tie -nt -3erg art boat -3in and take -3erg art scabbard -3in that
He tied his boat, took his scabbard, and looped it around

ɬəxʷpúsəms 212 uɬ ixíʔ sx̌íƛ̓əms, xʷuy kəɬqəltús 213 uɬ
ɬxʷ+p=us+m -s uɬ ixíʔ s -x̌iƛ̓+m -s xʷuy kɬ+qlt=us uɬ
loop_over_head -3erg and then nom -climb -3i go hill_top and
his neck. *He went up the hill, up the bank.*

t̓iʔ ilíʔ aɬíʔ i l skəɬqəltús kiʔ cwix səmx̌íkən 214 way̓ k̓ɬənɬaʔíp,
t̓iʔ ilíʔ aɬíʔ iʔ l s+kɬ+ql=t=us kiʔ c -wix s+mx̌=ikn way̓ k̓ɬ+n+ɬaʔ=íp
evid there so art at top rel hab -live grizzly yes be_next_to
Grizzly lived right there on the bank. *He got right close*

uɬ ilíʔ {l} kɬəxʷpəntís iʔ sənq̓ʷəɬtíʔstəns 215 way̓
uɬ ilíʔ k+ɬxʷ+p -nt -is iʔ s+n+q̓ʷɬ+t=iʔst+n -s way̓
and there hang_st_over -nt -3erg art scabbard -3in yes
to the door, and there he hung up his scabbard. 20:08 *He*

10 Madeline commented: "Gee, they must have a lot of boats."

kca?ca?álqʷəm i? l məlk̓ʷút, ałí? cənx̌ʷáyqn[m] sənk̓líp, {ay, ə}
k+ca?•ca?=álqʷ+m i? l mlk̓ʷ=ut ałí? c -n+x̌ʷay=qn+m s+n+k̓l̓=ip
knock_on_pole art on pole because hab -live_in_tipi Coyote
knocked on the pole, because Coyote, [correction] Grizzly lives in

səmx̌íkən 216 cus way̓ cən?úłxʷəxʷ, way̓ scən?úłxʷs
s+mx̌=ikn cu -s way̓ c+n+?ułxʷ -xʷ way̓ s -c+n+?ułxʷ -s
grizzly tell -3erg yes enter_cisl -isimptv yes nom -enter_cisl -3i
a tipi. *She said, "Come in," and he went in.*

217 cúntəm way̓ kʷu kícəntxʷ 218 lut qʷay i? sqilxʷ
cu -nt -m way̓ kʷu kic -nt -xʷ lut qʷay i? s+qilxʷ
tell -nt -psv well 1obj reach_st/sb -nt -2erg not often art person
She said to him, "You got to me. *People don't often,*

úłi? kʷu ał kícəntxʷ 219 way̓ kʷu x̌c̓íkstməntxʷ
uł i? kʷu ał kic -nt -xʷ way̓ kʷu x̌c̓=ikst+m -nt -xʷ
and_then 1obj compl reach_st/sb -nt -2erg yes 1obj surprise -nt -2erg
and now you got to me. *You surprise me."*

220 a·· cus, t̓əxʷ lut 221 uł t̓əxʷ way̓, way̓ ixí? mut ast̓əmk?ílt;
a cu -s t̓xʷ lut uł t̓xʷ way̓ way̓ ixí? mut a -s+t̓mk?=ilt
intj tell -3erg emph not and emph yes yes that sit_sg 2in -daughter
He said, "No. *Your daughter sitting there,*

222 ixí? ctxʷúymən kʷ isc̓awsənsucənmístəm 223 a·
ixí? c+t+xʷuy+m -n kʷ i -s -c+?aw+s+n+sw=cn+míst+m a
that come_toward -1erg 2kʷu 1i -intt -come_propose intj
that's why I came, to propose to you." *She*

cus way̓, way̓ ixí? ł akłcucín, way̓, way̓ n̓ín̓w̓i? kʷintxʷ
cu -s way̓ way̓ ixí? ł a -kł -cw=cin way̓ way̓ n̓ín̓w̓i? kʷin -t -xʷ
tell -3erg well yes that if 2i -to_be -talk yes well a_while take -nt -2erg
said, "Ah, that's what you have to say. You can take her."

224 uł ixí? cársəms axá? i? st̓əmk?ílts ks?ácqa?x 225 uł
uł ixí? cars+m -s axá? i? s+t̓mk?=ilt -s ks -?ácqa? -x uł
and then motion -3erg this art daughter -3in incp^ -go_out -^incp and
She motioned to her daughter to go out. 22:05 *And*

ixí? cúntəm t səmx̌íkən łə ?ácqa? i? st̓əmk?ílts 226 uł way̓
ixí? cu -nt -m t s+mx̌=ikn ł ?ácqa? i? s+t̓mk?=ilt -s uł way̓
then tell -nt -psv agInst grizzly when go_out art daughter -3in and yes
when her daughter goes out Grizzly tells him [what she wants]. *She*

ilí? x̌ilsts axá? i? cq̓íləns ixí? a ckła?[qín]
ilí? ?x̌il -st -s axá? i? cq̓=iln -s ixí? a c -ła?=qín
there do_like -st -3erg this art arrow -3in that art hab -lean_against
[the daughter] does the same thing with his arrows leaning there:

227 məʕʷmáʕʷłtəm i? snululmúsa?stəns 228 uł i? {a} ni?ák̓ʷ
mʕʷ•maʕʷ -łt -m i? s+n+wl•wlm=ús=a?st+n -s uł i? n=y̓ak̓ʷ
broken -łt -psv art arrow_points -3in and art across_water
she breaks their hard points. *Then she crosses and goes*

uɬ ixíʔ sx̌íƛ̓əms sʔawstəxʷcəncúts {təks} tə ksc̓íɬənsəlx
uɬ ixíʔ s -x̌iƛ̓+m -s s -ʔaw+s+txʷ=cn+cut -s t ksc -ʔiɬn -s -lx
and then nom -climb -3i nom -go_get_food -3i obj_itr futPerfi -eat -3i -pl
up the hill to get herself some grub,

saʕʷx̌ʷíp 229 cúntəm axáʔ t səmx̌íkən 230 way̓ aɬíʔ uɬ {kʷə}
s+ʕʷx̌ʷ=ip cu -nt -m axáʔ t s+mx̌=ikn way̓ aɬíʔ uɬ
roots tell -nt -psv this agInst grizzly well because and
roots. *Then Grizzly says to him:* *"You are going to be*

kʷ iksník̓əɬxʷ uɬ way̓ uɬ ixíʔ uɬ {kʷiɬs} 231 way̓ itlíʔ kən
kʷ i -k -s+nik̓=ɬxʷ uɬ way̓ uɬ ixíʔ uɬ way̓ itlíʔ kn
2kʷu 1i -to_be -son_in_law and yes and then and well from_there 1kn
my son-in-law. [tape ends] 22:47 *Well, I am going to*

ncəpq̓síwsəm axáʔ {t} t incaptíkʷɬ sənk̓líp 232 ixíʔ way̓ tkaʔkaʔɬís
n+c̓pq̓+s=iw̓s+m axáʔ t in -captíkʷɬ s+n+k̓lʼ=ip ixíʔ way̓ t=kaʔ•kaʔɬís
splice this obj_itr 1in -legends Coyote then yes three_persons
continue my story about Coyote. *Three sons*

iʔ sqʷəsqʷasíʔas iʔ ƛ̓axʷt 233 k̓im tk̓əsʔasíl 234 axáʔ mat
iʔ s+qʷs•qʷasíʔa -s iʔ ƛ̓axʷ+t k̓im tk=ʔas•ʔasíl axáʔ mat
art children -3in art dead_pl only two_persons this maybe
are already dead. *Only two are left.* *I don't know*

t̓əxʷ swit iʔ stʔiwtx iʔ skʷists k̓əɬtətiʔɬálqʷpxən {kəm}
t̓xʷ swit iʔ s+tʔiw+t=x iʔ s+kʷist -s k̓ɬ+t•tiʔɬ=álqʷp=xn
evidently somebody art young_one art name -3in Coyote's_son's_name
the youngest boy's name, maybe it's "k̓ɬtiʔɬálqʷpxn."

235 uɬ axáʔm iʔ sxʔitx iʔ skʷists iʔ skəlkʷtílts {a} sʔaʕníxʷ
uɬ axáʔ+m iʔ s+xʔit=x iʔ s+kʷist -s iʔ s+k+lkʷ=t=ilt -s s+ʕaňíxʷ
and this art oldest_one art name -3in art distant_child -3in Muskrat
And the oldest one, his distant son's name is "Muskrat."

236 ixíʔ k̓əm a cxʷəlxʷált 237 way̓ ksx̌əlpínaʔlx, ixíʔ
ixíʔ k̓m a c -xʷl•xʷal+t way̓ k+s+x̌l+p=ínaʔ -lx ixíʔ
that except art hab -alive well have_daylight -pl then
That's all that's left alive. *Daylight came,*

scúts axáʔ iʔ stʔiwtx 238 cus iʔ ƛ̓ax̌əx̌ƛ̓x̌áps way̓
s -cut -s axáʔ iʔ s+tʔiw+t=x cu -s iʔ ƛ̓x̌•x̌•ƛ̓x̌a+p -s way̓
nom -say -3i this art young_one tell -3erg art parents -3in well
and the youngest one said, *he said to his parents,*

ɬwíɬmən {a} kʷ inƛ̓ax̌əxƛ̓x̌áp 239 way̓ nk̓əwpílsmən
ɬwi -ɬm -n kʷ in -ƛ̓ax̌•x̌•ƛ̓x̌á+p way̓ n+k̓w+p=ils+m -n
leave -5obj -1erg 2kʷu 1in -elders yes be_lonesome_for -1erg
"I am leaving you, parents. *I am lonesome for my*

iɬəɬqíck 240 uɬ sc̓kinx ki əcksl̓ípla?lx
i -ɬɬ -qick uɬ sc -ʔkin -x kiʔ c -k+sl̓=ípla? -lx
1in -pl -older_brother and ipftvp^ -indef -^ipftvp rel hab -be_gone -pl
older brothers. 1:02 *How come they disappeared?*

241 waẏ mat laʔkín sc̓kinx
waẏ mat la+ʔkíṅ sc -ʔkin -x
yes must when ipftvp^ -indef -^ipftvp
Something must be the matter.

242 waẏ iksənʔúcxnəm
waẏ i -ks -n+ʔuc=xn -m
yes 1i -futi -track -apsv
I am going to track them,

iksmipnúnəm
i -ks -my+p -nun -m
1i -futi -learn -manage -apsv
I am going to find out.

243 ixíʔ uɬ kən nx̌əstəlsmíst
ixíʔ uɬ kn n+x̌s+t=ls+mist
then and 1kn satisfy_self
Then I'll be satisfied."

244 cúsəlx
cu -s -lx
tell -3erg -pl
His parents

iʔ t ƛ̓ax̌əx̌ƛ̓x̌áps, waẏ mat aspuʔús
iʔ t ƛ̓x̌•x̌•ƛ̓x̌a+p -s waẏ mat a -s+puʔ=ús
art agInst parents -3in well maybe 2in -heart
told him, "if that's how you feel...

245 nak̓ʷá
nak̓ʷ+á
indeed_not
We are not

kskʷulstmt, anwí aspuʔús
ks kʷulst[11] -m -t anwí a -s+puʔ=ús
futt^ send -2obj -4erg you 2in -heart
sending you, it's your wish.

246 waẏ uníxʷ mnímɬtət kʷu
waẏ wnixʷ mnimɬ+tt kʷu
yes true we 4kn
We too are bothered

nq̓aʔíls, {uɬ} uɬ aɬíʔ kʷu ʔaxknəmscút
n+q̓aʔ=íls uɬ aɬíʔ kʷu ʔax+kn+m+scút
concerned and so 4kn do_something
in the mind, but what can we do?

247 waẏ aɬíʔ uɬ kʷu
waẏ aɬíʔ uɬ kʷu
yes because and 4kn
We are

ƛ̓ax̌əx̌ƛ̓x̌áp {kʷu}
ƛ̓ax̌•x̌•ƛ̓x̌á+p
elders
old,

248 uɬ kʷu kɬtunəlsmíst ɬə ksƛ̓aʔƛ̓aʔntíməlx
uɬ kʷu kɬ+twn=ls+mist ɬ ks -ƛ̓aʔ•ƛ̓aʔ -nt -im -lx
and 4kn fall_short subord futt^ -look_for -nt -4erg -pl
and we can't trust ourselves to go looking for them.

249 uɬ anwí kʷ tətw̓ít, xʷuyx
uɬ anwí kʷ t•tw̓it xʷuy -x
and you 2kn boy go -isimptv
But you are a young boy, go."

250 waẏ ixíʔ sx̌əcmən̓cút, waẏ
waẏ ixíʔ s -x̌c+mncut -s waẏ
well then nom -get_ready -3i well
Then he got ready,

ixíʔ sxʷuys
ixíʔ s -xʷuy -s
then nom -go -3i
he went.

251 waẏ mat cənxƛ̓úsəlx kstáɬəm
waẏ mat c -n+xƛ̓=us -lx k+s+taɬm
well maybe hab -each -pl have_boat
I guess they each had a boat.

252 waẏ i
waẏ iʔ
well art
He went

l stáɬəms ki xʷuy, xʷu··y
l s+taɬm -s kiʔ xʷuy xʷuy
in boat -3in rel go go
in his boat, he went. 2:05

253 kyaʕcínəm səmx̌íkən ilíʔ cqaq
k+yaʕ=cín+m s+mx̌=ikn ilíʔ cq•aq
land_on_shore grizzly there land
He landed in front of Grizzly's house.

254 waẏ ʕacəntís iʔ stáɬəms, kʷis iʔ cq̓íləns, i[xíʔ]
waẏ ʕac -nt -is iʔ s+taɬm -s kʷi -s iʔ cq̓=iln -s ixíʔ
yes tie -nt -3erg art boat -3in take -3erg art arrow -3in that
He tied his boat, took his weapon, and slung it around

11 The root √kʷlst, so analyzed because of forms like t+kʷlst=ípla?-nt-s-n, where the sequence st cannot be viewed as the transitivizer, in this construction does treat the sequence st as a transitivizer. Alternatively, one can posit st + st > st. Cf. √kn-xit for a similar behavior.

ɬəxʷpúsəms 255 ixíʔ sx̌íƛ̓əms, way̓ kɬqəltús 256 way̓
ɬxʷ+p=us+m -s ixíʔ s -x̌iƛ̓+m -s way̓ kɬ+qlt=us way̓
loop_over_head -3erg then nom -climb -3i yes hill_top yes
his neck. *He went up the hill, and got up on the bank.* *That's*

ilíʔ ckɬwix səmx̌íkən 257 way̓ xʷuy k̓ɬənɬaʔíp uɬ i [l] tk̓əmkn̓íɬxʷ
ilíʔ c -kɬ+wix s+mx̌=ikn way̓ xʷuy k̓ɬ+n+ɬaʔ=íp uɬ iʔ l t+k̓m=kn=iɬxʷ
there hab -live grizzly well go be_next_to and art on outside
where Grizzly lives. *He went right up to the door, and he hung*

ɬəxʷpəntís iʔ sənq̓ʷɬtíʔstəns 258 way̓ kcaʔcaʔálqʷəm i l məlk̓ʷút
ɬxʷ+p -nt -is iʔ s+n+q̓ʷɬ+t=iʔst+n -s way̓ k+caʔ•caʔ=álqʷ+m iʔ l mlk̓ʷ=ut
hang -nt -3erg art scabbard -3in well knock_on_pole art in pole
his scabbard outside the door. *He knocked on the pole.*

259 cúntəm t səmx̌íkən cənʔúɬxʷəxʷ 260 way̓ nʔuɬxʷ iʔ ta
cu -nt -m t s+mx̌=ikn c+n+ʔuɬxʷ -xʷ way̓ n+ʔuɬxʷ iʔ t
tell -nt -psv obj_tr grizzly enter_cisl -isimptv yes enter art obl
Grizzly said "Come in!" *He went through*

nxárcən aɬíʔ sənx̌ʷáyqən 261 cúntəm t səmx̌íkən, way̓ uɬ
n+xar=cn aɬíʔ s+n+x̌ʷay=qn cu -nt -m t s+mx̌=ikn way̓ uɬ
curtain_in_front because tipi tell -nt -psv agInst grizzly well and
the curtain (because it's a tipi). *Grizzly said,*

kʷu x̌c̓íkstməntxʷ 262 way̓ lut qʷay iʔ sqilxʷ kʷu t̓a
kʷu x̌c̓=ikst+m -nt -xʷ way̓ lut qʷay iʔ s+qilxʷ kʷu t̓
1obj surprise -nt -2erg well not often art person 1obj negfac
"You surprise me; *It isn't often that people come*

ckícstəm 263 úɬi kʷu a ckícəntxʷ
c -kic -st -m uɬ iʔ kʷu a c -kic -nt -xʷ
cust^ -reach_st/sb -^cust -psv and_then 1obj art act -arrive -nt -2erg
to visit me. 3:03 *And then you got here to me."*

264 {a· t̓əxʷ lut t̓əxʷ is·} way̓ ixíʔ ast̓əmkʔílt iʔ mut k̓la nsək̓ʷtílp
way̓ ixíʔ a -s+t̓mkʔ=ilt iʔ mut k̓l n+s+k̓ʷt=ilp
well that 2in -daughter art sit_sg to across
"Your daughter sitting on the bed across there,

265 ixíʔ isctxʷúyəm, kən sənsucən̓místx 266 a· way̓, way̓
ixíʔ i -sc -t+xʷuy+m kn s -n+sw=cn+mist -x a way̓ way̓
that 1i -pftv -go_towards 1kn ipftv^ -propose -^ipftv intj Ok yes
that's what I came after, I am proposing for her." *"Oh, well.*

mʕ̓an límləmtx uɬ i kʷu nsíwcəntxʷ 267 lut uɬ t̓i
mʕ̓an lim•lm+t+x uɬ iʔ kʷu n+siw=cn -t -xʷ lut uɬ t̓iʔ
intj thank_you and art 1obj ask -nt -2erg not and evid
Thanks for asking me. *You didn't*

ascwíkʷm̓iʔst 268 uɬ caʔkʷ kʷu kʷánx̌əɬtxʷ ist̓əmkʔílt
a -sc -wíkʷ+miʔst uɬ caʔkʷ kʷu kʷan=x̌ -ɬt -xʷ i -s+t̓mkʔ=ilt
2i -pftv -hide_self and could 1obj kidnap -ɬt -2erg 1in -daughter
hide around, *and you didn't kidnap her from me,*

uɬ {kʷu kʷu} kʷu kʷiɬtxʷ 269 way̓ kʷu nsíwcəntxʷ kʷu
uɬ kʷu kʷi -ɬt -xʷ way̓ kʷu n+siw=cn -t -xʷ kʷu
and 1obj take -ɬt -2erg yes 1obj ask -nt -2erg 1obj
you didn't just take her. *You proposed to me, you showed*

misqílxʷstxʷ 270 way̓ cársəms ʔaxʷ iʔ st̓əmkʔílts
my+s+qilxʷ -st -xʷ way̓ cars+m -s ʔaxʷ iʔ s+t̓mkʔ=ilt -s
respect -caus -2erg well motion -3erg again art daughter -3in
respect to me." *Then she motioned to her daughter.*

271 uɬ nstils axáʔ iʔ tkəɬmílxʷ, way̓ uɬ lut t̓ sx̌asts {uɬ}
uɬ n+st=ils axáʔ iʔ tkɬ+m=ilxʷ way̓ uɬ lut t̓ s -x̌as+t -s
and think this art woman well and not negfac custˆ -good -3i
The woman [the daughter] thought, "It's no good. 4:03

272 {way̓ uɬ ta·} myaɬ xʷʔit iʔ sqilxʷ iʔ scƛ̓axʷs 273 a
myaɬ xʷʔi+t iʔ s+qilxʷ iʔ sc -ƛ̓axʷ -s a
too_much many art person art pftv -kill_many -3i intj
She is killing too many people. *And*

ckənxítən axáʔ inm̓ístəm̓ 274 uɬ aɬíʔ t̓əxʷ qʷən̓cín aɬíʔ
c -kn -xit -n axáʔ in -m̓ist+m uɬ aɬíʔ t̓xʷ qʷn̓=cin aɬíʔ
custˆ -1kn -xit -1erg this 1in -w's_father and so evid pity so
then I am helping my {father} [mother][12]*.* *It's a pity {he is my father}*

inm̓ístəm 275 uɬ lut scənpútəlsc iʔ l ksník̓əɬxʷs
in -m̓ist+m uɬ lut sc -n+put=ls -c iʔ l k -s+nik̓=ɬxʷ -s
1in -w's_father and not pftv -satisfied -3i art with to_be -son_in_law -3i
[she is my mother]. *She is not satisfied with her son-in-law to-be.*

276 incá way̓ uɬ t̓əxʷ {kən} kən npútəls, ixíʔ t̓əxʷ iwá qaʔɬsənk̓líp
in+cá way̓ uɬ t̓xʷ kn n+put=ls ixíʔ t̓xʷ iwá qɬ=s+nk̓l=íp
I yes and emph 1kn satisfied that emph even Coyote's_son
As for me, I am satisfied, even if it is just Coyote's son."

277 way̓ itíʔ ɬcársəms, way̓ ixíʔ səcʔácqaʔs,
way̓ itíʔ ɬ+cars+m -s way̓ ixíʔ sc -ʔácqaʔ -s
well from_that motion_again -3erg well that pftv -go_out -3i
She [the old Grizzly] made a motion to her, and she [the young Grizzly] just dragged

ncəkʷcəkʷmxán 278 uɬ ixíʔ cus axáʔ iʔ stʔawtílts sənk̓líp
n+ckʷ•ckʷ+m=xan uɬ ixíʔ cu -s axáʔ iʔ s+tʔaw+t=ílt -s s+n+k̓l̓=ip
drag_legs and then tell -3erg this art youngest_child -3in Coyote
her feet.[13] *Then she [old Grizzly] said to Coyote's youngest son:*

279 way̓, way̓ uɬ aɬíʔ taʔxʷsník̓əɬxʷməntsən 280 uɬ náx̌əmɬ way̓
way̓ way̓ uɬ aɬíʔ taʔxʷ+s+nik̓=ɬxʷ+m -nt -s -n uɬ nax̌mɬ way̓
well yes and so get_son_in_law -nt -2obj -1erg and so yes
"Well, I got you as a son-in-law now. *And I am going*

12 At the beginning of the story Pete announced that the Grizzly is a woman. Here the young grizzly talks about her "father." Later in the story there will be more evidence that the Grizzly is a woman.

13 i.e. she leaves begrudgingly.

kʷ iksk̓aʕʷmístəm 281 way̓ ik̓líʔ k̓a nsq̓ʷut k̓əl w̓íw̓aʔst
kʷ i -ks -k̓aʕʷ+míst -m way̓ ik̓líʔ k̓ n+s+q̓ʷut k̓l w̓í•w̓aʔs+t
2kʷu 1i -futi -hire -apsv well there to other_side to high_dim
to hire you. *Well, across the water, on the side hill,*

282 kiʔ kɬaʔksuxínk iʔ səmx̌íkən 283 way̓ ixíʔ kʷu ƛ̓aʔɬtíxʷ
kiʔ k̓ɬ+ʔaks+wx=ínk iʔ s+mx̌=ikn way̓ ixíʔ kʷu ƛ̓aʔ -ɬt -ixʷ
rel stand_on_side_hill art grizzly well that 1obj fetch -ɬt -2erg
that's where a grizzly is staying. *Go after it for me so I can put*

ikɬənqəqpáqstxən 284 way̓ myaˑˑɬ kən ck̓əɬk̓aʔk̓ʔá
i -kɬ -n+q•qp=aqst=xn way̓ myaɬ kn c -k̓ɬ+k̓aʔ•k̓ʔáʔ
1i -to_be -mat yes too_much 1kn hab -lumpy
it[s tanned hide] under my hip. 5:01 *When I go to bed I [lie on] too many*

kən ɬaʔ cpulx, ixíʔ iksxʷípəlp 285 cúntəm axáʔ {iʔ ts} iʔ
kn ɬaʔ c -pul+x ixíʔ i -k -s+xʷip=lp cu -nt -m axáʔ iʔ
1kn when hab -camp that 1i -to_be -mat tell -nt -psv this art
hard lumps. That [hide] is to put under me." *Her son-in-law*

t ksník̓əɬxʷs 286 way̓ {uɬ kin xaʔ way̓ kʷu ɬa} ixíʔ kʷu t
t k -s+nik̓=ɬxʷ -s way̓ ixíʔ kʷu t
agInst to_be -son_in_law -hab well that 1obj obl
said to her: *"Well, yes, just like*

cuntxʷ 287 uɬ way̓ {kʷ iks} kʷ iksyaʕyaʕ̓ncút[x]təm a[xáʔ]
cu -nt -xʷ uɬ way̓ kʷ i -ks -yaʕ̓•yaʕ̓+ncút -xt -m axáʔ
tell -nt -2erg and yes 2kʷu 1i -futi -russle -xit -apsv this
you asked me, *I'm going to rustle for you what you want,*

iʔ anx̌mínk {i} kʷu kskʷəlstúɬtxʷ 288 way̓ n̓ín̓wiʔ kən xʷuy, kəm̓a
iʔ an -x̌m=ink kʷu ks -kʷlst -uɬt -xʷ way̓ n̓ín̓wiʔ kn xʷuy km̓+a
art 2in -want 1oj futtˆ -send -tuɬt -2erg well a_while 1kn go not
what you send me for. *I will go, that's*

stim̓ 289 axáʔ iʔ tkəɬmílxʷ way̓ ʔácqaʔ, way̓ x̌íləm
stim̓ axáʔ iʔ tkɬ+m=ilxʷ way̓ ʔácqaʔ way̓ x̌il+m
something this art woman yes go_out yes do_like
nothing." *The woman [the young Grizzly] went out, and did the same thing:*

290 way̓ {nmyír̓k̓ʷɬtəm} [máʕʷɬtəm] iʔ sənululmúsaʔsts 291 ixíʔ uɬ
way̓ maʕʷ -ɬt -m iʔ s+n+wl•wlm=ús=aʔst -s ixíʔ uɬ
yes break -ɬt -psv art arrow_points -3in then and
she broke the hard points. *Then*

sic {i an} a niʔák̓ʷ {uɬ i}, iʔ k̓əɬqəltínk 292 way̓ axáʔ ʔácqaʔ qaʔɬsənk̓líp
sic a n=y̓ak̓ʷ iʔ k̓ɬ+qlt=ink way̓ axáʔ ʔácqaʔ qɬ=s+nk̓l=íp
then art across_water art hill_top well this go_out Coyote's_son
she went across, and got on the side hill. *Then Coyote's son went out.*

293 kʷis {iʔ} iʔ sənq̓ʷɬtíʔstəns {nɬxʷ} nʔuckláx̌nəms 294 uɬ lut t̓
kʷi -s iʔ s+n+q̓ʷɬ+t=iʔst+n -s n+ʔuckl=áx̌n+m -s uɬ lut t̓
take -3erg art scabbard -3in loop_over_arm -3erg and not negfac
He took his scabbard and looped it over his arm. 6:06 *It never came*

sk̓əktílsc lut uł sk̓əłmiʔpnúmts {uł} 295 stim̓ a
s -k•k̓t=ils -c lut uł s- k̓ł+my+p+numt -s stim̓ a
nom -close_to_mind -3i not and nom -think_about -3i what art
close to his mind, he never thought about [what might happen]. That's how

nƛ̓əxʷtans {iʔ} iʔ łəłqáqcaʔs 296 way̓ t̓áq̓əm t̓íxəlx,
n+ƛ̓xʷ+tan -s iʔ łł+qáqcaʔ -s way̓ t̓aq̓+m t̓ix+lx
death -3in art elder_brothers -3in well cross_stream come_to_shore
his brothers got killed. Well, he crossed, got on shore,

ʕacəntís iʔ stáləms 297 way̓ ixíʔ sx̌íƛ̓əms 298 lut uł
ʕac -nt -is iʔ s+tałm -s way̓ ixíʔ s -x̌iƛ̓+m -s lut uł
tie -nt -3erg art boat -3in well then nom -climb -3i not and
tied his boat, and went up the hill. He never

t̓ ʕác̓əs iʔ cq̓íləns ha x̌ast kəm c̓kin 299 a· {na} way̓ nixʷ
t̓ ʕac̓ -s iʔ cq̓=iln -s haʔ x̌as+t km̓ c+ʔkin a way̓ nixʷ
negfac look_at -3erg art arrow -3in inter good or how intj well also
even looked at his arrows [to see] if they are good or what. Oh, [I should

cúntəm t səmx̌íkən 300 cúntəm lut təl w̓íw̓aʔst
cu -nt -m t s+mx̌=ikn cu -nt -m lut tl w̓í•w̓aʔs+t
tell -nt -psv agInst grizzly tell -nt -psv not from high_dim
mention that the old] Grizzly also said to him, she said, "Don't shoot

mi t̓aʕpəntíxʷ 301 cəm̓ ləxʷpnúnts cəm̓
mi t̓aʕp -nt -ixʷ cm̓ lxʷ+p -nun -t -s cm̓
fut shoot -nt -2erg maybe hurt -manage -nt -3e2obj maybe
from above. She might hurt you, she might notice you

k̓əłníxəlmənts lúti aksk̓ík̓aʔt 302 tla lkʷut cəm̓ mi way̓
k̓ł+nixl+m -nt -s lút+i a -ks -k̓í•k̓aʔt tla lkʷ=ut cm̓ mi way̓
hear -nt -3e2obj before 2i -futi -near from far maybe fut yes
before you get close, she might notice you

k̓əłníxəlmənts 303 way̓ náx̌əmł tla ixʷút uł talí cəm̓
k̓ł+nixl+m -nt -s way̓ nax̌mł tla yxʷ=ut uł taʔlíʔ cm̓
hear -nt -3e2obj well but from below and very_much maybe
from afar. But [if you go] from below you might get

k̓aʔtmíntxʷ 304 ixíʔ mi t̓aʕpəntíxʷ uł tx̌əsíkxtxʷ
k̓aʔt+min -t -xʷ ixíʔ mi t̓aʕp -nt -ixʷ uł t+x̌s=ik -xt -xʷ
go_near -nt -2erg then fut shoot -nt -2erg and good_aim -xit -2erg
close to her. 7:00 And then you can shoot her, and you'll have a good aim."

305 cut way̓ way̓ x̌íləm 306 tla ixʷút [i]tíʔ sx̌íƛ̓əms
cut way̓ way̓ x̌il+m tla yxʷ=ut itíʔ s -x̌iƛ̓+m -s
say Ok yes do_like from below from_that nom -climb -3i
He said "Ok" and that's what he did. He went up from below.

307 x̌í··ƛ̓əm, wiks way̓ k̓əłʔaksuxínk 308 uł t̓i niʕíp
x̌iƛ̓+m wik -s way̓ k̓ł+ʔaks+wx=ínk uł t̓iʔ n+yʕ=ip
climb see -3erg yes stand_on_side_hill and evid always
He climbed, and he saw her [the grizzly] standing there. He kept going

tla ixʷút uɬ sx̌íƛ̓əms 309 way̓ t’i xʷu··y, k̓aʔk̓í··t cəm̓ uɬ
tla yxʷ=ut uɬ s -x̌iƛ̓+m -s way̓ t’iʔ xʷuy k̓aʔ•k̓ít cm̓ uɬ
from below and nom -climb -3i yes evid go softly maybe and
up from below. *He went, he stepped softly, and he got*

k̓aʔtmís 310 way̓ ƛ̓lap, a cutəntís iʔ cq̓íləns
k̓aʔt+mí -s way̓ ƛ̓la+p a c -wt -nt -is iʔ cq̓=iln -s
get_close -3erg yes stop intj act -place -nt -3erg art arrow -3in
close to her. *He stopped, he took out his arrows.*

311 ixíʔ {s} ksxət’əntís way̓ wiʔsksxət’əntís way̓ cúcm̓iʔs
ixíʔ k+s+xt’ -nt -is way̓ wy̓+s+k+s+xt’ -nt -is way̓ cucm̓ y̓ -s
then aim -nt -3erg yes finish_aiming -nt -3erg yes ? -nt -3erg
He started to aim. After he aimed he

t xʷiws 312 way̓ cʕác̓əntəm uɬ wíkəntəm 313 way̓
t xʷiw -s way̓ c -ʕac̓ -nt -m uɬ wik -nt -m way̓
obj_itr whistle -3in well act -look -nt -psv and see -nt -psv yes
whistled at her. *She looked at him, and she saw him.* *He*

t’aʕpəntís k̓əɬcəq̓cq̓áx̌s {axáʔ i ta n} 314 lut mat sənʔúɬxʷs iʔ
t’aʕp -nt -is k̓ɬ+cq̓•cq̓=ax̌ -s lut mat s -n+ʔuɬxʷ -s iʔ
shoot -nt -3erg hit_under_arm -3erg not maybe nom -enter -3i art
shot her right under the arm. 8:02 *[The point] didn’t even go through*

t {s} síp̓iʔ 315 uɬ maʕʷt a[xá]ʔ iʔ snululmús[aʔs]tən uɬ k̓aʔx̌í yaxʷt
t síp̓iʔ uɬ maʕʷ+t axáʔ iʔ s+n+wl•wlm=ús=aʔst+n uɬ k̓a+ʔx̌íʔ yaxʷ+t
obj_itr hide and broken this art arrow_points and there fall
her hide. *The hard point broke off and the arrow just*

iʔ cq̓ílən 316 ixíʔ e ctxʷət’pmíntəm, cacáʕypəm
iʔ cq̓=iln ixíʔ e c -t+xʷt’+p+min -t -m ca•cáʕy+p+m
art arrow then intj act -jump_on -nt -psv cry
fell there. *She jumped on him, she yelled and*

ctxʷət’pmíntəm, 317 nt’a aɬíʔ iwá t’ʕapəntís,
c -t+xʷt’+p+min -t -m nt’a aɬíʔ iwá t’aʕp -nt -is
act -jump_on -nt -psv intj so to_no_avail shoot -nt -3erg
jumped on him. *He tried to shoot her, kept shooting at her,*

ct’aʕpstí··s uɬ kícəntəm 318 uɬ t’qʷápqəntəm
c -t’aʕp -st -is uɬ kic -nt -m uɬ t’qʷ=ap=qn -t -m
cust^ -shoot -^cust -3erg and reach_st/sb -nt -psv and slap_on_head -nt -psv
and then she got to him. *She slapped him on*

məɬ ixíʔ púlstəm uɬ ksərqíntəm 319 {i·· way̓} ixíʔ
mɬ ixíʔ pul -st -m uɬ k+sr=qin -t -m ixíʔ
and then beat -st -psv and scalp -nt -psv then
the head, killed him, scalped him. *The woman*

ɬəɬsáx̌ʷts axáʔ iʔ tkəɬmílxʷ, cniʔák̓ʷ 320 ahá ixíʔ uɬ
ɬ -ɬ+sax̌ʷt -s axáʔ iʔ tkɬ+m=ilxʷ c -n=y̓ák̓ʷ ahá ixíʔ uɬ
nom -go_back_downhill -3i this art woman hab -swim intj then and
went back down the hill, crossed the river. *Coyote had*

ċəspílt sənk̓líp 321 k̓im knaqsəltílt, ixíʔ iʔ skləkʷtílts
ċs+p=ilt s+n+k̓lʼ=ip k̓im k=naqs=lt=ílt ixíʔ iʔ s+k+lkʷ=t=ilt -s
no_children Coyote only one_child that art distant_child -3in
no more children, except for his distant son

saʔʕníxʷ 322 k̓aw·· axáʔ iʔ stʔiwtx, iʔ stʔawtílts stʔawtílts
s+ʕaṅíxʷ k̓aw axáʔ iʔ s+tʔiw+t=x iʔ s+tʔaw+t=ílt -s s+tʔaw+t=ílt
Muskrat gone this art young_one art youngest_child -3in youngest_child
Muskrat. The oldest one is gone, and so is Coyote's

sənk̓líp {uɬ} 323 uɬ ksk̓əlxʷí··naʔ uɬ nkʷkʷʔác 324 way̓ cútəlx way̓
s+n+k̓lʼ=ip uɬ k -s+k̓lxʷ=ínaʔ uɬ n+kʷ•kʷʔac way̓ cut -lx way̓
Coyote and there_be -evening and dark well say -pl yes
youngest. It got late, it got dark. 9:01 Then they said,

way̓ ƛ̓lal nixʷ {iʔ} isqʷsíʔ 325 way̓ ixíʔ scaʕcáʕypəms sənk̓líp
way̓ ƛ̓l•al nixʷ i -s+qʷsiʔ way̓ ixíʔ s -ca•cáʕyp+m -s s+n+k̓lʼ=ip
yes dead also 1in -son well then nom -cry -3i Coyote
"Yes, my son died too." And Coyote started to bawl,

326 way̓ {uɬ mat} uɬ ksxʷíċəɬts axáʔ iʔ púlʼlaʔxʷs 327 cniɬc
way̓ uɬ ks -xʷiċ -ɬt -s axáʔ iʔ púlʼ=laʔxʷ -s cniɬ+c
well and futt^ -give -ɬt -3erg this art Gopher -3in (s)he
and I guess he blamed Gopher,[14] *as if*

cʔx̌iɬ ɬaʔ ksck̓ʷúlʼ úɬi ċəspílt 328 uɬ iwá
c+ʔx̌iɬ ɬaʔ ksc -k̓ʷulʼ uɬ iʔ ċs+p=ilt uɬ iwá
like the_one_that futPerfi -do and_then no_children and try_to
it were all her fault that the children are dead. Gopher

cúntəm iʔ t púlʼlaʔxʷs 329 lut {kʷ}, uɬ anwí, anwí iʔ kʷ
cu -nt -m iʔ t púlʼ=laʔxʷ -s lut uɬ anwí anwí iʔ kʷ
tell -nt -psv art agInst Gopher -3in not and you you art 2kn
tried to tell him: "No, you are the man,

sqəlʼtmíxʷ, anwí {aks} aksċx̌ʷám asqʷəsqʷasíʔa 330 uɬ
s+qlt=mixʷ anwí a -ks -ċx̌ʷa+m a -s+qʷs•qʷasíʔa uɬ
man you 2i -futi -instruct 2in -children and
you are supposed to guide your children. And

xiʔspuʔúsəntxʷ asqʷəsqʷasíʔa 331 lut x̌aʔntíxʷəlx, uɬ incá
xy̓+s+puʔ=ús -nt -xʷ a -s+qʷs•qʷasíʔa lut x̌aʔn -t -ixʷ -lx uɬ in+cá
go_along_with -nt -2erg 2in -children not stop -nt -2erg -pl and I
you went along with your children. 10:00 You didn't stop them, and now

iʔ kʷu aɬ ksxʷíċəɬtxʷ 332 ntʼa lut sənk̓líp {uɬ}, aɬíʔ way̓
iʔ kʷu aɬ ks -xʷiċ -ɬt -xʷ ntʼa lut s+n+k̓lʼ=ip aɬíʔ way̓
art 1kʷu compl futt^ -give -ɬt -2erg intj not Coyote because well
you put the blame on me." Heck no, Coyote.

14 Coyote typically shifts blame as he wants.

mat sənk̓əw[pílsx]
mat s -n+k̓ww+p=ils -x
maybe ipftv^ -lonesome -^ipftv
Maybe he got lonesome,

333 way̓ pulsts iʔ tkəɬm[ílxʷs]
way̓ pul -st -s iʔ tkɬ+m=ilxʷ -s
yes beat -st -3erg art wife -3in
so he beat his wife up.[15]

334 way̓ yiltmíntəm ɬəx̌ʷpnúntəm
way̓ ylt+min -t -m ɬx̌ʷ+p -nun -t -m
yes run_away_from -nt -psv escape -manage -nt -psv
She ran away from him, she got away.

335 way̓ uɬ
way̓ uɬ
well and
And Coyote is all

knáq[əq]s sənk̓líp
k=naq•q•s s+n+k̓l̓=ip
alone Coyote
by himself.[16]

336 kəmxáxəlx t̓əxʷ iʔ naʔɬ skəlkʷtílts
kmx•ax -lx t̓xʷ iʔ naʔɬ s+k+lkʷ=t=ilt -s
only -pl evidently art and distant_child -3in
He and his distant son are by themselves.

337 way̓ ksx̌əlpínaʔ, uɬ aɬíʔ axáʔ kʷəlstníman axáʔ{ɬ} saʔʕ̓níxʷ
way̓ k -s+x̌l+p=ínaʔ uɬ aɬíʔ axáʔ kʷls+tn+imn axáʔ s+ʕ̓an̓íxʷ
well there_be -daylight and because this sweat_bathe_often this Muskrat
Daylight came, and Muskrat likes to sweat bathe.

338 ixíʔ kʷəlstnímən saʔʕ̓níxʷ, way̓ caʕʷlxímən,
ixíʔ kʷls+tn+imn s+ʕ̓an̓íxʷ way̓ caʕʷ+lx+ímn
that sweat_bathe_often Muskrat yes bathe_often
Muskrat likes to sweat bathe, he likes to bathe. 11:00

339 way̓ taʔkín {i s}
way̓ ta+ʔkín̓
well from_where
Sometimes before

lúti sxəƛ̓ƛ̓úlaʔxʷs way̓ ʔawscáʕʷlx
lút+i s -xƛ̓•ƛ̓=úlaʔxʷ -s way̓ ʔaw+s+cáʕʷ+lx
before nom -daylight -3i yes go_bathe
daylight he goes bathing.

340 way̓ uɬ axáʔ t̓i kmix
way̓ uɬ axáʔ t̓iʔ kmix
yes and this evid only
And it's just

ckm̓máxəlx naʔɬ lʔiws {way̓}
c -km̓•m̓•ax -lx naʔɬ lʔiw -s
hab -only_dim -pl and m̓s_father -3in
he and his father.

341 uɬ aɬíʔ sisyús náx̌əmɬ sənk̓líp
uɬ aɬíʔ sy•sy=us nax̌mɬ s+n+k̓l̓=ip
and because smart so Coyote
Coyote is smart

i l sk̓ʷəlcəncút {i l s}
iʔ l s+k̓ʷl̓=cn+cut
art in cooking
at cooking.

342 lut náx̌əmɬ sənc̓aʔxʷíɬc̓aʔms, t̓i
lut nax̌mɬ s -n+c̓aʔxʷ=íɬc̓aʔ+m -s t̓iʔ
not but nom -make_hot_cakes -nom evid
He doesn't make hot cakes,

k̓ʷəlstóstəm
k̓ʷl̓+tost+m
make_toast
just toast,

343 sənʔacqʷúlaʔxʷ, uɬ ixíʔ a ck̓ʷulsts
s+n+ʔacqʷ=úlaʔxʷ uɬ ixíʔ a c -k̓ʷul̓ -st -s
bread and that art cust^ -make -^cust -3erg
bread roasted in the ashes, that's what he fixes,

kɬtost
kɬ -tost
to_be -toast
toast.[17]

344 way̓, way̓ wiʔcínəlx {uɬ xi}, {cus cunt} cus a
way̓ way̓ wy̓=cin -lx cu -s a
yes yes finish_eating -pl tell -3erg art
They got done eating, and he told his father,

15 Another reaction that fits Coyote's character.
16 Having made the situation even worse.
17 Coyote is making breakfast.

l?iws, way̓ l?iw, ɬwíntsən 345 way̓
l?iw -s way̓ l?iw ɬwi -nt -s -n way̓
m's_father -3in well m's_father leave -nt -2obj -1erg yes
"Father, I'm leaving you. *I am*

nq̓a?ílsmən axá? isk̓ʷíƛ̓təm 346 uɬ sc̓kinx
n+q̓a?=íls+m -n axá? i -s+k̓ʷiƛ̓+t+m uɬ sc -?kin -x
be_one's_business -1erg this 1in -others and ipftvp^ -indef -^ipftvp
troubled about my brothers. *Why it is that they*

uɬ {yaʕ} yayáʕtəlx uɬ aɬ cksl̓ípla?lx 347 lut̓ a
uɬ yaʕ•yáʕ+t -lx uɬ aɬ c -k+sl̓=ípla? -lx lut_t̓ a
and all -pl and compl hab -be_gone -pl neg_emph art
all disappeared? 12:01 *Not one*

kɬknáqs t̓a ɬckicx 348 way̓ mat la?kín
kɬ -k=naqs t̓ ɬ+c+kic+x way̓ mat la+?kíń
to_be -one_person negfac arrive_cisl_again yes must how
of them has come back. *Something must be wrong,*

sc̓kinx, way̓ iksmipnúnəm {uɬ} 349 a cus way̓,
sc -?kin -x way̓ i -ks -my+p -nun -m a cu -s way̓
ipftvp^ -indef -^ipftvp yes 1i -futi -learn -manage -apsv intj tell -3erg Ok
I am going to find out." *He [Coyote] said*

way̓ incá nixʷ kən nq̓a?íls uɬ aɬí? kən ks?axkənməscúta?x 350 {ɬ}
way̓ in+cá nixʷ kn n+q̓a?=íls uɬ aɬí? kn ks -?ax+kn+m+scút -a?x
yes I also 1kn concerned and so 1kn incp^ -do_something -^incp
to him, "I am troubled too, but what can I do? *I*

uɬ way̓ uɬ {k} talí kən ƛ̓əx̌ƛ̓x̌áp 351 uɬ anwí t̓əxʷ kʷ tətw̓ít, uɬ
uɬ way̓ uɬ ta?lí? kn ƛ̓x̌•ƛ̓x̌a+p uɬ anwí t̓xʷ kʷ t•tw̓it uɬ
and yes and very_much 1kn elder and you emph 2kn boy and
am too old. *You are young, and you can do*

kʷ nq̓a?íls 352 uɬ way̓ t̓i x̌ast 353 uɬ aɬí? axá? saʕníxʷ {uɬ aɬí?} uɬ
kʷ n+q̓a?=íls uɬ way̓ t̓i? x̌as+t uɬ aɬí? axá? s+ʕańíxʷ uɬ
2kn concerned and yes evid good and so this Muskrat and
something. *And that is good."* *And, as I said, Muskrat*

i? t cun kʷəlstnímən {uɬ} uɬ caʕʷlxímən 354 xík̓xək̓t uɬ {u} mat
i? t cu -n kʷls+tn+imn uɬ caʕʷ+lx+ímn xik̓•xk̓+t uɬ mat
art obl tell -1erg sweat_bathe_often and bathe_often spry and maybe
likes to sweat bathe and bathe. *He is spry and he has*

way̓ kscƛ̓x̌áp 355 {uɬ sc̓x̌ilx} uɬ mat way̓ k̓əɬukcút 356 mat way̓
way̓ ksc -ƛ̓x̌a+p uɬ mat way̓ k̓ɬ+wk+cut mat way̓
yes pperf -grow_sg and maybe yes see maybe yes
something to live for. *And I guess he had seen what was wrong,* *what had*

mipnús {il} stim̓ a {nƛ̓xʷ} nƛ̓əxʷtáns i? sk̓ʷíƛ̓təms
my+p -nu -s stim̓ a n+ƛ̓xʷ+tan -s i? s+k̓ʷiƛ̓+t+m -s
learn -manage -3erg what art death -3in art brothers -3in
caused his brothers' death;

357 mat waỷ {k̓əłq̓is} k̓əłqiʔsmíst 358 sc̓x̌ilx uł {i} iʔ
mat waỷ k̓ł+qỷs+mist sc+ʔx̌il+x uł iʔ
maybe yes dream_about reason_why and art
I guess he had a dream about it. 13:01 *That's why he is going*

ksƛ̓aʔƛ̓aʔntís iʔ sk̓ʷíƛ̓təms 359 uł {i} iʔ x̌əcməncút iʔ t
ks -ƛ̓aʔ•ƛ̓aʔ -nt -is iʔ s+k̓ʷiƛ̓+t+m -s uł iʔ x̌c+mncut iʔ t
futtˆ -look_for -nt -3erg art brothers -3in and art get_ready art obl
to look for his brothers, *and why he prepared what he is*

ksxʷilscúts 360 {uł ałíʔ} xʷilscút axáʔ saʔʕ̓níxʷ t t̓ic̓
k -s+xʷy=lscut -s xʷy=lscut axáʔ s+ʕ̓an̓íxʷ t t̓ic̓
to_be -things_to_take -3i take_along this Muskrat obj_itr pitch
going to take with him. *Muskrat took some pitch with him.*

361 {uł ixíʔ} uł ałíʔ mipnús ixíʔ {a n} a nƛ̓əxʷtáns axáʔ k̓əl
uł ałíʔ my+p -nu -s ixíʔ a n+ƛ̓xʷ+tan -s axáʔ k̓l
and so learn -manage -3erg that art death -3in this at
In his dream he figured out their

qiʔsmíst 362 i t {s} cmáʕʷłtməlx iʔ {snil}
qỷs+mist iʔ t c -maʕʷ -łt -m -lx iʔ
dream art obl custˆ -break -łt -psv -pl art
deaths. *Their hard points had been*

snululmúsaʔstsəlx 363 {kaʔc kaʔ cənƛ̓l} {inaud} uł iwá łaʔ
s+n+wl•wlm=ús=aʔst -s -lx uł iwá łaʔ
arrow_points -3in -pl and to_no_avail when
broken, *and when they do*

st̓aʕpstísəlx axáʔ iʔ səmx̌íkən 364 waỷ lut waỷ t̓a
s -t̓aʕp -st -is -lx axáʔ iʔ s+mx̌=ikn waỷ lut waỷ t̓
custˆ -shoot -ˆcust -3erg -pl this art grizzly well not yes negfac
shoot the grizzly *it doesn't even go*

cənʔúłxʷ iʔ t síp̓iʔs 365 məł maʕʷt axáʔ iʔ {snilil}
c+n+ʔułxʷ iʔ t síp̓iʔ -s mł maʕʷ+t axáʔ iʔ
enter_cisl art obj_itr hide -3in and break this art
through the hide, *and the hard point*

snululmúsaʔst[əns] 366 məł axáʔ iʔ cq̓ílən cləpláʕp 367 lut t̓a
s+n+wl•wlm=ús=aʔst+n -s mł axáʔ iʔ cq̓=iln c -lp•laʕp lut t̓
arrow_points -3in and this art arrow hab -fall_off not negfac
breaks, *and the arrow falls off.* *It doesn't*

cəlxʷáp axáʔ {i} iʔ səmx̌íkən qaʔłsəmx̌íkən 368 uł sc̓x̌ilx kiʔ
c -lxʷa+p axáʔ iʔ s+mx̌=ikn qł=s+mx̌=ikn uł sc+ʔx̌il+x kiʔ
hab -get_hurt this art grizzly grizzly's_child and reason_why rel
even hurt the grizzly, the grizzly's child. 14:00 *And that's why*

ksxʷuysts {axáʔ i} ksxʷyłt̓íc̓aʔx 369 məł ałíʔ kłəłk̓ʷúliʔs {i}
ks -xʷuy -st -s ks -xʷy+ł+t̓ic̓ -aʔx mł ałíʔ kł -ł+k̓ʷul̓ ỷ -s
futi -go -caus -3i incpˆ -take_pitch -ˆincp and so fut -do_again -nt -3erg
he is going to take pitch along. *Because he is going to repair*

iʔ {sn} snululmúsaʔstəns kɬc̓áʕnməsts 370 waẏ ixíʔ
iʔ s+n+wl•wlm=ús=aʔst+tn -s kɬ -c̓aʕn+m+st -s waẏ ixíʔ
art arrow_points -3in to_be -make_tight -3i yes then
the hard points solid. *Muskrat*

sk̓əwílxs saʔʕníxʷ 371 xʷu··y, kicx iʔ k̓əl səmx̌íkən
s -k̓w+ilx -s s+ʕan̓íxʷ xʷuy kic+x iʔ k̓l s+mx̌=ikn
nom -go_upstream -3i Muskrat go arrive art to grizzly
went upstream. *He went and he got right in front*

skiyaʕcínəms 372 waẏ ilíʔ cqaq 373 waẏ ʕacəntís iʔ stáɬəms,
s+k+yaʕ=cin+m -s waẏ ilíʔ cq•aq waẏ ʕac -nt -is iʔ s+taɬm -s
shore -3in yes there land yes tie -nt -3erg art boat -3in
of Grizzly's house. *He stopped there.* *He tied his boat and*

waẏ ɬəxʷpúsəms iʔ cq̓íləns 374 uɬ ilíʔ náx̌əmɬ {iʔ} iʔ
waẏ ɬxʷ+p=us+m -s iʔ cq̓=iln -s uɬ ilíʔ nax̌mɬ iʔ
yes loop_over_head -3erg art arrow -3in and there but art
looped his weapon around his neck, *but he left*

t̓ic̓s ilíʔ cután 375 kəm̓ mat ck̓əɬq̓aʔq̓ʔálqsəmsts
t̓ic̓ -s ilíʔ c -wta+n km̓ mat c -k̓ɬ+q̓aʔ•q̓ʔ=alqs+m -st -s
pitch -3in there hab -placed or maybe cust^ -put_under_clothes -^cust -3erg
his pitch there. *Or maybe he stuck it under his shirt,*

376 uɬ aɬí miná lut {ac} axáʔ iʔ t tkəɬmílxʷ
uɬ aɬíʔ miná lut axáʔ iʔ t tkɬ+m=ilxʷ
and because maybe_not not this art agInst woman
because the woman looks in his boat

cʕác̓ɬtməlx i l stáɬəmsəlx 377 c̓x̌ilx uɬ iʔ lut iʔ
c -ʕac̓ -ɬt -m -lx iʔ l s+taɬm -s -lx c+ʔx̌il+x uɬ iʔ lut iʔ
cust^ -look_at -ɬt -psv -pl art in boat -3in -pl how and art not art
to see what he has. *And so she can't see*

wíkɬtəməlx {iʔ} iʔ t̓ic̓s 378 waẏ xʷuy k̓ɬənɬaʔíp {k̓əl}, xʷuy
wik -ɬt -m -lx iʔ t̓ic̓ -s waẏ xʷuy k̓ɬ+n+ɬaʔ=íp xʷuy
see -ɬt -psv -pl art pitch -3in yes go be_next_to go
his pitch. 15:03 *He got right close to the door, he got on top*

kɬqəltús 379 waẏ cwi··x ixíʔ səmx̌íkən nák̓ʷəm citxʷs 380 xʷuy
kɬ+qlt=us waẏ c -wix ixíʔ s+mx̌=ikn nak̓ʷ+m citxʷ -s xʷuy
hill_top yes hab -live that grizzly evid house -3in go
of the bank. *There was a house there, that's Grizzly's house.* *He*

uɬ ilíʔ i l tk̓əmkn̓íɬxʷ {ilíʔ uɬ} 381 kɬəxʷpəntís {iʔ} iʔ
uɬ ilíʔ iʔ l t+k̓m=kn=iɬxʷ k+ɬxʷ+p -nt -is iʔ
and there art in outside hang_st_over -nt -3erg art
went there, got right outside the house, *hung up what he had looped*

sənʔuckláx̌əns, t̓əxʷ iʔ cq̓íləns 382 waẏ kcaʔcaʔálqʷəm i l
s+n+ʔuckl=áx̌n -s t̓xʷ iʔ cq̓=iln -s waẏ k+caʔ•caʔ=álqʷ+m iʔ l
looped_on_arm -3in evidently art arrow -3in yes knock_on_pole art in
around his arm, and his arrows. *He knocked on*

məl̓kʷúts 383 way̓ cúntəm t səmx̌íkən, way̓ cən?úɬxʷəxʷ
ml̓kʷ=ut -s way̓ cu -nt -m t s+mx̌=ikn way̓ c+n+?uɬxʷ -xʷ
pole -3in yes tell -nt -psv agInst grizzly well enter_cisl -isimptv
the poles. *Grizzly said "Come in!"*

384 way̓ nk̓ahcís ia nxárcən ixí? sən?úɬxʷs
way̓ n+k̓ah=cí -s i? n+xar=cn ixí? s -n+?uɬxʷ -s
yes raise -3erg art curtain_in_front then nom -enter -3i
He raised the curtain, he went in.

385 nak̓ʷá aɬiá pnicí? uɬ way̓ kɬbəŋəlolx, lut
nak̓ʷ+á aɬi+á pn+icí? uɬ way̓ kɬ+báŋgəlò -lx lut
indeed_not because_not at_that_time and yes have+bungalow -pl not
Because at that time they didn't have bungalows, no.

386 {ay in} nx̌ʷáyqən i? cítxʷsəlx 387 cúntəm t səmx̌íkən way̓
n+x̌ʷay=qn i? citxʷ -s -lx cu -nt -m t s+mx̌=ikn way̓
tipi art house -3in -pl tell -nt -psv agInst grizzly yes
Their houses are tipis. *Grizzly said, "Well,*

kʷu x̌əc̓íkstmənt[xʷ] 388 a[ɬí? l]ut kʷu t̓a
kʷu x̌c̓=ikst+m -nt -xʷ aɬí? lut kʷu t̓
1obj surprise -nt -2erg because not 1obj negfac
you surprise me. 16:00 *Nobody ever gets here,*

ckícəsts i? sqilxʷ ki? kʷu əɬ kícəntxʷ
c -kic -st -s i? s+qilxʷ ki? kʷu ɬ kic -nt -xʷ
cust^ -reach_st/sb -^cust -3erg art person rel 1obj subord reach_st/sb -nt -2erg
and then you got here."

389 a·, cus way̓, way̓ ixí? k̓l ast̓əmk?ílt ixí? i? mut ixí? i?
a cu -s way̓ way̓ ixí? k̓l a -s+t̓mk?=ilt ixí? i? mut ixí? i?
intj tell -3erg yes yes that for 2in -daughter that art sit_sg that art
"Ah," he said, "I came here for your daughter, the one

ctxʷúymən 390 x̌əl ixí? ki? cətxʷúyməntsən, way̓ kʷ
c+t+xʷuy+m -n x̌l ixí? ki? c+t+xʷuy+m -nt -s -n way̓ kʷ
come_toward -1erg for that rel come_toward -nt -2obj -1erg yes 2kʷu
sitting there. *That's what I come to you for, I'm going to*

iksənsucənmístəm 391 way̓ iwá t̓əxʷ lut ispapút i? k̓
i -ks -n+sw=cn+mist -m way̓ iwá t̓xʷ lut i -s+pa?•pút i? k̓
1i -futi -propose -apsv well even evidently not 1i -match art to
propose to you for her. *I am not a match for your*

ast̓əmk?ílt 392 uɬ aɬí?, aɬí? way̓ ikspúƛ̓əmstəm
a -s+t̓mk?=ilt uɬ aɬí? aɬí? way̓ i -ks -p̓uƛ̓+m -st -m
2in -daughter and so so yes 1i -futt^ -get_to_the_end -caus -apsv
daughter, *and so I want my thoughts to come to*

ispu?ús 393 way̓ {kən s} kən sk̓əɬq̇əmmíx i? k̓ ast̓əmk?ílt
i -s+pu?=ús way̓ kn s -k̓ɬ+q̇m -mix i? k̓ a -s+t̓mk?=ilt
1i -heart well 1kn ipftv^ -wish_for -^ipftv art to 2in -daughter
an end.[18] *I have been wishing for your daughter, and that's why*

uɬ {i} i ctxʷúyməntsən 394 a·, waẏ {sc̓kinx a} kʷu
uɬ iʔ c+t+xʷuy+m -nt -s -n a waẏ kʷu
and art come_toward -nt -2obj -1erg ntj well 1obj
I came to you." *"Ah, you are doing*

límkstməntxʷ, waẏ kʷ ikstaʔxʷsníḱəɬxʷ 395 waẏ myaɬ
lim=kst+m -nt -xʷ waẏ kʷ i -ks -taʔxʷ+s+níḱ=ɬxʷ waẏ myaɬ
do_st_good_for -nt -2erg yes 2kʷu 1i -futi -get_son_in_law yes too_much
something good for me, you are going to be my son-in-law. *My daughter*

q̓sápiʔ kiʔ sknánəqsaʔx axáʔ istʼəmkʔílt 396 uɬ mat
q̓sápiʔ kiʔ s -k=na•nqs -aʔx axáʔ i -s+tʼmkʔ=ilt uɬ mat
long_time rel ipftv^ -alone -^ipftvDim this 1i -daughter and maybe
has been single for too long. *I guess*

sc̓kinx uɬ aɬíʔ lut tʼa ksqílxʷ 397 mat
sc -ʔkin -x uɬ aɬíʔ lut tʼ k -s+qilxʷ mat
ipftvp^ -indef -^ipftvp and so not negfac there_be -person maybe
that's because there are no people here, *and*

sc̓kinx lut iwá sqícəlxs 398 waẏ cársəms iʔ
sc -ʔkin -x lut iwá s -qic+lx -s waẏ cars+m -s iʔ
ipftvp^ -indef -^ipftvp not try_to nom -run_sg -3i well motion -3erg art
she hasn't eloped yet." *She motioned to her*

stʼəmkʔílts 399 uɬ axáʔ tʼi wíkəntəm saʔʕ̓níxʷ axáʔ iʔ t
s+tʼmkʔ=ilt -s uɬ axáʔ tʼiʔ wik -nt -m s+ʕaṅíxʷ axáʔ iʔ t
daughter -3in and this evid see -nt -psv Muskrat this art agInst
daughter. 17:00 *The maiden saw*

stʼaʔḱmíx 400 waẏ uɬ npútəlsməntəm uɬ nstils 401 ntʼa··
s+tʼaʔḱ+míx waẏ uɬ n+put=ls+m -nt -m uɬ n+st=ils ntʼa
virgin well and be_satisfied_with -nt -psv and think intj
Muskrat. *She is plum satisfied with him, and she thought:* *"Gee, that's*

ixíʔ iksx̌ílwiʔ waẏ swiʔnúmtx, uɬ xíḱxəḱt 402 swit_aɬíʔ caʕʷlxímən
ixíʔ i -k -s+x̌ílwiʔ waẏ s+wẏ+numt=x uɬ xiḱ•xḱ+t swit_aɬíʔ caʕʷ+lx+ímn
that 1i -to_be -husband yes handsome and spry in_fact bathe_often
going to be my husband, and he's handsome, and he's spry." *Muskrat likes to*

kʷəlstnímən axáʔ {l} saʔʕ̓níxʷ 403 uɬ lut tʼa ckrar saʔʕ̓níxʷ,
kʷls+tn+imn axáʔ s+ʕaṅíxʷ uɬ lut tʼ c -kr•ar s+ʕaṅíxʷ
sweat_bathe_often this Muskrat and not negfac hab -mopey Muskrat
sweat bathe and to bathe; *Muskrat never gets mopey, he likes to hunt*

təxʷtəxʷcnúɬ 404 i· cársəms iʔ stʼəmkʔílts uɬ lutʼ
txʷ•txʷ=cn+uɬ i· cars+m -s iʔ s+tʼmkʔ=ilt -s uɬ lut_tʼ
provision_seeker intj motion -3erg art daughter -3in and neg_emph
for things to eat. *She motioned to her daughter but she*

18 "I may not be worthy of your daughter, but I want to find out if you will consent."

sxʷuys 405 wa y̓ {i} mat k̓ʷinx cársəms i? sť əmk?ílts
s -xʷuy -s wa y̓ mat k̓ʷin+x cars+m -s i? s+ť mk?=ilt -s
nom -go -3i well maybe a_few motion -3erg art daughter -3in
didn't go. *She motioned a few times,*

406 hoy uɬ nɬa?q̓ʷmqín 407 ixí? uɬ sic ?ácqa?, nlik̓k̓mníkst axá?
hoy uɬ n+ɬa?q̓ʷ+m=qín ixí? uɬ sic ?ácqa? n+lik̓•k̓+mn=ikst axá?
finish and audible that and then go_out be_forced this
finally she came out with words. *And then [the daughter] went out, the woman*

i? tkəɬmílxʷ 408 ixí? uɬ sic ?ácqa? 409 wa y̓ mumá?ʷɬtəm i?
i? tkɬ+m=ilxʷ ixí? uɬ sic ?ácqa? wa y̓ mw•ma?ʷ -ɬt -m i?
art woman then and then go_out yes break -ɬt -psv art
got forced. *She went out.* *She broke the arrows, and then*

cq̓íləns uɬ sic ni?ák̓ʷ uɬ ixí? sx̌íƛ̓əms 410 x̌í··ƛ̓əm uɬ
cq̓=iln -s uɬ sic n=y̓akʷ uɬ ixí? s -x̌iƛ̓+m -s x̌iƛ̓+m uɬ
arrow -3in and then across_water and then nom -climb -3i climb and
she crossed and went up the hill. 18:06 *She went up*

ixí? scíqəms 411 hoy, cúntəm a·, na?ɬcám,
ixí? s -ciq+m -s hoy cu -nt -m a naɬc•c•ám
then nom -dig -3i finish tell -nt -psv intj forget
the hill and started digging for roots. *She said, (I forgot to say), "There is one thing*

naqs isya?pcín 412 wa y̓ uɬ ixí? mat kʷ iksník̓əɬxʷ
naqs i -s+ya?+p=cín wa y̓ uɬ ixí? mat kʷ i -k -s+nik̓=ɬxʷ
one 1in -hardship well and then maybe 2kʷu 1i -to_be -son_in_law
I am hard up for. *I guess you are going to be my son-in-law,*

413 kʷ isník̓əɬxʷ uɬ axá? {ikɬ} ikɬnqəqpáqstxən kʷu
kʷ i -s+nik̓=ɬxʷ uɬ axá? i -kɬ -n+q•qp=aqst=xn kʷu
2kʷu 1i -son_in_law and this 1i -to_be -mat 1obj
you are my son-in-law and you are going to get me something to put

aksƛ̓a?ɬtím 414 ixí? ik̓lí? k̓a nsq̓ʷut i? k̓əl k̓əɬx̌sínk 415 ilí?
a -ks -ƛ̓a? -ɬt ixí? ik̓lí? k̓ n+s+q̓ʷut i? k̓l k̓ɬ+x̌s=ink ilí?
2i -futtˆ -fetch -ɬt that there to other_side art on side_hill there
under my hip. *Right across there on that bare side hill,* *that's*

səmx̌íkən ki? k̓əɬ?aksuxínk stəxʷcəncútx 416 ixí? kʷu
s+mx̌=ikn ki? k̓ɬ+?aks+wx=ínk s -txʷ=cn+cut -x ixí? kʷu
grizzly rel stand_on_side_hill ipftvˆ -get_food -ˆipftv that 1kʷu
where a grizzly hangs out getting things to eat. *That's what*

aksƛ̓a?ɬtím ikɬənqəqpáqstxən 417 wa y̓ myaɬ kən
a -ks -ƛ̓a? -ɬt -im i -kɬ -n+q•qp=aqst=xn wa y̓ myaɬ kn
2i -futtˆ -fetch -ɬt -apsv 1i -to_be -mat yes too_much 1kn
I want you to get me to put under my hip. *The floor is too hard*

ck̓əɬk̓ak̓?á? 418 uɬ kʷa ixí? sxʷípəlp ixí? l anqəqpáqstxən
c -k̓ɬ+k̓a?•k̓?á? uɬ kʷa ixí? s+xʷip=lp ixí? l an -q•qp=aqst=xn
hab -hard_surface and intj that mat that for 2in -lie_on
for me." *That's a mat for you to lie on, 19:00*

419 mat ixíʔ {sənk̓líp iʔ ə} səmx̌íkən iʔ mǽtrəsc 420 aˑˑ cúntəm
mat ixíʔ s+mx̌=ikn iʔ matrs -c a cu -nt -m
maybe that grizzly art mattress -3in intj tell -nt -psv
that is Grizzly's mattress. *Muskrat said:*

t saʔʕ̓níxʷ, way̓, ċkinx a kʷ isx̌aʔx̌á 421 uł
t s+ʕan̓íxʷ way̓ sc -ʔkin -x a kʷ i -s+x̌áʔ•x̌aʔ uł
agInst Muskrat yes ipftvpˆ -indef -ˆipftvp art 2kʷu 1in -father_in_law and
"It's like you are my {father-in-law} [mother-in-law]. *You*

way̓ {kʷ i} kʷu kʷulstxʷ i l stim̓ {uł} yaʕ̓pcínməntəxʷ 422 uł way̓
way̓ kʷu kʷulst -xʷ iʔ l stim̓ yaʕ+p=cín+m -nt -xʷ uł way̓
yes 1obj send -2erg art for what hard_up_for -nt 2erg and yes
can send me for whatever you are in need of, *and*

kʷ iksƛ̓aʔłtím 423 way̓ t̓əxʷ kən cənstíls kən put i
kʷ i -ks -ƛ̓aʔ -łt -im way̓ t̓xʷ kn c -n+st=ils kn put iʔ
2kʷu 1i -futtˆ -fetch -łt -apsv yes evidently 1kn hab -think 1kn exact art
I'll go get it for you. *I think I am a match [able enough] to get*

l stəxʷcəncút 424 way̓ n̓ín̓w̓iʔ ƛ̓aʔłtsín 425 ixíʔ
l s+txʷ=cn+cut way̓ n̓ín̓w̓iʔ ƛ̓aʔ -łt -s -in ixíʔ
for food yes a_while fetch -łt -2obj -1erg then
things to eat. *I'll go after it for you."* *Then*

sxʷət̓ílxs saʔʕ̓níxʷ 426 tkʷínksəm iʔ təl̓ slíp̓s axáʔ t {a}
s -xʷt̓+ilx -s s+ʕan̓íxʷ t+kʷin=ks+m iʔ tl̓ slip̓ -s axáʔ t
nom -get_up -3i Muskrat take art from wood -3in this agInstr
Muskrat got up, *and {Coyote} took a stick from*

sənk̓líp 427 uł ixíʔ {c} cúntəm t səmx̌íkən 428 way̓ ilíʔ uł
s+n+kl̓=ip uł ixíʔ cu -nt -m t s+mx̌=ikn way̓ ilíʔ uł
Coyote and then tell -nt -psv agInst grizzly yes there and
the fire. *Then Grizzly said,* *Grizzly started*

cacáʕypəm səmx̌íkən 429 cúntəm uł kʷ sċkinx uł {iʔ}
ca•cáʕy+p+m s+mx̌=ikn cu -nt -m uł kʷ sc -ʔkin -x uł
cry grizzly tell -nt -psv and 2kn ipftvpˆ -indef -ˆipftvp and
to howl, *she said, "What's the burning stick*

iʔ surísəlp̓ uł i kʷu əł tkʷínsəłtxʷ 430 aˑ cúntəm,
iʔ s+wr̓=islp̓ uł iʔ kʷu ł t+kʷin=s -łt -xʷ a cu -nt -m
art fire and art 1obj subord take_from_fire -łt -2erg intj tell -nt -psv
you took for?" 20:02 *He said,*

way̓, way̓ iksk̓ʷúl̓əm istáłəm 431 way̓ ixíʔ aláʔ iscəcqáq
way̓ way̓ i -k+s -k̓ʷul̓ -m i -s+tałm way̓ ixíʔ aláʔ i -sc -cq•aq
yes yes 1i -futtˆ -fix -apsv 1i -boat yes then here 1i -pftv -land
I am going to fix my boat. *Just when I got here on shore,*

mat kiʔ {iʔ} maʕʷt {i} incəp̓q̓mín iʔ t̓ic̓ 432 cut t̓əxʷ way̓
mat kiʔ maʕʷ+t i -n+c̓pq̓+min iʔ t̓ic̓ cut t̓xʷ way̓
maybe rel break 1i -glue art pitch say evidently yes
that's when my glue, my pitch came undone. *That's when it*

úłi a nċxʷaxʷ 433 cut put q̓ʷiċt uł i kən səcqáq 434 caʔkʷ
uł iʔ a n+ċxʷ•axʷ cut put q̓ʷiċ+t uł iʔ kn cq•aq caʔkʷ
and_then art leak say just full and art 1kn land if
[the boat] started to leak. *It got filled up when I landed.* *If*

t̓iʔx̌íł k̓la iʔ k̓la nqʷast way̓ uł ilíʔ kən nƛ̓əllítkʷ 435 lut t̓a
t̓i+ʔx̌íł k̓l iʔ k̓l n+qʷas+t way̓ uł ilíʔ kn n+ƛ̓l•l=itkʷ lut t̓
same_happen to art to deep yes and there 1kn drown not negfac
it had happened before, where it's deep I would have drowned. *I don't*

cmistín iʔ sk̓rám, 436 uł ixíʔ ikłəłk̓ʷúl̓əm
c -my -st -in iʔ s+k̓ra+m uł ixíʔ i -kł -ł+k̓ʷul̓+m
cust^ -know -^cust -1erg art swim and that 1i -futi -fix_again
know how to swim.[19] *That's what I am going to fix,*

iksċəpq̓ám {a} 437 uł ałíʔ lut t̓ qəłnún
i -ks -ċpq̓a+m uł ałíʔ lut t̓ qł -nu -n
1i -futi -glue and because not negfac able -manage -1erg
to glue back. *I can't*

ikst̓íxəlx 438 cəm̓ kən nƛ̓əllítkʷ, lut t̓a
i -ks -t̓ix+lx[20] cm̓ kn n+ƛ̓l•l=itkʷ lut t̓
1i -futi -come_to_shore maybe 1kn drown not negfac
sail. *I might drown, I don't know*

cmistín iʔ sk̓ram 439 uł ixíʔ {ikłəł mlam ik}
c -my -st -in iʔ s+k̓ram uł ixíʔ
cust^ -know -^cust -1erg art swim and that
how to swim. *That's what I am going*

[ikłəł]nmláʕsəm 440 cus, uł ha {kʷ kł kʷl} kʷ [kł]t̓iċ
i -kł -ł+n+ml=ʕas+m cu -s uł haʔ kʷ kł+t̓iċ
1i -futi -fill_with_clay_again tell -3erg and inter 2kn have_pitch
to fill with clay." *She asked: "And do you have some pitch?"*

441 way̓, ixíʔ náx̌əmł kən kłt̓iċ 442 ixíʔ uł sic iʔ xʷuy, nt̓aʔlíls
way̓ ixíʔ nax̌mł kn kł+t̓iċ ixíʔ uł sic iʔ xʷuy n+t̓aʔl=íls
yes that but 1kn have_pitch then and then art go satisfied
"Yes, I got some pitch." *Then he went. Grizzly got*

axáʔ səmx̌íkən 443 way̓ ʔácqaʔ łəxʷpúsəms {iʔ} iʔ cq̓íləns
axáʔ s+mx̌=ikn way̓ ʔácqaʔ łxʷ+p=us+m -s iʔ cq̓=iln -s
this grizzly well go_out loop_over_head -3erg art arrow -3in
satisfied. 21:02 *Muskrat wet out, he looped his bow and arrow,*

444 {nʔu i s nʔucklax̌n} nʔuckláx̌nəms {i} 445 hoy k̓ʷixʷs iʔ stáłəm,
n+ʔuckl=áx̌n+m -s hoy k̓ʷixʷ -s iʔ s+tałm
loop_over_arm -3erg well untie -3erg art boat
looped it around his arm. *He untied the boat,*

19 Ironic touch.
20 The choice of words is not clear to me.

uɬ ixíʔ sƛ̓áq̇əms
uɬ ixíʔ s -ƛ̓aq̇+m -s
and then nom -cross_stream -3i
and he went across.

446 way̓ uɬ ilíʔ {uɬ ə} kċaʔləmƛ̓íċaʔ axáʔ
way̓ uɬ ilíʔ k+ċaʔlmƛ̓=íċaʔ axáʔ
well and there get_chills this
The [old] grizzly got chills of

səmx̌íkən
s+mx̌=ikn
grizzly
premonition.

447 uɬ ʔácqaʔ uɬ kəɬtəɬxʷús uɬ cyaʔyáx̌aʔsts
uɬ ʔácqaʔ uɬ kɬ+tɬ+x=us uɬ c -yaʔ•yáx̌aʔ -st -s
and go_out and stand_on_bank and cust^ -watch -^cust -3erg
She went out, stood on the edge of the bank, and she watched him.

448 cƛ̓áq̇əm, way̓ axáʔ {c} cxʷukʷs iʔ cq̇íləns {uɬ ixíʔ}
c -ƛ̓aq̇m way̓ axáʔ c+xʷukʷ -s iʔ cq̇=iln -s
hab cross yes this pull -3erg art arrow -3in
He crossed, he started pulling out his arrows.

449 sta way̓ {c}
sta way̓
intj yes
Well,

cmuʔmáʕʷ axáʔ iʔ snululmúsaʔsts
c -mw•maʕʷ axáʔ iʔ s+n+wl•wlm=ús=aʔst -s
hab -break this art arrow_points -3in
the hard points were broken.

450 way̓ ixíʔ
way̓ ixíʔ
well then
He

ɬtəɬtəɬəmstí··s {uɬ ixíʔ ɬ}
ɬ+tɬ•tɬ+m -st -is
straighten_again -caus -3erg
straightened them out.

451 uɬ aɬíʔ axáʔ {c} cixs axáʔ iʔ ƛ̓iċ
uɬ aɬíʔ axáʔ cix -s axáʔ iʔ ƛ̓iċ
and so this warm -3erg this art pitch
Then he heated the pitch,

uɬ ixíʔ {ɬ} ɬməlməlntá··ʕs
uɬ ixíʔ ɬ+ml•ml -nt -aʕs
and then dab -nt -3erg
and dabbed it on. 22:00

452 uɬ way̓ cwaʔháʔ {səm} səmx̌íkən
uɬ way̓ c -wah•ah s+mx̌=ikn
and yes hab -holler grizzly
Grizzly started hollering.

453 cúntəm uɬ stim̓ ia ck̓ʷúl̓stxʷ
cu -nt -m uɬ stim̓ iʔ c -k̓ʷul̓ -st
tell -nt -psv and what art cust^ -do -^cust
She asked: "What it is you are fixing?"

454 a atláʔ ɬk̓əɬkʷíw[21]
a atláʔ ɬ+k̓ɬ+kʷiw
intj from_here answer_again
He started answering,

455 cus way̓, uɬ way̓ cúntsən {in} istáɬəm
cu -s way̓ uɬ way̓ cu -nt -s -n i -s+taɬm
tell -3erg yes and yes tell -nt -2obj -1erg 1in -boat
He said, "I told you, my boat.

456 uɬ aɬíʔ
uɬ aɬíʔ
and because
I was

kən sxʷúsəskaʔx, cəm̓ way̓ ɬənɬúxʷt iʔ səmx̌íkən
kn s -xʷús•s+kaʔ -x cm̓ way̓ ɬ+n+ɬuxʷ+t iʔ s+mx̌=ikn
1kn ipftv^ -be_in_hurry -^ipftv maybe yes enter_brush_again art grizzly
in a hurry, the grizzly might go back in the brush.

457 uɬ sċx̌ilx lut aláʔ [ilíʔ] iʔ k̓ʷúlən ki sic kən niʔák̓ʷ
uɬ sc+ʔx̌il+x lut aláʔ ilíʔ iʔ k̓ʷul̓ -n kiʔ sic kn n=y̓ak̓ʷ
and reason_why not here there art do -1erg rel then 1kn across_water
That's why I didn't fix it there, and then I crossed.

21 The expected form is ɬk̓ɬk̓ʷinxʷcn.

458 ɬaʔ kən cxʷuy ka ck̓ʷúl̓st[ən]
ɬaʔ kn c+xʷuy ka c -k̓ʷul̓ -st -n
when 1kn come rel cust^ -fix -^cust -1erg
When I come I'll fix it."

459 wal̓ ixíʔ put
wal̓ ixíʔ put
well then just
He fixed every

xəƛ̓pnús i? cq̓íləns uɬ maʕcnítkʷ
xƛ̓+p -nu -s iʔ cq̓=iln -s uɬ maʕ=cn=ítkʷ
complete -manage -3erg art arrow -3in and come_to_shore
one of the arrows, and he got to shore.

460 way̓ ixíʔ
way̓ ixíʔ
well then
He tied

ʕacəntís iʔ stáɬəms
ʕac -nt -is iʔ s+taɬm -s
tie -nt -3erg art boat -3in
his boat.

461 a ixíʔ ilíʔ wikɬts iʔ
a ixíʔ ilíʔ wik -ɬt -s iʔ
intj then there see -ɬt -3erg art
He saw

sk̓ʷíƛ̓təms iʔ stəɬtáɬəms
s+k̓ʷiƛ̓+t+m -s iʔ s+tɬ•taɬm -s
brothers -3in art boats -3in
his brothers' boats.

462 way̓ ilíʔ yayáʕt cʕaʕaccnítkʷ
way̓ ilíʔ yaʕ•yáʕ+t c -ʕa•ʕac=cn=ítkʷ
yes there all hab -tie_on_shore
They are all tied there,

músuʔɬ
mus=w̓ɬ
four_conveyances
four boats.

463 way̓ cniɬc ilíʔ nixʷ ʕacəntís, way̓ nstils
way̓ cniɬ+c ilíʔ nixʷ ʕac -nt -is way̓ n+st=ils
well (s)he there also tie -nt -3erg well think
He too tied his boat, and thought:

464 way̓ aláʔ way̓ way̓ uníxʷ isqíʔs
way̓ aláʔ way̓ way̓ wnixʷ i -s+qy̓s
yes here yes yes true 1in -dream
"Yes, yes, my dream was true.

465 way̓ {ax̌} ixíʔ mat ha k̓əl
way̓ ixíʔ mat haʔ k̓l
well then maybe inter to
It must be on this hill that

w̓íw̓aʔst {kiʔ} kiʔ ƛ̓áxʷtəlx axáʔ isk̓ʷíƛ̓təm
w̓í•w̓aʔs+t kiʔ ƛ̓axʷ+t -lx axáʔ i -s+k̓ʷiƛ̓+t+m
high_dim rel dead_pl -pl this 1in -brothers
my brothers died. 23:05

466 ƛ̓əxʷəntíməlx,
ƛ̓xʷ -nt -im -lx
kill_many -nt -psv -pl
They got killed,

uɬ i kʷa nʔaɬnaʔsqílxʷtən səmx̌íkən
uɬ iʔ kʷa n+ʔaɬn+aʔ+s+qílxʷ+tn s+mx̌=ikn
and art intj man_eater grizzly
Grizzly is a cannibal."

467 way̓ ixíʔ sx̌íƛ̓əms, a
way̓ ixíʔ s -x̌iƛ̓+m -s a
well then nom -climb -3i intj
He started to climb,

ta ck̓əlxʷmúlaʔxʷ uɬ x̌íƛ̓əm
t c -k̓lxʷ+m=úlaʔxʷ uɬ x̌iƛ̓+m
obl hab -out_of_sight and climb
he climbed sneaking.

468 aɬíʔ uɬ cúntəm t səmx̌íkən,
aɬíʔ uɬ cu -nt -m t s+mx̌=ikn
so and tell -nt -psv agInst grizzly
And Grizzly had told him, she

cúntəm
cu -nt -m
tell -nt -psv
had said,

469 way̓, way̓ lut aks {təl} təl w̓íw̓aʔst mi
way̓ way̓ lut a -ks tl w̓í•w̓aʔs+t mi
yes yes not 2i -futi from high_dim fut
"Don't go from above to come down

ctxʷúyməntxʷ
c+t+xʷuy+m -nt -xʷ
come_toward -nt -2erg
on her.

470 cəm̓ lúti akstk̓ík̓aʔt məɬ way̓
cm̓ lút+i a -ks -t+k̓í•k̓aʔt mɬ way̓
maybe before 2i -futi -get_near and yes
She'll notice you before

mipnúnts 471 taʔlíʔ pəx̌páx̌t iʔ səmx̌íkən 472 uɬ axáʔ
my+p -nun -t -s taʔlíʔ px̌•pax̌+t iʔ s+mx̌=ikn uɬ axáʔ
learn -manage -nt -3e2obj very_much smart art grizzly and this
you get near, *the Grizzly is very smart.* *But*

náx̌əmɬ tla ixʷút uɬ lut t̓ kswíkənts 473 uɬ cəm̓
nax̌mɬ tla yxʷ=ut uɬ lut t̓ ks -wik -nt -s uɬ cm̓
but from below and not negfac futt^ -see -nt -3e2obj and maybe
if you go from below, she won't see you. *You will get*

talíʔ k̓aʔtmíntxʷ mi_sic wíkənts 474 uɬ way̓
taʔlíʔ k̓aʔt+min -t -xʷ mi_sic wik -nt -s uɬ way̓
very_much go_near -nt -2erg then see -nt -3e2obj and yes
very close to her before she sees you. *You will*

miystxʷ pulstxʷ 475 ixíʔ náx̌əmɬ təl̓ w̓íwaʔst uɬ
miy -st -xʷ pul -st -xʷ ixíʔ nax̌mɬ tl̓ w̓í•w̓aʔs+t uɬ
be_sure_of -st -2erg kill_one -st -2erg then but from high_dim and
surely kill her. *But if you go from above you'll be*

cəm̓ t̓i kʷ miwsúlaʔxʷ 476 uɬ way̓ {mi} k̓əɬʔanwínts 477 uɬ
cm̓ t̓iʔ kʷ miw̓s=úlaʔxʷ uɬ way̓ k̓ɬ+ʔanwí -nt -s uɬ
maybe evid 2kn half_way and yes hear_st -nt -3e2obj and
just half way, *and she will notice you.* *Just*

way̓ {c} t̓i sic kʷ ɬʔiq̓ʷ uɬ way̓ wíkənts 478 uɬ aɬíʔ way̓
way̓ t̓iʔ sic kʷ ɬ[ʔ]iq̓ʷ uɬ way̓ wik -nt -s uɬ aɬíʔ way̓
yes evid then 2kn appear and yes see -nt -3e2obj and because yes
the minute you get in sight, she will see you. 24:03 *She has been*

ctk̓əlk̓əlstúms 479 a˙, cus way̓ 480 way̓ lut t̓a
c -t+k̓l•k̓l -st -um -s a cu -s way̓ way̓ lut t̓
cust^ -expect_so -^cust -2obj -3erg intj tell -3erg yes well not negfac
expecting you." *He said, "Yeah."* *He didn't*

nunxʷínaʔms, way̓ ta ck̓əlxʷmúlaʔxʷ uɬ x̌íƛ̓əm 481 a˙˙ məɬ
n+wnxʷ=ínaʔ+m -s way̓ t c -k̓lxʷ+m=úlaʔxʷ uɬ x̌iƛ̓+m a mɬ
believe_so -3erg yes obl hab -out_of_sight and climb intj and
believe her. He went out of sight and climbed. *And*

atláʔ wahám səmx̌íkən 482 kʷ isəscúnəm tla ixʷú˙˙t mi
atláʔ wahá+m s+mx̌=ikn kʷ i -ss -cun+m tla yxʷu+t mi
from_here holler grizzly 2kʷu 1i -pftv -tell from below fut
the Grizzly hollered: *"I have been telling you to go towards her*

txʷúyməntxʷ 483 cəm̓ ləxʷpnúnts təl̓ w̓íwaʔst
t+xʷuy+m -nt -xʷ cm̓ lxʷ+p -nun -t -s tl̓ w̓í•w̓aʔs+t
go_towards -nt -2erg maybe hurt -manage -nt -3e2obj from high_dim
from below. *She will hurt you from above."*

484 ə [lut] t̓ ntq̓aʔlsínaʔms, m[á]lx̌aʔs lut t̓
ə lut t̓ n+t+q̓aʔ=ls=ínaʔ+m -s málx̌aʔ -s lut t̓
intj not negfac pay_attention -3erg lie -3erg not negfac
He didn't pay any attention, he pretended not to

níxləms 485 xʷu··y {təl} təl̓ w̓íwaʔst {ki sic} t̓i k̓əłpaʔsəntís[22]
nixl+m -s xʷuy tl̓ w̓í•w̓aʔs+t t̓iʔ k̓ł+paʔs -nt -is
listen_to -3erg go from high_dim evid guess -nt -3erg
hear her. He went from above, he just guessed it,

486 uł ałíʔ way̓ wiks səmx̌íkən iʔ k̓əłʔaksuxínk 487 way̓ t̓i
uł ałíʔ way̓ wik -s s+mx̌=ikn iʔ k̓ł+ʔaks+wx=ínk way̓ t̓iʔ
and so yes see -3erg grizzly art stand_on_side_hill well evid
and he saw the grizzly standing on the side hill. He just

ck̓əłpaʔsəntís,[23] way̓ ixíʔ {s} sk̓aʔk̓ítxnəms 488 swit_ałíʔ
c -k̓ł+paʔs -nt -is way̓ ixíʔ s -k̓aʔ•k̓ít=xn+m -s swit_ałíʔ
act -guess -nt -3erg well then nom -step_lightly -3i in_fact
figured it out, then he started stepping lightly. He's always

kʷəlstnímən caʕʷlxímən uł t̓i k̓ək̓í··xʷ {ła} 489 uł t̓i lut {t̓a c}
kʷls+tn+imn caʕʷ+lx+ímn uł t̓iʔ k̓•k̓ixʷ uł t̓iʔ lut
sweat_bathe_often bathe_often and evid agile and evid not
sweating and bathing, and he is light on his feet. 25:04 He doesn't

t̓a nłíq̓ʷcən ła cxʷist łaʔ ck̓aʔk̓ítxnəm 490 way̓
t̓ n+łiq̓ʷ=cn łaʔ c -xʷist łaʔ c -k̓aʔ•k̓ít=xn+m way̓
negfac sound when hab -walk when hab -step_lightly well
make noise when he walks, sneaks. He

ck̓əłk̓ʷƛ̓áp way̓ wiks axáʔ iʔ {səmqi} səmx̌íkən, həłsəmx̌íkən
c -k̓ł+k̓ʷƛ̓a+p way̓ wik -s axáʔ iʔ s+mx̌=ikn hł=s+mx̌=ikn
hab -come_in_sight yes see -hab this art grizzly grizzly_group
came in sight, he saw the grizzly.

491 way̓ ctxʷu··yms, {uł a} way̓ ck̓aʔtmís 492 way̓ ixíʔ
way̓ c -t+xʷuy+m -s way̓ c -k̓aʔt+mí -s way̓ ixíʔ
yes act -go_toward -3erg yes act -get_close -3erg well then
He went straight towards her, got close. He

xʷiws, xʷíxʷuʔs 493 a uł way̓ məł səst̓əqʷcíns
xʷiw -s xʷi•xʷw̓ -s a uł way̓ mł ss -t̓qʷ=cin -s
whistle_at -3erg whistle_dim -3erg intj and yes and pftv -shout -3i
whistled, a small whistle. [The old] Grizzly has been hollering

səmx̌íkən {s sutəm} tla ixʷút 494 way̓ a taʔx̌íləm, k̓átqnəm axáʔ
s+mx̌=ikn tla yxʷ=ut way̓ a ta+ʔx̌íl+m k̓at=qn+m axáʔ
grizzly from below yes intj do_a_certain_way raise_head this
from below for nothing. The young Grizzly turned around,

iʔ qaʔłsəmx̌íkən way̓ wíkəntəm 495 way̓ ixíʔ nʕʷəyúsəntəm axáʔ iʔ
iʔ qł=s+mx̌=ikn way̓ wik -nt -m way̓ ixíʔ n+ʕʷy=us -nt -m axáʔ iʔ
art grizzly's_child yes see -nt -psv well then smile -nt -psv this art
raised her head, she saw him. The Grizzly girl gave

22 See 487.
23 See 485.

t xíxutəm qaʔłsmx̌íkən axáʔ saʔʕ̓níxʷ 496 way̓ {nixʷ} nstils saʔʕ̓nixʷ
t xi•xwt+m qł=s+mx̌=íkn axáʔ s+ʕ̓an̓íxʷ way̓ n+st=ils s+ʕ̓an̓íxʷ
agInst girl grizzly's_child this Muskrat well think Muskrat
Muskrat a smile. *Muskrat thought: 26:01*

497 {nixʷ axáʔ} nixʷ axáʔ x̌əláp ʕan iwá kʷ łənʕ̓ʷuy sqílxʷ
nixʷ axáʔ x̌la+p ʕan iwá kʷ ł+n+ʕʷuy s+qilxʷ
also this tomorrow onom to_no_avail 2kn smile_back person
"Tomorrow you won't be smiling at people.

498 t anwí kiʔ kʷu nc̓əspúlaʔxʷłtxʷ isk̓ʷíƛ̓təm 499 úłi
t anwí kiʔ kʷu n+c̓s+p=úlaʔxʷ -łt -xʷ i -s+k̓ʷiƛ̓+t+m uł iʔ
agInst you rel 1obj kill -łt -2erg 1in -brothers and_then
It was you that killed my brothers, *and then*

kʷu ał cənʕ̓ʷəyústxʷ {inaud} 500 [kʷ] ckəlq̓naʔncút iʔ kʷu
kʷu ał c -n+ʕʷuy -st -xʷ kʷ c -k+lq̓=naʔ+ncút iʔ kʷu
1obj compl cust^ -smile -^cust -2erg 2kn hab -cover_up art 1obj
you smile at me! *You are covering up now,*

ał cənʕ̓ʷuyústxʷ 501 nxt̓łq̓íts axáʔ iʔ səmx̌íkən
ał c -n+ʕʷuy -st -xʷ n+xt̓=łq̓it -s axáʔ iʔ s+mx̌=ikn
compl cust^ -smile -^cust -2erg let_arrow_go -3erg this art grizzly
and you smile at me." *He let the arrow go at Grizzly.*

502 uł axáʔ nis iʔ cq̓ílən uł {i k̓əl} iʔ k̓əl stəqpíʔstən {i kł kłaʔ} 503 hiʔ
uł axáʔ nis iʔ cq̓=iln uł iʔ k̓l s+tqp=iʔst+n hiʔ
and this sg_gone art arrow up_to art to feather intj
And the arrow went in all the way to the feather. *The*

ła nyq̓ísk̓itəm iʔ səmx̌íkən ki txʷət̓pmíntəm 504 uł ałíʔ
łaʔ n+yq̓=ísk̓it+m iʔ s+mx̌=ikn kiʔ t+xʷt̓+p+min -t -m uł ałíʔ
when grunt art grizzly rel chase -nt -psv and because
Grizzly let out a big grunt, she jumped at him. *And being*

cx̌əƛ̓mús, uł ałíʔ mat xərxrúlaʔxʷ 505 way̓ lut səkłcáwts
c -x̌ƛ̓+m=us uł ałíʔ mat xr•xr=úlaʔxʷ way̓ lut s -kł+cawt -s
hab -uphill and because maybe steep yes not nom -effort -3i
that it's uphill, and pretty steep, *the grizzly girl*

axáʔ qaʔłsəmx̌íkən i səcxʷúys 506 ixíʔ uł way̓ {s} ckłaʔpínk
axáʔ qł=s+mx̌=íkn iʔ sc -xʷuy -s ixíʔ uł way̓ c -k+łaʔ+p=ínk
this grizzly's_child art ipftvp^ -go -3i then and yes hab -close
had no show. *Muskrat got*

saʔʕ̓níxʷ 507 itlíʔ nixʷ nxət̓łq̓ítəm {t} axáʔ k̓əl sq̓ʷut 508 way̓ ixíʔ
s+ʕ̓an̓íxʷ itlíʔ nixʷ n+xt̓=łq̓it+m axáʔ k̓l s+q̓ʷut way̓ ixíʔ
Muskrat from_there again shoot this to across well then
very close. *He shot again at the other side. 27:01* *It's like*

uł cʔx̌iłt {ƛ̓əxʷƛ̓axʷ} ƛ̓əxʷƛ̓xʷáx̌ən axáʔ səmx̌íkən 509 way̓ t̓i ilíˑˑʔ uł {c}
uł c+ʔx̌ił+t ƛ̓xʷ•ƛ̓xʷ=ax̌n axáʔ s+mx̌=ikn way̓ t̓iʔ ilíʔ uł
and like paralized_arms this grizzly well evid there and
Grizzly is paralized in both arms. *Grizzly fell*

cɬəq̓q̓ílx samx̌íkən 510 uɬ aɬíʔ kmix_k̓əm t̓i iʔ sc̓uʔc̓uʔxáns
c -ɬq̓•q̓+ilx s+mx̌=ikn uɬ aɬíʔ kmix_k̓m t̓iʔ iʔ s+c̓w̓•c̓w̓=xan -s
hab -face_down grizzly and so that's evid art feet -3in
face down. *All what's alive is*

iʔ xʷəlxʷált 511 {cut} cɬq̓əq̓ílx 512 way̓ ctxʷət̓pmíntəm
iʔ xʷl•xʷal+t c -ɬq̓•q̓+ilx way̓ c -t+xʷt̓+p+min -t -m
art alive hab -face_down yes act -jump_on -nt -psv
her feet. *She fell down.* *Muskrat jumped*

t saʔʕníxʷ 513 kc̓əl̓l̓míntəm ixíʔ cənt̓ámuʔsqəntəm {k̓s}
t s+ʕan̓íxʷ k+c̓l•l+min -t -m ixíʔ c -n+t̓am+w̓s=qn -t -m
agInst Muskrat stand_close -nt -psv then act -grab_head -nt -psv
on her. *He got close to her, grabbed her by the top of the head,*

k̓əɬník̓{c}ntəm 514 aɬíʔ nak̓ʷá t̓ul̓ sx̌ʷəyx̌ʷáyts saʔʕníxʷ iʔ
k̓ɬ+nik̓ -nt -m aɬíʔ nak̓ʷ+á t̓ul̓ s -x̌ʷy•x̌ʷay+t -s s+ʕan̓íxʷ iʔ
cut_out -nt -psv because indeed_not fierce nom -sharp -3i Muskrat art
cut it off. *There is no question that Muskrat's knife*

n̓ínk̓m̓əns 515 nk̓ət̓pús, {a uɬ ixíʔ k} i wiʔsənk̓t̓úsəs 516 ixíʔ
ni•nk̓+mn n+k̓t̓+p=us iʔ wy̓+s+n+kt̓=us -s ixíʔ
knife cut_off_head art finish_cutting_head_off -3erg then
is sharp. *He cut off her head, got done cutting it off.* *The*

uɬ axáʔ ƛ̓lap {t} axáʔ iʔ qaʔɬsəmx̌íkən 517 uɬ aɬíʔ_swit ƛ̓lal, sənkt̓ús
uɬ axáʔ ƛ̓la+p axáʔ iʔ qɬ=s+mx̌=íkn uɬ aɬíʔ_swit ƛ̓l•al s+n+kt̓=us
and this stop this art grizzly's_child and in_fact dead decapitated
Grizzly girl lay still. 28:05 *She's dead, her head cut off.*

518 a ixíʔ c̓i··qʷs, t̓i taʔx̌í··ləm {i t}, way̓ t̓i kmix kckʷíc̓aʔs
a ixíʔ c̓iqʷ -s t̓iʔ ta+ʔx̌íl+m way̓ t̓iʔ kmix k+ckʷ=íc̓aʔ -s
intj then skin -3erg evid do_a_certain_way yes evid only pull_cover_off -3erg
He skinned her, just pulled off

iʔ t síp̓iʔ 519 i kmix iʔ {sip} síp̓iʔ {i} iʔ kʷis, way̓ ixíʔ
iʔ t síp̓iʔ i kmix iʔ síp̓iʔ iʔ kʷi -s way̓ ixíʔ
art obj_tr hide intj only art hide art take -3erg well that
her skin. *He just took her hide and threw it over*

nɬəqʷɬq̓ítəms 520 uɬ axáʔ iʔ c̓ásiqən stxríkstəms k̓əl
n+ɬqʷ=ɬq̓it+m -s uɬ axáʔ iʔ c̓asy=qn s -t+xr=ikst+m -s k̓l
throw_over_shoulder -3erg and this art head nom -dangle -3i to
his shoulder. And he packed her head on the

sq̓ʷut {uɬ} 521 uɬ axáʔ aɬíʔ cnʔucʔuckláx̌nəmsts iʔ
s+q̓ʷut uɬ axáʔ aɬíʔ c -n+ʔuc•ʔuckl=áx̌n+m[24] -st -s iʔ
across and this so cust^ -pack_over_arms -^cust -3erg art
other side. *And he also had his bow and arrow over his shoulder,*

24 The semantics of this form are not clear.

cq̓íləns uɬ aɬíʔ ksəńíńk̓məń 522 ixíʔ scʔucklípəm[s],
cq̓=iln -s uɬ aɬíʔ k+s+ni•ńk̓+mn ixíʔ s -c+ʔuckl=íp+m -s
arrow -3in and because have+knife_case then nom -run_downhill_cisl -3i
and he had a knife case. *He ran down the hill,*

cxʷu··ẏ iʔ k̓əl stáɬəms 523 sənt̓əqmís iʔ síp̓iʔ uɬ {c} iʔ
c+xʷuy iʔ k̓l s+taɬm -s s -n+t̓q+mi -s iʔ síp̓iʔ uɬ iʔ
come art to boat -3in nom -throw_st_sheet_like -3i art hide and art
he went to his boat. *He threw in the hide and threw in*

ċásiqən{səċəq̓} sənċəq̓mís 524 waẏ ixíʔ st̓áq̓əms 525 uɬ
ċasy=qn s -n+ċq̓+mi -s waẏ ixíʔ s -t̓aq̓+m -s uɬ
head nom -throw_in -3i well then nom -cross_stream -3i and
the head. 29:00 *He went back across.* *And*

aɬíʔ axáʔ mat {i c} iʔ ckmahqənmísts səmx̌íkən {t̓əxʷ iʔ c}
aɬíʔ axáʔ mat iʔ c -k+mah=qn+mí -st -s s+mx̌=ikn
so this maybe art cust^ -give_up -^cust -3erg grizzly
Grizzly must have already given up.

526 wiḿ iʔ st̓qʷcíns, uɬ ɬənʔúɬxʷ iʔ k̓əl citxʷ 527 ntils[25]
wiḿ iʔ s -t̓qʷ=cin -s uɬ ɬ+n+ʔuɬxʷ iʔ k̓l citxʷ nt=ils
in_vain art nom -shout -3i and enter_again art to house think
She hollered and hollered for nothing, then she went back into her house. *She*

kwaẏ yəʕʷpyáʕʷt ist̓əmkʔílt waẏ lut̓ {ks} t̓ə
k+waẏ yaw+p+yáʕʷ+t i -s+t̓mkʔ=ilt waẏ lut_t̓ t̓
well strong 1in -daughter yes neg_emph negfac
thought "My daughter can do wonders,

ksƛ̓əl·núntəm 528 ta ɬənʔúɬxʷ, waẏ maʕcnítkʷ axáʔ
ks -ƛ̓l•l -nun -t -m ta ɬ+n+ʔuɬxʷ waẏ maʕ=cn=ítkʷ axáʔ
futt^ -dead -manage -nt -psv intj enter_again yes come_to_shore this
he can't kill her." *She went in, and Muskrat got to*

saʔʕníxʷ 529 t̓i kyrəntís ilíʔ i l {i} ʕacmíns
s+ʕańíxʷ t̓iʔ k+yr -nt -is ilíʔ i l ʕac+mín -s
Muskrat evid tie_around -nt -3erg there intj at tying_place -3in
the shore. *At its tying place he only looped it.*

530 lut {t̓a} t̓ ʕacəntís cəḿ nstils cəḿ kən xárxərt
lut t̓ ʕac -nt -is cḿ n+st=ils cḿ kn xar•xr+t
not negfac tie -nt -3erg maybe think maybe 1kn waste_time
He didn't tie it because he thought, "It takes me too much time,

531 {mi kʷu} mi kʷu pulsts t səmx̌íkən, kʷu nkəcníkiʔs
mi kʷu pul -st -s t s+mx̌=ikn kʷu n+kc+n=íkiʔ -s
fut 1obj kill_one -st -3erg agInst grizzly 1obj catch_up_with -3erg
Grizzly might kill me, might overtake me.

25 ntils is a variant of nstils, with root √st. The reanalysis of ntils gives us √nt.

532 uɬ aɬíʔ təl iksxʷúsxʷəst kʷu ɬ ksɬəx̌ʷpn̓úyʔs
uɬ aɬíʔ tl i -ks -xʷus•xʷs+t kʷu ɬ ks -ɬx̌ʷ+p -nu y̓ -s
and so from 1i -futi -hurry 1obj subord futt^ -escape -manage -nt -3erg
I will do everything in a hurry and get away from her. 30:01

533 uc t̓əxʷ kʷu ɬ ksɬəx̌ʷpnúyʔs
uc t̓xʷ kʷu ɬ ks -ɬx̌ʷ+p -nu y̓ -s
dub emph 1obj subord futt^ -escape -manage -nt -3erg
Maybe I'll get away."

534 way̓ t̓i axáʔ
way̓ t̓iʔ axáʔ
well evid this
He threw

iʔ síp̓iʔ ixíʔ nɬqʷíknəms
iʔ síp̓iʔ ixíʔ n+ɬqʷ=ikn+m -s
art hide that carry_on_back -3erg
only her hide over his back,

535 ixíʔ stxrútəms, swit_aɬíʔ
ixíʔ s -t+xr=ut+m -s swit_aɬíʔ
then nom -run_uphill -3i in_fact
he ran up the bank. He's the one that

kʷəlstnímən uɬ píwput
kʷls+tn+imn uɬ piw•pw+t
sweat_bathe_often and lightweight
sweat bathes, he is light footed,

536 uɬ lut t̓a c̓ayx̌ʷt, x̌ast iʔ
uɬ lut t̓ c -ʔayx̌ʷ+t x̌as+t iʔ
and not negfac hab -tired good art
doesn't get tired, his breaths are good,

sɬəxʷncúts, cʕawlxímən
s+ɬxʷ+ncut -s caʕʷ+lx+ímn
breath -3in bathe_often
he likes to bathe.

537 xʷu·y kɬqəltús
xʷuy kɬ+qlt=us
go hill_top
He got up on the bank.

538 e· t̓əxʷ
e· t̓xʷ
intj evidently
Grizzly

cənkʷənkʷní··m səmx̌íkən
c -n+kʷn•kʷni+m s+mx̌=ikn
hab -sing grizzly
was humming a tune,

539 ixíʔ uɬ sclimtx {ixíʔ təs} ixíʔ uɬ
ixíʔ uɬ sc -lim+t -x ixíʔ uɬ
then and ipftvp^ -glad -^ipftvp that and
she was glad that Coyote's sons

nc̓əspúlaʔxʷɬts sənk̓líp {i} iʔ ɬəɬsqʷsíʔs
n+c̓s+p=úlaʔxʷ -ɬt -s s+n+k̓l̓=ip iʔ ɬɬ -sqʷsiʔ -s
kill -ɬt -3erg Coyote art pl -son -3in
are all gone,

540 naʔɬ s+k+lkʷ=t=ilt
naʔɬ s+k+lkʷ=t=ilt
and distant_child
[Muskrat] too.

541 i put ilíʔ cənʔax̌líls axáʔ, k̓ahəntís[26] {iʔ t̓əxʷ i i} iʔ k̓ɬənxárptən
i put ilíʔ c -n+ʔax̌l=íls axáʔ k̓ah -nt -is iʔ k̓ɬ+n+xar+p+tn
intj just there hab -think_so this raise -nt -3erg art door_flap
Just when she was thinking that, he [Muskrat] raised the door flap. 31:00

542 k̓la utəntís k̓ax̌ntís[27]
k̓l wt -nt -is k̓a+ʔx̌ -nt -is
to put_down -nt -3erg out_of_way -nt -3erg
He put it plum out of the way.

543 way̓
way̓
well
He

nt̓əqmíɬtəm axáʔ səmx̌íkən
n+t̓q+mí -ɬt -m axáʔ s+mx̌=ikn
throw_sheet_like_obj -ɬt -psv this grizzly
threw in the grizzly [hide].

544 cúntəm axáʔ iʔ kʷu
cu -nt -m axáʔ iʔ kʷu
tell -nt -psv this art 1obj
He said: "This is what you

26 Obscure form, may be related to √k̓hk̓ʷ *open.*
27 This analysis is tentative.

kskʷəlstúłtxʷ axáʔ akłənqəqpáqstxən 545 way̓ uł t̓əxʷ {t anwí}
ks -kʷlst -ułt -xʷ axáʔ a -kł -n+q•qp=aqst=xn way̓ uł t̓xʷ
futtˆ -send -tułt -2erg this 2i -to_be -mat well and emph
sent me for, for you to put under your hip. *Do*

t anwí kcutíkxtxʷ 546 naʔ łk̓əłylxʷíps ixíʔ {s}
t anwí k+cwt=ik -xt -xʷ naʔ ł+k̓ł+ylxʷ=ip -s ixíʔ
agInst you do_st_unpleasant -xit -2erg intj lower_flap_again -3erg then
as you please with it." *He put the flap back down,*

sʔax̌əlməncúts 547 cʔucklípəm iʔ k̓əl stáłəms 548 uł ałíʔ
s -ʔax̌l+mncút -s c+ʔuckl=íp+m iʔ k̓l s+tałm -s uł ałíʔ
nom -turn_around -3i run_downhill_cisl art to boat -3in and because
he turned around. *He ran down the hill to his boat.* *Because*

axáʔ t̓i {k} kyr̓əntís, way̓ {ti} tk̓ʷəƛ̓ntís 549 kiʔ
axáʔ t̓iʔ k+yr -nt -is way̓ t+k̓ʷƛ̓ -nt -is kiʔ
this evid tie_around -nt -3erg yes uncoil -nt -3erg rel
he had only looped it around, he unlooped it. *He*

[s]ənʔamúts ki ixíʔ {s sca·s} [s]sax̌ʷts 550 uł ałíʔ ƛ̓x̌itkʷ
s -n+ʔam=út -s kiʔ ixíʔ s -sax̌ʷ+t -s uł ałíʔ ƛ̓x̌=itkʷ
nom -sit_inside -3i rel then nom -go_downhill -3i and so fast_water
sat in his boat, went downstream. *It's swift water,*

k̓ʷək̓ʷnʔítaʔkʷ {kʷaʔ i s} 551 ƛ̓x̌itkʷ nx̌ʷyałpítkʷ łaʔ ck̓ʷək̓ʷn̓ítaʔkʷ
k̓ʷ•k̓ʷn̓=ítaʔkʷ ƛ̓x̌=itkʷ n+x̌ʷyaʔ=łp=ítkʷ łaʔ c -k̓ʷ•k̓ʷn̓=ítaʔkʷ
shallow_water fast_water Kettle_River when hab -shallow_water
shallow water, *the Kettle River is swift when it's shallow.*

552 way̓ ssax̌ʷts 553 níkna ł wiks axáʔ iʔ {síp̓iʔ}
way̓ s -sax̌ʷ+t -s níkxnaʔ ł wik -s axáʔ iʔ
well nom -go_downhill -3i goodness when see -3erg this art
He went down the river. *Gee, when Grizzly saw*

síp̓iʔs iʔ st̓əmkʔílts səmx̌íkən 554 nt̓a way̓ ixíʔ scacáʕypəm[s]
síp̓iʔ -s iʔ s+t̓mkʔ=ilt -s s+mx̌=ikn nt̓a way̓ ixíʔ s -ca•cáʕy+p+m -s
hide -3in art daughter -3in grizzly intj yes then nom -cry -3i
her daughter's hide 32:02 *she started bawling.*

555 nt̓a cacacáʕ uł {k} tałt kłcucín, cacacáʕ 556 way̓ {sc} cacacá··ʕ {in i}
nt̓a ca•ca•cáʕ uł tał+t kł+cw=cin ca•ca•cáʕ way̓ ca•caʕ•cáʕ
intj holler and surely cry holler well holler
She bawled and bawled, screamed, cried loudly. *She bawled,*

cʔx̌ił ta nt̓əkʷək̓ʷspuʔús səmx̌íkən 557 nstíls səmx̌íkən uł ałíʔ incá
c+ʔx̌ił t n+t̓kʷ•k̓ʷ+s+puʔ=ús s+mx̌=ikn n+st=ils s+mx̌=ikn uł ałíʔ in+cá
like obj_c+ʔx̌ił decide grizzly think grizzly and so I
it was like her mind was made up. *Grizzly thought,*

iskc̓áx̌ʷ 558 way̓ iwá cənpútəls axáʔ ist̓əmkʔílt
i -s+k+c̓ax̌ʷ way̓ iwá c -n+put=ls axáʔ i -s+t̓mkʔ=ilt
1in -one's_doing well to_no_avail hab -satisfied this 1in -daughter
"It's all my fault. *My daughter was satisfied.*

559 uɬ aɬíʔ kʷa kən nʔaɬnaʔsqílxʷ[tən], uɬ niʕíp ləkəmstín
uɬ aɬíʔ kʷa kn n+ʔaɬn+aʔ+s+qílxʷ+tn uɬ n+yʕ=ip lk+m -st -in
and because intj 1kn man_eater and always force -st -1erg
Here I am, a man-eater, and I always forced her,

560 {tli} ksmysxʷaʔtmíxaʔx iscƛ̓ax̌ʷ {uɬ} 561 ih tˈi náx̌əmɬ
ks -my+s+xʷaʔ+t -míx+aʔx i -sc+ƛ̓axʷ ih tˈiʔ nax̌mɬ
incp^ -more -^incp 1in -killing intj evid but
wanting to kill more and more. *But I am going*

ikspúlstəm {in} t iʔ kʷu pulɬts isťəmkʔílt 562 ixíʔ
i -ks -pul -st -m t iʔ kʷu pul -ɬt -s i -s+ťmkʔ=ilt ixíʔ
1i -futt^ -kill -st -apsv obj_itr art 1obj kill_one -ɬt -3erg 1in -daughter then
to kill the one who killed my daughter. *Then*

mi x̌ast ispuʔús 563 {sɬəx̌ʷp̓am} nustpálqsəm kiʔ ixíʔ
mi x̌as+t i -s+puʔ=ús n+ws+t+p=alqs+m kiʔ ixíʔ
fut good 1in -heart raise_dress rel then
I will be satisfied." *She raised her dress up, ran out*

scɬəx̌ʷp̓áms 564 {e c} iʔ k̓əl siwɬkʷ ckəɬcl̓ľús 565 nťa
s -c+ɬx̌ʷp̓a+m -s iʔ k̓l siwɬ=kʷ c -kɬ+c̓l•l=us nťa
nom -run_out_cisl -3i art to water hab -stand_on_bank intj
of the house. 33:00 *She got on the bank, facing the water.* *Well,*

kʷa uɬ ixíʔ sk̓əɬk̓láxʷs saʔʕníxʷ, csax̌ʷt 566 {nťa kata} uɬ
kʷa uɬ ixíʔ s -k̓ɬ+k̓laxʷ -s s+ʕaňíxʷ c -sax̌ʷ+t uɬ
intj and that nom -disappear -3i Muskrat hab -go_downhill and
Muskrat was just about out of sight, coming downstream. *The water*

aɬíʔ ixíʔ uɬ ctxəlkáqs iʔ siwɬkʷ 567 way̓ atáʔ k̓əɬk̓ʷítət
aɬíʔ ixíʔ uɬ c -t+xlk=aqs iʔ siwɬ=kʷ way̓ atáʔ k̓ɬ+k̓ʷiť•ť
because then and hab -around_a_bend art water well here shortcut
went around a bend. *Grizzly took*

səmx̌íkən 568 k̓əɬtɬílsəm iʔ stxəlkáqsc 569 way̓ ilíʔ {n} mi
s+mx̌=ikn k̓ɬ+tɬ=ils+m iʔ s+t+xlk=aqs -c way̓ ilíʔ mi
grizzly go_straight_for art bend_in_path -3in yes there fut
a shortcut, *went straight where the water bends.* *"I'll be waiting there,*

k̓əɬcahntín ilíʔ mi k̓əɬxaʔtətnún 570 xʷu··y k̓li kic[x]
k̓ɬ+cah -nt -in ilíʔ mi k̓ɬ+xaʔt•t -nu -n xʷuy ik̓líʔ kic+x
face_to_face -nt -1erg there fut be_ahead -manage -1erg go there arrive
I'll get ahead of him there." *She went, got there.*

571 kʷa itíʔ nťaq̓ʷpʔíwt saʔʕníxʷ iʔ sxʷúytən[s] 572 {həy, həy itlíʔ}
kʷa itíʔ n+ťaq̓ʷ+p=íwt s+ʕaňíxʷ iʔ s+xʷuy+tn -s
intj from_that riley_water Muskrat art track -3in
Muskrat's tracks are riley water.[28] *She looked*

28 Muskrat has already gone by.

ilíʔ t̓i ʕác̓əs iʔ siwɬkʷ, way̓ {i} nixʷ ctxəlkáqs
ilíʔ t̓iʔ ʕac̓ -s iʔ siwɬ=kʷ way̓ nixʷ c -t+xlk=aqs
there evid look_at -3erg art water well again hab -around_a_bend
at the water, there is another bend.

573 məɬ {k} itlíʔ k̓əɬtɬílsəm 574 wam̓ ik̓líʔ kicx, məɬ way̓ {t̓i}
mɬ itlíʔ k̓ɬ+tɬ=ils+m wam̓ ik̓líʔ kic+x mɬ way̓
and from_there go_straight_for no_avail there arrive and yes
She took another shortcut. *She got there, Muskrat's tracks*

t̓i nt̓aq̓ʷpíwt saʔʕ̓nixʷ iʔ cxʷúytəns 575 níkxna məɬ itlíʔ
t̓iʔ n+t̓aq̓ʷ+p=íwt s+ʕ̓an̓íxʷ iʔ s+xʷuy+tn -s níkxnaʔ mɬ itlíʔ
evid riley_water Muskrat art track -3in goodness and from_there
are riley water. 34:03 *Gee, she was mad!*

ʕímtəm l itlíʔ kswítmiʔst 576 {way̓ ixíʔ uɬ mat} way̓ nstils kway̓
ʕim+t+m l itlíʔ k+swít+miʔst way̓ n+st=ils k+way̓
be_angry_at at from_there do_one's_best well think yes
She went on, doing her best. *She thought,*

n̓ín̓wiʔ k̓əl citxʷs iʔ k̓la lʔiws 577 mi nkəcníkən' ɬ
n̓ín̓wiʔ k̓l citxʷ -s iʔ k̓l lʔiw -s mi n+kc+n=ikn -n ɬ
a_while to house -3in art to m's_father -3in fut overtake -1erg when
"At his father's house. *I will catch up with him when he*

kicx 578 ixíʔ məɬ nixʷ naʔɬ sənk̓líp, {naʔɬ t̓əxʷ n} naʔɬ púl̓laʔxʷ 579 uɬ
kic+x ixíʔ mɬ nixʷ naʔɬ s+n+k̓l̓=ip naʔɬ púl̓=laʔxʷ uɬ
arrive that and also and Coyote and Gopher and
gets there. *Then Coyote too, and Gopher.* *I*

yaʕyáʕtəlx iksənk̓áwlaʔxʷstəm 580 uɬ lut sʕanqílsc
yaʕ•yáʕ+t -lx i -ks -n+k̓áw=laʔxʷ -st -m uɬ lut s -ʕanq=íls -c
all -pl 1i -futtˆ -massacre -caus -apsv and not nom -satisfied -3i
will finish every one of them." *Grizzly wasn't*

səmx̌íkən 581 way̓ n̓k̓áwlaʔxʷɬtəm iʔ sqʷəsqʷasíʔas sənk̓líp
s+mx̌=ikn way̓ n+k̓áw=laʔxʷ -ɬt -m iʔ s+qʷs•qʷasíʔa -s s+n+k̓l̓=ip
grizzly well massacre -ɬt -psv art children -nom Coyote
satisfied. *She had killed all of Coyote's children,*

582 uɬ {nixʷ} nixʷ ksƛ̓əxʷəntíməlx həɬsənk̓líp {naʔɬ} naʔɬ púl̓laʔxʷ,
uɬ nixʷ ks -ƛ̓xʷ -nt -im -lx hɬ=s+n+k̓l̓=ip naʔɬ púl̓=laʔxʷ
and also futtˆ -kill_many -nt -psv -pl Coyote_group and Gopher
and she is also going to finish Coyote

naʔɬ ʕalapúl 583 ixíʔ iʔ sck̓əɬpáʔx̌s səmx̌íkən 584 uɬ aɬíʔm axáʔ
naʔɬ ʕalapúl ixíʔ iʔ sc -k̓ɬ+paʔx̌ -s s+mx̌=ikn uɬ aɬíʔ+m axáʔ
and Gopher that art pftv -think_about -3i grizzly and so this
and Gopher. *These are Grizzly's thoughts.* *And Gopher had*

way̓ yalt púl̓laʔxʷ 585 k̓əm t̓i sənk̓líp knánaʔqs 586 a uɬ
way̓ yal+t púl̓=laʔxʷ k̓m t̓iʔ s+n+k̓l̓=ip k+ná•naʔqs a uɬ
finish run_away Gopher except evid Coyote alone intj and
already run away from trouble, *there is only Coyote. 35:01* *So*

xʷu··y saʔʕ̓níxʷ, ckʷəntís iʔ k̓əɬnxárptən 587 cus a lʔiws
xʷuy s+ʕan̓íxʷ ckʷ -nt -is iʔ k̓ɬ+n+xar+p+tn cu -s a lʔiw -s
go Muskrat pull -nt -3erg art door_flap tell -3erg art m's_father -3in
Muskrat went,[29] *he pulled the curtain back.* *He said to his father:*

588 way̓ axáʔ iʔ c̓ásiqən atáʔ kiʔ ənc̓əspúlaʔxʷɬts asqʷəsqʷasíʔa
way̓ axáʔ iʔ c̓asy=qn atáʔ kiʔ n+c̓s+p=úlaʔxʷ -ɬt -s a -s+qʷs•qʷasíʔa
well this art head this rel kill -ɬt -3e2obj 2in -children
"Coyote, this is the head that wiped out

sənk̓líp, t̓əxʷ isk̓ʷíƛ̓təm 589 ixíʔ a[xáʔ] səmx̌íkən iʔ st̓əmkʔílts
s+n+k̓l̓=ip t̓xʷ i -s+k̓ʷiƛ̓+t+m ixíʔ axáʔ s+mx̌=ikn iʔ s+t̓mkʔ=ilt -s
Coyote emph 1in -brothers that this grizzly art daughter -3in
your children, my brothers. *This is Grizzly's daughter.*

590 ixíʔ axáʔ iʔ mílaʔs 591 cúntəm way̓ uɬ t akɬcáwt
ixíʔ axáʔ iʔ mílaʔ -s cu -nt -m way̓ uɬ t a -kɬ -cawt
that this art bait -3in tell -nt -psv well and obl 2i -to_be effort
She is her bait." *He [Muskrat] said, "Now what'll become of you?*

592 way̓ {kʷu} ckʷukʷ kʷu {t} cənʔúcxs, way̓ kʷu
way̓ ckʷ•ukʷ kʷu c -n+ʔuc=x -s way̓ kʷu
yes arrive 1obj act -follow -3erg yes 1obj
She is coming following my tracks, she is coming right

cənk̓aʔtíkiʔs 593 ixíʔ uɬ itlíʔ isyált 594 t̓əxʷ
c -n+k̓aʔt=ík y̓ -s ixíʔ uɬ itlíʔ i -s -yal+t t̓xʷ
act -near -nt -3erg then and from_there 1i -intt -run_away emph
behind me. *I am going to run away.* *What*

t akɬcáwt sənk̓líp 595 way̓ kʷis sənk̓líp axáʔ iʔ c̓ásyqən {ay e· t}
t a -kɬ+cawt s+n+k̓l̓=ip way̓ kʷi -s s+n+k̓l̓=ip axáʔ iʔ c̓asy=qn
obl 2i -effort Coyote well take -3erg Coyote this art head
will become of you?" *Coyote took the head.*

596 mat aɬíʔ ksəntk̓íwlxtən 597 way̓ tk̓i··wlx uɬ iʔ k̓əl
mat aɬíʔ k -s+n+t+k̓iw+lx+tn way̓ t+k̓iw+lx uɬ iʔ k̓l
maybe because there_be -ladder yes climb up_to art to
There must be something to climb on. *He climbed to where the poles*

sənlk̓qíns {iʔ s} iʔ sənx̌ʷáyqən 598 ilíʔ kiʔ cənʕacínks uɬ
s+n+lk̓=qin -s iʔ s+n+x̌ʷay=qn ilíʔ kiʔ s -n+ʕac=ínk -s uɬ
tied_ends -3in art tipi there rel nom -tie_to -3i and
of the tipi are tied. 36:01 *That's where he tied it [the head],*

ɬənʔúɬxʷ {tla} [k̓]a nixʷút i l sxʷuɬxʷ 599 ixíʔ uɬ ixíʔ {s} iʔ
ɬ+n+ʔuɬxʷ ka n+yxʷ=ut iʔ l s+xʷul=ɬxʷ ixíʔ uɬ ixíʔ iʔ
enter_again to inside art in tipi then and that art
then he went back in the tipi. *Then Coyote threw*

29 Having arrived at Coyote's.

sƛ̓əƛ̓úk̓ʷaʔ sənk̓lip ixíʔ kp̓əntís 600 way̓ uɬ yaʔx̌í kʷa iʔ
s+ƛ̓•ƛ̓úk̓ʷaʔ s+n+k̓l̓=ip ixíʔ k+p̓n -t -is way̓ uɬ yaʔx̌í kʷa iʔ
wood_pitch Coyote that place_on -nt -3erg well and that_one intj art
pitchwood on the fire. *And you know how pitchwood*

sƛ̓əƛ̓úk̓ʷaʔ {ɬiʔ kʷa} talí cq̓ʷuʔɬ {ɬaʔ c} ɬaʔ cuxʷáp 601 way̓ axáʔ
s+ƛ̓•ƛ̓úk̓ʷaʔ taʔlíʔ c -q̓ʷ[ʔ]uɬ ɬaʔ c -wxʷa+p way̓ axáʔ
wood_pitch very_much hab -black when hab -burn well this
gets black when it blazes. *When*

ɬaʔ wxʷap nt̓a aɬíʔ iʔ spuʔúl̓ iʔ sq̓ʷʔuɬ 602 ixíʔ uɬ
ɬaʔ wxʷa+p nt̓a aɬíʔ iʔ s+p[ʔ]ul̓ iʔ s+q̓ʷ[ʔ]uɬ ixíʔ uɬ
when burn intj so art smoke art black then and
it blazed the smoke was black. *Then*

sənkʷníms sənk̓líp 603 {i aɬ cus} scusts {iʔ t sənkʷmi} iʔ
s -n+kʷni+m -s s+n+k̓l̓=ip s -cu -st -s iʔ
nom -sing -3i Coyote cust^ -tell -^cust -3erg art
Coyote started to sing. *This is what his song*

sənkʷíns, 604 cus saʔlisáw saʔlisáw saʔlisáw saʔlisáw saʔlisáw
s+n+kʷin -s cu -s
song -3in tell -3erg
says, *it says "saʔlisáw saʔlisáw saʔlisáw saʔlisáw saʔlisáw*

saʔlisáw 605 aɬíʔ nak̓ʷá {ta} təl tan̓mús a kiʔ kən qʷəqʷáʕʷqʷut
aɬíʔ nak̓ʷ+á tl tanm̓=ús a kiʔ kn qʷ•qʷaʕʷ•qʷ=ut
because indeed_not of nothing intj rel 1kn crazy
saʔlisáw." 37:17 *"It isn't for nothing that I act crazy.*

606 iwá kʷ səmx̌íkən {kʷu c̓əsp kʷu c̓əsp} kʷu nk̓áwlaʔxʷɬtxʷ
iwá kʷ s+mx̌=ikn kʷu n+k̓áw=laʔxʷ -ɬt -xʷ
to_no_avail 2kn grizzly 1obj massacre -ɬt -2erg
Even if you are a Grizzly, you killed

isqʷəsqʷasíʔa 607 ixíʔ uɬ sqʷəlqʷəltuʔscəncúts sənk̓líp
i -s+qʷs•qʷasíʔa ixíʔ uɬ s -qʷl•qʷl+t=w̓s=cn+cut -s s+n+k̓l̓=ip
1in -children then and nom -talk_about_one's_thoughts -3i Coyote
all my children." *Then Coyote started to say how*

uɬ {c} cut 608 uɬ kʷ sqʷən̓mscútx uɬ nixʷ kʷ nstils kʷu
uɬ cut uɬ kʷ s -qʷn̓+m+scut -x uɬ nixʷ kʷ n+st=ils kʷu
and say and 2kn ipftv^ -pitiful -^ipftv and also 2kn think 1kʷu
he felt. *"You are pitiful that you think you are going*

akspúlstəm 609 uɬ axáʔ {in} inpúl̓laʔxʷ nixʷ kʷu
a -ks -pul -st -m uɬ axáʔ in -púl̓=laʔxʷ nixʷ kʷu
2i -futt^ -kill_one -st -apsv and this 1in -Gopher also 1obj
to kill me too, *and that you are going to kill*

aksƛ̓əxʷɬtím {way̓ kʷ qʷəqʷcənm} 610 ixíʔ uɬ {c} cktəɬəɬxníɬxʷ
a -ks -ƛ̓xʷ -ɬt -im ixíʔ uɬ c -k+tɬ•ɬ=xn=iɬxʷ
2i -futt^ -kill_many -ɬt -apsv then and hab -straight_to_door
my Gopher, too." *{Coyote}[30] [Grizzly] got to*

sənkl̓íp 611 uł ał̓í? alá? ck̓əkn̓ía?mstəm t səmx̌íkən
s+n+kl̓=ip uł ał̓í? alá? c -k̓•kníya?+m -st -m t s+mx̌=ikn
Coyote and so here cust^ -listen -^cust -psv agInst grizzly
the door. *All this time Grizzly was listening.*

612 ní··kxna tli? scʕimts {c} səmx̌íkən 613 way̓ {ixí? s} ixí?
níkxna? itlí? sc -ʕim+t -s s+mx̌=ikn way̓ ixí?
goodness from_there pftv -angry -3i grizzly well then
Boy did Grizzly get mad. 38:03 *She heard him,*

ck̓əł?an̓wís, cúntəm sənkl̓íp 614 kʷ sk̓a?knús, {kʷ} way̓
c -k̓ł+?anwí -st -s cu -nt -m s+n+kl̓=ip kʷ s+k̓a+?kn=ús way̓
cust^ -hear_st -^cust -3erg tell -nt -psv Coyote 2kn wherever yes
she said to Coyote: *"Wherever you are,*

kʷ ikspúlstəm 615 tanm̓ús ixí? i? kʷu acxəƛ̓cənmíst
kʷ i -ks -pul -st -m tanm̓=ús ixí? i? kʷu a -sc -xƛ̓=cn+mist
2kʷu 1i -futt^ -kill_one -st -psv nothing that art 1kʷu 2i -pftv -say_things
I will kill you. *You are saying all these things for nothing."*

616 way̓ níkxna sənkl̓ip way̓ ixí? {s} syaʕpcíns {n} way̓ uníxʷ
way̓ níkxna? s+n+kl̓=ip way̓ ixí? s -yaʕ+p=cín -s way̓ wnixʷ
well goodness Coyote yes then nom -scared -3i yes true
Boy, did Coyote get scared then, for sure.

617 {ałí?} uł ałí? way̓ ck̓łənk̓a?típəntəm 618 way̓ lut xkínəm
uł ałí? way̓ c -k̓ł+n+ka?t=íp -nt -m way̓ lut x+kin+m
and because yes act -close_to_door -nt -psv well not do_what
And she is right at the door. *There is nothing*

mi łx̌ʷap 619 way̓ {ixí? s} ixí? sq̓ʷa?stínkəms 620 way̓
mi łx̌ʷa+p way̓ ixí? s -q̓ʷa?s+t=ínk+m -s way̓
fut slipped_away well then nom -play_tricks -3i well
he can do to escape. *So then he pulled his old tricks*[31] *out.* *"p̓s*

p̓əs p̓əs p̓əs p̓əs k̓ʷƛ̓up, p̓əs p̓əs p̓əs p̓əs k̓ʷƛ̓up way̓
onom onom onom onom come_out onom onom onom onom come_out yes

kmúsəms {i? s i i} i? ?ácqa?sts, ksisyústəns 621 a··
k=mus•ms i? ?ácqa? -st -s k+sy•sy=us+tn -s a
four_persons art go_out -caus -3erg power -3in intj
p̓s p̓s p̓s k̓ʷƛ̓up, p̓s p̓s p̓s p̓s k̓ʷƛ̓up." Four of them came out, his powers. *They*

cúsəlx, way̓ kʷu csysúy̓kstməstxʷ, stim̓ ascənq̓a?íls
cu -s -lx way̓ kʷu c -sy•suy̓=kst+m -nt -xʷ stim̓ a -s+c+n+q̓a?=íls
tell -3erg -pl yes 1obj cust^ -get_chilled -nt -2erg what 2in -problem
said to him: "You are getting us chilled, what is troubling you?" 39:02

30 Grizzly is the one who arrived at Coyote's door.
31 The powers he summons when in need.

622 cut way̓ xʷústwi, kʷu k̓əłpaʔx̌xíti 623 {i·} way̓ kən
cut way̓ xʷus+t -wy kʷu k̓ł+paʔx̌ -xit -y way̓ kn
say well hurry -ipimptv 1obj figure_out -xit -tpimptv yes 1kn
He said to them, "Hurry up, think of something for me. I am going

ksƛ̓əlmíxaʔx t nʔałnaʔsqílxʷtən iʔ t səmx̌íkən 624 way̓
ks -ƛ̓l -míx+aʔx t n+ʔałn+aʔ+s+qílxʷ+tn iʔ t s+mx̌=ikn way̓
incpˆ -dead -ˆincp agInst man_eater art agInst grizzly yes
to die at the hand of the man-eater Grizzly. She

axáʔ {c kʷ} ck̓łənk̓aʔtíp 625 cúsəlx way̓ {k} uł ałíʔ {anwí kʷ m}
axáʔ c -k̓ł+n+k̓aʔt=íp cu -s -lx way̓ uł ałíʔ
this hab -close_to_door tell -3erg -pl yes and because
is right at my door." They said to him, "You are

myałm anwí uł kʷ sənxaʔcənmscútx 626 uł ałíʔ_swit
myał+m anwí uł kʷ s -n+xaʔ=cn+mscút[32] -x uł ałíʔ_swit
too_much you and 2kn ipftvˆ -put_self_first -ˆipftv and in_fact
always putting yourself ahead of everything. You have done

qʷn̓íkstməntxʷ st̓əmkʔílts 627 uł ixíʔ nʕacqíłtxʷ {i l} iʔ la
qʷn̓=ikst+m -nt -xʷ s+t̓mk?=ilt -s uł ixíʔ n+ʕac=qí -łt -xʷ iʔ l
do_st_pitiful -nt -2erg daughter -3in and then tie_at_end -łt -2erg art on
something pitiful to his daughter, you tied her [head] at the top of

nx̌ʷáyqən 628 cúntəm xʷústwi 629 a· cúntəm way̓, way̓ kən
n+x̌ʷay=qn cu -nt -m xʷus+t -wy a cu -nt -m way̓ way̓ kn
tipi tell -nt -psv hurry -ipimptv intj tell -nt -psv well yes 1kn
the tipi." He said, "Hurry up!" They [the first one] said, "I will

k̓ʷulˀl̓ t słiqʷ, x̌ast t słiqʷ 630 uł axáʔ iʔ knaqs cut way̓
k̓ʷul̓•l̓ t s+łiqʷ x̌as+t t s+łiqʷ uł axáʔ iʔ k=naqs cut way̓
turn_into obl meat good prttv meat and this art one_person say well
turn myself into meat, good meat." Another said,

incá {kən} kən k̓ʷulˀl̓ {t} t m̓áʕmlaʔ 631 uł axáʔ iʔ knaqs cut way̓
in+cá kn k̓ʷul̓•l̓ t m̓áʕmlaʔ uł axáʔ iʔ k=naqs cut way̓
I 1kn turn_into obl maggots and this art one_person say well
"I will turn into maggots." Another said, "I will turn into...,

incá kən k̓ʷulˀl̓ t iksəncq̓mnílsəm {il k il ks} kʷu ł kskímiʔs
in+cá kn k̓ʷul̓•l̓ t i -ks -n+cq̓+mn=ils+m kʷu ł ks -kim̓ y̓ -s
I 1kn turn_into obl 1i -futi -throw_thoughts 1obj subord futi -hate -nt -3erg
I am going to make it her business to hate me. 40:13

632 uł ałíʔ axáʔ n̓ín̓wiʔ iʔ słiqʷ 633 uł axáʔ n̓ín̓wiʔ iʔ máʕmlaʔntəm
uł ałíʔ axáʔ n̓ín̓wiʔ iʔ s+łiqʷ uł axáʔ n̓ín̓wiʔ iʔ m̓áʕmlaʔ -nt -m
and so this a_while art meat and this a_while art maggots -nt -psv
This meat, the meat will

32 xaʔ with loss of t becore c.

axáʔ iʔ słiqʷ 634 uł ixíʔ iwá scʕimts uł ixíʔ iwá
axáʔ iʔ s+łiqʷ uł ixíʔ iwá sc -ʕim+t -s uł ixíʔ iwá
this art meat and then even ipftvp^ -angry -3i and then even
maggot. *As mad as she is, she is going*

ksk̓ʷaʔntís ṅíṅwiʔ 635 {məł} məł łtkíl̓əms axáʔ iʔ
ks -k̓ʷaʔ -nt -is ṅíṅw̓iʔ mł ł+t+kil̓+m -s axáʔ iʔ
futi -bite -nt -3erg a_while and get_sick_of_again -3erg this art
to bite it, *and she'll get sick with*

ṁáʕmlaʔ 636 way̓ lut, ixíʔ məł ctaʔx̌íləm {way̓ məł i} ixíʔ məł way̓ anwí
ṁáʕmlaʔ way̓ lut ixíʔ mł c -ta+ʔx̌íl+m ixíʔ mł way̓ anwí
maggots well not then and hab -do_so then and yes you
the maggots. *'Heck no' [she will yell], she will turn, and you [can]*

kʷ łx̌ʷap 637 way̓ kʷ kəl̓l̓kʷákʷ, {inaud} itlíʔ mi
kʷ łx̌ʷa+p way̓ kʷ k+l̓•l̓kʷ•akʷ itlíʔ mi
2kn slip_away well 2kn far_dim from_there fut
get away. *You'll go quite a little ways, and then*

{ł}ctháhtməntxʷ 638 məł itlíʔ cəṁ txʷət̓pmínts
c -t+ḥa•ḥt+m -nt -xʷ mł itlíʔ cṁ t+xʷt̓+p+min -t -s
act -laugh_again -nt -2erg and from_there maybe chase -nt -3e2obj
you'll laugh at her. *Then she'll continue to run after you."*

639 way̓, {ayə} k̓łənłaʔíp, uł axáʔ ckʷənmíst səmx̌íkən [sənk̓líp],
way̓ k̓ł+n+łaʔ=íp uł axáʔ c -kʷn+mist s+mx̌=ikn s+n+k̓l̓=ip
well be_next_to and this hab -make_sound grizzly Coyote
She got right to the door, and Grizzly [Coyote] was singing about

cxəƛ̓cənmíst 640 ixíʔ k̓łənłaʔíp {s} səmx̌íkən, way̓ nłəx̌ʷṗam 641 uł ałíʔ
c -xƛ̓=cn+mist ixíʔ k̓ł+n+łaʔ=íp s+mx̌=ikn way̓ n+łx̌ʷṗa+m uł ałíʔ
hab -say_things then be_next_to grizzly well run_in and so
his power. 41:09 *Grizzly got right to the door, she went right in.* *And*

ixíʔ nixʷ iʔ scqʷəlqʷəlt[uʔs]cəncúts sənk̓lip 642 way̓
ixíʔ nixʷ iʔ sc -qʷl•qʷl+t=w̓s=cn+cut -s s+n+k̓l̓=ip way̓
then more art pftv -talk_about_one's_thoughts -3i Coyote yes
Coyote was saying these other things he had done. *"I*

nʕacqíłtən {i i lin} i l inx̌ʷáyqən axáʔ iʔ nʔałnaʔsqílxʷtən iʔ
n+ʕac=qí -łt -n iʔ l i -n+x̌ʷay=qn axáʔ iʔ n+ʔałn+aʔ+s+qílxʷ+tn iʔ
tie_at_end -łt -1erg art in 1in -tipi this art man_eater art
tied the Grizzly's bait on top of

mílaʔs 643 iʔ st̓əmkʔílts iʔ c̓ásyqəns 644 ixíʔ
mílaʔ -s iʔ s+t̓mk̓ʔ=ilt -s iʔ c̓asy=qn -s ixíʔ
bait -3in art daughter -3in art head -3in that
the tipi, *her daughter's head."* That's

scqʷəlqʷəltuʔscəncúts sənk̓líp 645 cut ałíʔ incá kən
sc -qʷl•qʷl+t=w̓s=cn+cut -s s+n+k̓l̓=ip cut ałíʔ in+cá kn
pftv -talk_about_one's_thoughts -3i Coyote say because I 1kn
what Coyote is saying he did. *He said,*

ła miyáw 646 ixíʔ ałíʔ mat {tixʷ} ta nt̓íxʷlcən ixíʔ
łaʔ myaw ixíʔ ałíʔ mat t n+t̓ixʷl=cn ixíʔ
the_one_that Coyote that because maybe agInst different_language that
"I am smiyaw" *(that's Coyote's name in a*

sənk̓líp skʷists 647 scúnəmslx sənk̓lip uł ixíʔ smiyáw
s+n+k̓l̓=ip s+kʷist -s s -cun+m -s -lx s+n+k̓l̓=ip uł ixíʔ s+myaw
Coyote name -3in nom -say -3i -pl Coyote and that Coyote
different language), *that means "Coyote," this "smiyáw." 42:00*

648 way̓ nłəx̌ʷp̓am səmx̌íkən, way̓ k̓aw 649 ta kway̓ əxʷ walmscút əxʷ
way̓ n+łx̌ʷp̓a+m s+mx̌=ikn way̓ k̓aw ta k+way̓ əxʷ wal̓+mscút əxʷ
well run_in grizzly yes gone intj well again do_magic again
Grizzly went right in, he [Coyote] is gone. *He did something magic*

səmx̌íkən [sənk̓líp] 650 way̓ mat əxʷ nak̓ʷá tanmús ha kiʔ sənk̓líp
s+mx̌=ikn s+n+k̓l̓=ip way̓ mat əxʷ nak̓ʷ+á tanm̓=ús haʔ kiʔ s+n+k̓l̓=ip
grizzly Coyote well maybe again indeed_not nothing inter rel Coyote
again. *He's not Coyote for nothing.*

651 a way̓ staʔx̌ílx ixíʔ {inaud} nłək̓ʷk̓ʷmís ƛ̓əm
a way̓ s -ta+ʔx̌íl -x ixíʔ n+łk̓ʷ•k̓ʷ+mi -s ƛ̓m
intj well ipftv^ -do_a_certain_way -^ipftv then think_about -3erg past
She did like that,[33] *and then she remembered what*

iʔ scqʷəlqʷəltuʔscúts sənk̓líp 652 níxləm[s], iwá
iʔ sc -qʷl•qʷl+t=w̓s+cut -s s+n+k̓l̓=ip nixl+m -s iwá
art pftv -brag -3i Coyote hear -3erg try_to
Coyote had been saying he did. *She heard him,*

staʔx̌íls, 653 ta kway̓ unixʷ cənʕacqníłxʷəmłtəm
s -ta+ʔx̌íl -s ta k+way̓ wnixʷ c -n+ʕac=qn=íłxʷ+m -łt -m
nom -do_a_certain_way -3i intj yes true cust^ -tie_to_top_of_house -łt -psv
she did like that. *It's true he had tied her daughter['s head] on top*

iʔ st̓əmkʔílts 654 way̓ uł i sq̓ʷʔułc way̓ uł tałt kłcawt
iʔ s+t̓mkʔ=ilt -s way̓ uł iʔ s -q̓ʷ[ʔ]uł -c way̓ uł tał+t kł+cawt
art daughter -cust^ yes and art nom -black -3i yes and surely effort
of the tipi. *And it's black beyond limit.*

655 ní··kxnaʔ səmx̌íkən {iʔ t sli} iʔ t łʕimt, ki 656 caʔkʷ iwá··
níkxnaʔ s+mx̌=ikn iʔ t ł+ʕim+t kiw caʔkʷ iwá
goodness grizzly art intj angry_again yes if even
Boy, was Grizzly angry, yes. *"No matter*

stim̓ uc sənk̓líp kʷ k̓ʷul̓l̓ 657 {k way̓} way̓ t̓i {kʷ iks} kʷ
stim̓ uc s+n+k̓l̓=ip kʷ k̓ʷul̓•l̓ way̓ t̓iʔ kʷ
whatever dub Coyote 2kn turn_into yes evid 2kʷu
what you turn into, *I will*

33 A motion or gesture might have accompanied this utterance.

iksk̓ʷʔám 658 kʷ ikspúlstəm {t in} t isplímcən
i -ks -k̓ʷʔa+m kʷ i -ks -pul -st -m t i -s+plim=cn
1i -futi -bite 2kʷu 1i -futi -kill_one -st -apsv agInst 1in -mouth
bite you. 43:00 *I am going to kill you*

mi {ƛ̓əl} ƛ̓əl·núntsən 659 ṅíṅẁiʔ
mi ƛ̓l•l -nun -t -s -n ṅíṅẁiʔ
fut dead -manage -nt -2obj -1erg a_while
with my mouth. *I am going*

ʕaƛ̓ʕaƛ̓s[c̓]í··məntsən 660 waẏ t̓i ƛ̓aʔƛ̓ʔám, t̓i xƛ̓úsəm ki
ʕaƛ̓•ʕaƛ̓+s+c̓í··m -nt -s -n waẏ t̓iʔ ƛ̓aʔ•ƛ̓ʔá+m t̓iʔ xƛ̓=us+m kiʔ
gnaw -nt -2obj -1erg well evid look_for evid look_around rel
to gnaw on you." *She looked around, all around,*

wiks nt̓a qʷá··mqʷəmt {iʔ s} iʔ sɬiqʷ 661 waẏ ixíʔ {wəs} əxʷ sənk̓líp,
wik -s nt̓a qʷam•qʷm+t iʔ s+ɬiqʷ waẏ ixíʔ əxʷ s+n+k̓l̓=ip
see -3erg intj excellent art meat well that again Coyote
and saw beautiful meat. *That's Coyote, he must have*

waẏ mat k̓ʷuľs[34] t sɬiqʷ 662 waẏ txʷət̓pmís, waẏ {i k}
waẏ mat k̓ʷul̓ -s t s+ɬiqʷ waẏ t+xʷt̓+p+mi -s waẏ
yes maybe make -3erg obj_tr meat well grab -3erg yes
turned into that meat. *She jumped at it, was going*

ksk̓ʷaʔntís ki {k} kmymypúsəms 663 nt̓a·· kmix máʕməlaʔ axáʔ
ks -k̓ʷaʔ -nt -is kiʔ k+my•my+p=us+m -s nt̓a kmix ṁáʕmlaʔ axáʔ
futtˆ -bite -nt -3erg rel realize -3erg intj only maggots this
to bite it, then she realized what it was. *The meat is nothing but*

iʔ sɬiqʷ 664 waẏ {ɬc ɬc} ɬcqəcpməncút səmx̌íkən, waẏ ixíʔ
iʔ s+ɬiqʷ waẏ ɬ+c+qc+p+mncut s+mx̌=ikn waẏ ixíʔ
art meat well draw_back grizzly well then
maggots. *Grizzly drew back, a thought*

nc̓q̓mnílsntəm 665 cut waẏ lut, {waẏ} waẏ myaɬ cəṁ kʷu
n+c̓q̓+mn=ils -nt -m cut waẏ lut waẏ myaɬ cṁ kʷu
throw_thought -nt -psv say well not yes too_much maybe 1obj
was thrown to her. *She said "No, I'm too sick to*

tkiľs 666 waẏ waẏ kən scpaʔpaʔsínkx uɬ
t+kil̓•l̓ -s waẏ waẏ kn sc -paʔ•paʔs=ínk -x uɬ
sick -3i yes yes 1kn ipftvpˆ -sad -ˆipftvp and
the stomach. *I am feeling*

itlíʔ {nixʷ kən unfin} 667 waẏ {n kʷa pul} púlstən cəṁ
itlíʔ waẏ pul -st -n cṁ
from_there yes kill_one -st -1erg maybe
bad. 44:00 *I'll kill him before*

34 Perhaps k̓ʷul+st?

ncaʔxʷúsən ixíʔ {k} 668 {i ta xʷ} təl kləl̓kʷú··t {ta ɬ} kiʔ chaht
n+caʔxʷ=ús -n ixíʔ tl k+l̓•l̓kʷ=ut kiʔ c -ḥa•ḥt
sicken -1erg then from far_dim rel hab -laugh
I get sick.” From a distance Coyote was

sənk̓líp 669 {a ɬc} {ɬ}ckáʔkaʔməntəm[35] səmx̌íkən 670 {m wa·· t}
s+n+k̓l̓=ip c -ká•kaʔ+m -nt -m s+mx̌=ikn
Coyote act -make_fun_of_again -nt -m_nt grizzly
laughing, making fun of Grizzly. No,

uc iʔ way̓ lut t̓a miyáw 671 təqəqnúnts 672 a ixíʔ
uc iʔ way̓ lut t̓ myaw tq•q -nun -t -s a ixíʔ
dub art well not negfac Coyote fool -manage -nt -3e2obj intj then
Coyote.[36] “He is making fun of you. You are

nx̌ílməntxʷ ɬ kswítənts {i} iʔ t máʕmlaʔ 673 i
n+x̌il+m -nt -xʷ ɬ k+swit -nt -s iʔ t m̓áʕmlaʔ i
fear -nt -2erg subord do_one's_best -nt -3e2obj art agInst maggots intj
scared that the maggots might beat you.” He

uɬ ixíʔ {ɬ} ɬ wiʔsənkʷním {ixíʔ ɬ} ixíʔ a ɬ
uɬ ixíʔ ɬ wy̓+s+n+kʷni+m ixíʔ a ɬ
and then subord finish_singing that art subord
got done singing, that's what he is saying he is going

cqʷəlqʷəltuʔscəncút 674 níkxnaʔ, itlíʔ sʕimts səmx̌íkən
c -qʷl•qʷl+t=w̓s=cn+cut níkxnaʔ itlíʔ s -ʕim+t -s s+mx̌=ikn
hab -talk_about_one's_thoughts goodness from_there nom -angry -3i grizzly
to do. 45:00 Goodness, Grizzly was madder than ever.

675 caʔkʷ iwá·· kʷ k̓ʷul̓l̓ t stim̓ way̓ t̓i kʷ
caʔkʷ iwá kʷ k̓ʷul̓•l̓ t stim̓ way̓ t̓iʔ kʷ
if even 2kn turn_into obl whatever yes evid 2kʷu
“Whatever you might turn into, I am going

ikspúlstəm 676 uɬ aɬíʔ axáʔ ck̓əɬxás axáʔ {iʔ} iʔ sɬiqʷ
i -ks -pul -st -m uɬ aɬíʔ axáʔ c -k̓ɬ+xas axáʔ iʔ s+ɬiqʷ
1i -futtˆ -kill_one -st -apsv and so this hab -disappear this art meat
to kill you.” Then the maggots

iʔ m̓áʕmlaʔ 677 níkxnaʔ ixíʔ itlíʔ ɬəxʷp̓ám tliʔ səmx̌íkən
iʔ m̓áʕmlaʔ níkxnaʔ ixíʔ itlíʔ ɬx̌ʷp̓a+m itlíʔ s+mx̌=ikn
art maggots goodness then from_there run_out from_there grizzly
disappeared. Gee, Grizzly bolted out of

itlíʔ 678 txʷət̓pəmsqílxʷ ik̓líʔ {ac} itlíʔ cníxəl 679 way̓
itlíʔ t+xʷt̓+p+m+s+qilxʷ ik̓líʔ itlíʔ c -nixl way̓
from_there run_after to_there from_there hab -hear well
there. She ran towards where she heard that. She

35 See 637 for a similar construction, not understood. Why ɬ+c+ in this order?
36 The rhetorical value of this utterance is not clear.

iklí? {utá} kəłƛ̓a?ƛ̓a?ús[xən] 680 nt'a kway̓ axá? i? sxʷúytəns sənk̓líp
iklí? kł+ƛ̓a?•ƛ̓a?=ús=xn nt'a k+way̓ axá? i? s+xʷuy+tn -s s+n+k̓l̓=ip
to_there look_for_tracks intj yes this art track -3in Coyote
went there and looked for tracks. *Yes, here are Coyote's tracks.*

681 nt'a ixí? nqíclxəms uł ałí? ƛ̓axt səmx̌íkən 682 way̓ lut
nt'a ixí? n+qic+lx+m -s uł ałí? ƛ̓ax̌+t s+mx̌=ikn way̓ lut
intj then run_after -3erg and because fast grizzly well not
She started running, Grizzly is fast. *And, no,*

sənk̓líp 683 way̓ iwá t'i kʷu ksənkcníki?s səmx̌íkən 684 way̓
s+n+k̓l̓=ip way̓ iwá t'i? kʷu ks -n+kc+n=íki? -s s+mx̌=ikn way̓
Coyote yes try_to evid 1obj futtˆ -catch_up_with -3erg grizzly well
Coyote. *"Grizzly is going to overtake me."* *He*

ck̓əłníxləms[ts] ałí? kʷa ałí? nak̓ʷá ck̓áwcən
c -k̓ł+nixl+m -st -s ałí? kʷa ałí? nak̓ʷ+á c -k̓aw=cn
custˆ -hear -ˆcust -3erg because intj because indeed_not hab -stop_talking
heard her, because a grizzly is never quiet

[ax]á? i? səmx̌íkən {ła?} ła? cən?úcxən 685 t'əscəncnílx ałí?
axá? i? s+mx̌=ikn ła? c -n+?uc=xn t's -cn=cn+ilx ałí?
this art grizzly when hab -track habCisl -roar so
when tracking something, 46:05 *she*

ła?c {unfin} 686 way̓ sənk̓líp way̓ uł nkəcníkəntəm 687 ixí? uł ła?
way̓ s+n+k̓l̓=ip way̓ uł n+kc+n=ik -nt -m ixí? uł ła?
well Coyote yes and overtake -nt -psv then and when
roars. *Coyote is going to be overtaken.* *While*

sk̓əłk̓láxʷs way̓ uł x̌əlíts {i s i sa·} i? ksisyústəns i?
s -k̓ł+k̓laxʷ -s way̓ uł x̌lit -s i? k+sy•sy=us+tn -s i?
nom -disappear -3i well and summon -3erg art power -3in art
she was out of sight he asked for his powers,

q̓ʷəsq̓ʷásc 688 way̓ ?am·útət ixí? uł 689 p̓əs p̓əs p̓əs p̓əs
q̓ʷs•q̓ʷas+t -s way̓ ?am•m=út•t ixí? uł p̓s p̓s p̓s p̓s
wish -3in well sit_down then and onom onom onom onom
his wishes. *He sat down.* *"p̓s p̓s p̓s p̓s*

k̓ʷƛ̓up 690 ixí? uł i? sx?itx 691 a uł itlí? ho··y uł
k̓ʷƛ̓up ixí? uł i? s+x?it=x a uł itlí? hoy uł
come_out then and art oldest_one intj and from_there finish and
k̓ʷƛ̓up" *Here is the first one,* *and then they all came,*

txƛ̓ap kmúsəms 692 cúsəlx way̓ kʷu csisúy̓kstəmstxʷ,
t+xƛ̓a+p k=mus•ms cu -s -lx way̓ c -sy•suy̓=kst+m -st -xʷ
complete four_persons tell -3erg -pl well custˆ -get_chilled -ˆcust -2erg
the four of them. *They said, "You are getting us chilled,*

uł stim̓ {an} asyaʕpcín 693 cúntməlx way̓ t'i kʷu
uł stim̓ a -s+yaʕ+p=cín cun -nt -m -lx way̓ t'i? kʷu
and what 2in -hardship tell -nt -psv -pl well evid 1obj
what do you want?" *He said, "Hurry up and*

xʷúskstməntxʷ 694 waẏ {kʷu} kʷu sənk̓aʔtíkiʔs ia
xʷus=kst+m -nt -xʷ waẏ kʷu s -n+k̓aʔt=íkiʔ -s iʔ
do_quickly -nt -2erg yes 1obj nom -near_back -3i art
do something for me, the man-eater is right on

nʔaɬnaʔsqílxʷtən 695 waẏ kʷu kspulsts səmx̌íkən 696 a··
n+ʔaɬn+aʔ+s+qílxʷ+tn waẏ kʷu ks -pul -st -s s+mx̌=ikn a
man_eater yes 1obj futt^ -kill_one -st -3erg grizzly intj
to me. Grizzly is going to kill me." 47:00 They

cúsəlx waẏ, waẏ ṅíṅẇiʔ kənxítəmt 697 waẏ ṅíṅẇiʔ kʷu
cu -s -lx waẏ waẏ ṅíṅẇiʔ kn -xit -m -t waẏ ṅíṅẇiʔ kʷu
tell -3erg -pl yes yes a_while help -xit -2obj -4erg yes a_while 4kn
said, "We will help you. We will turn

k̓ʷul̓st {t s} t sxʷaʔxʷʔankíɬp 698 lútəm axáʔ iʔ sxʷaʔxʷʔankíɬp
k̓ʷul̓+st t s+xʷaʔ•xʷaʔnk=íɬp lut+m axáʔ iʔ s+xʷaʔ•xʷaʔnk=íɬp
train obl thornbush no this art thornbush
ourselves into thorn bushes, not these thorn bushes,

axáʔ {indec} t̓qíɬəmlx 699 {iʔ} iʔ misx̌ʷyx̌ʷáyt {iʔ} iʔ ƛ̓qʷúməns
axáʔ t̓q=iɬmlx iʔ my+s+x̌ʷy•x̌ʷay+t iʔ ƛ̓qʷu+mn -s
this short_thorn_bushes art more_sharp art thorns -3in
the short ones, the ones with sharp thorns,

700 ixíʔ a scústsəlx iʔ x̌əx̌ʔíɬp, ixíʔ uɬ cʔx̌iɬt t
ixíʔ a s -cu -st -s -lx iʔ x̌•x̌ʔ=iɬp ixíʔ uɬ c+ʔx̌iɬ+t t
that art cust^ -tell -^cust -3erg -pl art thorn_bush that and like obj_c+ʔx̌iɬ
the ones they call red thorn bushes, just like

sənpəpl̓úlaʔxʷ 701 ixíʔ uɬ cəm̓ t̓i c̓apq̓, uɬ itíʔ iʔ t
s+n+p•pl̓=úlaʔxʷ ixíʔ uɬ cm̓ t̓iʔ c̓ap̓q̓ uɬ itíʔ iʔ t
sprouts that and maybe evid stick and from_that art obl
young brush. They'll be thick, right where

asxʷúytən 702 ilíʔ məɬ kʷu után ṅíṅẇiʔ 703 uɬ ilíʔ məɬ
a -s+xʷuy+tn ilíʔ mɬ kʷu wta+n ṅíṅẇiʔ uɬ ilíʔ mɬ
2in -track there and 4kn placed a_while and there and
you are moving. We'll settle right there, and she'll have

cəm̓ {ixim} talíʔ kɬcáwt mi itíʔ ksɬəx̌ʷṁúsaʔ 704 ixíʔ iwá
cm̓ taʔlíʔ kɬ+cawt mi itíʔ ks -ɬx̌ʷm=úsaʔ ixíʔ iwá
maybe very_much effort fut from_that futi -go_through that even
a tough time getting out of there. Even though

skəwpíc̓aʔs {səmx̌i} səmx̌íkən 705 uɬ waẏ cəm̓ talí sək̓sk̓ák̓, cəm̓
s -k+wp=íc̓aʔ -s s+mx̌=ikn uɬ waẏ cm̓ taʔlíʔ sk̓•sk̓•ak cm̓
nom -hairy_body -3i grizzly and yes maybe very_much torn_up maybe
Grizzly has a lot of wool, 48:02 she'll get all torn up, nothing

t̓i ƛ̓um̓ 706 mi ití ksxan {i ks} iʔ ksək̓sk̓ák̓s iʔ
t̓iʔ ƛ̓um̓ mi itíʔ k+sx̌a+n iʔ k -sk̓•sk̓•ak̓ -s iʔ
evid bloody fut from_that past art futi -torn_up -3i art
but blood. Before she gets through, she'll be all torn up,

ksm̓láľs 707 way̓ cúsəlx way̓ ixíʔ akłcawt
ks -mľ•aľ -s way̓ cu -s -lx way̓ ixíʔ a -kł -cawt
futi -bloody -3i well tell -3erg -pl yes that 2i -to_be -doing
bloody.” They said, “That's what's going to happen to you.

708 uł ťi ḱliʔ ṅíṅw̓iʔ {kʷ ł} cʔx̌iłt ał ƛ̓lap łə nťaʔlíls 709 mi
uł ťiʔ iḱlíʔ ṅíṅw̓iʔ c+ʔx̌ił+t ał ƛ̓la+p ł n+ťaʔl=íls mi
and evid there a_while like compl stop subord satisfied fut
And when she stops being mad then

tliʔ łthátməntxʷ, ixíʔ mi sic pulstxʷ 710 cut way̓
itlíʔ ł+t+ḥa•ḥt+m -nt -xʷ ixíʔ mi sic pul -st -xʷ cut way̓
from_there laugh_at_again -nt -2erg then then then kill_one -st -2erg say yes
you can laugh some more at her, that's when you can kill her.” He said

way̓ ixíʔ skľəľkʷákʷs sənḱlíp 711 way̓ ƛ̓lap, ḱəłʔíms iʔ
way̓ ixíʔ s -k+ľ•ľkʷ•akʷ -s s+n+ḱľ=ip way̓ ƛ̓la+p ḱł+ʔim -s iʔ
yes then nom -far_dim -3i Coyote well stop wait_for -3erg art
“Ok.” Then Coyote went a little ways, then he stopped, he waited for Grizzly.

səmx̌íkən, nťa səmx̌íkən ťi cənʔax̌ʷt {ca· na} 712 way̓ ixíʔ itlíʔ kən
s+mx̌=ikn nťa s+mx̌=ikn ťiʔ c -n+ʔax̌ʷ+t way̓ ixíʔ itlíʔ kn
grizzly intj grizzly evid hab -downriver well that from_there 1kn
Gee, Grizzly is coming downriver. [end of tape] 48:55 Well, I

ċəpq̓síw̓səm 713 ixíʔ əxʷ {skł} [s]ənkʷəncúts sənḱlíp uł ixíʔ
ċpq̓+s=iw̓s+m ixíʔ əxʷ s -n+kʷn+cut -s s+n+ḱľ=ip uł ixíʔ
glue then again nom -sing -3i Coyote and that
continue. Coyote started to sing his song again,

scuts 714 saʔlisáw saʔlisáw saʔlisáw saʔlisáw saʔlisáw 715 naḱʷá
s -cut -s naḱʷ+á
nom -say -3i indeed_not
and he went saʔlisáw saʔlisáw saʔlisáw saʔlisáw saʔlisáw “It isn't

ałiá təl taṅmús a kiʔ kən qʷəqʷáʕʷqʷut 716 ta kən sqəltmíxʷ,
ałi+á tl tanṁ=ús a kiʔ kn qʷ•qʷáʕʷ•qʷ=ut ta kn s+qlt=mixʷ
because_not from nothing intj rel 1kn crazy intj 1kn man
for nothing that I am tricky. I am a man,

ixíʔ iwá i sənḱlíp 717 way̓ iwá cmistín kən
ixíʔ iwá iʔ s+n+ḱľ=ip way̓ iwá c -my -st -in kn
that even art Coyote well even cust^ -know -^cust -1erg 1kn
even if I am a Coyote. Even if I know that I'm going

ksƛ̓əllmíxaʔx 718 uł ałíʔ ťəxʷ way̓ {kən ksq̓ʷəy} kən
ks -ƛ̓l•l -míx+aʔx uł ałíʔ ťxʷ way̓ kn
incp^ -dead -^incp and so emph yes 1kn
to die, I am going to sing

ksənkʷníxaʔx {kən ks} 719 way̓ axáʔ ckʷənmíst, uł way̓
ks -n+kʷni+x -aʔx way̓ axáʔ c -kʷn+mist uł way̓
incp^ -sing -^incp well this hab -make_sound and yes
anyway.” He was making noise singing,

ck̓əɬk̓ʷƛ̓áp səmx̌íkən 720 ní··kxna {əxʷ s} əxʷ sənk̓líp {axʷ a} ixíʔ a
c -k̓ɬ+k̓ʷƛ̓a+p s+mx̌=ikn níkxnaʔ əxʷ s+n+k̓l̓=ip ixíʔ a
hab -come_in_sight grizzly goodness again Coyote then art
and Grizzly came in sight. *Gee, Coyote makes noises*

ckʷənmíst {a ixíʔ ɬ} 721 cmay iksʕaƛ̓ʕaƛ̓scí··m caʔkʷ iwá ɬaʔ
c -kʷn+mist cmay i -ks -ʕaƛ̓•ʕaƛ̓+s+ċím caʔkʷ iwá ɬaʔ
hab -make_sound maybe 1i -futi -chew_up if even if
again. 1:04 *"I am going to chew him up, whatever*

ck̓ʷul̓l̓ t stim̓ 722 way̓ t̓i niʕíp̣ ikspúlstəm,
c -k̓ʷul̓•l̓ t stim̓ way̓ t̓iʔ n+yʕ=ip i -ks -pul -st -m
hab -turn_into obl something yes evid always 1i -futt^ -kill_one -st -apsv
he turns into. *I'm still going to kill him, I won't get*

nixʷ lut ikɬəɬtkíl̓lsəm 723 ńíńw̓iʔ kən ċənċənmáʕsəm
nixʷ lut i -kɬ -ɬ+t+kil̓=ls -m ńíńw̓iʔ kn ċn•ċnm=ʕas+m
again not 1i -futi -sick_to_stomach_again -apsv a_while 1kn eyes_closed
sick in the stomach again. *I'm going to kill him with my eyes*

iʔ púlstən 724 ay, sta axáʔ iʔ sxʷúytəns, a {cənʔus}
iʔ pul -st -n ay sta axáʔ iʔ s+xʷuy+tn -s a
art kill_one -st -1erg intj intj this art track -3in intj
shut tight. *Ah, here are his tracks,*

cənʔúcxstən 725 nt̓a·· {i s} iʔ x̌əx̌ʔíɬp, nt̓a way̓ uɬ itíʔ
c -n+ʔuc=x -st -n nt̓a iʔ x̌•x̌ʔ=iɬp nt̓a way̓ uɬ itíʔ
cust^ -follow -^cust -1erg intj art thorn_bush intj yes and from_that
I'm tracking him." *My, the thorn bushes. Coyote*

uɬ {i} iʔ xʷuy sənk̓líp 726 nstils {kʷ} uɬ aɬíʔ k̓ʷəm sənk̓líp kiʔ itíʔ
uɬ iʔ xʷuy s+n+k̓l̓=ip n+st=ils uɬ aɬíʔ k̓ʷm s+n+k̓l̓=ip kiʔ itíʔ
and art go Coyote think and so evid Coyote rel from_that
went through there. *And she thought, "Coyote went through*

iʔ xʷuy 727 uɬ axáʔ incá kən nʔaɬnaʔsqílxʷtən 728 uɬ {aɬ} aɬ
iʔ xʷuy uɬ axáʔ in+cá kn n+ʔaɬn+aʔ+s+qílxʷ+tn uɬ aɬ
art go and this I 1kn man_eater and compl
there, *and I am a man-eater.* *I am not going*

iksk̓əɬtər̓tər̓qəncút[37] kəmá ɬ ikstxəlkmínəm 729 pna ixíʔ əxʷ
i -ks -k̓ɬ+tr̓•tr̓=qn+cut km̓+á ɬ i -ks -t+xlk+min+m pnaʔ ixíʔ əxʷ
1i -futi -back_down or_not subord 1i -futi -go_around maybe that again
to back down, I am not going to go around it. *I suppose that's*

sənk̓líp {awxʷs} skɬcáwtx ʔəxʷ {uɬ y axa i} 730 caʔkʷ way̓ niʕíp̣
s+n+k̓l̓=ip s -kɬ+cawt -x ʔəxʷ caʔkʷ way̓ n+yʕ=ip
Coyote ipftv^ -effort -^ipftv intj should yes always
Coyote's doings, *but I am still going*

37 The Cv form is not a negative. Possibly "I am going to keep at it."

ikspúlstəm 731 t̓i itíʔ nʔuc[xs], itíʔ
i -ks -pul -st -m t̓iʔ itíʔ n+ʔuc=x -s itíʔ
1i -futt^ -kill_one -st -apsv evid from_that follow -3erg from_that
to kill him." She kept on tracking, walked right

nxʷəstíw̓s 732 ní¨kxna sək̓síkək̓ axáʔ səmx̌íkən, uɬ iwá tkəcxíls
n+xʷst=iw̓s níkxnaʔ sk̓•sik̓•k̓ axáʔ s+mx̌=ikn uɬ iwá t+kcx=ils
walk_through goodness scratched this grizzly and even be_in_pain
through. 2:03 Gee, Grizzly is all scratched up, she suffered.

733 uɬ aɬíʔ niʕíp scəlq̓məncútx scʕimtx 734 nay
uɬ aɬíʔ n+yʕ=ip sc -lq̓+mncut -x sc -ʕim+t -x nay
and so always ipftvp^ -go_strong -^ipftvp ipftvp^ -angry -^ipftvp intj
She is still going strong, angry. From

ʔəxʷ təl kl̓əl̓kʷút a[xáʔ] uɬ ixíʔ ɬəɬháʕts sənk̓líp
ʔəxʷ tl k+l̓•l̓kʷ=ut axáʔ uɬ ixíʔ ɬ -ɬ+ḥa•ḥt -s s+n+k̓l̓=ip
intj from far_dim this and then nom -laugh_again -3i Coyote
a little ways Coyote is laughing at her.

735 {nt̓a ixí ɬəɬ} ha¨ʕt, məɬ ixíʔ ɬəɬcúts 736 nt̓a səmx̌íkən,
ḥa•ḥt mɬ ixíʔ ɬ -ɬ+cut -s nt̓a s+mx̌=ikn
laugh and then nom -say_again -3i intj grizzly
He laughs, and then he'll say: "My, Grizzly

cx̌aʔx̌aʔscút nʔaɬnaʔsqílxʷtən 737 ixíʔ way̓ {ta miyanc} ta miyáw
c -x̌aʔ•x̌aʔ+scút n+ʔaɬn+aʔ+s+qílxʷ+tn ixíʔ way̓ t myaw
hab -self_important man_eater then yes agInst Coyote
thinks she's important, she's a man-eater." Coyote[38] scratched her all over

nc̓əlc̓əlx̌ʔú¨psəntəm {a} uɬ {iʔ} iʔ cksx̌an 738 níkxnaʔ itlíʔ
n+c̓l•c̓lx̌ʷ=ups -nt -m uɬ iʔ c -k+sx̌a+n níkxnaʔ itlíʔ
scratch_tail_end -nt -psv and art hab -pass_through goodness from_there
her hind end as she went through. My, did Grizzly

səmx̌íkən itlíʔ iʔ scʕimts {uɬ ilíʔ} 739 ixíʔ uɬ aɬíʔ nʔacqʔíw̓s
s+mx̌=ikn itlíʔ iʔ sc -ʕim+t -s ixíʔ uɬ aɬíʔ n+ʔacq̓ʔ=íw̓s
grizzly from_there art pftv -angry -3i then and so go_out_of_brush
get angry. Then she got out of the brush.

740 nt̓a kiʔ ixíʔ itlíʔ txʷət̓pmíntəm 741 way̓ a[xáʔ] itlíʔ
nt̓a kiʔ ixíʔ itlíʔ t+xʷt̓+p+min -t -m way̓ axáʔ itlíʔ
intj rel then from_there chase -nt -psv well this from_there
She went some more, went after him. Coyote

sənk̓líp it[líʔ] sxʷət̓t̓pnúmts, itlíʔ syalts
s+n+k̓l̓=ip itlíʔ s -xʷt̓•t̓+p+numt -s itlíʔ s -yal+t -s
Coyote from_there nom -jump -3i from_there nom -run_away -3i
started running, ran away from there. 3:02

38 By means of the thornbushes.

742 waẏ uɬ k̓əlxʷúsməntəm, waẏ itlíʔ nʔúcxəntəm
waẏ uɬ k̓lxʷ=us+m -nt -m waẏ itlíʔ n+ʔuc=xn -t -m
yes and get_out_of_sight_of -nt -psv yes from_there track -nt -psv
He got out of sight, she is tracking him again.

743 a məɬ itlíʔ c̓iʔpwíkstəm 744 məɬ ɬk̓əɬk̓láxʷ
a mɬ itlíʔ c -ʔip=wík -st -m mɬ ɬ+k̓ɬ+k̓laxʷ
intj and from_there cust^ -see_on_way -^cust -psv and out_of_sight_again
She gets a glimpse of him, *then Coyote gets*

axáʔ sənk̓líp 745 waẏ uɬ aɬíʔ ƛ̓ax̌t səmx̌íkən 746 {waẏ nkcníkəntəm}
axáʔ s+n+k̓l̓=ip waẏ uɬ aɬíʔ ƛ̓ax̌+t s+mx̌=ikn
this Coyote yes and because fast grizzly
out of sight again. *And because Grizzly is fast* *Grizzly*

waẏ t̓i ksənkcníkəntəm t səmx̌íkən 747 ixíʔ uɬ k̓əɬk̓láxʷ
waẏ t̓iʔ ks -n+kc+n=ikn -t -m t s+mx̌=ikn ixíʔ uɬ k̓ɬ+k̓laxʷ
yes evid futt^ -overtake -nt -psv agInst grizzly then and disappear
overtook him finally. *He is out of sight.*

na[x̌əmɬ] uɬ əxʷ ɬʔammútət sənk̓líp 748 waẏ ixíʔ
nax̌mɬ uɬ əxʷ ɬ+ʔam•m=út•t s+n+k̓l̓=ip waẏ ixíʔ
but and again sit_again Coyote well then
Coyote sat down again.

ɬəɬq̓ʷaʔstínkəms, waẏ ixíʔ ɬx̌əlíts axáʔ {iʔ} iʔ q̓ʷəsq̓ʷásts
ɬ -ɬ+q̓ʷaʔs+t=ínk+m -s waẏ ixíʔ ɬ+x̌lit axáʔ iʔ q̓ʷs•q̓ʷast -s
nom -do_magic_again -3i yes then summon_again this art wish -3in
Now he is going to make his tricks, he calls his tricks out again,

749 ixíʔ aɬíʔ ksysyústəns, kmúsc̓aʔ 750 waẏ x̌lits, uɬ
ixíʔ aɬíʔ k+sy•sy=us+tn -s k+mús=c̓aʔ waẏ x̌lit -s uɬ
that because power -3in four_packages yes summon -3erg and
they are his tricks, four packages. *He called them. They all*

axáʔ ixíʔ ɬtxƛ̓ap, kmúsc̓aʔ 751 cúsəlx waẏ kʷu
axáʔ ixíʔ ɬ+t+xƛ̓a+p k+mús=c̓aʔ cu -s -lx waẏ kʷu
this then all_again four_packages tell -3erg -pl yes 1obj
came out, four of them. 4:00 *They said to him,*

csysúẏkstəmst[xʷ], stim̓ uɬ ascənq̓aʔíls
c -sy•suẏ=kst+m -st -xʷ stim̓ uɬ a -sc -n+q̓aʔ=íls
cust^ -get_chilled -^cust -2erg what and 2in -pftv -concerned
"You are getting us chilled, what is your trouble?"

752 cúntməlx, xʷústwi waẏ mat ixíʔ sck̓əɬk̓ʷƛ̓aps {ikɬ}
cun -nt -m -lx xʷus+t -wy waẏ mat ixíʔ sc -k̓ɬ+k̓ʷƛ̓a+p -s
tell -nt -psv -pl hurry -ipimptv well maybe that pftv -come_in_sight -3i
He said to them, "Hurry. The one who is going to kill me is just about

ikɬpəlscútən 753 nʔaɬnaʔsqílxʷtən iʔ səmx̌íkən 754 waẏ ʕapná
i -kɬ -pl+scut+n n+ʔaɬn+aʔ+s+qílxʷ+tn iʔ s+mx̌=ikn waẏ ʕapnáʔ
1i -to_be -killer man_eater art grizzly yes now
in sight of me, *Grizzly the man-eater.* *Now she is*

sic kʷu kspulsts, kʷu ksƛ̓əlnúy̓ʔs 755 caʔkʷ
sic kʷu ks -pul -st -s kʷu ks -ƛ̓l•l[39] -nu y̓ -s caʔkʷ
then 1obj futt^ -kill_one -st -3erg 1obj futi -kill -manage -nt -3erg if
going to kill me, kill me dead, *even if*

iwá nixʷ itlíʔ kən ɬaʔ ɬk̓ʷúl̓l̓ t stim̓ 756 cúsəlx
iwá nixʷ itlíʔ kn ɬaʔ ɬ+k̓ʷul̓•l̓ t stim̓ cu -s -lx
even more from_there 1kn if turn_into_again obl something tell -3erg -pl
I turn into something else." *They told him,*

k aɬíʔ anwí swit nʔaɬnaʔsqílxʷtən 757 ka {ɬc} ɬ
k aɬíʔ anwí swit n+ʔaɬn+aʔ+s+qílxʷ+tn ka ɬ
intj so you who man_eater rel subord
"You know she is a man-eater, *and then*

ckákʔamstxʷ 758 cúntəm way̓, ńíńw̓iʔ ik̓líʔ {mi ɬ n}
c -ká•kaʔ+m -st -xʷ cu -nt -m way̓ ńíńw̓iʔ ik̓líʔ
cust^ -make_fun_of -^cust -2erg tell -nt -psv OK a_while there
you made fun of her again." *They said to him, "Ok," and then*

knaqs cúntəm iʔ t sxʔitx 759 ńíńw̓iʔ kən k̓ʷul̓l̓ t
k=naqs cu -nt -m iʔ t s+xʔit=x ńíńw̓iʔ kn k̓ʷul̓•l̓ t
one_person tell -nt -psv art agInst oldest_one a_while 1kn turn_into obl
the oldest one said to him: *"I'll turn into*

k̓ans 760 məɬ cúntəm i t knaqs incá kən k̓ʷul̓l̓ t
k̓ans mɬ cu -nt -m iʔ t k=naqs in+cá kn k̓ʷul̓•l̓ t
log_trap and tell -nt -psv art agInst one_person I 1kn turn_into obl
a trap." *And another one said, "I'll turn into*

mílaʔ 761 uɬ ixíʔ cúntəm iʔ t knaqs incá ńíńw̓iʔ kən
mílaʔ uɬ ixíʔ cu -nt -m iʔ t k=naqs in+cá ńíńw̓iʔ kn
bait and then tell -nt -psv art agInst one_person I a_while 1kn
bait." *Another one said, "I too will turn*

k̓ʷul̓l̓ t {ə¨} 762 t̓əxʷ t incá kʷin ńíńw̓iʔ 763 ɬə
k̓ʷul̓•l̓ t t̓xʷ t in+cá kʷi -n ńíńw̓iʔ ɬ
turn_into obl emph agInst I take -1erg a_while if
into... 5:00 *I'll grab her,* *if*

sk̓ʷəck̓ʷácts axáʔ iʔ k̓ans lut ksmáʕʷts 764 uɬ nixʷ mat
s -k̓ʷc•k̓ʷac+t -s axáʔ iʔ k̓ans lut ks -maʕʷ+t -s uɬ nixʷ mat
nom -strong -3i this art log_trap not futi -break -3i and also maybe
this trap is strong enough and won't break." *The youngest one*

tixʷkʷúnəm axáʔ iʔ stʔiwtx 765 ixíʔ uɬ {txl} txƛ̓ápəlx kmusms
tixʷ+kʷún+m axáʔ iʔ s+tʔiw+t=x ixíʔ uɬ t+xƛ̓ap -lx k=mus•ms
repeat this art young_one that and complete -pl four_persons
said the same thing. *That's all of them, four of them.*

39 It may be better to set up a stem ƛ̓l•l+nu *kill.*

766 waẏ ixíʔ əxʷ kləl̓lkʷákʷ sənk̓líp, ilíʔ uɬ cwíkʷmiʔst 767 waẏ
waẏ ixíʔ əxʷ k+l̓•l̓kʷ•akʷ s+n+k̓l̓=ip ilíʔ uɬ c -wíkʷ+miʔst waẏ
well then again far_dim Coyote there and hab -hide yes
Coyote went a little farther, he hid there. *And*

axáʔ ck̓əɬʔíq̓ʷ a[xáʔ] iʔ səmx̌íkən 768 wiṁ sƛ̓aʔƛ̓aʔúsəms
axáʔ c+k̓+ɬ[ʔ]iq̓ʷ axáʔ iʔ s+mx̌=ikn wiṁ s -ƛ̓aʔ•ƛ̓aʔ=ús+m -s
this come_in_sight this art grizzly in_vain nom -look_for -3i
Grizzly came in sight. *She looked around for*

sənk̓líp 769 waẏ t̓i cxʷuy cənʔúcxs 770 sta wiks
s+n+k̓l̓=ip waẏ t̓iʔ c -xʷuy c -n+ʔuc=x -s sta wik -s
Coyote yes evid hab -go act -follow -3erg intj see -3erg
Coyote. *She kept coming on his tracks.* *She saw*

axáʔ {iʔ} iʔ k̓ans 771 waẏ ixíʔ əxʷ sənk̓líp {əxʷ s} kʷu
axáʔ iʔ k̓ans waẏ ixíʔ əxʷ s+n+k̓l̓=ip kʷu
this art log_trap well that again Coyote 1obj
the trap. *"Well, that's Coyote playing tricks*

skənk̓əlpíkxtəm 772 waẏ ixíʔ əxʷ sənk̓líp {aw xa} iʔ walməscút
c -k+n+k̓l̓+p=ikxt+m waẏ ixíʔ əxʷ s+n+k̓l̓=ip iʔ wal+m+scút
hab -play_Coyote_tricks well that again Coyote art do_magic
on me. 6:00 *That's Coyote playing tricks again.*

773 kwaẏ lut t̓ iksnx̌íləm, kwaẏ t̓i niʕíp
k+waẏ lut t̓ i -ks -n+x̌il -m k+waẏ t̓iʔ n+yʕ=ip
well not negfac 1i -futi -fear -apsv well evid always
I am not afraid of him, I am still going

ikspúlstəm 774 uɬ aɬí nak̓ʷá t̓ul, k̓ʷəck̓ʷáct səmx̌íkən
i -ks -pul -st -m uɬ aɬíʔ nak̓ʷ+á t̓ul̓ k̓ʷc•k̓ʷac+t s+mx̌=ikn
1i -futi -kill_one -st -apsv and so indeed_not powerful strong grizzly
to kill him." *Grizzly is fierce and strong.*

775 uɬ {səc} nʔaɬnaʔsqílxʷtən 776 uɬ lut {t̓a kɬ} stiṁ t̓a
uɬ n+ʔaɬn+aʔ+s+qílxʷ+tn uɬ lut stiṁ t̓
and man_eater and not something negfac
She is a man-eater. *She fears*

kɬyáʕʷtəm 777 ixíʔ mat əxʷ sənk̓líp axáʔ {iʔ k} iʔ mílaʔ 778 {cnʕac̓}
kɬ+yaʕʷ+t+m ixíʔ mat əxʷ s+n+k̓l̓=ip axáʔ iʔ mílaʔ
best_s.o. that maybe again Coyote this art bait
nothing. *I suppose that bait is Coyote['s doing].* *The bait*

nt̓a qʷámqʷəmt aɬiʔ iʔ mílaʔ, {i} mat sɬiqʷ 779 mʕ̓an t̓i txiʔxá··n
nt̓a qʷam•qʷm+t aɬíʔ iʔ mílaʔ mat s+ɬiqʷ mʕ̓an t̓iʔ t+xẏ=xán
intj excellent because art bait maybe meat intj evid straight
is really good, maybe meat. *Grizzly went right up to it,*

səmx̌íkən uɬ i sənɬəx̌ʷṗáms 780 ixíʔ ck̓ʷaʔntís axáʔ {iʔ} iʔ
s+mx̌=ikn uɬ iʔ s -n+ɬx̌ʷṗa+m -s ixíʔ c -k̓ʷaʔ -nt -is axáʔ iʔ
grizzly and art nom -run_in -3i then act -bite -nt -3erg this art
went right into it. *She bit the bait, and the whole thing [trap]*

míla? ki ixíʔ kməɬqínaʔ 781 uɬ axáʔ tkʷəllínaʔsəlx {iʔ t} iʔ t
mílaʔ kiʔ ixíʔ k+mɬ=qín=aʔ uɬ axáʔ t+kʷl•l=ínaʔ -s -lx iʔ t
bait rel that fall_down_on and this pl_sit_on -3erg -pl art agInst
came down on her. *Two of them [the powers] sat down*

tk̓asʔasíl 782 way̓ uɬ lut t̓a kɬcawt 783 {uɬ aɬíʔ axáʔ iʔ} put
tk=ʔas•ʔasíl way̓ uɬ lut t̓ kɬ+cawt put
two_persons well and not negfac effort just
on her. *She had no show. 7:02* *It [the trap]*

axáʔ {i ts} iʔ t ʔásx̌əms iʔ t miw̓s iʔ sənk̓míkəns 784 itíʔ
axáʔ iʔ t ʔasx̌m -s iʔ t miw̓s iʔ s+n+k̓m=ikn̓ -s itíʔ
this art obl back -3in art obl middle art back -3in from_that
was right on her back, half way on her back. *The trap*

kiʔ {uɬ iʔ tk} a ntqəmnúlaʔxʷntəm axáʔ iʔ t k̓ans 785 way̓ uɬ
kiʔ a n+tq+mn=úlaʔxʷ -nt -m axáʔ iʔ t k̓ans way̓ uɬ
rel art hold_down -nt -psv this art agInst log_trap well and
just held her down. *Only*

k̓əm iʔ splips t̓i k̓əl tk̓əmkn̓íɬxʷ 786 way̓ ixíʔ sic sənk̓líp
k̓m iʔ s+pl=ip -s t̓iʔ k̓l t+k̓m=kn=iɬxʷ way̓ ixíʔ sic s+n+k̓l̓=ip
except art hind_end -3in evid to outside well then then Coyote
her hind end was outside [the trap]. *Then Coyote got*

ik̓líʔ ɬkícəntəm 787 way̓, way̓ ixíʔ sic ká··kaʔməntəm
ik̓líʔ ɬ+kic -nt -m way̓ way̓ ixíʔ sic ká•kaʔ+m -nt -m
to_there arrive_back -nt -psv well yes then then make_fun_of -nt -psv
there to her. *Then Coyote*

t sənk̓líp {way̓ ti} 788 lut_kəmʔíkxtəm {axáʔ iʔ} axáʔ iʔ pəptwínaʔxʷ iʔ
t s+n+k̓l̓=ip lut_km̓=ikxt+m axáʔ iʔ p•ptwínaʔxʷ iʔ
agInst Coyote do_things this art old_woman art
humiliated her. *He did all kinds of things to the old lady*

səmx̌íkən 789 lut uɬ {t̓a} t̓a nhiʔílsəntəm təl spəptwínaʔxʷs
s+mx̌=ikn lut uɬ t̓ n+hʔ=ils -nt -m tl s+p•ptwínaʔxʷ -s
grizzly not and negfac respect -nt -psv of old_ladyhood -3i
the Grizzly. *He showed no respect to her old ladyhood.*

790 way̓ ixíʔ wiʔskákaʔməntəm, way̓ {sic} sic ixíʔ {n} nsp̓úsəs
way̓ ixíʔ wy̓+s+ká•kaʔ+m -nt -m way̓ sic ixíʔ n+sp̓=us -s
well then finish_making_of -nt -psv yes then then hit_on_eye -3erg
When he got done humiliating her, he hit her in the eye.

791 {way̓ ixíʔ ɬ} itlíʔ nxátqnəms sənk̓líp 792 ixíʔ
itlíʔ n+xat=qn+m s+n+k̓l̓=ip ixíʔ
from_there sing Coyote then
Then Coyote started his song again. 8:03 *He*

wiʔsənk̓t̓úsəs ixíʔ wiʔspúlsts, ƛ̓əlnús {uɬ}
wy̓+s+n+k̓t̓=us -s ixíʔ wy̓+s+pul -st -s ƛ̓l•l -nu -s
finish_cutting_head -3erg then finish_fighting -st -3erg dead -manage -3erg
got done cutting her head off, fighting her, killed her dead.[40]

793 ixíʔ sənxátqnəms sənk̓líp {yat} 794 saʔlisá·w saʔlisá·w saʔlisá·w
ixíʔ s -n+xat=qn+m -s s+n+k̓l̓=ip
then nom -sing -3i Coyote
Coyote started singing his song *"saʔlisáw saʔlisáw saʔlisáw*

saʔlisá·w saʔlisá·w hu·y hu·y huyawá··w 795 huyawá··w huyawá··w huyawá··
saʔlisáw saʔlisáw hu·y hu·y huyawáw." *"huyawáw huyawáw huyawáw*

huyawá·· 796 way̓ ixíʔ sq^{w}əlq^{w}əltuʔscəncúts sənk̓líp
way̓ ixíʔ s -q^{w}l•q^{w}l+t=w̓s=cn+cut -s s+n+k̓l̓=ip
well then nom -talk_about_one's_thoughts -3i Coyote
huyawáw." *He started to say what he did to her. 9:00*

797 cut way̓, way̓ aɬíʔ k^{w} sq^{w}əňməscútx k^{w} səmx̌íkən, k^{w}
cut way̓ way̓ aɬíʔ k^{w} s -q^{w}ň+m+scut -x k^{w} s+mx̌=ikn k^{w}
say well yes because 2kn ipftv^ -pitiful -^ipftv 2kn grizzly 2kn
He said, "You are so pitiful, you

nʔaɬnaʔsqílx^{w}tən 798 x^{w}ʔi··t iʔ sqilx^{w} iʔ k̓awstx^{w} 799 uɬ nix^{w}
n+ʔaɬn+aʔ+s+qílx^{w}+tn x^{w}ʔi+t iʔ s+qilx^{w} iʔ k̓aw -st -x^{w} uɬ nix^{w}
man_eater many art person art gone -caus -2erg and also
man-eater. *You disposed of lots of people,* *and you*

k^{w}u ɬq^{w}əňíkstməntx^{w} {uɬ i} 800 iʔ {k^{w}u ɬc̓əs} k^{w}u
k^{w}u ɬ+q^{w}ň=ikst+m -nt -x^{w} iʔ k^{w}u
1obj do_pitiful_things_again -nt -2erg art 1obj
did pitiful things to me. *You wiped out*

nk̓áwlaʔx^{w}ɬtx^{w} isq^{w}əsq^{w}asíʔa 801 uɬ ʕapnáʔ k^{w}
n+k̓áw=laʔx^{w} -ɬt -x^{w} i -s+q^{w}s•q^{w}asíʔa uɬ ʕapnáʔ k^{w}
massacre -ɬt -2erg 1in -children and now 2k^{w}u
all my children. *Now I am getting*

iɬəɬʔíyksəm, sc̓x̌ilx kiʔ əcʔackňí··kstməntsən 802 ki
i -ɬ -ɬ+ʔiy=ks+m[41] sc+ʔx̌il+x kiʔ ʔac•ʔackn=íkst+m -nt -s -n kiʔ
1i -nom -pay_back reason_why rel play -nt -2obj -1erg rel
back on you, that's why I played tricks on you, *and*

sic iʔ púlstmən 803 uɬ aɬíʔ k^{w} q^{w}əňməscút, swit k^{w}
sic iʔ pul -st -m -n uɬ aɬíʔ k^{w} q^{w}ň+m+scut swit k^{w}
then art kill_one -st -2obj -1erg and because 2kn pitiful who 2kn
then I killed you. *You are pitiful, you are*

pəptwínaʔx^{w} k^{w} səmx̌íkən 804 axáʔ iʔ kən k̓əlsqəltmíx^{w} 805 ki k^{w}u
p•ptwínaʔx^{w} k^{w} s+mx̌=ikn axáʔ iʔ kn k̓l+s+qlt=mix^{w} kiʔ k^{w}u
old_woman 2kn grizzly this art 1kn better_man rel 1k^{w}u
an old lady Grizzly. *I am a better man.* *And then*

40 The logical order is "Coyote fought her, killed her, cut her head off."
41 The root may be √ys.

asənstíls kʷu akstk̓ʷəlqʷíksəm,[42] lu··t 806 sc̓x̌ilx uɬ iʔ {ay}
a -s+n+st=ils kʷu a -ks -t+k̓ʷaʔ=lqʷ=iks+m lut sc+ʔx̌il+x uɬ iʔ
2i -thought 1kʷu 2i -futi -bite_on_wrist not reason_why and art
you thought you were going to bite me on the wrist, no! *That's why*

káʔkaʔməntsən 807 lut t̓a nhʔílsən tl̓
ká•kaʔ+m -nt -s -n lut t̓ n+hʔ=ils -n tl̓
make_fun_of -nt -2obj -1erg not negfac respect -1erg from
I made fun of you. *I didn't even respect your*

aspəptwínaʔxʷ 808 ixíʔ sic iʔ púlstmən 809 cúntəm,
a -s+p•ptwínaʔxʷ ixíʔ sic iʔ pul -st -m -n cu -nt -m
2in -old_ladyhood then then art kill_one -st -2obj -1erg tell -nt -psv
old ladyhood. *That's why I killed you."* *He said [that],*

uɬ ixíʔ axáʔ aɬíʔ {s} sənk̓líp {t waẏ k waẏ a·} kcəkʷqíntəm səmx̌íkən
uɬ ixíʔ axáʔ aɬíʔ s+n+k̓l̓=ip k+ckʷ=qin -t -m s+mx̌=ikn
and then this so Coyote scalp -nt -psv grizzly
and then Coyote scalped Grizzly.10:04

810 wiʔsksərqíntəm 811. ixíʔ uɬ a[xáʔ] nʕacqíɬtəm
wẏ+s+k+sr=qin -t -m ixíʔ uɬ axáʔ n+ʕac=qí -ɬt -m
finish_scalping -nt -psv then and this tie_at_end -ɬt -psv
When he got done scalping her *he tied her scalp,*

axáʔ {iʔ} iʔ scksərqíns {a səm} səmx̌íkən iʔ qəpqíntəns 812 ixíʔ uɬ a
axáʔ iʔ sc -k+sr=qin -s s+mx̌=ikn iʔ qp=qin+tn -s ixíʔ uɬ a
this art pftv -scalp -3i grizzly art hair -3in then and art
Grizzly's hair. *Then he sang,*

ckʷənmíst, waẏ itlíʔ nxátqnəm 813 saʔlisá··w saʔlisá··w saʔlisá··w
c -kʷn+mist waẏ itlíʔ n+xat=qn+m
hab -make_sound yes from_there sing
started to sing again. *"saʔlisáw saʔlisáw saʔlisáw*

saʔlisá··w saʔlisá··w 814 cúnəlx waẏ, waẏ cxárkstmɬtsən
cu -n -lx waẏ waẏ c -xar=kst+m -ɬt -s -n
tell -1erg -pl yes yes cust^ -take_time -ɬt -2obj -1erg
saʔlisáw saʔlisáw" *I[43] say to them, "I am taking a lot of your time.*

815 waẏ naɬccám {kən s} kən sacṁaʔṁáʔyaʔx 816 aláʔ kʷu ɬ
waẏ naɬc•c•ám kn sc -ṁaʔ•ṁáya? -x aláʔ kʷu ɬ
yes forget 1kn ipftvp^ -teach -^ipftvp here 1obj subord
I just now realized I am teaching. *My pupil*

kmú··təms iscṁaʔṁáʔyaʔ 817 lútəm_swit a
k+mut+m -s i -sc+ṁaʔ•ṁáyaʔ lut+m_swit a
sit_by -3erg 1in -pupil not_anybody art
is sitting by me. *The one I am teaching*

42 Seymour hesitates in the middle of this word, making its recognition difficult.
43 Pete speaking now.

cṁa?•ṁáya?stən {ał}
c -ṁa?•ṁáya? -st -n
custˆ -teach -ˆcust -1erg
is not anybody.

818 lut tl isən?am?íma?t, sta
lut tl̓ i -s+n+?am•?íma?t sta
not from 1in -grand_children intj
The one getting taught is not

suyápix axá? i? cṁi?mẏa?ncút
s+wyapy=x axá? i? c -ṁẏ•ṁẏa?+ncút
white_person this art hab -get_taught
my grandchild, it's a white man. 11:01

819 waẏ kən nxixayápəlqs,
waẏ kn n+xy•xay=áplqs
well 1kn go_to_toilet
Well, I have to go

nċəyxʷápəlqs {that's all}
n+ċayxʷ=áplqs
end_of_story
to the toilet,[44] it's the end of the story. 11:10

44 This is what MD says the literal meaning of this closing formula is.

The two goats

1 way̓ ixíʔ axáʔ t̓əxʷ kʷu captíkʷləxts axáʔ isl̓áx̌t 2 axáʔ k̓əl
way̓ ixíʔ axáʔ t̓xʷ kʷu captíkʷl -xt -s axáʔ i -s+l̓áx̌+t axáʔ k̓l
well that this emph 1obj tell_stories -xit -3erg this 1in -friend this to
Well, my friend told me a fairy tale story. *At,*

t̓əxʷ lut t̓a cmistín iʔ t {s} sqilxʷ iʔ {skʷisc}
t̓xʷ lut t̓ c -my -st -in iʔ t s+qilxʷ iʔ
emph not negfac cust^ -know -^cust -1erg art agInst Indian art
I don't know the Indian name, the name of

skʷəstúlaʔxʷs 3 {uɬ i} kmix {ɬ} kən ksnuyápəxcnaʔx
s+kʷst=úlaʔxʷ -s kmix kn ks -n+uyapx=cn -aʔx
name_of_place -3in only 1kn incp^ -say_in_English -^incp
the country; *I'm going to say it only in English:*

4 c̓úms[ts]əlx {t} t mons 5 axáʔ {ia i} iʔ t̓ík̓ʷət {k̓} k̓
c -ʔum -st -s -lx t mons axáʔ iʔ t̓ikʷt k̓
cust^ -call -^cust -3erg -pl agInst Monse this art lake to
they call it "Monse." *This lake down*

ʔawtímtk {ut l} 6 {ki ixí} ixíʔ a nuknaqnítkʷ iʔ st̓əstiyáps
ʔawtím=tk ixíʔ a n+ukna=qn=ítkʷ iʔ s -t̓s+tiyá+p[1] -s
south that art Okanagan_River art nom -run_cisl -3i
south, *the Okanagan river runs this way, 1:04*

7 uɬ ixíʔ {iks} iʔ ksx̌an {ta} iʔ t uknaqín t tawn 8 ixíʔ uɬ itlíʔ
uɬ ixíʔ iʔ k+sx̌a+n iʔ t wkna=qín t tawn ixíʔ uɬ itlíʔ
and then art past art obl Okanagan obl town that and from_there
and goes past Okanagan town. *That's what*

c̓úmlaʔxʷstsəlx t mons 9 {ixíʔ uɬ itlíʔ} ilíʔ
c -ʔúm=laʔxʷ -st -s -lx t mons ilíʔ
cust^ -call_a_place -^cust -3erg -pl obl Monse there
they call "Monse." *And my friend*

sənʔamtlscítxʷəxʷ {axáʔ ixíʔ t} axáʔ isláx̌t 10 iwá {təm} kskʷist, uɬ aɬíʔ
s -n+ʔam=t+ls+cítxʷ -xʷ axáʔ i -s+l̓ax̌+t iwá k+s+kʷist uɬ aɬíʔ
ipftv^ -house_sit -^ipftv this 1in -friend even have_name and so
is just housekeeping. *He has a name,*

kən nɬəpɬəptúlaʔxʷ 11 uɬ ixíʔ nɬíptmən, {ɬə} nɬíptmɬtən iʔ skʷists
kn n+ɬp•ɬp+t=úlaʔxʷ uɬ ixíʔ n+ɬiptm -n n+ɬiptm -ɬt -n iʔ s+kʷist -s
1kn forgetful and that forget -1erg forget -ɬt -1erg art name -3i
but I am forgetful, *and I forget, I forget his name.*

1 Here t̓s- is derivational: the stem t̓s+tiyá+p receives the inflectional affixation.

12 ixíʔ x̌lítəntəm {a}, cúntəm way̓ caʔkʷ kʷu kəxəntíxʷ ik̓líʔ
ixíʔ x̌lit -nt -m cu -nt -m way̓ caʔkʷ kʷu kx+n -t -ixʷ ik̓líʔ
then call -nt -psv tell -nt -psv yes should 1obj follow -nt -2erg there
They asked him, they said, “You better come with me.

13 ksƛ̓aʔƛ̓aʔúlaʔxʷntəm təmxʷúlaʔxʷ 14 iʔ c̓úmstsəlx
ks -ƛ̓aʔ•ƛ̓aʔ=úlaʔxʷ -nt -m tmxʷ=úlaʔxʷ iʔ c -ʔum -st -s -lx
futt^ -look_for_place -nt -4erg country art cust^ -call -^cust -cust^ -pl
We are going to look for the place.” *They call it*

t {tə··} *Goose Lake* 15 uɬ mat ksʔum· t sqilxʷ 16 {uɬ aɬíʔ ta} aɬíʔ uɬ
t uɬ mat k+s+ʔum· t s+qilxʷ aɬíʔ uɬ
obl and must have_name obl Indian so and
“Goose Lake.” 2:05 *I expect it has an Indian name,* *but we'll talk*

way̓ uɬ {kʷu s} t̓i kʷu cnwyapxcən k̓im 17 uɬ t̓iʔ way̓ ixíʔ kəm̓ ixíʔ
way̓ uɬ t̓iʔ kʷu c -n+wyap=x=cn k̓im uɬ t̓iʔ way̓ ixíʔ km̓ ixíʔ
yes and evid 4kn hab -speak_English only and evid yes that or that
white man's talk. *That's all I remember,*

a cənɬək̓ʷɬək̓ʷtmístən {iʔ} iʔ *Goose Lake* 18 {axáʔ} axáʔ *Omak* [skʷant]
a c -nɬk̓ʷ•ɬk̓ʷt+mi -st -n iʔ axáʔ s+kʷant
art cust^ -remember -^cust -1erg art this Omak
“Goose Lake.” *Omak Lake is*

iʔ sílxʷa iʔ t̓ík̓ʷət 19 uɬ itlíʔ xʷu··y ta c̓utəmtkús 20 uɬ
iʔ sílxʷaʔ iʔ t̓ik̓ʷt uɬ itlíʔ xʷuy t c+ʔwtm=tk=us uɬ
art big art lake and from_there go obl southward and
a big lake. *From there it goes southward,* *and over*

ik̓líʔ nixʷ kɬt̓ək̓ʷt̓ík̓ʷaʔt 21 uɬ ixíʔ naqs ixíʔ a
ik̓líʔ nixʷ kɬ+t̓k̓ʷ•t̓ík̓ʷaʔt uɬ ixíʔ naqs ixíʔ a
to_there more have_small_lakes and that one that art
there there are some small lakes, *and one of them is*

scústsəlx {iʔ} iʔ *Goose Lake* *22* uɬ ixíʔ axáʔ x̌lítəntəm axáʔ
s -cu -st -s -lx iʔ uɬ ixíʔ axáʔ x̌lit -nt -m axáʔ
cust^ -tell -^cust -3erg -pl art and then this call -nt -psv this
what they call “Goose Lake.” *And they asked*

isl̓áx̌t 23 kən nstílsəm *Sam* iʔ skʷists 24 {uɬ i cut way̓} cut way̓
i -s+l̓áx̌+t kn n+st=ils+m iʔ s+kʷist -s cut way̓
1in -friend 1kn think art name -3in say well
my friend, *I think his name is Sam, 3:00* *he said,*

t̓əxʷ cwíklaʔxʷstən 25 {i} xʷaʔspíntk ki itíʔ kən
t̓xʷ c -wík=laʔxʷ -st -n xʷaʔ+s+pin=tk kiʔ itíʔ kn
emph cust^ -see_world -^cust -1erg many_years rel that 1kn
“I have seen that country; *but it's been many years since I traveled*

cxʷilwís {uɬ} 26 uɬ way̓ t̓əxʷ_mat n̓ín̓w̓iʔ kən ɬsúxʷlaʔxʷəm 27 way̓
c -xʷy+lwis uɬ way̓ t̓xʷ_mat n̓ín̓w̓iʔ kn ɬ+súxʷ=laʔxʷ+m way̓
hab -wander and yes maybe a_while 1kn recognize_place_again Ok
around there; *but maybe I'll remember the place.”* *“I'll*

kəxɫúlmən   28 {i uɫ} cúntəm   waẏ uɫ axáʔ incá kən kɫənx̌ʷúskʷ
kx -ɫulm -n   cu -nt -m   waẏ uɫ axáʔ in+cá kn kɫ+n=x̌ʷus=kʷ
follow -5obj -1erg   tell -nt -psv   well and this I 1kn have_beer
go with you."   *He said, "I have some beer."*

29 uɫ axáʔ isl̓áx̌t aɫíʔ lut t̓a {csiw̓} csiw̓st   30 cəwáylx iʔ
uɫ axáʔ i -s+l̓áx̌+t aɫíʔ lut t̓   c -siw+st   cway+lx iʔ
and this 1in -friend so not negfac   hab -drink   m's_name art
And my friend doesn't drink.   *His Indian*

skʷists iʔ ta nqílxʷcən   31 uɫ {m} axáʔ iʔ t
s+kʷist -s iʔ t n+qilxʷ=cn   uɫ axáʔ iʔ t
name -3in art obl Indian_language   and this art obl
name is "cəwáylx,"   *and with the white folks*

suyápix {uɫ} *Henry Nelson* {aɫí s} sək̓ʷtəmsqíltk   32 waẏ kʷu xʷuy {uɫ}, waẏ kʷu
s+wyapy=x   s+k̓ʷt+m+s+qil=tk   waẏ kʷu xʷuy   waẏ kʷu
white_person   half_blood   well 4kn go   well 4kn
"Henry Nelson," he's a half-breed.   *We went and we drank,*

caʔsíw̓st axáʔ naʔɫ isláx̌t myalíxʷtət   33 uɫ ixíʔ kʷu
c -saʔ•síw+st axáʔ naʔɫ i -s+l̓ax̌+t mya+líxʷ -tt   uɫ ixíʔ kʷu
hab -drink_pl this with 1in -friend guide -4in   and then 4kn
my friend and our guide.   *We came*

k̓əɫk̓ʷíƛ̓pt uɫ ixíʔ k̓la ncqʷut   34 uɫ {wíkən} wíkəntəm iʔ {s} sílxʷaʔ a
k̓ɫ+k̓ʷiƛ̓+p+t uɫ ixíʔ k̓l n+cq=ut   uɫ wik -nt -m iʔ sílxʷaʔ a
come_in_sight and then to woods   and see -nt -4erg art big art
in sight of the woods 4:05   *and we saw a big*

cmaq̓ʷ   35 ixíʔ uɫ ckp̓əƛ̓máqs ixíʔ a cmaq̓ʷ   36 uɫ ixíʔ
c+maq̓ʷ   ixíʔ uɫ c -k+p̓ƛ̓m=aqs ixíʔ a c+maq̓ʷ   uɫ ixíʔ
mountain   then and hab -end_of_mountain there art mountain   and then
mountain.   *At the end of the mountain there is another mountain.*   *I got*

nwaʔlílsmən uɫ siwn axáʔ {i s} iʔ xʷiscútəntət, {xʷi}
n+waʔl=íls+m -n uɫ siw -n axáʔ iʔ xʷy+scut+(t)n -tt
puzzle -1erg and ask -1erg this art travel_companion -4in
puzzled and I asked

myalíxʷtət   37 cun {uɫ} ha ixíʔ səcməq̓ʷmíx   38 uɫ
mya+líxʷ[2] -tt   cu -n ha ixíʔ sc -mq̓ʷ -mix   uɫ
guide -4in   tell -1erg intj that ipftvpˆ -mountain -ˆipftvp   and
our guide,   *I said, "Is that a mountain?"*   *That*

ilíʔ {uɫ i c} iʔ ckp̓ƛ̓maqs, uɫ way nwist   39 i kʷu kʕʷəyncútəms
ilíʔ iʔ c+k+p̓ƛ̓m=aqs uɫ waẏ n+wis+t   iʔ kʷu k+ʕʷy+ncut+m -s
there art end_of_mountain and yes high   art 1obj laugh -3erg
is the end of the mountain, and it's high.   *He laughed at me,*

2 Uncertain analysis.

uɬ_i kʷu cus 40 lut, lut ixíʔ {t̓ə} t̓ə {s⋅⋅} [sc]məq̓ʷmíx, {ixíʔ iʔ scə}
uɬ_iʔ kʷu cu -s lut lut ixíʔ t̓ sc -mq̓ʷ -mix
and_then 1obj tell -3erg not not that negfac ipftvp^ -mountain -^ipftvp
and he said to me: *"No, that's not a mountain.*

41 ixíʔ iʔ spíləm iʔ təmxʷúlaʔxʷ 42 uɬ axáʔm iʔ {t} ta nqílxʷcən
ixíʔ iʔ s+pil+m iʔ tmxʷ=úlaʔxʷ uɬ axáʔ+m iʔ t n+qilxʷ=cn
that art Big_Bend art country and this art obl Indian_language
That's the Big Bend [Wilbur]. *In Indian that's 'spíləm,'*

uɬ spíləm, axáʔ iʔ {iʔ} xíƛ̓laʔxʷ iʔ təmxʷúlaʔxʷ 43 uɬ axáʔm iʔ t
uɬ s+pil+m axáʔ iʔ xiƛ̓=laʔxʷ iʔ tmxʷ=úlaʔxʷ uɬ axáʔ+m iʔ t
and Big_Bend this art level_land art country and this art obl
that level ground country, 5:05 *and in English*

suyápəx uɬ aɬíʔ ksʔum⋅ ixíʔ iʔ *Big Bend Country* 44 scutx uɬ
s+wyapy=x uɬ aɬíʔ k+s+ʔum⋅ ixíʔ iʔ s -cut -x uɬ
English and so have_name that art ipftv^ -say -^ipftv and
it has the name 'Big Bend Country.'" *And he said,*

ilíʔ ki cp̓úƛ̓əm ck̓əɬʔálqʷaʔ 45 ixíʔ uɬ a ntx̌ʷitkʷ axáʔ
ilíʔ kiʔ c -p̓uƛ̓+m c -k̓+ɬʔ=álqʷaʔ ixíʔ uɬ a n+tx̌ʷ=itkʷ axáʔ
there rel hab -finish hab -next_to_shore that and art river this
"That's where it ends, right next to the river." *That's the main river,*

nx̌ʷəntkʷítkʷ 46 {púti} lúti ɬ tqípsəlx 47 {uɬ ixíʔ uɬ i}
n+x̌ʷn=tkʷ=itkʷ lút+i ɬ tq=ip -s -lx
Kettle_River before subord dam -3erg -pl
the Columbia, *that's before they put the dam in.* *And that's*

ixíʔ {ckp̓əƛ̓maq ə} cxílsəm ixíʔ təl {i təl} spíləm iʔ təl təmxʷúlaʔxʷ
ixíʔ c -xil=s -m ixíʔ tl s+pil+m iʔ tl tmxʷ=úlaʔxʷ
that hab -edge_of -mdl that of Big_Bend art of country
the edge of the level land,

48 uɬ c̓x̌iɬʔ a cmaq̓ʷ 49 uɬ yaʕyáʕt stim̓ ilíʔ {ks} ksp̓iʔqáɬq
uɬ c̓x̌iɬ+t aʔ c+maq̓ʷ uɬ yaʕ•yáʕ+t stim̓ ilíʔ ks -p̓y̓q=aɬq
and like art mountain and all thing there futi -ripe
and it's just like a mountain. *All kinds of things grow there,*

50 axáʔ iʔ t sqilxʷ iʔ t sp̓iʔqáɬq, sx̌ʷú⋅⋅səm, uɬ st̓xa⋅⋅ɬq 51 uɬ
axáʔ iʔ t s+qilxʷ iʔ t s+p̓y̓q=aɬq s+x̌ʷus+m uɬ s+t̓x=aɬq uɬ
this art prttv Indian art prttv fruit foam_berry and huckleberry and
Indian fruit, foam berries, huckleberries, *and*

axáʔ iʔ c̓x̌ʷl̓ú⋅⋅saʔ, uɬ ʔí⋅⋅tx̌ʷaʔ, t̓əxʷ yaʕyáʕt iʔ sqilxʷ iʔ sʔíɬən[s]
axáʔ iʔ c̓x̌ʷl̓=úsaʔ uɬ ʔítx̌ʷaʔ t̓xʷ yaʕ•yáʕ+t iʔ s+qilxʷ iʔ s+ʔiɬn -s
this art white_camas and camas emph all art Indian art food -3in
white camas, camas, all kinds of things the Indians eat. 6:12

52 uɬ ixíʔ ilíʔ {swit ixíʔ məɬ} kʷ ikscaptíkʷlxtəm 53 uɬ ilíʔ
uɬ ixíʔ ilíʔ kʷ i -ks -captíkʷl -xt -m uɬ ilíʔ
and then there 2kʷu 1i -futi -tell_stories -xit -apsv and there
And now I am going to tell you the fairy tale story. *Coyote*

cwix sənk̓líp uɬ ixíʔ sənk̓líp {uɬ} 54 uɬ nʔaɬnaʔsqílxʷtən uɬ
c -wix s+n+k̓l̓=ip uɬ ixíʔ s+n+k̓l̓=ip uɬ n+ʔaɬn+aʔ+s+qílxʷ+tn uɬ
hab -live Coyote and that Coyote and man_eater and
lived there, and Coyote was there. *A man-eater is killing*

səsƛ̓xʷáms iʔ sqilxʷ 55 uɬ ixíʔ ilíʔ a ilíʔ 56 uɬ i[líʔ] ɬaʔ
sc -ƛ̓xʷam -s iʔ s+qilxʷ uɬ ixíʔ ilíʔ a ilíʔ uɬ ilíʔ ɬaʔ
pftv -kill_many -3i art person and that there art there and there when
the people, *and that's why he is there.* *And when they get*

ckícsəlx 57 uɬ lut {itlíʔ tʼa c} itlíʔ tʼa
c+kic -s -lx uɬ lut itlíʔ tʼ
arrive_cisl -3erg -pl and not from_there negfac
there to him *they can't come away*

ckəlaʔkʷákʷəlx 58 itlíʔ təl sənk̓líp ksxʷəl·xʷál·tsəlx
c+k+laʔkʷ•ákʷ -lx itlíʔ tl s+n+k̓l̓=ip ks -xʷl••xʷal+t -s -lx
come_a_little_way_cisl -pl from_there from Coyote futi -alive_pl -3i -pl
from there. *They can't come away alive from Coyote.*

59 wa\u0079̓ kspúlstəməlx t sənk̓líp 60 {cut xit} ixíʔ iʔ captíkʷɬ[c]
way̓ ks -pul -st -m -lx t s+n+k̓l̓=ip ixíʔ iʔ captíkʷɬ -c
yes futt^ -beat -st -psv -pl agInst Coyote that art legends -3in
Coyote kills them. *That's the story of that. 7:05*

61 {uɬ axáʔ c} uɬ way̓ xʷʔit iʔ sqilxʷ a cƛ̓əxʷstís {i} sənk̓líp
uɬ way̓ xʷʔi+t iʔ s+qilxʷ a c -ƛ̓xʷ -st -is s+n+k̓l̓=ip
and yes many art person art cust^ -kill_many -^cust -3erg Coyote
And Coyote has already killed lots of people.

62 uɬ nák̓ʷəm ixíʔ iʔ mílaʔs sənk̓líp a kstʼəmkʔílts sənk̓líp
uɬ nak̓ʷ+m ixíʔ iʔ mílaʔ -s s+n+k̓l̓=ip a k -s+tʼmkʔ=ilt -s s+n+k̓l̓=ip
and evid that art bait -3in Coyote art to_be -daughter -3in Coyote
And Coyote's bait is Coyote's daughter.

63 swinú··mtx iʔ stʼəmkʔílts uɬ ixíʔ {i} iʔ mílaʔs sənk̓líp
s -wy̓+numt -x iʔ s+tʼmkʔ=ilt -s uɬ ixíʔ iʔ mílaʔ -s s+n+k̓l̓=ip
ipftv^ -handsome -^ipftv art daughter -3in and that art bait -3in Coyote
His daughter is good looking, and she is Coyote's bait.

64 ixíʔ uɬ {aɬ} ik̓líʔ {a} a cq̓əxʷáxʷəlx axáʔ {i s} iʔ splal
ixíʔ uɬ ik̓líʔ a c -q̓xʷ+axʷ -lx axáʔ iʔ s+pl•al
then and there art hab -flirt -pl this art young_growth
The young folks go over there to flirt with her;

65 məɬ ik̓líʔ {ə} a cxʷúy̓ilx 66 uɬ aɬíʔ scq̓əxʷəxʷmíxəlx iʔ k̓əl
mɬ ik̓líʔ a c+xʷuy•y -lx uɬ aɬíʔ sc -q̓xʷ•xʷ -mix -lx iʔ k̓l
and there art come_pl -pl and so ipftvp^ -flirt -^ipftvp -pl art to
they go there *and they flirt with*

sənk̓líp iʔ stʼəmkʔílts 67 ńíńwiʔ {ɬks} kscmər̓íma?xəlx 68 way̓ məɬ
s+n+k̓l̓=ip iʔ s+tʼmkʔ=ilt -s ńíńwiʔ ksc -mrim -aʔx -lx way̓ mɬ
Coyote art daughter -3in a_while ? -marry -^incp -pl yes and
Coyote's daughter *so they can marry her. 8:00* *They*

ixíʔ xkínməlx t̓əxʷ{a} tq̓ʷəq̓ʷúƛ̓aʔxnəməlx 69 t̓əxʷ lut_cmaylx {məɬ i}
ixíʔ x+ʔkiń+m -lx t̓xʷ t+q̓ʷ•q̓ʷúƛ̓+aʔ=xn+m -lx t̓xʷ lut_cmay -lx
then do_what -pl emph race -pl emph every_which_way -pl
do every which thing, they race, they do anything,

x̌əcnwíxʷəlx məɬ ixíʔ t sənk̓líp cúntməlx 70 ńíńw̓iʔ kʷu
x̌c+nwixʷ -lx mɬ ixíʔ t s+n+k̓l̓=ip cun -nt -m -lx ńíńw̓iʔ kʷu
bet -pl and then agInst Coyote tell -nt -psv -pl a_while 1obj
and they bet, and Coyote tells them: "If you beat me

ƛ̓xʷúpəntp uɬ ixíʔ kʷu ƛ̓xʷúpɬtəp ist̓əmkʔílt
ƛ̓xʷu+p -nt -p uɬ ixíʔ kʷu ƛ̓xʷu+p -ɬt -p i -s+t̓mkʔ=ilt
beat -nt -5erg then then 1kʷu win -ɬt -5erg 1in -daughter
you win my daughter.

71 náx̌əmɬ {kʷu} ƛ̓xʷúpɬmən ixíʔ uɬ p ƛ̓lal[3] púlɬmən
nax̌mɬ ƛ̓xʷu+p -ɬm -n ixíʔ uɬ p ƛ̓l•al pul -ɬm -n
but beat -5obj -1erg then and 5kn dead kill_one -5obj -1erg
But if I beat you, you'll be dead, I'll kill you."

72 {slx a·· uɬ i} uɬ ixíʔ {s a} təl tqəltkálqʷ uɬ cxʷuy tk̓asʔasíl {s} səncʔíw̓s
uɬ ixíʔ tl t+qlt=k=alqʷ uɬ c+xʷuy tk=ʔas•ʔasíl sncʔ=iw̓s
and then from across_line and come two_persons brothers
And from across the line came two brothers.

73 {ixíʔ s} ixíʔ {həɬ} həɬsx̌ʷƛ̓íʔ, ixíʔ səncʔíw̓s 74 {əy} sxʷúysəlx, cútəlx
ixíʔ hɬ=s+x̌ʷƛ̓iʔ ixíʔ sncʔ=iw̓s s -xʷuy -s -lx cut -lx
that goat_group that brothers nom -go -3i -pl say -pl
They are goats, brothers. 9:10 They went, they said,

way̓ sta {kʷu s} kʷu sənʔax̌ʷʔáx̌ʷtx ta nuknaqnítkʷ 75 məɬ
way̓ sta kʷu s -n+ʔax̌ʷ+ʔax̌ʷ+t -x t n+ukna=qn=ítkʷ mɬ
well intj 4kn ipftv^ -go_downstream -^ipftv obl Okanagan_River and
"Let's go downstream on the Okanagan River and

ik̓líʔ {kʷu} kʷu yaʕp {k̓əl i} k̓əl sənk̓líp {kʷu ʔaws} 76 cawts iʔ sqilxʷ
ik̓líʔ kʷu yaʕ+p k̓l s+n+k̓l̓=ip cawt -s iʔ s+qilxʷ
to_there 4kn arrive_pl to Coyote doing -3in art Indian
get to Coyote. That's the way people do.

77 aɬíʔ uɬ t̓əxʷ {kʷu} kʷu ksənx̌əstəlsmístaʔx 78 lut i məɬ {kʷu ks}
aɬíʔ uɬ t̓xʷ kʷu ks -n+x̌s+t=ls+mist -aʔx lut iʔ mɬ
so and emph 4kn incp^ -satisfy_self -^incp not art and
We are going to satisfy ourselves. They

kʷu ksənq̓əmscínməntəm 79 t̓əxʷ ixíʔ t̓əxʷ kʷu
kʷu ks -n+q̓m=s=cin+m -nt -m t̓xʷ ixíʔ t̓xʷ kʷu
3e4obj futt^ -pine_for -nt -3e4obj emph then emph 4kn
are not going to get stuck on us;[4] we are going to

3 ƛ̓lal has singular referent, but here it has plural inflection.

4 The sense is that the brothers take the initiative and do not wait for the woman to propose to them.

ksənx̌əstəlsmístaʔx 80 kʷu ksənsucənmístaʔx 81 ńíńẃiʔ t̓əxʷ
ks -n+x̌s+t=ls+mist -aʔx kʷu ks -n+sw=cn+mist -aʔx ńíńẃiʔ t̓xʷ
incp^ -satisfy_self -^incp 4kn incp^ -propose -^incp a_while emph
satisfy ourselves; we are going to propose. 10:00 If she

kʷu lútstəm, ixíʔ uɬ x̌ast iʔ spuʔústət 82 {a} cútəlx waẏ
kʷu lut -st -m ixíʔ uɬ x̌as+t iʔ s+puʔ=ús -tt cut -lx waẏ
3e4obj not -st -3e4obj then and good art heart -4in say -pl OK
turns us down, we're not going to feel bad." They said "Ok."

83 ixíʔ scənʔax̌ʷʔáx̌ʷtsəlx ta nuknaqnítkʷ 84 cxʷu··ylx, uɬ
ixíʔ sc -n+ʔax̌ʷ+ʔax̌ʷ+t -s -lx t n+ukna=qn=ítkʷ c -xʷuy -lx uɬ
then pftv -go_downstream -3i -pl obl Okanagan_River hab -go -pl and
Then they went downstream in the Okanagan River. They went,

waẏ ik̓líʔ {inaud} i l skiyláps iʔ nuknaqnítkʷ axáʔ iʔ {k̓əl}
waẏ ik̓líʔ iʔ l s+k+yla+p -s iʔ n+ukna=qn=ítkʷ axáʔ iʔ
yes there art at mouth_of_river -3in art Okanagan_River this art
and at the mouth of the Okanagan river into

k̓la nx̌ʷəntkʷítkʷ 85 ixíʔ {uɬ ac k̓ʷəlɬ} səlk̓əwsəmsəlx uɬ ixíʔ
k̓l n+x̌ʷn=tkʷ=itkʷ ixíʔ s+lk̓=ẃs+m -s -lx uɬ ixíʔ
to Kettle_River then make_raft -3erg -pl and then
the Columbia they made a raft,

st̓áq̓əmsəlx uɬ t̓íxəlxəlx k̓əl naɬáʔ 86 waẏ
s -t̓aq̓m -s -lx uɬ t̓ix+lx -lx k̓l na+ɬáʔ waẏ
nom -cross_water -3i -pl and come_to_shore -pl to other_side yes
and they crossed to the other side. They

t̓íxəlxəlx uɬ ixíʔ kɬqəlltúsəlx {uɬ i} 87 ixíʔ uɬ sxʷúysəlx,
t̓ix+lx -lx uɬ ixíʔ kɬ+ql•l•t=us -lx ixíʔ uɬ s -xʷuy -s -lx
come_to_shore -pl and then climb_on_bank -pl then and nom -go -3i -pl
came to shore and got on the bank. They went, they went,

xʷu··ylx, yáʕpəlx ik̓líʔ k̓əl sənk̓líp iʔ k̓əl cítxʷs 88 cúntməlx
xʷuy -lx yaʕ+p -lx ik̓líʔ k̓l s+n+k̓l̓=ip iʔ k̓l citxʷ -s cun -nt -m -lx
go -pl arrive_pl -pl there to Coyote art to house -3in tell -nt -psv -pl
and they arrived at Coyote's house. 11:05 Coyote said

t sənk̓líp 89 waẏ uɬ kʷu kícəntp p sqilxʷ
t s+n+k̓l̓=ip waẏ uɬ kʷu kic -nt -p p s+qilxʷ
agInst Coyote well and 1kʷu reach_st/sb -nt -5erg 5kn person
to them: "You got here, folks!

90 tlaʔkín uɬ p sqilxʷ 91 lut_sqʷays kʷu t̓a
tla+ʔkín uɬ p s+qilxʷ lut_s+qʷay+s kʷu t̓
from_there and 5kn person not_often 1obj negfac
Where are you folks from? It isn't often

ckícstsəlx t sqilxʷ 92 uɬ mnímɬəmp iʔ kʷu əɬ
c -kic -st -s -lx t s+qilxʷ uɬ mnimɬ+mp iʔ kʷu ɬ
cust^ -reach_st/sb -^cust -3erg -pl agInst person and you art 1obj comp
that people get here, and then you folks

kícəntp 93 cútəlx waẏ 94 t̓əxʷ aɬí? kʷu
kic -nt -p cut -lx waẏ t̓xʷ aɬí? kʷu
reach_st/sb -nt -5erg say -pl yes emph because 4kn
got to me." They said "Yes. We are just

səstəkʷtəkʷ?útx {uɬ} 95 uɬ i? kícəntsət {uɬ t̓əxʷ ixí?}
sc -tkʷ•tkʷ?=ut -x uɬ i? kic -nt -s -t
ipftvp^ -travel -^ipftvp and art reach_st/sb -nt -2obj -4erg
traveling around and we got here to you."

96 cúntəm waẏ stim̓ {uɬ is is} ya cktkʷtəkʷ?útəmstp
cu -nt -m waẏ stim̓ ya c -k+tkʷ•tkʷ?=ut -st -p
tell -nt -psv well what art cust^ -travel_for -^cust -5erg
He said to them, "What are you traveling around for?"

97 cúsəlx waẏ, waẏ t̓əxʷ kʷa ast̓əmk?ílt 98 kʷu níxəl aɬí? kʷ
cu -s -lx waẏ waẏ t̓xʷ kʷa a -s+t̓mk?=ilt kʷu nixl aɬí? kʷ
tell -3erg -pl well well emph intj 2in -daughter 4kn hear so 2kn
They said, "We're up to your daughter. We heard that you have

kst̓əmk?ílt {uɬ} 99 uɬ ast̓əmk?ílt ki? ctxʷúyməntst
k+s+t̓mk?=ilt uɬ a -s+t̓mk?=ilt ki? c+t+xʷuy+m -nt -s -t
have_daughter and 2in -daughter rel come_towards -nt -2obj -4erg
a daughter 12:00 and we came for your daughter.

100 {i} uɬ aɬí? t̓əxʷ {ks} kʷu ksənx̌əstəlsm̓ísta?x 101 kʷu
uɬ aɬí? t̓xʷ kʷu ks -n+x̌s+t=ls+mist -a?x kʷu
and so emph 4kn incp^ -satisfy_self -^incp 4kn
We are going to satisfy ourselves, we

ksənsəẁcənm̓ísta?x i k̓l ast̓əmk?ílt 102 cúntməlx t
ks -n+sw=cn+mist -a?x i? k̓l a -s+t̓mk?=ilt cun -nt -m -lx t
incp^ -propose -^incp art for 2in -daughter tell -nt -psv -pl agInst
are going to propose to your daughter." Coyote said

sənk̓líp 103 waẏ, waẏ t̓əxʷ lut {p t̓ iks} p t̓
s+n+k̓l̓=ip waẏ waẏ t̓xʷ lut p t̓
Coyote well well emph not 5kn negfac
to them: "I am not going to give you

ikskəɬkʷínxʷcnəm ʕapná? {t̓əxʷ} 104 {waẏ t̓əxʷ} mat talí
i -ks -k̓ɬ+kʷinxʷ=cn -m ʕapná? mat ta?lí?
1i -futi -answer -apsv now maybe very_much
the answer now. You have come

lkʷut i? scxʷúẏt[nəmp] 105 uɬ p ?ay?áyx̌ʷt uɬ p ?al?ílxʷt
lkʷ=ut i? sc -xʷuy+tn -mp uɬ p ?ay•?áyx̌ʷ+t uɬ p ?al•?ílxʷ+t
far art pftv -travel -5in and 5kn tired_pl and 5kn hungry
from long ways away; you are tired and hungry.

106 uɬ waẏ t̓əxʷ ńińẁi? {kʷa kʷ} kʷu wi?wi?cín kʷu
uɬ waẏ t̓xʷ ńińẁi? kʷu wẏ•wẏ=cin kʷu
and finish emph a_while 4kn finish_eating_pl 4kn
When we get done

wisəntx̌ʷəx̌ʷqínəm 107 ixíʔ mi_sic qʷəlqʷíłłmən 108 ixíʔ
wy̓+s+n+tx̌ʷ•x̌ʷ=qin -m ixíʔ mi_sic qʷl•qʷil -łm -n ixíʔ
finish_lunch -mdl then then talk_to -5obj -1erg then
eating our lunch *then I will talk to you, 13:00* *I will*

mi_sic {t̓əxʷ} k̓əłʔamcíłmən c̓x̌ił 109 cútəlx way̓ {way̓ ixí} 110 {i}
mi_sic k̓ał+ʔam=ci -łm -n c+ʔx̌ił cut -lx way̓
then answer -5obj -1erg like say -pl OK
give you your answer." *They said "Ok."* *Then*

ʔayxáxaʔ {uł} uł ałíʔ mat t sənk̓líp cus iʔ k̓ʷəlcəncútən
ʔayxáxaʔ uł ałíʔ mat t s+n+k̓l̓=ip cu -s iʔ k̓ʷl̓=cn+cut+(t)n
a_while and because maybe agInst Coyote tell -3erg art cook
maybe in a while Coyote told the cook...

111 way̓ {a} t k̓ʷəlcəncúts k̓ʷúlcəntəməlx, 112 a ʔayxáxaʔ uł
way̓ t k̓ʷl̓=cn+cut -s k̓ʷul̓=cn -t -m -lx a ʔayxáxaʔ uł
yes agInst cook -3in cook -nt -psv -pl intj a_while and
(The cook cooked for them.) *The cook*

p̓iʔqíltən axáʔ iʔ k̓ʷəlcəncútən uł kłsəlám 113 {uł ixíʔ cúntəm k way̓}
p̓y̓q=ilt+(t)n axáʔ iʔ k̓ʷl̓=cn+cut+(t)n uł kł+sla -m
cook this art cook and set_table -mdl
set the table, *then*

ixíʔ uł cúntəməlx axáʔ {ts} iʔ ta ilmíxʷəm 114 ałíʔ ilmíxʷəm
ixíʔ uł cu -nt -m -lx axáʔ iʔ t yl=mixʷ+m ałíʔ yl=mixʷ+m
then and tell -nt -psv -pl this art agInst chief because chief
the chief said *(and Coyote is*

sənk̓líp 115 cúntəm way̓ way̓ p̓iʔqíltən iʔ k̓ʷəlcəncútən 116 way̓
s+n+k̓l̓=ip cu -nt -m way̓ way̓ p̓y̓q=ilt+(t)n iʔ k̓ʷl̓=cn+cut+(t)n way̓
Coyote tell -nt -psv yes finish cook art cook yes
the chief), *he said, "The cook is done cooking. 14:00* *He*

uł kʷu x̌əlítəntəm kʷu ksʔałʔíłnaʔx 117 way̓ {i}
uł kʷu x̌lit -nt -m kʷu k+s -ʔał•ʔíłn -aʔx way̓
and 3e4obj call -nt -3e4obj 4kn incp^ -eat_pl -^incp yes
is asking us to go eat." *They*

sxʷúysəlx {a} kłkʷíl·əlx 118 way̓ {e} nwíluʔs {iʔ} iʔ sʔíłən
s -xʷuy -s -lx kł+kʷil•l -lx way̓ n+wil=w̓s iʔ s+ʔiłn
nom -go -3i -pl sit_pl -pl well lots art food
went and sat down. *There is all kinds of food,*

həłsp̓í·ƛ̓əm, həłʔí·tx̌ʷaʔ həłc̓əx̌ʷl̓ú·saʔ 119 lut_cmay axáʔ {a c} iʔ
hł=s+p̓iƛ̓+m hł=ʔítx̌ʷaʔ hł=c̓x̌ʷl̓=úsaʔ lut_cmay axáʔ iʔ
group_bitterroot group_camas group_camas every_which_way this art
bitterroot, camas, white camas... *All kinds of*

sqilxʷ iʔ sʔíłəns 120 way̓ ʔałʔí··łnəlx wiʔwiʔcínəlx {ə i}
s+qilxʷ iʔ s+ʔiłn -s way̓ ʔał•ʔíłn -lx wy̓•wy̓=cin -lx
Indian art food -3in well eat_pl -pl finish_eating_pl -pl
Indian food. *They ate, got done eating,*

cúntməlx {t sən} t sənk̓líp 121 cúntməlx way̓, way̓ p
cun -nt -m -lx t s+n+k̓l̓=ip cun -nt -m -lx way̓ way̓ p
tell -nt -psv -pl agInst Coyote tell -nt -psv -pl Ok finish 5kn
then Coyote said to them, he said, "Well, you are done

wiʔwiʔcín 122 uɬ way̓ sic c̓x̌iɬt p t ɬaʔɬaʔxʷísk̓it way̓ p {t p} t
wy̓•wy̓=cin uɬ way̓ sic c+ʔx̌iɬ+t p t ɬaʔ•ɬaʔxʷ=ísk̓it way̓ p t
finish_eating_pl and well then like 5kn ? well_rested 5kn res ?
eating. When you are rested, when

x̌əx̌əsmílx[5] way̓ 123 ixíʔ uɬ p ikscúnəm 124 way̓ t̓əxʷ kʷu
x̌•x̌s+m+ilx way̓ ixíʔ uɬ p i -ks -cun -m way̓ t̓xʷ kʷu
feel_better yes that and 5kn 1i -futi -tell -apsv yes emph 4kn
you feel better, 15:10 that's what I was going to tell you: we are going to

ksʔícəckna ʔx 125 uɬ ixíʔ ńińẃiʔ kʷu ʔícəckən kʷu wiʔsʔícəckən
ks -ʔic+c=kn -aʔx uɬ ixíʔ ńińẃiʔ kʷu ʔic•c•kn kʷu wy̓+s+ʔic•c•kn
incp^ -play -^incp and then a_while 4kn play 4kn finish_playing
play games. We play, and when we get done playing

126 kʷu ƛ̓xʷúpəntp ixíʔ uɬ kʷu ɬxʷuyɬtp isťəmkʔílt
kʷu ƛ̓xʷu+p -nt -p ixíʔ uɬ kʷu ɬ+xʷuy -ɬt -p i -s+ťmkʔ=ilt
1obj beat -nt -5erg then and 1obj go_back -ɬt -5erg 1in -daughter
if you beat me then you take back my daughter,

127 {ixíʔ uɬ aɬí} ixíʔ uɬ kɬnáx̌ʷnəx̌ʷəmp 128 {uɬ aɬíʔ mat i ac ki} x̌əl ixíʔ
ixíʔ uɬ kɬ -nax̌ʷ•nx̌ʷ -mp x̌l ixíʔ
then and to_be -wife -5in for that
and she will be your wife. I guess that's what you want

ki kʷu ckícəntp 129 kiʔ ckələkʷəkʷxənmíntəp
kiʔ kʷu c -kic -nt -p kiʔ c -k+lkʷ•kʷ=xn+mi -nt -p
rel 1obj act -arrive -nt -5erg rel act -travel_far -nt -5erg
and that's why you came to me, that's why you traveled so far,

130 tlaʔkín mat p sqilxʷ 131 cúntməlx, náx̌əmɬ ńińẃiʔ t
tla+ʔkín mat p s+qilxʷ cun -nt -m -lx nax̌mɬ ńińẃiʔ t
from_there maybe 5kn person tell -nt -psv -pl but a_while agInst
from wherever you are." 16:00 He said,

incá ƛ̓xʷúpɬmən, uɬ náx̌əmɬ way̓ t̓i p ƛ̓axʷt 132 ha way̓ ixíʔ
in+cá ƛ̓xʷu+p -ɬm -n uɬ nax̌mɬ way̓ t̓iʔ p ƛ̓axʷ+t ha way̓ ixíʔ
I beat -5obj -1erg and but yes evid 5kn dead_pl intj yes that
"But if I beat you, you are dead. Are you

ha x̌ast iʔ spuʔúsəmp ha 133 cútəlx way̓ {k aɬ} ixíʔ kʷu
ha x̌as+t iʔ s+puʔ=ús -mp ha cut -lx way̓ ixíʔ kʷu
intj good art heart -5in intj say -pl yes that 4kn
satisfied with the bargain?" They said, "Yes, that's why

5 This construction is unclear to me.

sċawsmúskstx 134 nak̓ʷá uɬ ha kʷu
sc -?aw+s+mús=kst -x nak̓ʷá uɬ ha kʷu
ipftvp^ -take_chance -^ipftvp indeed_not and intj 4kn
we came, to take a chance. *We didn't*

sənstílsx {a uɬ a} x̌əl tanm̓ús {kɬ} kʷiɬtst ast̓əmk?ílt
s -n+st=ils -x x̌l tanm̓=ús kʷi -ɬt -s -t a -s+t̓mk?=ilt
ipftv^ -think -^ipftv for nothing take -ɬt -2obj -4erg 2in -daughter
think we'd take your daughter for nothing.

135 uɬ t̓əxʷ ca?kʷ iwá kʷu ɬə ƛ̓axʷt 136 uɬ aɬí way̓ kʷu
uɬ t̓xʷ ca?kʷ iwá kʷu ɬ ƛ̓axʷ+t uɬ aɬí? way̓ kʷu
and emph if even 4kn if dead_pl and so yes 4kn
And if we die, *we*

nx̌əstəlsm̓íst i x̌əl ast̓əmk?ílt uɬ i kʷu ƛ̓axʷt
n+x̌s+t=ls+mist i? x̌l a -s+t̓mk?=ilt uɬ i? kʷu ƛ̓axʷ+t
satisfy_self art for 2in -daughter and art 4kn dead_pl
got our satisfaction for your daughter if we die."

137 {a cus} cúntməlx t sənk̓líp way, həhúy 138 cúsəlx axá?
cun -nt -m -lx t s+n+k̓l̓=ip way̓ hu•húy cu -s -lx axá?
tell -nt -psv -pl agInst Coyote yes OK tell -3erg -pl this
Coyote said "Ok." *The brothers*

i? t {s} sənc?íw̓s 139 uɬ stim̓ {i?} i? kɬən?íckəntəns {ti as} ascənstíls
i? t snc?=iw̓s uɬ stim̓ i? kɬ -n+?ickn+tn -s a -sc -n+st=ils
art agInst brothers and what art to_be -game -3in 2i -pftv -think
asked him: 17:03 *"And what is the game you figured?*

140 {a} i kʷ ilmíxʷəm kʷ sənk̓líp 141 cut way̓, way̓ t̓əxʷ kʷu
i? kʷ yl=mixʷ+m kʷ s+n+k̓l̓=ip cut way̓ way̓ t̓xʷ kʷu
art 2kn chief 2kn Coyote say well yes emph 4kn
You are the chief, Coyote." *He said, "We are going to*

ksq̓ʷəq̓ʷúƛ̓a?xna?x 142 o·· uɬ k̓a?kín {i s} i? səntxəlktán
ks -q̓ʷ•q̓ʷúƛ̓+a?=xn -a?x uɬ k̓a+?kín i? s+n+t+xlk+tan
incp^ -race -^incp and where_to art race_track
race." *"And where is the turn-around place?*

143 way̓ cúntməlx t sənk̓líp 144 t̓əxʷ way̓ ití {p cxʷ} p
way̓ cun -t -m -lx t s+n+k̓l̓=ip t̓xʷ way̓ ití? p
well tell -nt -psv -pl agInst Coyote emph yes from_that 5kn
Coyote said to them: *Coyote said, "Where you came*

cən?ax̌ʷ?áx̌ʷt 145 uɬ way̓ cwíkla?xʷəntp 146 ixí? a
c+n+?ax̌ʷ•?áx̌ʷ+t uɬ way̓ c -wík=la?xʷ -nt -p ixí? a
come_downriver and yes act -see_country -nt -5erg that art
downriver *you saw the country.* *They call it*

ċumstsəlx {i} t {s} a cxəlkíʔs[6], {ixíʔ} ixíʔ iʔ səntxəlktán
c -ʔum -st -s -lx t a c+xlk+iʔs ixíʔ iʔ s+n+t+xlk+tan
cust^ -call -^cust -incp^ -pl obl art turn_around that art race_track
"go around a tree," that's the turn around.

147 ití p cxəlkíʔs uɬ aláʔ p ɬciyáʕp 148 swit i
itíʔ p c+xlk+iʔs uɬ aláʔ p ɬ+c+y•yáʕ+p swit iʔ
from_that 5kn turn_around and here 5kn get_back_cisl who art
That's where you turn around and then you get back here. 18:00 *Whoever*

acxʔít, axáʔ mnímɬəmp p cxʔit 149 uɬ waẏ kʷu ƛ̓xʷúpəntp 150 uɬ
c+xʔit axáʔ mnimɬ+mp p c+xʔit uɬ waẏ kʷu ƛ̓xʷu+p -nt -p uɬ
first this you 5kn first and yes 1obj beat -nt -5erg and
is first, if you folks are first *then you beat me;* *but*

axáʔ incá náx̌əmɬ {iʔ} iʔ sƛ̓əx̌sqáx̌aʔtət cxʔit 151 uɬ waẏ
axáʔ in+cá nax̌mɬ iʔ s+ƛ̓x̌=sqáx̌aʔ -tt c+xʔit uɬ waẏ
this I but art race_horse -4in first and yes
if our race horse comes first *then I have*

ƛ̓xʷúpɬmən ixíʔ uɬ p ƛ̓axʷt 152 uɬ náx̌əmɬ kʷu ƛ̓xʷúpəntp
ƛ̓xʷu+p -ɬm -n ixíʔ uɬ p ƛ̓axʷ+t uɬ nax̌mɬ kʷu ƛ̓xʷu+p -nt -p
beat -5obj -1erg then and 5kn dead_pl and but 1obj beat -nt -5erg
beaten you and you are dead. *But if you beat me,*

məɬ kʷu ƛ̓xʷupɬtp isťəmkʔílt 153 a·· cútəlx waẏ, waẏ ixíʔ, waẏ
mɬ kʷu ƛ̓xʷu+p -ɬt -p i -s+ťmkʔ=ilt a cut -lx waẏ waẏ ixíʔ waẏ
and 1obj beat -ɬt -5erg 1in -daughter intj say -pl OK well that yes
then you win my daughter." *They said, "We are*

ixíʔ kʷu ksənx̌əstəlsmístaʔx 154 caʔkʷ iwá kʷu ɬ ƛ̓axʷt {l} nak̓ʷá
ixíʔ kʷu ks -n+x̌s+t=ls+mist -aʔx caʔkʷ iwá kʷu ɬ ƛ̓axʷ+t nak̓ʷá
that 4kn incp^ -satisfy_self -^incp if even 4kn if dead_pl indeed_not
going to be satisfied. *If we die, we aren't going*

kʷu kscútaʔx waẏ {n} kʷu ƛ̓xʷup 155 waẏ mi kʷu xƛ̓ap uɬ aɬíʔ ixíʔ
kʷu ks -cut -aʔx waẏ kʷu ƛ̓xʷu+p waẏ mi kʷu xƛ̓a+p uɬ aɬíʔ ixíʔ
4kn incp^ -say -^incp yes 4kn win well fut 4kn lose and so then
to say that we win. *[And if] we lose,*

kʷu ksənx̌əstəlsmístaʔx 156 kmátəm {kʷu a} sənq̓əmscínəmtət
kʷu ks -n+x̌s+t=ls+mist -aʔx kmatm s -n+q̓m=s=cin+m -tt
4kn incp^ -satisfy_self -^incp that's_why nom -pine_for -4i
we are [still] satisfied. *For sure we are stuck on your daughter,*

asťəmkʔílt ki ctxʷúyməntəm 157 {e} uɬ axáʔ sənk̓líp iʔ
a -s+ťmkʔ=ilt kiʔ c+t+xʷuy+m -nt -m uɬ axáʔ s+n+k̓l̓=ip iʔ
2in -daughter rel come_to -nt -4erg and this Coyote art
that's why we came." 19:00 *And Coyote's daughter*

6 This may be a fossilized lexical item derived from xlk-iʔ-s *turn around-nt-3erg "he turns around it."*

st’əmkʔílts 158 nt’a uɬ way̓ i·· t stanm̓ús {is} inm̓ístəm
s+t’mkʔ=ilt -s nt’a uɬ way̓ i·· t s+tanm̓=ús in -m̓ist+m
daughter -3in intj and yes intj obl for_nothing 1in -w’s_father
[thought]: *"My father is sure no good."*

159 {a uɬ aɬíʔ} way̓ xʔínaʔ axáʔ {iʔ k̓əl} iʔ k̓əl k̓əɬʔawtúsc axáʔ[7] iʔ k̓əl
way̓ xʔ=ínaʔ axáʔ iʔ k̓l k̓ɬ+ʔaw+t=ús -c axáʔ iʔ k̓l
well consent this art to antagonist -3in this art to
She had alredy consented to who she is running against, to the

sx̌ʷƛ̓iʔ 160 axáʔ uɬ way̓ nq̓əmscín axáʔ iʔ k̓əl sx̌ʷƛ̓iʔ {axáʔ iʔ} axáʔ iʔ
s+x̌ʷƛ̓iʔ axáʔ uɬ way̓ n+q̓m=s=cin axáʔ iʔ k̓l s+x̌ʷƛ̓iʔ axáʔ iʔ
goat this and yes be_stuck_on this art on goat this art
Goats. 20:00 *His daughter is stuck on*

st’əmkʔílts {ay} 161 way̓ ixíʔ st’wístsəlx, 162 way̓ cúntməlx
s+t’mkʔ=ilt -s way̓ ixíʔ s -t’wist -s -lx way̓ cun -nt -m -lx
daughter -3in well then nom -stand_pl -3i -pl well tell -nt -psv -pl
the Goats. *They got up,* *he said to them,*

way̓ ixíʔ uɬ p xítmiʔst {p} 163 p xʷu··y, məɬ ixíʔ k̓la cxəlkíʔs uɬ
way̓ ixíʔ uɬ p xít+miʔst p xʷuy mɬ ixíʔ k̓l c+xlk+iʔs uɬ
yes then and 5kn run 5kn go and then to turn_around and
"Go on, run. *You go, and when you get to*

aɬíʔ mat səcɬəkmíx 164 uɬ ixíʔ itíʔ {ti} məɬ p cxəlkíʔs
aɬíʔ mat sc -ɬk -mix uɬ ixíʔ itíʔ mɬ p c+xlk+iʔs
so maybe ipftvp^ -bushes -^ipftvp and then from_that and 5kn turn_around
the turn around point *that's where you turn around;*

165 ixíʔ iʔ səntxəlktán 166 uɬ {xʷe} swit ƛ̓xʷup məɬ ixíʔ ƛ̓xʷup
ixíʔ iʔ s+n+t+xlk+tan uɬ swit ƛ̓xʷu+p mɬ ixíʔ ƛ̓xʷu+p
that art race_track and who win and that win
that's the turn-around place. *Whoever wins wins;*

167 kʷu ƛ̓xʷúpəntp uɬ ixíʔ kʷu ƛ̓xʷupɬtp ist’əmkʔílt
kʷu ƛ̓xʷu+p -nt -p uɬ ixíʔ kʷu ƛ̓xʷu+p -ɬt -p i -s+t’mkʔ=ilt
1obj beat -nt -5erg and then 1obj win -ɬt -5erg 1in -daughter
and if you beat me you win my daughter.

168 ƛ̓xʷúpɬmən náx̌əmɬ uɬ ixíʔ p ƛ̓axʷt 169 way̓
ƛ̓xʷu+p -ɬm -n nax̌mɬ uɬ ixíʔ p ƛ̓axʷ+t way̓
beat -5obj -1erg but and then 5kn dead_pl OK
But if I win, you are dead." *"Ok." 21:00*

170 way̓ t’wístəlx, way̓ t’ʕapsqílxʷ {i} sənk̓líp 171 ixíʔ uɬ iʔ
way̓ t’wist -lx way̓ t’aʕp+s+qílxʷ s+n+k̓lʼ=ip ixíʔ uɬ iʔ
well stand_pl -pl yes fire_gun Coyote then and art
Coyote shot the [starting] gun *and they*

7 Here Pete chuckles and says "I'm forgetting the name of that animal, the goat." Seymour's narration has been uncharacteristically halting.

sxítmiʔstsəlx 172 xʷəm t̓i atláʔ ɫt̓pmístəlx 173 uɫ yaʔx̌í
s -xít+miʔst -s -lx xʷm t̓iʔ atláʔ ɫt̓+p+mist -lx uɫ yaʔx̌í
nom -run -3i -pl intj evid from_here jump_pl -pl and that_one
ran *When they first jumped,* *the girl,*

iʔ st̓aʔk̓míx {aɫ} iʔ tkəɫmílxʷ ƛ̓ax̌t {a ɫ} xaʔítət 174 {a ɫ t̓i} lúti
iʔ s+t̓aʔk̓+míx iʔ tkɫmilxʷ ƛ̓ax̌+t xaʔít•t lút+i
art virgin art woman fast be_first before
the woman, is fast, she has the lead.[8] *They hadn't*

smiw̓súlaʔxʷsəlx {iʔ t} iʔ t sk̓əlxʷmúlaʔxʷs 175 uɫ way̓ yaʔx̌í
s -miw̓s=úlaʔxʷ -s -lx iʔ t s -k̓lxʷ+m=úlaʔxʷ -s uɫ way̓ yaʔx̌í
nom -half_way -3i -pl art obl nom -out_of_sight -3i and yes that_one
gone halfway and she is out of sight, *the woman*

k̓əɫk̓láxʷ i tkəɫmílxʷ 176 uɫ aɫíʔ axáʔ {iʔ s} həɫsx̌ʷƛ̓íʔ way̓ t̓i kmix
k̓ɫ+k̓laxʷ iʔ tkɫmilxʷ uɫ aɫíʔ axáʔ hɫ=s+x̌ʷƛ̓iʔ way̓ t̓iʔ kmix
disappear art woman and so this goat_group yes evid only
is out of sight. *But the goats are*

scícəlm̓iʔstəlx 177 lut uɫ {t̓a} t̓a cq̓áʕpəlx, kmix
s -cí•cl+miʔst -lx lut uɫ t̓ c -q̓aʕ+p -lx kmix
hab -trot_slowly -pl not and negfac hab -move -pl only
just trotting. *They don't move [fast],*

scícəlm̓[iʔstsəlx] 178 xʷu··ylx uɫ {xiʔ k̓la} k̓a cxəlkíʔs
s -ci+cl+miʔst -s -lx xʷuy -lx uɫ k̓ c+xlk+iʔs
nom -trot_slowly -3i -pl go -pl and to turn_around
they just trot. 22:00 *They went and they went to the turn around place.*

179 uɫ aɫím ʕapnáʔ iʔ t suyápix ixíʔ uɫ *Ellisford* 180 ixíʔ {s}
uɫ aɫíʔ+m ʕapnáʔ iʔ t s+wyapy=x ixíʔ uɫ ixíʔ
and so now art agInst white_person that and that
And now in English they call it "Ellisford," *they*

cʔúmlaʔxʷ[stsəlx] ixíʔ a cxəlkíʔs
c -ʔúm=laʔxʷ -st -s -lx ixíʔ a c+xlk+iʔs
custˆ -call_a_place -ˆcust -3erg -pl that art turn_around
call it the "turn-around place."

181 cwíklaʔxʷ[st]n ixíʔ 182 way̓ ctxəlák axáʔ {iʔ} iʔ
c -wík=laʔxʷ -st -n ixíʔ way̓ c -t+xlak axáʔ iʔ
custˆ -see_country -ˆcust -1erg that finish hab -go_around this art
I have seen it. *The girl has already gone*

st̓aʔk̓míx 183 sənk̓líp iʔ st̓aʔk̓əmxílts 184 way̓
s+t̓aʔk̓+míx s+n+k̓l̓=ip iʔ s+t̓aʔk̓mx=ílt -s way̓
virgin Coyote art maiden_daughter -3in finish
around, *Coyote's daughter.* *She*

8 Coyote's daughter is the racer.

łcmiw̓súlaʔxʷ ki? łtkícəntməlx axáʔ iʔ ʔawʔawtúsc
ł+c+miw̓s=úlaʔxʷ kiʔ ł+t+kic -nt -m -lx axáʔ iʔ ʔaw•ʔaw+t=ús -c
come_halfway_again rel meet_with_again -nt -psv -pl this art opponents -3in
has come half way around again when she met her competitors,

həłsx̌ʷƛ̓íʔ 185 way̓ t̓iʔ scícəlm̓iʔstəlx {uł} 186 way̓ uł t̓i
hł=s+x̌ʷƛ̓iʔ way̓ t̓iʔ s -cí•cl+mist -lx way̓ uł t̓iʔ
goat_group well evid hab -trot -pl well and evid
the Goats. *They are just a-trotting along.* *She just*

cənʕʷəyúsəntməlx uł cənc̓áʕpsəntməlx {uł} 187 uł itlíʔ {c}
c -n+ʕʷy=us -nt -m -lx uł c -n+c̓aʕp=s -nt -m -lx uł itlíʔ
act -smile -nt -psv -pl and act -wink -nt -psv -pl and from_there
smiled at them, and she winked at them. *Coyote's daughter,*

cxʷt̓pəncút axáʔ iʔ st̓əmkʔílts sənk̓líp, sƛ̓əx̌sqáx̌aʔs 188 way̓ ixíʔ
c -xʷt̓+p+ncut axáʔ iʔ s+t̓mkʔ=ilt -s s+n+k̓l̓=ip s+ƛ̓x̌=sqáx̌aʔ -s way̓ ixíʔ
hab -run this art daughter -3in Coyote race_horse -3in well then
his race horse, kept running. *Then*

cus kin̓ mat t̓əxʷ iʔ sxʔitx {ə} iʔ cus iʔ
cu -s ʔkin̓ mat t̓xʷ iʔ s+xʔit=x iʔ cu -s iʔ
tell -3erg indef maybe evidently art oldest_one art tell -3erg art
he said to him, maybe the oldest said to his younger

síncaʔs 189 cus way̓ {im} uł kʷ sc̓kinx, way̓
síncaʔ -s cu -s way̓ uł kʷ sc -ʔkin -x way̓
younger_brother -3in tell -3erg well and 2kn ipftvp^ -indef -^ipftvp yes
brother, 23:10 *he said, "What's the matter with you, you are not doing*

lut uł askłcáwt 190 {inaud} mat t̓i kʷu ksƛ̓əxʷtmíxaʔx
lut uł a -s+kł+cawt mat t̓iʔ kʷu ks -ƛ̓xʷ+t -míx+aʔx
not and 2in -effort maybe evid 4kn incp^ -die_pl -^incp
anything. *We are going to be dead now."*

191 cúntəm uł stim̓ uł ikłcáwt {ikł} 192 way̓ uł kən
cu -nt -m uł stim̓ uł i -kł+cawt way̓ uł kn
tell -nt -psv and what and 1i -effort yes and 1kn
He said, "And what should I do? *I am*

sxʔimscútx 193 cúntəm lut, t̓əxʷ {lut atł} miná təl
s -xy̓+mscút -x cu -nt -m lut t̓xʷ miná tl
ipftv^ -be_at_limit -^ipftv tell -nt -psv not emph maybe_not of
at the limit." *He said "No, it isn't*

tanm̓ús ha {ki kʷu} ki kʷu c̓awsənsucənmíst 194 way̓ way̓ mat kʷ
tanm̓=ús haʔ kiʔ kʷu c+ʔaw+s+n+sw=cn+mist way̓ way̓ mat kʷ
nothing inter rel 4kn come_propose yes yes must 2kn
for nothing that we came here to propose. *You must be worth*

səkɬcáwtx 195 kʷ skəlmílsmistx [kʷ]
s -kɬ+cawt -x kʷ s -k+lm=íls+mist -x kʷ
ipftv^ -effort -^ipftv 2kn ipftv^ -think_highly_of_self -^ipftv 2kn
something. *You must think more[9] of*

csəlxʷaʔílsəm 196 cut lut, kʷu qʷəncínməntxʷ 197 waẏ t̓iʔ
c -slxʷaʔ=íls+m cut lut kʷu qʷn̓=cin+m -nt -xʷ waẏ t̓iʔ
hab -thing_highly_of_self say not 1obj pity -nt -2erg well evid
yourself.” *He said “No, pity me. 24:00* *I'm just*

kʷ iscəntkʷílsəm kiʔ ckəxəntsín kʷ isqpám
kʷ i -sc -n+t+kʷil=s+m kiʔ c -kx+n -t -s -in kʷ i -s+qpa+m
2kʷu 1i -pftv -keep_company rel act -follow -nt -2obj -1erg 2kʷu 1in -predicament
keeping you company that I came with you, I am in your same boat.

198 uɬ aɬíʔ waẏ místən waẏ t̓i {kʷ ksƛ̓} kʷ ɬ ƛ̓lal 199 lut
uɬ aɬíʔ waẏ mi -st -n waẏ t̓iʔ kʷ ɬ ƛ̓l•al lut
and so yes be_sure -st -1erg yes evid 2kn one_that dead not
I was sure you are going to die. *You*

t̓ akstk̓ík̓aʔt k̓əl sənk̓l̓íp aɬíʔ nʔaɬnaʔsqílxʷtən 200 uɬ ixíʔ
t̓ a -ks -t+k̓í•k̓aʔt k̓l s+n+k̓l̓=ip aɬíʔ n+ʔaɬn+aʔ+s+qílxʷ+tn uɬ ixíʔ
negfac 2i -futi -get_near to Coyote because man_eater and that
don't come close to Coyote, because he is a man-eater, *and*

iʔ st̓əmkʔílts ixíʔ ia nʕaʔcústəns 201 uɬ aɬíʔ lut t̓a cxƛ̓ap
iʔ s+t̓mkʔ=ilt -s ixíʔ iʔ n+ʕac=ús+tn -s uɬ aɬíʔ lut t̓ c -xƛ̓a+p
art daughter -3in that art trap -3in and so not negfac hab -lose
his daughter is his bait [lit. 'trap']. *He never loses.”*

202 waẏ itlíʔ ɬənʔawʔáwqəntəm iʔ t sl̓ax̌ts 203 ə··y
waẏ itlíʔ ɬ+n+ʔaw•ʔáw=qn -t -m iʔ t s+l̓ax̌+t -s
well from_there challenge_back -nt -psv art agInst friend -3in intj
Then his partner challenged him to do something. *He*

cus waẏ, cus waẏ n̓ín̓wiʔ t̓əxʷ kʷa kən múskstəm 204 náx̌əmɬ kʷ
cu -s waẏ cu -s waẏ n̓ín̓wiʔ t̓xʷ kʷa mus=kst+m nax̌mɬ kʷ
tell -3erg well tell -3erg OK a_while emph intj try but 2kn
said to him, “Ok, I will try to do something. *But you have*

txət̓mí··st 205 lut kʷu aksk̓ʷəɬtanm̓úsəm axáʔ {iʔ}
t+xt̓+mist lut kʷu a -ks -k̓ʷl̓+ɬ+tanm̓=ús -m axáʔ
be_careful not 1kʷu 2i -futi -minimize -apsv this
to look after yourself. 25:02 *Don't minimize what*

iʔ qʷəlqʷílstmən 206 waẏ c̓əx̌ʷc̓əx̌ʷəntsín 207 uɬ
iʔ qʷl•qʷil -st -m -n waẏ c̓x̌ʷ•c̓x̌ʷ -nt -s -in uɬ
art talk_to -st -2obj -1erg yes instruct -nt -2obj -1erg and
I tell you. *I am going to do some preaching to you.* *Then*

9 The sense is “try harder.”

ilíʔ kʷ x̌íləm axáʔ iʔ cúntsən 208 lut {aks}
ilíʔ kʷ x̌il+m axáʔ iʔ cu -nt -s -n lut
there 2kn do_like this art tell -nt -2obj -1erg not
you do what I tell you. *Don't*

aksənqələwtúɫtəm iʔ sxʷúytəns {kəm̓ t̓əxʷ aks} 209 way̓ niʕ̓íp t
a -ks -n+ql=wt -(t)uɫt -m iʔ s+xʷuy+tn -s way̓ nyʕ̓ip t
2i -futi -step_on -tuɫt -apsv art track -3in yes always obl
step on her tracks. *Keep staying*

tk̓əmɫníwts iʔ sxʷúytəns 210 kəm̓ lut akstk̓ʷít̓xəlx̣əmɫtəm
t+k̓m=ɫniwt -s iʔ s+xʷuy+tn -s km̓ lut a -ks -t+k̓ʷit̓=x+lx+m[10] -ɫt -m
alongside -3in art track -3in or not 2i -futi -walk_across -ɫt -apsv
alongside her tracks; *and don't cross her tracks,*

iʔ sxʷúytəns 211 ixíʔ {pna kʷu k pna} pna kʷu kɫcawt 212 pna {kʷu}
iʔ s+xʷuy+tn -s ixíʔ pnaʔ kʷu kɫ+cawt pnaʔ
art track -3in then maybe 4kn effort maybe
either. *We might be able to do something,* *we might*

kʷu ksulqnáɫq 213 cut way̓, way̓ ixíʔ ɫ akɫcəwcín 214 way̓
kʷu k+s+wl=qn=aɫq cut way̓ way̓ ixíʔ ɫ a -kɫ -cw=cin way̓
4kn have_a_chance say yes yes that one_that 2i -to_be -talk well
get the best of them." *He said "Now you are talking." 26:00* *He*

ck̓əɫk̓ʷƛ̓álqsəms axá iʔ 215 way̓ xiʔ ctxəlákəlx tl
c -k̓ɫ+k̓ʷƛ̓=alqs+m -s axáʔ iʔ way̓ ixíʔ c+t+xlak -lx tl̓
act -take_from_under_clothes -3erg this art well then go_around_cisl -pl from
took from under his clothes... [tape ends].[11] *They came around from around*

aʔ cxəlkíʔs 216 ixíʔ stxəlákəlx tl aʔ cxəlkíʔs uɫ xiʔ
aʔ c+xlk+iʔs ixíʔ s[12] -t+xlak -lx tl̓ aʔ c+xlk+iʔs uɫ ixíʔ
art turn_around then ? -turn_back -pl from art turn_around and then
the swamp. *They turned around and his partner*

cúntəm i t slax̌ts 217 huhúy kʷ sc̓kinx
cu -nt -m iʔ t s+l̓ax̌+t -s hu+húy kʷ sc -ʔkin -x
tell -nt -psv art agInst friend -3in OK 2kn ipftvp^ -indef -^ipftv
said to him: *"What is the matter with you?*

218 uɫ way̓ uɫ {ɫcmiw} cmiw̓súlaʔxʷ uɫ way̓ ɫtkícəntəm iʔ
uɫ way̓ uɫ c+miw̓s=úlaʔxʷ uɫ way̓ ɫ+t+kic -nt -m iʔ
and yes and half_way_cisl and yes meet_with_again -nt -4erg art
She had [already] come half way [back] when we met our opppontent

ʔawtústət 219 uɫ axáʔ t̓iʔ {kʷu c} kʷu cmúmsxnəm 220 uɫ way̓
ʔaw+t=ús -tt uɫ axáʔ t̓iʔ kʷu c -mu•ms=xn+m uɫ way̓
opponent -4in and this evid 4kn hab -drag_feet and yes
again, *and we are dragging our feet?* *We*

10 The sequence of suffixes is not clear. +x may be =x(n).

11 Usually Pete announces that he is "splicing" his story. This time he retraces the steps of his story without the announcement.

12 Possibly for c- *cisl.*

ťiʔ kʷu kɬƛ̓axʷt {uɬ kʷu ɬ} cmistím uɬ kʷu ƛ̓axʷt 221 uɬ lut
ťiʔ kʷu kɬ -ƛ̓axʷ+t c -my+st -im uɬ kʷu ƛ̓axʷ+t uɬ lut
evid 4kn to_be -dead_pl cust^ -know -4erg and 4kn dead_pl and not
are going to die, we know we are going to die. *And you*

asc̓axknəmscút 222 cut lut, pna anwí kʷ scmilsmístx
a -sc -ʔax+kn+m+scút cut lut pnaʔ anwí kʷ sc -mils+míst -x
2i -pftv -do_something say not maybe you 2kn ipftvp^ -make_plan -^ipftvp
don't try to do anything." *He said "No, maybe you' ll think about what to do."*

223 cut lut, waẏ ťiʔ kʷ iscqpám 224 aɬíʔ kʷ inx̌mínk,
cut lut waẏ ťiʔ kʷ i -sc -qpa+m aɬíʔ kʷ in -x̌m=ink
say not yes evid 2kn 1i -pftv -predicament because 2kʷu 1in -like
He said "No, I'm just going to stick by you, *because I like you, you're*

kʷ isláx̌t 225 uɬ waẏ cmistín kʷu kɬƛ̓axʷt
kʷ i -s+ľax̌+t uɬ waẏ c -my -st -in kʷu kɬ -ƛ̓axʷ+t
2kʷu 1i -friend and yes cust^ -know -^cust -1erg 4kn to_be -dead_pl
my friend. 1:00 *And I know we're going to die.*

226 uɬ aɬíʔ kʷ iscqpám kiʔ ckəxəntsín 227 uɬ
uɬ aɬíʔ kʷ i -sc -qpa+m kiʔ c -kx+n -t -s -in uɬ
and so 2kʷu 1i -pftv -predicament rel act -follow -nt -2obj -1erg and
But I was going to stick with you, that's why I came with you. *And*

waẏ anwí, waẏ anwí kchámstmən, mat waẏ kʷ
waẏ anwí waẏ anwí k+cha+m -st -m -n mat waẏ kʷ
yes you yes you facing -caus -2obj -1erg maybe yes 2kn
you, I'll put you before me, maybe you can do

smilsmístx 228 cus waẏ, waẏ kʷaʔ 229 waẏ
s -mils+míst -x cu -s waẏ waẏ kʷaʔ waẏ
ipftv^ -figure -^ipftv tell -3erg yes yes intj yes
something." *He said "Ok."* *He*

ck̓əɬk̓ʷƛ̓alqsəms {arc} ck̓əɬẇálqsəms iʔ {c}
c -k̓ɬ+k̓ʷƛ̓=alqs+m -s c -k̓ɬ+ɬw=alqs+m -s iʔ
act take_from_under_clothes -3erg act -pull_from_under_clothes -3erg art
took something wrapped up from under

ckəl·k̓íc̓aʔ 230 ixíʔ tk̓ʷí··xʷc̓aʔs ixíʔ 231 utəntís
c -k+lk̓=íc̓aʔ ixíʔ t+k̓ʷixʷ=c̓aʔ -s ixíʔ wt -nt -is
hab -bundle then unwrap -3erg that put_down -nt -3erg
his clothes, *he unwrapped it.* *He put it down, he got done*

wiʔstk̓ʷíxʷc̓aʔs 232 ilíʔ cənṗəṗníla?k̓, {tist} a[xáʔ] stəx̌ʷslíṗ,
wẏ+s+t+k̓ʷixʷ=c̓aʔ -s ilíʔ c -n+ṗ•ṗn=ílaʔk̓ axáʔ s+tx̌ʷ+s+liṗ
finish_unwrapping -3erg there hab -put_down_sticks this plain_wood
unwrapping it. *There are sticks there, just common*

sx̌əx̌c̓íʔ t̓əxʷ 233 ixíʔ nák̓ʷəm a ckəl·k̓íc̓aʔ {cut a cus cúntəm s} 234 cus
s+x̌•x̌c̓iʔ t̓xʷ ixíʔ nak̓ʷ+m a c -k+lk̓+ícaʔ cu -s
stick emph that evid art hab -bundle tell -3erg
wood sticks. That's what's wrapped up. He said

iʔ sl̓ax̌ts way̓ axáʔ {i a} ia ct̓k̓ʷílsmstən ki
iʔ s+l̓ax̌+t -s way̓ axáʔ iʔ c -t̓k̓ʷ=ils+m -st -n kiʔ
art friend -3in well this art cust^ -depend_on -^cust -1erg rel
to his partner, "That's what I depend on, that's

inksysyústən 235 t̓əxʷ axáʔ ṅíṅw̓iʔ lut kʷu kənxítəm, uɬ way̓
in -k+sy•sy=us+tn t̓xʷ axáʔ ṅíṅw̓iʔ lut kʷu kn+xit -m uɬ way̓
1in -power emph this a_while not 3e4obj help -3e4obj and yes
my power. 2:08 If this doesn't help us, we are

t̓iʔ kʷu ƛ̓axʷt 236 uɬ ixíʔ náx̌əmɬ iʔ {k} kʷ iksc̓x̌ʷám
t̓iʔ kʷu ƛ̓axʷ+t uɬ ixíʔ nax̌mɬ iʔ kʷ i -ks -c̓x̌ʷa+m
evid 4kn dead_pl and that but art 2kʷu 1i -futi -instruct
dead. And that's what I'm going to preach to you:

237 lut {aks akstk̓ʷít̓xəm} [aks]tk̓ʷít̓xəlxəmɬtəm axáʔ iʔ ʔawtústət
lut a -ks -t+k̓ʷit̓=x+lx+m -ɬt -m axáʔ iʔ ʔaw+t=ús-tt
not 2i -futi -walk_across -ɬt -apsv this art opponent-4in
you mustn't step over our opponent's

iʔ sxʷúytəns 238 way̓ t̓i niʕíp t {aɬ} tk̓əmɬníwts {mi} mi kʷ cxʷuy
iʔ s+xʷuy+tn -s way̓ t̓iʔ nyʕip t t+km=ɬniwt -s mi kʷ c+xʷuy
art track -3in well evid always obl alongside -3in fut 2kn come
tracks. Stay always on one side,

239 məɬ axáʔ incá ṅíṅw̓iʔ {təl} t k̓əlsq̓ʷút 240 c̓x̌iɬt
mɬ axáʔ in+cá ṅíṅw̓iʔ t k̓l+s+q̓ʷut[13] c+ʔx̌iɬ+t
and this I a_while obl other_side like
and I on the other side. That's what I am telling you:

txəmníw̓stəm 241 lut {ks t ks} kstk̓ʷít̓xəlxəmɬtəm iʔ
t+xmn=iw̓s -t -m lut ks -t+k̓ʷit̓=x+lx+m -ɬt -m iʔ
each_side -st -4erg not futt^ -walk_across -ɬt -4erg art
we're on each side of her, we won't cross her

sxʷúytən[s] 242 ixíʔ mi {kʷu} kʷu xʷəl·xʷált {lut} 243 náx̌əmɬ
s+xʷuy+tn -s ixíʔ mi kʷu xʷl·•xʷal+t nax̌mɬ
track -3in that fut 4kn alive_pl but
tracks. That's how we stay alive. But

tk̓ʷít̓xəlxəmɬtəm {iʔ} iʔ sxʷúytəns {uɬ} 244 uɬ kʷu
t+k̓ʷit̓=x+lx+m -ɬt -m iʔ s+xʷuy+tn -s uɬ kʷu
walk_across -ɬt -4erg art track -3in then 3e4obj
if we step over her tracks 3:02 my

13 I have not analyzed k̓l‿s+q̓ʷut because t‿ precedes it.

k̓ax̌əlməncútməntəm axáʔ i t istməlscút 245 uɬ
k+ʔax̌l+mncút+m -nt -m axáʔ iʔ t i -s+tm̓=lscut uɬ
turn_against -nt -3e4obj this art agInst 1in -beads and
good luck charm will go against us *and*

mnímɬtət {kʷu kʷu} kʷu ƛ̓axʷt {kʷu inaud} 246 waỷ ixíʔ
mnimɬ+tt kʷu ƛ̓axʷ+t waỷ ixíʔ
we 4kn dead_pl well then
we will die.” *He*

np̓núɬtəm axáʔ iʔ ƛ̓ax̌t axáʔ iʔ sxʷúytəns axáʔ {i l s i l s}
n+p̓n -uɬt -m axáʔ iʔ ƛ̓ax̌+t axáʔ iʔ s+xʷuy+tn -s axáʔ
put_long_objs_down -ɬt -psv this art fast this art track -3in this
put [sticks] down in the racer’s tracks,

i l naqs i l sqəl̓wítəms 247 ilíʔ nmáʕʷsəs axáʔ iʔ
iʔ l naqs iʔ l s+ql=wit+m -s ilíʔ n+maʕ=w̓s -s axáʔ iʔ
art in one art in footprints -3in there place_across -3erg this art
footprints. *He put one of the little sticks*

n̓əqsálaʔqʷ 248 uɬ itlíʔ naqs iʔ stxʷárqəns k̓əl sq̓ʷut 249 ixíʔ
n̓qs=álaʔqʷ uɬ itlíʔ naqs iʔ s+t+xʷar=qn -s k̓l s+q̓ʷut ixíʔ
stick_dim and from_there one art reach -3in to across then
across it *and then another on the other side.* *He*

nixʷ nmáʕwsəs 250 i·· waỷ ixíʔ xʷuy xʷuy {i} itlíʔ
nixʷ n+maʕ=w̓s -s i·· waỷ ixíʔ xʷuy xʷuy itlíʔ
also place_across -3erg intj well then time_go_by time_go_by from_there
also put one across there. *Then they started to run again,*

xítmiʔst {li} t̓i cícəlmiʔstəlx 251 xʷu··ylx, waỷ k̓əɬk̓ʷíƛ̓ptəlx
xít+miʔst t̓iʔ cí•cl+miʔst -lx xʷuy -lx waỷ k̓ɬ+k̓ʷiƛ̓+p+t -lx
run evid trot_slowly -pl go -pl yes come_in_sight -pl
they trotted. *They went and they came in sight. 4:02*

252 aʔ mu··t {ai} iʔ ʔawtúscəlx a[xáʔ] iʔ st̓aʔk̓míx 253 aỷ, aỷ cut
aʔ mut iʔ ʔaw+t=ús -c -lx axáʔ iʔ s+t̓aʔk̓+míx aỷ aỷ cut
intj sit_sg art opponent -3in -pl this art virgin intj intj say
Their opponent, the virgin, was sitting down. *His friend*

axáʔ iʔ slax̌ts 254 stim̓ mat qicks, kəm̓ mat
axáʔ iʔ s+l̓ax̌+t -s stim̓ mat qick -s km̓ mat
this art friend -3in something maybe older_brother -3in or maybe
said, *maybe it’s the older brother, maybe*

síncaʔs 255 axáʔ mat qicks 256 cus waỷ
síncaʔ -s axáʔ mat qick -s cu -s waỷ
younger_brother -3in this maybe older_brother -3in tell -3erg well
the younger brother... *Maybe the older brother:* *“What’s the matter*

uɬ {a} sc̓kinx a[xáʔ] iʔ ʔawtústət axáʔ nʔamtáqs 257 ha
uɬ sc -ʔkin -x axáʔ iʔ ʔaw+t=ús -tt axáʔ n+ʔam=t=áqs haʔ
and ipftvp^ -indef -^ipftvp this art opponent -4in this sit_on_road inter
with our opponent that she’s sitting in the middle of the road, *is*

mat kʷu sck̓əɬʔím·[14] 258 uɬ mat t̓iʔ kʷu sckákʔam·[15]
mat kʷu sc -k̓ɬ+ʔim•m uɬ mat t̓iʔ kʷu sc -ká•kaʔ+m
maybe 3e4obj nom -be_waited and maybe evid 4kn nom -be_made_fun_of
she waiting for us? *She must be making fun of us.*

259 ilíʔ kʷu əɬ ck̓əɬʔímstəm 260 {i·· uɬ itlíʔ c} ixíʔ uɬ
ilíʔ kʷu ɬ c -k̓ɬ+ʔim -st -m ixíʔ uɬ
there 3e4obj if cust^ -wait_for -^cust -3e4obj then and
Why would she wait for us?" *Because*

aɬíʔ t̓i scícəlmiʔstəlx axáʔ {i s} iʔ sx̌ʷƛ̓iʔ 261 way̓
aɬíʔ t̓iʔ s -cí•cl+miʔst -lx axáʔ iʔ s+x̌ʷƛ̓iʔ way̓
because evid hab -trot_slowly -pl this art goat yes
the Goats were just trotting. *They*

kícsəlx {uɬ iɬ}, way̓ ksəx̌əntísəlx 262 uɬ t̓iʔ
kic -s -lx way̓ k+sx̌+n -t -is -lx uɬ t̓iʔ
reach_st/sb -3erg -pl yes move_past -nt -3erg -pl and evid
got to her, they passed her. 5:03 *The girl,*

nʕayúsəntməlx axáʔ iʔ t st̓aʔk̓míx iʔ t ƛ̓ax̌t 263 uɬ niʕ̓íp
n+ʕay=us -nt -m -lx axáʔ iʔ t s+t̓aʔk̓+míx iʔ t ƛ̓ax̌+t uɬ nyʕ̓ip
smile_at -nt -psv -pl this art agInst virgin art agInst fast and always
the foot racer, gave them a pretty smile. *She didn't*

lut t̓ yúmiʔst ɬə kstiɬxs 264 {inaud} [itlíʔ]
lut t̓ yúm̓+miʔst ɬ ks -tiɬx -s itlíʔ
not negfac move subord futi -stand -3i from_there
move even to stand. *They*

ksx̌əntísəlx 265 uɬ ixíʔ scuts axáʔ {iʔ} iʔ knaqs,
k+sx̌+n -t -is -lx uɬ ixíʔ s -cut -s axáʔ iʔ k=naqs
move_past -nt -3erg -pl and then nom -say -3i this art one_person
passed her. *One of them said,*

mat {iʔ s} iʔ snəx̌ʷnəx̌ʷílsx 266 t̓əxʷ axáʔ {yakɬ} ia kstməlscút
mat iʔ s -nx̌ʷ•nx̌ʷ=ils -x t̓xʷ axáʔ iʔ k+s+tm̓=lscut
maybe art ipftv^ -want_wife -^ipftv evidently this art have_beads
maybe the one that wanted her, *the one that had the amulet,*

267 cut uɬ sc̓kinx uɬ haʔ ɬksəx̌əntím {i s} iʔ ʔawtústət
cut uɬ sc -ʔkin -x uɬ haʔ ɬ+k+sx̌+n -t -im iʔ ʔaw+t=ús -tt
say and ipftvp^ -indef -^ipftvp and inter pass_again -nt -4erg art opponent -4in
he said "How is it that we passed our opponent?

268 {mat} mat_laʔkín sc̓kinx 269 uɬ way̓ t̓iʔ x̌ast ɬə
mat_la+ʔkín sc -ʔkin -x uɬ way̓ t̓iʔ x̌as+t ɬ
somehow ipftvp^ -indef -^ipftvp and yes evid good if
There must be something the matter. *And it's better we wait for her,*

14 The suffix -s *3i* is expected here.
15 Length not clear.

k̓əɬʔíməntəm kʷu ɬ p̓əlk̓úsəm ɬ mipnúntəm sc̓kinx
k̓ɬ+ʔim -nt -m kʷu ɬ p̓lk̓=us+m ɬ my+p -nu -nt -m sc -ʔkin -x
wait_for -nt -4erg 4kn if turn_back if learn -manage -nt -4erg ipftvpˆ -indef -ˆipftv
we turn back, we find out what's wrong." 6:00

270 {a cus i} cúntəm iʔ t slax̌ts staʔk lut 271 kʷu ɬaʔ
cu -nt -m iʔ t s+ɬ̓ax̌+t -s staʔk lut kʷu ɬaʔ
tell -nt -psv art agInst friend -3in intj not 4kn when
His partner said "No sir. *We*

caʔkʷ {a} kʷa {m} mnímɬtət {kʷu} t̓iʔ kʷu cmiw̓súlaʔxʷ iʔ k̓əl səntxəlktán
caʔkʷ kʷa mnimɬ+tt t̓iʔ kʷu c+miw̓s=úlaʔxʷ iʔ k̓l s+n+t+xlk+tan
should intj we evid 4kn half_way_cisl art to race_track
are half way around the turn around point

272 uɬ_iʔ kʷu tkícəntəm 273 way̓ uɬ t̓iʔ {kʷuk} kʷu
uɬ_iʔ kʷu t+kic -nt -m way̓ uɬ t̓iʔ kʷu
and_then 3e4obj meet -nt -3e4obj yes and evid 3e4obj
and she's already met us. *She's just making fun*

kʕ̓ʷəyncútməntəm 274 uɬ itlíʔ cxʷət̓pəncút {l uɬ t̓iʔ cniɬc}
k+ʕ̓ʷy+ncut+m -nt -m uɬ itlíʔ c -xʷt̓+p+ncut
laugh_at -nt -3e4obj and from_there hab -run
of us. *Then she'll keep on running.*

275 lut kʷu t̓a nq̓aʔílsməntəm 276 cut lut
lut kʷu t̓ n+q̓aʔ+ils+m -nt -m cut lut
not 3e4obj negfac have_business_with -nt -3e4obj say not
She won't even bother with us." *He said "No.*

277 way̓ {t̓əxʷ ixíʔ kʷu} iwá t̓əxʷ kʷu ksƛ̓axʷt 278 uɬ aɬíʔ way̓ t̓əxʷ
way̓ iwá t̓xʷ kʷu ks -ƛ̓axʷt uɬ aɬíʔ way̓ t̓xʷ
well even emph 4kn to_be -dead_pl and so yes emph
Even if we are going to die, *we are*

ksmipnúntəm {iʔ s} 279 way̓ k̓əxʷkʷúnəms iʔ slax̌ts, way̓
k+s -my+p -nu -nt -m way̓ k+ʔxʷ+kʷun+m -s iʔ s+ɬ̓ax̌+t -s way̓
futtˆ -learn -manage -nt -4erg well coax -3erg art partner -3in well
going to find out." *He coaxed his partner, they stopped,*

ƛ̓lapəlx way̓ ɬp'əlk'úsəməlx 280 uɬ niʕ̓íp ilíʔ mut axáʔ iʔ tkəɬmílxʷ
ƛ̓la+p -lx way̓ ɬ+p'lk'=us+m -lx uɬ nyʕ̓ip ilíʔ mut axáʔ iʔ tkɬmilxʷ
stop -pl well turn_back_again -pl and always there sit_sg this art woman
they turned back. *That girl is still sitting there.*

281 way̓ ɬkícsəlx 282 cúsəlx way̓ uɬ kʷ
way̓ ɬ+kic -s -lx cu -s -lx way̓ uɬ kʷ
well arrive_back -3erg -pl tell -3erg -pl well and 2kn
They got back to her. *They said to her "What's the matter*

sc̓kinx {uɬ ha i kʷ} ha kʷ sx̌ʷəc̓pxənmíxaʔx 283 ha kʷ
sc -ʔkin -x haʔ kʷ s -x̌ʷc̓+p=xn -míx+aʔx haʔ kʷ
ipftvpˆ -indef -ˆipftvp inter 2kn incpˆ -break -ˆincp inter 2kn
with you, did you break your leg? *What*

sxkinx 284 lut, way̓ t̓i cəncəkʷcəkʷkʷíɬxən iʔ {kʷu} kʷu
s -x+kin -x lut way̓ t̓iʔ c -n+ckʷ•ckʷ•kʷ=iɬ=xn iʔ kʷu
ipftvˆ -do -ˆipftv not well evid hab -leg_cramp art 1obj
happened to you?" 7:00 *"No, it's just leg cramps*

kics {uɬ i} 285 i·· uɬ lut t̓ qəɬnún itlíʔ
kic -s i·· uɬ lut t̓ qɬ -nu -n itlíʔ
reach_st/sb -3erg intj and not negfac able -manage -1erg from_there
that got to me *and I couldn't keep on*

nixʷ {iks} iksxʷúy 286 ixíʔ uɬ aláʔ iʔ kən {a} ʔam·útət 287 a··
nixʷ i -ks -xʷuy ixíʔ uɬ aláʔ iʔ kn ʔam•m=út•t a
more 1i -futi -go then and here art 1kn sit_down intj
going. *I just had to sit down."* *They*

way̓, {way̓ ixíʔ} ixíʔ nq̓əlxʷáx̌nəmsəlx txəmniw̓slíwtsəlx
way̓ ixíʔ n+q̓lxʷ=ax̌n+m -s -lx t+xmn=iw̓s=ɬniwt -s -lx
yes then hook_under_arm -3erg -pl both_sides -3erg -pl
hooked her under the arms, on both sides.

288 axáʔ uɬ itlíʔ cícəlmiʔstəlx 289 xʷu··ylx, uɬ aɬíʔ axáʔ sənk̓líp {kɬ}
axáʔ uɬ itlíʔ cí•cl+miʔst -lx xʷuy -lx uɬ aɬíʔ axáʔ s+n+k̓l̓=ip
this and from_there trot_slowly -pl go -pl and so this Coyote
They started trotting along. *They went. And Coyote had*

kɬʕác̓mən 290 uɬ aɬíʔ {li} niʕíp {c} əckƛ̓aʔƛ̓ʔúsəmsts {iʔ s} axáʔ
kɬ+ʕac̓+mn uɬ aɬíʔ nyʕip c -k+ƛ̓aʔ•ƛ̓ʔ=ús+m -st -s axáʔ
have_binoculars and so always custˆ -watch -ˆcust -3erg this
binoculars *and he's been watching the foot racers*

iʔ scq̓ʷəq̓ʷúƛ̓aʔxnaʔx 291 ho··y {ɬ} ɬyiʕápəlx 292 ha
iʔ sc -q̓ʷ•q̓ʷúƛ̓+aʔ=xn -aʔx hoy ɬ+yaʕ+p -lx haʔ
art ipftvpˆ -race -? well arrive_again -pl inter
all the time. *They got there. 8:03* *What's*

sc̓kinx xaʔ {a} iʔ sƛ̓əx̌sqáx̌aʔs {a} sənk̓líp 293 axáʔ t
sc -ʔkin -x axáʔ iʔ s+ƛ̓x̌=sqáx̌aʔ -s s+n+k̓l̓=ip axáʔ t
ipftvpˆ -indef -ˆipftvp this art race_horse -3in Coyote this agInst
the matter with Coyote's racer? *The two*

sənq̓əlq̓əlxʷáx̌nəmsəlx axáʔ iʔ t səncʔíw̓s 294 ixíʔ aɬíʔ put {cxaʔxaʔ t}
s+n+q̓l·q̓lxʷ=ax̌n+m -s -lx axáʔ iʔ t sncʔ=iw̓s ixíʔ aɬíʔ put
one_arm_in_arm -3in -pl this art agInst brothers then so just
brothers hooked her under her arms. *Then so...*

295 way̓ ixíʔ kstk̓ʷít̓xaʔxəlx iʔ t ɬp̓úlaʔxʷtən
way̓ ixíʔ ks -t+k̓ʷit̓=x -aʔx -lx iʔ t ɬp̓=úlaʔxʷ+tn
well then incpˆ -step_over -ˆincp -pl art obl border
Just before they crossed the finish line

296 ɬuníkstəmsəlx axáʔ {i} iʔ ƛ̓ax̌t iʔ st̓aʔk̓míx 297 ixíʔ sənk̓líp
ɬwn=ikst+m -s -lx axáʔ iʔ ƛ̓ax̌+t iʔ s+t̓aʔk̓+míx ixíʔ s+n+k̓l̓=ip
let_go_of -3erg -pl this art fast art virgin that Coyote
they dropped the fast girl, *Coyote's*

i? ƛ̓əx̌sqáx̌a?s, ɬuníkstəm[səlx] 298 a· uɬ t̓i? ilí? ɬpt̓aʕt̓
i? ƛ̓x̌=sqáx̌a? -s ɬwn=ikst+m -s -lx a uɬ t̓i? ilí? ɬ+p̓t̓•aʕt̓
art race_horse -3in let_go_of -3erg -pl intj and evid there fall_flat_again
race horse, they dropped her. *She fell down flat.*

299 ?ammútət aɬí lut̓ qəɬnús t cniɬc
?am•m=út•t aɬí? lut_t̓ qɬ -nu -s t cniɬ+c
sit_down because neg_emph accomplish -manage -3erg agInst (s)he
She sat down as she couldn't even

ksxʷists 300 səncəkʷcəkʷkʷíɬxən {uɬ axá? t̓i həɬ həɬ həɬ}[16] 301 i?
ks -xʷist -s s+n+ckʷ•ckʷ•kʷ=iɬ=xn i?
futi -walk -3i cramps art
walk, *she had cramps. 10:00* And

həɬsx̌ʷƛ̓í? {a nɬəxʷ} nɬəx̌ʷmíw̓səlx i t ɬp̓úla?xʷtən 302 i·· way̓
hɬ=s+x̌ʷƛ̓i? n+ɬx̌ʷ+m=iw̓(s) -s -lx i? t ɬp̓=úla?xʷ+tn i·· way̓
goat_group go_over -3erg -pl art obj_tr border intj well
the Goats went over the mark on the ground, the finish line. Coyote

cúntməlx t sənk̓líp 303 way̓, way̓ kʷu ƛ̓xʷupɬtp
cun -nt -m -lx t s+n+k̓l̓=ip way̓ way̓ kʷu ƛ̓xʷu+p -ɬt -p
tell -nt -psv -pl agInst Coyote yes yes 1obj win -ɬt -5erg
said to them: *"You won my daughter*

ist̓əmk?ílt 304 kʷu ƛ̓xʷupəntp 305 way̓ ixí? uɬ {pɬ pɬ}
i -s+t̓mk?=ilt kʷu ƛ̓xʷu+p -nt -p way̓ ixí? uɬ
1in -daughter 1obj beat -nt -5erg yes that and
from me." *"You beat me.* *You take her*

ɬxʷuystp 306 ixí? uɬ lut uɬ sənʕíc̓pəms sənk̓líp {s} i?
ɬ+xʷuy -st -p ixí? uɬ lut uɬ s -n+ʕic̓+p+m -s s+n+k̓l̓=ip i?
go_back -caus -5erg then and not and nom -argue_over -3i Coyote art
back." *Coyote didn't argue about*

sənx̌cípəms 307 kmix uɬ kmax̌qənmíst sənk̓líp 308 ixí? nc̓ayxʷápəlqs
s+n+x̌c=ip+m kmix uɬ k+mah=qn+míst s+n+k̓l̓=ip ixí? n+c̓ayxʷ=áplqs
bet only and give_up Coyote that end_of_story
his bet. *Coyote just gave up.* *That's*

nxixayápəlqs
n+xy•xay=áplqs
end_of_story
the end of the story. 10:47

16 Here is a long pause, then Pete chuckles and says "dang... simple word and I can't remember them goats, oh."

Lynx and the virgin

1 {a} xʷʔit iʔ sqilxʷ, uɬ {kɬya} kɬxaʔtúsəlx, kɬilmíxʷməlx {uɬ ə} 2 náx̌əmɬ
xʷʔi+t iʔ s+qilxʷ uɬ kɬ+xaʔt=ús -lx kɬ+yl=mixʷ+m -lx nax̌mɬ
many art person and have_leader -pl have_chief -pl but
There were lots of people and they had a leader, a boss, *but*

lut t’a cmiɬtín swit iʔ skʷists 3 ixíʔ xaʔtúscəlx
lut t’ c -my -ɬt -in swit iʔ s+kʷist -s ixíʔ xaʔt=ús -c -lx
not negfac custˆ -know -ɬt -1erg who art name -3in that leader -3in -pl
I don’t know his name. *He’s their leader,*

ia ilmíxʷəmsəlx 4 uɬ kst’əmkʔílt way̓ uɬ t’aʔk̓əmxəwílx 5 way̓ uɬ
iʔ yl=mixʷ+m -s -lx uɬ k+s+ť mkʔ=ilt way̓ uɬ t’aʔk̓+mx+wílx way̓ uɬ
art chief -3in -pl and have_daughter yes and maiden yes and
their boss, *and he had a daughter, she was in her puberty.* *His*

tkəɬmílxʷ iʔ st’əmkʔílts, uɬ swiʔnúmtx 6 níkna uɬ {iʔ} iʔ tuʔtw̓ít uɬ
tkɬmilxʷ iʔ s+ťmkʔ=ilt -s uɬ s+wy̓+numt=x níkxnaʔ uɬ iʔ tw̓•tw̓it uɬ
woman art daughter -3in and handsome goodness and art boys and
daughter is already a woman, and good looking, *and the boys and the young men*

iʔ splal iʔ scənsucənmístx iʔ k̓əl tkəɬmílxʷ uɬ iʔ k̓la
iʔ s+pl•al iʔ sc -n+sw=cn+mist -x iʔ k̓l tkɬmilxʷ uɬ iʔ k̓l
art young_growth art ipftvpˆ -propose -ˆipftvp art to woman and art to
are proposing for that girl to

ilmíxʷəm 7 uɬ {cútəlx} cúntməlx i ta ilmíxʷəm 8 aɬíʔ lut t
yl=mixʷ+m uɬ cun -t -m -lx iʔ t yl=mixʷ+m aɬíʔ lut t
chief and tell -nt -psv -pl art agInst chief so not agInst
the boss. *And the boss says to them:* *“I am not*

incá {ikst} iksk̓ʷínmʔam axáʔ ist’əmkʔílt 9 ńíńw̓iʔ
+cá i -ks -k̓ʷín=maʔ+m axáʔ i -s+ťmkʔ=ilt ńíńw̓iʔ
I 1i -futi -choose this 1in -daughter a_while
going to choose for my daughter 1:07 *if*

npútəlsəmɬmən {way̓ t’əxʷ} 10 way̓ məɬ iwá nmiʔcís axáʔ iʔ
n+put=ls+m -ɬm -n way̓ mɬ iwá n+my=ci -s axáʔ iʔ
be_satisfied_with -5obj -1erg well and to_no_avail interpret -3erg this art
I am satisfied with you.” *And he reported for nothing what*

sənsucənmístx {iʔ} 11 cus iʔ st’əmkʔílts 12 way̓ axáʔ kʷ
s -n+sw=cn+mist -x cu -s iʔ s+ťmkʔ=ilt -s way̓ axáʔ kʷ
ipftvˆ -propose -ˆipftv tell -3erg art daughter -3in well this 2kn
the suitors said. *He said to his daughter:* *“They are*

scənsucənmístx 13 náx̌əmɬ yaʔx̌í, pkʷúsəm yaʔx̌í iʔ
sc -n+sw=cn+mist -x nax̌mɬ yaʔx̌í pkʷ=us+m yaʔx̌í iʔ
ipftvpˆ -propose -ˆipftvp but that_one shake_head that_one art
proposing for you.” *But the woman would shake*

tkəłmílxʷ 14 cut lut, sťa?ḱmíx 15 lúti? kən ťa cənstíls ca?kʷ
tkłmilxʷ cut lut s+ťa?ḱ+míx lút+i kn ť c -n+st=ils ca?kʷ
woman say not virgin not_yet 1kn negfac hab -think should
her head, the virgin says "No, I haven't thought yet about

waẏ kən cmrim 16 uł waẏ ixí? slutx {ə} 17 ixí? cúntəm
waẏ kn c -mrim uł waẏ ixí? s -lut -x ixí? cu -nt -m
yes 1kn hab -marry and yes then ipftv^ -not -^ipftv then tell -nt -psv
marrying." And she refused. The boss

axá? i? {t} ta ilmíxʷəm 18 waẏ ałí?, waẏ cúntsən, waẏ ťi
axá? i? t yl=mixʷ+m waẏ ałí? waẏ cu -nt -s -n waẏ ťi?
this art agInst chief well because yes tell -nt -2obj -1erg yes evid
said to them: "I've told you, she's got to boss

cniłc spu?úsc 19 lut ť iksənləḱmníksəm {uł} 20 uł lut ť
cnił+c s+pu?=ús -c lut ť i -ks -n+lḱ+mn=iks+m uł lut ť
(s)he heart -3in not negfac 1i -futi -force and not negfac
her own self, I am not going to force her, 2:00 and I'm not

iksḱəłpa?x̌xítəm 21 hoy, ho··y uł txƛ̓ap i? sqilxʷ ilí? {i s}
i -ks -kł+pa?x̌ -xit -m hoy hoy uł t+xƛ̓a+p i? s+qilxʷ ilí?
1i -futi -deliberate -xit -apsv well well and complete art person there
going to do the thinking for her." The whole tribe

i? scənsucənmístx 22 hoy uł axá?, ḱim nałcəcám wápupxən
i? sc -n+sw=cn+mist -x hoy uł axá? ḱim nałc•c•ám wap•wp=xn
art ipftvp^ -propose -^ipftvp well and this but forget lynx
proposed, except (I forgot) Lynx who

i? lúti? {s} 23 uł ałí? skm̓əlsmístx wápupxən {uł i} i?
i? lút+i uł ałí? s -km=ls+mist -x wap•wp=xn i?
art not_yet and because ipftv^ -not_good_enough -^ipftv lynx art
hadn't yet... Lynx is not good enough, and he put himself

?íwtmi?st 24 uł lúti a cənsucənmíst 25 waẏ
?íwt+mi?st uł lút+i a c -n+sw=cn+mist waẏ
stay_behind and not_yet art hab -propose well
back, and doesn't propose. Lynx

ksḱəłpa?x̌x̌í?sts wápupxən 26 waẏ uł ałí? {ə ałí? uł ə} naḱʷá {s}
ks -kł+pa?x̌•x̌=í?st -s wap•wp=xn waẏ uł ałí? naḱʷá
futi -think_of_something -3i lynx well and because indeed_not
is going to think of something. They are not

suyápixəlx {ə ťəxʷ əs} 27 sqilxʷ {axá? i ac} axá? ła? kłcáwtəlx,
s+wyapy=x -lx s+qilxʷ axá? ła? kł -cawt -lx
white -pl Indian this the_one_that ła?_pos -doing -pl
white people, 3:02 that's the Indian way,

lut {ťəs} ť sáma? 28 uł sc̓x̌ilx uł wa?xútya? uł
lut ť sáma? uł sc+?x̌il+x uł wa?x=útya? uł
not negfac white_person and reason_why and dwelling_dim and
it isn't French. That's why they have tipis, buckskin tipis,

səp̓ʔíɬxʷəlx, cxʷúl̓ɬxʷ 29 uɬ aɬíʔ axáʔ {ks ə··} ksk̓əlxʷínaʔlx 30 məɬ {axáʔ}
sp̓iʔ=íɬxʷ -lx c+xʷul=ɬxʷ uɬ aɬíʔ axáʔ k+s+k̓lxʷ=ínaʔ -lx mɬ
tipi -pl tipi and so this have_evening -pl and
and tipis. *When night comes* *the chief*

axáʔ ilmíxʷəm {k̓ɬən} k̓əɬnəx̌p̓íps {i iə} a nxárcən 31 ixíʔ uɬ aɬíʔ
axáʔ yl=mixʷ+m k̓ɬ+n+x̌p̓=ip -s a n+xar+cn ixíʔ uɬ aɬíʔ
this chief fasten_door -3erg art curtain_in_front then and so
ties the curtain with a string *and*

laklís 32 uɬ aɬíʔ tla nixʷút {ki c} kiʔ ckʕacacstís
laklí -s uɬ aɬíʔ tla n+yxʷ=ut kiʔ c -k+ʕac•ʕac -st -is
lock -3erg and so from inside rel cust^ -tie -^cust -3erg
he locks it, *and he ties it from inside.*

33 ixíʔ uɬ lut_səwít ksnʔúɬxʷməntəm 34 uɬ aɬíʔ {k̓ʷnaʔ} k̓ʷnaʔ cəm̓
ixíʔ uɬ lut_swit ks -n+ʔuɬxʷ+m -nt -m uɬ aɬíʔ k̓ʷnaʔ cm̓
then and nobody futt^ -enter -nt -psv and because intj maybe
And nobody can get in. 4:02 *Because they might*

k̓əɬʔatətxnúm̓t axáʔ iʔ laʔɬ tkəɬmílxʷ 35 mi {c}
k̓ɬ+ʔat•t•x+númt axáʔ iʔ laʔɬ tkɬmilxʷ mi
fall_asleep this art with woman fut
fall in bed with the woman,

ckiʕamɬtíməlx iʔ st̓aʔk̓əmxíltsəlx 36 ixíʔ uɬ
c -k+yaʕ+m[1] -ɬt -im -lx iʔ s+t̓aʔk̓+mx=ílt -s -lx ixíʔ uɬ
cust^ -crawl_in_bed_with -ɬt -psv -pl art virgin_daughter -3in -pl that and
and they'll crawl in bed with the virgin. *That's why*

əctxət̓íltməlx 37 way̓ ixíʔ k̓əɬpaʔx̌x̌íʔst a wápupxən
c -t+xt̓=ilt+m -lx way̓ ixíʔ k̓ɬ+paʔx̌•x̌=íʔst a wap•wp=xn
hab -protect_child -pl well then think_of_something art lynx
they have to watch their daughter. *And Lynx thought of something.*

38 uɬ aɬíʔ ilíʔ ik̓líʔ mat {əc} cm̓il̓t wápupxən {uɬ} 39 uɬ way̓
uɬ aɬíʔ ilíʔ ik̓líʔ mat c -m̓il+t wap•wp=xn uɬ way̓
and so there there maybe hab -visit lynx and yes
I guess Lynx goes visiting over there *and*

wikɬts {i s} iʔ cítxʷsəlx 40 t̓əxʷ {i s} iʔ sənɬq̓ʷútənsəlx 41 uɬ
wik -ɬt -s iʔ citxʷ -s -lx t̓xʷ iʔ s+n+ɬq̓ʷ=ut+n -s -lx uɬ
see -ɬt -3erg art house -3in -pl evidently art bed -3in -pl and
he's seen the house *and their beds.* *And*

axáʔ {i} iʔ st̓aʔk̓míx {k̓la} k̓la niríp {t̓xʷ} k̓la nsək̓ʷtílp {ki c} kiʔ cɬq̓ilx
axáʔ iʔ s+t̓aʔk̓+míx k̓l n+yr=ip k̓l n+s+k̓ʷt=ilp kiʔ c -ɬq̓+ilx
this art virgin to back_of_tipi to across_bed rel hab -lie
the virgin, way in the back on one side is where she lays. 5:01

1 This analysis is uncertain.

42 uɬ axáʔ {i} ia ilmíxʷəm {kəl} axáʔ atláʔ iʔ təl̓ scənʔúɬxʷs
uɬ axáʔ iʔ yl=mixʷ+m axáʔ atláʔ iʔ tl̓ s -c+n+ʔuɬxʷ -s
and this art chief this from_here art from nom -enter_cisl -3i
And the boss, as soon as you get in the door

43 ilíʔ uɬ {k̓ɬən} kiʔ sənɬq̓ʷútənslx 44 uɬ aɬíʔ
ilíʔ uɬ kiʔ s+n+ɬq̓ʷ=ut+n -s -lx uɬ aɬíʔ
there and rel bed -3in -pl and so
that's where he lays. *They lay*

ck̓ɬənɬəq̓ʷluʔtíplx 45 uɬ aɬíʔ səstxət̓íltxəlx
c -k̓ɬ+n+ɬq̓ʷ=lut=íp -lx uɬ aɬíʔ s -t+xt̓=ilt -x -lx
hab -lie_in_front_of_door -pl and because ipftv^ -protect_child -^ipftv -pl
right in front of the door *because they got to watch her.*

46 way̓ ixíʔ ksk̓əlxʷínaʔlx 47 way̓ ixíʔ sʔawskiʕáms
way̓ ixíʔ k+s+k̓lxʷ=ínaʔ -lx way̓ ixíʔ s -ʔaw+s+kyáʕm -s
well then have_evening -pl well then nom -go_crawl_in_bed_with -3i
Night time comes. *That's when Lynx is going to crawl in bed*

wápupxən 48 xʷu··y ik̓líʔ uɬ aɬíʔ way t q̓sápiʔ sənkʷəkʷʔác
wap•wp=xn xʷuy ik̓líʔ uɬ aɬíʔ way̓ t q̓sápiʔ s+n+kʷ•kʷʔac
lynx go there and so well from long_ago night
with her. *He went there, it's long after dark*

49 aɬíʔ kʷaʔ {i s} iʔ sqílxʷ {i s} iʔ splal lut xʷus[2] t̓a
aɬíʔ kʷaʔ iʔ s+qilxʷ iʔ s+pl•al lut xʷus t̓
because intj art person art young_growth not early negfac
because the people, the young people don't go to bed

ċatxílxəlx {əy} 50 ksʔícəckiʔsəlx məɬ {q} q̓sápiʔ sənkʷkʷʔác
c -ʔatx+ílx -lx ks -ʔíc•c•kiʔ -s -lx mɬ q̓sápiʔ s+n+kʷ•kʷʔac
hab -sleep_pl -pl futi -play -3i -pl and long_time night
early. *They play, the last ones go to sleep*

ċíwtəlx mi_sic ʔatxílxəlx 51 way̓ csisiʕá··lxəlx 52 uɬ axáʔ
c+ʔiwt -lx mi_sic ʔatx+ílx -lx way̓ c -sy•sy+ʕalx -lx uɬ axáʔ
last -pl then sleep_pl -pl well hab -make_noise -pl and this
long after dark, *and they make all kinds of noise.* *And*

wápupxən way̓ i[xíʔ] sʔawskiʕáms 53 xʷu··y kɬaʔkn̓íɬxʷ
wap•wp=xn way̓ ixíʔ s -ʔaw+s+kyáʕm -s xʷuy k+ɬaʔ=kn̓=íɬxʷ
lynx well then nom -go_crawl_in_bed_with -3i go edge_of_house
Lynx went there to crawl in bed with her. 6:03 *He got right to the edge.*

54 way̓ k̓níʔams axáʔ {i} a ilmíxʷəm 55 way̓ cx̌ʷáq̓ʷəlqsəm a
way̓ k̓níyaʔ+m -s axáʔ a yl=mixʷ+m way̓ c -x̌ʷaq̓ʷ=lqs+m a
well listen -3erg this art chief yes hab -snore art
He listened for the chief. *The chief was snoring,*

2 This may be xʷust.

ilmíxʷəm, waỷ ʔitx 56 uɬ axáʔ {ḱla} iʔ ḱla nsəḱʷtílp iʔ ḱəl sťaʔḱmíx
yl=mixʷ+m waỷ ʔitx uɬ axáʔ iʔ ḱl n+s+ḱʷt=ilp iʔ ḱl s+ťaʔḱ+míx
chief yes sleep and this art to across_bed art to virgin
he's asleep. *He listened for the one on the other side,*

ixíʔ ḱníʔams 57 waỷ nixʷ cx̌ʷáq̓ʷəlqsəm 58 uɬ aɬíʔ nḱəḱaʔlícəň
ixíʔ ḱníyaʔ+m -s waỷ nixʷ c -x̌ʷaq̓ʷ=lqs+m uɬ aɬíʔ n+ḱ•ḱaʔlí=cn
that listen -3erg yes also hab -snore and so soft_talk
the girl. *She's snoring too.* *It's a soft sound*

ɬaʔ cx̌ʷáq̓ʷəlqsəm, lut č̓x̌iɬt iʔ t m̓ístəms 59 iʔ
ɬaʔ c -x̌ʷaq̓ʷ=lqs+m lut c+ʔx̌iɬ+t iʔ t m̓ist+m -s iʔ
when hab -snore not like art obj_č̓x̌iɬ w's_father -3in art
when she snores, not like her father; *her*

m̓ístəms talí nƛ̓əx̌cín ɬaʔ cx̌ʷáq̓ʷəlqsəm 60 waỷ {ḱəɬḱʷiʔi}
m̓ist+m -s taʔlíʔ n+ƛ̓x̌=cin ɬaʔ c -x̌ʷaq̓ʷ=lqs+m waỷ
w's_father -3in very_much loud when hab -snore well
father is very loud when he snores. *He figured*

əɬḱʷiʔínmaʔs, hoy ixíʔ stḱiwlxs 61 uɬ aɬíʔ mat iʔ l
ḱɬ+ḱʷ[ʔ]ín=maʔ -s hoy ixíʔ s -t+ḱiw+lx -s uɬ aɬíʔ mat iʔ l
figure_out -3erg well then nom -climb -3i and because maybe art for
where she would be, and started climbing. 7:06 *He must have had*

stḱiwlx {i} iʔ q̓aʔxáns 62 ixíʔ iʔ xʷuysts iʔ q̓aʔxáns
s+t+ḱiw+lx iʔ q̓aʔ=xán -s ixíʔ iʔ xʷuy+st -s iʔ q̓aʔ=xán -s
climbing art shoes -3in then art take_st -3erg art shoes -3in
climbing shoes. *He took his shoes,*

63 axáʔ {t} stḱiwlxs axáʔ iʔ t məlḱʷút {li·· ḱəl} 64 yaʔx̌í ḱla
axáʔ s -t+ḱiw+lx -s axáʔ iʔ t mlḱʷ=ut yaʔx̌í ḱl
this nom -climb -3i this art obl pole that_one to
he climbed on the tipi poles *right to*

nḱəmqníɬxʷ ilíʔ {ki c} kiʔ cƛ̓lpúlaʔxʷ 65 waỷ ixíʔ {s waỷ ixíʔ sc}
n+ḱm=qn=iɬxʷ ilíʔ kiʔ c -ƛ̓l+p=úlaʔxʷ waỷ ixíʔ
ceiling there rel hab -settle well then
the top of the tipi; he settled there. *Lynx*

scxʷəxʷc̓xínəms wápupxən 66 uɬ aɬíʔ axáʔ ncc̓əqqúsəs 67 uɬ
sc -xʷ•xʷc̓=xin+m[3] -s wap•wp=xn uɬ aɬíʔ axáʔ n+c+cq•q=ús+s uɬ
pftv -raise_leg -3i lynx and because this lie_head_up and
raised his leg. 8:23 *She was lying with her head up.* *It*

aɬíʔ ťi_č̓x̌iɬ {tsə ə·· ts} t suʔq̓ím 68 uɬ ťiʔ nkʷkʷl̓al axáʔ iʔ
aɬíʔ ťiʔ_č̓x̌iɬ t s+wq̓im uɬ ťiʔ n+kʷ•kʷl̓•al̓ axáʔ iʔ
because like obj_č̓x̌iɬ moonlight and evid light_dim this art
was like moonlight *and there was dim light*

3 =xin (for expected =xan) is otherwise unattested.

sxʷulɬxʷ {axʷ a} 69 xʷu¨y iʔ sxʷəxʷc̓xíns 70 uɬ aláʔ ncəqqúsəs iʔ
s+xʷul+ɬxʷ xʷuy iʔ s+xʷ•xʷc̓=xin -s uɬ aláʔ n+cq•q=us+s iʔ
tipi go art pee -3in and here face_up art
in the tipi. *His pee traveled.*[4] *The girl was there*

sťaʔk̓míx sáq̓əq̓cəns sc̓ítxəx 71 a put iʔ t məlk̓ʷút
s+ťaʔk̓+míx saq̓•q̓=cn -s sc -ʔitx -x a put iʔ t mlk̓ʷ=ut
virgin open_wide -3in ipftvp^ -sleep -^ipftvp intj just art agInst pole
head up mouth wide open; she was asleep. *The drop dropped*

itíʔ {k} t kcaʕwáp 72 nʕawpáɬq̓ʷəlt axáʔ {iʔ} iʔ sťaʔk̓míx,
itíʔ t k+caʕʷá+p n+ʕaw+p=áɬq̓ʷlt axáʔ iʔ s+ťaʔk̓+míx
from_that agInst dribble drip_in_mouth this art virgin
right down the pole, *it dropped in the virgin's mouth, it spilled in*

nc̓əxʷxʷáɬq̓ʷəlt 73 way̓ uɬ aɬíʔ q̓əmcínəm, uɬ lut ť
n+c̓xʷ•xʷ=aɬq̓ʷlt way̓ uɬ aɬíʔ q̓m=cin+m uɬ lut ť
spill_in_mouth yes and so swallow and not negfac
her mouth. 9:00 *And so she swallowed, and she never*

snanaqnúm̓ts {e¨ ɬ} 74 lut_sq̓sápiʔs {uɬ} way̓ uɬ ixíʔ səlxʷaʔtwílxs
s -na+naq+númt -s lut_s+q̓sápiʔ+s way̓ uɬ ixíʔ slxʷaʔ+t+wílx -s
nom -feel_full -3i not_long_after yes and then get_big -3i
felt anything. *Not long after that she started to get big.*

75 uɬ txəťťíʔst 76 uɬ axáʔ {n} nstils axáʔ iʔ sťaʔk̓míx uɬ ha
uɬ t+xť•ť=iʔst uɬ axáʔ n+st=ils axáʔ iʔ s+ťaʔk̓+míx uɬ haʔ
and pregnant and this think this art virgin and inter
She was carrying. *And the virgin thought, "And what is*

sc̓kinx ha 77 uɬ ťəxʷ nwaʔlílsmsəlx nixʷ ixíʔ iʔ t
sc+ʔkin+x haʔ uɬ ťxʷ n+waʔl=íls+m -s -lx nixʷ ixíʔ iʔ t
why_is_it inter and emph admire -3erg -pl also that art agInst
the matter?" *And her parents got puzzled*

ƛ̓ax̌əx̌ƛ̓ƛ̓x̌áps 78 way̓ ixíʔ suwsíwsəlx qʷaʔqʷaʔləmstísəlx {e}
ƛ̓x̌•x̌•ƛ̓x̌a+p -s way̓ ixíʔ sw•siw -s -lx qʷaʔ•qʷaʔl+m+st -is -lx
parents -3in well then ask_rep -3erg -pl interrogate -3erg -pl
too. *And they started asking her questions, put her on trial.*

79 cúsəlx iʔ sťəmkʔílts uɬ ha kʷ skícəms ha iʔ t
cu -s -lx iʔ s+ťmkʔ=ilt -s uɬ haʔ kʷ s -kic+m -s haʔ iʔ t
tell -3erg -pl art daughter -3in and inter 2kʷu nom -reach -3i inter art agInst
They asked her daughter "Did somebody get

sqilxʷ 80 ha uɬ{i kʷ}_iʔ kʷ txəťťíʔst 81 lu¨t 82 cúsəlx lut
s+qilxʷ haʔ uɬ_iʔ kʷ t+xť•ť=iʔst lut cu -s -lx lut
person inter and_then 2kn pregnant not tell -3erg -pl not
to you *that then you got pregnant?"* *"No".* *They said*

4 The form is not clear and it probably is a euphemism. The root seems to be √xʷc̓ *give*.

aksmálx̌aʔ 83 ixíʔ cut lut, uɬ sc̓kinx ha mi {kən ɬ} kən ɬ
a -ks -málx̌aʔ ixíʔ cut lut uɬ sc+ʔkin+x haʔ mi kn ɬ
2i -futi -lie then say not and why_is_it inter fut 1kn compl
"Don't lie." 10:02 *She said "No, and why should I make up*

cmál·x̌aʔ 84 uɬ caʔkʷ iwá kən ɬ mál·x̌aʔ uɬ way̓ kən
c -mál•l•x̌aʔ uɬ caʔkʷ iwá kn ɬ mál•l•x̌aʔ uɬ way̓ kn
hab -lie and if even 1kn if lie and yes 1kn
a lie? *And even if I did lie, I'd get caught*

ksmiʔpmíxaʔx 85 uɬ way̓ uníxʷ lut kʷu t̓a
ks -my+p -míx+aʔx uɬ way̓ wnixʷ lut kʷu t̓
incp^ -learn -^incp and yes true not 1obj negfac
anyway. *It's the truth,*

ckicsts iʔ t sqílxʷ 86 ilíʔ isknánaʔqs
c -kic -st -s iʔ t s+qilxʷ ilíʔ i -s -k=ná•naʔqs
cust^ -reach_st/sb -^cust -3erg art agInst person there 1i -nom -alone
no man ever got to me, *I have been alone."*

87 uɬ kʷa sc̓kinx {kʷa} kiʔ kʷ aɬ txət̓t̓íʔst 88 scutx uɬ
uɬ kʷa sc+ʔkin+x kiʔ kʷ aɬ t+xt̓•t̓=iʔst s -cut -x uɬ
and intj why_is_it rel 2kn compl pregnant ipftv^ -say -^ipftv and
"Well, how is it that you are carrying?" *She said,*

aɬíʔ {mat l} lut t̓a cmistín laʔkín {lut} 89 lut kʷu t̓a
aɬíʔ lut t̓ c -my -st -in la+ʔkíń lut kʷu t̓
so not negfac cust^ -know -^cust -1erg how not 1obj negfac
"Well, I don't know how. *Nobody got to me*

ckicsts {i t s} iʔ t sqilxʷ {ɬ iks} ɬ
c -kic -st -s iʔ t s+qilxʷ ɬ
cust^ -reach_st/sb -^cust -3erg art agInst person compl
for me to know

ikscminám ɬ ikstxət̓t̓íʔst 90 way̓, way̓
i -ksc -my+na+m ɬ i -ks -t+xt̓•t̓=iʔst way̓ way̓
1i -futPerfi -find_out if 1i -futi -pregnant well well
I am pregnant." *They got*

nwaʔlílsəmsəlx 91 ixíʔ uɬ lut_sq̓sápiʔs {way uɬ} hoy k̓ʷəl̓líl̓əlt
n+waʔl=íls+m -s -lx ixíʔ uɬ lut_s+q̓sápiʔ+s hoy k̓ʷl̓•l̓=il̓t
puzzle -3erg -pl then and not_long_after well child_born
puzzled. *It wasn't long a child was*

[k̓ʷəl̓lílt] 92 ixíʔ uɬ aɬíʔ kʷa swit smisqílxʷ a ilmíxʷəm
k̓ʷl̓•l̓=ilt ixíʔ uɬ aɬíʔ kʷa swit s+my+s+qilxʷ a yl=mixʷ+m
have_baby that and because intj somebody important_people art chief
born. 11:03 *Because the chief is way up in society*

93 uɬ kʷa nc̓íxc̓əxls 94 uɬ aɬíʔ cəm̓ kʕ̓ʷəy̓məncútmsəlx
uɬ kʷa n+c̓ix•c̓x=ls uɬ aɬíʔ cm̓ k+ʕ̓ʷy+mncut+m -s -lx
and intj shameful and because maybe laugh_about -3erg -pl
and it's shameful *and they might laugh about it,*

95 cəm̓ cútəlx way̓ a ilmíxʷəm {yə··} nt̓k̓ʷíltəm, 96 taʔxʷsqʷəsqʷsíʔ way̓
cm̓ cut -lx way̓ a yl=mixʷ+m n+t̓k̓ʷ=ilt+m taʔxʷ+s+qʷs•qʷsíʔ way̓
maybe say -pl well art chief have_a_baby get_baby yes
they might say "The boss got a child, *got a child who is*

təl̓ sl̓iksts 97 cəm̓ uɬ talí·· c̓ʔáxəlx {uɬ n} 98 ixíʔ uɬ k̓ʷul̓l̓
tl̓ sl̓=ikst -s cm̓ uɬ taʔlíʔ c̓[ʔ]ax -lx ixíʔ uɬ k̓ʷul̓•l̓
from bastard -3in maybe and very_much shame_inch -pl then and born
a bastard," *they might get ashamed.* *Then the baby*

axáʔ iʔ uʔx̌tílaʔt 99 ixíʔ uɬ nstils axáʔ ilmíxʷəm way̓
axáʔ iʔ w̓x̌t=ílaʔt ixíʔ uɬ n+st=ils axáʔ yl=mixʷ+m way̓
this art newborn then and think this chief well
was born. 12:00 *And the boss thought:*

100 {uɬ aɬíʔ way̓ t̓əxʷ} uɬ aɬí {lut} lut t̓a cmistím {iʔ} swit iʔ
uɬ aɬíʔ lut t̓ c -my+st -im swit iʔ
and so not negfac cust^ -know -4erg who art
"We don't know who

kɬƛ̓ax̌ƛ̓x̌áps {uɬ aɬí} 101 uɬ talí nixʷ kʷu c̓ʔax ɬə
kɬ -ƛ̓x̌•ƛ̓x̌a+p -s uɬ taʔlíʔ nixʷ kʷu c̓[ʔ]ax ɬ
to_be -parent -3i and very_much also 4kn shame_inch compl
his father is, *and also we are very ashamed*

kstxət̓ntím {ɬ ks} axáʔ iʔ st̓əmkʔíltət 102 uɬ way̓ t̓iʔ_x̌ast {ɬə}
ks -t+xt̓ -nt -im axáʔ iʔ s+t̓mkʔ=ilt -t uɬ way̓ t̓iʔ_x̌as+t
futt^ -watch_so -nt -4erg this art daughter -4in and yes as_well
to take care of our daughter. *It's better that*

ɬ xʷíc̓xməntəm 103 way̓ ixíʔ {s} st̓qʷcins {i s} iʔ səxʷwahwáhm
ɬ xʷic̓+x+m -nt -m way̓ ixíʔ s -t̓qʷ=cin -s iʔ sxʷ=wah•wáh+m
compl give_to -nt -4erg well then nom -holler -3i art announcer
we give her away." *The announcers started to holler.*

104 ixíʔ ɬ k̓laxʷ uɬ cútəlx way̓ x̌lítɬəms iʔ ta ilmíxʷəm
ixíʔ ɬ k̓laxʷ uɬ cut -lx way̓ x̌lit -ɬm -s iʔ t yl=mixʷ+m
then ? evening and say -pl well summon -5obj -3erg art agInst chief
In the evening they said, "The chief is calling you,

105 yaʕyáʕt iʔ p sqilxʷ, lut_ksluts 106 yaʕyáʕt {p}
yaʕ•yáʕ+t iʔ p s+qilxʷ lut_k+s+lut+s yaʕ•yáʕ+t
all art 5kn person there_is_no_no_about_it all
all of you people, there is no no about it. 13:02 *He is*

x̌lítɬəms {i} [ks]m̓ayxtwíxʷaʔx 107 kəm̓ {ks··} t sx̌ʷúsəm
x̌lit -ɬm -s ks -m̓ay+xt+wíxʷ -aʔx km̓ t s+x̌ʷus+m
summon -5obj -3erg incp^ -have_meeting -^incp or prttv foam_berry
asking all of you to have a meeting. *Or maybe you'll eat some*

p ksʔíɬnaʔx 108 way̓ {ə s} k̓ɬəmcínəlx iʔ sqilxʷ 109 way̓ ixíʔ
p ks -ʔiɬn -aʔx way̓ k̓ɬ+ʔm=cin -lx iʔ s+qilxʷ way̓ ixíʔ
5kn incp^ -eat -^incp well agree -pl art person well then
foam berries." *The people agreed.* *They got*

sx̌əcmənc̓útsəlx waẏ ixíʔ sxʷúẏysəlx 110 waẏ niʕ̓áʔlx {uɬ} uɬ
s -x̌c+mncut -s -lx waẏ ixíʔ s -xʷuẏ•y -s -lx waẏ n+yʔaʕ̓[5] -lx uɬ
nom -get_ready -3i -pl well then nom -go_pl -3i -pl well gather_in -pl and
ready, they all went. *They all are gathered*

aɬíʔ mat a nmásqən {a i} iʔ silmxʷíɬxʷ 111 uɬ aɬíʔ {s} sílxʷaʔ {əɬ əɬ}
aɬíʔ mat a n+mas=qn iʔ s+yl=mxʷ=iɬxʷ uɬ aɬíʔ sílxʷaʔ
so maybe art four_head art chief's_house and so big
there, and the chief's house is four tipis together, *it's big.*

112 kʷli··wt axáʔ iʔ sqilxʷ uɬ nxəl̓lákək 113 uɬ axáʔ iʔ la
kʷl=iwt axáʔ iʔ s+qilxʷ uɬ n+xl̓•l̓•ak•k uɬ axáʔ iʔ l
sit this art person and in_circle and this art in
The people sat down in a circle, *and right in the*

nq̓aqʔíẇs {uɬ uɬ axáʔ ilil} 114 aɬí uɬ sc̓iwtx wápupxən
n+q̓a•q̓ʔ=íẇs aɬíʔ uɬ sc -ʔiwt -x wap•wp=xn
center so and ipftvp^ -behind -^ipftvp lynx
center... [unfinished]14:06 *Lynx was the last one.*

115 axáʔ {i l s} iʔ l k̓ɬənk̓míp ilíʔ t̓i_kmix ilíʔ kiʔ cx̌əx̌áq
axáʔ iʔ l k̓ɬ+n+k̓m=ip ilíʔ t̓iʔ_kmix ilíʔ kiʔ c -x̌•x̌aq
this art at door there only there rel hab -empty_dim
There is only a little place by the door,

116 waẏ {ilíʔ uɬ} ilíʔ uɬ smuts wápupxən 117 waẏ
waẏ ilíʔ uɬ s -mut -s wap•wp=xn waẏ
well there and nom -sit_sg -3i lynx well
and Lynx sat there. *They*

wiʔsmáńxʷəlx waẏ cúntməlx i ta ilmíxʷəm 118 waẏ nak̓ʷá kʷu
wẏ+s+mańxʷ -lx waẏ cun -t -m -lx iʔ t yl=mixʷ+m waẏ nak̓ʷá kʷu
finish_smoking -pl well tell -nt -psv -pl art agInst chief well not 4kn
finished smoking, the chief said to them: *"It's not that*

kscaptíkʷlaʔx [nak̓ʷ]á kʷu ksəxkínaʔx {i} kiʔ x̌lítɬmən
ks -captíkʷl -aʔx nak̓ʷá kʷu ks -x+kin -aʔx kiʔ x̌lit -ɬm -n
incp^ -tell_stories -^incp not 4kn incp^ -do -^incp rel call -5obj -1erg
we are going to tell stories, or do something else that I called you.

119 waẏ {axáʔ} axáʔ ist̓əmkʔílt {waẏ ta} taʔxʷsqʷəsqʷsíʔ 120 uɬ iwá
waẏ axáʔ i -s+t̓mkʔ=ilt taʔxʷ+s+qʷs•qʷsíʔ uɬ iwá
well this 1in -daughter get_baby and to_no_avail
My daughter got a baby. 15:00 *And we*

síwəntəm swit iʔ kɬƛ̓əx̌ƛ̓x̌áps {uɬ} 121 uɬ ɬínəm, cut waẏ lut t̓a
siw -nt -m swit iʔ kɬ -ƛ̓x̌•ƛ̓x̌a+p -s uɬ ɬin+m cut waẏ lut t̓
ask -nt -4erg who art to_be -parent -3i and deny say well not negfac
asked her who its father is for nothing. *She denied it, she said*

5 Phonetics uncertain.

cmistín 122 lut{k}swit kʷu t̓a ckicsts
c -my -st -in lut_swit kʷu t̓ c -kic -st -s
cust^ -know -^cust -1erg nobody 1obj negfac cust^ -reach_st/sb -^cust -3erg
'I don't know, *no man*

iʔ t sqəl̓tmíxʷ 123 lut t̓a cmistín swit iʔ
iʔ t s+qlt=mixʷ lut t̓ c -my -st -in swit iʔ
art agInst man not negfac cust^ -know -^cust -1erg who art
got to me. *I don't know who*

kłƛ̓əx̌ƛ̓x̌áps 124 uł ixíʔ kən ksnx̌əstəlsmístaʔx kiʔ
kł -ƛ̓x̌•ƛ̓x̌a+p -s uł ixíʔ kn ks -n+x̌s+t=ls+mist -aʔx kiʔ
to_be -parent -3i and then 1kn incp^ -satisfy_self -^incp rel
its father is.' *And I am going to satisty myself, that's why*

x̌əlítłmən 125 uł ixíʔ swit ńíńw̓iʔ {i} 126 uł ałíʔ
x̌lit -łm -n uł ixíʔ swit ńíńw̓iʔ uł ałíʔ
call -5obj -1erg and then who a_while and because
I called you. *And when somebody... [unfinished]* *The baby*

yaʔx̌í {i sc} iʔ uʔx̌tílaʔt {t̓i uł i} scacacáʕs 127 swit ńíńw̓iʔ mi
yaʔx̌í iʔ w̓x̌t=ílaʔt s -ca•ca•cáʕ -s swit ńíńw̓iʔ mi
that_one art newborn nom -holler -3i who a_while fut
is crying. *Whoever holds it*

xʷaʔntís k̓əwáp 128 uł {ixíʔ} ixíʔ nák̓ʷəm łaʔ ksqʷəsqʷsíʔ
xʷaʔ -nt -is k̓wa+p uł ixíʔ nak̓ʷ+m łaʔ k+s+qʷs•qʷsiʔ
pick_up -nt -3erg quiet and that evid the_one_that have_son
and it stops, *that's his son, he takes*

ixíʔ uł kʷis ist̓əmkʔílt 129 way̓ ixíʔ {s} níkxnaʔ {way̓ ixíʔ ə¨ s}
ixíʔ uł kʷi -s i -s+t̓mkʔ=ilt way̓ ixíʔ níkxnaʔ
that and take -3erg 1in -daughter well then goodness
my daughter." 16:03 *The people*

sxʷʔíltəmsəlx iʔ sqílxʷ {i ya i tla ck̓əł inaud} 130 itlíʔ uł
s -xʷʔ=ilt+m -s -lx iʔ s+qilxʷ itlíʔ uł
nom -hold_baby -3i -pl art person from_there and
started holding the baby. *They went*

cənxəlkmstísəlx 131 ak̓láʔ sənk̓líp kcahhám məł {indec}
c -n+xlk+m -st -is -lx ak̓láʔ s+n+k̓l̓=ip k+cah•há+m mł
cust^ -go_in_circle -^cust -3erg -pl here Coyote have_turn and
in a circle. *It was Coyote's turn and he held the baby,*

cxʷíltəm, iwá łaʔ cyáʕtkstms {indec} 132 nt̓a məł sic yaʔx̌í iʔ
cxʷ=ilt+m iwá łaʔ c -yaʕ+t=kst+m -s nt̓a mł sic yaʔx̌í iʔ
hold_child try_to if cust^ -all_kinds -3erg intj and then that_one art
he tried to humor it. *The child*

sk̓ʷk̓ʷíməlt t̓kap c̓qʷaqʷ {məł} 133 way̓ uł ixíʔ ncaq̓ʷs {i ta} iʔ t
s+k̓ʷ•k̓ʷiy=m̓+l̓t t̓ka+p c̓qʷ•aqʷ way̓ uł ixíʔ n+caq̓ʷ -s iʔ t
child cry (?) cry well and then stick_in -3erg art agInst
cries and cries. *He sticks his index finger*

cúq̓ʷmaʔs 134 ixíʔ uɬ {ks} ksk̓əwpmíxaʔx {wa} iʔ sk̓ʷk̓ʷíməlt {ta}
cúq̓ʷ=maʔ -s ixíʔ uɬ ks -k̓wp -míx+aʔx iʔ s+k̓ʷ•k̓ʷiy=m̓+l̓t
index_finger -3in then and incpˆ -stop_talking -ˆincp art child
[in its mouth] so the baby will be quiet. 17:00

135 uɬ lut yaʔx̌í iʔ sk̓ʷk̓ʷíməlt 136 way̓ t̓iʔ_wim̓ uɬ cúsəlx
uɬ lut yaʔx̌í iʔ s+k̓ʷ•k̓ʷiy=m̓+l̓t way̓ t̓iʔ_wim̓ uɬ cu -s -lx
and not that_one art child well powerless and tell -3erg -pl
But no the baby. The people tried

yaʔx̌í iʔ t sqilxʷ 137 way̓ uyá tkʷpxíxməntxʷəlx iʔ {qʷs}
yaʔx̌í iʔ t s+qilxʷ way̓ uyá t+kʷp+xix+m -nt -xʷ -lx iʔ
that_one art agInst person well intj pass_along -nt -2erg -pl art
to tell him. "Coyote,

sqʷəsqʷsíʔsəlx əxʷ sənk̓líp {a ɬ} 138 lut akskəwápəp, {tkʷpxitx}
s+qʷs•qʷsiʔ -s -lx əxʷ s+n+k̓l̓=ip lut a -ks -kwap•p
child -3in -pl intj Coyote not 2i -futi -dog
pass their child on, don't be a dog,

tkʷpxíxmənt 139 way̓ itlíʔ xʷíc̓xəms 140 way̓ itlíʔ
t+kʷp+xixm -nt way̓ itlíʔ xʷic̓+x+m -s way̓ itlíʔ
pass_along -nt well from_there give_to -3erg well from_there
pass it on." Then he gave it to them. They took it

kʷíɬtsəlx sənk̓líp, {məɬ} məɬ itlíʔ k̓əl knaqs 141 məɬ axáʔ
kʷi -ɬt -s -lx s+n+k̓l̓=ip mɬ itlíʔ k̓l k=naqs mɬ axáʔ
take -ɬt -3erg -pl Coyote and from_there to one_person and this
from Coyote, and then to another, and

sənk̓líp ɬtxlak nxəlkíkiʔsəlx iʔ sqilxʷ {ik̓líʔ k̓əl k̓əl xaʔt unfin}
s+n+k̓l̓=ip ɬ+t+xlak n+xlk=íkiʔ -s -lx iʔ s+qilxʷ
Coyote around_again pass_around -3erg -pl art person
Coyote goes back around another person

142 ik̓líʔ məɬ ɬtmut[6] 143 axáʔ məɬ ɬckícxsəlx axáʔ iʔ
ik̓líʔ mɬ ɬ+t+mut axáʔ mɬ ɬ+c+kic+x -s -lx axáʔ iʔ
there and sit_again this and arrive_cisl_again -3erg -pl this art
and sits down again.[7] Then the baby

sk̓ʷk̓ʷíməlt 144 məɬ ixíʔ ɬxʷʔíltmsəlx 145 məɬ cúsəlx
s+k̓ʷ•k̓ʷiy=m̓+l̓t mɬ ixíʔ ɬ+xʷʔ=ilt+m -s -lx mɬ cu -s -lx
child and then hold_child_again -3erg -pl and tell -3erg -pl
comes back and he takes it again. And they say

sənk̓líp uɬ ha kʷ sk̓ʷənɬxʷʔíltaʔx ha {ɬ way̓} 146 way̓ kʷ
s+n+k̓l̓=ip uɬ haʔ kʷ s -kʷn+ɬ+xʷʔ=ilt -aʔx haʔ way̓ kʷ
Coyote and inter 2kn incpˆ -hold_baby_indef -ˆincp inter yes 2kn
"Coyote, how many times are you holding it? You've

6 t+ is not understood.
7 To get another turn at holding the baby. He wants the young woman.

xʷʔíltəm {lut} 147 ho··y uɬ txƛ̓ápəlx nxəl̓ákəkəlx 148 way̓
xʷʔ=ilt+m hoy uɬ t+xƛ̓a+p -lx n+xl̓•l•ak•k -lx way̓
hold_baby well and complete -pl in_circle -pl well
already held him." 18:05 *They all went around.* *Nobody*

lut_swit k̓əwpstísəlx iʔ sk̓ʷk̓ʷíməlt {cúsəlx a} 149 cúntməlx
lut_swit k̓wp -st -is -lx iʔ s+k̓ʷ•k̓ʷiy=m̓+l̓t cun -t -m -lx
nobody stop_talking -caus -3erg -pl art child tell -nt -psv -pl
made the baby be quiet. *The boss*

iʔ ta ilmíxʷəm 150 ha way̓ ha p txƛ̓ap 151 way̓, cútəlx, way̓,
iʔ t yl=mixʷ+m haʔ way̓ haʔ p t+xƛ̓a+p way̓ cut -lx way̓
art agInst chief inter yes inter 5kn complete yes say -pl yes
asked them: *"Did you all [hold him]?"* *"Yes," they said,*

mat kʷu txƛ̓ap 152 way̓ kʷu nxəl̓ákək {ə ɬə ilíʔəlx} 153 ilíʔ náx̌əmɬ lut
mat kʷu t+xƛ̓a+p way̓ kʷu n+xl̓•l•ak•k ilíʔ nax̌mɬ lut
maybe 4kn complete yes 4kn in_circle there but not
"Yes, we all did, *we've gone around."* *I don't know who*

t̓a {ɬ} cmistín swit {iʔ k̓am} iʔ tk̓ík̓ətməntəm wápupxən iʔ
t̓ c -my -st -in swit iʔ t+k̓i•k̓t+m -nt -m wap•wp=xn iʔ
negfac cust^ -know -^cust -1erg who art be_near -nt -psv lynx art
the one next to Lynx was,

l k̓ɬənk̓míp 154 ah, ixíʔ cut ixíʔ iʔ {s} tk̓ík̓tməntəm wápupxən
l k̓ɬ+n+k̓m=ip ah ixíʔ cut ixíʔ iʔ t+k̓i•k̓t+m -nt -m wap•wp=xn
at door intj that say that art be_near -nt -psv lynx
by the door, *the one next to Lynx. 19:00*

155 cut a·, way̓ wápupxən lútiʔ xʷʔíltəm 156 way̓ istk̓ík̓təm
cut a way̓ wap•wp=xn lút+i xʷʔ=ilt+m way̓ i -s -t+k̓i•k̓t+m
say intj well lynx not_yet hold_baby yes 1i -nom -be_near
He said, "Ah, Lynx never held it. *I was close to him.*

157 incá iʔ kən xʷʔíltəm uɬ {cn} cniɬc iwá xʷíc̓ɬtən uɬ lut
in+cá iʔ kn xʷʔ=ilt+m uɬ cniɬ+c iwá xʷic̓ -ɬt -n uɬ lut
I art 1kn hold_baby and (s)he try_to give -ɬt -1erg and not
I held him, I tried to give it to him, but no.

158 nt̓aʔ uɬ axáʔ uɬ iʔ sk̓ʷk̓ʷíməlt niʕíp scacacáʕ[s] 159 a·
nt̓a uɬ axáʔ uɬ iʔ s+k̓ʷ•k̓ʷiy=m̓+l̓t nyʕip s -ca•ca•cáʕ -s a
intj and this and art child always nom -holler -3i intj
And the baby is still a-crying." *They*

cútəlx way̓ xʷíc̓əɬti wápupxən 160 way̓ kən cut yaʕyáʕt_swit
cut -lx way̓ xʷic̓ -ɬt -y wap•wp=xn way̓ kn cut yaʕ•yáʕ+t_swit
say -pl well give -ɬt -tpimptv lynx yes 1kn say everybody
said "Give it to Lynx." *"I said everybody is going to*

ksxʷʔíltaʔx 161 ixíʔ n̓ín̓w̓iʔ swit mi k̓əwpstís uɬ
ks -xʷʔ=ilt -aʔx ixíʔ n̓ín̓w̓iʔ swit mi k̓w+p -st -is uɬ
incp^ -hold_baby -^incp then a_while who fut stop_talking -caus -3erg and
hold the baby, *and whoever makes it stop,*

ixíʔ łaʔ ksqʷəsqʷsíʔ 162 ixíʔ uł kʷis axáʔ {is} isťəmkʔílt
ixíʔ łaʔ k+s+qʷs•qʷsiʔ ixíʔ uł kʷi -s axáʔ i -s+ťmkʔ=ilt
that the_one_that have_child that and take -3erg this 1in -daughter
that's his baby, *and he's going to take my daughter."*

163 waẏ xʷúystsəlx wápupxən 164 waẏ cúsəlx {waẏ} waẏ kʷ
waẏ xʷuy+st -s -lx wap•wp=xn waẏ cu -s -lx waẏ kʷ
well take_st -3erg -pl lynx well tell -3erg -pl well 2kʷu
They took it to Lynx, *they said to him,*

scúnəms iʔ ta ilmíxʷəm kʷ ksxʷʔíltaʔx 165 waẏ uyá
s -cun+m -s iʔ t yl=mixʷ+m kʷ ks -xʷʔ=ilt -aʔx waẏ uyá
nom -tell -3i art agInst chief 2kn incp^ -hold_baby -^incp well intj
"The chief told you, you have to hold the baby." 20:03 *"Heck,*

waẏ kʷu cqʷəṅcínəmstp, waẏ lut 166 cúsəlx lut, kwaẏ
waẏ kʷu c -qʷṅ=cin+m -st -p waẏ lut cu -s -lx lut k+waẏ
yes 1obj cust^ -pity -^cust -5erg well not tell -3erg -pl not well
have pity on me." *They said to him "No,*

scutx a ilmíxʷəm 167 ṅíṅẇiʔ lut kʷ xʷʔíltəm {i}
s -cut -x a yl=mixʷ+m ṅíṅẇiʔ lut kʷ xʷʔ=ilt+m
ipftv^ -say -^ipftv art chief a_while not 2kn hold_baby
you've got to, the chief said so. *If you don't hold the baby,*

nx̌ʷílcəntxʷ ya ilmíxʷəm 168 mi kʷ kčx̌ʷx̌ʷípla? 169 waẏ
n+x̌ʷil=cn -t -xʷ ya yl=mixʷ+m mi kʷ k+čx̌ʷ•x̌ʷ=íplaʔ waẏ
disregard_order -nt -2erg art chief fut 2kn be_sentenced well
if you don't listen to the chief, *you'll be sentenced."* *Then*

ixíʔ sənx̌íłc wápupxən 170 waẏ ixíʔ sxʷʔíltəms {haya}
ixíʔ s -n+x̌ił -c wap•wp=xn waẏ ixíʔ s -xʷʔ=ilt+m -s
then nom -afraid -3i lynx well then nom -hold_baby -3i
Lynx got scared, *and he held the baby.*

171 kʷis wápupxən, ťiʔ {indec} sǩəwáṗs yaʔx̌í iʔ sǩʷǩʷíməlt
kʷi -s wap•wp=xn ťiʔ s -ǩwa+p -s yaʔx̌í iʔ s+ǩʷ•ǩʷiy=ṁ+ľt
take -3erg lynx evid nom -quiet -3i that_one art child
Lynx took it, the baby stopped.

172 hi hawhíwiʔst{a} iʔ sǩʷǩʷíməlt, waẏ ixíʔ{s} sʔitxs 173 cut a
hi haw•híw=iʔst iʔ s+ǩʷ•ǩʷiy=ṁ+ľt waẏ ixíʔ s -ʔitx -s cut a
intj yawn art child well then nom -sleep -3i say art
The baby yawned, went to sleep. 21:00 *And*

ilmíxʷəm 174 waẏ, waẏ {i nikʷ a} ṅíṅẇiʔ {indec} ł ťalaʔxwílx axáʔ
yl=mixʷ+m waẏ waẏ ṅíṅẇiʔ ł ťalaʔ+x+wílx axáʔ
chief well well a_while when next_generation this
the chief said: *"When the human beings come*

i? sťəlsqílxʷ {xʷa məɬ} 175 məɬ kɬswi?númtx[8] {i} ťəxʷ cpu?ḱsús {i k} i?
i? s+ťl+s+qilxʷ mɬ kɬ+s+wẏ+numt=x ťxʷ c -pu=ḱs=ús i?
art earth_people and have_handsome emph hab -ugly_spouse art
on earth *there will be good looking people, and anyone*

knaqs i? {i s} swi?númtx {waẏ ixí? mat c} 176 ixí? uɬ waẏ kʷu
k=naqs i? s+wẏ+numt=x ixí? uɬ waẏ kʷu
one_person art handsome that and yes 1obj
good looking can have an ugly mate.[9] *He won*

ƛ̓xʷupɬts isťəmk?ílt, waẏ cniɬc nák̓ʷəm ɬa? ksqʷəsqʷsí?
ƛ̓xʷu+p -ɬt -s i -s+ťmk?=ilt waẏ cniɬ+c nak̓ʷ+m ɬa? k+s+qʷs•qʷsi?
win -ɬt -3erg 1in -daughter well (s)he evid the_one_that have_child
my daughter, that's his child."

177 waẏ cúntməlx waẏ ixí? {uɬ waẏ ťəxʷ} kʷu px̌ʷməncút
waẏ cun -t -m -lx waẏ ixí? kʷu px̌ʷ+mncut
well tell -nt -psv -pl well then 4kn scatter
He said "We'll scatter.

178 waẏ {axá? i? i} axá? i? tkəɬmílxʷ {ixí? uɬ intkɬ} isťəmk?ílt ixí? uɬ waẏ
waẏ axá? i? tkɬmilxʷ i -s+ťmk?=ilt ixí? uɬ waẏ
well this art woman 1in -daughter that and yes
This woman my daughter

cmrím 179 i waẏ kʷis wápupxən axá?{i} isťəmk?ílt
c -mrim i waẏ kʷi -s wap•wp=xn axá? i -s+ťmk?=ilt
hab -marry intj well take -3erg lynx this 1in -daughter
is married. 22:00 *Lynx took my daughter.*

180 ixí? uɬ waẏ kʷu px̌ʷməncút 181 waẏ {ə} swit {mat aɬí?} mat səmx̌íkən
ixí? uɬ waẏ kʷu px̌ʷ+mncut waẏ swit mat s+mx̌=ikn
then and yes 4kn scatter well somebody maybe grizzly
Let's scatter." *Maybe Grizzly*

ya cx?it {ik ya yəc} 182 i? cpicxʷts smx̌íkən {ə} 183 aɬí? nstils
ya c+x?it i? s -picxʷt -s smx̌=ikn aɬí? n+st=ils
art first art nom -disgusted -3i grizzly because think
was first, *and Grizzly was disgusted* *because*

waẏ cniɬc ksƛ̓xʷúpi?s {i?} i? qa?ɬilmíxʷəm {i} 184 i? kɬtkəɬmílxʷs
waẏ cniɬ+c ks -ƛ̓xʷu+p ẏ -s i? qa?ɬ=yl=míxʷ+m i? kɬ -tkɬ+m=ilxʷ -s
well (s)he fut -win -nt -3i art chief's_children art to_be -wife -3i
he thought he was going to win the chief's daughter, *and that's going to be his*

uɬ lut, {ay} 185 wápupxən i? ksən?íwt ka? ɬƛ̓xʷups {i} ia ilmíxʷəm
uɬ lut wap•wp=xn i? k+s+n+?iwt ki? ɬ+ƛ̓xʷu+p -s i? yl=mixʷ+m
and not lynx art have_end rel win_again -3erg art chief
wife, but no. *Lynx at the end won the chief's*

8 The s is unexpected.
9 Lynx is considered ugly.

i? sť̓əmk?ílts 186 waỷ xʷťilx səmx̌íkən {a is indec} s?ácqa?s {indec}
i? s+ťmk?=ilt -s waỷ xʷť+ilx s+mx̌=ikn s -?ácqa? -s
art daughter -3in well get_up grizzly nom -go_out -3i
daughter. *Grizzly got up and he went out;*

187 xƛ̓məntís[10] wápupxən, [w]aỷ ḱəɬtraqspu?úsəs 188 uɬ ya?x̌í
xƛ̓+m -nt -is wap•wp=xn waỷ ḱɬ+traq+s+pu?=ús -s uɬ ya?x̌í
go_by -nt -3erg lynx well kick_heart -3erg and that_one
as he passed Lynx he kicked him where his heart should be, 23:05 *and Lynx*

cəqqínk t wápupxən, 189 uɬ ilí? mənm̓ínxən̓mi?səlx uɬ
cq•q=ink t wap•wp=xn uɬ ilí? mn•min=xn+mi -s -lx uɬ
fall_on_back agInst lynx and there rub_feet -3erg -pl and
fell on his back. *He [Grizzly] just rubbed his feet on him and*

itlí? ?ácqa? 190 náx̌əmɬ itlí? knaqs, ití? x̌í··lməlx uɬ
itlí? ?ácqa? nax̌mɬ itlí? k=naqs ití? x̌il+m -lx uɬ
from_there go_out so from_there one_person that do_like -pl and
then he went out. *And then another one, they all did the*

txƛ̓ápəlx {uɬ} 191 ɬʕáťxənmsəlx axá? {ixí? a·h} 192 axá? ilmíxʷəm
t+xƛ̓a+p -lx ɬaʕť=xn+m -s -lx axá? axá? yl=mixʷ+m
complete -pl smash -3erg -pl this this chief
same thing, *they smashed him all up.* *The chief*

kc̓sá··lxʷs i? sť̓əmk?ílts {ť} 193 uɬ miná laswá {i} i?
k+c̓sa=lxʷ -s i? s+ťmk?=ilt -s uɬ miná laswá i?
strip -3erg art daughter -3in and maybe_not silk art
took the clothes off his daughter.[11] *I don't suppose it was a silk*

wedding dress, mat waỷ səp̓i?álqs {uɬ ixí?} 194 waỷ uɬ ťi_kmix
mat waỷ sp̓i?=álqs waỷ uɬ ťi?_kmix
maybe yes buckskin_dress well and only
wedding dress, maybe buckskin. *All the girl had on*

cənɬəɬqʷípu?stxən axá? i? tkəɬmílxʷ 195 waỷ ixí? uɬ c̓sápəlx {i s ah}
c -n+ɬ•ɬqʷ=íp=ẃstxn axá? i? tkɬmilxʷ waỷ ixí? uɬ c̓sa+p -lx
hab -loin_cloth this art woman well then and gone -pl
was the breech cloth. 24:02 *They were all gone.*

196 cúntməlx i? ta ilmíxʷəm 197 waỷ uɬ ixí? uɬ kʷu ?imx
cun -t -m -lx i? t yl=mixʷ+m waỷ uɬ ixí? uɬ kʷu ?imx
tell -nt -psv -pl art agInst chief well and then and 4kn move
The chief said: *"We're going to move."*

198 ?úmla?xʷəm ḱa?kín {i k i··} i? ksənƛ̓lpúla?xʷtənsəlx 199 ixí?
?úm=la?xʷ+m ḱa+?kín i? k -s+n+ƛ̓l+p=úla?xʷ+tn -s -lx ixí?
name_place to_where art to_be -settling_place -3i -pl that
He named the place where they were goint to settle. *They*

10 The sense here might be "(first) in a row."
11 To shame her.

nixʷ {sən} səncítxʷtənsəlx, {ku} sqəlxʷúlaʔxʷ iḱlíʔ 200 i
nixʷ s+n+citxʷ+tn -s -lx s+qlxʷ=úlaʔxʷ iḱlíʔ i
also camping_place -3in -pl Indian_land there intj
had lived there before, it's an Indian campground. *They*

[s]x̌əcməncúts[əlx] 201 waẏ uɬ aɬíʔ naḱʷáʔ {c} cq̓sápiʔlx ɬaʔ
s -x̌c+mncut -s -lx waẏ uɬ aɬíʔ naḱʷ+á c -q̓sápiʔ -lx ɬaʔ
nom -get_ready -3i -pl well and so not hab -long_time -pl when
started getting ready. *It didn't take long to*

cx̌əcməncútəlx 202 uɬ aɬíʔ axáʔ iʔ smaʔmʔím {i··} iʔ səc̓síc̓əm ixíʔ
c -x̌c+mncut -lx uɬ aɬíʔ axáʔ iʔ s+maʔ•mʔím iʔ sc̓•sic̓m ixíʔ
hab -get_ready -pl and so this art women art blankets that
get ready. *The women fixed the blankets*

ḱʷúl̓səlx úɬi ksq̓ʷíɬtsəlx 203 uɬ axáʔ iʔ {a i}
ḱʷul̓ -s -lx uɬ iʔ ks -q̓ʷiɬ+t -s -lx uɬ axáʔ iʔ
fix -3erg -pl and_then futi -pack_on_back -3i -pl and this art
for their packs *and the men*

sqəlqəltmíxʷ məɬ axáʔ {iʔ ə··} kcəkʷntísəlx iʔ səṗʔíɬxʷ 204 ṫiʔ
s+ql•qlt=mixʷ mɬ axáʔ k+ckʷ -nt -is -lx iʔ sṗʔ=iɬxʷ ṫiʔ
men and this take_down -nt -3erg -pl art tipi evid
took down the buckskin tipis. 25:06 *In*

ixíxiʔ məɬ wiʔlscútəlx wiʔskʕacíknməlx 205 məɬ ixíʔ
ix•íxiʔ mɬ wẏ=lscut -lx wẏ+s+k+ʕac=íkn+m -lx mɬ ixíʔ
in_a_while and finish_clothes -pl finish_tying -pl and then
a little while things are ready tied with strings around. *They*

[s]tkʷʔútsəlx, ʔímxəlx 206 uɬ axáʔ ḱáwxənmsəlx wápupxən
s -tkʷʔ=ut -s -lx ʔim+x -lx uɬ axáʔ ḱaw=xn+m -s -lx wap•wp=xn
nom -walk_pl -3i -pl move -pl and this destroy_w_feet -3erg -pl lynx
started walking, they moved. *They had smashed Lynx to death when*

ɬaʔ ctərqxənmístsəlx 207 a· kmix_ḱəm {s s} spumts uɬ
ɬaʔ c -trq=xn+mi -st -s -lx a kmix_ḱm s+pumt -s uɬ
when cust^ -kick -^cust -3erg -pl intj only fur -3in and
they kicked him around; *only his fur was left;*

nixʷ ixíʔ klək̓ʷk̓ʷmíntəm mat 208 uɬ ḱim ṫəxʷ stim̓s mat
nixʷ ixíʔ k+lkʷ•kʷ+mi -nt -m mat uɬ ḱim ṫxʷ stim̓ -s mat
also that remove -nt -psv maybe and left evidently what -3in maybe
maybe they busted that too. *I don't know what else,*

209 ḱim ilíʔ ki {c} ḱim ṫi sc̓ims 210 nṫa uɬ paʔpaʔsínk axáʔ {iʔ}
ḱim ilíʔ kiʔ ḱim ṫiʔ s+c̓im -s nṫa uɬ paʔ•paʔs=ínk axáʔ
only there rel only evid bone -3in intj and sad this
only his bones...[12] *And the virgin started*

12 All that's left of Lynx is a pile of bones.

iʔ st̓aʔk̓míx 211 lut k̓im t̓ st̓aʔk̓míx t̓əxʷ uɬ aɬíʔ
iʔ s+t̓aʔk̓+míx lut k̓im t̓ s+t̓aʔk̓+míx t̓xʷ uɬ aɬíʔ
art virgin not but negfac virgin evidently and because
feeling bad. 26:00 *She is not a virgin any more, because she had a*

k̓əɬt̓aʔk̓mxínkəm {təl x̌ʷilst} 212 təl x̌ʷílstəm iʔ t ƛ̓ax̌əx̌ƛ̓x̌áps
k̓ɬ+t̓aʔk̓+mx=ínk+m tl x̌ʷil -st -m iʔ t ƛ̓x̌•x̌•ƛ̓x̌a+p -s
have_baby_young ? discard -st -psv art agInst parents -3in
virgin-baby. *Her parents and the people*

t̓əxʷ aɬíʔ iʔ t sqilxʷ 213 i· uɬ k̓laxʷ uɬ {cúntəm ə··uɬ c cus} aɬíʔ
t̓xʷ aɬíʔ iʔ t s+qilxʷ i· uɬ k̓laxʷ uɬ aɬíʔ
evidently so art agInst person intj and evening and so
threw her away. *Night came, and she was*

sc̓qʷaqʷ 214 uɬ ixíʔ {c t axáʔ i ta c} k̓im iʔ t sc̓ims {mat i s} kʷm̓iɬ
s -c̓qʷ•aqʷ uɬ ixíʔ k̓im iʔ t s+c̓im -s kʷm̓iɬ
hab -cry and that only art from bone -3in suddenly
crying. *Just from that pile of bones*

ixíʔ qʷəlqʷílstəm 215 cúntəm way̓, way̓ lut myaɬ
ixíʔ qʷl•qʷil -st -m cu -nt -m way̓ way̓ lut myaɬ
that talk_to -st -psv tell -nt -psv well well not too_much
words come out. *He said: "Don't feel*

akspaʔpaʔsínk 216 way̓ kʷ xʷuy ik̓líʔ {k̓l in} k̓ incítxʷ 217 ilíʔ
a -ks -paʔ•paʔs=ínk way̓ kʷ xʷuy ik̓líʔ k̓ in -citxʷ ilíʔ
2i -futi -sad well 2kn go there to 1in -house there
too bad. *Go to my house.* *There*

iʔ l is{ə·}t̓qílp ilíʔ {t̓əxʷ l} iʔ l isxʷípəlp ilíʔ i l k̓ɬixʷút {i l is}
iʔ l i -s+t̓q=ilp ilíʔ iʔ l i -s+xʷip=lp ilíʔ iʔ l k̓ɬ+yxʷ=ut
art in 1in -mattress there art in 1in -rug there art in underneath
in my bed mattress are my sheets; under that 27:15

218 ilíʔ way̓ {a} aksttəm̓tím̓ 219 ixíʔ {kʷ} km̓əntíxʷ, ixíʔ məɬ {i}
ilíʔ way̓ a -k -s+t•tm̓•tim̓ ixíʔ km̓ -nt -ixʷ ixíʔ mɬ
there yes 2i -to_be -clothes that take -nt -2erg that and
there you'll find some clothes. *Take them, put them*

iʔ kʷ x̌əcməncút 220 lut maɬ akspaʔpaʔsínk {way̓ axáʔ kʷa uɬ} 221 t̓i
iʔ kʷ x̌c+mncut lut maɬ a -ks -paʔ•paʔs=ínk t̓iʔ
art 2kn get_dressed not too_much 2i -futi -sad evid
on yourself.[13] *Don't feel too bad."* *The*

paʕs axáʔ iʔ tkəɬmílxʷ {uɬ ə} 222 way̓ k̓ʷəl̓skəwkwíkəms, swit_aɬíʔ kmix
paʕs axáʔ iʔ tkɬmilxʷ way̓ k̓ʷl̓+s+kw•kwik+m -s swit_aɬíʔ kmix
paʕs this art woman well turn_ghost -3in in_fact only
woman got surprised. *It's his ghost that's talking to her,*

13 She had been stripped.

sc̓im axáʔ a cqʷəlqʷílstəm 223 cúntəm xʷuyx, lut kʷu
s+c̓im axáʔ a c -qʷl•qʷil -st -m cu -nt -m xʷuy -x lut kʷu
bone this art custˆ -talk_to -ˆcust -psv tell -nt -psv go isimptv not 1kʷu
a pile of bones. *He told her "Go, don't be*

aksənx̌íləm 224 way̓ ixíʔ {ałíʔ uł} qʷən̓cín 225 way̓ xʷuy axáʔ iʔ
a -ks -n+x̌il+m way̓ ixíʔ qʷn̓=cin way̓ xʷuy axáʔ iʔ
2i -futi -fear well that pity well go this art
afraid of me. *I sympathize with you." 28:01* *The woman*

tkəłmílxʷ 226 way̓ xʷuy ik̓líʔ k̓əl citxʷs wápupxən 227 way̓ { i l} i l
tkłmilxʷ way̓ xʷuy ik̓líʔ k̓l citxʷ -s wap•wp=xn way̓ i l
woman well go there to house -3in lynx yes art in
went. *She went to Lynx's house.* *Under*

sənk̓ʔínaʔs ixíʔ {cuł} utłtís 228 way̓ ilíʔ {k} tətəm̓tím̓s
s+n+k̓ʔ=ínaʔ -s ixíʔ wt -łt -is way̓ ilíʔ t•tm̓•tim̓ -s
pillow -3in that put_down -łt -3erg yes there clothes -3in
the pillow where he put it *that's where her clothes are,*

ksəpiʔálqsc 229 nt̓a łəxʷpəntís nt̓a t̓iʔ pu··t {xʷəm t̓i}
k -sp̓iʔ=álqs -c nt̓a łxʷ+p -nt -is nt̓a t̓iʔ put
to_be -buckskin_dress -3i intj hang -nt -3erg intj evid exact
her buckskin dress. *She put it on and it fit perfectly,*

230 xʷəm̓_t̓i scsúxʷmaʔ 231 way̓ {ł} [s]x̌əcməncúts
xʷm_t̓iʔ sc -súxʷ=maʔ way̓ s -x̌c+mncut -s
evid ? -measure well nom -get_dressed -3i
just like fitted. *She put it on, [then]*

kłq̓aʔxáns {ay łcxʷuy əy n} 232 nx̌əsəlswílx axáʔ iʔ tkəłmílxʷ
kł -q̓aʔ=xán -s n+x̌s=ls+wilx axáʔ iʔ tkłmilxʷ
to_be -shoes -3in mood_improves this art woman
her shoes. *The woman got in a better humor.*

233 cúntəm way̓ ha way̓ kʷ wiʔsx̌əcməncút ha 234 cut way̓.
cu -nt -m way̓ haʔ way̓ kʷ wy̓+s+x̌c+mncut haʔ cut way̓
tell -nt -psv well inter finish 2kn finish_dressing inter say yes
He asked "Are you done dressing?" *She said "Yes."*

235 cúntəm way̓, huhúy uł {kʷu} kʷu ʔúluʔłt {is} isqiltk 236 axáʔ
cu -nt -m way̓ hu+húy uł kʷu ʔulw̓ -łt i -s+qiltk axáʔ
tell -nt -psv OK OK and 1obj gather -łt 1in -body this
He said, "Ok, gather my body, 29:05 *all*

yaʕyáʕt lut_ksluts 237 uł axáʔ n̓ín̓w̓iʔ {axáʔ i t sə} iʔ t
yaʕ•yáʕ+t lut_k+s+lut+s uł axáʔ n̓ín̓w̓iʔ iʔ t
all there_is_no_no_about_it and this a_while art agInst
of it, don't leave anything. *And that*

sq̓ʷəłqnísəlp̓ t̓əxʷ iʔ t scx̌ʷil axáʔ ia nk̓əmqníłxʷ 238 ałíʔ
s+q̓ʷl=qn=islp̓ t̓xʷ iʔ t sc+x̌ʷil axáʔ iʔ n+k̓m=qn=iłxʷ ałíʔ
smoked_tipi evidently art agInst discarded this art ceiling because
smoked piece of tipi thrown away" *(because*

uɬ ixíʔ cḱəɬníḱstsəlx
uɬ ixíʔ c -ḱɬ+niḱ -st -s -lx
and that cust^ -cut_out -^cust -3erg -pl
they cut that off

239 məɬ ilíʔ x̌ʷílstsəlx axáʔ
mɬ ilíʔ x̌ʷil -st -s -lx axáʔ
and there discard -st -3erg -pl this
and they throw away the

iʔ səṗʔíɬxʷ
iʔ sṗʔ=iɬxʷ
art tipi
buckskin tipis)

240 ixíʔ ṅíṅẇiʔ kʷintxʷ
ixíʔ ṅíṅẇiʔ kʷin -t -xʷ
that a_while take -nt -2erg
“you take that

241 məɬ axáʔ kʷu
mɬ axáʔ kʷu
and this 1obj
and put a curtain

ḱəɬxárəntxʷ
ḱɬ+xar -nt -xʷ
curtain -nt -2erg
in front of me.

242 cúntəm lut {aks} aksxʷúsəskaʔ
cu -nt -m lut a -ks -xʷús•s+kaʔ
tell -nt -psv not 2i -futi -be_in_hurry
Don’t be in a hurry.

243 ṅíṅwiʔ {kən ɬ} kʷ ɬ níxəl t stiṁ
ṅíṅẇiʔ kʷ ɬ nixl t s+tiṁ
a_while 2kn if hear obj_itr something
If you hear something

244 uɬ lut aksənx̌íləm
uɬ lut a -ks -n+x̌il+m
and not 2i -futi -fear
don’t get scared,

uɬ lut aksxʷúsəskaʔ
uɬ lut a -ks -xʷús•s+kaʔ
and not 2i -futi -be_in_hurry
and don’t get in a hurry. 30:04

245 ṅíṅẇiʔ ċx̌iɬ cúntsən
ṅíṅẇiʔ c+ʔx̌iɬ cu -nt -s -n
a_while like tell -nt -2obj -1erg
I’ll let you know

246 mi_sic {kʷu kʷ} lkʷílxstxʷ axáʔ inḱəɬxármən
mi_sic lkʷ+ilx+st -xʷ axáʔ in -ḱɬ+xar+mn
then remove -2erg this 1in -curtain
when you can take away my curtain.

247 ixíʔ mi_sic {kə ɬ}
ixíʔ mi_sic
then then
Then

kʷu asx̌ílwiʔ
kʷu a -s+x̌ílwiʔ
1kʷu 2in -husband
I’ll be your husband.”

248 nstils axáʔ iʔ tkəɬmílxʷ
n+st=ils axáʔ iʔ tkɬmilxʷ
think this art woman
The woman thought

249 na·· nt̓a mat aɬíʔ mat
na nt̓a mat aɬíʔ mat
intj intj must so must
“Lynx sure

waẏ yaʕʷpyáwt {aɬ}[14] wápupxən
waẏ yaw+p+yáʕʷ+t wap•wp=xn
yes powerful lynx
must be powerful.

250 uɬ aɬíʔ lut kʷu t̓
uɬ aɬíʔ lut kʷu t̓
and because not 1obj negfac
He never did

kics
kic -s
reach_st/sb -3erg
get to me.

251 uɬ laʔkín kiʔ uɬ xkínəm kiʔ {kʷu kən nʔaɬtxət̓} kən
uɬ la+ʔkíṅ kiʔ uɬ x+kin+m kiʔ kn
and how rel and do_what rel 1kn
I wonder how it happened that I got

naʔɬtxət̓stíʔst[15] təl cniɬc
naʔɬ+t+xt̓+st=íʔst tl cniɬ+c
become_pregnant from (s)he
pregnant from him.

252 lut kʷu t̓a ckics
lut kʷu t̓ c+kic -s
not 1obj negfac arrive_cisl -3erg
He never got to me.

253 waẏ
waẏ
well
He’s

14 Could this be the lexical prefix haɬ= which, therefore, goes with the following utterance producing haɬwápupxən *the Lynx group*?

15 The make-up of this word is not clear.

mat iʔ sq̓ʷíɬq̓ʷəɬtx {cut ə} 254 way̓ ixíʔ ú··luʔɬtəm iʔ sqiltks
mat iʔ s -q̓ʷiɬ•q̓ʷɬ+t -x way̓ ixíʔ ʔulw̓ -ɬt -m iʔ s+qil=tk -s
must art ipftv^ -strong -^ipftvp well then gather -ɬt -psv art body -3in
sure smart." 31:06 *She gathered all his body parts and*

iʔ spumts {uɬixíʔ} 255 ixíʔ ilíʔ tx̌ʷáyqɬtəm {i s} 256 ixíʔ
iʔ s+pumt -s ixíʔ ilíʔ t+x̌ʷay=q -ɬt -m ixíʔ
art fur -3in that there pile -ɬt -psv then
his fur, *she put it all in a pile.* *She*

sƛ̓aʔƛ̓ʔáms axáʔ iʔ t sq̓ʷəlqnísəlp̓ {i t} iʔ t scx̌ʷíl·səlx {i s}
s -ƛ̓aʔ•ƛ̓ʔá+m -s axáʔ iʔ t s+q̓ʷl=qn=islp̓ iʔ t sc+x̌ʷil•l -s -lx
nom -look_for -3i this art obj_itr smoked_tipi art obj_itr discarded -3in -pl
started looking for the smoked top of the tipi they had thrown away,

257 a nk̓əmqníɬxʷ iʔ sxʷulɬxʷ iʔ {k̓əɬ} k̓əɬk̓ərəntísəlx {aɬíʔ uɬ ay i} 258 ixíʔ
a n+k̓m=qn=iɬxʷ iʔ s+xʷul+ɬxʷ iʔ k̓ɬ+k̓r -nt -is -lx ixíʔ
art ceiling art tipi art cut_off -nt -3erg -pl then
the old top of the tipi that they cut off. *She*

k̓əɬxárəntəm {way̓} 259 way̓ uɬ {naɬ} sqáqsəsc 260 way̓, way̓
k̓ɬ+xar -nt -m way̓ uɬ s -qa•qs•s -c way̓ way̓
curtain -nt -psv well and nom -dusk -3i well well
put the curtain in front of him. *It was getting dark;* *a little*

ʔayxáxaʔ təl sqáqsəsc t̓əxʷ_mat k̓əl sənsúxʷxʷcəns {way̓} 261 way̓
ʔayxáxaʔ tl s -qa•qs•s -c t̓xʷ_mat k̓l s -n+suxʷ•xʷ=cn -s way̓
a_while from nom -dusk -3i maybe to nom -light_leaves -3i yes
after dark, when light disappears *some*

ɬaʔq̓ʷcín {i s} iʔ skəkáʕkaʔ {i} 262 siməncáʕt axáʔ {i l} tla
ɬaʔq̓ʷ=cín iʔ s+k•kʕá•kaʔ sy+mncʕat axáʔ tla
audible art bird make_noise this from
birds could be heard. 32:07 *They were making noise from behind the*

ck̓əɬxár̓ {way̓ uɬ a c̓x̌iɬ t s} 263 way̓ qʷim̓m axáʔ {i s} iʔ kɬtkɬmílxʷs
c -k̓ɬ+xar way̓ qʷim̓•m̓ axáʔ iʔ kɬ -tkɬ+m=ilxʷ -s
hab -curtain well surprised this art to_be -wife -3i
curtain [tape ends]. 32:24 *His wife got in a hurry.*

264 uɬ aɬíʔ way̓ uɬ k̓əwk̓əwpnúmt təl̓ sknánaqs {uɬ} 265 xʷúsəskaʔms
uɬ aɬíʔ way̓ uɬ k̓w•k̓w+p+numt tl̓ s+k=ná•naqs xʷús•skaʔ+m -s
and so yes and lonesome from being_alone be_in_hurry -3erg
She got lonesome because she's alone. *She's in a hurry*

axáʔ {iʔ} iʔ sqəl̓tmíxʷs 266 cus way̓ xʷustx way̓ {kən} kən
axáʔ iʔ s+qlt=mixʷ -s cu -s way̓ xʷus+t -x way̓ kn
this art man -3in tell -3erg well hurry -isimptv yes 1kn
for her man. *She said to him "Hurry,*

qʷim̓m kən nk̓əwpíls {way̓ u} 267 cus lútiʔ {t is} t iswiʔnúmt {t isc} iʔ
qʷim̓•m̓ kn n+k̓w+p=ils cu -s lút+i t i -s+wy̓+numt iʔ
surprised 1kn lonesome tell -3erg not_yet ? 1in -put_together art
I'm in a hurry, I'm lonesome." *"I'm not put together yet, I am not finished*

t iscmrímst
t i -sc+mrim+st
? 1in -recovery
with my medicine."

268 waẏ ixíʔ sta waẏ put
waẏ ixíʔ sta waẏ put
well that intj yes just
"That's good enough."

269 cúntəm waẏ, waẏ
cu -nt -m waẏ waẏ
tell -nt -psv well well
He said "Well, if you think so.

aspuʔús, mat kʷ sxʷúsəskaʔ
a -s+puʔ=ús mat kʷ c -xʷús•s+kaʔ
2in -heart maybe 2kn -be_in_hurry
You must be in a hurry.

270 waẏ {kʷu a kł} kʷu k̓əł{c}ckʷánt
waẏ kʷu k̓ł+ckʷa -nt
well 1obj take_down -nt
Take down

axáʔ a nxárcən
axáʔ a n+xar+cn
this art curtain_in_front
the curtain." 1:02

271 waẏ ixíʔ lkʷilxsts a nxárcən
waẏ ixíʔ lkʷ+ilx+st -s a n+xar+cn
well then remove -3erg art curtain_in_front
She took the curtain off,

272 uł waẏ k̓əm axáʔ iʔ sk̓ʷəƛ̓úsc {a}
uł waẏ k̓m axáʔ iʔ s+k̓ʷƛ̓-us -c
and yes except this art face -3in
and it's only his face

273 lútiʔ ixíʔ
lút+i ixíʔ
not_yet that
that wasn't

sx̌asəsmílxs úłiʔ sxʷúsəskaʔməntəm
s -x̌as•s+m+ilx -s uł iʔ s+xʷús•s+kaʔ+m -nt -m
nom -heal -3i and_then rush -nt -psv
healed up yet.

274 sc̓x̌ilx uł
sc+ʔx̌il+x uł
reason_why and
That's why

scútxəlx wápupxən uł cqəqcús
s -cut -x -lx wap•wp=xn uł c -q•qc=us
ipftv^ -say -^ipftv -pl lynx and hab -wrinkled_face
they say Lynx is "wrinkled face."

275 uł caʔkʷ lut
uł caʔkʷ lut
and if not
And if

xʷərrápəp axáʔ iʔ kłtkəłmílxʷs
xʷr•ra+p•p axáʔ iʔ kł -tkł+m=ilxʷ -s
anxious this art to_be -wife -3i
his wife hadn't got anxious

276 uł lut ksc̓x̌ilts {i s} iʔ
uł lut ks -c+ʔx̌ił+t -s iʔ
and not futi -like -3i art
his face wouldn't be

sk̓ʷəƛ̓úsc kscqəqcúsc
s+k̓ʷƛ̓=us -c ksc -q•qc=us -c
face -3in futPerfi -wrinkled_face -3i
puckered like that.

277 nt'a waẏ swiʔnúmtx axáʔ iʔ
nt'a waẏ s+wẏ+numt=x axáʔ iʔ
intj yes handsome this art
This woman's man was

staʔxʷsqəl̓tmíxʷs axáʔ iʔ tkəłmílxʷ
s -taʔxʷ+s+qlt=mixʷ -s axáʔ iʔ tkłmilxʷ
nom -get_husband -3i this art woman
a real handsome man.

278 waẏ npútəls axáʔ iʔ tkəłmílxʷ
waẏ n+put=ls axáʔ iʔ tkłmilxʷ
yes satisfied this art woman
The woman is well

waẏ
waẏ
yes
satisfied.

279 cúntəm waẏ huhúy cxʷuyx ik̓líʔ k̓ incítxʷ
cu -nt -m waẏ hu+húy c+xʷuy -x ik̓líʔ k̓ in -citxʷ
tell -nt -psv well OK come -isimptv there to 1in -house
She said "Come on now to my bed." 2:05

280 waẏ ixíʔ xʷʔíltəms axáʔ iʔ sqəl̓tmíxʷ
waẏ ixíʔ xʷʔ=ilt+m -s axáʔ iʔ s+qlt=mixʷ
well so hold_baby -3erg this art man
The man took the baby.

281 tətw̓ít ałíʔ iʔ
t•tw̓it ałíʔ iʔ
boy because art
They had

staʔxʷsqʷsíʔsəlx 282 xʷʔíltəms wáy̓ uɬ ixíʔ {s}
s -taʔxʷ+s+qʷsíʔ -s -lx xʷʔ=ilt+m -s wáy̓ uɬ ixíʔ
nom -get_son -3i -pl hold_baby -3erg well and then
a baby boy. He took the baby and his wife

sənq̓əlxʷáx̌əntəm axáʔ iʔ t tkəɬmílxʷ 283 iʔ ka stkʷnims
c -n+q̓lxʷ=ax̌n -t -m axáʔ iʔ t tkɬmilxʷ iʔ ka s -t+kʷni+m -s
act -link_arms -nt -psv this art agInst wife art rel nom -grab_at -3i
hooked up with him in the arm, *she took*

iʔ k̓əl {s} sək̓ʷtáx̌əns 284 axáʔ iʔ sxʷuys 285 xʷu··y̓ilx iʔ k̓əl
iʔ k̓l s+k̓ʷt=ax̌n -s axáʔ iʔ s -xʷuy -s xʷuy•y -lx iʔ k̓l
art to other_arm -3in this art nom -go -3i go -pl art to
his other arm. *They went.* *They went to...*

286 aɬíʔ uɬ axáʔ yaʕyáʕt ʔimx iʔ sqilxʷ {uɬ k̓im t̓i} 287 k̓im cniɬc ilíʔ
aɬíʔ uɬ axáʔ yaʕ•yáʕ+t ʔimx iʔ s+qilxʷ k̓im cniɬ+c ilíʔ
because and this all move art person only (s)he there
All the people had moved away. *Only*

iʔ citxʷs {cwi} cw̓íwaʔx 288 cxʷuylx uɬ wáy̓ npəpílxəlx {ə}
iʔ citxʷ -s c -w̓í•w̓aʔx c -xʷuy -lx uɬ wáy̓ n+p•pilx -lx
art house -3in hab -dwell_dim hab -go -pl and yes enter_pl -pl
her little tipi is left. *They went and they went in.*

289 xʷʔit ct̓ík̓əlsts axáʔ t wápupxən 290 aɬíʔ {s} q̓ʷíɬq̓ʷəɬt
xʷʔi+t c -t̓ik̓l -st -s axáʔ t wap•wp=xn aɬíʔ q̓ʷiɬ•q̓ʷɬ+t
much cust^ -grub -^cust -3erg this agInst lynx because strong
Lynx had gotten lots of grub, *because*

i l stəxʷcəncút {mat i t s} 291 axáʔ i l spíx̌əm, uɬ axáʔ i l {s}
iʔ l s+txʷ=cn+cut axáʔ iʔ l s+pix̌+m uɬ axáʔ iʔ l
art at food this art at hunting and this art in
he was smart at getting grub, 3·00 *in hunting,*

siwɬkʷ i l stəxʷcəncút iʔ t qáqxʷəlx 292 uɬ ixíʔ {s} iʔ st̓ík̓əls
siwɬ=kʷ iʔ l s+txʷ=cn+cut iʔ t qa•qxʷ+lx uɬ ixíʔ iʔ s+t̓ik̓l -s
water art at food art prttv fish and that art grub -3in
and getting fish. *And that's his grub,*

xʷʔit st̓ík̓əls 293 wáy̓ qʷámqʷəmt axáʔ iʔ spuʔúsc iʔ tkɬmílxʷ
xʷʔi+t s+t̓ik̓l -s wáy̓ qʷam•qʷm+t axáʔ iʔ s+puʔ=ús -c iʔ tkɬ+m=ílxʷ
much grub -3in yes excellent this art heart -3in art woman
lots of grub. *The woman was happy.*

294 wáy̓ ksx̌əlpínaʔlx məɬ ixíʔ spíx̌əms wápupxən 295 uɬ aɬíʔ
wáy̓ k+s+x̌lp=ínaʔ -lx mɬ ixíʔ s -pix̌+m -s wap•wp=xn uɬ aɬíʔ
well have_daylight -pl and then nom -hunt -3i lynx and because
It got daylight, and Lynx is ready to go hunting. *Lynx*

wápupxən ałíʔ q̓ʷíłq̓ʷəłt {wa} 296 nák̓ʷəm ckminíplaʔsts {iʔ s}[16]
wap•wp=xn ałíʔ q̓ʷił•q̓ʷł+t nak̓ʷ+m c -k+my+n=íplaʔ -st -s
lynx because strong evid cust^ -know_about -^cust -3erg
is really smart, he knows all

iʔ sƛ̓aʔcínəm 297 ixíʔ paʔsmís axáʔ {i sʔi} iʔ sʔímxəx
iʔ s+ƛ̓aʔ=cín+m ixíʔ paʔs+mí -s axáʔ iʔ s -ʔimx -x
art deer then think_about -3erg this art ipftv^ -move -^ipftvp
about deer. *He had wished bad luck hunting for those*

atláʔ ik̓líʔ {s} kspíx̌aʔxəlx 298 uł ʔax̌líkstəm iʔ
atláʔ ik̓líʔ ks -pix̌ -aʔx -lx uł ʔax̌l=íkst+m iʔ
from_here there incp^ -hunt -^incp -pl and turn_toward art
that moved from there, *and he turned the deer*

sƛ̓aʔcínəm {ta c} k̓əl cniłc 299 uł axáʔ lut t̓a cwíkłts
s+ƛ̓aʔ=cín+m k̓l cnił+c uł axáʔ lut t̓ c -wik -łt -s
deer to (s)he and this not negfac cust^ -see -łt -3erg
towards him.[17] *And the chief and his tribe*

axáʔ {iʔ} ia ilmíxʷəm iʔ laʔł sqʷəsqʷasíʔas ik̓líʔ spíx̌xəlx
axáʔ iʔ yl=mixʷ+m iʔ laʔł s+qʷs•qʷasíʔa -s ik̓líʔ s -pix̌ -x -lx
this art chief art and children -3in there ipftv^ -hunt -^ipftv -pl
don't see them when they hunt. 4:05

300 way̓ uł lut t̓a ct̓aʕpáməlx t sƛ̓aʔcínəm {tə} 301 ho··y uł
way̓ uł lut t̓ c -t̓aʕpá+m -lx t s+ƛ̓aʔ=cín+m hoy uł
well and not negfac hab -shoot -pl obj_itr deer well and
They never get to shoot deer. *They*

c̓əspcínəlx 302 uł axáʔ wápupxən ʔax̌lásq̓ət scpíx̌əx
c̓s+p=cin -lx uł axáʔ wap•wp=xn ʔax̌l=ásq̓t sc -pix̌ -x
run_out_of_food -pl and this lynx every_day ipftvp^ -hunt -^ipftvp
ran out of grub. *Lynx goes hunting every day*

303 yaʕyáʕt səsƛ̓xʷáms iʔ sƛ̓aʔcínəm 304 uł way̓ {ya} yaʕpqín
yaʕ•yáʕ+t sc -ƛ̓xʷam -s iʔ s+ƛ̓aʔ=cín+m uł way̓ yaʕ+p=qín
all pftv -kill_many -3i art deer and yes lots
and he kills lots of deer, *lots*

iʔ sƛ̓aʔcínəm 305 uł way̓ uł xʷaʔtíls axáʔ {iʔ} iʔ tkəłmílxʷ 306 ałíʔ
iʔ s+ƛ̓aʔ=cín+m uł way̓ uł xʷaʔ+t=íls axáʔ iʔ tkłmilxʷ ałíʔ
art deer and yes and have_enough this art woman so
of deer. *The woman has enough.* *She*

uł ʔax̌əlásq̓ət scx̌əw̓íłc̓aʔx 307 uł ałíʔa pnicíʔ uł ałíʔ
uł ʔax̌l=ásq̓t sc -x̌w̓=íłc̓aʔ -x uł ałi+á pn+icíʔ uł ałíʔ
and every_day ipftvp^ -dry_meat -^ipftvp and so_not at_that_time and so
dries meat every day. *At that time they didn't have*

16 I do not recognize the n of this form.
17 Lynx insured the group's failure and his success hunting.

(i)wá akɬ*fridgidaire* kəm̓ kɬ*deepfreeze* {yə} 308 t̓i_kmix
iwá kɬ+*fridgidaire* km̓ kɬ+*deepfreeze* t̓iʔ_kmix
even have_refridgerator or have_freezer only
fridge or freezer; they

cx̌əw̓stísəlx iʔ sɬiqʷ kiʔ lut ck̓əstwílx 309 way̓ uɬ
c -x̌w̓ -st -is -lx iʔ s+ɬiqʷ kiʔ lut c -k̓st+wilx way̓ uɬ
cust^ -dry -^cust -3erg -pl art meat rel not hab -become_bad well and
only dried the meat and it didn't spoil. She

cus iʔ sqəl̓tmíxʷs 310 way̓ uɬ kən xʷaʔtíls iʔ t
cu -s iʔ s+qlt=mixʷ -s way̓ uɬ kn xʷaʔ+t=íls iʔ t
tell -3erg art man -3in yes and 1kn have_enough art obj_itr
said to her man: "I have enough meat, and what

sɬíqʷtət, uɬ laʔkín mi xkístən 311 uɬ way̓ iʔ tx̌əlíwstət
s+ɬiqʷ -tt uɬ la+ʔkíǹ mi x+ki[18] -st -n uɬ way̓ iʔ t+x̌l=iw̓s -tt
meat -4in and how fut do_something -st -1erg and well art cache -4in
will I do with it? 5:02 The cache where

iʔ sənkʷúmcəntət 312 way̓ uɬ tq̓aʔíw̓s iʔ t x̌əw̓áw̓ 313 cus
iʔ s+n+kʷum=cn -tt way̓ uɬ t+q̓aʔ=íw̓s iʔ t x̌w̓•aw̓ cu -s
art storage -4in well and stuffed art agInst dried tell -3erg
we store our food is getting crowded with dry meat." He said

lut, lut ilíʔ akstixʷkʷúnəm 314 way̓ {i ay} k̓l anƛ̓ax̌əx̌ƛ̓x̌áp
lut lut ilíʔ a -ks -tixʷ+kʷún+m way̓ k̓l an -ƛ̓ax̌•x̌•ƛ̓x̌á+p
not not there 2i -futi -talk yes for 2in -elders
"No, don't say that. That's for your people.

315 ixíʔ xʷíc̓xtxʷəlx t ksɬíqʷsəlx i l tx̌əlíw̓scəlx {ilíʔ mi}
ixíʔ xʷic̓ -xt -xʷ -lx t k -s+ɬiqʷ -s -lx iʔ l t+x̌l=iw̓s -c -lx
then give -xit -2erg -pl obj_tr to_be -meat -3i -pl art for cache -3in -pl
You'll give them some meat for their cache.

316 ik̓líʔ mi ckʷúmɬtxʷəlx i {a} l {i} sənkʷúmcəntənsəlx
ik̓líʔ mi c -kʷum -ɬt -xʷ -lx iʔ l s+n+kʷum=cn+tn -s -lx
there fut cust^ -store -ɬt -2erg -pl art in storage_place -3in -pl
You can store it in their cache.

317 məɬ axáʔ ixíʔ ńíńw̓iʔ {x xʷa} kʷ nstils way̓ put xʷʔit 318 məɬ
mɬ axáʔ ixíʔ ńíńw̓iʔ kʷ n+st=ils way̓ put xʷʔi+t mɬ
and this then a_while 2kn think yes just enough and
And if you think it's enough then

itlíʔ k̓la nəqsíɬxʷ 319 yaʕyá··t ixíʔ {iʔ s} iʔ tx̌əlíw̓scəlx ixíʔ
itlíʔ k̓l nqs=iɬxʷ yaʕ•yáʕ+t ixíʔ iʔ t+x̌l=iw̓s -c -lx ixíʔ
from_there to next_door all that art cache -3in -pl that
put it in another one. Put it in

18 Root-initial ʔ is lost.

utxítxʷəlx ilíʔ 320 yaʕyáʕt iʔ sqilxʷ ya kɬtx̌əlíw̓s
wt -xit -xʷ -lx ilíʔ yaʕ•yáʕ+t iʔ s+qilxʷ ya kɬ+t+x̌l=iw̓s
put_down -xit -2erg -pl there all art person art have_cache
all the caches *(everybody has got caches). 6:00*

321 ń̓íń̓w̓iʔ ixíʔ {pna} pna kʷu ɬctxʷúyməntəm 322 yaʕyáʕt
ń̓íń̓w̓iʔ ixíʔ pnaʔ kʷu ɬ+c+t+xʷuy+m -nt -m yaʕ•yáʕ+t
a_while then maybe 3e4obj come_back_to -nt -3e4obj all
They might come back to us, *it's*

kʷa səncítxʷtənsəlx 323 nʕayapcínəlx nak̓ʷáʔ {xʷuəm} ʔax̌lásq̇ət
kʷa s+n+citxʷ+tn -s -lx na+yaʕ+p=cín -lx nak̓ʷ+á ʔax̌l=ásq̇t
intj camping_place -3in -pl hard_up -pl indeed_not every_day
their homes. *They are hard up, they won't get*

a mi {kɬ} ksqʷaqʷícsəlx iʔ t sc̓íɬən 324 way̓, way̓
a mi ks -qʷa•qʷíc -s -lx iʔ t sc+ʔiɬn way̓ way̓
intj fut futi -get_enough -3i -pl art obj_itr food well yes
what they want to eat every day." *The woman*

itlíʔ {ɬ} ɬx̌əw̓íɬc̓aʔms axáʔ iʔ tkəɬmílxʷ 325 uɬ axáʔ {iʔ}
itlíʔ ɬ+x̌w̓=íɬc̓aʔ+m -s axáʔ iʔ tkɬmilxʷ uɬ axáʔ
from_there dry_meat_again -3erg this art woman√ʕc̓ and this
kept on drying meat, *and Lynx*

wápupxən ʔax̌lásq̇ət scpíx̌əx 326 st̓aʕpáms iʔ
wap•wp=xn ʔax̌l=ásq̇t sc -pix̌ -x s -t̓aʕpá+m -s iʔ
lynx every_day ipftvp^ -hunt -^ipftvp nom -shoot -3i art
hunts every day. *He shoots*

sƛ̓aʔcínəm {i} kəm̓ iʔ skəm̓xíst 327 ʔax̌lásq̇ət scyaʕkínx
s+ƛ̓aʔ=cín+m km̓ iʔ s+kmx+ist ʔax̌l=ásq̇t sc -yaʕ=kíń -x
deer or art bear every_day ipftvp^ -all_on_back -^ipftvp
deer or bear; *every day he gets stuff off his back.*[19]

328 ho··y uɬ {aʔ} cut iʔ tkəɬmílxʷ 329 way̓, way̓ uɬ, way̓ yaʕyáʕt {iʔ} iʔ
hoy uɬ cut iʔ tkɬmilxʷ way̓ way̓ uɬ way̓ yaʕ•yáʕ+t iʔ
well and say art woman well well and well all art
Then the wife said: *"Well, all the people's caches are*

sqilxʷ iʔ tx̌líw̓scəlx utxítnəlx t ksc̓íɬənsəlx
s+qilxʷ iʔ t+x̌l=iw̓s -c -lx wt -xit -n -lx t ksc -ʔiɬn -s -lx
person art cache -3in -pl put_down -xit -1erg -pl obj_tr futPerfi -eat -3i -pl
full with grub; 7:05

330 uɬ way̓ {xə·} xʷaʔtíls 331 cúntəm way̓ {way̓ t̓əxʷ iʔ} way̓
uɬ way̓ xʷaʔ+t=íls cu -nt -m way̓ way̓
and yes have_enough tell -nt -psv well yes
it's already lots." *He said*

19 Back from hunting he unloads his pack.

mat {k̓ík̓ə} k̓ík̓əm mi kʷu kícəntəm 332 i kʷu
mat k̓i•k̓m mi kʷu kic -nt -m iʔ kʷu
maybe soon fut 3e4obj reach_st/sb -nt -3e4obj art 3e4obj
"Pretty soon they'll get to us; *they're going to*

kspqʷílxəntəm 333 ixíʔ n̓ín̓w̓iʔ {ckic ckicx} kʷu
ks -pqʷ+ilx -nt -m ixíʔ n̓ín̓w̓iʔ kʷu
futt^ -visit -nt -3e4obj then a_while 3e4obj
come and see what's happened to us. *When your cousins,*

ckícəntəm aláʔ stim̓ a səntxʷús {kʷa} t̓əxʷ asnəqsílxʷ
c+kic -nt -m aláʔ s+tim̓ a s+n+txʷ+us t̓xʷ a -s+nqs=ilxʷ
arrive_cisl -nt -3e4obj here what art cousin emph 2in -relative
your relation come to us

334 ixíʔ {s} kʷu {spqʷílxəm t̓əxʷ} kspqʷílxəmsəlx 335 n̓ín̓w̓iʔ {ɬa cxʷ}
ixíʔ kʷu ks -pqʷ+ilx+m -s -lx n̓ín̓w̓iʔ
then 3e4obj futt^ -visit -3erg -pl a_while
they'll want to find out what's happened to us, *if you're*

uc ɬ ascxʷəlxʷált kəm̓ way̓ kʷ ɬ ƛ̓lal 336 úɬiʔ {c i cpqʷilx} iʔ
uc ɬ a -sc -xʷl+xʷál+t km̓ way̓ kʷ ɬ ƛ̓l•al uɬ iʔ iʔ
dub if 2in -pftv -alive or yes 2kn if dead and_then art
alive or if you're dead." *Their elders*

ckʷúlstməlx iʔ t ƛ̓ax̌əx̌ƛ̓x̌ápsəlx {iʔ} iʔ cpqʷílxəmsəlx
c -kʷulst+m -lx iʔ t ƛ̓ax̌•x̌•ƛ̓x̌á+p -s -lx iʔ c -pqʷ+ilx+m -s -lx
cust^ -send -pl art agInst elders -3in -pl art act -visit -3erg -pl
sent them to come over and see them.[20] *8:04*

337 uɬ n̓ín̓w̓iʔ ckícəntsəlx aláʔ uɬ n̓ín̓w̓iʔ x̌ast k̓ʷúl̓əntxʷəlx
uɬ n̓ín̓w̓iʔ c+kic -nt -s -lx aláʔ uɬ n̓ín̓w̓iʔ x̌as+t k̓ʷul̓ -nt -xʷ -lx
and a_while arrive_cisl -nt -2obj -pl here and a_while good treat -nt -2erg -pl
"And whenever they get here to you, treat your cousins

asəntxʷtxʷús 338 uɬ ʔamtíxʷəlx 339 uɬ n̓ín̓w̓iʔ ixíʔ {ɬ}
a -s+n+txʷ•txʷus uɬ ʔam -t -ixʷ -lx uɬ n̓ín̓w̓iʔ ixíʔ
2in -cousins and feed -nt -2erg -pl and a_while then
well *and feed them.* *And when*

kɬəɬxʷúyaʔxəlx 340 məɬ ɬt̓ík̓ləntxʷəlx a[xáʔ] t
kɬ -ɬ+xʷuy -aʔx mɬ ɬ+t̓ik̓l -nt -xʷ -lx axáʔ t
incp^ -go_back -^incp and give_provisions_again -nt -2erg -pl this obj_tr
they're ready to go back *give them grub,*

sƛ̓aʔcínəm t ksq̓ʷíɬtsəlx put, t ksq̓ʷíɬtsəlx
s+ƛ̓aʔ=cín+m t k -s+q̓ʷiɬ+t -s -lx put t k -s+q̓ʷiɬ+t -s -lx
deer obj_tr to_be -load -3i -pl just obj_tr to_be -load -3i -pl
deer to pack, just to pack.

20 A delegation of two will be sent.

341 uɬ ṅíṅẇiʔ cúntxʷəlx 342 ṅíṅẇiʔ axáʔ p ɬiyáʕ̣p 343 uɬ
uɬ ṅíṅẇiʔ cu -nt -xʷ -lx ṅíṅẇiʔ axáʔ p ɬ+yaʕ+p uɬ
and a_while tell -nt -2erg -pl a_while this 5kn arrive_again and
And then you tell them *'When you get back* *you*

cúntxʷəlx {ə an} [iʔ] λ̓ax̌əx̌λ̓x̌áptət talí k[ən] scx̌əstmíx {mʕan ɬ c s x̌s}
cu -nt -xʷ -lx iʔ λ̓ax̌+x̌+λ̓x̌a+p -tt taʔlíʔ kn sc -x̌st -mix
tell -nt -2erg -pl art elders -4in very_much 1kn ipftvp^ -good -^ipftvp
tell our elders I am doing real good,

344 cx̌əstmín uɬ waẏ kʷu wíkəntp axáʔ {i} 345 talí
c -x̌st+mi -n uɬ waẏ kʷu wik -nt -p axáʔ taʔlíʔ
habnt -like -1erg and yes 1obj see -nt -5erg this very_much
I'm doing good, you see me. *Look,*

ʕ̣áċənt {kən} kən t̓ x̌ast, kən ċíɬən 346 uɬ ʕ̣aċənt {kən} t̓i kən
ʕ̣aċ -nt kn t̓ x̌as+t kn c -ʔiɬn uɬ ʕ̣aċ -nt t̓iʔ kn
look_at -nt 1kn evid good 1kn hab -eat and look_at -nt evid 1kn
I'm well, and I eat; 9:01 *and look, I feel well,*

x̌is kən q̓ʷuct {uɬ kən} 347 uɬ cúntəp axáʔ anλ̓ax̌əx̌λ̓x̌áp uɬ
x̌is kn q̓ʷuċ+t uɬ cu -nt -p axáʔ an -λ̓ax̌•x̌•λ̓x̌á+p uɬ
feel_well 1kn fat and tell -nt -5erg this 2in -elders and
I am fat. *And you tell the elders*

waẏ iɬəɬcx̌lítməlx 348 waẏ nk̓əwpílsmnəlx 349 waẏ
waẏ i -ɬ -ɬ+c+x̌lit+m -lx waẏ n+k̓wp=ils+m -n -lx waẏ
yes 1i -nom -invite_again_cisl -pl yes be_lonesome_for -1erg -pl yes
I'm asking them back, *I am lonesome for them.* *Come*

kʷu kɬckṁíltməntp, waẏ kʷu kɬctxʷúyməntp
kʷu k -ɬ+c+k+ṁil+m -nt -p waẏ kʷu k -ɬ+c+t+xʷuy+m -nt -p
1obj futt^ -visit_again_cisl -nt -5erg yes 1obj futt^ -come_back_to -nt -5erg
and visit us again, come see us again.'"

350 waẏ cútəlx waẏ, waẏ ɬxʷúẏilx 351 xʷú¨ẏilx ɬyáʕpəlx
waẏ cut -lx waẏ waẏ ɬ+xʷuẏ•y -lx xʷuẏ•y -lx ɬ+yaʕ+p -lx
well say -pl yes well go_back_pl -pl go_pl -pl arrive_again -pl
They said "Ok," they went back.[21] *They went, they got back home.*

352 waẏ xʷʔit aɬíʔ {px} iʔ sq̓ʷíɬtsəlx iʔ x̌əẇáẇ {tk̓asəl}
waẏ xʷʔi+t aɬíʔ iʔ s+q̓ʷiɬ+t -s -lx iʔ x̌ẇ•aẇ
yes much so art load -3in -pl art dried
And they packed lots of dried meat.

353 tk̓asʔasíl·x aɬíʔ {uɬ mət} uɬ tk̓asəlmístəlx {p} ksq̓ʷíɬtəlx {put} 354 put
tk=ʔas•ʔasíl -lx aɬíʔ uɬ tk=ʔasl+míst -lx k+s+q̓ʷiɬ+t -lx put
two_persons -pl so and two_persons -pl have_load -pl just
Two of them and both had packs, 10:02 *just*

21 It's implied that the events took place as Lynx foretold.

sq̓ʷiɬts iʔ sq̓ʷíɬtsəlx, yaʕyáʕt x̌əw̓áw̓ 355 way̓ cúntməlx {uy} iʔ
s+q̓ʷiɬ+t -s iʔ s+q̓ʷiɬ+t -s -lx yaʕ•yáʕ+t x̌w̓•aw̓ way̓ cun -t -m -lx
load -3in art load -3in -pl all dried well tell -nt -psv -pl
enough for a big pack, all dried meat. *And their elders*

t ƛ̓ax̌əx̌ƛ̓x̌ápsəlx 356 uɬ sctl̓aʔkínəmp[22] axáʔ {uɬ i}
t ƛ̓ax̌•x̌•ƛ̓x̌á+p -s -lx uɬ sc -tla+ʔkín -mp axáʔ
agInst elders -3in -pl and pftv -from_there -5in this
asked them: *"And where did you get this?"*

357 cútəlx way̓ {s¨ cə} ixíʔ təl̓ sɬəx̌míltət, ixíʔ təl̓ sɬəx̌míltət {ta˙}
cut -lx way̓ ixíʔ tl̓ s+ɬx̌m=ilt -t ixíʔ tl̓ s+ɬx̌m=ilt -t
say -pl well that from relative -4in that from relative -4in
They said "From our relative, from our relative.

358 talí¨ sx̌əstmíx iʔ sɬəx̌míltət 359 way̓ yaʕ̓pqín
taʔlíʔ s -x̌s+t -mix iʔ s+ɬx̌m=ilt -t way̓ yaʕ+p=qín
very_much ipftv^ -good -^ipftv art relative -4in yes many_gathered
Our young relative is very good, *she has lots*

i {s} sɬiqʷs 360 ʔax̌lásq̓ət sx̌əw̓íɬc̓aʔx, ʔax̌lásq̓ət
iʔ s+ɬiqʷ -s ʔax̌l=ásq̓t s -x̌w̓=íɬc̓aʔ -x ʔax̌l=ásq̓t
art meat -3in every_day ipftv^ -dry_meat -^ipftv every_day
of meat, 11:00 *she dries meat*

sqlíɬc̓aʔx 361 uɬ axáʔ {i kʷu} iʔ kʷu kɬəɬcxʷúyaʔx
s -ql=íɬc̓aʔ -x uɬ axáʔ iʔ kʷu kɬ -ɬ+c+xʷuy -aʔx
ipftv^ -raw_meat -^ipftv and this art 4kn incp^ -come_again -^incp
every day. *And we were coming back,*

362 uɬ axáʔ iʔ kʷu cʔamtím uɬ iʔ {kʷu c} kʷu
uɬ axáʔ iʔ kʷu c -ʔam -t -im uɬ iʔ kʷu
and this art 3e4obj habnt -feed -nt -3e4obj and art 3e4obj
and they fed us, and they

cúntəm 363 way̓ ńíńwiʔ p ikscúnəm axáʔ {i}
cu -nt -m way̓ ńíńwiʔ p i -ks -cun+m axáʔ
tell -nt -3e4obj well a_while 5kʷu 1i -futi -tell this
told us *'Now I'm going to tell you something.*

364 cuntp {indec} inƛ̓ax̌əx̌ƛ̓x̌áp, kʷu kɬəɬckm̓íltməntp 365 way̓
cu -nt -p in -ƛ̓ax̌•x̌•ƛ̓x̌á+p kʷu kɬ -ɬ+c+k+m̓il+m -nt -p way̓
tell -nt -5erg 1in -elders 1obj futt^ -visit_again_cisl -nt -5erg yes
Tell my elders to come and visit me.' *She*

talí¨ nk̓əwpílsəms [nk̓əwpílsmɬms] {uɬ kə˙} 366 uɬ aɬíʔ {ə}
taʔlíʔ n+k̓wp=ils+m -s n+k̓wp=ils+m -ɬm -s uɬ aɬíʔ
very_much be_lonesome_for -3e2obj be_lonesome_for -5obj -3erg and so
is lonesome for you. *'And*

22 Here the amalgam tla+ʔkín functions as a stem.

axáʔ iʔ {i sc} nixʷ kswíkəntp iʔ sənʔímaʔtəmp 367 uɬ aɬíʔ wa̓y
axáʔ iʔ nixʷ ks -wik -nt -p iʔ s+n+ʔím+aʔ+t -mp uɬ aɬíʔ wa̓y
this art more futt^ -see -nt -5erg art grandchild -5in and so yes
another thing, I want you to see your grandchild'" (the child

uɬ ƛ̓x̌ap axáʔ {iʔ} iʔ sk̓ʷk̓ʷíməlt 368 uɬ aɬíʔ captíkʷɬ uɬ wa̓y
uɬ ƛ̓x̌a+p axáʔ iʔ s+k̓ʷ•k̓ʷiy=m̓+l̓t uɬ aɬíʔ captíkʷɬ uɬ wa̓y
and grow_sg this art child and because legends and yes
is already growing). 12:01 And it's a fairy tale, and he's already

cqəcqícəlx {eʔ} 369 wa̓y ixíʔ st̓əqʷcíns axáʔ { i s} ia ilmíxʷəm
c -qc•qic+lx wa̓y ixíʔ s -t̓qʷ=cin -s axáʔ iʔ yl=mixʷ+m
hab -run well then nom -holler -3i this art chief
running around. Then the boss started hollering.

370 ʔácqaʔ uɬ ixíʔ t̓qʷcín {əy} x̌əlíts iʔ snəqsílxʷs 371 uɬ {aɬíʔs}
ʔácqaʔ uɬ ixíʔ t̓qʷ=cin x̌lit -s iʔ s+nqs=ilxʷ -s uɬ
go_out and then holler summon -3erg art relative -3in and
He went out and hollered, he called his people. And

aɬíʔ ilmíxʷəm, sílxʷaʔ ilmíxʷəm 372 uɬ lut t̓a cənx̌ʷílcən
aɬíʔ yl=mixʷ+m sílxʷaʔ yl=mixʷ+m uɬ lut t̓ c -n+x̌ʷil=cn
because chief big chief and not negfac hab -disregard_order
he's the boss, a big boss; they don't dispute his words.

373 cúntməlx wa̓y x̌lítɬmən 374 wa̓y {kʷu ks} ɬciyáʕp
cun -t -m -lx wa̓y x̌lit -ɬm -n wa̓y ɬ+c+y•yáʕ+p
tell -nt -psv -pl well summon -5obj -1erg yes get_back_cisl
He said to them "I'm asking you to come. My children

axáʔ {i s} isqʷəsqʷasíʔa 375 t̓əxʷ iɬəɬsqʷsí spqʷílxəmsəlx
axáʔ i -s+qʷs•qʷasíʔa t̓xʷ i -ɬɬ -s+qʷsiʔ s -pqʷ+ilx+m -s -lx
this 1in -children evidently 1in -pl -son nom -visit -3i -pl
got back. My sons went to check up on

iʔ {s} səntxʷúscəlx 376 wa̓y sx̌əstmíx i səntxʷúscəlx
iʔ s+n+txʷus -c -lx wa̓y s -x̌s+t -mix i s+n+txʷus -c -lx
art cousin -3in -pl yes ipftv^ -good -^ipftv art cousin -3in -pl
their sister. 13:04 Their sister is doing all right

377 uɬ ixíʔ ksm̓ayncútaʔxəlx 378 wa̓y ixíʔ uɬ nyaʕ̓mísəlx {iʔ}
uɬ ixíʔ ks -m̓ay+ncút -aʔx -lx wa̓y ixíʔ uɬ n+yaʕ̓+mí -s -lx
and then incp^ -tell_story -^incp -pl well then and gather -3erg -pl
and they're going to tell their story." They gathered.

379 uɬ aɬíʔ scksq̓əmltnáwlaʔxəlx[23] {əy} 380 niyá⋅ʕ̓lx {uɬ ax}
uɬ aɬíʔ sc -k+s+q̓m=lt+n=áwlaʔ -x -lx n+y•yáʕ -lx
and so ipftvp^ -starve -^ipftvp -pl gather_in -pl
They were starving. They all gathered

23 Unclear analysis.

txƛ̓apəlx 381 uɬ aɬíʔ mat nmásqən swit_aɬíʔ ilmíxʷəm, nmásqən
t+xƛ̓a+p -lx uɬ aɬíʔ mat n+mas=qn swit_aɬíʔ yl=mixʷ+m n+mas=qn
complete -pl and because maybe four_head in_fact chief four_head
in there. *Maybe there are four tipis together, because he's the boss,*

iʔ sxʷulɬxʷ 382 waẏ snq̓ʷíc̓txəlx 383 waẏ {indec} lut axáʔ
iʔ s+xʷul+ɬxʷ waẏ s -n+q̓ʷic̓+t -x -lx waẏ lut axáʔ
art tipi yes ipftv^ -full -^ipftv -pl well not this
four tipis. *It's jam full.* *He didn't untie*

t̓a ck̓ʷəxʷk̓ʷíxʷsts {iʔ} a ckʕacʕacíkn axáʔ iʔ sq̓ʷiɬts
t̓ c -k̓ʷxʷ•k̓ʷixʷ -st -s a c -k+ʕac•ʕac=íkn̓ axáʔ iʔ s+q̓ʷiɬ+t -s
evid cust^ -untie -^cust -3erg art hab -bundles this art load -3in
his sons'

iʔ ɬəɬsqʷsíʔs 384 waẏ ixíʔ tk̓ʷíxʷc̓aʔs iʔ naqs 385 cut
iʔ ɬɬ -sqʷsiʔ -s waẏ ixíʔ t+k̓ʷíxʷ=c̓aʔ -s iʔ naqs cut
art pl -son -3in well then unwrap -3erg art one say
bundles. 14:04 *They unwrapped one.* *He*

waẏ {axáʔ t̓əxʷ} waẏ ha p txƛ̓ap 386 cúntməlx waẏ, cútəlx waẏ,
waẏ waẏ haʔ p t+xƛ̓a+p cu -nt -m -lx waẏ cut -lx waẏ
well well inter 5kn complete tell -nt -psv -pl yes say -pl yes
said, "Are you all here?" *They said, "Yes, yes,*

waẏ kʷu txƛ̓ap {kʷu wi} 387 cúntməlx waẏ axáʔ t̓əxʷ
waẏ kʷu t+xƛ̓a+p cu -nt -m -lx waẏ axáʔ t̓xʷ
yes 4kn complete tell -nt -psv -pl well this emph
we're all here." *He said "This was given*

sənc̓əx̌ʷx̌ʷíkstət iʔ təl̓ sník̓əɬxʷtət 388 iʔ t st̓əmkʔíltət
s+n+c̓x̌ʷ•x̌ʷ=ikst -t iʔ tl̓ s+nik̓=ɬxʷ -tt iʔ t s+t̓mkʔ=ilt -t
what_was_promised -4in art from son_in_law -4in art agInst daughter -4in
to us by our son-in-law. *Our daughter*

kʷu ck̓əɬʔamtím 389 uɬ lut iksknáqscən, uɬ
kʷu c -k̓ɬ+ʔam -t -im uɬ lut i -ks -k=naqs=cn uɬ
3e4obj habnt -feed -nt -3e4obj and not 1i -futi -eat_alone and
fed it to us. *And I'm not going to eat it alone,*

sc̓x̌ilx kiʔ x̌əlítɬmən 390 waẏ kʷu ksənʔaɬncín 391 kʷu
sc+ʔx̌il+x kiʔ x̌lit -ɬm -n waẏ kʷu k+s+n+ʔaɬn=cín kʷu
reason_why rel call -5obj -1erg yes 4kn have_food_to_share 4kn
and that's why I called you. *We are going to share.* *We*

yaʕyáʕt {kʷu ks} kʷu ksk̓ʷək̓ʷaʔmíxaʔx iʔ təl̓ sənc̓əx̌ʷx̌ʷíkstət
yaʕ•yáʕ+t kʷu ks -k̓ʷ•k̓ʷaʔ -míx+aʔx iʔ tl̓ s+n+c̓x̌ʷ•x̌ʷ=ikst -tt
all 4kn incp^ -chew -^incp art from what_was_promised -4in
all are going to chew from what's given to us."

392 uɬ aɬíʔ_swit {ə sks} ksq̓məltnáwlaʔxəlx 393 uɬ aɬíʔ kʷa
uɬ aɬíʔ_swit s -k+s+q̓m=ltn=áwlaʔ -x -lx uɬ aɬíʔ kʷa
and in_fact ipftv^ -starve -^ipftv -pl and because intj
They were all starving *because*

lut t̓a ct̓aʕpáməlx t sƛ̓aʔcínəm 394 wim̓ scpíx̌əms
lut t̓ c -t̓aʕpá+m -lx t s+ƛ̓aʔ=cín+m wim̓ sc -pix̌+m -s
not evid hab -shoot -pl obj_itr deer in_vain pftv -hunt -3i
they never got any deer 15:03 *[though] they tried to hunt.*

395 way̓, way̓ wiʔstk̓ʷíxʷkiʔs axáʔ iʔ nəqsíkən̓ 396 way̓ {ixíʔ} ixíʔ
way̓ way̓ wy̓+s+t+k̓ʷíxʷ=kiʔ -s axáʔ iʔ nqs=ikn̓ way̓ ixíʔ
well well finish_untying -3erg this art one_bundle well then
He untied a bundle; *he passed it*

nxƛ̓íksəntməlx {həy} 397 xʷí··c̓xtməlx uɬ mat tx̌ʷoʔsúlaʔxʷ {it s}
n+xƛ̓=iks -nt -m -lx xʷic̓ -xt -m -lx uɬ mat tx̌ʷ=w̓s=úlaʔxʷ
do_to_all -nt -psv -pl give -xit -psv -pl and maybe half_way_around
around in their hands. *He gave it to them, and maybe went half way around*

398 ixíʔ uɬ {lə} c̓sap axáʔ {iʔ} iʔ nəqsíkən̓ 399 way̓ {itlíʔ nə} itlíʔ {nə}
ixíʔ uɬ c̓sa+p axáʔ iʔ nqs=ikn̓ way̓ itlíʔ
then and gone this art one_bundle well from_there
and the first bundle was all gone. *Then*

nəqsíkən̓, ixíʔ itlíʔ mil̓s 400 mi··l̓s uɬ
nqs=ikn̓ ixíʔ itlíʔ mil̓ -s mil̓ -s uɬ
one_bundle then from_there pass_around -3erg pass_around -3erg and
another bundle, he passed it around. *He passed it around and joined*

xət̓t̓uʔsús, x̌əw̓áw̓ iʔ sɬiqʷ 401 way̓ cúntməlx way̓ 402 way̓ axáʔ
xt̓•t̓=w̓s=us x̌w̓•aw̓ iʔ s+ɬiqʷ way̓ cu -nt -m -lx way̓ way̓ axáʔ
join_in_middle dried art meat well tell -nt -psv -pl OK well this
where he started from, dry meat. *He said to them “Well,* *when*

kʷu ksx̌əlpínaʔ 403 ixíʔ uɬ ʕ̓ant way̓ {p} p nxʷaʔxʷaʔƛ̓íɬc̓aʔ
kʷu k+s+x̌l+p=ínaʔ ixíʔ uɬ ʕac̓ -nt way̓ p n+xʷaʔ•xʷaʔƛ̓=íɬc̓aʔ
4kn have_daylight then and look_at -nt yes 5kn have_enough_to_eat
daylight comes 16:00 *(you got enough to eat)*

404 ixíʔ uɬ {kʷu ɬəɬʔim} kʷu sʔimxs 405 kʷu sx̌lítəm iʔ
ixíʔ uɬ kʷu s -ʔim+x -s kʷu s+x̌lit+m iʔ
then and 4kn nom4ˆ -move -ˆnom4 4kn one_invited art
we’re going to move. *Our daughter asked us*

t st̓əmkʔíltət, kmíl̓tməntəm 406 kʷu ksʔawswíkəltaʔx iʔ
t s+t̓mkʔ=ilt -t k+m̓il+t+m -nt -m kʷu ks -ʔaw+s+wík=lt -aʔx iʔ
agInst daughter -4in visit_so -nt -4erg 4kn incpˆ -go_see -ˆincp art
to come back, and we are going to visit her; *we are going over*

t sənʔímaʔtət 407 way̓ uɬ scutx axáʔ {iʔ s iʔ ɬəssíʔt} iʔ
t s+n+ʔím+aʔ+t -t way̓ uɬ s -cut -x axáʔ iʔ
obj_itr grandchild -4in well and ipftvˆ -say -ˆipftv this art
to see our grandchild. *Their uncles*

ɬəɬsəsíʔsəlx 408 uɬ cútəlx way̓ cqəcqícəlx, kʷu
ɬɬ+s•siʔ -s -lx uɬ cut -lx way̓ c -qc•qic+lx kʷu
uncles -3in -pl and say -pl yes hab -run 4kn
are saying, *they said he’s already running around. We are going to go*

ksʔawscxʷíltaʔx {indec} 409 swit_aɬíʔ sksq̓məltnáwlaʔxəlx
ks -ʔaw+s+cxʷ=ílt -aʔx swit_aɬíʔ s -k+s+q̓m=ltn=áwlaʔ -x -lx
incp^ -go_hold_baby -^incp in_fact ipftv^ -starve -^ipftv -pl
and make over him." *They're all starving,*

410 uɬ lut t̓ sʔatxílxsəlx {uɬ} uɬ x̌lap 411 cxʷuy sx̌lap
uɬ lut t̓ s -ʔatx+ílx -s -lx uɬ x̌la+p c+xʷuy s+x̌la+p
and not negfac nom -sleep_pl -3i -pl until morning come morning
and they didn't sleep until daylight. *Daylight came,*

way̓ uɬ ixíʔ sur̓ur̓ísəlp̓msəlx uɬ ixíʔ ncíxəmsəlx mat
way̓ uɬ ixíʔ s -wr̓•wr̓=islp̓+m -s -lx uɬ ixíʔ n=cix+m -s -lx mat
well and then nom -light_fire -3i -pl and then warm_liquid -3erg -pl maybe
and maybe they warmed up some

t *cocoa* {kəm̓ mat} 412 way̓ wiʔwiʔcínəlx uɬ ixíʔ {uɬ i}
t way̓ wy̓•wy̓+cin -lx uɬ ixíʔ
obj_tr well finish_eating_pl -pl and then
cocoa. 17:07 *They got done eating, they started tying their stuff*

skʕackən̓lscútsəlx 413 way̓ ixíʔ ɬəɬʔímxsəlx 414 way̓
s -k+ʕac=kn̓=lscút -s -lx way̓ ixíʔ ɬ -ɬ+ʔim+x -s -lx way̓
nom -tie_in_bundles -3i -pl well then nom -move_back -3i -pl well
in bundles, *and they started moving back.* *They*

ɬxʷú··y̓ilx ɬk̓əɬk̓ʷƛ̓ápəlx 415 nt̓a·· iʔ spaʔl̓ísəlp̓[s] uɬ
ɬ+xʷuy̓•y -lx ɬ+k̓ɬ+k̓ʷƛ̓ap -lx nt̓a iʔ s -paʔl̓=íslp̓ -s uɬ
go_back_pl -pl come_in_sight_again -pl intj art nom -wood_smoke -3i and
went and got in sight. *My, there is smoke at*

axáʔ iʔ sɬəx̌míltsəlx 416 way̓ ɬiyáʕpəlx way̓
axáʔ iʔ s+ɬx̌m=ilt -s -lx way̓ ɬ+yaʕ+p -lx way̓
this art relative -3in -pl well arrive_again -pl well
their daughter's. *They got back,*

cʔax̌əx̌lílxsts scx̌əw̓íɬc̓aʔx axáʔ {iʔ} iʔ
c -ʔax̌•x̌•l+ílx -st -s sc -x̌w̓=íɬc̓aʔ -x axáʔ iʔ
cust^ -busy_with -^cust -3i ipftvp^ -dry_meat -^ipftvp this art
their daughter is busy

st̓əmkʔíltsəlx 417 níkxnaʔ ɬtkʷúpxnəmsəlx iʔ
s+t̓mkʔ=ilt -s -lx níkxnaʔ ɬ+t+kʷup=xn+m -s -lx iʔ
daughter -3in -pl goodness rush_to_again -3erg -pl art
drying meat. *Gee, they rushed to their*

sənʔímaʔtsəlx 418 way̓ cxʷíltməlx axáʔ {iʔ} ia ilmíxʷəm iʔ naʔɬ
s+n+ʔím+aʔ+t -s -lx way̓ cxʷ=ilt+m -lx axáʔ iʔ yl=mixʷ+m iʔ naʔɬ
grandchild -3in -pl well hold_child -pl this art chief art and
grandchild. *The boss and his wife started*

tkəɬmílxʷs 419 way̓ axáʔ iʔ sqilxʷ iwá ɬyaʕmísəlx {iʔ iʔ} iʔ
tkɬ+m=ilxʷ -s way̓ axáʔ iʔ s+qilxʷ iwá ɬ+yaʕ+mí -s -lx iʔ
wife -3in well this art person try_to return_to -3erg -pl art
loving him. 18:04 *The people tried to get back*

cətcíxʷsəlx t̓əxʷ i? sənpúlxtənsəlx 420 waẏ ixí?
ct•citxʷ -s -lx t̓xʷ i? s+n+pul+x+tn -s -lx waẏ ixí?
houses -3in -pl evidently art camping_place -3in -pl well then
to their houses, their camping places, and because

c?awsksíw uɬ aɬí? sɬiqʷ x̌əẁaẁ i? l tx̌líẁscəlx ilí?
c+?aw+s+k+síw uɬ aɬí? s+ɬiqʷ x̌ẁ•aẁ i? l t+x̌l=iẁs -c -lx ilí?
come_ask and because meat dried art in cache -3in -pl there
there is meat in the dry cache where they had put it,

cutáns 421 waẏ ixí? c?awsíwsəlx axá? {i?} i? tkəɬmílxʷ
c -wta+n -s waẏ ixí? c -?aw+síw -s -lx axá? i? tkɬmilxʷ
act -put -3erg well then habnt -go_ask -3erg -pl this art woman
they went to ask.[24] *They asked the woman,*

422 cúsəlx waẏ uɬ la?kín məɬ kʷu t̓qlimx
cu -s -lx waẏ uɬ la+?kíṅ mɬ kʷu t̓ql=imx
tell -3erg -pl well and wherever and 4kn settle
they asked "And where shall we put our place to stay?"

423 kʕoyncútməntməlx {uɬ i t} i? t tkəɬmílxʷ 424 cúntməlx uɬ ha
k+ʕʷy+ncut+m -nt -m -lx i? t tkɬmilxʷ cu -nt -m -lx uɬ ha?
laugh_at -nt -psv -pl art agInst woman tell -nt -psv -pl and inter
The woman laughed at them. *She said "What*

p sċintx ha 425 sc̓kinx a cítxʷəmp ka?
p s -ċint -x ha? sc+?kin+x a citxʷ -mp ki?
5kn ipftv^ -say_what -^ipftv inter why_is_it intj house -5in rel
are you saying? 19:00 *This is your own place and*

ɬcyaʕ̓místp 426 uɬ ixí? t̓əxʷ {i? l} i? l səncítxʷtnəmp
ɬ+c+yaʕ+mí -st -p uɬ ixí? t̓xʷ i? l s+n+citxʷ+tn -mp
be_backward_about -st -5erg and that evidently art in camping_place -5in
you are backward. *It's your own place to stay."*

427 cútəlx uɬ ixí? i? sɬiqʷ {uɬ i} pna swit ixí? {indec} [ɬa?
cut -lx uɬ ixí? i? s+ɬiqʷ pna? swit ixí? ɬa?
say -pl and that art meat maybe somebody that the_one_that
They said "And the meat? Maybe it's somebody

ksɬiqʷ] 428 cúntməlx uɬ ha p sċintx 429 ixí?
k+s+ɬiqʷ cu -nt -m -lx uɬ ha? p s -ċint -x ixí?
have_meat tell -nt -psv -pl and inter 5kn ipftv^ -say_what -^ipftvp that
else's." *She said "What are you saying?* *That*

mnímɬəmp i? {sənkʷúmcnəmp} sənkʷúmcəntnəmp tx̌líẁsəmp 430 uɬ ixí?
mnimɬ+mp i? s+n+kʷum=cn+tn -mp t+x̌l=iẁs -mp uɬ ixí?
you art storage_place -5in cache -5in and that
is your storage cache, *that's*

24 The camping spots are presumed occupied and the full caches to belong to others.

mnímɬəmp sɬíqʷəmp {ili a cu} ka? ɬcyaʕ̓místp 431 níkna··
mnimɬ+mp s+ɬiqʷ -mp ki? ɬ+c+yaʕ̓+mí -st -p níkxna?
you meat -5in rel be_backward_about -st -5erg goodness
your meat, and then you're backward." They're sure

taɬt límtəlx {inaud} uɬ ktpíɬxʷmsəlx {a i} 432 k̓əl sk̓laxʷ way̓ {ɬc}
taɬ+t lim+t -lx uɬ k+tp=iɬxʷ+m -s -lx k̓l s+k̓laxʷ way̓
surely glad -pl and build_house -3erg -pl at evening yes
tickled, and they started setting up their houses. 20:02 In the evening

ɬckicx wápupxən 433 cq̓mənkíń̓əm {i t} i? tla nyrip i?
ɬ+c+kic+x wap•wp=xn c̓q̓+mn=kiń̓+m i? tla n+yr=ip i?
arrive_cisl_again lynx throw_pack art from back_of_tipi art
Lynx came back. He threw his pack in the back, with deer,

sƛ̓a?cínəm t qlíɬc̓a? 434 ixí? nc̓ayxʷápəlqs
s+ƛ̓a?=cín+m t ql=íɬc̓a? ixí? n+c̓ayxʷ=áplqs
deer obl raw_meat that end_of_story
fresh meat. That's the end of the story. 20:48

BlueJay and Wolf

1 way̓ axáʔ qʷásqiʔ naʔł nkʷəl̓múts nc̓íʔcən, ixíʔ ikscaptíkʷləm.
way̓ axáʔ qʷásqiʔ naʔł n+kʷl̓mut -s ixíʔ ixíʔ i -ks -captíkʷl+m
well this BlueJay and brother_in_law -3in that that 1i -futi -tell_stories
Well, this here BlueJay and his brother-in-law Wolf, that's what I'm going to talk about.

2 {*all right*} axáʔ nc̓íʔcən ixíʔ i l sxʔítx kiʔ cmrim. 3 uł ixíʔ
axáʔ n+c̓iʔ=cn ixíʔ iʔ l s+xʔit=x kiʔ c -mrim uł ixíʔ
this wolf that art with oldest_one rel hab -marry and that
Wolf was married with the oldest one. *And*

xaʔtúscəlx axáʔ iʔ nək̓ʷcwílxʷtn 4 ʔəxʷ qaʔłilmíxʷəm, ilmíxʷəm iʔ
xaʔt=ús -c -lx axáʔ iʔ nk̓ʷ+cw=ilxʷ+tn ʔəxʷ qaʔł=yl=míxʷ+m yl=mixʷ+m iʔ
leader -3in -pl this art one_group intj chief's_children chief art
he was the leader of this group. *There were also others, such as the chief's*

sənłəx̌mtáns 5 uł ałíʔ {ixíʔ iʔ} q̓sápiʔ iʔ sqílxʷ ixíʔ
s+n+łx̌m+tan -s uł ałíʔ q̓sápiʔ iʔ s+qilxʷ ixíʔ
in_law -3in and so long_ago art Indian that
children, and the chief's law relations. *And so, long ago that's what comes first for*

iʔ xʔítsəlx 6 {iʔ} iʔ qʷyúlaʔxʷsəlx iʔ sysyús i l stəxʷcəncút;
iʔ xʔit -s -lx iʔ qʷy=úlaʔxʷ -s -lx iʔa sy•sy=us iʔ l s+txʷ=cn+cut
art first -3in -pl art riches -3in -pl art smart art at food
the people; *their riches, those who are good providers 1:03*

7 axáʔ i l qáqxʷəlx, kəm̓ axáʔ {i l} i l sƛ̓aʔcínəm 8 uł ałíʔ nak̓ʷáʔ
axáʔ iʔ l qa•qxʷ+lx km̓ axáʔ iʔ l s+ƛ̓aʔ=cín+m uł ałíʔ nak̓ʷ+á
this art at fish or this art at deer and because not
of fish, or deer. *At that time*

cmystísəlx pnicíʔ a[xáʔ] iʔ sqláw̓, məł ixíʔ
c -my -st -is s+qlaw pn+icíʔ ixíʔ iʔ s+qlaw mł that
custˆ -know -ˆcust -3erg money at_that_time this art money and that
they didn't know what money was, so they put them

cxaʔtəmstísəlx. 9 uł way̓ t̓i axáʔ iʔ stəxʷcəncút, ixíʔ {a} a
c -xaʔt+m -st -is -lx uł way̓ t̓iʔ axáʔ iʔ s+txʷ=cn+cut ixíʔ a
custˆ -first -ˆcust -3erg -pl and yes evid this art food then art
above all else. *Obtaining food, yes indeed, they put above all else*

cxaʔtəmstísəlx. ixíʔ {i} iʔ xʔítsəlx. 10 uł scʔx̌ílx
c -xaʔt+m -st -is -lx ixíʔ iʔ xʔit -s -lx uł sc+ʔx̌il+x
custˆ -first -ˆcust -3erg -pl that art first -3in -pl and reason_why
these providers, they are the highest. *And that's why*

úłiʔ nsucənmístməntəm ta nc̓íʔcən axáʔ ya ilmíxʷəm i l
uł iʔ n+sw=cn+mist+mn -t -m t n+c̓iʔ=cn axáʔ ya yl=mixʷ+m iʔ l
and_then propose_for -nt -psv agInst wolf this art chief art for
when Wolf proposed to the chief for his daughter, he consented,

sť̓əmkəʔílts, úłiʔ xəʔína?, ałíʔ sysyús [a]tá nc̓íʔcən i l
s+ť̓mkʔ=ilt -s uł iʔ xʔ=ínaʔ ałíʔ sy•sy=us atáʔ n+c̓iʔ=cn iʔ l
daughter -3in and_then consent because smart this wolf art at
because Wolf is smart at getting food,

stəxʷcəncút, axáʔ i l sƛ̓aʔcínəm. 11 ixíʔ uł {ya} cúntəm: "wáy̓" uł
s+txʷ=cn+cut axáʔ iʔ l s+ƛ̓aʔ=cín+m ixíʔ uł cu -nt -m way̓ uł
food this art at deer then and tell -nt -psv yes and
deer. *He was told: "All right." And so*

ixíʔ uł a cmrímәlx naʔł sť̓əmkəʔílts. 12 way̓ uł ixíʔ łaʔ
ixíʔ uł a c -mrim -lx naʔł s+ť̓mkʔ=ilt -s way̓ uł ixíʔ łaʔ
then and intj hab -marry -pl with daughter -3in well and then when
he and the [chief's] daughter got married. 2:00 *And when*

cpíx̌əm ł xaʔtúsəmsəlx nc̓íʔcən 13 uł ałíʔ {p} iʔ sqílxʷ
c -pix̌+m xaʔt=ús+m -s -lx n+c̓iʔ=cn uł ałíʔ iʔ s+qilxʷ
hab -hunt ? make_leader -3erg -pl wolf and so art people
they go hunting they put Wolf at the head. *Because*

pnicíʔ uł nak̓ʷáʔ {ałíʔ ť̓i} ckmax, way̓ ixíʔ a nək̓ʷcwílxʷtn. 14 uł
pn+icíʔ uł nak̓ʷ+á c -kmax way̓ ixíʔ a nk̓ʷ+cw=ilxʷ+tn uł
at_that_time and not hab -only ye that art group and
at that time the people didn't stay alone, but in a group. *And*

way̓ ť̓i ilíʔ cʔul̓úsəlx i l sʔístk[əm] 15 cʔístkməlx,
way̓ ť̓iʔ ilíʔ c -ʔul=w̓s -lx iʔ l s+ʔistk+m c -ʔistk+m -lx
yes evid there hab -gather -pl art in winter hab -winter -pl
they stick together in winter. *They winter,*

cúsəlx sənʔístktn. 16 {ixíʔ uł} lútəm t sip̓əʔíłxʷəlx, {i t}
cu -s -lx s+n+ʔis=tk+tn lut+m t sip̓ʔ=íłxʷ -lx
tell -3erg -pl wintering_pla no agInst tipi -pl
they call it "wintering place;" *They don't have buckskin tipis,*

x̌líłxʷməlx, kəm̓ axáʔ tkʷtan. 17 x̌líłxʷməlx axáʔ iʔ t k̓ilílxʷ
x̌l=iłxʷ+m -lx km̓ axáʔ tkʷ+tan x̌l=iłxʷ+m -lx axáʔ iʔ t k̓yl=ilxʷ
board_house -pl or this tule board_house -pl this art agInst tree_bark
board houses or tule [houses]. *They cover houses with tree bark*

18 kəm̓ iʔ t {iʔ t} sutn, iʔ t qʷílcən, axáʔ iʔ ʔastkʷ iʔ {iʔ ə}
km̓ iʔ t sut+n iʔ t qʷil=cn axáʔ iʔ ʔastkʷ iʔ
or art agInst thing art agInst fir_boughs this art cedar_wood art
or anything, boughs, cedar

[mxʷíłp] 19 ť̓əxʷ way̓ skpəllíksts iʔ stkəlkəlxmíkstn, uł ixíʔ a
mxʷ=iłp ť̓xʷ way̓ s+k+pl•l=ikst -s iʔ s+t+kl•klx+m=ikst+n uł ixíʔ a
cedar_boughs emph yes sprout -3in art sticks and that art
boughs. 3:00 *Those which sprout from the limbs, these they call*

ccústsəlx {indec} 20 təl ʔastkʷ kiʔ sckpəllíks[tx].
c -cu -st -s -lx tl ʔastkʷ kiʔ sc -k+pl•l=ikst -x
cust^ -tell -^cust -3erg -pl from cedar_wood rel ipftvp^ -sprout -^ipftvp
"palm boughs," *they grow from cedar trees.*

21 scʔx̌ílx ʕáċənt axáʔ {i} iʔ cq̓iɬp; 22 uɬ ixíʔ scústsəlx
sc+ʔx̌il+x ʕaċ -nt axáʔ iʔ cq̓=iɬp uɬ ixíʔ s -cu -st -s -lx
reason_why look -nt this art fir and then cust^ -tell -^cust -3erg -pl
That's why, look at fir trees; these they call "fir boughs;"

kcq̓əɬpíkst, uɬ itíʔ ċx̌iɬ kpəllíkst. 23 uɬ axáʔ iʔ {iʔ} ʔastkʷ iʔ
k+cq̓=ɬp=ikst uɬ itíʔ c+ʔx̌iɬ k+pl•l=ikst uɬ axáʔ iʔ ʔastkʷ iʔ
fir_boughs and from_that like sprout and this art cedar_wood art
that's how it grows. And that which grows

skpəllíksts {false starts}; 24 waẏ lut iksʔaməm̓núnəm, ixíʔ
s+k+pl•l=ikst -s waẏ lut i -ks -ʔam•m -nun -m ixíʔ
sprout 3in well not 1i -futi -name -manage -apsv that
on the cedar... Well, no, I can't name [i.e. remember its name]

ʔastkʷ ɬaʔ ckpəllíkst. 25 ixíʔ məɬ ixíʔ ɬ
ʔastkʷ ɬaʔ c -k+pl•l=ikst ixíʔ mɬ ixíʔ
cedar_wood the_one_that hab -sprout that and that ?
what grows on cedar. That's how they

cqʷyíɬxʷəmstsəlx. 26 uɬ lut t̓ə cɬʕát̓əlx, uɬ kʷal̓t.
c -qʷy=iɬxʷ+m -st -s -lx uɬ lut t̓ c -ɬaʕt̓ -lx uɬ kʷal̓+t
cust^ -cover_house -^cust -3erg -pl and not negfac hab -wet -pl and warm
cover their houses. And they don't get wet, and it's warm.

27 uɬ axáʔ iʔ sx̌líɬxʷ, {i} sutn k̓ilílxʷ; 28 ixíʔ a
uɬ axáʔ iʔ s+x̌l=iɬxʷ sut+n k̓yl=ilxʷ ixíʔ a
and this art board_house thing tree_bark that art
And those that are board houses that's bark; they

cx̌əlstísəlx, məɬ kɬx̌əlstísəlx. 29 uɬ ixíʔ a
c -x̌l -st -is -lx mɬ kɬ+x̌l -st -is -lx uɬ ixíʔ a
cust^ -cover -^cust -3erg -pl and cover_on_top -^cust -3erg -pl and that art
board these up, and they board them on top. 4:00 And they

scústsəlx sx̌líɬxʷ. 30 waẏ {a} kícəntməlx t
s -cu -st -s -lx s+x̌l=iɬxʷ waẏ kic -nt -m -lx t
cust^ -tell -^cust -3erg -pl board_house well reach_st/sb -nt -psv -pl agInst
call them "boarded houses." Well, BlueJay got

qʷásqiʔ. 31 waẏ nsucənmístməntəm axáʔ aʔ ilmíxʷəm. 32 waẏ uɬ
qʷásqiʔ waẏ n+sw=cn+mist+mn -t -m axáʔ aʔ yl=mixʷ+m waẏ uɬ
BlueJay well propose_for -nt -psv this art chief yes and
to them. Well, he proposed to the chief. Yes,

aɬíʔ axáʔ iʔ stʔiwtx waẏ uɬ nixʷ ƛ̓x̌ap. 33 cakʷ cus a
aɬíʔ axáʔ iʔ s+tʔiw+t=x waẏ uɬ nixʷ ƛ̓x̌a+p caʔkʷ cu -s a
because this art young_one yes and also grow_sg as tell -3erg art
since the youngest one also had grown up. One should say

nqílxʷcən waẏ uɬ st̓aʔk̓míx, st̓aʔk̓əmxwílx. 34 waẏ uɬ nx̌əluʔíls,
n+qilxʷ=cn waẏ uɬ s+t̓aʔk̓+míx s+t̓aʔk̓+mx+wílx waẏ uɬ n+x̌lwʔ=ils
Indian_language yes and virgin young_woman yes and want_husband
in Indian she was a young maiden, she had grown up. Yes, she wants a man. Well,

waẏ q̓ʷaxʷ. 35 x̌minks axáʔ {iʔ} iʔ st̓əmkəʔílts axáʔ {a ilmíxʷəm}
waẏ q̓ʷ•axʷ x̌m=ink -s axáʔ iʔ s+t̓mkʔ=ilt -s axáʔ
yes flirt want -3erg this art daughter -3in this
he began to flirt. *BlueJay likes his daughter,*

iʔ axáʔ qaʔɬilmíxʷəm, qʷásqiʔ. 36 nq̓əmscínəms, uɬ cus iʔ
iʔ axáʔ qaʔɬ=yl=míxʷ+m qʷásqiʔ n+q̓m=s=cin+m -s uɬ cu -s iʔ
art this chief's_children BlueJay pine_for -3erg and tell -3erg art
the chief's daughter. *He got stuck on her, and she said to her father:*

místəms: waẏ kʷ xəʔínaʔ. 37 iwáʔ cúntəm iʔ t místəms:
ṁist+m -s waẏ kʷ xʔ=ínaʔ iwá cu -nt -m iʔ t ṁist+m -s
w's_father -3in yes 2kn consent try_to tell -nt -psv art agInst w's_father -3in
"Well, you had better consent." *To no avail her father said to her:*

uɬ aɬíʔ lut t̓a csúxʷstəm. 38 lut t̓a
uɬ aɬíʔ lut t̓ c -suxʷ -st -m lut t̓
and so not negfac custˆ -recognize -ˆcust -4erg not negfac
"But we don't know him. 5:02 *We don't*

cmystím {i siʔ} i l stiṁ sisyús; 39 i l stəxʷcəncút, pnaʔ
c -my -st -im iʔ l s+tiṁ sy•sy=us iʔ l s+txʷ=cn+cut pnaʔ
custˆ -know -ˆcust -4erg art at what smart art at food maybe
know in what things he is smart, *in getting things to eat,*

cmay ixíʔ akɬqʷəṅqʷəṅtán. 40 cəṁ t̓i lut məɬ {kʷɬ} kʷ ɬ
cmay ixíʔ a -kɬ -qʷṅ•qʷṅ+tan cṁ t̓iʔ lut mɬ kʷ ɬ
maybe then 2i -to_be -suffer maybe evid not and 2kn compl
maybe you'll suffer from it. *It might not be long and you will throw him*

x̌ʷlíɬc̓aʔ ṅíṅẇiʔ sx̌ʷupts. 41 uɬ axáʔ t
x̌ʷl=íɬc̓aʔ ṅíṅẇiʔ s+x̌ʷup+t -s uɬ axáʔ t
throw_away_person a_while worthlessness -3in and this obl
away if it turns out that he's good for nothing. *One who will do us*

kɬənx̌stántət, mi t aksqəl̓tmíxʷ [kʷ kʷnim iʔ t
kɬ -n+x̌s+tan -tt mi t a -k -s+qlt=mixʷ kʷ kʷni+m iʔ t
to_be -well_being -4i fut obl 2i -to_be -husband 2kn take art obl
good, take him for

aksqəltmíxʷ]. 42 lut, axáʔ iʔ st̓əmkəʔílts. 43 ta incá
a -k -s+qlt=mixʷ lut axáʔ iʔ s+t̓mkʔ=ilt -s ta in+cá
2i -to_be -man not this art daughter -3in intj I
your husband." *But no, his daughter.* *"He's*

iksx̌ílwiʔ, nak̓ʷáʔ anwí aks[x̌ílwiʔ]; 44 iwá kən ɬ
i -k -s+x̌ílwiʔ nak̓ʷ+á anwí a -k -s+x̌ílwiʔ iwá kn ɬ
1i -to_be -husband not you 2i -to_be -husband even 1kn compl
going to be MY husband, not your husband; *even if I get hard up,*

nqʷəṅqʷəṅtmín, uɬ incá iʔ kən ksqʷəṅqʷáṅta[ʔx]. 45 cúntəm: waẏ,
n+qʷṅ•qʷṅ+t+min uɬ in+cá iʔ kn ks -qʷṅ•qʷṅ+t -aʔx cu -nt -m waẏ
hard_up and I art 1kn incpˆ -hard_up -ˆincp tell -nt -psv well
it is I who would be hard up." *He told her:*

way̓, mat aspu?ús. 46 ixí? k̓ɬ?əm̓cíntəm qʷásqi?. 47 way̓
way̓ mat a -s+pu?=ús ixí? k̓ɬ+?m=cin[1] -t -m qʷásqi? way̓
Ok maybe 2in -heart then answer -nt -psv BlueJay well
"Well, if that's how you feel." That was that, BlueJay got his answer. So

ixí? cmrím. 48 ixí? uɬ síscəlqʷəm t{a} qʷásqi?. 49 uɬ aɬí? t̓i
ixí? c -mrim ixí? uɬ si•sc=lqʷ+m t qʷásqi? uɬ aɬí? t̓i?
then hab -marry then and honeymoon agInst BlueJay and so evid
he got married. So BlueJay honeymooned. So they were

ilí? c̓ul̓úsəlx; 50 axá? nc̓í?cən na?ɬ tkɬmílxʷs, uɬ axá? qʷásqi?
ilí? c -?ul=w̓s -lx axá? n+c̓i?=cn na?ɬ tkɬ+m=ilxʷ -s uɬ axá? qʷásqi?
there hab -gather -pl this Wolf and wife -3in and this BlueJay
gathered together; Wolf and his wife, and BlueJay and

na?ɬ tkɬmílxʷs; 51 uɬ axá? {i} i? sənɬəx̌mtáns, ya nəx̌ʷnx̌ʷíw̓s
na?ɬ tkɬ+m=ilxʷ -s uɬ axá? i? s+n+ɬx̌m+tan -s ya nx̌ʷ•nx̌ʷ=iw̓s
and wife -3in and this art in_law -3in art married_couple
his wife, 6:06 and his law-relations, the couple

a? ilmíxʷəm. 52 uɬ t̓i ilí? c̓ul̓úsəlx, nəqsíɬxʷəlx, mat
a? yl=mixʷ+m uɬ t̓i? ilí? c -?ul=w̓s -lx nqs=iɬxʷ -lx mat
art chief and evid there hab -gather -pl one_house -pl maybe
of the chief. And there they are all together, in one house, I don't know in

nk̓ʷánxqnəlx, [mat] nmásqnəlx; 53 [ma]t nka?ɬálqən, uɬ aɬí?
n+k̓ʷan+x=qn -lx mat n+mas=qn -lx mat n+ka?ɬál=qn uɬ aɬí?
several_tipis -pl maybe four_head -pl maybe three_tipis and because
how many tipis put together, maybe four, maybe three, since there are

ka?ɬəl̓nəx̌ʷnx̌ʷíw̓səm. 54 way̓ axá? qʷásqi? {tik way} t̓i_kmix {c}
ka?ɬl+nx̌ʷ•nx̌ʷ=iw̓s+m way̓ axá? qʷásqi? t̓i?_kmix
three_couples well this BlueJay only
three couples. Well, all BlueJay does is play

cpu?acki?scút. 55 a ks?í··t[x] cəm̓ la ntx̌ʷəx̌ʷqín, mi uɬ
c -pu=?acki?+scút a ks -?itx cm̓ l n+tx̌ʷ•x̌ʷ=qin mi uɬ
hab -play_with_wife intj futi -sleep maybe at noon then and
with his wife. He sleeps until noon, then he wakes, then

xʷt̓lílxəlx axá? na?ɬ tkɬmílxʷs; 56 way̓ aɬí? uɬ
xʷt̓+lilx -lx axá? na?ɬ tkɬ+m=ilxʷ -s way̓ aɬí? uɬ
get_up_pl -pl this and wife -3in well because and
he and his wife get up, because they are

csíscəlqʷa?x. 57 alá? a[xá?] pnicí? way̓ súxʷəxʷ, i?
c -si•sc=lqʷ -a?x alá? axá? pn+icí? way̓ suxʷ•xʷ i?
hab -honeymoon -? here this at_that_time yes leave_pl art
honeymooning. By that time the others are gone,

1 Expected here (and elsewhere) is k̓ɬ+?am=cín. In this form often the glottal stop disappears altogether.

scpíx̌əx, iʔ sctəxʷcəncútxəlx. 58 uɬ axáʔ nc̓íʔcən {iʔ}
sc -pix̌ -x iʔ sc -txʷ=cn+cut -x -lx uɬ axáʔ n+c̓iʔ=cn
ipftvp^ -hunt -^ipftvp art ipftvp^ -get_food -^ipftvp -pl and this wolf
those that hunt, and get things to eat. *And Wolf is their*

iʔ xaʔtúsc aɬíʔ wnixʷ sisyús {i l} i l stəxʷcəncút.
iʔ xaʔt=ús -c aɬíʔ wnixʷ sy•sy=us iʔ l s+txʷ=cn+cut
art leader -3in because true smart art at food
leader because he sure is smart at getting things to eat. 7:04

59 cmistís laʔkín iʔ sənʔístktns iʔ sƛ̓aʔcínəm;
c -my -st -is la+ʔkíń iʔ s+n+ʔis=tk+tn -s iʔ s+ƛ̓aʔ=cín+m
cust^ -know -^cust -3erg wherever art wintering_place -3in art deer
He knows where the deer's wintering places are,

60 uɬ sisyús i l syríwaxən. 61 waẏ ɬaʔ cqíxʷstsəlx
uɬ sy•sy=us iʔ l s+yr=íwaʔ=xn waẏ ɬaʔ c -qixʷ -st -s -lx
and smart art at snowshoes yes when cust^ -drive -^cust -3erg -pl
and he's smart with snowshoes. *When they make a drive for the deer,*

iʔ sƛ̓aʔcínəm, kíləntməlx ta nc̓íʔcən. 62 lut {ks ks} kscxʷuys
iʔ s+ƛ̓aʔ=cín+m kil -nt -m -lx t n+c̓iʔ=cn lut ksc -xʷuy -s
art deer chase -nt -psv -pl agInst wolf not futPerfi -go -3i
Wolf chases them. *The deer don't go far,*

iʔ sƛ̓aʔcínəm, məɬ nkcníkəńtməlx; 63 məɬ ixíʔ ƛ̓xʷəntí··məlx {a nqilt}
iʔ s+ƛ̓aʔ=cín+m mɬ n+kc+n=ikn -t -m -lx mɬ ixíʔ ƛ̓xʷ -nt -im -lx
art deer and overtake -nt -psv -pl and then kill_many -nt -psv -pl
and he catches up with them, *and then he slaughters*

kəm̓ nk̓áwlaʔxʷ. 64 mi_sic nkcníkəń axáʔ {i} iʔ sənɬəx̌mtáns, iʔ k̓ʷíƛ̓ət
km̓ n+k̓áw=laʔxʷ mi_sic n+kc+n=ikn axáʔ iʔ s+n+ɬx̌m+tan -s iʔ k̓ʷiƛ̓+t
or massacre then catch_up this art in_law -3in art others
them. *Then he overtakes his law relations, the other*

iʔ sqílxʷ. 65 waẏ məɬ ixíʔ mílxətməlx t sƛ̓aʔcínəm. 66 waẏ məɬ
iʔ s+qilxʷ waẏ mɬ ixíʔ mil̓ -xt -m -lx t s+ƛ̓aʔ=cín+m waẏ mɬ
art people well and then gift -xit -psv -pl obj_tr deer well and
people. *And then he gives them the deer.* *And then*

ixíʔ sckʷíɬc̓aʔsəlx, lut t̓a ct̓ʕapáməlx, məɬ waẏ taʔxʷsɬíqʷ[əlx].
ixíʔ s -ckʷ=íɬc̓aʔ -s -lx lut t̓ c -t̓aʕp+ám -lx mɬ waẏ taʔxʷ+s+ɬíqʷ -lx
then nom -drag_body -3i -pl not negfac hab -shoot -pl and yes get_meat -pl
they drag the meat home, they don't even have to shoot,

67 ixíʔ ɬaʔ cʔamstíməlx {t} ta nc̓íʔcən. 68 uɬ aɬíʔ x̌aʔ•x̌áʔ,
ixíʔ ɬaʔ c -ʔam -st -im -lx t n+c̓iʔ=cn uɬ aɬíʔ x̌aʔ•x̌áʔ
that when cust^ -feed -^cust -psv -pl agInst wolf and because great
and that's how Wolf feeds them. *Because he's great,*

sisyús i l spíx̌əm. 69 sc̓x̌ilx úɬiʔ {xaʔ} xaʔtústsəlx.
sy•sy=us iʔ l s+pix̌+m sc+ʔx̌il+x uɬ iʔ xaʔt=ús -t -s -lx
smart art at hunting reason_why and_then leader -st -3erg
smart at hunting. 8:02 *That's why he was their leader.*

70 {waẏ} waẏ uɫ axáʔ nk̓ʷaʔlsncút axáʔ iʔ sxʔitx iʔ sťəmkʔílt;
waẏ uɫ axáʔ n+k̓ʷaʔ=ls+ncút axáʔ iʔ s+xʔit=x iʔ s+ťmkʔ=ilt
well and this cranky this art oldest_one art daughter
Well, the oldest daughter started eating her feelings (getting cross),

71 ťəxʷ axáʔ nc̓íʔcən iʔ tkɫmilxʷs. 72 uɫ ťiʔ kiwúsəms iʔ
ťxʷ axáʔ n+c̓iʔ=cn iʔ tkɫ+m=ilxʷ -s uɫ ťiʔ k+yw=us+m -s iʔ
emph this wolf art wife -3in and evid watch -3erg iʔ
Wolf's wife. *She's always*

saʔstáms, uɫ cxʷətxʷtnústs iʔ saʔstáms.
saʔ•stám -s uɫ c -xʷt•xʷt -nu -st -s iʔ saʔ•stám -s
saʔ•stám -s uɫ cust^ -unhappy_with -manage -^cust -3erg art brother_in_law -3in
watching her brother-in-law.

73 uɫ iwá cus {i} iʔ ɬcəcʔúpsc: waẏ uɫ kʷ sc̓kinx
uɫ iwá cu -s iʔ ɬ+c•cʔ=ups -c waẏ uɫ kʷ sc -ʔkin -x
and try_to tell -3erg art younger_sister -3in well and 2kn ipftvp^ -indef -^ipftvp
She even said to her younger sister: "What's the matter?

74 waẏ uɫ xʷəʔásq̓ət, uɫ {a} pútiʔ p csíscəlqʷəm. 75 waẏ uɫ caʔkʷ
waẏ uɫ xʷʔ=asq̓t uɫ pút+iʔ p c -si•sc=lqʷ+m waẏ uɫ caʔkʷ
well and many_days and still 5kn hab -honeymoon yes and should
It's been many days, and still you two are honeymooning. *You should be*

kʷ ks{p̓aʕp̓ʕa}p̓aʕp̓ʕawmənwíxʷaʔx, 76 uɫ waẏ caʔkʷ ctəxʷcəncút
kʷ ks -p̓a•p̓aʕʷ+m+nwíxʷ -aʔx uɫ waẏ caʔkʷ c -txʷ=cn+cut
2kn incp^ -tire_recip -^incp and yes should hab -get_food
getting tired of one another. *And your husband should*

ixíʔ {as} asqəl̓tmíxʷ. 77 waẏ uɫ ťi_kmix p c̓ícəckən̓. 78 uɫ lut
ixíʔ a -s+qlt=mixʷ waẏ uɫ ťiʔ_kmix p c -ʔic•c•kn uɫ lut
that 2in -husband well and only 5kn hab -play and not
get things to eat. 9:00 *And all you do is play.*

waẏ {pause} cmistíxʷ axáʔ {an} asastám talí·· waẏ
waẏ c -my -st -ixʷ taʔlíʔ a -saʔ•stám taʔlíʔ waẏ
yes hab -know -^cust -2erg this 2in -brother_in_law very_much yes
But no. You know that your brother-in-law gets

mat c̓ayx̌ʷt; 79 uɫ waẏ ťi_kmix p c̓ícəckən̓, lut ťa
mat c -ʔayx̌ʷ+t uɫ waẏ ťiʔ_kmix p c -ʔic•c•kn lut ť
maybe hab -tired and well only 5kn hab -play not hab
very tired. *All you do is play, and he doesn't get*

ctəxʷcəncút. 80 ixíʔ caʔkʷ ťi ckəxstís, caʔkʷ iwá lut
c -txʷ=cn+cut ixíʔ caʔkʷ ťiʔ c -kx -st -is caʔkʷ iwá lut
hab -get_food that should evid cust^ -follow -^cust -3erg should even not
things to eat. *Even if he doesn't shoot, just so*

sťaʕpám, uɫ itíʔ ckxan 81 uɫ ťi x̌ast iʔ spuʔúsc axáʔ {i}
s -ťaʕpá+m uɫ itíʔ c -kxa+n uɫ ťiʔ x̌as+t iʔ s+puʔ=ús -c axáʔ
hab -shoot and that hab go along and evid good art heart -3in this
he goes along. *And his brother-in-law would sure*

ya nkʷəl̓múts. 82 uɬ mat way̓ talí
ya n+kʷl̓mut -s uɬ mat way̓ taʔlíʔ
art brother_in_law -3in and maybe yes very_much
feel good.” I guess she has all kinds of

cxʷaʔɬk̓əɬpaʔx̌áms. 83 way̓ k̓əxʷkʷú··nəms {i} iʔ ɬcəcʔúpsc.
c -xʷaʔ+ɬ+k̓ɬ+paʔx̌á+m -s way̓ k+ʔxʷ+kʷun+m -s iʔ ɬ+c•cʔ=ups -c
act -think_much -3erg well nag -3erg art younger_sister -3in
different thoughts. Well, she kept nagging at her younger sister.

84 way̓ ixíʔ {ixíʔ cx̌ɬ} snunxʷínaʔs. 85 la_cxʔít iwáʔm k̓əɬqíxʷs
way̓ ixíʔ s -n+wnxʷ=ínaʔ -s la_c+xʔít iwá+m k̓ɬ+qixʷ -s
well then nom -believe -3i at_first try_to take_up_for -3erg
Well, she believed her. At first she tried to take up for

iʔ sx̌ílwiʔs; 86 way̓ ixíʔ uɬ sic nun·xʷínaʔ, nsúxʷnaʔ uɬ
iʔ s+x̌ílwiʔ -s way̓ ixíʔ uɬ sic n+wn•n•xʷ=ínaʔ n+súxʷ=naʔ uɬ
art husband -3in yes then and then believe recognize_talk and
her husband; finally she believed, she

nun·xʷínaʔ. 87 way̓ wnixʷ, scuníxʷəxʷ {iɬcəcʔúps} [iɬkíkxaʔ].
n+wn•n•xʷ=ínaʔ way̓ wnixʷ sc -wnixʷ -xʷ i -ɬ+kí•kxaʔ
believe well true ipftvp^ -true -^ipftvp 1in -older_sister
understood. 10:00 “That's true, my older sister is telling the truth.”

88 uɬ axáʔ iʔ ƛ̓ax̌əx̌ƛ̓x̌áp lut {t̓ə} t̓a cc̓íntəlx {t̓a c}. 89 wím̓
uɬ axáʔ iʔ ƛ̓ax̌•x̌•ƛ̓x̌á+p lut t̓ c -c̓int -lx wim̓
and this art parents not negfac hab -say_what -pl in_vain
The parents never say anything. They

cx̌aʔəncístsəlx axáʔ iwáʔ iʔ sxaʔtmíxəltsəlx {ɬa} ɬaʔ
c -x̌aʔn=cí -st -s -lx axáʔ iwá iʔ s+xaʔt+míx=lt -s -lx ɬaʔ
cust^ -silence -^cust -3erg -pl this try_to art first_child -3in -pl when
tried to stop their oldest daughter when

ckim̓sts {i} iʔ saʔstáms, wíkʷcnəms. 90 way̓ ixíʔ
c -kim̓ -st -s iʔ saʔ•stám -s wikʷ=cn+m -s way̓ ixíʔ
cust^ -hate -^cust -3erg art brother_in_law -3in backbite -3erg well then
she hates her brother-in-law, and she backbites him. Well,

cus iʔ qʷásqiʔs: way̓ uyáʔ. 91 {way̓ uɬ} way̓ myaɬ xʷʔásq̓ət,
cu -s iʔ qʷásqiʔ -s way̓ uyá way̓ myaɬ xʷʔ=asq̓t
tell -3erg art BlueJay -3in well listen well too_much many_days
she said to BlueJay: “Listen here. It's been too many days,

nyʕ̓íp kʷu scsíscəlqʷaʔx. 92 way̓ uyáʔ, k̓əɬpáx̌x iʔ
nyʕip kʷu sc -si•sc=lqʷ -aʔx way̓ uyá k̓ɬ+pax̌ -x iʔ
always 4kn ipftvp^ -honeymoon -^ipftvp well listen thinking -isimptv art
and we're still honeymooning. Listen, think about getting

l akstəxʷcəncút. 93 way̓ myaɬ kʷu ɬaʔ cənʔaɬncín.
l a -k -s+txʷ=cn+cut way̓ myaɬ kʷu ɬaʔ c -n+ʔaɬn=cín
about 2i -to_be -food yes too_much 4kn comp hab -sponge_food
something to eat. We have sponged too much.

94 waẏ mat {kʷu} kʷu nxiʔílsməntəm.
waẏ mat kʷu n+xẏ=íls+m -nt -m
yes maybe 3e4obj tire_of -nt -3e4obj
Maybe they are getting tired of us.11:00

95 mʕan axáʔ iʔ t
mʕan axáʔ iʔ t
intj this art agInst
Just look at your

asaʔstám {uɬ}, waẏ taʔlíʔ kʷu nxiʔílsməntəm.
a -saʔ•stám waẏ taʔlíʔ kʷu n+xẏ=íls+m -nt -m
2in -sister_in_law yes very_much 3e4obj tire_of -nt -3e4obj
sister-in-law. They hate us very much.

96 uɬ kmix
uɬ kmix
and only
And

axaʔ iʔ {ta} t asənɬəx̌mtán iwáʔ ck̓əɬqíxʷstəmsəlx.
axáʔ iʔ t a -s+n+ɬx̌m+tan iwá c -k̓ɬ+qixʷ -st -m -s -lx
this art agInst 2in -in_law try_to cust^ -take_up_for -^cust -2obj -3erg -pl
your law relations tried to take up for you.

97 ixíʔ iwáʔ cx̌aʔncístsəlx iʔ stʼəmkʔíltsəlx, axáʔ iʔ
ixíʔ iwá c -x̌aʔn=cí -st -s -lx iʔ s+tʼmkʔ=ilt -s -lx axáʔ iʔ
then to_no_avail cust^ -stop_talk -^cust -3erg -pl art daughter -3in -pl this art
They tried to stop their daughter,

sxʔítx.
s+xʔit=x
oldest_one
the oldest one.

98 cúsəlx: waẏ uyáʔ, k̓əwpmínt asaʔstám.
cu -s -lx waẏ uyá k̓w+p+mi -nt a -saʔ•stám
tell -3erg -pl well listen stop_asking -nt 2in -brother_in_law
They said to her: 'Listen, leave your brother-in-law alone.'"

99 waẏ, waẏ cus iʔ tkɬmílxʷs: waẏ {kʷu kʷa kʷu} kʷu xʷíc̓əxtxʷ
waẏ waẏ cu -s iʔ tkɬ+m=ilxʷ -s waẏ kʷu xʷic̓ -xt -xʷ
well well tell -3erg art wife -3in OK 1obj give -xit -2erg
He said to his wife: "Give me a piece of

t síp̓iʔ;
t síp̓iʔ;
obj_tr hide
skin,

100 aɬíʔ uɬ kʷu qʷəńcínməntxʷ.
aɬíʔ uɬ kʷu qʷń=cin+m -nt -xʷ
because and 1obj pity -nt -2erg
since you complain with me.

101 waẏ lut kən
waẏ lut kn
well not 1kn
I haven't

tʼa {kən tʼa kɬ} ksyríwaxən kəm̓ lut kən tʼa kɬcq̓ílən.
tʼ k+s+yr=íwaʔ=xn km̓ lut kn tʼ kɬ+cq̓=iln
negfac have_snowshoes or not 1kn negfac have+arrow
any snowshoes, or bow and arrow.

102 waẏ tʼəxʷ
waẏ tʼxʷ
OK emph
I'm

ixíʔ istəxʷəlscút.
ixíʔ i -s -txʷ=lscut
then 1i -intt -get_ready
going to prepare myself."

103 waẏ ixíʔ stəxʷɬckʷíńkəms[2] qʷásqiʔ.
waẏ ixíʔ s -txʷ+ɬ+ckʷ=ink+m -s qʷásqiʔ
well then nom -obtain_bow -3i BlueJay
Well, BlueJay got a bow. 12:01

104 waẏ iwá sk̓ʷəl̓ckʷíńks, uɬ lut itíʔ, iʔ sk̓ásts.
waẏ iwá s+k̓ʷl̓+ckʷ=ink -s uɬ lut itíʔ iʔ s -kas+t -s
well try_to bow_one_makes -3in and not that art nom -bad -3i
Well, the bow he made wasn't even that, it was awful.

105 lu··t
lut
not
It

2 The -m suffix seems to exclude the analysis of this construction as a nominalization. See forms in 104 and 106.

úɬəm txíxiʔ. 106 uɬ axáʔ {iʔ sck̓ʷəlc̓əq̓} iʔ stəxʷɬcq̓íləns way̓ nixʷ
uɬ+m t+xí•xiʔ uɬ axáʔ iʔ s+txʷ+ɬ+cq̓=iln -s way̓ nixʷ
and fall_short and this art arrow_one_gets -3in well also
wasn't any good. *And the arrows he got are just*

t̓i put c̓x̌iɬt{s}[3]. 107 uɬ axáʔ nixʷ iwá {ɬ} ɬ utəntís iʔ
t̓iʔ put c+ʔx̌iɬ+t uɬ axáʔ nixʷ iwá ɬ wt -nt -is iʔ
evid just like and this also to_no_avail compl put_down -nt -3erg art
the same. *And when he put the feathers*

kstqpíʔstn axáʔ [iʔ] l cq̓ílən; 108 kc̓əpq̓əntís, way̓ uɬ lut
k -s+tqp=iʔst+n axáʔ iʔ l cq̓=iln k+c̓p̓q̓ -nt -is way̓ uɬ lut
to_be -feather this art on arrow glue -nt -3erg well and not
on the arrows, *he just sticks them on. And his arrows*

txíxiʔ axáʔ iʔ kɬcq̓íləns. 109 way̓ k̓səlscút, uɬ axáʔ i l
t+xí•xiʔ axáʔ iʔ kɬ -cq̓=iln -s way̓ k̓s=lscut uɬ axáʔ iʔ l
fall_short this art to_be -arrow -3i well bad_outfit and this art for
are not good enough. *His things are bad;*

syríwaxəns {i sc}; 110 way̓ uɬ lut itíʔ, ck̓əsk̓sálqʷ. 111 uɬ sic
s+yr=íwaʔ=xn -s way̓ uɬ lut itíʔ c -k̓s•k̓s=alqʷ uɬ sic
snowshoes -3in well and not that hab -bad_rd_object and then
the snowshoes, *no, they're bad, they weren't much.* *Well,*

təltútəm, {unclear} swit_aɬíʔ sp̓p̓aʔc̓ʕálaʔqʷ aɬíʔ scyryárk̓ʷəs. 112 way̓
tlt•ut+m swit_aɬíʔ s+p̓•p̓aʔc̓=ʕálaʔqʷ aɬíʔ sc -yr•yark̓ʷ -s way̓
worthless in_fact new_shoots because pftv -round -3i well
they are not fit, he made the frame with new shoots. 13:03 *Well,*

uɬ lut ití myútyaʔ. 113 way̓ ixíʔ x̌litxts axáʔ {iʔ} iʔ
uɬ lut itíʔ my=útyaʔ way̓ ixíʔ x̌lit -xt -s axáʔ iʔ
and not that unfit well then call -xit -3erg this art
it's not even fit. *She asked her mother*

tum̓s {ta} t nʔíyxəntəns t síp̓iʔ 114 cúntəm: uɬ haʔ
tum̓ -s t n+ʔiy=xn+tn -s t síp̓iʔ cu -nt -m uɬ haʔ
wo's_mother -3in obl shoe_lacing -3in obl hide tell -nt -psv and inter
for some lacing skin. *She asked her: "And what*

kstim̓ 115 cus: way̓ asník̓əɬxʷ, isənkʷəɬmrím, way̓ {ks}
k -s+tim̓ cu -s way̓ a -s+nik̓=ɬxʷ i -s+nkʷ+ɬ+mrim way̓
to_be -what tell -3erg well 2in -son_in_law 1in -spouse well
is it for?" *She said: "Your son-in-law, the one I'm married to,*

kskxənmíxaʔx ɬ kspíx̌aʔx; 116 uɬ lut t̓a
ks -kx+n -míx+aʔx ɬ ks -pix̌ -aʔx uɬ lut t̓
incpˆ -follow -ˆincp and incpˆ -hunt -ˆincp and not negfac
he's going with the hunters *and he doesn't have*

3 A complement is expected here.

ksyríwaxən, uɬ waẏ ʕapnáʔ xʷíƛ̓xnəm; 117 uɬ waẏ
k+s+yr=íwaʔ=xn uɬ waẏ ʕapnáʔ xʷiƛ̓=xn+m uɬ waẏ
have_snowshoes and yes now make_snowshoe_sticks and yes
snowshoes, and now he's prepared sticks, *and made*

yrík̓ʷəxnəm uɬ lut nax̌əmɬ t̓a kɬənʔíyxən {uɬ}. 118 [s]c̓x̌íl[x] kiʔ
yrik̓ʷ=xn+m uɬ lut nax̌mɬ t̓ kɬ+n+ʔiy=xn sc+ʔx̌il+x kiʔ
make_snowshoes and not but negfac have+shoe_lace reason_why rel
frames, but he doesn't have anything to lace them with. *That's why*

kʷu cus uɬ a nmycíntsən, pnaʔ kʷ ksíp̓iʔ. 119 a
kʷu cu -s uɬ a n+my=cin -t -s -n pnaʔ kʷ k+asíp̓iʔ a
1obj tell -3erg and art interpret -nt -2obj -1erg maybe 2kn have_hide intj
he told me, and I interpret him to you, maybe you have some hide." *She*

cúntəm: waẏ, waẏ t̓əxʷ kən ck̓əɬccəx̌ʷəncút. 120 waẏ t̓əxʷ ixíʔ
cu -nt -m waẏ waẏ t̓xʷ kn c -k̓ɬ+c•cx̌ʷ+ncut waẏ t̓xʷ ixíʔ
tell -nt -psv yes yes emph 1kn hab -in_stock yes emph that
said to her: "Yes, I keep some in stock. 14:03 *I'll*

xʷíc̓əɬtsən. 121 waẏ ixíʔ k̓ərəntí··s qʷásqiʔ, waẏ ixíʔ
xʷic̓ -ɬt -s -n waẏ ixíʔ k̓r -nt -is qʷásqiʔ waẏ ixíʔ
give -ɬt -2obj -1erg well then cut -nt -3erg BlueJay well then
give you some." *She started cutting it. BlueJay started stringing*

sənʔíyxn[əms]. 122 waẏ ksk̓əlxʷəmstís axáʔ iʔ
s -n+ʔiy=xn+m -s waẏ ks -k̓lxʷ+m -st -is axáʔ iʔ
nom -lace_shoe -3i well futt^ -evening -caus -3erg this art
the shoes. *It took him one day to fix his*

sck̓ʷúl̓aʔsts; 123 {uɬ} uɬ axáʔ {iʔiʔksiri} iʔ ksyríwaxəns.
sc -k̓ʷul̓=aʔst -s uɬ axáʔ iʔ k -s+yr=íwaʔ=xn -s
pftv -make_weapon -3i and this art to_be -snowshoes -3i
bow and arrow *and his snowshoes.*

124 uɬ {tam} axáʔ yaʔ ksqʷaʔmíkst, 125 {ta} k̓ʷənxá··sq̓ət mi uʔyúsxən
uɬ axáʔ iʔ k+s+qʷaʔm=íkst k̓ʷn+x=asq̓t mi wẏ=us=xn
and this art have_familiarity a_few_days fut finish_shoe_work
And it takes those who are used to it, *several days to finish shoe work*

kəm̓ wiʔsck̓ʷəl̓scq̓ílən. 126 cniɬc t̓i [i] l ksk̓laxʷ uɬ waẏ wiʔstís
km̓ wẏ+sc+k̓ʷl̓+s+cq̓=iln cniɬ+c t̓iʔ iʔ l k+s+k̓laxʷ uɬ waẏ wẏ -st -is
or finish_arrow (s)he evid art in all_day and yes finish -st -3erg
or arrow work. *But he in one day already had finished his arrows and*

iʔ kɬcq̓íləns {iʔ kɬ} iʔ ksyríwaxəns. 127 uɬ aɬíʔ lut txíxiʔ.
iʔ kɬ -cq̓=iln -s iʔ k -s+yr=íwaʔ=xn -s uɬ aɬíʔ lut t+xí•xiʔ
art to_be -arrow -3i art to_be -snowshoes -3i and so not fall_short
his snowshoes. *They can't be good enough.*

128 {axá} axáʔm scx̌síkstəmsəlx aʔ ksqʷaʔmíkst. 129 x̌əẇẇálqʷ
axáʔ axáʔ+m sc -x̌s=ikst+m -s -lx aʔ k+s+qʷaʔm=íkst x̌ẇ•ẇ=alqʷ
this this pftv -do_well -3erg -pl art have_familiarity dry_sticks
Those who know how to fix them take pains. 15:00 *The sticks*

iʔ kɬcq̓ílən[səlx], mi uɬ tələntí··səlx [tələmstísəlx MD].
iʔ kɬ -cq̓=iln -s -lx mi uɬ tɬ -nt -is -lx tɬ+m -st -is -lx
art to_be -arrow -3i -pl then and straight -nt -3erg -pl tɬ+m -st -is -lx
for the arrows have to be dry, and then they straighten them.

130 mi_sic tk̓ʷúl̓aʔstməlx, tk̓ʷəlk̓ʷúl̓sts axáʔ iʔ cq̓ílən, 131 məɬ axáʔ
mi_sic t+k̓ʷúl̓=aʔst+m -lx t+k̓ʷl̓•k̓ʷul̓ -st -s axáʔ iʔ cq̓=iln mɬ axáʔ
then attach_feathers -pl make_how -st -3erg this art arrow and this
Then they fix the feathers on, they fix the arrows, *and*

iʔ ckʷín̓k ilíʔ cʔx̌iɬ. 132 x̌ẁəntí··səlx x̌əẁẁá··lqʷ, xʷƛ̓əntí··səlx
iʔ ckʷ=ink ilíʔ c+ʔx̌iɬ x̌ẁ -nt -is -lx x̌ẁ•ẁ=alqʷ xʷƛ̓ -nt -is -lx
art bow there like dry -nt -3erg -pl dry_sticks whittle -nt -3erg -pl
the bow the same way. *They dry the sticks dry, they whittle them, and they*

məɬ ʔíp̓əs. 133 {mat t̓əxʷ yat lut t̓a cmistín i} ya
mɬ ʔip̓ -s ya
and wipe -3erg art
dry them. *They make it shine*

cktíqʷəlqʷstsəlx axáʔ iʔ la nq̓aʔq̓ʔíẁs; 134 məɬ ixíʔ
c -k+tiqʷ=lqʷ -st -s -lx axáʔ iʔ l n+q̓aʔ•q̓ʔ=íẁs mɬ ixíʔ
cust^ -shine -^cust -3erg -pl this art in in_middle and then
in the center of the bow, *and*

kəlk̓álqʷsəlx iʔ t tinx, məɬ ixíʔ iʔ t t̓ic̓; 135 t̓íɬsəlx,
k+lk̓=alqʷ -s -lx iʔ t tinx mɬ ixíʔ iʔ t t̓ic̓ t̓iɬ -s -lx
tie_stick -3erg -pl art agInst sinew and then art agInst pitch glue -3erg -pl
then they wrap it with sinew, and with pitch; *they glue it,*

məɬ lut kstk̓ʷáxʷxʷəlqʷs, uɬ t̓i yʕac̓; 136 ixíʔ uɬ a cyuʔyáʕʷt
mɬ lut ks -t+k̓ʷaxʷ•xʷ=lqʷ -s uɬ t̓iʔ yaʕc̓ ixíʔ uɬ a c -yw•yaʕʷ+t
and not futi -unravel -3i and evid solid then and art hab -strong
and it doesn't come loose, and it's solid, *the bow is good*

iʔ ckyuyuwínk. 137 uɬ {axáʔ ta} qʷásqiʔ uɬ aɬíʔ mat
iʔ c -k+yw•yw=ink uɬ qʷásqiʔ uɬ aɬíʔ mat
art hab -strong_bow and BlueJay and because maybe
and strong. *But because BlueJay maybe has*

sx̌ʷptáx̌ənx; 138 uɬ waẏ {t̓i lut} ck̓səlscút {uɬ waẏ}. 139 waẏ
s -x̌ʷp+t=ax̌n -x uɬ waẏ c -k̓s=lscut waẏ
ipftv^ -weak_arm -^ipftv and yes hab -bad_thing well
weak arms, 16:05 *what he made is no good.* *The*

x̌lap, waẏ t̓i pútiʔ k̓ímlaʔxʷ, waẏ t̓əqʷcín axáʔ nc̓íʔcən; 140 waẏ cəm
x̌la+p waẏ t̓iʔ pút+iʔ k̓ím=laʔxʷ waẏ t̓qʷ=cin axáʔ n+c̓iʔ=cn waẏ cm̓
morning well evid still dark well holler this wolf well maybe
next day it was still dark when Wolf hollered: *"Daylight*

kʷu k̓əɬx̌əlx̌láp, kʷu nwaʔsnúxʷ; 141 lkʷut iʔ ksxʷúytntət, waẏ
kʷu k̓ɬ+x̌l•x̌la+p kʷu nwaʔs=núxʷ lkʷ=ut iʔ k -s+xʷuy+tn -tt waẏ
4kn daylight 4kn late far art to_be -travel -4i yes
will overtake us, we will be late, *we are going far,*

xʷt̓líl xʷwi. 142 níkxnaʔ axáʔ iʔ sqílxʷ xʷt̓lílx iʔ splal.
xʷt̓+lilx -wy níkxnaʔ axáʔ iʔ s+qilxʷ xʷt̓+lilx iʔ s+pl•al
get_up_pl -ipimptv goodness this art people get_up_pl art young_growth
get up." *Goodness, the people, the young people, got up.*

143 way̓ uɬ ʔíɬnəlx way̓ ɬʕápməlx, way̓ ixíʔ uɬ wiʔnúmtəlx. 144 way̓
way̓ uɬ ʔiɬn -lx way̓ ɬaʕp+m -lx way̓ ixíʔ uɬ wy̓+numt -lx way̓
well and eat -pl yes drink -pl well then and ready -pl well
They ate, they drank, they were all ready. *Wolf*

t̓əqʷcín, {t} wahwáhm nc̓íʔcən. 145 way̓, wáy̓ kʷu təkʷʔút. 146 way̓ uɬ
t̓qʷ=cin wh•wáh+m n+c̓iʔ=cn way̓ way̓ kʷu tkʷʔ=ut way̓ uɬ
holler holler wolf yes yes 4kn walk_pl well and
hollered, he was proclaiming. *"All right. We are going."* *The*

c̓ácqaʔlx axáʔ iʔ splal. 147 way̓ uɬ nixʷ qʷásqiʔ t̓i c̓ácqaʔ.
c+ʔácqaʔ -lx axáʔ iʔ s+pl•al way̓ uɬ nixʷ qʷásqiʔ t̓iʔ c+ʔácqaʔ
come_out -pl this art young_growth well and also BlueJay evid come_out
young folks started coming out. 17:01 *BlueJay came out too.*

148 way̓ axáʔ qʷásqiʔ tla nyxʷút, uɬ ixíʔ k̓ʕəwqənmístəms axáʔ iʔ
way̓ axáʔ qʷásqiʔ tla n+yxʷ=ut uɬ ixíʔ k̓aʕʷ=qn+míst+m -s axáʔ iʔ
well this BlueJay from inside and then coax -3erg this art
From inside BlueJay coaxed

tkɬmílxʷs 149 ksláʕ̓ʷɬtəm[4] iʔ syríwaxəns; 150 uɬ aɬíʔ
tkɬ+m=ilxʷ -s ks -laʕ̓ʷ -ɬt -m iʔ s+yr=íwaʔ=xn -s uɬ aɬíʔ
wife -3in futi -put_on -ɬt -psv art snowshoes -3in and because
his wife *to put his snowshoes on him,* *because*

lut t̓a cmystís ɬ kskʕacəntís iʔ sc̓uʔxans,
lut t̓ c -my -st -is ɬ ks -k+ʕac -nt -is iʔ s+c̓w̓=xan -s
not negfac cust^ -know -^cust -3erg how futt^ -tie -nt -3erg art shoe -3in
he doesn't even know how to tie his shoes, the loops around the ankle,

ɬəqʷcínxən, c̓úmstəm. 151 way̓ {ci} [t] iʔ tkɬmílxʷs t̓i
ɬqʷ=cin=xn c -ʔum -st -m way̓ t iʔ tkɬ+m=ilxʷ -s t̓iʔ
ankle_loops cust^ -name -^cust -4erg well agInst art wife -3in evid
that's what we call it. *Well, it was his woman who put*

láʕ̓ʷɬtəm iʔ syríwaxəns; 152 way̓ t̓i tla nixʷút uɬ way̓
laʕʷ -ɬt -m iʔ s+yr=íwaʔ=xn -s way̓ t̓iʔ tla n+yxʷ=ut uɬ way̓
put_on -ɬt -psv art snowshoes -3in yes evid from inside and yes
his snowshoes on him, *right from inside he put his*

cyríwaxən. 153 uɬ axáʔm iʔ splal aʔ ksqʷʔam {unclear}
c -yr=íwaʔ=xn uɬ axáʔ+m iʔ s+pl•al aʔ k+s+qʷʔam
hab -snow_shoe and this art young_growth art have_familiarity
snowshoes on. *These young folks that are used to it...,*

4 Here the root √lʕ̓ʷ functions as a strong (stressed) root; not elsewhere.

kəlkʷákʷəlx; 154 sc̓x̌iɬ lut l aʔkɬxəwíɬ,[5] məɬ sic yríwaxən[məlx].
k+lkʷ•akʷ -lx sc+ʔx̌iɬ lut l aʔkɬ -xwiɬ mɬ sic yr=íwaʔ=xn+m -lx
far -pl like not at there_is -road and then snowshoes -pl
they go far, like where there is no road, and then they put their snowshoes on.

155 níknaʔ ɬ kákaʔmsəlx; 156 k̓ʕʷəyncútəmsəlx uɬ aɬíʔ
níkxnaʔ ɬ ká•kaʔ+m -s -lx k+ʕʷy+ncut+m -s -lx uɬ aɬíʔ
goodness and make_fun_of -3erg -pl laugh_at -3erg -pl and because
Goodness, they made fun of him. The people laughed at him because

t sqílxʷ tla nyxʷút iʔ l syríwax[ns]. 157 way̓ t̓i
t s+qilxʷ tla n+yxʷ=ut iʔ l s+yr=íwaʔ=nx -s way̓ t̓iʔ
agInst people from inside art in snowshoe -3in well evid
he put his snowshoes on from inside. 18:01 BlueJay

nəqsí··ʔpustxən məɬ tq̓əlq̓əlxʷúsxən {ə} qʷásqiʔ {məɬ a}; 158 {a} məɬ kəlkílxs {ə}
nqs=ípuʔst=xn mɬ t+q̓l•q̓lxʷ=us=xn qʷásqiʔ mɬ kl•kilx -s
one_step and hook_on BlueJay and hands -3in
takes just one step and he hooks on something, and he has to protect

k̓əɬtqəncútəms. 159 way̓ uɬ mat iʔ t̓əxʷ iʔ t
k̓ɬ+tq+ncut+m -s way̓ uɬ mat iʔ t̓xʷ iʔ t
protect_self -3erg well and maybe art evidently art agInst
himself with his hands. It must have been that his hands

smík̓ʷət uɬ aɬíʔ k̓əyʔí··kst; 160 uɬ aɬíʔ miná kspíkst, miná
s+mik̓ʷ+t uɬ aɬíʔ k̓y̓=ikst uɬ aɬíʔ miná k+sp=ikst miná
snow_on_ground and so cold_hands and because futNeg have_glove futNeg
got cold from the snow, because I don't suppose he has gloves,

t *wool gloves.* 161 məɬ ixíʔ c̓əm̓c̓m̓əntʕás iʔ kəlkílx[s] t̓i {indec}
t mɬ ixíʔ c̓m̓•c̓ -nt -ʕas iʔ kl•kilx -s t̓iʔ
obl and then suck -nt -3erg art hands -3in evid
wool gloves. He started sucking his fingers because they are

k̓əy̓íkst. 162 way̓ uɬ cútəlx axáʔ iʔ splal: way̓ lút. {unclear}
k̓y̓=ikst way̓ uɬ cut -lx axáʔ iʔ s+pl•al way̓ lut
cold_hands well and say -pl this art young_growth well not
cold. Then the young ones said: "Well, no,

163 cəm̓ uc k̓əɬk̓ək̓láxʷ cəm̓ itlíʔ mi ɬcp̓əlk̓úsəm, uɬ aɬíʔ
cm̓ uc k̓ɬ+k̓•k̓laxʷ cm̓ itlíʔ mi ɬ+c+p̓lk̓=us+m uɬ aɬíʔ
maybe dub out_of_sight maybe from_there then turn_bacl_cisl and because
maybe he'll get out of sight and then he'll come back, because BlueJay is way

c̓iwt qʷásqiʔ; 164 cəm̓ mi kəmahqənmíst, mi ɬcp̓əlk̓úsəm, way̓ staʔ kʷu
c+ʔiwt qʷásqiʔ cm̓ mi k+mah=qn+míst mi ɬ+c+p̓lk̓=us+m way̓ staʔ kʷu
last BlueJay maybe fut give_up then turn_bacl_cisl well intj 4kʷu
behind, there he will give up, he'll come back. He's making us

5 aʔ kɬ+xwiɬ is possible.

a cxárkstəms. 165 ixíʔ təkʷʔútəlx, uł axáʔ atáʔ nc̓íʔcən ałíʔ
a c -xar=kst+m -s ixíʔ tkʷʔ=ut -lx uł axáʔ atáʔ n+c̓iʔ=cn ałíʔ
art act -take_time -3erg then walk_pl -pl and this this wolf so
lose time.” *They walked away, and Wolf is way ahead,*

scxaʔtmíx ixíʔ sk̓əłq̓əx̌əncút; 166 k̓əłq̓əx̌ntís iʔ
sc -xaʔt -mix ixíʔ s -k̓ł+q̓x̌+ncut k̓ł+q̓x̌ -nt -is iʔ
ipftvp^ -first -^ipftvp that hab -trail_blaze trail_blaze -nt -3erg art
he breaks the trail for his friends. 19:00 *He breaks the trail for*

sl̓əx̌l̓áx̌ts. 167 ixíʔ ńíńẃiʔ k̓liʔ mi k̓əłwíkxnəlx, 168 ixíʔ məł
s+l̓x̌•l̓ax̌t -s ixíʔ ńíńẃiʔ ik̓líʔ mi k̓ł+wik=xn -lx ixíʔ mł
friends -3in then a_while there then see_tracks -pl then and
his friends. *Then they find tracks,* *then*

px̌ʷməncútəlx, c̓áq̓ʷl̓aʔxʷəm nc̓íʔcən. 169 uł axáʔ ta[6] nc̓íʔcən [u]ł ixíʔ
px̌ʷ+mncut -lx c̓áq̓ʷ=laʔxʷ+m n+c̓iʔ=cn uł axáʔ t n+c̓iʔ=cn uł ixíʔ
scatter -pl point_the_way wolf and this wolf and that
they scatter. Wolf'll point to where to go. *This Wolf is the leader,*

xaʔtús {iʔ} iʔ sənsisyúscəlx; 170 uł ixíʔ a ck̓əłxʷúy {iʔ k̓əl s} iʔ k̓əl
xaʔt=ús iʔ s+n+sy•sy=us -c -lx uł ixíʔ a c -k̓ł+xʷuy iʔ k̓l
leader art smart_ones -3in -pl and then art hab -go art to
the smartest of all; *and then he goes where*

ksxʷúytəns iʔ sƛ̓aʔcínəm. 171 uł ałíʔ təl sisyúsc
k -s+xʷuy+tn -s iʔ s+ƛ̓aʔ=cín+m uł ałíʔ tl sy•sy=us -c
to_be -travel -3in art deer and because from smart -3in
the deer go. *Because he's smart and strong.*

k̓ʷəck̓ʷáct, uł ƛ̓ax̌t łaʔ cxʷúy. 172 way̓ cxʷú··yəlx, way̓
k̓ʷc•k̓ʷac+t uł ƛ̓ax̌+t łaʔ c -xʷuy way̓ c -xʷuy -lx way̓
strong and fast when hab -go yes hab -go -pl yes
And he can go fast. *They were going. Then they*

k̓əłwíkxəns {ic}. 173 way̓ xʷʔit sƛ̓aʔcínəm, sənʔíłəntəns. 174 ixíʔ uł
k̓ł+wik=xn -s way̓ xʷʔi+t s+ƛ̓aʔ=cín+m s+n+ʔiłn+tn -s ixíʔ uł
see_tracks -3erg yes many deer feeding_place -3in then and
see the tracks. *Lots of deer where they are feeding.* *They*

px̌ʷməncút, uł taʔlíʔ way̓ xʷʔit iʔ sƛ̓aʔcínəm. 175 way̓ ƛ̓lap, way̓
px̌ʷ+mncut uł taʔlíʔ way̓ xʷʔi+t iʔ s+ƛ̓aʔ=cín+m way̓ ƛ̓la+p way̓
scatter and very_much yes many art deer yes stop well
scattered. There were very many deer. 20:01 *He stopped.*

mat axáʔ cənqʷəʔúl̓axʷ, səlxʷʔúl̓axʷ. 176 way̓ aláʔ mat iʔ sƛ̓aʔcínəm.
mat axáʔ c -n+qʷʔ=úlaʔxʷ slxʷʔ=úlaʔxʷ way̓ aláʔ mat iʔ s+ƛ̓aʔ=cín+m
maybe this hab -ground_pocket big_place yes here must art deer
There's a hollow place, it's a big place. *The deer must be there:*

6 This particle intrudes, marking emphasis.

177 lut qíxʷəntəm axáʔ iʔ stəkʷtəkʷʔútn[səlx], mat iʔ
lut qixʷ -nt -m axáʔ iʔ s+tkʷ•tkʷʔ=ut+n -s -lx mat iʔ
not drive -nt -4erg this art tracks -3in -pl maybe art
"We didn't scare them. Here are their tracks, they might

sc̓íɬənxəlx. 178 ixíʔ uɬ way̓ xƛ̓púl̓aʔxʷ {uɬ i}. 179 way̓ ƛ̓lap
sc -ʔiɬn -x -lx ixíʔ uɬ way̓ xƛ̓+p=úlaʔxʷ way̓ ƛ̓la+p
ipftvpˆ -eat -ˆipftvp -pl then and yes daylight well stop
still be eating." *It was broad daylight.* *They*

uɬ ixíʔ cúntməlx: haʔ way̓ haʔ p cyáʕ̓ʔ 180 cútəlx: way̓, way̓
uɬ ixíʔ cu -nt -m -lx haʔ way̓ haʔ p c -yaʕ cut -lx way̓ way̓
and then tell -nt -psv -pl inter yes inter 5kn hab -arrive say -pl yes yes
stopped and he asked them: "Are you all gathered here?" *They said: "Yes,*

kʷu cyaʕ̓, kmíx ankʷəl̓mút qʷásqiʔ, lútiʔ t̓a {təc} ck̓əɬ·ʔíq̓ʷ.
kʷu c+yaʕ kmix a -n+kʷl̓mut qʷásqiʔ lút+i t̓ c+k̓+ɬʔiq̓ʷ
4kn all only 2in -brother_in_law BlueJay not_yet negfac come_in_sight
we are all here. Just your brother-in-law BlueJay hasn't yet come in sight.

181 {aɬəm} aɬíʔ t̓i ixíʔ kʷu ctəkʷʔút, ixíʔ uɬ cənɬəpɬʕapáq;[7]
aɬíʔ t̓iʔ ixíʔ kʷu c -tkʷʔ=ut ixíʔ uɬ c -n+ɬp•ɬʕapák
because evid then 4kn hab -walk then and hab -fall_in_snow
Just as we left, he was falling around,

182 uɬ aɬíʔ lut t̓a cmistís iʔ syríwaxən, uɬ way̓
uɬ aɬíʔ lut t̓ c -my -st -is iʔ s+yr=íwaʔ=xn uɬ way̓
and because not negfac custˆ -know -ˆcust -3erg art snowshoes and well
because he doesn't know anything about snowshoes, he might have

mat ɬp̓əlk̓úsəm; 183 way̓ lut ksk̓əɬʔímәntəm, kʷu
mat ɬ+p̓lk̓=us+m way̓ lut ks -k̓ɬ+ʔim -nt -m kʷu
maybe turn_back well not futtˆ -wait_for -nt -4erg 4kʷu
turned back. *Let's not wait for him. We are*

xárkstməntəm. 184 cut nc̓íʔcən: way̓, way̓ uníxʷ, 185 way̓
xar=kst+m -nt -m cut n+c̓iʔ=cn way̓ way̓ wnixʷ way̓
take_time -nt -3e4obj say wolf yes yes true well
wasting time." *Wolf said: "Well, that's right, 21:04* *we*

wíkəntəm axáʔ iʔ sxʷúytns iʔ sƛ̓aʔcínəm, sícxən. 186 lut mat
wik -nt -m axáʔ iʔ s+xʷuy+tn -s iʔ s+ƛ̓aʔ=cín+m sic=xn lut mat
see -nt -4erg this art track -3in art deer new_tracks not maybe
saw tracks of deer, fresh tracks. *I don't*

k̓aʔkín, axáʔ mət aláʔ cənqʷəʔúl̓axʷ, aláʔ csciẋʷ. 187 way̓
k̓a+ʔkín axáʔ mat aláʔ c -n+qʷʔ=úlaʔxʷ aláʔ c -sciẋʷ way̓
to_where this maybe here hab -ground_pocket here hab -slate_rocks well
think they went anywhere far. Maybe they're in that hollow, in those slate rocks. *We*

7 I have recorded this form with a final q, as here, and with a final k, as in sentence 221, with a difference in meaning that parallels Sh ʔs-t-ɬəpek *to fall in the snow*, ʔs-t-ɬəpeq *to fall in the mud*. The pharyngeal intrusion in the Ok form is not clear.

axáʔ kʷu kspx̌ʷməncútaʔx. 188 {li} ik̓líʔ k̓əl sqilt
axáʔ kʷu ks -px̌ʷ+mncut -aʔx ik̓líʔ k̓l s+qilt
this 4kn incpˆ -scatter -ˆincp be_there to top
are going to scatter. *There on the top there's a hollow.*

cənxʷəxʷrús, ik̓líʔ mi kʷu ɬúl·us. 189 n̓ín̓w̓iʔ itíʔ ɬ
c -n+xʷ•xʷr̓=us ik̓líʔ mi kʷu ɬ+ʔúl•l=us n̓ín̓w̓iʔ itíʔ ɬ
hab -hollow there fut 4kn gather_again a_while from_that if
That's where we will get back together. *If they've gone over,*

scqíltsəlx, məɬ itlíʔ k̓əɬpx̌əntím nixʷ itlíʔ {iʔ} iʔ
sc -qilt -s -lx mɬ itlíʔ nixʷ -nt -im nixʷ itlíʔ iʔ
pftv -top -3i -pl and from_there figure_out -nt -4erg again from_there art
then we'll think more how they're going

kspx̌məncúts."[8] 190 cútəlx: way̓. 191 way̓ cúntməlx,
ks -px̌ʷ+mncut -s cut -lx way̓ way̓ cu -nt -m -lx
futi -scatter -3i say -pl OK well tell -nt -psv -pl
to scatter." *They agreed: "Yes."* *He pointed for them*

miyú··l̓aʔxʷɬtməlx iʔ ksyx̌ísaʔx; 192 uɬ axáʔ {i ks ə} iʔ
my=úlaʔxʷ -ɬt -m -lx iʔ ks -yx̌=iʔs -aʔx uɬ axáʔ iʔ
point_to_a_place -ɬt -psv -pl art incpˆ -drive_herd -ˆincp and this art
where to drive the deer. 22:02 *"And those on*

kstk̓máx̌ən; 193 sk̓ʷút {i ks} iʔ ksʔáwsk̓əɬcahmíxaʔx,
k -s+t+k̓m=áx̌n s+k̓ʷut iʔ ks -ʔaw+s+k̓ɬ+cah -míx+aʔx
to_be -outside half art incpˆ -go_wait -ˆincp
the outside, *half of them will go where they'll be watching (for deer)*

ksk̓əɬxʷúyaʔx uɬ aɬíʔ ctk̓asʔasíl; 194 uɬ axáʔ cut incáʔ axáʔ
ks -k̓ɬ+xʷuy -aʔx uɬ aɬíʔ c -tk=ʔas•ʔasíl uɬ axáʔ cut incá axáʔ
incpˆ -go_under -ˆincp and so hab -two_persons and this say I this
to walk under: there will be two of them; *and as for me, I'll be from*

təl sk̓ʷút; 195 {i} kən k̓əɬtk̓máx̌ən, ixíʔ kən ksk̓əɬxʷúyaʔx.
tl s+k̓ʷut kn k̓ɬ+t+k̓m=ax̌n ixíʔ kn ks -k̓ɬ+xʷuy -aʔx
from other_side 1kn outside then 1kn incpˆ -walk_under -ˆincp
this half, *I will be on the outside, I am going to walk under."*

196 uɬ aɬíʔ axáʔ iʔ sisyús iʔ tk̓máx̌ən; 197 uɬ aɬíʔ ixíʔ
uɬ aɬíʔ axáʔ iʔ sy•sy=us iʔ t+k̓m=ax̌n uɬ aɬíʔ ixíʔ
and because this art smart art go_outside and because that
Only the smart ones can be on the outside, *because they're*

sckswitmístxəlx iʔ {k̓əl k̓əl} k̓əl sxʷúytns sƛ̓aʔcínəm {aɬi}.
sc -k+swít+miʔst -x -lx iʔ k̓l s+xʷuy+tn -s s+ƛ̓aʔ=cín+m
ipftvpˆ -do_one's_best -ˆipftvp -pl art to track -3in deer
going to have to work hard to get to where the deer go.

8 Expected here is "we are going to scatter."

198 ixíʔ sxʷaʔxʷúytəns a cənxʷəxʷṙús iʔ sƛ̓aʔcínəm. 199 uł ałíʔ
ixíʔ s+xʷaʔ•xʷúy+tn -s a c -n+xʷ•xʷr=us iʔ s+ƛ̓aʔ=cín+m uł ałíʔ
that usual_tracks -3in art hab -hollow art deer and so
That's where they always go, it's a low place where the deer go. *And*

axáʔ iʔ scix̌ísx, axáʔ qam·scútəlx; 200 waẏ məł iʔ
axáʔ iʔ sc -yx̌is -x axáʔ qam•m+scút -lx waẏ mł iʔ
this art ipftvp^ -drive_herd -^ipftvp this slow -pl yes and art
these who drive the deer take their time; *when*

k̓əłwíkxsəlx, məł t̓i nʔaʔú··cxsəlx, hoy məł qíxʷsəlx.
k̓ł+wik=x -s -lx mł t̓iʔ n+ʔa•ʔúc=x -s -lx hoy mł qixʷ -s -lx
see_tracks -3erg -pl and evid follow_tracks -3erg -pl finish and drive -3erg -pl
they see tracks they follow them, they drive them. 23:00

201 məł t̓i ik̓líʔ təłməncút axáʔ iʔ sƛ̓aʔcínəm ixíʔ k̓əl
mł t̓iʔ ik̓líʔ tł+mncut axáʔ iʔ s+ƛ̓aʔ=cín+m ixíʔ k̓l
and evid to_there go_straight_(up) this art deer then to
The deer tracks go straight to the

sxʷaʔxʷúytəns 202 uł waẏ ilíʔ axáʔ iʔ sʔawsk̓əłcahmíx, ixíʔ
s+xʷaʔ•xʷúy+tn -s uł waẏ ilíʔ axáʔ iʔ s -ʔaw+s+k̓ł+cah -mix ixíʔ
many_tracks -3in and yes there this art ipftv^ -go_wait -^ipftv that
low pass, *and those who went to watch, these*

məł ƛ̓xʷəntís. 203 laʔkín t̓əxʷ łaʔ cʔipuksqílxʷ axáʔ
mł ƛ̓xʷ -nt -is la+ʔkíṅ t̓xʷ łaʔ c -ʔip=wk+sqílxʷ axáʔ
and kill_many -nt -3erg whenever evidently when hab -happen_to_see this
will kill them. *When he who drives the deer accidentally*

iʔ scix̌íʔstx məł t̓ʕapám; 204 kəṁá yaʔx̌í łctqʷáẏ
iʔ sc -yx̌=iʔs+t -x mł t̓aʕp+ám kṁ+a yaʔx̌í ł+c+t+qʷay
art ipftvp^ -drive_herd -^ipftvp and shoot or yonder come_back_down
catches a glimpse of it, he shoots it, *or when they come down and*

łcṗəlk̓úsəm, 205 wíksəlx iʔ sk̓əłcahmíx, uł
ł+c+ṗlk̓=us+m wik -s -lx iʔ s -k̓ł+cah -mix uł
turn_bacl_cisl see -3erg -pl art ipftv^ -face_to_face -^ipftv and
turn around, *they see the ones who are watching, and they come down*

łcənxiʔstxəncútəlx, 206 ixíʔ məł cahəntíməlx, ixíʔ məł t̓ʕapsqílxʷəlx.
ł+c+nx=iʔst=xn+cut[9] -lx ixíʔ mł cah -nt -im -lx ixíʔ mł t̓aʕp+s+qílxʷ -lx
back_track pl then and face -nt -psv -pl then and fire_gun -pl
on their same tracks, *they run across the others, then they kill them.*

207 ilíʔ kiʔ ct̓ʕappíʔstəlx axáʔ {iʔ sc} iʔ scix̌íʔst[x].
ilíʔ kiʔ c -t̓aʕp•p=íʔst -lx axáʔ iʔ sc -yx̌=iʔst -x
there rel hab -get_so_killed -pl this art ipftvp^ -drive_herd -^ipftvp
That's when the ones that are driving kill their own deer.

9 This analysis is tentative.

208 uɬ ixíʔ axáʔ iʔ sʔums[10] iʔ ta nqʷəlqʷíltn iʔ
uɬ ixíʔ axáʔ iʔ s+ʔum -s iʔ t n+qʷl•qʷil+tn iʔ
and then this art name -3in art agInst language art
And that's what's called in the language "the ones that go

sck̓awsk̓əɬcahmíx; 209 axáʔ iʔ sysyús, səlxʷúsəm. 210 way̓,
sc -k+ʔaw+s+k̓ɬ+cah -mix axáʔ iʔ sy•sy=us s+lxʷ=us+m way̓
ipftvp^ -go_watch -^ipftvp this art smart watch well
and set watch," 24:00 the smart ones, those who watch. They

way̓ cútəlx: way̓ mat qʷásqiʔ way̓ ixíʔ mi ck̓əɬkláxʷ {unclear} mi
way̓ cut -lx way̓ mat qʷásqiʔ way̓ ixíʔ mi c -k̓ɬ+klaxʷ mi
well say -pl well maybe BlueJay yes then fut hab -disappear fut
said: "Maybe when BlueJay comes out of sight he gets

cʔayx̌ʷt; 211 {unclear} mi c{k̓ay}k̓ay̓ʔíks, itlíʔ mi ɬp̓əlk̓úsəm.
c -ʔayx̌ʷ+t mi c -k̓ay̓=íks itlíʔ mi ɬ+p̓lk̓=us+m
hab -tired fut hab -cold_hands from_there fut turn_back_again
tired, his hands'll get cold, he might turn back.

212 nák̓ʷəm lut t̓a cmystís iʔ syríwaxən. 213 way̓ uɬ
nak̓ʷ+m lut t̓ c -my -st -is iʔ s+yr=íwaʔ=xn way̓ uɬ
evid not negfac cust^ -know -^cust -3erg art snowshoes well and
He doesn't know anything about snowshoes. We'll

myaɬ cəm̓ kʷu xárkstməntəm ɬ k̓əɬʔíməntəm. 214 ixíʔ uɬ
myaɬ cm̓ kʷu xar=kst+m -nt -m ɬ k̓ɬ+ʔim -nt -m ixíʔ uɬ
too_much maybe 3e4obj take_time -nt -3e4obj if wait_for -nt -4erg then and
waste too much time if we wait for him." They

spəx̌ʷməncútsəlx. 215 cúntməlx: way̓ cmystíp iʔ
s -px̌ʷ+mncut -s -lx cu -nt -m -lx way̓ c -my -st -ip iʔ
nom -scatter -3i -pl tell -nt -psv -pl well cust^ -know -^cust -5erg art
scattered. He told them: "You know the place where I told you to go,

miyúl̓aʔxʷɬmən, ik̓líʔ mi kʷu yaʕmílx. 216 ixíʔ uɬ
my=úlaʔxʷ -ɬm -n ik̓líʔ mi kʷu yaʕ+m+ílx ixíʔ uɬ
point_to_a_place -5obj -1erg to_there fut 4kn together then and
we will gather there." They

[s]px̌ʷməncútsəlx. 217 uɬ axáʔ nák̓ʷəm ck̓əɬx̌əx̌lʕásəm qʷásqiʔ.
s -px̌ʷ+mncut -s -lx uɬ axáʔ nak̓ʷ+m c -k̓ɬ+x̌•x̌l=ʕas+m qʷásqiʔ
nom -scatter -3i -pl and this evid hab -watch_for BlueJay
scattered. BlueJay's been watching for them.

218 way̓ wiks px̌ʷməncút {iʔ} iʔ səl̓x̌l̓áx̌ts. 219 uɬ aɬíʔ mat {kyuyiwnə}
way̓ wik -s px̌ʷ+mncut iʔ s+l̓x̌•l̓ax̌t -s uɬ aɬíʔ mat
well see -3erg scatter art friends -3in and so maybe
He saw his friends scatter. 25:03 He must have good hearing,

10 Perhaps sʔum·s.

kyuyuwínaʔ, uɬ aɬíʔ stxəxƛ̓ínaʔmsts. 220 way̓ iʔ
k+yw•yw=ínaʔ uɬ aɬíʔ s -t+x•xƛ̓=ínaʔ+m -st -s way̓ iʔ
good_hearing and so cust^ -hear_all -^cust -3erg well art
he heard every word of it. *His*

nkʷəl̓múts {iʔs} iʔ ksəlxʷúsaʔx. 221 nák̓ʷəm t̓i
n+kʷl̓mut -s iʔ ks -lxʷ=us -aʔx nak̓ʷ+m t̓iʔ
brother_in_law -3in art incp^ -set_watch -^incp evid evid
brother-in-law is the one who's going to watch. *BlueJay*

sck̓ʷaʔk̓ʷúl̓əms qʷásqiʔ, ixíʔ uɬ a {c} cənɬpɬʕapák[11] {yac}, 222 lut
sc -k̓ʷaʔ•k̓ʷúl̓+m -s qʷásqiʔ ixíʔ uɬ a c -n+ɬp•ɬʕapák lut
pftv -practice -3i BlueJay then and art hab -fall_around_in_snow not
was just putting on, and that's why he fell deep in the snow, *like*

cmistís yríwa[xən]. 223 {inaud) nwísəlx qʷásqiʔ {k}
c -my -st -is yr=íwaʔ=xn n+wis+lx qʷásqiʔ
cust^ -know -^cust -3erg showshoe jump BlueJay
he didn't know snowshoeing. *BlueJay rose,*

ktər̓qíksəs a sc̓əlc̓ál. 224 nt̓a kiʔ niw̓t, taɬ[t] st̓r̓aq̓ʷ {iʔ s} iʔ
k+trq=iks -s a s+c̓l•c̓al nt̓a kiʔ niw̓+t taɬ+t s[12] -t̓raq̓ʷ iʔ
kick -3erg art trees intj rel wind surely ? -come_down art
he kicked the trees. *The wind started blowing, it came off the trees,*

skəm̓kʷúqən iʔ {s} smik̓ʷt iʔ k̓əl təmxʷúlaʔxʷ {unclear};
s+k+m̓kʷu=qn iʔ s+mik̓ʷt iʔ k̓l tmxʷ=úlaʔxʷ
snow_on_trees art snow_on_ground art to ground
the snow to the ground.

225 qʷaʔɬməncút iʔ təmxʷúlaʔxʷ. ixíʔ stxrútəms. 226 uɬ aɬíʔ
qʷaʔɬ+mncút iʔ tmxʷ=úlaʔxʷ ixíʔ s -t+xr=ut+m -s uɬ aɬíʔ
snow_dust art land then nom -run_uphill -3i and so
The snow was floating around the earth. He went up the hill. 26:00 *The deer...*

axáʔ iʔ sƛ̓aʔcínəm ilíʔ x̌íləm iʔ təmxʷúlaʔxʷ. 227 məɬ ixíʔ
axáʔ iʔ s+ƛ̓aʔ=cín+m ilíʔ x̌il+m iʔ tmxʷ=úlaʔxʷ mɬ ixíʔ
this art deer there do_like art land and then
The same thing there, the earth... *They*

skswitmístsəlx {iʔ k̓əl} iʔ k̓əl sənk̓əɬq̓ʷúystənsəlx; 228 c̓x̌iɬt {əs} iʔ
s -k+swít+miʔst -s -lx iʔ k̓l s+n+k̓ɬ+q̓ʷuy=s+tn -s -lx c+ʔx̌iɬ+t iʔ
nom -do_one's_best -3i -pl art to shelter -3in -pl like art
did their best to get where they could get shelter, *to a place*

sənt̓əwsqáx̌aʔtən,[13] uɬ aɬíʔ q̓ʷuyq̓ʷúylaʔxʷ. 229 lut ilíʔ t̓a ckicx
s+n+t̓w=sqáx̌aʔ+tn uɬ aɬíʔ q̓ʷuy•q̓ʷúy=laʔxʷ lut ilíʔ t̓ c -kic+x
barn and so still_air not there negfac hab -arrive
for shelter, and there is no air there. *The snow didn't reach there,*

11 I have recorded this form with a final k, as here, and with a final q, as in 181.
12 Possibly s- *cisl.*
13 A shortened form of sn+t̓wst=sqáx̌aʔ+tn.

iʔ {s} smik̓ʷt, {təm is} t̓əxʷ iʔ sniw̓t q̓ʷuyq̓ʷúylaʔxʷ. 230 way̓
iʔ s+mik̓ʷt t̓xʷ iʔ s+niw̓+t q̓ʷuy•q̓ʷúy=laʔxʷ way̓
art snow_on_ground evidently art wind still_air well
the wind is still. *BlueJay went*

txrútəm qʷásqiʔ; 231 xʷu··y, kicx ik̓líʔ nqəltús iʔ k̓la cənxʷəxʷr̓ús.
t+xr=ut+m qʷásqiʔ xʷuy kic+x ik̓líʔ n+qlt=us iʔ k̓l c -n+xʷ•xʷr=us
run_uphill BlueJay go arrive there summit art to hab -hollow
up the hill. 27:01 *He went, got to the top of the mountain where that low place is.*

232 way̓ itíʔ iʔ sƛ̕aʔcínəm iʔ sxʷúyʔitəns. 233 way̓ itíʔ {iʔ s} iʔ
way̓ itíʔ iʔ s+ƛ̕aʔ=cín+m iʔ s+xʷuy•y+tn -s way̓ itíʔ iʔ
yes from_that art deer art tracks -3in well from_that art
The deer had already gone over. *His partner,*

sl̓ax̌ts way̓ [n]kʷəl̓múts, way̓ kskəlkəlnwíxʷtən[14] t_sʔiwt. 234 way̓
s+l̓ax̌+t -s way̓ n+kʷl̓mut -s way̓ ks -kl•kl+nwixʷ+tn t_s+ʔiwt way̓
friend -3in yes brother_in_law -3in yes ? -chase behind well
his brother-in-law has already gone over behind. *He*

itlíʔ nʔucxs, nqíclxəms {iʔ s} a nkʷəl̓múts. 235 t̓i lut
itlíʔ n+ʔuc=x -s n+qic+lx+m -s a n+kʷl̓mut -s t̓iʔ lut
from_there follow -3erg run_after -3erg art brother_in_law -3in evid not
started following, he was right on the tracks of his brother-in-law. *Wolf*

skscxʷuys axáʔ nc̓íʔcən, {xaʔ i} way̓ k̓əɬníxəl {inaud}, ksəxpíc̓aʔ.
s -ksc -xʷuy -s axáʔ n+c̓iʔ=cn way̓ k̓ɬ+nixl k+sx+p=íc̓aʔ
nom -pperf -go -3i this wolf yes hear have_chills
hadn't gone very far, he heard something. He got the chills.

236 nʕac̓əx̌kən̓cút sta kway, cənkcníkən̓təm iʔ ta
n+ʕac̓x̌=kn̓+cút sta k+way̓ c -n+kc+n=ikn -t -m iʔ t
look_behind intj yes act -reach -nt -psv art agInst
He looked behind him, well, he was being overtaken by

nkʷəl̓múts, t qʷásqiʔ 237 ih, {itlíʔ} itlíʔ qícəlx, kswitmíst.
n+kʷl̓mut -s t qʷásqiʔ ih itlíʔ qic+lx kswít+miʔst
brother_in_law -3in agInst BlueJay intj from_there run_sg do_one's_best
his brother-in-law BlueJay. *Then he runs, he's doing his best. 28:00*

238 nstils: t̓a··, nt̓aʔ uɬ a{xáʔ} ck̓əɬtun̓ilxtəm.
n+st=ils nt̓a nt̓a uɬ axáʔ c -k̓ɬ+twnil -xt -m
think intj intj and this cust^ -fall_short -xit -4erg
He thinks: "Ah. And we thought he couldn't make it.

239 {uɬ iʔ kʷu ta xikən} kən xʔit {iʔ l} iʔ l spíx̌əm úɬiʔ kʷu
kn xʔit iʔ l s+pix̌+m uɬ iʔ kʷu
1kn first art at hunting and_then 1obj
And I am the best in hunting, and then he

14 Unclear form.

ɬcənkcníki?s. 240 waẏ ńińẃi? aḱlá? mi ks?ayx̌ʷtáyn." 241 put
ɬ+c+n+kc+n=íki? -s waẏ ńińẃi? aḱlá? mi k+s+?ayx̌ʷ+t+áyn put
overtake_cisl_again -3erg yes a_while here fut have_tiredeness just
overtakes me. *It won't be far he will give out."* *Until*

nkcníki?s aɬí? i? sƛ̓a?cínəm, ka? t̓əcṕəlḱúsəm axá? a nći?cən.
n+kc+n=íki? -s aɬí? i? s+ƛ̓a?=cín+m ki? t̓c -ṕlḱ=us+m axá? a n+ċi?=cn
catch_up_with -3erg so art deer rel habCisl -turn_back this art wolf
he overtakes the deer, that's when Wolf'll turn back.

242 hi, itlí? ?ucklípəm axá? a nći?cən. 243 qʷuɬ qʷuɬ qʷuɬ qʷuɬ qʷuɬ
hi itlí? ?uckl=íp+m axá? a n+ċi?=cn qʷuɬ qʷuɬ qʷuɬ qʷuɬ qʷuɬ
intj from_there run_downhill this art wolf dust dust dust dust dust
Well, Wolf ran down the hill. *"Dust, dust, dust, dust, dust"*

i? {s} syríwaxəns. 244 uɬ nuknapána?qnəms[15] ya
i? s+yr=íwa?=xn -s uɬ n+wk+nap=ána?=qn+m -s ya
art snowshoes -3in and see_with_corner_of_eye -3erg art
go his snowshoes. *And with the corner of his eye he saw*

nkʷəl̓múts. 245 nixʷ waẏ t̓i c?x̌iɬ̯t qʷuɬ, qʷuɬ, qʷuɬ, i?
n+kʷl̓mut -s nixʷ waẏ t̓i? c+?x̌iɬ̯t qʷuɬ qʷuɬ qʷuɬ i?
brother_in_law -3in also yes evid like dust dust dust art
his brother-in-law. *"Dust, dust, dust" go his*

syríwax̌ən[s]. 246 waẏ uɬ qʷa?mmís i? syríwaxən[s].
s+yr=íwa?=xn -s waẏ uɬ qʷa?m+mí -s i? s+yr=íwa?=xn -s
snowshoes -3in yes and familiar -3erg art snowshoes -3in
snowshoes. *He had got used to his snowshoes.*

247 waẏ {əy} lut {s} səntíkɬc, ixí? uɬ ks?ayx̌ʷtáyn, 248 uɬ aɬí?
waẏ lut s -n+tikɬ -c ixí? uɬ k-s+?ayx̌ʷ+t+áyn uɬ aɬí?
well not nom -bottom -3i then and have_tiredeness and because
He didn't get to the bottom and he got give out,[16] 29:04 *because it*

miná tanḿús {ki?} ki? qʷásqi?. 249 uɬ ixí? uɬ aɬí? ƛ̓əm lut t̓a
miná tanḿ=ús ki? qʷásqi? uɬ ixí? uɬ aɬí? ƛ̓m lut t̓
futNeg nothing rel BlueJay and that and so past not negfac
isn't for nothing that he's BlueJay. *Wolf used to not*

c?ayx̌ʷt a nći?cən {indec}. 250 put [n]kcníki?s i? sƛ̓a?cínəm,
c -?ayx̌ʷ+t a n+ċi?=cn put n+kc+n=íki? -s i? s+ƛ̓a?=cín+m
hab -tired art wolf just catch_up_with -3erg art deer
get tired. *He just overtakes the deer,*

ƛ̓xʷəntis, 251 uɬ nixʷ lut t̓a c?ayx̌ʷt, məɬ ɬckícx.
ƛ̓xʷ -nt -is uɬ nixʷ lut t̓ c -?ayx̌ʷ+t mɬ ɬ+c+kic+x
kill_many -nt -3erg and also not negfac hab -tired and arrive_cisl_again
he slaughters them, *and he doesn't get tired, and he gets back.*

15 I cannot confirm the correctness of +nap.
16 BlueJay has the power to cause Wolf to get tired. See 253.

252 uɬ aɬí? mat s?ax̌líkstəm {ta} t qʷásqi?, úɬi? i? ?ayx̌ʷt.
uɬ aɬí? mat s -?ax̌l=íkst+m t qʷásqi? uɬ i? i? ?ayx̌ʷ+t
and because maybe hab -turn_toward agInst BlueJay and_then art tired
I suppose BlueJay changed him around, that's why he's tired.

253 waẏ t'i wim̓, uɬ ixí? s?ax̌əlməncúts axá? nc̓í?cən. 254 waẏ uɬ
waẏ t'i? wim̓ uɬ ixí? s -?ax̌l+mncút -s axá? n+c̓i?=cn waẏ uɬ
well evid in_vain and then nom -turn_around -3i this wolf well and
Wolf tried but could't do it, and he turned around. *He*

aɬí? n?ayx̌ʷtíls. 255 cus a nkʷəl'múts: xʷúyx, pna?
aɬí? n+?ayx̌ʷ+t=íls cu -s a n+kʷl'mut -s xʷuy -x pna?
because get_tired tell -3erg art brother_in_law -3in go -isimptv maybe
was too tired. *He told his brother-in-law: "Go ahead, maybe you are*

anwí kʷ c̓a?knúl'axʷ. 256 waẏ uɬ kən ksx?i? {kən ks} i? t
anwí kʷ c -?akn=úla?xʷ waẏ uɬ kn k+s+x[?]ẏ i? t
you 2kn hab -be_better_off yes and 1kn have_extreme_tiredeness art agInst
a little better off. *I am plum to the end with*

s?ayx̌ʷt {la} 257 anwí kʷ yaʕ̓ʷpyáwt. 258 ah cus waẏ. 259 uɬ
s+?ayx̌ʷ+t anwí kʷ yaw+p+yáʕʷ+t ah cu -s waẏ uɬ
tiredness you 2kn strong intj tell -3erg Ok and
tiredness. 30:02 *You are stronger."* *He said, "Ok."* *And*

aɬí? {k̓əɬx̌əqəntís} k̓əɬx̌qəntím ta nc̓í?cən. 260 itlí? nwísəlx
aɬí? k̓ɬ+x̌q -nt -im t n+c̓i?=cn itlí? n+wis+lx
so step_aside -nt -psv agInst wolf from_there jump
Wolf gave him the way. *BlueJay*

qʷásqi?. 261 {waẏ təm} xʷəm t'i lut itli? t'ə syum̓míst
qʷásqi? xʷm t'i? lut itlí? t' s -yúm+mi?st
BlueJay intj evid not from_there negfac hab -move
jumped. *Like Wolf didn't*

axá? {qʷásqi?} t nc̓í?cən. 262 itlí? waẏ xʷúy, {unclear} t'i ta_?x̌íləm,
axá? t n+c̓i?=cn itlí? waẏ xʷuy t'i? ta+?x̌íl+m
this agInst wolf from_there yes go evid like_that
make a move.[17] *He started to go. Just like that BlueJay*

uɬ k̓əɬk̓láxʷ qʷásqi?. 263 waẏ kswitmí··st, ixí? uɬ ntikɬ nc̓í?cən,
uɬ k̓ɬ+k̓laxʷ qʷásqi? waẏ k+swít+mi?st ixí? uɬ n+tikɬ n+c̓i?=cn
and disappear BlueJay yes do_one's_best then and bottom wolf
was out of sight. *He tried his best, finally Wolf got to the bottom,*

264 axá? aɬí? nyʕ̓íp cən?ucxsts axá? i? sƛ̓a?cínəm.
axá? aɬí? nyʕip c -n+?uc=x -st -s axá? i? s+ƛ̓a?=cín+m
this because always cust^ -follow -^cust -3erg this art deer
because he always tracks the deer.

17 BlueJay outdistances Wolf as though Wolf weren't moving.

265 nyʕ̓íp itíʔ sxʷúytəns qʷásqiʔ. 266 {ə} uɬ way̓ nkʷəkʷʔác,
nyʕ̓ip itíʔ s+xʷuy+tn -s qʷásqiʔ uɬ way̓ n+kʷ•kʷʔac
always from_that track -3in BlueJay and yes dark
BlueJay's tracks are right along. It got dark, it was dusk when

kiʔpúl̓aʔxʷ, kiʔ ntikɬ. 267 {taʔk} way̓ {axá t} qəqmənʔí¨waʔt iʔ sƛ̓aʔcínəm.
ky+p=úlaʔxʷ kiʔ n+tikɬ way̓ q•qm+n=íwaʔt iʔ s+ƛ̓aʔ=cín+m
dusk rel bottom well lie_around art deer
he got to the bottom. There are deer laying all over. 31:03

268 way̓ axáʔ ʔax̌əx̌lílx {ta}, ixíʔ uɬ ya cʔíwt uɬ wiʔsəntəlkʷíɬc̓aʔs
way̓ axáʔ ʔax̌•x̌l+ílx ixíʔ uɬ ya c+ʔiwt uɬ wy̓+s+n+tlkʷ=iɬc̓aʔ -s
well this busy_with that and art last and finish_gutting -3erg
Well, he was busy doing something. That was the last. And BlueJay got done taking

qʷásqiʔ 269 ixíʔ úɬiʔ a nkəckn̓áɬq. 270 way̓ nk̓áwl̓axʷsts
qʷásqiʔ ixíʔ uɬ iʔ a n+kc=kn=aɬq way̓ n+k̓áw=laʔxʷ -st -s
BlueJay then and_then art catch_up yes massacre -st -3erg
the guts out. That's when [Wolf] overtook him. He has the deer all

nák̓ʷəm iʔ sƛ̓aʔcínəm. 271 ah, n[s]tíls nc̓íʔcən: axáʔ təl isck̓ʷúl̓, təl
nak̓ʷ+m iʔ s+ƛ̓aʔ=cín+m ah n+st=ils n+c̓iʔ=cn axáʔ tl i -s+c -k̓ʷul̓•l̓ tl
evid art deer intj think wolf this from 1i -pftv -born from
killed. Wolf thought: "From the time I was born, from the time

istaʔxʷspx̌páx̌t 272 lut_swit kʷu t̓a ck̓əɬxaʔtxtís.
i -s+taʔxʷ+s+px̌•páx̌+t lut_swit kʷu t̓ c -k̓ɬ+xaʔt -xt -is
1in -becoming_conscious nobody 1obj negfac cust^ -be_in_front_of -xit -3erg
I got my senses, there is not anybody who could step in front of me.

273 ʕapnáʔ axáʔ t inkʷəl̓mút kiʔ kʷu aɬ k̓əɬxaʔtəntís.
ʕapnáʔ axáʔ t i -n+kʷl̓mut kiʔ kʷu aɬ k̓ɬ+xaʔt -nt -is
now this agInst 1in -brother_in_law rel 1obj compl be_in_front_of -nt -3erg
Now this brother-in-law of mine steps in front of me.

274 uɬ way̓, way̓ c̓x̌iɬ lut iksnunxʷínaʔ. 275 way̓ mat haʔ kən
uɬ way̓ way̓ c+ʔx̌iɬ lut i -ks -n+wnxʷ=ínaʔ way̓ mat haʔ kn
and yes yes like not 1i -futi -believe yes maybe inter 1kn
I'm not going to believe it. Maybe I am just

scpúlpəltx. 276 {cúntəm t t qʷásqiʔ ah cus qʷás} cúntəm t
sc -pul•pl+t -x cu -nt -m t
ipftvp^ -dream -^ipftvp tell -nt -psv agInst
dreaming." BlueJay said to him: "Hurry,

qʷásqiʔ: huhúy, kʷu p̓əlk̓úsəm. 277 way̓ {a} cəm̓ talíʔ kʷu ɬ
qʷásqiʔ hu•húy kʷu p̓lk̓=us+m way̓ cm̓ taʔlíʔ kʷu
BlueJay OK 4kn turn_back yes maybe very_much 4kn ?
let's turn back. 32:05 We might be very

nkʷaʔcnúxʷ. 278 lkʷut kʷaʔ {i s} iʔ smaʔməʔímtət, iʔ snilíʔtntət.
n+kʷaʔc=núxʷ lkʷ=ut kʷaʔ iʔ s+ma•mʔím -tt iʔ s+n+ilíʔ+tn -tt
get_dark far intj art women -4in art dwelling_place -4in
late. Our women and our staying place are far away."

279 cúntəm {ta} ta nc̓íʔcən, uɬ aɬíʔ miyílsəms; 280 uɬ yayʕát
cu -nt -m t n+c̓iʔ=cn uɬ aɬíʔ my=ils+m -s uɬ yaʕ•yáʕ+t
tell -nt -psv agInst wolf and because figure -3erg and all
Wolf told him, and he figured, *it's all*

cx̌əƛ̓mús, uɬ tqəltíkən̓ ixíʔ uɬ sic cx̌ʷəx̌ʷstús iʔ{k̓əl} cítxʷsəlx;
c -x̌ƛ̓+m=us uɬ t+qlt=ikn ixíʔ uɬ sic c+x̌ʷ•x̌ʷst=us iʔ citxʷ -s -lx
hab -uphill and top_of_ridge then and then downhill art house -3in -pl
uphill to the top, then it's downhill to their houses,

281 cus: way̓ lút, way̓ kən ʔimmscút. 282 ixí··ʔ uɬ kən c̓əspísk̓it iʔ
cu -s way̓ lut way̓ kn ʔim+mscút ixíʔ uɬ kn c̓s+p=ísk̓it iʔ
tell -3erg well not yes 1kn fear then and 1kn out_of_breath art
he said: "No. I fear it. *I have no more breath from*

t sʔayx̌ʷt. 283 t̓a uníxʷ k axáʔ iʔ cənkcníkən̓tsən.
t s+ʔayx̌ʷ+t nt̓a wnixʷ kiʔ axáʔ iʔ c -n+kc+n=ikn -t -s -n
agInst tiredness intj true rel this art act -overtake -nt -2obj -1erg
fatigue. *All I could do was catch up with you.*

284 uɬ way̓ lut t̓ə qəɬnún axáʔ ɬ kɬəɬx̌íƛ̓əm, uɬ
uɬ way̓ lut t̓ qɬ -nu -n axáʔ ɬ i -kɬ -ɬ+x̌iƛ̓+m uɬ
and yes not negfac able -manage -1erg this compl 1i futi -climb_back and
I can't make it up the hill. I am going to camp

way̓ t̓i aláʔ kən pulx. 285 a··, cúntəm way̓, uɬ aɬíʔ way̓
way̓ t̓iʔ aláʔ kn pul+x a cu -nt -m way̓ uɬ aɬíʔ way̓
yes evid here 1kn camp intj tell -nt -psv well and so yes
here." 33:00 *"Ah." He said: "Ok," and BlueJay had already*

wiʔsk̓əɬpáʔx̌s qʷásqiʔ. 286 way̓, iʔ sxʔimɬsílxʷaʔ iʔ xaʔtús iʔ
wy̓+s+k̓ɬ+paʔx̌ -s qʷásqiʔ way̓ iʔ s+xʔim+ɬ+sílxʷaʔ iʔ xaʔt=ús iʔ
finish_deliberating -3erg BlueJay well art biggest art leader art
figured out what to do. *The biggest, the leader of the deer*

sƛ̓aʔcínəm, ixíʔ pulsts, 287 uɬ aɬíʔ {k} taʔlíʔ ksq̓ʷísəs a
s+ƛ̓aʔ=cín+m ixíʔ pul -st -s uɬ aɬíʔ taʔlíʔ k+s+q̓ʷis•s a
deer that kill_one -st -3erg and so very_much have+fat art
that he had killed, *there was very much fat in the inside*

nyxʷtíɬc̓aʔ. 288 way̓ nstils; way̓ ixíʔ t̓k̓ʷəɬtís {i ks} iʔ
n+yxʷ=t=íɬc̓aʔ way̓ n+st=ils way̓ ixíʔ t̓k̓ʷ -ɬt -is iʔ
inside_body well think well that put_down -ɬt -3erg art
of it, *he thought; he lay down*

ksənq̓ʷəɬtáqsc. 289 way̓ ixíʔ kcíqnaʔsəlx ixíʔ yaʔx̌í {ɬc}
k -s+n+q̓ʷɬ+t=aqs -c way̓ ixíʔ k+cíq=naʔ -s -lx ixíʔ yaʔx̌í
to_be -share_one_carries -3i well that dig -3erg -pl then yonder
the deer gift. *They dug until the deer*

ɬʔiq̓ʷ iʔ sƛ̓aʔcínəm. 290 way̓ ɬmʕáwɬts axáʔ iʔ
ɬʔiq̓ʷ iʔ s+ƛ̓aʔ=cín+m way̓ ɬ+maʕʷ -ɬt -s axáʔ iʔ
appear art deer well break_again -ɬt -3erg this art
came in sight. *He broke up the stitches*

kɬúʔx^{w}uɬts iʔ sƛ̓aʔcínəm {i k}, 291 aɬíʔ í·lwəm, ixíʔ
k+ɬuʔx^w=w̓ -ɬt -s iʔ s+ƛ̓aʔ=cín+m aɬíʔ yilw+m ixíʔ
stitch -ɬt -3erg art deer because stitch that
on the deer, *because he had*

kɬúʔx^{w}usəs iʔ sƛ̓aʔcínəm. 292 cus {i} a nk^{w}əl̓múts: way̓, way̓
k+ɬúʔx^w=w̓s -s iʔ s+ƛ̓aʔ=cín+m cu -s a n+k^{w}l̓mut -s way̓ way̓
stitch -3erg art deer tell -3erg art brother_in_law -3in well yes
stitched the deer up. *He told his brother-in-law: "Here,*

aláʔ k^{w}aʔ k^w nʔuɬx^w, axáʔ i l sƛ̓aʔcínəm. 293 cúntəm ixíʔ mi k^w
aláʔ k^{w}aʔ k^w n+ʔuɬx^w axáʔ iʔ l s+ƛ̓aʔ=cín+m cu -nt -m ixíʔ mi k^w
here intj 2kn enter this art in deer tell -nt -psv then fut 2kn
get into this deer." 34:00 *He said to him, "And then you*

x^{w}əlx^{w}ált. 294 nt̓aʔ {la}, ʕác̓ənt k^{w}aʔ itíʔ, kiyc̓ásq̓ət {iʔ}, talíʔ c̓aɬt.
x^{w}l•x^{w}al+t nt̓a ʕac̓ -nt k^{w}aʔ itíʔ ky=c̓a=sq̓t[18] taʔlíʔ c̓aɬ+t
alive intj look -nt intj that clear_sky very_much cold
will live. *Well, look how clear it is, it's very cold.*

295 way̓ t̓i k^w ksc̓áɬəɬt, k^w xʔkínəm mi k^w wr̓ísəlp̓əm, 296 k^w
way̓ t̓iʔ k^w ks -c̓aɬ•ɬ+t k^w x+kin+m mi k^w wr̓=islp̓+m k^w
yes evid 2kn futi -freeze 2kn do_what fut 2kn build_fire 2kn
You will freeze. What can you do to make fire, *what*

xʔkínəm mi k^w kslip̓ axáʔ, {iʔ} muk^w iʔ smík̓^{w}ət.
x+kin+m mi k^w k+slip̓ axáʔ muk^w iʔ s+mik̓^{w}+t
do_what fut 2kn have_fire_wood this snow_on_trees art snow_on_ground
can you do to get wood. There's snow on trees, lots of snow.

297 k^w xʔkínəm mi k^w təx^{w}sq^{w}ílpəm axáʔ i l sənk^{w}ək^{w}ác, uɬ way̓ k^w
k^w x+kin+m mi k^w tx^w+s+q^{w}il=p+m axáʔ iʔ l s+n+k^w•k^{w}ʔac uɬ way̓ k^w
2kn do_what fut 2kn gather_boughs this art in night and yes 2kn
What can you do to get fir boughs in the dark. And you are tired

ʔáyx̌^{w}t. 298 way̓ ixíʔ axáʔ akɬənx^{w}əlx^{w}əltán. 299 lut
ʔayx̌^{w}+t way̓ ixíʔ axáʔ a -kɬ -n+x^{w}l•x^{w}l+tan lut
tired well that this 2i -to_be -livelyhood not
besides. *That's the only way you can save your life.* *Don't*

akslútəm, n̓[in̓w̓iʔ] k^w lútəm, mi {k^w} k^w ƛ̓lál. 300 lut haʔ
a -ks -lut+m n̓ín̓w̓iʔ k^w lut+m mi k^w ƛ̓l•al lut haʔ
2i -futi -refuse a_while 2kn refuse fut 2kn dead not inter
refuse. If you refuse, you will die. *Don't you*

q̓íx̌əx̌məntx^w haʔ antkɬmílx^w, k^w nx^{w}əlx^{w}əltíls. 301 way̓
q̓ix̌•x̌+m -nt -x^w haʔ an -tkɬ+m=ilx^w k^w n+x^{w}l•x^{w}lt=ils way̓
be_stingy_of -nt -2erg inter 2in -wife 2kn want_to_live well
get stingy of your wife? You want to stay alive." *He*

18 This analysis is uncertain.

k̓əxʷkʷúnəms a nkʷəl̓mút[s], way̓ nunxʷínaməntəm.
k+ʔxʷ+kʷun+m -s a n+kʷl̓mut -s way̓ n+wnxʷ=ína?+m -nt -m
coax -3erg art brother_in_law -3in yes believe_so -nt -psv
coaxed his brother-in-law. He believed him.

302 nstils: {unclear} way̓ myáɬ kən ʔáyx̌ʷt, way̓ lut qəɬnún
n+st=ils way̓ myaɬ kn ʔayx̌ʷ+t way̓ lut qɬ -nu -n
think yes too_much 1kn tired yes not able -manage -1erg
He thought: "Well, I am too tired. I can't even try

ɬ iksuŕísəlp̓əm {t'i k}; 303 cakʷ iwá kən ɬaʔ uŕísəlp̓əm, uɬ way̓ kən
ɬ i -ks -wŕ=islp̓+m caʔkʷ iwá kn ɬaʔ wŕ=islp̓+m uɬ way̓ kn
compl 1i -futi -build_fire if even 1kn if build_fire and yes 1kn
to get fire; *and if even I make fire, I still have to*

ksksliṕaʔx. 304 uɬ way̓ lut, sic i l sənkʷəkʷʔác, uɬ way̓ kən
ks -k+slip̓ -aʔx uɬ way̓ lut sic iʔ l s+n+kʷ•kʷʔac uɬ way̓ kn
incp^ -have_wood -^incp and well not then art in night and yes 1kn
get wood. *No. It's still early in the night, and I have got to have*

ksksqʷílpaʔx. 305 uɬ way̓ kən hoy t sʔayx̌ʷt, uɬ way̓
ks -k+s+qʷil=p -aʔx uɬ way̓ kn hoy t s+ʔayx̌ʷ+t uɬ way̓
incp^ -have_bedding -^incp and yes 1kn finish agInst tiredness and yes
something under me. 35:02 *And I am done in from being tired. What he*

wnixʷ a[xáʔ] iʔ kʷu k̓əɬpaʔx̌xíts {indec}. 306 cut way̓, way̓, way̓
wnixʷ axáʔ iʔ kʷu k̓ɬ+paʔx̌ -xit -s cut way̓ way̓ way̓
true this art 1obj figure_out -xit -3erg say yes yes yes
figured out for me is true." *He said:*

kʷíɬtsən asck̓əɬpáʔx̌. 307 cúntəm: kʷaʔ nʔúɬxʷəxʷ.
kʷi -ɬt -s -n a -sc -k̓ɬ+paʔx̌ cu -nt -m kʷaʔ n+ʔuɬxʷ -xʷ
take -ɬt -2obj -1erg 2i -pftv -figure_out tell -nt -psv intj enter -isimptv
"I'll take your advice." *He told him: "Get in."*

308 way̓ i[xíʔ] sənʔúɬxʷs i l sƛ̓aʔcínəm, uɬ aɬíʔ sílxʷaʔ.
way̓ ixíʔ s -n+ʔuɬxʷ -s iʔ l s+ƛ̓aʔ=cín+m uɬ aɬíʔ sílxʷaʔ.
well then nom -enter -3i art in deer and because big
He went into the deer, because it's big.

309 way̓ i[xíʔ] ɬk̓ɬənx̌p̓í··ps axáʔ iʔ sƛ̓aʔcínəm, məɬ ixíʔ ɬkcmínaʔs.
way̓ ixíʔ ɬ+k̓ɬ+n+x̌p̓=ip -s axáʔ iʔ s+ƛ̓aʔ=cín+m mɬ ixíʔ ɬ+k+cm=ínaʔ -s
well then stitch_back -3erg this art deer and then cover_back -3erg
He stitched the deer back, and he put snow back on it.

310 way̓ axáʔ nc̓íʔcən axáʔ {tiɬ) i[xíʔ] wiʔskcmínaʔs ixíʔ uɬ kʷʔal̓
way̓ axáʔ n+c̓iʔ=cn axáʔ ixíʔ wy̓+s+k+cm=ínaʔ -s ixíʔ uɬ kʷ[ʔ]al̓
well this wolf this then finish_covering -3erg that and get_warm
After he got snow on top of him, Wolf got warmed

axáʔ. 311 uɬ aɬíʔ t'əxʷ lútiʔ t sk̓íy̓ts {əɬ}, talíʔ kskʷal̓t;
axáʔ. uɬ aɬíʔ t'xʷ lút+i s -k̓iy̓+t -s taʔlíʔ k+s+kʷal̓+t
this and because emph not_yet ? nom -cold -3i much have_warmth
up. *Because he still wasn't too cold, he was warm;*

312 lut t̓ə sú?its. 313 ixí? uɬ x̌əstmís i? skʷ?ál̓s,
lut t̓ suy̓+t -s ixí? uɬ x̌st+mi -s i? s+kʷ[?]al̓[19] -s
not negfac chilled -3i then and like -3erg art warmth -3in
he hadn't gotten cold. *He really liked how he was getting warm.*

talí? uɬ cíx̌cəx̌t. 314 ixí? nax̌əmɬ ?ilxʷt. 315 way̓ təl stím̓ axá? i?
ta?lí? uɬ cix̌•cx̌+t ixí? nax̌mɬ ?ilxʷ+t way̓ tl stim̓ axá? i?
very_much and hot then but hungry well from what this art
It was very warm. *But he's very hungry.* *He felt something,*

məssíkst, a[xá?] i t sq̓ʷísəs. 316 way̓ itlí? sckník̓əms,
ms•s=ikst axá? i? t s+q̓ʷis•s way̓ itlí? sc -k+nik̓+m -s
feel_with_hand this art obj_itr fat well from_there ipftvp^ -cut_off -3i
fat. 36:00 *He cut some off.*

way̓ uɬ ixí? s?íɬəns {i a}, t qʷámqʷəm[qs]. 317 way̓ nc̓əspínks {i?}
way̓ uɬ ixí? s -?iɬn -s t qʷam•qʷm=qs way̓ n+c̓s+p=ink -s
yes and then nom -eat -3i obj_itr delicious_food well clean_inside -3erg
And then he ate it. It was delicious. *He cleaned off the inside*

i? ksənq̓ʷəɬtáqsc. 318 way̓ ?ayxáxa? way̓, swit_aɬí? síc̓ɬc̓a?, way̓
i? k -s+n+q̓ʷɬ+t=aqs -c way̓ ?ayxáxa? way̓ swit_aɬí? síc=ɬc̓a? way̓
art to_be -share_one_carries -3in well a_while well in_fact fresh_meat yes
of his deer gift. *In a little while since it's fresh meat, he got*

nc̓a?ṙínk. 319 way̓, way̓ lut x?kínəm mi ?ácqa?, uɬ aɬí? a
n+c̓a?r=ínk way̓ way̓ lut x+kin+m mi ?ácqa? uɬ aɬí? a
diarrhea well well not do_what fut go_out and because intj
diarrhea. *He couldn't do anything to get out, because he's*

ck̓ɬənx̌p̓íp. 320 way̓ t̓i ilí? uɬ qʷəńkstmíst axá? nc̓í?cən, ƛ̓əm
c -k̓ɬ+n+x̌p̓=ip way̓ t̓i? ilí? uɬ qʷń=kst+mist axá? n+c̓i?=cn ƛ̓m
hab -fasten_door well evid there and do_pitiful_thing this wolf past
sewn up in there. *Then Wolf did something pitiful, he that used to be*

xa?tús. 321 way̓ axá? ɬtxrútəm aɬí? qʷásqi?. 322 ɬtxrú¨təm, qilt,
xa?t=ús way̓ axá? ɬ+txr=ut+m aɬí? qʷásqi? ɬ+txr=ut+m qilt
leader well this run_back_uphill so BlueJay run_back_uphill top
boss. *BlueJay ran up the hill.* *He ra¨n, got to the top,*

ixí? ɬ?ucklípəm [tape ends] 323 way̓ itlí? kən nc̓əpq̓síẃsəm i? t
ixí? ɬ+?uckl=íp+m way̓ itlí? kn n+c̓p̓q̓s=iws+m i? t
then run_back_downhill well from_there 1kn splice art obj_itr
he ran down the hill. 36:57 *Now I am going to splice*

incaptíkʷɬ. 324 axá? həɬqʷásqi? na?ɬ nc̓í?cən {ə}, nkʷl̓əmtíẃsəlx.
in -captíkʷɬ axá? hɬ=qʷásqi? na?ɬ n+c̓i?=cn n+kʷl̓mt=iẃs -lx
1in -legends this BlueJay_family with wolf be_brothers_in_law -pl
my story. *The BlueJay group with Wolf, they are brothers-in-law.*

19 Notice the inchoative infix in this nominal form.

325 waẏ ałí? scpíx̌xəlx úłi? ks?ayx̌ʷtáyn axá? nc̓í?cən.
waẏ ałí? sc -pix̌ -x -lx uł i? k+s+?ayx̌ʷ+t+áyn axá? n+c̓i?=cn
well so ipftvp^ -hunt -^ipftvp -pl and_then have_tiredeness this wolf
They were hunting when Wolf got tired. 0:33

326 waẏ uł axá? qʷásqi? ałí? {sic} síscəlqʷ {uł}. 327 uł lut ?áyx̌ʷt, uł
waẏ uł axá? qʷásqi? ałí? si•sc=lqʷ uł lut ?ayx̌ʷ+t uł
well and this BlueJay so honeymoon and not tired and
And BlueJay was newly wed. *And he wasn't tired,*

nk̓əwpíls, lut x̌minks kskpúlxmi?s {i} ya nkʷəl̓múts.
n+k̓w+p=ils lut x̌m=ink -s ks -k+púl+x+mi -s i? n+kʷl̓mut -s
lonesome not want -3erg futt^ -camp_by -3erg art brother_in_law -3in
and he was lonesome.[20] *He didn't like to camp by his brother-in-law.*

328 uł ixí? t̓i nk̓ʷa?k̓ʷíni?s {i?} i? sílxʷa? i? q̓ʷuct i? sƛ̓a?cínəm.
uł ixí? t̓i? n+k̓ʷa?•k̓ʷín+i? -s i? sílxʷa? i? q̓ʷuc̓+t i? s+ƛ̓a?=cín+m
and then evid pick -3erg art big art fat art deer
And he picked out the biggest fattest deer.

329 ilí? ki? n?úłxʷsts {i?} a nkʷəl̓múts. 330 uł {i?} cus:
ilí? ki? n+?ułxʷ -st -s a n+kʷl̓mut -s uł cu -s
there rel enter -caus -3erg art brother_in_law -3in and tell -3erg
That's where he put his brother-in-law. 1:03 *And he said:*

waẏ cəm̓ kʷ ksc̓áłəłt, uł waẏ {kʷ} kʷ ?ayx̌ʷt, 331 la?kín kʷ x?kínəm
waẏ cm̓ kʷ k+s+c̓ał•ł+t uł waẏ kʷ ?ayx̌ʷ+t la+?kín̓ kʷ x+kin+m
well maybe 2kn have_freeze and yes 2kn tired how 2kn do_what
"You might freeze, you are tired, *what can you do*

mi kʷ ur̓ísəlp̓əm, kəm̓ kʷ kslíp̓əm, kəm̓ kʷ təxʷsqʷílpəm. 332 waẏ
mi kʷ wr̓=islp̓+m km̓ kʷ k+slip̓+m km̓ kʷ txʷ+s+qʷil=p+m waẏ
fut 2kn build_fire or 2kn get_wood or 2kn gather_boughs yes
to make fire, or to get wood, or to get the boughs. *It's*

myał c̓ałt, waẏ t̓i kʷ ksc̓áłəłt; 333 waẏ axá? kʷəl̓úl̓a?xʷ
myał c̓ał+t waẏ t̓i? kʷ k+s+c̓ał•ł+t waẏ axá? kʷl̓=úla?xʷ
too_much cold yes evid 2kn have_freeze yes this warm_place
too cold. You will freeze. *The place for you here is*

aksnilí?tn. 334 waẏ nstíls {nc̓il} nc̓í?cən: kwáẏ,
a -k -s+n+ilí?+tn waẏ n+st=ils n+c̓i?=cn k+waẏ
2i -to_be -dwelling_place well think wolf yes
nice and comfortable." *Wolf thought: "Yes, he's telling*

swníxʷəxʷ, cus: waẏ. 335 waẏ n?úłxʷstəm {il} i l sílxʷa?
s -wnixʷ -xʷ cu -s waẏ waẏ n+?ułxʷ -st -m i? l sílxʷa?
ipftv^ -true -^ipftv tell -3erg Ok well enter -caus -psv art in big
the truth." He said: "Ok." *He put him in the*

20 Lonesome for his wife and eager to get back to camp.

i l sƛ̓aʔcínəm. 336 ixíʔ tx̌p̓í··w̓səntəm axáʔ iʔ {t} t syílwiʔ;
iʔ l s+ƛ̓aʔ=cín+m ixíʔ t+x̌p̓=iw̓s -nt -m axáʔ iʔ t s+yílwiʔ
art in deer then stitch -nt -psv this art agInst twig
biggest deer. He sewed him up there with a twisted twig,

337 axáʔ sic kcmí··naʔntəm, way̓ t̓i ʔayxáxaʔ ta nc̓íʔcən uɬ ʔanwís
axáʔ sic k+cm=ínaʔ -nt -m way̓ t̓iʔ ʔayxáxaʔ n+c̓iʔ=cn uɬ ʔanwí -s
this then cover -nt -psv well evid a_while ? wolf and feel -3erg
then he covered it with snow. In a little while Wolf

iʔ scʔixs, 338 axáʔ mat iʔ {təl s} təl sɬəxʷɬəxʷəncúts uɬ
iʔ s -c[ʔ]ix -s axáʔ mat iʔ tl s+ɬxʷ•ɬxʷ+ncut -s uɬ
art nom -get_warm -3i this maybe art from breath -3in and
felt warm, I guess from his breath, from where else could

aɬíʔ tlaʔkín mi x̌ʕap, 339 uɬ aɬíʔ axáʔ iʔ sƛ̓aʔcínəm la
aɬíʔ tla‿ʔkín mi x̌aʕ+p uɬ aɬíʔ axáʔ iʔ s+ƛ̓aʔ=cín+m l
because from_there fut draft and because this art deer in
the air come, the deer in his insides, and besides

nixʷúts, uɬ sic ckcmínaʔ. 340 way̓ axáʔ qʷásqiʔ txrú··təm, qilt,
n+yxʷ=ut -s uɬ sic c -k+cm=ínaʔ way̓ axáʔ qʷásqiʔ t+xr=ut+m qilt
inside -3in and then hab -cover well this BlueJay run_uphill top
he had snow on it. 2:03 BlueJay ran up the hill, got to the top;

way̓ ʔucklí··pm {əm}. 341 way̓ miw̓súl̓[aʔxʷ], t̓əxʷ k̓aʔtúl̓aʔxʷ.
way̓ ʔuckl=íp+m way̓ miw̓s=úlaʔxʷ t̓xʷ k̓aʔt=úlaʔxʷ
well run_down_canyon well half_way evidently close_to_home
he ran down the hill. He got half way, closer to home.

342 way̓ ixíʔ st̓aʔqʷcíns, ixíʔ aɬíʔ cawts iʔ scpíx̌əx
way̓ ixíʔ s -t̓aʔqʷ=cín -s ixíʔ aɬíʔ cawt -s iʔ ɬaʔ -pix̌ -x
well then nom -holler -3i that because doing -3in art when -hunt -ˆipftvp
He hollered repeatedly, because that's the way the hunters go

ɬaʔ cənkʷaʔcnúxʷ; 343 uɬ aɬíʔ lut t̓a c̓atxílxəlx ɬaʔ
ɬaʔ c -n+kʷaʔc=núxʷ uɬ aɬíʔ lut t̓ c -ʔatx+ílx -lx ɬaʔ
when hab -get_dark and because not negfac hab -sleep_pl -pl when
when they get late. They don't go to sleep when they have

ksnəqsílxʷəlx; 344 nyʕ̓ip ctk̓əlstísəlx, k̓əɬkʷləwtúsx[nəlx].
k+s+nqs=ilxʷ -lx n+yʕ̓=ip c -t+k̓l -st -is -lx k̓ɬ+kʷl=wt=us=xn -lx
have_relative -pl always custˆ -wait_up -ˆcust -3erg -pl sit_around -pl
relatives. They always wait up for them. They sit around.

345 lu··t k̓ɬkicx, məɬ x̌lap məɬ ixíʔ sic ƛ̓aʔƛ̓aʔntísəlx. 346 way̓
lut k̓ɬ+kic+x mɬ x̌la+p mɬ ixíʔ sic ƛ̓aʔ•ƛ̓aʔ -nt -is -lx way̓
not arrive and morning and then then look_for -nt -3erg -pl well
If nobody shows up, then the next daylight they go looking for them. And

mət səxʔkín[xəlx], 347 [s]x̌ənnúmt[x] kəm̓
mat s -x+kin -x -lx s -x̌n̓+numt -x km̓
maybe ipftvˆ -do_what -ˆipftv -pl ipftvˆ -get_hurt -ˆipftv or
something could have happened to them, they're either hurt or

sksʔayx̌ʷtáyn. 348 way̓ níxəl̓, t̓əqʷt̓aʔqʷcín. 349 way̓
s k+s+ʔayx̌ʷ+t+áyn way̓ nixl t̓qʷ•t̓aʔqʷ=cín way̓
? have+tiredeness yes hear holler_repeatedly well
give out. *They heard. He was hollering.* *They*

k̓əɬk̓ʷínxʷcsəlx {way̓ cut a}, nstílsəlx: way̓ ixíʔ [a]táʔ nc̓íʔcən. {eˑʔ}
k̓ɬ+k̓ʷinxʷ=c -s -lx n+st=ils -lx way̓ ixíʔ atáʔ n+c̓iʔ=cn
answer -3erg -pl think -pl yes that this wolf
answered him. They thought: "That's Wolf." 3:02

350 yrəntís axáʔ {iʔ} nc̓íʔcən iʔ tkɬmílxʷs, {il} yrəntís iʔ
yr -nt -is axáʔ n+c̓iʔ=cn iʔ tkɬ+m=ilxʷ -s yr -nt -is iʔ
push -nt -3erg this wolf art wife -3in push -nt -3erg art
Wolf's wife pushed her. She pushed her

ɬcəcʔúpsc. 351 ah cus: way̓ k̓ɬur̓úsxənt,[21] way̓ mat ixíʔ
ɬ+c•cʔ=ups -c ah cu -s way̓ k̓ɬ+wr̓=usx -nt way̓ mat ixíʔ
younger_sister -3in intj tell -3erg well make_fire -nt yes must that
younger sister. *She said: "Fix the fire. That might be*

asqəltmíxʷ {unclear} ct̓əqʷt̓aʔqʷcín. 352 uɬ kcqúsəntxʷ iʔ
a -s+qlt=mixʷ c -t̓qʷ•t̓aʔqʷ=cín uɬ k+cq=us -nt -xʷ iʔ
2in -man hab -holler_repeatedly and put_on_the_fire -nt -2erg art
your husband that is hollering. *Put the coffee pot on the fire.*

sənlkapítn, mat way̓ iʔ t sq̓míltən. 353 uɬ sckákaʔms iʔ
s+n+lkapí+tn mat way̓ iʔ t s+q̓m=ilt+n uɬ sc -ká•kaʔ+m -s iʔ
coffee_pot must yes art agInst hunger and pftv -deride -pftv art
He must be awful hungry." *Now she's making fun of*

ɬcəcʔúpsc, 354 uɬ aɬíʔ t̓iʔ kʷaʔ atláʔ [t]la nixʷút kiʔ a
ɬ+c•cʔ=ups -c uɬ aɬíʔ t̓iʔ kʷaʔ atláʔ tla n+yxʷ=ut kiʔ a
younger_sister -3in and so evid intj from_here from inside rel intj
her younger sister, *because BlueJay put his snowshoes on*

yríwaxnəm qʷásqiʔ. 355 lut t̓a cmistís iʔ
yr=íwaʔ=xn+m qʷásqiʔ lut t̓ c -my -st -is iʔ
wear_snowshoes BlueJay not negfac cust^ -know -^cust -3erg art
from inside. *He didn't know his*

syríwaxən. 356 t̓i t̓k̓ʷək̓ʷlwíˑs úɬiʔ k̓əɬk̓láxʷ. 357 uɬ aɬíʔ
s+yr=íwaʔ=xn t̓iʔ t̓k̓ʷ•k̓ʷ+lwis uɬ iʔ k̓ɬ+k̓laxʷ uɬ aɬíʔ
snowshoes evid fall_around and_then disappear and because
snowshoes. *He was falling around and then he got out of sight.* *Because*

axáʔ iʔ sxʔitx uɬ aɬíʔ miysts sisyús iʔ sqəltmíxʷs.
axáʔ iʔ s+xʔit=x uɬ aɬíʔ miy -st -s sy•sy=us iʔ s+qlt=mixʷ -s
this art oldest_one and because be_sure_of -st -3erg smart art man -3in
the oldest one is sure that the smartest one is her husband.

21 This form seems incorrect. k̓ɬur̓úsx would be an intransitive command; k̓ɬur̓úsənt would be a transitive command. Madeline did not correct it, and I leave it as is.

358 sc?x̌ilx úɬi? káka?ms axá? i? ɬcəc?úpsc. 359 way̓
sc+?x̌il+x uɬ i? ká•ka?+m -s axá? i? ɬ+c•c?=ups -c way̓
reason_why and_then deride -3erg this art younger_sister -3in well
That's why she was making fun of her younger sister. *The*

axá? {i? isxʷ} sxʷt̓ilxs {axá?}, tiɬx axá? i? {i?} ɬcəc?úpsc. 360 i[xí?]
axá? s -xʷt̓+ilx -s tiɬ+x axá? i? ɬ+c•c?=ups -c ixí?
this nom -get_up -3i stand_sg this art younger_sister -3in then
younger sister jumped up, stood up. 4:07 *She*

tk̓ʷú··l̓səs axá? i? sur̓ísəlp̓ uɬ ixí? skcqúsəms {axá? i?}; 361 t̓əxʷ
t+k̓ʷul̓=s -s axá? i? s+wr̓=islp̓ uɬ ixí? s -k+cq=us+m -s t̓xʷ
fix_fire -3erg this art fire and then nom -put_on_the_fire -3i emph
fixed the fire. And she started supper. *She*

kcqúsəs i? skəmʕaw̓áqs axá? i? [s]t̓xítkʷ, i? k̓əɬk̓ʷúl̓cəntəm,
k+cq=us -s i? s+k+maʕʷ=áqs axá? i? s+t̓x=itkʷ i? k̓ɬ+k̓ʷul̓=cn -t -m
put_on_the_fire -3erg art left_overs this art soup art cooked_food -nt -psv
warmed up some leftovers, some soup, what was cooked for them.

ncixs. 362 way̓, way̓ itlí? ɬct̓aqʷcínəm, way̓
n=cix -s way̓ way̓ itlí? ɬ+c+t̓aqʷ=cin+m way̓
warm_water -3erg well well from_there holler_again yes
She warmed it over. *The hollering continued.*

ɬk̓əɬk̓ʷínxʷcsəlx. 363 way̓ itlí? sxʷsma?cínəms i?
ɬ+k̓ɬ+k̓ʷinxʷ=c -s -lx way̓ itlí? s -xʷs=ma?=cín+m -s i?
answer_back -3erg -pl well from_there nom -rush -3i art
They answered it. *Then she rushed her*

ɬcəc?úpsc. 364 cus {a}: tk̓ʷúl̓sənt {a} way̓ ixí? asqəltmíxʷ.
ɬ+c•c?=ups -c cu -s t+k̓ʷul̓=s -nt way̓ ixí? a -s+qlt=mixʷ
younger_sister -3in tell -3erg fix_fire -nt yes that 2in -man
younger sister. *She said: "Fix that fire, that's your man."*

365 way̓ wim̓ uɬ tx̌?anípla?səlx axá? i? t ƛ̓ax̌əx̌ƛ̓x̌ápsəlx;
way̓ wim̓ uɬ t+x̌a?n=ípla? -s -lx axá? i? t ƛ̓ax̌•x̌•ƛ̓x̌á+p -s -lx
well in_vain and keep_from -3erg -pl this art agInst parents -3in -pl
Their parents tried to stop her,

366 aɬí? uɬ way̓ míystsəlx {sckák?amsəlx} sckáka?ms i?
aɬí? uɬ way̓ miy -st -s -lx sc -ká•ka?+m -s i?
because and yes be_sure_of -st -3erg -pl pftv -deride -3i art
their parents are sure she's making fun of her younger sister when she says:

ɬcəc?úpsc uɬ a scusts ixí? way̓ asqəltmíxʷ.
ɬ+c•c?=ups -c uɬ a s -cu -st -s ixí? way̓ a -s+qlt=mixʷ
younger_sister -3in and art cust^ -tell -^cust -3erg that yes 2in -man
"That's your husband." 5:01

367 aɬí? lut t̓ə ck̓ək̓tílscəlx, way̓ nstílsəlx;
aɬí? lut t̓ c -k̓•k̓t=ils -t -s -lx way̓ n+st=ils -lx
because not negfac cust^ -close_to_mind -^cust -3erg -pl well think -pl
Because it never came close to their minds. They thought,

368 waẏ t'i ksʔayx̌ʷtáyn qʷásqiʔ, ałíʔ sic ixíʔ ł kspíx̌əms,
waẏ t'iʔ k+s+ʔayx̌ʷ+t+áyn qʷásqiʔ ałíʔ sic ixíʔ ł ks -pix̌+m -s
well evid have_tiredeness BlueJay because new that compl futi -hunt -3i
"The one who gave up is BlueJay, because he's new at hunting, since he

təl słəx̌mám[s]. 369 ho⋅⋅y, ck̓əłníxl̓əms, {a} ałíʔ nƛ̓əx̌cín iʔ
tl s+łx̌m•am -s hoy c -k̓ł+nixl+m -s ałíʔ n+ƛ̓x̌=cin iʔ
from in_laws -3in well ? -hear -3erg because loud art
got married." *Well. They heard him, because the snowshoes*

syríwaxən, ałíʔ mat súsəlt. 370 t'i pəx̌, pəx̌, pəx̌, pəx̌, pəx̌, pəx̌, waẏ
s+yr=íwaʔ=xn su•sl+t mat su•sl+t t'iʔ px̌ px̌ px̌ px̌ px̌ px̌ waẏ
snowshoes frozen must frozen evid px̌ px̌ px̌ px̌ px̌ px̌ yes
are loud, because it's frozen. *"px̌, px̌, px̌, px̌, px̌, px̌." That's*

ixíʔ {s} syríwaxən. 371 waẏ t'i nx̌əscín {i s} iʔ słaq̓ʷcíns iʔ
ixíʔ s+yr=íwaʔ=xn waẏ t'iʔ n+x̌s=cin iʔ s -łaq̓ʷ=cín -s iʔ
that snowshoes yes evid good_sound art nom -clear_sound -3i art
snowshoes. *The snowshoes make a good,*

syríwaxən. 372 hu⋅⋅y a cənʔúłxʷ, waẏ {nix} taʔx̌ílsts a
s+yr=íwaʔ=xn huy a c+n+ʔułxʷ waẏ ta+ʔx̌íl -st -s a
snowshoes intj intj enter_cisl well do_a_certain_way -st -3erg art
clear sound. *He came in. He raised*

nxárcən. 373 waẏ cənʔúłxʷ, t'i ilíʔ cyríwaxən {unclear} uł
n+xar=cn waẏ c+n+ʔułxʷ t'iʔ ilíʔ c -yr=íwaʔ=xn uł
curtain_in_front well enter_cisl evid there hab -snow_shoe and
the curtain. *He came in. He had snowshoes still on.*

[s]ʔam·útəts. 374 {waẏcusiʔtkłmílxʷsaił} txʷət'pmíntəm iʔ t
s -ʔam•mút•t -s t+xʷt'+p+min -t -m iʔ t
nom -sit_down -3i rush_to -nt -psv art agInst
And he sat down. *His wife rushed*

tkłmílxʷs; 375 nt'aʔ nkəlxúsəntəm, uł k̓əłt'əmʕásəntəm.
tkł+m=ilxʷ -s nt'a n+klx=us -nt -m uł k̓ł+t'mʕ=as -nt -m
wife -3in intj arms_around -nt -psv and kiss -nt -psv
to him. *She hugged him and kissed him on the face.*

376 cúntəm: wa⋅⋅ẏ mat kʷ ʔayx̌ʷt. 377 cut: waẏ, waẏ, kən ʔayx̌ʷt, lkʷut
cu -nt -m waẏ mat kʷ ʔayx̌ʷ+t cut waẏ waẏ kn ʔayx̌ʷ+t lkʷ=ut
tell -nt -psv well must 2kn tired say yes yes 1kn tired far
She said to him: "I bet you are tired." *He said: "Yes, yes, I am tired.*

ałíʔ isxʷylwístn. {i} 378 kən sxiẏmscútx uł kən ckicx.
ałíʔ i -s+xʷy+lwis+tn kn s -xẏ+mscut -x uł kn c+kic+x
because 1in -travel 1kn ipftv^ -done_in -^ipftv and 1kn arrive_cisl
I have travelled far. *I was done in when I got back.*

379 waẏ kʷu k̓ʷíƛ̓əłt {iʔ} isyríwaxən. 380 waẏ k̓ʷíƛ̓əłtəm iʔ
waẏ kʷu k̓ʷiƛ̓ -łt i -s+yr=íwaʔ=xn waẏ k̓ʷiƛ̓ -łt -m iʔ
well 1obj take_off -łt 1in -snowshoes yes take_off -łt -psv art
Take off my snowshoes." *She took off his snowshoes,*

syríwaxəns, uɬ ixíʔ cús 381 nixʷ inq̓aʔxán, uɬ aɬíʔ kən
s+yr=íwaʔ=xn -s uɬ ixíʔ cu -s nixʷ in -q̓aʔ=xán uɬ aɬíʔ kn
snowshoes -3in and then tell -3erg also 1in -shoes and because 1kn
and then he said: *"Also my moccasins, because my feet*

ɬaʔɬaʔt̓xʕán 382 uɬ aɬíʔ t sp̓síp̓iʔxən, 383 {kəm̓} ɬaʔ
ɬaʔ•ɬaʔt̓=xán uɬ aɬíʔ sp̓•síp̓iʔ=xn ɬaʔ
wet_feet and because ? moccasin when
got wet *(because he had moccasins on)* *when*

ccəmstín iʔ sƛ̓aʔcínəm ixíʔ {uɬ ac} iʔ t smík̓ʷət."
c -cm -st -in iʔ s+ƛ̓aʔ=cín+m s+mik̓ʷ+t iʔ t s+mik̓ʷ+t
cust^ -cover -^cust -1erg art deer then art agInst snow_on_ground
I covered the deer with snow."

384 way̓, i[xíʔ] k̓ʷíƛ̓ɬtəm iʔ q̓aʔxáns, ixíʔ x̌əw̓x̌əw̓ɬtím. 385 a
way̓ ixíʔ k̓ʷiƛ̓ -ɬt -m iʔ q̓aʔ=xán -s ixíʔ x̌w̓•x̌w̓ -ɬt -im a
well then take_off -ɬt -psv art shoes -3in then dry -ɬt -psv intj
Well, she took his moccasins off, she dried them. *She*

ɬxʷíc̓əɬtəm {iʔ l} iʔ l sɬq̓ilx iʔ q̓aʔxáns; 386 a
ɬ+xʷic̓ -ɬt -m iʔ l s+ɬq̓+ilx iʔ q̓aʔ=xán -s a
give_again -ɬt -psv art for bedroom art shoes -3in art
gave him bedroom slippers. *They*

scústsəlx iʔ *house slippers* t suyápix[cən]. 387 way̓, way̓
s -cu -st -s -lx iʔ t s+wyap=x=cn way̓ way̓
cust^ -tell -^cust -3erg -pl art agInst white_man well well
say in English "house slippers." 7:00 *She*

kəɬsəlxítəm nak̓ʷáʔ uɬ aɬíʔ aʔkɬlatáp məɬ kɬsəlxítəm;
kɬ+sl -xit -m nak̓ʷ+á uɬ aɬíʔ aʔkɬ -latáp mɬ kɬ+sl -xit -m
set_table -xit -4erg not and because there_is -table and set_st_down -xit -psv
set dishes up. They don't have a table, she set down dishes for him.

388 t̓əxʷ k̓əɬxʷípxtəm, ixíʔ uɬ sic kɬsəlxítəm; 389 məɬ ixíʔ
t̓xʷ k̓ɬ+xʷip -xt -m ixíʔ uɬ sic kɬ+sl -xit -m mɬ ixíʔ
evidently spread -xit -psv then and then set_st_down -xit -psv and then
She just spread something down for him. *And then*

cqɬtim iʔ ksc̓íɬəns. 390 way̓ ixíʔ {c i} ksʔíɬnaʔx,
cq -ɬt -im iʔ k -sc+ʔiɬn -s way̓ ixíʔ ks -ʔiɬn -aʔx
place_down -ɬt -psv art to_be -food -3i well then incp^ -eat -^incp
she put a whole pot of food for him. *BlueJay was about to eat*

ck̓əɬk̓ʷəƛ̓álqsəms axáʔ atáʔ qʷásqiʔ 391 ixíʔ
c -k̓ɬ+k̓ʷƛ̓=alqs+m -s axáʔ atáʔ qʷásqiʔ ixíʔ
act -pull_from_under_clothes -3erg this this BlueJay that
and he pulled something from his vest. *And*

cəq̓məntúɬts iʔ sx̌áʔx̌aʔs. 392 cus: axáʔ {ma}
c̓q̓+mn -tuɬt -s iʔ s+x̌áʔ•x̌aʔ -s cu -s axáʔ
throw_at -tuɬt -3erg art father_in_law -3in tell -3erg this
he threw it at his father-in-law. *He said, "Look at this.*

ʕ̓ac̓ʕác̓əntxʷ axáʔ {mi} mipnúntxʷ stim̓ axáʔ, sc̓kinx
ʕac̓•ʕác̓ mi -xʷ axáʔ my+p -nu -nt -xʷ s+tim̓ axáʔ, sc+ʔkin+x
look fut -2erg this learn -manage -nt -2erg what this why_is_it
Then you'll know what this is, you'll wonder what

axáʔ {i}. 393 way̓ kʷis axáʔ iʔ sx̌áʔx̌aʔs, ixíʔ tk̓ʷíxʷc̓aʔs.
axáʔ way̓ kʷi -s axáʔ iʔ s+x̌áʔ•x̌aʔ -s ixíʔ t+k̓ʷíxʷ=c̓aʔ -s
this well take -3erg this art father_in_law -3in that unwrap -3erg
it is." *His father-in-law took it. He started to unwrap it.*

394 haʔ stim̓ {a} sƛ̓aʔcínəmʔ 395 way̓ ixíʔ qəmís,
haʔ s+tim̓ s+ƛ̓aʔ=cín+m way̓ ixíʔ qmi -s
inter what deer well that put_down -3erg
What part of the deer is it? 8:02 *He laid it down, he did like that,*

taʔx̌ílsts, pkʷmstis, uɬ ixíʔ qmis, uɬ
ta+ʔx̌íl -st ixíʔ pkʷ+m -st -is uɬ ixíʔ qmi -s uɬ
do_a_certain_way -st -3erg shake -st -3erg and then put_down -3erg and
shook it, and put it down; he can't figure out

iwá kcəhcəhmstís. 396 way̓ lut t̓a kskchahám.
iwá k+cah•cah+m -st -is way̓ lut t̓ ks -k+cah•ahá+m
to_no_avail match -st -3erg well not negfac futi -match
what it is. *It doesn't come out right.*

397 way̓ uɬ axáʔ ʔíɬən, ʔí··ɬən qʷásqiʔ, way̓ wiʔcín. 398 nt̓aʔ axáʔ iʔ
way̓ uɬ axáʔ ʔiɬn ʔiɬn qʷásqiʔ way̓ wy̓=cín nt̓a axáʔ iʔ
well and this eat eat BlueJay well finish_eating intj this art
He started to eat. BlueJay ate. He got done eating. *My, his*

saʔstáms, way̓ {t̓i} t̓i ckíl̓kəl̓s axáʔ {its} iʔ t
saʔ•stám -s t̓iʔ t̓iʔ c -kil̓•kl̓ -s axáʔ iʔ t
sister_in_law -3in evid evid act -frown -3erg this art agInst
sister-in-law, the one that made fun of him,

kákaʔms{is} iʔ saʔstáms. 399 uɬ axáʔ cniɬc uníxʷ cniɬc yə
ká•kaʔ+m -s iʔ saʔ•stám -s uɬ axáʔ cniɬ+c wnixʷ cniɬ+c i
deride -3erg art sister_in_law -3in and this (s)he true (s)he art
had a frown on her face. *And sure enough her older sisters*

ɬcənʔúɬxʷ úɬəm t̓i sckákʔəms axáʔ iʔ ɬcəcʔúpsc.
ɬ+c+n+ʔuɬxʷ uɬ+m t̓iʔ sc -ká•kaʔ+m -s axáʔ iʔ ɬ+c•cʔ=ups -c
come_back_in and evid ipftvp^ -deride -3erg this art younger_sister -3in
was making fun of him, and it was he who came in.

400 uɬ {ɬaʔc} cus {ts}: asx̌ílwiʔ a t̓əcxʷúy, {k̓əɬk̓əɬk̓ʷ} k̓ɬur̓úsxənt.
uɬ cu -s a -s+x̌ílwiʔ a t̓c -xʷuy k̓ɬ+wr̓=usx -nt
and tell -3erg 2in -husband art habCisl -go fix_fire -nt
She was saying: "Your husband is coming. Fix that fire." 9:00

401 uɬ uníxʷ qʷásqiʔ cənʔúɬxʷ, way̓ uɬ ixíʔ uɬ aɬ[íʔ] ɬpicxʷt axáʔ
uɬ wnixʷ qʷásqiʔ c+n+ʔuɬxʷ way̓ uɬ ixíʔ uɬ aɬíʔ ɬ+picxʷ+t axáʔ
and true BlueJay enter_cisl well and then and so disgusted_again this
And true enough, BlueJay came in. His sister-in-law was

i? saʔstáms {uɬá}. 402 ċəʔáx náx̌əmɬ kċaʔxqín təl kákaʔms
i? saʔ•stám -s ċ[ʔ]ax nax̌mɬ k+ċaʔx=qín tl ká•kaʔ+m -s
art sister_in_law -3in shame_inch but be_ashamed from deride -3erg
disappointed. *She got ashamed, felt cheap for making fun of her*

i? saʔstám[s]. 403 waẏ wiʔcín qʷásqiʔ. 404 waẏ axáʔ ʔácqaʔ iʔ
i? saʔ•stám -s waẏ wẏ=cín qʷásqiʔ waẏ axáʔ ʔácqaʔ iʔ
art sister_in_law -3in well finish_eating BlueJay well this go_out art
brother-in-law. *BlueJay got done eating.* *The old man*

ƛ̓əx̌ƛ̓x̌áp, uɬ aɬíʔ ilmíxʷəm, waẏ ixíʔ sť̓əqʷcíns. 405 ť̓əqʷcín{s}
ƛ̓x̌•ƛ̓x̌a+p uɬ aɬíʔ yl=mixʷ+m waẏ ixíʔ s -ť̓qʷ=cin -s ť̓qʷ=cin
elder and because chief yes then nom -holler -3i holler
went out, and because he's chief he yelled. *He hollered,*

swit_aɬíʔ ťi kyúnaʔ iʔ sqilxʷ. 406 hi, cyaʕ̓ {təl} kiʔ cútəlx: aʔ, waẏ
swit_aɬíʔ ťiʔ k+yúw=naʔ iʔ s+qilxʷ hi c+yaʕ̓ kiʔ cut -lx aʔ waẏ
in_fact evid listen art people intj all rel say -pl intj yes
and everybody is listening. *It was all of them and they said:*

ť̓əqʷcín a ilmíxʷəm. 407 waẏ x̌əċċənmíst. 408 cúntməlx: p
ť̓qʷ=cin a yl=mixʷ+m waẏ x̌ċ=cn+mist cu -nt -m -lx p
holler art chief well important tell -nt -psv -pl 5kn
"Ah, the chief is talking. *It's important."* *He said to them: "I am calling*

isx̌lítəm. 409 waẏ ɬckicx isníḱəɬxʷ qʷásqiʔ. 410 uɬ
i -s -x̌lit+m waẏ ɬ+c+kic+x i -s+niḱ=ɬxʷ qʷásqiʔ uɬ
1i -intt -summon yes arrive_cisl_again 1in -son_in_law BlueJay and
all of you. *My son-in-law BlueJay came back.* *And*

axáʔ kʷu xʷíċəxts ta cḱəɬláḱ. 411 uɬ waẏ wiṁ
axáʔ kʷu xʷiċ -xt -s t c -ḱɬ+laḱ uɬ waẏ wiṁ
this 1obj give -xit -3erg obj_tr hab -tie_up and well in_vain
he gave me this thing that is tied up. *And I can't*

ckcahcahmstín uɬ lut ťa
c -k+cah•cah+m -st -in uɬ lut ť
cust^ -make_fit -^cust -1erg and not evid
get them together, and I can't

ckcahhamnústən. 412 uɬ ixíʔ kʷu
c -k+cah•ah+m -nu -st -n uɬ ixíʔ kʷu
cust^ -make_fit -manage -^cust -1erg and that 1obj
get it right. 10:03 *I want you to*

ksḱəɬpaʔx̌ɬtíp kiʔ x̌lítɬmən. 413 níkxnaʔ {n} cxíʔtmist
ks -ḱɬ+paʔx̌ -ɬt -ip kiʔ x̌lit -ɬm -n níkxnaʔ c -xít+miʔst
futt^ -figure_out -ɬt -5erg rel summon -5obj -1erg goodness hab -run
figure it for me, that's why I am calling you." *My, the people ran over*

iʔ sqílxʷ, aɬíʔ ḱʷəɬxcínməntəm. 414 waẏ cənyáʕ̓lx, uɬ i ḱl aʔ
iʔ s+qilxʷ aɬíʔ ḱʷɬx=cin+m -nt -m waẏ c -n+yaʕ̓ -lx uɬ iʔ ḱl aʔ
art people so surprising_news -nt -psv well hab -gather -pl and art to art
there, because that's surprising news. *They all came in, at the chief's.*

ilmíxʷəm, nt̓aʔ uɬ nq̓ʷíc̓təlx iʔ splal 415 way̓ ixíʔ xʷíc̓əɬtməlx iʔ
yl=mixʷ+m nt̓a uɬ n+q̓ʷic̓+t -lx iʔ s+pl•al way̓ ixíʔ xʷic̓ -ɬt -m -lx iʔ
chief intj and full -pl art youth well that give -ɬt -psv -pl art
It was a house full with young folks. *The old man gave it*

t ƛ̓əx̌ƛ̓x̌áp. 416 way̓ ixíʔ iwá kcahamstísəlx. 417 way̓ lut
t ƛ̓x̌•ƛ̓x̌a+p way̓ ixíʔ iwá k+cah+m -st -is -lx way̓ lut
agInst elder well that try_to figure_out -caus -3erg -pl well not
to them. *They tried to figure it out.* *No,*

t̓a kskcahahám axáʔ iʔ t̓ínaʔ. 418 way̓ míystsəlx sƛ̓aʔcínəm
t̓ ks -k+cah•há+m axáʔ iʔ t̓ínaʔ way̓ miy -st -s -lx s+ƛ̓aʔ=cín+m
evid futi -figure_out this art ear yes know -st -3erg -pl deer
they couldn't figure out the ears. *They knew it's deer's ears;*

t̓ínaʔ[s], uɬ náx̌əmɬ way̓ lut t̓a kskcahhám. 419 iwá
t̓ínaʔ -s uɬ nax̌mɬ way̓ lut t̓ ks -k+cah•ahá+m iwá
ear -3in and but well not negfac futi -figure_out to_no_avail
but they didn't match. *They even*

qmísəlx, {iwá} lut k̓əl sk̓ʷut axáʔ iʔ naqs uɬ k̓əl sk̓ʷut;
qmi -s -lx lut k̓l s+k̓ʷut axáʔ iʔ naqs s+k̓ʷut k̓l s+k̓ʷut
put_down -3erg -pl not to other_side this art one and to other_side
laid them out. One half doesn't fit with the other.

420 uɬ way̓ lut, lut̓ skcahhám[s]. 421 way̓ ixíʔ sic
uɬ way̓ lut lut_t̓ s -k+cah•ahá+m -s way̓ ixíʔ sic
and well not neg_emph nom -figure_out -3i well then then
Well, no, it doesn't match. *Then they*

síwsəlx qʷásqiʔ. 422 cúsəlx: way̓ uɬ kʷu sl̓al̓. 423 uɬ laʔkín
siw -s -lx qʷásqiʔ cu -s -lx way̓ uɬ kʷu sl̓•al̓ uɬ la+ʔkín̓
ask -3erg -pl BlueJay tell -3erg -pl yes and 4kn puzzle and how
asked BlueJay. *They said: "We are puzzled. 11:04* *What is*

sc̓kinx axáʔ iʔ t̓ínaʔ, uɬ lut t̓a kskcahhám?
sc+ʔkin+x axáʔ iʔ t̓ínaʔ uɬ lut t̓ ks -k+cah•ahá+m
why_is_it this art ear and not negfac futi -figure_out
wrong with this ear that it doesn't match?"

424 kʕʷəyncútməntməlx t qʷásqiʔ, uɬ cúntməlx: way̓, a way̓
k+ʕʷy+ncut+m -nt -m -lx t qʷásqiʔ uɬ cu -nt -m -lx way̓ a way̓
laugh_at -nt -psv -pl agInst BlueJay and tell -nt -psv -pl yes intj yes
BlueJay laughed at them, and he said to them:

p cpspsʕáyaʔ. 425 uɬ cmistíp lut t̓a
p c -ps•ps=ʕáyaʔ uɬ c -my -st -ip lut t̓
5kn hab -goofy and cust^ -know -^cust -5erg not negfac
"You got no sense. *You know that it won't*

kskcahhám. 426 uɬ way̓ t̓əxʷ {t̓ixʷtis} snaqsx ixíʔ
ks -k+cah•ahá+m uɬ way̓ t̓xʷ s -naqs -x ixíʔ
futi -figure_out and yes emph ipftv^ -one -^ipftv that
match. *And each deer has*

ɬaʔ kɬťínaʔ. 427 uɬ aɬíʔ yayʕát tq̓y̓ínaʔn, ťi way̓ k̓əl
ɬaʔ kɬ+ťínaʔ uɬ aɬíʔ yaʕ•yáʕ+t t+q̓y̓=ínaʔ -n ťiʔ way̓ k̓l
the_one_that have+ear and so all mark -1erg evid yes to
one ear. *I marked all of them*

sksk̓ʷtínaʔ. 428 uɬ aɬíʔ ṅíṅẇiʔ {kʷ na} kcəhhám, uɬ aɬíʔ
s+k+s+k̓ʷt=ínaʔ uɬ aɬíʔ ṅíṅẇiʔ k+cah•há+m uɬ aɬíʔ
one_side and so a_while match and so
to one side. *And if it comes out right,*

ksɬíq̓ʷtaʔx. 429 uɬ ixíʔ ťíťim i l sc̓kaks. 430 way̓ ixíʔ kiʔ
ks -ɬiq̓ʷ+t -aʔx uɬ ixíʔ ťi•ťym iʔ l s+c̓k•ak -s way̓ ixíʔ kiʔ
incp^ -appear -^incp and that easy art for count -3in well then rel
it will show. *And it will be easy to count."* *That's*

uɬ sic mypcín[əlx], nsúxʷnaʔmsəlx; 431 mypnúsəlx
uɬ sic my+p=cin -lx n+súxʷ=naʔ+m -s -lx my+p -nu -s -lx
and then agree -pl understand -3erg -pl learn -manage -3erg -pl
when they all agreed. They understood; *and they knew*

ťəxʷ axáʔ iʔ ťínaʔ. 432 way̓ {ixíʔ} ixíʔ c̓kəntísəlx, nťaʔ uɬ
ťxʷ axáʔ iʔ ťínaʔ way̓ ixíʔ c̓k -nt -is -lx nťa uɬ
evidently this art ear well that count -nt -3erg -pl intj and
the ears. *They counted them. There were lots of deer*

yaʕpqín sƛ̓aʔcínəm axáʔ ɬaʔ kɬťínaʔ. 433 {cúsəlx uɬ} cúntəm
yaʕ+p=qín s+ƛ̓aʔ=cín+m axáʔ ɬaʔ kɬ+ťínaʔ cu -nt -m
lots deer this the_one_that have_ear tell -nt -psv
if there are so many ears. 12:04 *The brother-in-law*

axáʔ iʔ ta nkʷəl̓mútn.[22] 434 {ə} ixíʔ uɬ aɬíʔ way̓ mat nťaʔlíls axáʔ
axáʔ iʔ t n+kʷl̓mut ixíʔ uɬ aɬíʔ way̓ mat n+ťaʔl=íls axáʔ
this art agInst brother_in_law then and so yes must satisfied this
told them this. *Because maybe the oldest one*

iʔ t sc̓ʔaxs axáʔ iʔ sxʔitx; 435 way̓ ixíʔ {siws} siws iʔ
iʔ t s+c̓ʔax -s axáʔ iʔ s+xʔit=x way̓ ixíʔ siw -s iʔ
art obl shame -3in this art oldest_one well then ask -3erg art
got over her shame, *his sister-in-law*

saʔstáms; 436 cúntəm: uɬ xʔkínəm ankʷəl̓mút, lut haʔ
saʔ•stám -s cu -nt -m uɬ x+kin+m a -n+kʷl̓mut lut haʔ
brother_in_law -3in tell -nt -psv and do_what 2in -brother_in_law not inter
asked him, *she said: "And what became of your brother-in-law? Didn't*

wíkəntxʷ 437 cut: way̓, ixíʔ qíxʷəntəm iʔ sƛ̓aʔcínəm {uɬi};
wik -nt -xʷ cut way̓ ixíʔ qixʷ -nt -m iʔ s+ƛ̓aʔ=cín+m
see -nt -2erg say yes that drive -nt -4erg art deer
you see him?" *He said: "Yes, we scared the deer,*

22 For intended nkʷl̓mut.

438 úɬiʔ kən kswitmíst {iʔ k̓əl} iʔ k̓əl ksxʷuytns, 439 iʔ k̓la
uɬ iʔ kn kswít+miʔst iʔ k̓l k -s+xʷuy+tn -s iʔ k̓l
and_then 1kn do_one's_best art to there_be -track -3in art to
and then I did my best to where they're going, *to*

cp̓əp̓sʕáwaʔs {iʔ l sa} [s]txt̓át̓əs {iʔ} iʔ məm̓kʷíwaʔt, 440 itíʔ aɬíʔ
c -p̓•p̓s=ʕáwaʔs s -t+xt̓•at̓ -s iʔ m•m̓kʷ=íwaʔt itíʔ aɬíʔ
hab -low_place nom -join -3i art mound_dim from_that so
a low place where it joins the little mounds, *that's where*

sxʷuytns iʔ sƛ̓aʔcínəm, uɬ cniɬc k̓əɬxʷúy iʔ k̓əl cix̌íʔst. 441 way̓
s+xʷuy+tn -s iʔ s+ƛ̓aʔ=cín+m uɬ cniɬ+c k̓ɬ+xʷuy iʔ k̓l c -yx̌=iʔst way̓
track -3in art deer and (s)he go art to hab -drive well
the deer went. And he went to the outside of those who drive. 13:05 *I*

ik̓líʔ kən kicx, way̓ itíʔ súxʷəxʷ iʔ sƛ̓aʔcínəm, qíll̓t. 442 way̓
ik̓líʔ kn kic+x way̓ itíʔ suxʷ•xʷ iʔ s+ƛ̓aʔ=cín+m qil•l•t way̓
there 1kn arrive well from_that leave_pl art deer get_to_top yes
got there. The deer had left, gone over the mountain. *I*

ƛ̓mípst[ən], way̓ itíʔ nixʷ cniɬc ksxʷuytn t sʔiwts.[23]
ƛ̓mi+p -st -n way̓ itíʔ nixʷ cniɬ+c -s+xʷuy+tn t s+ʔiwt -s
be_late -st -1erg well from_that also (s)he ? -track agInst one_behind ?
was late. He also was tracking behind.

443 uɬ way̓ lut mat t̓a ksənt̓ʕapsqílxʷtn t̓a ksnuksqílxʷ.
uɬ way̓ lut mat t̓ k+s+n+t̓aʕp+s+qílxʷ+tn t̓ k+s+n+wk+s+qilxʷ
and well not maybe negfac have_shot negfac have_look
I guess he didn't even get a shot at it,

444 ixíʔ uɬ kəlkəlnwíxʷsts iʔ sƛ̓aʔcínəm, axáʔ iʔ xʷʔit. 445 way̓ uɬ
ixíʔ uɬ kl•kl+nwixʷ -st -s iʔ s+ƛ̓aʔ=cín+m axáʔ iʔ xʷʔi+t way̓ uɬ
then and chase -st -3erg art deer this art many well and
and then he started chasing the deer, many of them. *And*

ixíʔ nixʷ incá iskəlkəlnwíxʷ, nʔúcxənn. 446 uɬ lútiʔ
ixíʔ nixʷ in+cá i -s -kl•kl+nwixʷ n+ʔuc=xn -n uɬ lút+i
then also I 1i -intt -chase track -1erg and not_yet
I started chasing too. I followed the tracks. *They hadn't got to the*

səntkɬlílxs {k̓əl naɬáʔ ə} k̓aɬʔús. 447 ixíʔ uɬ aɬíʔ itlíʔ
s -n+tkɬ+lilx -s k̓a+ɬʔ=ús ixíʔ uɬ aɬíʔ itlíʔ
nom -get_to_bottom -3i other_side_of_mntn then and so from_there
bottom yet on the other side of the mountain. *There was a bigger valley*

k̓aɬʔús, uɬ itlíʔ sílxʷaʔ ya cənt̓áq̓əm. 448 lútiʔ
k̓a+ɬʔ=ús uɬ itlíʔ sílxʷaʔ ya c -n+t̓aq̓+m[24] lút+i
other_side_of_mntn and from_there big art hab -cross_valley not_yet
from there to the other side. *They hadn't yet*

23 The construction ksxʷuytn t sʔiwts is not understood.
24 This form may be cəntáq̓əm.

sənṫkɬlílxsəlx ki? miẃsúl̓axʷ ki? nkcníkəńn
s -n+tkɬ+lilx -s -lx ki? miẃs=úla?xʷ ki? n+kc+n=ikn -n
nom -get_to_bottom -3i -pl rel half_way rel overtake -1erg
got to the bottom, they were gone half way when I overtook my

inkʷəl̓mút. 449 waẏ ṫi lut səlkʷúts, uɬ ixí?
i -n+kʷl̓mut waẏ ṫi? lut s -lkʷ=ut -s uɬ ixí?
1in -brother_in_law well evid not nom -far -3i and then
brother-in-law. 14:00 *He didn't go far, and he made room,*

s?ax̌əlməncúts, kʷu cus: 450 waẏ uɬ kən ?ayx̌ʷtíls, waẏ lut
s -?ax̌l+mncút -s kʷu cu -s waẏ uɬ kn ?ayx̌ʷ+t=íls waẏ lut
nom -turn_around -3i 1obj tell -3erg yes and 1kn tired yes not
he told me: *'I am getting tired. I will never*

ikstḱíḱa?t, huy uɬ t anwí 451 cut: waẏ ixí?
i -ks -t+ḱí•ḱa?t huy uɬ t anwí cut waẏ ixí?
1i -futi -get_near intj and agInst you say Ok then
get near them. You go ahead.' *He said: 'Ok.'*

ḱəɬxa?təntín, waẏ ixí? uɬ ɬwin. 452 put ntkɬlílx i?
ḱɬ+xa?t -nt -ian waẏ ixí? uɬ ɬwi -n put n+tkɬ+lilx i?
be_in_front_of -nt -1erg well then and leave -1erg just get_to_bottom art
I went ahead of him. I left him. *The deer just got*

sƛ̓a?cínəm ki? nkcníkəńn. 453 ƛ̓xʷəntí··n uɬ
s+ƛ̓a?=cín+m ki? n+kc+n=ikn -n ƛ̓xʷ -nt -in uɬ
deer rel overtake -1erg kill_many -nt -1erg and
to the bottom and I overtook them. *I killed them,*

nḱáwl̓a?xʷstən, uɬ ixí? axá? yayʕát ɬa? kɬṫína?{i?} 454 uɬ
n+ḱáw=la?xʷ -st -n uɬ ixí? axá? yaʕ•yáʕ+t ɬa? kɬ-ṫína? uɬ
massacre -st -1erg and that this all the_one_that have_ear and
finishem them all, and these are their ears. *And*

put wi?səntəltəlkʷíɬċa?n, ikslíq̓məlx ki? kʷu nkcníki?s axá?
put wẏ+s+n+tl•tlkʷ=íɬċa? -n i -ks -liq̓+m -lx ki? kʷu n+kc+n=íki? -s axá?
just finish_gutting -1erg 1i -futi -cover -pl rel 1obj catch_up_with -3erg this
I just had got done gutting them, I was going to bury them when my brother-in-law

inkʷəl̓mút. 455 waẏ uɬ huy i? t s?ayx̌ʷt, ḱim ṫi {ta} t
i -n+kʷl̓mut waẏ uɬ hoy i? t s+?ayx̌ʷ+t ḱim ṫi?
1in -brother_in_law well and finish art agInst tiredness only evid ?
overtook me. *He's played out with fatigue, he's just*

cxʷstútya?. 456 {unclear} úɬi? kʷu cús:
c -xʷst=útya? uɬ i? kʷu cu -s
hab -go_on_foot and_then 1obj tell -3erg
walking. *Then he told me: 'You cleaned*

waẏ {uɬ nċəspúl̓axʷ nkəcníkəntxʷ} nċəspúla?xʷstxʷ i? sƛ̓a?cínəm.
waẏ n+ċs+p=úla?xʷ -st -xʷ i? s+ƛ̓a?=cín+m
well kill -st -2erg art deer
the deer all out.' 15:00

457 cun: way̓, kʷu cus: way̓, uɫ incá_kən way̓ kən ʔáyx̌ʷt, kən
cu -n way̓ kʷu cu -s way̓ uɫ incá_kn way̓ kn ʔayx̌ʷ+t kn
tell -1erg yes 1obj tell -3erg well and I yes 1kn tired 1kn
I said: 'Yes.' And he said to me: 'Well, with me,

ksʔayx̌ʷtáyn. 458 uɫ way̓ kən kɫp̓ap̓ {kʷu uɫ t} ikɫəɫxʷúy. 459 uɫ
k+s+ʔayx̌ʷ+t+áyn uɫ way̓ kn k+ɫp̓•ap̓ i -kɫ -ɫ+xʷuy uɫ
have_tiredeness and yes 1kn discouraged 1i -futi -go_back and
I got tired. And I am discouraged to go back. And

t̓əxʷ way̓, way̓ t̓i aláʔ kpúlxmən iʔ sƛ̓aʔcínəm. 460 úɫiʔ
t̓xʷ way̓ way̓ t̓iʔ aláʔ k+pul+x+m -n iʔ s+ƛ̓aʔ=cín+m uɫ iʔ
emph yes yes evid here camp_with -1erg art deer and_then
I'll camp here with these deer.' And

cun: lut, kʷu cus: uɫ aɫíʔ way̓ myaɫ kən ʔayx̌ʷt.
cu -n lut kʷu cu -s uɫ aɫíʔ way̓ myaɫ kn ʔayx̌ʷ+t
tell -1erg not 1obj tell -3erg and because yes too_much 1kn tired
I said to him: 'No.' He told me: 'I am too tired.'

461 cun: uɫ way̓ t̓i kʷ ksc̓áɫəɫt. 462 ixíʔ uɫ aɫíʔ {way̓} way̓
cu -n uɫ way̓ t̓iʔ kʷ ks -c̓aɫ•ɫ+t ixíʔ uɫ aɫíʔ way̓
tell -1erg and yes evid 2kn futi -freeze then and so yes
And I said: 'No. You will freeze to death. It's late and

k̓laxʷ, nkʷəkʷʔác. 463 nt̓a uɫ t̓i c̓ix̌ʷ iʔ skʷkʷúsənt. 464 cun:
k̓laxʷ n+kʷ•kʷʔac nt̓a uɫ t̓iʔ c̓ix̌ʷ iʔ s+kʷ•kʷusnt cu -n
evening dark intj and evid spark art stars tell -1erg
dark. Gee, the stars are bright.' I said

uɫ axáʔ kʷ cut kʷ ksʔayx̌ʷtáyn, kʷ ʔayx̌ʷt. 465 uɫ laʔkín kʷ
uɫ axáʔ kʷ cut kʷ k+s+ʔayx̌ʷ+t+áyn kʷ ʔayx̌ʷ+t uɫ la+ʔkín̓ kʷ
and this 2kn say 2kn have_tiredeness 2kn tired and how 2kn
to him: 'You just said you are tired, tired. And what

xʔkínəm mi kʷ ur̓r̓íʔst. 466 uɫ cakʷ iwá kʷ ɫ ur̓r̓íʔst, uɫ laʔkín kʷ
x+kin+m mi kʷ wr̓•r̓=iʔst uɫ caʔkʷ iwá kʷ ɫ wr̓•r̓=iʔst uɫ la+ʔkín̓ kʷ
do_what fut 2kn make_fire and if even 2kn if make_fire and how 2kn
can you do to make fire. And if even you did make fire, what can you do

xʔkínəm mi kʷ kslíp̓əm uɫ axáʔ i l sənkʷəkʷʔác? 467 uɫ axáʔ nixʷ kʷ
x+kin+m mi kʷ k+slip̓+m uɫ axáʔ iʔ l s+n+kʷ•kʷʔac uɫ axáʔ nixʷ kʷ
do_what fut 2kn get_wood and this art in night and this also 2kn
to get wood in this dark night? And also

təxʷsqʷílpəm {uɫ cəm ta} way̓ t̓i kʷ ksc̓áɫəɫt. 468 cúntəm way̓ kʷ
txʷ+s+qʷil=p+m way̓ t̓iʔ kʷ ks -c̓aɫ•ɫ+t cu -nt -m way̓ kʷ
gather_boughs yes evid 2kn futi -freeze tell -nt -psv yes 2kn
things to put under you? You will freeze to death. 16:02 You want to camp,

sənpəlxílsx, uɫ way̓ axáʔ aláʔ{mik} mi kʷúməntsən,
s -n+pl+x=ils -x uɫ way̓ axáʔ aláʔ mi kʷum -nt -s -n
ipftvˆ -want_to_camp -ˆipftv and well this here fut store -nt -2obj -1erg
and I will store you here,

i? sx?imłsílxʷa? i l sƛ̓a?cínəm{ixí?}; 469 ałí? way̓ cyaʕ
i? s+x?im+ł+sílxʷa? i? l s+ƛ̓a?=cín+m ałí? way̓ c+yaʕ
art biggest art in deer because yes all
in the biggest of the deer, because they are all

ckt̓liw̓s. 470 {way̓ ilí?} cúntəm alá? n?úłxʷstmən uł
c -k+t̓l=iw̓s cu -nt -m alá? n+?ułxʷ -st -m -n uł
hab -split_lengthwise tell -nt -psv here enter -st -2obj -1erg and
cut open. I will put you here and you won't

way̓ lut {aksc} akskscáłəłt. 471 talí? kʷal̓t axá? i? sƛ̓a?cínəm,
way̓ lut a -ks -k+s+cał•ł+t ta?lí? kʷal̓+t axá? i? s+ƛ̓a?=cín+m
yes not 2i -futi -have_freeze very_much warm this art deer
freeze to death. The deer is quite warm,

púti? cəc?íx. 472 uł ṅíṅw̓i? klíq̓ən[tsən], uł lut
pút+i? c -c[?]ix uł ṅíṅw̓i? k+liq̓ -nt -s -n uł lut
still hab -get_warm and a_while bury -nt -2obj -1erg and not
still warm. And then I'll bury you, and you won't

akskscáłəłt. 473 {indec} way̓ ilí? kʷúmən, uł {i} [ix]í? uł
a -ks -ks+cał•ł+t way̓ ilí? kʷum -n uł ixí? uł
2i -futi -have_freeze yes there store -1erg and then and
freeze to death.' I put him there, and I

tx̌p̓í··w̓[sən]. 474 kən yilw[m] i? sx̌əx̌c̓í?, ixí? kłu?xʷxʷúsən axá? i?
t+x̌p̓=iw̓s -n kn yilw+m i? s+x̌•x̌c̓i? ixí? k+łú?xʷ•xʷ=w̓s -n axá? i?
stitch -1erg 1kn twist art stick then sew_up -1erg this art
sewed him up. I twisted a stick. I sewed up

sƛ̓a?cínəm. 475 {i} tər̓qəntí··n i? smík̓ʷət, uł i l nłəx̌ʷx̌ʷúl̓axʷ
s+ƛ̓a?=cín+m trq -nt -in i? s+mik̓ʷ+t uł i? l n+łx̌ʷ•x̌ʷ=úla?xʷ
deer kick -nt -1erg art snow_on_ground and art in hole_in_ground
the deer. I stamped on the snow and it made a hole there. I stuck him there,

ilí? nləʕ̓ʷúl̓axʷən,{i} klíq̓na?n i? t smík̓ʷət. 476 ixí?
ilí? n+lʕ̓ʷ=úla?xʷ -n k+líq̓=na? -n i? t s+mik̓ʷ+t ixí?
there stick_into_gr -1erg bury -1erg art agInst snow_on_ground then
and I buried him with snow.17:04 And

úłi? kən cqəlwítəm. 477 cúntəm axá? a ilmíxʷəm, cus
uł i? kn c -ql=wit+m cu -nt -m axá? a yl=mixʷ+m cu -s
and_then 1kn hab -step tell -nt -psv this art chief tell -3erg
then I stepped away." He told the chief. He told his

i? sx̌á?x̌a?s; 478 cúntəm t qʷásqi?, cúntməlx, ṅíṅw̓i?
i? s+x̌á?•x̌a? -s cu -nt -m t qʷásqi? cu i? -m -lx ṅíṅw̓i?
art father_in_law -3in tell -nt -psv agInst BlueJay tell art -psv -pl a_while
father-in-law, BlueJay told them: "All of you that are related

axá? {as} [i? p] ksnəqsílxʷ kskʷʕácta?xəlx; 479 na?ł sma?mə?í··m,
axá? i? p k+s+nqs=ilxʷ ks -kʷaʕct -a?x -lx na?ł s+ma•m?ím
this art 5kʷu have_relative incp^ -early -^incp -pl and women
will get up early, also the women folks,

kʷu ksmíc̓aʔx, uɬ aɬíʔ lkʷut. 480 {a u} cútəlx: way̓.
kʷu ks -míc̓aʔ -x uɬ aɬíʔ lkʷ=ut cut -lx way̓
4kn incp^ -dead_game -^incp and because far say -pl Ok
we are going to get the dead deer. Because it's far." They said: "Ok."

481 {way̓ ixíʔ} way̓ lut sʔatxílxs iʔ sqílxʷ {way̓ t̓i}. 482 cxʷuy i
way̓ lut s -ʔatx+ílx -s iʔ s+qilxʷ c+xʷuy iʔ
well not nom -sleep_pl -3i art people come art
The folks didn't go to sleep. Came

sx̌lap, uɬ qíɬəɬtəlx, t̓əxʷ t̓əqʷcínəlx úɬi xʷət̓lílxəlx. 483 way̓ t̓i
s+x̌la+p uɬ qiɬ•ɬ+t -lx t̓xʷ t̓qʷ=cin -lx uɬ iʔ xʷt̓+lilx way̓ t̓iʔ
morning and wake_up_pl -pl emph holler -pl and_then get_up_pl well evid
morning, and they woke up, and started hollering. 18:00 They

taʔx̌í¨lməlx uɬ wiʔwiʔcínəlx {uɬ i}. 484 ixíʔ sʔácqaʔs a
ta+ʔx̌íl+m -lx uɬ wy̓•wy̓=cin -lx ixíʔ s -ʔácqaʔ -s a
do_a_certain_way -pl and finish_eating_pl -pl then nom -go_out -3i art
did that, and got done eating. Then the chief went out.

ilmíxʷəm, cut "hu•húy, kʷu təkʷʔút. 485 way̓ cúsəlx: way̓, way̓ kʷu
yl=mixʷ+m cut hu+húy kʷu tkʷʔ=ut way̓ cu -s -lx way̓ way̓ kʷu
chief say OK 4kn walk_pl well tell -3erg -pl yes yes 4kn
He said, "Now we will walk." They said: "We are all

wiʔnúmt. 486 way̓ {naʔɬs} naʔɬ ksxƛ̓ƛ̓úl̓axʷs. 487 way̓ p həɬsmaʔməʔím
wy̓+numt way̓ naʔɬ k -s+xƛ̓•ƛ̓=úlaʔxʷ -s way̓ p hɬ=s+ma•mʔím
ready well and ? -full_daylight ? well 5kn women_group
ready." It got broad daylight. "You women folks whose

pukxəncútəlx. 488 uɬ aɬíʔ sisyús iʔ smaʔməʔím i l
pu=kx+n+cut -lx uɬ aɬíʔ sy•syus iʔ s+ma•mʔím iʔ l
wife_follow -pl and because smart art women art in
husbands have gone along." Because the women are smart with snowshoes,

syríwaxən, uɬ aɬíʔ ixíʔ t̓i a ntəkʷtəkʷʔútənsəlx; 489 aɬíʔ
s+yr=íwaʔ=xn uɬ aɬíʔ ixíʔ t̓iʔ a n+tkʷ•tkʷʔ=ut+n -s -lx aɬíʔ
snowshoes and so then evid art means_of_travel -3in -pl because
and that's the only way they can travel anyway, they

nak̓ʷáʔ ɬ kɬkaw̓ápəlx, swit iʔ l sʔistk {uɬ}. 490 ixíʔ t̓iʔ a
nak̓ʷ+á ɬ kɬ+kw̓•w•áp -lx swit iʔ l s+ʔis=tk ixíʔ t̓iʔ a
indeed_not compl have_horses -pl who art in winter that evid art
don't have horses, who does in wintertime. That's all they

ntkʷtkʷʔútnsəlx iʔ siríwaxən, axáʔ pútəm iʔ sənʕíckstx. 491 way̓
n+tkʷ•tkʷʔ=ut+n -s -lx iʔ s+yr=íwaʔ=xn axáʔ put+m iʔ s+n+ʕic=kst=x way̓
means_of_travel -3in -pl art snowshoes this just art Lakes well
travel on, snowshoes. Especially the North Halfs. They

xʷúy̓ilx, way̓ k̓əɬxaʔtəntíməlx t qʷásqiʔ. 492 níknaʔ qʷásqiʔ,
xʷuy̓•y -lx way̓ k̓ɬ+xaʔt -nt -im -lx t qʷásqiʔ níkxnaʔ qʷásqiʔ
go_pl -pl yes be_preceded -nt -psv -pl agInst BlueJay goodness BlueJay
went. And they got a leader, BlueJay. BlueJay is

waẏ q̓ʷíɬq̓ʷəɬt iʔ l siríwaxən; 493 ƛ̓əm lut t̓a cmistís,
waẏ q̓ʷiɬ•q̓ʷɬ+t iʔ l s+yr=íwaʔ=xn ƛ̓m lut t̓ c -my -st -is
yes strong art on snowshoes past not negfac custˆ -know -ˆcust -3erg
really smart on snowshoes. 19:04 *He didn't used to know how.*

a ckákaʔmstsəlx. 494 waẏ nixʷ axáʔ iʔ t təkɬmílxʷs
a c -káʔkaʔ+m -st -s -lx waẏ nixʷ axáʔ iʔ t tkɬ+m=ilxʷ -s
intj custˆ -deride -ˆcust -custˆ -pl yes also this art agInst wife -3in
And they made fun of him. *BlueJay's wife had*

pukxəncút {a} qʷásqiʔ. 495 uɬ t̓iʔ ilíʔ nk̓ək̓tíkəntəm iʔ t
pu=kx+n+cút qʷásqiʔ uɬ t̓iʔ ilíʔ n+k̓•k̓t=ikn -t -m iʔ t
wife_follow BlueJay and evid there right_behind -nt -psv art agInst
gone along. *And his sister-in-law was right*

saʔstáms; {uɬ} 496 uɬ axáʔ iʔ {tɬcic} t sx̌aʔ•x̌áʔs naʔɬ
saʔ•stám -s uɬ axáʔ iʔ t s+x̌áʔ•x̌aʔ -s naʔɬ
sister_in_law -3in and this art agInst father_in_law -3in and
behind him, *his father-in-law and mother-in-law*

ɬcicks t̓i iliʔ ċíwtəlx. 497 {m} uɬ sic iʔ k̓ʷíƛ̓ət iʔ
ɬ+ci•ck -s t̓iʔ ilíʔ c+ʔiwt -lx uɬ sic iʔ k̓ʷiƛ̓+t iʔ
mother_in_law -3in evid there last -pl and then art others art
are also behind. *And then the rest of the folks*

sqilxʷ ɬ ʔawtpáɬq. 498 waẏ xʷu··ylx uɬ axáʔ uɬ cləʕʷútəm {i}
s+qilxʷ ɬ ʔaw+t+p=áɬq waẏ xʷuy -lx uɬ axáʔ uɬ c -lʕ̓ʷ=ut+m
people compl follow well go -pl and this and hab -valley
string along. *They went there in a big valley, and at the end*

uɬ k̓əl skəmq̓ʷáq̓ʷəs; 499 ixíʔ kiʔ cənxʷəxʷṙús, itíʔ kiʔ
uɬ k̓l s -k+mq̓ʷ•aq̓ʷ -s ixíʔ kiʔ c -n+xʷ•xʷr=us itíʔ kiʔ
and to nom -mountain -3i there rel hab -hollow from_that rel
a little mountain, *that's where the low place is. They went right*

qíl̓ltəlx. 500 waẏ itlíʔ {n} saʕməncútəlx. 501 waẏ xʷuylx, waẏ
qil•l•t -lx waẏ itlíʔ saʕ+mncút -lx waẏ xʷuy -lx waẏ
get_to_top -pl well from_there go_downhill -pl well go -pl yes
over that hill. *Then they went down the hill.* *They went. They got to*

ntkɬəl̓ílxəlx. 502 waẏ cúntməlx, waẏ axáʔ, ixíʔ uɬ t̓iʔ {t̓iʔ}
n+tkɬ+lilx -lx waẏ cu -nt -m -lx waẏ axáʔ ixíʔ uɬ t̓iʔ
get_to_bottom -pl well tell -nt -psv -pl well this that and evid
the bottom. *He told them: "It's right here." There are snow mounds*

məkʷʔíw+t {i s} iʔ sƛ̓aʔcínəm iʔ scliq̓.[25] 503 {waẏ ixíʔ cúntəm axáʔ i t}
mkʷ=iwt iʔ s+ƛ̓aʔ=cín+m iʔ sc -liq̓ -s
lump_pl art deer art pftv -bury -3i
all over where the deer are buried. 20:06

25 The suffix is expected here.

cus i? sx̌a?•x̌á?s way̓ anwí kʷ ilmíxʷəm i? kʷ
cu -s i? s+x̌á?•x̌a? -s way̓ anwí kʷ yl=mixʷ+m i? kʷ
tell -3erg art father_in_law -3in yes you 2kn chief art 2kʷu
He told his father-in-law: "You are the boss, my

isx̌a?•x̌á?; 504 way̓ uɬ pəx̌ʷəmstíxʷ axá? i? sɬiqʷ, ilí?
i -s+x̌a?•x̌á? way̓ uɬ px̌ʷ+m -st -ixʷ axá? i? s+ɬiqʷ ilí?
1in -father_in_law well and distribute -st -2erg this art meat there
father-in-law. *You distribute the meat. That's the*

cmalk̓ʷ. 505 cut axá? i? sx̌a?•x̌á?, lut, iwá t̓əxʷ kən ilmíxʷəm {uɬ};
c -malk̓ʷ cut axá? i? s+x̌á?•x̌a? lut iwá t̓xʷ kn yl=mixʷ+m
hab -entire say this art father_in_law not even emph 1kn chief
whole catch." *The father-in-law said: "No, even if I am the chief.*

506 uɬ anwí {kʷ ɬa kscaxʷ} kʷ ɬa? ksc̓ƛ̓axʷ, anwí kʷ
uɬ anwí kʷ ɬa? ksc -ƛ̓axʷ anwí kʷ
and you 2kn the_one_that pperf -kill_many you 2kn
It's you that killed them, you're the one that worked hard.

ɬa? kɬk̓áyx̌ʷtn, way̓ t anwí mi pəx̌ʷmstíxʷ. 507 uɬ
ɬa? kɬ+k+?ayx̌ʷ+t+n way̓ t anwí mi px̌ʷ+m -st -ixʷ uɬ
the_one_that have_tiredness yes agInst you fut distribute -st -2erg and
You pass it around. *And*

axá? incá t̓i kmix kən mu··t, kən səcqínk, kən sləqpa?səncút,
axá? in+cá t̓i? kmix kn mut kn s -cq=ink kn s -lq=pa?s+ncút
this I evid only 1kn sit_sg 1kn hab -lie_on_back 1kn hab -pull_whiskers
here I only was sitting around, lying on my back, pulling my whiskers with tweezers,

508 mi ɬ stkʷínpla?stən ɬ cpəx̌ʷmstín,
mi ɬ s -t+kʷín=pla? -st -n ɬ c -px̌ʷ+m -st -in
fut compl cust^ -take_the_lead -^cust -1erg compl cust^ -distribute -^cust -1in
and for me to take the lead to pass it around... You

anwí. 509 ah, way̓, way̓ pəx̌ʷmstís. 510 {way̓ axá?i?sa?stáms}
anwí ah way̓ way̓ px̌ʷ+m -st -is
you intj Ok well distribute -st -3erg
do it." 21:05 *He said: "Ok," and he passed it around.* *He knew*

ixí? uɬ aɬí? way̓ cmystis la?kín {ki?} ki? kʷums axá?
ixí? uɬ aɬí? way̓ c -my -st -is la+?kíṅ ki? kʷum -s axá?
that and because yes cust^ -know -^cust -3erg where rel store -3erg this
what deer he

i? l sƛ̓a?cínəm. 511 cus axá? i? sa?stáms: way̓ axá? anwí {a}
i? l s+ƛ̓a?=cín+m cu -s axá? i? sa?•stám -s way̓ axá? anwí
art in deer tell -3erg this art sister_in_law -3in well this you
put him in. *He told his sister-in-law: That's what*

aksənq̓ʷəɬtáqs, 512 ixí? axá? {as i} anmkʷíwt, ixí? uɬ
a -k -s+n+q̓ʷɬ+t=aqs ixí? axá? an -mkʷ=iwt ixí? uɬ
2i -to_be -share_one_carries that this 2in -mound that and
I'm going to give you, *this is your lump. You dig that out,*

cíqəntxʷ uɬ xʔkistxʷ; 513 kʷ ɬckʷíɬċaʔm, kəm̓ ċíqʷəntxʷ,
ciq -nt -xʷ uɬ x+ki -st -xʷ kʷ ɬ+ckʷ=íɬċaʔ+m km̓ ċiqʷ -nt -xʷ
dig -nt -2erg and do_what -st -2erg 2kn drag_body_back or skin -nt -2erg
do what you please, *drag it home, or skin it,*

ɬq̓ʷíɬtməntxʷ, xʔkistxʷ; 514 {unclear} t̓i kpaʔsəntíxʷ
ɬ+q̓ʷiɬ+t+m -nt -xʷ x+ki -st -xʷ t̓iʔ k+paʔs -nt -ixʷ
pack_back -nt -2erg do_what -st -2erg evid think_about -nt -2erg
pack it back, do what you want. *Whatever you*

anwí. 515 níkxnaʔ iʔ saʔstáms limt. 516 mat k̓əɬt̓əmʕásəs {i s a}
anwí níkxnaʔ iʔ saʔ•stám -s lim+t mat k̓ɬ+t̓m=ʕas -s
you goodness art sister_in_law -3in glad maybe kiss -3erg
think .” *My, his sister-in-law was glad.* *I suppose his sister-in-law*

qʷásqiʔ iʔ t saʔstáms iʔ t slimt. 517 ƛ̓əm axáʔ
qʷásqiʔ iʔ t saʔ•stám -s iʔ t s+limt ƛ̓m axáʔ
BlueJay art agInst sister_in_law -3in art from gladness past this
kissed BlueJay, she was so tickled. 22:02 *His*

sʕaʕímaʔ iʔ t saʔstáms təl sx̌ʷupts. 518 hi,
s -ʕa•ʕím+aʔ iʔ t saʔ•stám -s tl s+x̌ʷup+t -s hi
? -hate art agInst sister_in_law -3in from worthlessness -3in intj
sister-in-law used to hate him because he was good for nothing. *She*

kcíqnaʔs axáʔ iʔ sƛ̓aʔcínəm uɬ {a} kəlkʷkʷínaʔ iʔ t smik̓ʷət,
k+cíq=naʔ -s axáʔ iʔ s+ƛ̓aʔ=cín+m uɬ k+lkʷ•kʷ=ínaʔ iʔ t s+mik̓ʷt
dig -3erg this art deer and uncover art obl snow_on_ground
started digging the deer. She took off the snow,

519 way̓ k̓əɬkícxs iʔ sƛ̓aʔcínəm. 520 way̓ {əck} ckɬúʔxʷuʔs
way̓ k̓ɬ+kic+x -s iʔ s+ƛ̓aʔ=cín+m way̓ c -k+ɬuʔxʷ=w̓s
well manage_to_arrive -3erg art deer well hab -sewn_up
she got to the deer. *It was sewn up twisted*

iʔ t syílwiʔ iʔ t sx̌əx̌ċíʔ. 521 way̓ {ixíʔ} ixíʔ ktrí··w̓səs
iʔ t s+yílwiʔ iʔ t s+x̌•x̌ċiʔ way̓ ixíʔ k+tr=iw̓s -s
art agInst twig art agInst stick well then unstitch -3erg
with the sprig. *She undid the stictches,*

ixíʔ, {c ay u} taʔx̌ílsts, 522 tx̌qíw̓səs axáʔ iʔ {unclear}
ixíʔ ta+ʔx̌íl -st -s t+x̌q=iw̓s -s axáʔ iʔ
that do_a_certain_way -st -3erg open -3erg this art
she did like that, *she opened it where*

ckt̓liw̓s a ckɬúʔxʷuʔs. 523 way̓ tx̌qíw̓səs, t̓i kʷm̓iɬ
c -k+t̓l=iw̓s a c -k+ɬuʔxʷ=w̓s way̓ t+x̌q=iw̓s -s t̓iʔ kʷm̓iɬ
hab -split_lengthwise art hab -sewn_up well open -3erg evid suddenly
it was cut open and sewn up. *She opened it. All of a sudden*

uɬ ċácqaʔ {iʔ s} iʔ sqəltmíxʷs. 524 nt̓a way̓ uɬ kmix mənksqáx̌aʔ.
uɬ c+ʔácqaʔ iʔ s+qlt=mixʷ -s nt̓a way̓ uɬ kmix mnk=sqáx̌aʔ
and come_out art man -3in intj well and only shit_covered_body
out came her husband. *He's nothing but shit.*

525 níkxnaʔ ncq̓áqsəntəm axáʔ iʔ tkɬmílx^{w}. 526 way̓ uɬ lut_itíʔ,
níkxnaʔ n+cq̓=aqs -nt -m axáʔ iʔ tkɬ+m=ilx^{w} way̓ uɬ lut_itíʔ
goodness hit_nose -nt -psv this art woman well and good_about_one
Goodness, the stench hit the woman's nose. 23:02 *Her husband*

sqy̓ax^{w}s {iʔ s} iʔ sqəltmíx^{w}s. 527 way̓ {uyu} utəntís iwá
s -qy̓ax^{w} -s iʔ s+qlt=mix^{w} -s way̓ wt -nt -is iwá
nom -stink -3i art man -3in well put_down -nt -3erg try_to
really stank. *She tried. She's going to try*

uɬ {ks} ksc̓íq^{w}iʔs, way̓ lut. 528 way̓ uɬ t̓i kmix
uɬ ks -c̓iq^{w} y̓ -s way̓ lut way̓ uɬ t̓iʔ kmix
and futt^ -skin -nt -3erg well not well and evid only
to skin it. She couldn't stand it. *The deer is*

mníkɬc̓aʔ nák̓^{w}əm axáʔ {unclear} iʔ sƛ̓aʔcínəm. 529 uɬ aɬíʔ
mník=ɬc̓aʔ nak̓^{w}+m axáʔ iʔ s+ƛ̓aʔ=cín+m uɬ aɬíʔ
body_covered_in_shit evid this art deer and because
nothing but shit. *Her*

axáʔ [iʔ] sqəltmíx^{w} c̓x̌iɬt aɬíʔ iʔ ksʔayx̌^{w}táyn; uɬ aɬíʔ sʔilx^{w}t,
axáʔ iʔ s+qlt=mix^{w} c+ʔx̌iɬ+t aɬíʔ iʔ k+s+ʔayx̌^{w}+t+áyn uɬ aɬíʔ s+ʔilx^{w}+t
this art man like because nt have_tiredeness and so hunger
husband got tired and hungry,

530 kiʔ sqilx^{w} sʔilx^{w}t {ka} kaʔ c̓ayx̌^{w}t. 531 way̓ uɬ ixíʔ t̓i {s}
kiʔ s+qilx^{w} s+ʔilx^{w}+t kiʔ c -ʔayx̌^{w}+t way̓ uɬ ixíʔ t̓iʔ
rel person hunger rel hab -tired well and then evid
and people get hungry when they get tired. *He got warmed up there*

scʔi··xs ilíʔ, uɬ {c} ɬaʔx^{w}ísk̓it c̓x̌iɬt 532 way̓ uɬ ixíʔ
s -c[ʔ]ix -s ilíʔ uɬ ɬaʔx^{w}=ísk̓it c+ʔx̌iɬ+t way̓ uɬ ixíʔ
nom -get_warm -3i there and rest like well and then
when he got rested *and then*

nɬək̓^{w}ək̓^{w}mís {iʔ s} iʔ sksq̓míltəns. 533 way̓ t̓i·· məsməlwís {unclear}
n+ɬk̓^{w}•k̓^{w}+mi -s iʔ s k+s+q̓m=ilt+n way̓ t̓iʔ ms+m+lwis
think_about -3erg nt ? have_hunger well evid feel_around
he realized he was hungry. *He felt around,*

məssíkstəms axáʔ {iʔ} iʔ sq̓^{w}ísəs. 534 way̓ uɬ t̓i ixíʔ {c}
ms•s=ikst+m -s axáʔ iʔ s+q̓^{w}is•s way̓ uɬ t̓iʔ ixíʔ
feel_with_hands -3erg this nt fat well and evid then
he felt the fat. 24:02 *He cut off*

ckník̓əms itlíʔ, uɬ {aɬ} ixíʔ {c} sʔíɬəns
c -k+nik̓+m -s itlíʔ uɬ ixíʔ s -ʔiɬn -s
act -cut_off -3erg from_there and that nom -eat -3i
from there and he ate it.

535 sənmaʔmúk^{w}ək^{w}pnaʔms, swit_aɬíʔ sícɬc̓aʔ. 536 a t̓i ʔayxáxaʔ
s -n+maʔ•múk^{w}•k^{w}+pnaʔm[26] -s swit_aɬíʔ síc=ɬc̓aʔ a t̓iʔ ʔayxáxaʔ
nom -bulge -3i in_fact fresh_meat intj evid a_while
It's fresh meat that bulged here and there. *Soon after*

təl swiʔcíns, waẏ, waẏ nkcnínkəntəm iʔ [t sə]nc̓aʔrínk.
tl s -wẏ=cin -s waẏ waẏ n+kc+n=ikn -t -m iʔ t s+n+c̓aʔr=ínk
from nom -finish_eating -3i well yes overtake -nt -psv art agInst diarrhea
he had eaten he started to ache with diarrhea.

537 waẏ ksʔácqaʔx, waẏ lut. 538 təl tk̓əmkníɬxʷ waẏ kiʔ
waẏ ks -ʔácqaʔ -x waẏ lut tl t+k̓m=kn=iɬxʷ waẏ kiʔ
well incp^ -go_out -^incp well not from outside yes rel
He tried to get out. He couldn't. *It's sewn from the outside,*

ck̓ɬənx̌p̓ip, uɬ lut xʔkínəm {mi} mi ʔacəcqaʔíʔst. 539 waẏ uɬ
c -k̓ɬ+n+x̌p̓=ip uɬ lut x+kin+m mi ʔác•c•qaʔ=iʔst waẏ uɬ
hab -fasten_door and not do_what fut struggle_to_exit well and
and there isn't anything to do to get out. *He came*

xiẏmscút, waẏ t̓i ilíʔ {uɬ} uɬ np̓c̓əntʕás {iʔ} axáʔ iʔ sƛ̓aʔcínəm. 540 waẏ
xẏ+mscut waẏ t̓iʔ ilíʔ uɬ n+p̓c̓ -nt -ʕas axáʔ iʔ s+ƛ̓aʔ=cín+m waẏ
done_in well evid there and squirt -nt -3erg this art deer well
to the end. He crapped right in there, in the deer. *He*

ksx̌lap np̓c̓əntʕás iʔ sƛ̓aʔcínəm. 541 scʔx̌ilx uɬ aɬíʔ {kmix kmix}
k+s+x̌la+p n+p̓c̓ -nt -ʕas iʔ s+ƛ̓aʔ=cín+m sc+ʔx̌il+x uɬ aɬíʔ
all_night squirt -nt -3erg nt deer reason_why and so
crapped in the deer until daylight. *That's why it stank,*

kmix mnik iʔ sqẏaxʷs. 542 níknaʔ, waẏ t̓i ckíl̓kəl̓s axáʔ iʔ
kmix mnik iʔ s+qẏaxʷ -s níkxnaʔ waẏ t̓iʔ c -kil̓•kl̓ -s axáʔ iʔ
only shit art stink -3in goodness well evid act -frown -3erg this nt
it's nothing but shit. 25:00 *Goodness. the woman just*

təkɬmílxʷ. 543 nt̓aʔ xʷaẏsts iʔ sqəltmíxʷs. 544 cus: waẏ
tkɬ+m=ilxʷ nt̓a xʷaẏ -st -s iʔ s+qlt=mixʷ -s cu -s waẏ
woman intj reproach -st -3erg nt man -3in tell -3erg well
frowned. *She got after her husband.* *She said:*

myáɬəm anwí kʷ kɬp̓əmscút. 545 scʔkinx aʔ kscʔíɬəntət {ta uɬ a} aʔ ɬ
myaɬ+m anwí kʷ k+ɬp̓+mscut sc+ʔkin+x aʔ k -sc+ʔiɬn -tt aʔ ɬ
too_much you 2kn awful why_is_it art to_be -food -4in art compl
"You have done something awful. *Why, that's our eats, and you*

k̓əɬx̌ʷílən[txʷ]. 546 a cus iʔ tkɬmilxʷs: waẏ kʷ
k̓ɬ+x̌ʷil -nt -xʷ a cu -s iʔ tkɬ+m=ilxʷ -s waẏ kʷ
drive_off -nt -2erg intj tell -3erg nt wife -3in yes 2kn
messed it up." *He told his wife:*

sqʷəńcənmístx, nak̓ʷáʔ t ink̓əɬcútn. 547 waẏ aɬí kən
s -qʷń=cn+mist -x nak̓ʷ+á t in -k̓ɬ+cut+n waẏ aɬíʔ kn
ipftv^ -pitiful_thing -^ipftvp indeed_not obl 1in -manners yes because 1kn
"You talk pitifully. I didn't do it on purpose. *I got*

26 This suffix is not known to me.

sksʔayx̌ʷtáynx, kən sʔayx̌ʷt[x]{uɬ}. 548 uɬ caʔkʷ lut ilíʔ
s -k+s+ʔayx̌ʷ+t+áyn -x kn s -ʔayx̌ʷ+t -x uɬ caʔkʷ lut ilíʔ
ipftv^ -have_tiredness -^ipftv 1kn ipftv^ -tired -^ipftv and if not there
give out, I was tired. *If I hadn't*

kən pulx iʔ l sƛ̓aʔcínəm, axáʔ kʷu k̓əɬpaʔx̌xíts inkʷəl̓mút
kn pul+x iʔ l s+ƛ̓aʔ=cín+m axáʔ kʷu k̓ɬ+paʔx̌ -xit -s i -n+kʷl̓mut
1kn overnight art in deer this 1obj decide -xit -3erg 1in -brother_in_law
slept inside the deer (my brother-in-law did my thinking)

549 uɬ waẏ kən ksċáɬəɬt, uɬ ixíʔ kʷu ɬwis. 550 ʔayxáxaʔ {kən c}
uɬ waẏ kn ks -ċaɬ•ɬ+t uɬ ixíʔ kʷu ɬwi -s ʔayxáxaʔ
and yes 1kn futi -freeze and then 1obj leave -3erg a_while
I would have frozen to death. He left me. *In a while*

kən ɬaʔxʷísk̓it {ċx̌iɬtwa}, aɬíʔ ʔanwín isksq̇mílt[n]. 551 [s]cutx,
kn ɬaʔxʷ=ísk̓it aɬíʔ ʔanwí -n i -s+k+s+q̇m=ilt+n s -cut -x
1kn rest so feel -1erg 1i -being_hungry ipftv^ -say -^ipftv
I got rested, and that's when I felt hungry." *He said: "And I*

uɬ aɬíʔ {i} [kən] ʔiɬən {i a} iʔ sq̇ʷísəs. 552 ixíʔ aʔ ɬ nk̓əstmín
uɬ aɬíʔ kn ʔiɬn iʔ s+q̇ʷis•s ixíʔ aʔ ɬ n+k̓s+t+mi -n
and so 1kn eat art fat that art one_that harm -1erg
ate the fat. *That's what did me bad, and then*

iʔ kən {a ɬ} nċaʔrínk. 553 uɬ aɬíʔ lut kən xʔkínəm mi kən
iʔ kn n+ċaʔr=ínk uɬ aɬíʔ lut kn x+kin+m mi kn
art 1kn diarrhea and because not 1kn do_what fut 1kn
I got diarrhea. 26:02 *There isn't any way for me*

ʔacəcqaʔíʔst {wa uɬ}. 554 ixíʔ uɬ ilíʔ {iʔ} kən qʷənəmscút ilíʔ la_nyxʷút,
ʔác•c•qaʔ=iʔst ixíʔ uɬ ilíʔ kn qʷṅ+mscut ilíʔ la_n+yxʷ=ut
struggle_to_exit then and there 1kn pitiful there inside
to get out. *That's when I did that pitiful thing inside there,*

nak̓ʷáʔ inkċáx̌ʷ." 555 waẏ ixíʔ [sʔəkʷ]ʔəkʷíɬċaʔmsəlx.
nak̓ʷ+á in -k+ċax̌ʷ waẏ ixíʔ s -ʔkʷ•ʔkʷ=íɬċaʔ+m -s -lx
indeed_not 1in -willfully well then nom -pack_meat -3i -pl
I didn't do it on purpose." *They started packing the deer.*

556 waẏ, ilmxʷílx {uɬ qʷa} qʷásqiʔ, yaʕ̓íɬċaʔlx {waẏ}. 557 ixíʔ uɬ cəqʔíɬċaʔm
waẏ yl=mxʷ+ilx qʷásqiʔ yaʕ̓=íɬċaʔ -lx ixíʔ uɬ cqʔ=íɬċaʔ+m
well become_chief BlueJay gather_meat -pl then and dry_meat
BlueJay became boss. They got the meat home. *The men folks*

[scəqʔíɬcaʔmsəlx MD], e t̓əxʷ q̇ʷláməlx axáʔ iʔ sqəlqəltmíxʷ. 558 uɬ
s -cqʔ=íɬċaʔ+m -s -lx e• t̓xʷ q̇ʷla+m -lx axáʔ iʔ s+ql•qlt=mixʷ uɬ
nom -dry_meat -3i -pl intj evidently roast -pl this art men and
started drying meat, roasting it. *And*

axáʔ iʔ smaʔməʔím ixíʔ uɬ skəṅkṅámsəlx, ixíʔ uɬ
axáʔ iʔ s+ma•mʔím ixíʔ uɬ s -kṅ•kṅa+m -s -lx ixíʔ uɬ
this art women that and nom -cut_open -3i -pl that and
the women started cutting it open, they started drying it

scəqʔíɬċaʔsəlx. 559 yaʕpqín sƛ̓aʔcínəm, malk̓ʷíɬċaʔməlx. 560 uɬ
s -cqʔ=íɬċaʔ -s -lx yaʕ+p=qín s+ƛ̓aʔ=cín+m malk̓ʷ=íɬċaʔ+m -lx uɬ
nom -dry_meat -3i -pl lots deer get_whole_deer -pl and
over the fire. *Lots of deer, each one gets a whole deer.* *And*

t'əxʷ axáʔ {qʷasqiʔ} nċíʔcən axáʔ iʔ tkɬmilxʷs, uɬ aɬíʔ miná
t'xʷ axáʔ n+ċiʔ=cn axáʔ iʔ tkɬ+m=ilxʷ -s uɬ aɬíʔ miná
evidently this wolf this art wife -3in and because futNeg
Wolf's woman, she will not

ɬ ksx̌ʷilsts, 561 uɬ mat talí xʔkin[sts] {unclear}
ɬ ks -x̌ʷil -st -s uɬ mat taʔlíʔ x+kin -st -s
compl futt^ -discard -st -3erg and maybe very_much do_what -st -3erg
throw it away, *whatever she did with it,*

ċíw̓əs mat a[xáʔ] iʔ sƛ̓aʔcínəm{əx}. 562 səxəntís kiʔ úɬiʔ
ċiw̓ -s mat axáʔ iʔ s+ƛ̓aʔ=cín+m sx -nt -is kiʔ uɬ iʔ
wash -3erg maybe this art deer air_out -nt -3erg rel and_then
maybe she washed the deer. 27:08 *She aired it out and when*

csxap uɬ sic {iʔ} iʔ q̓ʷləntís. 563 uɬ aɬíʔ t'əxʷ captíkʷɬ,
c -sxa+p uɬ sic iʔ q̓ʷl -nt -is uɬ aɬíʔ t'xʷ captíkʷɬ
hab -aired_out and then art roast -nt -3erg and because emph legends
it had no more smell then she roasted it. *And because it's fairy tales*

ixíʔ uɬ cúnəlx: 564 way̓ sta, way̓ kən waʔsnúxʷ, way̓ {kən} kən
ixíʔ uɬ cu -n -lx way̓ sta way̓ kn waʔs=núxʷ way̓ kn
then and tell -1erg -pl well intj yes 1kn late yes 1kn
I tell them: *"The sun is coming high on me, I am going to end,*

xixaʔyápəlqs, caʔkʷ cus aʔ nxaʔmxʷcín. 565 axáʔm ta mnímɬtət
xy•xaʔy=áplqs caʔkʷ cu -s aʔ n+xaʔmxʷ=cín axáʔ+m t mnimɬ+tt
end_story should tell -3erg art Moses_language this agInst us
as they say in Moses language (Columbian). *With us we say*

uɬ cúntəm nċəyxʷʕápəlqs"
uɬ cu -nt -m n+ċayxʷ=ʕáplqs
and tell -nt -4erg finish_story
'It's the end of the story'. That's the end." 27:42

Index of stems and inflectional affixes

Entries in this index, approximately 4,500, are of the stems and inflectional affixes found in the anthology. The entry of each lexical headword (in boldface) consists of the stem followed by the consonant skeleton (vowelless) of the root on which it is based. A simple gloss (in italics) follows. The first occurrence of each form in each text is listed with an appropriate abbreviation followed by the number of the utterance where it is found. The order of the abbreviations follows the chronology of the texts (see "Index and chronology of Pete Seymour's narrations").

1 Probably related to √cʕ.

2 Not the only example of an alternation l with ɬ.

3 Laryngealization of w is not certain. Cf. Th √suw, √səw *moisture, wet, dewy,* n√sy=cín *saliva;* Sp sus-t *to drink*; Sh t-sw-suʔ-t *wet.*

4 See RnTrp 65.

5 I have recorded obviously related forms as containing a root √ċq̓ or √cq̓ with meaning *hit, throw*. The situation is not entirely clear. Cf. Sp √ċq̓, Th √ċq̓, Sh √cq̓. Shuswap does not allow a sequence of two glottalized consonants (Kuipers 1974 p. 23). Ok may be in the process of developing a similar deglottalization or an original √ċq̓ may be evolving into two roots. I have written all forms with reference to *hit* as √cq̓, and those with reference to *throw* as √ċq̓ but I have left the forms in the phonetic line as I heard and recorded them.

6 I have recorded this root as √ht as well as √ḥt.

7 The expected root is √ɬx^{w}.

8 I have recorded this also as √mx̌. But see Sp č=mš-qn-mist *he gave up*.

9 +st in this root may be traced to an old reflexive suffix *+sut.

10 This form needs confirmation.

k+s+t̓ik̓l (√t̓k̓l). *have grub.* In HnTrp 82, GD2 175.

k+s+t̓mkʔ=ilt (√t̓mkʔ). *have daughter.* In CoGr 12, Whal 65, Lynx 4, 2gts 98.

k+s+t̓m=ʕalt (√t̓ʕm). *have cow.* In Hrvst 102, Marry 73, Aut 287.

k+swit (√swt). *do one's best.* In CoGr 672, GDd2 460.

k+swít+miʔst (√swt). *do one's best.* In CoGr 575, BJ 197, HnTrp 200, Nams 94.

k+s+wl=qn=ałq (√wl). *have a chance.* In 2gts 212.

k+s+wl•wlm=ink (√wlm). *have gun.* In HnTrp 13.

k+s+wp=úlaʔxʷ (√wp). *have hay.* In Hrvst 121, Aut 260.

k+s+wyapy+x (√wyp) *have, there are whites.* In Marry 5.

k+sx+p=iċaʔ (√sx). *have chills.* In BJ 235.

ks+xt̓ (√xt̓). *aim.* In CoGr 311, HnTrp 169.

k+s+x[ʔ]ẏ (√xẏ). *have extreme tiredness.* In BJ 256.

k+sxʷ=k+ʕac=qáx̌aʔ+m (√ʕc). *have packer.* In Hrvst 214.

k+sxʷ=k̓ʷul̓+m (√k̓ʷl̓). *have worker.* In Hrvst 58.

k+sxʷ=nik̓=ẇs+m (√nk̓). *have cutter.* In Aut 211.

k+s+xʷuy+nt (√xʷy). *have ice.* In Dvl 199.

k+s+xʷuy+tn (√xʷy). *have tracks.* In GD2 152, Dvl 305.

k+sx̌+n (√sx̌). *move past.* In 2gts 261.

k+sx̌a+n (√sx̌). *past.* In CoGr 706, Hrvst 51, Aut 43, RHorse 159, 2gts 7.

k+s+x̌c-ut (√sx̌). *have companion.* In GDd2 698.

k+s+x̌la+p (√x̌l). *all night, towards daylight, have morning.* In BJ 540, GDd1 220, GDd2 278, Aut 361.

ks+x̌l+p (√x̌l). *all night.* In GDd2 433.

k+s+x̌l+p=ínaʔ (√x̌l). *have daylight.* In blkpg 105, CoGr 18, GDd1 450, HnTrp 11, Hrvst 115, Lynx 294, Nams 25, Whal 67.

k+sx̌ʷ+p=ínaʔ (√sx̌ʷ). *have runoff.* In Dvl 285.

k+s+x̌ʷy•x̌ʷay+t (√x̌ʷy). *have sharpness.* In RnTrp 36.

k+s+yaʕ+p=cín (√yʕ̓). *have hardship.* In Nams 202.

k+s+yr=íwaʔ=xn (√yr). *have snowshoes.* In BJ 101, HnTrp 28.

k+sy•sy=us (√sy). *have power(s).* In Nams 249.

k+sy•sy=us+tn (√sy). *power(s).* In CoGr 620, Nams 168, Whal 13, 2gts 234.

k+s+yum (√ym). *curse.* In Brth 39.

k+s+yum=cn (√ym). *have curse.* In Brth 9.

k+sy=ups (√sy). *have tail.* In Dvl 84.

k+s+ʔas=tk=ína ʔ (√ʔs). *have winter.* In Dvl 106.

ks+ʔatx+ílx (√ʔtx). *sleepy.* In GDd1 387.

k+s+ʔayx̌ʷ+táyn (√ʔyx̌ʷ). *have tiredness.* In BJ 240, GDd1 251, GDd2 742.

ks+ʔitx (√ʔtx). *sleepy.* In Nams 37.

k+s+ʔum• (√ʔm). *have name.* In 2gts 15.

k+tał•ł (√tł). *in front of.* In GDd1 273.

k+taxʷ (√txʷ). *addition.* In Whal 540.

k+til+m (√tl). *entrust.* In GDd1 502, GDd2 321.

k+tił+x+m (√tł). *stand by.* In Nams 133, Dvl 357.

k+tiqʷ=lqʷ (√tqʷ). *shine.* In BJ 133.

k+tíw=ċaʔ (√tw). *buy clothes.* In GDd1 76.

k+tk̓=us+tn (√tk̓). *gun sights.* In Prov 22.

k+tkʷ•tkʷʔ=ut (√tkʷʔ). *travel for.* In 2gts 96.

k+tl+mn (√tl). *put in custody of.* In GDd1 478, GDd2 245.

k+tlt=ípla ʔ (√tlt). *orphan.* In GDd1 229.

k+tł•ł=xn=iłxʷ[11] (√tł). *straight to door.* In CoGr 610.

k+tł+mncut+m (√tł). *go straight.* In GDd1 45, GDd2 57.

k+tma=lxʷ (√tm). *naked.* In RnTrp 44.

k+tmxʷ=íċaʔ (√tmxʷ). *clothes wear out.* In GDd1 35, GDd2 39.

k+tp=iłxʷ+m (√tp). *build house.* In Lynx 431.

k+tp=ínaʔ (√tp). *cover.* In GDd2 371.

k+tq=ínaʔ (√tq). *hold down.* In Nams 39.

k+tq•q=ínaʔ (√tq). *hold down.* In Nams 41.

k+tq=s+ncut (√tq). *press eye.* In Nams 42.

k+tr=iẇs (√tr). *unstitch.* In BJ 521.

k+trq=íċaʔ (√trq). *kick body.* In GDd1 55, GDd2 67.

k+trq=iks (√trq). *kick.* In BJ 223.

k+tw=ċaʔ+ncút+n (√tw). *buy clothes.* In GDd1 35.

11 The n is unexplained.

12 May be related to √k̓hk̓ʷ *open.*

13 This analysis is tentative.

14 It is unclear what the best analysis of this stem might be. The Sp cognate is analyzed as a compound ʔeč√s-wiš. *CPD He is standing* (Carlson, Flett & Black p. 218)

15 This root, posited √ʔmn, loses its n before the transitivizers in the entire paradigm.

16 The expected for is k̓ɬ+ʔam=cín. In this stem often the ʔ disappears altogether.

17 The root √k̓ʷn is the result of a re-analysis of k̓ʷ•k̓ʷy=naʔ into k̓ʷ•k̓ʷín=aʔ. See √k̓ʷy *small*.

18 This and the forms that follow beginning with ɬ+c+ force the analysis of c+ as *cisl.* An alternative would be to allow for c+ to be identified as the *hab* prefix, in which case we would have an inflectional prefix to the right of a derivational prefix.

19 The t+ of this stem is problematic.

20 The root is unclear.

21 ml+ of this form is indeterminate. See also ml+pul+st+m (Nams 241).

Hrvst 14, Dvl 106.

mq̓ʷ (√mq̓ʷ). *mountain.* In 2gts 37.

mq̓ʷ•maq̓ʷ (√mq̓ʷ). *mountains.* In Nams 22.

mrim (√mrm). *marry; doctor.* In blkpg 9, BJ 2, Hrvst 166, Marry 7, Aut 217, GDd2 488, Lynx 15, 2gts 67.

mrim+st (√mrm). *doctor.* In Brth 59, Whal 268.

mrm•mrim (√mrm). *marry pl.* In Aut 371.

ms+ɬ+ʔupn=kst (√ms, √ʔpn). *forty.* In Aut 349.

ms+m=iẇs (√ms). *fourth layer.* In GDd2 402.

ms+m+lwis (√ms). *feel around.* In BJ 533.

ms•s=ikst (√ms). *feel with hand.* In BJ 315.

mukʷ (√mkʷ). *snow on trees.* In BJ 296.

mulx (√mlx). *cottonwood.* In Hrvst 87.

mu•ms=xn+m (√ms). *drag feet.* In 2gts 219.

mus (√ms). *four.* In HnTrp 132, Hrvst 15, RHorse 103, Whal 204.

mus=kst+m (√ms). *try.* In 2gts 203.

mus=ls (√ms). *hope.* In CoGr 133.

mus=ẇɬ (√ms). *four conveyances.* In CoGr 462.

mut (√mt). *sit sg, be home.* In blkpg 90, CoGr 51, BJ 507, GDd1 8, HnTrp 310, Marry 60, Aut 118, Lynx 116, Nams 37, Whal 321, 2gts 251.

mut+st (√mt). *set down.* In Nams 96.

mw•maʕʷ (√mʕʷ). *break.* In CoGr 409.

mxʷ=iɬp (√mxʷ). *cedar boughs.* In BJ 18.

my (√my). *know, remember.* In blkpg 31, CoGr 4, BJ 8, GDd1 24, Prov 29, Hrvst 61, Aut 5, RHorse 5, GDd2 36, Lynx 2, Nams 219, Whal 60, 2gts 2, Dvl 37.

my+m (√my). *pile.* In Dvl 81.

mya+líxʷ (√my). *guide.* In 2gts 32.

myaɬ. *too much.* In blkpg 81, CoGr 272, BJ 91, GDd1 216, HnTrp 246, Hrvst 112, Marry 61, Aut 64, GDd2 165, Lynx 215, Dvl 292.

myaɬ+m. *too much.* In CoGr 625, BJ 544.

(√myw). *Coyote.* In CoGr 645, Whal 514.

my=ils+m (√my). *figure, deem.* In CoGr 77, BJ 279.

my+ɬ+s+wẏ+numt+x (√my, √wẏ). *more beautiful.* In blkpg 56.

my+ɬ+sy•sy=us (√my, √sy). *smart comptv.* In RHorse 178, GDd2 428, Whal 24.

my+ɬ+x̌m=ink (√my, √x̌m). *like better.* In Aut 163.

my•my (√my). *know pl.* In Prov 40.

my•my=ikst (√my). *skilled.* In Aut 290.

my+n+am (√my). *find out.* In Lynx 89.

my+n=úlaʔxʷ (√my). *know the country.* In HnTrp 25, Whal 331.

my+n=úlaʔxʷ+m (√my). *know country.* In GDd1 191, HnTrp 221.

my+p (√my). *learn.* In CoGr 2201, BJ 392, Prov 14, Marry 35, Aut 65, RHorse 121, Lynx 84, Nams 114, Whal 36, 2gts 269.

my+p=cin (√my). *agree.* In BJ 430.

my+scut (√my). *know how.* In RnTrp 20.

my+s+kʷum (√my, √kʷm). *store well.* In GDd2 402.

my+s+ɬaʔ•ɬaʔxʷ=ísk̓it (√my, √ɬxʷ). *rest more pl.* In GDd1 620.

my+s+qilxʷ (√my, √qlxʷ). *respect.* In CoGr 269.

my+st (√my). *know.* In Whal 146.

my+s+xʷaʔ+t (√my, √xʷʔ). *more.* In CoGr 560.

my+s+x̌ʷy•x̌ʷay+t (√my, √x̌ʷy). *more sharp.* In CoGr 699.

my+s+ʔiɬn (√my, √ʔɬn). *eat more.* In GDd1 351.

my=úlaʔxʷ (√my). *point to a place.* In BJ 191.

my=útyaʔ (√my).[22] *heterogeneous, unfit, uneven.* In BJ 112.

mʕan. *mind you, intj.* In CoGr 28, BJ 95, GDd1 580, HnTrp 319, Hrvst 61, Brth 38, Marry 46, Aut 158, Nams 221, Whal 571.

mʕʷ•maʕʷ (√mʕʷ). *broken.* In CoGr 107.

ṁáʕmlaʔ (√mmlʕʔ). *maggots.* In CoGr 630.

ṁay (√ṁy). *tell.* In GDd1 564, Aut 142.

ṁáyaʔ (√ṁy). *tell, teach.* In GDd1 98, Marry 77, Aut 2, RHorse 65, GDd2 106, Whal 18.

ṁáyaʔ+m[23] **(√ṁy).** *tell, teach.* In Aut 4.

ṁay+ncút (√ṁy). *tell story.* In HnTrp 62, Hrvst 1, Aut 154, Lynx 377.

ṁay+ncút+mi (√ṁy). *tell confidentially.* In Aut 155.

ṁay+xt+wíxʷ (√ṁy). *tell stories rec., have*

22 Not clear with which of the √my roots this form is best connected.

23 I am uncertain how to analyze aʔ of this and related forms.

24 Not clear that this is a root (and not a particle).

25 The root is probably √nx̌ʷ (cf. Thompson nox̣ʷ, Sh nux̌ʷ).

26 xa? with loss of t before c.

27 This root is certain to be related to √pt *enough, just.*

28 The connections between √q̓ʷt and √k̓ʷt are not clear.

29 A variant of nstils, prevalent in Penticton.

30 +st may go back to *-sut *refl.*

31 xaʔ with loss of t before c.
32 xaʔ with loss of t before c.

33 Phonetics uncertain.

34 ʔuc=xn when root stressed, ʔac=xn+cút when suffix stressed.

35 Analysis unclear, particularly with reference to +s.

36 Analysis unclear, particularly with reference to +ls.

37 This form appears to have a reduplicative prefix, which I do not represent.

38 Variant of paq.

39 The root has a (regional) variant with an unrounded pharyngeal. Some speakers use the forms interchangeably.

40 Laryngealization not certain.

41 This form may involve the lexical suffix =alqʷ.

42 This root is related to √ɬq̓, with the rounding of q̓ before u, giving rise to √ɬq̓^{w}. Reduplicated forms confirm this analysis.

43 A shortened form of sn+t̓wst=sqáx̌aʔ+tn.

44 Cf Sp s=q̓tim *a scar.* n-q̓t̓t̓-m=aqs *the road is all scarred up and rutted.* Sh c-qit̓ *a scar.* This is another example that points to the tendency in Ok to deglottalize the first of a pair of ejectives.

45 See also 2gts 54.

-t. *^cust.* In Marry 36.
-t. *nt tr.* Variant of -nt after stems ending in n. In BJ 10, GDd1 59, Butch 14, Aut 79, RHorse 87, GDd2 322, Lynx 7, Nams 68, Whal 25, 2gts 111, Dvl 65.
-t. *nt tr.* Variant of -nt with the stem ʔam *feed.* In Hrvst 136.
-t. *st tr.* Variant of -st after stems ending in s. In Hrvst 33, RHorse 73, Whal 362, 2gts 240, Dvl 48.
‿t. *obj c+ʔx̌iƚ.* In CoGr 40, GDd1 44, HnTrp 268, RnTrp 36, GDd2 594.
t‿s+piʔ+s+c̓íƚt (√pʔ, √c̓ƚt). *yesterday.* In Hrvst 131.
t‿s+ʔiwt (√ʔwt). *behind.* In BJ 233.
ta. *intj.* In CoGr 528, Aut 118.
ta‿c+k̓. *in the direction of.* In HnTrp 71.
ta‿c+k̓l. *in the direction of.* In HnTrp 35.
ta‿c+k̓líʔ (√k̓lʔ). *in that direction, that way.* In GDd1 42, GDd2 125.
tah. *intj.* In GDd1 400.
ta+ʔkín (√ʔkn). *from there.* In BJ 339.
takʷʔ=út (√tkʷʔ). *walk pl.* In GDd2 307.
taƚ+t (√tƚ). *surely.* In CoGr 555, BJ 224, Hrvst 74, Marry 23, Aut 136, Lynx 431, Whal 150.
taƚ+t uƚ (√tƚ). *my goodness!* In GDd2 225.
tanm̓=s=úlaʔxʷ (√tnm̓). *walk aimlessly.* In GDd2 48.
tanm̓=ús (√tnm̓). *nothing.* In CoGr 605, BJ 248, GDd1 193, Aut 256, GDd2 508, Nams 170, Whal 382, 2gts 134.
ta‿n+yʕ=ip (√yʕ). *keep on, forever.* In Whal 396.
taqí (√tq). *?.* In Whal 406.
tawn. *town.* In blkpg 30, GDd1 203, 2gts 7.
tawn+m (√twn). *go to town.* In HnTrp 9.
taxʷ=ƚq (√txʷ). *harvest.* In Aut 316, Dvl 57.
taxʷ=ƚq+m (√txʷ). *harvest.* In Aut 257, Dvl 44.
ta+ʔkíń (√ʔkn). *from where; sometimes; how far.* In CoGr 339, GDd1 347, HnTrp 169.
taʔkʷʔ=ut (√tkʷʔ). *walk pl.* In GDd1 566.
taʔlíʔ. *very much.* In blkpg 55, CoGr 205, BJ 78, GDd1 21, Prov 24, HnTrp 172, Hrvst 88, Aut 77, RHorse 24, GDd2 14, Lynx 59, Whal 164, 2gts 104, Dvl 115.
taʔ+ƚ+wl•wlím (√tʔ, √wlm). *blacksmithing.* In Brth 19.
taʔm=úlaʔxʷ (√tm). *snow melt.* In HnTrp 80, Hrvst 21, Aut 330.
taʔxʷ+l̓x̌•l̓áx̌+t (√txʷ, √l̓x̌). *have friends.* In HnTrp 279.
taʔxʷ+ƚ+cítxʷ (√txʷ, √ctxʷ). *get house.* In Dvl 263.
taʔxʷ+ƚ+cq̓=íln (√txʷ, √cq̓). *get arrow.* In Whal 2.
taʔxʷ+ƚ+k̓ƚ+xʷip+mn (√txʷ, √xʷp). *get liner.* In Dvl 181.
taʔxʷ+ƚ+ní•nk̓+mn (√txʷ, √nk̓). *have knives.* In Whal 204.
taʔxʷ+ƚ+n+t+kʷil (√txʷ, √kʷl). *have company.* In GDd1 257.
taʔxʷ+ƚ+n+t̓aʕp+m=útyaʔ (√txʷ, √t̓ʕp). *have gun loaders.* In Aut 71.
taʔxʷ+ƚ+n+wnxʷ=ínaʔ+tn (√txʷ, √wnxʷ). *get belief.* In Marry 79.
taʔxʷ=ƚq+m (√txʷ). *get crop.* In Marry 77, Aut 225.
taʔxʷ+ƚ+sn+kƚ+c̓aʔ=sqáx̌aʔ (√txʷ, √c̓ʔ). *get horses.* In Hrvst 255.
taʔxʷ+ƚ+tkƚ+m=ilxʷ (√txʷ, √tkƚ). *get wife.* In Marry 2.
taʔxʷ+ƚ+xwíƚ (√txʷ, √xwƚ). *have road.* In GDd1 179, GDd2 124.
taʔxʷ+ƚ+x̌ʷíc̓=laʔxʷ+tn (√txʷ, √x̌ʷc̓). *get mowers.* In Hrvst 227.
taʔxʷ+s+l̓áx̌+t+m (√txʷ, √l̓x̌). *get friend.* In RHorse 80.
taʔxʷ+s+ƚíqʷ (√txʷ, √ƚqʷ). *get meat.* In BJ 66.
taʔxʷ+s+ma•mʔím (√txʷ, √mʔm). *get wives.* In Marry 54.
taʔxʷ+s+mík̓ʷt (√txʷ, √mk̓ʷt). *get snow.* In HnTrp 2.
taʔxʷ+s+ník̓=ƚxʷ (√txʷ, √nk̓). *get son-in-law.* In CoGr 394.
taʔxʷ+s+nik̓=ƚxʷ+m (√txʷ, √nk̓). *get son-in-law.* In CoGr 279.
taʔxʷ+sn+ilíʔ+tn (√txʷ, √lʔ). *get place.* In Aut 223.
taʔxʷ+sn+kʷum=cn+tn (√txʷ, √kʷm). *get storage device.* In Prov 14.
taʔxʷ+sn+ƚx̌m+tán (√txʷ, √ƚx̌m). *get in-laws.* In Whal 549.
taʔxʷ+s+n+q̓ʷic̓+tn (√txʷ, √q̓ʷc̓). *get new mate.* In Marry 83.
taʔxʷ+s+puʔ=ús (√txʷ, √pʔ). *gain feelings.* In Hrvst 2.
taʔxʷ+s+px̌•páx̌+t (√txʷ, √px̌). *get senses.* In

46 Uncertain form.

47 tixʷ may not be a root, but a prefix with a function or meaning that I do not understand. Cf. Sp ʔexʷ-kʷún-m *he said it, he talks in this manner*. Further, the connections between this stem and tixʷ+kʷun+m (q.v.) are not clear.

48 Surely there is a connection with s+t·tm̓·tím̓.

49 This stem does not have the ? I have posited for √?x̌l.

50 In this form, s-t̓c+xʷuy-x (*ipftv^-come-^ipftv*) t̓c- is derivational.

51 The segmentation t̓=ínaʔ is pointless. =ínaʔ historically derives from t̓ínaʔ.

52 The form probably has a reduplicative affix.

53 Possibly xaʔtmaʔsqílx^{w}.

54 Irregular reduplicative prefix. See yw•yaʕʷ+t.

55 yw < yʕʷ is the result of pharyngeal movement (to the stressed syllable).
56 Unclear form.

57 This root, posited √ʔmn, loses its n before the transitivizers in the entire paradigm.

58 The suffix =ẇstxn may be further segmentable.

59 For the moment I am not segmenting this form, even though it has a reduplicative suffix.

60 The analysis of this form is not clear.

Index of roots

Here I list in three columns all the roots found in the anthology. The vowelless root skeleton is in the first column; one or more representative stems are in the second; and one or more English glosses or translations are in the third. In my lists of roots (and lexical affixes), I use vowelles skeleta because the consonants, and not the vowels, are determinant—not only it is easier to find the forms in indices and other lists, but also it is easier to search for cognates.

In footnotes I provide some of the cognates in the other Interior Salish languages, primarily those of the Southern Interior languages, listed in order of what I perceive as their proximity to Cv-Ok: Sp-Ka-Fl (Spokane, Kalispel, Flathead), Cm (Moses Columbian), Cr (Coeur d'Alene), Sh (Shuswap), Th (Thompson), and Li (Lillooet). My listing of cognates is not exhaustive, but a start in what I envision as an eventual comprehensive compilation.

Two of my primary sources, the Spokane and the Columbian, are drafts, the first of a revised edition of the 1989 *Spokane dictionary* (with third author, Deirdre Black), and the second of a preliminary version of a Moses-Columbian dictionary. The draft of the revised *Spokane dictionary* is strewn with Pauline Flett's important handwritten notes, of which I have made use in this index.

The Cm speakers who participated in the project chose to use č, š, s for conventional c, s, ṣ, but I have transliterated the Cm forms I quote into the standard Salish orthography, except for retracted vowels which are written as sequences of two identical vowels. And I hope I have not overlooked anything.

The third source, based on Lawrence Nicodemus's two-volume dictionary, is John Lyon and Rebecca Green-Wood's *Lawrence Nicodemus's Coeur d'Alene dictionary in root format*. This work is a transliteration and re-organization of Nicodemus's practical orthography into the standard Salish orthography.

Nicodemus had not marked stress consistently in his original work, and neither have Flett and al., nor the Cm group. As a consequence of the original compilers' neglect to mark stress consistently, in all three sources the vowels of mono-vocalic words may or may not have a stress marked; and neither do polyvocalic words always have a stress marked. Lyon and Greene-Wood have remained faithful to the practice of the original works, and I have also done my best to be faithful to these sources.

Another matter is the use of the symbols x̣, x̣^{w} (Sp) / x̌ x̌^{w} (Cm, Cr). However trivial this matter, I have regularly used x̌ x̌^{w} when quoting a cognate form.

I add this note about some of the work that remains to be done: cases like Sp tix^{w} *to get, to obtain*, tux^{w}(ú) *to add*, Cm c̓əɬt, c̓aɬ *to cool down*, Cr *c̓ep airtight*, c̓ip̓ *pinch*. tag^{w} *buy*, teg^{w} *buy, sell*, point to the need to map out the ablaut which is common to all the interior languages.

(√ch)[1]	cah	face, turn, figure out, fit, match, in front of, watch for, straight, match, face, take turn, sit and watch, set watch
(√ch)[2]	s+k+ch=ikst	right hand
(√ck)[3]	ł+ci•ck	mother-in-law
(√ck̓)[4]	ck̓=iłp	rib
(√ck̓)	s+kł+ck̓a+p	cream
(√ckʷ)	ca?kʷ+mscút	hard to get
(√ckʷ)[5]	ckʷa-[6]	pull, haul, take down, pull off, drag, hold back, pull back, pull (buggy), wagon, bow, cramp
(√ckʷ)[7]	ckʷ=ink	bow
(√ckʷ)	sn+ckʷ+min	ton
(√cl)	cí•cl+mi?st	trot slowly
(√cl)[8]	cil=kst	five
(√cly)	culáy	(4th of) July
(√cłm)[9]	s+cł•cułm	bulls
(√cm)	k+cm=ína?	cover
(√cṁ)[10]	c•cáṁ+a?t	small, children
(√cn)[11]	cn•cn+ilx	roar
(√cn)[12] See √ct	cun+m	tell, account
(√cnł)[13]	cnił+c	that one
(√cptkʷl) ~ (√cptkʷł)	captíkʷl	legends, tell stories
(√cpx̌ʷ)	cp•cipx̌ʷ+t	break through
(√cq)[14]	ciq	dig
(√cq)[15]	cq•aq, c+k̓ł+n+ca?q•q=íp, cq•q•=cn=itkʷ	come close (to the door, shore ...), place down on, place on, lie, rest, face up, put down, land, lie
(√cq)[16]	n+cq=ut	woods
(√cq?)	cq?=íłċa?	dry (meat)
(√cq̇) (see √ċq̇)	cq̇a+m	hit
(√cq̇)[17]	cq̇=iłp	fir tree, fir boughs

1 Sp √ceh(é). See Cm ch-aẇs *middle*.
2 See Sp s-čh=éčst; Cm k-ch-akst *right side, right hand.*
3 Sp ł-cécč; Cm cak *female's mother-in-law.*
4 Cm ck̓-ałp.
5 Sp ckʷ(ú); Cm ckʷ-nt-xʷ *you pull s.t.*; Cr cekʷ.
6 A vowelless root with excrescent a when no suffix takes the stress.
7 Probably the same root as the preceding. Cm ckʷ-ikn.
8 Sp cil; Cm cil-kst; Cr cil=čt.
9 Sp s-cúł-m; Cm s-cułm; Cr s+cúł+m.
10 Sp √ciṁ *tiny*; Cm c-cṁ-a?-t *be little, small (pl)*; Cr ci+ceṁe?.
11 Sp √cn *sing, hum, whisper.*
12 Cm cu(n)-nt-xʷ *you tell s.o., say s.t.*; Cr cun *indicate, point, show.*
13 Sp cníłc; Cm cnil; Cr cénel.
14 Sp ciq; Cm ciq-m.
15 Sp caq(é) *put, placed, set*; Cm cq-q-cin *to land on shore*; Cr caq-nt-s *park (... a car), put down or place ...*
16 Cr caq *solid object stands upright*; Ka caq.
17 Sp ċq̇=éłp; Cm ċq̇-ałp.

(√cqʷ)[18]	n+cqʷ•caqʷ=qn	stuck on, point, stick in
(√crs)	cars+m	motion to, indication
(√ct)[19] (see √cn)	c̓ut	say
(√ct)[20] See √cwt	k̓ɬ+cut+n	manners, training
(√ctxʷ)[21]	citxʷ	house
(√cw)	cw=cin[22] n+cw•cw=iks	talk, cry, good word, loud, do the same
(√cw)	k+cw=ína?	cover
(√cw)	nk̓ʷ+cw=ilxʷ+tn	group, live, tribe
(√cwl)	k+cwil	give to eat
(√cwt)[23] See √ct	cawt	do, ways, effort, deed, doings
(√cwx)[24]	cwix	creek
(√cwyl)	cway+lx	m's name
(√cx)[25]	c[ʔ]ix, k+caʔx=ísxn	warm, hot, heat, glow
(√cx)	n+k+cx=iw̓s	fall back in
(√cxʷ)[26]	s+caxʷ	pat, hold (child), affection
(√cxʷ)[27]	c[ʔ]axʷ	tired, sicken
(√cxʷʔ)	cíxʷaʔ	fool(ed), fool, deceive
(√cx̌)[28]	cix̌•cx̌+t	hot
(√cx̌)	cix̌+lx	move, relocate
(√cx̌ʷ)[29]	k̓ɬ+c•cx̌ʷ+ncut	stock, store
(√cʕ)[30] (see √cʕy)	ca•ca•cáʕ	holler
(√cʕn)	caʕn+m+st	tight
(√cʕw)[31]	k+cw=ʕakst=xn[32]	fringe(d), chaps
(√cʕy) (see √cʕ)	ca•cáʕy+p+m	cry
(√cʕycwp)	s+cʕaycwp	Kettle Falls
(√cʕʷ)[33]	caʕʷ+lx, k+caʕʷá+p	bathe; dribble
(√cʔ)[34]	ciʔ	stop
(√cʔ)[35]	k̓ɬ+n+cʔ=ip	knock, hit, elbow s.o.
(√cʔ)[36]	ɬ+c•cʔ=ups	younger sister
(√cʔ)	s+cʔ=ikst	front (leg)

18 Sp caqʷ; Cr caqʷ *insert (a long object in a tube)...*
19 Sp hes-cú-t-i *he is saying things*; Cm cút *to say.*
20 Sp √cut *to act in a certain way.*
21 Sp citxʷ; Cr cétxʷ.
22 This may be cw(t)=cin.
23 Cr cegʷ+t *behave, character...*
24 Cm c-cw̓ax-aʔ.
25 Cm na-cix; Cr ciš.
26 Cm cuxʷ-nt-xʷ *you pet, caress s.o.*; Cr cexʷ.
27 Sp cexʷ *to feel vaguely ill...*; Cm caʔxʷ *to ache from fever; to feel bad physically.*
28 Cm cəx̌ *bright red.* ʔal-cx̌ *to make s.t. hot again.* See also čix-nt-xʷ *you warm s.t. up [food or object].*
29 Sp cax̌ʷ *to round up or herd livestock*
30 Sp cácácá *wailing sound...*, caʕ *cry*; Cm caḥ-caḥ-ap-m *to scream*; Cr caʕ.
31 Sp √co (coʔ) (coʕʷ) (caw); Cm s-cʕʷ-ʕʷ; Cr caʕʷ; cugʷ *feathered.*
32 With pharyngeal movement.
33 The northern Ok root is √caʕ, with a not uncommon unrounded counterpart. Sp √caw (caʕʷ); Cm ciʕʷ-lx.
34 Cm ciʔ *(right) here; stop!*
35 Sp √cu(ú); Cm cuw̓-nt-xʷ *you punch s.o.*; Cr cuw̓ *punch.*
36 Sp √cʔ, ɬ-ccʔ=úps.

(√cʔlm)	n+caʔlím	Inchelium
(√cʔqʷ)	s+cʔaqʷ	summer
(√ċk)[37]	s+ċk•ak	charge, count, name price, figure
(√ċkʷʔ)[38]	s+k+ċíkʷaʔ	left hand
(√ċl)	ċl•ċal+p+t	fierce, spooky
(√ċl)[39]	ċl•ċal	stand, trees, erector, stand up; bundling scythe, reach up
(√ċlmt̓)[40]	k+ċaʔlmt̓=íċaʔ	chills
(√ċlx̌ʷ)[41]	ċl•ċlx̌ʷ=úlaʔxʷ+m	scratch, prongs, point extend
(√ċɬ)[42]	ċaɬ+t	cold, freeze
(√ċɬt)	s+piʔ+s+ċíɬt	yesterday
(√ċm)[43]	s+ċim	bone
(√ċṁ)[44]	ċm•ċuṁ	suck
(√ċn)[45]	ċin	say what, worry, preoccupied
(√ċpq̇)[46]	ċpaq̇	glue, stick, splice together
(√ċṗ)[47] See √ċʕp	n+ċiṗ•ċṗ=s+m	closed tight
(√ċq̇)[48]	ċq̇+mi	throw
(√ċqʷ)[49]	ċiqʷ	skin, butcher
(√ċqʷ)[50]	ċqʷ•aqʷ	cry
(√ċq̇ʷ)	ċaq̇ʷ•ċq̇ʷ=ɬp	wire bush
(√ċq̇ʷ)[51]	ċaq̇ʷ	point
(√ċr)[52]	n+ċaʔr=ínk, n+ċaʔr=qín	ache, diarrhea, sour
(√ċrs)[53]	s+ċrs=iɬmlx	Oregon grape
(√ċs)[54]	ċsa+p	gone, rid of, strip, finished, clean, killed, all gone, run out, out of
(√ċsy)	ċasy=qn	head
(√ċw)[55]	ċiẇ	wash, wash (dishes), towel
(√ċw)	s+k+ċiw=lps	mane
(√ċẇ)[56]	s+ċẇ•ċẇ=xan	feet, legs, hind leg, shoe

37 Cm ċk-nt-xʷ *you count s.t.*; Cr ċeč̣.
38 Sp ċikʷ(i); Cm k-ċikʷ-aʔ; Cr ċik̓ʷeʔ.
39 Sp ċil; Cm √ċl; Cr ċel.
40 See Sp ċil̓ *ghostly, spooky*.
41 Sp calx̌ʷ(ú) *clustered, propped up like a tripod*; Cm ċlx̌-nt-xʷ *you scratch s.o. with nails*; Cr ċalx̌ʷ *claw*.
42 Sp ċeɬ *cool down, cool off*; Cm ċəɬt; ċaɬ *to cool down*; Cr ċiɬ *cool*.
43 Sp s-ċoṁ; Cr s + ċam.
44 Cm ċəṁ-m; Cr ċo[ṁ].
45 Sp heċiṅt *what did he say?*
46 Sp ċaṗaq̇ *sticky, gooey, syrupy*; Cm k-ċq̇-p *to stick to s.t.*; Cr ċaṗq̇, ċaṗq.
47 Sp ċaṗ *snap shut*, ċiṗ *pinch, nip in a vise*; Cm ċiṗ-nt-xʷ *you pinch s.t.*; Cr *ċep airtight*, ċiṗ *pinch*.
48 Sp ċaq̇; Cm ċq̇al̓n *arrow, bullet*.
49 Cm ċiq̇ʷ-nt-xʷ *you skin s.t. with a knife [animal]*.
50 Sp ċqʷáqʷ.
51 Sp ċoq̇ʷ; Cm ċuq̇ʷ-m. See Cr ċuq̇ʷn pronounce ...
52 Sp ċer (ċal); Cm ċər, ċaʔar *ache, hurt*; ċor *salt, sour*.
53 Cm ċr-s-aɬp *gooseberry bush*.
54 Sp ċs-íp *it's all gone*; Cr ċes+p *gone (It is all...)*.
55 Sp ċeẇ; Cm ċaẇ-m.
56 Sp s-ċuʔ=šín; Cm s-ċuʔ-xn.

(√ċwq)[57]	ċwq+m	fall behind
(√ċx)[58]	ċ[ʔ]ax	shame, ashamed, embarrass
(√ċxʷ)[59]	ċxʷ•axʷ	pour, spill liquid, make pancake, sleak, enema, pancake
(√ċx̌ʷ)[60]	ċix̌ʷ	spark
(√ċx̌ʷ)[61]	ċx̌ʷa+m	instruct, promise, appoint, willful, promise, judge, train, order, show, law, arrangement, guide, one's doing
(√ċx̌ʷ)	k+ċi•ċx̌ʷ=s+m	peek
(√ċx̌ʷl̓)	√ċx̌ʷl̓	camas, white camas
(√ċyxʷ)	n+ċayxʷ=áplqs	end of story
(√ċʕn)[62]	ċn•ċaʕn+t	closed tight
(√ċʕp) See √ċp̓	c+n+ċaʕp=s	wink
(√ċʔ)[63]	n+ċiʔ=cn	wolf
(√ċʔ)[64]	sn+kł+ċaʔ=sqáx̌aʔ	horse
(√ċʔk̓ʷ)[65]	ċʔak̓ʷ+m s+ċaʔk̓ʷ=áłq	blossom, flower
(√hw)[66]	haw•híw=iʔst	yawn
(√hʔ)[67]	n+hʔ=ils	respect
(√hʕʷ)	ha•háʕʷ+mist	loose
(√ḥt)	ḥa•ḥt	laugh
(√kc)[68]	kic, kaʔ•kíc	meet, arrive, reach, meet with, run across, meet, get together, in midst, catch up, overtake, go meet, take, bring, find
(√kc)[69]	s + kic + w	Idaho
(√kċ)	kċ+ilx=kn	woodtick
(√kcx)	t+kcx=ils	be in pain
(√kl)	kil	chase, follow
(√klx)[70]	kilx	arm, hand, sticks
(√kl̓)	kil̓•kl̓, t+kil̓+m	frown, sick (of)
(√kł)[71]	kł=iẇs, k̓ł+kł+m=ikst	divide, separate, one side
(√kłcw)	k̓ł+kłcaw	under shed

57 Sp ċẇáq *pull out*; Cr ċaẇq *extract, pull out ...*
58 Sp ċeš *bahful, shy, embarrassed*; Cm ċa-ċaʔx-t *be ashamed.*
59 Cm ċxʷ-nt-xʷ *you pour s.t. out [liquid]*; Cm ċxʷ-xʷ. See Cr hn+ċéxʷ+t *channel, creek, stream.*
60 Sp ċix̌ʷċx̌ʷ-t *glowing embers.*
61 Sp ċox̌ʷ *intend, mean to*; Cm ċəx̌ʷ-ċx̌ʷ-m *to advise, lecture*; Cr ċax̌ʷ+ċux̌ʷn *admonish, advise, counsel.*
62 Sp ċan(á).
63 Sp n-ċiʔ=cn.
64 Sp s-n-č̓ł-ċaʔ=sqáx̌eʔ.
65 Sp ċaʔák̓ʷ *to bloom*; Cm ċaʔák̓ʷ *to bloom.*
66 Sp hew; Cm hẇ-haẇ-nct.
67 Sp heʔ.
68 Sp čic, čičš; Cm c-kic-x *to arrive here*, k-kic *to find*; Cr čic.
69 Sp sčícẇiʔ *Coeur d'Alene reservation.*
70 Sp čelš; Cm kalx.
71 Sp č̓łim. See Cm kał-x-twaxʷ *to exchange gifts with one another*, kł-aẇs *be separate*; Cr čeł.

(√kmn)[72]	kmn=kin̓	turn one's back
(√kmx)[73]	kmax, kmix	only
(√kmxst)	s+kmxist	(black) bear
(√km̓)[74]	kim̓	hate
(√km̓)	km=ls+mist, km̓=ik	not good enough, any which way
(√km̓)[75]	km̓a+m	hold, take, grab pl. obj., kidnap pl.
(√kn)[76]	kn + xit	help
(√kn̓)	kn̓•kn̓a+m, s+t+kn̓=plaʔ=sqáx̌aʔ	cut open; lead horse
(√kp̓)	kip̓=w̓s	pinch
(√kr)[77]	kr•ar	mopey
(√ksqm)	ksqm=qin+m	drive team
(√kt̓)	k̓ł+kt̓a+m	burst, cut open, cut off, decapitated
(√kw)[78]	kł+kiw	open area
(√kwk)	kw•kwik+m	be ghosted
(√kwp)	-kwap, k•kw̓áp+aʔ	horse, dog
(√kw̓)	kw̓+t+wilx	lose weight
(√kx)[79]	kxa+m	follow, travel, accompany on foot
(√kxʔ)[80]	ł+kí•kxaʔ	older sister
(√ky)	ky=c̓=asq̓t	dusk; clear (sky)
(√kyʕm)[81]	ʔaw+s+kyáʕm	crawl in bed
(√kʕ)	s+kaʕ=cín+m	landing place
(√kʕ)	kaʕ=ílsxn+m	cut hair
(√kʕʔ)	s+k•kʕá•kaʔ	bird, animal, chicken
(√kʕ^{w})	kʕ^{w}a+p	slide
(√kʔ)	sn+kaʔ•kʔ=íw̓s	soul
(√kʔ)[82]	ká•kaʔ+m	make fun of, ridicule, deride
(√kʔłs)[83]	kaʔłís	three
(√kʔn)	kaʔ•kaʔn=xán	sore feet
(√k̓h)	k̓ah	raise
(√k̓hk̓^{w})[84]	k̓ł+n+k̓ahk̓^{w}=íp	open
(√k̓l)	t+k̓l•k̓l+am	wait up, expect
(√k̓l̓)[85]	sn+k̓l̓=ip	Coyote, coyote, buffoon
(√k̓lx^{w})	s+k̓lax^{w}	disappear, out of sight, dark, be late, all day, evening

72 See Cr č+čmin Lit *throw one object.*
73 Sp čmiš; Cm kməx *be the only one*. See Cr u tmiš *only, but.*
74 Cr čim̓ *disdain*.
75 Cm km̓-nt-x^{w} *you carry things [pl]*; Cr čem̓ *grab, grasp*.
76 Sp čn̓-š-cút *he called for help.*
77 See Cm kir̓-nt-x^{w} *you look, glance at s.t.*
78 Sp čł-čéw-šiš *he went out on the water*, čł-čéw-m *meadow, prairie ...*; Cr čig^{w}-š Lit *go out on the prairie.*
79 Cm na-kəx-t *to walk on road, or trail*, kxap-nt-x^{w} *you chase, pursue s.t.*; Cr češ *accompany*.
80 Sp ł-číčš-eʔ; Cm kəx *female's older sister.*
81 Analysis unclear.
82 Cm k-ka-kaʔ-mn-(n)t-x^{w} *you make fun of, mock s.o.*
83 Sp čeʔłés; Cm kaʔłás; Cr čiʔłes.
84 Cm kł-n-k̓ah-ap-nt-x^{w} *you open s.t. [door].*
85 Sp s-n-č̓l=éʔ.

(√k̓lʔ)	ak̓láʔ, ik̓líʔ	here, there, in that direction, that way
(√k̓m)[86]	k̓ím=laʔxʷ	dark
(√k̓m)[87]	k̓i•k̓m	near, soon
(√k̓m)[88]	k̓ɬ+n+k̓m=ip, k̓m=ikn̓, k̓ɬ+k̓m=cn=ikst	root that participates in constructions with lexical affixes, wrist, door, outside, end, side of
(√k̓np̓)[89]	k̓np̓=qin	ring, circle
(√k̓ns)	k̓ans	log trap
(√k̓nt)[90]	s+k̓int+m	fear, afraid
(√k̓nyʔ)	k̓ɬ+k̓níyaʔ+m	listen, hear
(√k̓p̓)[91]	k̓ip̓•p̓	pinch(ed)
(√k̓r)[92]	n+k̓r=iw̓s	cut, cut off, cut open
(√k̓r)[93]	s+k̓ra+m	swim
(√k̓s)[94]	k̓as+t, k̓s•k̓as•s	bad, sick, ill, ugly, quarrel, angry
(√k̓spn)[95]	k̓span	nape of neck
(√k̓t)[96]	t+k̓í•k̓aʔt, t+k̓aʔt=ús+m	close (to), near, right behind, catch up, still have time
(√k̓t)	k̓at=qn+m	raise (head)
(√k̓t)	k̓aʔ•k̓ít, k̓aʔ•k̓ít=xn+m	soft(ly)
(√k̓t̓)	k̓t̓+p=iys	stop (snowing)
(√k̓t̓)[97]	t+k̓it̓=ks	get cut (off)
(√k̓w)[98]	k̓aw, k̓wa + p, k̓w•k̓w + p + numt	go, gone, not there, stopped, quiet, destroy; lonesome, miss, massacre
(√k̓w)[99]	k̓iw+lx, k̓w+ilx, k̓ɬ+k̓aw+ílx	old; ladder, climb, go upstream, upriver
(√k̓wʔ)[100]	k̓í•k̓waʔ	mother's father
(√k̓xʷ)[101]	k̓•k̓ixʷ	agile, light
(√k̓xʷm)	s+t+k̓•k̓xʷum	ball, round
(√k̓y̓)[102]	k̓iy̓+t	cold; fall hunt, autumn
(√k̓yl)	k̓yl=ilxʷ	tree bark
(√k̓ʕʷ)[103]	k̓aʕʷ+mn, k̓aʕʷ+míst	coax, pray, hire

86 Cm k̓əm̓; Cr č̓em̓.
87 This may be a particle.
88 Cm kat-k̓m-akst *back side of the hand*; Cr √č̓m.
89 Cm s-k̓ɬ-k̓np̓-cn-akst *bracelet*; Cr č̓enp̓ *clasp, encircle*.
90 Cm k̓in̓-k̓in̓-t *be dangerous*; Cr č̓in *dangerous*.
91 Cm k̓ip̓-nt-xʷ *you pinch s.t.*, k̓ip̓-mn *tongs*, see also k̓-a-k̓ip̓-mn *scissors*; Cr č̓ip̓ *pinch*.
92 Cm k̓r̓-(nt)-n *I cut s.t.*; Cr č̓ar.
93 Cm na-k̓r-m *to swim*; Cr č̓ar.
94 Cm k̓əst, k̓as-s-(nt)-n *I argue, quarrel with s.o.*; Cr č̓es *bad*.
95 Cm k̓əspn.
96 Cm k̓i(t)-l̓x *be close, be near*; Cr č̓íteʔ *near*.
97 Cm k̓ɬ-k̓t̓-p *to break off*, k̓ɬ-k̓t̓-nt-xʷ *you trim s.t. off [branches or threads]*; Cm č̓et̓ *chop (off), cut (off completely)...*
98 Cm k̓uw; Cr č̓ew *nostalgic*, č̓u *absent, away ...*
99 Cm t-k̓iw-lx *to climb up*; Cr t+č̓igʷl Lit *he climbed*.
100 Cm k̓-k̓aw̓-aʔ *great grandfather; great grandson*; Cr č̓íweʔ *father (...of deceased mother)*.
101 Cm k̓-k̓axʷ *be light in weight*.
102 Cm s-k̓aʔ-iʔ *November (fall)*.
103 √k̓ʕʷ is the southern form, √k̓ʕ the northern. Cm k̓iʕʷ-m *to pray*; Cr č̓eʕʷ *pray*, s+t+č̓érw+um *pray, prayer*.

(√k̓ʔ)	k̓aʔ=qín=xn	knee(s)
(√k̓ʔ)	k̓ɬ+k̓aʔ•k̓ʔáʔ	hard surface
(√k̓ʔ)	sn+k̓ʔ=ínaʔ	pillow
(√k̓ʔlʔ)[104]	k̓•k̓aʔlíʔ	soft, slow
(√kʷkʷ)	k̓ɬ+kʷukʷ, kʷkʷ+scut	benefit, grateful, lucky
(√kʷl)	kʷil, kʷl=iwt, n+t+kʷil=s	pl. sit (around), live, company,
(√kʷl)[105]	kɬ+kʷil=lxʷ	red, (dark) sorrel
(√kʷl)	kʷl+x=úlaʔxʷ, n+kʷl+x=úlaʔxʷ[106]	leave
(√kʷls)	kʷils+tn	sweat bath(e)
(√kʷlst)[107]	kʷulst	send (on errand)
(√kʷl̓)[108]	s+kʷal̓+t, kʷ[ʔ]al̓, kʷl̓=úlaʔxʷ	sun, sunshine, warm(th), sweat; visibility, sunshine, light
(√kʷl̓)[109]	kʷl̓•kʷl̓=alxʷ	calf (cow)
(√kʷl̓mt)	n+kʷl̓mut	brother-in-law
(√kʷɬn)[110]	kʷuɬn	lend (out), borrow
(√kʷm)[111]	kʷum	store, (keep in) store, save, storage
(√kʷn)[112]	c+kʷan=x̌; kʷin	take sg. obj., kidnap sg., shake hands, receive, grab, hold
(√kʷn)[113]	k+ʔxʷ+kʷun+m, k̓ɬ+ʔaxʷ•ʔaxʷ+kʷú=kst	coax, sound
(√kʷn)[114]	n+kʷni+m	sing, song
(√kʷnt)	s+kʷant	Omak
(√kʷp)[115]	t+kʷup=xn, t+kʷp+xix+m	pass along, rush (to)
(√kʷr)[116]	kʷ•kʷr̓iʔ+t, kʷ•kʷar̓•kʷr̓=xn+m	yellow, Rogers Bar
(√kʷs)	kʷis•kʷs	hold (on to)
(√kʷs)[117]	kʷs•s=cin	joke
(√kʷs)	kʷu•kʷús	pig, bacon
(√kʷsnt)	s+kʷ•kʷusnt	stars
(√kʷst)[118]	s+kʷist	name
(√kʷst) (?)	kʷus·s·t+m	lend, pay
(√kʷw) (?)	k̓ɬ+kʷiw	answer

104 Cm k̓al̓áʔ *be slow*.
105 Cm kʷil *dark red*, kʷa-kʷil-aʔ *bay horse*; Cr kʷil *red*.
106 n+ in the second form is not understood.
107 Cm kʷuls-(s)t-xʷ *you send s.t.*
108 Cm kʷaʔl *be warm*; Cr kʷel̓ *hot, sunny, warm*.
109 Cm kʷl̓kʷl̓-alxʷ *calf*.
110 Cm kʷuɬ-nt-xʷ *you lend s.t. to s.o.; you borrow s.t. from s.o.*; Cr kʷuɬ *borrow, lend*.
111 Cm na-kʷum *large bowl*.
112 Cm c̣-kʷn-am *to get s.t.*; Cr kʷin *grasp (a small object), hold (a small object)*.
113 Cm k̓ɬ-kʷan̓-c(n)-nt-xʷ *you interpret, translate s.t.*
114 Cm n-kʷan-cin-tn *song, hymn; s.t. used to play music*; Cr kʷin *sing*.
115 Cm tkʷupxnt-xʷ *you rush toward s.t.*
116 Cm kʷ-kʷr̓iʔ -t *gold, copper*, kʷar-(nt)-n *I apply yellow paint*; Cr kʷar *yellow*; Cr qʷ+qʷár̓eʔ+t *gold*.
117 Cm kʷs-s-cin-m *to joke, tease*.
118 Cr kʷis *name*.

(√kʷʕc)	kʷaʕc+t	early morning, rise early
(√kʷʕst)[119]	s+kʷ•kʷaʕst, syɬ+kʷ•kʷ=ʕast	early morning
(√kʷʕt)	kʷaʕtá	quarter
(√kʷʔ)	s+kʷ•kʷʔ=iɬp	rose hip
(√kʷʔ)	kʷú•kʷaʔ	different, strange
(√kʷʔc)[120]	n+kʷaʔc=núxʷ	dark, night
(√k̓ʷc)[121]	k̓ʷc•k̓ʷac+t	strong, strength, stiffness
(√k̓ʷl̓)[122]	k̓ʷul̓	work, do, make, train, practice, be born, turn into, origin, doll up, birth, cook
(√k̓ʷlk̓)	k̓ʷlk̓=itkʷ+m	roll (around), roiling
(√k̓ʷɬx)[123]	k̓ʷɬax, k̓ʷɬx=cin+m	startle, surprise
(√k̓ʷƛ̓)[124]	c+k̓ɬ+k̓ʷiƛ̓+p+t	come in sight, take from under, pull out, appear
(√k̓ʷƛ̓)	s+k̓ʷƛ̓=us; s+t+k̓ʷƛ̓•k̓ʷƛ̓=us	face; eyes
(√k̓ʷƛ̓)	k̓ʷiƛ̓+t, s+k̓ʷiƛ̓+t+m	others, brothers, the rest
(√k̓ʷn)	s+k̓ʷan=ɬq	harvest, flower, grow, garden, plant, crop
(√k̓ʷn)[125]	k̓ʷin, k̓ɬ+k̓ʷin+st	pick, choose, figure out, try, decide, select
(√k̓ʷn)[126]	k̓ʷin+x	indef. number, how many, a few, some
(√k̓ʷn)[127]	k̓ʷ•k̓ʷn̓=ítaʔkʷ	shallow water (little water)
(√k̓ʷnxʷ)	k̓ɬ+k̓ʷinxʷ=c	answer
(√k̓ʷr)	k̓ʷar•r	crooked
(√k̓ʷs)	k̓ʷas	singe
(√k̓ʷt)[128]	s+k̓ʷut, k+s+k̓ʷt=us	one, half, across
(√k̓ʷt̓)	k̓ɬ+k̓ʷit̓•t̓	shortcut, step over, walk across
(√k̓ʷxʷ)[129]	k̓ʷixʷ, t+k̓ʷaxʷ•xʷ=lqʷ	take off, apart, remove, unwrap, untie, unravel, pull off, uncoil, pull out
(√k̓ʷy)	k̓ʷ•k̓ʷy=ínaʔ, k̓ʷ•k̓ʷy=úmaʔ, s+k̓ʷ•k̓ʷiy=m=lt	small, baby, child
(√k̓ʷy)[130]	s+k̓ʷuy	man's mother
(√k̓ʷʔ)[131]	c+k̓ʷaʔ. n+k̓ʷaʔ=ls+ncút	chew, bite, cranky
(√lkl)	laklí	lock, key

119 Cf. Sp s-kʷékʷs-t; Cm ʔikʷ-kʷaast *early morning* (aa confirms an earlier pharyngeal). Ok siɬ+ is not understood.
120 Cr kʷiʔc *dusk, evening, nightfall.*
121 Cm k̓ʷac̓.
122 Cm k̓ʷul̓-ɬqʷ-nt-xʷ *you plant s.t.*; Cr k̓ʷul̓ *do, fix, make, to produce.*
123 Cm k̓ʷəɬx *be startled*; Cr k̓ʷeɬš *startle, surprise.*
124 Cm k̓ʷƛ̓-ƛ̓ *to show up, turn up, be found*; Cr k̓ʷet̓ *evident, exposed, plain, take off (clothes)...*
125 Cm k̓ʷan̓-nt-xʷ *you try s.t.*; Cr k̓ʷin̓ *choose, consider, try.*
126 Cm k̓ʷin̓-x *how many, much*; Cr k̓ʷinš *how many?*
127 The root √k̓ʷn is the result of a re-analysis of k̓ʷ•k̓ʷy=naʔ into k̓ʷ•k̓ʷín=aʔ. See √k̓ʷy *small.*
128 Sp s-č̓ut *half*; Cm s-k̓ʷut *half, equal parts.*
129 Cm k̓ʷaxʷ-nt-xʷ *you open s.t.*
130 Cm s-k̓ʷuy.
131 Cm k̓ʷaʔ-m *to take a bite*, n-k̓ʷaʔ-lwas *to hate, be angry with s.o.*, k̓ʷiʔ *bite.*

(√lklt)[132]	lkalát	biscuits
(√lkp)[133]	lkapú	coat
(√lkp)[134]	lkapí	coffee
(√lkst)	lkasát	box
(√lk̓)[135]	lak̓, lk̓=iẇs	tie, jail, bundle, force, strap, bale, tied
(√lk̓)[136]	ł+k+lk̓a+m	take (?)
(√lkʷ)[137]	k+lkʷ•akʷ, lkʷ=ut	far; remove, leave, distant
(√lm)[138]	lim+t, k+lm=íls+mist	glad, pleased, thank you, glad(ness), glad with oneself
(√lmn)[139]	limnó	watermelon
(√lmx)	k+lmx=qin+m	love song
(√lpl)	lapál	shovel
(√lpl)[140]	liplí	corn
(√lpm)	lipúm	apple
(√lṗ)[141]	s+liṗ	firewood
(√lq)[142]	n+lq=iẇs, lq=úlaʔxʷ+m	pull, pluck, uproot, pull (weeds, whiskers)
(√lq̇)[143]	liq̇	bury, hill the ground, cover
(√lq̇)[144]	lq̇a+m, k+lq̇=ísxiʔ	peel (off)
(√lq̇)[145]	lq̇+mncut	go strong
(√lqʷ)[146]	laqʷn, ẇẏ+s+láqʷ=naʔ+m[147]	shed hair
(√lq̇ʷ)[148]	lq̇ʷa+m, lq̇ʷ•lq̇ʷ=iẇs	break in two
(√lsl)	laslí	sleigh
(√lsmst)	lasmís, lasmíst	shirt
(√lsw)	laswá	silk
(√lt)[149]	lut	no(t), refuse
(√ltp)	latáp	table
(√lw)[150]	lw•liw, lw=iẇs	ringing sound
(√lwn)[151]	lawán	granary, oats
(√lxʷ)[152]	lxʷa+p[153]	hurt, get hurt

132 Ka lqelét *bread*.
133 Sp lkepú.
134 Cr lka·pí.
135 Sp leč̓, lič̓(í); Cm k-lk̓-iċaʔ-m *to tie a bundle*; Cr leč̓.
136 Uncertain form.
137 Sp lkʷu-t; Cm k̓lkʷut *further away*; Cr lekʷ.
138 Sp lem; Cm lam-t *be glad*; Cr lim.
139 See Cr la·mná *honey, syrup*.
140 Sp liplí.
141 Cm qt:kas-laṗ *to gather firewood*; Cr qt:sliṗ *woody*.
142 Sp liq; Cm liq-(nt)-n *I break s.t. [string]*; Cr laq.
143 Sp laq̇; Cm ka(t)-liq̇-naʔ-nt-xʷ *you bury s.o. with dirt*; Cr leq̇.
144 Cm k-lq-iċaʔ-nt-xʷ *you pluck s.t. [feathers]*.
145 Uncertain form.
146 Sp loqʷ.
147 Cf. Sh luqʷ; Cr laq *pull out plants*. See also Ok √lq.
148 Sp loq̇ʷ *torn loose from*; Cm lq̇ʷ-nt-xʷ *you break s.t.*; Cr hn+loq̇ʷ=íẇes *divorced, split*.
149 Cm lut; Cr lut *mischievous, negative, no, not*.
150 Sp liw; Cm liw-kst-mn-(n)t-xʷ *you ring s.t. [a bell]*; Cr liw.
151 Sp lewén.
152 Sp lxʷ(ú) *to feel pain, to ache, hurt*; Cm lxʷ-p *be injured*; Cr lexʷ.
153 Cf. Sp lxʷup.

(√lxʷ)	lxʷ=us	set watch, watch
(√lʕp)[154]	c+lp•laʕp	fall off
(√lʕ̓ʷ)[155]	laʕ̓ʷ, c+lʕ̓ʷ=ut+m	fit (around), valley, fit, gulch, fit, insert, match, fasten, hitch, wear
(√lʔ)	aláʔ, ilíʔ	here, there, dwell, place, stay
(√lʔw)[156]	lʔiw	m's father
(√l̓x̌)[157]	s+l̓ax̌+t	friend
(√łc̓)[158]	łc̓•ac̓	whip, hit
(√łc̓)[159]	łic̓=k	cut off
(√łk)[160]	ł•łak, c+łak	bushes, brush, vegetation, swamp
(√łkp)[161]	łkap	bucket
(√łkʷ)	łúkʷ=laʔxʷ	dirt
(√łk̓ʷ)[162]	n+łk̓ʷ•k̓ʷ+mi	think about, remember, recall
(√łm)	n+łm=ils+m	pet, touch, be nice to
(√łmn)	łmn=iw̓s	side by side, tied together
(√łn)[163]	łin+m	deny
(√łp)	k+łip=w̓s	Republic
(√łp)[164]	n+łip+t+m	forget
(√łp)[165]	łup	suck in
(√łpk)	n+łpak[166]	fall in snow, stuck in snow
(√łp̓)[167]	k+łp̓•ap̓, k+łp̓+mscut	discouraged, awful
(√łp̓)[168]	łp̓=úlaʔxʷ+tn	border
(√łq̓)[169] see √łq̓ʷ	łq̓+ilx	lie, recline, in bed, lie on back, bedroom, pajamas
(√łqʷ)	s+łiqʷ	meat
(√łqʷ)[170]	łqʷ=cin=xn	carry on back, pack, throw over shoulder, loop, loin cloth
(√łq̓ʷ)[171] see √łq̓	k+sn+łq̓ʷ+ut+n	lie, bed, lay, lie down

154 See Sp lʕap *emerge, come out, float*. See Cm liʕ̓-iʔ *to become loose*.
155 Sp hec-l̓aʕʷ-n̓-t-én̓ *I keep on fitting it together*, liʕ̓ʷ *fit loosely*, loʕʷ(ó) *to fit together*; Cm ka(t)-l̓aʕʷ-ikn-xn *button-hook*; Cr hn+láʕʷ-nt-m *he was ... inserted into a sheath*, leʕʷ *adjust, fit*, loʔ+loʔ+ótm *valley*.
156 Sp lʔéw; Cm ləʔáw.
157 Cr s+l̓ax̌+t.
158 Sp łic̓ *thrash, whip*; Cm k-łc̓-alqʷ-nt-xʷ *you hit s.t. with a stick*.
159 Sp łec̓ *ripped along the seams*; Cr łuc̓ *break (sticklike objects)*.
160 Cm łak-l̓əxʷ *swamp*.
161 Sp łčep; Cm łkap; Cr łčíp.
162 Sp n-łk̓ʷk̓ʷ-mí-n *I remembered it accidentally*; Cm n-łk̓ʷ-k̓ʷ-mi(n)-nt-xʷ *you remember s.t.*; Cr łuk̓ʷ.
163 See Sp łen *straight faced*.
164 Sp łep.
165 Sp łup.
166 Sp n-łpič, n-łepč.
167 Cm ka(t)-łip̓-cn *to pout*; Cr łep̓ *disappoint, distasteful*.
168 Sp łip̓(í); Cr łip̓.
169 Sp qt:łq̓-íl̓š *he lay down*; Cr qt:łaq̓ *crouch, lie (on one's stomach)*.
170 Cm k-łqʷ-aw̓s-(s)t-xʷ *you hang s.t. up*; Sh t-łqʷ-ew̓s-n-s *to throw something over a line*.
171 Sp łq̓ʷut; Cm ka(t)-łq̓ʷ-ut *to lie down on a bed, bench, cot*.

(√ɬq̓ʷ)[172]	ɬaq̓ʷ=cín, ɬ[ʔ]iq̓ʷ	clear sound, appear, perceptible, audible, come in sight, show
(√ɬt̓)	s+ɬ•ɬt̓a+m	fishing
(√ɬt̓)[173]	ɬt̓a+p, ɬt̓ + p+mist	jump pl., fly off, jump off
(√ɬw)[174]	s+ɬw=ilt	niece
(√ɬw)[175]	k+ɬw+scut, c+k̓ɬ+ɬw=alqs+m	pull away, separate, part ways
(√ɬwn)[176]	ɬwin	leave, abandon
(√ɬw̓)[177]	ɬw̓•ɬw̓=ikst	prick, stab, puncture
(√ɬxʷ)	n+ɬuxʷ+t	brush (vegetation), enter brush, go in the bushes
(√ɬxʷ)[178]	k+ɬúʔxʷ=w̓s	stitch, sew
(ɬxʷ)[179]	s+ɬxʷ+ncut, ɬáʔxʷ=sk̓it, ɬaʔxʷ=ísk̓it	rest, catch your breath
(√ɬxʷ)[180]	ɬ•ɬaxʷ, k+ɬxʷ+p, ɬxʷ+p=us	dress, hang, drape over, rope (a horse), slip on
(√ɬxʷ)	n+ɬxʷ+p=us	boil
(√ɬx̌m)[181]	s+ɬx̌m•am, s+ɬx̌m=ilt	in-laws, relative
(√ɬx̌ʷ)[182]	k+ɬx̌ʷ+m=úsaʔ, ɬx̌ʷa+p[183] ɬaʔ•ɬaʔx̌ʷ=úlaʔxʷ+m	hole, dig hole, slip away, go through, run to the finish, cross, get across, go over
(√ɬx̌ʷp̓)[184]	ɬx̌ʷp̓a+m, ɬix̌ʷp̓+t	run out, run in
(√ɬʕp)	ɬaʕp+m	drink
(√ɬʕt̓)[185]	ɬaʕt̓, ɬaʔ•ɬaʔt̓=xán	wet
(√ɬʕt̓)	ɬaʕt̓=xn+m[186]	smash
(√ɬʔ)[187]	ɬaʔ=íys, k̓a+ɬáʔ	close (to), near, next to, on that side, other side, edge, lean against, at that point
(√ɬʔ)	s+k+ɬaʔ=ásq̓t	Saturday
(√ƛ̓k)[188]	ƛ̓k=s=ups+m	sprout
(√ƛ̓k̓ʷʔ)	s+ƛ̓•ƛ̓úk̓ʷaʔ	wood pitch
(√ƛ̓l)[189]	ƛ̓l•al, ƛ̓la+p, ƛ̓íl+miʔst	lifeless, stop, stay put, still, dead, settled, sg. die, loss, kill

172 Sp ɬaq̓ʷ; Cr ɬaq̓ʷ *peel, skin.*
173 Sp ɬit̓, ɬt̓-íp *it lept suddenly, it bounced*; Cm ɬit̓pt *be bouncing (pl)*; Cr ɬet̓+p.
174 Cm sɬwalt *male's brother's child; male's nephew.*
175 See Cr ɬuwis+tn Lit. *uncle of a person whose parent is dead.*
176 Sp ɬw-ént *a person who has ben left*; Cm k̓(ɬ)-ɬwan *to move.*
177 Sp ɬu(ú).
178 Cm ɬxʷ-nt-xʷ *you sew s.t.*; Cr ɬexʷ.
179 Cm ɬxʷ-ašk̓it *to take a deep breath, catch one's breath.*
180 Sp ɬxʷ-p=ús-n-t *rope it!*; Cm k-ɬxʷp *to hang up.*
181 Sp ɬx̌-m-ím *he is leaving with his in-laws*; Cm ɬax̌m.
182 Sp ɬix̌ʷ, ɬox̌ʷ(ú); Cr č+ ɬ+ ɬx̌ʷ=ál̓qʷ Lit. *holes bored on a hollow stick, log, etc.*, ɬáx̌ʷ+p *escape.*
183 See √ɬx̌ʷp̓.
184 Sp ɬix̌ʷp̓ *run recklessly*, ɬx̌ʷup *escape, dash out*; Cm ɬəx̌ʷp *to escape, take off*; Cr ɬax̌ʷp̓ *rush (to ... out).*
185 Cm ɬət̓ *be wet*, ɬa-ʔ-at̓ *to become wet*, k-ɬt̓ *dew.*
186 The connection, if any, with √ɬʕt̓ *wet* is not understood.
187 Sp ɬeʔ(é); Cm k-ɬaʔ-m *be close to, close by*; Cr ɬiʔ *border, edge (close to the ...).*
188 Sp ƛ̓eč / ƛ̓eč̓ s-ƛ̓eč̓č̓=s-m̓ *a sprout*; Sh t̓ek *stick out, protrude*; Cr t̓ič̓ *protrude.*
189 Sp ƛ̓il(í) *still, unmoving, stopped, quiet.*

(√ƛ̓m)[190]	ƛ̓mi+p, ƛ̓m=us	be late, left behind
(√ƛ̓m̓)[191]	ƛ̓um̓	bloody
(√ƛ̓q)[192]	ƛ̓áq=naʔ	sack, pocket, bag
(√ƛ̓q)[193]	s+ƛ̓aq̣	dig
(√ƛ̓qʷ)[194]	ƛ̓qʷ•ƛ̓qʷu+mn	thorn
(√ƛ̓xʷ)[195]	ƛ̓xʷa+m	kill many, dead many, pl. die, paralized
(√ƛ̓xʷ)[196]	ƛ̓xʷu+p	beat, win, earn
(√ƛ̓x̌)[197]	ƛ̓ax̌+t, ƛ̓x̌=itkʷ	fast, race, speed
(√ƛ̓x̌)[198]	ƛ̓x̌a+p, s+ƛ̓x̌•ƛ̓x̌a+p	elders, parents, age, grown
(√ƛ̓x̌)[199]	n+ƛ̓x̌=cin	loud, strong
(√ƛ̓ʕm)	n+ƛ̓ʕam=cn	thirsty
(ƛ̓ʔ)[200]	k+ƛ̓aʔ•ƛ̓ʔ=ús+m; k+ƛ̓ʔam	look for, search, watch; fetch
(√ƛ̓ʔ)	s+ƛ̓aʔ=cín+m	deer
(√ƛ̓ʔ)	k+ƛ̓ʔ=íplaʔ[201]	make trouble
(√ƛ̓ʔ)[202]	ƛ̓ʔiʔ	canoe
(√mc̓ʔ)	míc̓aʔ	(fetch) dead game
(√mh)[203]	k+mah=qn+míst	give up
(√mkʷ)[204]	mukʷ, mkʷ=iwt	snow on trees, lump, mound, bulge
(√mk̓ʷt)[205]	s+mik̓ʷt	snow on ground, snowed in
(√ml)[206]	ml+pul+st+m	want to beat
(√ml)[207]	ml=qn=ups	golden eagle
(√ml)[208]	mul+m	dip (water)
(√mlk̓ʷ)[209]	malk̓ʷ; mlk̓ʷ=ápaʔst, mlk̓ʷ=ut	whole, entire, stallion, pole
(√mls)[210]	mils+míst	confident; make plans
(√mlx)[211]	mulx	cottonwood

190 Cf the particle ƛ̓əm *past*. Cm k-ƛ̓m̓-t *to pass by; be past, after, beyond*, ƛ̓m̓-ap *be late, miss s.t.*
191 Sp ƛ̓um̓ *bloody, red like blood*.
192 Sp n-ƛ̓áq=neʔ *pocket, bag*; Cr t̓áq=ney̓ Lit *a sack*.
193 Sp n̩-ƛ̓q-ém *he dug to the bottom of it*; Cm ƛ̓q-nt-xʷ *you dig s.t. up*.
194 Sp ƛ̓oqʷ(ú) *poke*.
195 Cm ƛ̓xʷ-nt-xʷ *you kill many others*; Cr t̓exʷ *to die (people only), kill (people)*.
196 Sp ƛ̓xʷup *win*, ƛ̓xʷup *to win*; Cr t̓u·xʷp *to win*.
197 Sp ƛ̓ax̌+ t; Cm ƛ̓x̌-t *be fast, quick*; Cr t̓ax̌ *swift*.
198 Cm ƛ̓əx̌p *to grow up*, ƛ̓ix̌pt lx *they grew up*.
199 Cm n-ƛ̓x̌-cin.
200 Sp ƛ̓eʔ(é̜); Cm ka-ƛ̓ʔ-uš-m *to watch for*.
201 Cf. Sp č-ƛ̓ʔ=éplʔe-n *I caused him to get in trouble*.
202 Sp ƛ̓yéʔ; Cr t̓édeʔ.
203 Sp č-mš=qn-míst; Cm kmahahcínxn *to give out;* k-mx̌-qn-min-ct *to lose heart, give up*.
204 Sh t-mukʷ-tm̓ *snow on trees*.
205 Sp s-mek̓ʷ-t *snow on the ground*; Cm š-mak̓ʷ-t *snow on the ground*; Cr s+mik̓ʷ+t *snow*.
206 The root is unclear.
207 Sp n-mlq-n=úps *golden eagle*; Cr ml=qn=ups.
208 Sp mul; Cm mul *to dip with a ladle*; Cr mul.
209 Sp milkʷ *solid, whole*; Cm məlk̓ʷ *be round (pole)*; n-mlk̓ʷ-ap-aʔšt *stallion*; Cr melk̓ʷ *complete, intact, whole*.
210 This root is the source of =ils *stomach, feelings*. See also miw̓s > =iw̓s.
211 Sp mulš; Cr mulš.

(√mlx̌ʔ)[212]	málx̌aʔ	tell lies, pretend
(√mlʔ)[213]	mílaʔ	bait
(√ml̓)[214]	ml̓•al̓	bloody
(√ml̓)[215]	mil̓	give as gift, pass around
(√ml̓t)[216]	ml̓•ml̓t=iɬp	poplar
(√mɬ)[217]	k+mɬ•ɬ=ínaʔ	cave in, fall down on
(√mɬk̓yʔ)[218]	mɬk̓íyaʔ	blood
(mƛ̓)[219]	miƛ̓	smear, paint, mixed
(√mmlʕʔ)[220]	ṁáʕmlaʔ	maggots
(√mn)[221]	(maʔ•mín), mn+min=xn+mi	rub
(√mnk)[222]	mnik	excrement, shit
(√mnmɬ)[223]	mnimɬ+tt	they, we, you pl. (pl. person marker)
(√mns)	mons	Monse (place name)
(√mṅxʷ)[224]	s+maṅxʷ	tobacco, smoke
(√mq)[225]	maq	stop someone from
(√mq̇)[226]	mq̇•mq̇=ink	full (stomach)
(√mqʷ)	mqʷ•aqʷ, k+mqʷ=ínaʔ	falling snow
(√mq̇ʷ)[227]	c+maq̇ʷ	mountain, mountains, mounds
(√mrm)[228]	mrim	doctor, medicine, mix, recover, marry, marriage, spouse
(√mṙ)[229]	k+máṙ=naʔ	fill a hole
(√mṙwʔ)[230]	máṙwiʔ	season, dress
(√ms)[231]	mus	four
(√ms)[232]	ms•mus+m, mu•ms=xn+m	feel with hand, drag (feet)
(√ms)	mus=kst+m, mus=ls	try, hope
(√mt)[233]	mut	sg. sit, be home
(√mtln)	matlán	Madeline

212 Cm mlx̌aʔ-ncut *to tell a lie.*
213 Cr ṁel̓eʔ.
214 Sp ml̓(í) *to bleed, to flow.*
215 Cr mil̓ *distribute, pass around (food).*
216 Sp ṁl̓ṁl̓-t=éɬp *trembling aspen.*
217 Sp meɬ *topple over*; Cm maɬ-m *to rest*; Cm miɬ *rest.*
218 Cm mɬk̓-ayaʔ *blood.* See Cr mít̓č=edeʔ *blood.*
219 Sp miƛ̓ *covered with a liquid (like paint)*; meƛ *mix, shuffle, deal cards*; Cm maƛ̓-nt-xʷ *you spread, smear s.t.*, miƛ̓-nt-xʷ *you smear s.t.*
220 Further analyzable?
221 Cm min-nt-xʷ *you rub s.t.*
222 Sp mneč; Cm mnak.
223 Cm nmniml *we; us.*
224 Sp s-meṅxʷ; Cm maṅxʷ-m; Cr s-mil̓xʷ; Sh s-menx.
225 Sp maq *to convince, to urge.*
226 Sp maq̇ *full, sated*; moqʷ *full, sated, too much*; Cm mq̇-ank *be full.*
227 Sp moq̇ʷ; Cm ac-mq̇ʷ *hill, mountain*; Cr maq̇ʷ *pile, stack.*
228 Sp √mry (malí) *to heal*; Cm mryam *medicine*; Cr marim *treatment*, marare·m=íẇes *couple.*
229 Sp mal *dirt, earth.*
230 See √mṙ. Sp mérwiʔ *to season in cooking*; Cr mar=kʷe *flavor, season.*
231 Sp mus; Cm mus; Cr mus.
232 Sp mus *to feel (with the hand)*; Cm ṁs-ṁus-m *to feel around, grope*; Cr mus *feel about.*
233 Sp ʔemút.

(√mw̓s)	miw̓s	middle, half way, midway
(√mxʷ)[234]	mxʷ=iłp	cedar boughs
(√mx̌)[235]	s+mx̌=ikn	she grizzly
(√my)[236]	my+st, mya+líxʷ, my=ils+m, my+n+am, my+n=úlaʔxʷ, my+p, n+my=cin, n+my•my+p+mist[237]	know, realize, learn, be sure, figure, deem, know, interpret, guide, skilled, agree, confess
(√my)[238]	s+my+s+qilxʷ	important, better, more, excellent
(√my)	my+m	pile
(√myw)[239]	(s+)myaw	Coyote
(√mʕ)	n+maʕ=ítkʷ, n+maʕ=w̓s, kł+maʕ=ítkʷ	fall in, cave in, lay across, float, come to rest ... (to shore)
(√mʕl)[240]	ł+ml•ml	fill with clay, dab, smear
(√mʕʷ)[241]	maʕʷ, s+k+maʕʷ=áqs	break, left overs
(√mʕʷt)	maʕʷt•t	man's name
(√mʔ)[242]	maʔ=cín+m, maʔ+mín	bother, be bothered, send away, run away, discourage
(√mʔm)[243]	s+ma•mʔím	women, wives
(√mʔqʷ)	maʔqʷ=áln	knife
(√m̓cxn)[244]	s+m̓u•m̓cxn	mare
(√m̓l)	k+m̓il+t+m	visit
(√m̓st)[245]	m̓istm	w's father
(m̓y̓)[246]	m̓áyaʔ+m, s+m̓aʔ•m̓áy+m, m̓ay+xt+wíxʷ	story, know, tell, teach, school, pupil, teacher, find out, news, report,
(√nc)	incá	I
(√nc̓ʔ)[247]	nc̓iʔ=cn	wolf
(√nk̓)[248]	k̓ł+nik̓	saw, cut, knife
(√nk̓)[249]	s+nik̓=łxʷ	son-in-law

234 See Sp mš=éɬp.
235 Sp s-mx̌=éy̓=čn *grizzly bear*; Cm míx̌ał *black bear*.
236 Sp miy, *to know, to tell, to repeat, fact*; Cm may̓-xit-xʷ *you tell s.t. [a story]*; Cr may *foresee, foretell, predict*.
237 Sp n-m̓ey̓-p-m̓íst *he confessed to the* priest. Cf. Cr s+n+my=ep+mí+ncut *confession*.
238 Cm my-my-akst *to be good with one's hands*; Cr s+miyes+čínt *aristocracy ... bigwig ...*
239 Sp smyéw; Cm s-miyaw; Cr s+miyíw.
240 Sp mal *dirt, earth*.
241 √mʕʷ has a northern variant √mʕ. Sp √maw, s-č-maʔw=áqs *leftovers of food*; Cm maʕʷ-nt-xʷ *you break s.t.*; Cr meʕʷ *broken*.
242 Sp meʔ *bother, pester*; Cm c-k-maʔ-m *to act rudely, incorrectly*; Cr miʔ *annoy, bore*, meʔ+eʔ *send away*.
243 Sp s-m-ʔem *woman*; Cr s+míʔyem *bride, wife, woman*, s+mí+mʔeʔem *women*.
244 Sp s-m̓úm̓c=šn̓.
245 Sp m̓éstm̓; Cm maʔástm.
246 Sp meyeʔ *to show, to teach, to preach, to tell*; Cm may̓aʔ-ɬt-xʷ *you speak for s.o.; you teach, explain to s.o.*
247 Sp n-c̓íʔ=cn.
248 Sp nič̓; Cm n-nik̓-mn *knife*; Cr nič̓.
249 Sp s-néč̓=lxʷ; Cm snak̓łxʷ *daughter's husband; son-in-law*.

(√nk̓ʷ)[250]	nk̓ʷ+cw=ilxʷ+tn	one, co-, fellow ...
(√nɬcm)	naɬc•c•ám	forget
(√nm)[251]	k+nm=qin	blind
(√nq)[252]	na+naq+númt, na+naʕ•nq=cín, nq=ils	filled up, satisfied
(√nqs)[253]	naqs	one, alone; relative, neighbor
(√nq̓ʷ)	k̓ɬ+nq̓ʷ+mist	run away
(√nq̓ʷ)[254]	naq̓ʷ+m	steal, rob
(√ns)	nis	sg gone
(√nw)[255]	anwí	you sg.
(√nw̓)[256]	(s+)niw̓+t[257]	wind
(√nx)	c+nx=iʔst=xn+cut	back track
(√nxl)	k̓ɬ+nixl	hear, listen, understand, mind
(√nx̌ʷ)	náx̌ʷ=aʔst	game gets away, almost gain
(√nx̌ʷ)[258]	nax̌ʷ•nx̌ʷ	married, wife
(√nys)	nyas	Eneas, Ignace
(√nʕm)	c+naʕm	deaf mute
(√nʕs)[259]	naʕs+t	one pound (weight), heavy
(√nʕ̓p)[260]	nyʕip	always, continuously, still
(√nʔq̓)	naʔ•naʔq̓+nwís	witness
(√nʔx̌ʷ)[261]	naʔ•naʔx̌ʷ+t	lope, gallop
(√pcs)	pacís	Baptiste
(√pcxʷ)[262]	picxʷ+t	disgusted
(√pk)[263]		board, plank
(√pkʷ)[264]	n+pakʷ, pkʷ=us+m	pour loose material, pile solids, pour solids, sow, shake
(√pl)[265]	sn+p•pul+x, pul+x,[266] sn+paʔ•púl+x+tn	overnight, camp, guest, overnighter, go to bed
(√pl)	pl•al, s+k+pl•l=ikst, sn+pl̓•l̓=iw̓s	weeds, grow, sprout, youth, young

250 Sp nk̓ʷuʔ; Cm s-nk̓ʷ+ s-kint *one's Indian people*; Cr nek̓ʷ *one, unit,* s+nukʷ(-) *fellow, together, with*
251 Sp č-ṅṁ=qin.
252 Sp naq *the water has reached the marker along the river's edge*; Cr naq *satiated (with food).*
253 Sp čnáqs *one person*; Cm naqs.
254 Sp naq̓ʷ; Cr naq̓ʷ.
255 Sp √hanwí.
256 Sp new̓; Cr e·+ niw̓+ t *the wind blows.*
257 Sp s-new̓-t; Sh s-new-t.
258 Sp nóx̌ʷnox̌ʷ *wife*; Cm nux̌ʷ-nux̌ʷ *wife.*
259 Also recorded without the pharyngeal. Cm nəəṣ-t *be heavy.*
260 Cm niʕáp *always.*
261 Cf. √nx̌ʷ.
262 Sp picxʷ; Cm picxʷ-t *be disgusted, disappointed*; Cr picxʷ *disappointed, disgusted.*
263 Sp s-c-pič *lumber, a board.*
264 Sp pukʷ(ú) *round objects lying in a pile or lying about in a general area*; Cr pekʷ *lay (round objects).*
265 Cm pulx *to camp, stay overnight.*
266 Sh pul(t) *to lie.*

(√pl)[267]	p•pil̓, n+s+pil+m	Nespelem, bare ground, flat, flat land, Big Bend
(√pl)[268]	pul+st	kill, beat, fight, hit
(√pl)[269]	pul•pl+t	dream
(√pl)	s+paʔ•pʔúl	man's name
(√pl)	s+pl=ip	hind end, rump
(√plm)[270]	s+plim=cn	mouth
(√plx)[271]	n+p•pilx	pl. enter
(√pl̓)[272]	púl̓=laʔx^{w}	Gopher
(√pl̓)	s+p[ʔ]ul̓, paʔl=íslp̓	smoke (with wood)
(√pɬn)[273]	puɬn	Portland
(√pƛ̓m)	s+kɬ+pu•p•ƛ̓m	Meyers Falls
(√pmt)[274]	s+pumt	fur
(√pn)[275]	s+pin=tk	time, year, always
(√pn)[276]	n+pn=w̓s+cut	buck, jump, fold
(√pnh)[277]	pnh=iw̓s	on time; get caught
(√pq)[278]	piq, payq, c+n+paʔq=cín	white, dawn
(√pq^{w})[279]	pq^{w}+ilx+m	go visit, go find out
(√pq̓^{w})[280]	kɬ+p•pq̓^{w}=úsaʔ, k+pq̓^{w}=ínaʔ+m, n+pq̓^{w}+min	fill a hole, fill, spill or pour solids on top; black powder
(√psx)[281]	paʔsíx+m	load, carry (on back)
(√pt)[282]	put, n+put=ls, paʔ•pút	match, enough, just, exact, satisfied with, still
(√ptk̓)	ptk̓=ink	gut, disembowel
(√ptq)[283]	patáq	potato
(√ptwnx^{w})[284]	p•ptwínaʔx^{w}	old woman
(√ptʔ)[285]	n+pútaʔ+tn	respect
(√pw)[286]	piw•pw+t	lightweight

267 Sp pil *flat and thin*; Cm pəl *be flat*, nspilm *Nespelem*.
268 Sp puls *to kill, fight*; Cr púlut *harm, injure*.
269 Cm pl-pul-t *to dream*.
270 269 Sp s-pl-im̓=cn; Cr s+ plim̓=cn *lips*.
271 Sp n-pilš.
272 Sp pul̓ *fluff up the dirt*, púl̓yeʔ *gopher*, púl̓yaʔ *Mrs. Coyote*; Cm pul̓-yaʔ *gopher, mole*; Cr pul̓ye.
273 Cr puɬn.
274 Sp s-pum; Cr spum.
275 Sp pén=tč *always*; Cm pan-tk *always, forever, often;* Cr pin=tč *always*.
276 Sp pin̓ *bent, crooked, dented, folded*; Cm pn̓-n̓ *be bent over*; Cr pen̓ *bent, bend*.
277 Sp √penx^{w} (pnh), pnh=éw̓s-m *he met someone halfway*.
278 Sp piq (paq); Cm payq *be white*; Cr peq *white, bleached, silver*.
279 Sp pq^{w}-ilš *he visited an ill person in an attempt to spread good cheer*; Cr puq^{w}+ilš *spy*.
280 Cm na-puq̓^{w}-m *to fill with powder or granular substance*, n-puq̓^{w}-min *gunpowder*.
281 Sp pseš *to carry wood on one's back*; Cm psax-nt-x^{w} *you bundle, gather s.t. [sticks]*.
282 Sp put (puteʔ) *be exact, be able, be correct*; Cm put *just, only, exact; fit*, na-put-aʔ-tn *special observance; spirituality*.
283 Sp patáq; Cr pa·táq.
284 Cr s+ptwínx^{w} *hog (mother...)*.
285 Certainly related to √pt. Sp put (puteʔ) *be exact, be able, be correct*; Cm na-put-aʔ-tn *special observance; spirituality*; Cr puteʔ *honor, respect, worship*.
286 Sp pew̓ *lightweight*; Cm paw̓ *be light weight*; Cr piw̓ *light (in weight)*.

(√pw)[287]	pw•piw+t	blister
(√pwn)	wẏ+ipwn	bury
(√px̌)	pix̌+m	hunt
(√px̌)[288]	px̌•pax̌+t	smart, think, aware, consciousness, smarts, senses, deliberate
(√px̌^{w})[289]	px̌^{w}a+m	distribute, scatter
(√px̌^{w})	px̌^{w}•px̌^{w}•x̌^{w}=ils	Hunters (place name)
(√pyr)	pyar	Peter
(√pyrs)	pyarís	man's name
(√pʕ)[290]	paʕ, n+paʕ=íẃs	bleached, grey
(√pʕs)[291]	ps=ʕáyaʔ	goofy, feeble minded
(√pʕs)[292]	paʕs	surprised
(√pʔ)[293]	s+puʔ=ús	heart, feelings, feel
(√pʔ, √c̓ɬt)	s+piʔ+s+c̓íɬt[294]	yesterday
(√pʔs)[295]	k̓ɬ+paʔs, paʔ•paʔs=ínk, ɬ+paʔs+mí	guess, think, worry, thinking, wish (by magic), desire, sad
(√p̓c̓n)	s+p̓ic̓n	rope
(√p̓lk)[296]	p̓lk=us+m	turn, turn back, turn around
(√p̓ƛ̓)[297]	s+p̓iƛ̓+m	bitterroot
(√p̓ƛ̓)[298]	n+p̓uƛ̓+m, s+p̓aƛ̓+m=qn	come out, get to the end, finish; head of (river, gulch...)
(√p̓n)[299]	p̓na+m	put down long objects
(√p̓q̓s)	p̓i•p̓q̓s	weasel
(√p̓s)[300]	p̓•p̓s=ʕáwaʔs	low place
(√p̓sƛ̓ʔ)[301]	p̓ísƛ̓aʔ	big, large pl.
(√p̓x^{w})[302]	n+p̓aʔ•p̓aʔx^{w}=ús	bright, shine
(√p̓ẏq)[303]	sc+p̓ayq, p̓ẏq=aɬq	cooked, ripe, cook, ready to eat, fruit
(√p̓ʕc̓)[304]	s+p̓ʕac̓	plant shoots, squirt, soft excrement

287 Sp pew *to inflate, to swell*; Cr pig^{w} *breathe, whole*.
288 Sp pax̌; Cm pəx̌px̌t px̌-px̌-t *be intelligent, wise*, k̓ɬ-paʔx̌ -m *to think, plan*.
289 Sp px̌^{w}-úm *he distributed something*; Cm pux̌^{w}-m *be scattered*; Cr pax̌^{w} *distribute (in order)*.
290 Sp paʕ; Cm pəḥ *gray*, paʕ-uš-m *to powder one's face*; Cr par *to be white (with powder)*.
291 Cm pəəṣ *be empty-headed, blank*, pṣ-ayaʔ *dumb, incompetent*; Cr psáye *foolish*.
292 Sp pas *amazed, wide-eyed, speechless;* Cr pas *amazed, astonished, bewildered*.
293 Sp puʔs-mi-n *I thought fondly of him*; Cr puʔs *heart, desire*.
294 Sp spiʔsc̓éʔ.
295 Probably related to √pʔ and segmentable pʔ=u(s). Cm s-c-puʔ-s *heart*, k̓ɬ-puʔs-m *to think*, puʔ-puʔ-s-ank *be sad*.
296 Cm l-c-p̓lk-us-m *to turn around and come back*; Cr p̓elč̓ *turn (a flat object), to turn flat things over*; p̓ulk^{w} *fold*.
297 Cr s+p̓ít̓em.
298 Cm pƛ̓-nt-x^{w} *you dismantle, take s.t. apart*; Cr p̓et̓ *dislodge, slip (out of place)...*
299 Cm p̓n-nt-x^{w} *you lay s.t. down [long objects]*; Cr p̓en *lie (long objects)*.
300 Sp p̓s *crushed, dented, bent*. hec-p̓s-ám *it's crushed. It's dented.*
301 Cm p̓isƛ̓aʔ-t *be big (pl)*; Cr s+pist̓=eẏt *(of things)*.
302 Cm p̓aʔx^{w} *be bright, shiny*, k-p̓aʔx^{w}-anaʔ *be covered in light, shined on*; Cr p̓ix^{w} *agleam, flashed, glow ...*
303 Sp hec-p̓aẏq *it's ripe, it's baked*; Cm p̓iʔq *be cooked, ripe*.
304 Sp s-p̓ʕac̓ *diarrhea, excrement, feces*. p̓ac̓(á) *loose bowels*; Cm s-p̓əəc̓ *soft excrement*; Cr p̓ac̓ *defecate, squirt*.

(√p̓ʕt̓)[305]	p̓t̓•aʕt̓	fall flat, slushy substance falls
(√p̓ʕʷ)[306]	p̓aʕʷ	tire(d), bored
(√p̓ʔ)[307]	k̓ł+p̓aʔ•p̓áʔ, k̓ł+p̓aʔ•p̓ʔá+m	milk cow, squeeze
(√qc)[308]	qa•qc+lx, qic+lx	run, trot, elope, rail
(√qc)[309]	q•qc=us, qc+p+mncut	wrinkled, shrink, draw back
(√qck)[310]	qick	older brother
(√qcʔ)	ł+qá•qcaʔ	older brother
(√ql)	sn+t+ql+ł+xwil+tn	place name
(√ql)[311]	ql=íłc̓aʔ	fresh, raw meat
(√ql)[312]	ql=wit+m, ql=wat=q	step on, thresh, footprint
(√ql)[313]	s+qil=tk, sk̓ʷ=t+m+s+qil=tk	body, (half)breed
(√qlt)[314]	qilt,qa•qlt, s+qlt=mixʷ, s+kł+qlt=us, n+qilt, t+qlt=k=alqʷ	top, man, husband, summit, hilltop, ridge, go over falls, Canada
(√qlw)[315]	s+qlaw, s+qlw=íc̓aʔ	money, beaver pelt, raw hide
(√qlxʷ)	s+qilxʷ	Indian, human, person, reflection, image
(√qł)[316]	qił+t	awake
(√qł)[317]	qł+nu	able, accomplish
(√qm)[318]	qmi, ł+qma+p, n+qm=ils+m	lay out, place down, calm, at ease, slow, rest, give up
(√qm)	s+qm•qm•min	man's name
(√qnʔ)[319]	qá•qnaʔ	paternal grandmother
(√qp)[320]	qp=qin+tn	hair
(√qp)	qpa+m	predicament, be in the same situation as
(√qp)[321]	sn+qp=íłc̓aʔ	cupboard

305 Sp p̓at̓(á) *substance in gravy-like form ...*, p̓t̓-m-cot *she became limp*. The o of cot is the result of an earlier pharyngeal. Cm p̓t̓-(nt)-s *he dumped s.t.*, p̓aat̓-t̓ *be gooey, mushy*, p̓ét̓ət̓ *be overflowing*; Cr p̓et *fall (to ground of own weight as grain)*; p̓at̓ *dream*, t+p̓at̓+t̓ *a sticky substance clinging to something*.

306 The root has a (regional) variant with an unrounded pharyngeal. Some speakers use the forms interchangeably. Sp p̓aw *bored, unconcerned, uncaring*; Cr s+p̓aʕʷ *apathy*.

307 Sp č̓ł-p̓eʔp̓-ém *he milked the cow*; Cr p̓eʔ *to squeeze in orgasm*.

308 Sp qec.

309 Sp qc-ip *it shrank*; Cm qəcp *to shrink, be shrunken*; Cr qec *dwindle, shrink (in quantity)*.

310 Sp qéčč; Cr qicč; Cm qack *male's older brother; male's older male cousin*.

311 Cm ql-t *be fresh, raw (meat, fish)*; Cr qel *meat (raw...)*.

312 Sp ql̓wet *to stand on, to step on*.

313 Sp qel *body, mass*; Cm c-k-s-qal-t-(t)k-m *body (whole)*.

314 Sp qél-t *he got on top of something*; Cm kat-qalt-(t)k *be on top*, s-qlt-mixʷ *man*; Cr s+qil̓=tmxʷ *husband, male ...*

315 Sp s-ql=éw̓ *beaver, money*; Cm s-qlaw̓ *beaver; money*.

316 Sp qił; Cr qeł.

317 Cr qeł *awake, overcome, succeed*.

318 Sp qmin *to lay something down*, qem (qim) *calm, serene*; Cm qm-m-p *be calm*; Cr qem *home..., unconcerned, uninterested...*

319 Sp qén=eʔ; Cm q-qan̓aʔ *father's mother; father's parent's sister; father's parent's female cousin; female's son's child*; Cr qíneʔ *grandmother (paternal...)*.

320 Cm qap-qn *hat*; qt:s-n-qa-qap-qn *beret, soft cap*.

321 Cr qa+qépeʔ *bag (corn husk...)*.

(√qp)	n+q•qp=aqst=xn[322]	mat, mat under the hip
(√qs)[323]	qa•qs•s	dusk
(√qt̓)	s+qt̓a+m[324]	scar
(√qw)	qa•qw=lp̓	driftwood
(√qxʷ)	qa•qxʷ+lx	fish
(√qxʷ)[325]	qixʷ, k̓ɬ+qixʷ	drive a herd, training, whip, drive, take up for
(√qx̌)[326]	k̓ɬ+qax̌	clear of
(√qy̓s)[327]	qy̓s+mist	dream
(√qy̓xʷ)[328]	qy̓axʷ	stink
(√qʔm)[329]	s+qʔim	milk, breast
(√q̓l)[330]	q̓il+t, s+q̓l+x=alq	sick, hurt, hospital gown
(√q̓lxʷ)[331]	n+q̓lxʷ=ax̌n	hook, link, hooked, arm in arm, trip (hook on something)
(√q̓m)[332]	s+q̓m•am, s+q̓m=ilt+n, s+k̓ɬ+q̓am	hunger, wish, swallow, wish, pine for, get stuck on
(√q̓pnʔxʷ)	s+q̓aʔpínaʔxʷ	sand
(√q̓p̓xʷ)[333]	q̓p̓axʷ	tied up (of stomach)
(√q̓spʔ)[334]	q̓sápiʔ	long time, long time past
(√q̓t)	q̓it	rain
(√q̓xʷ)[335]	q̓xʷ•axʷ	flirt, be smitten
(√q̓x̌)[336]	q̓ax̌	trail blaze, clear up, clear, clean
(√q̓x̌)[337]	q̓ix̌+m	be stingy of, keep close, want to
(√q̓y)[338]	q̓iy=w̓s, q̓y=w̓=ɬtiɬn	doubt
(√q̓y)[339]	s+q̓iy+mn	tipi poles
(√q̓y̓)[340]	q̓ay̓, q̓y̓+min, k̓ɬ+q̓y̓•ay̓	paper, mark, pencil, write, picture, book
(√q̓y̓k)	q̓y̓•q̓y̓ik	colt
(√q̓y̓pywt)	q̓y̓pyawt	man's name
(√q̓ʕ)[341]	q̓aʕ+p	move

322 Sp qep *soft*; č-qp=ew̓s *a blanket to pad your seat.*
323 Cm qiʔs *dusk.*
324 Sp s=q̓tim *a scar*; n-q̓t̓t̓-m=aqs *the road is all scarred up and rutted*; Sh c-qit̓ *a scar.*
325 Sp qixʷ *to drive away.*
326 See √x̌q.
327 Sp qey̓s; Cr qiʔs *he had a dream, nightmare, vision*; Sh qeys *to have a nightmare.*
328 Cm qiʔxʷ-nu(n)-nt-xʷ *you smell s.t.*; Cr qiʔxʷ *smell, stink.*
329 Sp qʔ-em *suck, nurse*; Sh qʔem *to suck, take the breast.*
330 Cm q̓il-t *to ache, be sick.*
331 Sp q̓l̓uxʷ *hooked together, strung together*; Cr q̓el̓xʷ *to hook, snag.*
332 Cm n-q̓m-s-cin-m(n)-nt-xʷ *you wish for s.t.*; Cr q̓em *covet, desire, long for, swallow.*
333 Sp q̓ep̓xʷ *the angry snap snap of a horse's teeth on empty air (as it tries to bite).*
334 Sp q̓sípiʔ; Cm q̓əsp *long ago*; Cr q̓es+p *ancient, chronic, long ago*; Sh q̓ʔes *to take a long time.*
335 Sp q̓ʷxʷuxʷ *he flirted*; Cr q̓exʷ *covetous, desire, longing, proud.*
336 Sp q̓ax̌ *cleared, marked.*
337 Sp q̓ix̌ *loathe to give up*; Cm q̓íx̌-q̓ix̌-t *be precious, carefully guarded.*
338 Cf. Sp q̓ey=uʔs-n-t-m *they doubted him*; Cr q̓ey=úʔs-nt-m *disbelieved.*
339 Sp s-n-q̓ey-mn-tn *tipi poles.*
340 Cm q̓iy̓-m *to write*; Cr q̓ey̓ *design, graphics, writing.*
341 Sh q̓ʕeʕ *to move, keep going.*

(√q̓ʔ)[342]	q̓aʔ=xán	shoe, stick in, insert, stick, put in, go between, sandwich, middle, stuff, center, stab
(√q̓ʔ)[343]	n+q̓aʔ=íls	concerned, one's business, problem, pay attention
(√qʷc)	qʷa•qʷíc	enough
(√qʷc)[344]	s+qʷaʔc=ínaʔ	warm weather
(√qʷl)[345]	qʷl•qwil+t	talk (to), phone, insult, brag, word, agree, interrogate
(√qʷl)[346]	qʷil=cn	fir boughs
(√qʷl)	s+qʷil=p	bedding
(√qʷl)[347]	qʷil+m	cheat
(√qʷl)[348]	s+qʷl=cn=ink	belly
(√qʷl̓)[349]	sn+qʷl̓=us	bannock
	s+qʷl̓=ip	moss
(√qʷɬ)[350]	qʷuɬ, n+qʷuɬ=qn	dust
(√qʷm)[351]	qʷam•qʷm+t	excellent
(√qʷm̓)[352]	qʷim̓•m̓	surprise, prance
(√qʷn̓)[353]	qʷn̓=cin	pity, hard up, sorry, suffer
(√qʷs)[354]	n+qʷas+t	deep
(√qʷsp)[355]	qʷsp=íc̓aʔ	buffalo
(√qʷsqʔ)[356]	qʷásqiʔ	blue jay
(√qʷsʔ)[357]	s+qʷsiʔ	son
(√qʷy)[358]	qʷay	often, enough, riches
(√qʷy)	t+qʷay	discend, run down
(√qʷʕʷ)[359]	qʷaʕʷ•qʷw+t	crazy
(√qʷʔ)[360]	n+qʷʔ=úlaʔxʷ	(ground) pocket
(√qʷʔm)[361]	qʷʔam	get used to, familiar, train, accustomed

342 Cm q̓aʔ-aʔ *be stuck*, na-q̓aʔ-nt-xʷ *you put s.t. into a bag or container*; Cr q̓iʔ *clasp, grasp, penetrate*.
343 Cm n-q̓aʔ-lwas *be concerned*.
344 Sp qʷec; Cm qʷaʔc; Cr qʷic.
345 Sp qʷel; Cr √qʷl, qʷaʔ+qʷel̓ *speak*.
346 This and the following root are probably one and the same. Sp qʷel=cn *grand fir*; Cm qʷalcn *tree boughs*
347 Sp qʷil; Cm qʷil-m; Cr qʷil.
348 Sp qʷl̓in̓ *gall*; Cm qʷéəll-iʔ *spleen, gall bladder*
349 Sp s-n-qʷl̓-p=úleʔxʷ *bread baked in the ashes*; Cr qʷel̓ *kindle, light*.
350 Sp qʷuɬ; Cm qʷuɬ-t; Cr qʷuɬ.
351 Sp qʷam *wonderful*; Cm qʷam-qʷam-t *be beautiful, very good*; Cr qʷam *attractive, pleasant …*
352 Sp qʷim̓ *always in a hurry*.
353 Sp qʷin̓; Cm n-qʷn̓-n̓-mi(n)-nt-xʷ *you are merciful, kind to s.o.*; Cr qʷay̓ *impoverished, pitiable, poor*.
354 Sp qʷes; Cm qʷaast *be deep* (aa suggests a pharyngeal in an earlier form), na-qʷast; Cr √qʷs *deepen*.
355 Cm qʷisp *cow; buffalo*.
356 Probably qʷás=qiʔ. Sp qʷásqʷiʔ; Cm qʷas-qʷy̓; Cr qʷás=qn̓ *blue jay (lit. blurred head)*.
357 Sp s-qʷs=éʔ; Cm s-qʷs-aʔ *female's sister's child*, ʔas-qʷs-aʔ *son*.
358 Sp qʷey *frequently, easily, plenty*; Cm qʷay; Cr qʷiy *to abound*.
359 Sp qʷew (qʷaw); Cm na-qʷaʕʷ-qn; Cr qʷeʕʷ *drunk, insane*.
360 Sp č-qʷeʔ=ɬc̓ép *a pouch-like pocket …*; Cm qʷaʔ-ap *duffle bag; pocket*; Cr qʷiʔ *hollow*.
361 Sp qʷʔem; Cm na-qʷaʔ-m *to linger, overstay a visit*; Cr qʷiʔ *accustomed*.

(√q̓ʷc̓)[362]	q̓ʷuc̓+t, q̓ʷic̓, n+q̓ʷic̓+tn[363]	full, lard, fat, fill up, replacement spouse
(√q̓ʷl)[364]	q̓ʷla+m, s+q̓ʷl=qn=islp̓	roast; smoked tipi
(√q̓ʷɬ)[365]	q̓ʷiɬ+t+m, q̓ʷaɬ+t=sqáx̌aʔ	pack, carry, strong, prowess, load, quiver
(√q̓ʷɬ)	q̓ʷ[ʔ]uɬ	black
(√q̓ʷƛ̓)[366]	q̓ʷ•q̓ʷúƛ̓+aʔ=xn+m	race
(√q̓ʷm)[367]	sn+q̓ʷma+m	feeder, pile up
(√q̓ʷm)[368]	n+q̓ʷim+p	take from
(√q̓ʷs)	s+q̓ʷis•s	fat
(√q̓ʷs)	q̓ʷs•q̓ʷas+t	wish, do magic, play tricks
(√q̓ʷt)[369]	n+s+q̓ʷut	other side
(√q̓ʷxʷ)[370]	q̓ʷixʷ	untie
(√q̓ʷy̓)[371]	q̓ʷy̓+mncut	dance
(√q̓ʷy)[372]	q̓ʷuy•q̓ʷúy=laʔxʷ	still air, shelter
(√q̓ʷʕy)[373]	q̓ʷaʕy	black, dirty
(√q̓ʷʔ)[374]	n+q̓ʷaʔ•q̓ʷʔ=ápaʔst[375]	gelding
(√q̓ʷʔ)[376]	n+q̓ʷʔ=itkʷ, n+q̓ʷaʔ=tkʷ=lscut	launder, wash
(√sc)[377]	sic, síc=ɬc̓aʔ, si•sc=lqʷ	one's best, new, fresh; honeymoon
(√scx̌ʷ)	scix̌ʷ	slate rocks
(√sc̓m)[378]	sic̓m	blanket
(√sk̓)	sk̓•sik̓•k̓, sk̓•sk̓•ak̓	scratched, torn up
(√sk̓ʷt)[379]	sk̓ʷt+lilx	float down
(√sl)[380]	sla+m, kɬ+sal	set, laid out, set table
(√sl)[381]	sul+t	frozen, cold
(√slp̓)[382]	slip̓	fire wood, wood.
(√slxʷ)	k+slxʷ	hit target

362 Cm q̓ʷac̓-st-xʷ *you fill s.t.*; Cr q̓ʷic̓ *full, replete.*
363 Sp n-q̓ʷic̓-tn *deceased brother or sister's living spouse.*
364 Sp q̓ʷl-im *roast, barbeque;* Cm q̓ʷl-m *to roast over a fire*; Cr q̓ʷal *char, singe*; Sh q̓ʷel.
365 Cm q̓ʷáɬt *to backpack, pack*; Cr q̓ʷeɬ *endurance (to have ...).*
366 Cm q̓ʷaʔ-q̓ʷuƛ̓-aʔ-xn-m *foot or horse race.*
367 Sp q̓ʷum(í) *piled up, stuffed.*
368 Sp q̓ʷum̓ *take, grab.*
369 Sp q̓ʷut, č-s-q̓ʷút=šn *one foot, one stocking, one shoe, one-legged*; Sh s-q̓ʷut *a half.*
370 Sp q̓ʷixʷ *slide, glide, unravel.*
371 Cr q̓ʷey̓ *dance, bounce.*
372 Cm q̓ʷuy̓ *be calm (wind).*
373 Sp q̓ʷay *black*; q̓ʷy=os *black face* (this form confirms an earlier pharyngeal); Cm q̓ʷiy *black*, q̓ʷay-l̓qs *priest*; Cr qʷiy=os *Negro*, q̓ʷid *blacken*; Sh q̓ʷiy, q̓ʷey - qʷy-q̓ʷiy-t *black* [no glottalization ?].
374 This and the following root may be one and the same.
375 Sp n-q̓ʷaq̓ʷ=épl=s-n-t-m *it was castrated.* See also Cr anqʷaʔqʷaʔepeʔst *geld[ing].*
376 Sp n-q̓ʷʔ=etkʷ-m *She laundered the clothes.*
377 Sp sic *new, right now.*
378 Sp sic̓m.
379 Cm nasúk̓ʷt *float on water*; Cr suk̓ʷ *float (... with current).*
380 Sp sil *to place more than one object*; č-sl-im *he set the table.*
381 Sp sul *cold*; Cr sul.
382 Cr slip̓ *woody.*

(√slxʷʔ)	sílxʷaʔ	big sg.
(√sl̓)	k+sl̓=íc̓aʔ	dappled grey
(√sl̓)[383]	sal̓+m, k+sl̓=íplaʔ, n+sl̓+p=qin	lost, distracted, puzzle, lose, dizzy, bastard, deceived
(√sɬqʷ)	sɬiqʷ	meat
(√smcxn)[384]	s+sm̓•m̓cxn=sqáx̌aʔ	mare
(√smpyr)	simupyár	man's name
(√smʔ)[385]	sámaʔ	white person
(√sn)[386]	sun=kʷ	island
(√sncʔ)[387]	sincaʔ	younger brother, brothers
(√sp)	sp=ikst	glove
(√spn)[388]	sipn	daughter-in-law
(√sp̓)[389]	sap̓+m=útyaʔ, sp̓=qin, sp̓=us+tn	thresh, hit, whip, club, sword, scythe, wheat
(√sp̓lk̓)[390]	si•sp̓lk̓	seven
(√sp̓ʔ)[391]	síp̓iʔ	hide, skin, buckskin
(√sq̓)[392]	siq̓+m, saq̓•q̓=cn	split, cut across, open wide
(√sr)[393]	k+sr=qin	scalp
(√st)[394]	n+st=ils	think, thought
(√st)	sut+n	thing
(√stm)[395]	saʔ•stám	brother-in-law, sister-in-law (of opposite sex).
(√sw) ?	swp=ilxʷ	itchy
(√sw)[396]	siw+st	drink
(√sw)[397]	siw, sw=ɬtiɬn, k+síw=plaʔ	ask, propose,ask for information
(√swɬ)[398]	siwɬ=kʷ	water
(√swt)[399]	swit	who (+ idiom), one, some one, somebody
(√swt)[400]	k+swít+miʔst	do one's best
(√sw̓)[401]	sw̓•aw̓	dry, water recedes
(√sw̓)	sn+si•sw̓=xn	socks

383 Sp sil̓ *wrong, lost, confused*; Cr sel *hazy, obscure ... complex, complicated, confused, intricate...*
384 Sp s-m̓úm̓c=šn *mare*.
385 Sp sém=eʔ *the French. French-Canadian Indian, taboo*; Cr hemeʔ *Frenchman*.
386 Sp čsúnkʷ; Cm k-sun-kʷ; Cr č+sún=kʷeʔ.
387 Sp sín=ceʔ; Cr sínceʔ; Sh síncе *younger sibling of opposite sex*.
388 Sp sépn; Sh sepn; Cr sipn.
389 Sp sp̓(í) *to hit with a stick, to beat, to club*.
390 Sp sisp̓l̓.
391 Sp síp̓y̓ *tanned hide*; Cr sip̓ey̓ *buckskin*; Sh səsp̓ey *skin*.
392 Sp saq̓(é) *cracked, split*; Cr saq̓ *split*; Sh siq̓-m *to break, crack*.
393 Sp sr̓, č-sr̓=álqʷ-n-t-xʷ *peel the bark off*; Cm k-sr-nt-xʷ *you skin, peel s.t.*; Sh sel, x-sl-qin-s *to scalp*.
394 Sp nt=éls *he thought*.
395 Sp seʔstém.
396 Cf √swɬ. See Sp n-soʔ-p-nú-n-t-xʷ *drink it all (sg)!*, sus *to drink*.
397 Sp sew; Cr sigʷ.
398 Cf √sw. Sp séwɬ=kʷ *water*.
399 Sp swet.
400 Sp č-s-w̓iʔt-m̓íst *he did his level best*.
401 Cf ? Sh t-sw-suw̓-t *dew*.

(√sx)[402]	sxa+p, sx+p=íc̓a?	air out, get the chills
(√sx^{w})[403]	súx^{w}=la?x^{w}+m, sx^{w}+nwix^{w}	recognize, acquaint, know, recognize, acquaintance
(√sx^{w})	súx^{w}=maʔ	measure, mile, map
(√sx^{w})[404]	sux^{w}•x^{w}	pl. leave
(√sx̌)[405]	k+sx̌a+n, ɬ+six̌+lx	move past, pass, move location, move, move something, pass through
(√sx̌^{w})[406]	ɬ+sax̌^{w}+t	downhill, runoff, go downhill, run off
(√sy)[407]	sy•sy=us	smart(s), power, smart, powerful
(√sy)[408]	sy=ups	tail
(√sẏ)[409]	sy•suẏ=kst+m	chilled, cold
(√sʕ)	saʕ+mncút, saʕ•sáʕ+t	dismount, descend, go down, go downhill, fall off
(√sʕnx^{w})	saʕ̓níx^{w}	Muskrat
(√sʕy)	n+saʕy=cn	interrupt
(√sʕy)[410]	sy+mncaʕt, sy•syaʕ+lx	make noise
(√sʔ)[411]	s•siʔ	uncle
(√th)[412]	thim	benefit
(√tkɬ)	n+tikɬ, tkɬ+m=ilx^{w},	bottom, down, bring down; woman, wife
(√tk̓)	k+tk̓=us+tn	gun sight
(√tk^{w})[413]	tk^{w}a+p	choke(d), breathe hard
(√tk^{w})[414]	t[ʔ]ik^{w}	spark
(√tk^{w}tn)	tk^{w}tan	tules
(√tk^{w}ʔ)[415]	tak^{w}ʔ=út	pl. walk, run, walk, travel, tracks
(√tl)[416]	k+til+m	entrust
(√tlk^{w})[417]	n+tlk^{w}=íɬc̓aʔ, n+tlk^{w}=ip	disembowel, uproot, gut, clean
(√tlt)[418]	k+tlt=íplaʔ	orphan, fail, worthless, weak
(√tlx^{w})[419]	til•tlx^{w}+t	difficult
(√tlʔ)	atláʔ, itlíʔ	from here, from there

402 Sp seš *to cool*; Cm sxxip *evening breeze*.
403 Sp sux^{w} *to know, to understand*; Cr sux^{w} *acquainted ...*
404 Sp hi súx^{w} *Everyone is suddenly gone!*; Cr súx^{w}+x^{w} *empty, vacated...*
405 Sp sax̌ *near*.
406 Sp n-sx̌^{w}-p=cín *saliva dribbled*; Cm na-sx̌^{w}-p *to leak (roof)*; Cr saʔx̌^{w} *dissolve, melt*.
407 Sp sy *smart, able, industrious*; Cr siy+siy=ús *astute, capable, clever, intelligent...*
408 Sp sups *tail*.
409 Sp suẏ *chilly*.
410 Sp say *the sound of voices*.
411 Sp síʔ; Cr s+síʔ *maternal uncle*.
412 Uncertain root and stem.
413 Sp tk^{w}-úp *he ran out of breath*; Cm tək^{w}p *to choke, smother, suffocate*; Cr tek̓^{w} *choke, smother ...* (also written as √tk^{w}); Sh ʔs-tuk^{w} *fall silent*; Th tək^{w}-p=áqs *smother, suffocate*.
414 Cm s-tiʔk^{w} *spark, tiny ember*; Sh tʔik^{w} *fire*.
415 Sp tk^{w}ʔú-t *they walked*.
416 Sp tel *to leave something in a safe place*; Cm k-talm-nt-x^{w} *you leave s.t. with s.o. for a while*.
417 See Sp s-n-tl=énč-m *gutted fish*.
418 Cr cəntluutíl̓š *he became an orphan*.
419 Sp til̓x^{w}; Cm tíl̓til̓x^{w}t.

(√tɬ)[420]	tiɬ+x, taɬ+t	stand (by), upright, straight, shorten, straighten, shortcut, rights, surely, in front of
(√tɬm)[421]	s+taɬm	boat
(√tm)[422]	k+tma=lxʷ, kɬ+tm=lxʷ+ncut, s+taʔm=ína?, taʔm=úlaʔxʷ	bare, strip, naked, clear, spring, springtime, snow melt
(√tm)[423]	s+tm=áliʔs	relatives
(√tmɬ)	timɬ	eight
(√tmnʔ)[424]	tm•tmniʔ	corpse, graveyard
(√tmxʷ)[425]	tmxʷ=úlaʔxʷ	land, country
(√tmxʷ)[426] see √tm	tmxʷ=lscut	wear out
(√tmxʷ)[427]	tmixʷ	creature
(√tm̓)[428]	s+tim, s+tim̓, sn+tim̓+tn	(some)thing, storage, what
(√tm̓)[429]	s+t•tm̓•tim̓, sn+t•tm̓•tim̓+tn, s+tm̓=lscut	wardrobe, clothing, clothes, regalia, stock, wealth, beads
(√tm̓)[430]	tum̓	w's mother
(√tnm̓)[431]	s+tanm̓=ús	for nothing, aimless, nothing, minimize
(√tnx)	s+tunx	beaver hide, beaver
(√tnx)[432]	tinx	sinew, muscle
(√tp)[433]	k+tp=ínaʔ, k̓ɬ+tap,k+tp=iɬxʷ+m	cover, (behind) curtain, build (cover?)
(√tq)[434]	k+tq=ínaʔ, tqa+m, tq=ip, tq+mi, tq•q+nun+m[435]	hold down, press, touch, protect, stack, place, dam, cheat, fool
(√tqp)[436]	k̓ɬ+tqp=ils+m	worry
(√tqp)[437]	s+tqp=iʔst+n	feather, wings

420 Sp teɬ *to lie face down*; Cm təɬ *be straight*. See also Cm ka(t)-tɬ *be level on top*; Cr teɬ *straight*.
421 Sp s-tíɬ-m; Cm s-təɬ-m; Cr s+téɬm.
422 Cm tam-wil̓x *s.t. disappears*; Sp č-tm=élxʷ *he's nude*, tiʔm=úleʔxʷ *spring season. The snow melted away off the ground*; Cr tim̓ *ground is clear of snow*; Th √tem *lack*.
423 Sp √tem, tétm̓-tn̓ *one's children's relatives*; Cm s-k-tam-qn *kin, relative*.
424 Sp tmtm-n=éẏ; Cm tm-tmn-aẏ; Cr tm+tmníʔ; Sh tumn *to get a dream-vision*.
425 Sh tmixʷ *land, country, world*; Th tmixʷ.
426 Cf ? Th tm̓əx ... *disappeared, vanished*.
427 Cr t+tm̓íxʷ *animal, beast, bird, cattle*.
428 Sp tem̓; Cm stam̓; Cr s+tim̓ *device*; Sh s-tem, s-tem̓y *what, something*.
429 Cm tm̓-tm̓-ut-(t)n, n-tm̓-tm̓-utn-tn *dresser*, s-tm̓-luscut *seed beads*; Sh s-tm-stitm̓; Th √tem̓ *dentalium*.
430 Sp tum (tum̓) *mother, suck*; Cm tum̓ *female's mother*.
431 Sp tnm̓ús *nothing*.
432 Cm tinx.
433 Cm k-tp-anaʔ-tn *comforter, coverlet*, n-tp-s-aɬxʷ-tn *curtain*; Cr taq *cover (with hand), deceive, fool, touch*.
434 Sp s-tq=ép, *a dam*, n-tq=ítkʷ-n-t-m *he was held underwater*, čɬ-tq=éneʔ-tn *piano, organ, typewriter, calculator*; Cm tq-nt-xʷ *you touch s.t.*, n-tq-aẁs *dam*, tq-anaʔ *to press down*; Sh tq-em.
435 Sp tqq-nu-n-c *he caught you off guard;* Cr taq, taqaqnúnn *I fooled him*.
436 Probably tq+p. See Sh tq-p-min-s *to wonder at stg*.
437 Cm s-tqp-aʔs-(t)-(t)n *feather*.

(√tqʷ)	k+tiqʷ=lqʷ	shine
(√tr)[438]	k+tr=iẁs	unravel, unstitch
(√trq)[439]	k+trq=iks	kick, dance
(√trwyʔ)	tríwyaʔ+m	react
(√tr̓)	k̓ɬ+tr̓•tr̓=qn+cut	not back down (?), keep at it (?)
(√tr̓)[440]	tr̓+mncut	form a line
(√tw)[441]	tiw=cn, s+tw+mist	trade, buy, store, grocery, merchandise, get groceries, sell
(√twn)[442]	k̓ɬ+twin, twn=asq̇t, s+tawn=qínaʔ=kst	short, (fall) short; "Short Day", little finger
(√twn)	tawn	town
(√tw(t))[443]	tẁ•tẁit	boy, baby s.o.
(√tx)	s+tx+min, tx•txa+m	comb
(√tx)[444]	txa+m	insert
(√txr)	txr=ut+m	run uphill
(√txʷ)[445]	tixʷ+kʷú=kst+m	say, utter, repeat
(√txʷ)[446]	tixʷ, taxʷ=ɬq	more, acquire, obtain, harvest, gather, contribution
(√txʷ)	sn+txʷ=us	cousin
(√tx̌)	tx̌=ilps	gray
(√tx̌ʷ)[447]	tx̌ʷ=iẁs	middle, divide, half, straight (up), normal, center, river, noon, lunch, straight, plain
(√tx̌ʷ)	kɬ+tx̌ʷ=wt=iẁs	Colville river
(√ty)[448]	tya+p	water runs
(√tyqʷ)[449]	tyaqʷ+m	fight
(√tʔ)	atáʔ, itíʔ	this, here, from here, that, there, from that
(√tʔ)[450]	taʔ+ɬ+wl•wlím	forge, pound
(√tʔ)[451]	tuʔ	herd
(√tʔw)[452]	s+tʔiw+t=x	youngest
(√tʔ)	t•tʔ=iwl=tk	on shore
(√t̓ċ)[453]	t̓iċ	wood pitch
(√t̓k)[454]	t̓kap	cry (?)

438 Sp √ter *come untied, feed, loosened*; Cm √tr; Cr tar *loosen, stretch out, extend, untie.*
439 Sp √taraq (talaq); Cm √tr̓q.
440 Th ʔes/tə̣̓l=qs *a lot of people strung out in a long line.*
441 Sp tew; Cm taw-ɬt-n *I buy s.t. from s.o.*; Cr tagʷ *buy* tegʷ *buy, sell.*
442 Sp tẁiṅ; Cr tegʷ *fail (to reach).*
443 Sp tew *little*, tʔew *younger, following*, ttẁ-ít; Cm tẁit; Cr ttẁít, tíweʔ *indulge*; Sh twit *to grow up.*
444 I see no clear cognate forms in the other Interior Salish languages, except perhaps Li √tixaʔ *narrow*, and Th √tx *thin, narrow.*
445 Sp ʔexʷ-kʷún-m *he said it, he talks in this manner.*
446 Sp tixʷ *to get, to obtain*, tuxʷ(ú) *to add*; Cr tíxʷ+m *obtain*; Sh s-təxʷ-st-es *to add to.*
447 Sp tox̌ʷ.
448 Cm tiyáx *to swim (fish).*
449 Sp tyaqʷ; Cr tiy̓eqʷ.
450 Sp teʔ(é); Cm taʔ-nt-xʷ *you pound food*; Cr tiʔ *hit, pound.*
451 Sp tuʔ *stuffed, crowded.*
452 Sp s-ttʔíẁ-t-i *the youngest*; Cm s-taʔaw-t *be youngest.*
453 Cm t̓iċ *pitch of a tamarack tree.*
454 See Cr t̓ekʷ *cry out, whinny.*

(√ťk)[455]	ťk=ikst+n, k+ťk•ťk=us	cane, prop, support
(√ťk̓l)[456]	ťik̓l	grub, provisions, lunch
(√ťk̓)[457]	s+ťik̓+t	high water, flood
(√ťkʷ)	c+ťkʷ•ťakʷ	bush
(√ťk̓ʷ)[458]	ťak̓ʷ, kɫ+ťk̓ʷ•ak̓ʷ, n+ťk̓ʷ+min	place something on, put down, settle, put (in), enter, saddle, envelope, post office, coffin, rest, resting place, fall, lie on
(√ťk̓ʷt)[459]	ťik̓ʷt	lake
(√ťl)[460]	ťl=úlaʔxʷ+tn	plow, tear, split lengthwise, burst, rip
(√ťl)	ťalaʔ+x+wílx[461]	next generation, come to life
(√ťl) See √ťɫ	s+ťúl=c̓aʔ[462]	mule
(√ťlt)	s+ťilt=x	Kutenai
(√ťlx̌ʷ) See √ťl	ťilx̌ʷ	tear apart
(√ťl̓)	ťul̓	fierce
(√ťɫ)[463]	ťiɫ, k+ť•ťɫ•ťaɫ	stick, glue
(√ťɫ)[464]	s+k+ťɫ•ɫ=íc̓aʔ	dirty
(√ťɫ)[465] See √ťl	s+ťúɫ=c̓aʔ	mule
(√ťm)[466]	c+n+ťam=ẃs=qn	grab
(√ťm)[467]	k̓ɫ+ťm=ʕas	suck, kiss
(√ťmkʔ)[468]	s+ťmkʔ=ilt	daughter
(√ťnʔ)[469]	ťínaʔ	ear
(√ťp)	n+ťp=qs+am	tip, bend
(√ťp)[470]	ťap	object lies, place on, load, stack, lie on, lump
(√ťp)[471]	s+n+ťp=ink	gun
(√ťpʔ)[472]	ťaʔ•ťúpaʔ	great grandfather
(√ťq)[473]	kɫ+ťaq, kɫ+ťqa+m, n+ťq=cin, n+ťq+mi, s+ťq=ilp	lie, throw sheet-like object, mattress, load, stack, full
(√ťq)	ťq=iɫmlx	thorn bushes

455 Cm k̓ɫ-ťk-cin *to prop up, brace,* ťk-aks(t)-(t)n *cane*; Sh s-ťək-st-es *to support, prop up.*
456 Sp ťečl̓ *lunch*; Cm s-ťk̓ʷal-tn *travel food, packed lunch*; Cr s+ťíčl̓ *provisions (travelling...).*
457 Sp ťeč̓ *to flood*; Sh x-tek̓-m *to fill with liquid.*
458 Cr u+ťék̓ʷ *bedridden...* (lit. *he just lies down all the time).*
459 Cm ťak̓ʷt.
460 Sp ťil̓; Cm ʔacťél ʔac-ťl *be torn,* ťal̓-nt-xʷ *you slice s.t.*; Cr ťel̓ *rip, tear*; Sh ťl-úleʔxʷ-m *to plough.*
461 Sp s-ťll√s-qéliʔxʷ *the beginning of the two legged people world and the ending of the animal world.*
462 Sp s-ťul=c̓eʔ *muledeer*; Cm s-ťul-ɫc̓aʔ *mule.*
463 Cr ťoɫ *lumpy, sticky*; Sh ťeɫ-n-s *to stick on, paste, glue.*
464 Sp ťiɫ; Cm ťəɫ *be dirty*; Cr s+ťéɫ+ɫ *blotch.*
465 See Cr s-ťún=ɫc̓eʔ
466 Sp č-ťám=q-n *I grabbed his hair.*
467 Sp ťm=ós-n (the o confirms the earlier pharyngeal); Cm ťum-nt-xʷ *you suck s.t. out*; Cr ťaṁ *kiss, lick.* See also Cr tum *pump, suck (e.g. through a tube)...* (xref √ťṁ).
468 Probably analyzable √ťm=kʔ. Sp s-ťm=čʔ=élt *daughter, niece (woman's sister's daughter)*; Cm s-ťámk-aʔ *daughter*; Cr s+ťímčeʔ *daughter.*
469 Sp ťéneʔ; Cm ťánaʔ; Cr ť(=)íneʔ *ear.*
470 Sp ťp(í) *upright (pl)...*; Cm ʔacťép ʔac-ťəp *be lying there.*
471 This may be √ťp *object lies.*
472 Sp ťeťúpeʔ; Cr ťupye *great grandfather.*
473 Cr ťaq *lie (bushy objects).*

(√ťql)[474]	ťql=imx	settle, make camp, stop, move to
(√ťq̓)	ťaq̓m	cross (a stream), six
(√ťq̓)	ť•ťáʔq̓aʔ+t	short
(√ťq̓)	n+ťaq̓+m	valley, six (cross), cross stream
(√ťq^{w})[475]	k̓ł+ťaq̓^{w}	sew
(√ťq^{w})	ťiq^{w}=lq^{w}	tall
(√ťq^{w})[476]	ťiq^{w}=kst+m	shoot, explosion
(√ťq^{w})[477]	ťaʔq^{w}=cín, ťq^{w}=cin	honk, holler, yell at
(√ťq^{w})[478]	ťq^{w}=ap=qn	slap
(√ťq̓^{w})[479]	n+ťaq̓^{w}+p=íwt	riley (water)
(√trq̓^{w})[480]	ťraq̓^{w}	come down
(√ťsq̓^{w})[481]	ťsaq̓^{w}	bored
(√ťws) ?	ťiws	flat
(√ťwst)	ťwist	horse stall, barn, stand (up), stand in line
(√ťx)	s+ťx=ałq, s+ťx=itk^{w}	huckleberry, soup
(√ťx)	ťix+lx	come to shore
(√ťx^{w}l)[482]	ťix^{w}•x^{w}+l+m	different
(√ťx^{w}t)[483]	ťux^{w}+t	fly
(√ťx̌)	ťx̌iw+t+wilx	next year
(√ťy)[484]	ťiyá+m, ťy+ťy+m+uł	dispute, disobey, refuse to, lazy
(√ťym)	ťi•ťym	easy
(√ťʕm)[485]	s+ťm=ʕalt	cow
(√ťʕp)[486]	ťaʕp, ťaʕp+sqílx^{w}, sn+ťp=ink	shoot, (load to) shoot
(√ťʔ)	ťaʔ•ťʔ=úlaʔx^{w}	level (ground)
(√ťʔk)[487]	s+ťaʔk̓+míx	virgin, maiden
(√ťʔl)	n+ťaʔl=íls[488]	satisfied, settle one's feelings
(√ťʔʔ)	s+ťʔiʔ	grass
(√wh)[489]	wahá+m, sx^{w}=wah•wáh+m	holler, announce(r)
(√wk)[490]	wik	look, see
(√wkn)[491]	wkna=qín	Okanagan

474 Cf. Cm ťq-t+ ał+ ʔim̓x *to move camp, relocate.*
475 Sp ťoq̓^{w}(ú); Sh ťəq^{w}ʔ-um.
476 Cr ťeq^{w} *explode, burst.* See Cm ťk^{w}-p *to burst, explode.*
477 Possibly one root √ťq^{w} *holler, sound of (slap).* Cm ťq^{w}-čin.
478 Cm ťq^{w}-nt-x^{w} *you slap s.t.*; Cr ťaq^{w} *slap.*
479 Sp ťiq̓^{w} *roiled up, muddy looking water*; Sh x-təq^{w}-tiq̓^{w} *dirty, muddy (of water).*
480 See Sp ťroq̓^{w} *to run from danger*; Cr s+ťark^{w} *flee, fleeing.*
481 Cr ťasq̓^{w} *weary (with waiting).*
482 Cr ťix^{w}l *abnormal, different.*
483 Sp ťux^{w}t; Sh ťux^{w}t.
484 Cm ťiy-m *to not want to do s.t.; to refuse.*
485 Sp s-ťm̓=áʔ; Cr s+ ťm̓a *buffalo, cow.*
486 Sp ťap(í); Cm ťəpm *to thunder*; Cr ťap *shoot*; Sh ťap(í).
487 Cr s+ťiyč+miš.
488 Cf? Th ƛ̓[ʔ]lúý ...*keep calm...*; Li ƛ̓ul̓ *calm.*
489 Sp weʔ; Cm wahm *to bark (dog)*; Cr wih *bark*; Sh x-wey-m *to bark (at).*
490 Sp wič; Cm wik-ɬ-nt-x^{w} *you see s.o.*
491 Sp sʔučnaʔqíni.

(√wkʷ)[492]	wikʷ	hide, backbite, secret
(√wl)[493]	wla+p, k+wl=us	light, burn
(√wl)	n+wil=ẇs	lots
(√wl)	wil=qn, wl=qn=ałq	have a chance
(√wl)	k+w•wl=ína?, wl•wl=qin	cover, canned goods
(√wlm)[494]	wl•wlim, n+wl•wlm=ús=a?st, s+wl•wlm=ink, sn+ta?+ł+wl•wlím+tn	arrow points, hard points, gun, iron, blacksmith, forge, nail
(√wl?xʷ)	s+wa?•wíla?xʷ	man's name
(√wľ)[495]	waľ=cn+míst, waľ=íkst+m, n+wa?l=íls+m	talk funny, trick, do magic, puzzle, admire
(√wnx)[496]	s+wanx	war dance
(√wnxʷ)[497]	wnixʷ, n+wn•n•xʷ=ína?	believe, true, religion, belief, sure
(√wp)[498]	wp=cin, s+wp=úla?xʷ, k+wp=íċa?, n+wap=áqs; wap•wp=xn	thick growth, beard, hay, body hair, grassy; lynx
(√wp)[499]	n+wi•wp+m	back up
(√wq̓m)[500]	wq̓im	moonlight
(√wṙ)[501]	waṙ, k̓ł+wṙ=usx, s+wṙ=islṗ	fire, burn, stove, fireplace
(√ws)[502]	wis+t, wa?s=núxʷ, kł+n+ws+lx+ilx	mountains, (sun) up high, morning, late, off the ground, brag, high, rise, upward, jump, raise
(√ws)[503]	wis=xn	long(est)
(√ws?)[504]	wása?	aunt
(√wt)[505]	c+wta+n	place, put (down)
(√wt)[506]	s+wit	someone
(√wx)[507]	wix, ẇí•ẇa?x, wa?x=útya?	dwell, live
(√wxʷ)[508]	n+wxʷ•xʷ=ink	hang uneven
(√wxʷ)	wxʷa+p	burn

492 Sp wekʷ; Cm wakʷ.
493 Sp s-?ul-ip, √wir (wil) *to burn*; Sh wl-em.
494 Cm s-wlm-ink *gun*; Cr wl+wlím *aluminum, argent, capital, coin, metal, money, silver*.
495 Sp wiľ *strange, silly, foolish*; Cm n-wľ-łċa?-nčut *to fantasize, imagine*; Cr ẇeľ *clownish, silly, unnatural*.
496 Sp wenš; Cr winš.
497 Sp winxʷ *plainly visible*.
498 Sp wup *hairy, fuzzy*.
499 Sp n-wéw-p-m *he backed up*.
500 Cr sgʷaq̓íṁ *moonlight*.
501 Sp wir (wil) *to burn*.
502 Sp n-wis-t *it's up high*.
503 Sp wis=šn *it's long*.
504 Cm łwasn *aunt or uncle when connecting parent is dead*.
505 Cm swətn *thing; place*.
506 Sp swét; Cm s-wat; Sh s-wet-(ẏ) *who, somebody*.
507 Cr wiš *build, raise poles*.
508 Sp wuxʷ *hung up*, nwíxʷ=ne? *her hair has come unbraided.*

(√wx̌t)[509]	wx̌t=íłaʔt	baby
(√wx̌ʷ)	n+wx̌ʷ•x̌ʷ+t=iʔst	gallop
(√wy̓)[510]	way̓, s+wy̓+numt	yes, complete, finish, ready, stop; handsome, put together
(√wyp)[511]	s+wyapy=x	white person, English, white man
(√wʕ)	waʕ+m=úlaʔxʷ	thaw
(√wʔ)[512]	waʔ•wáʔ+m	announce
(√w̓k)[513]	s+w̓•w̓ík=iʔst	electricity
(√xk̓)[514]	xik̓•k̓	miss, mistake
(√xk̓)	xik̓•xk̓+t	spry
(√xl)[515]	xʔal, n+xil=s	about to appear, soon, edge of
(√xl)	n+xl=aw̓s=qn	chop, cut off
(√xlk)[516]	t+xlak, xlk+iʔs	go around, turn around, (pass) around, go in a circle, race track, bend in path, go around curves
(√xƛ̓)[517]	xiƛ̓, xƛ̓a+p, xƛ̓+p=úlaʔxʷ, n+xƛ̓=iks, xƛ̓•aƛ̓	all, complete, full, entire, even, level, mature, grown, all kinds of, in a row
(√xƛ̓)[518]	xƛ̓a+p	lose, beat, win
(√xmn)	n+xmn=iw̓s[519]	two sides, both sides, each side
(√xn)	k̓ł+xn•xn=ink	side hill, place name
(√xn)[520]	n+xn=s=iłxʷ+tn	window
(√xp)[521]	t+xp=alqʷ	chew, gnaw
(√xp)	xəp	suck in
(√xr)[522]	k̓ł+xar, k̓ł+n+xar+p+tn	curtain, door flap, dangle, drape
(√xr)[523]	t+xir•r+p, t+xr=ut+m, xr•xr=úlaʔxʷ	run uphill, climb,steep
(√xr)[524]	xar=kst+m	take, waste time

509 Cm wx̌t-alt *infant*; Cr gʷáx̌-t-elt *a young offspring, a young person*.
510 Sp wiy̓ *to finish*, s-wiʔ-núm̓t-i *she is beautiful, he is handsome*; Cm ʔac-wy̓ *be finished*, s-wy̓-num-t-əxʷ *be handsome, beautiful*; Cr s+wiʔ *goodlooking, handsome (ref to persons only)*.
511 Sp suyépi *whiteman*; Cr s+wiyép+mš=mš *acculturation, civilization*.
512 Sp weʔ *call, shout, holler*; Cr wiʔ *announced ... (Lit. town crier in Indian village)*; Sh wew-m *to call, holler to sb.*
513 Sp s-ʔuw̓éč-ń-t.
514 Sp šič̓ *to miss*; Cm s-xik̓-k̓-əxʷ *be making a mistake*; Cr šič̓ *miss (the target)*; Sh xik̓-m *to miss a target*.
515 Sp šʔel *to draw near to*.
516 Cm xəlk *to go around*.
517 Sp šiƛ̓ *straight, lined up in a row*; Cr šiƛ̓ *flat, smooth, level, even*.
518 Sp šƛ̓(i) *to beat in a competition, to win*; Cm xƛ̓-p *be defeated; to lose a bet*.
519 Sp šm=ń=uʔs=ús *a double bitted axe*, šmšm=n=oʔs=áyaʔ=qn *a double-headed snake*.
520 Sp šiń *sheet (of solid, flat material)*, s-n-šń=s=éłxʷ-tn *a window pane*.
521 Sp √šp(í) *gnaw*; Cm xp-nt-xʷ *you eat, chew on s.t.*
522 Sp šer (šal) *to hang*; Cm n-xr-s-ałxʷ-tn *curtain*; Sh xal-m *to partition off by hanging up a mat, curtain, etc.*
523 Cm xr̓-xr̓-t *be steep; steep bank*; Cr šár+šar+t *arduous, difficult, steep*.
524 Sh xal *short of breath*.

(√xs)	k̓ɬ+xas[525]	disappear
(√xs)	xs-nú-	miss
(√xt)	n+xat=qn+m	sing
(√xt)[526]	xít+mi?st	pl run, run around
(√xt̓)[527]	k̓ɬ+xt̓•xt̓=ax̌, n+xt̓=ɬq̓it	hit (with bullet), let arrow go, shoot
(√xt̓)[528]	t+xt̓a+m, t+xt̓+mist, t+xt̓•t̓=i?st	take care of, care for, join in, protect, pregnant, watch, be careful, owe, aim
(√xt̓)[529]	t+xt̓•at̓	join
(√xt̓)	xat̓=ls+míst	be fooled
(√xwl)	sn+t+ql+ɬ+xwil+tn	place name
(√xwɬ)[530] See √xwl	xwiɬ	road
(√xwtm)[531]	xi•xwtm	girl
(√xy)	n+xy•xay=áplqs	end of story
(√xy̓)[532]	xy̓+mscut, xy̓+wílx, n+xy̓=íls+m, k̓ɬ+xy̓=us+s+t, t+xy̓=xán	done in, tired of; pass by, conform, be mixed with, amidst, straight through
(√x?)[533]	axá?, ixí?	this, that
(√x?)	k+n+xa?=cín+m	on the way
(√x?)[534]	s+xi?+míx	whatever
(√x?)	t+xí•xi?	fall short
(√x?)	x?=ína?	consent, go along with
(√x?l)[535]	xa?l+s+qíɬ+t	near, almost
(√x?m)[536]	x?im+scút, s+x?im+ɬ+sílx^{w}a?	at the limit; best, superlative (in compounds)
(√x?mx^{w})[537]	n+xa?mx^{w}=cín	Moses Columbia language
(√x?t)[538]	c+xí?t+mist	run
(√x?t)[539]	c+x?it, xa?t=ús, n+xa?=cín	first, ancestor, go first, first, original, leader, oldest, older relative. in front, ahead
(√x?y)[540]	n+xa?y=áwa?	in the midst
(√x?y)	xy•xa?y=áplqs	end story; go to the bathroom
(√x^{w}ċ)[541]	x^{w}iċ	give

525 Th s[?]éx *[of odor, smell] get (very) weak; fade away, dissipate, disappear.*
526 Sp šet *run in every direction*; Sh xət-xn-em *to walk around.*
527 Cf? Cr šet̓ *beat, win.*
528 Sp čšt̓(í), šit(í) *to care for, to tend to, to nurse*, hec-č-št̓-mí *she's pregnant*; Cm txt̓-nt-x^{w} *you take care of, look after s.o.*; Cr šet̓; Sh c-xet̓ ... *guard (e.g. at open fence-gate)*,
529 Sh xet̓ t-xət̓et̓(-m) *to join, fall in with (a herd).*
530 Sp šu?šẃ=éɬ *a road, a route*; Cm xwal *road, trail*; Cr hnšég^{w}el *path, trail* ...; Th xwéɬ, xẃeɬ.
531 Sp šéẃ-t-m; Cr šiẃtm.
532 Sp šy̓ús *to pass by, to take a route*; š?el *to draw near to.*
533 Cm l-xa? *here*, ?i-xa? *this one here.*
534 Sp ši?-miš.
535 Sp š?el *to draw near to.*
536 Cm mi?áš *most, might.*
537 Cm nxa?amxcín.
538 Sp šet-ṁí?st *they (a couple of people or so) ran in every direction*; Sh xet *go, walk, be energetic.*
539 Sp š?-ít *he's the first one*; Cm s-c-x?it *be first*; Cr ši?t *firstborn, oldest.*
540 Sp (?) šey̓ *that, together, grouped.*
541 Sp x^{w}iċš. See also Cr x^{w}iċ *indicate, point out*; Sh x^{w}iċ-n-s *to show.*

(√xʷċ)	xʷ•xʷċ=xin+m, s+xʷ•xʷċ=xin[542]	raise up (leg), pee (Reverse of ċxʷ)
(√xʷkʷ)[543]	c+xʷukʷ	pull
(√xʷkʷ)[544] See xʷk̓ʷ	xʷikʷ	tan hides
(√xʷk̓ʷ)[545]	n+xʷuk̓ʷ=ẁs	clean (up), deserted
(√xʷl)[546]	xʷl•xʷal+t	(a)live, livelyhood
(√xʷl)	s+xʷul=łxʷ	tipi
(√xʷl)[547]	xʷl•xʷilt	debt, owe
(√xʷl)[548]	xʷ[ʔ]ul	steam
(√xʷƛ̓)	n+xʷaʔ•xʷaʔƛ̓=íłċaʔ	have enough
(√xʷƛ̓)[549]	xʷiƛ̓=xn+m	whittle
(√xʷṁ)	t+xʷṁ=qn+cut[550]	forget
(√xʷp)[551]	k̓ł+xʷip, s+xʷip=lp	mat, rug, spread on ground, liner
(√xʷr)	n+xʷ•xʷr̓=us	hollow, low place
(√xʷr)[552]	s+t+xʷar=qn	reach
(√xʷr)[553]	xʷr•ra+p	nervous, anxious
(√xʷs)[554]	s+xʷús•s+kaʔ+m, xʷs=maʔ=cín+m, xʷs•xʷus+lx	rush, in a hurry, quick, early
(√xʷst)[555]	xʷist	walk, travel around, go on foot
(√xʷt)[556]	xʷt•xʷt	unhappy with
(√xʷt')[557]	c+xʷt'u+p, xʷt'+p=us, xʷt'+ilx	jump, run, chase, grab, run after, get up, hurry, run
(√xʷw)[558]	xʷiw	whistle
(√xʷy)[559]	xʷuy	go, vehicle, travel, walk, step, wander, tracks, time go by, behave, take s.t.
(√xʷy)[560]	s+xʷuy+nt	ice
(√xʷẏ)[561]	xʷaẏ	reproach

542 Sh t-xʷəċ-xn-ten *dog-piss*.
543 Sp xʷukʷ *to pull out*; Sh xʷukʷ *to pull something out of a pile*. Also Sh (s)-t-xʷuk̓ʷ-m *to pull out (e.g. nail, feather)*.
544 Recorded also as xʷk̓ʷ. Cf. Li xʷík̓ʷ-iṅ *to polish s.t. (by rubbing polish on it); to spread ointment, medicine on s.t.*
545 Sp xʷuk̓ʷ(ú) *clean, clear*; Cm na-xʷuk̓ʷ *be clean, clear, empty*; Cr qt:xʷek̓ʷ *clean, sweep*.
546 Sp hec-xʷlxʷíl-t *he's alive*; Cm s-xʷl-xʷl-t *life*; Cr xʷel *alive*; Sh xʷl-xʷel-t *well, allright*.
547 Sp xʷlxʷi'lt *a debt*; Cr xʷel-xʷl-t *debt*.
548 Sp xʷul̓.
549 Sp xʷƛ̓(í); Cm xʷƛ̓-xʷaƛ̓-ákst-m *to whittle*; Sh xʷiƛ̓-n-s *to cut (up)...*
550 Sp hec-xʷṁ=qn-cút-i *he's deep in thought*.
551 Sp xʷep; Cm xʷṗ-nt-xʷ *you unfold s.t.*; Sh xʷep-n-s *to unfold...*
552 Sp xʷer̓ *to hand over*.
553 Sp xʷrxʷér-t *he's always trembling with excitement*; Cr xʷar *to quiver, tremble*.
554 Cm xʷus-s *be in a hurry*.
555 Sp xʷist.
556 Sp xʷet (xʷit) *to hate, to be mean*; Cm n-xʷt-xʷt-lwas *be hateful, bad tempered*.
557 Sp xʷt'(í) *to run, to arise*; Cm xʷət'p *to escape, run away, take off*.
558 Cm xʷiw-m; Sh xʷiw-m.
559 Sp xʷuy; Cr xʷuy.
560 Sp s-xʷúy-n=tkʷ; Cm s-xʷuy-n-tk; Cr s+x̌ʷdent *ice cream, ice*; Sh s-xʷuy-nt.
561 Sp xʷeẏ *to scold severely*.

(√xʷʔ)[562]	xʷʔi+t,[563] xʷʔ=asq̇t, xʷaʔ+s+mík̓ʷt	lots, many, much, big, several
(√xʷʔ)[564]	xʷaʔ, xʷʔ=ilt+m	hold in hands, hold a baby, pick st up
(√xʷʔ)	n+xʷ•xʷʔ=ítaʔkʷ	Meteor
(√xʷʔ)[565]	s+xʷaʔ•xʷaʔ=nk=íɬp	thornbush
(√x̌c)[566]	s+x̌ac, x̌ca+m, sn+x̌c=ip+m	bet
(√x̌c)[567]	n+x̌c=ip+m	cut low (to the ground)
(√x̌c)[568]	s+x̌c+mncut, n+x̌c=ilst+n	attire, dress, get ready, dressed, ready (weapon)
(√x̌c)[569]	x̌c•c=ikst	hundred
(√x̌c)[570]	s+x̌c+ut, x̌c+twixʷ	companion
(√x̌c̓)[571]	x̌c̓•x̌ac̓+t, x̌c̓=cn+mist, x̌c̓=ikst+m	sacred, serious, important, surprise
(√x̌c̓ʔ)[572]	s+x̌•x̌c̓iʔ	stick, stalk
(√x̌l)[573]	t+x̌l=iẇs	cache, cover, board, porch, plank, bridge, side board, platform, floor
(√x̌l)[574] See √x̌ɬ	n+x̌il+m, n+x̌la+wlx	fear, scare(d)
(√x̌l)[575]	x̌la+p, s+x̌l•x̌aʕl+t, n+x̌l=s=ʕáɬc̓aʔ+tn, k̓ɬ+x̌•x̌l=ʕas+m	day, daylight, morning, bright, glitter, tomorrow, window, clear, red hot, watch for
(√x̌lt)[576]	x̌lit	call, summon, invite, ask
(√x̌lwʔ)[577]	s+x̌ílwiʔ	husband
(√x̌ɬ)[578] See √x̌l	n+x̌iɬ	afraid
(√x̌ƛ̓)[579]	x̌iƛ̓+m, s+x̌iƛ̓=xn[580]	climb, uphill, trousers, incline, hill
(√x̌m)[581]	x̌m=ink	love(r), want, like

562 Sp xʷeʔí *many*.
563 Cm xʷiʔít *many, lots.*
564 Sh xʷʔ-im *to lift up.*
565 Cm sxʷaʔník *thornberry.*
566 Sp √x̌c(í) *to gamble*; Cr x̌ac; Sh x̌c-em.
567 Cf. Sp √x̌ect *to dig roots.*
568 Sp √x̌c(í) *to get dressed, to get ready*; Cr x̌ec.
569 Cm x̌c-c-akst *one hundred.*
570 Sp √x̌c(í), s-x̌c-út.
571 Sp x̌ic̓ *staring wide-eyed, awed,* x̌c̓x̌éc̓-t *it is to be held in awe*; Cr x̌ac̓ *extraordinary, outstanding.*
572 Possibly √x̌c̓y̓. Sh s-x̌c̓ey *wood, log, stick.*
573 Sp x̌el *long objects (poles or logs) are laid next to each other,* x̌l-ém *he built a cover*; Cm n-x̌l-aẇš *bridge.*
574 Sp x̌el.
575 Many stems based on this root show pharyngeal intrusion, e.g. s+x̌l•x̌aʕl+t *day*. Sp x̌al(í) *to be light, to be clear*; Cm x̌əl *be clear, lit.*
576 Cm x̌lit-nt-xʷ *you invite, call s.o.*
577 Sp s-x̌élwiʔ; Sh sx̌élwe.
578 Sp n-x̌eɬ *he was afraid.*
579 Li x̌aƛ̓-əm *to climb a hill or ladder.*
580 Sp s-x̌éƛ̓=iʔ=šn *trousers*; Cm s-x̌aƛ̓-u-xn *trousers.*
581 Sp x̌m=énč-m *he likes something*; Cm x̌m-ank-nt-xʷ *you like s.t. or s.o.*; Cr x̌em=inč *to like, love.*

(√x̌ṅ)[582]	x̌ṅ+numt	get hurt
(√x̌ṅt)[583]	x̌•x̌ṅut	nine
(√x̌pʔ)[584]	s+x̌á•x̌paʔ	grandfather
(√x̌p̓)[585]	t+x̌p̓=iẁs, k̓ɬ+n+x̌p̓=ip	fasten, stitch
(√x̌q)[586]	x̌•x̌aq, t+x̌q=iẁs	step aside, empty, open, clear
(√x̌q̓)[587]	s+x̌aq̓•q̓, t+x̌áq̓=plaʔ	wages, pay, reward
(√x̌s)[588]	x̌as+t, x̌is,[589] k̓ɬ+x̌s=ink, x̌aʔs=íkst+miʔ	good, (get) well, satisfy, lucky, good (aim), side hill
(√x̌ẁ)[590]	x̌ẁa+p, x̌ẁ•aẁ	dry
(√x̌ẁ)[591]	x̌ẁ•x̌ẁ=us	eager
(√x̌yɬ)	x̌•x̌yaɬ=nxʷ	month, sun, moon, sundown, menstruate, hour, clock, watch
(√x̌ʕ)[592]	x̌aʕ+p	cool draft
(√x̌ʔ)	n+x̌aʔ•x̌ʔ=ítkʷ[593]	(water) monster
(√x̌ʔ)	s+x̌áʔ•x̌aʔ[594]	father-in-law
(√x̌ʔ)	x̌aʔ•x̌áʔ, x̌aʔ•x̌aʔ+scút[595]	sacred, great, self important
(√x̌ʔ)	x̌•x̌ʔ=iɬp[596]	thorn bush
(√x̌ʔn)[597]	x̌aʔn, s+x̌aʔn=úxʷ+m, t+x̌aʔn=cn+míst, t+x̌aʔn=íplaʔ	stop, keep from
(√x̌ʷc̓)[598]	x̌ʷc̓a+m, x̌ʷc̓a+p, x̌ʷíc̓=laʔxʷ+tn, sn+x̌ʷuc̓•c̓+tn	mow, cut, break (in two)
(√x̌ʷckʷ)[599]	n+x̌ʷ•x̌ʷickʷ	slice, cut
(√x̌ʷl)[600]	x̌ʷil, k̓ɬ+x̌ʷil, x̌ʷl=úlaʔxʷ+m	drive off, discard, abandon, leave, disregard, devil, throw away, garbage

582 Sp x̌ṅ, čn x̌ṅ-núṁt *I had an accident, I hurt myself*; Sh x̌éne *to be hurt.*
584 Cr x̌ípeʔ *grandfather (paternal)*; Sh x̌péʔe.
583 Sp x̌x̌ṅut; Cm x̌-x̌ṅut; Cr x̌a+x̌aṅ+út.
585 Sp x̌ep̓(í) *to lace, to weave, to baste*; Cm x̌əp̓-nt-xʷ *you join, stitch together s.t.*; Cr x̌ep̓ *button, fasten, sew*; Sh x̌p̓-em *to stitch up, join together.*
586 Sp x̌aq *to make room.*
587 Cm x̌aq̓-nt-xʷ *you pay s.o.*
588 Th √x̌əs *favorable*, x̌s=ékst *good with one's hands, skillful.*
589 Sp x̌es (x̌is); Cm x̌əst; Cr x̌es.
590 This root may be cognate with √x̌w-like roots in the other IS language, all glossed as *raw*.
591 See Sp hi x̌ʷuʔ *he's eager to please*.
592 Sp hec-x̌aʕ-p-mí *it's beginning to cool off*; Cm s-x̌aʕ-p *breeze, wind.*
593 Cm n-x̌aʔ-x̌aʔ-atkʷ *water monster.*
594 Cm ʔas-x̌aʔ-x̌aʔ.
595 Cm x̌aʔ-x̌aʔ *be powerful.*
596 See ? Cm x̌x̌iẏ *thornberry*.
597 Sp x̌eʔn *to warn, to caution, to forbid, taboo*; Sh x̌ʔen *to forbid, scold.*
598 Cm x̌ʷc̓am *to break (stick)*.
599 The root may be √x̌ʷc̓kʷ. Sp x̌ʷic *to cut in a swath.*
600 Sp x̌ʷel.

(√x̌ʷλ̓)[601]	k̓ł+x̌ʷiλ̓, x̌ʷλ̓•x̌ʷiλ̓=xn	whittle, shuck, break
(√x̌ʷλ̓ʔ)[602]	s+x̌ʷλ̓iʔ	goat
(√x̌ʷn)	s+x̌ʷn=itkʷ,[603] n+x̌ʷn=tkʷ=itkʷ	Colville, Columbia River, Kettle River
(√x̌ʷp)[604]	x̌ʷup+t	worthless, weak
(√x̌ʷq̓ʷ)[605]	x̌ʷaq̓ʷ+mn, t+x̌ʷaq̓ʷ=lqs	mill, grind; snore
(√x̌ʷs)[606]	n+x̌ʷus=kʷ, t+x̌ʷus•s	beer, foam, soapberry
(√x̌ʷst)	c+x̌ʷ•x̌ʷst=us	downhill
(√x̌ʷy)	x̌ʷy•x̌ʷy+s+c̓im	man's name
(√x̌ʷy)[607]	x̌ʷy•x̌ʷay+t	sharp
(√x̌ʷy)	n+x̌ʷay=qn[608]	poles tied together, tipi
(√x̌ʷy)[609]	t+x̌ʷay=qn	pile
(√x̌ʷyʔ)[610]	n+x̌ʷyaʔ=łp=ítkʷ	Kettle Falls
(√x̌ʷʔ)[611]	s+x̌ʷʔ=iłp=x	Colville
(√yk̓ʷ)[612]	n+y̓ak̓ʷ, s+yaʔk̓ʷ=áqs	across, mid (winter)
(√yl)[613]	yl=mixʷ+m	chief
(√yl)[614]	yla+p, yl+p=iʔst, s+k+yla+p	be hit, hit target, mouth or junction of rivers
(√yl)[615]	yul+t, s+yl̓•yúl̓+aʔt	big around, circumference
(√yl)[616]	yal+t, c+yl•yl+min	run away, drive, send
(√yl)	yil	force something
(√ylq)	ylq	uncover
(√ylw)[617]	yilw, k+ylw=íc̓aʔ, s+yílw+iʔ	stitch, twist, bushel
(√ylxʷ)[618]	k̓ł+ylxʷ=ip	lower door flap
(√yl̓)	sn+yal̓+mn	Montana
(√ym)[619]	s+yum=cn	curse
(√ym)[620]	yúm+miʔst, ym̓•m̓+scut	move, make a motion, helpless

601 Sp x̌ʷiλ̓-t *it's splintered into pieces.*
604 Sp x̌ʷup *lazy, unskilled, weak*; Cm x̌ʷupt; Cr x̌ʷup *careless, inefficient*; Sh s-x̌ʷup-t-x *dumb, stupid, good-for-nothing.*
603 Cm s-x̌ʷní-tkʷ-əxʷ *Kettle Falls Indians*; Cr s-x̌ʷen=ítkʷeʔ *rapids, hurrying water.*
602 Sp s-xʷλ̓=éy̓ *mountain goat.* See Cm s-x̌ʷiy-awt-əxʷ *mountain goat.*
605 Sp x̌ʷaq̓ʷ *to pulverize, to grind, grinding sound*, x̌ʷoq̓ʷ ... *sound of snoring*; Cm x̌ʷaq̓ʷ-mn *grinder*, x̌ʷuq̓ʷ-m *to snore*; Cr x̌ʷaq̓ʷ; Sh x̌ʷuq̓l-əqs *to snore.*
606 Sp x̌ʷus *soapy, foamy*; Cm s-x̌ʷuš-m *foamberries*; Cr x̌ʷus; Sh x̌ʷus *foam.*
607 Sp x̌ʷiy; Cm x̌ʷiy-x̌ʷiy-t *be sharp (edge)*; Sh x̌ʷey sharp.
608 Cm n-x̌ʷaʔ-x̌ʷ-ayaʔ-qn *tipi.*
609 Cm t-x̌ʷay-qn-(n)t-xʷ *you pile up s.t.*
610 Not clear how this root is related to √x̌ʷʔ.
611 Cm sx̌ʷuy̓áłpm *people from Ft. Colville area (now known as Colvilles)*; Cr s+x̌ʷiy=íʔłp=mš *Colville tribes.*
612 Sp yek̓ʷ(ú) *passed, to take across*; Cm n-yk̓ʷ-lx-us *to cross a road.*
613 Sp yl=mixʷ-m; Cm yl-mixʷ-m; Cr yilmíxʷ+m.
614 Sp yil(í), yl-p-nú-n *I accidentally hit it*, s-č-yl-íp *junction of two rivers (or roads).*
615 Sp yúl-t *it's thick at its circumference.* See Sh yulqʷ *thick (of cylindrical objects).*
616 Cm ylam *to run (pl).*
617 Sp yilw *twisted.*
619 Sp √yum̓ *superstition.*
620 See Sp √yum̓ *to move involuntarily*, yúm̓-miʔst *he moved suddenly after being asleep (or still) for quite a while*; Cm yum̓ *to move slightly.*

(√yp)[621]	c+yip	tree
(√yq̓)[622]	n+yq̓=ísk̓it+m	groan
(√yq̓)	yq̓=ip[623]	belt
(√yr)[624]	s+yr=íwa?=xn, k̓ɬ+yr̓=cin, n+yr=ip, k̓ɬ+yr+mn=ils	snowhoes (round), tie around, kerchief ((a)round), back (of tipi), turn down
(√yr)	yir	push
(√yrk̓ʷ)[625]	yark̓ʷ, n+yrk̓ʷ=ip+tn, k̓ɬ+yrk̓ʷ=cn=ikst, yrik̓ʷ=xn+m	hoop, wrist band, crooked, circle, make snowshoes, round
(√yskr)	yasukrí	Jesus Christ
(√ytkʷ)[626]	n+ytkʷ=ip	rotten
(√yw)[627]	k+yw•yw=ína?, k+yúw=na?, k+yw=us+m	strong, clear, listen,
(√yw)	k̓ɬ+ya?wá+m	wait
(√yx?)	n+yx?=úla?xʷ+m+s	place name(√yxʷ)
(√yxʷ)[628]	yxʷ=ut, yaxʷ+t, sc+yxʷ=itkʷ, n+yaxʷ+t	fall or get off, down, under, below, fall in, inside(s), underneath, deep, basement, underground, waterfall, lower, downstream
(√yxʷ)[629]	n+yxʷ•xʷ+mi	imitate
(√yx̌)[630]	yx̌=i?s	drive stock, drag, drive into
(√yx̌?)	ya?•yáx̌a?	watch
(√yʕ)[631]	iyáʕ+p, k+yaʕ=cín+m	arrive pl., shore
(√yʕ)[632]	yaʕ•yáʕ+t, c+yaʕ,[633] yaʕ+mncút, yaʕ+m+ílx, yaʕ+p=qín,[634] n+yaʕ=sqáx̌a?+m, yaʕ•yaʕ+ncút, yaʕ=kín̓	all, together, many, lots, complete, gather all, corral, all on back
(√yʕ)	yaʕ=cín,[635] k+yaʕ=cin+m	shore

621 Cf. northern Ok cɣip. See also Sh s-cɣ-ep *tree* ... "The word cɣep is prob. originally the status form of yep-m *to put up (e.g. a pole)*; in the pl scɣcɣep *trees*, cɣ- is treated as a root and -ep can be identified with the suffix." Kuipers 1974:173.

623 See Th q̓ip̓ *belt, waistband.*

622 Sp y̓iq̓ *sound of creaking bones, sound of creaking timbers*; Cr yq̓ , is+yáq̓+yaq̓+iš *creak.*

618 Sp č̓ɬ-n-y̓l̓xʷ=p-n-cút-n *it's his tipi flap door;* √yel̓xʷ covered. draped, wrapped around, wound; Cr qt:yél̓xʷ cover (to...with cloth).

624 Sp √yir̹(é) (yal̹(é)) *(Ka) round*; Cr yar *roll*; Sh yel, yal *be wound around*; Li zəl *to turn.*

625 Sp yerk̓ʷ (yalk̓ʷ) *bent, crooked*; Cr yark̓ʷ *crooked, curved.*

626 Cr yetkʷ *decay, decompose, putrify, rot.*

627 Sp √yo? (yo yu? yu) *strong*; Cr √yʕgʷ *able, capable...*; Sh yʕʷ-ilx *to exert oneself, do one's outmost.* Sp o suggests cognacy with Ok √yʕʷ (see below). Ok has two roots, √yw and √yʕʷ.

628 Sp yšut *bottom, below*; Cm k-yxʷ-m-s-akst *downriver, down below*; Sh yuxʷ *descend.*

629 Cm yuxʷ-xʷ, na-yxʷ-xʷ *to imitate, copy.*

630 Sp yx̌=sqáx̌a? *hedrove the horses away. He herded the animals*; Sp yx̌en *to chase fish into fishtrap*; Cm s-ya?x̌ *to chase, herd.*

631 Sh c-yʕ-ep *to arrive (from far).*

632 Sp hecy̓áʕ̓ (?ecyáʕ̓) cyáʕ̓ *all, everything, everyone;* √yaʕ̓ *(ya?) gathered, accumulated*; Cm yaʕ-yaʕ-tu *all, whole*; Cr a·yáʕ *all, everyone;* Th zaʕ, zaʕ•záʕ-t *[of pelple] assembled, gotten together, having arrived at a place*, zaʕ-m-ə́m *asemble, collect, gather (things) in a particular place]*; Li zí?•zəʕ̓ *each one, every one*, n.zí?•zəʕ̓-s *to go to everybody...*

633 Sp yiʕa?p *they all arrived together*; Cr c+yaʕ̓ *all arrived.*

634 Cm yaʕ̓-p-qin *many, lots.*

635 Th zaʕ=cín *walk along the waterline on the beach next to the water.*

(√yʕ)	k+yaʕ+m[636]	crawl in bed with
(√yʕc̓)[637]	yaʕc̓	solid
(√yʕ̓)	n+yʕ̓=ip[638]	always.
(√yʕ̓)[639]	c+n+yaʕ̓	gather, assemble, arrive, gather
(√yʕ̓)[640]	yaʕ̓+p=cín, c+yaʕ̓+mí	scared, hard up, in need, be backward, bashful, hardship
(√yʕʷ)	n+yʕʷ•yʕʷ=us	stiff neck
(√yʕʷ)[641]	sn+yaʕʷ+t, yw•yaʕʷ+t, n+yʕʷ=lscut, s+yʕʷp•yaw+t, yaw+p+yáʕʷ+t	strength, powerful, strong, best someone, control temper
(√yʔx̌)	yaʔx̌í	that one yonder
(√y̓k̓ʷ)[642]	c+n=y̓ák̓ʷ, y̓aʔk̓ʷ=áqs	swim across
(√y̓l)[643]	k̓ł+y̓l•al	lose
(√y̓l̓w̓)	s+y̓al̓w̓=ánk[644]	cricket, Cricket
(√ʕc)[645]	ʕac, s+k+ʕac•ʕac=qín=xn, ʕac•c=qn+mnwíxʷ	tie, trap, pack, loin cloth, leggings, corral, go head to head
(√ʕc)	sn+ʕic=kst+x	Lakes (tribe)
(√ʕc̓)[646]	n+ʕic̓+p+m	argue over, insist
(√ʕl)	ʕalá+p,[647] ʕal+p+ncút	lose, lose gambling
(√ʕlpl)	ʕalapúl	Gopher
(√ʕl̓)[648]	k̓ł+ʕal̓, k̓ł+n+ʕal̓=íp, k̓ł+ʕal̓+mín, n+ʕal̓=qí	shut, fence, cover, partition
(√ʕƛ̓)[649]	ʕaƛ̓•ʕaƛ̓+s+c̓ím	gnaw, chew up
(√ʕm)[650]	ʕamá+p	melt, thaw
(√ʕm)[651]	ʕim+t, ʕa•ʕím+aʔ	hate, angry
(√ʕnq)[652]	ʕanq=íls	satisfied

636 Probably the root is √yʕ *all.*
637 Sp yac̓ *tight*; Cr yec̓, u yc̓+op (the o of the lexical suffix confirms an earlier pharyngeal).
638 Sp n-yiʕ-áp *always, forever, still, yet.*
639 Sp yaʕ̓ (yaʕ) *gathered, accumulated*; Cm syáʕ̓-ʕ̓ *gathering, meeting* (also s-yaʕ̓ʷ-ʕ̓ʷ *to meet, gather*); Cr yaʕ *assemble, crowd, gather*; Th yəʕ̓ *assemble*, zʕ ~ zʕ̓, √zəʕ *group*, zʕ-ə́m *assemble, collect, gather things*, zʕə́p *pl. persons come, arrive, assemble, gather at a particular place [esp. just arrived].*
640 Sp yaʕ *apprehensive, afraid*, hec-yaʕ̓-p=cín *they're poor people*; Cm y̓aʕ̓-p-cin *be in need, without*; Cr yaʕ *hesitant, shy, timid*, yaʕ̓+t+mí-nt-s *needed, required.*
641 Sp n-yaw=ls *he's strong headed*; Cm yʕ̓ʷ-yʕ̓ʷ-t *be hard, difficult*, yaʕ̓-p-y-awt *be well endowed, powerful, psychic.*
642 Sp yekʷ(ú) *passed, to take across*; Cm na-yak̓ʷ-lx *to cross over water.*
643 This form is uncertain. The connection with √ʕl, if any, is unclear.
644 Sp s-y̓el̓w̓=énč.
645 Sp ʕac(í) *to tie*; Cm ḥac-łt-xʷ *you tie s.t. of s.o.'s*, nḥcusm *trap animals*; Cr hec; Sh ʕec *to tie up, knit (nets).*
646 Cr ʕic̓ *persistene, tenacious*; Sh ʕec̓-t *tough (of hide).*
647 Sp ʔal-íp *he lost it all*; Cr s+ʕel+p *demerit*, ʕel+p+mí-nt-s *confiscate (lit. he forfeited it (to public use)).*
648 Sp ʕal̓ *to be fenced in*; Cr ʕel̓ *block, obstruct, fence, curtain.*
649 Sp √x̌ƛ̓(í) *to chew, to eat*; Cm s-ḥ-ḥƛ̓-mix *to be gnawing.*
650 Sp ham-íp; Cm ḥəm-p *become damp, dissolve, melt*; Cr ʕem *dissolve, melt, waste away.*
651 Sp ʕaymt; Cm ḥímt ḥim-t.
652 Sp √ʕanq, n-ʕanq=cín *he finally got enough to eat.*

(√ʕpnʔ)[653]	ʕapnáʔ	now
(√ʕw)[654]	n+ʕaw+p=áɬq̓ʷlt	drip
(√ʕx̌)	ʕáx̌=laʔxʷ[655]	harrow
(√ʕy)[656] See √ʕʷy	n+ʕay=us[657]	smile
(√ʕy)	sn+ʕáyu	remainder
(√ʕ̓c̓) See √ʕ̓c̓x̌	sc+ʕ̓ac̓, x̌s+ʕ̓ac̓•c̓	look (behind), read
(√ʕ̓c̓x̌)[658] See √ʕ̓c̓	n+ʕ̓ac̓x̌=kn̓+cút, ʕ̓ac̓x̌+ɬ+q̓ẏ+mín+m	look, looks, watch, look at
(√ʕ̓n̓xʷ)[659]	s+ʕ̓an̓íxʷ	Muskrat
(√ʕʷc̓)	ʕʷc̓a+p	waste
(√ʕʷx̌ʷ)[660]	n+ʕʷx̌ʷ=iw̓s	drag across
(√ʕʷx̌ʷ)[661]	s+ʕʷx̌ʷ=ip[662]	roots
(√ʕʷy) See √ʕy	n+ʕʷuy, c+n+ʕʷy=us, k+ʕʷy+ncut+m[663]	smile, laugh
(√ʔc)[664]	n+ʔuc=xn, n+ʔac=xn+cút	follow
(√ʔckl)	ʔuckl=íp+m, n+ʔuckl=áx̌n+m	run downhill, go down a slope, run down canyon, loop over, looped on ..., drape over
(√ʔckn)[665]	n+ʔickn+tn, pu=ʔackiʔ+scút	play, game
(√ʔcl)	ʔucl+m[666]	paddle
(√ʔcqʔ)[667]	ʔácqaʔ	go out, anus, bathroom
(√ʔcqʷ)	sn+ʔacqʷ=úlaʔxʷ[668]	bread
(√ʔkn)[669]	kin̓, c+ʔkin, c+ʔkn=útyaʔ, k̓a+ʔkín	do what, how, indef., bad state, when, how, wherever, be better off, from somewhere, how far, sometimes
(√ʔks, √wx)[670]	ʔaks+wíx	stand (on hillside ...)

653 Sh ʕép *until dusk*; Th ʕáp *dusk*. Cf. Li ʕap *(late) evening sets in (part of the night before)*, ɬ‿ʕáp-as *tonight*.
654 Sp √ʕaw; Cr ʕaw, ʕ̓ew+ p *dripped*.
655 Sp ʕax̌=leʔxʷ-m *he harrowed and raked the field for seeding*; Cm ʔix̌-l̓əxʷ-tn.
656 Northern variant of √ʕʷy.
657 Sp n-oẏ=ús-m̓ *he smiled*.
658 Sp ʔác̓x̌-m; Cr ʔac̓x̌; Cm ʔac̓x̌-nt-xʷ *you look at, watch s.t.*
659 Cm ḥan̓áxʷ.
660 Sp √ʕʷox̌ʷ, hec-ʕʷóx̌ʷ *it's strung up (as is telephone line...)*.
661 Probably a single root √ʕʷx̌ʷ.
662 Sp s-ox̌ʷ=ép, s-ʕʷóx̌ʷ=ép; Cm sx̌ʷ-ap *plant root(s)*.
663 Sp hoẏ-n̓-cút (ʔoẏ-n̓-cút) *he smiled*.
664 Sp √ʔuc *follow the tracks of*.
665 Cr ʔičč.
666 See Sp č hi yeʔc lʕapmí *I paddled the canoe... I'm floating downriver*.
667 Sp ʔócqeʔ; Cr ʔácqeʔ.
668 Sh ʔecqʷ-m; Th n-ʔecqʷ=uym̓xʷ *bake bread ... in ashes ...*
669 Sp čen̓; Cr e=čín+ m *happen*.
670 Sp ʔeč√s-wiš *he stands*; Cr ec-wiš *stand*.

(√ʔkʷ)[671]	ʔukʷ, n+ʔakʷ+t=áqs	take, bring, transport, carry, bring, take around, hoard, car (take, haul), truck, deliver, haul
(√ʔkʷt)[672] See √kʷ	ʔakʷt+lílx	crawl
(√ʔl)[673]	ʔuľ=ẁs, ʔal=ẁs=íkst+m	gather, collect
(√ʔl)[674]	n+ʔal=ks+nwíxʷ+m	fight over
(√ʔlk̓ʷ)	ʔalk̓ʷ=ús	sharpen
(√ʔlpl)[675] See √pľ	ʔalapúl	Gopher
(√ʔlqʷʔ)[676]	k̓ɬ+ʔál·qʷaʔ	border, Marcus
(√ʔlxʷ)	ʔilxʷ+t	hungry
(√ʔɬn)[677]	ʔiɬn	eat, food, manger
(√ʔɬxʷ)	n+ʔuɬxʷ, n+ʔaɬxʷ=íɬxʷ	enter
(√ʔƛ̓)	n+ʔiƛ̓=tk	north
(√ʔm)[678]	ʔúm=laʔxʷ, k+ʔam=plaʔ+ncút+m, k̓ɬ+ʔam=ci, k̓ɬ+ʔm=cin	name, call, announce, agree, answer
(√ʔm) See √mt	k+ʔam=t=íẁs[679]	sg. sit, set, sit down, ride, saddle horse, horseback riding, jockey
(√ʔm)	k̓ɬ+ʔim[680]	wait (for)
(√ʔm)	ʔim•m+scút, ʔama+s+n+sp̓=íliʔs	fear, threaten
(√ʔmn)[681]	ʔamn=sqáx̌aʔ	feed, manger
(√ʔmt)[682]	sn+ʔímaʔt	grandchild, grandparent
(√ʔmx)[683]	ʔimx	move, relocate
(√ʔnwn)[684]	k̓ɬ+ʔanwín+m	hear, feel, notice
(√ʔpn)[685]	ʔupn=kst, ʔapn=kst=ásq̓t	ten
(√ʔp̓)[686]	ʔip̓, k+ʔap̓=c̓aʔ+ncút	wipe (dry)
(√ʔq̓ʷ)[687]	ʔaq̓ʷ=s+m	scrape, shave
(√ʔs)[688]	ʔis=tk+m, s+ʔas=tk=ínaʔ	winter, wintering place

671 Sp ʔúkʷuʔ *bring, take*; Cm s-n-ʔukʷ-mn *truck*; Cr y+ʔúkʷ+m *to move something yonder*.
672 Cr ʔukʷ+t *crawled*.
673 Sp ʔul *meet*, n-ʔúl=uʔs-m *they're united, they're joined, they're merged...*; Li √ʔuľus *to get together, to have a meeting*.
674 See Cr ʔél+m-s-n *to move, stir, rouse*. See also Sp ʔeľ *try, test, experiment with*.
675 Sp púľyeʔ; Cm puľ-yaʔ *gopher, mole*.
676 See Sp ʔólqʷeʔ *go down towards the water, go down towards the river*.
677 Sp ʔiɬn; Cm ʔiɬn; Cr ʔiɬn; Sh ʔiɬn; Th ʔiɬn; Li ʔíɬən.
678 See Sp hec-ʔáw-s-t-m *he was (customarily) named, called by them*; Sh ʔəm(e)t *to call, name, mention*; Th ʔúm *name*.
679 Sp ʔemút, n-ʔem̓t=íčn̓ *he rode bareback*; Sh ʔəmut *to sit down, sg*.
680 Cm k̓ɬ-ʔam *to wait*; Cr ce·n+ʔím-nt-s ... *he waited for him*.
681 Sp ʔem̓, ʔam-i=sqáx̌ʔe *he fed his animals*; Cm ʔəm-t-xʷ *you feed s.o.*; Cr ʔem-t-s *feed*; Li ʔam *to feed*.
682 Cm ʔa-ʔim̓ac *grandchild*; Sh ʔimc *(great-)grandchild*; Th √ʔímec *grandchild*.
683 Sp ʔim̓š; Cm ʔím̓x.
684 Sp ʔenwén *feel, sense*.
685 Sp ʔupn; Cr ʔúpen.
686 Cm ʔap̓-nt-xʷ *you wipe s.t.*
687 Cm ʔaq̓ʷ-nt-xʷ *you scrape s.t.*, ʔaq̓ʷ-s-m *to shave oneself*; Sh ʔiq̓ʷ *to scrape, to drag stg. over stg.*; Th ʔíq̓ʷ; Li ʔiq̓ʷ.
688 Sp s-ʔístč; Cm s-ʔistkʷ *December (early winter)*; Sh s-ʔistk; Li s.ʔístkən *winter dwelling*.

(√ʔsl)[689]	ʔasíl	two, twins
(√ʔstkʷ)[690]	ʔastkʷ	cedar
(√ʔsx̌m)[691]	ʔasx̌m	back(bone)
(√ʔsʔ)[692]	ʔaʔúsaʔ	egg
(√ʔtx)[693]	ʔitx	sleep
(√ʔtx̌ʷʔ)[694]	ʔítx̌ʷaʔ	camas
(√ʔw)	ʔaw+s+k+síw	go ... (in compounds)
(√ʔw)[695]	n+ʔaw=cín+m	upstream
(√ʔw)[696]	ʔaw+t=ús,[697] n+ʔaw=qn,[698] ʔaw+t+s=iẃs	opponent, challenge, antagonist
(√ʔw)	ʔaw•ʔaw=cí, k̓ł+ʔaẃ[699]	wait, watch (for)
(√ʔwt)	sn+ʔaw·t=iłxʷ+tn	name of river
(√ʔwt)[700]	sn+ʔiwt, s+ʔawt=íłc̓aʔ, ʔawt=íp,[701] c+ʔiwt, ʔawt+p=áłq,[702] ʔawt=maʔ+s+qílxʷ[703]	end, back side, behind, last, behind, follow, sneak up, last, youngest, inhabitants, contemporaries
(√ʔwtm)[704]	ʔawtím=tk	south
(√ʔẃ)[705]	s+ʔẃ=íkiʔ+st	electricity
(√ʔxʷ, √kʷn)	k+ʔxʷ+kʷun+m[706]	coax, nag
(√ʔx̌l)[707] see √ʔx̌ł	ta+ʔx̌íl+m, c+ʔx̌il+x,[708] ʔax̌l+lwís, ʔax̌•x̌•l+ílx, sn+ʔax̌l=íls, ʔax̌l=áqs+m	(do) a certain way, act so, how, reason why, similar, matched, (do) like, same, as, happen, mill about, busy with, want to do, push aside
(√ʔx̌l)	ʔax̌l+mncút,[709] ʔax̌l=íkst+m	turn (around)

689 Sp ʔesél; Cr ʔésel; Sh səséle.
690 Sh ʔestqʷ.
691 Sp ʔásx̌-m̓ *spine, backbone.*
692 Sp ʔuʔús=eʔ; Cr ʔúseʔ; Sh ʔúʔse; Li ʔú•saʔ.
693 Sp ʔitš; Cr ʔitš; Cm s-ʔitx; Sh ʔitx.
694 Sp ʔítx̌ʷeʔ; Cm ʔitx̌ʷáʔ *black camas*; Cr ʔétx̌ʷeʔ.
695 Cf. Sh t-ʔiwl-tk *upstream area, interior.*
696 Sp ʔewt=ús *enemy, rival, opponent, challenger.*
697 Sp ʔewt=ús, ʔeẃt=ús *enemy, rival, opponent, challenger*; Cm q:ʔaw-t–us *opponent*; Cr ʔew + t=ús ... *contestant.*
698 Sp n-ʔawq-n *I encouraged her, I urged her.*
699 Cm ? k̓łʔam.
700 Sh ʔəwit *the last, behind*; Li ʔaẃ-t *to get behind...*
701 Cm ʔaẃ-t-ap-nt-xʷ *you follow s.o.*
702 Sp ʔaẃt=p=áłq *he followed in the footsteps of someone*; Cm ʔac-ʔaw-t *be last, behind.*
703 Sp ʔawt-m=a√sqél=ixʷ *Indian in name only. "Apple Indian" (red on the outside and white on the inside, describing one who is visibly indian but does not care to practice the Indian customs or chooses not to learn the Indian ways).*
704 Sp ʔutémtč *away from bank of river.*
705 Sp s-ʔuẃéč-ń-t.
706 Sp ʔexʷ-kʷún-m *he said it. He talks in this manner,* qʷu č̓-xʷ-kʷún-m-i-s *he coaxed me. He tried to persuade me* (where the prefix č has coalesced with the initial glottal stop of ʔəxʷ.
707 Sp ʔax̌íl *be a certain way, do a certain way*; Cm ʔac-ʔx̌il *be the same, similar; to resemble; to do like*; Cr ʔax̌el *thus (to do...)*; Sh x̌il-m *act thus.*
708 Sp he-c̓x̌íl-i *it seems like that, it's the same.*
709 Sp čn ʔax̌l-m-n-cút *I turned myself around.*

710 Cr naʔ+x̌íɬ *maybe, possibly.*
711 Sp ʔax̌ʷ *scooping motion, scraping motion.*
712 Sp cn n-ʔáx̌ʷ-t *I paddled downriver, I went downstream*; Cr n+ʕax̌ʷ.
713 Sp ʔey *to buy, to exchange money, to cross.*
714 Sp n-ʔéy=s-n *I bought it*; Sh ʔey *exchange, give in return, meet.*
715 Sp ʔey̓xʷ.
716 Sp ʔáyx̌ʷ-t; Cr ʔayx̌ʷ; Cm ʔayx̌ʷt.

Lexical affixes

In the tables that follow I list the lexical affixes found in the anthology, first the prefixes, then the suffixes, and then the combinations of two suffixes. The sequences of lexical suffixes do not always form a complex suffix with its own meaning. For example, while =qin=kst, the combination of =qin *head* and =ikst *hand* equals *finger*, a form like s+x̌ʷʔ=iɬp=x *Colville* should not be viewed as =iɬp *tree* and =x *person*, with some meaning *tree person*. I provide examples of all sequences of lexical suffixes, but glosses only for those sequences I am reasonably sure constitute lexical units.

I list lexical affixes by consonant skeleta alphabetized ignoring vowels and intrusive pharyngeals. In the first column, I list each affix with its allomorphs arranged alphabetically. In the second column I give each affix a simple gloss. In the third column I list one or more examples, and in the fourth column the translation of the example. When I list multiple examples, I start with the one representing the most basic sense of the affix and end with one the sense of which is least transparent.

Prefixes			
hɬ=	group	hɬ=c+kic	group arrives.
k=	person	k=mus•ms	four persons.
t=	person	t=kaʔ•kaʔɬís	three persons.
tk=	person	tk=ʔasl+míst	two persons.
n=	water	n=cix	warm water.
pu=	wife	pu=kx+ncút c-pu=t=xʷaʔxʷʔít	wife follows. many wives.
qɬ=	offspring	qɬ=s+mx̌=íkn	grizzly's child.
sxʷ=	one who	sxʷ=k+ʕac=qáx̌aʔ+m sxʷ=c̓aľá+m	packer. one who stands it.
ʔip=	on the way	ʔip=píx̌+m	hunt on the way.

Suffixes			
=cin	mouth	c+n+paʔq=cín cw=cin c̓s+p=cin k+nxaʔ=cín+m kɬ+cw=cin	dawn cisl. talk. run out of food. on the way. cry, good word.
=c		k̓ɬ+kʷinxʷ=c	answer.
=cí		c+kɬ+ʕac=cí	tie around neck cisl.
=cn		s+yum=cn kɬ+k̓ʷľ=cn+cut+n k=naqs=cn	curse. have cook. eat alone
=íc̓aʔ	body	k+ckʷ=íc̓aʔ kɬ+k+lk̓=íc̓aʔ+t	pull cover off. have baler.
=ác̓aʔ		k̓ɬ+nqs=ác̓aʔ	sleep alone.

=ċaʔ		k+číw=ċaʔ k+míƛ̓=ċaʔ k+mús=ċaʔ	wash body. smear. four packages.
=k	?	kʷn•kʷan=k t+qilt=k	hold. top.
=ikn[1]	back	t+qlt=ikn kɬ+lk̓=ikn	top of ridge. tie on back.
=íkiʔ		s+ʔẇ=íkiʔ+st k+ʕac=íkiʔ	electricity. tie to post.
=ikṅ		kɬ+qc+lx=ikṅ k+ʕac•ʕac=íkṅ	run on crust. bundles.
=kiʔ		wẏ+s+t+k̓ʷíxʷ=kiʔ	finish untying.
=kn		kċ+ilx=kn	woodtick.
=kiṅ[2]	back	cq̓+mn=kiṅ+m c+k+mn=kíṅ	throw pack turn one's back
=ikst	hand	c+n+lʕʷ=ikst+m k+pl•l=ikst sl=ikst	stick hand in cisl. sprout. bastard.
=ik		t+x̌s=ik c+n+k̓aʔt=ík	good aim. near cisl.
=ks		cl=ks+pin=tk c+t+kʷin=ks	five years. take by hand.
=iks		k+trq=iks k̓aẏ=íks	kick. cold hands.
=kst		sy•suy=kst+m cil=kst	get chilled. five.
=ʕakst		yw•yw=ʕakst	strong hand.
=ikxt	hand	k+n+k̓l+p=ikxt+m	play Coyote tricks.
=il	?	k̓ɬ+twn=il	think one falls short.
=líls	?	ɬ+n+waʔ=líls+m	puzzle again.
=áln	weapon	maʔqʷ=áln	knife.
=iln		cq̓=iln	arrow, bullet.
=ilp	floor	s+x̌l=ilp s+t̓q=ilp	floor. mattress.
=ilps	coat	tx̌=ilps	gray horse.
=lps		s+k+čiw=lps	mane.
=lp̓	wood	qa•qw=lp̓	driftwood.
=lqs	?	x̌ʷaq̓ʷ=lqs+m	snore.
=álq	clothes	sip̓iʔ=álq	buckskin clothes.
=alqs		c+kɬ+kʷƛ̓=alqs+m	take from under clothes cisl.
=alqʷ	cylindrical object	t+qlt+k=alqʷ c+kɬʔ=al·qʷ s+x̌•x̌ċiʔ+m=álqʷ k+caʔ•caʔ=álqʷ+m	Canada, across the line. next to shore cisl. stalk. knock on pole.
=lqʷ		k+tiqʷ=lqʷ t+k̓ʷaxʷ•xʷ=lqʷ	shine rd obj. unravel.
=álaʔqʷ		ṅqs=álaʔqʷ	stick dim.

1 See =kiṅ.
2 See =ikn.

=ʕálaʔqʷ		s+p̓•p̓aʔc̓=ʕálaʔqʷ	new shoots.
=ils	stomach	(t+)ks=ils klm=íls+mist k̓ɬ+tɬ=ils+m	bad stomach. think highly of self. go straight for.
=ls		kɬ+twn=ls+mist	fall short.
=lscut	clothes	s+x̌s=lscut	good clothes.
=ilst	weapon	n+x̌c=ilst+n	bow and arrow, weapon.
=ilsxn	forehead	qaʕ=ilsxn+m	cut hair.
=lut	place	ɬq̓ʷ=lut	lie down pl.
=ʕalt	?	s+t̓m=ʕalt	cow
=ilt	child	cxʷ=ilt+m k+s+q̓m=ilt+n	hold child. have hunger.
=ílaʔt		wx̌t=ílaʔt	baby.
=il̓t		c•cm̓=il̓t	children.
=l̓t		s+k̓ʷ•k̓ʷim̓=l̓t	baby.
=alxʷ[3]	coat	kʷl̓•kʷl̓=alxʷ	calf.
=lxʷ		c̓s=lxʷ+ncut kɬ+kʷil=lxʷ	strip. dark sorrel.
=álaʔxʷ		kʷ•kʷl̓•kʷl̓=álaʔxʷ	little calves.
=ilxʷ[4]	people	t̓xʷl+m=ilxʷ kɬ+k̓yl=ilxʷ nqs=ilxʷ	different tribe. have tree bark. suit.
=ílaʔk̓	?	n+p̓•p̓n=ílaʔk̓	sticks.
=íliʔs	relative	kt̓=íliʔs ɬ+ʔamas+n+sp̓=íliʔs sncaʔ•cʔ=íliʔs	stomachs burst. threaten to beat again. brothers.
=áliʔs	relative	s+tm=áliʔs	relatives.
=úlaʔxʷ	country	sx̌+lx=úlaʔxʷ	change country.
=laʔxʷ		cíq=laʔxʷ+m	dig.
=íɬc̓aʔ	body	s+ʔawt=íɬc̓aʔ ckʷ=íɬc̓aʔ	back side. drag body, take breath.
=ɬc̓aʔ		mník=ɬc̓aʔ	body covered in shit.
=ʕáɬc̓aʔ		n+x̌ls=ʕáɬc̓aʔ+tn	window.
=iɬmlx	bush	s+c̓rs=iɬmlx t̓q=iɬmlx	Oregon grape. thornbushes
=iɬm		t̓q=iɬm	short thorn bushes.
=ɬniwt	side	t+k̓m=ɬniwt	alongside.
=iɬp	tree	ck̓•ck=iɬp cq̓=iɬp	ribs. fir.
=ɬp		c̓aq̓ʷ•c̓q̓ʷ=ɬp	wire brush.
=aɬq	fruit	p̓y̓q=aɬq	ripe.
=ɬq		s+kʷan=ɬq	harvest.
=ɬq̓it	shoulder	n+ɬqʷ=ɬq̓it+m	throw over shoulder.
=aɬq̓ʷlt	throat	n+c̓xʷ•xʷ=aɬq̓ʷlt	spill in mouth.
=ɬtíɬn	informatio n	maʔ=cn+m=ɬtíɬn	bother with talk.
=iɬn		qʷl•qʷl+t=iɬn	talk.

3 See =ilxʷ.
4 See =alxʷ.

=iɬxʷ	house	s+x̌l=iɬxʷ	board house.
=ɬxʷ		c+xʷul=ɬxʷ	tipi.
=íɬaʔxʷ		k̓ʷ•k̓ʷym=íɬaʔxʷ	small house.
=imx	?	t̓ql=imx[5]	stop, settle, move.
=mixʷ	person	ɬ+k̓ʷl̓+s+qlt=mixʷ+m	get second husband.
=úmaʔ	small	k̓ʷ•k̓ʷy=úmaʔ	small.
=maʔ	?	c̓úq̓ʷ=maʔ k̓ɬ+k̓ʷʔín=maʔ k̓ʷín=maʔ+m n+ʔakʷ=maʔ+s=cín ʔaw+t=maʔ+s+qílxʷ	index finger. figure out. choose. hoard food. people, inhabitants, contemporaries
=ink	back	ckʷ=ink k̓ɬ+qc+lx=ink c+k+ɬaʔ+p=ínk cq•q=ink	bow. run on hill. close cisl. fall on back.
=ánk		s+yal̓w=ánk	Cricket.
=núxʷ	weather	waʔs=núxʷ s+x̌aʔ=núxʷ+m n+kʷaʔc=núxʷ	late. stop weather. get dark.
=nxʷ		x̌yaɬ=nxʷ	sun.
=uxʷ		x̌aʔn=úxʷ+m	stop the weather.
=ínaʔ	ear, surface	k+pq̓ʷ=ínaʔ+m sx̌ʷ+p=ínaʔ c+k+mɬ•ɬ=ínaʔ k+mqʷ=ínaʔ k+ʔastk=ínaʔ s+x̌lp=ínaʔ	fill in a hole. run off. cave in cisl. snow cover. winter supply daylight.
=naʔ		wál̓=naʔ k+cíq=naʔ k+lq̓=naʔ+ncút k+már̓=naʔ	talk smart. dig. cover up. fill hole.
=ip	door	c+k̓ɬ+n+k̓ahk̓ʷ=íp c+ʔuckl=íp+m c+k̓ɬ+n+k̓ahk̓ʷ=íp c+ʔuckl=íp+m	lower bottom. open door cisl. open door cisl. run downhill cisl.
=p		k̓ɬ+n+maʕʷ=p	break door.
=up[6]	?	c+xʷt̓=up	jump up.
=íplaʔ	handle	k+c̓x̌ʷ=íplaʔ k+ƛ̓ʔ=íplaʔ	judge. make trouble.
=plaʔ		t+x̌áq̓=plaʔ k+síw=plaʔ	reward. ask about.
=áplqs	story	n+c̓ayxʷ=áplqs	end of story.
=ʕáplqs		n+c̓ayxʷ=ʕáplqs	end of story.
=ups	tail	sy=ups ɬ+c•cʔ=ups	tail. younger sister.
=paʔs	?	lq=paʔs+ncút	pull whiskers.
=ápaʔst	testicle	n+mlk̓ʷ=ápaʔst	stallion.

5 Cf. √ʔimx *move.*
6 See ? =ups.

=qin	head	k+ckʷ=qin k+lmx=qin+m k+nm=qin k+c̓aʔx=qín	scalp. love song. blind. be ashamed.
=q		t+x̌ʷay=q	pile.
=qi		wl=qi k+ɬaʔ=qí	cover. lean st against.
=qn		t+x̌ʷay=qn c̓asy=qn	pile. head.
=qsa[7]	?	n+t̓p=qsa+m	tip head.
=aqs	road	cah•ch=aqs n+ckʷ+mn=aqs k+p̓ƛ̓m=aqs s+yaʔk̓ʷ=áqs k+t̓aʔk̓+mx=áqs	face direction. wagon road. end of the mountain. mid winter. taste of maiden.
=áqaʔs		n+k̓•k̓t=áqaʔs	close to the road.
=qs	food	s+x̌ʷal=qs	garbage, food thrown away.
=us	eye, fire	sy•sy=us xaʔ+t=ús s+x̌s=us c+kɬ+c̓l•l=us c+p̓lk̓=us+m k+cq=us	power, smart. leader. good looks. stand on bank cisl. turn around cisl. put on fire.
=s		c+n+c̓aʕp=s	wink cisl.
=ʕas		c̓n•c̓nm=ʕas+m k̓ɬ+t̓m=ʕas	eyes closed. kiss.
=ísk̓it	breath	c̓sp=ísk̓it	out of breath.
=sk̓it		ɬáʔxʷ=sk̓it	rest.
=islp̓	firewood	wr̓=islp̓+m	build fire.
=sqáx̌aʔ	horse	s+ʔamn=sqáx̌aʔ	animal fed.
=qáx̌aʔ		sxʷ=k+ʕac=qáx̌aʔ+m	packer.
=asq̓t	sky	twn=asq̓t kaʔɬl=ásq̓t	Tonasket. three days.
=sq̓t		k+yic̓=sq̓t	clear sky.
=usx[8]	?	k̓ɬ+wr̓=usx	make fire.
=ísxn	small rock	kaʔx=ísxn k+caʔx=ísxn saʔx=ísxn	warm st. glow. glow.
=sxiʔ		k+c̓íw̓=sxiʔ	wash rd object.
=ísxiʔ		k+lq̓=ísxiʔ	peel st.
=ʕásxn		s+t+x̌al=ʕásxn t+x̌al=ʕásxn	brightness. red hot.
=úsaʔ	?	c̓x̌ʷl=úsaʔ kɬ+p+pq̓ʷ=úsaʔ k+ɬx̌ʷm=úsaʔ	white camas. good on top. hole trough.

7 The a of =qsa forms +m verbs of weak stems. Such verb forms could be segmented *stem+ám* but I have preferred *stemá+m*, giving a vowel to the stem.

8 Unclear.

=tk	surface	t+qil=tk cl=ks+pin=tk n+ʔiƛ̓=tk	height, top. five years. north.
=aʔtk		nk̓ʷ•nk̓ʷ+s+pín=aʔtk	yearlings dim.
=itkʷ	water	s+x̌ʷn=itkʷ kɬ+cq•q=itkʷ	Colville. top of water.
=kʷ		n+qʷam•qʷm=kʷ k+siwɬ=kʷ (√swɬ)	excellent water. have, there is water
=ítaʔkʷ		k̓ʷ•k̓ʷn̓=ítaʔkʷ	shallow water.
=útyaʔ	makeshift	waʔx=útyaʔ kʷniʔ=útyaʔ	dwelling dim. grab.
=ú(tyaʔ)		xʷs•xʷaʔst=ú	walk floor.
=u		n+ckʷ=u	pull back.
=ẇɬ	conveyanc e	mus=ẇɬ	four conveyances.
=iwt[9]	place	kɬ+kʷl=iwt	sit in.
=íwaʔt		m•m̓kʷ=íwaʔt qmn=íwaʔt	mound dim. lying around.
=ut[10]	place	tx̌ʷ+m=ut c+lʕ̓ʷ=ut+m c+tkʷʔ=ut	straight, normal. valley. walk cisl.
=wit[11]	place	c+ql=wit+m	step cisl.
=wt		kʷl=wt+lwis	sit around.
=áwaʔ	?	s+x̌m=nk=áwaʔ n+xaʔy=áwaʔ	lover. in the midst.
=iẇs	middle	c̓p̓q̓+s=iẇs+m k+tr=iẇs	splice. unstitch.
=íẇ		k+ʔamt=íẇ	ride.
=ẇ		k+ɬuʔxʷ=ẇ	stitch.
=ẇs		kip̓=ẇs	pinch middle.
=ʕáwaʔs		p̓•p̓s=ʕáwaʔs	low place.
=x	person	s+x̌ʷʔ=iɬp=x s+xʔit=x s+tʔiwt=x	Colville. oldest one. youngest one.
=aʔx		s+x•xʔít=aʔx s+t•tʔíw+t=aʔx	oldest dim. youngest.
=xan	foot	kaʔ•kaʔn=xán	sore feet.
=x		c+n+ʔuc=x	follow cisl.
=xn		s+x̌iƛ̓=xn s+yr=íwa=xn k+lxʷp=xn	trousers. snowshoes. hurt foot.
=xna		k̓ɬ+xát=xna+m	go first, ahead.
=xiʔ		n+ʔuc=xiʔ	follow.
=xin	?	s+xʷ•xʷc̓=xin	pee.

9 See =wit.
10 The allomorphy is not entirely clear. See =iwt.
11 See =iwt.

=axn	arm	ḱɬ+c̓q̓=axn	hit under arm.
=x̌		c+kʷan=x̌	kidnap.
=áya	pretend, play	wyp=áya+m	play white man.
=ʕáyaʔ[12]		ps•ps=ʕáyaʔ	goofy, feeble minded.
=iys	snow	kt̓+p=iys ɬaʔ=íys	stop snowing. near edge.
=iʔ	?	ḱ•kaʔl=íʔ	go slow.
=iʔs(t)	?	yx̌=iʔs(t) wr̓•r̓=iʔst haw•híw=iʔst s+n+q̓ʷɬt=iʔst+n ɬt̓•ít̓=iʔst+m n+wx̌ʷ•x̌ʷ+t=iʔst	drive stock, herd. make fire. yawn. quiver. jump. gallop.
=aʔst	?	t+ḱʷúl̓=aʔst+m s+ḱʷúl̓=aʔst	attach feathers. handywork.

Sequences of lexical suffixes			
=cn+m=íc̓aʔ[13]		s+ƛ̓aʔ=cn+m=íc̓aʔ	deer hide.
=cn=iks	wrist	ḱɬ+kʷƛ̓=cn=iks	pull off of wrist.
=cn=ikst	wrist	c+ḱɬ+lʕʷ=cn=ikst+m	fit on wrist cisl.
=cn=lúp		n+yaʕ̓+p=cn=lúp	need a place.
=cn=ink	belly	s+qʷl=cn=ink	belly.
=cn=itkʷ	shore	t̓q=cn=itkʷ	lie on shore
=cin=xn	ankle	ɬqʷ=cin=xn	ankle loops
=kn=aɬq		n+kc=kn=aɬq	catch up.
=kn=iɬxʷ	outside	t+ḱm=kn=iɬxʷ	outside.
=kń=lscút		k+ʕac=kń=lscút	tie in bundles.
=kń=íɬxʷ		k+ɬaʔ=kń=íɬxʷ	edge of house.
=kst=íc̓aʔ		k+ʔapn=kst=íc̓aʔ	ten packages.
=kst+m=ɬtíɬn		maʔ=kst+m=ɬtíɬn	bother people.
=kst=asq̓t		t̓q̓m=kst=asq̓t	six days.
=ʕakst=xn	leg	k+cw=ʕakst=xn	chaps.
=kiʔ=sqáx̌aʔ		n+kʷxʷ=kiʔ=sqáx̌aʔ+m	take saddle off.
=ln=útyaʔ		cq̓=ln=útyaʔ	bow and arrow.
=lqs=íkst	elbow	n+caʔ=lqs=íkst+m	elbow someone.
=lqʷ=iks	wrist	t+ḱʷm=lqʷ=iks+m	bite on wrist.
=álqʷp=xn[14]		ḱɬ+t+tiʔɬ=álqʷp=xn	Coyote's son's name.
=ls=ínaʔ		n+t+q̓aʔ=ls=ínaʔ+m	pay attention.
=lt=ílt	child	k=naqs=lt=ílt	one child
=lt=ílaʔt	child	k=nqs=lt=ílaʔt s+k=ńqs=l̓t=ílaʔt	only child. only child dim.
=lt+n=áwlaʔ		k+s+q̓m=lt+n=áwlaʔ	starve.

12 The glottal stop may be a mishearing.
13 I ignore the +m in the alphabetization in this and other cases where some element intervenes between the lexical suffixes.
14 The p is unexplained.

=lut=ip		k̓ɬ+n+ɬq̓ʷ=lut=ip	lie in front of door.
=laʔxʷ=ílp	bed	kʷl̓=laʔxʷ=ílp+m =laʔxʷ=ilp	fix, prepare a surface. bed.
=ɬp=ikst	boughs	k̓+cq̓=ɬp=ikst	fir boughs.
=ɬp=ítkʷ		n+xʷyaʔ=ɬp=ítkʷ	Kettle River.
=ɬp=ítkʷ=x		s+nxʷyaʔ=ɬp=ítkʷ=x	Kettle people.
=iɬp=x		s+x̌ʷʔ=iɬp=x	Colville.
=iɬ=xn	leg	s+n+ckʷ•ckʷ•kʷ=iɬ=xn n+ckʷ•ckʷ•kʷ=iɬ=xn	leg cramps.
=ʕáɬxʷ=c̓aʔ		n+x̌ls=ʕáɬxʷ=c̓aʔ+m	glass house.
=mxʷ=sqáx̌aʔ		s+ql•qlt=mxʷ=sqáx̌aʔ	male horses.
=nk=íɬp		s+xʷaʔ•xʷaʔ=nk=íɬp	thorn bushes.
=nk=áwaʔ		s+x̌m=nk=áwaʔ	lover.
=ánaʔ=qn		n+wk+nap=ánaʔ=qn+m	see with corner of eye.
=íp•p=laʔxʷ		xʷp•xʷp=íp•p=laʔxʷ	spread on floor.
=plaʔ=sqáx̌aʔ		s+t+kn̓=plaʔ=sqáx̌aʔ	lead horse.
=ap=qn	top of head	t̓q̓ʷ=ap=qn	slap on head.
=íp=w̓stxn		ʔasl=íp=w̓stxn n+ɬ•ɬqʷ=íp=w̓stxn	two steps. loin cloth.
=qin=kst	finger	k̓n•k̓np̓=qin=kst+n	rings.
=qn=aɬq		wl=qn=aɬq	upset.
=qn=iɬxʷ	top of house	n+k̓m=qn=iɬxʷ	ceiling.
=qn=ups		ml=qn=ups	golden eagle.
=qn=islp̓		s+q̓ʷl=qn=islp̓	smokey tipi.
=qn=ítkʷ		n+wkna=qn=ítkʷ	Okanagan River.
=qín=xn	leg	s+k+ʕac•ʕac=qín=xn	leggings.
=qn=iʔ		c̓s+p=qn=iʔ	bullets, shots finish.
=qínaʔ=kst	finger	s+tawn=qínaʔ=kst	little finger.
=qs=íɬaʔxʷ		t+k̓•k̓m=qs=íɬaʔxʷ	small house by itself.
=aqst=xn	hip	s+n+q•qp=aqst=xn	under hip mat.
=s=úlaʔxʷ		tanm̓=s=úlaʔxʷ	travel aimlessly.
=ús=xn		k̓ɬ+ƛ̓aʔ•ƛ̓aʔ=ús=xn	look for tracks.
=ús=aʔst		n+wl•wlm=ús=aʔst	hard (arrow) points.
=t=lscut		k̓ɬ+yxʷ=t=lscut	underwear.
=t=ilt		s+k+lkʷ=t=ilt	distant child
=t=úlaʔxʷ		n+yxʷ=t=úlaʔxʷ	basement.
=t=íɬc̓aʔ		s+n+yxʷ=t=íɬc̓aʔ	insides.
=t=ínk		k̓ɬ+tkʷaʔ=t=ínk	walk side hill
=tk=us		c+ʔwtm=tk=us	southward.
=tkʷ=lscut		n+q̓ʷaʔ=tkʷ=lscut	wash clothes.
=tkʷ=itkʷ		n+x̌ʷn=tkʷ=itkʷ	Columbia / Kettle River.
=t=aqs		n+ʔakʷ=t=áqs n+ʔam=t=áqs	car. sit on road.
=iwl=tk		t•tʔ=iwl=tk	up on shore
=wt=álaʔqʷ		n+m̓kʷ=wt=álaʔqʷ	little lump in woods.

=wat=qn		t+ql=wat=qn+tn	threshing horse.
=wt=us=xn		k̓ɬ+kʷl=wt=us=xn	sit around.
=íwa=xn		s+yr=íwa=xn	snowshoes.
=ẇs=cín		n+ʔayxʷ=ẇs=cín+m	trade for groceries.
=ẇs=cn		qʷl•qʷl+t=ẇs=cn+cut	talk about one's thoughts.
=iẇs=íkn̓		n+m=iẇs=íkn̓	middle.
=ẇs=íkst		ʔal=ẇs=íkst+m	collect.
=iẇs=álqʷ		mi•m=iẇs=álqʷ	half way up tree.
=ẇs=ílxʷ		ʔax̌•x̌•l=ẇs=ílxʷ	matched coats.
=iẇs=úlaʔxʷ		ɬ+c+m=iẇs=úlaʔxʷ	come halfway again.
=ẇs=úlaʔxʷ		tx̌ʷ=ẇs=úlaʔxʷ	half way around.
=ẇs=ɬniwt		t+xmn=ẇs=ɬniwt	both sides.
=aẇs=q(n)		n+xl=aẇs=qn	chop head.
=ẇs=qn		c+n+t̓am=ẇs=qn	grab head cisl.
=ẇs=us		xt̓•t̓=ẇs=us xt̓=ẇs=us	join in middle. complete, full.
=x=cn		n+wyap=x=cn	English language.
=xn=iɬxʷ		c+k+tɬ•ɬ=xn=iɬxʷ	straight to door cisl.
=iʔst=xn		ɬ+c+nx=iʔst=xn+cut	back track.

Index and chronology of Pete Seymour's narrations

I list in tabular form all the texts Pete Seymour narrated and I recorded. The dates (Column 1) are followed by a reference I gave to the tape on which the narration was recorded (Column 2). Copies of some of these tapes are deposited in the archives of the University of Washington. I have digitized the tapes in mp3 form, and the Colville Tribes have posted the mp3s at http://www.colvilletribes.com/mattina.php. I list the titles Pete gave to the narratives first, followed in square brackets by the title I have choses for this anthology (Column 3). If it was I who suggested and named a topic, I list such in square brackets. We can infer that Pete did not ascribe any special importance or significance to the titles, by noting the variations of the titles he gave to the various parts of some of the narratives, and of the titles (if so they can be called) he gave the autobiographical and ethnographic texts and of the texts of European origin. Finally, I indicate the length of each narration, except The Golden Woman, (Column 4).

Date	Tape	Text	Length of audio files
July 30, 1968	68-01	Black Pig	10:11
August 2, 4, 5, 6 1968	68-02	The Golden Woman Parts I -VII	
August 6, 1968	68-08	Coyote and his family [Coyote and Grizzly] Part 1	22:48
August 8, 1968	68-09	Coyote and his sons [Coyote and Grizzly] Part 2	48:54
August 8, 1968	68-10	Coyote and his family [Coyote and Grizzly] Part 3	11:09
August 8, 1968	68-10	BlueJay and his brother-in-law the Wolf [BlueJay and Wolf] Part 1	36:57
August 9, 1968	68-11	BlueJay and his brother-in-law the Wolf [BlueJay and Wolf] Part 2	27:42
August 9, 1968	68-11	The king with one boy [The grateful dead version 1 (unfinished)] Part 1	20:49
August 9, 1968	68-12	The king with one boy [The grateful dead version 1 (unfinished)] Part 2	47:37
June 26, 1969	69-07	[The attainment of provisions]	6:23
July 1, 1969	69-07	A hunting trip Part 1	9:39
July 1, 1969	69-09	A hunting trip Part 2	24:54
July 1, 1969	69-09	Partnership butchering	3:12
July 9, 1969	69-09	The rainy hunting trip Part 1	4:51
July 10, 1969	69-10	The rainy hunting trip Part 2	2:28
July 16, 1969	69-10	Harvesting (unfinished)	29:09
July 21, 1969	69-12	Man's activities after the birth of a child	8:01
July 21, 1969	69-12	Marriage customs	10:33
July 21, 1969	69-12	Autobiography Part 1	12:59
July 31, 1969	69-14	Autobiography Part 2	29:55

August 4, 1969	69-16	Racing horses (unfinished)	20:36
July 30, 1970	70-08	The chief's family Part 1 [The grateful dead version 2]	25:52
July 30, 1970	70-08[1]	The Chief's family Part 2 [The grateful dead version 2]	27:39
July 30, 1970	70-20	The Chief's family Part 3 [The grateful dead version 2]	17:59
July 28, 1970	70-18	Lynx and the virgin Part 1	32:24
July 28, 1970	70-19[2]	Lynx and the virgin Part 2	20:48
July 14, 1971	71-03	How Coyote got his powers[3]	26:53
July 19, 1971	71-05	Coyote and Whale Part 1	32:47
August 2, 1971	71-06	Coyote and Buffalo Woman [Coyote and Whale Part 2]	32:37
August 2, 1971	71-07	Coyote and Buffalo Woman [Coyote and Whale Part 3]	5:32
August 2, 1971	71-07	The two goats Part 1	26:09
August 2, 1971	71-08	The two goats Part 2	10:46
July 19, 1974	74-02	The Devil and the Black Man	53:36

1 Side two.
2 This is side two of tape 1970-18.
3 This text is commonly referred to as "How Coyote got his name."

References

Aarne, Antti. 1961. *The types of the folktale: A Clcssification and bibliography*. The Finnish Academy of Science and Letters, Helsinki.

Andrist, John E., ed. 1971. *Coyote and the Colville*. Material collected and prepared by Eileen Yanan. St Mary's Mission, Omak, Washington.

Bierhorst, John 1985. *The mythology of North America.* Quill William Morrow, New York.

Boas, Franz, ed. 1917. *Folk-tales of Salishan and Sahaptin tribes*. Collected by James A. Teit, Livingston Farrand, Marian K. Gould, Herbert J. Spinden. American Folklore Society, Lancaster, Pa, and New York.

----. 1927-28. *The Salishan Tribes of the Western Plateaus*. 45th Bureau of American Ethnology Annual Report. Smithsonian Institution.

Carlson, Barrry F. and Pauline Flett 1989. *Spokane dictionary. University of Montana Occasional Papers in Linguistics No. 6,* Missoula.

Carlson, Barry F., Pauline Flett and Deirdre Black. ND. *Spokane Dictionary*. MS.

Greenway, John 1964. *Literature among the primitives.* Folklore Associates, Hatbory, Pennsylvania.

Hill-Tout 1911. *Report on the Ethnology of the Okanák•ēn of British Columbia, an Interior Division of the Salish Stock*. In Maud, Ralph, ed. 1978. *The Salish people. The local contribution of Charles Hill-Tout. Volume I: The Thopson and the Okanagan*. Talonbooks, Vancouver.

Kinkade, M. Dale 1982. "Transitive inflection in (Moses) Columbian Salish. *Kansas Working Papers in Linguistics.* Vol. 7, pp. 49-62.

Kuipers, Aert H. 1974. *The Shuswap language. Grammar, texts, dictionary.* Mouton, The Hague, Paris.

----. 2002. *Salish etymological dictionary. University of Montana Occasional Papers in Linguistics No. 16,* Missoula.

Lyon, John and Rebecca Green-Wood, eds. 2007. *Lawrence Nicodemus's Coeur d'Alene dictionary in root format. University of Montana Occasional Papers in Linguistics No. 20,* Missoula.

Mattina, Anthony 1987. *Colville-Okanagan dictionary. University of Montana Occasional Papers in Linguistics No. 5,* Missoula.

----. ND. *matlán kʷu̯ m̓ay̓xíts. Madeline told me*. MS.

Mattina, Anthony and Madeline DeSautel, eds. 2002. *Dora Noyes DeSautel ɬaʔ kɬcaptíkʷɬ. University of Montana Occasional Papers in Linguistics No. 15,* Missoula.

Mattina, Anthony and Clara Jack 1992. "Okanagan-Colville kinship terms." *Anthropological Linguistics*. Vol. 34, Nos 1-4, pp. 117-137.

Mattina, Nancy J. 1996. *Aspect and category in Okanagan word formation*. PhD dissertation, Simon Fraser University.

----, ed. ND. *Nxaʔamxčín Nwwawlxtnt: Moses-Columbia dictionary.* Compiled by Moses-Columbia Language Program, Colville Confederated Tribes. MS.

Maud, Ralph, ed. 1978. *The Salish people. The local contribution of Charles Hill-Tout. Volume I: The Thompson and the Okanagan.* Talonbooks, Vancouver.

Mourning Dove 1933. *Coyote stories.* Ed and illus. Heister Dean Guie, with notes by Lucullus V. McWhorter (Old Wolf) and a foreword by Chief Standing Bear. Caxton Printers, Caldwell, Idaho.

Ray, Verne F. 1933a. *The Sanpoil and Nespelem: Salishan Peoples of Northeastern Washington.* University of Washington Publications in Anthropology.

Ray, Verne F. 1933b. "Sanpoil folk tales." In *Journal of American Folklore* Vol 46, pp. 129-187.

Reichard, Gladys A. 1933-1938. "Coeur d'Aleme." In *Handbook of American Indian languages* Part 3. Ed. Franz Boas. J.J. Augustin.

Robinson, Harry.1989. *Write It on Your heart: The Epic World of an Okanagan Storyteller*. Compiled and edited by Wendy Wickwire. Talonbooks/Theytus, Vancouver.

----. 1992. *Nature Power: In the Spirit of an Okanagan Storyteller.* Compiled and edited by Wendy Wickwire. Douglas & McIntyre Vancouver/Toronto; University of Washington Press, Seattle.

----. 2005. *Living by stories. A journey of landscape memory*. Compiled and edited by Wendy Wickwire. Talonbooks, Vancouver.

Seymour, Peter J. 1985. *The Golden Woman: The Colville Narrative of Peter J. Seymour*. Edited by Anthony Mattina. The University of Arizona Press.

Speck, Brenda J. 1980. *An edition of Father Post's Kalispel grammar.University of Montana Occasional Papers in Linguistics* No 1. Missoula.

Spier, Leslie, ed. 1938. *The Sinkaietk or Southern Okanagon of Washington*. By Walter Cline, Rachel S. Commons, May Mandelbaum, Richard H. Post, and L. V. W. Walters. General Series in Anthropology No. 6. Contributions from the laboratory of anthropology. George Banta Publishing Company, Menasha, Wisconsin.

Teit, James 1930. *The Salishan Tribes of the Western Plateaus*. Edited by Franz Boas. 45th Annual Report, Bureau of American Ethnology, pp. 23-396.

Thompson, Laurence C. and M. Terry Thompson. 1996. *Thompson River Salish Dictionary. University of Montana Occasional Papers in Linguistics* No 12. Missoula.

Thompson, Stith 1955. *Motif-index of folk-literature*. Revised and Enlarged Edition. Indiana University Press.

Turner, Nancy J, Randy Bouchard and Dorothy I. D. Kennedy. 1980. *Ethnootany of the Okanagan-Colville Indians of British Columbia and Washington.* Occasional Papers of the British Columbia Provincial Museum, No. 21.

van Eijk, Jan P. 1987. *Dictionary of the Lillooet language.* MS.

Vogt, Hans 1940. *The Kalispel language*. Det Norske Videnskaps. Akademi I Oslo.

In the Native Literatures of the Americas Series

Pitch Woman and Other Stories: The Oral Traditions of Coquelle Thompson, Upper Coquille Athabaskan Indian
Edited and with an introduction by William R. Seaburg
Collected by Elizabeth D. Jacobs

Inside Dazzling Mountains: Southwest Native Verbal Arts
Edited by David L. Kozak

The Complete Seymour: Colville Storyteller
Peter J. Seymour
Compiled and edited by Anthony Mattina
Translated by Madeline DeSautel and Anthony Mattina

Algonquian Spirit: Contemporary Translations of the Algonquian Literatures of North America
Edited by Brian Swann

Born in the Blood: On Native American Translation
Edited and with an introduction by Brian Swann

Sky Loom: Native American Myth, Story, and Song
Edited and with an introduction by Brian Swann

Voices from Four Directions: Contemporary Translations of the Native Literatures of North America
Edited by Brian Swann

Salish Myths and Legends: One People's Stories
Edited by M. Terry Thompson and Steven M. Egesdal

To order or obtain more information on these or other University of Nebraska Press titles, visit nebraskapress.unl.edu.

www.ingramcontent.com/pod-product-compliance
Lightning Source LLC
Chambersburg PA
CBHW081130300726
48982CB00005B/919

* 9 7 8 0 8 0 3 2 7 7 0 5 2 *